Lecture Notes in Computer Science 8373

Commenced Publication in 1973
Founding and Former Series Editors:
Gerhard Goos, Juris Hartmanis, and Jan van Leeuwen

Shusaku Iida   José Meseguer
Kazuhiro Ogata (Eds.)

Specification, Algebra, and Software

Essays Dedicated to Kokichi Futatsugi

 Springer

Volume Editors

Shusaku Iida
Senshu University
School of Network and Information
2-1-1 Higashi-mita, Tama-ku, Kawasaki, Kanagawa 214-8580, Japan
E-mail: iida@isc.senshu-u.ac.jp

José Meseguer
University of Illinois at Urbana-Champaign (UIUC)
Department of Computer Science
Thomas M. Siebel Center for Computer Science
201 N. Goodwin Avenue, MC 258, Urbana, IL 61801, USA
E-mail: meseguer@illinois.edu

Kazuhiro Ogata
Japan Advanced Institute of Science and Technology (JAIST)
School of Information Science
1-1 Asahidai, Nomi, Ishikawa 923-1292, Japan
E-mail: ogata@jaist.ac.jp

ISSN 0302-9743   e-ISSN 1611-3349
ISBN 978-3-642-54623-5   e-ISBN 978-3-642-54624-2
DOI 10.1007/978-3-642-54624-2
Springer Heidelberg New York Dordrecht London

Library of Congress Control Number: 2014932844

LNCS Sublibrary: SL 1 – Theoretical Computer Science and General Issues

Typesetting: Camera-ready by author, data conversion by Scientific Publishing Services, Chennai, India

Printed on acid-free paper

Springer is part of Springer Science+Business Media (www.springer.com)

Kokichi Futatsugi

Preface

During his entire professional life, Prof. Kokichi Futatsugi has worked in the intersection of formal methods and software engineering. He has made fundamental scientific contributions to both of these areas and is recognized as an international leader in both of them.

In formal methods he is one of the founding fathers of the field of algebraic specification and verification. In 1980 he designed and implemented the first Japanese algebraic specification language (HISP), one of the very first such languages in the world with powerful module operations. And in the mid-1980s he co-designed the OBJ algebraic specification language, at the time the most advanced language of its type in the world, which has had an enormous impact in the field of formal methods. In the 1990s he greatly expanded the reach and impact of algebraic specification and verification by supporting reasoning and executable formal specification of systems involving algebraic data types, objects, states, and concurrency through the seamless and elegant integration of equational, hidden, and rewriting logic in the so-called CafeOBJ "cube."

The CafeOBJ language and the range of verification methods and tools it supports —including its support for inductive theorem proving, verification of behavioral specifications, deductive invariant proof, and reachability analysis of concurrent systems— has played a key role in both extending and bringing algebraic specification techniques into contact with many software engineering applications. In the most recent years, the CafeOBJ approach to formal specification and verification has been further advanced under his leadership to achieve a more intimate integration between theorem proving and model checking, reach greater automation of proofs, and make further breakthroughs in deductive invariant verification.

One of the most appealing strong points of the vision brought to fruition by Kokichi Futatsugi through all these efforts is the advancement of a style of executable specification that is in fact, simultaneously, a very simple and intuitive form of declarative programming, and therefore considerably easier to understand and use by software engineers than other, more arcane formalisms. This, together with all the above-mentioned formal verification methods and tools based on such executable specifications, has brought formal methods considerably closer to software engineering practice.

His leadership in the software engineering field includes, but has not been limited to, all the above-mentioned scientific contributions: He has furthermore carried out a sustained and impressive effort to connect his formal methods work with other key areas of software engineering such as object-oriented design and model-based software development. Furthermore, with his collaborators he has developed a very impressive array of case studies showing the practical usefulness of these methods. He has also been a leading figure in the ICSE community

as its main Japanese representative over the years, has played a key role in promoting other important international research initiatives such as the ICFEM
conferences that bring together researchers in formal methods and software engineering all over the word, has promoted and edited the proceedings of many
other scientific events, and has served as program chair and/or on steering and
program committees of numerous prestigious international scientific conferences.

In Japan his leadership and influence in formal methods and software engineering have been immense, not only among researchers, but also in bringing
formal methods closer to industrial software practice.

For us it is both an honor and a pleasure to have been able to organize
this event and have edited this volume. The response from the internationally
leading researchers in formal methods and software engineering that we have
invited has been enthusiastic. Thanks to them we have been able to assemble a
remarkable body of research papers that, in different ways, bring out both the
vibrancy of research in this frontier and allude to Kokichi Futatsugi's remarkable
impact on it. Indeed, we believe that this festive volume and event to honor
Kokichi Futatsugi afford a rather special opportunity for leading researchers at
the intersection of formal methods and software engineering to reflect on and
discuss some of the main research directions in this frontier in the context of the
life-long ideas of one of its leading contributors.

We wish to thank all the contributors to this Festschrift volume and all the
researchers who, through their careful refereeing of the papers, have allowed us
to assemble a volume of very high scientific quality. We also wish to thank Alfred
Hofmann and all the staff at Springer for their warm support and encouragement
of this project from its very inception and for their excellent technical help.
Finally, we are grateful to the Kanazawa Convention Bureau for supporting this
event.

January 2014   Shusaku Iida
                                                                    José Meseguer
                                                                    Kazuhiro Ogata

Organization

Program Chairs

Shusaku Iida	Senshu University, Japan
José Meseguer	UIUC, USA
Kazuhiro Ogata	JAIST, Japan

Publicity/Publication Chair

Yuki Chiba	JAIST, Japan

Reviewers

María Alpuente
Takahito Aoto
Christian Attiogbé
Yasuhito Arimoto
Kyungmin Bae
Dines Bjørner
Roberto Bruni
Ştefan Ciobâcă
Manuel Clavel
Răzvan Diaconescu
Marina Egea
Santiago Escobar
Bertram Felgenhauer
Daniel Găină
Carlo Ghezzi

Michael R. Hansen
Shigenori Ioroi
Alexander Knapp
Koichi Kobayashi
Weiqiang Kong
Hironobu Kuruma
Keiichirou Kusakari
Dorel Lucanu
Narciso Martí-Oliet
Kazuhiro Minami
Till Mossakowski
Shin Nakajima
Masaki Nakamura
Peter Ölveczky
Leon Osterweil

Iakovos Ouranos
Adrián Riesco
Camilo Rocha
Grigore Roşu
Ralf Sasse
Stephen Skeirik
Mark-Oliver Stehr
Andrzej Tarlecki
Tatsuhiro Tsuchiya
Martin Wirsing
Jianwen Xiang
Hirokazu Yatsu
Min Zhang

Bibliography of Kokichi Futatsugi

(Major English publications in anti-chronological order)

Books Authored or Edited

[1] Futatsugi, K., Jouannaud, J.-P., Meseguer, J. (eds.): Algebra, Meaning, and Computation. LNCS, vol. 4060. Springer, Heidelberg (2006)

[2] Futatsugi, K., Mizoguchi, F., Yonezaki, N. (eds.): ISSS 2003. LNCS, vol. 3233. Springer, Heidelberg (2004)

[3] Futatsugi, K., Nakagawa, A.T., Tamai, T. (eds.): CAFE: An Industrial-Strength Algebraic Formal Method. Elsevier B.V. (2000) ISBN: 978-0-444-50556-9

[4] Futatsugi, K., Goguen, J., Meseguer, J. (eds.): OBJ/CafeOBJ/Maude at Formal Methods 1999, Formal Specification, Proof and Applications. THETA, Bucharest (1999) ISBN 973-99097-1-X

[5] Diaconescu, R., Futatsugi, K.: CafeOBJ Report - The Language, Proof Techniques, and Methodologies for Object-Oriented Algebraic Specification, p. 196. World Scientific (1998) ISBN 978-981-02-3513-0 (hardcover)

[6] Torii, K., Futatsugi, K., Kemmerer, R.A. (eds.): Forging New Links, Proceedings of the 1998 International Conference on Software Engineering, ICSE 1998, Kyoto, Japan, April 19-25. IEEE Computer Society (1998) ISBN 0-8186-8368-6

[7] Futatsugi, K., Matsuoka, S. (eds.): ISOTAS 1996. LNCS, vol. 1049. Springer, Heidelberg (1996)

Journal Articles

[1] Gaina, D., Futatsugi, K.: Initial semantics in logics with constructors. Journal of Logic and Computation (2013), doi:10.1093/logcom/exs044

[2] Zhang, M., Ogata, K., Futatsugi, K.: Formalization and Verification of Behavioral Correctness of Dynamic Software Updates. Electr. Notes Theor. Comput. Sci. 294, 12–23 (2013)

[3] Ogata, K., Futatsugi, K.: Compositionally Writing Proof Scores of Invariants in the OTS/CafeOBJ Method. J. UCS 19(6), 771–804 (2013)

[4] Arimoto, Y., Iida, S., Futatsugi, K.: Formal Verification of Effectiveness of Control Activities in Business Processes. IEICE Transactions 95-D(5), 1342–1354 (2012)

[5] Gâinâ, D., Futatsugi, K., Ogata, K.: Constructor-based Logics. J. UCS 18(16), 2204–2233 (2012)

[6] Futatsugi, K., Gâinâ, D., Ogata, K.: Principles of proof scores in CafeOBJ. Theor. Comput. Sci. 464, 90–112 (2012)

[7] Li, Y., Kan, H., Futatsugi, K.: A Note on "On the Construction of Boolean Functions with Optimal Algebraic Immunity". IEICE Transactions 94-A(9), 1877–1880 (2011)

[8] Kong, W., Ogata, K., Futatsugi, K.: Towards Reliable E-Government Systems with the OTS/CafeOBJ Method. IEICE Transactions 93-D(5), 974–984 (2010)

[9] Ogata, K., Futatsugi, K.: Proof Score Approach to Analysis of Electronic Commerce Protocols. International Journal of Software Engineering and Knowledge Engineering 20(2), 253–287 (2010)

[10] Nakamura, M., Ogata, K., Futatsugi, K.: Reducibility of operation symbols in term rewriting systems and its application to behavioral specifications. J. Symb. Comput. 45(5), 551–573 (2010)

[11] Nakamura, M., Ogata, K., Futatsugi, K.: User-Defined On-Demand Matching. IEICE Transactions 92-D(7), 1401–1411 (2009)

[12] Ogata, K., Futatsugi, K.: Simulation-based Verification for Invariant Properties in the OTS/CafeOBJ Method. Electr. Notes Theor. Comput. Sci. 201, 127–154 (2008)

[13] Nakamura, M., Kong, W., Ogata, K., Futatsugi, K.: A Specification Translation from Behavioral Specifications to Rewrite Specifications. IEICE Transactions 91-D(5), 1492–1503 (2008)

[14] Ogata, K., Futatsugi, K.: Proof Score Approach to Verification of Liveness Properties. IEICE Transactions 91-D(12), 2804–2817 (2008)

[15] Ogata, K., Futatsugi, K.: Comparison of Maude and SAL by Conducting Case Studies Model Checking a Distributed Algorithm. IEICE Transactions 90-A(8), 1690–1703 (2007)

[16] Ogata, K., Futatsugi, K.: State Machines as Inductive Types. IEICE Transactions 90-A(12), 2985–2988 (2007)

[17] Kong, W., Ogata, K., Futatsugi, K.: Specification and Verification of Workflows with Rbac Mechanism and Sod Constraints. International Journal of Software Engineering and Knowledge Engineering 17(1), 3–32 (2007)

[18] Nakano, M., Ogata, K., Nakamura, M., Futatsugi, K.: CrÈme: An Automatic Invariant Prover of Behavioral Specifications. International Journal of Software Engineering and Knowledge Engineering 17(6), 783–804 (2007)

[19] Ogata, K., Futatsugi, K.: Modeling and verification of real-time systems based on equations. Sci. Comput. Program. 66(2), 162–180 (2007)

[20] Futatsugi, K., Jouannaud, J.-P., Meseguer, J.: Joseph Goguen (1941-2006). Bulletin of the EATCS 90, 199–201 (2006)

[21] Seino, T., Ogata, K., Futatsugi, K.: A Toolkit for Generating and Displaying Proof Scores in the OTS/CafeOBJ Method. Electr. Notes Theor. Comput. Sci. 147(1), 57–72 (2006)

[22] Nakamura, M., Watanabe, M., Futatsugi, K.: A Behavioral Specification of Imperative Programming Languages. IEICE Transactions 89-A(6), 1558–1565 (2006)

[23] Kondoh, H., Futatsugi, K.: To use or not to use the goto statement: Programming styles viewed from Hoare Logic. Sci. Comput. Program. 60(1), 82–116 (2006)

[24] Seino, T., Ogata, K., Futatsugi, K.: Mechanically supporting case analysis for verification of distributed systems. Int. J. Pervasive Computing and Communications 1(2), 135–146 (2005)

[25] Diaconescu, R., Futatsugi, K., Ogata, K.: CafeOBJ: Logical Foundations and Methodologies. Computers and Artificial Intelligence 22(3-4), 257–283 (2003)

[26] Ogata, K., Futatsugi, K.: Flaw and modification of the iKP electronic payment protocols. Inf. Process. Lett. 86(2), 57–62 (2003)

[27] Ogata, K., Futatsugi, K.: Rewriting-Based Verification of Authentication Protocols. Electr. Notes Theor. Comput. Sci. 71, 208–222 (2002)

[28] Diaconescu, R., Futatsugi, K.: Logical foundations of CafeOBJ. Theor. Comput. Sci. 285(2), 289–318 (2002)

[29] Futatsugi, K.: Preface. Electr. Notes Theor. Comput. Sci. 36, 1 (2000)

[30] Diaconescu, R., Futatsugi, K.: Behavioural Coherence in Object-Oriented Algebraic Specification. J. UCS 6(1), 74–96 (2000)
[31] Matsumoto, M., Futatsugi, K.: Test set coinduction - Toward automated verification of behavioural properties. Electr. Notes Theor. Comput. Sci. 15, 242–262 (1998)
[32] Diaconescu, R., Futatsugi, K.: An overview of CafeOBJ. Electr. Notes Theor. Comput. Sci. 15, 285–298 (1998)

Conference and Workshop Papers

[1] Yatsu, H., Ando, T., Kong, W., Hisazumi, K., Fukuda, A., Aoki, T., Futatsugi, K.: Towards Formal Description of Standards for Automotive Operating Systems. In: ICST Workshops 2013, pp. 13–14 (2013)
[2] Zhang, M., Ogata, K., Futatsugi, K.: An Algebraic Approach to Formal Analysis of Dynamic Software Updating Mechanisms. APSEC 2012, 664–673 (2012)
[3] Komoto, T., Taguchi, K., Mouratidis, H., Yoshioka, N., Futatsugi, K.: A Modelling Framework to Support Internal Control. SSIRI (Companion), 187–193 (2011)
[4] Futatsugi, K.: Fostering Proof Scores in CafeOBJ. In: Dong, J.S., Zhu, H. (eds.) ICFEM 2010. LNCS, vol. 6447, pp. 1–20. Springer, Heidelberg (2010)
[5] Ogata, K., Futatsugi, K.: A Combination of Forward and Backward Reachability Analysis Methods. In: Dong, J.S., Zhu, H. (eds.) ICFEM 2010. LNCS, vol. 6447, pp. 501–517. Springer, Heidelberg (2010)
[6] Izumida, T., Futatsugi, K., Mori, A.: A Generic Binary Analysis Method for Malware. In: Echizen, I., Kunihiro, N., Sasaki, R. (eds.) IWSEC 2010. LNCS, vol. 6434, pp. 199–216. Springer, Heidelberg (2010)
[7] Găină, D., Futatsugi, K., Ogata, K.: Constructor-Based Institutions. In: Kurz, A., Lenisa, M., Tarlecki, A. (eds.) CALCO 2009. LNCS, vol. 5728, pp. 398–412. Springer, Heidelberg (2009)
[8] Kong, W., Ogata, K., Cheng, J., Futatsugi, K.: Trace anonymity in the OTS/CafeOBJ method. In: CIT 2008, pp. 754–759 (2008)
[9] Xiang, J., Bjørner, D., Futatsugi, K.: Formal digital license language with OTS/CafeOBJ method. In: AICCSA 2008, pp. 652–660 (2008)
[10] Arimoto, Y., Kudo, M., Watanabe, Y., Futatsugi, K.: Checking assignments of controls to risks for internal control. In: ICEGOV 2008, pp. 98–104 (2008)
[11] Ogata, K., Futatsugi, K.: Formal Analysis of the Bakery Protocol with Consideration of Nonatomic Reads and Writes. In: Liu, S., Araki, K. (eds.) ICFEM 2008. LNCS, vol. 5256, pp. 187–206. Springer, Heidelberg (2008)
[12] Chen, X., Kong, W., Futatsugi, K.: Formal support for e-government system design with transparency consideration. In: ICEGOV 2007, pp. 20–29 (2007)
[13] Masaki, N., Kokichi, F.: On Equality Predicates in Algebraic Specification Languages. In: Jones, C.B., Liu, Z., Woodcock, J. (eds.) ICTAC 2007. LNCS, vol. 4711, pp. 381–395. Springer, Heidelberg (2007)
[14] Kong, W., Ogata, K., Futatsugi, K.: Algebraic Approaches to Formal Analysis of the Mondex Electronic Purse System. In: Davies, J., Gibbons, J. (eds.) IFM 2007. LNCS, vol. 4591, pp. 393–412. Springer, Heidelberg (2007)
[15] Ogata, K., Futatsugi, K.: Some Tips on Writing Proof Scores in the OTS/CafeOBJ Method. Essays Dedicated to Joseph A. Goguen 2006, 596–615 (2006)
[16] Ogata, K., Nakano, M., Kong, W., Futatsugi, K.: Induction-Guided Falsification. In: Liu, Z., Kleinberg, R.D. (eds.) ICFEM 2006. LNCS, vol. 4260, pp. 114–131. Springer, Heidelberg (2006)

[17] Futatsugi, K.: Verifying Specifications with Proof Scores in CafeOBJ. In: ASE 2006, pp. 3–10 (2006)

[18] Nakano, M., Ogata, K., Nakamura, M., Futatsugi, K.: Automating Invariant Verification of Behavioral Specifications. In: QSIC 2006, pp. 49–56 (2006)

[19] Ogata, K., Kong, W., Futatsugi, K.: Falsification of OTSs by Searches of Bounded Reachable State Spaces. In: SEKE 2006, pp. 440–445 (2006)

[20] Xiang, J., Kong, W., Futatsugi, K., Ogata, K.: Analysis of Positive Incentives for Protecting Secrets in Digital Rights Management. In: WEBIST, vol. (2), pp. 5–12 (2006)

[21] Ogata, K., Futatsugi, K.: Analysis of the Suzuki-Kasami Algorithm with SAL Model Checkers. In: CIT 2005, pp. 937–943 (2005)

[22] Kong, W., Seino, T., Futatsugi, K., Ogata, K.: A Lightweight Integration of Theorem Proving and Model Checking for System Verification. In: APSEC 2005, pp. 59–66 (2005)

[23] Ogata, K., Futatsugi, K.: Analysis of the Suzuki-Kasami Algorithm with the Maude Model Checker. In: APSEC 2005, pp. 159–166 (2005)

[24] Ogata, K., Futatsugi, K.: Equational Approach to Formal Analysis of TLS. In: ICDCS 2005, pp. 795–804 (2005)

[25] Ogata, K., Nakano, M., Nakamura, M., Futatsugi, K.: Chocolat/SMV: A Translator from CafeOBJ into SMV. In: PDCAT 2005, pp. 416–420 (2005)

[26] Kong, W., Ogata, K., Futatsugi, K.: Formal Analysis of Workflow Systems with Security Considerations. In: SEKE 2005, pp. 531–536 (2005)

[27] Ogata, K., Futatsugi, K.: Proof Score Approach to Verification of Liveness Properties. In: SEKE 2005, pp. 608–613 (2005)

[28] Senachak, J., Seino, T., Ogata, K., Futatsugi, K.: Provably Correct Translation from CafeOBJ into Java. In: SEKE 2005, pp. 614–619 (2005)

[29] Futatsugi, K., Goguen, J., Ogata, K.: Verifying Design with Proof Scores. In: Meyer, B., Woodcock, J. (eds.) VSTTE 2005. LNCS, vol. 4171, pp. 277–290. Springer, Heidelberg (2008)

[30] Seino, T., Ogata, K., Futatsugi, K.: Supporting Case Analysis with Algebraic Specification Languages. In: CIT 2004, pp. 1073–1080 (2004)

[31] Kong, W., Ogata, K., Xiang, J., Futatsugi, K.: Formal Analysis of an Anonymous Fair Exchange E-Commerce Protocol. In: CIT 2004, pp. 1100–1107 (2004)

[32] Xiang, J., Futatsugi, K., He, Y.: Fault Tree and Formal Methods in System Safety Analysis. In: CIT 2004, pp. 1108–1115 (2004)

[33] Xiang, J., Futatsugi, K., He, Y.: Formal fault tree construction and system safety analysis. In: IASTED Conf. on Software Engineering 2004, pp. 378–384 (2004)

[34] Xiang, J., Futatsugi, K., He, Y.: Formal construction model and specification of fault tree. In: IASTED Conf. on Software Engineering and Applications 2004, pp. 374–381 (2004)

[35] Sriharee, N., Senivongse, T., Teppaboot, C., Futatsugi, K.: Adding Semantics to Attribute-Based Discovery of Web Services. In: International Conference on Internet Computing 2004, pp. 790–794 (2004)

[36] Ogata, K., Yamagishi, D., Seino, T., Futatsugi, K.: Modeling and Verification of Hybrid Systems Based on Equations. In: DIPES 2004, pp. 43–52 (2004)

[37] Ogata, K., Futatsugi, K.: Equational Approach to Formal Verification of SET. In: QSIC 2004, pp. 50–59 (2004)

[38] Sawada, T., Kishida, K., Futatsugi, K.: Past, Present, and Future of SRA Implementation of CafeOBJ: Annex. In: Araki, K., Gnesi, S., Mandrioli, D. (eds.) FME 2003. LNCS, vol. 2805, pp. 7–17. Springer, Heidelberg (2003)

[39] Ogata, K., Futatsugi, K.: Proof Scores in the OTS/CafeOBJ Method. In: Najm, E., Nestmann, U., Stevens, P. (eds.) FMOODS 2003. LNCS, vol. 2884, pp. 170–184. Springer, Heidelberg (2003)

[40] Ogata, K., Futatsugi, K.: Formal Analysis of the NetBill Electronic Commerce Protocol. In: Futatsugi, K., Mizoguchi, F., Yonezaki, N. (eds.) ISSS 2003. LNCS, vol. 3233, pp. 45–64. Springer, Heidelberg (2004)

[41] Ogata, K., Futatsugi, K.: Formal Verification of the Horn-Preneel Micropayment Protocol. In: Zuck, L.D., Attie, P.C., Cortesi, A., Mukhopadhyay, S. (eds.) VMCAI 2003. LNCS, vol. 2575, pp. 238–252. Springer, Heidelberg (2002)

[42] Tapabut, C., Senivongse, T., Futatsugi, K.: Defining Attribute Templates for Descriptions of Distributed Services. In: APSEC 2002, pp. 425–434 (2002)

[43] Futatsugi, K.: Formal Methods in CafeOBJ. In: Hu, Z., Rodríguez-Artalejo, M. (eds.) FLOPS 2002. LNCS, vol. 2441, pp. 1–20. Springer, Heidelberg (2002)

[44] Ogata, K., Futatsugi, K.: Formal Analysis of Suzuki & Kasami Distributed Mutual Exclusion Algorithm. In: Jacobs, B., Rensink, A. (eds.) FMOODS V. IFIP, vol. 81, pp. 181–195. Springer, Heidelberg (2002)

[45] Hasebe, K., Okada, M.: Formal Analysis of the iKP Electronic Payment Protocols. In: Okada, M., Babu, C. S., Scedrov, A., Tokuda, H. (eds.) ISSS 2002. LNCS, vol. 2609, pp. 441–460. Springer, Heidelberg (2003)

[46] Mori, A., Futatsugi, K.: CafeOBJ as a Tool for Behavioral System Verification. In: Okada, M., Babu, C. S., Scedrov, A., Tokuda, H. (eds.) ISSS 2002. LNCS, vol. 2609, pp. 461–470. Springer, Heidelberg (2003)

[47] Ogata, K., Futatsugi, K.: Formally Modeling and Verifying Ricart&Agrawala Distributed Mutual Exclusion Algorithm. In: APAQS 2001, pp. 357–366 (2001)

[48] Ogata, K., Futatsugi, K.: Specifying and verifying a railroad crossing with CafeOBJ. In: IPDPS 2001, p. 150 (2001)

[49] Ogata, K., Futatsugi, K.: Modeling and Verification of Distributed Real-Time Systems Based on CafeOBJ. In: ASE 2001, pp. 185–192 (2001)

[50] Matsumoto, M., Futatsugi, K.: The support tool for highly reliable component-based software development. In: APSEC 2000, pp. 172–179 (2000)

[51] Matsumoto, M., Futatsugi, K.: Highly Reliable Component-Based Software Development by Using Algebraic Behavioral Specification. In: ICFEM 2000, pp. 35–44 (2000)

[52] Ogata, K., Futatsugi, K.: Operational Semantics of Rewriting with the On-demand Evaluation Strategy. In: SAC 2000, vol. (2), pp. 756–764 (2000)

[53] Matsumoto, M., Futatsugi, K.: Simply Observable Behavioral Specification. In: APSEC 1999, pp. 460–467 (1999)

[54] Ogata, K., Futatsugi, K.: Formal verification of the MCS list-based queuing lock. In: Thiagarajan, P.S., Yap, R.H.C. (eds.) ASIAN 1999. LNCS, vol. 1742, pp. 281–293. Springer, Heidelberg (1999)

[55] Mori, A., Futatsugi, K.: Verifying Behavioural Specifications in CafeOBJ Environment. In: Wing, J.M., Woodcock, J., Davies, J. (eds.) FM 1999. LNCS, vol. 1709, pp. 1625–1643. Springer, Heidelberg (1999)

[56] Diaconescu, R., Futatsugi, K., Iida, S.: Component-Based Algebraic Specification and Verification in CafeOBJ. In: Wing, J.M., Woodcock, J., Davies, J. (eds.) FM 1999. LNCS, vol. 1709, pp. 1644–1663. Springer, Heidelberg (1999)

[57] Ogata, K., Ioroi, S., Futatsugi, K.: Optimizing Term Rewriting Using Discrimination Nets With Specialization. In: SAC 1999, pp. 511–518 (1999)

[58] Ogata, K., Hirata, H., Ioroi, S., Futatsugi, K.: Experimental Implementation of Parallel TRAM on Massively Parallel Computer. In: Pritchard, D., Reeve, J.S. (eds.) Euro-Par 1998. LNCS, vol. 1470, pp. 846–851. Springer, Heidelberg (1998)

[59] Ishikawa, H., Watanabe, T., Futatsugi, K., Meseguer, J., Nakashima, H.: On the Semantics of GAEA. In: Fuji International Symposium on Functional and Logic Programming 1998, pp. 123–142 (1998)

[60] Ogata, K., Kondo, M., Ioroi, S., Futatsugi, K.: Design and Implementation of Parallel TRAM. In: Lengauer, C., Griebl, M., Gorlatch, S. (eds.) Euro-Par 1997. LNCS, vol. 1300, pp. 1209–1216. Springer, Heidelberg (1997)

[61] Futatsugi, K., Nakagawa, A.T.: An Overview of CAFE Specification Environment - An Algebraic Approach for Creating, Verifying, and Maintaining Formal Specifications over Networks. In: ICFEM 1997, pp. 170–181 (1997)

[62] Nakajima, S., Futatsugi, K.: An Object-Oriented Modeling Method for Algebraic Specifications in CafeOBJ. In: ICSE 1997, pp. 34–44 (1997)

[63] Ogata, K., Futatsugi, K.: Implementation of Term Rewritings with the Evaluation Strategy. In: PLILP 1997, pp. 225–239 (1997)

[64] Ogata, K., Ohhara, K., Futatsugi, K.: TRAM: An Abstract Machine for Order-Sorted Conditioned Term Rewriting Systems. In: RTA 1997, pp. 335–338 (1997)

[65] Nakagawa, A.T., Futatsugi, K.: Formalizing humans in software processes. In: ISPW 1994, pp. 60–61 (1994)

[66] Ohmaki, K., Takahashi, K., Futatsugi, K.: A LOTOS Simulator in OBJ. In: FORTE 1990, pp. 535–538 (1990)

[67] Futatsugi, K.: Trends in Formal Specification Methods Based on Algebraic Specification Techniques - From Abstract Data Types to Software Processes: A Personal Perspective. In: Proc. InfoJapan 1990: Information Technology Harmonizing with Society, IPSJ (Tokyo), pp. 59–66 (1990)

[68] Ohmaki, K., Futatsugi, K., Takahashi, K.: A Basic LOTOS Simulator in OBJ. In: Proc. InfoJapan 1990: Information Technology Harmonizing with Society, IPSJ (Tokyo), pp. 497–504 (1990)

[69] Nakagawa, A.T., Futatsugi, K.: Software Process à la Algebra: OBJ for OBJ. In: ICSE 1990, pp. 12–23 (1990)

[70] Futatsugi, K.: Product-centered process description = algebraic specification of environment + SCRIPT. In: ISPW 1990, pp. 95–98 (1990)

[71] Nakagawa, A.T., Futatsugi, K.: Stepwise Refinement Process with Modularity: An Algebraic Approach. In: ICSE 1989, pp. 166–177 (1989)

[72] Nakagawa, A.T., Futatsugi, K.: Product-based process models. In: ISPW 1989, pp. 101–105 (1989)

[73] Nakagawa, A.T., Futatsugi, K., Tomura, S., Shimizu, T.: Algebraic Specification of Macintosh's Quickdraw Using OBJ2. In: ICSE 1988, pp. 334–343 (1988)

[74] Futatsugi, K., Goguen, J.A., Meseguer, J., Okada, K.: Parameterized Programming in OBJ2. In: ICSE 1987, pp. 51–60 (1987)

[75] Futatsugi, K., Goguen, J.A., Jouannaud, J.-P., Meseguer, J.: Principles of OBJ2. In: POPL 1985, pp. 52–66 (1985)

[76] Futatsugi, K., Okada, K.: A Hierarchical Structuring Method for Functional Software Systems. In: ICSE 1982, pp. 393–402 (1982)

[77] Futatsugi, K., Okada, K.: Specification Writing as Construction of Hierarchically Structured Clusters of Operators. In: IFIP Congress 1980, pp. 287–292 (1980)

Book Chapters

[1] Diaconescu, R., Futatsugi, K., Iida, S.: CafeOBJ Jewels. In: Futatsugi, K., Nakagawa, A.T., Tamai, T. (eds.) CAFE: An Industrial-Strength Algebraic Formal Method, pp. 33–60. Elsevier B.V. (2000)

[2] Goguen, J.A., Winkler, T., Meseguer, J., Futatsugi, K., Jouannaud, J.-P.: Introducing OBJ. In: Goguen, J., Malcolm, G. (eds.) Software Engineering with OBJ, pp. 3–167. Springer (2000) ISBN: 978-1-4419-4965-3 (Print)

[3] Nakagawa, A.T., Futatsugi, K.: Constructing a Graphics System with OBJ2: A Practical Guide. In: Goguen, J., Malcolm, G. (eds.) Software Engineering with OBJ, pp. 193–247. Springer (2000) ISBN: 978-1-4419-4965-3 (Print)

[4] Ohmaki, K., Takahashi, K., Futatsugi, K.: A LOTOS Simulator in OBJ. In: Goguen, J., Malcolm, G. (eds.) Software Engineering with OBJ, pp. 363–392. Springer (2000) ISBN: 978-1-4419-4965-3 (Print)

[5] Diaconescu, R., Futatsugi, K., Iida, S.: Component-based Algebraic Specification and Verification in CafeOBJ. In: Futatsugi, K., Goguen, J., Meseguer, J. (eds.) OBJ/CafeOBJ/Maude at Formal Methods 1999, pp. 17–33. THETA, Bucharest (1999) ISBN 973-99097-1-X

[6] Kuruma, H., Futatsugi, K.: Incremental Specification Based on the Combination of Data and Types. In: Futatsugi, K., Goguen, J., Meseguer, J. (eds.) OBJ/CafeOBJ/Maude at Formal Methods 1999, pp. 95–114. THETA, Bucharest (1999) ISBN 973-99097-1-X

[7] Matsumoto, M., Futatsugi, K.: Object Compositions and Refinement by using Non-Observable Projection Operators: A Case Study of the Automated Teller Machine system. In: Futatsugi, K., Goguen, J., Meseguer, J. (eds.) OBJ/CafeOBJ/Maude at Formal Methods 1999, pp. 133–157. THETA, Bucharest (1999) ISBN 973-99097-1-X

[8] Ogata, K., Futatsugi, K.: Specification and Verification of Some Classical Mutual Exclusion Algorithm with CafeOBJ. In: Futatsugi, K., Goguen, J., Meseguer, J. (eds.) OBJ/CafeOBJ/Maude at Formal Methods 1999, pp. 159–177. THETA, Bucharest (1999) ISBN 973-99097-1-X

[9] Ishikawa, H., Futatsugi, K., Watanabe, T.: An Operational Semantics of GAEA in CafeOBJ. In: Futatsugi, K., Goguen, J., Meseguer, J. (eds.) OBJ/CafeOBJ/Maude at Formal Methods 1999, pp. 213–225. THETA, Bucharest (1999) ISBN 973-99097-1-X

[10] Matsumiya, C., Iida, S., Futatsugi, K.: A Component-based Algebraic Specification of ODP Trading Function and the Interactive Browsing Environment. In: Futatsugi, K., Goguen, J., Meseguer, J. (eds.) OBJ/CafeOBJ/Maude at Formal Methods 1999, pp. 227–241. THETA, Bucharest (September 1999) ISBN 973-99097-1-X

[11] Futatsugi, K.: Hierarchical Software Development in HISP. In: Kitagawa, T. (ed.) Computer Science and Technologies 1982. Japan Annual Review in Electronics, Computers and Telecommunications Series, pp. 151–174. OHMSHA, Tokyo and North-Holland, Amsterdam (1982)

Table of Contents

Domain Endurants

An Analysis and Description Process Model

Dines Bjørner

Fredsvej 11, DK-2840 Holte, Danmark
DTU, DK-2800 Kgs. Lyngby, Denmark
bjorner@gmail.com
www.imm.dtu.dk/~dibj

Laudatio

Futatsugi says he's known me since the IFIP World Gongress in Tokyo, Japan, September 1980. I can certainly and clearly remember having met Kokichi in the late Joseph Goguen's SRI office in July 1984. He was there; so was José Meseguer and Jean-Pierre Jouannaud. They were **clear**ly onto something, **OBJ**ectively speaking, very exciting! Nothing really "destined" us for one another. Kokichi was into algebraic specifications and I into model-oriented ones. Mathematicians versus engineers — some would say. Well, the RAISE, [25], specification language RSL, [24], does "mix" traditional model-oriented expressivity with sorts, observers and axioms — borrowed very specifically from early work on **OBJ** [27]. So maybe we were destined. At least I have enjoyed, tremendously, our acquaintance. Had we lived closer, geographically, I might even have been able to claim the kind of friendship that survives sitting together, not saying a word, for hours. That's not difficult in our case: Kokichi has his mother tongue, hopelessly isolated out here, in the Far East, and I have my mother tongue, hopelessly isolated back here! Kokichi and his work has become an institution [26]. First ETL and then JAIST became firmly implanted in the universe of the communities of algebraic semantics and formal specification scientists. Not many Japanese computer scientists have become so well-known abroad as has Kokichi. One thing that has paved the way for this is Kokichi's personality. A Japanese at ease also in the Western World. Westerners being so very kindly accepted and welcome by Kokichi and his colleagues here in the beautiful, enigmatic Land of the Rising Sun. One thing I always do complain about when seeing Kokichi in my world is that he should bring his wife, charming Junko, there more often — well every time! So, Kokichi, thanks for your scientific contributions; thanks for your being a fine Doctors Father; thanks for hosting one of my former students, Dr. Anne Elisabeth Haxthausen for half a year at ETL; thanks for hosting me here at JAIST for a whole year, 2006; and thanks for helping us "barbarian" Westerners getting to love Japan and all things Japanese.

Abstract: We present a summary, Sect. 2, of a structure of domain analysis and description concepts: techniques and tools. And we link, in Sect. 3, these concepts, embodied in *domain analysis prompts* and *domain description prompts*, in a model of how a diligent domain analyser cum describer would use them. We claim that both sections, Sects. 2–3, contribute to a methodology of software engineering.

S. Iida, J. Meseguer, and K. Ogata (Eds.): Futatsugi Festschrift, LNCS 8373, pp. 1–34, 2014.
© Springer-Verlag Berlin Heidelberg 2014

1 Introduction

A Context for Domains: Before software can be designed we must have a reasonably good grasp of its requirements. Before requirements can be prescribed we must have a reasonably good grasp of the domain in which the software is to reside. So we turn to domain analysis & description as a means to obtain and record that 'grasp'. In this paper we summarise an approach to domain analysis & description recorded in more detail in [12]. Thus this paper is based on [12].

Related Papers: This paper is one in a series of papers on domain science & engineering. In [6] we present techniques related to the analysis and description of domain facets. In [4] we investigate some research issues of domain science. The paper [13] examines possible contributions of domain science & engineering to *computation for the humanities*. It is expected that the present paper may be followed by respective ("spin-off") papers on *Perdurants* [10], *A Formal Model of Prompts* [11], *Domain Facets* (cf. [6]) [9], and *On Deriving Requirements From Domain Descriptions* (cf. [5]) [14].

A `TripTych` of Software Engineering: The first 3+ lines above suggest an "idealised", the `TripTych`, approach to software development: first a phase of domain engineering in which is built a domain model; then a phase of requirements engineering in which is built a requirements model; and finally a phase of software design in which the code is developed. We show in [5] how to systematically "transform" domain descriptions into requirements prescriptions.

Structure of this Paper: The structure of this paper is as follows: First, in Sect. 2 we present a terse summary of a system of domain analysis & description concepts focused on endurants. This summary is rather terse, and is a *"tour de force"*. Section 2 is one of the two main sections of this paper. Section 3 suggests a formal-looking model of the structure of *domain analysis prompts* and *domain description prompts* introduced in Sect. 2. It is not a formalisation of domains, but of the domain analysis & description process. Domains are usually not computationally tractable. Less so is the domain analysis & description processes. Finally, Sect. 4 concludes this paper. An appendix, Appendix A, presents a domain description of a [class of] *pipeline systems*. Some seminars over the underlying paper may start by a brief presentation of this model. The reader is invited to browse this *pipeline system* model before, during and/or after reading Sects. 2–3.

2 The Domain Analysis Approach

2.1 Hierarchical versus Compositional Analysis and Description

In this paper we choose, what we shall call, a 'hierarchical analysis' approach which is based on decomposing an understanding of a domain from the "overall domain" into its components, and these, if not atomic, into their sub-components • In contrast we could have chosen a 'compositional analysis' approach which starts with an understanding of a domain from its atomic endurants and composes these into composite ones, finally ending up with an "overall domain" description •

2.2 Domains

A 'domain' is characterised by its observable, i.e., manifest *entities* and their *qualities* • [1] *Example 1*. Domains: *a road net, a container line, a pipeline, a hospital*■ [2]

2.3 Sorts, Types and Domain Analysis

By a 'sort' (or 'type' which we take to be the same) we shall understand the largest set of entities all of which have the same qualities[3] • *Example 2*. Sorts: Links of any road net constitute a sort. So does hubs. The largest set of (well-formed) collections of links constitute a sort. So does similar collections of hubs. The largest set of road nets (containing well-formed collections of hubs and links) form a sort■

By 'domain analysis' we shall understand a process whereby a domain analyser groups entities of a domain into sorts (and types) • The rest of this paper will outline a class of domain analysis principles, techniques and tools.

2.4 Entities and Qualities

Entities: By an 'entity' we shall understand a phenomenon that can be observed, i.e., be seen or touched[4] by humans, or that can be conceived as an abstraction of an entity[5] • The method can thus be said to provide the *domain analysis prompt*: is_entity where is_entity(θ) holds if θ is an entity. *Example 3*. Entities: *(a) a road net, (b) a link[6] of a road net, (c) a hub[7] of a road net;* and *(d) insertion of a link in a road net, (e) disappearance of a link of a road net,* and *(f) the movement of a vehicle on a road net*■

---

[1] Definitions start with a single quoted 'term' and conclude with a •

[2] Examples conclude with a ■

[3] Taking a sort (type) to be *the largest set of entities all of which have the same qualities* reflects Ganter & Wille's notion of a 'formal concept' [23].

[4] An entity which can be seen or touched is thus a physical phenomenon. If an entity has the quality the colour red, it is not the red that is an entity.

[5] There is no "infinite loop" here: a concept can be an abstraction of (another) concept, etc., which is finally an abstraction of a physical phenomenon.

[6] A link: a street segment between two adjacent hubs.

[7] A hub: an intersection of street segments.

Qualities: By a 'quality' of an entity we shall understand a property that can be given a name and precisely measured by physical instruments or otherwise identified • *Example 4*. Quality Names: *cadestral location of a hub, hub state*[8], *hub state space*[9], etcetera■ *Example 5*. Quality Values: *the name of a road net, the ownership of a road net, the length of a link, the location of a hub*, etcetera■

2.5   Endurants and Perdurants

Entities are either endurants or are perdurants.

Endurants: By an 'endurant entity' (or just, an endurant) we shall understand that can be observed or conceived, as a "complete thing", at no matter which given snapshot of time. Were we to "freeze" time we would still be able to observe the entire endurant • Thus the method provides a *domain analysis prompt*: is_endurant where is_endurant(e) holds if entity e is an endurant. *Example 6*. Endurants: Items (a–b–c) of Example 2.4 are endurants; so are the pipes, valves, and pumps of a pipeline.

Perdurants: By a 'perdurant entity' (or just, an perdurant) we shall understand an entity for which only a fragment exists if we look at or touch them at any given snapshot in time, that is, were we to freeze time we would only see or touch a fragment of the perdurant • Thus the method provides a *domain analysis prompt*: is_perdurant where is_perdurant(e) holds if entity e is a perdurant. *Example 7*. Perdurants: Items (d–e–f) of Example 2.4 are perdurants; so are the insertion of a hub, removal of a link, etcetera■

2.6   Discrete and Continuous Endurants

Entities are either discrete or are continuous.

Discrete Endurants: By a 'discrete endurant' we shall understand something which is separate or distinct in form or concept, consisting of distinct or separate parts • We use the term 'part' for discrete endurants, that is: is_part(p)≡ is_endurant(p)∧is_discrete(p) • Thus the method provides a *domain analysis prompt*: is_discrete where is_discrete(e) holds if entity e is discrete. *Example 8*. Discrete Endurants: The examples of Example 2.5 are all discrete endurants■

Continuous Endurants: By a 'continuous endurant' we shall understand something which is prolonged without interruption, in an unbroken series or pattern • We use the term 'material' for continuous endurants • Thus the method provides a *domain analysis prompt*: is_continuous where is_continuous(e) holds if entity e is continuous. *Example 9*. Continuous Endurants: The pipes, valves, pumps,

---

[8] From which links can one reach which links at a given time.

[9] Set of all hub states over time.

etc., of Example 2.5 may contain oil; water of a hydro electric power plant is also a material (i.e., a continuous endurant) ∎

2.7   Discrete and Continuous Perdurants

We are not covering perdurants in this paper.

2.8   Atomic and Composite Discrete Endurants

Discrete endurants are either atomic or are composite.

Atomic Endurants: By an 'atomic endurant' we shall understand a discrete endurant which in a given context, is deemed to *not* consist of meaningful, separately observable proper sub-parts ● The method can thus be said to provide the *domain analysis prompt*: is_atomic where is_atomic(p) holds if p is an atomic part. *Example 10.* Atomic Parts: Examples of atomic parts of the above mentioned domains are: aircraft (of air traffic), demand/deposit accounts (of banks), containers (of container lines), documents (of document systems), hubs, links and vehicles (of road traffic), patients, medical staff and beds (of hospitals), pipes, valves and pumps (of pipeline systems), and rail units and locomotives (of railway systems) ∎

Composite Endurants: By a 'composite endurant' we shall understand a discrete endurant which in a given context, is deemed to *indeed* consist of meaningful, separately observable proper sub-parts ● The method can thus be said to provide the *domain analysis prompt*: is_composite where is_composite(p) holds if p is an a composite part. *Example 11.* Composite Parts: Examples of composite parts of the above mentioned domains are: airports and air lanes (of air traffic), banks (of a financial service industry), container vessels (of container lines), dossiers of documents (of document systems), routes (of road nets), medical wards (of hospitals), pipelines (of pipeline systems), and trains, rail lines and train stations (of railway systems) ∎

It is the domain analysers who decide whether an endurant is atomic or composite. In the context of air traffic an aircraft might very well be described as an atomic entity; whereas in the context of an airline an aircraft might very well be described as a composite entity consisting of the aircraft 'body', the crew, the passengers, their luggage, the fuel, etc.

2.9   Part Observers

From atomic parts we cannot observe any sub-parts. But from composite parts we can.

Composite Sorts: For composite parts, p, the *domain description prompt*

observe_part_sorts(p)

yields some *formal description text* according to the following *schema*:

type P_1, P_2, ..., P_n;[10]
value obs_P_1: $P \rightarrow P_1$, **obs_P_2**: $P \rightarrow P_2$,...,**obs_P_n**: $P \rightarrow P_n$;[11]

where sorts P_1, P_2, ..., P_n must be disjoint. A proof obligation may need be discharged to secure disjointness.

Sort Models: A part sort is an abstract type. Some part sorts, P, may have a concrete type model, T. Here we consider only two such models: one model is as sets of parts of sort A: T = A-**set**; the other model has parts being of either of two or more alternative, disjoint sorts: T=P1|P2|...|PN. The *domain analysis prompt*: has_concrete_type(p) holds if part p has a concrete type. In this case the *domain description prompt*

observe_concrete_type(p)

yields some *formal description text* according to the following *schema*,

* either
      type   P1, P2, ..., PN, T = $\mathcal{E}$(P1,P2,...,PN)[12]
      value obs_T: P $\rightarrow$ T[13]

  where $\mathcal{E}$(...) is some type expression over part sorts and where P1,P2,...,PN are either (new) part sorts or are auxiliary (abstract or concrete) types[14];
* or:
      type
          T = P1 | P2 | ... | PN[15]
          P_1, P_2, ..., P_n
          P1 :: mkP1(P_1), P2 :: mkP2(P_2), ..., PN :: mkPN(P) [16]
      value
          obs_T: P $\rightarrow$ T[17]

---

[10] This RSL **type** clause defines P_1, P_2, ..., P_n to be types.

[11] Thus RSL **value** clause defines n function values. All from type P into some type P_i.

[12] The concrete type definition T = $\mathcal{E}$(P1,P2,...,PN) define type T to be the set of elements of the type expressed by type expression $\mathcal{E}$(P1,P2,...,PN).

[13] **obs_T** is a function from any element of P to some element of T.

[14] The *domain analysis prompt*: sorts_of(t) yields a subset of {P1,P2,...,PN}.

[15] A|B is the union type of types A and B.

[16] Type definition A :: mkA(B) defines type A to be the set of elements mkA(b) where b is any element of type B.

[17] **obs_T** is a function from any element of P to some element of T.

2.10   Material Observers

Some parts p of sort P may contain material. The *domain analysis prompt* has_material(p) holds if composite part p contains one or more materials. The *domain description prompt*

observe_material_sorts(p)

yields some *formal description text* according to the following *schema*:

type M_1, M_2, ..., M_m;
value obs_M_1: P → M_1, **obs_M_2**: P → M_2, ..., **obs_M_m**: P → M_m;

where values, m_i, of type M_i satisfy is_material(m) for all i; and where M_1, M_2, ..., M_m must be disjoint sorts. *Example 12*. Part Materials: The pipeline parts p pipes, valves, pumps, etc., contains some either liquid material, say crude oil. or gaseous material, say natural gas∎

Some material m of sort M may contain parts. The *domain analysis prompt* has_parts(m) holds if material m contains one or more parts. The *domain description prompt*

observe_part_sorts(m)

yields some *formal description text* according to the following *schema*:

type P_1, P_2, ..., P_n;
value obs_P_1: M→P_1, **obs_P_2**: M→P_2,...,**obs_P_m**: M→P_m;

where values, p_i, of type P_i satisfy is_part(p_i) for all i; and where P_1, P_2, ..., P_n must be disjoint sorts. *Example 13*. Material and Part Relations: A global transport system can, for example, be described as primarily containing navigable waters, land areas and air — as three major collections of parts. Navigable waters contain a number of "neighbouring" oceans, channels, canals, rivers and lakes reachable by canals or rivers from other navigable waters (all of which are parts). The part sorts of navigable waters has water materials. All water materials has (zero or more) parts such as vessels and sea-ports. Land areas contain continents, some of which are neighbouring (parts), while some are isolated (that is, being islands not "border–"connected to other continents). Some land areas contain harbour. Harbours and seaports are overlapping parts sharing many attributes. And harbours and seaports are connected to road and rail nets. Etcetera, etcetera∎ The above example, Example 2.10, help motivate the concept of mereology (see below).

2.11   Endurant Properties

External and Internal Qualities: We have already, above, treated the following properties of endurants: is_discrete, is_continuous, is_atomic, is_composite and has_material. We may think of those properties as external qualities. In contrast we may consider the following internal qualities: has_unique_identifier (parts), has_mereology (parts) and has_attributes (parts and materials).

2.12   Unique Identifiers

Without loss of generality we can assume that every part has a unique identifier[18]. A 'unique part identifier' (or just unique identifier) is a further undefined, abstract quantity. If two parts are claimed to have the same unique identifier then they are identical, that is, their possible mereology and attributes are (also) identical • The *domain description prompt*:

   observe_unique_identifier(p)

yields some *formal description text* according to the following *schema*:

   type PI;
   value uid_P: P → PI;

Example 14. Unique Identifiers: A road net consists of a set of hubs and a set of links. Hubs and links have unique identifiers. That is: **type** HI, LI; **value uid_H**: H→HI, **uid_L**: L→LI; ∎

2.13   Mereology

By 'mereology' [35] we shall understand the study, knowledge and practice of parts, their relations to other parts and "the whole" •

   Part relations are such as: two or more parts being connected, one part being embedded within another part, and two or more parts sharing (other) attributes. *Example 15.* Mereology: The mereology of a link of a road net is the set of the two unique identifiers of exactly two hubs to which the link is connected. The mereology of a hub of a road net is the set of zero or more unique identifiers of the links to which the hub is connected∎ The *domain analysis prompt*: has_mereology(p) holds if the part p is related to some others parts $(p_a, p_b, \ldots, p_c)$. The *domain description prompt*:

   observe_mereology(p)

can then be invoked and yields some *formal description text* according to the following *schema*:

   type MT = $\mathcal{E}$(PI$_A$,PI$_B$,...,PI$_C$);
   value mereo_P: P → MT;

where $\mathcal{E}(\ldots)$ is some type expression over unique identifier types of one or more part sorts. Mereologies are expressed in terms of structures of unique part identifiers. Usually mereologies are constrained. Constraints express that a mereology's unique part identifiers must indeed reference existing parts, but also that these mereology identifiers "define" a proper structuring of parts. *Example 16.* Mereology Constraints: We continue our line of examples of road net endurants, cf. Example 2.4 but now a bit more systematically: A road net, n:N, contains

---

[18] That is, has_unique_identifier(p) for all parts p.

a pair, (HS,LS), of sets Hs of hubs h:H and sets Ls of links. The mereology of links must identify exactly two hubs of the road net, the mereology of hubs must identify links of the road net, so connected hubs and links must have commensurate mereologies■ Two parts, $p_i:P_i$ and $p_j:P_j$, of possibly the same sort (i.e., $P_i \equiv P_j$) are said to 'refer one to another' if the mereology of p_i contains the unique identifier of p_j and vice-versa● The parts p_i and p_j are then said to enjoy 'part overlap' ● We refer to the concept of shared attributes covered at the very end of this section.

2.14   Attributes

Attributes are what really endows parts with qualities. The external properties[19] are far from enough to distinguish one sort of parts from another. Similarly with unique identifiers and the mereology of parts. We therefore assume, without loss of generality, that every part, whether discrete or continuous, whether, when discrete, atomic or composite, has at least one attributes.

By a 'part attribute', or just an 'attribute', we shall understand a property that is associated with a part p of sort P, and if removed from part p, that part would no longer be part p but may be a part of some other sort P'; and where that property itself has no physical extent (i.e., volume), as the part may have, but may be measurable by physical means ● *Example 17.* Attributes: Some attributes of road net hubs are location, hub state[20], hub state space[21], and of road net links are location, length, link state[22], link state space[23], etcetera■ The *domain description prompt*

```
observe_attributes(p)
```

yields some *formal description text* according to the following *schema*:

> **type** A_1, A_2, ..., A_n, ATTR;
> **value attr_**A_1:P→A_1, **attr_**A_2:P→A_2, ..., **attr_**A_n:P→A_n,
>   **attr_ATTR**:P→ATTR;

where **for** $\forall$ p:P, **attr_**A_i(**attr_ATTR**(p)) $\equiv$ **attr_**A_i(p).

Shared Attributes: A final quality of endurant entities is that they may share attributes. Two parts, $p_i:P_i, p_j:P_j$, of different sorts are said to enjoy 'shared attributes' if P_i and P_j have at least one attribute name in common● In such cases the mereologies of p_i and p_j are expected to refer to one another, i.e., be 'commensurable'.

---

[19] `is_discrete,is_continuous,is_atomic,is_compositehas_material`.
[20] Hub state: a set of pairs of unique identifiers of actually connected links.
[21] Hub state space: a set of hub states that a hub states may range over.
[22] Link state: a set of pairs of unique identifiers of actually connected hubs.
[23] Link state space: a set of link states that a link state may range over.

3 A Model of the Analysis and Description Process

3.1 A Summary of Prompts

In the previous section we outlined two classes of prompts: the domain [endurant] analysis prompts:[24]

a. is_entity
b. is_endurant
c. is_perdurant
d. is_part
e. is_discrete
f. is_continuous
g. is_atomic
h. is_composite

i. has_concrete_type
j. sorts_of
k. has_material
l. has_parts
m. has_unique_ identifier
n. has_mereology
o. has_attributes

and the domain [endurant] description prompts:

1. observe_part_sorts
2. observe_concrete_type
3. observe_material_sorts

4. observe_unique_identifier
5. observe_mereology
6. observe_attributes

These prompts are imposed upon the domain analyser cum describer. They are "figuratively" applied to the domain. Their orderly, sequenced application follows the method hinted at in the previous section and expressed in a pseudo-formal notation in this section. The notation looks formal but since we have not formalised these prompts it is only pseudo-formal. In [11] we shall formalise these prompts.

3.2 Preliminaries

Let P be a sort, that is, a collection of endurants. By ηP we shall understand a syntactic quantity: the name of P. By ιp:P we shall understand the semantic quantity: an (arbitrarily selected) endurant in P. And by $\eta^{-1}\eta$P we shall understand P. To guide the TripTych domain analysis & description process we decompose it into steps. Each step "handles" a sort p:P or a material m:M. Steps handling discovery of composite sorts generate a set of sort names ηP$_1$, ηP$_2$, ..., ηP$_n$ and ηM$_1$, ηM$_2$, ..., ηM$_n$. These are put in a reservoir for sorts to be inspected. The handled sort ηP or ηM is removed from that reservoir. Handling of material sorts concerns only their attributes. Each domain description prompt results in domain specification text (here we show only the formal texts) being deposited in the domain description reservoir, a global variable τ. The clause: domain_description_prompt(p) : τ := $\tau \oplus$ ["text ; "] means that the formal

---

[24] The prompts are sorted in order of appeareance. The one or two digits following the prompt names refer to page numbers minus the number of the first page of this paper + 1.

text "text ; " is joined to the global variable τ where that "text ; " is prompted by `domain_description_prompt(p)`. The meaning of $\oplus$ will be discussed at the end of this section.

3.3 Initialising the Domain Analysis and Description Process

We remind the reader that we are dealing only with endurant domain entities. The domain analysis approach covered in Sect. 2 was based on decomposing an understanding of a domain from the "overall domain" into its components, and these, if not atomic, into their subcomponents. So we need to initialise the domain analysis & description by selecting (or choosing) the domain Δ.

Here is how we think of that "initialisation" process. The domain analyser & describer spends some time focusing on the domain, maybe at the "white board"[25], rambling, perhaps in an un-structured manner, across its domain, Δ, and its subdomains. Informally jotting down more-or-less final sort names, building, in the domain analysers' & describers' mind an image of that domain. After some time, doing this, the domain analyser & describer is ready. An image of the domain is in the form of "a domain" endurant, $\delta{:}\Delta$. Those are the quantities, $\eta\Delta$ (name of Δ) [Item 1] and ιp:P (for $(\delta{:}\Delta)$) [Item 8], referred to below.

Thus this initialisation process is truly a creative one.

3.4 A Domain Analysis and Description State

1. A global variable αps will accumulate all the sort names being discovered.
2. A global variable νps will hold names of sorts yet to be analysed and described.
3. A global variable τ will hold the (so far) generated (in this case only) formal domain description text.

variable
1. αps $:= [\eta\Delta]$ ηP-set or ηP*
2. νps $:= [\eta\Delta]$ $(\eta$P$|\eta$M)-set or $(\eta$P$|\eta$M)*
3. $\tau := []$ **Text-set** or **Text***

We shall explain the use of [...]s and the operations of $\backslash$ and $\oplus$ on the above variables in Sect. 3.6.

3.5 Analysis and Description of Endurants

4. To analyse and describe endurants means to first
5. examine those endurant which have yet to be so analysed and described
6. by selecting and removing from νps (Item 11.) an as yet unexamined sort (by name);

---

[25] Here 'white board' is a conceptual notion. It could be physical, it could be yellow "post-it" stickers, or it could be an electronic conference "gadget".

7. then analyse and describe an endurant entity (ιp:P) of that sort — this analysis, when applied to composite parts, leads to the insertion of zero[26] or more sort names[27];
8. then to analyse and describe the mereology of each part sort,
9. and finally to analyse and describe the attributes of each sort.

value

4. analyse_and_describe_endurants: **Unit** $\rightarrow$ **Unit**
4. analyse_and_describe_endurants() $\equiv$
5. **while** $\sim$is_empty(νps) **do**
6. **let** ηS = select_and_remove_ηS() **in**
7. analyse_and_describe_endurant_sort(ιs:S) **end end** ;
8. **for all** ηP • ηP $\in \alpha$ps **do** analyse_and_describe_mereology(ιp:P) **end**
9. **for all** ηP • ηP $\in \alpha$ps **do** analyse_and_describe_attributes(ιp:P) **end**

The ι of Items 7, 8 and 9 are crucial. The domain analyser is focused on sort S (and P) and is "directed" (by those items) to choose (select) an endurant ιs (ιp) of that sort. The ability of the domain analyser to find such an entity is a measure of that person's professional creativity.

As was indicated in Sect. 2, the mereology of a part may involve unique identifiers of any part sort, hence must be done after all such part sort unique identifiers have been identified. Similarly for attributes which also may involve unique identifiers. Each iteration of analyse_and_describe_endurant_sort(ιp:P) involves the selection of a sort (by name) (which is that of either a part sort or a material sort) with this sort name then being removed.

10. The selection occurs from the global state (hence: ()) and changes that (hence **Unit**).
11. The affected global state component is that of the reservoir, νps.

value

10. select_and_remove_ηS: **Unit** $\rightarrow \eta$P
10. select_and_remove_ηS() $\equiv$
11. **let** ηS • ηS $\in \nu$ps **in** νps := νps $\setminus \{\eta$S$\}$; ηS **end**

The analysis and description of all sorts also performs an analysis and description of their possible unique identifiers (if part sorts) and attributes. The analysis and description of sort mereologies potentially requires the unique identifiers of any set of sorts. Therefore the analysis and description of sort mereologies follows that of analysis and description of all sorts.

12. To analyse and describe an endurant

---

[26] If the sub-parts of p are all either atomic or already analysed, then no new sort names are added to the repository νps.

[27] These new sort names are then "picked-up" for sort analysis &c. in a next iteration of the while loop.

13. is to find out whether it is a part.
14. If so then it is to analyse and describe it as a part,
15. else it is to analyse and describe it as a material.

12. analyse_and_describe_endurant_sort: $(P|M) \rightarrow$ **Unit**
12. analyse_and_describe_endurant_sort(e:(P|M)) $\equiv$
13.   **if** is_part(e)
13.   **assert:** is_part(e) $\equiv$ is_endurant(e)$\wedge$is_discrete(e)
14.   **then** analyse_and_describe_part_sort(e:P)
15.   **else** analyse_and_describe_material_parts(e:M)
12.   **end**

Analysis and Description of Part Sorts:

16. The analysis and description of a part sort
17. is based on there being a set, ps, of parts[28] to analyse —
18. of which an archetypal one, p$'$, is arbitrarily selected.
19. analyse and describe part p$'$

16. analyse_and_describe_part_sort: $P \rightarrow$ **Unit**
16. analyse_and_describe_part_sort(p:P) $\equiv$
17.   **let** ps = observe_parts(p) **in**
18.   **let** p$'$:P $\bullet$ p$'$ $\in$ ps **in**
19.   analyse_and_describe_part(p$'$)
16.   **end end**

20. The analysis (&c.) of a part
21. first analyses and describes its unique identifiers.
22. If atomic
23. and
24. if the part embodies materials,
25. we analyse and describe these.
26. If not atomic then the part is composite
27. and is analysed and described as such.

20. analyse_and_describe_part: $P \rightarrow$ **Unit**
20. analyse_and_describe_part(p) $\equiv$
21.   analyse_and_describe_unique_identifier(p) ;
22.   **if** is_atomic(p)
23.   **then**

---

[28] We can assume that there is at least one element of that set. For the case that the sort being analysed is a domain Δ, say *"The Transport Domain"*, p$'$ is some representative *"transport domain"* δ. Similarly for any other sort for which ps is now one of the sorts of δ.

24.   **if** has_materials(p)
25.   **then** analyse_and_describe_part_materials(p) **end**
26.   **else assert:** is_composite(p)
27.   analyse_and_describe_composite_endurant(p) **end**
20.   **pre:** is_discrete(p)

We do not associate materials with composite parts.

Analysis and Description of Part Materials:

28. The analysis and description of the material part sorts, one or more, of atomic parts p of sort P containing such materials,
29. simply observes the material sorts of p,
30. that is, generates the one or more continuous endurants
31. and the corresponding observer function text.
32. The reservoir of sorts to be inspected is augmented by the material sorts — except if already previously entered (the $\setminus$ αps clause).

28.   analyse_and_describe_part_materials: P $\rightarrow$ **Unit**
28.   analyse_and_describe_part_materials(p) $\equiv$
29.   observe_material_sorts(p) :
30. $\tau := \tau \oplus [\,$"**type** $M_1,M_2,...,M_m$;
31.   **value obs_M_1:P$\rightarrow M_1$,obs_M_2:P$\rightarrow M_2$,...,obs_M_m:P$\rightarrow M_m$;**"$\,]$
32. νps := νps $\oplus$ ($[\, M_1,M_2,...,M_m \,] \setminus \alpha$ps)
28.   **pre:** has_materials(p)

Analysis and Description of Material Parts:

33. To analyse and describe materials, m, i.e., continuous endurants,
34. is only necessary if m has parts.
35. Then we observe the sorts of these parts.
36. The identified part sort names update both name reservoirs.

33.   analyse_and_describe_material_parts: M $\rightarrow$ **Unit**
33.   analyse_and_describe_material_parts(m:M) $\equiv$
34.   **if** has_parts(m)
35.   **then** observe_part_sorts(m):
35. $\tau := \tau \oplus [\,$" **type**   P1,P2,...,PN ;
35.   **value** obs_Pi: M$\rightarrow$Pi i:{1..N};"$\,]$
36. $\|$ νps := νps $\oplus$ ($[\, \eta$P1,ηP2,...,ηPN $]\setminus \alpha$ps)
36. $\|$ αps := αps $\oplus [\, \eta$P1,ηP2,...,ηPN $]$
33.   **end**
33.   **assert:** is_continuous(m)

Analysis and Description of Composite Endurants:

37. To analyse and describe a composite endurant of sort P
38. is to analyse and describe the unique identifier of that composite endurant,
39. then to analyse and describe the sort. If the sort has a concrete type
40. then we analyse and describe that concrete sort type
41. else we analyse and describe the abstract sort.

37. analyse_and_describe_composite_endurant: P → **Unit**
37. analyse_and_describe_composite_endurant(p) ≡
38.   analyse_and_describe_unique_identifier(p) ;
39. **if** has_concrete_type(p)
40.   **then** analyse_and_describe_concrete_sort(p)
41.   **else** analyse_and_describe_abstract_sort(p)
39. **end**

Analysis and Description of Concrete Sort Types:

42. The concrete sort type being analysed and described
43. is either
44. expressible by some compound type expression
43. or is
45. expressible by some alternative type expression.

42. analyse_and_describe_concrete_sort: P → **Unit**
42. analyse_and_describe_concrete_sort(p:P) ≡
44.   analyse_and_describe_concrete_compound_type(p)
43.   ⌷
45.   analyse_and_describe_concrete_alternative_type(p)
42.   **pre**: has_concrete_type(p)

46. The concrete compound sort type
47. is expressible by some simple type expression, $T=\mathcal{E}(Q,R,...,S)$ over either concrete types or existing or new sorts Q, R, ..., S.
48. The emerging sort types are identified
49. and assigned to both νps
50. and αps.

44. analyse_and_describe_concrete_compound_type: P → **Unit**
44. analyse_and_describe_concrete_compound_type(p:P) ≡
46.   observe_part_type(p):
46. $\tau := \tau \oplus$ [″**type** Q,R,..,S, T = $\mathcal{E}$(Q,R,...,S);
46.   **value obs_T**: P → T ;″] ;
47.   **let** $\{P_a, P_b,...,P_c\}$ = sorts_of($\{Q,R,...,S\}$)
48.   **assert**: $\{P_a, P_b,...,P_c\} \subseteq \{Q,R,...,S\}$ **in**
49. νps := νps $\oplus$ [$\eta P_a, \eta P_b, ..., \eta P_c$] ∥
50. αps := αps $\oplus$ ([$\eta P_a, \eta P_b, ..., \eta P_c$] \ αps) **end**
44.   **pre**: has_concrete_type(p)

51. The concrete alternative sort type expression
52. is expressible by an alternative type expression T=P1|P2|...|PN where each
    of the alternative types is made disjoint wrt. existing types by means of the
    description language Pi::mkPi(s_u:P_i) construction.
53. The emerging sort types are identified and assigned
54. to both νps
55. and αps.

45. analyse_and_describe_concrete_alternative_type: P → **Unit**
45. analyse_and_describe_concrete_alternative_type(p:P) ≡
51.   observe_part_type(p):
52. τ := τ ⊕ ["**type** T=P1 | P2 | ... | PN, Pi::mkPi(s_u:P_i) (1≤i≤N);
52.   **value obs_T**: P→T ;"] ;
53.   **let** {P_a,P_b,...,P_c} = sorts_of({P_i|1≤i≤n})
53.   **assert**: {P_a,P_b,...,P_c} ⊆ {P_i|1≤i≤n} **in**
54. νps := νps ⊕ ([ηP_a, ηP_b, ..., ηP_c] \ αps) ||
55. αps := αps ⊕ [ηP_a, ηP_b, ..., ηP_c] **end**
42.   **pre**: has_concrete_type(p)

Analysis and Description of Abstract Sorts:

56. To analyse and describe an abstract sort
57. amounts to observe part sorts and to
58. update the sort name repositories.

56. analyse_and_describe_abstract_sort: P → **Unit**
56. analyse_and_describe_abstract_sort(p:P) ≡
57.   observe_part_sorts(p):
57. τ := τ ⊕ ["**type** P_1, P_2, ..., P_n;
57.   **value obs_**P_i:P→P_i (0≤i≤n);"]
58. || νps := νps ⊕ ([ηP_1, ηP_2, ..., ηP_n] \ αps)
58. || αps := αps ⊕ [ηP_1, ηP_2, ..., ηP_n]

Analysis and Description of Unique Identifiers:

59. To analyse and describe the unique identifier of parts of sort P is
60. to observe the unique identifier of parts of sort P
61. where we assume that all parts have unique identifiers.

59. analyse_and_describe_unique_identifier: P → **Unit**
59. analyse_and_describe_unique_identifier(p) ≡
60.   observe_unique_identifier(p):
60. τ := τ ⊕ ["**type** PI; **value uid_P**:P→PI;"]
61.   **assert**: has_unique_identifier(p)

Analysis and Description of Mereologies:

62. To analyse and describe a part mereology
63. if it has one
64. amounts to observe that mereology
65. and otherwise do nothing.
66. The analysed quantity must be a part.

62. analyse_and_describe_mereology: P → **Unit**
62. analyse_and_describe_mereology(p) ≡
63.   **if** has_mereology(p)
64.   **then** observe_mereology(p) :
64. $\tau := \tau \oplus$ "**type** MT = $\mathcal{E}(\text{PI}_a, \text{PI}_b, ..., \text{PI}_c)$;
64.   **value mereo_P**: P→MT ;"
65.   **else skip end**
62.   **pre**: is_part(p)

Analysis and Description of Part Attributes:

67. To analyse and describe the attributes of parts of sort P is
68. to observe the attributes of parts of sort P
69. where we assume that all parts have attributes.

67. analyse_and_describe_part_attributes: P → **Unit**
67. analyse_and_describe_part_attributes(p) ≡
68.   observe_attributes(p):
68. $\tau := \tau \oplus$ ["**type** $A_1, ..., A_m$;
68.   **value attr_A_1**:P→A_1,,...,**attr_A_m**:P→A_m;"]
69.   **assert**: has_attributes(p)

3.6   Discussion of the Model

The above model lacks a formal understanding of the individual prompts as listed in Sect. 3.1. Such an understanding is attempted in [11].

Termination: The sort name reservoir νps is "reduced" by one name in each iteration of the **while** loop of the analyse_and_describe_endurants, cf. Item 6, and is augmented, in each iteration of that loop, by sort names – if not already dispensed of iterations of in earlier itetrations, cf. formula Items 32, 36, 49, 54 and 49. We take it as a dogma that domains contain a finite number of differently typed parts and matyerials. This introduction and removal of sort names and the finiteness of sort names is then the basis for a proper proof of terminaton of the the analysis & description process.

Axioms and Proof Obligations: We have omitted from the above treatment of axioms concerning well-formedness of parts, materials and attributes and proof obligations concerning disjointness of observed part and material sorts and attribute types. A more proper treatment would entail adding a line of proof obligation text right after Item lines 65 and 68, and of axiom text right after Item lines 31, 35, 46, 48, 60, 68, No axiom is needed in connection with Item line 52.

[12] covers axioms and proof obligations in some detail.

Order of Analysis and Description: A Meaning of '$\oplus$': The variables αps, νps and τ are defined to hold either sets or lists. The operator $\oplus$ can be thought of as either set union ($\cup$ and $[,]\equiv\{,\}$) — in which case the domain description text in τ is a set of domain description texts or as list concatenation ($\widehat{}$ and $[,]\equiv\langle,\rangle$) of domain description texts. The operator $\ell_1 \oplus \ell_2$ now has at least two interpretations: either $\ell_1\widehat{}\ell_2$ or $\ell_2\widehat{}\ell_1$. In the case of lists the $\oplus$ (i.e., $\widehat{}$) does not (suffix or prefix) append ℓ_2 elements already in ℓ_1. The select_and_remove_ηP function on Page 12 applies to the set interpretation. A list interpretation is:

value
6.   select_and_remove_ηP: **Unit** $\rightarrow \eta$P
6.   select_and_remove_ηP() $\equiv$
6.   **let** ηP = **hd** νps **in** νps := **tl** νps; ηP **end**

In the first case ($\ell_1\widehat{}\ell_2$) the analysis and description process proceeds from the root, breadth first, In the second case ($\ell_2\widehat{}\ell_1$) the analysis and description process proceeds from the root, depth first.

Laws of Description Prompts: The domain 'method' outlined in the previous section suggests that many different orders of analysis & description may be possible. But are they? That is, will they all result in "similar" descriptions? That is, if $\mathcal{D}_a$ and $\mathcal{D}_b$ are two domain description prompts where $\mathcal{D}_a$ and $\mathcal{D}_b$ can be pursued in any order will that yield the same description? And what do we mean by 'can be pursued in any order', and 'same description'? Let us assume that sort P decomposes into sorts P_a and P_b (etcetera). Let us assume that the domain description prompt $\mathcal{D}_a$ is related to the description of P_a and $\mathcal{D}_b$ to P_b. Here we would expect $\mathcal{D}_a$ and $\mathcal{D}_b$ to commute, that is $\mathcal{D}_a;\mathcal{D}_b$ yields same result as does $\mathcal{D}_b;\mathcal{D}_a$. In [7] we made an early exploration of such laws of domain description prompts.

To answer these questions we need a reasonably precise model of domain prompts. We attempt such a model in [11].

4   Conclusion

Domains can be studied, that is, analysed and described, without any thoughts of possible, subsequent phases of requirements and software development. To study domains includes, for proper studies. the establishment of domain theories, that is, of theorems about what is being described. This paper does not, unfortunately, show even "top of the iceberg" domain theorems. Such theories are necessary in order to develop a trust in domain desxcriptions. Theorems can then be held up against the actual domain and it can then be checked whether that domain satisfy the theorems. We know that such domain theories can be established as a result of domain modelling. A domain description can be said to be the description of the language spoken by practitioners of the domain, that is, by its stake-holders, hence of a semantics of that language.

4.1   Comparison to other Work

Domain Analysis: Section 2 outlined the `TripTych]` approach to the analysis & description of domain endurants. We shall now compare that approach to a number of techniques and tools that are somehow related — if only by the term 'domain'!

[1] Ontological and Knowledge Engineering: Ontological engineering [3] build ontologies. Ontologies are *"formal representations of a set of concepts within a domain and the relationships between those concepts"* — expressed usually in some logic. Published ontologies usually consists of thousands of logical expressions. These are represented in some, for example, low-level mechanisable form so that they can be interchanged between ontology research groups and processed by various tools. There does not seem to be a concern for "deriving" such ontologies into requirements for software. Usually ontology presentations either start with the presentation of, or makes reference to its reliance on, an upper ontology. Instead the ontology databases appear to be used for the computerised discovery and analysis of relations between ontologies.

The aim of knowledge engineering was formulated, in 1983, by an originator of the concept, Edward A. Feigenbaum [20]: knowledge engineering is an engineering discipline that involves integrating knowledge into computer systems in order to solve complex problems normally requiring a high level of human expertise. A seminal text is that of [19]. Knowledge engineering focus on continually building up (acquire) large, shared data bases (i.e., knowledge bases), their continued maintenance, testing the validity of the stored 'knowledge', continued experiments with respect to knowledge representation, etcetera. Knowledge engineering can, perhaps, best be understood in contrast to algorithmic engineering: In the latter we seek more-or-less conventional, usually imperative programming language expressions of algorithms whose algorithmic structure embodies the knowledge required to solve the problem being solved by the algorithm. The former seeks to solve problems based on an interpreter inferring possible solutions from logical data. This logical data has three parts: a collection that "mimics" the semantics of, say, the imperative programming language, a collection that formulates the problem, and a collection that constitutes the knowledge particular to the problem. We refer to [15].

The concerns of our form of domain science & engineering is based on that of algorithmic engineering. Domain science & engineering is not aimed at letting the computer solve problems based on the knowledge it may have stored. Instead it builds models based on knowledge of the domain. Our form of domain science & engineering differs from conventional ontological engineering in the following, essential ways: Our domain descriptions rely essentially on a "built-in" upper ontology: types, abstract as well as model-oriented (i.e., concrete) and actions, events and behaviours. Domain science & engineering is not, to a first degree, concerned with modalities, and hence do not focus on the modelling of knowledge and belief, necessity and possibility, i.e., alethic modalities, epistemic modality (certainty), promise and obligation (deontic modalities), etcetera.

[2] Domain Analysis: Domain analysis, or product line analysis (see below) — as it was then conceived in the early 1980s by James Neighbors — is the analysis of related software systems in a domain to find their common and variable parts. It is a model of a wider business context for the system. This form of domain analysis turns matters "upside-down": it is the set of software "systems" (or packages) that is subject to some form of inquiry, albeit having some domain in mind, in order to find common features of the software that can be said to represent a named domain. In this section ([2]) we shall mainly be comparing the TripTych approach to domain analysis to that of Reubén Prieto-Dĩaz's approach [40,41,42]. Firstly, the two meanings of domain analysis basically coincide. Secondly, in, for example, [40], Prieto-Dĩaz's domain analysis is focused on the very important stages that precede the kind of domain modelling that we have described: major concerns are selection of what appears to be similar, but specific entities, identification of common features, abstraction of entities and classification. Selection and identification is assumed in the TripTych approach, but we suggest to follow the ideas of Prieto-Dĩaz. Abstraction (from values to types and signatures) and classification into parts, materials, actions, events and behaviours is what we have focused on. All-in-all we find Prieto-Dĩaz's work very relevant to our work: relating to it by providing guidance to pre-modelling steps, thereby emphasising issues that are necessarily informal, yet difficult to get started on by most software engineers. Where we might differ is on the following: although Prieto-Dĩaz does mention a need for domain specific languages, he does not show examples of domain descriptions in such DSLs. We, of course, basically use mathematics as the DSL. In the TripTych approach we do not consider requirements, let alone software components, as do Prieto-Dĩaz, but we find that that is not an important issue.

[3] Domain Specific Languages Martin Fowler[29] defines a *Domain-specific language* (DSL) *as a computer programming language of limited expressiveness focused on a particular domain* [21]. Other references are [38,45]. Common to [45,38,21] is that they define a domain in terms of classes of software packages; that they never really "derive" the DSL from a description of the domain; and that they

---

[29] http://martinfowler.com/dsl.h

certainly do not describe the domain in terms of that DSL, for example, by formalising the DSL.

[4] Feature-oriented Domain Analysis (FODA): FODA is a domain analysis method which introduced feature modelling to domain engineering FODA was developed in 1990 following several U.S. Government research projects. Its concepts have been regarded as critically advancing software engineering and software reuse. The US Government supported report [34] states: *"FODA is a necessary first step"* for software reuse. To the extent that domain engineering with its subsequent requirements engineering indeed encourages reuse at all levels: domain descriptions and requirements prescription, we can only agree. Another source on FODA is [18]. Since FODA "leans" quite heavily on 'Software Product Line Engineering' our remarks in that section, next, apply equally well here.

[5] Software Product Line Engineering [SPLE]: SPLE earlier known as domain engineering, is the entire process of reusing domain knowledge in the production of new software systems. Key concerns of SPLE are reuse, the building of repositories of reusable software components, and domain specific languages with which to more-or-less automatically build software based on reusable software components. These are not the primary concerns of our form of domain science & engineering. But they do become concerns as we move from domain descriptions to requirements prescriptions. But it strongly seems that software product line engineering is not really focused on the concerns of domain description — such as is our form of domain engineering. It seems that software product line engineering is primarily based, as is, for example, FODA, on analysing features of software systems. Our [8] puts the ideas of software product lines and model-oriented software development in the context of the TripTych approach.

[6] Problem Frames [PF]: The concept of PF is covered in [32]. Jackson's prescription for software development focus on the "triple development" of descriptions of the problem world, the requirements and the machine (i.e., the hardware and software) to be built. Here domain analysis means, the same as for us, the problem world analysis. In the PF approach the software developer plays three, that is, all the rôles: domain engineer, requirements engineer and software engineer, "all at the same time", iterating between these rôles repeatedly. So, perhaps belabouring the point, domain engineering is done only to the extent needed by the prescription of requirements and the design of software . These, really are minor points. But in "restricting" oneself to consider only those aspects of the domain which are mandated by the requirements prescription and software design one is considering a potentially smaller fragment [31] of the domain than is suggested by the TripTych approach. At the same time one is, however, sure to consider aspects of the domain that might have been overlooked when pursuing domain description development in the "more general" three stage development approach outlined above.

[7] Domain Specific Software Architectures (DSSA): It seems that the concept of DSSA was formulated by a group of ARPA[30] project "seekers" who also

---

[30] ARPA: The US DoD Advanced Research Projects Agency.

performed a year long study (from around early-mid 1990s); key members of the DSSA project were Will Tracz, Bob Balzer, Rick Hayes-Roth and Richard Platek [46]. The [46] definition of domain engineering is *"the process of creating a DSSA: domain analysis and domain modelling followed by creating a software architecture and populating it with software components."* This definition is basically followed also by [39,44,36]. Defined and pursued this way, DSSA appears, notably in these latter references, to start with the analysis of software components, "per domain", to identify commonalities within application software, and to then base the idea of software architecture on these findings. Thus DSSA turns matter "upside-down" with respect to our requirements development by starting with software components, assuming that these satisfy some requirements, and then suggesting domain specific software built using these components. This is not what we are doing: we suggest that requirements can be "derived" systematically from, and related back, formally to domain descriptionss without, in principle, considering software components, whether already existing, or being subsequently developed. Of course, given a domain description it is obvious that one can develop, from it, any number of requirements prescriptions and that these may strongly hint at shared, (to be) implemented software components; but it may also, as well, be the case two or more requirements prescriptions "derived" from the same domain description may share no software components whatsoever! It seems to this author that had the DSSA promoters based their studies and practice on also using formal specifications, at all levels of their study and practice, then some very interesting insights might have arisen.

[8] Domain Driven Design [DDD] DDD[31] *"is an approach to developing software for complex needs by deeply connecting the implementation to an evolving model of the core business concepts; the premise of domain-driven design is the following: placing the project's primary focus on the core domain and domain logic; basing complex designs on a model; initiating a creative collaboration between technical and domain experts to iteratively cut ever closer to the conceptual heart of the problem."*[32] We have studied some of the DDD literature, mostly only accessible on the Internet, but see also [29], and find that it really does not contribute to new insight into domains such as we see them: it is just "plain, good old software engineering cooked up with a new jargon.

[9] Unified Modelling Language (UML) Three books representative of UML are [16,43,33]. The term domain analysis appears numerous times in these books, yet there is no clear, definitive understanding of whether it, the domain, stands for entities in the domain such as we understand it, or whether it is wrought up, as most of the 'approaches' treated in this section, to wit, Items [3–8], with either software design (as it most often is), or requirements prescription. Certainly, in UML, in [16,43,33], as well as in most published papers claiming "adherence" to UML, domain analysis usually is manifested in some UML text which "models" some requirements facet. Nothing is necessarily wrong with that, but it is therefore not really our form of domain analysis with its concepts of abstract

---

[31] Eric Evans: http://www.domaindrivendesign.org/

[32] http://en.wikipedia.org/wiki/Domain-driven_design

representations of endurant and perdurants, and with its distinctions between domain and requirements, and with its possibility of "deriving" requirements prescriptions from domain descriptions. The UML notion of class diagrams is worth relating to our structuring of the domain. Class diagrams appear to be inspired by [2, Bachman, 1969] and [17, Chen, 1976]. It seems that each part sort — as well as other than part (or material) sorts — deserves a class diagram (box), that (assignable) attributes — as well as other non-part (or material) types — are written into the diagram box — as are action signatures — as well as other function signatures. Class diagram boxes are line connected with annotations where some annotations are as per the mereology of the part type and the connected part types and others are not part related. The class diagrams are said to be object-oriented but it is not clear how objects relate to parts as many are rather implementation-oriented quantities. All this needs looking into a bit more, for those who care.

• • •

Summary of Comparisons: It should now be clear from the above that basically only Jackson's *problem frames* really take the same view of domains and, in essence, basically maintain similar relations between requirements prescription and domain description. So potential sources of, we should claim, mutual inspiration ought be found in one-another's work — with, for example, [28,31], and the present document, being a good starting point.

But none of the referenced works make the distinction between discrete endurants (parts) and their qualities, with their further distinctions between unique identifiers, mereology and attributes. And none of them makes the distinction between parts and materials.

Domain Analysis and Philosophy: Many readers may have felt somewhat queasy about our definitions of, for example, the notions of domain, entity, endurant, perdurant, discrete, continuous, part and material. Perhaps they thought that these were not proper definitions. Well, the problem is that we are encroaching upon the disciplines of epistemology[33], in particular ontology[34]. Thus we have to thread carefully: On one hand we cannot and do not pretend to formalise philosophical notions. On the other hand we do wish to "get as close to such formalisations as possible" ! In the context of a philosophical inquiry our

---

[33] Epistemology is the branch of philosophy concerned with the nature and scope of knowledge and is also referred to as "theory of knowledge". It questions what knowledge is and how it can be acquired, and the extent to which any given subject or entity can be known. Much of the debate in this field has focused on analyzing the nature of knowledge and how it relates to connected notions such as truth, belief, and justification[1,30].

[34] Ontology is the philosophical study of the nature of being, becoming, existence, or reality, as well as the basic categories of being and their relations. Traditionally listed as a part of the major branch of philosophy known as metaphysics, ontology deals with questions concerning what entities exist or can be said to exist, and how such entities can be grouped, related within a hierarchy, and subdivided according to similarities and differences [1,30].

definitions are acceptable as witnessed by two work on which we draw [37,22]. In the context of classical computer science they are not. In computer science we would expect precise, mathematical definitions. But that would defeat our purpose, namely to get "as close" to actual domains as possible! So we have opted for a compromise: To keep our 'philosophical-inquiry-acceptable' definitions, while, as in Sect. 3, beginning a journey of formalising such processes of 'philosophical-inquiry-processes'.

4.2   What Have We Achieved

Domain Analysis: In Sect. 2 we have presented a terse, seven+ page, summary of a novel approach to domain analysis. That this approach is different from other 'domain analysis' approaches is argued in [12, Sect. 6.2]. The new aspects are: the distinction between parts and materials, the distinction between external and internal properties (Sect. 2.11), the introduction of the concept of mereologies and the therefrom separate treatment of attributes. It seems to us that "conventional" domain analysis treated all endurant qualities as attributes. The many concepts, endurants and perdurants, discrete and continuous, hence parts and materials, atomic and composite, uniqueness of parts, mereology, and shared attributes, we claim, are forced upon the analysis by the nature of domains: existing in some not necessarily computable reality. In this way the proposed domain analysis & description approach is new.

Methodology: By a 'method' we shall understand a set of principles for selecting and applying techniques and tools in order to analyse and construct an artifact. Section 3 presents a partially instantiated framework for a formal model of a 'method' for domain analysis & description: Some principles are abstraction (sorts in preference for concrete types), separation of concerns (tackling endurants before perdurants), commensurate narratives and formalisations, tackling domain analysis either "top-down", hierarchically from composite endurants, or "bottom-up", compositionally, from atomic endurants, or in some orderly combination of these; etcetera. Some techniques are expressing axioms concerning well-formedness of mereologies and attribute values; stating (and discharging) proof obligations securing disjointness of sorts; etcetera. And some tools are the *domain analysis prompts*, the *domain description prompts* and the description language (here RSL [24]). We claim that we have sketched a formalisation of a method for domain analysis and description.

What is really new here is, as for domain analysis, that the analysis & description process is applied to a domain, that is, to our image of that domain, something not necessarily computable, and that our description therefore must not reduce the described domain to a computable artefact.

4.3   Future Work

There remains to conclude studies of, that is, to document and publish treatments of the following related topics: (i) domain analysis of perdurants (actions, events and behaviours [12, Sect. 5]) — including related *domain analysis prompts* and *domain description prompts*[35], (ii) model(s) of prompts[36], (iii) domain facets, cf. [6][37], and (iv) derivation of requirements from domain descriptions, cf. [5][38]. And there remains to actually establish theories of specific domains.

Acknowledgements. The author thanks three referees for their careful reading and comments. I think that I have dealt with all their remarks.

Bibliographical Notes

Concerning Sect. 3, A Model of The Analysis & Description Process: we could not find — and were therefore not influenced or inspired by — publications of formalised process models for software development.

References

1. Audi, R.: The Cambridge Dictionary of Philosophy. Cambridge University Press, The Pitt Building (1995)
2. Bachman, C.: Data structure diagrams. Data Base, Journal of ACM SIGBDP 1(2) (1969)
3. Benjamins, V., Fensel, D.: The Ontological Engineering Initiative (KA)2. Internet publication + Formal Ontology in Information Systems, University of Amsterdam, SWI, Roetersstraat 15, 1018 WB Amsterdam, The Netherlands and University of Karlsruhe, AIFB, 76128 Karlsruhe, Germany (1998), http://www.aifb.uni-karlsruhe.de/WBS/broker/KA2.htm
4. Bjørner, D.: Domain Theory: Practice and Theories, Discussion of Possible Research Topics. In: Jones, C.B., Liu, Z., Woodcock, J. (eds.) ICTAC 2007. LNCS, vol. 4711, pp. 1–17. Springer, Heidelberg (2007)
5. Bjørner, D.: From Domains to Requirements. In: Degano, P., De Nicola, R., Meseguer, J. (eds.) Montanari Festschrift. LNCS, vol. 5065, pp. 278–300. Springer, Heidelberg (2008)
6. Bjørner, D.: Domain Engineering. In: Boca, P., Bowen, J. (eds.) Formal Methods: State of the Art and New Directions, pp. 1–42. Springer, London (2010)
7. Bjørner, D.: Domain Science & Engineering – From Computer Science to The Sciences of Informatics Part II of II: The Science Part. Kibernetika i Sistemny Analiz (2), 100–120 (2011)
8. Bjørner, D.: Domains: Their Simulation, Monitoring and Control – A Divertimento of Ideas and Suggestions. In: Calude, C.S., Rozenberg, G., Salomaa, A. (eds.) Maurer Festschrift. LNCS, vol. 6570, pp. 167–183. Springer, Heidelberg (2011)
9. Bjørner, D.: Domain Analysis & Description: Modelling Facets (Writing to begin Summer 2013) (paper[39], slides [40]). Research Report 2013-7, DTU Compute and Fredsvej 11, DK-2840 Holte, Denmark. A first draft of this document might be written late summer of 2013 (Summer/Fall 2013)

---

[35] See forthcoming [10].
[36] See forthcoming [11].
[37] See forthcoming [9].
[38] See forthcoming [14].
[39] http://www.imm.dtu.dk/~dibj/da-facets-p.pdf
[40] http://www.imm.dtu.dk/~dibj/da-facets-s.pdf

10. Bjørner, D.: Domain Analysis & Description: Perdurants (Writing to begin Summer 2013) (paper [41], slides [42]). Research Report 2013-7, DTU Compute and Fredsvej 11, DK-2840 Holte, Denmark. A first draft of this document might be written late summer of 2013 (Summer/Fall 2013)
11. Bjørner, D.: Domain Analysis: A Model of Prompts (Writing of crucial final section yet to begin) (paper [43], slides [44]). Research Report 2013-6, DTU Compute and Fredsvej 11, DK-2840 Holte, Denmark. A first draft of this document will be written over the summer of 2013) (Summer 2013)
12. Bjørner, D.: Domain Analysis (paper [45], slides [46]). Research Report 2013-1, DTU Compute and Fredsvej 11, DK-2840 Holte, Denmark (April 2013)
13. Bjørner, D.: Domain Science and Engineering as a Foundation for Computation for Humanity. In: Zander, J., Mosterman, P.J. (eds.) Computational Analysis, Synthesis, and Design of Dynamic Systems, ch. 7, pp. 159–177. CRC (Francis & Taylor) (2013)
14. Bjørner, D.: On Deriving Requirements from Domain Specifications (Writing to begin Summer 2013) (paper [47], slides [48]). Research Report 2013-8, DTU Compute and Fredsvej 11, DK-2840 Holte, Denmark. A first draft of this document might be written late summer of 2013 (Summer/Fall 2013)
15. Bjørner, D., Nilsson, J.F.: Algorithmic & Knowledge Based Methods — Do they "Unify" ? In: International Conference on Fifth Generation Computer Systems: FGCS 1992, June 1-5, pp. 191–198. ICOT (1992)
16. Booch, G., Rumbaugh, J., Jacobson, I.: The Unified Modeling Language User Guide. Addison-Wesley (1998)
17. Chen, P.P.: The Entity-Relationship Model - Toward a Unified View of Data. ACM Trans. Database Syst. 1(1), 9–36 (1976)
18. Czarnecki, K., Eisenecker, U.W.: Generative Programming: Methods, Tools, and Applications. Addison-Wesley (2000)
19. Fagin, R., Halpern, J.Y., Moses, Y., Vardi, M.Y.: Reasoning about Knowledge, 2nd printing. The MIT Press, Cambridge, 02142 (1996)
20. Feigenbaum, E.A., McCorduck, P.: The fifth generation, 1st edn. Addison-Wesley, Reading (1983)
21. Fowler, M.: Domain Specific Languages. Signature Series. Addison-Wesley (October 2012)
22. Fox, C.: The Ontology of Language: Properties, Individuals and Discourse. CSLI Publications, Stanford University (2000)
23. Ganter, B., Wille, R.: Formal Concept Analysis — Mathematical Foundations, 300 pages. Springer (January 1999) Amazon price: US$ 44.95. ISBN: 3540627715
24. George, C.W., Haff, P., Havelund, K., Haxthausen, A.E., Milne, R., Nielsen, C.B., Prehn, S., Wagner, K.R.: The RAISE Specification Language. The BCS Practitioner Series. Prentice-Hall, Hemel Hampstead (1992)
25. George, C.W., Haxthausen, A.E., Hughes, S., Milne, R., Prehn, S., Pedersen, J.S.: The RAISE Development Method. The BCS Practitioner Series. Prentice-Hall, Hemel Hampstead (1995)

[41] http://www.imm.dtu.dk/~dibj/perd-p.pdf
[42] http://www.imm.dtu.dk/~dibj/perd-s.pdf
[43] http://www.imm.dtu.dk/~dibj/da-mod-p.pdf
[44] http://www.imm.dtu.dk/~dibj/da-mod-s.pdf
[45] http://www.imm.dtu.dk/~dibj/da-p.pdf
[46] http://www.imm.dtu.dk/~dibj/da-s.pdf
[47] http://www.imm.dtu.dk/~dibj/da-fac-p.pdf
[48] http://www.imm.dtu.dk/~dibj/da-fac-s.pdf

26. Goguen, J.A., Burstall, R.M.: Introducing institutions. In: Clarke, E., Kozen, D. (eds.) Logics of Programs. LNCS, vol. 164, pp. 221–256. Springer, Heidelberg (1984)

27. Goguen, J.A., Winkler, T., Meseguer, J., Futatsugi, K., Jouannaud, J.-P.: Introducing OBJ. In: J. A. Goguen and G. Malcolm, editors, Software Engineering with OBJ: Algebraic Specification in Action. Kluwer Press, 2000. Also Technical Report SRI-CSL-88-9, SRI International (August 1988)

28. Gunter, C.A., Gunter, E.L., Jackson, M.A., Zave, P.: A Reference Model for Requirements and Specifications. IEEE Software 17(3), 37–43 (2000)

29. Haywood, D.: Domain-Driven Design Using Naked Objects. The Pragmatic Bookshelf (an imprint of 'The Pragmatic Programmers, LLC.') (2009), http://pragprog.com/

30. Honderich, T.: The Oxford Companion to Philosophy. Oxford University Press, Oxford (1995)

31. Jackson, M.: Program Verification and System Dependability. In: Boca, P., Bowen, J. (eds.) Formal Methods: State of the Art and New Directions, pp. 43–78. Springer, London (2010)

32. Jackson, M.A.: Problem Frames — Analyzing and Structuring Software Development Problems. ACM Press, Pearson Education. Addison-Wesley, England (2001)

33. Jacobson, I., Booch, G., Rumbaugh, J.: The Unified Software Development Process. Addison-Wesley (1999)

34. Kang, K.C., Cohen, S.G., Hess, J.A., Novak, W.E., Peterson, A.S.: Foda: Feature-oriented domain analysis. Feasibility Study CMU/SEI-90-TR-021. Software Engineering Institute. Carnegie Mellon University (November 1990), http://www.sei.cmu.edu/library/abstracts/reports/90tr021.cfm

35. Luschei, E.: The Logical Systems of Leśniewksi. North Holland, Amsterdam (1962)

36. Medvidovic, N., Colbert, E.: Domain-Specific Software Architectures (DSSA). Power Point Presentation, found on The Internet. Absolute Software Corp., Inc.: Abs[S/W] (March 5, 2004)

37. Mellor, D.H., Oliver, A. (eds.): Properties. Oxford Readings in Philosophy, 320 pages. Oxford Univ. Press (May 1997) ISBN: 0198751761

38. Mernik, M., Heering, J., Sloane, A.M.: When and how to develop domain-specific languages. ACM Computing Surveys 37(4), 316–344 (2005)

39. Mettala, E., Graham, M.H.: The Domain Specific Software Architecture Program. Project Report CMU/SEI-92-SR-009, Software Engineering Institute Carnegie Mellon University Pittsburgh, Pennsylvania 15213 (June 1992)

40. Prieto-Díaz, R.: Domain Analysis for Reusability. In: COMPSAC 1987. ACM Press (1987)

41. Prieto-Díaz, R.: Domain analysis: an introduction. Software Engineering Notes 15(2), 47–54 (1990)

42. Prieto-Díaz, R., Arrango, G.: Domain Analysis and Software Systems Modelling. IEEE Computer Society Press (1991)

43. Rumbaugh, J., Jacobson, I., Booch, G.: The Unified Modeling Language Reference Manual. Addison-Wesley (1998)

44. Shaw, M., Garlan, D.: Software Architecture: Perspectives on an Emerging Discipline. Prentice Hall (1996)

45. Spinellis, D.: Notable design patterns for domain specific languages. Journal of Systems and Software 56(1), 91–99 (2001)

46. Tracz, W.: Domain-specific software architecture (DSSA) frequently asked questions (FAQ). Software Engineering Notes 19(2), 52–56 (1994)

A   Pipeline Endurants

Our example is an abstraction of pipeline system endurants. The presentation of the example reflects a rigorous use of the domain analysis & description method outlined in Sect. 2, but is relaxed with respect to not showing all — one could say — intermediate analysis steps and description texts, but following stoichiometry ideas from chemistry makes a few short-cuts here and there. The use of the "stoichiometrical" reductions, usually skipping intermediate endurant sorts, ought properly be justified in each step — and such is adviced in proper, tool-supported industry-scale domain analyses & descriptions.

A.1   Parts

70. A pipeline system contains a set of pipeline units and a pipeline system monitor.
71. The well-formedness of a pipeline system depends on its mereology (cf. Sect. A.2) and the routing of its pipes (cf. Sect. A.3).
72. A pipeline unit is either a well, a pipe, a pump, a valve, a fork, a join, or a sink unit.
73. We consider all these units to be distinguishable, i.e., the set of wells, the set pipe, etc., the set of sinks, to be disjoint.

type
70.   PLS', U, M
71.   PLS = {| pls:PLS'•wf_PLS(pls) |}
value
71.   wf_PLS: PLS → **Bool**
71.   wf_PLS(pls) ≡ wf_Mereology(pls) ∧ wf_Routes(pls)
70.   obs_Us: PLS → U-**set**
70.   obs_M: PLS → M
type
72.   U = We | Pi | Pu | Va | Fo | Jo | Si
73.   We :: Well
73.   Pi :: Pipe
73.   Va :: Valv
73.   Fo :: Fork
73.   Jo :: Join
73.   Si :: Sink

A.2   Part Identification and Mereology

Unique Identification:

74. Each pipeline unit is uniquely distinguished by its unique unit identifier.

type
74.   UI
value
74.   uid_UI: U → UI
axiom
74.   ∀ pls:PLS,u,u':U•{u,u'}⊆obs_Us(pls)⇒u≠u'⇒uid_UI(u)≠uid_UI(u')

Unique Identifiers:

75. From a pipeline system one can observe the set of all unique unit identifiers.

value
75. xtr_UIs: PLS → UI-set
75. xtr_UIs(pls) ≡ {uid_UI(u)|u:U•u ∈ obs_Us(pls)}

76. We can prove that the number of unique unit identifiers of a pipeline system equals that of the units of that system.

theorem:
76.   ∀ pls:PLS•**card** obs_Us(pl)=**card** xtr_UIs(pls)

Mereology:

77. Each unit is connected to zero, one or two other existing input units and zero, one or two other existing output units as follows:
   a A well unit is connected to exactly one output unit (and, hence, has no "input").
   b A pipe unit is connected to exactly one input unit and one output unit.
   c A pump unit is connected to exactly one input unit and one output unit.
   d A valve is connected to exactly one input unit and one output unit.
   e A fork is connected to exactly one input unit and two distinct output units.
   f A join is connected to exactly two distinct input units and one output unit.
   g A sink is connected to exactly one input unit (and, hence, has no "output").

type
77.   MER = UI-set × UI-set
value
77.   mereo_U: U → MER
axiom
77.   wf_Mereology: PLS → **Bool**
77.   wf_Mereology(pls) ≡
77.   ∀ u:U•u ∈ obs_Us(pls)⇒
77.   **let** (iuis,ouis) = mereo_U(u) **in** iuis ∪ ouis ⊆ xtr_UIs(pls) ∧
77.   **case** (u,(**card** uius,**card** ouis)) **of**
77a.   (mk_We(we),(0,1)) → **true**,
77b.   (mk_Pi(pi),(1,1)) ⟩ **truo**,
77c.   (mk_Pu(pu),(1,1)) → **true**,
77d.   (mk_Va(va),(1,1)) → **true**,
77e.   (mk_Fo(fo),(1,1)) → **true**,
77f.   (mk_Jo(jo),(1,1)) → **true**,
77g.   (mk_Si(si),(1,1)) → **true**,
77.   _ → **false end end**

A.3   Part Concepts

An aspect of domain analysis & description that was not covered in Sect. 2 was that of derived concepts. Example pipeline concepts are routes, acyclic or cyclic, circular, etcetera. In expressing well-formedness of pipeline systems one often has to develop subsidiary concepts such as these by means of which well-formedness is then expressed.

Pipe Routes:

78. A route (of a pipeline system) is a sequence of connected units (of the pipeline system).
79. A route descriptor is a sequence of unit identifiers and the connected units of a route (of a pipeline system).

type
78. $R' = U^\omega$
78. $R = \{| \ r{:}Route'\bullet wf\_Route(r) \ |\}$
79. $RD = UI^\omega$
axiom
79. $\forall \ rd{:}RD \bullet \exists \ r{:}R\bullet rd{=}descriptor(r)$
value
79.   descriptor: $R \to RD$
79.   descriptor(r) $\equiv \langle uid\_UI(r[\,i\,])|i{:}\mathbf{Nat}\bullet 1{\leq}i{\leq}\mathbf{len} \ r\rangle$

80. Two units are adjacent if the output unit identifiers of one shares a unique unit identifier with the input identifiers of the other.

value
80.   adjacent: $U \times U \to \mathbf{Bool}$
80.   adjacent(u,u') $\equiv$
80.   **let** (,ouis)=mereo_U(u),(iuis,)=mereo_U(u') **in**
80.   ouis $\cap$ iuis $\neq \{\}$ **end**

81. Given a pipeline system, *pls*, one can identify the (possibly infinite) set of (possibly infinite) routes of that pipeline system.
    a The empty sequence, $\langle\rangle$, is a route of *pls*.
    b Let u, u' be any units of *pls*, such that an output unit identifier of u is the same as an input unit identifier of u' then $\langle u, u'\rangle$ is a route of *pls*.
    c If r and r' are routes of *pls* such that the last element of r is the same as the first element of r', then $r\hat{\ }\mathbf{tl}r'$ is a route of *pls*.
    d No sequence of units is a route unless it follows from a finite (or an infinite) number of applications of the basis and induction clauses of Items 81a–81c.

value
81.   Routes: PLS $\to$ RD-**infset**
81.   Routes(pls) $\equiv$
81a.   **let** rs = $\langle\rangle \ \cup$
81b. $\{\langle uid\_UI(u),uid\_UI(u')\rangle|u,u'{:}U\bullet\{u,u'\}{\subseteq}obs\_Us(pls) \wedge adjacent(u,u')\}$
81c. $\cup \ \{r\hat{\ }\mathbf{tl} \ r'|r,r'{:}R\bullet\{r,r'\}{\subseteq}rs\}$
81d.   **in** rs **end**

Well-Formed Routes:

82. A route is acyclic if no two route positions reveal the same unique unit identifier.

value
82. acyclic_Route: R → **Bool**
82. acyclic_Route(r) ≡ ∼∃ i,j:**Nat**•{i,j}⊆**inds** r ∧ i≠j ∧ r[i]=r[j]

83. A pipeline system is well-formed if none of its routes are circular (and all of its routes embedded in well-to-sink routes).

value
83. wf_Routes: PLS → **Bool**
83. wf_Routes(pls) ≡
83.   non_circular(pls) ∧ are_embedded_in_well_to_sink_Routes(pls)

83. non_circular_PLS: PLS → **Bool**
83. non_circular_PLS(pls) ≡
83.   ∀ r:R•r ∈ routes(p)∧acyclic_Route(r)

84. We define well-formedness in terms of well-to-sink routes, i.e., routes which start with a well unit and end with a sink unit.

value
84. well_to_sink_Routes: PLS → R-set
84. well_to_sink_Routes(pls) ≡
84.   **let** rs = Routes(pls) **in**
84.   {r|r:R•r ∈ rs ∧ is_We(r[1]) ∧ is_Si(r[**len** r])} **end**

85. A pipeline system is well-formed if all of its routes are embedded in well-to-sink routes.

85. are_embedded_in_well_to_sink_Routes: PLS → **Bool**
85. are_embedded_in_well_to_sink_Routes(pls) ≡
85.   **let** wsrs = well_to_sink_Routes(pls) **in**
85.   ∀ r:R • r ∈ Routes(pls) ⇒
85.   ∃ r′:R,i,j:**Nat** •
85.   r′ ∈ wsrs
85.   ∧ {i,j}⊆**inds** r′∧i≤j
85.   ∧ r = ⟨r′[k]|k:**Nat**•i≤k≤j⟩ **end**

Embedded Routes:

86. For every route we can define the set of all its embedded routes.

value
86. embedded_Routes: R → R-set
86. embedded_Routes(r) ≡
86.   {⟨r[k]|k:**Nat**•i≤k≤j⟩ | i,j:**Nat**• i {i,j}⊆**inds**(r) ∧ i≤j}

A Theorem:

87. The following theorem is conjectured:
      a the set of all routes (of the pipeline system)
      b is the set of all well-to-sink routes (of a pipeline system) and
      c all their embedded routes

theorem:
87. $\forall$ pls:PLS •
87.   let rs = Routes(pls),
87.   wsrs = well_to_sink_Routes(pls) **in**
87a.   rs =
87b.   wsrs $\cup$
87c. $\cup$ {{r'|r':R • $r' \in$ embedded_Routes(r'')} | r'':R • $r'' \in$ wsrs}
86.   **end**

A.4   Materials

88. The only material of concern to pipelines is the gas[49] or liquid[50] which the pipes transport[51].

type
88.   GoL
value
88.   obs_GoL: U $\rightarrow$ GoL

A.5   Attributes

Part Attributes:

89. These are some attribute types:
      a estimated current well capacity (barrels of oil, etc.),
      b pipe length,
      c current pump height,
      d current valve open/close status and
      e flow (e.g., volume/second).

type
89a.   WellCap
89b.   LEN
89c.   Height
89d.   ValSta == open | close
89e.   Flow

---

[49] Gaseous materials include: air, gas, etc.
[50] Liquid materials include water, oil, etc.
[51] The description of this document is relevant only to gas or oil pipelines.

90. Flows can be added (also distributively) and subtracted, and
91. flows can be compared.

value

90. $\oplus, \ominus$: Flow×Flow → Flow
90. $\oplus$: Flow-**set** → Flow
91. $<, \leq, =, \neq, \geq, >$: Flow × Flow → **Bool**

92. Properties of pipeline units include
    a estimated current well capacity (barrels of oil, etc.),
    b pipe length,
    c current pump height,
    d current valve open/close status,
    e current $\mathcal{L}$aminar in-flow at unit input,
    f current $\mathcal{L}$aminar in-flow leak at unit input,
    g maximum $\mathcal{L}$aminar guaranteed in-flow leak at unit input,
    h current $\mathcal{L}$aminar leak unit interior,
    i current $\mathcal{L}$aminar flow in unit interior,
    j maximum $\mathcal{L}$aminar guaranteed flow in unit interior,
    k current $\mathcal{L}$aminar out-flow at unit output,
    l current $\mathcal{L}$aminar out-flow leak at unit output,
    m maximum guaranteed $\mathcal{L}$aminar out-flow leak at unit output.

value

92a.   attr_WellCap: We → WellCap
92b.   attr_LEN: Pi → LEN
92c.   attr_Height: Pu → Height
92d.   attr_ValSta: Va → VaSta
92e.   attr_In_Flow$_{\mathcal{L}}$: U → UI → Flow
92f.   attr_In_Leak$_{\mathcal{L}}$: U → UI → Flow
92g.   attr_Max_In_Leak$_{\mathcal{L}}$: U → UI → Flow
92h.   attr_body_Flow$_{\mathcal{L}}$: U → Flow
92i.   attr_body_Leak$_{\mathcal{L}}$: U → Flow
92j.   attr_Max_Flow$_{\mathcal{L}}$: U → Flow
92k.   attr_Out_Flow$_{\mathcal{L}}$: U → UI → Flow
92l.   attr_Out_Leak$_{\mathcal{L}}$: U → UI → Flow
92m.   attr_Max_Out_Leak$_{\mathcal{L}}$: U → UI → Flow

A.6   Flow Laws

93. "What flows in, flows out !". For $\mathcal{L}$aminar flows: for any non-well and non-sink unit the sums of input leaks and in-flows equals the sums of unit and output leaks and out-flows.

Law:

93. $\forall$ u:U\We\Si •
93.   sum_in_leaks(u) $\oplus$ sum_in_flows(u) $=$
93.   attr_body_Leak$_{\mathcal{L}}$(u) $\oplus$
93.   sum_out_leaks(u) $\oplus$ sum_out_flows(u)

value

> sum_in_leaks: U → Flow
> sum_in_leaks(u) ≡
>   **let** (iuis,) = mereo_U(u) **in**
>   ⊕ {attr_In_Leak$_\mathcal{L}$(u)(ui)|ui:UI•ui ∈ iuis} **end**
> sum_in_flows: U → Flow
> sum_in_flows(u) ≡
>   **let** (iuis,) = mereo_U(u) **in**
>   ⊕ {attr_In_Flow$_\mathcal{L}$(u)(ui)|ui:UI•ui ∈ iuis} **end**
> sum_out_leaks: U → Flow
> sum_out_leaks(u) ≡
>   **let** (,ouis) = mereo_U(u) **in**
>   ⊕ {attr_Out_Leak$_\mathcal{L}$(u)(ui)|ui:UI•ui ∈ ouis} **end**
> sum_out_flows: U → Flow
> sum_out_flows(u) ≡
>   **let** (,ouis) = mereo_U(u) **in**
>   ⊕ {attr_Out_Leak$_\mathcal{L}$(u)(ui)|ui:UI•ui ∈ ouis} **end**

94. "What flows out, flows in !". For $\mathcal{L}$aminar flows: for any adjacent pairs of units the output flow at one unit connection equals the sum of adjacent unit leak and in-flow at that connection.

Law:

94. ∀ u,u′:U•adjacent(u,u′) ⇒
94.   **let** (,ouis)=mereo_U(u), (iuis′,)=mereo_U(u′) **in**
94.   **assert:** uid_U(u′) ∈ ouis ∧ uid_U(u) ∈ iuis ′
94.   attr_Out_Flow$_\mathcal{L}$(u)(uid_U(u′)) =
94.   attr_In_Leak$_\mathcal{L}$(u)(uid_U(u))⊕attr_In_Flow$_\mathcal{L}$(u′)(uid_U(u)) **end**

On Formal Definition and Analysis of Formal Verification Processes

Leon J. Osterweil ˙

Lab. For Advanced Software Engineering Research
(laser.cs.umas.edu)
School of Computer Science
University of Massachusetts
Amherst, MA 01003
ljo@cs.umass.edu

Abstract. This paper suggests that there is considerable value in creating precise and formally-defined specifications of processes for carrying out formal verification, and in then subjecting those processes to rigorous analysis, and using the processes to guide the actual performance of formal verification. The paper suggests that some of the value could derive from widening the community of verifiers by having a process definition guide the performance of formal verification by newcomers or those who may be overawed by the complexities of formal verification. The paper also suggests that formally-defined process definitions can be of value both to novices and more experienced verifiers by serving as subjects of both dynamic and static analyses, with these analyses helping to build the confidence of various stakeholder groups (including the verifiers themselves) in the correct performance of the process and hence the correctness of the verification results. This paper is a status report on early work aimed at developing such processes, and demonstrating the feasibility and value of such analyses. The paper provides an example of a formally-defined verification process and suggests some kinds of dynamic and static analyses of the process. The process incorporates specification of both the nominal, ideal process as well as how the process must be iterated in response to such verification contingencies as incorrect assertions, incorrectly stated lemmas, and failed proofs of lemmas. In demonstrating how static analyses of this process can demonstrate that it assures certain kinds of desirable behaviors, the paper demonstrates an approach to providing effective verification guidance that assures sound verification results.

1   Introduction

Society is becoming ever more dependent upon systems that rely importantly upon the reliably correct functioning of software. Air travel is now heavily dependent upon software that is pervasive both in the cockpit and on the ground. Automobiles are similarly increasingly dependent upon software. Health care devices and systems also increasingly employ software in critical roles. Because of this it is correspondingly important that the software in these systems performs correctly, across the

S. Iida, J. Meseguer, and K. Ogata (Eds.): Futatsugi Festschrift, LNCS 8373, pp. 35–52, 2014.

increasingly broad spectrum of situations in which it is relied upon. There are many approaches to assuring the correct functioning of software, including dynamic testing and various forms of static analysis. But perhaps the strongest assurances of correct functioning of software are provided by formal verification. This paper describes an approach that is currently being developed for making the performance of formal verification accessible to more practitioners by providing explicit proactive process guidance to this performance.

In addition, we note that while it is essential that critical software reliably function correctly in all circumstances and situations, it is also most important that those who rely upon such correct functioning have a sound basis for believing that that is the case. In short, it is not enough for software to perform correctly, but it is also important that all of the software's stakeholders have access to satisfactory evidence of this correct performance. This paper also suggests that the explicit process guidance provided by the approaches presented in this paper can also be the basis for providing importance forms of evidence that the formal verification process has been performed correctly. Evidence of correct functioning that is provided by testing and many forms of static analysis can be relatively accessible to broad communities of stakeholders, but it seems important to also consider how it might be possible to provide broadly accessible evidence of correct performance of formal verification. It is the position of this paper that the formal verification community has made good progress towards the goal of understanding how to reason about the correct performance of software (although it would be desirable to make formal verification processes more accessible to more practitioners), but that more progress should be made towards the second goal of being able to provide convincing assurances to stakeholders that a formal verification process has actually been carried out correctly.

Over the past several decades many approaches to reasoning about the correct performance of software have been developed. The most widely recognized and employed approach has been testing, where the program is run using a large number of diverse input datasets. Typically the results can be examined by diverse stakeholder communities to provide these stakeholders assurances that the program behaves correctly. While this approach allows for the in-depth exploration of the behavior of a program under actual runtime conditions, testing results do not extrapolate. Thus, even if a program has been run successfully millions of times on different datasets, there is no assurance that it might not fail on the next test execution. Consequently testing is unable to offer the kinds of ironclad assurances of correct performance that are required by many stakeholders in software for critical applications.

Static analysis approaches such as finite state verification [3] and model checking [1] can offer some kinds of more definitive assurances, however, and thus serve as a useful complement to dynamic testing. The static analysis approach makes it possible to prove that all possible executions of a program must necessarily always satisfy certain classes of properties. Typically these kinds of properties are modeled as sequences of events, often represented by finite state machines. Insofar as these properties are modeled by relatively accessible diagrams such as finite state machines, and anomalous execution sequences can be presented as statement execution traces, these kinds of analyses can provide relatively accessible evidence of correct program performance to relatively broad classes of stakeholders. A principal drawback of this approach, however, is that the need to represent these properties by formalisms such as finite state machines limits the kinds of properties for which it is useful. In particular these static analysis approaches are generally not useful in supporting demonstrations that the program will always necessarily demonstrate the desired functional behavior.

Especially in view of the foregoing, formal verification [2,4,7] occupies a very important position among the many approaches to reasoning about the behavior of programs. Formal verification can be used to prove that all possible executions of a program must necessarily always deliver specified functional behavior. Doing so, however, requires a considerable amount of effort and resources. The program to be formally verified must be written in a language whose semantics have been defined formally, the specified behavior must be defined in the form of formally specified assertions, and human verifiers are invariably required to create large numbers of proofs, each of which may be quite complex and must be meticulously reasoned. Because the reasoning process is complex and lengthy, errors of many kinds can be committed. The structure of lemmas to be proven may be flawed, the assertions essential to the statements of the lemmas may also be flawed, and the details of the actual proofs may be incorrect. All of these difficulties have in the past served as obstacles to the broader adoption of formal verification by practitioners, and to the accessibility of formal verification results by broader stakeholder communities. Novices, in particular, have all too often been daunted by the complexities of performing formal verification. And the complexity of the work of formal verification experts has at times seemed to be beyond the grasp of some stakeholders, suggesting the desirability of additional forms of visibility into how the formal verification process was carried out. In both cases, the continued evolution of software systems creates additional difficulties. Once modified in any way, a previously-verified program must be reverified. If modifications are minor and quarantined to a small program locality, the reverification of the entire program may not be necessary. But it can be difficult to determine which reverifications are necessary, and which are not. Automated tool support can be quite useful in guiding both novices and experts to the correct determination.

Especially since formal verification is employed most commonly to offer the most solid assurances of correct performance to the most demanding stakeholders, it then seems appropriate that these stakeholders have the most definitive assurances that the verification results are trustworthy. In large-scale industrial contexts, these assurances are often obtainable using verification assistants and checkers such as Isabelle [12]. But even in these contexts, the need to reverify software as it continues to evolve can lead to uncertainty about just which portions of which versions of a program have been subjected to which verification activities. In other contexts, especially where verification is done informally or by novices, these assurances are harder to obtain, and necessarily less reliable.

A variety of directions have been taken in order to address the many difficulties inherent in formal verifications of programs. Of particular interest in the context of this event, we note that Futatsugi [5, 6] has suggested the value of verifying designs rather than code, inventing the notion of Proof Scores. Another approach has advocated the use of automated proof checkers and proof assistants to support humans in carrying out the formal verification process. The first tool to provide such support, a verification assistant, was developed in 1969 by James King [8]. Many such systems have been developed subsequently. Currently Isabelle/HOL [12] seems particularly popular and effective in supporting the verification process and the checking of needed proofs. It is important to note, however, that the participation of humans is typically essential, especially at the higher levels of lemma specification, and that considerable amounts of iteration and rework are typically required to successfully complete an entire formal verification. Typically humans must create and place assertions, and guide the proof of many lemmas derived from the assertions and program code. As noted above, iteration is typically necessary, requiring and responding to assertion modifications, lemma regeneration, and proof defects. As also noted above, program evolution necessitates reverification that can be expedited by lemma reuse, but can also lead to configuration management issues leading to mistakenly thinking that an incorrect verification is correct.

One approach to addressing these problems is to formally define formal verification processes that incorporate specifications of these various kinds of iteration, and then to apply the various forms of reasoning just summarized to this process definition. In short, we advocate formally defining realistic iterative formal verification processes, and then applying dynamic testing, finite state verification, and other forms of analysis to such processes in order to generate analysis results that can lead to greater insight into these processes, and increased credence in the results they deliver. The purpose of this paper is to indicate that such formal definitions and analyses of formal verification processes are feasible, and should be increasingly important additions to the formal verification enterprise. To that end, this paper describes early work that is developing formal definitions of iterative formal verification processes such as Floyd's Method. The paper presents one such process definition that has been written in a rigorously-defined process definition language. Because of the language's semantic definition in terms of a rigorous notation (in this case it is Finite State Machines) we are able to demonstrate the feasibility of applying rigorous analysis to these processes, thereby obtaining definitive analytic results.

2   A Process-Centric View of Formal Verification

A formal verification of a program is essentially a proof that all possible executions of the program must necessarily deliver functional results that are consistent with a specification. The program and a precise specification of desired functionality are taken as input to the verification process, and the desired result of the process is a proof of a theorem that the program meets its specification. The process of producing the proof consists of creating and then proving a carefully constructed set of lemmas. We will use Floyd's Method of Inductive Assertions [4] as an example of an approach to formal verification.

2.1   Floyd's Method of Inductive Assertions

Floyd's Method begins by creating a set of assertions, each of which is a statement that characterizes what should be true at a specific point in the execution of a program. These assertions must then be placed so that every program loop is "broken" or "cut" by an assertion (i.e. every iteration of every loop in the program must necessarily encounter at least one assertion). Initial and Final Assertions are also placed at the beginning and end of the program to capture the desired functional behavior of the program. The placement of these assertions assures that every possible execution of the program is a sequence of loop-free statement execution sequences, each of which is bounded at each end by an assertion. Because any program has a finite number of statements there are only a finite number of places where assertions can be positioned. Thus there are a finite number, N, of assertions placed in any program, and there can therefore be at most N^2 pairs of assertions. Assuming that there are at most C different paths between any pair of adjacent assertions, then any execution of the program can be viewed as a sequence that consists of at most $C*N^2$ different loop-free statement execution sequences that are bounded at each end by an assertion. Assuming that there are in fact L such different loop-free execution sequences (where $L <= C*N^2$), then the essence of Floyd's Method is to prove L lemmas, each of which consists of demonstrating that, assuming the assertion at the start of the loop-free execution sequence is true, the execution of the loop-free execution sequence then assures that the assertion at the end of the loop-free execution sequence must also be true. If all such lemmas can be proven, then by induction, for any possible program execution, the truth of the initial assertion guarantees the truth of the final assertion assuming that the execution of the program reaches the final assertion. The verification of the program then requires a proof that the program must actually terminate.

This elegant approach to reasoning about the functionality of a program provides an excellent intellectual framework for understanding and reasoning about a program. The need to be sure that the final assertion is implied by all of its possible predecessor assertions makes it imperative that all of these previous assertions address the real functional substance of the program (e.g. trivial assertions such as *true = true ∧ true* will not help imply the final assertion). Thus there is strong pressure for intermediate assertions that are placed inside of loops to be specifications of the quintessential contribution that each loop iteration makes to the overall work of the program. As such, creating these so-called *loop invariant assertions, or loop breakers,* compels the human verifier to come to grips with the nature of the program being verified, and to develop a deep understanding of the program. This discipline is widely regarded as being of at least as much value and importance as the actual completed proof itself, suggesting that it is particularly important for novice programmers to understand and practice the discipline. One key motivation of the work described here is to suggest an approach to helping novices feel comfortable in carrying out formal verifications of their programs.

2.2   Pragmatic Issues

While the conceptual basis for Floyd's Method is beautiful and elegant, the actual execution of the method is fraught with difficulties and perils. Ultimately the human verifier would like to either prove all of the lemmas, thereby verifying that the program must always produce the correct functional results, or in failing to do so come to the realization of the existence of a program error that must be fixed. But simply failing to be able to prove all lemmas may result from difficulties in performing the verification, rather than from the presence in the program of an error that must be fixed. Specifically, the following are some of the difficulties that a human verifier may encounter in performing the verification:

- An assertion may be incorrect or inadequate: As noted above, a loop invariant assertion must capture the essence of what each loop is quintessentially all about and what it contributes to the overall functioning of the program. All too often programmers have only a fuzzy grasp of this and may build loops whose actual functioning lacks this sharp focus. In such cases, the verifier will understandably have difficulty in enunciating simple and elegant loop-breaker assertions. Sometimes this lack of clarity of purpose causes a loop indeed to be programmed incorrectly, but often it simply creates an intellectual challenge that requires the verifier to iterate the specification of the loop invariant or modify the program code, seeking code and assertion that will suffice. Thus, lack of success in proving a needed lemma may well indicate ways in which a loop invariant specification may need improvement or code should be modified. When any code or assertion is changed, then it becomes necessary to repeat the proof of any previously-proven lemma that involved that assertion or code.

- An assertion may be positioned in the wrong place in the program: In a similar way, it may be the case that the verifier understands the essential nature of the performance of a loop, but may position a needed loop invariant in a location where the specification of the invariant it not true under all circumstances. Here too failure to prove one or more lemmas may lead to a clearer understanding of where the assertion needs to be positioned. And here too, any change in the position of an assertion requires that any lemma involving that assertion be reproven.

- The proof of a lemma may be incorrect: The proof of a lemma requires that the contribution of every statement in the loop-free execution sequence be characterized as a specific change that the execution of that statement makes to the overall state of the program's execution. The statement's contribution may be to change the value of one or more program variables, or the concurrency state of the program, for example. The semantics of the language in which the program is written provide a template for determining the contribution of a statement, and the specifics of each statement can then be used to elaborate the template into a precise and detailed specification of the contribution of the statement. Proving a lemma entails composing the contributions of each of the statements in the loop-free execution sequence, and proving that their combined behaviors must always cause the final assertion to be true, given that the initial assertion is true. Because the semantics of a typical programming language are defined using non-trivial mathematics, proofs of lemmas about programs written in such languages require good facility with such mathematics. Even a very minor error in inference can cause a verifier to incorrectly conclude that a correct lemma is incorrect, or that an incorrect lemma is correct. Either of these errors invalidates the entire verification. Because of this, proof checking tools are typically used to review the proofs of lemmas. If the proof of a lemma is found to be incorrect, the proof must be corrected.

- The lemma may be correct, but too difficult for the verifier to prove: As noted above, a proof typically requires reasoning meticulously about the combined behaviors of all of a sequence of program statements. When the sequence of statements gets long, the combined behaviors of these statements can become quite complex, requiring the verifier to create a long and complex lemma. The very size and complexity of the lemma may make the proof too difficult for the verifier to carry out. In such cases, the verifier may expedite the verification process by creating new assertions, modifying some of the existing assertions, moving the locations of some of the existing assertions, or modifying the underlying program to be verified. In each of these cases, the changes to assertions or to program statements will require reconsideration of the previously developed lemmas and proofs.

The foregoing suggests why many novices may be daunted by the prospect of carrying out the formal verification of a program. But it also suggests the value of proactive process guidance through the different kinds of iterations that may be necessary, and the prospect that such guidance could increase the accessibility and appeal of formal verification to novices. In particular, because the formal verification of a program is likely to require a considerable amount of trial and error, leading to a considerable amount of iteration, guidance through these iterations could be of considerable value. Some iteration might be minor, requiring only a minor modification to a slightly flawed proof of a single lemma. But some iteration, such as the need to modify an assertion that is a part of several different lemmas, may require a very considerable amount of effort. In cases where considerable effort seems required, it is reasonable for the verifier to think carefully about which lemmas need to be reproven, and which need not be reproven. In the case of lemmas to be reproven, it is reasonable for the verifier to seek to reuse as much of the previous proof as possible. All of this reasoning is error-prone and can lead to the incorporation into the final set of lemmas of one or more lemmas whose correctness might be incorrectly assumed, leading to an incorrect verification. Therefore, proactive support for reasoning about he reuse of lemmas would be of great value to the verifier.

Documentation of the reasoning about lemma reuse can also be of considerable value to stakeholders. The possibility that a formal verification of a program is incorrect should be a concern for all of the stakeholders of that program. All of these stakeholders should be insistent upon having access to evidence that the verification has indeed delivered correct results. Among the kinds of stakeholders that should have this concern and should require such evidence are:

- Customers who have paid for the program and should expect that they are receiving what they have paid for.
- Users who need the functionality that has been promised.
- Innocent bystanders (e.g. passengers on a software-guided airplane) whose safety might be jeopardized by software that performs in an incorrect and/or unsafe way.
- Developers whose pride and professional reputations derive from their demonstrated ability to create software that meets the needs of stakeholders.

There are some differences in the ways in which the needs of these different stakeholders should be met. But all are seeking assurances that the process by which the formal verification of the program was carried out is itself correct, and was carried out correctly. Our view is that these assurances can be derived from appropriate examinations of a sufficiently precise and detailed definition of the formal verification process, and of a sufficiently precise and detailed history its execution. Thus, for example, it would be important to be able to show definitive evidence that a proof checker has been run on each of the lemmas. And to show that none of the assertions or code involved in a lemma that is incorporated as part of a final program verification has been modified subsequent to the running of a check of its proof. As noted above, automated tool systems such as Isabelle can help to provide these kinds of evidence. But as a less expensive and more accessible alternative, an appropriately complete and detailed definition of the formal verification process could be used to provide some of these forms of evidence as well. Moreover, a trace of the execution of the process could provide evidence that all proofs were indeed checked, and no changes were made subsequently. Human verifiers' efforts could be augmented by such a process if the process were to specify that the human verifier could not declare the program to be verified until and unless all lemmas were proof-checked. These examples suggest ways in which an appropriate formal verification process definition could be used to provide desired assurances of different kinds to different stakeholder groups.

3   An Example Formalization of a Formal Verification Process

To demonstrate the feasibility of creating a formal definition of a formal verification process, we now use Little-JIL, a semantically well-defined language [13,14], to define precisely and in some detail Floyd's Method of Inductive Assertions. We have chosen to use Little-JIL as the vehicle for the definition of this process for a number of reasons. First, the semantic scope of Little-JIL seems particularly well-matched to the needs of an iteration-intensive formal verification process definition in that Little-JIL provides particularly strong support for such features as abstraction, exception management, rigorously-defined artifact flow, and human choice, all of which seem to be important in formal verification processes. Thus, for example, Petri Nets seem particularly poorly suited to the concise specification of such processes in that they lack strong features for modeling artifacts and their flow, and are particularly clumsy in dealing with exception management. In their lack of hierarchical structure they make it hard to deal with abstraction. Other specification languages have other patterns of weakness in specifying these critical features of iteration-intensive formal verification processes.

3.1   About Little-JIL

We now provide some minimal level of details about the Little-JIL language. More complete details about the language can be found in [13] and will also be introduced in the context of our explanation of the definition of Floyd's Method. Little-JIL is a visual language, depicting processes as hierarchies of steps. But Little-JIL is also semantically well-defined, with its semantics being based upon finite state machines. The semantics are sufficiently strongly defined to support the execution of processes defined in Little-JIL. A presentation of the finite state machines used to define Little-JIL semantics is well beyond the scope of this paper. But these finite state machine definitions have been used to support various forms of reasoning about processes from many diverse domains that have been defined in Little-JIL. In this section we build upon that process reasoning experience to apply it to reasoning about formal verification processes.

A Little-JIL process definition looks initially somewhat like a task decomposition graph, in which processes are decomposed hierarchically into steps, with the order of execution of child steps being specified by the parent. Steps can be thought of as procedures, especially in that they incorporate specifications of argument flow. When a Little-JIL process definition is executed, its various steps are elaborated at run time into step instances.

Figure 1 is a visualization of a step, where the black bar represents the step. Little-JIL steps are connected to each other with edges that represent both hierarchical decomposition and artifact flow. These edges are shown emanating from the left side of the step bar in Figure 1. The left side of a non-leaf step bar contains an iconic representation of the order in which the step's substeps are to be executed. Little-JIL incorporates four different step execution sequencing specifications: sequential (indicated by a right facing arrow), which specifies that substeps are to executed sequentially from left to right; parallel (indicated by an = sign), which specifies fork-and-join for its substeps; choice (indicated by a circle slashed through the middle), which specifies that only one of the step's substeps is to be executed, with the choice being made by the parent step; and try (indicated by a right facing arrow with an X on its tail), which specifies that the step's substeps are to be executed in left-to-right order until one of them succeeds by failing to throw an exception.

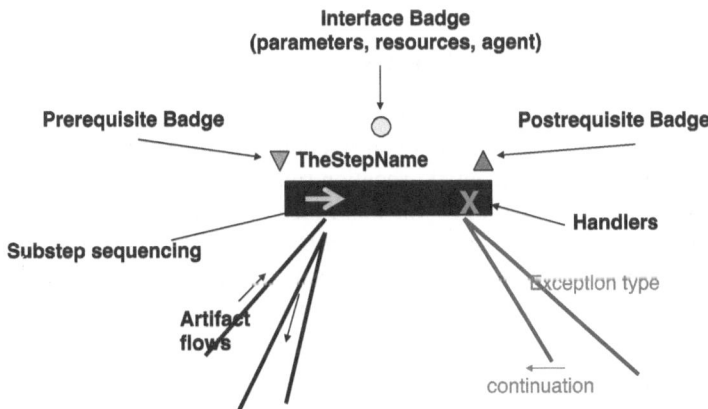

Fig. 1. A visualization of a Little-JIL step showing its key semantic features

Each step definition contains an interface specification, represented in Figure 1 by the small blue ball over the step bar. The interface specification consists of a specification of the step's arguments and its resource requirements. An argument specification incorporates both type information and information about whether the argument is an input, an output, or both. Step invocation parameter-passing semantics are essentially copy-and-restore. A step's resource requirement specification details the types of resources needed in order to perform the task associated with that step. In Little-JIL, moreover, one resource is always designated as the step's agent, namely the resource responsible for the performance of the step. Thus, for example, in Floyd's Method, the agent for a step such as the specification of a loop invariant would be a human, but the agent for a step that checks the details of a proof would probably be an automated proof-checker.

Exception handling is a particularly strong and important feature of Little-JIL. Steps can be preceded by a prerequisite check (indicated by a green triangle to the left of the step bar in Figure 1) and followed by a postrequisite check (indicated by a red triangle to the right of the step bar in Figure 1). Each of these can represent an entire step structure that evaluates to true or false. If a requisite evaluates to false then an exception is thrown. The agent for a step can also throw an exception during the execution of the step. Exceptions are typed objects, and are handled by handlers for that exception type that are above the step that has thrown the exception in the step decomposition hierarchy. Every step can contain one or more exception handlers, each of which may itself be an entire step hierarchy. A step's exception handlers are attached to the step by edges that emanate from the right side of the step bar. When a step contains exception handlers, a red X appears inside the right side of the step bar. Non-leaf steps are sometimes introduced into the step hierarchy specifically for the purpose of creating a scope of applicability for a particular exception handler. Little-JIL's exception management facilities seem particularly well suited to support the clear and concise specification of various kinds of iteration that must occur in realistic formal verification activities.

3.2   A Little-JIL Definition of Floyd's Method

Figure 2 depicts a Little-JIL definition of Floyd's Method. As might be expected, the process consists, at the highest level of abstraction (represented by the substeps of the root step in Figure 2), of sequential execution (indicated by the right-facing arrow in *Floyds Method,* the root step) of *Define and Place Initial and Final Assertions,* a step to create and place all needed assertions, then *Define and Place All Invariants,* a step to create all of the needed loop-breaker invariants, *Create Lemmas,* a step to build all of the lemmas whose proofs are needed to complete the formal verification of the program, *Prove Lemmas,* a step to actually carry out the proofs of all of the lemmas, and then *Prove Program Termination,* a step to prove that program execution must terminate.

While these top level steps capture the nominal process of performing Floyd's Method, our process is designed to support the actual process that a verifier most typically goes through, including the recovery from errors and speculative approaches that do not work out, and supporting verifiers' efforts to determine when such recoveries are need, and how to carry out the recoveries. In the lower levels of this process definition we will show some examples of such error detection and recovery. At the top level, though, we can already see such an example. Hanging from the right end of the step bar of the root step, *Floyds Method*, is an exception handler that shows that the entire *Floyds Method* process will be reexecuted in response to an appropriately typed exception thrown at any time during the execution of the process. This presumably would happen in response to a realization that the execution of the process has become hopelessly entangled (we shall see shortly how easily this can happen). In this case the process definition specifies that the hopelessly entangled verification process execution will be abandoned and the entire *Floyds Method* process will be restarted. We note that the reinvocation of *Floyds Method* is essentially a recursion, indicating that the new process invocation takes place in the context created by this exception handler, where that context (communicated perhaps through arguments thrown with the exception) may incorporate important information about what has been tried previously and why it has not worked out well. Other examples of exception management will be shown in the elaboration of the top level steps that we address now.

To provide further examples of the power of our process definition to describe and guide the details of a realistic performance of Floyd's Method, we now describe elaborations of some top level steps, starting with *Define and Place All Invariants*. This step is an iteration over all of the invariants needed to support the complete proof.

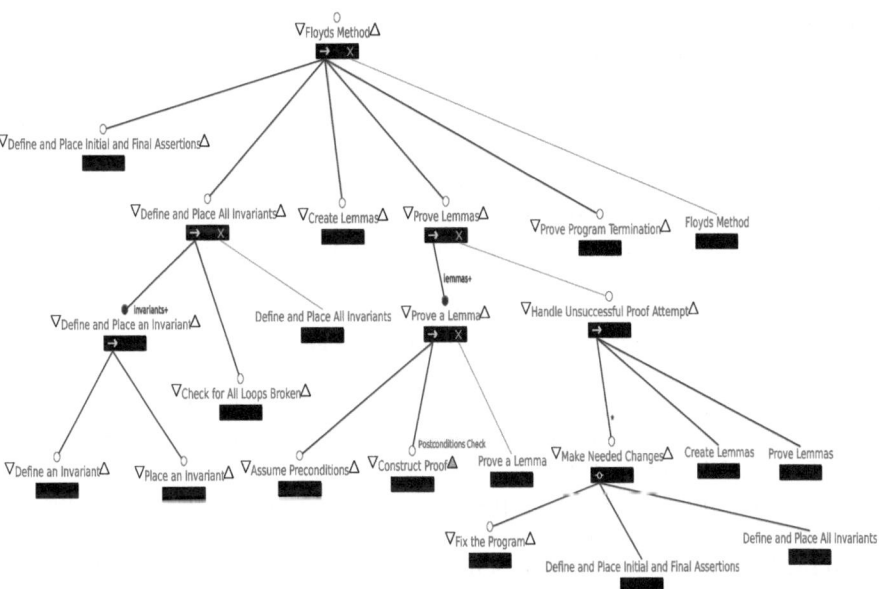

Fig. 2. An Example of a Little-JIL definition of a process for performing Floyd's Method of Inductive Assertions

The iteration is indicated by the annotation *invariants+* positioned on the edge between *Define and Place All Invariants* and *Define and Place an Invariant*. The *invariants+* annotation on the edge indicates that the lower level step is to be instantiated one or more times (the Kleene +), once for each invariant that the verifier wishes to create. The lower level step, *Define and Place an Invariant*, is decomposed into two further substeps, namely the defining of the invariant and the placement of the invariant in the program source text. Following performance of the iterative definition and placement of all invariants, is a substep of *Define and Place All Invariants, Check for All Loops Broken*, that is imbedded in the process here to assure that enough invariants have been created and that they have been appropriately placed. It is expected that this step is to be executed by some kind of automated tool, and that can be specified as part of the Little-JIL definition of this process, although this visualization of the definition does not include that annotation in order to reduce visual clutter. If the checking to assure that all loops are broken by an assertion reveals that this critical requirement has not been met, then the checker will throw an appropriately typed exception. This exception is to be handled by the *Define and Place All Invariants* step, which consists of reinvoking *Define and Place All Invariants*. Here too, this is a recursive invocation of the step in which the new execution context will presumably contain information about the cause of the exception, most likely a specification of all of the loops that have not yet been broken. This information would presumably be of considerable value to the verifier in identifying just where additional assertions are needed. As the entire *Define and Place All Invariants* step is reinstantiated, however, the verifier will in this case also be free to edit, remove, or replace any existing assertions. The reinstantiations of the *Define and Place All Invariants* step will continue until checking confirms that all loops have been broken.

The elaboration of the *Prove Lemmas* step incorporates other interesting details. *Prove Lemmas* is also an iteration whose nature is specified by the *lemmas+* annotation on the edge from *Prove Lemmas* to its substep, *Prove a Lemma*, which will be instantiated once for each of the lemmas to be proven. The list of lemmas to be proven will have been generated by *Create Lemmas*, the immediate predecessor sibling of *Prove Lemmas*, and then passed as an argument from *Create Lemmas* to *Prove Lemmas*. *Prove a Lemma* consists of the sequential execution of *Assume Preconditions* and then *Construct Proof*. Certainly most of the time and effort in verification is spent in the *Construct Proof* step, which we do not elaborate here. This is the heart of program verification, and is often a highly creative activity. Some guidance in how to carry out that activity could be provided by elaborations of this Little-JIL step, perhaps emphasizing the details of how humans and proof assistants might collaborate. Thus, further elaboration of this step would seem to be particularly important if this process is to be used to train and support formal verification novices. Elaborations of this kind will be pursued in future work on this ongoing project.

To see how this process definition does help support assurance about the correctness of the proof, note that the *Construct Proof* step has a postrequisite, presumably (but not necessarily) carried out by an automated proof checker, whose job is to confirm that what has been created is indeed a valid proof of the lemma. If the postrequisite determines that the proof is not valid, then two different exceptions might be thrown. One exception, suggesting a defect in the proof, would be handled by the *Prove a Lemma* step, and would cause the *Prove the Lemma* step to be reinvoked recursively thereby causing the verifier to examine the report of the defect in the proof thereby expediting the process of correcting the defect.

The postrequisite in this definition is also able to throw a different exception, this one to be handled by *Handle Unsuccessful Proof Attempt*, an exception handler attached to the higher level *Prove Lemmas* step. *Handle Unsuccessful Proof Attempt* is to be thrown when a failed proof attempt has indicated that there is a more fundamental problem with the verification. It is not uncommon, for example, for an assertion to have been incorrectly stated, or inconveniently placed, or indeed for the program that is being verified to contain a defect (a principal reason for doing the verification). Each of these three possible difficulties is to be addressed by a different substep of *Make Needed Changes*, the first substep of *Handle Unsuccessful Proof Attempt*. *Make Needed Changes*, is defined to be a choice step, indicating that the verifier is free to choose whichever of its three substeps (each supporting a different kind of change) is to be performed. Of particular note is the fact that the edge from *Handle Unsuccessful Proof Attempt* to *Make Needed Changes*, is annotated with a Kleene *, indicating that this step can be instantiated as many times as the verifier might wish, in order to support the possibility that the verifier may need to make more than one change (e.g. perhaps to modify more than one assertion, and perhaps also change some program source text). Regardless of the number of instantiations of *Make Needed Changes*, the process next mandates that *Create Lemmas* and *Prove Lemmas* be executed next. The reexecution of *Create Lemmas* is to assure that all lemmas continue to be consistent with the current set of loop-breaker assertions (some of which might have been changed during the execution of *Make Needed Changes*). The reexecution of *Prove Lemmas* requires that all lemmas be proven. In cases where neither the assertions nor code have been changed, the proof would not need to be modified, and the postcondition on *Construct Proof* would reconfirm the validity of the previous proof. In other cases, *Prove a Lemma* would entail creating a new proof, and would require the successful execution of the *Construct Proof* postcondition. Failure of the postcondition would cause the throwing of an exception and might cause another recursive invocation of *Prove Lemmas*.

It is clear that continued recursive invocations of this step, perhaps multiple times in response to multiple postcondition failures, can create a situation in which several different proof failures are being investigated and corrected essentially simultaneously, perhaps even in ways where progress in addressing one difficulty creates new difficulties for other proof correction activities. All of this creates a potentially very confusing environment for the human verifier. Little-JIL's hierarchical structure, and its ability to support recursive invocations, each of which can carry considerable amounts of contextual information, seems to have the clear potential to provide guidance that could be very useful to the verifier in this sort of complex situation. Still, however, it is not hard to envisage situations in which there are so many recursive reconsiderations of so many lemmas that the verifier might feel it is best to simply start all over again. In that case, this process definition supports the ability of the human verifier to throw the exception this is handled by the top level *Floyds Method* step, causing the entire process to be started anew (although still in a context that might make information about the previous verification attempts available).

4 Analysis of a Formal Verification Processes

As noted above, we feel that it is not sufficient only to verify a program, but that it is also important to be able to provide to stakeholders (including the human verifier—especially a novice human verifier) credible evidence that the program has indeed been verified, and verified correctly. In this section we demonstrate how a formal definition of a formal verification process such as the one just presented can be effective in supporting the creation of such evidence. To provide some initial examples, we suggest some fundamental assurances are that: all loops have been shown to have been broken by at least one assertion, that all necessary lemmas have been created, that each lemma is stated based upon the most recently created assertions and current code, and that each lemma that has been verified is indeed a lemma based upon current assertions and code. The nominal execution of Floyd's Method as a straight un-iterated sequence of the top level substeps of *Floyds Method* makes it clear that a verification cannot terminate until and unless all lemmas have been created and proven. But experience suggests that the verification of a real program is almost never as simple as following that nominal uniterated straight path, because errors in creating assertions, placing them, creating lemmas and (especially) proving lemmas successfully are to be expected, necessitating backtracking, and iterations of various kinds. As noted above, all of these difficulties are further complicated when reverifying a program that has been modified. In such a case some assertions, lemmas, and proofs can be reused, but others cannot. We suggest that proactive process support can be quite useful both to verifiers and other stakeholders, in providing guidance about which assertions, lemmas, and proofs are safe to reuse and which are not. The example process presented above is a suggestion of one way in which needed backtracking and iteration might be organized systematically, hopefully providing structure and artful integration of automated tools that can be of real assistance to a human verifier, especially a novice human verifier. But this process definition also makes it clear that the specification of backtracking and iteration also make it more difficult to be sure that all needed lemmas have been created and then proven successfully, with no changes to any assertions or program text taking place between the conclusion of all of these proofs and the end of the execution of this process.

In earlier work we have argued that a process that is defined in a rigorously specified language can be thought of as a kind of software that is, in particular, amenable to analysis using existing software analysis approaches, such as testing, static analysis, and formal verification [9,10]. That suggests to us that it should be possible to apply these kinds of analyses to formally defined formal verification process definitions such as the one presented above in order to produce assurances to stakeholders of the correctness, and the correct execution, of such processes.

We begin by observing that the executability of a Little-JIL process supports the ability to do dynamic analyses of executions of the process. Little-JIL processes are executed using a system, Juliette [14], that assures that steps are executed in orders that are consistent with Little-JIL semantics, and that arguments are correctly collected from completed steps and delivered to steps that are defined to be their users. Juliette also delivers to agents, both human and automated, the work that they have been assigned as per the specifications in the process definition. These work assignments are delivered to the agendas of the agents, who signal the completion of assigned work by making appropriate annotations to their agendas. Clearly the history of inputs received, assignments of steps to agents, the completion statuses of those steps, and the values of artifacts both consumed and generated, comprises an articulate record of how the process has been executed for any given input program. This record, generated in the form of a Data Derivation Graph (DDG) [11], seems to be an excellent basis for reasoning about whether key properties have been adhered to by any execution of the process. Thus, for example, if we wish to be sure that all lemmas have been proven successfully and correctly, we should be able to verify this by examining the DDG to see that no changes have been made either to a lemma's assertions, or to the lemma's code subsequent to the last successful verification of that lemma, and prior to the completion of the execution of the entire process. By confirming that this is indeed the case for each lemma, we then confirm that all of the component parts of the verification have been proven. If the postcondition of the *Construct Proof* step has been executed by an automated proof checker, then this will be observable from an examination of the DDG, and reportable as part of the assurances provided to stakeholders.

As is the case with other kinds of software, however, this sort of dynamic analysis of a single formal verification process execution may provide useful assurance about the trustworthiness of a single verification, but provides no assurances about any other verification process execution. More generally, in addition to knowing that a single verification has satisfied some key properties, it is also quite important to know that any verification that follows the same process must also always satisfy these key properties. Thus, we believe it is important to be able to analyze a given formal verification process definition to verify properties such as that all lemmas have been proven correctly prior to the termination of the verification process. This can be done by applying finite state verification [3] to a rigorously defined verification process specification such as the one just presented. As an example, we indicate how this property can be verified for the specific process shown in Figure 2.

A finite state verification of the property that all lemmas have been successfully proven before the process terminates should be based upon analysis of a flow graph derived from the Little-JIL process definition. Because Little-JIL's semantics are rigorously defined based upon finite state machines, such a flowgraph can be automatically generated (and indeed we have developed a tool for automatically generating such process definitions into the Bandera intermediate representation, which incorporates all needed data and control flow information [3]). The verification of this property then entails verifying that no modifications to a lemma's statement or to the program text used by the lemma can occur between the end node of the process flowgraph and the most immediately proximate prior successful execution of the proof checker's confirmation of the correctness of the proof. An informal inspection of the process definition strongly supports a surmise that this is the case, as the termination of the execution of the process occurs only after the successful completion of the *Prove Lemmas* step (regardless of how many times this step might have been called recursively), and the successful completion of the *Prove Lemmas* step occurs only after all of the proofs of the individual lemmas have been confirmed as being correct.

Certainly, however, this informal argument should be supplanted by a rigorous proof of the consistency of the process with this property. To cite a specific suggestive reason, suppose that the *Create Lemmas* step had been omitted from the list of children of the *Handle Unsuccessful Proof Attempt* exception handler step. If that were the case, it might then be possible that the *Define and Place All Invariants* step might have been performed as part of the response to an unsuccessful proof attempt, thereby potentially necessitating the modification of some prior lemma statements. But, with the *Create Lemmas* step missing, the process now no longer assures that those new lemmas would be created, and thus does not assure that the needed new proofs would be completed. Determining whether the needed proofs have been correctly created and proven would have to be determined based upon a careful analysis that included precise specification of the flow of arguments between these process steps. Certainly this is eminently possible, based upon the semantics of Little-JIL. But the purpose of this thought-exercise is to suggest that just this kind of careful and precise mathematically sound static analysis of processes such as this one is necessary—but possible. Similar kinds of concerns about the soundness of a proof arise in being sure that a reverification has not relied upon lemmas that are no longer valid, or upon lemmas that have been incorrectly constructed using assertions that are no longer valid.

Indeed, going a step further, the kind of analysis that is probably of most value is a full formal verification of this formal verification process definition. We suggest that it is not only possible, but actually highly desirable, to apply Floyd's Method to the verification that this process for the performance of Floyd's Method necessarily always produces a correct outcome. Thus, for example, we would like to use Floyd's Method to verify formally that all lemmas needed for a verification have been created correctly, and that every one of these lemmas has been proven correctly. Doing this requires, obviously, the creation of at least one loop-breaking invariant assertion for each of the loops in our process definition. As in the case of the verification of any other kind of program, this requires a firm understanding of the essential goals and natures of each of the loops, which is perhaps the most valuable product of any verification effort. In the case of the iteration in the *Prove Lemmas* step, for example, a component of the needed invariant would certainly have to assert that at the end of the ith iteration all lemmas up to and including $lemma_i$ have been proven successfully.

We have not, at present, undertaken the formal verification of a formal verification process, as this work is currently ongoing. But we expect that the somewhat intricate structure of exceptions and exception handling in this example verification process might make the proof of all needed lemmas difficult, perhaps suggesting the advisability of creating a more straightforwardly understandable and provable process. This is very much in line with what our community has learned about the value of verifying programs, namely that proof attempts often lead to the kinds of deeper understandings that point the way to useful simplifications.

The fact that program verifications currently are often carried out (e.g. by novices or those having to work in environments that lack powerful proof assistant tools) without benefit of a formally defined process to guide them raises the risk that reported successes in verification may not be supportable by acceptably rigorous arguments and acceptably definitive evidence. The example we have just presented makes it clear that the expectable need to incorporate various kinds of iteration and rework into real verification processes can make it difficult to assemble such rigorous and definitive evidence. To address this worrisome problem this paper has suggested an approach that should seem quite natural to those who have developed the admirable science and technology of testing, analysis, and verification.

5   Conclusions

We have argued that it is quite important to be able to assure all stakeholders that a formal verification of a program has been carried out correctly. This seems particularly important in consideration of the fact that formal verifications typically entail extensive amounts of rework and iteration that can raise doubts about whether all necessary lemmas have really been generated and proven. We have then demonstrated that the process of performing just such an iteration-intensive formal verification can be defined precisely in a rigorously defined process definition language. We then indicated how classical dynamic, static, and formal verification approaches can be applied to such a process definition thereby creating the kinds of assurances of verification correctness that should be desired by stakeholders. But our work is still in a relatively early stage, and so in this paper we describe the application of these analysis approaches to only one specific desirable property. Future work must address far more properties.

In addition, this paper has suggested the applicability of only a few analysis approaches. But in future work it seems useful to consider how to apply other approaches. For example, dynamic monitoring could be used to help identify proof bottlenecks and sticking points and to suggest possible approaches to resolving such problems, perhaps aided by the results of automated proof assistants that might be automatically invoked. Moreover, timing analyses might be carried out as well to attempt to project the amount of time needed to complete a verification. Most important, perhaps, is this paper's suggestion that formal verification has applicability to more than just programs, but also is a valuable technology to apply to processes as well, even the processes that should be used to carry out formal verification.

Acknowledgments. The author wishes to thank Xiang Zhao for developing the Little-JIL definition of Floyd's Method shown as Figure 2 in this paper. This work described in this paper has been supported by the National Science Foundation under grants IIS-1239334, CNS-1258588, and IIS-0705772.

References

1. Clarke Jr., E.M., Grumberg, O., Peled, D.A.: Model Checking. MIT Press, Cambridge (1999)
2. Dijkstra, E.W.: A Discipline of Programming. Prentice Hall, Englewood Cliffs (1976)
3. Dwyer, M.B., Clarke, L.A., Cobleigh, J.M., Naumovich, G.: Flow Analysis for Verifying Properties of Concurrent Software Systems. ACM Transactions on Software Engineering and Methodology 13(4), 359–430 (2004)
4. Floyd, R.W.: Assigning Meanings to Programs. In: Schwartz, J.T. (ed.) Proceedings of a Symposium on Applied Mathematics, vol. 19, pp. 19–31 (1967)
5. Futatsugi, K.: Verifying Specifications with Proof Scores in CafeOBJ. In: Intl. Conf. on Automated Software Engineering, Tokyo, Japan, pp. 3–10 (2006)
6. Futatsugi, K.: Fostering Proof Scores in CafeOBJ. In: Intl. Conference on Formal Engineering Methods, Shanghai, China, pp. 1–20 (2010)
7. Hoare, C.A.R.: An Axiomatic Basis for Computer Programming. Communications of the ACM 12(10), 576–580 (1976)
8. King, J.C.: A Program Verifier., PhD Thesis, Carnegie Mellon University (1969)
9. Osterweil, L.J.: Software Processes are Software Too. In: ACM SIGSOFT/IEEE 9th International Conference on Software Engineering (ICSE 1987), Monterey, CA, pp. 2–13 (March 1987)
10. Osterweil, L.J.: Software Processes Are Software Too, Revisited. In: ACM SIGSOFT/IEEE 19th International Conference on Software Engineering (ICSE 1997), Boston, MA, pp. 540–548 (May 1997)
11. Osterweil, L.J., Clarke, L.A., Podorozhny, R., Wise, A., Boose, E., Ellison, A.M., Hadley, J.: Experience in Using a Process Language to Define Scientific Workflow and Generate Dataset Provenance. In: Proceedings of the ACM SIGSOFT 16th International Symposium on Foundations of Software Engineering, Atlanta, GA, pp. 319–329 (2008)
12. Paulson, L.C.: The foundation of a generic theorem prover. Journal of Automated Reasoning 5(3), 363–397 (1989)
13. Wise, A.: Little-JIL 1.5 Language Report. Department of Computer Science, University of Massachusetts, Amherst, UM-CS-2006-51 (2006)
14. Wise, A., Cass, A.G., Lerner, B.S., McCall, E.K., Osterweil, L.J., Sutton Jr., S.M.: Using Little-JIL to coordinate agents in software engineering. In: Proceedings of the Automated Software Engineering Conference (ASE 2000), Grenoble, France (2000)

CafeOBJ Traces

Răzvan Diaconescu

Simion Stoilow Institute of Mathematics of the Romanian Academy
Razvan.Diaconescu@imar.ro

Abstract. We survey two important distinctive features of CafeOBJ, namely behavioural specification based upon coherent hidden algebra and heterogeneous specification based upon Grothendieck institutions. Both of them represent seminal contributions to formal specification culture that go much beyond the realm of CafeOBJ. Our presentation includes rather detailed explanations of the motivations and of the process leading to the inception of these concepts and theories. The paper is dedicated to Professor Kokichi Futatsugi, the leader of the CafeOBJ project, and also close friend and collaborator, on the occasion of his retirement.

1   Introduction

In the early nineties the lifespan of OBJ [28], the iconic language of algebraic specification, was nearing its end. This was much due to several important theoretical developments that had happened at the time, and that were calling for a new generation of algebraic specification languages. Three offsprings of OBJ were thus born, CASL [1], Maude [5], and CafeOBJ [17]. All of them are now mature specification languages, each of them with its own identity. I would like to confess: from all OBJ offsprings, I see the fate of CafeOBJ and its associated activities over next one or two decades as uncertain. The CafeOBJ definition [17] (that was the fruit of intense collaboration between me and Professor Futatsugi between 1996–2000) lacks the theoretical rigor and clarity of CASL, and the quality of the JAIST/SRA implementation is far from the impecable and powerful Maude rewrite engine. Moreover the current activities around CafeOBJ are rather weak compared to the other two. Although CafeOBJ does not have many regular users outside JAIST, its semantics continues to this day to pose challenging research questions (e.g. [16,12,15] etc.). The effort put into the design of CafeOBJ between 1996–2000 had left traces in the algebraic specification culture that in my opinion will continue to have a great impact for a long time.

In this survey, I would like to share with you, the reader, two of the traces left by CafeOBJ, what they mean, their impact so far, and especially an insider perspective about how they appeared and how they developed.

S. Iida, J. Meseguer, and K. Ogata (Eds.): Futatsugi Festschrift, LNCS 8373, pp. 53–65, 2014.

2   Modern Behavioural Specification through Coherent Hidden Algebra

2.1   From Rewriting Logic to Behavioural Specification

When I arrived at JAIST in January 1996, being hired by Professor Futatsugi on a recommendation of Joseph Goguen, the CafeOBJ project was at the beginning and it looked very much that it will become a kind of copy of Maude, and extension of OBJ towards rewriting logic. At that moment I was under the strong influence of the work on behavioural specification that I had been doing in the early nineties with Joseph Goguen, my Oxford D.Phil. supervisor. This very promising specification and verification paradigm introduced first time perhaps by Horst Reichel in the early eighties [37] had undergone a new development within Joseph Goguen's research group at Oxford, the most representative paper from that period being [26].

It was not very difficult to convince Professor Futatsugi, the head of the CafeOBJ project, that we need to realize behavioural specification directly as part of the CafeOBJ definition and implementation. This was meant to provide CafeOBJ an unique identity, and after all behavioural specification was an extremely promising specification paradigm, very worth to explore through an executable specification language. Thus CafeOBJ was to become the first language directly implementing behavioural specification. Later on there was BOBJ [38] that after several more years evolved into the CIRC behavioural verification tool [39]. By contrast, the design team of CASL decided to have behavioural specification at the methodology level rather than at the language definition level.

2.2   The Birth of Non-monadic Hidden Algebra

The process of rethinking hidden algebra, the logic underlying behavioural specification, this time fuelled by the design of a real language, led in 1998 to a profound extension of the definition of hidden algebra [6] (its journal version being [18]). This was called 'coherent hidden algebra', a way to point out the single most important aspect of this reform, the so-called coherence property that opened the door for allowing algebraic operations with more than one hidden sort in their arity.

The main idea behind the coherence property was that the actual specification practice may require operations that have no behavioural meaning, but that have the flavour of constructors and that preserve the behavioural equivalence determined by the operations that are explicitly specified as 'behavioural'. I still remember the original example of a coherent operator, given by the following specification of a non-deterministic choice function on natural numbers.

```
mod* NNAT-HSA {
  protecting(NAT)
  *[ NNat ]*
  op [_] : Nat -> NNat
```

```
  op _|_ : NNat NNat -> NNat {coherent}
  bop _->_ : NNat Nat -> Bool
  vars S1 S2 : NNat
  vars M N : Nat
  eq [M] -> N = M == N .
  eq (S1 | S2) -> N = (S1 -> N) or (S2 -> N) .
}
```

In this specification NNat models behaviourally the set of the non-deterministic naturals, and _|_ looks like a state constructor and carries no behavioural meaning. But on the other hand, _|_ preserves the behavioural equivalence $\sim$ determined by the choice predicate _->_. This means each model of NNAT-HSA satisfies

$$(\forall s_1, s_1', s_2, s_2') \, (s_1 \sim s_1') \wedge (s_2 \sim s_2') \Rightarrow (s_1 \mid s_2) \sim (s_1' \mid s_2').$$

The idea to allow for operations with more than one hidden sort in the arity meant a dramatic breakthrough the monadic world of the hidden algebra at the time, a departure from the final semantics (in its strict sense) and the ideology of co-algebra [31]. Within Goguen's inner circle of collaborators there was already an understanding that co-algebra was not technically adequate for real software specification mainly because of its inability to integrate well data types. On the contrary, hidden algebra looked already much better in this respect and at this new level even "more divorced" from co-algebra. Later on, Grigore Roşu, in his San Diego Ph.D. thesis under Joseph Goguen's supervision [38], took another step forward and explored behavioural operations with more than one hidden sort in the arity. He came up with a very interesting finding . While of course final semantics in its literal sense is lost (no more chance to have a final algebra for the signature, in a category theoretic sense), its congruence theoretic essence is still there in the form of the existence of the largest hidden congruence. The way I present these important results these days is as follows.

Definition 1 (Signatures). *A $\underline{HA}$ signature is a tuple (H, V, F, BF) where*

- *$(H \cup V, F)$ is a many sorted signature with $H \cap V = \emptyset$; the sorts in V are called* visible *sorts and the sorts in H are called* hidden *sorts; and*
- *$(H \cup V, BF)$ is a sub-signature of $(H \cup V, F)$; the operations of BF are called* behavioural *operations.*

Definition 2 (Hidden algebras). *Given a signature (H, V, F, BF), an (H, V, F, BF)-algebra is just an $\underline{MSA}$ $(H \cup V, F)$-algebra.*

Definition 3 (Hidden congruence). *Given a (H, V, F, BF)-algebra A, a hidden (H, V, F, BF)-congruence $\sim$ on A is just an $(H \cup V, BF)$-congruence which is identity on the visible sorts.*

Definition 4 (Behavioural equivalence). *The largest hidden (H, V, F, BF)-congruence $\sim_A$ on a (H, V, F, BF)-algebra A is called the* behavioural equivalence *on A.*

Theorem 1. *Behavioural equivalence exists for any (H, V, F, BF)-algebra.*

2.3   Behavioural Specification of Hierarchical Object Composition

In spite of its great promises, behavioural specification has remained to this day marginal among CafeOBJ activities. For some it was still too sophisticated to be of real use. I think this is one of the major failures of the CafeOBJ project so far. However the start of a new era of behavioural specification given by CafeOBJ has a major impact on CASL behavioural specification methodologies and its ideas have been taken over and developed to very advanced stages by CIRC. I think CIRC shows very clearly that the original great promises of behavioural specification as formal method paradigm were not empty.

There was a very notable exception to the inability of the CafeOBJ community to cultivate behavioural specification. This was the so-called 'hierarchical object composition' methods that was the subject of Shusaku Iida's JAIST Ph.D. thesis [30] and that had a further semantic development stage in [10]. The roots of behavioural approaches to object composition can be traced to [26], but that was an initial semantics approach. By contrast the method put forward by Shusaku Iida was a final semantics one (as shown in [10]), very much true to the spirit of behavioural specification. A great benefit of this specification method is that its associated verification method is fully automatic, and moreover the debugging process is linear. In spite of all these promises the CafeOBJ behavioural object composition has not yet been developed as a tool, an easy step from the point of view of implementation, but absolutely mandatory for a real industrial usage of the method.

2.4   Structuring Behavioural Specifications

The structuring of behavioural specifications poses particular challenging problems. Unfortunately specification in-the-large in CafeOBJ has been defined rather sketchy in [17], and at the level of the details there are problems that only now are being addressed.

A peculiarity of hidden algebra that prevents a direct application of the very mature general theory on structuring specifications (e.g. [40,20,16]) is that in general one does not have unions of any hidden algebra signatures. This is due to the encapsulation condition on the hidden algebra signature morphisms, which is absolutely necessary to ensure the so-called Satisfaction Condition from institution theory [25] for hidden algebra. In its absence no decently working modularization system would be possible. Let us recall the definition of hidden algebra signature morphisms.

Definition 5. *A* quasi-morphism of *HA* signatures

$$\varphi \colon (H, V, F, BF) \to (H', V', F', BF')$$

is just a morphism of many sorted algebra signatures $\varphi \colon (H \cup V, F) \to (H' \cup V', F')$ *such that*

- $\varphi(H) \subseteq H'$ *and* $\varphi(V) \subseteq V'$, *and*

– *the restriction of φ to $(H \cup V, BF)$ is morphism of many sorted algebra signatures $(H \cup V, BF) \to (H' \cup V', BF')$.*

A *quasi-morphism* $\varphi \colon (H, V, F, BF) \to (H', V', F', BF')$ is a signature morphism *if and only if the following 'encapsulation' condition holds:*

for any $\sigma' \in BF'_{w \to s}$, if $w \cap \varphi(H) \neq \emptyset$ (i.e. w contains an 'old' hidden sort) then there exists σ in BF such that $\sigma' = \varphi(\sigma)$.

The connection between the encapsulation condition for <u>HA</u> signature morphisms and the Satisfaction Condition from institution theory has been discovered in [23], where it had been noted for the first time this strong interdependency between the logic and engineering levels of behavioural specification. Work on the semantics and methodologies of structuring specifications directly motivated by CafeOBJ semantics is currently under development [15].

3   Heterogeneous Specification through Grothendieck Institutions

3.1   The CafeOBJ Cube

When a decision was made to shift the CafeOBJ focus from rewriting logic to behavioural specification, there was also the decision not to abandon completely rewriting logic. Without rewriting logic inside CafeOBJ, the language would have had a simpler semantics based upon hidden algebra. The way rewriting logic is realized in CafeOBJ is quite different from Maude, and in fact these days it is called differently, namely *preordered algebra* [11,12]. Firstly, CafeOBJ rewriting logic has a clear institution theoretic semantics based upon preordered algebra [19], which supports only unlabelled transitions.[1] Second, unlike in Maude rewriting logic, the equations and the transitions live at the same conceptual level. Consequently, in CafeOBJ it is possible to have equations conditioned by transitions. Some applications have showed that this is a very useful feature which is not possible in Maude where the level of the transitions is built on top of the equational logic level.

CafeOBJ not being anymore an orthodox rewriting logic language, and having also the other dimension of behavioural specification, it began to look more like a heterogeneous specification language. However in the mid nineties there was not yet a clear thinking about what heterogeneity really means and how to deal with it. Therefore it was desirable to have, at least at the level of the semantics, a conventional approach based upon institutions. But there was a serious obstacle given by the presence of rewriting logic which may be easily understood through the following very simple example of a specification of the order between natural numbers as transitions.

---

[1] This is one aspect that is incorrectly addressed in [17] and had been fixed in [19].

```
mod! TWO {
  [ s ]
  ops 0 1 : -> s .
}
mod! TRANS {
  protecting(TWO)
  trans 0 => 1 .
}
```

The semantics of TRANS is given by the preordered algebra that consists of the two elements Boolean partial order. But if we look at what happens with TWO then we see that if we treat its semantics as a preordered algebra then it is not protected anymore since the reduct from TRANS to TWO is not able to get rid off the order $0 \leq 1$ in order to obtain a discrete algebra (set) for TWO.

The dramatic implication of this example is that it does not suffice to work only within one logic, namely preordered algebra (eventually enhanced with hidden algebra things). It is rather necessary that each of the paradigms involved maintain the identities of their underlying logics, that we cannot just work within only a big one obtained as a combination of logics corresponding to the primitive specification paradigms. Instead we have to consider a *system of logics* in which the component logics are linked by their embedding relationships. In this system of logics, in order to have a smooth module structuring system for CafeOBJ, any two logics must have a least upper bound. That implied that everything had to be combined with everything else, which resulted in the following system of logics, known as the 'CafeOBJ cube'.

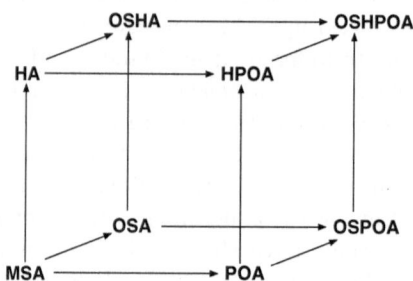

(In the cube 'OS' stands for 'order sorted', 'H' for 'hidden', and 'PO' for 'pre-ordered', 'A' for 'algebra' and 'MS' means many sorted.) Above we have given a modern version of the CafeOBJ cube that differs from the original one (e.g. from [17]) in two ways: rewriting logic is replaced by preordered algebra, and also the direction of the arrows is inverse. Below we will understand the significance of the latter aspect.

3.2   Logic Combination in CafeOBJ

The CafeOBJ cube represents a 3D system of logics, one dimension being the order sorted algebra, another hidden algebra, and the third one being preordered algebra. Then all possible combinations between these, the ultimate one being order sorted hidden preordered algebra. In the logic communities, logic combination has been for long time a hot research topic, the main result so far being the so-called fibring method [4]. However logic combination in CafeOBJ is quite different from fibring in that it is rather ad-hoc and based upon the intuitive combinations of the respective model theories. Because of the strong emphasis on model theory, this is beyond what fibring generally proposes. Fibring cannot capture properly combinations of model theories, and the consequence relations of the model theoretic logic combinations are in general stronger than those of the fibring theoretic logic combinations. On the other hand, of course, fibring is a general method, while the model theoretic combinations are still quite ad-hoc.

However logic combinations in CafeOBJ follow a general pattern, that although does not enjoy a full theoretical support, that appears also in other works such as [22,21,32,14] etc., and that may be described in general terms as follows. Given a logic L_1 and another logic L_2

1. we develop the essential features of L_2 at an abstract institution theory level, the result being a generalized abstract version of L_2, denoted $\mathcal{I}(L_2)$;
2. then the combination $L_1 \star L_2$ is obtained by instantiating the abstract parts of $\mathcal{I}(L_2)$ to L_1.

This is obviously a hierarchical asymmetric combination in which L_2 is developed on top of L_1. For example, in CafeOBJ the combination between hidden algebra and preordered algebra is a development of former on top of the latter [12].

It is worth mentioning that this method has been first realized and applied in [3] in order to achieve a combination between order sorted algebra and hidden algebra. A refinement of [3] that accommodates non-monadic hidden algebra has been developed in [36].

3.3   Grothendieck Institutions

Since the eighties the foundations of modern algebraic specification is based upon the theory of institutions of Goguen and Burstall [25]. Moreover other logic-based computing science areas are increasingly based upon institutions, most notably ontologies [24,35]. In the recent ISO standard 17347 Ontology Integration and Interoperability (OntoIOp) institution theory plays a core role. As a side comment, the enormous success of institution theory has extended beyond computing science, as it has become a major and perhaps the most developed trend of the so-called 'universal logic' in the sense envisaged by Béziau [2]. The monograph [11] includes some of the works on institutional abstract model theory, that are not necessarily computing science motivated.

So, the design ideology of modern logic-based specification languages is that there is an underlying logic, captured as an institution, such that all of the respective language constructs can be explained rigorously as mathematical concepts in the underlying institution. Then one may use the rather rich and advanced body of logic and specification concepts and results that have been developed over the past three decades at the general level of abstract institutions. The effort is rather minimal, just have to instantiate those to the concrete details of the actual institution underlying the respective language. Of course, this process requires that the designer of the language makes sure that the logic involved enjoys several institution theoretic properties that constitute the conditions for the development of the general results. The best example of a concrete realization of this ideology is constituted by the design of CASL [1]. At this stage it is useful to recall the definition of institutions.

Definition 6 (Institutions). *An institution* $\mathcal{I} = (Sig^{\mathcal{I}}, Sen^{\mathcal{I}}, Mod^{\mathcal{I}}, \models^{\mathcal{I}})$ *consists of*

1. *a category* $Sig^{\mathcal{I}}$, *whose objects are called* signatures,
2. *a functor* $Sen^{\mathcal{I}} : Sig^{\mathcal{I}} \to \mathbf{Set}$, *giving for each signature a set whose elements are called* sentences *over that signature,*
3. *a functor* $Mod^{\mathcal{I}} : (Sig^{\mathcal{I}})^{\mathrm{op}} \to \mathbf{CAT}$ *giving for each signature* Σ *a category whose objects are called* Σ-models, *and whose arrows are called* Σ-(model) homomorphisms, *and*
4. *a relation* $\models^{\mathcal{I}}_{\Sigma} \subseteq |Mod^{\mathcal{I}}(\Sigma)| \times Sen^{\mathcal{I}}(\Sigma)$ *for each* $\Sigma \in |Sig^{\mathcal{I}}|$, *called* Σ-satisfaction,

such that for each morphism $\varphi \colon \Sigma \to \Sigma'$ *in* $Sig^{\mathcal{I}}$, *the* satisfaction condition

$$M' \models^{\mathcal{I}}_{\Sigma'} Sen^{\mathcal{I}}(\varphi)(\rho) \quad \text{if and only if} \quad Mod^{\mathcal{I}}(\varphi)(M') \models^{\mathcal{I}}_{\Sigma} \rho$$

holds for each $M' \in |Mod^{\mathcal{I}}(\Sigma')|$ *and* $\rho \in Sen^{\mathcal{I}}(\Sigma)$.

The heterogeneous logical nature of CafeOBJ represented the single strongest obstacle that initially prevented CafeOBJ to benefit from the institution theoretic design ideology. Confronted with such difficulty, my first reaction was to begin a process of lifting the huge body of institution theoretic concepts and results supporting the specification theory and practice from the framework of a single institution to that of a system of institutions, and then to apply the fruits of this process to the CafeOBJ cube. The general results obtained in the process, reported in [7], may have constituted a first foundational theory of heterogeneous specification. When talking about 'systems of institutions' this does not mean a discrete collection of institutions but rather a diagram of homomorphisms linking the various component institutions. For this in [7] I considered the projection-styled institution homomorphisms as defined in [25].

Definition 7 (Institution morphism). *An* institution morphism (Φ, α, β) $: \mathcal{I}' \to \mathcal{I}$ *consists of*

1. *a functor* $\Phi \colon Sig' \to Sig$,
2. *a natural transformation* $\alpha \colon \Phi; Sen \Rightarrow Sen'$, *and*
3. *a natural transformation* $\beta \colon Mod' \Rightarrow \Phi^{\mathrm{op}}; Mod$

such that the following satisfaction condition *holds*

$$M' \models'_{\Sigma'} \alpha_{\Sigma'}(e) \quad \text{iff} \quad \beta_{\Sigma'}(M') \models_{\Phi(\Sigma')} e$$

for each signature $\Sigma' \in |Sig'|$, *for each* Σ'-*model* M', *and each* $\Phi(\Sigma')$-*sentence* e.

After [7] was published I have had a brief correspondence with Martin Hoffman who was working on a review of the paper for Mathematical Reviews. He raised one remark that triggered the hope about the possibility to come up with a general procedure to flatten a system of institutions back to a single institution that would maintain the substance of the heterogeneity but within a technically homogeneous situation. So I come up with the definition of the concept of Grothendieck institution which replicates the flattening construction from category theory invented by the famous algebraic geometrician Alexandre Grothendieck [29], to the much more refined framework of institutions. As shown in [8] both the original construction of Grothendieck and the Grothendieck institutions arise as a 2-categorical co-limit, the former in **CAT**, the 2-category of categories and functors, and the later in **INS**, the 2-category of institutions and institution morphisms. Let us recall the original definition from [8].

Definition 8. *Given a category I of indices, an* indexed institution $\mathcal{J}$ *is a functor* $\mathcal{J}: I^{\mathrm{op}} \to \mathbf{INS}$. *For each index* $i \in |I|$ *we denote the institution* $\mathcal{J}^i$ *by* $(\mathrm{Sig}^i, \mathrm{Mod}^i, \mathrm{Sen}^i, \models^i)$ *and for each index morphism* $u \in I$ *we denote the institution morphism* $\mathcal{J}^u$ *by* $(\varPhi^u, \alpha^u, \beta^u)$.

The Grothendieck institution $\mathcal{J}^\sharp = (\mathrm{Sig}^\sharp, \mathrm{Sen}^\sharp, \mathrm{Mod}^\sharp, \models^\sharp)$ *of an indexed institution* $\mathcal{J}: I^{\mathrm{op}} \to \mathbf{INS}$ *is defined as follows:*

1. *Let* $\mathrm{Sig}: I^{\mathrm{op}} \to \mathbb{C}\mathrm{at}$ *be the indexed institution mapping each index i to Sig^i and each index morphism u to $\varPhi^u$; then the category of the signatures of $\mathcal{J}^\sharp$ is the Grothendieck category $\mathrm{Sig}^\sharp$. Thus the signatures of $\mathcal{J}^\sharp$ consist of pairs $\langle i, \varSigma \rangle$ with i index and $\varSigma \in |\mathrm{Sig}^i|$ and signature morphisms $\langle u, \varphi \rangle: \langle i, \varSigma \rangle \to \langle i', \varSigma' \rangle$ consists of index morphisms $u: i \to i'$ and signature morphisms $\varphi: \varSigma \to \varPhi^u(\varSigma')$.*
2. *The model functor $\mathrm{Mod}^\sharp: (\mathrm{Sig}^\sharp)^{\mathrm{op}} \to \mathbb{C}\mathrm{at}$ is given by*
   - $\mathrm{Mod}^\sharp(\langle i, \varSigma \rangle) = \mathrm{Mod}^i(\varSigma)$ *for each index $i \in |I|$ and signature $\varSigma \in |\mathrm{Sig}^i|$, and*
   - $\mathrm{Mod}^\sharp(\langle u, \varphi \rangle) = \beta^u_{\varSigma'}; \mathrm{Mod}^i(\varphi)$ *for each* $\langle u, \varphi \rangle: \langle i, \varSigma \rangle \to \langle i', \varSigma' \rangle$.
3. *The sentence functor $\mathrm{Sen}^\sharp: \mathrm{Sig}^\sharp \to \mathbf{Set}$ is given by*
   - $\mathrm{Sen}^\sharp(\langle i, \varSigma \rangle) = \mathrm{Sen}^i(\varSigma)$ *for each index $i \in |I|$ and signature $\varSigma \in |\mathrm{Sig}^i|$, and*
   - $\mathrm{Sen}^\sharp(\langle u, \varphi \rangle) = \mathrm{Sen}^i(\varphi); \alpha^u_{\varSigma'}$ *for each* $\langle u, \varphi \rangle: \langle i, \varSigma \rangle \to \langle i', \varSigma' \rangle$.
4. *The satisfaction relation is given by*
   $$M \models^\sharp_{\langle i, \varSigma \rangle} e \quad \text{if and only if} \quad M \models^i_{\varSigma} e$$
   for each index $i \in |I|$, signature $\varSigma \in |\mathrm{Sig}^i|$, model $M \in |\mathrm{Mod}^\sharp(\langle i, \varSigma \rangle)|$, and sentence $e \in \mathrm{Sen}^\sharp(\langle i, \varSigma \rangle)$.

It is important to point out a crucial aspect of the Grothendieck construction. In a Grothendieck institution the individual identities of the original component institutions is preserved, it is not melted like in the case of the logic combinations. For example, in the case of the Grothendieck institution obtained from flattening of the CafeOBJ cube the result is very different from the upper bound of the logics in the cube, namely order sorted hidden preordered algebra. Unfortunately all these developments happened two years after the official CafeOBJ definition was published [17], however a corresponding upgrade of this was published in [19].

3.4   Morphisms or Co-morphisms?

Besides the definition of the Grothendieck institutions and the proof of their universal property, [8] also resumed from [7] the theme of lifting several properties important for specification theory from the local level of component institutions to the global level of the Grothendieck institution. From these properties model amalgamation was really difficult to prove and it required rather strong conditions. Joseph Goguen told me that Till Mossakowski was doing a replica of Grothendieck institutions using embedding-styled rather than projection-styles institution homomorphisms, called *co-morphisms* in [27].

Definition 9 (Institution co-morphisms). *An* institution co-morphism

$$(\Phi, \alpha, \beta) \colon \mathcal{I} \to \mathcal{I}'$$

consists of

1. *a functor* $\Phi \colon \mathrm{Sig} \to \mathrm{Sig}'$,
2. *a natural transformation* $\alpha \colon \mathrm{Sen} \Rightarrow \Phi; \mathrm{Sen}'$, *and*
3. *a natural transformation* $\beta \colon \Phi^{\mathrm{op}}; \mathrm{Mod}' \Rightarrow \mathrm{Mod}$

such that the following satisfaction condition *holds*

$$M' \models'_{\Phi(\Sigma)} \alpha_\Sigma(e) \quad \textit{iff} \quad \beta_\Sigma(M') \models_\Sigma e$$

for each signature $\Sigma \in |\mathrm{Sig}|$, *for each* $\Phi(\Sigma)$-*model* M', *and each* Σ-*sentence* e.

Till Mossakowski was claiming that obtaining model amalgamation in co-morphism-based Grothendieck institutions [34] was rather smooth. After overcoming an initial feeling of skepticism I came to understand what Till Mossakowski meant, and in fact the rather strong conditions of [8] for model amalgamation to hold in Grothendieck institutions were exactly the conditions required to turn a morphism-based Grothendieck construction into a co-morphism-based one. What happens is that, roughly speaking, any adjunction between the categories of signatures of institutions $\mathcal{I}$ and $\mathcal{I}'$ determines a canonical bijection between co-morphisms $\mathcal{I} \to \mathcal{I}'$ and morphisms $\mathcal{I}' \to \mathcal{I}$. Moreover, in a diagram of institutions, if any of the edges corresponds to an adjunction at the level of the categories of the signatures, then the morphism-based and the co-morphism-based Grothendieck constructions yield isomorphic results. This is also the case of the CafeOBJ institution, it can be obtained by flattening the CafeOBJ cube either considered with institution morphisms or with co-morphisms.

In any case Till Mossakowski was right, heterogeneous specification through Grothendieck institution is more convenient, and has more applications by co-morphisms rather than by morphisms. In fact my next paper dedicated to Grothendieck institutions [9] was already using the co-morphism-based construction. Moreover since several years all my references to the CafeOBJ cube are to its co-morphism-based version (e.g. [13]) rather to its morphism-based original version of [17,19].

3.5 The Wider Impact of Grothendieck Institutions

The Grothendieck construction on institutions did CafeOBJ a great service, it provided an underlying institution for CafeOBJ. The CafeOBJ institution is just the Grothendieck flattening of the CafeOBJ cube. But the impact of the Grothendieck institution concept has gone far beyond the world of CafeOBJ. Grothendieck institution have become a quite standard way to approach heterogeneity in logic-based contexts. They have been adopted as foundations for Hets, the heterogeneous environment around CASL [33], and recently for heterogeneous ontologies [35] (an idea already suggested by Goguen several years ago [24]). Surprising applications also happened in model theory, such as a general method to extend Craig interpolation to Craig-Robinson interpolation in logics without implication [11]. Grothendieck institutions have also inspired and called for the Grothendieck construction on inclusion systems [13] that provide an important technical device for the structuring of heterogeneous specifications.

4 Conclusions

We have discussed coherent hidden algebra, logic combination, and Grothendieck institutions. These are theoretical achievements coming originally from the CafeOBJ project, and they have played and continue to play a major role in my scientific career. I think even in the absence of the CafeOBJ project these would have been developed by others. Serious thinking about Grothendieck institutions was going in parallel from Till Mossakowski and I am also sure that eventually Grigore Roşu and Joseph Goguen would have had discovered by themselves alone the possibility of non-monadic hidden algebra. However the CafeOBJ project gave me the opportunity to get involved and work with these wonderful bits of math, logic and computer science; and this is not the only way Professor Futatsugi has contributed positively to my scientific career.

References

1. Astesiano, E., Bidoit, M., Kirchner, H., Krieg-Brückner, B., Mosses, P., Sannella, D., Tarlecki, A.: CASL: The common algebraic specification language. Theoretical Computer Science 286(2), 153–196 (2002)
2. Béziau, J.-Y.: 13 questions about universal logic. Bulletin of the Section of Logic 35(2/3), 133–150 (2006)
3. Burstall, R., Diaconescu, R.: Hiding and behaviour: An institutional approach. In: William Roscoe, A. (ed.) A Classical Mind: Essays in Honour of C.A.R. Hoare, pp. 75–92. Prentice-Hall, 1994. Also in Technical Report ECS-LFCS-8892-253, Laboratory for Foundations of Computer Science, University of Edinburgh (1992)
4. Carnielli, W., Coniglio, M., Gabbay, D.M., Gouveia, P., Sernadas, C.: Analysis and Synthesis of Logics How to Cut and Paste Reasoning Systems. Applied Logic —Series, vol. 35. Springer (2008)
5. Clavel, M., Durán, F., Eker, S., Lincoln, P., Martí-Oliet, N., Meseguer, J., Talcott, C.: All About Maude - A High-Performance Logical Framework. LNCS, vol. 4350. Springer, Heidelberg (2007)

6. Diaconescu, R.: Behavioural coherence in object-oriented algebraic specification. Technical Report IS-RR-98-0017F, Japan Advanced Institute for Science and Technology (June 1998)
7. Diaconescu, R.: Extra theory morphisms for institutions: Logical semantics for multi-paradigm languages. Applied Categorical Structures 6(4), 427–453 (1998). A preliminary version appeared as JAIST Technical Report IS-RR-97-0032F in 1997
8. Diaconescu, R.: Grothendieck institutions. Applied Categorical Structures 10(4), 383–402 (2002); Preliminary version appeared as IMAR Preprint 2-2000 (February 2000) ISSN 250-3638
9. Diaconescu, R.: Interpolation in Grothendieck institutions. Theoretical Computer Science 311, 439–461 (2004)
10. Diaconescu, R.: Behavioural specification of hierarchical object composition. Theoretical Computer Science 343(3), 305–331 (2005)
11. Diaconescu, R.: Institution-independent Model Theory. Birkhäuser (2008)
12. Diaconescu, R.: Coinduction for preordered algebras. Information and Computation 209(2), 108–117 (2011)
13. Diaconescu, R.: Grothendieck inclusion systems. Applied Categorical Structures 19(5), 783–802 (2011)
14. Diaconescu, R.: Quasi-varieties and initial semantics in hybridized institutions. Journal of Logic and Computation, doi:10.1093/logcom/ext016
15. Diaconescu, R., Țuțu, I.: Foundations for structuring behavioural specifications. Journal of Logic and Algebraic Programming (to appear)
16. Diaconescu, R., Țuțu, I.: On the algebra of structured specifications. Theoretical Computer Science 412(28), 3145–3174 (2011)
17. Diaconescu, R., Futatsugi, K.: CafeOBJ Report: The Language, Proof Techniques, and Methodologies for Object-Oriented Algebraic Specification. AMAST Series in Computing, vol. 6. World Scientific (1998)
18. Diaconescu, R., Futatsugi, K.: Behavioural coherence in object-oriented algebraic specification. Universal Computer Science 6(1), 74–96 (2000); First version appeared as JAIST Technical Report IS-RR-98-0017F (June 1998)
19. Diaconescu, R., Futatsugi, K.: Logical foundations of CafeOBJ. Theoretical Computer Science 285, 289–318 (2002)
20. Diaconescu, R., Goguen, J., Stefaneas, P.: Logical support for modularisation. In: Huet, G., Plotkin, G. (eds.) Logical Environments, pp. 83–130. Cambridge (1993). Proceedings of a Workshop held in Edinburgh, Scotland (May 1991)
21. Diaconescu, R., Stefaneas, P.: Ultraproducts and possible worlds semantics in institutions. Theoretical Computer Science 379(1), 210–230 (2007)
22. Finger, M., Gabbay, D.M.: Adding a temporal dimension to a logic system. Journal of Logic, Language and Information 1(3), 203–233 (1992)
23. Goguen, J.: Types as theories. In: Reed, G.M., Roscoe, A.W., Wachter, R.F. (eds.) Topology and Category Theory in Computer Science, pp. 357–390. Oxford (1991). Proceedings of a Conference held at Oxford (June 1989)
24. Goguen, J.: Data, schema, ontology and logic integration. Journal of IGPL 13(6), 685–715 (2006)
25. Goguen, J., Burstall, R.: Institutions: Abstract model theory for specification and programming. Journal of the Association for Computing Machinery 39(1), 95–146 (1992)
26. Goguen, J., Diaconescu, R.: Towards an algebraic semantics for the object paradigm. In: Ehrig, H., Orejas, F. (eds.) Abstract Data Types 1992 and COMPASS 1992. LNCS, vol. 785, pp. 1–34. Springer, Heidelberg (1994)

27. Goguen, J., Roşu, G.: Institution morphisms. Formal Aspects of Computing 13, 274–307 (2002)
28. Goguen, J., Winkler, T., Meseguer, J., Futatsugi, K., Jouannaud, J.-P.: Introducing OBJ. In: Goguen, J., Malcolm, G. (eds.) Software Engineering with OBJ: Algebraic Specification in Action. Kluwer (2000)
29. Grothendieck, A.: Catégories fibrées et descente. In: Revêtements Étales et Groupe Fondamental, Séminaire de Géométrie Algébrique du Bois-Marie 1960/61, Exposé VI. Lecture Notes in Mathematics, vol. 224. Institut des Hautes Études Scientifiques (1963); Reprinted in Lecture Notes in Mathematics, vol. 224, pp. 145–194. Springer (1971)
30. Iida, S.: An Algebraic Formal Method for Component based Software Developments. PhD thesis, Japan Advanced Institute for Science and Technology (1999)
31. Jacobs, B., Rutten, J.M.: A tutorial on (co)algebras and (co)induction. Bulletin of EATCS 62, 222–259 (1997)
32. Martins, M.A., Madeira, A., Diaconescu, R., Barbosa, L.S.: Hybridization of institutions. In: Corradini, A., Klin, B., Cîrstea, C. (eds.) CALCO 2011. LNCS, vol. 6859, pp. 283–297. Springer, Heidelberg (2011)
33. Mossakowski, T., Maeder, C., Lüttich, K.: The heterogeneous tool set. In: Grumberg, O., Huth, M. (eds.) TACAS 2007. LNCS, vol. 4424, pp. 519–522. Springer, Heidelberg (2007)
34. Mossakowski, T.: Comorphism-based Grothendieck logics. In: Diks, K., Rytter, W. (eds.) MFCS 2002. LNCS, vol. 2420, pp. 593–604. Springer, Heidelberg (2002)
35. Mossakowski, T., Kutz, O., Lange, C.: Semantics of Distributed Ontology Language: Institutes and institutions. In: Martí-Oliet, N., Palomino, M. (eds.) WADT 2012. LNCS, vol. 7841, pp. 212–230. Springer, Heidelberg (2013)
36. Popescu, A., Roşu, G.: Behavioral extensions of institutions. In: Fiadeiro, J.L., Harman, N.A., Roggenbach, M., Rutten, J. (eds.) CALCO 2005. LNCS, vol. 3629, pp. 331–347. Springer, Heidelberg (2005)
37. Reichel, H.: Behavioural equivalence – a unifying concept for initial and final specifications. In: Proceedings, Third Hungarian Computer Science Conference, Akademiai Kiado, Budapest (1981)
38. Roşu, G.: Hidden Logic. PhD thesis, University of California at San Diego (2000)
39. Roşu, G., Lucanu, D.: Circular coinduction: A proof theoretical foundation. In: Kurz, A., Lenisa, M., Tarlecki, A. (eds.) CALCO 2009. LNCS, vol. 5728, pp. 127–144. Springer, Heidelberg (2009)
40. Sannella, D., Tarlecki, A.: Foundations of Algebraic Specifications and Formal Software Development. Springer (2012)

Parchments for **CafeOBJ** Logics[*]

Till Mossakowski[1], Wiesław Pawłowski[2],
Donald Sannella[3], and Andrzej Tarlecki[4]

[1] Faculty of Computer Science, University of Magdeburg
[2] Institute of Informatics, University of Gdańsk
[3] Laboratory for Foundations of Computer Science, University of Edinburgh
[4] Institute of Informatics, University of Warsaw

Abstract. This paper addresses issues arising in the systematic construction of large logical systems. We rely on a model-theoretic view of logical systems, captured by *institutions* that are in turn presented by *parchments*. We define their categories, and study constructions that may be carried out in these categories. In particular we show how limits of parchments may be used to combine features involved in various logical systems, sometimes necessarily augmenting the universal construction by additional systematic adjustments. We illustrate these developments by sketching how the logical systems that form the logical foundations of CafeOBJ may be built in this manner.

1 Introduction

This paper is written as a tribute to Professor Kokichi Futatsugi, the leader of the algebraic specification community in Japan, whom we have had a chance to meet many times over the years. One of his major undertakings was the very successful CafeOBJ project [DF98], which led to the development of a system that implements and executes algebraic specifications, in the tradition of the OBJ family [GWM+00]. The system is based on solid logical foundations given by a family of logical systems linked by a number of logic morphisms, referred to as the *CafeOBJ cube* [DF02]:

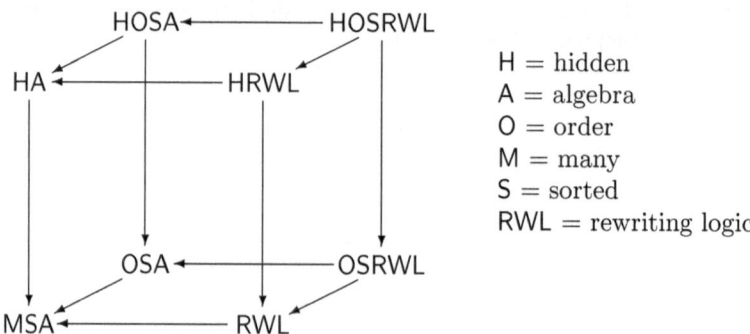

H = hidden
A = algebra
O = order
M = many
S = sorted
RWL = rewriting logic

[*] This work has been partially supported by the Polish Ministry of Science and Higher Education, grant N206 493138 (AT).

S. Iida, J. Meseguer, and K. Ogata (Eds.): Futatsugi Festschrift, LNCS 8373, pp. 66–91, 2014.

The eight logical systems listed above and the twelve arrows that link them are formalised as, respectively, *institutions* and *institution morphisms* [GB92]. The institution diagram above may be viewed as an *indexed institution*; the actual logical system that underlies CafeOBJ is given as the *Grothendieck institution* [Dia02] built out of it. Even if we prefer to think of the cube above as a heterogeneous logical environment [MT09] and work with heterogeneous specifications, technically the differences are negligible and the main point is to understand properly the CafeOBJ cube of institutions and their morphisms.

As far as we are aware, while the CafeOBJ literature presents the institutions involved in a manner that is sufficient to understand and work with them well, there is no document that presents the institutions involved formally in complete detail; this applies even more to the institution morphisms that link them. In a way, this is rather expected, as the details appear to be quite obvious, largely routine and repetitive from one institution to another, and from one morphism to another. So, the CafeOBJ authors present the interesting aspects of the institutions, leaving out the details.[1]

The main point of the present paper concerns the methodology of logic definitions. [DF02] defines the CafeOBJ cube in a top-down manner. Although in the literature, the concepts of order-sorting, rewriting logic and hidden algebra have been defined and studied (and integrated) separately, the technical presentation in [DF02] starts with a large combined institution, from which suitable subinstitutions are obtained subsequently. A drawback of this approach is the difficulty of changing individual feature components in a simple way. For example, [Dia07] claims that the base institution of equational logic could be replaced by membership equational logic, but to our knowledge, this has never been worked out. Indeed, working this out would imply a lot of tedious repetition of the original CafeOBJ definitions. However, even if the details seem routine and repetitive, one cannot just leave them out without a risk of unforeseen interactions between the modifications and the other features.

We therefore propose a bottom-up approach to the CafeOBJ cube. We present each of the features separately, and obtain the combined institution via a general universal construction. At each step of the combination, the details may be finetuned, if needed. This approach has the benefit of increased modularity: we can change certain feature components and then automatically re-generate the whole picture by repeating the universal constructions involved. In this paper, we concentrate on the methodology of this approach and therefore take the liberty of deviating from some details of the CafeOBJ institutions as defined in [DF02].

Like CafeOBJ, we follow Goguen and Burstall [GB92] and work within the theory of institutions as a formal framework to study and use logical systems. We will, however, look more closely at the structure of logical sentences and their semantics, and consider institutions to be presented by *parchments* [GB86]. We employ the version of parchments introduced in [MTP98] to avoid the technically

---

[1] We should stress though that this point may be due to our lack of complete knowledge of the CafeOBJ literature.

unnecessary and methodologically dubious blending of models into the syntactic aspects of logical systems.

We study various ways to extend, combine and modify these *model-theoretic parchments*, thus obtaining new logical systems and morphisms between them. We sketch how the logical systems in the CafeOBJ cube and morphisms between them may be obtained in such a way.

We start by recalling some standard algebraic notions (Sect. 2) and the basic concepts of the theory of institutions (Sect. 3). Then the less standard notions of model-theoretic parchment and parchment morphism are recalled in Sect. 4. The crucial property here is that when such parchments and their morphisms are *institutional*, they present institutions and institution morphisms, respectively. In Sect. 5 we discuss some simple ways to extend, combine and modify model-theoretic parchments and their morphisms, and in particular the use of limits in various parchment categories to combine institutions presented by parchments. We show how this works on some simple examples, sketching how the institutions and morphisms in the CafeOBJ cube may arise.

2 Algebraic Preliminaries

We briefly recall the key concepts and notations used throughout this paper; we refer to [ST12] for details omitted here.

First-order signatures are triples $\Theta = \langle S, \Omega, \Pi \rangle$, consisting of a set S of sorts, set Ω of operation names classified by their profiles (we write $f: s_1 \times \cdots \times s_n \to s$, $n \geq 0$, to indicate that f has the arity $s_1 \ldots s_n \in S^*$ and result sort $s \in S$) and set Π of predicate names classified by their profiles (we write $p: s_1 \times \cdots \times s_n$, $n \geq 0$, to indicate that the predicate p has arity $s_1 \ldots s_n \in S^*$). *First-order signature morphisms* map sorts, operation and predicate names to sorts, operation and predicate names, respectively, preserving their arities and result sorts. This yields the category **FOSig**.

Given a first-order signature $\Theta = \langle S, \Omega, \Pi \rangle$, a Θ-*structure* A consists of an S-sorted carrier set $|A| = \langle |A|_s \rangle_{s \in S}$, for each operation name $f: s_1 \times \cdots \times s_n \to s$, a function $f_A: |A|_{s_1} \times \cdots \times |A|_{s_n} \to |A|_s$, and for each predicate name $p: s_1 \times \cdots \times s_n$, a relation $p_A \subseteq |A|_{s_1} \times \cdots \times |A|_{s_n}$. A Θ-*homomorphism* $h: A \to B$ between two such Θ-structures is a family of maps $h = \langle h_s: |A|_s \to |B|_s \rangle_{s \in S}$ that preserves results of operations and predicate relations; h is *closed* if it also reflects predicate relations. $\mathbf{Str}(\Theta)$ is the category of Θ-structures and their (not necessarily closed) homomorphisms. For any first-order morphism $\theta: \Theta \to \Theta'$, we have the usual *reduct* functor $\mathbf{Str}(\theta): \mathbf{Str}(\Theta') \to \mathbf{Str}(\Theta)$, often written as $\_|_\theta$. This yields a functor $\mathbf{Str}: \mathbf{FOSig}^{op} \to \mathbf{Cat}$.[2]

---

[2] **Cat** denotes the (quasi-)category of all categories. We will gloss over fine foundational distinctions between categories at various levels of the hierarchy of universes [Mac71], and use the same term *category* to refer to (quasi-)categories of all categories, of all institutions, etc.

For any signature morphism $\theta\colon \Theta \to \Theta'$, the θ-reduct has a left adjoint $F_\theta\colon \mathbf{Str}(\Theta) \to \mathbf{Str}(\Theta')$; for any $A \in |\mathbf{Str}(\Theta)|$, $F_\theta(A) \in |\mathbf{Str}(\Theta')|$ is its *free extension* with unit $\eta_\theta\colon A \to F_\theta(A)|_\theta$.

Logic denotes a special signature with $*$ as the only sort, no operations and a unique predicate $\mathsf{D}\colon *$. $\mathbf{FOSig}_*$ is the subcategory of $\mathbf{FOSig}$ that has signatures that extend *Logic* and signature morphisms that are identities on *Logic*.

The category $\mathbf{FOSig}$ is cocomplete, with the standard colimit construction. The functor $\mathbf{Str}$ is continuous, which in particular implies that the amalgamation property holds. This carries over to $\mathbf{FOSig}_*$ and the restriction of $\mathbf{Str}$ to $\mathbf{FOSig}_*$.

For any signature Θ, Θ-terms and their evaluation in Θ-structures are defined as usual. In particular, the algebra T_Θ of terms with predicates interpreted as empty relations is initial in $\mathbf{Str}(\Theta)$. For any (ground) term $t \in |T_\Theta|$ and structure $A \in |\mathbf{Str}(\Theta)|$, we write $t_A \in |A|$ for the value of t in A (which is the value of the unique homomorphism $!_A\colon T_\Theta \to A$ on t).

Θ-equations and predicate applications, as well as their satisfaction in Θ-structures, are defined as usual.

Any signature morphism $\theta\colon \Theta \to \Theta'$ determines the obvious translation of Θ-terms to Θ'-terms, given by $\theta\colon T_\Theta \to T'_\Theta|_\theta$. This translation further extends to Θ-equations and predicate applications. Then for any term $t \in |T_\Theta|$, and Θ'-structure A', the crucial property is that $\theta(t)_{A'} = t_{A'|_\theta}$. This yields the famous *satisfaction condition* for equations and predicate applications: given any Θ-equation or predicate application φ and structure $A' \in |\mathbf{Str}(\Theta')|$, $A' \models_{\Theta'} \theta(\varphi)$ iff $A'|_\theta \models_\Theta \varphi$.

3   Institutions

Goguen and Burstall [GB92] formalised the notion of a logical system as an *institution*, thus starting a line of important developments of adequately abstract and general approaches to the foundations of software specifications and formal system development (as envisaged by the work on CLEAR [BG80], and carried forward by [ST88], see [ST12]), as well as a modern and elegant version of very abstract model theory (as proposed in [Tar86], see [Dia08]). Another important line of work which exploits institutions and their various morphisms [GR02] aims at moving between logical systems within a heterogeneous logical environment, comparing logical systems, and building complex logical systems in a systematic manner. In our view, in spite of work on various aspects of this area [Tar96, MTP97, MTP98, Tar00, CMRS01, CGR03, Mos03, Mos05, MT09], there is much to add here. The current paper is a contribution to this field.

An *institution* $\mathbf{INS} = \langle \mathbf{Sign}, \mathbf{Sen}, \mathbf{Mod}, \langle \models_\Sigma \rangle_{\Sigma \in |\mathbf{Sign}|} \rangle$ consists of:

- a category $\mathbf{Sign}$ of *signatures*;
- a functor $\mathbf{Sen}\colon \mathbf{Sign} \to \mathbf{Set}$ which for any signature $\Sigma \in |\mathbf{Sign}|$ yields a set $\mathbf{Sen}(\Sigma)$ of *sentences*, and for any signature morphism $\sigma\colon \Sigma \to \Sigma'$, a σ-*translation of sentences*, often written as $\sigma\colon \mathbf{Sen}(\Sigma) \to \mathbf{Sen}(\Sigma')$;

- a functor **Mod**: **Sign**^{op} → **Class**[3] which for any signature Σ yields a class **Mod**(Σ) of *models*, and for any morphism $\sigma: \Sigma \to \Sigma'$, a σ-*reduct of models* often written as $\_|_\sigma: \mathbf{Mod}(\Sigma') \to \mathbf{Mod}(\Sigma)$; and
- a *satisfaction relation* $\models_\Sigma \subseteq \mathbf{Mod}(\Sigma) \times \mathbf{Sen}(\Sigma)$ for any signature $\Sigma \in |\mathbf{Sign}|$

such that the following *satisfaction condition* holds: for any signature morphism $\sigma: \Sigma \to \Sigma'$, sentence $\varphi \in \mathbf{Sen}(\Sigma)$ and model $M' \in \mathbf{Mod}(\Sigma')$, $M' \models_{\Sigma'} \sigma(\varphi)$ iff $M'|_\sigma \models_\Sigma \varphi$.

For simplicity of presentation, we will look at examples of logical systems drawn from the CafeOBJ cube in their *ground* versions, without variables:

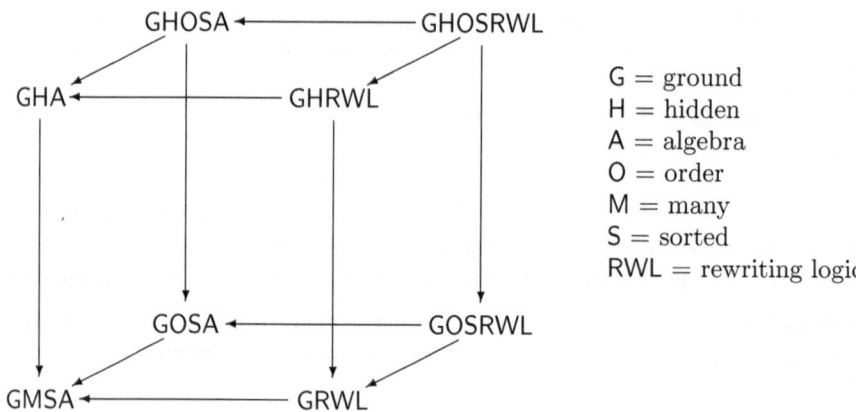

G = ground
H = hidden
A = algebra
O = order
M = many
S = sorted
RWL = rewriting logic

Variables and (universal) quantification may be introduced in a rather standard way, see Sect. 6 for some hints. Moreover, we will simplify all of the logical systems involved by disregarding the fact that all statements in CafeOBJ may be conditional [DF02] — hence there are no conditional statements in the logics below. Adding conditions to the sentences of each of the logics considered is straightforward. Thus, we consider ground atomic sentences of CafeOBJ logics.

Furthermore, we will only attempt to capture the essential features of the logics in the CafeOBJ cube, rather than follow their published definitions. Consequently, the exact details of the logics presented below may depart from their CafeOBJ inspirations.

Finally, the logics of CafeOBJ seem to be set up incrementally, so that for instance strict equations, behavioural (hidden) equations and rewriting statements coexist rather than replacing one another [DF02]. So, the version of rewriting logic we consider covers equations (inherited from many-sorted equational logic)

---

[3] **Class** is the quasi-category of all classes (or discrete categories). The standard definition of institution puts **Cat** here. There would be no problem in doing the same, and we realise that this is important for the semantics of CafeOBJ specifications. However, since model morphisms are orthogonal to the issues discussed in this paper, we decided to leave them out to simplify the technicalities and notation somewhat.

as well as rewriting statements. For presentation purposes, we will introduce another logical system, GPRWL, capturing ground rewriting statements only.[4]

Example 3.1. A trivial algebraic institution: A = $\langle \mathbf{AlgSig}, \mathbf{Sen}^{\emptyset}, \mathbf{Alg}, \models^{\emptyset} \rangle$, with *algebraic signatures* (i.e., first-order signatures with no predicates, so that **AlgSig** is the full subcategory of **FOSig**), with *algebras* (i.e., structures over algebraic signatures) as models (with reducts inherited from the definition of algebras as first-order structures, so that **Alg** is a "subfunctor" of **Str**), and with no sentences whatsoever (so that $\mathbf{Sen}^{\emptyset}(\Sigma) = \emptyset$).

Example 3.2. Ground equational institution: GMSA = $\langle \mathbf{AlgSig}, \mathbf{GEQ}, \mathbf{Alg}, \models \rangle$, where for each algebraic signature $\Sigma \in |\mathbf{AlgSig}|$, $\mathbf{GEQ}(\Sigma)$ is the set of ground (no variables) Σ-equations, with the translations along signatures morphisms and the satisfaction of equations in algebras defined in the standard way (as recalled in Sect. 2).

Example 3.3. The institution of ground order-sorted equational logic: GOSA = $\langle \mathbf{OSSig}, \mathbf{GOSEQ}, \mathbf{OSAlg}, \models \rangle$, where

- An order-sorted signature $\langle \Sigma, \leq \rangle$ is an algebraic signature Σ with a partial ordering $\leq$ on its set of sorts. Order-sorted signature morphisms are like algebraic signature morphisms which in addition must preserve the ordering. This yields the category **OSSig** of order-sorted signatures and their morphisms.
- For each order-sorted signature $\langle \Sigma, \leq \rangle$:
  - $\langle \Sigma, \leq \rangle$-terms are built as usual, except that in addition to the operations in Σ, a subsort inclusion $\iota_{s \leq s'} : s \to s'$ and retract $r_{s \leq s'} : s' \to s$ is available when $s \leq s'$. Then $\mathbf{Sen}^{\mathsf{GOSA}}(\langle \Sigma, \leq \rangle)$ contains equations between such ground terms.
  - An order-sorted $\langle \Sigma, \leq \rangle$-algebra A is a Σ-algebra where for any sorts $s \leq s'$, $|A|_s \subseteq |A|_{s'}$.
  - Evaluation of order-sorted $\langle \Sigma, \leq \rangle$-terms is as usual, except that the inclusions $\iota_{s \leq s'}$ are interpreted as inclusions from $|A|_s$ to $|A|_{s'} \supseteq |A|_s$, and retracts $r_{s \leq s'}$ as maximal partial identities from $|A|_{s'}$ to $|A|_s \subseteq |A|_{s'}$. So, term evaluation is *partial*.[5] A ground order-sorted equation $t = t'$ holds in an order-sorted algebra A, written as usual $A \models t = t'$, if the values in A of both t and t' are defined and equal.

Example 3.4. Ground rewriting institution GPRWL = $\langle \mathbf{AlgSig}, \mathbf{GRW}, \mathbf{RAlg}, \models \rangle$ with algebraic signatures, and then for each signature $\Sigma \in |\mathbf{AlgSig}|$,

- sentences in $\mathbf{GRW}(\Sigma)$ are *rewritings* (or *transitions*) $t \Rightarrow t'$ between (ground) terms of a common sort,

---

[4] P stands for "pure".

[5] We depart here from CafeOBJ, which to handle partiality either refers to the order-sorted [GM92] tradition, relying on the use of "error supersorts", with retracts yielding "erroneous terms" rather than being undefined, or vaguely mentions membership equational logic [Mes98].

- models in $\mathbf{RAlg}(\Sigma)$ are *rewriting algebras*[6], i.e., Σ-algebras $A \in \mathbf{Alg}(\Sigma)$ additionally equipped with a *rewriting relation* $\preceq_s \subseteq |A|_s \times |A|_s$ on the carrier of each sort s in Σ, where the family of the rewriting relations is required to be a *precongruence* on A, i.e., a preorder that is preserved (in the obvious sense) by all of the operations in A,
- a Σ-rewriting $t \Rightarrow t'$ holds in a rewriting algebra $A \in \mathbf{RAlg}(\Sigma)$, written as usual $A \models t \Rightarrow t'$, if $t_A \preceq t'_A$.

Example 3.5. The institution of ground behavioural equational logic GHA $=$ $\langle \mathbf{BehSig}, \mathbf{GBEQ}, \mathbf{Alg}, \models \rangle$, where:[7]

- A *behavioural signature* $\langle \Sigma, OBS \rangle$ consists of an algebraic signature Σ together with the indicated set OBS of *observable* sorts in Σ. Behavioural signature morphisms are those algebraic signature morphisms that preserve the sets of observable and of non-observable sorts and, stating the extra condition somewhat informally, add no new terms leading from an "old" non-observable sort to an observable sort. This defines the category of behavioural signatures $\mathbf{BehSig}$.
- For each behavioural signature $\langle \Sigma, OBS \rangle$,
  - sentences are pairs of (ground) terms of a common sort, just like Σ-equations, but we write them here as $t \sim t'$,
  - models are just Σ-algebras,
  - for each Σ-algebra A, let $\approx_A$ be the *indistinguishability* relation, i.e., the largest congruence on the subalgebra of A generated by the sorts in OBS that is the identity on the carriers of sorts in OBS (so that $a \approx_A b$ iff, relying on standard concepts and notation, for all contexts C of an observable sort, $C_A[a] = C_A[b]$). A ground Σ-equation $t \sim t'$ *behaviourally* holds in A, written $A \models t \sim t'$, if $t_A \approx_A t'_A$.

Given institutions $\mathbf{INS} = \langle \mathbf{Sign}, \mathbf{Sen}, \mathbf{Mod}, \langle \models_\Sigma \rangle_{\Sigma \in |\mathbf{Sign}|} \rangle$ and $\mathbf{INS}' = \langle \mathbf{Sign}', \mathbf{Sen}', \mathbf{Mod}', \langle \models'_{\Sigma'} \rangle_{\Sigma' \in |\mathbf{Sign}'|} \rangle$, an *institution morphism* $\mu \colon \mathbf{INS} \to \mathbf{INS}'$ consists of

- a functor $\mu^{Sig} \colon \mathbf{Sign} \to \mathbf{Sign}'$,
- a natural transformation $\mu^{Sen} \colon \mu^{Sig};\mathbf{Sen}' \to \mathbf{Sen}$, and
- a natural transformation $\mu^{Mod} \colon \mathbf{Mod} \to (\mu^{Sig})^{op};\mathbf{Mod}'$

such that the following *satisfaction condition* holds: for any signature $\Sigma \in |\mathbf{Sign}|$, sentence $\varphi' \in \mathbf{Sen}'(\mu^{Sig}(\Sigma))$ and model $M \in \mathbf{Mod}(\Sigma)$, $M \models_\Sigma \mu^{Sen}_\Sigma(\varphi')$ iff $\mu^{Mod}_\Sigma(M) \models'_{\mu^{Sig}(\Sigma)} \varphi'$.

---

[6] This terminology follows [DF02], even though recently some CafeOBJ authors go back to the more traditional term *(pre)ordered algebras*.

[7] This is a crude version of the behavioural (hidden) equational logic of CafeOBJ presented in [DF02], which has a more subtle treatment of observability, specifying the set of operations that may be used as observers rather than indicating observable sorts, much in the style of constructor observational logic COL [BH06], going back perhaps to [SW83, ST87]. We omit here *coherence* statements, which are trivial in our behavioural institution.

Institution morphisms compose in the obvious, component-wise manner. We thus have a category $\mathcal{INS}$ of institutions and their morphisms.

Example 3.6. There are evident institution morphisms from the institutions GMSA, GOSA, GPRWL, GHA given in Examples 3.2, 3.3, 3.4 and 3.5, respectively, to the institution A of Example 3.1; in each case signatures are mapped to their underlying algebraic signatures, and models to their underlying algebras (some of these mappings are identities, of course).

Example 3.7. The trivial morphism from GOSA to A of Example 3.6 extends easily to a morphism from GOSA to GMSA, with the translation of (ground) equations in GMSA to order-sorted equations being the identity.

Example 3.8. The trivial morphism from GHA to A of Example 3.6 does not extend to an institution morphism from GHA to GMSA — one may try to map equations $t = t'$ to behavioural equations $t \sim t'$ and check that one implication of the satisfaction condition would in general fail.

However, we may construct a different morphism, based on a signature functor that maps any behavioural signature $\langle \langle S, \Omega \rangle, OBS \rangle$ to the algebraic signature $\langle OBS, \Omega_{OBS} \rangle$ with observable sorts only and operations limited to *observable operations*, i.e., operations with observable arity and result sorts. Algebras are then mapped to their appropriate reducts, and (ground) equations over such limited signatures are mapped to their behavioural versions. It is easy to see that the satisfaction condition holds for such equations.

It is relatively easy to show completeness of the category $\mathcal{INS}$ of institutions and their morphisms:

Theorem 3.9 ([Tar86]). $\mathcal{INS}$ *is complete.*

In essence, the limit of a diagram of institutions is built by first defining the category of signatures as the limit of the categories of signatures of the institutions in the diagram. Signatures so defined in essence combine individual signatures in the institutions in the diagram linked by the signature functors of the institution morphisms involved. Then for each such "combined" signature, the set of sentences is defined as the colimit of the sets of sentences over the corresponding individual signatures with sentence translations between them given by the institution morphisms. Dually, the class of models is defined as the limit of the model classes over the corresponding individual signatures with model translations between them given by the institution morphisms. Finally, the satisfaction relation is defined uniquely so that the satisfaction condition holds for each of the resulting projection morphisms.

Example 3.10. The institution GRWL is defined as a pullback of GMSA and GPRWL over A (via the trivial morphisms of Example 3.6). It has algebraic signatures (common to GMSA and GPRWL), rewriting algebras of GPRWL as models (mapped onto the class of algebras of GMSA) and sentences that are either equations (coming from GMSA) or rewritings (from GPRWL), with satisfaction inherited from the appropriate component institutions.

Example 3.11. Similarly, we may consider a pullback of GMSA and GHA over A (via the morphisms of Example 3.6). It has behavioural signatures as signatures, behavioural algebras as models, and sentences that are either (ground) equations of GMSA or behavioural equations of GHA. The morphism from GHA to GMSA of Example 3.8 is not involved here, and the two sets of sentences remain separate, even though one might want to identify equations between terms of observable sorts with their behavioural versions.

Example 3.12. We may also form a pullback of GOSA and GRWL over GMSA (via the morphism of Example 3.7 and the morphism given by the pullback construction of GRWL in Example 3.10). This would not be quite satisfactory though: in such a pullback institution, sentences would be either equations between order-sorted terms, as expected, or rewritings, but only between ordinary many-sorted terms. There would be no rewritings between order-sorted terms that involve subsort inclusions and retracts, which we would like to include in a combination of order-sorted algebra and rewriting logic as well. On the positive side: as expected, equations between the terms we have in GRWL would be glued together with their corresponding order-sorted equations.

Example 3.13. Another interesting pullback that is not adequate as a logic combination is the pullback of GHA and GRWL over GMSA (via the morphism of Example 3.8 and the morphism given by the pullback construction of GRWL in Example 3.10). The pullback institution has behavioural signatures as signatures (that map to the algebraic signatures in GRWL as in the morphism given in Example 3.8), and as models algebras with carriers equipped with a rewriting preorder on observable sorts only, preserved by observable operations. As sentences, we would get behavioural equations, here including standard equations between terms built using solely observable operations, and rewritings between such terms only. Clearly, what would be "missing" are rewritings between terms involving operations with non-observable result sorts.

4   Model-Theoretic Parchments

Examples 3.12 and 3.13 illustrate a major problem with using institutions and their limits as a tool for combining logical systems. Since logical sentences in institutions are regarded as unstructured entities, this works as expected only when we put together logical systems with sentences that capture distinct properties that do not interact with each other, as in Examples 3.10 and 3.11. Otherwise, we would prefer to combine the ways sentences are built, rather than sets of sentences as such. Consequently, we have to look more closely at sentence construction. To capture this, Goguen and Burstall [GB86] introduced *parchments*, an algebraic way to present institutions, where the syntax of sentences is given by the initial (term) algebra over a signature that lists the operations for constructing sentences and other auxiliary syntactic phrases. Parchments also presented models as signature morphisms into a special "large" signature, naming all potential denotations for signature components, with an indicated

Procrustean structure comprising all these denotations. Semantics of syntactic phrases is then captured by mapping the initial syntax to the corresponding reduct of the Procrustean algebra. The disadvantage is not only the need to use such "large" objects (with all the foundational worries they bring) but also that we inherently mix together model-theoretic and syntactic aspects of logical systems presented in such a way. To avoid this, in [MTP98] we proposed a version of parchments that keeps the models separate and splits the Procrustean semantic object into smaller objects appropriate for each model considered.

This means that model-theoretic parchments comprise signatures and models in the same way as institutions do. However, while in institutions sentences are given directly by the sentence functor, model-theoretic parchments feature a language functor that maps each signature of the model-theoretic parchment to a first-order signature with an algebraic part representing the abstract syntax of sentences[8]; sentences are then generated as terms of the distinguished sort $*$. Moreover, instead of a satisfaction relation, model-theoretic parchments, for each signature and model, feature an *evaluation structure* that gives interpretation for the syntactic constructs used to build sentences. The interpretation of terms in the evaluation structure determines the meaning of syntactic phrases used in sentences, and of sentences themselves. A sentence holds in a model when in the evaluation structure for this model the sentence as a term evaluates to a logical value designated by the special predicate D. Finally, the satisfaction condition is ensured by suitable coherence homomorphisms between evaluation structures.

A *model-theoretic parchment* (or briefly: *parchment*) $\mathbf{P} = \langle \mathbf{Sign}, \mathbf{L}, \mathbf{Mod}, \mathcal{G} \rangle$ consists of:

- a category **Sign** of signatures;
- a functor $\mathbf{L} \colon \mathbf{Sign} \to \mathbf{FOSig}_*$ that for any signature $\Sigma \in |\mathbf{Sign}|$ yields a first-order signature $\mathbf{L}(\Sigma)$ that gives the abstract syntax for sentences;
- a functor $\mathbf{Mod} \colon \mathbf{Sign}^{op} \to \mathbf{Class}$ (as for institutions); and
- a family $\mathcal{G}$ that in turn consists of:[9]
  - for any signature $\Sigma \in |\mathbf{Sign}|$ and model $M \in \mathbf{Mod}(\Sigma)$, an $\mathbf{L}(\Sigma)$-structure $\mathcal{G}_\Sigma(M) \in |\mathbf{Str}(\mathbf{L}(\Sigma))|$; and
  - for any signature morphism $\sigma \colon \Sigma \to \Sigma'$ and model $M' \in \mathbf{Mod}(\Sigma')$, an $\mathbf{L}(\Sigma)$-homomorphism $\mathcal{G}_\sigma(M') \colon \mathcal{G}_\Sigma(M'|_\sigma) \to \mathcal{G}_{\Sigma'}(M')|_{\mathbf{L}(\sigma)}$

  such that for any signature morphisms $\sigma_1 \colon \Sigma_0 \to \Sigma_1$, $\sigma_2 \colon \Sigma_1 \to \Sigma_2$ and model $M_2 \in \mathbf{Mod}(\Sigma_2)$, $\mathcal{G}_{\sigma_1;\sigma_2}(M_2) = \mathcal{G}_{\sigma_1}(M_2|_{\sigma_2}); \mathcal{G}_{\sigma_2}(M_2)|_{\mathbf{L}(\sigma_1)}$.

Informally, for any signature $\Sigma \in |\mathbf{Sign}|$ and model $M \in \mathbf{Mod}(\Sigma)$, the *evaluation structure* $\mathcal{G}_\Sigma(M)$ determines semantic evaluation of $\mathbf{L}(\Sigma)$-phrases in the model M. Then the *mediating homomorphisms* $\mathcal{G}_\sigma(M') \colon \mathcal{G}_\Sigma(M'|_\sigma) \to$

---

[8] This relies on the usual correspondence between context-free grammars and algebraic signatures.

[9] $\mathcal{G}$ may be viewed as a signature-preserving functor between Grothendieck categories built by "flattening" $\mathbf{Mod} \colon \mathbf{Sign}^{op} \to \mathbf{Class}$ and $\mathbf{L}^{op}; \mathbf{Str} \colon \mathbf{Sign}^{op} \to \mathbf{Cat}$, respectively, cf. [TBG91]. We prefer to indicate the components of $\mathcal{G}$ explicitly, so we refrain from spelling out and using this alternative formulation.

$\mathcal{G}_{\Sigma'}(M')|_{\mathbf{L}(\sigma)}$ ensure that this evaluation changes smoothly when we move from one signature to another, and so is in a sense uniform for the entire logical system presented by the parchment. However, the uniformity as captured by the mediating homomorphisms implies that semantic properties are preserved, but not necessarily reflected, by model reducts w.r.t. signature morphisms.

We think of the set $|\mathcal{G}_{\Sigma}(M)|_*$ as the set of logical values for evaluation of Σ-sentences in $M \in \mathbf{Mod}(\Sigma)$. By allowing arbitrary sets of values here we naturally accommodate various forms of many-valued logics, with non-standard logical values permitted. Then the predicate $\mathsf{D}\colon *$ designates the logical values that indicate which sentences "hold" in the model, thus enabling a classical two-valued understanding of satisfaction on top of possibly many-valued sentence evaluation.

A parchment as above is *institutional* if for any signature morphism $\sigma\colon \Sigma \to \Sigma'$ and model $M' \in \mathbf{Mod}(\Sigma')$, $\mathcal{G}_{\sigma}(M')\colon \mathcal{G}_{\Sigma}(M'|_{\sigma}) \to \mathcal{G}_{\Sigma'}(M')|_{\mathbf{L}(\sigma)}$ is a closed $\mathbf{L}(\Sigma)$-homomorphism on the subsignature *Logic*, that is $|\mathcal{G}_{\sigma}(M')|_*$ preserves and reflects the predicate $\mathsf{D}\colon *$.[10] Then, such an institutional parchment is *Boolean* if for any signature $\Sigma \in |\mathbf{Sign}|$ and model $M \in \mathbf{Mod}(\Sigma)$, $|\mathcal{G}_{\Sigma}(M)|_* = Bool$, where $Bool = \{tt, f\!f\}$, and $\mathsf{D}_{\mathcal{G}_{\Sigma}(M)} = \{tt\}$ (it follows that the homomorphisms $\mathcal{G}_{\sigma}(M')$ are identities on the sort $*$). We say that a parchment is *strict* if for any signature morphism $\sigma\colon \Sigma \to \Sigma'$ and model $M' \in \mathbf{Mod}(\Sigma')$, $\mathcal{G}_{\sigma}(M')\colon \mathcal{G}_{\Sigma}(M'|_{\sigma}) \to \mathcal{G}_{\Sigma'}(M')|_{\mathbf{L}(\sigma)}$ is the identity; in particular, all strict parchments are institutional.

Any institutional parchment $\mathbf{P} = \langle \mathbf{Sign}, \mathbf{L}, \mathbf{Mod}, \mathcal{G} \rangle$ *presents* the institution $\mathcal{J}(\mathbf{P}) = \langle \mathbf{Sign}, \mathbf{Sen}, \mathbf{Mod}, \langle \models_{\Sigma} \rangle_{\Sigma \in |\mathbf{Sign}|} \rangle$, which inherits signatures and models directly from $\mathbf{P}$, and

- for $\Sigma \in |\mathbf{Sign}|$, $\mathbf{Sen}(\Sigma) = |T_{\mathbf{L}(\Sigma)}|_*$, where $T_{\mathbf{L}(\Sigma)}$ is the initial $\mathbf{L}(\Sigma)$-structure (so that Σ-sentences are ground $\mathbf{L}(\Sigma)$-terms of sort $*$),
- for $\sigma\colon \Sigma \to \Sigma'$, $\mathbf{Sen}(\sigma) = (!_{\sigma})_*$, where $!_{\sigma}\colon T_{\mathbf{L}(\Sigma)} \to T_{\mathbf{L}(\Sigma')}|_{\mathbf{L}(\sigma)}$ is the unique $\mathbf{L}(\Sigma)$-homomorphism given by the initiality of $T_{\mathbf{L}(\Sigma)}$, and
- for $\Sigma \in |\mathbf{Sign}|$, $\varphi \in |T_{\mathbf{L}(\Sigma)}|_*$, and $M \in \mathbf{Mod}(\Sigma)$, $M \models_{\Sigma} \varphi$ iff $\varphi_{\mathcal{G}_{\Sigma}(M)} \in \mathsf{D}_{\mathcal{G}_{\Sigma}(M)}$ (i.e., in $\mathcal{G}_{\Sigma}(M)$ the predicate D holds on the value of φ viewed as a $\mathbf{L}(\Sigma)$-term of sort $*$).

One can check now that $\mathcal{J}(\mathbf{P})$ so defined is indeed an institution, where for $\sigma\colon \Sigma \to \Sigma'$, $\varphi \in \mathbf{Sen}(\Sigma)$ and $M' \in \mathbf{Mod}(\Sigma')$, the satisfaction condition follows since the homomorphism $\mathcal{G}_{\sigma}(M')$ preserves and reflects the predicate $\mathsf{D}\colon *$.

A parchment $\mathbf{P} = \langle \mathbf{Sign}, \mathbf{L}, \mathbf{Mod}, \mathcal{G} \rangle$ is *atomic* if for all $\Sigma \in |\mathbf{Sign}|$, the first-order signature $\mathbf{L}(\Sigma)$ has no operations with $*$ in their arity. In that case, no sentence is constructed out of other sentences, and so, informally, all the sentences are atomic.

Example 4.1. A Boolean parchment that presents the institution A of Example 3.1 is $\mathbf{P}_{\mathsf{A}} = \langle \mathbf{AlgSig}, \mathbf{L}^{\mathsf{A}}, \mathbf{Alg}, \mathcal{G}^{\mathsf{A}} \rangle$ with algebraic signatures, with algebras as models, and where for any $\Sigma \in |\mathbf{AlgSig}|$, $\mathbf{L}^{\mathsf{A}}(\Sigma)$ extends *Logic* by

---

[10] This requirement is deliberately weaker than that imposed on "logical" parchments in [MTP98].

adding (the sorts and operations of) Σ, and then for any algebra $A \in \mathbf{Alg}(\Sigma)$, $\mathcal{G}_\Sigma^A(A) \in \mathbf{Str}(\mathbf{L}^A(\Sigma))$ coincides with A on Σ, with identity mediating homomorphisms.

Example 4.2. A Boolean parchment that in essence presents the institution GMSA of Example 3.2 is $\mathbf{P}_{\mathsf{GMSA}} = \langle \mathbf{AlgSig}, \mathbf{L}^{\mathsf{GMSA}}, \mathbf{Alg}, \mathcal{G}^{\mathsf{GMSA}} \rangle$, with algebraic signatures, with algebras as models, and where for any $\Sigma \in |\mathbf{AlgSig}|$:

- $\mathbf{L}^{\mathsf{GMSA}}(\Sigma)$ extends *Logic* by adding Σ and for each sort s in Σ, a binary operation $eq\colon s \times s \to *$;
- for any algebra $A \in \mathbf{Alg}(\Sigma)$, $\mathcal{G}_\Sigma^{\mathsf{GMSA}}(A) \in \mathbf{Str}(\mathbf{L}^{\mathsf{GMSA}}(\Sigma))$ is A on Σ, and interprets eq as the diagonal function, yielding tt if its two arguments coincide, and $f\!f$ if they are distinct; and
- mediating homomorphisms are identities.

Now, $\mathbf{L}^{\mathsf{GMSA}}(\Sigma)$-terms of sort $*$ are of the form $eq(t, t')$, for Σ-terms t and t' of a common sort. Such a term evaluates to tt in $\mathcal{G}_\Sigma^{\mathsf{GMSA}}(A)$ if the terms t and t' evaluate in $\mathcal{G}_\Sigma^{\mathsf{GMSA}}(A)$ (or equivalently, in A) to equal values. Consequently, the parchment $\mathbf{P}_{\mathsf{GMSA}}$ presents the institution GMSA, modulo the details of the actual notation used for sentences (we will disregard such differences from now on).

Example 4.3. A Boolean parchment that presents the institution GOSA of Example 3.3 is $\mathbf{P}_{\mathsf{GOSA}} = \langle \mathbf{OSSig}, \mathbf{L}^{\mathsf{GOSA}}, \mathbf{OSAlg}, \mathcal{G}^{\mathsf{GOSA}} \rangle$, with order-sorted signatures, with order-sorted algebras as models, and then for any order-sorted signature $\langle \Sigma, \le \rangle$:

- $\mathbf{L}^{\mathsf{GOSA}}(\langle \Sigma, \le \rangle)$ extends *Logic* by Σ and all the subsort inclusions and retracts, as well as the operation $eq\colon s \times s \to *$ for each sort s in Σ;
- for each order-sorted algebra $A \in \mathbf{OSAlg}(\langle \Sigma, \le \rangle)$, $\mathcal{G}_{\langle \Sigma, \le \rangle}^{\mathsf{GOSA}}(A)$ expands A on Σ by adding an "undefined" element $\bot$ to the carrier of each sort s in Σ and extending the interpretation of all operations in A so that they are strict on $\bot$ (yield $\bot$ as the result on any tuple of arguments that contains $\bot$), and interprets subsort inclusions and retracts in the obvious way (retracts map to $\bot$ the elements of the supersort that are not in the subsort) and the eq operations as the diagonal on the "defined" elements in $|A|$ and yielding $f\!f$ when any of its arguments is $\bot$; and
- mediating morphisms are identities again.

Now, an order-sorted $\langle \Sigma, \le \rangle$-term with a defined value in an order-sorted $\langle \Sigma, \le \rangle$-algebra A evaluates to the same value in $\mathcal{G}_{\langle \Sigma, \le \rangle}^{\mathsf{GOSA}}(A)$; if it is undefined in A then in $\mathcal{G}_{\langle \Sigma, \le \rangle}^{\mathsf{GOSA}}(A)$ it has the value $\bot$. Hence, $eq(t, t')$ evaluates to tt in $\mathcal{G}_{\langle \Sigma, \le \rangle}^{\mathsf{GOSA}}(A)$ iff the values of t and t' in A are defined and equal. Consequently, the parchment $\mathbf{P}_{\mathsf{GOSA}}$ indeed presents the institution GOSA.

Example 4.4. A Boolean parchment that presents the institution GPRWL of Example 3.4 is $\mathbf{P}_{\mathsf{GPRWL}} = \langle \mathbf{AlgSig}, \mathbf{L}^{\mathsf{GPRWL}}, \mathbf{RAlg}, \mathcal{G}^{\mathsf{GPRWL}} \rangle$, with algebraic signatures, with rewriting algebras as models, and where for any $\Sigma \in |\mathbf{AlgSig}|$:

- $\mathbf{L}^{\mathsf{GPRWL}}(\Sigma)$ extends *Logic* by adding Σ and for each sort s in Σ a binary operation $rwrt\colon s \times s \to *$,
- for any rewriting algebra $A \in \mathbf{RAlg}(\Sigma)$, $\mathcal{G}^{\mathsf{GPRWL}}_{\Sigma}(A) \in \mathbf{Str}(\mathbf{L}^{\mathsf{GPRWL}}(\Sigma))$ is the standard algebra part of A on Σ, and interprets each $rwrt$ so that it yields tt if its two arguments are in the rewriting precongruence, and $f\!f$ otherwise, and
- mediating homomorphisms are identities.

Example 4.5. A Boolean parchment that presents the institution GHA of Example 3.5 is $\mathbf{P}_{\mathsf{GHA}} = \langle \mathbf{BehSig}, \mathbf{L}^{\mathsf{GHA}}, \mathbf{Alg}, \mathcal{G}^{\mathsf{GHA}} \rangle$, with behavioural signatures and algebras as models, and where for any $\Sigma \in |\mathbf{AlgSig}|$:

- $\mathbf{L}^{\mathsf{GHA}}(\Sigma)$ extends *Logic* by adding Σ and for each sort s in Σ a binary operation $beq\colon s \times s \to *$, and
- for any algebra $A \in \mathbf{Alg}(\Sigma)$, $\mathcal{G}^{\mathsf{GHA}}_{\Sigma}(A) \in \mathbf{Str}(\mathbf{L}^{\mathsf{GHA}}(\Sigma))$ is A on Σ, and interprets beq to capture the indistinguishability relation, yielding tt if its two arguments are related by $\approx_A$, and $f\!f$ otherwise, and
- mediating homomorphisms are identities.[11]

Clearly, all parchments in Examples 4.1–4.5 are atomic and strict.

Given two parchments $\mathbf{P} = \langle \mathbf{Sign}, \mathbf{L}, \mathbf{Mod}, \mathcal{G} \rangle$ and $\mathbf{P}' = \langle \mathbf{Sign}', \mathbf{L}', \mathbf{Mod}', \mathcal{G}' \rangle$, a *parchment morphism* $\gamma\colon \mathbf{P} \to \mathbf{P}'$ consists of:

- a functor $\gamma^{Sig}\colon \mathbf{Sign} \to \mathbf{Sign}'$,
- a natural transformation $\gamma^{Lan}\colon \gamma^{Sig};\mathbf{L}' \to \mathbf{L}$,
- a natural transformation $\gamma^{Mod}\colon \mathbf{Mod} \to (\gamma^{Sig})^{op};\mathbf{Mod}'$,
- a family of homomorphisms $\gamma^{\mathcal{G}}_{\Sigma,M}\colon \mathcal{G}'_{\gamma^{Sig}(\Sigma)}(\gamma^{Mod}_{\Sigma}(M)) \to \mathcal{G}_{\Sigma}(M)|_{\gamma^{Lan}_{\Sigma}}$, for $\Sigma \in |\mathbf{Sign}|$ and $M \in \mathbf{Mod}(\Sigma)$, such that for any signature morphism $\sigma\colon \Sigma_1 \to \Sigma_2$ in $\mathbf{Sign}$ and model $M_2 \in \mathbf{Mod}(\Sigma_2)$ we have

$$\gamma^{\mathcal{G}}_{\Sigma_1,M_2}\big|_{\sigma};\mathcal{G}_{\sigma}(M_2)\big|_{\gamma^{Lan}_{\Sigma_1}} = \mathcal{G}'_{\sigma'}(\gamma^{Mod}_{\Sigma_2}(M_2));\gamma^{\mathcal{G}}_{\Sigma_2,M_2}\big|_{\mathbf{L}'(\sigma')}$$

where $\sigma' = \gamma^{Sig}(\sigma)\colon \Sigma'_1 \to \Sigma'_2$.

The naturality condition in the last item captures the identity of two composed $\mathbf{L}'(\Sigma'_1)$-homomorphisms of type

$$\mathcal{G}'_{\Sigma'_1}(\gamma^{Mod}_{\Sigma_1}(M_2|_{\sigma})) = \mathcal{G}'_{\Sigma'_1}(\gamma^{Mod}_{\Sigma_2}(M_2)|_{\sigma'}) \to \mathcal{G}_{\Sigma_2}(M_2)|_{\gamma^{Lan}_{\Sigma_1};\mathbf{L}(\sigma)} = \mathcal{G}_{\Sigma_2}(M_2)\big|_{\mathbf{L}'(\sigma');\gamma^{Lan}_{\Sigma_2}}.$$

This may look scary, but we encourage the reader to "type" the morphisms in question and make sure that the condition is not only correctly stated, but is indeed natural.[12]

---

[11]   The extra condition imposed in Example 3.5 on signature morphisms in $\mathbf{BehSig}$ plays a crucial role here: for signature morphisms that add new contexts to "observe" old sorts, the identity map indicated here as the mediating homomorphism may fail to preserve the operation beq.

[12]   In fact, $\gamma^{\mathcal{G}}$ is a natural transformation between suitably re-indexed functors $\mathcal{G}'$ and $\mathcal{G}$, see footnote 9.

As with parchments, where only institutional parchments presented institutions, not every parchment morphism presents an institution morphism. We say that a parchment morphism as above is *institutional* if all homomorphisms $\gamma^{\mathcal{G}}_{\Sigma,M}$ are closed on the subsignature *Logic*.[13] It follows that in institutional parchment morphisms[14] between Boolean parchments, the homomorphisms $\gamma^{\mathcal{G}}_{\Sigma,M}$ are identities on the subsignature *Logic*. If all homomorphisms $\gamma^{\mathcal{G}}_{\Sigma,M}$ are identities, we say that the parchment morphism is *strict*.

For institutional parchments **P** and **P**′ as above, each institutional parchment morphism $\gamma = \langle \gamma^{Sig}, \gamma^{Lan}, \gamma^{Mod}, \gamma^{\mathcal{G}} \rangle \colon \mathbf{P} \to \mathbf{P}'$ presents an institution morphism $\mathcal{J}(\gamma) \colon \mathcal{J}(\mathbf{P}) \to \mathcal{J}(\mathbf{P}')$, defined as follows:

- $(\mathcal{J}(\gamma))^{Sig} = \gamma^{Sig}$,
- $(\mathcal{J}(\gamma))^{Mod} = \gamma^{Mod}$,
- for $\Sigma \in |\mathbf{Sign}|$, let $\Sigma' = \gamma^{Sig}(\Sigma)$; then $(\mathcal{J}(\gamma))^{Sen}_{\Sigma} \colon |T_{\mathbf{L}'(\Sigma')}|_* \to |T_{\mathbf{L}(\Sigma)}|_*$ is given as the $*$ component of the unique $\mathbf{L}'(\Sigma')$-homomorphism $!_{\Sigma} \colon T_{\mathbf{L}'(\Sigma')} \to T_{\mathbf{L}(\Sigma)}|_{\gamma^{Lan}_{\Sigma}}$.

One can check now that $\mathcal{J}(\gamma)$ so defined is indeed an institution morphism $\mathcal{J}(\gamma) \colon \mathcal{J}(\mathbf{P}) \to \mathcal{J}(\mathbf{P}')$. In particular, the satisfaction condition follows since for any signature $\Sigma \in |\mathbf{Sign}|$ and $M \in \mathbf{Mod}(\Sigma)$, the homomorphism $\gamma^{\mathcal{G}}_{\Sigma,M}$ reflects and preserves the predicate $\mathsf{D} \colon *$.

Example 4.6. There are evident parchment morphisms from the parchments $\mathbf{P}_{\mathsf{GMSA}}$, $\mathbf{P}_{\mathsf{GOSA}}$, $\mathbf{P}_{\mathsf{GPRWL}}$, $\mathbf{P}_{\mathsf{GHA}}$, given in Examples 4.2, 4.3, 4.4, and 4.5, respectively, to $\mathbf{P}_{\mathsf{A}}$ given in Example 4.1, presenting the corresponding institution morphisms from Example 3.6. In each case signatures are mapped to their underlying algebraic signatures, models are mapped to the underlying algebras, and the maps on abstract syntax signatures are simply inclusions. All these parchment morphisms are strict (i.e., all the $\gamma^{\mathcal{G}}$ homomorphisms are identities) except for the morphism from $\mathbf{P}_{\mathsf{GOSA}}$ to $\mathbf{P}_{\mathsf{A}}$, where for any order-sorted signature $\langle \Sigma, \leq \rangle$ and $A \in \mathbf{OSAlg}(\langle \Sigma, \leq \rangle)$, $\gamma^{\mathcal{G}}_{\langle \Sigma, \leq \rangle, A} \colon \mathcal{G}^{\mathsf{A}}_{\Sigma}(A) \to \mathcal{G}^{\mathsf{GOSA}}_{\langle \Sigma, \leq \rangle}(A)|_{\mathbf{L}^{\mathsf{A}}(\Sigma)}$ is identity on $*$ and inclusion on sorts from Σ ("adding" undefined elements $\bot$).

Example 4.7. The parchment morphism from $\mathbf{P}_{\mathsf{GOSA}}$ to $\mathbf{P}_{\mathsf{A}}$ extends to the obvious strict parchment morphism from $\mathbf{P}_{\mathsf{GOSA}}$ to $\mathbf{P}_{\mathsf{GMSA}}$, where the abstract syntax signatures are mapped by inclusions. This parchment morphism presents the institution morphism from GOSA to GMSA given in Example 3.7.

Example 4.8. The institution morphism from GHA to GMSA given in Example 3.8 is presented by a strict parchment morphism from $\mathbf{P}_{\mathsf{GHA}}$ to $\mathbf{P}_{\mathsf{GMSA}}$: signatures and models are mapped as in the institution morphism (so, forgetting about non-observable parts of behavioural signatures and their algebras), and abstract syntax signatures are mapped essentially by inclusions, except that the *eq* operations are renamed to *beq*.

---

[13] Again, this is weaker than the corresponding condition imposed in [MTP98].

[14] To clarify: *institutional parchment morphism* refers to a parchment morphism that is institutional (rather than to an institutional-parchment morphism, i.e., a morphism between institutional parchments).

5   Constructions in Parchment Categories

The rather straightforward composition of parchment morphisms $\gamma_1 \colon \mathbf{P}_0 \to \mathbf{P}_1$ and $\gamma_2 \colon \mathbf{P}_1 \to \mathbf{P}_2$ is the parchment morphism $\gamma \colon \mathbf{P}_0 \to \mathbf{P}_2$ defined as follows:

- $\gamma^{Sig} = \gamma_1^{Sig}; \gamma_2^{Sig}$,
- $\gamma^{Lan} = (\gamma_1^{Sig}.\gamma_2^{Lan}); \gamma_1^{Lan}$,
- $\gamma^{Mod} = \gamma_1^{Mod}; ((\gamma_1^{Sig})^{op}.\gamma_2^{Mod})$,
- for any $\mathbf{P}_0$-signature Σ_0 and any Σ_0-model M_0, let $\Sigma_1 = \gamma_1^{Sig}(\Sigma_0)$ and $M_1 = (\gamma_1^{Mod})_{\Sigma_0}(M_0)$; then $\gamma^{\mathcal{G}}_{\Sigma_0, M_0} = (\gamma_2^{\mathcal{G}})_{\Sigma_1, M_1}; (\gamma_1^{\mathcal{G}})_{\Sigma_0, M_0}|_{(\gamma_2^{Lan})_{\Sigma_1}}$.

This defines a category $\mathcal{PAR}$ of parchments and their morphisms. $\mathcal{IPAR}$ denotes the subcategory of institutional parchments with institutional parchment morphisms. The construction of institutions and institutions morphisms from institutional parchments and their institutional morphisms, respectively, as given in Sect. 4, yields a functor $\mathcal{J} \colon \mathcal{IPAR} \to \mathcal{INS}$.

We can combine parchments using limits:

Theorem 5.1 ([MTP98]). $\mathcal{PAR}$ *is complete.*

Instead of a detailed proof (which may be found in the full version of [MTP98]), let us just mention that the construction of limits in $\mathcal{PAR}$ essentially follows the same idea as for institutions, see Thm. 3.9, and illustrate how this works for pullbacks.

Given parchments $\mathbf{P}_0 = \langle \mathbf{Sign}_0, \mathbf{L}_0, \mathbf{Mod}_0, \mathcal{G}_0 \rangle$, $\mathbf{P}_1 = \langle \mathbf{Sign}_1, \mathbf{L}_1, \mathbf{Mod}_1, \mathcal{G}_1 \rangle$, $\mathbf{P}_2 = \langle \mathbf{Sign}_2, \mathbf{L}_2, \mathbf{Mod}_2, \mathcal{G}_2 \rangle$ and parchment morphisms $\gamma_1 \colon \mathbf{P}_1 \to \mathbf{P}_0$ and $\gamma_2 \colon \mathbf{P}_2 \to \mathbf{P}_0$, we sketch the construction of their pullback in $\mathcal{PAR}$ as a parchment $\mathbf{P} = \langle \mathbf{Sign}, \mathbf{L}, \mathbf{Mod}, \mathcal{G} \rangle$ with morphisms $\gamma_3 \colon \mathbf{P} \to \mathbf{P}_1$ and $\gamma_4 \colon \mathbf{P} \to \mathbf{P}_2$:

- The category $\mathbf{Sign}$ of signatures with $\gamma_3^{Sig} \colon \mathbf{Sign} \to \mathbf{Sign}_1$ and $\gamma_4^{Sig} \colon \mathbf{Sign} \to \mathbf{Sign}_2$ is obtained as a pullback of $\gamma_1^{Sig} \colon \mathbf{Sign}_1 \to \mathbf{Sign}_0$ and $\gamma_2^{Sig} \colon \mathbf{Sign}_2 \to \mathbf{Sign}_0$ in $\mathbf{Cat}$.
- For each signature $\Sigma \in |\mathbf{Sign}|$, with $\Sigma_1 = \gamma_3^{Sig}(\Sigma)$, $\Sigma_2 = \gamma_4^{Sig}(\Sigma)$ and $\Sigma_0 = \gamma_1^{Sig}(\Sigma_1) (= \gamma_2^{Sig}(\Sigma_2))$:
  - the abstract syntax signature $\mathbf{L}(\Sigma)$ with $(\gamma_3^{Lan})_{\Sigma} \colon \mathbf{L}_1(\Sigma_1) \to \mathbf{L}(\Sigma)$ and $(\gamma_4^{Lan})_{\Sigma} \colon \mathbf{L}_2(\Sigma_2) \to \mathbf{L}(\Sigma)$ is given as a pushout of $(\gamma_1^{Lan})_{\Sigma_1} \colon \mathbf{L}_0(\Sigma_0) \to \mathbf{L}_1(\Sigma_1)$ and $(\gamma_2^{Lan})_{\Sigma_2} \colon \mathbf{L}_0(\Sigma_0) \to \mathbf{L}_2(\Sigma_2)$ in $\mathbf{FOSig}_*$,
  - the class of models $\mathbf{Mod}(\Sigma)$ with $(\gamma_3^{Mod})_{\Sigma} \colon \mathbf{Mod}(\Sigma) \to \mathbf{Mod}_1(\gamma_3^{Sig}(\Sigma))$ and $(\gamma_4^{Mod})_{\Sigma} \colon \mathbf{Mod}(\Sigma) \to \mathbf{Mod}_2(\gamma_4^{Sig}(\Sigma))$ is obtained as a pullback of $(\gamma_1^{Mod})_{\Sigma_1} \colon \mathbf{Mod}_1(\Sigma_1) \to \mathbf{Mod}_0(\Sigma_0)$ and $(\gamma_2^{Mod})_{\Sigma_2} \colon \mathbf{Mod}_2(\Sigma_2) \to \mathbf{Mod}_0(\Sigma_0)$ in $\mathbf{Class}$, and
  - for each model $M \in \mathbf{Mod}(\Sigma)$, in an attempt to make the construction of $\mathcal{G}_\Sigma(M)$ readable, let us introduce a number of abbreviations:
    * $M_1 = (\gamma_3^{Mod})_{\Sigma}(M)$, $M_2 = (\gamma_4^{Mod})_{\Sigma}(M)$ and $M_0 = (\gamma_1^{Mod})_{\Sigma_1}(M_1)$ $(= (\gamma_2^{Mod})_{\Sigma_2}(M_2))$,
    * $G_1 = (\mathcal{G}_1)_{\Sigma_1}(M_1)$, $G_2 = (\mathcal{G}_2)_{\Sigma_2}(M_2)$, and $G_0 = (\mathcal{G}_0)_{\Sigma_0}(M_0)$,

* $\theta_1 = (\gamma_1^{Lan})_{\Sigma_1} \colon \mathbf{L}_0(\Sigma_0) \to \mathbf{L}_1(\Sigma_1)$, $\theta_2 = (\gamma_2^{Lan})_{\Sigma_2} \colon \mathbf{L}_0(\Sigma_0) \to \mathbf{L}_2(\Sigma_2)$, $\theta_3 = (\gamma_3^{Lan})_\Sigma \colon \mathbf{L}_1(\Sigma_1) \to \mathbf{L}(\Sigma)$, $\theta_4 = (\gamma_4^{Lan})_\Sigma \colon \mathbf{L}_2(\Sigma_2) \to \mathbf{L}(\Sigma)$, and $\theta = \theta_1;\theta_3 \ (= \theta_2;\theta_4)$.

We have two $\mathbf{L}_0(\Sigma_0)$-homomorphisms $(\gamma_1^{\mathcal{G}})_{\Sigma_1,M_1} \colon G_0 \to G_1|_{(\gamma_1^{Lan})_{\Sigma_1}}$ and $(\gamma_2^{\mathcal{G}})_{\Sigma_2,M_2} \colon G_0 \to G_2|_{(\gamma_2^{Lan})_{\Sigma_2}}$. Using freeness, we get $(\gamma_1^{\mathcal{G}})^{\#}_{\Sigma_1,M_1} \colon F_{\theta_1}(G_0) \to G_1$ in $\mathbf{Str}(\mathbf{L}_1(\Sigma_1))$ and $(\gamma_2^{\mathcal{G}})^{\#}_{\Sigma_2,M_2} \colon F_{\theta_2}(G_0) \to G_2$ in $\mathbf{Str}(\mathbf{L}_2(\Sigma_2))$. Then, since (up to natural isomorphism) $F_{\theta_3}(F_{\theta_1}(G_0))$ and $F_{\theta_4}(F_{\theta_2}(G_0))$ coincide with $F_\theta(G_0)$, we may assume that $F_{\theta_3}((\gamma_1^{\mathcal{G}})^{\#}_{\Sigma_1,M_1}) \colon F_\theta(G_0) \to F_{\theta_3}(G_1)$ and $F_{\theta_4}((\gamma_2^{\mathcal{G}})^{\#}_{\Sigma_2,M_2}) \colon F_\theta(G_0) \to F_{\theta_4}(G_2)$. Let now $\mathcal{G}_\Sigma(M)$ with $\mathbf{L}(\Sigma)$-homomorphisms $g_1 \colon F_{\theta_3}(G_1) \to \mathcal{G}_\Sigma(M)$ and $g_2 \colon F_{\theta_4}(G_2) \to \mathcal{G}_\Sigma(M)$ be their pushout in $\mathbf{Str}(\mathbf{L}(\Sigma))$. Finally, put $(\gamma_3^{\mathcal{G}})_{\Sigma,M} = (\eta_{\theta_3})_{G_1};g_1|_{\theta_3} \colon G_1 \to \mathcal{G}_\Sigma(M)|_{\theta_3}$ and $(\gamma_4^{\mathcal{G}})_{\Sigma,M} = (\eta_{\theta_4})_{G_2};g_2|_{\theta_4} \colon G_2 \to \mathcal{G}_\Sigma(M)|_{\theta_4}$.

Then, for each signature morphism $\sigma \colon \Sigma \to \Sigma'$:

- $\mathbf{L}(\sigma) \colon \mathbf{L}(\Sigma) \to \mathbf{L}(\Sigma')$ is given by the pushout property of $\mathbf{L}(\Sigma)$,
- $\mathbf{Mod}(\sigma) \colon \mathbf{Mod}(\Sigma') \to \mathbf{Mod}(\Sigma)$ is given by the pullback property of $\mathbf{Mod}(\Sigma)$, and
- for any model $M' \in \mathbf{Mod}(\Sigma')$, $\mathcal{G}_\sigma(M') \colon \mathcal{G}_\Sigma(M'|_\sigma) \to \mathcal{G}_{\Sigma'}(M')|_{\mathbf{L}(\Sigma)}$ is given by the pushout property of $\mathcal{G}_\Sigma(M'|_\sigma)$.

It is routine (but very tedious!) to check that the above indeed defines a parchment $\mathbf{P} = \langle \mathbf{Sign}, \mathbf{L}, \mathbf{Mod}, \mathcal{G} \rangle$ with parchment morphisms $\gamma_3 \colon \mathbf{P} \to \mathbf{P}_1$ and $\gamma_4 \colon \mathbf{P} \to \mathbf{P}_2$ which form a pullback of $\gamma_1 \colon \mathbf{P}_1 \to \mathbf{P}_0$ and $\gamma_2 \colon \mathbf{P}_2 \to \mathbf{P}_0$.

Proposition 5.2. *The limit in $\mathcal{PAR}$ of a diagram of institutional parchments and institutional parchment morphisms is not necessarily an institutional parchment, but the limiting cone consists of institutional parchment morphisms.*

This is the first sign of worry that a programme to "just" use the standard limit construction to put together logical systems presented by institutional parchments linked by institutional parchment morphisms is doomed. Here is another negative result, perhaps expected after Prop. 5.2, to show that this idea cannot work in general:

Proposition 5.3 ([MTP98]). *The category $\mathcal{IPAR}$ of institutional parchments and their institutional morphisms is not complete.*

The source of these negative results is that the free constructions involved in building the evaluation structures in the limit parchment in general add new values, possibly also new logical values (of sort $*$). The predicate $\mathsf{D} \colon *$ does not hold on these new values over a given signature (so that the limit projection morphisms are institutional). However, there may be extensions of the signature considered where the new logical values are glued together with "old" logical values (due to identification of some parts of syntax) and when $\mathsf{D} \colon *$ holds on them, the mediating homomorphism is not closed — which yields the negative part of Prop. 5.2. Then, even when this does not happen and the limit parchment is institutional, there may be common compatible extensions of the parchments in the diagram (institutional cones over this diagram) that designate the predicate $D: *$ to hold for some of the new logical values. Consequently, the unique parchment morphism from such a cone to the limit in $\mathcal{PAR}$ need not be institutional. This shows that for a parchment diagram in $\mathcal{IPAR}$, even if its limit given by Thm. 5.1 is an institutional parchment and so the limit cone fits entirely into $\mathcal{IPAR}$, it still does not have to be a limit of this diagram in $\mathcal{IPAR}$.

In fact, this is as expected: there is nothing like a free lunch, we cannot get meanings for essentially new combinations of syntactic constructs involved for free. The upshot is that the new logical values added by the free constructions involved in the limits in $\mathcal{PAR}$ indicate the need for some decision concerning the meaning of such new phrases. Technically, this may take the form of consistently choosing a family of congruences on the evaluation structures that glue together new and old logical values.

Example 5.4. One can easily construct the combination of $\mathbf{P}_{\text{GOSA}}$ and $\mathbf{P}_{\text{GPRWL}}$ as a pullback of $\mathbf{P}_{\text{GOSA}}$ and $\mathbf{P}_{\text{GPRWL}}$ over $\mathbf{P}_A$, via the parchment morphisms given in Example 4.6. The pullback parchment has order-sorted signatures as signatures, and order-sorted algebras as models. For any order-sorted signature $\langle \Sigma, \leq \rangle$, the abstract syntax signature extends *Logic* by Σ and subsort inclusions and retracts, as well as by $eq: s \times s \to *$ and $rwrt: s \times s \to *$ for each sort s in Σ. So, in contrast to Example 3.12, the abstract syntax here covers rewritings between all order-sorted terms. Then, for any order-sorted algebra $A \in \mathbf{OSAlg}(\langle \Sigma, \leq \rangle)$, the evaluation structure will comprise the carriers of A extended with the undefined element $\bot$, operations from Σ and eq interpreted as in $\mathbf{P}_{\text{GOSA}}$, and operations $rwrt$ interpreted as in $\mathbf{P}_{\text{GPRWL}}$ on arguments from $|A|$, but on pairs of arguments containing $\bot$ interpreted as new "free" logical values. It is now our decision to define how to interpret rewritings between terms with undefined values. The obvious choice — though technically not the only one possible — is to identify the freely added logical values with *ff* (thus setting rewritings between undefined terms to never hold) which would complete an adequate combination of the logical systems given by $\mathbf{P}_{\text{GOSA}}$ and $\mathbf{P}_{\text{GPRWL}}$.

The above example captures well a general situation; let's have a closer look at the issue of when a parchment combination is "satisfactory".

Consider a family $\mathcal{P} = \langle \mathbf{P}_i = \langle \mathbf{Sign}_i, \mathbf{L}_i, \mathbf{Mod}_i, \mathcal{G}_i \rangle \rangle_{i \in \mathcal{I}}$ of parchments. A parchment $\mathbf{P} = \langle \mathbf{Sign}, \mathbf{L}, \mathbf{Mod}, \mathcal{G} \rangle$ with parchment morphisms $\gamma_i: \mathbf{P} \to \mathbf{P}_i$, $i \in \mathcal{I}$, is a *complete joint extension* of $\mathcal{P}$ if for all signatures $\Sigma \in |\mathbf{Sign}|$ and models $M \in \mathbf{Mod}(\Sigma)$, the homomorphisms $(\gamma_i^{\mathcal{G}})_{\Sigma, M}: (\mathcal{G}_i)_{\Sigma_i}(M_i) \to \mathcal{G}_\Sigma(M)|_{(\gamma_i^{Lan})_\Sigma}$, $i \in \mathcal{I}$ (where $\Sigma_i = \gamma_i^{Sig}(\Sigma)$, $M_i = (\gamma_i^{Mod})_\Sigma(M)$) are jointly surjective on the sort $*$. So, informally, a parchment $\mathbf{P}$ gives a complete joint extension of a family of parchments if each logical value in $\mathbf{P}$ corresponds to some logical value in at least one of the parchments jointly extended. If all of the parchments in $\mathcal{P}$ are institutional, then the complete joint extension is *institutional* if $\mathbf{P}$ is institutional and all morphisms γ_i are institutional as well.

Proposition 5.5. *If a limit in $\mathcal{PAR}$ of a diagram of institutional parchments and institutional parchment morphisms is a complete joint extension of the parchments in the diagram, then it is a limit in $\mathcal{IPAR}$ as well.*

Things work particularly easily when the parchment extensions involved in the diagram do not interfere with each other. To keep the presentation relatively simple, we look at pullbacks only.

We say that institutional parchment morphisms $\gamma_1 \colon \mathbf{P}_1 \to \mathbf{P}_0$ and $\gamma_2 \colon \mathbf{P}_2 \to \mathbf{P}_0$ in $\mathcal{IPAR}$ *do not interfere*, if for any signatures $\Sigma_1 \in |\mathbf{Sign}_1|$ and $\Sigma_2 \in |\mathbf{Sign}_2|$ such that $\gamma_1^{Sig}(\Sigma_1) = \gamma_2^{Sig}(\Sigma_2) = \Sigma_0$, we have that the term algebra over the pushout (in $\mathbf{FOSig}_*$) signature of $(\gamma_1^{Lan})_{\Sigma_1} \colon \mathbf{L}_0(\Sigma_0) \to \mathbf{L}_1(\Sigma_1)$ and $(\gamma_2^{Lan})_{\Sigma_2} \colon \mathbf{L}_0(\Sigma_0) \to \mathbf{L}_2(\Sigma_2)$ has as the carrier of sort $*$ the pushout in $\mathbf{Set}$ of $!_{\Sigma_1} \colon T_{\mathbf{L}_0(\Sigma_0)} \to T_{\mathbf{L}_1(\Sigma_1)}|_{(\gamma_1^{Lan})_{\Sigma_1}}$ and $!_{\Sigma_2} \colon T_{\mathbf{L}_0(\Sigma_0)} \to T_{\mathbf{L}_2(\Sigma_2)}|_{(\gamma_2^{Lan})_{\Sigma_2}}$ restricted to the functions on the carriers of sort $*$.

Informally, this condition captures the fact that the new syntactic constructs added in $\mathbf{P}_1$ and $\mathbf{P}_2$, respectively, do not interact with each other to build new sentences that would not come from either $\mathbf{P}_1$ or $\mathbf{P}_2$. In particular, it requires both parchments to be atomic (except for some degenerate cases). It is rather obvious that in such a situation we can put the two parchments together without further ado:

Proposition 5.6. *If two morphisms $\gamma_1 \colon \mathbf{P}_1 \to \mathbf{P}_0$ and $\gamma_2 \colon \mathbf{P}_2 \to \mathbf{P}_0$ in $\mathcal{IPAR}$ do not interfere then their pullback in $\mathcal{PAR}$ is also a pullback in $\mathcal{IPAR}$. Moreover the functor $\mathcal{I} \colon \mathcal{IPAR} \to \mathcal{INS}$ maps this pullback to a pullback in $\mathcal{INS}$.*

Example 5.7. Define a parchment $\mathbf{P}_{\mathsf{GRWL}}$ as the pullback of $\mathbf{P}_{\mathsf{GMSA}}$ and $\mathbf{P}_{\mathsf{GPRWL}}$ over $\mathbf{P}_{\mathsf{A}}$ (via the morphisms sketched in Example 4.6). It is easy to see that the two parchment morphisms do not interfere, and the pullback presents the pullback of the corresponding institutions given in Example 3.10; in particular, $\mathbf{P}_{\mathsf{GRWL}}$ presents GRWL.

Example 5.8. Similarly, $\mathbf{P}_{\mathsf{GHA}}$ and $\mathbf{P}_{\mathsf{GMSA}}$ over $\mathbf{P}_{\mathsf{A}}$ (via the morphisms of Example 4.6) do not interfere. Their pullback presents the institution sketched in Example 3.11, where standard ground equations and ground behavioural equations coexist.

Before we return to the general case of an arbitrary combination of institutional parchments, let's have a look at a simpler situation, when given a parchment $\mathbf{P} = \langle \mathbf{Sign}, \mathbf{L}, \mathbf{Mod}, \mathcal{G} \rangle$, we want to add to it some new syntactic constructs, as captured by a natural transformation $\alpha \colon \mathbf{L} \to \mathbf{L}'$ between functors from $\mathbf{Sign}$ to $\mathbf{FOSig}_*$. We may now build another parchment $\mathcal{F}_\alpha(\mathbf{P}) = \langle \mathbf{Sign}, \mathbf{L}', \mathbf{Mod}, \mathcal{G}' \rangle$, with the same signatures and models as $\mathbf{P}$, with the richer abstract syntax signatures given by $\mathbf{L}'$, with the evaluation structures that freely extend the evaluation structures of $\mathbf{P}$, i.e., for $\Sigma \in |\mathbf{Sign}|$ and $M \in \mathbf{Mod}(\Sigma)$, $\mathcal{G}'_\Sigma(M) = F_{\alpha_\Sigma}(\mathcal{G}_\Sigma(M))$, and with the mediating homomorphisms defined as follows. For $\sigma \colon \Sigma_1 \to \Sigma_2$ and $M_2 \in \mathbf{Mod}(\Sigma_2)$, with $M_2|_\sigma = M_1$, we have morphisms $\mathcal{G}_\sigma(M_2) \colon \mathcal{G}_\Sigma(M_1) \to \mathcal{G}_{\Sigma_2}(M_2)|_{\mathbf{L}(\sigma)}$ and $\eta_{\alpha_{\Sigma_2}} \colon \mathcal{G}_{\Sigma_2}(M_2) \to$

$F_{\alpha_{\Sigma_2}}(\mathcal{G}_{\Sigma_2}(M'))|_{\alpha_{\Sigma_2}} = \mathcal{G}'_{\Sigma_2}(M_2)|_{\alpha_{\Sigma_2}}$, which yield $\mathcal{G}_\sigma(M_2);\eta_{\alpha_{\Sigma_2}}|_{\mathbf{L}(\sigma)}\colon \mathcal{G}_{\Sigma_1}(M_1) \to$
$(\mathcal{G}'_{\Sigma_2}(M_2)|_{\alpha_{\Sigma_2}})|_{\mathbf{L}(\sigma)} = (\mathcal{G}'_{\Sigma_2}(M_2)|_{\mathbf{L}'(\sigma)})|_{\alpha_{\Sigma_1}}$. Since $\mathcal{G}'_\Sigma(M_1) = F_{\alpha_{\Sigma_1}}(\mathcal{G}_{\Sigma_1}(M_1))$,
we can now define $\mathcal{G}'_\sigma(M_2)\colon \mathcal{G}'_{\Sigma_1}(M_1) \to \mathcal{G}'_{\Sigma_2}(M_2)|_{\mathbf{L}'(\sigma)}$ as the unique morphism
such that $\eta_{\alpha_{\Sigma_1}};\mathcal{G}'_\sigma(M_2)|_{\alpha_{\Sigma_1}} = \mathcal{G}_\sigma(M_2);\eta_{\alpha_{\Sigma_2}}|_{\mathbf{L}(\sigma)}$. It is routine now to verify further compatibility condition, so that we get:

Proposition 5.9. *Given any parchment* $\mathbf{P} = \langle \mathbf{Sign}, \mathbf{L}, \mathbf{Mod}, \mathcal{G} \rangle$ *and natural transformation* $\alpha\colon \mathbf{L} \to \mathbf{L}'$, $\mathcal{F}_\alpha(\mathbf{P}) = \langle \mathbf{Sign}, \mathbf{L}', \mathbf{Mod}, \mathcal{G}' \rangle$ *as defined above is a parchment with an institutional parchment morphism* $\gamma_\alpha = \langle Id_{\mathbf{Sign}}, \alpha, Id_{\mathbf{Mod}}, \gamma_\alpha^\mathcal{G} \rangle$ *from* $\mathcal{F}_\alpha(\mathbf{P})$ *to* $\mathbf{P}$*, where* $Id_{\mathbf{Sign}}$ *is the identity functor,* $Id_{\mathbf{Mod}}$ *is the identity natural transformation, and for* $\Sigma \in |\mathbf{Sign}|$ *and* $M \in \mathbf{Mod}(\Sigma)$*,* $(\gamma_\alpha^\mathcal{G})_{\Sigma,M} = (\eta_{\alpha_\Sigma})_M$.

In general, $\mathcal{F}_\alpha(\mathbf{P})$ need not be institutional, even if $\mathbf{P}$ is so. The problem is similar to that indicated for Prop. 5.2: new logical values freely added over one signature may become identified with some old logical values over another signature, and if D: ∗ holds for those, the resulting mediating homomorphism is not closed. For typical extensions this does not happen though.

A natural transformation $\alpha\colon \mathbf{L} \to \mathbf{L}'$ (between functors from $\mathbf{Sign}$ to $\mathbf{FOSig}_*$) is *clean* if new parts of syntax are never identified with old parts of syntax, i.e., for any signature morphism $\sigma\colon \Sigma_1 \to \Sigma_2$, for any symbol x (sort, operation or predicate name) in $\mathbf{L}'(\Sigma_1)$ that is not in the image of $\alpha_{\Sigma_1}\colon \mathbf{L}(\Sigma_1) \to \mathbf{L}'(\Sigma_1)$, the symbol $\mathbf{L}'(\sigma)(x)$ is not in the image of $\alpha_{\Sigma_2}\colon \mathbf{L}(\Sigma_2) \to \mathbf{L}'(\Sigma_2)$.

Proposition 5.10. *Given any institutional parchment* $\mathbf{P} = \langle \mathbf{Sign}, \mathbf{L}, \mathbf{Mod}, \mathcal{G} \rangle$ *and clean natural transformation* $\alpha\colon \mathbf{L} \to \mathbf{L}'$, $\mathcal{F}_\alpha(\mathbf{P}) = \langle \mathbf{Sign}, \mathbf{L}', \mathbf{Mod}, \mathcal{G}' \rangle$ *as defined above is an institutional parchment.*

This is promising, but we have not ensured that $\mathcal{F}_\alpha(\mathbf{P})$ is a *complete* (joint) extension of $\mathbf{P}$ — there may be, and typically there are, new logical values of sort ∗ freely added by the construction above. To complete the extension, we need to identify these new logical values with some old ones, used already in $\mathbf{P}$. To carry this out, another concept is useful.

Given a parchment $\mathbf{P} = \langle \mathbf{Sign}, \mathbf{L}, \mathbf{Mod}, \mathcal{G} \rangle$, a *coherent family of semantic congruences for* $\mathbf{P}$ is a family $\langle \cong_{\Sigma,M} \rangle_{\Sigma \in |\mathbf{Sign}|, M \in \mathbf{Mod}(\Sigma)}$, where for $\Sigma \in |\mathbf{Sign}|$ and $M \in \mathbf{Mod}(\Sigma)$, $\cong_{\Sigma,M}$ is a congruence on $\mathcal{G}_\Sigma(M)$ that is preserved by the mediating homomorphisms, i.e., for any signature morphism $\sigma\colon \Sigma \to \Sigma'$ and $M' \in \mathbf{Mod}(\Sigma')$ with $M'|_\sigma = M$, we have $\mathcal{G}_\sigma(M')(\cong_{\Sigma,M}) \subseteq \cong_{\Sigma',M'}|_{\mathbf{L}(\sigma)}$. Given such a family, we may build another parchment $\mathbf{P}/\cong = \langle \mathbf{Sign}, \mathbf{L}, \mathbf{Mod}, \mathcal{G}^\cong \rangle$, where for $\Sigma \in |\mathbf{Sign}|$ and $M \in \mathbf{Mod}(\Sigma)$, $\mathcal{G}_\Sigma^\cong(M) = \mathcal{G}_\Sigma(M)/\cong_{\Sigma,M}$ and for $\sigma\colon \Sigma \to \Sigma'$ and $M' \in \mathbf{Mod}(\Sigma')$ with $M'|_\sigma = M$, $\mathcal{G}_\sigma^\cong(M')\colon \mathcal{G}_\Sigma^\cong(M) \to \mathcal{G}_{\Sigma'}^\cong(M')|_{\mathbf{L}(\sigma)}$ is defined by $\mathcal{G}_\sigma^\cong(M')([a]_{\cong_{\Sigma,M}}) = [\mathcal{G}_\sigma(M')(a)]_{\cong_{\Sigma',M'}}$ (the coherence condition ensures that this is well-defined).

Proposition 5.11. *Given any parchment* $\mathbf{P} = \langle \mathbf{Sign}, \mathbf{L}, \mathbf{Mod}, \mathcal{G} \rangle$ *and coherent family* $\cong$ *of semantic congruences for* $\mathbf{P}$*,* $\mathbf{P}/\cong = \langle \mathbf{Sign}, \mathbf{L}, \mathbf{Mod}, \mathcal{G}^\cong \rangle$ *as defined above is a parchment, with a parchment morphism* $\gamma_\cong = \langle Id_{\mathbf{Sign}}, Id_{\mathbf{L}}, Id_{\mathbf{Mod}}, \gamma_\cong^\mathcal{G} \rangle$ *from* $\mathbf{P}/\cong$ *to* $\mathbf{P}$*, where* $Id_{\mathbf{Sign}}$ *is the identity functor,* $Id_{\mathbf{L}}$ *and* $Id_{\mathbf{Mod}}$ *are the* *identity natural transformations, and for any* $\Sigma \in |\mathbf{Sign}|$ *and* $M \in \mathbf{Mod}(\Sigma)$, $(\gamma_{\cong}^{\mathcal{G}})_{\Sigma,M} = [\_]_{\cong_{\Sigma,M}}$.

The construction above simplifies considerably when the parchment is atomic: instead of considering congruences on the evaluation structures, it is sufficient to consider equivalence relations on the carriers of sort $*$ of these structures (which together with identities on other sorts then form congruences).

Now, given a family $\mathcal{P} = \langle \mathbf{P}_i = \langle \mathbf{Sign}_i, \mathbf{L}_i, \mathbf{Mod}_i, \mathcal{G}_i \rangle\rangle_{i \in \mathcal{I}}$ of parchments, consider a parchment $\mathbf{P} = \langle \mathbf{Sign}, \mathbf{L}, \mathbf{Mod}, \mathcal{G} \rangle$ with parchment morphisms $\gamma_i: \mathbf{P} \to \mathbf{P}_i$, $i \in \mathcal{I}$. A coherent family $\cong$ of semantic congruences for $\mathbf{P}$ is *complete* for $\mathcal{P}$, if for any signature $\Sigma \in |\mathbf{Sign}|$ and $M \in \mathbf{Mod}(\Sigma)$, for any $a \in |\mathcal{G}_{\Sigma}(M)|_*$, for some $i \in \mathcal{I}$ and $a_i \in |(\mathcal{G}_i)_{\gamma_i^{Sig}(\Sigma)}((\gamma_i^{Mod})_{\Sigma}(M))|_*$, we have $a \cong_{\Sigma,M} (\gamma_i^{\mathcal{G}})_{\Sigma}(M)(a_i)$.

Proposition 5.12. *Consider any family* $\mathcal{P} = \langle \mathbf{P}_i = \langle \mathbf{Sign}_i, \mathbf{L}_i, \mathbf{Mod}_i, \mathcal{G}_i \rangle\rangle_{i \in \mathcal{I}}$ *of parchments, parchment* $\mathbf{P} = \langle \mathbf{Sign}, \mathbf{L}, \mathbf{Mod}, \mathcal{G} \rangle$ *with parchment morphisms* $\gamma_i: \mathbf{P} \to \mathbf{P}_i$, $i \in \mathcal{I}$, *and coherent family* $\cong$ *of semantic congruences for* $\mathbf{P}$ *that is complete for* $\mathcal{P}$. *Then the parchment* $\mathbf{P}/\cong$ *with parchment morphisms* $\gamma_{\cong};\gamma_i: \mathbf{P}/\cong \to \mathbf{P}_i$, $i \in \mathcal{I}$, *is a complete joint extension for the family* $\mathcal{P}$.

Furthermore, a coherent family $\cong$ of semantic congruences for $\mathbf{P}$ is *institutional* for $\mathcal{P}$, if for any signature $\Sigma \in |\mathbf{Sign}|$ and $M \in \mathbf{Mod}(\Sigma)$, whenever for any $i, j \in \mathcal{I}$, with $\gamma_i^{Sig}(\Sigma) = \Sigma_i$, $\gamma_j^{Sig}(\Sigma) = \Sigma_j$, $(\gamma_i^{Mod})_{\Sigma}(M) = M_i$ and $(\gamma_j^{Mod})_{\Sigma}(M) = M_j$, we have $a_i \in |(\mathcal{G}_i)_{\Sigma_i}(M_i)|_*$, $a_j \in |(\mathcal{G}_j)_{\Sigma_j}(M_j)|_*$, $(\gamma_i^{\mathcal{G}})_{\Sigma,M}(a_i) \cong_{\Sigma,M} (\gamma_j^{\mathcal{G}})_{\Sigma,M}(a_j)$ and $a_i \in \mathsf{D}_{(\mathcal{G}_i)_{\Sigma_i}(M_i)}$, then $a_j \in \mathsf{D}_{(\mathcal{G}_j)_{\Sigma_j}(M_j)}$ as well. Informally: we can glue together only those "old" logical values that either both designate sentences to hold, or both designate them not to hold.

Theorem 5.13. *Consider any family* $\mathcal{P} = \langle \mathbf{P}_i = \langle \mathbf{Sign}_i, \mathbf{L}_i, \mathbf{Mod}_i, \mathcal{G}_i \rangle\rangle_{i \in \mathcal{I}}$ *of institutional parchments, parchment* $\mathbf{P} = \langle \mathbf{Sign}, \mathbf{L}, \mathbf{Mod}, \mathcal{G} \rangle$ *with institutional parchment morphisms* $\gamma_i: \mathbf{P} \to \mathbf{P}_i$, $i \in \mathcal{I}$, *and coherent family* $\cong$ *of semantic congruences for* $\mathbf{P}$ *that is complete and institutional for* $\mathcal{P}$. *Then the parchment* $\mathbf{P}/\cong$ *with parchment morphisms* $\gamma_{\cong};\gamma_i: \mathbf{P}/\cong \to \mathbf{P}_i$, $i \in \mathcal{I}$, *is a complete institutional joint extension for the family* $\mathcal{P}$.

One strength of the above result is that we show the quotient parchment to be institutional without assuming that $\mathbf{P}$ is so. This follows since the parchments in the family are institutional, and the coherent family of congruences is complete and institutional as well.

Example 5.14. Consider a pullback of $\mathbf{P}_{\mathsf{GOSA}}$ and $\mathbf{P}_{\mathsf{GRWL}}$ over $\mathbf{P}_{\mathsf{CMSA}}$ via the morphisms given by Example 4.7 and the pullback construction of $\mathbf{P}_{\mathsf{GRWL}}$ in Example 5.7, respectively. In fact, the pullback parchment is the same as the pullback parchment for $\mathbf{P}_{\mathsf{GOSA}}$ and $\mathbf{P}_{\mathsf{GPRWL}}$ over $\mathbf{P}_{\mathsf{A}}$ described in Example 5.4. The problem is that it is not a complete joint extension of $\mathbf{P}_{\mathsf{GOSA}}$ and $\mathbf{P}_{\mathsf{GRWL}}$, as evaluation structures carry freely added logical values, corresponding to rewriting statements between terms with undefined values. To fix this, consider a family of equivalences on the carriers of sort $*$ that glue values of the operations *rwrt* on pairs of arguments containing $\perp$ with $f\!f$. Since the parchment is atomic, this family extends to a family of congruences by adding identities on the carriers of other sorts. It is easy to check now that this family is coherent as well as complete and institutional for $\mathbf{P}_{\mathsf{GOSA}}$ and $\mathbf{P}_{\mathsf{GRWL}}$. Consequently, by Thm. 5.13, quotienting the pullback parchment by this family yields an institutional complete joint extension of $\mathbf{P}_{\mathsf{GOSA}}$ and $\mathbf{P}_{\mathsf{GRWL}}$ — this is an institutional parchment $\mathbf{P}_{\mathsf{GOSRWL}}$ that presents the institution GOSRWL, and the institutional parchment morphisms from $\mathbf{P}_{\mathsf{GOSRWL}}$ to $\mathbf{P}_{\mathsf{GOSA}}$ and $\mathbf{P}_{\mathsf{GRWL}}$, respectively, present the corresponding institution morphisms in the CafeOBJ cube.

Example 5.15. Consider now a pullback $\mathbf{P}_0 = \langle \mathbf{Sign}_0, \mathbf{L}_0, \mathbf{Mod}_0, \mathcal{G}_0 \rangle$ of $\mathbf{P}_{\mathsf{GHA}}$ and $\mathbf{P}_{\mathsf{GRWL}}$ over $\mathbf{P}_{\mathsf{GMSA}}$ via the parchment morphisms given by Example 4.8 and the pullback construction of $\mathbf{P}_{\mathsf{GRWL}}$ in Example 5.7, respectively. As in Example 3.13, $\mathbf{Sign}_0$ is the category of behavioural signatures, and $\mathbf{Mod}_0(\langle \Sigma, OBS \rangle)$ is the class of Σ-algebras with a rewriting preorder $\preceq_o \subseteq |A|_o \times |A|_o$ on observable sorts $o \in OBS$ only, preserved by observable operations. For any behavioural signature $\langle \Sigma, OBS \rangle$, the abstract syntax signature $\mathbf{L}_0(\langle \Sigma, OBS \rangle)$ extends *Logic* by Σ, operations $beq\colon s \times s \to *$ for all sorts s in Σ, and operations $rwrt\colon o \times o \to *$ for observable sorts $o \in OBS$. Perhaps surprisingly, $\mathbf{P}_{\mathsf{GHA}}$ and $\mathbf{P}_{\mathsf{GRWL}}$ over $\mathbf{P}_{\mathsf{GMSA}}$ do not interfere, and so $\mathbf{P}_0$ is a pullback of $\mathbf{P}_{\mathsf{GHA}}$ and $\mathbf{P}_{\mathsf{GRWL}}$ over $\mathbf{P}_{\mathsf{GMSA}}$ in $\mathcal{JPAR}$, and in fact is their complete institutional joint extension. But we still "miss" rewritings on non-observable sorts!

So, let us add them: consider the natural inclusion $\alpha\colon \mathbf{L}_0 \to \mathbf{L}^{\mathsf{GHRWL}}$, for any behavioural signature $\langle \Sigma, OBS \rangle$, $\mathbf{L}^{\mathsf{GHRWL}}(\langle \Sigma, OBS \rangle)$ adding to $\mathbf{L}_0(\langle \Sigma, OBS \rangle)$ operations $brwrt\colon s \times s \to *$ for non-observable sorts $s \notin OBS$. Now, by Prop. 5.9, we obtain the parchment $F_\alpha(\mathbf{P}_0)$, which is institutional by Prop. 5.10. However, it is not a complete joint extension of $\mathbf{P}_{\mathsf{GHA}}$ and $\mathbf{P}_{\mathsf{GRWL}}$, with new logical values added for behavioural rewritings between terms of non-observable sorts. Of course, it is now our decision how to interpret such rewritings.

For any signature $\langle \Sigma, OBS \rangle$ and $\langle A, \langle \preceq_o \rangle_{o \in OBS} \rangle \in \mathbf{Mod}_0(\langle \Sigma, OBS \rangle)$, let $\precsim \subseteq |A| \times |A|$ be the largest precongruence on A such that $\precsim_o \subseteq \preceq_o$ for all observable sorts $o \in OBS$.[15] Now, consider a family of equivalences on the carriers of sort $*$ of the evaluation structures in $F_\alpha(\mathbf{P}_0)$ that glue values of the operations $brwrt$ on arguments a, b with tt if $a \precsim b$ and with $f\!f$ otherwise. Since the parchment is atomic, this family extends to a family of congruences by adding identities on the carriers of other sorts. Given the conditions on behavioural signature morphisms, it is easy to check now that this family is coherent as well as complete and institutional for $\mathbf{P}_{\mathsf{GHA}}$ and $\mathbf{P}_{\mathsf{GRWL}}$. Consequently, by Thm. 5.13, quotienting $F_\alpha(\mathbf{P}_0)$ by this family yields an institutional complete joint extension of $\mathbf{P}_{\mathsf{GHA}}$ and $\mathbf{P}_{\mathsf{GRWL}}$ — this is an institutional parchment $\mathbf{P}_{\mathsf{GHRWL}}$ that presents institution GHRWL, and the institutional parchment morphisms from $\mathbf{P}_{\mathsf{GHRWL}}$ to $\mathbf{P}_{\mathsf{GHA}}$ and $\mathbf{P}_{\mathsf{GRWL}}$, respectively, present the corresponding institution morphisms in the CafeOBJ cube.

---

[15] So that $a \precsim b$ iff, relying on the standard concepts and notation, for all contexts C of an observable sort, $C_A[a] \preceq C_A[b]$.

Example 5.16. Consider now a pullback of $\mathbf{P}_{\mathsf{GHA}}$ and $\mathbf{P}_{\mathsf{GOSA}}$ over $\mathbf{P}_{\mathsf{GMSA}}$ via the morphisms of Examples 4.8 and 4.7, respectively. Somewhat similarly to the initial construction in Example 5.15, a signature in the resulting parchment is a behavioural signature with ordering on the set of sorts that is non-trivial on observable sorts only, and models over such signature are order-sorted algebras over the obvious order-sorted signature extracted from it. For any such signature $\langle \Sigma, OBS, \le \rangle$, the abstract syntax signature extends *Logic* by Σ, operations $beq: s \times s \to *$ for all sorts s in Σ, and subsort inclusions and retracts as determined by the subsorting relation on the observable sorts. No need to discuss evaluation structures — they are given by the obvious amalgamation of the evaluation structures in $\mathbf{P}_{\mathsf{GHA}}$ and $\mathbf{P}_{\mathsf{GOSA}}$.

For the purposes of this presentation we stop at this point and set this parchment to be $\mathbf{P}_{\mathsf{GHOSA}}$, presenting an institution that corresponds to GHOSA. Note though that we thus neglect adding subsorting on non-observable sorts – this could be done much in the style of adding rewritings on non-observable sorts in Example 5.15, except that we would need a slightly more general form of Prop. 5.9 and Thm. 5.13, with extension of signatures (and models) permitted.

Example 5.17. Finally, let $\mathbf{P}_{\mathsf{GHOSRWL}}$ be a pullback of $\mathbf{P}_{\mathsf{GHRWL}}$ and $\mathbf{P}_{\mathsf{GOSRWL}}$ over $\mathbf{P}_{\mathsf{GRWL}}$ via the morphisms constructed in Examples 5.15 and 5.14, respectively. Equivalently, $\mathbf{P}_{\mathsf{GHOSRWL}}$ is the limit of the parchments and their morphisms constructed so far. It is a complete joint extension of the parchments considered so far, and so by Prop. 5.5, it is the limit in $\mathcal{JPAR}$ of the diagram constructed so far. $\mathbf{P}_{\mathsf{GHOSRWL}}$ presents an institution that corresponds to GHOSRWL in the cube, inheriting the comments on the lack of subsorting for non-observable sorts from Example 5.16.

6   Final Remarks

In this paper we study the problems of systematic combination of logical systems in the framework of the theory of institutions and their presentations as parchments. To begin with, we recall the notion of institution and institution morphism [GB92], and the construction of limits in the category they form [Tar86]. Then we introduce a new notion of model-theoretic parchment, modifying the original notions defined in [GB86] and [MTP98]. We sketch again how limits in the category of such parchments are built, and argue that they do not always offer a satisfactory way of putting logical systems together. We present a new understanding of this phenomena via Props. 5.2 and 5.3, and the new notion of a complete joint extension of a family of parchments. We suggest some simple situations when the use of limits yields a desired result, as for instance captured by Prop. 5.6. We also develop constructions that adjust such limits to a more desired form, Props. 5.9, 5.11 and Thm. 5.13.

All these developments are extensively illustrated by referring to various logical systems that underlie CafeOBJ [DF02]. We start from simple parchments that capture equational logic, order-sorted equational logic, behavioural equational logic and rewriting logic, respectively, and show how to systematically combine and modify them to obtain the remaining logical systems of the CafeOBJ cube.

To keep the presentation relatively simple and hopefully understandable, in places we depart from the details of the logical systems as used in CafeOBJ. In particular, we deal with their ground versions only (no variables). Adding variables would be simple: in essence, we would have to multiply the sorts in the abstract syntax signatures by the sets of variables considered, and to parametrise non-logical values in the evaluation structures by valuations of variables, as is done in [Mos96]. We foresee no major difficulties with this, but it is worth spelling out the details, of course. Another departure from the logics of CafeOBJ is elimination of conditions in statements – adding those should pose no difficulties whatsoever, although the abstract syntax signatures and the evaluation structures would again become somewhat more complex. We also simplify the view of behavioural satisfaction, by using a set of observable sorts rather than a designated set of observer operations. The changes required to capture the more refined view of CafeOBJ are rather obvious as well. To deal with order-sorted algebra, we introduce explicit subsort inclusions and (partial) retracts, again somewhat departing from what is sketched in [DF02]. The combination of behavioural equations with subsorting, omitted here, requires further careful study in our view, perhaps building on [BD94].

To keep the paper to a reasonable size, we entirely omitted notions of comorphisms for institutions and parchments, even though there seems to have been a shift in the presentation of the CafeOBJ cube from institution morphisms to comorphisms [Dia11]. In the case of the logical systems considered here, these are simple, as all the morphisms in use are based on signature functors having left adjoints — and in such cases well-known results about duality between institution morphisms and comorphisms [FC96] carry over to parchments as well. In general, however, the use of comorphisms in this context is not immediate. First, there are formal problems: for instance, the category of institutions and their comorphisms is not cocomplete due to foundational reasons, and some size limitations have to be imposed on the institutions considered. Second, and perhaps more to the point, comorphisms capture a different intuition concerning the relationship between the institutions they link. Informally, while institution morphisms indicate how a richer logical system is built over a simpler one, institution comorphisms show how a simpler logical system is encoded in a richer one. Consequently, it is not obvious at all that comorphisms offer a proper technical framework for the modular construction of logical systems we aim at here. We leave this as a worthwhile topic for further investigation though, as comorphisms open the way to the study of parchment representations in universal logics we began in [MTP98], and link to other frameworks based on heterogeneous logical environments like HETS [MML07] and LATIN [CHK+11], which admit logic definitions in a modular manner [CHK+12].

An interesting, far-reaching and difficult problem is how to capture in our framework the operational ideas that underlie the CafeOBJ implementation and are closely linked with the logical systems involved.

Acknowledgements. Thanks to the anonymous referees for valuable feedback.

References

[BD94]   Burstall, R., Diaconescu, R.: Hiding and behaviour: An institutional approach. In: Roscoe, A.W. (ed.) A Classical Mind: Essays in Honour of C.A.R. Hoare, pp. 75–92. Prentice-Hall (1994)

[BG80]   Burstall, R.M., Goguen, J.A.: The semantics of Clear, a specification language. In: Bjørner, D. (ed.) Abstract Software Specifications. LNCS, vol. 86, pp. 292–332. Springer, Heidelberg (1980)

[BH06]   Bidoit, M., Hennicker, R.: Constructor-based observational logic. Journal of Logic and Algebraic Programming 67(1-2), 3–51 (2006)

[CGR03]   Caleiro, C., Gouveia, P., Ramos, J.: Completeness results for fibred parchments: Beyond the propositional base. In: Wirsing, M., Pattinson, D., Hennicker, R. (eds.) WADT 2003. LNCS, vol. 2755, pp. 185–200. Springer, Heidelberg (2003)

[CHK+11]   Codescu, M., Horozal, F., Kohlhase, M., Mossakowski, T., Rabe, F.: Project abstract: Logic atlas and integrator (LATIN). In: Davenport, J.H., Farmer, W.M., Urban, J., Rabe, F. (eds.) MKM 2011 and Calculemus 2011. LNCS, vol. 6824, pp. 289–291. Springer, Heidelberg (2011)

[CHK+12]   Codescu, M., Horozal, F., Kohlhase, M., Mossakowski, T., Rabe, F., Sojakova, K.: Towards logical frameworks in the heterogeneous tool set HETS. In: Mossakowski, T., Kreowski, H.-J. (eds.) WADT 2010. LNCS, vol. 7137, pp. 139–159. Springer, Heidelberg (2012)

[CMRS01]   Caleiro, C., Mateus, P., Ramos, J., Sernadas, A.: Combining logics: Parchments revisited. In: Cerioli, M., Reggio, G. (eds.) WADT 2001 and CoFI WG Meeting 2001. LNCS, vol. 2267, pp. 48–70. Springer, Heidelberg (2002)

[DF98]   Diaconescu, R., Futatsugi, K.: CafeOBJ Report: The Language, Proof Techniques, and Methodologies for Object-Oriented Algebraic Specification. AMAST Series in Computing, vol. 6. World Scientific (1998), See also http://www.ldl.jaist.ac.jp/cafeobj/

[DF02]   Diaconescu, R., Futatsugi, K.: Logical foundations of CafeOBJ. Theoretical Computer Science 285, 289–318 (2002)

[Dia02]   Diaconescu, R.: Grothendieck institutions. Applied Categorical Structures 10(4), 383–402 (2002)

[Dia07]   Diaconescu, R.: A methodological guide to the CafeOBJ logic. In: Bjørner, D., Henson, M.C. (eds.) Logics of Specification Languages, Monographs in Theoretical Computer Science, pp. 153–240. Springer, Heidelberg (2007)

[Dia08]   Diaconescu, R.: Institution-independent Model Theory. Birkhäuser (2008)

[Dia11]   Diaconescu, R.: Grothendieck inclusion systems. Applied Categorical Structures 19(5), 783–802 (2011)

[FC96]   Fiadeiro, J.L., Costa, J.F.: Mirror, mirror in my hand: A duality between specifications and models of process behaviour. Mathematical Structures in Computer Science 6(4), 353–373 (1996)

[GB86]   Goguen, J.A., Burstall, R.M.: A study in the functions of programming methodology: Specifications, institutions, charters and parchments. In: Pitt, D., Abramsky, S., Poigné, A., Rydeheard, D. (eds.) Category Theory and Computer Programming. LNCS, vol. 240, pp. 313–333. Springer, Heidelberg (1986)

[GB92]   Goguen, J.A., Burstall, R.M.: Institutions: Abstract model theory for specification and programming. Journal of the Association for Computing Machinery 39(1), 95–146 (1992)

[GM92]   Goguen, J., Meseguer, J.: Order-sorted algebra I: Equational deduction for multiple inheritance, overloading, exceptions and partial operations. Theoretical Computer Science 105(2), 217–273 (1992)

[GR02]   Goguen, J.A., Roşu, G.: Institution morphisms. Formal Aspects of Computing 13(3-5), 274–307 (2002)

[GWM+00]   Goguen, J., Winkler, T., Meseguer, J., Futatsugi, K., Jouannaud, J.-P.: Introducing OBJ3. In: Goguen, J., Malcolm, G. (eds.) Software Engineering with OBJ: Algebraic Specification in Action. Kluwer (2000)

[Mac71]   Mac Lane, S.: Categories for the Working Mathematician. Springer (1971)

[Mes98]   Meseguer, J.: Membership algebra as a logical framework for equational specification. In: Parisi-Presicce, F. (ed.) WADT 1997. LNCS, vol. 1376, pp. 18–61. Springer, Heidelberg (1998)

[MML07]   Mossakowski, T., Maeder, C., Lüttich, K.: The heterogeneous tool set, HETS. In: Grumberg, O., Huth, M. (eds.) TACAS 2007. LNCS, vol. 4424, pp. 519–522. Springer, Heidelberg (2007), See also http://www.informatik.uni-bremen.de/cofi/hets/

[Mos96]   Mossakowski, T.: Using limits of parchments to systematically construct institutions of partial algebras. In: Haveraaen, M., Owe, O., Dahl, O.-J. (eds.) WADT 1995 and COMPASS 1995. LNCS, vol. 1130, pp. 379–393. Springer, Heidelberg (1996)

[Mos03]   Mossakowski, T.: Foundations of heterogeneous specification. In: Wirsing, M., Pattinson, D., Hennicker, R. (eds.) WADT 2003. LNCS, vol. 2755, pp. 359–375. Springer, Heidelberg (2003)

[Mos05]   Mossakowski, T.: Heterogeneous Specification and the Heterogeneous Tool Set. Habilitation thesis, Universität Bremen (2005)

[MT09]   Mossakowski, T., Tarlecki, A.: Heterogeneous logical environments for distributed specifications. In: Corradini, A., Montanari, U. (eds.) WADT 2008. LNCS, vol. 5486, pp. 266–289. Springer, Heidelberg (2009)

[MTP97]   Mossakowski, T., Tarlecki, A., Pawłowski, W.: Combining and representing logical systems. In: Moggi, E., Rosolini, G. (eds.) CTCS 1997. LNCS, vol. 1290, pp. 177–196. Springer, Heidelberg (1997)

[MTP98]   Mossakowski, T., Tarlecki, A., Pawłowski, W.: Combining and representing logical systems using model-theoretic parchments. In: Parisi-Presicce, F. (ed.) WADT 1997. LNCS, vol. 1376, pp. 349–364. Springer, Heidelberg (1998)

[ST87]   Sannella, D., Tarlecki, A.: On observational equivalence and algebraic specification. Journal of Computer and System Sciences 34, 150–178 (1987)

[ST88]   Sannella, D., Tarlecki, A.: Specifications in an arbitrary institution. Information and Computation 76(2-3), 165–210 (1988)

[ST12]   Sannella, D., Tarlecki, A.: Foundations of Algebraic Specification and Formal Software Development. Monographs in Theoretical Computer Science. An EATCS Series. Springer (2012)

[SW83]   Sannella, D., Wirsing, M.: A kernel language for algebraic specification and implementation. In: Karpinski, M. (ed.) FCT 1983. LNCS, vol. 158, pp. 413–427. Springer, Heidelberg (1983)

[Tar86]   Tarlecki, A.: Bits and pieces of the theory of institutions. In: Pitt, D.H., Abramsky, S., Poigné, A., Rydeheard, D.E. (eds.) Category Theory and Computer Programming. LNCS, vol. 240, pp. 334–360. Springer, Heidelberg (1986)

[Tar96]   Tarlecki, A.: Moving between logical systems. In: Haveraaen, M., Owe, O., Dahl, O.-J. (eds.) WADT 1995 and COMPASS 1995. LNCS, vol. 1130, pp. 478–502. Springer, Heidelberg (1996)

[Tar00]   Tarlecki, A.: Towards heterogeneous specifications. In: Gabbay, D., de Rijke, M. (eds.) Frontiers of Combining Systems 2. Studies in Logic and Computation, pp. 337–360. Research Studies Press (2000)

[TBG91]   Tarlecki, A., Burstall, R.M., Goguen, J.A.: Some fundamental algebraic tools for the semantics of computation. Part 3: Indexed categories. Theoretical Computer Science 91(2), 239–264 (1991)

Incremental Proofs of Termination, Confluence and Sufficient Completeness of OBJ Specifications

Masaki Nakamura[1], Kazuhiro Ogata[2], and Kokichi Futatsugi[2]

[1] Toyama Prefectural University,
5180 Kurokawa, Imizu, Toyama, Japan
[2] Japan Advanced Institute of Science and Technology,
1-1 Asahidai, Nomi, Ishikawa, Japan

Abstract. OBJ languages support semi-automated verification for algebraic specifications based on equational reasoning by term rewriting systems (TRS). Termination, confluence and sufficient completeness are important fundamental properties for the equational reasoning. In this article, we give light-weight methods for checking those properties in a modular way. We formalize the notion of hierarchical extension for constructor-based conditional algebraic specifications, and give sufficient conditions for those fundamental properties, which can be used for proving them incrementally [1].

Keywords: conditional term rewriting systems, algebraic specifications, termination, confluence, sufficient completeness, incremental proofs.

1 Introduction

There are three fundamental properties of OBJ algebraic specifications: termination, confluence and sufficient completeness. Termination guarantees that a normal form exists and computable. Confluence guarantees the uniqueness of normal forms. Sufficient completeness guarantees the well-definedness of a function. Those fundamental properties are undecidable in general. There are several methods and tools to prove termination, confluence and sufficient completeness, which can be proved automatically for some class of TRSs. We may apply those established methods to OBJ specifications directly, however, for a large and complex system, its specification may involve lots of equations and we may face a limitation of time and space for proving the properties by those methods. To make the task easy, incremental approaches are effective. In an incremental approach, those properties are proved in a modular way. To prove termination (or confluence, sufficient completeness), first prove it for the imported modules, and then prove it for the importing module, which guarantee the whole specification to satisfy the property. Unfortunately, termination is not modular in general. Even if two sets E_0 and E_1 of equations have no shared operators, termination of each

---

[1] The preliminary version of a part of this article appeared in the short paper [14].

S. Iida, J. Meseguer, and K. Ogata (Eds.): Futatsugi Festschrift, LNCS 8373, pp. 92–109, 2014.
© Springer-Verlag Berlin Heidelberg 2014

E_0 and E_1 does not imply termination of the union $E_0 \cup E_1$. The following is a famous example of Toyama's counter-example: $E_0 = \{f(0, 1, X) = f(X, X, X)\}$ and $E_1 = \{g(X, Y) = X, g(X, Y) = Y\}$ where f, g are operators, $0, 1$ are constants, and X, Y are variables. E_0 and E_1 are terminating respectively, however, $E_0 \cup E_1$ is not terminating since $f(0, 1, g(0, 1)) \rightarrow f(g(0, 1), g(0, 1), g(0, 1)) \rightarrow f(0, g(0, 1), g(0, 1)) \rightarrow f(0, 1, g(0, 1))$. Thus, we need to give an appropriate condition such that the fundamental properties can be proved in a modular way and the condition covers practically used specifications. In [20,18], incremental approaches for proving termination (and confluence, sufficient completeness) have been proposed. However, they do not deal with conditional equations. Conditional equations in OBJ specifications are useful to describe the meaning of an operator by case splitting, and used in lots of practical case studies, including OTS/CafeOBJ specifications in [15,9,17], for example. The main contribution of our work is to give incremental approaches to prove fundamental properties for specifications with conditional equations.

2 Preliminaries

In this section, we introduce the notion of algebraic specifications [1,3] and term rewriting systems [19,16]. Though we take CafeOBJ notations in this article, our approaches and results can be applied to other OBJ specification languages.

2.1 Algebraic Specifications

A sort is a name of entities of the same type. For a partial order $\leq$ on a set S of sorts, $\equiv_{\leq}$ is defined as the equivalence relation. The quotient of S under $\equiv_{\leq}$ is denoted by $\hat{S} = S/\equiv_{\leq}$. The element of $\hat{S}$ which contains $s \in S$ is denoted by $[s] \in \hat{S}$, and called a connected component. In CafeOBJ, S and $\leq$ are declared with the square brackets and the symbol <. For example, when declaring [Zero NzNat < Nat], the corresponding set S_n is $\{\text{Zero}, \text{NzNat}, \text{Nat}\}$ and the partial order $\leq_n$ on S is the reflexive and transitive closure of <, that is, $\leq_n = \{(\text{Zero}, \text{Zero}), (\text{NzNat}, \text{NzNat}), (\text{Nat}, \text{Nat}), (\text{Zero}, \text{Nat}), (\text{NzNat}, \text{Nat})\}$. An operator is an element of an S^+-sorted set Σ, where S^+ (or S^*) is the set of all non-empty strings (or all strings) on S. An operator $f \in \Sigma_{ws}$ is denoted by $f : w \rightarrow s$, and $w \in S^*$, $s \in S$ and $ws \in S^+$ are called the arity, the sort and the rank of f respectively. The empty string is denoted by $[]$. A constructor-based order-sorted signature is denoted by $(S, \leq, \Sigma, \Sigma^C)$ (abbr. $(S, \leq, \Sigma)$ or Σ) where a set S of sorts, a poset $\leq$ on S, a S^+-sorted set Σ of operators, and a set $\Sigma^C \subseteq \Sigma$ of constructors, where we use set notations for A-sorted set B with natural extension such that $B \subseteq B'$ means $B_a \subseteq B'_a$ for all $a \in A$, $e \in B$ means $e \in B_a$ for some $a \in A$, and so on. In CafeOBJ, $f \in \Sigma_{ws}$ (or $f_0, f_1, \ldots \in \Sigma_{ws}$) is declared as op $f : w \rightarrow s$ (or ops $f_0 f_1 \cdots : w \rightarrow s$ for plural ones of a same rank). Constructors are declared with the operator attribute {constr}. For example, ops (_+_) (_-_) : Nat Nat -> Nat is a declaration of two operators. op 0 : -> Zero {constr} and op s_ : Nat -> NzNat {constr} are declarations of constructors on S_n. Underlines in operators indicate the positions of their arguments in term expression, defined below. We assume $(S, \leq, \Sigma, \Sigma^C)$ is sensible, that is, for each $f \in \Sigma_{ws} \cap \Sigma_{w's'}$, $w \equiv_{\leq} w'$ implies $s \equiv_{\leq} s'$. A sort $s \in S$ is called constrained if (1) there exists $f \in \Sigma_{ws}^C$ or (2) there exists a constrained sort $s' \leq s$. We denote the set of all constrained sorts in S by S^{CT}. A non-constrained sort is called loose, and denoted by $S^{LS} = S \setminus S^{CT}$. A term is a tree whose nodes are operators and leaves are variables. For a given signature $(S, \leq, \Sigma, \Sigma^C)$ and an S-sorted set X of variables, the S-sorted set $T_\Sigma(X)$ (abbr. T) of (Σ, X)-terms is defined as the smallest set satisfying that (1) $X_s \subseteq T_s$ for each $s \in S$, (2) $T_s \subseteq T_{s'}$ for each $s \leq s'$, and (3) $f(\bar{t}_n) \in T_s$ for each $f \in \Sigma_{\bar{s}_n\, s}$ and $t_i \in T_{s_i}$ ($i \in \{\bar{n}\}$) [2]. Term $t \in T_s$ is called a term of s. We write c instead of a term $c()$ for a constant $c \in \Sigma_s$. Variables are declared with var and vars in CafeOBJ, for example, vars M N : Nat means that M, N $\in X_{\text{Nat}}$. The followings are examples of terms: $0 \in T_{\text{Zero}}$, $0 \in T_{\text{Nat}}$, s $0 \in T_{\text{NzNat}}$, s $0 \in T_{\text{Nat}}$, M + (N + s 0) $\in T_{\text{Nat}}$ and so on. A position of a term is given by the string of positive integers, where the empty string is denoted by ε. The set $O(t)$ of positions of a term t is defined as $O(x) = \{\varepsilon\}$ and $O(f(\bar{t}_n)) = \{\varepsilon\} \cup \{i.p \in \mathcal{N}_+^* \mid i \in \{\bar{n}\}, p \in O(t_i)\}$. The root symbol of a term t, denoted by $root(t)$, is defined as $root(t) = f$ if $t = f(\cdots)$ and $root(t) = x$ if $t = x \in X$. The subterm of a term t at position $p \in O(t)$, denoted by $t|_p$, is defined as $t|_\varepsilon = t$ and $f(\bar{t}_n)|_{i.p} = t_i|_p$. The subterm relation $\geq_{sub}$ is defined as follows: $t \geq_{sub} t'$ if and only if $t' = t|_p$ for some $p \in O(t)$. We call it the strict subterm relation, denoted by $>_{sub}$, when $p \neq \varepsilon$.

An equation, denoted by $t = t'$, on a signature Σ and a variable set X is a pair of (Σ, X)-terms $t, t' \in T_s$ of a same sort s. In CafeOBJ, an equation $t = t'$ is declared like eq $t = t'$. A conditional equation, denoted by $t = t'$ if c, on a signature Σ and a variable set X is a pair of an equation $t = t'$ on them and a (Σ, X)-term $c \in T_{\text{Bool}}$ [3]. A conditional equation is declared like ceq $t = t'$ if c. For example, eq N + 0 = N is an equation since both N + 0 and N are of the sort Nat, and ceq even (s N) = true if not (even N) is a conditional equation for op even_ : Nat -> Bool. Hereafter, we may regard an equation eq l = r as a conditional equation ceq l = r if c, and call just an equation for both unconditional and conditional equations if no confusion arises.

A pair of (Σ, E) is a specification if each $e \in E$ is an equation on Σ and a variable set X. CafeOBJ supports a module system for describing a large specification effectively. A CafeOBJ module consists of imports, a signature and axioms. We only treat equational specifications in this article, that is, axioms are equations. A module may import other modules. When a module M' imports a module M, the sorts and the operators in M can be used to declare sorts, operators and equations in M'. There are three kinds of imports in CafeOBJ: protecting, extending and using imports, denoted by pr(M), ex(M) and us(M). By

---

[2]   Hereafter we may write $\bar{a}_n$ instead of $a_1, \ldots, a_n$, and $\bar{n}$ instead of $1, \ldots, n$.

[3]   Bool is a special sort of CafeOBJ, which is declared in a built-in module BOOL, where constants true, false and logical operators not_, _and_, _or_, ... are declared with some equations like eq false and A = false with var A : Bool. In default, each CafeOBJ module implicitly imports BOOL.

using those notions, we can describe algebraic specifications in various abstract levels. For more details of semantics, see the literatures [1,3]. Note that in this article, we focus on equational reasoning by the TRS, and the TRS ignores the difference between import modes.

Example 1. We show CafeOBJ modules NAT-OP specifying natural numbers with addition, subtraction and comparison operators, and ACCOUNT specifying a bank account system with balance, deposit and withdraw operators (Fig.1).

```
mod! NAT-OP{
  [Zero NzNat < Nat]
  op 0 : -> Zero          {constr}
  op s_ : Nat -> NzNat   {constr}
  ops (_+_) (_-_) : Nat Nat -> Nat
  ops (_>=_) (_>_) : Nat Nat -> Bool
  vars M N : Nat
  eq N + 0 = N .                    eq M + s N = s (M + N) .
  eq 0 - N = 0 .                    eq M - 0 = M .
  eq s M - s N = M - N .
  eq N >= N = true .                eq M >= 0 = true .
  eq 0 >= s N = false .             eq s M >= s N = M >= N .
  eq N > M = not (M >= N) .
}
mod* ACCOUNT{
  pr(NAT-OP)
  [Account]
  op balance_ : Account -> Nat
  ops (deposit_ _) (withdraw_ _) : Nat Account -> Account  {constr}
  op init : -> Account  {constr}
  var A : Account
  var N : Nat
  eq balance init = 0 .
  eq balance (deposit N A) = balance A + N .
 ceq balance (withdraw N A) = balance A - N if balance A >= N .
 ceq withdraw N A           = A            if N > balance A .
}
```

Fig. 1. CafeOBJ modules NAT-OP and ACCOUNT

In NAT-OP, the sorts Zero, NzNat and Nat are declared with the subsort relation Zero < Nat and NzNat < Nat. The set $S_{\text{NAT-OP}}$ is {Zero, NzNat, Nat} and the partial order $\leq_{\text{NAT-OP}}$ on $S_{\text{NAT-OP}}$ is the reflexive and transitive closure of <, that is, $\leq_{\text{NAT-OP}} = \{(\text{Zero}, \text{Zero}), (\text{NzNat}, \text{NzNat}), (\text{Nat}, \text{Nat}), (\text{Zero}, \text{Nat}), (\text{NzNat}, \text{Nat})\}$. The constant 0 stands for zero, and s_ stands for the Peano style successor function. Constructors are declared with {constr}. The terms 0, s 0, s s 0, ... are regarded as $0, 1, 2, \ldots$ respectively. The operators _+_, _-_, _>=_, and _>_ stand for the addition, the subtraction, $\geq$ and $>$ on natural numbers respectively. Those operators are defined by the equations in NAT-OP inductively.

In ACCOUNT, the module NAT-OP is imported with the protect mode. The sort Account is declared. A term of Account stands for a state of the account. The operator balance_ returns the balance of a state. The term deposit N A is the result state of depositing N into A, and the term withdraw N A is the result state of withdrawing N from A. The constant init stands for the initial state. The first equation means that the initial balance is zero. The second equation means that after depositing N, the balance increases by N. The third one means that after withdrawing N, the balance decreases by N when the current balance is greater than or equal to N. The last one means that the state does not change, and thus the balance also does not change, when trying to withdraw more than the current balance.

2.2   Term Rewriting Systems

OBJ languages support specification execution based on the theory of term rewriting systems (TRS). In the TRS, an equation is regarded as a left-to-right rewrite rule. An instance of a left-hand side of an equation is called a redex (of the equaiton). A term is rewritten by replacing a redex of an equation with the corresponding instance of the right-hand side of the equation. A term is reduced by rewriting a given term until it cannot. A conditional equation is regarded as a conditional rewrite rule, which can be applied when the instance of the condition is reduced into true.

For a given binary relation $\rightarrow$, the transitive closure and the reflexive and transitive closure are written by $\rightarrow^{+}$ and $\rightarrow^{*}$ respectively. A map $\theta \in T^X$ from a set of variable X to a set of terms T is called a substitution, and the instance of a term t by θ, denoted by $t\theta$, is defined as $x\theta = \theta(x)$ and $f(\bar{t}_n)\theta = f(\overline{t_n\theta})$. For a given set E of equations, the rewrite relation $\rightarrow_E$ is defined as follows:

$$
\begin{aligned}
t \rightarrow_E t' &\iff \exists i \in \mathcal{N}.t \rightarrow_{E,i} t' \\
t \rightarrow_{E,<i} t' &\iff \exists j < i.t \rightarrow_{E,j} t' \\
t \rightarrow_{E,0} t' &\iff \exists \mathsf{eq}\ l = r \in E.\theta \in T^X.p \in O(t).t|_p = l\theta \wedge t' = t[r\theta]_p \\
t \rightarrow_{E,i} t' &\iff \exists \mathsf{ceq}\ l = r\ \mathsf{if}\ c \in E.\theta \in T^X.p \in O(t).t|_p = l\theta \wedge t' = t[r\theta]_p \\
&\qquad\qquad\qquad\qquad\qquad\qquad\qquad\qquad\qquad \wedge\ c\theta \rightarrow^{*}_{E,<i} \mathsf{true}
\end{aligned}
$$

A term t is called an E-normal form if there is no u such that $t \rightarrow_E u$. A term is called E-reducible if it is not an E-normal form. We may omit E and write a normal form and a reducible term if no confusion. When $t \rightarrow_E t'$ is obtained by applying an equation e, we write $t \rightarrow_e t'$. Hereafter, we assume each specification satisfies the following conditions: (1) the number of equations is finite, (2) the left-hand side is not a variable for each equation, and (3) all variables in the right-hand side and the condition term are included in the left-hand side for each equation [4]. Then, for each unconditional equation e : eq $l = r$ and each

---

[4] A conditional TRS for a CafeOBJ specification is categorized into strongly deterministic oriented 1-CTRS[16], where a conditional equation $l = r$ if c of CafeOBJ corresponds to a conditional rewrite rule $l \rightarrow r \Leftarrow c \rightarrow$ true of 1-CTRS.

redex t, that is, $t = l\theta$ for some θ, there exists the unique t' such that $t \to_e t'$. For each conditional equation e : ceq $l = r$ if c and each redex t, there exists the unique $c\theta$ to be checked, and there exists the unique t' such that $t \to_e t'$ when $c\theta \to^*$ true. We may write $\to_M$ instead of $\to_{E_M}$ where E_M is the set of all equations declared in a module M and the all modules imported by M. We may omit the subscript E in $\to_E$ (or $\to_{E,i}$) and write $\to$ (or $\to_i$) if no confusion arises.

Example 2. Equational reasoning in CafeOBJ is done by the reduction command. The following is an example of the reduction with the input term s 0 + s s 0 in NAT-OP:

```
CafeOBJ> red in NAT-OP : s 0 + s s 0 .
s (s (s 0)) : NzNat
```

This input and output mean that s 0 + s s 0 $\to^*_{\text{NAT-OP}}$ s s s 0. When $t \to^*_M t'$, the terms t and t' are equivalent, i.e. $t = t'$ can be deduced from the axioms. Thus, the above execution is a proof of $1 + 2 = 3$ in NAT-OP. The trace of the above reduction is <u>s 0 + s s 0</u> $\to_0$ s(<u>s 0 + s 0</u>) $\to_0$ s s(<u>s 0 + 0</u>) $\to_0$ s s s 0, where a redex $(l\theta)$ is underlined for each rewrite relation. First and second rewrites are obtained by the second equation eq M + s N = s(M + N) in NAT-OP and the last one is obtained by the first equation eq M + 0 = M.

Example 3. The following is an example of reduction with the input term balance (withdraw (s s 0) (deposit (s 0) init)) in ACCOUNT:

```
CafeOBJ> red in ACCOUNT : balance (withdraw (s s 0) (deposit (s 0) init)) .
(s 0):NzNat
```

The input term means that the result state of depositing 1 to the initial state and then withdrawing 2 from that state. The result is 1 since the deposit succeeds and the balance increases 1, however the withdrawal does not succeed because of $1 \not\geq 2$. The trace is balance(<u>withdraw (s s 0) (deposit (s 0) init)</u>) $\to_1$ balance (<u>deposit (s 0) init</u>) $\to_0$ <u>balance init</u> + s 0 $\to_0$ <u>0 + s 0</u> $\to^*_0$ s 0. The first rewrite is obtained by the last equation ceq withdraw N A = A if N > balance A in ACCOUNT. To apply the equation, the condition part should be reduced into true. The corresponding instance of the condition is s s 0 > balance (deposit (s 0) init). The right-hand side of > is reduced into s 0, and s s 0 > s 0 $\to$ not (s 0 >= s s 0) $\to$ not (0 >= s 0) $\to$ not false $\to_{\text{BOOL}}$ true.

3   Hierarchical Extension

In this section, we introduce the notion of hierarchical extension proposed in [20,13] to give incremental proof methods for termination, confluence and sufficient completeness.

A module $[\Sigma \mid E]$ is a pair of a signature and a set of equations. Note that a module may not be a specification (or a TRS), which means that E may involve operators not involved in Σ. For a given CafeOBJ module M, we write Σ_M for the set of all operators declared in M, and E_M for the set of all equations in

M. For example, the set E_{ACCOUNT} involves eq balance init = 0, declared in ACCOUNT, but does not involve eq N + 0 = N, declared in NAT-OP. The equation eq balance init = 0 $\in E_{\text{ACCOUNT}}$ involves the constant 0, which is declared in NAT-OP, that is, $0 \in \Sigma_{\text{NAT-OP}}$ but $0 \notin \Sigma_{\text{ACCOUNT}}$.

To obtain a sufficient condition under which we can try to prove termination (or confluence, sufficient completeness) by checking some conditions on each module, we give the notion of hierarchical extension, which originally proposed in [20] for unconditional TRSs and extended to conditional TRSs in [13].

Definition 1. [20,13] Let $M_0 = (\Sigma_0, E_0)$ be a specification and $M_1 = [\Sigma_1 \mid E_1]$ be a module. A pair of M_0 and M_1 is called a hierarchical extension (or M_1 is called a module extending M_0 in [20]), denoted by $M_0 \leftarrow M_1$, if (1) $\Sigma_0 \cap \Sigma_1 = \emptyset$ [5], (2) $(\Sigma_0 \cup \Sigma_1, E_1)$ is a specification, and (3) $D_{E_1} \subseteq \Sigma_1$, where D_E is the set of the root symbols of the left-hand sides of all equations in E, that is, $D_E = \{f \in \Sigma \mid f(\cdots) = r \text{ if } c \in E\}$, and $f \in D_E$ is called a defined symbol of E.

The union of M_0 and M_1 is a specification when $M_0 \leftarrow M_1$. We denote $M_0 \leftarrow M_1 \leftarrow M_2$ when $M_0 \leftarrow M_1$ and $M_0 \cup M_1 \leftarrow M_2$. A specification (Σ_0, E_0) can be regarded as a module $[\Sigma_0 \mid E_0]$ extending the empty specification $(\emptyset, \emptyset)$. Hereafter we may use the module expression for both specifications and modules if no confusion arises.

Example 4. NAT-OP $\leftarrow$ ACCOUNT is a hierarchical extention since (1) there are no shared operators, (2) all equations in ACCOUNT are defined on $\Sigma_{\text{NAT-OP}} \cup \Sigma_{\text{ACCOUNT}}$, and (3) balance and withdraw $\in D_{E_{\text{ACCOUNT}}}$ are included in Σ_{ACCOUNT}.

4   Incremental Proofs

In the following subsections, we give a sufficient condition for each of termination, confluence and sufficient completeness, which can be proved incrementally. For each property, we give two kinds of conditions. The first condition is a sufficient condition for each property, which can be checked automatically. The second condition enables us to check the first condition incrementally.

4.1   Termination

For unconditional equations, termination is defined as the absence of infinite reduction sequences $t_0 \to_0 t_1 \to_0 t_2 \to_0 \cdots$. In the case of conditional equations, the absence of infinite reduction sequences is not enough to obtain termination of computation. Let $E = \{\text{ceq } a = b \text{ if } a\}$, and try to reduce a term a. To apply the conditional equation to a, we need to reduce the condition term a again. To avoid such infinite condition calls as well as infinite reduction sequences, the notion of operational termination has been proposed [10].

---

[5]   This means that they have no shared operations, i.e. $\Sigma_0' \cap \Sigma_1' = \emptyset$ when $\Sigma_0 = (S_0, \leq_0, \Sigma_0')$ and $\Sigma_1 = (S_1, \leq_1, \Sigma_1')$. In this article, we mean that operator *names* are not shared in Σ_0 and Σ_1. Thus, overloaded operators between M_0 and M_1 are not allowed. For example, op _+_ : Nat Nat -> Nat in M_0 and op _+_ : Int Int -> Int with [Nat < Int] in M_1 do not satisfy the condition.

Reflexive	Transitive	Congruence	Replacement
$\dfrac{}{t \to^* t}$	$\dfrac{t_0 \to t_1 \quad t_1 \to^* t_2}{t_0 \to^* t_2}$	$\dfrac{u_i \to u_i'}{f(\bar{u}) \to f(\bar{u}')}$ where $f \in \Sigma$ and $\forall j \neq i.u_i = u_i'$	$\dfrac{c\theta \to^* \mathbf{true}}{l\theta \to r\theta}$ where $l = r$ if $c \in E$

Fig. 2. Inference rules

We give a definition of operational termination for CafeOBJ, which can be obtained from the definitions in [10] straightforwardly [6]. The operational termination is defined by the absence of infinite chains of well-formed proof trees on some inference rules. Inference rules for the CafeOBJ reduction are given as Figure 2. We call $t \to t'$ or $t \to^* t'$ a formula. The set of (finite) proof trees and the head of a proof tree are defined inductively. A proof tree is either an open goal G, which is a formula, where we denote $head(G) = G$, or a derivation tree with G as its head, denoted as

$$\frac{T_1 \quad \cdots \quad T_n}{G} \ (R)$$

where G is a formula, R is an inference rule, and $T_1, \ldots, T_n$ are proof trees such that

$$\frac{head(T_1) \quad \cdots \quad head(T_n)}{G}$$

is an instance of R. Let T and T' be proof trees. We denote $T \subset T'$ when T has open goals G_i and T' is obtained by replacing the G_i with a derivation tree T_i whose head is G_i.

A proof tree is closed if it is finite and has no open goals. A proof tree is well-formed if it is either an open goal, a closed proof tree, or a derivation tree of the form

$$\frac{T_1 \quad \cdots \quad T_i \quad \cdots \quad T_n}{G} \ (R)$$

where all $T_1 \ldots, T_n$ are well-formed, $T_1, \ldots, T_{i-1}$ are closed, T_i is not closed, and $T_{i+1}, \ldots, T_n$ are open goals. Operation termination is defined as follows.

Definition 2. [10] A specification is operationally terminating if there is no infinite chain $T_0 \subset T_1 \subset T_2 \cdots$ of well-formed finite proof trees.

Operational termination is shown to be equivalent to the notion of quasi-decreasingness [10].

---

[6] The results of Section 4.1 have been published in our preliminary work [14], however the definitions and the proofs are rough in [14]. Thus, we give precise definitions and proofs for constructor-based order-sorted specifications in this article.

Definition 3. [16] A specification (Σ, E) is quasi-decreasing if there is a well-founded partial ordering $>$ on T such that (1) $\to_E \subseteq >$, (2) $>_{sub} \subseteq >$, and (3) for each ceq $l = r$ if c and $\theta \in T^X$, if $c\theta \to^*$ true then $l\theta > c\theta$.

Proposition 1. [10] A specification is quasi-decreasing if and only if it is operationally terminating.

By Proposition 1, operational termination can be proved by finding an appropriate well-founded partial ordering on terms. Recursive path ordering (RPO) is one of the classical approaches to make a well-founded partial ordering on terms.

Definition 4. [19] Let Σ be a signature, X a set of variables, and $\unrhd \subseteq \Sigma \times \Sigma$ a quasi-order on operators. RPO $>_{rpo} \subseteq T_\Sigma(X) \times T_\Sigma(X)$ is defined as follows:

$$t >_{rpo} t' \overset{def}{\iff} t = f(\bar{t}_m) \text{ and}$$

$$(1)\ \exists i \in \{\bar{m}\}.t_i \geq_{rpo} t',\ \text{or}$$
$$(2)\ t' = g(\bar{t}'_n) \wedge f \rhd g \wedge \forall j \in \{\bar{n}\}.t >_{rpo} t'_j,\ \text{or}$$
$$(3)\ t' = g(\bar{t}'_n) \wedge f \sim g \wedge \{\bar{t}_m\} >^{mul}_{rpo} \{\bar{t}'_n\},$$

where $a \rhd b \Leftrightarrow a \unrhd b \wedge b \ntrianglerighteq a$, $a \sim b \Leftrightarrow a \unrhd b \wedge b \unrhd a$. $\{\ldots\}$ stands for a multiset[7]. The partial order $>^{mul}$ is a multiset order w.r.t. $>$ [8].

The following property holds.

Proposition 2. [19] Let (Σ, E) be a specification. If there exists $\unrhd$ such that $\rhd$ is well-founded, then $>_{sub} \subseteq >_{rpo}$, $>_{rpo}$ is well-founded, and closed under contexts and substitutions, i.e. $l >_{rpo} r$ implies $f(\ldots, l\theta, \ldots) >_{rpo} f(\ldots, r\theta, \ldots)$ for each $f \in \Sigma$ and $\theta \in T^X$.

To give a well-founded order $\unrhd$ on operators declared in a module, we introduce the notion of recursive dependency on operators [18,14]. Let (Σ, E) be a specification. The relations $\succeq^1_E, \succeq_E \subseteq \Sigma \times \Sigma$ are defined as follows: $f \succeq^1_E g \iff \exists\ f(\cdots) = r$ if $c \in E.$ ($\exists p \in O(r).\ r|_p = g(\cdots) \vee \exists p \in O(c).\ c|_p = g(\cdots)$), and $\succeq_E \subseteq \Sigma \times \Sigma$ is the reflexive and transitive closure of $\succeq^1_E$. The strict part and the equivalent part of $\succeq_E$ is defined as $\succ_E = \succeq_E \setminus \preceq_E$ and $\sim_E = \succeq_E \cap \preceq_E$ respectively. We have the following property.

Lemma 1. Let $(\Sigma_0, E_0) \leftarrow [\Sigma_1 \mid E_1]$ and $f, g \in \Sigma_0 \cup \Sigma_1$. If $f \in D_{E_0 \cup E_1}$ and $g \sim_{E_0 \cup E_1} f$ then (1) $g \in D_{E_0 \cup E_1}$ and (2) either $g \sim_{E_0} f$ or $g \sim_{E_1} f$.

Proof. From the definition of $\sim_E$, we have $g \succeq_{E_0 \cup E_1} f$ and $f \succeq_{E_0 \cup E_1} g$. First, we prove the claim (1). From the definition of $\succeq_E$, either $g = f$ or $g \succeq^{1+}_{E_0 \cup E_1} f$ holds. The former case is trivial from the assumption $f \in D_{E_0 \cup E_1}$. For the latter

---

[7]   A multiset is a collection where duplicated elements are allowed. For example, $\{a, a, b\}$ and $\{a, b\}$ are different. $FM(A)$ is the set of all finite multisets whose elements are of a given set A, e.g. $\{0, 2, 2\} \in FM(\mathcal{N})$.

[8]   A multiset order $>^{mul} \subseteq FM(A) \times FM(A)$ w.r.t. a partial $> \subseteq A \times A$ is defined as follows: $M_1 >^{mul} M2 \Leftrightarrow \exists X, Y \in FM(A).[X \neq \emptyset \wedge X \subseteq M_1 \wedge M_2 = (M_1 \setminus X) + Y \wedge \forall y \in Y.\exists x \in X.x > y]$. For example, $\{2, 2, 3\} >^{mul} \{1, 1, 2, 3\}$ holds, where $X = \{2\}$ and $Y = \{1, 1\}$.

case, there exists $g(\cdots) = r$ if $c \in E_0 \cup E_1$. Thus, $g \in D_{E_0 \cup E_1}$. Next, we prove the claim (2). There are the following two cases: $g \in D_{E_0}$ and $g \in D_{E_1}$. Consider the case of $g \in D_{E_0}$. It is trivial for the case of $g = f$. We assume $g \succeq^{1+}_{E_0 \cup E_1} f$ and decompose the sequence as follows: $g = f_0 \succeq^1_{E_0 \cup E_1} f_1 \succeq^1_{E_0 \cup E_1} \cdots \succeq^1_{E_0 \cup E_1} f_n = f$ $(n > 0)$. All f_i are defined symbols of $E_0 \cup E_1$ from the definition of $\succeq^1_E$ and the assumption of $f \in D_{E_0 \cup E_1}$. If $h \succeq^1_{E_0 \cup E_1} h'$ and $h \in D_{E_0}$ then there exists $h(\cdots) = r$ if $c \in E_0$ and $h' \in \Sigma_0$ since $(\Sigma_0, E_0) \leftarrow [\Sigma_1 \mid E_1]$. Thus, all f_i are defined symbols of E_0 and $g = f_0 \succeq^1_{E_0} f_1 \succeq^1_{E_0} \cdots \succeq^1_{E_0} f_n = f$. The opposite side $f \succeq^1_{E_0} g$ can be proved from the definition of $\succeq^1_E$ and (1) in the same way. Therefore, we have $f \sim_{E_0} g$. Consider the case of $g \in D_{E_1}$. Assume there exists $f_i \in D_{E_0}$ in $g = f_0 \succeq^1_{E_0 \cup E_1} f_1 \succeq^1_{E_0 \cup E_1} \cdots \succeq^1_{E_0 \cup E_1} f_n = f$. We have $f \in D_{E_0}$ from the same reason as above, and then we have $g \in D_{E_0}$ from $f \succeq^{1+}_{E_0 \cup E_1} g$. It contradicts $g \in D_{E_1}$ and $(\Sigma_0, E_0) \leftarrow [\Sigma_1 \mid E_1]$. Thus, all f_i are defined symbols of E_1 and we have $f \sim_{E_1} g$. □

We introduce the notion of decreasing rules [18,14]. Let $g \in \Sigma$. An equation $f(\bar{t}_m) = r$ if c is g-argument decreasing if for each subterm $g(\bar{u}_n)$ of r or c, $\{\!\{\bar{t}_m\}\!\} >^{mul}_{sub} \{\!\{\bar{u}_n\}\!\}$. Then, we have the following sufficient condition for operational termination.

Lemma 2. [14] Let (Σ, E) be a specification. If each equation $f(\bar{t}_m) = r$ if $c \in E$ is g-argument decreasing for each operator $g \sim_E f$, then (Σ, E) is operationally terminating.

Proof. For any operator h included in r or c, either $f \succ_E h$ or $f \sim_E h$ holds from the definition of $\succeq_E$. From the definition of RPO, $>_{rpo}$ w.r.t. $\succeq_E$ satisfies $l >_{rpo} r$ and $l >_{rpo} c$. Since RPO is closed under substitution and contexts, all conditions in Definition 3 hold. The specification is quasi-decreasing, and thus operationally terminating. □

Lemma 3. Let $(\Sigma_0, E_0) \leftarrow [\Sigma_1 \mid E_1]$. Assume (0) each equation $f(\bar{t}_m) = r$ if $c \in E_0$ is g-argument decreasing for each operator $g \sim_{E_0} f$, and (1) each equation $f(\bar{t}_m) = r$ if $c \in E_1$ is g-argument decreasing for each operator $g \sim_{E_1} f$. Then, each equation $f(\bar{t}_m) = r$ if $c \in E_0 \cup E_1$ is g-argument decreasing for each operator $g \sim_{E_0 \cup E_1} f$.

Proof. Let $f(\bar{t}_m) = r$ if $c \in E_0 \cup E_1$. Consider the case of $f(\bar{t}_m) = r$ if $c \in E_0$. If $g \sim_{E_0 \cup E_1} f$, then $g \sim_{E_0} f$ or $g \sim_{E_1} f$ from Lemma 1. If $g \sim_{E_1} f$, then $g \succeq_{E_1} f$ and $f \succeq_{E_1} g$. If $f \succeq_{E_1} g$, then $f \in D_{E_1}$, and it contradicts the assumption of hierarchical extension. Thus, $g \sim_{E_0} f$ and the equation is g-argument decreasing from the assumption (0). Similarly, when $f(\bar{t}_m) = r$ if $c \in E_1$, it is g-argument decreasing. □

We have the following theorem of an incremental proof of operational termination.

Theorem 1. [14] Let $(\Sigma_0, E_0) \leftarrow [\Sigma_1 \mid E_1]$. Assume (0) and (1) in Lemma 3. Then, $(\Sigma_0 \cup \Sigma_1, E_0 \cup E_1)$ is operationally terminating.

Proof. From Lemmata 2 and 3. □

4.2 Confluence

Confluence is another important property of TRSs. A specification is confluent if all terms reduced from a same term are joinable. We write $t_0 \uparrow_E t_1$ if there exists t such that $t \to^* t_0$ and $t \to^* t_1$. Terms t_0 and t_1 are called joinable, denoted by $t_0 \downarrow_E t_1$, if there exists u such that $t_0 \to^* u$ and $t_1 \to^* u$. Then, confluence is defined as $\uparrow_E \subseteq \downarrow_E$. Confluence guarantees the uniqueness of normal forms. If u_0 and u_1 are normal forms of t then $t \to^* u_0$ and $t \to^* u_1$ and there should be u such that $u_0 \to^* u$ and $u_1 \to^* u$. Since u_0, u_1 are normal forms, we have $u_0 = u = u_1$.

The congruence relation $=_E$ obtained from E is defined as the smallest equivalence relation on terms satisfying that (1) $f(\bar{t}_n) =_E f(\bar{t}'_n)$ whenever $t_i =_E t'_i$ for each $i \in \{\bar{n}\}$, and (2) $l\theta =_E r\theta$ whenever $c\theta =_E$ true for each ceq $l = r$ if $c \in E$. Equational reasoning is to prove or disprove $t_0 =_E t_1$ for given t_0, t_1 and E. For terminating and confluent E, $t_0 \downarrow_E t_1$ can be checked in finite time, and $t_0 \downarrow_E t_1$ if and only if $t_0 =_E t_1$.

The notion of critical pairs is useful to prove confluence of terminating specifications. Our approach to prove confluence is first to prove termination and then to prove confluence by checking the joinability of critical pairs. We give a definition of conditional critical pairs for CafeOBJ specifications.

Definition 5. [16] Let $l_0 = r_0$ if c_0 and $l_1 = r_1$ if c_1 be renamed equations of E such that they do not share variables. If $l_0|_p = t \notin X$ and $t\sigma = l_1\sigma$ for a most general unifier σ, then the triple $(l_0[r_1]\sigma, r_0\sigma)$ if $c_0\sigma$ and $c_1\sigma$ of terms is called a conditional critical pair (CCP) of E. If these equations are renamed ones of the same equation of E, p should be non-empty string ($p \neq \varepsilon$). A CCP (t, t') if c is joinable if $t\sigma \downarrow t'\sigma$ for any substitution σ satisfying $c\sigma \to^*$true. It is called feasible if there exists σ such that $c\sigma \to^*$true, infeasible if no such σ exists, and trivial if $t = t'$. The set of all CCPs of E is denoted by $CCP(E)$.

Note that _and_ : Bool Bool -> Bool is an operator of the built-in module BOOL. Infeasible (or trivial) CCPs are joinable. We have the following proposition.

Proposition 3. [16] If a specification is operationally terminating and every CCPs are joinable, then it is confluent.

Checking Joinability of CCPs. In this section, we give a sufficient condition for joinability of CCPs. For unconditional TRSs, it is known that non-overlapping and left-linear TRSs are confluent. However, the non-overlapping is too strong for conditional ones. A typical use of conditional equations is to describe equations with a same left-hand side with disjoint conditions, like ceq $l = r_0$ if c, and ceq $l = r_1$ if not c . Instead of non-overlapping, we adopt infeasibility of CCPs [16]. Unfortunately, infeasibility is undecidable since we need to check the absence of σ such that $c\sigma \to^*$ true. Thus, for automated checker, we should take an approximation for it.

We first give a sufficient condition for trivial CCPs. [**C0**] A CCP is a pattern of (t, t) if c. Next, we give three conditions for checking infeasibility automatically. The first one is that [**C1**] the condition c is a pattern of t and not t. The condition can be checked by just pattern matching. This approach may be extended by adding other typical unsatisfiable patterns, like t and not $(t$ or $t')$ made from the combination of ceq $l = r_0$ if c_0, ceq $l = r_1$ if c_1, and ceq $l = r_2$ if not $(c_0$ or $c_1)$. Instead of enumerating conceivable patterns, we may use CafeOBJ reduction as follows. The second one is that [**C2**] c is reduced into false by the Hsiang's TRS of Boolean algebra, which reduces a Boolean formula into its exclusive-or normal form (with the associative and commutative and, or and xor) [6]. The following is (a part of) the built-in module BOOL in CafeOBJ, which implements a Hsiang's TRS [4]:

```
vars A B C : Bool
eq (false and A) = false .    eq (true and A) = A .
eq (A and A) = A .
eq (A or A) = A .             eq (false or A) = A .
eq (true or A) = true .
eq (A or B) = ((A and B) xor (A xor B)) .
eq (A xor A) = false .        eq (false xor A) = A .
eq (A and (B xor C)) = ((A and B) xor (A and C)) .
eq (not A) = (A xor true) .
```

It is known that the exclusive-or normal form is true if the input term is valid, and false if it is unsatisfiable. Thus, for example, the above Boolean terms t and not t, and t and not $(t$ or $t')$ can be reduced into false by the CafeOBJ reduction command. In this case, although reduction of a term is needed, the complexity can be estimated since only the equations in BOOL are used in the reduction, and it depends on the form of the condition terms (mainly depends on the number of or). The last one is that [**C3**] c can be reduced into false by all rewrite rules (with the evaluation strategy implemented in CafeOBJ [1]). This covers the case of the CCP (balanceA, balanceA − N) if balance A >= N and N > balance A from the module ACCOUNT. The condition part balance A >= N and N > balance A can be written into balance A >= N and not balance A >= N by the equation eq N > M = not (M >= N), and reduced into false by BOOL's equations. By [C3], we may prove infeasibility of more CCPs than the other conditions. For operationally terminating specifications, [C3] can be checked in finite time, however, it is hard to estimate its computation complexity since it depends on not only the size of the condition part but also the equations of the specifications.

Non-overlapping Modules. To obtain a light-weight proof of confluence, we give a condition for the hierarchical extension to avoid CCPs between different modules. A TRS (Σ, E) is called a constructor system if every left-hand side has no defined symbols except at the root position, i.e., $\forall f(\bar{t}_n) = r$ if c. $\forall i \in \{\bar{n}\}$. $t_i \in T_{\Sigma \backslash D_E}(X)$ [16]. If $(\Sigma_0, M_0) \leftarrow [\Sigma_1 \mid M_1]$ and $(\Sigma_0 \cup \Sigma_1, E_0 \cup E_1)$ is a constructor TRS, there is no CCPs between $e_0 \in E_0$ and $e_1 \in E_1$ since for a constructor system, only root position can be overlapped and the root symbol of the left-hand side of each equation should be an operator declared in the module from the definition of the hierarchical extension. Constructor TRSs seem to be reasonable to describe a specification since a term constructed by constructors denotes an element of the sort and the meaning of an operator defining some function is often defined for patterns of such terms constructed by constructors. However, there is a difference of the meaning of the constructor between constructor TRSs and constructor operators of CafeOBJ. In constructor TRSs, the constructor means non-defined symbols, i.e. it does not appear as the root symbol of the left-hand side of any equation. In CafeOBJ, an operator with the attribute {constr} may appear as the root symbol, like ceq withdraw N A = A if N > balance A in the module ACCOUNT. Thus, $\Sigma^C \neq \Sigma \setminus D_E$ in general. Another typical example is a specification of integers described by extending Peano-style natural numbers as follows:

```
mod! BASIC-INT{
  [Zero < Int]    op 0 : -> Zero    op (s_) (p_) : Int -> Int
  var X : Int     eq s p X = X .    eq p s X = X .  }
```

We give a condition such that there are no CCPs between different modules although non-constructor systems like ACCOUNT and BASIC-INT are allowed.

Definition 6. A hierarchical extension $(\Sigma_0, E_0) \leftarrow [\Sigma_1 \mid E_1]$ is called non-overlapping if for each $l = r$ if $c \in E_1$, the left-hand side l does not involve any defined symbol of E_0, that is, $l \in T_{(\Sigma_1 \cup \Sigma_0) \setminus D_{E_0}}(X)$.

Unlike constructor TRSs, a left-hand side of an equation may have a defined symbol at non root positions if the symbol is declared in the module itself in a non-overlapping hierarchical extension.

For a non-overlapping hierarchical extension, there are no CCPs between $e_0 \in E_0$ and $e_1 \in E_1$. The following lemma holds straightforwardly.

Lemma 4. Let $(\Sigma_0, E_0) \leftarrow [\Sigma_1 \mid E_1]$ be a non-overlapping hierarchical extension. Then, $CCP(E_0) \cup CCP(E_1) = CCP(E_0 \cup E_1)$.

We have the following theorem for an incremental proof of confluence.

Theorem 2. Let $(\Sigma_0, E_0) \leftarrow [\Sigma_1 \mid E_1]$ be a non-overlapping hierarchical extension such that $(\Sigma_0 \cup \Sigma_1, E_0 \cup E_1)$ is operationally terminating. If every CCPs of $CCP(E_0) \cup CCP(E_1)$ satisfy either [C0] or [C1] (or [C2], [C3]), then $(\Sigma_0 \cup \Sigma_1, E_0 \cup E_1)$ is confluent.

Proof. From Lemma 4, $CCP(E_0) \cup CCP(E_1) = CCP(E_0 \cup E_1)$. Let $ccp \in CCP(E_0 \cup E_1)$. If ccp satisfies [C0], it is trivial. If ccp satisfies [C1] (or [C2], [C3]), it is infeasible. Thus every CCPs are joinable, and $(\Sigma_0 \cup \Sigma_1, E_0 \cup E_1)$ is confluent from Proposition 3.   □

Example 5.

Since $M_{\text{NAT-OP}} \leftarrow M_{\text{ACCOUNT}}$ is a non-overlapping hierarchical extension, $CCP(E_{\text{NAT-OP}})$ is empty, $CCP(E_{\text{ACCOUNT}})$ has only the CCP

(balanceA, balanceA − N) if balance A >= N and N > balance A,

which satisfies [C3], i.e., is infeasible, ACCOUNT is confluence.

4.3   Sufficient Completeness

Sufficient completeness is an important property of algebraic specifications [5]. Roughly speaking, sufficient completeness guarantees the existence of solutions, where a solution means a term constructed by constructors.

Definition 7. [3] Let $((S, \leq, \Sigma, \Sigma^C), E)$ be a specification, $S^{CT} = \{s \in S \mid f \in \Sigma^C_{ws} \vee (f \in \Sigma^C_{ws'} \wedge s' \leq s)\}$ the set of constrained sorts, $S^{LS} = S \setminus S^{CT}$ the set of loose sorts, $\Sigma^{S^{CT}} = \{f \in \Sigma_{ws} \mid w \in S^*, s \in S^{CT}\}$ and Y an S^{LS}-sorted set of variables of loose sorts. We call E sufficiently complete if for each term $t \in T_{\Sigma^{S^{CT}}}(Y)$, there exists a term $u \in T_{\Sigma^C}(Y)$ such that $t =_E u$.

Sufficient completeness of terminating specifications can be proved by checking reducibility as follows: Assume that (Σ, E) is operationally terminating. If each term $t \in T_{\Sigma^{S^{CT}}}(Y)$ is reducible whenever t has an operator $\Sigma^{S^{CT}} \setminus \Sigma^C$, then there exists a normal form $u \in T_{\Sigma^C}(Y)$, and thus $t =_E u$. We give the notion of quasi-C-reducibility, which is a straightforward extension of the notion of quasi-reducibility.

Definition 8. A term $f(\bar{t}_n)$ is basic if $f \in \Sigma^{S^{CT}} \setminus \Sigma^C$ and $\bar{t}_n \in T_{\Sigma^C}(Y)$. A specification is quasi-C-reducible if every basic terms are reducible.

Lemma 5. If a specification is operationally terminating and quasi-C-reducible, then it is sufficiently complete.

Proof. Let $t \in T_{\Sigma^{S^{CT}}}(Y)$. If t has an operator $f \in \Sigma^{S^{CT}} \setminus \Sigma^C$, t is E-reducible. From the operational termination, t has a normal form $u \in T_{\Sigma^C}(Y)$.   □

In this section, we give a sufficient condition for checking quasi-C-reducibility of basic terms. A basic term t is reducible when (1) it has a redex, that is, $t|_p = l\theta$ for some $l = r$ if c, and (2) the redex can be rewritten, that is, $c\theta \rightarrow^* \text{true}$.

Cover Sets. It is known that whether a basic term is a redex or not is decidable and can be checked by using the notion of cover sets [8,12]. We define the notion of cover sets for the quasi-C-reducibility.

Definition 9. The height of a term t, denoted by $\#(t)$, is defined as $\#(x) = 0$ and $\#(f(\bar{t}_n)) = 1 + max\{\#(t_i) \mid i \in \{\bar{n}\}\}$. The height of $f \in \Sigma^{S^{CT}}$ in E, denoted by $\#(E, f)$, is defined as $\#(E, f) = max\{\#(f(\bar{l}_n)) \mid f(\bar{l}_n) = r \text{ if } c \in E\}$.

Definition 10. A cut function $cut(i, t)$, which cuts a term t whose height is more than i and returns a term whose height is less than or equal i, is defined as follows: $cut'(0, t) = \square_s$ for a term $t \in T_s$, $cut'(n + 1, x) = x$ for a variable $x \in X$, and $cut'(n + 1, f(\bar{t}_n)) = f(\overline{cut'(n, t_i)})$. $cut(i, t)$ is obtained by replacing the occurrence of $\square$ by fresh variables in $cut'(i, t)$.

Definition 11. A cover set $CS(M, f)$ of an operator $f \in \Sigma^{S^{CT}} \setminus \Sigma^C$ in a module $M = [(S, \leq, \Sigma, \Sigma^C) \mid E]$ is defined as follows:

$$CS(M, f)_{\leq i} = \{f(\bar{t}_n) \mid t_i \in T_{\Sigma^C}(Y), \#(f(\bar{l}_n)) \leq i\}$$
$$CS(M, f) = \{cut(\#(E, f), f(\bar{t}_n)) \mid f(\bar{t}_n) \in CS(M, f)_{\leq \#(E, f) + 1}\}$$

We have the following property.

Lemma 6. Let $M = [(S, \leq, \Sigma, \Sigma^C) \mid E]$ be a specification. If all $cs \in CS(M, f)$ for all $f \in \Sigma^{S^{CT}} \setminus \Sigma^C$ are reducible, then M is quasi-C-reducible.

Proof. It is trivial that every basic term is an instance of some cs.   □

Example 6. For NAT-OP, we have #(NAT-OP, +) $= 2$ and CS(NAT-OP, +) $=$ {0 + 0, 0 + s X, s X + 0, s X + s Y}. For ACCOUNT, we have CS(ACCOUNT, balance) $=$ {balance init, balance (deposit X Y), balance (withdraw X Y)}.

Checking Reducibility of Cover Sets. In this section, we give three sufficient conditions under which $cs \in CS(M, f)$ is reducible.

Definition 12. Let $cs \in CS(M, f)$. The disjunction of conditions of equations applicable to cs, denoted by c_{cs}, is defined as follows:

$$C_{cs} = \{c\theta \mid l = r \text{ if } c \in E, l\theta \leq_{sub} cs\}$$
$$c_{cs} = \begin{cases} \text{false} & \text{if } C_{cs} = \emptyset \\ t_1 \text{ or } t_2 \text{ or } \cdots \text{ or } t_n & \text{if } C_{cs} = \{\bar{t}_n\} \end{cases}$$

where an unconditional equation $l = r$ is regarded as $l = r$ if true.

Example 7. Let $cs =$ balance (withdraw X Y) $\in CS$(ACCOUNT, balance). Then, $c_{cs} =$ balance A >= X or X > balance A.

Similar to Section 4.2, we give three conditions for $cs \in CS(M, f)$. **[S1]** Let $c_{cs} = t_1$ or t_2 or $\cdots$ or t_n. Either (1) $t_i = $ **true** for some t_i or (2) $t_i = $ **not** t_j for some t_i and t_j [9], **[S2]** c_{cs} is reduced into **true** by the Hsiang's TRS, and **[S3]** c_{cs} is reduced into **true** by all equations.

Let $M = [\Sigma, E]$ and $f \in \Sigma^{S^{CT}} \setminus \Sigma^C$. If each $cs \in CS(M, f)$ satisfies [S1] (or [S2], [S3]), then cs is reducible, and M is quasi-C-reducible from Lemma 6.

Constructor Preserving. To prove sufficient completeness incrementally, we give a condition for the hierarchical extension to keep $T_{\Sigma^C}(Y)$ unchanged by module imports.

Definition 13. A hierarchical extension $((S_0, \leq_0, \Sigma_0), E_0) \leftarrow [(S_1, \leq_1, \Sigma_1) \mid E_1]$ is called constructor-preserving if (1) $s \notin S_0$ for each $f \in \Sigma^C_{1\,ws}$, and (2) there is no $s_1 \in S_1$ such that $s_1 \leq_1 s_0$ for each $s_0 \in S_0$ [10].

We have the following property for constructor-preserving specification.

Lemma 7. If $((S_0, \leq_0, \Sigma_0, \Sigma^C_0), E_0) \leftarrow [(S_1, \leq_1, \Sigma_1, \Sigma^C_1) \mid E_1]$ is constructor-preserving, then (1) #$(E_0, f) = $ #$(E_0 \cup E_1, f)$ for each $f \in \Sigma^{S^{CT}}_0$ and (2) $T_{\Sigma^C_0 \cup \Sigma^C_1}(Y)_{s_0} = T_{\Sigma^C_0}(Y)_{s_0}$ for each $s_0 \in S_0$.

---

[9] Here, the operator **or** is associative and commutative.

[10] For example, introducing a subsort of an existing sort may specify an inheritance in the sense of object oriented modeling [7].

Proof. (1) E_1 does not include $f(\bar{l}_n) = r$ if $c \in E_1$ from the definition of the hierarchical extension. (2) Let $t \in T_{\Sigma_0^C \cup \Sigma_1^C}(Y)_{s_0}$. Assume t has $f : \bar{s}_i \to s \in \Sigma_1^C$. From the definition of constructor-preserving, $s \in S_1$ and all operators between the root and f are of Σ_1^C. Thus, $t \in T_{s_1}$, which contradicts $t \in T_{\Sigma_0^C \cup \Sigma_1^C}(Y)_{s_0}$. Therefore, t does not have $f \in \Sigma_1^C$ and $T_{\Sigma_0^C \cup \Sigma_1^C}(Y)_{s_0} = T_{\Sigma_0^C}(Y)_{s_0}$. $\square$

We have the following theorem for an incremental proof of sufficient completeness.

Theorem 3. Let $M_0 = ((S_0, \leq_0, \Sigma_0, \Sigma_0^C), E_0) \leftarrow [(S_1, \leq_1, \Sigma_1, \Sigma_1^C) \mid E_1] = M_1$ be a constructor-preserving hierarchical extension such that $(\Sigma_0 \cup \Sigma_1, E_0 \cup E_1)$ is operationally terminating. If

1. each $cs \in CS(M_0, f)$ satisfies [S1] (or [S2], [S3]) for each $f \in \Sigma_0^{S_0^{CT}} \setminus \Sigma_0^C$ and
2. each $cs \in CS(M_1, f)$ satisfies [S1] (or [S2], [S3]) for each $f \in \Sigma_1^{S_0^{CT} \cup S_1^{CT}} \setminus \Sigma_1^C$,

then $(\Sigma_0 \cup \Sigma_1, E_0 \cup E_1)$ is sufficiently complete.

Proof. From Lemmata 5 and 6, it suffices to show that each $cs \in CS(M_0 \cup M_1, f)$ satisfies [S1] (or [S2], [S3]) (and thus reducible) for each $f \in (\Sigma_0 \cup \Sigma_1)^{(S_0 \cup S_1)^{CT}} \setminus (\Sigma_0 \cup \Sigma_1)^C$. From the definition of constructor-preserving, $(\Sigma_0 \cup \Sigma_1)^C = \Sigma_0^C \cup \Sigma_1^C$, and $(\Sigma_0 \cup \Sigma_1)^{(S_0 \cup S_1)^{CT}} = \Sigma_0^{S_0^{CT}} \cup \Sigma_1^{S_0^{CT} \cup S_1^{CT}}$. For $f \in \Sigma_0^{S_0^{CT}}$, $CS(M_0, f) = CS(M_0 \cup M_1, f)$ from Lemma 7. For $f \in \Sigma_1^{S_0^{CT} \cup S_1^{CT}}$, $CS(M_1, f) = CS(M_0 \cup M_1, f)$ since M_0 does not have f. Therefore, for each $f \in (\Sigma_0 \cup \Sigma_1)^{(S_0 \cup S_1)^{CT}} \setminus (\Sigma_0 \cup \Sigma_1)^C$, $cs \in CS(M_0 \cup M_1, f)$ satisfies [S1] (or [S2], [S3]) from the assumptions 1 and 2. $\square$

Example 8. $M_{\texttt{NAT-OP}} \leftarrow M_{\texttt{ACCOUNT}}$ is a constructor-preserving hierarchical extension. For $\texttt{NAT-OP}$, each element in the cover sets made from $\texttt{+}$, $\texttt{-}$, $\texttt{>=}$ and $\texttt{>}$ satisfies [S1]. For $\texttt{ACCOUNT}$, each element in the cover sets made from $\texttt{balance}$ satisfies [S3]. Thus, $\texttt{ACCOUNT}$ is sufficiently complete.

5   Conclusion

We proposed methods to prove termination, confluence and sufficient completeness incrementally by checking syntactical conditions of specifications and reducing terms. Among termination, confluence and sufficient completeness, our proof methods assume different conditions: hierarchical extension for termination, non-overlapping extension for confluence, and constructor-preserving extension for sufficient completeness.

We give several kinds of conditions for checking infeasibility (or quasi-C-reducibility). Our example $\texttt{ACCOUNT}$ satisfies only [C3] (or [S3]) and does not satisfy [C1] (or [C2], [S1], [S2]). If we give the condition $\texttt{not (balance A >= N)}$ for the conditional equation $\texttt{ceq withdraw N A = A if N > balance A}$, then $\texttt{ACCOUNT}$ satisfies [C1]. One solution may be to give a guideline to describe specifications satisfying the condition [C1] (or [C2], [S1], [S2]) for CafeOBJ specifiers, which not only gives a lighter checker of the conditions but also may help reduce the mistake when giving appropriate case-splitting.

When using our methods, we may take a different class of modules for each property. For example, consider the case of specifying ACCOUNT on BASIC-INT given in Section 4.2 instead of NAT-OP, for example, BASIC-INT ← INT-OP ← ACCOUNT-Z. Each of them may satisfy the constructor-preserving condition, however, INT-OP may not satisfy the non-overlapping condition with M + s N = s (M + N) where s_ is a defined symbol of BASIC-INT. For such cases, termination and sufficient completeness are proved incrementally according to BASIC-INT ← INT-OP ← ACCOUNT-Z, and confluence is proved according to (BASIC-INT ∪ INT-OP) ← ACCOUNT-Z where the union of BASIC-INT and INT-OP is regarded as a single module.

In this article, we focus to formalize proof methods for conditional equations. As future work, other important notions should be covered for the practical use: associative and commutative (AC) attributes of operators, parameterized modules, built-in modules, and so on. Our methods can be extended for dealing with AC operators straightforwardly if we restrict no defined symbols are AC operators. Then, our method covers practical case studies of OTS/CafeOBJ specifications like [9,17]. The literatures [11,18] deal with AC operators, which can be defined symbols. In addition, overlorded operators with order-sorts are allowed in [18]. We may apply these techniques for conditional systems. The literature [2] presents a sufficient completeness checker for conditional systems with inductive theorem proving based on a tree grammars. The technique may improve our sufficient completeness checker by extending applicable specifications.

Acknowledgement. We thank the anonymous reviewers whose comments and suggestions helped improve this paper. This work was supported in part by Grant-in-Aid for Scientific Research (S) 23220002 from Japan Society for the Promotion of Science (JSPS).

References

1. CafeOBJ, http://www.ldl.jaist.ac.jp/cafeobj/
2. Bouhoula, A., Jacquemard, F.: Sufficient Completeness Verification for Conditional and Constrained Term Rewriting Systems. Journal of Applied Logic 10(1), 127–143 (2012)
3. Futatsugi, K., Găină, D., Ogata, K.: Principles of proof scores in CafeOBJ. Theor. Comput. Sci. 464, 90–112 (2012)
4. Goguen, J.A., Winkler, T., Meseguer, J., Futatsugi, K., Jouannaud, J.-P.: Software Engineering with OBJ: Algebraic Specification in Action. In: Introducing OBJ*. Kluwers Academic Publishers (2000)
5. Guttag, J.V.: The specification and application to programming of abstract data types. PhD thesis, University of Toronto, Toronto, Ont., Canada, Canada (1975)
6. Hsiang, J.: Refutational theorem proving using term-rewriting systems. Artif. Intell. 25(3), 255–300 (1985)
7. Jouannaud, J.-P., Kirchner, C., Kirchner, H., Mégrelis, A.: OBJ: Programming with equalities, subsorts, overloading and parameterization. In: Grabowski, J., Lescanne, P., Wechler, W. (eds.) ALP 1988. LNCS, vol. 343, pp. 41–52. Springer (1988)

8. Kapur, D., Narendran, P., Rosenkrantz, D.J., Zhang, H.: Sufficient-completeness, ground-reducibility and their complexity. Acta Inf. 28(4), 311–350 (1991)
9. Kong, W., Ogata, K., Futatsugi, K.: Towards reliable e-government systems with the OTS/CafeOBJ method. IEICE Transactions 93-D(5), 974–984 (2010)
10. Lucas, S., Marché, C., Meseguer, J.: Operational termination of conditional term rewriting systems. Inf. Process. Lett. 95(4), 446–453 (2005)
11. Marché, C., Urbain, X.: Modular and incremental proofs of ac-termination. J. Symb. Comput. 38(1), 873–897 (2004)
12. Nakamura, M., Ogata, K., Futatsugi, K.: Reducibility of operation symbols in term rewriting systems and its application to behavioral specifications. J. Symb. Comput. 45(5), 551–573 (2010)
13. Nakamura, M., Ogata, K., Futatsugi, K.: On proving operational termination incrementally with modular conditional dependency pairs. IAENG International Journal of Computer Science 40(2), 117–123 (2013)
14. Nakamura, M., Ogawa, K., Futatsugi, K.: A hierarchical approach to operational termination of algebraic specifications. In: Proceedings of the International Conference on Electronics, Information and Communication, ICEIC 2013, pp. 144–145 (2013)
15. Ogata, K., Futatsugi, K.: Proof scores in the OTS/CafeOBJ Method. In: Najm, E., Nestmann, U., Stevens, P. (eds.) FMOODS 2003. LNCS, vol. 2884, pp. 170–184. Springer, Heidelberg (2003)
16. Ohlebusch, E.: Advanced Topics in Term Rewriting, 1st edn. Springer Publishing Company, Incorporated (2010)
17. Ouranos, I., Ogata, K., Stefaneas, P.: Formal analysis of tesla protocol in the timed OTS/CafeOBJ method. In: Margaria, T., Steffen, B. (eds.) ISoLA 2012, Part II. LNCS, vol. 7610, pp. 126–142. Springer, Heidelberg (2012)
18. Schernhammer, F., Meseguer, J.: Incremental checking of well-founded recursive specifications modulo axioms. In: Schneider-Kamp, P., Hanus, M. (eds.) PPDP, pp. 5–16. ACM (2011)
19. Terese: Term Rewriting Systems. Cambridge Tracts in Theoretical Computer Science, vol. 55. Cambridge University Press (2003)
20. Urbain, X.: Modular & incremental automated termination proofs. J. Autom. Reasoning 32(4), 315–355 (2004)

The Versatile Synchronous Observer

John Rushby

Computer Science Laboratory
SRI International
333 Ravenswood Avenue
Menlo Park, CA 94025 USA

Abstract. A synchronous observer is an adjunct to a system model that monitors its state variables and raises a signal flag when some condition is satisfied. Synchronous observers provide an alternative to temporal logic as a means to specify safety properties but have the advantage that they are expressed in the same notation as the system model—and thereby lower the mental hurdle to effective use of model checking and other techniques for automated analysis of system models. Model checkers that do use temporal logic can nonetheless employ synchronous observers by checking for properties such as "never(flag raised)."

The use of synchronous observers to specify properties is well-known; rather less well-known is that they can be used to specify assumptions and axioms, to constrain models, and to specify test cases. The idea underlying these applications is that the basic model generates more behaviors than are desired, the synchronous observer recognizes those that are interesting, and the model checker is constrained to just the interesting cases. The efficiency in this approach is that it is usually much easier to write recognizers than generators.

The paper describes and illustrates several applications of synchronous observers.

1 Introduction

Model checkers are called that because, in their basic form, they *check* whether a system defined as a finite state machine is a Kripke *model* of a specification expressed in a temporal logic. The selection of finite state machines for the system description and (branching time) temporal logic for their specification has pragmatic benefits: in this form, the model checking problem can be fully automated and its complexity is linear in the size of both system and specification (although the size of the system is often exponential in the number of its components).

However, the term *model checking* has grown beyond this precise usage and now refers to any highly automated method for formal analysis of systems and their specifications—as contrasted, for example, to methods that use interactive theorem provers. Under this looser usage, specification methods other than temporal logic may be employed, and one example is the *synchronous observer*. Here, the system is described as a state machine, as before, and its specification is likewise described by a state machine that observes the state variables of the

S. Iida, J. Meseguer, and K. Ogata (Eds.): Futatsugi Festschrift, LNCS 8373, pp. 110–128, 2014.
© Springer-Verlag Berlin Heidelberg 2014

system and sets a Boolean "flag" variable *true* as long as the required properties hold. The "model checker" then verifies that the flag variable is always *true*. Obviously, the flag variable can be used in either "parity": we can choose to set it *true* when the required property is satisfied or, alternatively, if it is violated. For consistency in the examples, we will use state variables whose names are a variant on `ok` for the former case and a variant on `alarm` for the latter.

Both the concept and the term "synchronous observer" were introduced in the context of the *synchronous languages* developed in France and, in particular, by the Lesar model checker for the language Lustre [1,2]. However, the idea is readily adapted for use with temporal logic model checkers: we simply model check for the temporal property `always(ok)` or `always(NOT alarm)` (this expresses the `never` construct used in the abstract to this paper); the "always" operator may be written as `AG` in a specification language based on the branching time logic CTL (Computation Tree Logic), or as `G` or $\Box$ in one based on Linear Temporal Logic, LTL. If the model checker allows liveness properties (e.g., its specification language provides the operator `eventually`, which may be written `AF`, `F`, or $\Diamond$) then synchronous observers can likewise be extended to liveness properties.

An advantage claimed for synchronous observers over temporal logic specifications is that a single language is used to describe both the system and its required properties (and, as we will see later, also its assumptions). Furthermore, engineers readily understand the method, since it is like adding a runtime check to an executable program. In contrast, when using temporal logic specifications, the engineer is required to learn and use one language and method for describing the system, and another for specifying its properties. As we will see, many simple specification constructs are quite difficult to write as temporal logic formulas and intermediate "pattern languages" have arisen to ease this difficulty [3].

The purpose of this paper is to describe and illustrate the uses and benefits of synchronous observers. We begin with their familiar use in the specification of properties and assumptions, and then proceed to less familiar uses where they enable the specification of relational constraints and of axioms for uninterpreted functions. We then turn from applications in verification to their use in the construction of test cases. These illustrations of the versatility of synchronous observers constitute Section 2 of the paper; brief conclusions are presented in Section 3.

2   Synchronous Observers and Their Applications

In the subsections that follow, we introduce several applications for synchronous observers.

2.1   Specification

We begin by describing the standard use of synchronous observers to specify properties and assumptions, as in Lesar [2], but we do so in the framework of model checkers that ordinarily use temporal logic specifications. To make our illustrations concrete, we use the syntax and tools of the SAL suite of model checkers from SRI [4].

In SAL, systems are specified as synchronous or asynchronous compositions of modules that read and write state variables of various (not necessarily finite) types. Thus, an `observer` module can be written as follows.

```
observer: MODULE =
BEGIN
  INPUT
    <state variables>
  OUTPUT
    ok: BOOLEAN
  INITIALIZATION
    ok = TRUE
  TRANSITION
  [
    <property> --> ok' = TRUE
  []
    ELSE --> ok' = FALSE
  ]
END;
```

Here, `<state variables>` represents declaration of the observed state variables and their types, and `<property>` represents a Boolean expression over these state variables that specifies the desired property. The observer sets the Boolean flag variable `ok` to `TRUE` or `FALSE` according to whether the property is satisfied or not: "primed" variables in SAL represent values in the "new" state, and "unprimed" in the "old" state; the symbol `-->` indicates that the assignments are "guarded" by the Boolean expression appearing to its left.

If the system is specified in a module `system` (which may itself be the composition of other modules), then the "observed system" is the synchronous composition of this with the `observer`, which is written as follows (in SAL, the symbol `||` represents synchronous composition).

```
observed: MODULE = (system || observer);
```

We can then specify the theorem `correctness`, which states that `ok` is always true in the observed system.

```
correctness: THEOREM observed |- G(ok);
```

Depending on the types of the state variables in `system`, we can examine `correctness` using the symbolic, bounded, or infinite-bounded model checkers of SAL using shell commands such as the following.

```
sal-smc example.sal correctness

sal-bmc example.sal correctness -d 17 -it

sal-inf-bmc example.sal correctness -i -d 2 -ice
```

The first of these invokes SAL's symbolic (BDD-based) model checker on the theorem `correctness` in the file `example.sal`; this will prove the theorem if it is true, or provide a counterexample if it is not (of course, it may also run out of memory or time). The second invokes the bounded (SAT-based) model checker to search for a counterexample up to depth 17, operating iteratively (i.e., depth 1, depth 2,...); the third invokes the infinite-bounded (SMT-based) model checker to attempt proof by k-induction at depth 2 (i.e., 2-induction), and to provide an inductive counterexample if this fails.

The basic construction illustrated above allows checking of invariants over the state variables of the system; it can be extended to general safety properties, including bounded liveness properties and properties on transitions, by adding new variables to the state of the observer that act as "history variables" to remember the values of system state variables some time in the past.

2.2   Assumptions

Systems are seldom expected to satisfy their specifications in an unconstrained environment; usually there are assumptions about the environment and the system is required to satisfy its specification only in cases where the assumptions are satisfied.

Like properties, assumptions also can be described by synchronous observers and the verification method can be suitably adjusted to ensure that the required properties are satisfied for all those reachable states that satisfy the assumptions.

In SAL, we could use an `assumptions` module, defined in a similar way to the `observer` module in the previous section, but using a flag variable `aok` (for "assumptions OK") whose assignments are guarded by Boolean expressions over the state variables that specify the assumptions. We then form the synchronous composition of the `system`, `assumptions`, and `observer` and state the `requirement` that the correctness property should be true whenever the assumptions are satisfied (the symbol `=>` represents implication in SAL).

```
constrained: MODULE = (system || assumptions || observer);

requirement: THEOREM constrained |- G(aok => ok);
```

Actually, the LTL formula suggested above `G(aok => ok)` raises some interesting issues. Consider the trace of some imaginary system shown below, which displays the values of `aok` and `ok` in the first six steps (where T represents *true*, and F *false*).

step	1	2	3	4	5	6
aok:	T	T	T	F	T	T
ok:	T	T	T	T	F	T

This fails to satisfy the formula `G(aok => ok)` because `ok` is *false* at step 5 while `aok` is *true*. But `aok` itself was *false* at step 4 and usually we do not care what happens after the assumptions have been violated.

To specify this different requirement in LTL, it is convenient to use the "weak until" operator W, which is usually defined in terms of the "strong" variant U as follows (where ∨ indicates disjunciton):

$$\mathtt{W}(p, q) \stackrel{\text{def}}{=} \mathtt{G}(p) \vee \mathtt{U}(p, q).$$

Intuitively, $\mathtt{U}(p, q)$, which is primitive in most formulations of LTL, requires that q eventually becomes *true*, and that p is *true* until (and possibly beyond) that point; W is the same but relaxes the requirement for q to become true if p is invariantly *true*. A subtle point is that LTL formulas are defined only on infinite traces; however, most model checkers extend interpretation of G and W (but not F or U) to finite traces. Using the W operator, our adjusted requirement can be written in SAL as follows.

```
requirement_alt1: THEOREM constrained |- W(ok, NOT aok);
```

Intuitively, this says that ok must be *true* until aok is *false*, and it accepts the trace we saw earlier, and also the following one.

step	1	2	3	4	5	6
aok:	T	T	T	F	T	T
ok:	T	T	T	F	F	T

Here, both aok and ok go *false* at step 4. There are several formulations of compositional reasoning (e.g., [5,6]) that require the assumptions to fail *before* the property. The trace above does not satisfy this requirement, but the first one does. An LTL formula that specifies the "fails before" requirement uses the strong until operator U and is expressed in SAL as follows.

```
requirement_alt2: THEOREM constrained |- NOT U(aok, NOT ok);
```

Most readers will surely agree that it is not easy to see that this formula captures exactly the informal requirement that aok fails before ok; neither is it straightforward to comprehend the difference between this formula and the earlier one using W, nor why the positions of ok and aok are reversed in the arguments to W and U.

We are employing a "hybrid" approach here: using synchronous observers to specify properties and assumptions, and temporal logic to combine them. This is rather unnatural and was done to illustrate some of the complexities in writing temporal logic specifications.

Exploiting synchronous observers more fully, it becomes straightforward to say what we mean. First, we adjust the **assumptions** module so that it does nothing if the <assumption> is satisfied and "latches" aok as soon as it becomes *false*.

```
assumptions: MODULE =
BEGIN
  INPUT
    <state variables>
  OUTPUT
    aok: BOOLEAN
  INITIALIZATION
    aok = TRUE
  TRANSITION
  [
    <assumption> -->
  []
    ELSE --> aok' = FALSE
  ]
END;
```

Then we modify the observer module so that it takes `aok` as an input and latches `ok` to *false* if the desired `<property>` ever goes *false* when `aok` is *true*.

```
observer: MODULE =
BEGIN
  INPUT
    aok: BOOLEAN,
    <state variables>
  OUTPUT
    ok: BOOLEAN
  INITIALIZATION
    OK = TRUE
  TRANSITION
  [
    aok AND NOT <property> --> ok' = FALSE
  []
    ELSE -->
  ]
END;
```

Now we use the model checker simply to verify that `ok` is invariantly *true*.

```
requirement_simplified: THEOREM constrained |- G(ok);
```

This combination of observers requires the assumptions to fail before the property; if we wish to allow the assumptions to fail at the same time as the property, then we can simply replace the appearance of `aok` in the observer guard by `aok'`.

As always when theorems have the form of an implication, as these implicitly do, it is prudent to check that they are not vacuously *true*: that is, we should check that the antecedent is not invariantly *false*. There is a large literature on the related problem of *vacuity detection* in LTL formulas (e.g., [7]) and the necessary tests become quite difficult. However, this difficulty is a result of the complex LTL formulas used to state the basic property of interest. If we use synchronous observers of the form described above, then all we need to do is check that each of the positive flag variables can remain *true* and each of the negative ones can remain *false* at least one step beyond its initialization. In the example, this is accomplished by seeking a counterexample to the following formula, which asserts that aok is *false* in the second step.

```
check_simple: CLAIM constrained |- X(NOT aok);
```

Of course, an alternative is to prove the positive claim X(aok), but this is computationally more demanding (with a bounded model checker, it requires k-induction).

2.3   Expressivity

Model checkers in which the system is specified by state machines generally provide some way to describe how the values of state variables are updated on a state transition. For example, in SAL, the expression

```
x' = x + y
```

indicates that the "new" value of the state variable x is the sum of the current values of itself and the state variable y. Nondeterministic assignments are often supported as well, as in the following example, where x is nondeterministically assigned a value between 25 and 50, inclusive.

```
x' IN { a: nat | a >= 25 AND a <= 50 }
```

Now, suppose we wish to specify that the new value of x can be any value *larger* than its current value. In SAL we could write

```
x' IN { a: nat | a > x }
```

but not all model checkers provide this expressivity. Another option, available in those languages that provide guarded commands is the following.

```
(x' > x) --> x' IN { a: nat | TRUE }
```

But notice this requires a primed variable to appear in the guard, and not all model checker state machine languages allow this.

In this simple case, an alternative would be to use an auxiliary variable that is nondeterministically set to the amount by which x should be incremented. However, this does not solve the general problem, which is that of updating (possibly several variables of) the state so that some *constraint* is satisfied—such as to nondeterministically update real variables x and y so that they lie on a unit circle (i.e., x*x + y*y = 1).

However, one method that is almost always feasible uses a synchronous observer. Returning to the simple example of nondeterministically incrementing x: in the main system specification, we make an unconstrained nondeterministic assignment to x as follows.

```
x' IN { a: nat | TRUE }
```

Then, in a synchronous observer module, we enforce the desired relation using cok (for "constraints OK") as our flag variable as follows.

```
TRANSITION
[
  (x' > x) -->
[]
  ELSE --> cok' = FALSE
]
```

If the language does not allow primed variables in the guards, then we will need to introduce a history variable oldx to remember the previous value of x.

```
TRANSITION
oldx' = x;
[
  (x > oldx) -->
[]
  ELSE --> cok' = FALSE
]
```

Then we model check for whatever property p we had in mind, but only in cases where cok is *true*.

```
constrained_prop: THEOREM (system || constraints) |- G(cok => p)
```

Or, if the required property is specified by a synchronous observer with flag variable ok, we would use the following variant.

```
constrained_req: THEOREM
    (system || observer || constraints) |- G(cok => ok)
```

Rather than the explicit implication G(cok => ok), we can also use the methods of the previous section. Note that if we are using a history variable in the constraints module, then the property p or flag ok must also be defined in a similar way, or should reference oldx rather than x, as otherwise the property will be out of step with the constraint.

Sometimes, we may we wish to consider only traces in which the constraints are satisfied globally. For example, in the following trace the constraint is violated at step 6, but it may be that some earlier decisions made this violation inevitable.

step	1	2	3	4	5	6
cok:	T	T	T	T	T	F
ok:	T	T	T	F	F	T

Hence, although the required property is violated at steps 4 and 5, we consider this entire scenario invalid because the constraint is not globally *true*. If desired, although it is seldom appropriate, we can specify this interpretation as follows (and, of course, we can do the same for other kinds of assumptions as well).

```
globally_constrained_req: THEOREM
   (system || observer || constraints) |- G(cok) => G(ok)
```

Note that this is a liveness property and cannot be verified by bounded model checkers, although they can find counterexamples.

Using observers to specify constraints is especially useful when we wish to update multiple variables in a way that enforces a *relation* on them as, for example, the case mentioned earlier of points constrained to lie on a circle. This finds particular application in specifying *relational abstractions* for hybrid automata [8]. Unlike other methods for abstracting hybrid automata, which typically abstract the state space, relational abstraction retains the state space (i.e., continuous variables continue to range over the reals) but simplifies the transition relation.

Generally, we start with a true hybrid automaton (i.e., a state machine plus differential equations) and calculate a relational abstraction in the manner described by Sankaranarayanan and Tiwari and mechanized in the HybridSAL Relational Abstractor [9]. But another approach, suitable when we have or need only a crude model of the dynamical system, is to *assert* a relational abstraction as the model. An example is described in [10]; there, the basic task is analysis of human-machine interaction and only crude models of the aircraft automation and dynamics are needed, such as "when automation is in a climb mode, the pitch angle must be positive" and "when the pitch angle is positive, the altitude increases." These are specified in a constraints module as follows.

```
INITIALIZATION
    cok = TRUE;
TRANSITION
[  actual_mode = op_des AND pitch > 0 --> cok' = FALSE;
[] actual_mode = op_clb AND pitch < 0 --> cok' = FALSE;
[] actual_mode = vs_fpa AND fcu_fpa <= 0 AND pitch > 0
     --> cok' = FALSE;
[] actual_mode = vs_fpa AND fcu_fpa >= 0 AND pitch < 0
     --> cok' = FALSE;
[] pitch > 0 AND altitude' < altitude --> cok' = FALSE;
[] pitch < 0 AND altitude' > altitude --> cok' = FALSE;
[] pitch=0 AND altitude' /= altitude --> cok' = FALSE;
[] ELSE -->
] END;
```

Observe that each guard is the *negation* of a desired constraint (e.g., the first guard is the negation of the natural constraint actual_mode = op_des => pitch <= 0). This is because we generally require *all* assumptions or constraints to be satisfied—i.e., they are conjoined together—whereas guarded commands are disjoined. Hence, we apply De Morgan's rule and disjoin the negations. An alternative is to conjoin all the (unnegated) constraints together in the guard of a single command.

This subsection has shown how synchronous observers provide expressivity that can assist in the construction of *system models*. This is a different topic than their expressivity with respect to the classes of *properties* that can be specified, which will be considered in Section 3. In the following subsection, we continue our examination of the use of synchronous observers in the construction of system models by considering the case of very abstract models that employ uninterpreted functions.

2.4   Axioms for Uninterpreted Functions

Traditional model checkers require the system model to be totally explicit—effectively, a program or hardware circuit—and this is one of the reasons that interactive theorem provers are preferred for some verification tasks. For reasons of efficiency or generality, we often wish to abstract some parts of a design prior to verification. One way to do this is to replace parts of the design by a nondeterministic component (this is feasible with traditional model checkers) but a more general and attractive method is to use *uninterpreted functions* constrained by suitable axioms.

One standard example in model checking is to verify correctness of the bypass logic in a model of a processor pipeline [11]. The pipeline feeds values into an arithmetic logic unit (ALU) and a standard way to verify its correctness is to prove that the outputs of the ALU are the same in a processor design with and without the pipeline. In traditional model checking we need to provide some implementation for the ALU; if this is fully accurate the verification complexity may be very high, but if it is simplified (e.g., every operation is an addition) some flaws in the bypass logic may be masked by the simplification (e.g., a flaw that transposes arguments will be masked by the commutativity of addition); and if the simplification is excessive (e.g., nondeterministic) then the property may become unverifiable. A much more attractive solution is to model the ALU by an uninterpreted function ALU(x, y): that is, a function about which we know nothing. If we did wish the function to be commutative for some reason, we would add the following axiom.

$$\forall x, y : \text{ALU}(x,\ y) = \text{ALU}(y,\ x)$$

First order logic provides uninterpreted functions and, when restricted to the unquantified case (i.e., all variables are implicitly universally quantified), the theory of uninterpreted functions with equality is decidable. Interactive theorem provers provide uninterpreted functions and often a decision procedure to automate the unquantified case and, for this reason (among others), they may be preferred to conventional (i.e., finite-state or explicit-state) model checkers for some verification tasks.

However, the theory of uninterpreted functions is one of the core theories automated in modern solvers for satisfiability modulo theories (SMT) [12] and bounded model checking can be generalized to use these solvers, yielding *infinite* bounded model checkers, abbreviated as inf-BMC [13] ("infinite" because SMT includes theories of infinite cardinality such as the integers and rationals).

Inf-BMC blurs the line between model checking and theorem proving and is widely used for verification of models that use linear arithmetic, arrays, and other theories decided by SMT. It would also be very attractive to incorporate uninterpreted functions into inf-BMC models, but we must then find a way to convey any axioms about the functions to the underlying SMT solver. By now, readers will not be surprised to learn that synchronous observers provide a way to do this. The method is basically the same as that described in the previous section.

For example, suppose we have a system with one integer-valued state variable called `count` and that the behavior of the system is simply to apply an uninterpreted function `f` to this variable at each step. This can be specified in SAL as follows.

```
f(x: int): int;

system: MODULE =
BEGIN
  OUTPUT
    count: int
  INITIALIZATION
    count = 0
  TRANSITION
    count' = f(count)
END;
```

Now suppose we wish to assert the axiom $\forall x : f(x) \geq x$ and then prove that `count` is always non-negative. We introduce a synchronous observer called `constraints` that does nothing as long as the axiom about `f` is satisfied, but sets the flag variable `cok` to *false* when it is violated.

```
constraints: MODULE =
BEGIN
  INPUT
    count: integer
  OUTPUT
    cok: BOOLEAN
  INITIALIZATION
    cok = TRUE
  TRANSITION
  [
    f(count) >= count -->
  []
    ELSE --> cok' = FALSE
  ]
END;
```

We then synchronously compose the system and the observer and state the theorem that `count` is non-negative provided the axiom flagged by `cok` is satisfied.

```
nonneg: THEOREM (system || constraints) |- G(cok => count >= 0);
```

The SAL inf-BMC can prove this by 1-induction.

```
sal-inf-bmc increments.sal nonneg -i -d 1
```

If we modify the guard encoding the axiom to read as follows, so that `f(x)`

```
f(count) >= count - 375 -->
```

can be less than `x`, then the SAL inf-BMC constructs a 1-step counterexample in which `f(0) = -1`.

This ability of SMT solvers, and hence of inf-BMC, to construct witnesses for uninterpreted functions is very useful: it helps us to discover necessary constraints, as described in the following section.

2.5   Discovering Assumptions

The previous sections have described how synchronous observers can be used to specify assumptions, axioms, and constraints. The descriptions assume we know these beforehand and merely need to formalize them in a way that is feasible and effective for model checking. A variant problem is that of *discovering* suitable assumptions and constraints. Synchronous observers are very convenient for this purpose. We can start with an "empty" assumptions observer of the following form, where `aalarm` is a flag for "assumption alarm" and is set *true* when the assumptions are violated. (It is "empty" because the command with guard `FALSE` can never be taken.) Incidentally, we are using a "negative" flag variable here simply for variety.

```
assumptions: MODULE =
BEGIN
  OUTPUT
    aalarm: BOOLEAN
  INPUT
      <state variables>
  INITIALIZATION
    aalarm = FALSE
  TRANSITION
  [
  assumption_violation:
    FALSE --> aalarm' = TRUE
  assumptions_ok:
    [] ELSE -->
  ]
END;
```

Then we model check for the property of interest `p` when `aalarm` is *false*.

```
learn_assumptions: LEMMA (system || assumptions) |- G((NOT aalarm) => p)
```

If this formula is violated, the counterexample should suggest a missing assumption, which we add to the assumptions module (below the `FALSE` guard).

```
[] NOT <new assumption> --> aalarm' = TRUE
```

We proceed in this way until all necessary assumptions have been discovered. The use of counterexamples to guide discovery of assumptions can be employed no matter how the assumptions are represented. But this form of synchronous observer is a particularly attractive representation because it allows each newly discovered assumption to be added as a new guard: it is truly incremental. By contrast, a more tightly integrated representation of the assumptions might require substantial revision at each step.

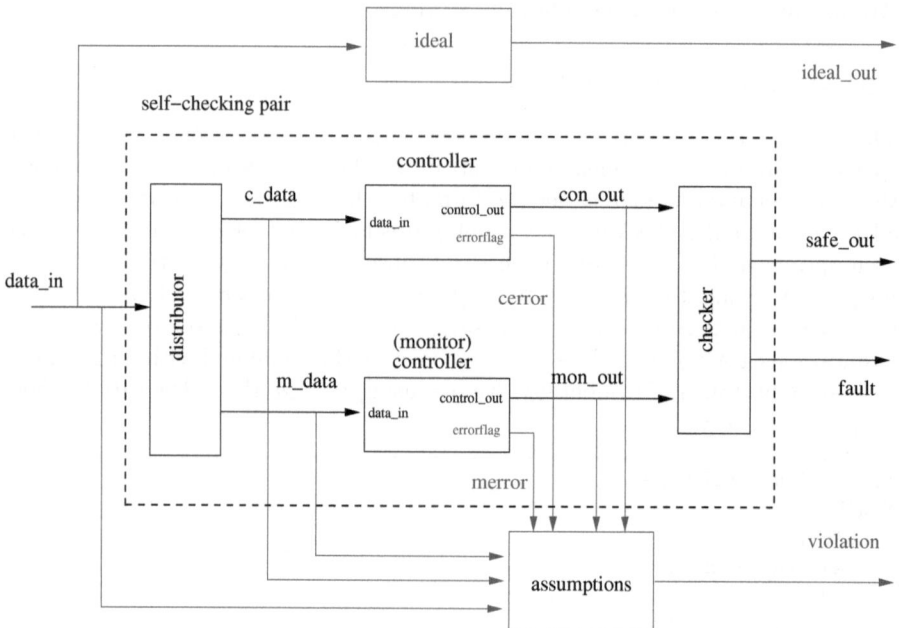

Fig. 1. "Box and Arrow" Diagram of a Self-Checking Pair

This approach combines very well with that of the previous subsection. Uninterpreted functions are very attractive for the highly abstract modeling that is appropriate for the upper levels of system design, where systems are often represented by "box and arrow" diagrams. Flaws at this level of design are a major cause of incidents in aircraft software [14]. Traditionally, it has been difficult to apply any mechanized analysis to this level of description, so often they are prematurely "prototyped" in a simulation environment like Simulink and the prototype then becomes the requirement. However, uninterpreted functions can be used to provide suitably abstract semantics for a box and arrow diagram and the methods of this and the previous subsection can then be used to analyze it and to discover its properties and required assumptions.

An example, taken from [15] and shown in Figure 1 illustrates this. Here, the goal is to deduce the assumptions under which a "self-checking pair" works correctly. Self-checking pairs are used quite widely in safety-critical systems to provide protection against random hardware faults: two identical controllers perform the same calculations and their results are compared; if they differ the pair shuts down (thereby becoming a "fail-stop" processor [16]) and some higher-level fault management activity takes over. Obviously, this does not work if both controllers become faulty and compute the *same* wrong result. We would like to learn if there are any other scenarios that can cause a self-checking pair to deliver the wrong result; we can then assess their likelihood (for example, the double fault scenario just described may be considered extremely improbable) and calculate the overall reliability of this architecture.

In the SAL model corresponding to the box and arrow diagram shown in Figure 1, the `controllers` simply compute some uninterpreted function f of their inputs, unless they are faulty—in which case the produce some nondeterministic (but incorrect) output. The components shown in red are synchronous observers (the arrows represent the state variables that they observe). The `ideal` box serves as a correctness specification: it computes the same function f as the real controllers but never fails. The requirement is that if the (as yet undetermined) assumptions are not violated, and if the checker component does not signal a fault, then the output of the self-checking pair should be the same as that of the ideal controller.

Among the assumptions discovered (see [15] or [17] for fuller descriptions) is one that says a faulty distributor component must not relay different, incorrect values x and y to the two controllers such that $f(x) = f(y)$ (x and y correspond to c_data and m_data in the diagram). This would be a Byzantine fault on the part of the distributor (this can occur—even when the implementation of the distributor is as simple as a solder joint—if voltages or timing are close to their boundaries) and is unlikely to be discovered in simulation experiments. This is because we would first have to anticipate the possibility of Byzantine faults and build this into the simulation model for the distributor, and would also have to supply some concrete instantiation for $f(x)$ (e.g., x+1) and are unlikely to choose one that can produce the same output for different inputs. In contrast, the SMT solver underneath inf-BMC synthesizes whatever behavior of the distributor and whatever instantiation of f are needed to construct a counterexample.

2.6   Test Cases

All the applications of synchronous observers that we have seen so far concern their use in verification. A quite different application is their use in test generation. It is well-known that model checkers can be used to construct test cases: if we seek a test characterized by a property p then we model check for G(NOT p) and the counterexample provides a test case.

One difficulty in exploitation of this idea is to decide what properties p correspond to good test cases, and how to specify such p. Often, tests are based on structural coverage of the source program or specification: that is, we aim to find a suite of tests that exercises each statement or branch (or visits each state or transition). This can be accomplished by adding "trap variables" that are set *true* when some coverage target is encountered, and then using these variables in definition of **p** [18]. Unfortunately, model checkers are so good at finding counterexamples that the tests produced by this method are often short and very similar to each other [19].

A better approach uses a synchronous observer to indicate whether the trace seen so far satisfies some "test purpose." The observer merely has to *recognize* tests satisfying its purpose, then raise a flag **tok** (for "test OK"). We then model check for **G(NOT tok)** and the model checker effectively performs constraint satisfaction to generate tests satisfying that purpose. This approach is very effective. Several examples are given in the manual for the SAL test generator **sal-atg** [20]. One concerns the "shift scheduler" for the automatic gearbox of a car.

The inputs to this component are **torque**, **velocity**, and **gear**; its outputs drive actuators that change clutch pressures and thereby influence the gearbox to select a different gear. The goal of test generation in this example is to find sequences of inputs that drive the state machine of the shift scheduler through all its transitions and this is easily accomplished by **sal-atg**. However, the test cases have many "discontinuities" in the **gear** input: that is, the currently selected gear may go from 2 to 4 to 1 in successive inputs. We might suppose that a more realistic test sequence would not have these discontinuities, and therefore propose a test purpose in which the **gear** input changes by at most one at each step. We can implement this purpose by adding the following observer to the SAL specification of the shift scheduler.

```
purpose: MODULE =
BEGIN
  INPUT
    gear: [1..4]
  OUTPUT
    continuous: BOOLEAN
  INITIALIZATION
    continuous = (gear=1);
  TRANSITION
    continuous' = continuous AND (gear - gear' <= 1)
                AND (gear' - gear <= 1);
END;

monitored_system: MODULE = (scheduler || purpose);
```

Here, the **purpose** module takes **gear** as input and produces the Boolean output **continuous**: this output remains TRUE as long as the sequence of inputs changes by at most 1 at each step (and starts at 1). The **purpose** module is then synchronously composed with the existing **scheduler** to yield the **monitored_system**. We then repeat test generation, but indicate to **sal-atg** that the flag **continuous**, representing the test purpose, must remain *true*.

It turns out that the test generated holds the **gear** input constant for long periods (e.g., the first ten inputs that it generates are 1, 1, 1, 1, 1, 1, 2, 3, 3, 3) so we might adjust the test purpose to additionally require that the **gear** input *always* changes value from one step to the next. It is easy to add this to the **purpose** module and we then obtain a single test of length 51 that discharges all the coverage goals while satisfying the enlarged test purpose (the first ten **gear** inputs are 1, 2, 3, 2, 3, 2, 3, 2, 3, 2).

3   Discussion and Conclusion

I hope the examples in this paper serve to alert readers to the utility and versatility of synchronous observers. The first examples that we considered were focused on the use of observers to specify properties and assumptions. The main advantage that we claim for this application of synchronous observers is convenience: it is generally easier and less error-prone to specify properties and assumptions in this way than to write temporal logic formulas. But convenience aside, do we give up any expressiveness in using synchronous observers rather than temporal logic?

In the "hybrid" case where we use observers to define flag variables and temporal logic to combine them, the answer is obviously "no," because we have the full resources of both methods at our disposal. So let us focus on the case where flag variables are used only in formulas of the form G(ok) and G(aok => ok), and compare these to general temporal logic formulas over "natural" state variables (i.e., state variables that are intrinsically part of the system model, not those introduced as observers). The main loss with synchronous observers is that they are restricted to safety properties and therefore cannot specify general liveness properties. However, most applications are not concerned with possibilities in the indefinite future (e.g., "every request eventually receives a response"), but with explicit bounds (e.g., "every request receives a response within 8 steps, or returns an error"), and these are safety properties.

On the other hand, synchronous observers can specify properties that LTL cannot (an example is "p is true on every alternate state"). Industrial specifications languages such as the Accellera/IEEE Property Specification Language (PSL) [21] and SystemVerilog Assertions (SVA) [22] extend LTL with regular expressions and thereby achieve approximate expressive parity with synchronous observers.[1] CTL and LTL are mutually incomparable and some properties that are in CTL but not LTL may also be beyond the reach of synchronous observers (because CTL can specify nondeterministic possibilities whereas synchronous observers monitor single threads).

In general, it is safe to assume that synchronous observers have approximately the same expressive power as industrial assertion languages based on LTL, when

---

[1] We say "approximate" because, although regular expressions are equivalent to finite automata, the comparison here is complicated by the presence of state variables ranging over possibly infinite types and constrained by theories and, in the case of SVA, local variables.

the latter are restricted to safety properties. Hence, selecting between the two approaches can be based on user preferences, tool capabilities, and overall workflows, rather than fundamental limitations.

The later examples that we considered focussed on the use of observers to enhance the class of system models that can be defined conveniently. These include models where updates to state variables must maintain some constraint, and those where axioms are applied to uninterpreted functions. The methods used in these examples were later used to facilitate the discovery of suitable constraints, and the specification of test purposes.

The idea underlying these applications is that the basic system model generates more behaviors than are desired, the synchronous observer recognizes those that are "good" (or "bad," depending on the parity) and raises a flag appropriately, and the model checker is constrained to scenarios where the flag is raised. The value in this approach derives from the fact that it is usually much easier to specify systems that recognize desired behavior than those that generate it. Of course, the approach is "inefficient" in that the basic system model generates many scenarios that are rejected and "thrown away" by the observer and this may make it unsuitable for explicit-state model checkers, which really do have to enumerate all behaviors. But there is no comparable penalty when using symbolic model checkers, whether based on BDDs, SAT, or SMT: the observer simply adds to the constraints that must be solved by the underlying symbolic method.

Despite their versatility, synchronous observers are intuitive and easy to use: the system, its requirements, assumptions, axioms, and test plans are all written using the same state-machine notation, and this reduces the learning burden for verification and test engineers. Furthermore, it eliminates the need to use a property specification language (apart from "canned" formulas such as $G(p)$): in traditional model checking, the need to learn a property language based on temporal logic is often a major obstacle to adoption and effective use.

Synchronous observers closely correspond to runtime monitors for executable programs, and this also is a familiar concept to most engineers. Furthermore, assumptions for high-level models, possibly discovered in the manner described in Section 2.5, can provide the basis for runtime monitors that deliver significant benefit in system reliability [23]. These monitors could even be formally synthesized directly from the model and this is an attractive direction for future research.

Acknowledgments. Some of this material was developed for a talk at JAIST in 2007 and I am grateful to Kokichi Futatsugi for facilitating that visit and for the many interesting discussions that we have enjoyed since first meeting as visitors to SRI in the early 1980s.

This paper is based on an invited talk presented at the 15th Brazilian Symposium on Formal Methods (SBMF) in Natal on 25 September 2012. The abstract was published in the proceedings of the symposium [24].

I am grateful to Ashish Tiwari for showing me several ways to represent the constraints for relational abstractions in a model checker, to N. Shankar for helpful discussions on observers and LTL, and to Moshe Vardi for information on industrial specification languages. Comments by the anonymous referees helped improve the presentation.

This work was supported by NASA under contracts NNA13AB02C with Drexel University and NNL13AA00B with the Boeing Company, and by SRI International. The content is solely the responsibility of the author and does not necessarily represent the official views of NASA.

References

1. Halbwachs, N., Lagnier, F., Ratel, C.: Programming and verifying real-time systems by means of the synchronous data-flow language LUSTRE. IEEE Transactions on Software Engineering 18, 785–793 (1992)
2. Halbwachs, N., Lagnier, F., Raymond, P.: Synchronous observers and the verification of reactive systems. In: Algebraic Methodology and Software Technology (AMAST 1993). Workshops in Computing, pp. 83–96. Springer, Enschede (1994)
3. Dwyer, M.B., Avrunin, G.S., Corbett, J.C.: Patterns in property specifications for finite-state verification. In: International Conference on Software Engineering, pp. 411–420. IEEE Computer Society, Los Angeles (1999)
4. SAL home page, http://sal.csl.sri.com/
5. McMillan, K.L.: Circular compositional reasoning about liveness. In: Pierre, L., Kropf, T. (eds.) Advances in Hardware Design and Verification: IFIP WG10.5 International Conference on Correct Hardware Design and Verification Methods (CHARME 1999). LNCS, vol. 1703, pp. 342–346. Springer, Heidelberg (1999)
6. Rushby, J.: Formal verification of McMillan's compositional assume-guarantee rule. Technical report, Computer Science Laboratory, SRI International, Menlo Park, CA (2001)
7. Kupferman, O., Vardi, M.Y.: Vacuity detection in temporal model checking. International Journal on Software Tools for Technology Transfer 4, 224–233 (2003)
8. Sankaranarayanan, S., Tiwari, A.: Relational abstractions for continuous and hybrid systems. In: Gopalakrishnan, G., Qadeer, S. (eds.) CAV 2011. LNCS, vol. 6806, pp. 686–702. Springer, Heidelberg (2011)
9. Tiwari, A.: HybridSAL relational abstracter. In: Madhusudan, P., Seshia, S.A. (eds.) CAV 2012. LNCS, vol. 7358, pp. 725–731. Springer, Heidelberg (2012)
10. Bass, E.J., Feigh, K.M., Gunter, E., Rushby, J.: Formal modeling and analysis for interactive hybrid systems. In: Fourth International Workshop on Formal Methods for Interactive Systems: FMIS 2011, Limerick, Ireland. Electronic Communications of the EASST, vol. 45 (2011)
11. Burch, J.R., Clarke, E.M., McMillan, K.L., Dill, D.L., Hwang, L.J.: Symbolic model checking: 10^{20} states and beyond. Information and Computation 98, 142–170 (1992)
12. de Moura, L., Rueß, H.: Lemmas on demand for satisfiability solvers. In: Proceedings of the Fifth International Symposium on the Theory and Applications of Satisfiability Testing (SAT 2002), Cincinnati, OH (2002)
13. de Moura, L., Rueß, H., Sorea, M.: Lazy theorem proving for bounded model checking over infinite domains. In: Voronkov, A. (ed.) CADE 2002. LNCS (LNAI), vol. 2392, pp. 438–455. Springer, Heidelberg (2002)
14. Rushby, J.: New challenges in certification for aircraft software. In: Baruah, S., Fischmeister, S. (eds.) Proceedings of the Ninth ACM International Conference On Embedded Software: EMSOFT, pp. 211–218. Association for Computing Machinery, Taipei (2011)

15. Rushby, J.: A safety-case approach for certifying adaptive systems. In: AIAA Infotech@Aerospace Conference, Seattle, WA. American Institute of Aeronautics and Astronautics, AIAA paper 2009-1992 (2009)
16. Schlichting, R.D., Schneider, F.B.: Fail-stop processors: An approach to designing fault-tolerant computing systems. ACM Transactions on Computer Systems 1, 222–238 (1983)
17. Rushby, J.: Composing safe systems. In: Arbab, F., Ölveczky, P.C. (eds.) FACS 2011. LNCS, vol. 7253, pp. 3–11. Springer, Heidelberg (2012)
18. Gargantini, A., Heitmeyer, C.: Using model checking to generate tests from requirements specifications. In: Nierstrasz, O., Lemoine, M. (eds.) ESEC/FSE 1999. LNCS, vol. 1687, pp. 146–162. Springer, Heidelberg (1999)
19. Hamon, G., de Moura, L., Rushby, J.: Generating efficient test sets with a model checker. In: 2nd International Conference on Software Engineering and Formal Methods (SEFM), Beijing, China, pp. 261–270. IEEE Computer Society (2004)
20. Hamon, G., de Moura, L., Rushby, J.: Automated test generation with SAL. Technical note, Computer Science Laboratory, SRI International, Menlo Park, CA (2005), http://www.csl.sri.com/users/rushby/abstracts/sal-atg
21. IEEE Standard 1850–2010: Property Specification Language, PSL (2010)
22. IEEE Standard 1800–2012: SystemVerilog—Unified Hardware Design, Specification, and Verification Language (2012)
23. Littlewood, B., Rushby, J.: Reasoning about the reliability of diverse two-channel systems in which one channel is "possibly perfect". IEEE Transactions on Software Engineering 38, 1178–1194 (2012)
24. Rushby, J.: The versatile synchronous observer (abstract only). In: Gheyi, R., Naumann, D. (eds.) SBMF 2012. LNCS, vol. 7498, p. 1. Springer, Heidelberg (2012)

Model Checking TLR* Guarantee Formulas on Infinite Systems*

Óscar Martín, Alberto Verdejo, and Narciso Martí-Oliet

Facultad de Informática, Universidad Complutense de Madrid, Spain
{omartins,jalberto,narciso}@ucm.es

Abstract. We present the implementation of a model checker for systems with a potentially infinite number of reachable states. It has been developed in the rewriting-logic language Maude. The model checker is explicit-state, that is, not symbolic. In infinite systems, we cannot expect it to finish in every case: it provides a semi-decision algorithm to validate guarantee formulas (or, equivalently, to falsify safety ones). To avoid getting lost in infinite paths, search is always performed within bounded depth. The properties to be checked are written in the Temporal Logic of Rewriting, TLR*, a generalization of CTL* that uses atomic propositions both on states and on transitions, providing, in this way, a richer expressive power. As an intermediate step, a strategy language is used. Guarantee formulas are first translated into strategy expressions and, then, the system and the strategy *evolve* in parallel searching for computations that satisfy the strategy and, thus, the formula. An example on verifying cache coherence protocols is presented, showing the usefulness of the tool.

Keywords: Infinite-state system, rewriting logic, Maude, model checking, strategy, temporal logic, TLR*, guarantee formula, cache coherence.

1 Introduction

Rewriting logic is a language for the specification of concurrent systems [19]. It is also an executable logic, which makes it a very useful formalism. Maude is a language and development system that incorporates both equational logic and rewriting logic [11]. Parallelism and nondeterminism are natural features of rewriting logic and Maude.

We now describe a very simple system that we use to introduce some important concepts in this paper. There are a number of counting devices in the system. Each time some external event happens, one and only one device detects it and increases its own counter. In order to be able to share data, the devices are organized as a ring, so that each device knows to whom it must send its messages, that are then resent until they have visited the whole ring. As we do

---

* Research supported by MINECO Spanish project StrongSoft (TIN2012–39391–C04–04) and Comunidad de Madrid program PROMETIDOS (S2009/TIC-1465).

S. Iida, J. Meseguer, and K. Ogata (Eds.): Futatsugi Festschrift, LNCS 8373, pp. 129–150, 2014.

not care about the nature of the events being counted, in our model each device is able by itself to increase its counter by one and immediately send a message to its *next* device. Here is the complete Maude specification:

```
mod COUNTING is
  protecting NAT .
  sort Id .
  subsort Nat < Id .
  sort Device .
  op [_,_,_] : Id Id Nat -> Device [ctor] .
  sort Message .
  op _|>_ : Id Id -> Message [ctor] .
  sort State .
  subsorts Device Message < State .
  op nullState : -> State [ctor] .
  op __ : State State -> State [ctor comm assoc id: nullState] .
  vars I J N : Id .  var A : Nat .
  rl [change] : [I, N, A] => [I, N, s(A)] (I |> N) .
  crl [resend] : [I, N, A] (J |> I) => [I, N, s(A)] (J |> N) if I =/= J .
  rl [remove] : (I |> I) => nullState .
endm
```

Types are introduced in Maude by the keyword `sort`. A `Device` is built by enclosing between square brackets three natural numbers: the device's `Id`, the `Id` of the next device in the ring, and the counter. A `Message` is given by two `Id`s: the first argument is the sender's `Id`, and the second the addressee's `Id`. The last sort we need is the `State` of the system. Maude uses an order-sorted type system. Thus, we declare that any `Device` or `Message`, by itself, constitutes a `State`. We also provide an operator with empty syntax, `__`, that allows to juxtapose any number of `States` to get a new one. Note that the `comm` and `assoc` attributes given to the operator allow commutative and associative matching. This way of defining states is a usual idiom in Maude. We have also declared a `nullState` to be used as identity element for states.

The three rewrite rules represent the different ways the system can evolve. Rule `change` represents the counting of an event and the sending of the associated message. Rule `resend` states that when device I sees a message addressed to itself, it updates its counter and resends the message to the next device. It is a conditional rule, because this should only happen for devices other than the original one. Rule `remove` just drops a message whose sender and addressee coincide—that is, the message has already visited the whole ring. Notice that the variable I is used twice: this rule should only be applied when both arguments of a message are equal.

A nice property of rewriting logic is that both states and transitions between states can be represented by terms. In the example, states are represented by terms of sort `State`, like `[0, 1, 5] [1, 0, 5]`. Transitions are represented by terms on a larger signature, so-called *proof terms* [19]. For instance, the transition

$$[0, 1, 5] \ [1, 0, 5] \longrightarrow [0, 1, 5] \ [1, 0, 6] \ (1 \ |> \ 0)$$

is represented by this proof term:

```
{[0, 1, 5] [] | 'change : ('I \ 1) ; ('N \ 0) ; ('A \ 5)}
```

This is a triple of a context (a term with a hole symbol [] showing where the rewrite took place), the name of the rule that has been applied, and the substitution used. (The leading quotes are a syntactic requirement of Maude.)

Atomic propositions on states and on transitions can be declared, and their satisfaction relations be defined, based on the shape of the term representing them. Once defined, they can be used to formally express temporal properties by means of temporal-logic formulas. For the example system, a proposition selfMsg that asserts that some message has completed its trip around the ring, and another parametric proposition rule that asserts that the transition is executing the rule whose label is given in its argument can be defined like this:

```
var I : Id .    var S : State .    var Cn : Context$State .
var L : Qid .   var Sb : Subst .   var T : Trans .


op selfMsg : -> StateProp [ctor] .
eq (I |> I) S |= selfMsg = true .
eq S |= selfMsg = false [owise] .


op rule : Qid -> TransProp [ctor] .
eq {Cn | L : Sb} |= rule(L) = true .
eq T |= rule(L) = false [owise] .
```

Thus, a State satisfies selfMsg iff it matches the pattern (I |> I) S.

The Temporal Logic of Rewriting TLR* [20] has been designed to take profit of this strength of rewriting logic. The logic CTL* allows only propositions on states; TLR* extends CTL* by allowing also propositions on transitions. Some interesting properties of systems are only naturally expressible using both state and transition propositions. For instance, the TLR* formula $\mathbf{G}$(selfMsg $\to$ rule('remove)) asserts that each time a message has completed its trip around the ring it must be immediately removed.

The model checker we have implemented accepts guarantee formulas of TLR*. Guarantee formulas assert that some property is going to hold in the future. For instance, $\mathbf{F}$ selfMsg asserts that, at some future time, the system will arrive to a state satisfying selfMsg. The model checker explores all possible evolutions of the given system in search for that future time in which the property holds. If the formula happens to be false for the given system, the algorithm may not terminate: thus, for infinite systems, it only provides a semi-decision algorithm (but a complete decision one for finite systems). Bounded-depth search is necessary to avoid getting lost into an infinite branch when, perhaps, the answer is on another. Our implementation provides a way to specify the maximum depth to be explored. Also, it provides a command to ask the system to explore some more levels based on the open branches left by a previous model-checking command. Note that any tool that can verify guarantee formulas can also be used to falsify safety ones through the duality trick of verifying their (guarantee) negations.

Internally, the model checker uses strategies. Strategies [22,8,17] applied to system specifications are a means of guiding their evolution and restricting their nondeterminism. The strategy "any^{+} . selfMsg", for instance, accepts only executions that, after some positive number of steps, land on a state that satisfies `selfMsg`. And the strategy "`(rule('change) ; rule('resend)+ ; rule('remove))+`" guides the system in such a way that once a message is added to the system, it is processed by all the devices and removed before a new event can be counted.

We will describe below a strategy language and show how TLR* guarantee formulas can be translated into it. We internally implement the strategies and use this implementation to model check TLR* guarantee formulas.

In the rest of the paper we first review rewrite systems, proof terms, TLR* and its semantics, and the strategy language and its semantics, following [20], and then we show how all of them are used to implement the model checker. Then we present an example on verifying the MSI cache coherence protocol. We finish with some related work and conclusions. An extended version of this paper can be found in [18]. Also, the complete Maude specifications for the model checker as well as for some examples, including the MSI cache coherence protocol, are available for download at `http://maude.sip.ucm.es/ismc`.

2   Rewrite Systems

Formally, a rewrite system [19] is a triple $\mathcal{R} = (\Sigma, E, R)$, where Σ is an order-sorted signature, E a set of equations, and R a set of rewrite rules of the form $l : q \to q'$, with l a label, and q, q' terms of the same sort and such that all variables in q' appear also in q. Such a triple specifies a concurrent, nondeterministic system in which the states of the system are E-equivalence classes of ground terms $[t]_E$; that is, the initial algebra $T_{\Sigma/E}$ constitutes the state space. The dynamics of the system are given by the rewrite rules in R. As states are equivalence classes of terms, rewriting happens also at this level. Thus, a transition from state $[t]_E$ to state $[t']_E$, denoted by $[t]_E \longrightarrow^1_{\mathcal{R}} [t']_E$, is possible in $\mathcal{R}$ iff there exist $u \in [t]_E$ and $u' \in [t']_E$ such that u can be rewritten to u' using some rule $l : q \to q'$ in R.

For arbitrary E and R, whether $[t]_E \longrightarrow^*_{\mathcal{R}} [t']_E$ holds is undecidable in general.

Definition 1 (computable rewrite system [20]). *A rewrite system $\mathcal{R} = (\Sigma, E \cup A, R)$ (where the set of equations has been split into two disjoint subsets) is computable if E, A and R are finite and the following conditions hold:*

1. *Equality modulo A is decidable, and there exists a matching algorithm modulo A, producing a finite number of A-matching substitutions or failing otherwise, that can implement rewriting in A-equivalence classes.*
2. *$(\Sigma, E \cup A)$ is ground terminating and confluent modulo A. That is: (i) there are no infinite sequences of reductions with E modulo A; and (ii) for each $[t]_A \in T_{\Sigma/A}$ there is a unique A-equivalence class $[\text{can}_{E/A}(t)]_A \in T_{\Sigma/A}$, called the E-canonical form of $[t]_A$ modulo A, such that the last term, which cannot be further reduced with E modulo A, of any terminating sequence beginning at $[t]_A$ is necessarily $[\text{can}_{E/A}(t)]_A$.*

3. The rules R are ground coherent *relative to the equations E modulo A. That is, if $[t]_A$ is rewritten to $[t']_A$ by a rule $l \in R$, then $[\mathrm{can}_{E/A}(t)]_A$ is also rewritten by l to some $[t'']_A$ such that $[\mathrm{can}_{E/A}(t')]_A = [\mathrm{can}_{E/A}(t'')]_A$.*

These three conditions imply that for each sort $S \in \Sigma$ the relation $\longrightarrow^1_{\mathcal{R},S}$ is computable: one can decide $[t]_{E\cup A} \longrightarrow^1_{\mathcal{R}} [t']_{E\cup A}$ by generating the finite set of all one-step R-rewrites modulo A of $\mathrm{can}_{E/A}(t)$ and testing if any of them has the same E-canonical form modulo A as $[\mathrm{can}_{E/A}(t')]_A$.

The three conditions are quite natural and are typically met in practical rewriting-logic specifications. In Maude, the set of equations A is given by *operator attributes* like `comm` and `assoc` used in the example of Section 1, for which Maude knows specific matching algorithms.

3   Proof Terms and Computations

In rewriting logic computation and proof are equivalent. Given a system $\mathcal{R} = (\Sigma, E \cup A, R)$, the state $[u]_{E\cup A}$ can be rewritten to $[u']_{E\cup A}$ if and only if the inference rules of rewriting logic [19,9] allow to prove $\mathcal{R} \vdash [u]_{E\cup A} \rightarrow^+ [u']_{E\cup A}$. Single rewritings are witnessed by so-called *one-step proof terms*. One-step proof terms can be characterized in an algebraic fashion. We define the signature $\mathrm{Trans}(\Sigma)$ (Trans for "transition"), on which one-step proof terms are built, extending Σ in this way:

- For each sort $S \in \Sigma$, we add a new sort $\mathrm{Trans}(S)$ to $\mathrm{Trans}(\Sigma)$, and state that $S < \mathrm{Trans}(S)$, that is, S is a subsort of $\mathrm{Trans}(S)$. Terms of sort $\mathrm{Trans}(S)$ represent one-step rewrites between terms of sort S.
- Given a rule $l : q \to q'$ in R, let S be the sort of q and q', and let the variables appearing in q, taken in their textual order of appearance, have sorts $S_1, \ldots, S_n$. Then, for each such rule $l \in R$, we add to $\mathrm{Trans}(\Sigma)$ a new function symbol $l : S_1 \times \cdots \times S_n \to \mathrm{Trans}(S)$.
- For each function symbol $f : S_1 \times \cdots \times S_n \to S$ in Σ and each $i = 1, \ldots, n$, we add to $\mathrm{Trans}(\Sigma)$ an overloaded function symbol (with the same attributes as the original f) $f : S_1 \times \cdots \times \mathrm{Trans}(S_i) \times \cdots \times S_n \to \mathrm{Trans}(S)$.

In this paper, we assume that the sort of the terms that represent states of the system is called `State`. In that case, $\mathrm{Trans}(\mathtt{State})$ is the sort of one-step proof terms. We declare `Trans` as a convenient synonym for $\mathrm{Trans}(\mathtt{State})$.

Thus, a proof term has the form $v[l(\bar{u})]_p$: a term v of sort `State` whose subterm at position p has been replaced by $l(\bar{u})$. In such a proof term, $v[\ ]_p$ shows the *context* in which the rewrite is taking place, l is the rule being executed, and the substitution $\bar{x} \mapsto \bar{u}$ is being used, where $\bar{x}$ is the tuple of all the variables in q in the textual order in which they appear.

Now consider the rewrite system $\mathrm{Trans}(\mathcal{R}) = (\mathrm{Trans}(\Sigma), E \cup A, R)$. There are no new equations and no new rules. Thus, if $\mathcal{R}$ is computable (as defined in Section 2), so is $\mathrm{Trans}(\mathcal{R})$. In particular, every term has a unique E-canonical form modulo A. For each sort S, let $(\mathrm{Can}_{\mathrm{Trans}(\Sigma)/E\cup A})_S$ denote the set of all

A-equivalence classes of the form $[\mathrm{can}_{E/A}(t)]_A$, where t is a ground-term of sort S. Thus, $(\mathrm{Can}_{\mathrm{Trans}(\Sigma)/E\cup A})_{\mathrm{Trans}}$ describes the set of all transitions between States in the system specified by $\mathcal{R}$ in their canonical form representation. And $(\mathrm{Can}_{\Sigma/E\cup A})_{\mathrm{State}} = (\mathrm{Can}_{\mathrm{Trans}(\Sigma)/E\cup A})_{\mathrm{State}}$ describes the set of all States.

Definition 2. *[20] A computation (s,t) in $\mathcal{R}$ is a pair of functions*

$$s : \mathbb{N} \to (\mathrm{Can}_{\Sigma/E\cup A})_{\mathrm{State}} \qquad and \qquad t : \mathbb{N} \to (\mathrm{Can}_{\mathrm{Trans}(\Sigma)/E\cup A})_{\mathrm{Trans}}$$

such that for all $n \in \mathbb{N}$ we have $s(n) \xrightarrow{t(n)} s(n+1)$. Usually, we write $s_i = s(i)$ and $t_i = t(i)$, and we consider s and t as sequences. Thus, the computation $s_0 \xrightarrow{t_0} s_1 \xrightarrow{t_1} s_2 \xrightarrow{t_2} \cdots$ is represented as $(s,t) = (s_0 s_1 s_2 \ldots, t_0 t_1 t_2 \ldots)$.

Note that we only consider infinite computations. This allows an easier definition of the semantics, and it is not at all a strong restriction. See [20] for details.

Computations are the semantic entities on which the truth of TLR* formulas is evaluated.

4   Temporal Logics and TLR* Guarantee Formulas

Temporal logics, in their different flavors, are a usual formalism to express the properties we expect a system to satisfy as it evolves in time. Usually, temporal logics fall in one of two classes according to the kind of atomic propositions they use: state-based or action-based. State-based logics, like LTL, CTL and CTL*, can only talk directly about states [10]. Action-based logics, like A-CTL* [12] and Hennessy-Milner logic [16], can only talk directly about actions (that is, transitions). Rewriting logic provides algebraic structure both to states and to actions and TLR* was designed to form a good tandem with it [20].

The formulas our model checker understands are guarantee formulas with a leading path quantifier, either universal or existential. They constitute a sublogic of TLR*. We define its syntax now, with σ denoting an atomic state proposition and τ an atomic transition proposition:

$$\phi ::= \top \mid \bot \mid \sigma \mid \neg\sigma \mid \tau \mid \neg\tau \mid \phi_1 \vee \phi_2 \mid \phi_1 \wedge \phi_2 \mid \mathbf{X}\,\phi \mid \phi_1\,\mathbf{U}\,\phi_2 \mid \mathbf{F}\,\phi$$
$$\varphi ::= \mathbf{A}\,\phi \mid \mathbf{E}\,\phi$$

The definition of the semantics, following [20], is given below. Remember that s_0 and t_0 always denote the first state and transition in the sequences s and t, respectively. Also, for a computation (s,t), its suffix resulting by removing the first k elements from s and from t is denoted by $(s,t)^k$.

- $\mathcal{R}, (s,t) \models \top$;
- $\mathcal{R}, (s,t) \not\models \bot$;
- $\mathcal{R}, (s,t) \models \sigma \Leftrightarrow \mathcal{R}, s_0 \models \sigma$;
- $\mathcal{R}, (s,t) \models \tau \Leftrightarrow \mathcal{R}, t_0 \models \tau$;

- $\mathcal{R}, (s,t) \models \neg\phi \Leftrightarrow \mathcal{R}, (s,t) \not\models \phi;$
- $\mathcal{R}, (s,t) \models \phi_1 \vee \phi_2 \Leftrightarrow \mathcal{R}, (s,t) \models \phi_1 \text{ or } \mathcal{R}, (s,t) \models \phi_2;$
- $\mathcal{R}, (s,t) \models \mathbf{X}\,\phi \Leftrightarrow \mathcal{R}, (s,t)^1 \models \phi;$
- $\mathcal{R}, (s,t) \models \phi_1 \mathbf{U} \phi_2 \Leftrightarrow \exists k \text{ s.t. } \mathcal{R}, (s,t)^k \models \phi_2 \text{ and } \forall i \in [0,k), \mathcal{R}, (s,t)^i \models \phi_1;$
- $\mathcal{R}, (s,t) \models \mathbf{F}\,\phi \Leftrightarrow \exists k \text{ s.t. } \mathcal{R}, (s,t)^k \models \phi;$
- $\mathcal{R}, s_0 \models \mathbf{A}\,\phi \Leftrightarrow \text{for all computations } (s,t) \text{ we have } \mathcal{R}, (s,t) \models \phi;$
- $\mathcal{R}, s_0 \models \mathbf{E}\,\phi \Leftrightarrow \text{for some computation } (s,t) \text{ we have } \mathcal{R}, (s,t) \models \phi.$

Thus, an existentially quantified formula, $\mathbf{E}\,\phi$, represents a reachability predicate, while a universally quantified one, $\mathbf{A}\,\phi$, has the semantics of a linear temporal formula.

5   A Strategy Language

There exists a rich strategy language for Maude [17]. Now we describe another such strategy language, proposed in [20], designed with the construction of the model checker in sight. As above, we denote by σ and τ generic atomic propositions on states and transitions. The syntax contains three syntactic categories: *Test* (tests on states), *Strat* (strategy expressions), and *StratForm* (strategy formulas). Here, e, e_1, e_2 are strategy expressions, and b, b_1, b_2 are tests.

- *Test:* $b ::= \top \mid \bot \mid \sigma \mid \neg b \mid b_1 \vee b_2 \mid b_1 \wedge b_2$
- *Strat:* $e ::= \text{idle} \mid \tau \mid \neg\tau \mid \text{any} \mid e_1 \wedge e_2 \mid (e_1 \mid e_2) \mid e_1 \,;\, e_2 \mid e^+ \mid e_1 \mathcal{U} e_2 \mid e.b$
- *StratForm:* $f ::= \mathbf{A}\,e \mid \mathbf{E}\,e$

Formal semantics are given below. A few informal explanations follow on the operators that may not be trivial:

- The strategy idle does nothing, is always satisfied, and leaves the system in the same state it was.
- The expression $e_1 \,;\, e_2$ means sequential composition, that is, the system is first guided by e_1 and then, when e_1 has finished its job, by e_2.
- The strategy $e_1 \mathcal{U} e_2$ is an *until* operator: e_1 holds for subcomputations beginning at the first state, at the second, and so on, until a subcomputation beginning at state $n \geq 0$, and then e_2 holds from state $n+1$.
- The strategy $e.b$ combines e with a test b. It holds iff e holds and the test b succeeds for the last state reached.

Our model checker internally works with strategies, but we want the user to introduce TLR* guarantee formulas. So a semantically appropriate translation from the former to the latter is needed. It is given by the function [20]

$$\beta : \text{TLR* guarantee formulas} \rightarrow \textit{Strat}$$

defined by

$\beta(\phi) = \text{idle} . \phi$ for $\phi = \top, \bot, \sigma, \neg\sigma$

$\beta(\phi) = \phi$ for $\phi = \tau, \neg\tau$

$\beta(\phi_1 \vee \phi_2) = \beta(\phi_1) \mid \beta(\phi_2)$

$\beta(\phi_1 \wedge \phi_2) = \beta(\phi_1) \wedge \beta(\phi_2)$

$\beta(\mathbf{X} \phi) = \text{any} ; \beta(\phi)$

$\beta(\phi_1 \mathbf{U} \phi_2) = \beta(\phi_1) \mathcal{U} \beta(\phi_2)$

$\beta(\mathbf{F} \phi) = (\text{idle} \mid \text{any}^+) ; \beta(\phi)$

In the next section we define a semantics for strategy expressions with the aim of making ϕ and $\beta(\phi)$ semantically equivalent for each formula ϕ.

6 Strategy Semantics

Our semantics is different, but equivalent, to the one defined in [20] (see also [18]). Two nice features of our semantics are:

1. That it is bounded by definition. We are defining the relation $\mathcal{R}, (s,t) \models_k e$ with the intuitive meaning that the computation (s,t) needs to perform at most k steps before satisfying e. (This is in the same spirit as the bounded semantics defined in [7].)
2. That it allows a step-by-step implementation. That is, we are able to check whether $\mathcal{R}, (s,t) \models_k e$ by, first, checking whether (s_0, t_0) is a step *compatible* with e, and, second, checking whether the rest of the computation $(s,t)^1$ satisfies *the rest* of e in at most $k-1$ steps.

The semantics uses two auxiliary functions with these intuitive meanings:

fail(e) = does e always fails, for any computation and with no need to take any step? *A posteriori*, fail(e) means that e is semantically equivalent to idle . $\bot$.

tick(e) = is e always satisfied, for any computation and with no need to take any step? *A posteriori*, tick(e) means that e is semantically equivalent either to idle or to idle $\mid e'$ for some e'.

Definition 3 (fail **and** tick). *The functions* fail, tick : *Strat* $\rightarrow$ *Bool are defined as shown in this table:*

e	fail(e)	tick(e)
idle	*false*	*true*
τ	*false*	*false*
$\neg\tau$	*false*	*false*
any	*false*	*false*
$e_1 \wedge e_2$	fail(e_1) $\vee$ fail(e_2)	tick(e_1) $\wedge$ tick(e_2)
$e_1 \mid e_2$	fail(e_1) $\wedge$ fail(e_2)	tick(e_1) $\vee$ tick(e_2)
$e_1 ; e_2$	fail(e_1) $\vee$ fail(e_2)	tick(e_1) $\wedge$ tick(e_2)
e_1^+	fail(e_1)	tick(e_1)
$e_1 \mathcal{U} e_2$	fail(e_1) $\wedge$ fail(e_2)	tick(e_2)
$e_1 . b$	fail(e_1) $\vee$ $b \equiv \bot$	tick(e_1) $\wedge$ $b \equiv \top$

The most important function in the definition of the semantics is $\text{rest}_{s_0,t_0}(e)$. It answers the question: what strategy, derived from e, remains to be satisfied after step (s_0, t_0)? For instance, $\text{rest}_{s_0,t_0}(\text{idle} \,|\, (\tau \,;\, \text{any})) = \text{any}$ if t_0 satisfies τ. We define this function below, based on the structure of the formula.

In some cases, the result of $\text{rest}_{s_0,t_0}(e)$ is a disjunction, showing the different ways in which a step can be taken. For instance, $e_1 \,;\, e_2$ can take a step in two nonexclusive ways: (i) e_1 takes a step to become $\text{rest}_{s_0,t_0}(e_1)$, with e_2 still pending behind, or (ii) e_1 is already satisfied and then e_2 takes a step to become $\text{rest}_{s_0,t_0}(e_2)$. In cases like this, we use a convenient shorthand notation, showing each possible first step on a different line.

Definition 4. *The notation*

$$e_1$$
$$|\, e_2 \; if \; B$$

where e_1 and e_2 are strategies and B is a Boolean expression, is equal to just (e_1) if B evaluates to false, and is equal to $((e_1) \,|\, (e_2))$ if B evaluates to true.

Definition 5 (rest_{s_0,t_0}). *Given s_0 and t_0 (a state and a transition from it), the function $\text{rest}_{s_0,t_0} : Strat \to Strat$ is defined by:*

e	$\text{rest}_{s_0,t_0}(e)$
idle	idle $.\perp$
τ	*if* $\mathcal{R}, t_0 \models \tau$ *then* idle *else* idle $.\perp$
$\neg\tau$	*if* $\mathcal{R}, t_0 \models \tau$ *then* idle $.\perp$ *else* idle
any	idle
$e_1 \wedge e_2$	$\text{rest}_{s_0,t_0}(e_1) \wedge \text{rest}_{s_0,t_0}(e_2)$ $\mid \text{rest}_{s_0,t_0}(e_1)$ *if* $\text{tick}(e_2)$ $\mid \text{rest}_{s_0,t_0}(e_2)$ *if* $\text{tick}(e_1)$
$e_1 \,|\, e_2$	*if* $\text{fail}(e_1)$ *then* $\text{rest}_{s_0,t_0}(e_2)$ *if* $\text{fail}(e_2)$ *then* $\text{rest}_{s_0,t_0}(e_1)$ *otherwise* $\text{rest}_{s_0,t_0}(e_1) \,|\, \text{rest}_{s_0,t_0}(e_2)$
$e_1 \,;\, e_2$	$\text{rest}_{s_0,t_0}(e_1) \,;\, e_2$ $\mid \text{rest}_{s_0,t_0}(e_2)$ *if* $\text{tick}(e_1)$
$e_1{}^+$	$\text{rest}_{s_0,t_0}(e_1) \,;\, (\text{idle} \,|\, e_1{}^+)$ $\mid$ idle *if* $\text{tick}(e_1)$
$e_1 \,\mathcal{U}\, e_2$	$\text{rest}_{s_0,t_0}(e_2)$ $\mid$ idle *if* $\text{tick}(e_2)$ $\mid e_1 \,\mathcal{U}\, e_2$ *if* $\text{tick}(e_1)$ $\mid \text{rest}_{s_0,t_0}(e_1) \wedge (c_1 \,\mathcal{U}\, c_2)$ *if* $\neg\text{fail}(e_1)$
$e_1 \,.\, b$	$\text{rest}_{s_0,t_0}(e_1) \,.\, b$ $\mid$ idle *if* $\text{tick}(e_1) \wedge \mathcal{R}, s_0 \models b$

Note that $\text{rest}_{s_0,t_0}(e)$ is never called with an e such that $\text{fail}(e)$, and thus we avoid some cases in the definition.

The last case in this definition uses the semantics for *Test*, that follows the usual definition for Boolean expressions, as shown next.

Definition 6 (*Test* **semantics**). *Given a rewrite system $\mathcal{R}$, a state s_0, and a Test on states b:*

$\mathcal{R}, s_0 \models \top$

$\mathcal{R}, s_0 \not\models \bot$

$\mathcal{R}, s_0 \models \sigma$ *according to the definition of σ, i.e., iff $E \cup A \vdash (s_0 \mathbin{|} = \sigma) = \texttt{true}$*

$\mathcal{R}, s_0 \models \neg b \Leftrightarrow \mathcal{R}, s_0 \not\models b$

$\mathcal{R}, s_0 \models b_1 \vee b_2 \Leftrightarrow \mathcal{R}, s_0 \models b_1$ *or* $\mathcal{R}, s_0 \models b_2$

$\mathcal{R}, s_0 \models b_1 \wedge b_2 \Leftrightarrow \mathcal{R}, s_0 \models b_1$ *and* $\mathcal{R}, s_0 \models b_2$

The semantics for strategies and strategy formulas are given in the following two definitions:

Definition 7 (*Strat* **semantics**). *Given a rewrite system $\mathcal{R}$, a strategy e, a computation (s,t), and an integer k, we define the bounded semantic relation $\models_k$, whose value can be true, false or uncertain, by case distinction:*

If $\mathrm{fail}(e)$ *then*	$\mathcal{R}, (s,t) \models_k e$ *is false for every k*
else if $\mathrm{tick}(e)$ *then*	$\mathcal{R}, (s,t) \models_k e$ *is true for every k*
else if $k = 0$ then	$\mathcal{R}, (s,t) \models_0 e$ *is uncertain*
else	$\mathcal{R}, (s,t) \models_k e = \mathcal{R}, (s,t)^1 \models_{k-1} \mathrm{rest}_{s_0,t_0}(e)$

Definition 8 (*StratForm* **semantics**). *Given a rewrite system $\mathcal{R}$, a strategy e, a computation (s,t) (with s_0 always denoting the first state in s), and an integer k, we define the bounded semantic relation $\models_k$, whose value can be true, false or uncertain, by case distinction:*

$\mathcal{R}, s_0 \models_k \mathbf{A}\, e$ *is true*	$\Leftrightarrow$	$\mathcal{R}, (s,t) \models_k e$ *is true for all (s,t)*
$\mathcal{R}, s_0 \models_k \mathbf{A}\, e$ *is false*	$\Leftrightarrow$	$\mathcal{R}, (s,t) \models_k e$ *is false for some (s,t)*
$\mathcal{R}, s_0 \models_k \mathbf{A}\, e$ *is uncertain*	*otherwise*	

$\mathcal{R}, s_0 \models_k \mathbf{E}\, e$ *is true*	$\Leftrightarrow$	$\mathcal{R}, (s,t) \models_k e$ *is true for some (s,t)*
$\mathcal{R}, s_0 \models_k \mathbf{E}\, e$ *is false*	$\Leftrightarrow$	$\mathcal{R}, (s,t) \models_k e$ *is false for all (s,t)*
$\mathcal{R}, s_0 \models_k \mathbf{E}\, e$ *is uncertain*	*otherwise*	

Theorem 1. *[20,18] Given a computable rewrite system $\mathcal{R}$, a TLR* guarantee formula ϕ and a computation (s,t) in $\mathcal{R}$, we have*

$$\mathcal{R}, (s,t) \models \phi \Leftrightarrow \exists k \in \mathbb{N} \text{ such that } \mathcal{R}, (s,t) \models_k \beta(\phi) \text{ is true}$$
$$\mathcal{R}, s_0 \models \mathbf{A}\, \phi \Leftrightarrow \exists k \in \mathbb{N} \text{ such that } \mathcal{R}, s_0 \models_k \mathbf{A}\, \beta(\phi) \text{ is true}$$
$$\mathcal{R}, s_0 \models \mathbf{E}\, \phi \Leftrightarrow \exists k \in \mathbb{N} \text{ such that } \mathcal{R}, s_0 \models_k \mathbf{E}\, \beta(\phi) \text{ is true}$$

Proof (sketch). Based on the definition, semantic equivalences $e \equiv e'$ between strategy expressions e and e' can be proved just by proving that $\mathrm{fail}(e) = \mathrm{fail}(e')$,

$\text{tick}(e) = \text{tick}(e')$, and $\text{rest}_{s_0,t_0}(e) \equiv \text{rest}_{s_0,t_0}(e')$. In this way, we get some intuitive and useful equivalences. For instance:

$$e \,|\, e' \equiv e' \text{ if } \text{fail}(e)$$
$$\text{idle} \,;\, e \equiv e$$

With equivalences like these, a proof of the theorem by structural induction is straightforward. We review just the case for the **X** operator:

$$
\begin{array}{ll}
\mathcal{R}, (s,t) \models \mathbf{X}\,\phi & \Leftrightarrow \text{(TLR* semantics)} \\
\mathcal{R}, (s,t)^1 \models \phi & \Leftrightarrow \text{(induction hypothesis)} \\
\exists k \text{ s.t. } \mathcal{R}, (s,t)^1 \models_k \beta(\phi) \text{ is true} & \Leftrightarrow \text{(semantic equivalence)} \\
\exists k \text{ s.t. } \mathcal{R}, (s,t)^1 \models_k \text{idle}\,;\, \beta(\phi) \text{ is true} & \Leftrightarrow \text{(definition of rest}_{s_0,t_0}) \\
\exists k \text{ s.t. } \mathcal{R}, (s,t)^1 \models_k \text{rest}_{s_0,t_0}(\text{any}\,;\, \beta(\phi)) \text{ is true} & \Leftrightarrow \text{(strategy semantics)} \\
\exists k \text{ s.t. } \mathcal{R}, (s,t) \models_{k+1} \text{any}\,;\, \beta(\phi) \text{ is true} & \Leftrightarrow \text{(definition of }\beta) \\
\exists k \text{ s.t. } \mathcal{R}, (s,t) \models_{k+1} \beta(\mathbf{X}(\phi)) \text{ is true} &
\end{array}
$$

7   The Implementation

Maude has reflective capabilities through its *metalevel* [11]. That means, for instance, that using the Maude language we can ask Maude itself about the possible rewrites from some given state, so that we can manipulate them in our code. We use the metalevel to compute and explore all evolutions of the system.

Functions equivalent to tick, fail, and rest_{s_0,t_0} have been coded into Maude. With this we make the strategy evolve at the same time as the system. To avoid getting lost in infinite branches, we use a bounded depth-first search. The depth is a parameter the user provides. The tool includes a command to search some additional levels when the previous search has not been conclusive. This shows a scheme of the algorithm:

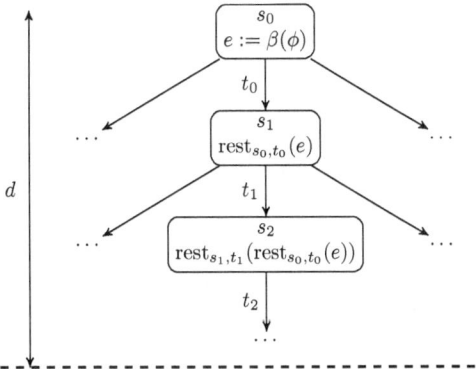

At each node, the algorithm checks whether the state definitively satisfies the strategy, or it definitively does not, or more states have to be explored. It has to take care of a few more points not mentioned yet:

– Whether the quantifier is `forall` or `exists` to stop or continue the search when a satisfying or falsifying node is found.

- Storing the path from the initial state to the current one for loop detection and witness reporting. This is achieved by means of an ordered list of (state, strategy) pairs. At present, we do not store the whole set of visited nodes, so that our tests for repetitions are limited to the current path.
- Storing the open branches of the computation tree, in case they are later needed for a deeper search. It is not enough to store the set of leaves open at the depth bound, but whole paths to all of the open leaves are needed, so that a new, deeper search will be able to do loop detection and witness reporting properly from the original initial state.

The model checker, as it is, does not show an industrial-level performance and, although we show its usefulness below, it must be rather seen as a prototype.

The tool's user interface has two components: some commands related to model checking (described later), and an operator on modules, called `EXTENDED`. Given a system module—let us call it `UserMod`—our tool is able to generate the module `EXTENDED[UserMod]` and put it at the user's disposal. The operator `EXTENDED` assumes and needs that `UserMod` has a sort named `State`. The module `EXTENDED[UserMod]` adds to `UserMod` the following (syntax largely borrowed from [3,5]):

- New sorts `Trans`, `StateProp`, and `TransProp`, and satisfaction operators

  `op |= : State StateProp -> Bool .     op |= : Trans TransProp -> Bool .`
- For each sort `S` in `UserMod`, a new sort `Context$S`, a subsort declaration `S < Context$S`, and an overloaded constant `op [] : -> Context$S`.
- For each constructor operator, say `op f : S1 S2 ... Sn -> S`, new operators

  `op f : Context$S1 S2 ... Sn -> Context$S .`
  ...
  `op f : S1 S2 ... Context$Sn -> Context$S .`
- The constructor for proof terms

  `op {_|_:_} : Context$State Qid Subst -> Trans .`

  Note that this is not the algebraic syntax proposed in Section 3, but is equivalent to it and more convenient for implementation.
- New sorts `Assign` and `Subst`, with the subsort relation `Assign < Subst`.
- For each sort `S` in `UserMod`, an operator `op _\_ : Qid S -> Assign`.
- New operators to build substitutions:

  `op noSubst : -> Subst .`
  `op _;_ : Subst Subst -> Subst [comm assoc id: noSubst] .`
- An operator `op _instanceOf_ : Subst Subst -> Bool` and equations to define the `instanceOf` relation as true when the first argument, taken as a set of assignments, is a subset of the second.

Users need to write at least two modules:

```
(mod UserMod is                    (mod UserMod-FULL is
    sort State .                       extending EXTENDED[UserMod] .
    ...                                op foo : -> StateProp .
endm)                                  ...
                                   endm)
```

The first one, UserMod, has the whole specification of the system in the usual Maude way. Of course, it can import other modules as needed. The other module has to include the instruction extending EXTENDED[UserMod]. In this second module the users—having at their disposal all the infrastructure on proof terms, satisfaction, etc.—can define their own atomic propositions to be used in TLR* formulas, as we did in the example of Section 1. The definition of initial states is usually included in this second module as well.

The main model-checking command the user can issue is

```
(ismc [d] s |= q φ .)
```

Here, d is a natural number that specifies the maximum depth in the system's state space to which the search has to be performed; s is a term of sort State; q is a quantifier, either the literal exists or forall; and ϕ is a TLR* guarantee formula.

The concrete syntax for TLR* guarantee formulas is:

$$\phi ::= \text{TRUE} \mid \text{FALSE} \mid \sigma \mid \text{NOT } \sigma \mid \tau \mid \text{NOT } \tau \mid \phi_1 \text{ AND } \phi_2 \mid \phi_1 \text{ OR } \phi_2 \mid$$
$$\text{X } \phi \mid \text{F } \phi \mid \phi_1 \text{ U } \phi_2$$

The possible answers to a model-checking command are Yes or No, with a witness computation when appropriate, or DontKnow when the search was not conclusive, followed in this case by the number of open tasks left. Witnesses and counterexamples can be, in particular, looping computations. In the DontKnow case, the tool keeps in its memory all the open tasks, so that this new command can be issued:

```
(ismc deeper [d] .)
```

This asks the model checker to search d more levels for each open task remaining after the latest ismc or deeper command.

There are also two set commands:

- (ismc set loops on / off .)
- (ismc set contexts on / off .)

The first instructs the tool to look (or not) for possible looping computations as it searches. It must be noted that in a loop not only states have to repeat, but also the strategies coupled with them. Detecting loops is not for free, as it involves the storing of information and the comparison of terms. Some model-checking tasks in which loops happen to be rare benefit notably from disabling loop detection. However, in many cases the effort is worthwhile—it may even be the only way to reach a final answer.

The command about contexts instructs the tool to generate (or not) contexts for proof terms. Contexts tend to be seldom used in practice; when they are not used, one gains some performance by setting contexts off (about 10% to 20% according to our measures).

8   Verification of the MSI Cache Coherence Protocol

As an example to test our tool, we have chosen cache coherence protocols, a problem that does not seem to have been previously modeled in rewriting logic. In multiprocessor computers it is frequently the case that a small cache memory is attached to each processor. This cache memory, or just *cache*, holds a copy of a part of the main memory. A processor only reads from and writes to its cache, improving in this way the overall computer's performance. The cache coherence problem arises because several caches may hold copies of the same main-memory address, and the respective processors may write different data on them.

To avoid this problem, cache coherence protocols have been devised, that dictate the actions a cache must perform according to the orders that arrive to it. Here we consider one of the best-known protocols: MSI. In this protocol, like in most others, each cache line is marked with a *mode* that determines the validity of the information it stores. A cache line is the smallest chunk of memory that can be moved between the main memory and a cache. In MSI a cache line can be in one of three modes:

Modified: the line has been modified in this cache, so other copies of the same memory address, both in caches and in main memory, are unreliable;
Shared: the line is valid and so is every other copy of the line stored in any cache and in main memory;
Invalid: the line is not valid, presumably because it has been modified elsewhere.

The initials of these three modes give its name to the protocol. We abbreviate the three modes as mdf, shr, and inv.

There is usually a bus through which all communication between caches and main memory happens. MSI was designed for buses that do not allow direct communication of data from cache to cache. However, the caches are able to *snoop* the bus, that is, to monitor it to detect when another cache is trying to access a certain main-memory address. By snooping, a cache cannot see the data being read or written by another cache, but only its address in main memory.

To simplify the model, operations on the bus are taken to be atomic, that is, they are fully dealt with before the system does anything else. Reality is usually not that simple, but considering technicalities on the bus side would make the model unnecessarily complex. Also, we assume that each cache only contains one line of information. This turns out to be an unrealistic but sensible simplification: each operation happens to a particular line, all other lines in the cache being irrelevant to this operation.

A computer is a finite object. Although the number of processors and the size of the memory are not limited in principle, once a computer is built and running, these numbers are fixed. Or this was so until the advent of virtual machines. Virtualization software allows running operating systems on virtual hardware that is not mapped in a one-to-one fashion to actual hardware. The online manual for VMware vSphere 5.1 [23] states: "When the virtual machine is turned on [...] you can hot add virtual CPUs to the running virtual machine." Thus, we include in our model the possibility of adding new processors *on the fly*, which turns the number of states reachable from a given one into infinite.

First, we need the data structures. A `Line` consists of two natural numbers representing the address and the data stored. Caches and processors are independent entities, identified and coupled by its `ChipId` (a `Nat`). A CPU, or processor, contains just its `ChipId` and a Boolean that indicates whether it sent a message to its cache and is waiting for the answer. A cache registers its `ChipId`, its mode and its only line of information.

```
sorts Mode Line CPU Cache .
ops mdf shr inv : -> Mode [ctor] .
op line : Address Data -> Line [ctor] .
op cpu : ChipId Bool -> CPU [ctor] .
op cache : ChipId Mode Line -> Cache [ctor] .
```

Main memory is declared as a set of lines enclosed in double curly brackets:

```
sort MemContents .   subsort Line < MemContents .
op mtMemContents : -> MemContents [ctor] .
op __ : MemContents MemContents -> MemContents
        [ctor comm assoc id: mtMemContents] .
eq MC:MemContents MC:MemContents = MC:MemContents .
sort Memory .
op {{_}} : MemContents -> Memory [ctor] .
```

The bus is not a distinct entity in our model: there are `BusMessage`s loose in the state. There are also `LocalMessage`s, that is, messages between a processor and its cache, whose means of transmission is of no concern to us either.

```
sorts BusMessage LocalMessage .
op bus-read : ChipId Address -> BusMessage [ctor] .
op bus-hereur : ChipId Line -> BusMessage [ctor] .
op read : ChipId Address -> LocalMessage [ctor] .
op hereur : ChipId Line -> LocalMessage [ctor] .
op write : ChipId Line -> LocalMessage [ctor] .
```

We want to control the amount of memory addresses and of possible data values available, so that they can be kept to the minimum we need in each moment. We do so by defining a sort of sets on natural numbers, `NatSet`, and these two sorts:

```
sorts AddressRange DataRange .
op aRange : NatSet -> AddressRange [ctor] .
op dRange : NatSet -> DataRange [ctor] .
```

A `State` is defined as a *soup* of elements, enclosed in curly brackets:

```
sort StateContents .
subsorts CPU Cache Memory BusMessage LocalMessage
         AddressRange DataRange ChipId < StateContents .
```

```
op mtStateContents : -> StateContents [ctor] .
op __ : StateContents StateContents -> StateContents
        [ctor comm assoc id: mtStateContents] .
sort State .
op {_} : StateContents -> State [ctor] .
```

We also store in the state the maximum ChipId currently used, so that adding new caches is easier. Some provisos are missing that are important. For instance, one and only one Memory, AddressRange, and DataRange should exist in a given State, and there should be as many Caches as CPUs, coupled by id. These and others will be enforced in the initial states we use and in the rules that govern the system.

Let us consider now the dynamics of the system. A processor starts sending a read or write order. Its cache, and maybe others, reacts in a number of ways, depending on where the information is stored. There are ten possible cases a cache must be ready to react to: from its processor it can receive a read or a write order; from the bus it can snoop a read or a write being performed on another cache, or also an invalidate signal (to be explained soon). Each of these five cases unfolds into two, as we need to separately consider a *hit*, that happens when the order the cache receives refers to the memory address that the cache is already storing, and a *miss*, which is the opposite.

First, this is the way a new processor and cache may come into existence:

```
var Id : ChipId .  var SC : StateContents .
crl [add] : { Id SC }
          => { s(Id) cpu(s(Id), false) cache(s(Id), inv, line(0, 0)) SC }
          if allCpusBusy(SC) .
```

The function allCpusBusy checks that each existing processor is waiting for an answer. So, we can only add a processor when all others are busy. These are the ways a processor sends an order to its cache:

```
vars N N' : Nat .       vars NS NS' : NatSet .  var Md : Mode .
vars A A' : Address .   var  MM : Memory .
crl [read] : { cpu(Id, false) aRange(N ; NS) SC }
           => { cpu(Id, true) read(Id, N) aRange(N ; NS) SC }
           if not hasBusMsg(SC) .
crl [write] : { cpu(Id, false) aRange(N ; NS) dRange(N' ; NS') SC }
            => { cpu(Id, true) write(Id, line(N, N'))
                 aRange(N ; NS) dRange(N' ; NS') SC }
            if not hasBusMsg(SC) .
```

The condition in the rules ensures that bus messages are dealt with before any other action takes place.

We review next some of the ways in which the system can react to an order. Specially simple are the cases for bus misses. On snooping these, a cache would think: "Someone is reading from or writing to or invalidating an address I don't have stored, so I have nothing to do." Therefore, we include no rule for this case. For a more complex case, consider the "processor write hit." On detecting this, a cache in mode shr would think: "My processor needs to write to a line I already have stored. I will just write the new data. But, as this is the first time I modify this line, I will ask the bus to send an *invalidate* signal, so that other caches are aware that some change has happened. And I will change to mdf."

```
crl [write-hit] :
    { cpu(Id, true) cache(Id, Md, line(A, D)) write(Id, line(A, D')) SC }
 => { cpu(Id, false) cache(Id, mdf, line(A, D'))
      (if Md == shr then invalidate(Id, A, SC) else SC fi) }
 if not hasBusMsg(SC) .
```

The invalidate function simulates the workings of the bus and the snooping caches, running through the state to find caches that need to be invalidated:

```
op invalidate : ChipId Address StateContents -> StateContents .
ceq invalidate(Id, A, cache(Id', Md, line(A, D)) SC) =
    cache(Id', inv, line(0, 0)) invalidate(Id, A, SC) if Id =/= Id' .
eq invalidate (Id, A, SC) = SC [owise] .
```

For a "processor read miss" the cache must react like this:

```
crl [read-miss] : { MM cache(Id, Md, line(A, D)) read(Id, A') SC }
              => { (if Md == mdf then update(MM, line(A, D)) else MM fi)
                   cache(Id, Md, line(A, D)) bus-read(Id, A') SC }
              if A =/= A' /\ not hasBusMsg(SC) .
```

The processor needs to read an address A' that is not the one stored now in its cache. The cache puts in the system a message bus-read, asking for the needed data. When the answer is finally received, cache contents are going to be overwritten, so if cache was in mode mdf, that is, if it had the only valid copy of its data, it has to copy its line to main memory (*eviction* is the technical term for this action). That is what the update function is for.

Now, when a mdf cache sees a bus-read order for the address it is storing, it copies its data to main memory and produces the answer.

```
crl [bus-read-hit] : { MM cache(Id', mdf, line(A, D)) bus-read(Id, A) SC }
                  => { update(MM, line(A, D)) cache(Id', shr, line(A, D))
                       bus-hereur(Id, line(A, D)) SC }
                  if Id =/= Id' .
```

In case no mdf cache has the data, it is the main memory who must answer to the bus-read, through a rule not shown here. By the way, the previous rule is a simplification of the standard MSI, as caches cannot usually communicate directly data to each other. The reading cycle ends with these two rules:

```
rl [bus-read-done] : { cache(Id, Md, L) bus-hereur(Id, L') SC }
                  => { cache(Id, shr, L') hereur(Id, L') SC } .
rl [read-done] : { cpu(Id, true) hereur(Id, L) SC }
             => { cpu(Id, false) SC } .
```

To begin with model-checking tasks, we wonder first whether invalidating is really needed. Namely: if we remove invalidation from our system, is coherence still guaranteed? This is more intuitive if viewed as a question about the safety formula **A G** coherent, but we use its negation, as our model checker only accepts guarantee formulas. We redefine invalidate to an identity in its third argument, and define a coherent proposition (after importing EXTENDED[MSI]):

```
op coherent : -> StateProp [ctor] .
```

```
ceq { cache(Id, shr, line(A, D)) cache(Id', shr, line(A, D')) SC }
    |= coherent = false if D =/= D' .
ceq { cache(Id, shr, line(A, D)) {{line(A, D')}} SC }
    |= coherent = false if D =/= D' .
eq { SC } |= coherent = true [owise] .
```

We ask our brand-new model checker whether coherence can be violated

```
(ismc [8] init |= exists F NOT coherent .)
```

from this initial state:

```
op init : -> State .
eq init = { cpu(1, false) cache(1, mdf, line(1, 2))
            cpu(2, false) cache(2, inv, line(0, 0))
            2 {{line(1, 1)}} aRange(1 ; 2) dRange(1 ; 3) } .
```

We get a Yes and a witness computation ending in this state:

```
{ {{line(1, 1)}} aRange(1 ; 2) dRange(1 ; 3) 2
  cpu(1, true) cpu(2, true) cache(1, mdf, line(1, 1))
  cache(2, shr, line(1, 2)) bus-read(1, 2) hereur(2, line(1, 2)) }
```

So, yes, invalidating is necessary, and we restore it to go on. The question in this example is a reachability one and does not use propositions on transitions, so its result can be achieved as well with Maude's `search` command.

Next, we consider this initial state:

```
op init2 : -> State .
eq init2 = { cpu(1, false) cache(1, mdf, line(1, 3))
             cpu(2, true) cache(2, inv, line(0, 0)) read(2, 1)
             2 {{line(1, 1)}} aRange(1) dRange(4) } .
```

Processor 2 wants to read the contents of memory address 1. That information is stored in the main memory, but it is cache 1 who has the only valid value. We want to check that, eventually, cache 2 receives `line(1, 3)`. With `aRange(1)` and `dRange(4)`, we include the possibility for processors to initiate new reads or writes to address 1 with a different value 4; this is not a big range of possibilities, but it is all we need to try to interfere with the reading.

We model check this:

```
(ismc [10] init2 |= forall F readdone(2, line(1, 3)) .)
```

for this parametric proposition on transitions:

```
var Ln : Line .   var C : Context$State .   var L : Qid .   var Sb : Subst .
op readdone : ChipId Line -> TransProp [ctor] .
eq {Cn | 'read-done : ('Id \ Id) ; ('L \ Ln) ; Sb}
    |= readdone(Id, Ln) = true .
eq {C | L : Sb} |= readdone(Id, Ln) = false [owise] .
```

Unfortunately, it produces a No after finding a looping computation in just four steps. The problem is clearly unfairness: the system is only paying attention to processor 1, or creating new processors. This example shows model checking with an infinity of reachable states and with a proposition on transitions, which puts it out of the scope of other existing tools. Some other model-checking tasks at different levels of abstraction are shown in [18].

Unfortunately, slight increases in the number of caches tend to cause large increases in the time needed for the checking to complete. On the other hand, it is known that most design flaws can often be found using small systems.

9   Related Work

Model Checking TLR*. The papers [6,3,4,5] are all related to model checking Maude modules with LTLR formulas. The logic LTLR is the linear sublogic of TLR*, that is, formulas with no path quantifiers taken to be universally quantified on paths. In [6] the authors implement a translation, already described in [20], that allows the use of Maude's LTL model checker (see [11] for explanations on this model checker). The idea is the following: we are given a rewrite system $\mathcal{R}$, with an initial state on it, and a LTLR formula as parameters to perform model checking on them. From $\mathcal{R}$ we produce a new system, equivalent to $\mathcal{R}$ in an appropriate way, whose states store, in addition to its own information, also data on the transition that took the system to them. In parallel, we translate the given LTLR formula to a LTL formula with equivalent semantics. The produced system satisfies the produced formula iff the given system satisfies the given formula [20]. Looking for better performance, [3] implements a different algorithm for LTLR model checking in C++, by modifying the implementation of Maude's LTL model checker.

The papers [4,5] show how fairness constraints can be included in the system specification, and how to model check LTL or LTLR formulas taking these constraints into account in the very algorithm. Moreover, these papers show how to use *parameterized* fairness properties, that allow the user to specify which entities of the system have to be treated with fairness and which others we do not care about.

None of these model checkers works for systems with an infinity of reachable states.

Infinite Systems. Model checking on infinite systems has been the subject of many studies. Most of them look for either an abstraction that turns the system finite, or a way to finitely represent the elements that compose the system.

Abstraction is a well-known mechanism to make the size of a system smaller, where *smaller* can even mean finite from infinite. See [21] for an approach within rewriting logic. The idea of abstraction is grouping together states that, though different, are indistinguishable to the formula we are model checking. In this respect, model checking on timed systems often uses *time regions* with the same idea: instead of using time *instants*, use well-chosen time *intervals*, taking care that the given temporal formula is not able to tell apart two instants on the same interval.

In the way of finite representability, the method of *well-structured transition systems* has proved useful [1,15]. A well-structured transition system is one in whose infinite set of states a well-quasi-ordering has been defined. A well-quasi-ordering is a reflexive and transitive relation such that no infinite strictly decreasing sequence exists. In a well-structured system certain sets (so called *upward-closed sets*) of states are finitely representable. These sets are enough to provide algorithms to solve some model-checking problems. The reference [15] lists a collection of natural examples for which a well-quasi-ordering exists.

The papers [13,2] describe a narrowing-based approach to model checking rewrite systems in which terms with variables are used as patterns to represent and let evolve whole sets of states. Also, abstraction and *folding relations* (similar to the quasi-orderings of well-structured transition systems) are used.

As explained below, the advantage of our own method is that it does not need to find relations and prove they are appropriate, but uses the raw system as it is given.

Strategies. Strategies do not seem to have been used as a means to model checking before. However, they are present in several languages. In Maude, there is a rich strategy language; see [17], for instance. In some sense, that is a more powerful strategy language than the one presented in this paper, although none of them contains the other. In [22] strategies are used in the framework of program transformation (like for refactoring, compiling, optimization). In particular, they use Stratego, a language for program transformation based on rewriting and strategies. ELAN, described for instance in [8], is a rewriting-logic language. Both ELAN and Stratego have strategies included in the language, while in Maude system modules and strategy modules are separated syntactic entities.

10   Conclusions and Future Work

Several subjects related to system specification and verification have got roles in this work: rewriting logic (and Maude) as a specification formalism, rewriting logic (and Maude) as a software development tool, state-based and action-based temporal logics and TLR*, guarantee and safety properties, strategies applied to nondeterministic systems, and model checking on infinite systems. We have introduced all of them. We have implemented a strategy language and shown how it can be used to model check TLR* guarantee formulas on possibly infinite systems by first translating them into strategy expressions. Finally, we have proved the usefulness of the tool verifying the MSI cache coherence protocol.

Our model checker has a unique combination of three ingredients: it admits propositions on transitions (and states), bounded search on finite or infinite systems (even with an infinity of reachable states), and existential or universal quantification on paths. Maude's `search` command works in a bounded way, but lacks the other ingredients; Maude's built-in model checker for LTL does not have any of the three; and the LTLR model checkers cited above allow propositions on transitions, but not the other two.

An explicit-state model-checking procedure on infinite systems cannot be expected to produce a definitive answer in all cases, and cannot be expected either to provide the best performance. However, the point is that our model-checking procedure is available almost for free as soon as the system is specified. Quoting

Meseguer, talking about an example presented in [20], "all such efforts to obtain a tractable finite-state abstraction, and the associated theorem proving work to check confluence, coherence and preservation of state predicates for the abstraction, are not even worth it; since this simpler analysis of the system specification has already uncovered a key flaw." Thus, we think explicit-state model checking deserves a place in an infinite-system verification toolbox.

Several improvements and lines for additional work are possible. A C++ implementation in search for better performance is an obvious thing to do. In a different line, we already have loop detection, that is, detection of repeated (state, strategy) pairs on the same path. But, when repetition occurs in different branches, we are not ready to detect it. For some systems, this would provide a drastically improved performance. Also some other tools can be offered to the user: abstraction, well-structured transition systems, and partial order reduction. To this end, means should be implemented to allow the user specify, respectively, when two different states can be considered equivalent to the current model-checking task, or when they are related by the well-quasi-ordering, or when two transitions are independent, so that only one way to order and perform them has to be taken into account. The reference [14] has proposals on how to implement partial order reduction in rewrite systems.

Acknowledgments. We thank José Meseguer for motivating this research and showing us its initial foundations; Fernando Rosa for answering our questions about model checking and suggesting us readings and examples; and the anonymous referees for their helpful suggestions to improve this paper.

References

1. Abdulla, P.A., Cerans, K., Jonsson, B., Tsay, Y.-K.: General decidability theorems for infinite-state systems. In: LICS, pp. 313–321. IEEE Computer Society Press (1996)
2. Bae, K., Escobar, S., Meseguer, J.: Abstract logical model checking of infinite-state systems using narrowing. In: van Raamsdonk, F. (ed.) RTA. LIPIcs, vol. 21, pp. 81–96. Schloss Dagstuhl - Leibniz-Zentrum fuer Informatik (2013)
3. Bae, K., Meseguer, J.: The linear temporal logic of rewriting Maude model checker. In: Ölveczky, P.C. (ed.) WRLA 2010. LNCS, vol. 6381, pp. 208–225. Springer, Heidelberg (2010)
4. Bae, K., Meseguer, J.: State/event-based LTL model checking under parametric generalized fairness. In: Gopalakrishnan, G., Qadeer, S. (eds.) CAV 2011. LNCS, vol. 6806, pp. 132–148. Springer, Heidelberg (2011)
5. Bae, K., Meseguer, J.: Model checking LTLR formulas under localized fairness. In: Durán, F. (ed.) WRLA 2012. LNCS, vol. 7571, pp. 99–117. Springer, Heidelberg (2012)
6. Bae, K., Meseguer, J.: A rewriting-based model checker for the linear temporal logic of rewriting. Electr. Notes Theor. Comput. Sci. 290, 19–36 (2012)
7. Biere, A., Cimatti, A., Clarke, E.M., Strichman, O., Zhu, Y.: Bounded model checking. Advances in Computers 58, 117–148 (2003)

8. Borovanský, P., Kirchner, C., Kirchner, H., Moreau, P.-E.: ELAN from a rewriting logic point of view. Theoretical Computer Science 285(2), 155–185 (2002)
9. Bruni, R., Meseguer, J.: Semantic foundations for generalized rewrite theories. Theoretical Computer Science 360(1-3), 386–414 (2006)
10. Clarke, E.M., Grumberg, O., Peled, D.: Model checking. MIT Press (2001)
11. Clavel, M., Durán, F., Eker, S., Lincoln, P., Martí-Oliet, N., Meseguer, J., Talcott, C.L.: All About Maude - A High-Performance Logical Framework, How to Specify, Program and Verify Systems in Rewriting Logic. LNCS, vol. 4350. Springer, Heidelberg (2007)
12. De Nicola, R., Vaandrager, F.W.: Action versus state based logics for transition systems. In: Guessarian, I. (ed.) Semantics of Systems of Concurrent Processes. LNCS, vol. 469, pp. 407–419. Springer, Heidelberg (1990)
13. Escobar, S., Meseguer, J.: Symbolic model checking of infinite-state systems using narrowing. In: Baader, F. (ed.) RTA 2007. LNCS, vol. 4533, pp. 153–168. Springer, Heidelberg (2007)
14. Farzan, A.: Static and Dynamic Formal Analysis of Concurrent Systems and Languages: A Semantics-Based Approach. PhD thesis, Department of Computer Science, University of Illinois at Urbana-Champaign (2007)
15. Finkel, A., Schnoebelen, P.: Well-structured transition systems everywhere! Theor. Comput. Sci. 256(1-2), 63–92 (2001)
16. Hennessy, M., Milner, R.: Algebraic laws for nondeterminism and concurrency. Journal of the ACM 32(1), 137–161 (1985)
17. Martí-Oliet, N., Meseguer, J., Verdejo, A.: Towards a strategy language for Maude. In: Martí-Oliet, N. (ed.) Proceedings of the Fifth International Workshop on Rewriting Logic and its Applications, WRLA 2004, Barcelona, Spain, March 27-April 4. Electronic Notes in Theoretical Computer Science, vol. 117, pp. 417–441. Elsevier (2004)
18. Martín, Ó.: Model checking TLR* guarantee formulas on infinite systems. Master's thesis, Facultad de Informática, Universidad Complutense de Madrid (July 2013), http://maude.sip.ucm.es/ismc
19. Meseguer, J.: Conditional rewriting logic as a unified model of concurrency. Theoretical Computer Science 96(1), 73–155 (1992)
20. Meseguer, J.: The temporal logic of rewriting. Technical Report UIUCDCS-R-2007-2815, Department of Computer Science, University of Illinois at Urbana-Champaign (2007)
21. Meseguer, J., Palomino, M., Martí-Oliet, N.: Equational abstractions. Theoretical Computer Science 403(2-3), 239–264 (2008)
22. Visser, E.: A survey of strategies in program transformation systems. Electr. Notes Theor. Comput. Sci. 57, 109–143 (2001)
23. VMware. vSphere Virtual Machine Administration (update 1, ESXi 5.1, vCenter Server 5.1), http://pubs.vmware.com/vsphere-51/topic/com.vmware.ICbase/PDF/vsphere-esxi-vcenter-server-511-virtual-machine-admin-guide.pdf

Towards a Combination of CafeOBJ and PAT

Yongxin Zhao[1], Jinsong Dong[1], Yang Liu[2], and Jun Sun[3]

[1] School of Computing, National University of Singapore, Singapore
[2] Nanyang Technological University, Singapore
[3] Singapore University of Design and Technology, Singapore

Abstract. In the quest for tractable formal methods to improve the practice of software engineering, both CafeOBJ [7] and PAT[1] [12] have made great achievements based on different formal techniques. CafeOBJ has an evident advantage in specifying concurrent systems with object-oriented methods and proving behavioral properties based on reusability of proof. However, it is difficult to be applied to automatically verify some LTL based properties which involve complex state updates and finite path of states. Conversely, PAT offers great flexibility to simulate system behaviors and support modeling checking various properties, but it is difficult to prove behavioral properties directly, the definition of which is based on the structure of contexts. In the paper, we attempt to combine the two approaches by modeling specifications and verifying properties in CafeOBJ and PAT. A keyless car system is provided to illustrate our approach.

1 Introduction

Formal methods with rigorously mathematical description and verification techniques are considered as approaches to ensure system requirements always correct and satisfied in the full development process from specification to implementation [9]. In the quest for tractable formal methods to improve the practice of software engineering, both CafeOBJ [7] and PAT [12] have made great achievements based on different formal techniques. CafeOBJ is a multi-paradigm specification language equipped with verification methodologies based on algebraic specification technique [5] while PAT [11] is a self-contained framework to support composing, simulating and verifying software systems based on model checking technique.

Object-oriented technique is one of the most promising modeling and programming techniques for complex and critical system development. CafeOBJ enhances formal methods with object-oriented techniques to achieve the modularity and reusability power. Thus it has an evident advantage in specifying concurrent systems with object-oriented methods. Further, CafeOBJ supports not only the reusability of specification code but also the reusability of proofs. The behavioral equivalence of composing object can be proved by reusing the

---

[1] PAT represents Process Analysis Toolkit.

S. Iida, J. Meseguer, and K. Ogata (Eds.): Futatsugi Festschrift, LNCS 8373, pp. 151–170, 2014.
© Springer-Verlag Berlin Heidelberg 2014

proof of that for the composing objects, which facilitates to prove behavioral properties of the system.

However CafeOBJ is not designed to be applied to automatically verify LTL based properties which involve complex state updates and finite path of states. Some safety properties like invariant properties can be done by structural induction on module operators using an interactive approach. LTL based properties may be verified based on observational transition systems (OTSs) which can be used as mathematical models of designs for systems. In some situations, more complex types of hidden objects are needed, such as semantic configuration, path of states and sequence of actions. All of them are usually expected to be constructed from scratch by the users. Further, the LTL formula are not directly verified since its syntax are not supported in CafeOBJ. For these reasons, users often need to encode the algorithm by themselves. Thus it is necessary to incorporate other tools for effective verification of the LTL properties.

PAT is an extensible and modularized framework [11,12,13], which allows user to build customized model checkers easily. It provides a library of model checking algorithms as well as the support for customizing language syntax, semantics, model checking algorithms and reduction techniques, graphic user interfaces, and domain specific abstraction techniques. At present, PAT has successfully modeled and verified a variety of systems, which shows that PAT is capable of verifying systems with a number of states and outperforms the popular model checkers in many cases. But it is difficult to prove behavioral properties directly, the definition of which is based on the structure of contexts. For some specified behavioral properties, PAT may handle with them by adding extra processes.

Consequently, we attempt to combine the two approaches by modeling and verifying specification using CafeOBJ and PAT. The combination leverages their respective advantages of CafeOBJ and PAT. On one hand, the combination supports describing object-oriented specification and prove behavioral properties easily using CafeOBJ's capability. On the other hand, it facilitates analyzing and verifying the specification based on the simulation and verification power of PAT. The key point of combination depends on the translation from CafeOBJ specification to a CSP# [11] model. We propose a semantic link that can identify a CafeOBJ module with a CSP# process and the object composition with process composition operators. Further, following the OTSs' method in [3], for each method in CafeOBJ module, we describe its behaviors by a conditional transition rule and the corresponding *effective* condition. The former is generally expressed as a data operation attaching to an event and the latter is described as boolean guard in CSP#. In sum, all of these contribute to the generation of CSP# model from the CafeOBJ specification.

The remainder of the paper is organized as follows. Section 2 briefly introduces CafeOBJ and PAT and describes the push-button keyless system. In Section 3, the object-oriented algebraic specification of the keyless car system is described and specified in CafeOBJ, and then we prove behavioral properties in CafeOBJ in Section 4. Section 5 verifies the related temporal properties of the specified specification, which provides a possibility of combining CafeOBJ and PAT. Finally, Section 6 presents the future work and concludes the paper.

2   Preliminaries

In this section, we firstly give a brief description of CafeOBJ and PAT respectively, by covering their most important and distinct features used in this paper. Complete details are available in their respective documents [1,13]. And then, we explain the push-button keyless system.

2.1   CafeOBJ

As a successor of OBJ [10,8,14], CafeOBJ is an executable formal algebraic specification language, which provides an elegant declarative way of algebraic programming to incorporate several algebraic specification paradigms such as equational specification, rewriting logic specification and behavior specification. The underlying logics of CafeOBJ consist of *many sorted algebra*, *order sorted algebra*, *hidden algebra* and *rewriting logic*, which form the so called CafeOBJ cube with respect to institution embedding, i.e., the Grothendieck institution of the indexed institution [2].

CafeOBJ has a natural advantage in specifying concurrent systems with object-oriented methods due to its modularity and reusability power. Inherits from OBJ, CafeOBJ has a powerful module system which supports several kinds of imports, shared for multiple imports, parameterized modules and module expression. More importantly, depending on where one module appears or what it contains, the users can choose different semantics for the module, i.e., tight (initial) and loose semantics. The former, declared by module!, denotes a unique model while the latter, denoted by module*, indicates a class of models which is generally employed to act as a parameter or define behavioral properties.

In actual, each module denotes order-sorted algebra, each of which embodies several kinds of objects and operators defined among them, whose meanings are specified by equational specification. A set of objects with some common properties is defined as a *sort*. CafeOBJ provides two kinds of sorts called *visible sorts* and *hidden sorts*. A visible sort is declared with [name] and it is generally used to define data type. A hidden sort is introduced by *[name]* and the corresponding hidden algebra over the hidden sort facilitates users to specify encapsulated objects. Further, models can be imported by using protecting, extending, using and including. A simple example is listed in the following.

```
module* OWNER-ID {
    -- declarations of sorts
    [ Oid ]
    -- declarations of operators
    op defoid : -> Oid
```

}

This defines a loose module named OWNER − ID, which specifies a visible sort Oid and an operator (actually a constant) defoid. No more property of Oid is defined except that it at least contains a constant defoid. The lines that start with −− are comments which will be displayed when the module is input to the CafeOBJ tool. The examples which contain more basic constructs of a module will be illustrated in subsequent sections. In summary, we list the subset of CafeOBJ that is sufficient for writing a specification in this paper.

1 . Module (loose and tight)
2 . Parameterized module
3 . Comment
4 . Import feature
5 . Sort declaration (visible and hidden)
6 . Operator and behavior operator
7 . Attribute and method
8 . Variable declaration
9 . Equation declaration and its label
10 . Predicate and transition

2.2 Process Analysis Toolkit (PAT)

PAT is a self-contained framework to support composing, modeling, simulating and verifying concurrent, real-time systems and other possible domains. It offers featured model editor, animated simulator and various verifiers. The editor provides a user friendly editing environment to develop system models. The simulator enables users to interactively and visually simulate system behaviors using facilities such as by random simulation, user-guided step-by-step simulation, complete state graph generation, trace playback, counterexample visualization, etc. The verifiers implement various model checking techniques catering for different properties such as deadlock-freeness, divergence-freeness, reachability, LTL properties with fairness assumptions, refinement checking and probabilistic model checking [17]. Further, to achieve good performance, advanced optimization techniques are implemented in PAT, e.g., partial order reduction, symmetry reduction, process counter abstraction, parallel model checking.

CSP#[11,15,16], as PAT's specification language, offers great modeling flexibility and efficient system verification by integrating high level CSP-like operators with low level sequential programs constructs such as assignments and while loops. A CSP# model may consist of definitions of constants, variables and processes. A constant is declared with keyword #define followed by a name and a value, e.g., #define *off* 0. A variable is defined with keyword #var followed by a name and an initial value, which may be either a scalar or an array. For example, var *mst* = off indicates a variable *mst* with initial value off and var *opos*[2] : {0..2} defines an array *opos* with 2 elements and each of which ranges over the set 0..2. Part of the syntax of a CSP# process is shown below with short descriptions.

$$
\begin{array}{lll}
P ::= & skip & \text{– termination} \\
& | \ e\{prog\} \rightarrow P & \text{– data operation prefixing} \\
& | \ [b]P & \text{– state guard} \\
& | \ P[\,]Q & \text{– general choices} \\
& | \ P;\ Q & \text{– sequential composition} \\
& | \ P \ ||| \ Q & \text{– interleaving} \\
& | \ ||| \ i : \{m..n\}@P(i) & \text{– indexed interleaving}
\end{array}
$$

where P and Q are processes, e is an event, $prog$ is a sequential program updating global shared variables, b is a Boolean expression and $m..n$ defines a set of natural numbers from m to n. The process $skip$ terminates and does nothing. In process $e\{prog\} \rightarrow P$, $prog$ is executed atomically with the occurrence of event e. Process $[b]P$ waits until condition b becomes $true$ and then behaves as P. For process $P;\ Q$, Q starts only when P has finish. In process $P[\,]Q$, either process P or process Q may execute. $P \ ||| \ Q$ allows processes P and Q to run in parallel, except they communicate with shared variables or synchronous events. In particular, the indexed interleaving extends the interleaving to apply to more than two processes.

PAT supports a number of different assertions to query about system behaviors or properties, denoted by keyword #assert.

- Deadlock: given P as a process, the assertion #assert P deadlockfree checks whether P is deadlock-free or not.
- Reachability: the assertion #assert P reach $cond$ asks whether P can reach a state at which some given condition $cond$ is satisfied.
- Linear Temporal Logic (LTL): PAT supports the full set of LTL syntax, such as $\square$ (*always*) and $\diamond$ (*eventually*). In general, the assertion $P \models F$ checks whether P satisfies the LTL formula F.

2.3   Keyless Car System

One of the latest automotive technologies, push-button keyless system, allows you to start your car's engine without the hassle of key insertion and offers great convenience. Push-button keyless system allows owner with key-fob in her pocket to unlock the door when she is very near the car. The driver can slide behind the wheel, with the key-fob in her pocket (briefcase or purse or anywhere inside the car), she can push the start/stop button on the control panel. Shutting off the engine is just as hassle-free, and is accomplished by merely pressing the start/stop button.

These systems are designed so it is impossible to start the engine without the owner's key-fob and it cannot lock your key-fob inside the car because the system will sense it and prevent the user from locking them in. However, the keyless system can also surprise you as it may allow you to drive the car without key-fob. This has happened to someone when his wife dropped him to his office on the way to a shopping mall but the key-fob was in his pocket. At the shopping mall, when the engine was turned off, the car could not be locked or re-started again. The man had to take a taxi to the mall to pass the key-fob.

3   Modeling Specification in CafeOBJ

In the section, we use CafeOBJ to describe and model the behaviors in the algebraic specification of the keyless car system with object-oriented techniques. Following the method advocated by S. Iida et al. in [6], the keyless system will be divided into six composing objects, i.e., Key, Door, Motor, Cardr, Fuel and Owner[2] which represents the (unique) push-button key-fob, the door of the car, the motor system, the drive state of the car, the fuel and the owner (or user) of the car, respectively. The object Owner will be defined in a parameterized module, which facilitates to prepare a generic reusable module. All these objects, regarded as static objects, can be composed by synchronized concurrent connection.

3.1   Definitions of Modules for Composing Objects

We first show how to specify the module Key in detail. The module KEY−POS is declared to indicate the location status of the key with respect to tight semantics. Constant faralone indicates the key is put outside and far from the car while constant incar represents the key is in the car.

```
module!  KEY− POS {
    [ Kpos ]
    op  faralone :   −> Kpos
    op  incar :   −> Kpos
}
```

Next, we specify a loose module KEY to describe the specification and the behaviors of a key. The clause protecting(KEY−POS + OWNERS−ID) imports the predefined modules KEY−POS and OWNER−ID. According to the manual [1], protecting imports cannot collapse elements or add new elements to the models of the imported modules KEY−POS and OWNERS−ID.

The hidden sort Key, declared with *[Key]*, specifies an encapsulated object of which we can observe the state only by using some operators kowner and kpos. From a methodological perspective from object-oriented techniques, it makes a hidden object look like a *black box*: the insides of the box are hidden from view and operators are on the outside of the box. In general, specifications referring to hidden algebra are called *behavioral* (or *observational*) specifications.

Behavioral operators, denoted as bop, have exactly a hidden sort in their domain, and when the sort in their codomain is hidden they are named method and

---

[2] This kind of decomposition are considered for simplification. Multi-hierarchy decomposition is also supported in our approach.

when it is visible they are named **attributes**. Attributes kowner and kpos indicate the holder and the position of the key respectively. The sort Key provides two methods putincar and putaway to update the position of key and method getkey to change the holder of the key. Using eq or ceq clauses, the equations describe the specification and behaviors of operators. Further, this kind of equational specification is the underlying foundation of algebraic programming and term rewriting system.

All operators defined in CafeOBJ modules are well formed, each of which has a given *rank* defined by its domain and codomain. Actually, all terms in CafeOBJ have a type, which facilitates to do runtime type checking and error handling. Note that for each operator in composing module, we only describe the effect when it occurs and do not specify the condition under which it may do. This approach is significant for our combination of CafeOBJ and PAT, of which the advantages will be interpreted later.

```
module*  KEY {
    − − import modules

    protecting(KEY−POS + OWNERS−ID)

    * [ Key ] *

    op  init−key :   −> Key                − − initial state
    bop putincar : Key −> Key              − − method
    bop putaway : Key −> Key               − − method
    bop getkey :  Oid Key −> Key           − − method
    bop kowner : Key −> Oid                − − attribute
    bop kpos : Key −> Kpos                 − − attribute

    − − declarations of variables

    var ID : Oid
    var K : Key

    − − declarations of equations

    eq kowner(init−key) = defoid .
    eq kpos(init−key) = faralone .
    eq kowner(putincar(K)) = kowner(K) .
    eq kowner(putaway(K)) = kowner(K) .
    eq kowner(getkey(ID, K)) = ID .
    eq kpos(putincar(K)) = incar .
    eq kpos(putaway(ID, K)) = faralone .
    eq kpos(getkey(ID, K)) = kpos(K) .
}
```

Due to the reason of space, for other static objects, we only list their declarations of sorts and operators and the declarations for variables and equations are omitted. The modules DOOR−ST, ENGINE and CAR−ST define the possible status of the door, the motor and the car, which are listed in the Appendix. The module DOOR introduces a hidden sort Door and provides attribute dst to observe the status of every door of Door. Given a state d : Door, method close(d) makes the door closed but unlocked; similarly method open(d) opens the door while lock locks the door.

```
module*  DOOR {
    protecting(DOOR−ST)
    * [ Door ] *
    op init−door :  −> Door
    bop open : Door −> Door
    bop close : Door −> Door
    bop lock : Door −> Door
    bop dst : Door −> Dst
}
```

The module FUEL describes the amount of fuel when the car is used. The attribute fst tells the amount of fuel and the initial amount of fuel is 10 units. The behavior operator longdrive costs 5 units of fuel each time while shortdrive consume 1 unit. Method refill will refuel 10 units of fuel when it is empty.

```
module*  FUEL {
    protecting(INT)
    * [ Fuel ] *
    op init−fuel :  −> Fuel
    bop longdrive : Fuel −> Fuel
    bop shortdrive : Fuel −> Fuel
    bop refill : Fuel −> Fuel
    bop fst : Fuel −> Nat
}
```

The module MOTOR describes the specification and behaviors of the motor of car. The attribute mst gives the status of a motor and the initial state of motor should be off. Methods turnon and turnoff can launch and shut down the engine respectively.

```
module*  MOTOR {
    protecting(ENGINE)
    * [ Motor ] *
    op init−motor :  −> Motor
    bop turnon : Motor −> Motor
    bop turnoff : Motor −> Motor
    bop mst : Motor −> Egn
```

}

The module CARDR describes the specification and behaviors of a car. The attribute cst shows the status of a car and the initial state of car is stopped. Method startdrive can drive a car while method stop stops the car but the engine may be still launched.

```
module∗  CARDR {
    protecting(CAR−ST)

    ∗ [ Cardr ] ∗

    op  init−cardr  :   −> Cardr
    bop  startdrive  :  Cardr  −> Cardr
    bop  stop  :  Cardr  −> Cardr
    bop  cst  :  Cardr  −> Cst
}
```

3.2   Parameterized Module

In this subsection, we will show how to define a generic parameterized module, which can be instantiated by the actual parameter. We first specify the parameterized module USER with formal parameter module TRIV, which is a build-in module in CafeOBJ. The module USER contains three methods gonear, gofar and getin, by which the user can approach a car, go far away from a car or get in a car. The initial operator init−user associates a given element of Elt with a user, which is far from the car initially.

```
module∗  USER(X :: TRIV) {
    protecting(OWNER−POS + OWNER+ID)

    ∗ [ User ] ∗

    op  init−user  :  Elt  −> User
    bop  opos  :  User  −> Opos
    bop  gofar  :  USER  −> USER
    bop  gonear  :  USER  −> USER
    bop  getin  :  USER  −> USER

    var I  :  Oid
    var U  :  USER

    eq  opos(init−user(ID))  =  far  .
    eq  opos(gofar(O))  =  far  .
    eq  opos(gonear(O))  =  near  .
    eq  opos(getin(O))  =  in  .
}
```

After that we can easily declare the module OWNERS by instantiating the formal parameter Elt with Oid and rename the initial operator into init−owner. Note that the actual parameter should be a member of class of algebras defined by module TRIV.

```
mod∗ OWNER {
    protecting(USER (X  <=  view to OWNER−ID { sort Elt  −>  Oid })
                    ∗{ hsort User  −>  Owner,
                        op init−user  −>  init−owner } )
}
```

3.3   Object Composition

In this subsection, we will show how to compose the keyless car system from the objects defined above using *projection* operators. Due to space limit, we only give the specification for some of the operators involving the owner and the key; the others can be similarly defined.

Inspired by the approach advocated in [3], we specify the composed object Keyless in terms of a restricted type of coherent hidden algebra, i.e., observational transition system (OTS) [4]. Every operator defines the conditional transition rule while the corresponding predicate describes the *effective* condition of the operator. When the effective condition is not satisfied, the corresponding operator would not change the state. For example, operator k−putaway defines a transition rule, denoted in equation $[k-3]$, stating that the key would be put far away from the car and the predicate c−putaway indicates the effective condition of k−putaway. The case that the predicate is not satisfied is shown in equation $[k-4]$.

The operators of the composing objects are now reused in describing the equation specification for operators of composed specification. Note that the descriptions of effective conditions in composing objects are undesired since the effective condition for the new operator of the composed objection often depends on the states of several composing objects. In addition, the dependent relation may not be orthogonal. Thus the reusability of effective conditions for composing objects are quite difficult. The separation of behavior and effective condition facilitates to easily express the corresponding model in the PAT framework based on CafeOBJ specification[3] and this can be seen in Section 5.

```
module∗  KEYLESS {
    protecting(OWNER + KEY + DOOR + MOTOR + FUEL + CARDR)
    ∗ [ Keyless ] ∗
    op  init−keyless :  −> Keyless
    bop  k−owner : Oid Keyless  −> Owner
    bop  k−key : Keyless  −> Key
```

---

[3] Actually, this separation is helpful to construct the transition system in CafeOBJ.

bops k−towards k−goaway k−getin k−goout : Oid Keyless −> Keyless
preds c−towards c−goaway c−getin c−goout : Oid Keyless
bops k−putincar k−putaway k−getkey : Oid Keyless −> Keyless
preds c−putincar c−putaway c−getkey : Oid Keyless

vars I I′ : Oid
var K : Keyless

eq [o−1] : k−owner(I, init−keyless) = init−owner(I) .
ceq [o−2] : k−owner(I′, k−towards(I, K)) =
            (if I′ == I then gonear(k−owner(I′, K)) else k−owner(I′, K) fi)
                                        if c−towards(I, K) .
ceq [o−3] : k−towards(I, K) = K if not c−towards(I, K) .
ceq [o−4] : k−owner(I′, k−putaway(I, K)) = k−owner(I′, K) .
ceq [o−a] : c−towards(I, K) = opos(k − owner(I, K)) == far .
eq [k−1] : k−key(init−keyless) = init−key .
ceq [k−2] : k−key(k−towards(I, K)) = k−key(I, K) .
ceq [k−3] : k−key(k−putaway(I, K)) = putaway(k−key(K))
                                        if c−putaway(I, K) .
ceq [k−4] : k−putaway(I, K) = K if not c−putaway(I, K) .
ceq [k−a] : c−putaway(I, K) =
            kowner(k−key(K)) == I and opos(I, k−owner(K)) == far .
}

At last, we list the main steps of specifying the composed module KEYLESS.

1. import the component objects OWNER, KEY, DOOR, MOTOR, FUEL and CARDR.

2. declare a new hidden sort Keyless and several behavior projection operations to connect with the hidden sorts of all the components respectively. The operators are k−owner, k−key, k−door, k−motor, k−fuel, and k−cardr. For example, given a K ∈ Keyless, method k−owner(K) can obtain the object of Owner.

3. define operators on Keyless which describes the behaviors of the keyless car system, such as k−towards and k−putaway. All these operators are related to the corresponding methods of component objects by equations. For example, in clause $o - 2$, the method k−towards of Keyless changes the position of owner I by the method gonear of its component object Owner.

4. introduce predicates to describe the effective conditions under which all the corresponding operators of object Keyless could occur, for instance, when c−putincar is satisfied, it indicates the operator k−putaway could occur, i.e., the key can be put away from the car. Based on projection operations, all the predicates can be checked. For example, in clause $k - a$, it will establish the predicate c−putincar when the holder of the key is far away from the car. Note that the operators k − key and k − owner are projection operations.

4   Proving Behavioral Properties in CafeOBJ

Behavioral properties based on hidden objects are independent from the concrete implementation, whose underlying foundation is so called *behavioral equivalence*, denoted as $=*=$. Informally, two behavioral equivalent states of sort cannot be distinguished under all the observations on attributes after applying any method. Behavioral equivalence is weaker than strict equivalence, and actually it is the largest hidden congruence with respect to behavioral operators.

In previous section, we reuse the code specifications by importing composing objects. Here, we apply a technique of *reusability of proofs* to establish behavioral equivalence of the composed object Keyless, which is supported by the following theorem [5,6].

Theorem 1. *The behavioral equivalence of the composed object T is the conjunction via all the projection operations of the behavioral equivalences of its component objects, i.e., $\forall t_1, t_2 : T \bullet t_1 =*= t_2$ if $\bigwedge\limits_{a \in A} a(t_1) =*_a= a(t_2)$.*

where A defines the set of attributes of composed object and $=*_a=$ is the corresponding behavioral equivalence on attribute a.

Thus we first demonstrate all behavioral equivalence for composing objects. Considering object Key and a relation $=*_k=$ such that $\forall k_1, k_2 : \text{Key} \bullet k_1 =*_k= k_2$ if $\text{kowner}(k_1) = \text{kowner}(k_2) \wedge \text{kpos}(k_1) = \text{kpos}(k_2)$. Thus we can obtain the theorem below.

Theorem 2. *The relation $=*_k=$ is the behavioral equivalence of Key.*

We give the proof using the following CafeOBJ code.

```
module*  BEQ − KEY {

   protecting(KEY)

   op _ =*k= _ : Key Key −> Bool
   vars K1, K2 : Key

   eq K1 =*k= K2 = kowner(K1) == kowner(K2) ∧ kpos(K1) == kpos(K2) .
}


open BEQ−KEY .

   ops k1, k2 : −> Key .
   op id : −> Oid .

   −− hypothesis
   eq kowner(k1) = kowner(k2) .
   eq kpos(k1) = kpos(k2) .

   −− prove  =*k= is a congruence
   red putaway(k1) =*k= putaway(k2) .
   −− excepted to return true
```

```
red putincar(k₁)  =*ₖ= putincar(k₂) .
— — excepted to return true

red getkey(id, k₁)  =*ₖ= getkey(id, k₂) .
— — excepted to return true
```

}

Similarly, we can establish behavioral equivalences for other objects. For each hidden object, the CafeOBJ tool will try to prove behavioral equivalence predicate automatically. If it is satisfied, the system will add the ceq clause for behavioral equivalence predicate; otherwise, we should complete that which is the same as above. According to Theorem 1, we obtain the following theorem below about the behavioral equivalence of Keyless.

Theorem 3. *The relation $R[id]$, derived from composing objects based on projection operations, is the behavioral equivalence of* Keyless *with respect to id.*

Now we can prove a behavioral property stating that given a K ∈ Keyless embodying two owners at least, the result states are not distinguishable no matter who firstly tries to get in the car without respect of their positions, the state of door or the state of car. This property can be denoted as:

$$k-\text{getin}(l, k-\text{getin}(l', K))\ R[I]\ k-\text{getin}(l', k-\text{getin}(l, K))\ \text{and}$$
$$k-\text{getin}(l, k-\text{getin}(l', K))\ R[I']\ k-\text{getin}(l', k-\text{getin}(l, K))$$

where I, I' are the user identifiers.

There are several case analysis involved and we only give one proof of them using the following CafeOBJ code.

open KEYLESS .

```
ops i, i' :  —> Oid .
op k :  —> KEYLESS .
ops d :  —> Door .
ops c :  —> Cardr .

— — hypothesis
eq i =/= i' = true .
eq opos(k — owner(i, k))  = far .
eq opos(k — owner(i', k))  = near .
eq dst(k — door(k))  = opened .
eq cst((k — cardr(i', k))  = stopped .

— — prove the property
red k−getin(l, k−getin(l', K))  R[i]  k−getin(l', k−getin(l, K)) .
— — excepted to return true

red k−getin(l, k−getin(l', K))  R[i']  k−getin(l', k−getin(l, K)) .
— — excepted to return true
```

}

5   Verifying Specification in PAT

In previous sections, we present an algebraic specification for the keyless car system and establish the behavioral equivalence of **Keyless**. Now, we construct the corresponding model in PAT and verifying some properties in the PAT framework.

Table 1. Declaration of constants and variables

#define *far* 0;	#define *near* 1;	#define *in* 2;
#define *incar* − 1;	#define *faralone* − 2;	
#define *unlocked* 0;	#define *locked* 1;	#define *opened* 2;
#define *off* 0;	#define *on* 1;	#define *defoid* 0;
#define *stopped* 0;	#define *moving* 1;	var *opos*[*N*];
var *kpos* = *faralone*;	var *kowner* = *defoid*;	var *dst* = *locked*;
var *mst* = *off*;	var *cst* = *stopped*;	var *fst* = 10;

The construction process can be easily carried out in these steps blew.

1. declare constants in CSP# to correspond with the constants in basic objects such as **KEYPOS** and **ENGINE**.
2. define variables and arrays to correspond with the attributes in modules, for example, declare variable *kowner* for attribute **kowner** and array *opos*[*N*] for attribute **k−owner**., where variable N indicates the current number of owners; then initialize all variables and arrays according to initial operators in CafeOBJ module.
3. for each composing object, we construct a corresponding parameterized CSP# process and the concrete construction method refers to step 4 and 5. These processes are *owner*(i), *key*(i), *door*(i), *motor*(i), *fuel*(i) and *cardr*(i), where i represents the identifier of owner and $P(i)$ indicates the process is related to owner i.
4. considering all pairs of method (k−) and condition (c−) with the same suffix name in object **Keyless**; then divide them into six groups according to their corresponding composing object.
5. for each pair (k−operator, c−operator) in the same group $P(i)$, we first build the CSP# prefix [b]*operator*.i{*prog*}, where b is the corresponding effective condition c−operator and program *prog* describes the corresponding behaviors of k−operator when c−operator is satisfied. Then, we obtain a subprocess branch [b]*operator*.i{*prog*} → $P(i)$. At last, the process for each composing object can be completed by combining all these branches using general choice.
6. combine all the processes using interleaving and indexed interleaving into process *keyless*.

Here, we give the CSP# declarations of variables and constants in Table 1 which correspond to the initial operators and basic visible objects in CafeOBJ. In

PAT, the constants belong to the same sort are distinguished by different values, such as $faralone = -2$ and $in = -1$. The variables derived from the attributes of modules and their initial values are deployed according to the initial operator of modules, for instant, $kpos = faralone$. In particular, array $opos[N]$ is defined and each element is initialized as far.

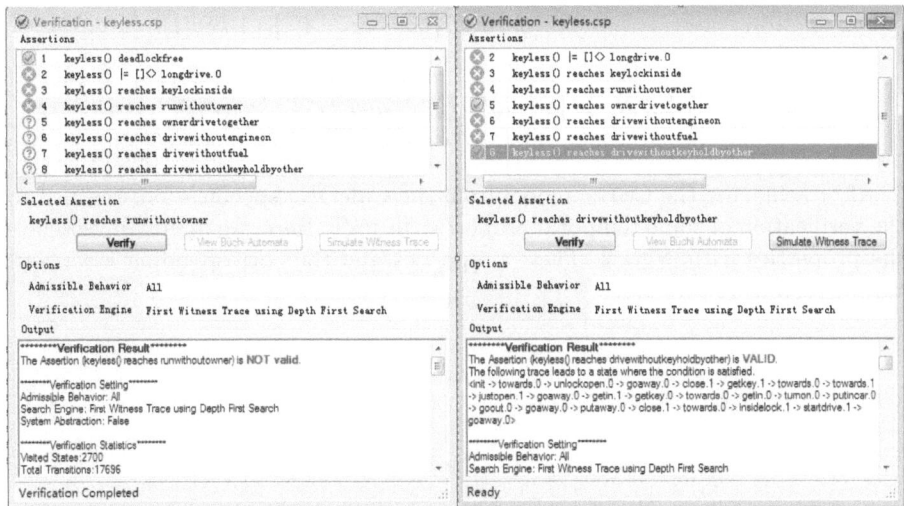

Fig. 1. The verification results

According to steps 3-5 of the construction process described above, 6 corresponding sub-processes are generated from the composing modules and the process $keyless$ are combined by these sub-processes using CSP# operators indexed interleaving. Part of the CSP# processes are listed in the following and others can be found in Appendix. Process $owner(i)$ describes the behaviors of owner with identifier i. Each choice branch denotes one method of object Owner; state guard and data operation respectively define the effective condition and transition rule in CafeOBJ.

$$owner(i) = [opos[i] == far]towards.i\{opos[i] = near; \} \to owner(i)$$
$$[\,]$$
$$[opos[i] == near]goaway.i\{opos[i] = far; \} \to owner(i)$$
$$[\,]$$
$$[opos[i] == near \&\& dst == opened \&\& cst == stopped]$$
$$getin.i\{opos[i] = in; \} \to owner(i)$$
$$[\,]$$
$$[opos[i] == in \&\& dst == opened \&\& cst == stopped]$$
$$goout.i\{opos[i] = near; \} \to owner(i);$$

$$key(i) = [kowner == i\&\&opos[i] == in]$$
$$putincar.i\{keypos = incar; \} \rightarrow key(i)$$
$$[\,]$$
$$[kowner == i\&\&opos[i] == far]$$
$$putaway.i\{keypos = faralone; \} \rightarrow key(i)$$
$$[\,]$$
$$[(keypos == faralone\&\&opos[i] == far) \;||$$
$$(keypos == incar\&\&opos[i] == in)]$$
$$getkey.i\{kowner = i; \} \rightarrow key(i);$$

$$keyless = (|||\; i : \{0..N - 1\}@(motor(i) \;|||\; door(i) \;|||\; key(i) \;|||$$
$$owner(i) \;|||\; fuel(i) \;|||\; cardr(i)));$$

After achieving the CSP# model from the CafeOBJ specification, we turn to the verification of some temporal properties in PAT. Here, we mainly investigate the properties with $N = 2$. These properties and the corresponding assertions can be seen in Figure 2.

```
#define runwithoutowner (cst==moving && opos[0] == far && opos[1] == far);
//can car moving without owner
#define ownerdrivetogether (cst==moving && opos[0] == in && opos[1] == in);
//can ower drives the car
#define keylockinside (kpos == incar && dst == locked && opos[0] != in &&
                                                          opos[1] != in);
  // can key be locked inside
#define drivewithoutengineon (cst==moving && mst==off);
//can car move when engine is off
#define drivewithoutfuel (cst==moving&&fst==0);
//can car move without fuel
#define drivewithoutkeyholdbyother (cst==moving && opos[1] == in &&
                                    opos[0] == far && kowner == defoid);
//car can be driven without key

#assert keyless deadlockfree;
#assert keyless |= []<> longdrive.0;
#assert keyless reaches keylockinside;
#assert keyless reaches runwithoutowner;
#assert keyless reaches ownerdrivetogether;
#assert keyless reaches drivewithoutengineon;
#assert keyless reaches drivewithoutfuel;
#assert keyless reaches drivewithoutkeyholdbyother;
```

Fig. 2. Some properties and assertions in PAT

All these properties can be automatically checked in PAT and the results of the verification are shown in Figure 1. From the result, we can conclude that the keyless car system would be deadlock-free. There may exist a path such that the first owner cannot drive the car for a long time. Actually, the PAT gives one of these paths as a counterexample. It cannot lock your key-fob inside the car and it is impossible to start the engine without the owner's key-fob, which are shown by the unsatisfaction of properties keylockinside and runwithoutowner respectively. The *keyless* model allows the two owner drive the car together. Obviously, it cannot drive the car when the engine is off or the fuel is exhausted. At last, we state that it is possible to drive the car without key-fob in the *keyless* model.

6   Conclusion

In this paper, we give the algebraic specification of the keyless car system in CafeOBJ and investigate the behavioral equivalence of the composed object Keyless and its composing objects, which can be used to prove behavioral properties. Further, the CafeOBJ specification can be transformed into CSP# model and several LTL properties can be automatically verified in PAT.

In the future, a more thorough comparsion of CafeOBJ and PAT will be investigated and we will combine them to model and verify the specification in a consistent and effective way. The transformation from CafeOBJ specification to CSP# will be implemented in a tool.

References

1. Nakagawa, A.T., Sawada, T., Futatsugi, K.: CafeOBJ User's Manual (1997)
   http://ldl.jaiat.ac.jp:8080/cafeobj
2. Goguen, J., Burstall, R.: Institutions: Abstract Model Theory for Specification and Programming. Journal of the Association for Computing Machinery 39(1), 95–146 (1992)
3. Diaconescu, R., Futatsugi, K., Ogata, K.: CafeOBJ: Logical Foundations and Methodologies. Journal of Computers and Artificial Intelligence 22(3-4), 257–283 (2003)
4. Chandy, K.M., Misra, J.: Parallel Program Design: A Foundation. Addison Wesley, Reading, MA (1988)
5. Futatsugi, K.: Formal Methods in CafeOBJ. In: Hu, Z., Rodríguez-Artalejo, M. (eds.) FLOPS 2002. LNCS, vol. 2441, pp. 1–20. Springer, Heidelberg (2002)
6. Iida, S., Matsumoto, M., Diaconescu, R., Futatsugi, K., Lucanu, D.: Concurrent object composition in CafeOBJ. Technical Report IS-RR-98-0009S, Japan Advanced Institue for Science and Technology (1998) (Submitted to publication)
7. Diaconescu, R., Futatsugi, K.: CafeOBJ report. AMAST Series in Computing, vol. 6. World Scientific, Singapore (1998)
8. Futatsugi, K.: An Overview of OBJ2. In: Proc. of Franco Japancse Symp. on Programming of Future Generation Computers, pp. 139C160 (1988)
9. Nissanke, N.: Real time systems. Prentice Hall series in computer science. Prentice Hall (1997)
10. Futatsugi, K., Goguen, J.A., Jouannaud, J.P., Meseguer, J.: Principles of OBJ2. In: Proceedings of the 12th ACM Symposium on Principles of Programming Languages, pp. 55–66. ACM (1985)
11. Sun, J., Liu, Y., Dong, J.S., Chen, C.: Integrating Specification and Programs for System Modeling and Verification. In: TASE, pp. 127–135 (2009)

12. Sun, J., Liu, Y., Dong, J.S., Pang, J.: PAT: Towards Flexible Verification under Fairness. In: Bouajjani, A., Maler, O. (eds.) CAV 2009. LNCS, vol. 5643, pp. 709–714. Springer, Heidelberg (2009)
13. Liu, Y., Sun, J., Dong, J.S.: PAT 3: An EXtensible Architecture for Building Multi-domain Model Checkers. In: ISSRE, pp. 190–199. IEEE (2011)
14. Goguen, J., Winkler, T., Meseguer, J., Futatsugi, K., Jouannaud, J.P.: Introducing OBJ. In: Goguen, J., Malcolm, G. (eds.) Software Engineering with OBJ, pp. 3–167. Kluwer Academic Publishers (2000)
15. Chen, C.Q., Sun, J., Liu, Y., Dong, J.S., Zheng, M.C.: Formal modeling and validation of Stateflow diagrams. Journal of STTT 14(6), 653–671 (2012)
16. Shi, L., Zhao, Y., Liu, Y., Sun, J., Dong, J.S., Qin, S.: A UTP Semantics for Communicating Processes with Shared Variables. In: Groves, L., Sun, J. (eds.) ICFEM 2013. LNCS, vol. 8144, pp. 215–230. Springer, Heidelberg (2013)
17. Sun, J., Song, S., Liu, Y.: Model Checking Hierarchical Probabilistic Systems. In: Dong, J.S., Zhu, H. (eds.) ICFEM 2010. LNCS, vol. 6447, pp. 388–403. Springer, Heidelberg (2010)

Appendix

Some CabeOBJ Specification

```
-- --------------------------------------------
-- Values of OWNER
-- --------------------------------------------
module!  OWNER - POS {
   [ Opos ]

   op  far  :   -> Opos
   op  near :   -> Opos
   op  in   :   -> Opos
}


-- --------------------------------------------
-- Values of DOOR
-- --------------------------------------------
module!  DOOR - ST {
   [ Dst ]

   op  opened   :   -> Dst
   op  unlocked :   -> Dst
   op  locked   :   -> Dst
}


-- --------------------------------------------
-- Values of MOTOR
-- --------------------------------------------
module!  ENGINE {
   [ Egn ]

   op  on  :   -> Egn
   op  off :   -> Egn
}
```

```
-- -----------------------------------
-- Values of CARDR
-- -----------------------------------
module!  CAR - ST {
   [ Cst ]
   op  moving  :  -> Cst
   op  stopped  :  -> Cst
}


-- -----------------------------------
-- KEYLESS
-- -----------------------------------
module*  KEYLESS {
   protecting(OWNER + KEY + DOOR + MOTOR + FUEL + CARDR)
   * [ Keyless ] *
   op  init-keyless  :  -> Keyless
   bop  k-owner  : Oid Keyless  -> Owner
   bop  k-key  : Keyless  -> Key
   bop  k-door  : Keyless  -> Door
   bop  k-motor  : Keyless  -> Motor
   bop  k-fuel  : Keyless  -> Fuel
   bop  k-cardr  : Keyless  -> Cardr
   bops  k-towards k-goaway k-getin k-goout : Oid Keyless  -> Keyless
   preds  c-towards c-goaway c-getin c-goout : Oid Keyless
   bops  k-putincar k-putaway k-getkey : Oid Keyless  -> Keyless
   preds  c-putincar c-putaway c-getkey : Oid Keyless
   bops  k-unlockopen k-justopen k-insideopen : Oid Keyless  -> Keyless
   preds  c-unlockopen c-justopen c-insideopen : Oid Keyless
   bops  k-close k-insidelock k-outsidelock : Oid Keyless  -> Keyless
   preds  c-close c-insidelock c-outsidelock : Oid Keyless
   bops  k-turnon k-turnoff : Oid Keyless  -> Keyless
   preds  c-turnon c-turnoff : Oid Keyless
   bops  k-startdrive k-stop : Oid Keyless  -> Keyless
   preds  c-startdrive c-stop : Oid Keyless
   bops  k-refill k-longdrive k-shortdrive : Oid Keyless  -> Keyless
   preds  c-refill c-longdrive c-shortdrive : Oid Keyless
}


-- -----------------------------------
-- The other CSP proceses
-- -----------------------------------
```

$$door(i) = [kowner == i\&\&opos[i] == near\&\&dst == locked\&\&$$
$$kpos! = incar\&\&cst == stopped]$$
$$unlockopen.i\{dst = opened; \} \to door(i)$$
$$[\,]$$
$$[opos[i] == near\&\&dst == unlocked\&\&cst == stopped]$$
$$justopen.i\{dst = opened; \} \to door(i)$$
$$[\,]$$
$$[dst! = opened\&\&opos[i] == in]$$
$$insideopen.i\{dst = opened; \} \to door(i)$$
$$[\,]$$
$$[dst == opened]close.i\{dst = unlocked; \} \to door(i)$$
$$[\,]$$
$$[dst == unlocked\&\&opos[i] == in]$$
$$insidelock.i\{dst = locked; \} \to door(i)$$
$$[\,]$$
$$[dst == unlocked\&\&opos[i] == near\&\&kowner == i\&\&$$
$$kpos! = incar]outsidelock.i\{dst = locked; \} \to door(i);$$

$$motor(i) = [opos[i] == in\&\&(kowner == i \,\|\, kpos == incar)\&\&$$
$$mst == off\&\&fuel! = 0]$$
$$turnon.i\{mst = on; \} \to motor(i)$$
$$[\,]$$
$$[mst == on\&\&cst == stopped\&\&opos[i] == in]$$
$$turnoff.i\{mst = off; \} \to motor(i);$$

$$fuel(i) = [cst == moving\&\&fst > 1]shortdrive.i\{fst = fst - 1; \} \to fuel(i)$$
$$[\,]$$
$$[cst == moving\&\&fst == 1]shortdrive.i$$
$$\{fst = fst - 1; \; mst = off; \; cst = stopped\} \to fuel(i)$$
$$[\,]$$
$$[cst == moving\&\&fuel > 6]longdrive.i\{fst = fst - 5; \} \to fuel(i)$$
$$[\,]$$
$$[cst == moving\&\&fst == 5]longdrive.i$$
$$\{fst = fst - 1; \; mst = off; \; cst = stopped\} \to fuel(i)$$
$$[\,]$$
$$[fst == 0\&\&mst == off]refill\{fst = 10; \} \to fuel(i);$$

$$cardr(i) = [mst == on\&\&opos[i] == in\&\&cst == stopped]$$
$$startdrive.i\{cst = moving; \} \to cardr(i)$$
$$[\,]$$
$$[mst == on\&\&cst == moving\&\&opos[i] == in]$$
$$stop.i\{cst = stopped; \} \to cardr(i)$$

Negative Variables and the Essence of Object-Oriented Programming

Bertrand Meyer[1] and Alexander Kogtenkov[2]

[1] ETH Zurich
and Eiffel Software (Santa Barbara)
and ITMO National Research University (Saint Petersburg)
Bertrand.Meyer@inf.ethz.ch
[2] ITMO National Research University (Saint Petersburg)
and Eiffel Software (Moscow)
alexk@eiffel.com

Abstract. Reasoning about object-oriented programs requires an appropriate technique to reflect a fundamental "general relativity" property of the approach: every operation is relative to a current object, which changes with every qualified call; such a call needs access to the context of the client object. The notion of negative variable, discussed in this article, provides a framework for reasoning about OO programs in any semantic framework. We introduce a fundamental rule describing the semantics of object-oriented calls, its specific versions for such frameworks as axiomatic (Hoare-style) logic and denotational semantics, and its application to such problems as alias analysis and the consistency of concurrent programs. The approach has been implemented as part of a verification environment for a major object-oriented language and used to perform a number of proofs and analyses.

Keywords: Program logic, operational semantics, object-oriented language.

1 Preamble: The Need for Coordinate Transform

The concept of negative variable, discussed in this article, addresses a specific but important aspect of reasoning about object-oriented programs: the need to obtain reverse access to the context of your caller. Current verification approaches miss it, and hence cannot express certain important properties, let alone verify them. Even for properties that can be expressed otherwise, the negative variable technique provides a simpler and more elegant framework, making automatic verification easier.

A little non-technical example illustrates the issue (all person names are fictitious). Eri likes to party, and has many followers who send her lots of invitations on Twitter, but she is selective. A typical tweet says *"Restaurant Komatsu Yasuke, today at 19:30, Shin also coming"*. But she would like to know more: how many people are invited? Is Junko coming? (If so Eri will stop at home on the way, to pick up a nice bracelet that she has bought for her.) Now whoever is inviting Eri — today Kokichi, say, and tomorrow Taku — could answer these questions; but Eri's procedure for

S. Iida, J. Meseguer, and K. Ogata (Eds.): Futatsugi Festschrift, LNCS 8373, pp. 171–187, 2014.

accepting or skipping an invitation can only be based on the message she has received; she would need access to information available only to the tweet's author.

All she does know is the content of the tweet: place, time, and possibly the name of another person who is also invited. Maybe that person has the other information; but maybe not. The only way to answer the pending questions would be to reach the original tweeter.

This setup, including lack of access to the tweeter's own context, exactly mirrors what happens in the execution of a routine (method) on a target object in an object-oriented programming language. We are considering a "qualified call"

$$\text{call } Eri\text{.}invite \ (Komatsu\_Yasuke, \ [Today, \ ``19:30"], \ Shin) \tag{1}$$

(using an explicit **call** keyword for clarity, although it usually does not appear in programming languages). This call executes the procedure *invite* on the "target object" denoted by *Eri*, with the arguments given. The procedure is declared with the corresponding arguments:

invite (p: PLACE; d: DATE; other_invitee: PERSON)
require ... **do** ... **ensure** ... **end**

To do its work, the procedure can only use the arguments it has; but then it lacks context. For example it cannot answer Eri's question, which we can rephrase in software terms. The question applies to a given object such as the restaurant, accessible to the procedure as the formal argument *p*:

- Is x (some person) also invited to p today? (2)
- How many people are invited to p today? (3)

In a particular call, such as (1), this information is accessible to the calling object, but not to the object on which the call executes.

In the *writing* of object-oriented programs, this restriction is not a major obstacle (otherwise people would have been complaining about it loudly). In fact one can argue that not knowing the caller helps write self-contained, reusable code.

For *reasoning* about OO programs, however, the restriction also exists, and it hurts. For example Müller [13] states, in presenting a proof rule for OO routines:

Req-clauses [shared precondition components] *and* [the rest of the] *preconditions may refer to formal* [arguments], *the object store, and the current universe, whereas the postcondition may only refer to the object store and **result*** [denoting the result of a function].

This information does not identify the caller, and hence does not make it possible to *express* properties such as the above.

The usual technique for modelling qualified calls is to treat the target as if it were a supplementary argument, understanding (1), for example, as **call** *invite*$_C$ (*Eri, Komatsu_Yasuke*, [*Today*, "19:30"], *Shin*) where *invite*$_C$ is the non-OO equivalent to *invite*, extended with one argument, as it would be written for example in the C language (or in the C output of an Eiffel compiler generating C code). Verification techniques will then handle the target just as it handles other arguments, through proof rules that transpose any property of the routine to a property of a call by substituting actual arguments for the formal arguments. This standard approach, however, will fail for properties such as (2) and (3) above, because it ignores the distinctive object-oriented style of programming, detailed in the next section: the target of an OO call is more than just another argument.

The gist of the present paper is a simple notation that addresses the issue: for any call $x.r$ $(args)$, one may use x', called the "negation" of x, to represent a back reference to the calling object, making it accessible to the target object (the object on which r is executed). Negative variables enjoy simple mathematical properties, such as $x.x' = $ **Current** where **Current** denotes the "current object" of execution.

Through the negative variable, any analysis of the call has access to the caller context, enabling it to answer questions such as those in our example: if the caller has (as it must) a list *invited* of persons invited, the call can use the integer $Eri'.invited.count$ and the test $Junko \in Eri'.invited$. More generally, the basic rule for reasoning about calls makes it possible to establish any property for the call $x.r$ $(args)$ by:

- Establishing the property for r $(x'.args)$, that is to say, a call executed locally in the context of the target object, but with access to the caller's context through x'.
- Transposing the result back to the caller's context by prefixing it with "$x.$"; occurrences of x' will normally disappear through the rule just mentioned.

The negative variable technique is an application to formal program analysis of a well-established mathematical technique: coordinate transform. Reasoning about the effect of a call is easier if we transpose the coordinates to the context of the target; then we interpret the results back in the caller context by performing the reverse coordinate transformation.

2   Overview: General Relativity

2.1   In the Space Capsule

The negative variable technique is a response to the special nature of object-oriented programming, based on what has been called a principle of "General Relativity" [10]. This style sets OO programming apart from all other approaches even before one considers inheritance and other advanced techniques (which require it).

What is relative is the meaning of every operation in the program text: it applies to a "current object" ("this", **"Current"**, "self") known only at the time of each execution. In a non-OO language, $x = 3$ states a property of a variable of the program; in an OO language, it states a property of "the x of the current object". The name x by itself is meaningless except with respect to that context.

We can think of the execution of an OO program (see fig. 1 on the next page) as occurring, at any given time, in a space vehicle that operates in its own set of coordinates (the current object). The cosmonauts responsible for executing these operations, and the operations themselves, do not see the larger context in which the vehicle exists. In fact the vehicle was launched from another, itself launched from yet another and so on up to the   initial event that started the entire execution ("root procedure").

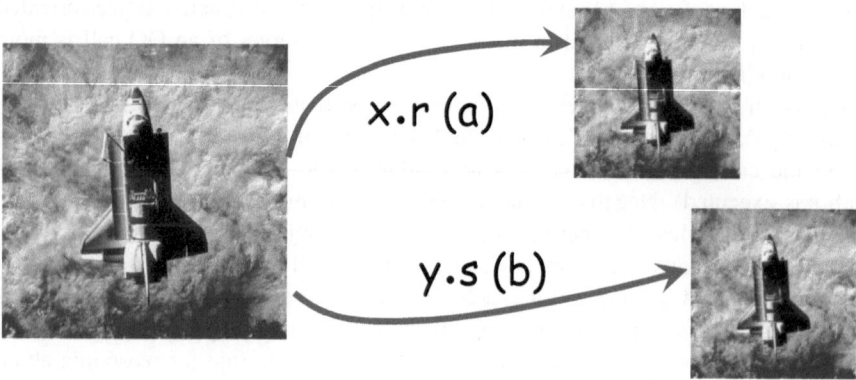

Fig. 1. Objects as space vehicles

2.2   The Execution of an Object-Oriented Program

In an OO language the operations are of two kinds: basic operations (assignments and such, sequenced by control structures such as conditionals and loops) and routine calls.

Every basic operation is relative to a designated object, the "current object" at the time of the operation's execution.

Routine calls have two variants:

- An **unqualified** call, written **call** r (*args*), executes the body of r on the current object, with the given arguments.

- A **qualified** call, written **call** $t.r$ (*args*) causes another object, the **target** of the call, to execute the body of the routine on itself. The target is the object denoted by t at the time of execution. (The term "target" denotes both a static notion, the variable or expression t in the program text, and a dynamic one, the object attached to t in a particular call.)

For all operations of all kinds except one, the current object remains current: such operations execute within the current spacecraft. This is true in particular for unqualified calls. The one exception is qualified call. More precisely:

- At the start of a qualified call, the target object (the object attached to t in **call** $t.r$ (*args*)) becomes the new current object. All the operations of the body of r will treat it as their current object.

- At the end of the execution of the qualified call, the formerly current object becomes current again.

This process is recursive since the execution of the routine can execute qualified calls on new targets.

The names of all variables occurring in an operation are understood in relation to the current object; the name t means "the t of the current object". This property applies to basic operations, such as the assignment $t := u$, but also to qualified calls: to determine the target object (target in the dynamic sense) in the call $t.r$ (*args*) requires finding out the value of t (the target in the static sense) relative to the current object.

For generality we assume the Eiffel convention for executing entire programs: the execution consists of creating an instance of a designated "root class" and executing a designated "root procedure" on that target. (In languages with a more traditional "main program" we can posit a fictitious root object and consider the main program as the root procedure. Global variables do not fit well in the OO paradigm and do not exist in Eiffel, but their presence in other languages does not fundamentally affect the discussion.) Any operation is executed as part of a **current call**: the qualified call last started and not yet terminated (or, if there is no such call, meaning that we are at the top level of the execution flow, the root object). The target of that call serves as current object during the execution of the call; we may call it the **current target**, or just "the target", of the current call. The object that was current at the time of the call is the **caller object**, or just "the caller". In the root call the target is the root object and there is no caller (in all other cases there is a caller).

Object-oriented programming languages do not provide access to the caller object. The cosmonauts are in their own vehicle, and may launch new vehicles, but have no information or access to the vehicle that launched them.

For reasoning and verification purposes, we may need such access. If the current call is of the form $x.r$ $(args)$, the negative variable, written x' (x negated), denotes a backward reference to the caller.

2.3   Negative Variable Basics

From an implementation perspective, negative variables are only a fiction, as no backward reference exists in the execution-time structure. Their role is to support reasoning and verification.

The notion was introduced in [11] and [12], in the context of developing the "alias calculus" for automatic may-alias analysis of OO programs; the calculus needs negative variables in the rules for qualified calls. The present work generalizes the original concept, showing that beyond alias analysis it can provide a framework for reasoning about a wide variety of properties of object-oriented programs.

The traditional approach, as noted, treats the target as if it were just one more argument, then applying the usual technique for dealing with arguments to calls: substitution of actuals for formals. This approach ignores the specific role of the target in object-oriented programming. As we have seen, it precludes the very expression of some important properties of the object store; aliasing properties are an example.

Negative variables define a basic semantic rule for handling qualified call, the fundamental operation of object-oriented programming. A simplified version of the rule (the full version appears in Section 5) is, for any property Π of program elements:

$$\Pi\ (x.r\ (args)) = x.\Pi\ (r\ (x'.args)) \tag{4}$$

meaning, informally, that to derive a property of the qualified call $x.r$ (...) we start from a property of the unqualified call r (...), where we interpret the arguments in relation to the calling context, hence the prefixing by x', then plunge the result back into that calling context by prefixing it with x.

We may, as noted, view the technique as coordinate transform. The rule tells us that to reason about a call, we first transport ourselves to the new spacecraft, evaluating Π for an unqualified call to r; in this evaluation, we may need back-access to the caller spacecraft's context, which we obtain by prefixing arguments with x'. Then we perform the reverse coordinate transform, getting everything back to the original context, by prefixing the results with x. As a result the property Π of the unqualified call, be it a value, a set, a list, a relation or a function is reinterpreted in the caller's context. In normal usage the result will no longer contain any occurrence of negative variables, thanks to rules stating that x and x' cancel each other out.

Section 3 further illustrates, through examples, the need for negative variables. Section 4 introduces the notations and conventions. Section 5 introduces the basic rules. Section 6 presents a number of applications; Section 7 provides comparison to previous work and Section 8 describes opportunities for further development.

3   Examples

The usual modes of reasoning about programs cannot be transposed to OO programs without adaptation. Even simple examples bring out the need for different techniques.

Consider classes C (client) and S (supplier). S has a simple argument-less procedure r with the postcondition $m = n$, where m and n are attributes (fields) of S. The procedure may be written as

r

       -- Among other possible effects, make sure that the fields m and n
       -- of the current object have equal values.
  do
       ... Appropriate implementation, including the assignment $m := n$ ...
  ensure
       $m = n$
  end

In C, with x declared of type S, we may call $x.r$. We may deduce properties of such a call from the properties of the routine simply by prefixing the latter with "$x.$"; in this case the postcondition $m = n$ tells us, after actual-formal argument substitution, that the following will hold after the call:

$$x_{\bullet}m = x_{\bullet}n$$

To cover such cases it would suffice to use a naïve adaptation to object-oriented programming of the standard Hoare rule for procedures [6]:

$$\frac{\{P\,(f)\}\ \mathbf{call}\ r\,(f)\ \{Q\,(f)\}}{\{x_{\bullet}P\,(a)\}\ \mathbf{call}\ x_{\bullet}r\,(a)\ \{x_{\bullet}Q\,(a)\}}$$

     -- *Warning*: naïve rule,
     -- corrected in (6) below.

(Conventions: f stands for the list of formal arguments, a for the list of actual arguments; P and Q are explicitly parameterized by arguments, as an alternative to using substitution; we ignore recursion, which can be handled as described in [6]; we also ignore the role of class invariants, essential in practice for OO programs but not directly related to this discussion.)

The "$\textbf{.}$" operator is a "distributed dot" which distributes the period of OO programming, used for calls and "path expressions" such as $x\textbf{.}y\textbf{.}z$ (which in fact are a special case of calls, resulting in this example from applying z to the result of applying y to x) over:

- An equality: $x\textbf{.}(u = v)$ denotes the equality $x\textbf{.}u = x\textbf{.}v$
- A set: $x\textbf{.}\{a, b, c\}$ denotes $\{x\textbf{.}a, x\textbf{.}b, x\textbf{.}c\}$.
- A pair: $x\textbf{.}[y, z]$ denotes $[x\textbf{.}y, x\textbf{.}z]$.
- More generally, a list: $x\textbf{.}[u, v, w]$ denotes the list $[x\textbf{.}u, x\textbf{.}v, x\textbf{.}w]$.
- A relation (a set of pairs): $x\textbf{.}\{[a, b], [c, d]\}$ denotes $\{[x\textbf{.}a, x\textbf{.}b], [x\textbf{.}c, x\textbf{.}d]\}$.
- A function (a special case of relations): if $f(u) = v$ then $x\textbf{.}(f(u)) = x\textbf{.}v$. Another way of denoting this property is to state that $x\textbf{.}(f(\underline{u})) = x\textbf{.}f(x\textbf{.}\underline{u})$. Note the double application of the dot; the reason is that stating that $f(u) = v$ means, if we look at f as a relation, that $[u, v] \in f$. This rule (like the preceding ones) is recursive: u could be, for example, a list.

As soon as we move on to less trivial properties, however, the simple device of prefixing properties by "$x\textbf{.}$" no longer works. Assume that r now has an argument and new postconditions:

$r(u: T)$
   do

      ...

   ensure
      $m\textbf{.}count > 0$
      $u = m$
   end

and we call $x\textbf{.}r(a)$, for a of type T. Application of the naïve rule would give us meaningless properties for the call: $x\textbf{.}m\textbf{.}count > x\textbf{.}0$, where it makes no sense to prefix the constant 0 with "$x\textbf{.}$"; and $x\textbf{.}a = x\textbf{.}m$, where $x\textbf{.}a$ also makes no sense since a is an expression defined in the calling context, C, and prefixing it with x is pointless. We can get away in the first case through a general rule that identifies $x\textbf{.}const$, for any constant $const$, with $const$; but such tricks would not work for more significant properties such as the second postcondition. The problem is not syntactical but conceptual: every expression needs to be interpreted in the right object context (the right space vehicle). The actual argument a belongs to the **client** context (C) whereas m, an attribute of S, makes sense in the context of the **supplier** object.

With negative variables, the correct consequent for the procedure rule, replacing $\{x\textbf{.}P(a)\}$ **call** $x\textbf{.}r(a)$ $\{x\textbf{.}Q(a)\}$ above, is

$$\{x\textbf{.}P(x'\textbf{.}a)\} \textbf{ call } x\textbf{.}r(a) \{x\textbf{.}Q(x'\textbf{.}a)\}$$

stating that the arguments must be interpreted relative to the caller's context, accessible through the (fictitious) back-pointer x'. Applying this rule gives, as the second postcondition of the call:

$$x{\scriptstyle\bullet}x'{\scriptstyle\bullet}a = x{\scriptstyle\bullet}m$$

Then we apply two of the fundamental rules listed below: $x{\scriptstyle\bullet}x' = $ **Current**, and **Current**${\scriptstyle\bullet}e = e$ for any expression e, giving

$$a = x{\scriptstyle\bullet}m$$

which correctly describes the effect of the call.

The example remains sufficiently simple to suggest that other rules could do the job, for example a set of ad hoc rules stating that $x{\scriptstyle\bullet}v = v$ for various kinds of elements v in the caller context. But such an approach fails to capture the "general relativity" property of object-oriented programming discussed in section 2, which implies that every program element or program property makes sense only with respect to a well-defined context. For a call, in particular, a property belongs to the context of either the caller (client) or the supplier. Consider the following new variant of our example routine, now with a precondition:

```
r (u: T)
    require
        u.p + q > 0
    do
        u.set_m (n + 1)
            -- The procedure set_m, in T, sets the value of the attribute m.
    ensure
        u.m = n + 1
    end
```

Consider the call $x{\scriptstyle\bullet}r\ (a)$. By applying the rule we get as a postcondition of the call

$$x{\scriptstyle\bullet}(x'{\scriptstyle\bullet}a){\scriptstyle\bullet}m = x{\scriptstyle\bullet}n + x{\scriptstyle\bullet}1$$

(distributing "$\bullet$" over addition, as justified in Section 4). Simplifying, this yields

$$a{\scriptstyle\bullet}m = x{\scriptstyle\bullet}n + 1$$

Similarly, the precondition making this call legal (assuming, as implied by the example, that p and q are integer attributes of classes T and S respectively) is

$$x{\scriptstyle\bullet}(x'{\scriptstyle\bullet}a){\scriptstyle\bullet}p + x{\scriptstyle\bullet}q > x{\scriptstyle\bullet}0$$

or, after simplification:

$$a{\scriptstyle\bullet}p + x{\scriptstyle\bullet}q > 0$$

Note how $u.p$ refers to a property of the client context and q to a property of the supplier context. The general rule makes it possible to switch back and forth effortlessly between these contexts:

- As stated in the routine, the properties (here a precondition and a postcondition, but the same rules will apply to any kind of a property) are expressed relative to the supplier context. T has access to the client context through the formal arguments which, however, describe an unknown caller.
- When the caller is known, here x, the formal arguments can be transposed back to the client context through prefixing by x', representing a fictitious back pointer.
- The resulting properties are also transposed back to the client context, but in this case through prefixing by x.

This example illustrates only one of the applications of the general approach: the Hoare-style rule. We will now explore the general framework and the general rules.

4   Notations and Conventions

The discussion is applicable to any object-oriented language. We assume an imperative language, with an assignment instruction written *target* := *source*, and routines (methods) that can be functions (returning a result) or procedures (changing the state). Examples of such languages include Java, Eiffel and C#. The imperative character of the language has no influence on the discussion, so the results are also applicable to a functional (applicative) object-oriented language.

We make the assumption that (as in Eiffel) no direct assignment is permitted to fields of an object: rather than $x.a := v$, the programmer must write a procedure call $x.set\_a\ (v)$, with the appropriate setter procedure set_a declared in the corresponding class. (Some languages, such as Eiffel, allow the syntax $x.a := v$ provided the class author has marked the setter procedure as "assigner"; but this instruction is not an assignment, only a different syntactical form of the explicit call $x.set\_a\ (v)$. C#'s "properties" have a similar role.) This restriction, justified by information hiding principles, does not limit the application of the approach to languages that permit direct field assignments: one should simply replace such assignments, for the purpose of program analysis or verification, by the application of a suitable setter.

Among routines we will only consider procedures, with the understanding that a function call can be handled as a procedure call followed by assignment of the result.

Calls, qualified and unqualified, are as discussed in Section 2.2, which also introduced the notions of target and caller objects.

Since the matter of defining the semantics of unqualified calls is independent from the problem tackled in this article, we assume that such a semantic definition exists. The simplest way to define it (depending on the rules of argument passing) is that the semantics of call $r\ (a)$ is the semantics of the *body* of the routine r, after substitution of actual arguments a for formals.

The notation **old** e, for an expression e, denotes the value that e had at the start of the current call. **Current** denotes the current object.

The dot operator is generalized as explained in Section 3, complemented by the convention that if c is a constant then $x.c$ is c. The combination of all the variants allows us to generalize the distributive dot to a wide class of operators:

$$x.(u \boxtimes v) \text{ is } (x.u) \boxtimes (x.v)$$

where $\boxtimes$ is any operator that can be defined from functions, relations, sets, pairs, lists and equality; for example, in a pure OO language, $u + v$ on numerical arguments is simply an abbreviation for the function call $u.plus\ (v)$, so that by application of the second case $x.(u + v)$ is $(x.u) + (x.v)$.

Thus generalized, the dot operator covers, in our experience so far, all the kinds of properties that one may want to express about a program.

5   Negative Variables: Definitions and Rules

For any variable x that may be used as target of a qualified call, the "negation" of x, written x', denotes a reference, defined during the execution of a qualified call of target x, to the object that started this call. (The existence of such an object is traditionally checked at run time, through "null pointer" exceptions, but in some recent languages it has become a static property enforced by the compiler, as in Eiffel's "void safety" mechanism [9]. The present discussion assumes that all calls are void-safe, i.e. pointers are not null.)

The following rules are applicable to any variable x and its negation x', and to any expression e of the target programming language[1]:

N1   **Current'** = **Current**
N2 e.**Current** = e
N3   **Current**.e = e
N4 $x.x'$ = **Current**[2]
N5 $x'.(\textbf{old } x)$ = **Current**
N6   **old** x' = x'

N1 enables us, by application of the call rules that follow, to treat a qualified call of the form **Current**.$r\ (a)$ as equivalent to the unqualified call $r\ (a)$. In N5, note the use of **old**, without which the rule would be unsound since it is in principle possible for a routine r, during the execution of $x.r\ (a)$, to modify (through callbacks) the value of the very variable x that the client object used as target of the current call. Such a setup is of course error-prone; we say that a routine is *nonprodigal* if it cannot modify the target of its own call. For a nonprodigal routine, N5 yields a more practical variant (symmetric with N4):

$$x'.x = \textbf{Current}$$

---

[1] Depending on the rules of the programming language, occurrences of e may have to be enclosed in parentheses to avoid syntactic ambiguity.

[2] Depending on the context $x.x'$ can also be replaced with an implicit current object that is usually omitted, for example, $x.x'.y$ simplifies to y.

N6 expresses that the back link to a routine's caller cannot be changed: your spacecraft was launched by a given spacecraft, and there is nothing you can do about it.

In the application to aliasing, rules N4 and N5 may produce an over-approximation for some cyclic structures. Adding integer indexes can improve the precision. This issue has no influence on the rest of the discussion and is hence not considered further in this article.

The fundamental rule was previewed in Section 3 and will now be given in full. It considers an arbitrary property Π applicable to a program element such as an instruction, an expression, a class or an entire program.

In the initial version, Π had just one argument, the program element. In practice, any realistic framework for reasoning about programs involves properties of *two* arguments: a program element, and an **environment** representing what is already known, or assumed, about the context of the program element's current execution. In static analysis, for example, we may compute the "defined" and "used" variables of a block in relation to the values of these properties for the context in which it is executed. As another example, the alias calculus [11] is a set of rules giving the value of $a » p$ for the various constructs p of an OO programming language; a is an alias relation, consisting of a set of pairs of expressions that may be aliased to each other (denote the same object) at a given program point, and $a » p$ is the new alias relation that results from executing p when the original alias relation is a. In this case the alias relation is the environment.

With this convention, the fundamental rule for reasoning about properties Π of object-oriented programming languages is

$$\Pi \text{ (call } x.r \text{ } (args), env) = x.\Pi \text{ (call } r \text{ } (x'.args), x'.env) \qquad (4)$$

The rule enables us to deduce, from a property of the unqualified call (that is to say, a property that makes sense in the context of the supplier object), the corresponding property of a qualified call (in the client context).

The prefixing by "$x'.$" must be applied to the environment as well as to the actual arguments, since both are relative to the client context.

The rule is applicable to properties for which the prefixing by "$x'.$" is defined, as discussed in section 4. It appears to cover all properties used in existing frameworks for semantics and verification of programs, from static analysis to denotational and axiomatic semantics.

In denotational (and operational) semantics, a common scheme is to define a program construct such as an instruction as a function (usually partial) in *Environment* $\rightarrow$ *State* $\rightarrow$ *State*, preceded by *Arguments* $\rightarrow$ for a routine. The Fundamental Rule applied to this framework gives[3]:

$$\text{call } x.r = \lambda \text{ } args \text{ | } \lambda \text{ } env \text{ | } x.(\text{call } r \text{ } (x'.args) \text{ } (x'.env)) \qquad (5)$$

---

[3] It is common practice to define the semantics through a "meaning function" M, which for any program element p yields a mathematical function M $[p]$, the "denotation" of p. The alternative, used here for simplicity, is to define every construct directly as a mathematical function, skipping the meaning function. The "M" variant is easy to deduce from this form.

In axiomatic semantics, the environment does not need to be explicitly stated since it is embedded in the precondition, postcondition and invariant[4]:

$$\frac{\{P\ (f)\ \textbf{and}\ INV\}\ \textbf{call}\ r\ (f)\ \{Q\ (f)\ \textbf{and}\ INV\}}{\{x_\bullet P\ (x'_\bullet a)\ \textbf{and}\ x.INV\}\ \textbf{call}\ x_\bullet r\ (a)\ \{x_\bullet Q\ (x'_\bullet a)\ \textbf{and}\ x.INV\}} \qquad (6)$$

6   Applications

We now show some potential uses of the rules given.

The alias calculus rule given in [11] is a direct application of the fundamental rule (4). The purpose of the alias calculus is to answer, for any two reference (pointer) expressions e and f and any program point pp at which they are both defined, the question: "can e and f, at any time execution reaches pp, have as their values references to the same object?". To this end, the calculus is a set of rules to compute $a \gg p$ for every programming language construct p, where a is an alias relation, containing all pairs of expressions that may be aliased to each other. If a is the alias relation before execution of p, $a \gg p$ will be the alias relation after that execution. The rule for qualified calls, where l denotes a list of actual arguments, is:

$$a \gg \textbf{call}\ x_\bullet r\ (l) = x_\bullet((x'_\bullet a) \gg \textbf{call}\ r\ (x'_\bullet l\ )) \qquad (7)$$

This rule shows a typical use of the negative variable technique in its full extent. Both the initial alias relation a and the list of arguments l are defined on the client's side (the caller's context). To apply the unqualified call rule on the right side of (7), we must be able to interpret a and l on the supplier side; this is achieved by prefixing both of them with "$x'_\bullet$" to interpret them in the context of the callee. The expression $(x'_\bullet a) \gg \textbf{call}\ r\ (x'_\bullet l\ )$ then gives us the resulting alias relation, but still in the supplier context. To transpose it back to the client context, which is where we need the final result, we prefix that supplier-side relation with "$x_\bullet$", yielding a client-side property.

Here now are examples of application of the axiomatic rule (6). Consider a routine *sign* used to sign a message with a signature computed from a key, according to the specification:

$$\{is\_valid\_key\ (k)\}\ \textbf{call}\ sign\ (k, s)\ \{signed\ (k, s)\}$$

where k is a key and s a message to be signed. Applying the rule (6) to a qualified call

$$\textbf{call}\ x_\bullet sign\ (y, z)$$

where y and z are local variables or attributes, we get

$$\{x_\bullet(is\_valid\_key\ (x'_\bullet y))\}\ \textbf{call}\ x_\bullet sign\ (y, z)\ \{x_\bullet(signed\ (x'_\bullet y, x'_\bullet z))\}$$

which rules N4 and N3 from Section 5 allow us to simplify into

---

[4] This rule implies some conditions on callbacks (to ensure that they satisfy the invariant), an issue separate from the theme of this article.

$$\{x_\bullet is\_valid\_key\ (y)\}\ \textbf{call}\ x_\bullet sign\ (y,\ z)\ \{x_\bullet signed\ (y,\ z)\}$$

reflecting the intuitive result.

Another application area is purity. A routine is pure if it does not modify the state. In the case of *weak* purity [3] it may, however, create and modify new objects. Consider a pure routine r and purity (strong or weak) for r relative to an expression e:

$$\{\ldots\}\ \textbf{call}\ f\ (t)\ \{e == \textbf{old}\ e\}$$

where == expresses deep equality (equality not only of the values themselves but of all reachable objects). Rule (6) yields

$$\{\ldots\}\ \textbf{call}\ x_\bullet f\ (a)\ \{x_\bullet(x'_\bullet e == \textbf{old}\ x'_\bullet e)\}$$

The postcondition can be simplified through distributivity to

$$x_\bullet x'_\bullet e == x_\bullet(\textbf{old}\ x'\ )_\bullet e$$

which through N4, N3 and N6 gives

$$e == \textbf{old}\ e$$

In other words, a qualified call to a pure routine (weak or strong) is itself pure.

The same approach generalizes to a full-fledged frame rule. A frame rule is a specification of which properties an operation may modify; it is typically stated by listing the possibly affected expressions in a **modifies** or **only** clause. (Purity is a special case, expressed as a frame clause with an empty list of attributes.) Consider a routine with such a specification:

$f\ (p\colon X\ ;\ q\colon Y)$
 ...
 ensure
  $a = p$
  $p_\bullet b = q$
  $g_\bullet v = \textbf{old}\ g_\bullet v + 1$
 only
  $a,\ p_\bullet b,\ g_\bullet v$
 end

Ignoring the rest of the postcondition, we may write the frame property in Hoare style as

$$\{\ldots\}\ \textbf{call}\ f\ (p,\ q)\ \{\textbf{only}\ a,\ p_\bullet b,\ g_\bullet v\}$$

The transposition to a qualified call through (6) is

$$\{\ldots\}\ x_\bullet\textbf{call}\ f\ (p,\ q)\ \{x_\bullet(\textbf{only}\ a,\ x'_\bullet p_\bullet b,\ g_\bullet v)\}$$

which after simplification yields

$$\{\dots\}\ x.\mathbf{call}\ f\ (p,\ q)\ \{\mathbf{only}\ x.a,\ p.b,\ x.g.v\}$$

SCOOP, a concurrency model developed for simple and reliable concurrent programming through the safe use of shared resources ([14]), provides another example of application of negative variables. SCOOP binds the concurrency structure to the object-oriented structure by partitioning the object space into a number of "regions", each associated with a given thread of control or "processor", the "handler" of these objects, so that a qualified call $x.r$ $(args)$ is always processed by the handler of the target object (the object denoted by x). If a variable x may denote an object in another region (so that calls $x.r$ $(args)$ will be handled by a different processor), it must be declared **separate**. The SCOOP type system includes a set of rules to ensure consistent semantics. The rules imply in particular that if x is separate the formal arguments corresponding to $args$ must also be declared separate. The reason for this rule is that if the call is executed on behalf of processor A and the processor of x is B, $args$ denotes objects in A, which for B are separate and hence must be declared accordingly. In other words, the notion of separateness is always relative.

Applying this observation to negative variables yields the rule that if the variable x is separate, its negation x' is also separate (if the supplier S is separate from the client C, then C is separate from S).

Then in the application of any semantic rule, for example the axiomatic rule (6), to a call

$$\mathbf{call}\ x.r\ (args)$$

the formal arguments will be prefixed with "$x'.$", since the rules deduce properties of the qualified call from the properties of its unqualified version **call** r $(x'.args)$. This observation indicates that, in the program text, the formal arguments should themselves be declared as **separate** for consistency. This is indeed one the rules of the SCOOP type system. Here we see it arising as a consequence of the general properties of negative variables, without any domain-specific reasoning.

7   Related Work

Even before OO came to the scene, back pointers were used to simplify and optimize the implementation of algorithms working on complex data structures. Such back-pointers, however, are physically present in the corresponding data structures and usually take up memory (although some algorithms, such as the Deutsch-Schorr-Waite stack-free technique for tree or graph traversal, reuse other fields for the temporary representation of back pointers). Any reasoning about and manipulation of such back pointers follows the same rules as for other references and makes no use of their specific nature. Negative variables as discussed in this article are a conceptual mechanism to reason about OO programs; it is not necessary (but of course not prohibited) to turn them into physical components of the data structure representations.

Operating systems have used back pointers for a long time. They serve in particular to keep references to the parent directory in a file system, making it possible to use "..."to refer to the parent directory without knowing the current directory's actual location. OO languages usually do not support such a mechanism for their run-time data structures, since this would require keeping track of the invocation structure. Negative variables give us the concept without requiring its implementation.

Usually the axiomatic semantics of a method call is described using substitution rules of actual arguments to formal arguments, target of a call as the current object, and return value as a result after the call; see in particular the work of Müller, Leino and their colleagues [13] [8] [4]. Negative variables are not explicitly used in these approaches and are not available for formal reasoning on program properties. Meyer's "Calculus of Object Programs" [12] is an exception, integrating the alias calculus [11] and negative variables. Schoeller's path-based alias analysis [16] comes close to the need to use negative variables, but still uses the standard substitution technique to describe the semantics of a qualified method call. Other semantic descriptions of object-oriented languages, such as algebraic specifications [5], also use substitution.

The specifications and subtleties of pure functions are described by Darvas, Müller and Leino in [3] and [4]. We used a simplified version of the specification.

Nienaltowski provides in [14] an analysis of the type requirements for safe concurrent programming and the resulting design of a type system for SCOOP. The approach covers both the attachment (non-nullness) status and the separateness status of the target and arguments of a call. The target's attachment status ensures that a call cannot lead to an exception at run-time. Meyer, Kogtenkov and Stapf address this issue in [9]; in the examples we have taken the assumption of attachment for granted. The other key property presented in [14] can be deduced, as we have seen, from the general rules for negative variables.

Shield [17] makes the current object explicit through a variable *self*. He treats every qualified call as an operation that saves the value of the current object to a stack, and assigns the call's target to *self*. After the call, the original value is restored. The author notes that this technique works for recursive calls only when the stack stores a reference to the current object, not the object itself, on the stack. The present work makes a similar assumption for negative variables.

Research in automatic program verification, particularly around the ESC/Java and JML languages and verification systems, uses the notion of *model fields* [1] or *ghost variables* [2]: variables used only for verification, without influence on the generated code, as in the classic Owicki-Gries approach [15] to the verification of concurrent programs. The variables should be specified by the developer and should be kept in sync with the rest of the program in the annotation sections. The verifier can use the properties of these variables to perform the verification of the actual code. Negative variables have a similar status: useful for reasoning and verification, but not used directly in the program.

Kassios [7] proposes an extension to ghost fields by introducing implicit backpointers that are automatically added to the explicit ghost fields as soon as the corresponding forward field is marked as **tracked**. The back-pointers are really object sets and are used to turn unstable class invariants into stable ones by making sure that data reflecting the references to the given object are always synchronized with the references themselves (the example in [7] uses reference count for this purpose). This approach makes it possible to apply separation logic rules to cases when actual object disjointness is replaced by *observable* disjointness.

Wei Ke at al [18] use a special $-edge in object state graphs to denote a call stack. Whenever a qualified call is made, a new $-edge that points to the current root is created and points from the new root object node. On return the $-edge is removed and the current object is popped from it. Our approach is quite similar but goes beyond graph-based framework and state representation. Moreover, it allows using both – normal and reverse edges indistinguishably in cases when caller's and callee's contexts are to be taken into account, as in alias calculus.

8   Implementation, Discussion and Future Work

We have proposed a simple concept, negative variables, reflecting an essential property of object-oriented computation: the relativity of all program constructs to a "current object" known only at the very last moment during execution. The corresponding fundamental rule, (4), provides a general framework for reasoning about object-oriented programs regardless of the programming language and semantic framework; directly applicable versions of the general rule have been shown for specific frameworks such as denotational (5) and Hoare-style axiomatic (6) semantics, as well as alias analysis. Other examples, such as the application to concurrency, show the generality of the approach.

The mechanisms for dealing with negative variables, particularly in the axiomatic and alias calculus applications, have been implemented in EVE, the research version of the EiffelStudio IDE (integrated development environment) and have been used to prove a number of properties of example programs.

The discussion has not considered some important OO mechanisms such as inheritance, polymorphism, genericity, expanded (value) types, closures (C# delegates, Eiffel agents) and the full extent of concurrency; specific rules may (or not) be needed to handle them. More generally, the use of negative variables in the verification of ever larger object-oriented programs may lead to generalizations of the techniques described here.

Acknowledgments. This work was performed in the ITMO Software Engineering Laboratory, made possible by a grant from the mail.ru group. It also benefited from the ERC Advanced Investigator Grant "Concurrency Made Easy" (ERC no. 291389.)

We are grateful to the anonymous referees for their very useful comments.

It is a pleasure to dedicate this article to Professor Kokichi Futatsugi in celebration of thirty-five years of friendship with the first author (going back to lectures in the same session of the IFIP 78 World Computer Congress in Tokyo under the aegis of Harlan Mills) and of his seminal contribution to the science and practice of software specification as reflected in particular in the CaféOBJ language and system.

References

1. Chalin, P., Kiniry, J.R., Leavens, G.T., Poll, E.: Beyond Assertions: Advanced Specification and Verification with JML and ESC/Java2. In: de Boer, F.S., Bonsangue, M.M., Graf, S., de Roever, W.-P. (eds.) FMCO 2005. LNCS, vol. 4111, pp. 342–363. Springer, Heidelberg (2006)
2. Cohen, E., Moskal, M., Schulte, W., Tobies, S.: Local Verification of Global Invariants in Concurrent Programs. In: Touili, T., Cook, B., Jackson, P. (eds.) CAV 2010. LNCS, vol. 6174, pp. 480–494. Springer, Heidelberg (2010)
3. Darvas, Á., Leino, K.R.M.: Practical reasoning about invocations and implementations of pure methods. In: Dwyer, M.B., Lopes, A. (eds.) FASE 2007. LNCS, vol. 4422, pp. 336–351. Springer, Heidelberg (2007)
4. Ádám, D., Müller, P.: Reasoning about Method Calls in Interface Specifications. Journal of Object Technology 5(5); Special Issue: ECOOP 2005 Workshop FTfJP, pp. 59–85 (June 2006), http://www.jot.fm/issues/issues200606/article3
5. Fronk, A.: An Approach to Algebraic Semantics of Object-Oriented Languages. – Software-Technology. University of Dortmund, Germany (2003), doi:2003/2682
6. Hoare, C.A.R.: Procedures and Parameters, An Axiomatic Approach. In: Symposium on Semantics of Algorithmic Languages, pp. 102–116 (1971), doi:10.1007/BFb0059696
7. Kassios, I.T., Kritikos, E.: A Discipline for Program Verification based on Backpointers and its Use in Observational Disjointness. ETH Zurich, Department of Computer Science (2012), http://dx.doi.org/10.3929/ethz-a-007560318
8. Rustan, K., Leino, M.: Ecstatic: An object-oriented programming language with an axiomatic semantics. Digital Equipment Corporation Systems Research Center (1996)
9. Meyer, B., Kogtenkov, A., Stapf, E.: Avoid a Void: The Eradication of Null Dereferencing. In: Jones, C.B., Roscoe, A.W., Wood, K.R. (eds.) Reflections on the Work of C.A.R. Hoare, pp. 189–211. Springer (2010)
10. Meyer, B.: Object-Oriented Software Construction, 2nd edn. Prentice Hall (1997)
11. Meyer, B.: Steps Towards a Theory and Calculus of Aliasing. International Journal of Software and Informatics (2011)
12. Meyer, B.: Towards a Calculus of Object Programs. In: Festschrift, J.B., Breitman, K., Horspool, N. (eds.). Springer (2012)
13. Müller, P.: Modular Specification and Verification of Object-Oriented Programs. LNCS, vol. 2262. Springer, Heidelberg (2002)
14. Nienaltowski, P.: Practical framework for contract-based concurrent object-oriented programming. – PhD dissertation 17061, Department of Computer Science, ETH Zurich (February 2007). Other SCOOP references at http://se.inf.ethz.ch/research/cme/
15. Owicki, S., Gries, D.: An axiomatic proof technique for parallel programs. Acta Informatica 6(4), 319–340 (1976)
16. Schoeller, B.: Aliased-based Reasoning for Object-Oriented Programs. Tech. Report, ETH Zurich (2005), http://se.ethz.ch/people/schoeller/pdfs/10-Annual_Report_CSE_ETHZ_2005.pdf
17. Shield, J.: Towards an Object-Oriented Refinement Calculus. - PhD Thesis, The University of Queensland (2004)
18. Ke, W., Liu, Z., Wang, S., Zhao, L.: A graph-based generic type system for object-oriented programs. Frontiers of Computer Science 7(1), 109–134 (2013), doi:10.1007/s11704-012-1307-8

Reasoning (on) Service Component Ensembles in Rewriting Logic*

Lenz Belzner[1], Rocco De Nicola[2], Andrea Vandin[2], and Martin Wirsing[1]

[1] LMU Munich, Chair for Programming and Software Engineering
{belzner,wirsing}@pst.ifi.lmu.de
[2] IMT Institute for Advanced Studies Lucca, Italy
{rocco.denicola,andrea.vandin}@imtlucca.it

Dedicated to Kokichi Futatsugi.

Abstract. Programming autonomic systems with massive number of heterogeneous components poses a number of challenges to language designers and software engineers and requires the integration of computational tools and reasoning tools. We present a general methodology to enrich SCEL, a recently introduced language for programming systems with massive numbers of components, with reasoning capabilities that are guaranteed by external reasoners. We show how the methodology can be instantiated by considering the MAUDE implementation of SCEL and a specific reasoner, PIRLO, implemented in MAUDE as well. Moreover we show how the actual integration can benefit from the existing analytical tools of the MAUDE framework. In particular, we demonstrate our approach by considering a simple scenario consisting of a group of robots moving in an arena aiming at minimising the number of collisions.

1 Introduction

The increasing complexity, heterogeneity and dynamism of current computational and information infrastructures is calling for new ways of designing and managing computer systems and applications. *Adaptation,* namely "the capability of a system to change its behavior according to new requirements or environment conditions" [18], has been largely proposed as a powerful means for taming the ever-increasing complexity of today's computer systems and applications. Besides, a new paradigm, named *autonomic computing* [19], has been advocated that aims at making modern distributed IT systems *self-manageable,* i.e. capable of continuously self-monitoring and selecting appropriate operations.

More recently, to capture the relevant features and challenges, the 'Interlink WG on software intensive systems and new computing paradigms' [20] has proposed to use the term *ensembles* to refer to:

---

* Research supported by the European Integrated Project 257414 ASCENS and by the MIUR COFIN Project CINA.

S. Iida, J. Meseguer, and K. Ogata (Eds.): Futatsugi Festschrift, LNCS 8373, pp. 188–211, 2014.

The future generation of software-intensive systems dealing with massive numbers of components, featuring complex interactions among components and with humans and other systems, operating in open and non-deterministic environments, and dynamically adapting to new requirements, technologies and environmental conditions.

The notions of *service components* (SCs) and *service-component ensembles* (SCEs) have been put forward as a means to structure a system into well-understood, independent and distributed building blocks that interact in specified ways. SCs are autonomic entities that can cooperate, with different roles, in open and non-deterministic environments. SCEs are instead sets of SCs with dedicated knowledge units and resources, featuring goal-oriented execution. Most of the basic properties of SCs and SCEs are already guaranteed by current service-oriented architectures; the novelty lays in the notions of goal-oriented evolution and of self-awareness and context-awareness.

These notions of SCs and SCEs are the starting point of the EU project AS-CENS [3,31] that aims at investigating different issues ranging from languages for modelling and programming SCEs to foundational models for adaptation, dynamic self-expression and reconfiguration, from formal methods for the design and verification of reliable SCEs to software infrastructures supporting deployment and execution of SCE-based applications. The aim is to develop formal tools and methodologies supporting the design of self-adaptive systems that can autonomously adapt to, also unexpected, changes in the operating environment, while keeping most of their complexity hidden from administrators and users.

To this end, the SCEL language [13] has been proposed to deal with *service component ensembles*. The language supports attribute-based communication and sharing of (local) knowledge repositories to model interactions, and allows to express behaviours in terms of process calculi. While SCEL is sufficiently powerful for dealing with coordination and interaction issues, it does not provide advanced tools for specifying components that take decisions about the action to perform while taking into account the context they are currently in. Obviously, the language could be extended in order to encompass such possibilities, and one could have specific reasoning phases when decisions need to be taken because changes of context have been noticed.

In our view, it is however preferable to have separate reasoning components that SCEL programs can invoke whenever they need to take decisions. Having two different languages, one for computation and coordination and one for "reasoning", does guarantee *separation of concerns*, a fundamental property to obtain reliable and maintainable specifications. Also, it may be beneficial to have a methodology for integrating different reasoners, designed and optimised for specific purposes, with a specific programming language. What we envisage is having SCEL programs that whenever have to take decisions have the possibility of invoking an external reasoner by providing it information about the relevant knowledge they have access to and receiving in exchange informed suggestions about how to proceed.

In this paper, we start our investigation towards the actual integration of SCEL components and reasoners and describe a possible approach to the design of interfaces and methodologies for building up systems consisting of separated components concerned with computations and with decision taking. In particular we show how a specific implementation of SCEL, that we call MISSCEL, can be integrated with a specific reasoner that we call PIRLO [5]. The integration is simplified by the fact that both MISSCEL and PIRLO are based on rewriting logic and developed in MAUDE. We can thus specify: *reasoning service component ensembles.*

The use of the MAUDE framework as basic tools for the implementation of the two main components of our system paves also the way towards the exploitation of tools and techniques for analysing the behaviour of SCEs, and we can thus *reason on reasoning service component ensembles.* Indeed, all analytical tools that have been developed for MAUDE, can now be exploited to analyse or simulate the behaviour of SCEs. As an example we will show how MULTIVESTA[26], a recently proposed statistical analyser for probabilistic systems, can be used to evaluate the implementation of a simple scenario consisting of a group of robots moving in an arena paying attention at minimising the number of collisions.

Indeed, this robotics scenario will be used throughout the paper to explain the role of the different components. In particular, we will discuss the role of SCEL and PIRLO in the modelling and reasoning phases and will assess the impact of different perception ranges on the actual behaviour of the robots and on the number of collisions.

The scenario is depicted in Figure 1, and is concerned with a group of robots moving in an arena. The arena is abstracted as a discrete grid (the grey dashed lines), while robots (the white or black circles) are situated in cells intersections. Several robots can reside in the same position, in which case they collide. Robots are labelled with their current number of collisions. Robots perform one-cell movements following a dashed line (up, right, down or left), or stay idle. We consider two kinds of robots distinguished by how the choice of action is performed: *nor-*

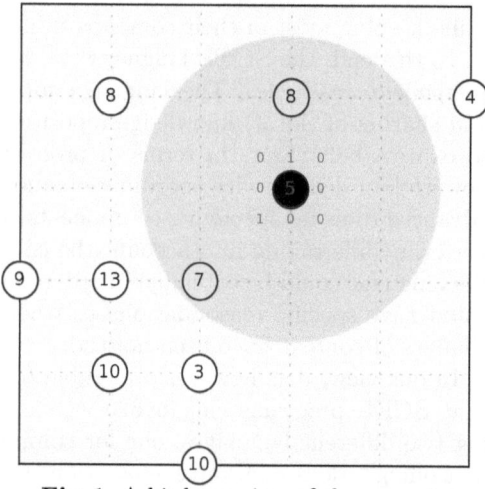

Fig. 1. A bird-eye view of the scenario

mal robots, depicted as white circles, and *informed robots*, represented as black circles. Normal robots randomly choose the action to be executed among the five listed above, i.e. they perform a random walking or stay idle. The informed robots monitor their surrounding environment by relying on proximity sensors and exploit this information to choose an action that exhibits the minimal probability of colliding with other robots. The amount of environment perceived by an informed robot depends on its perception range (depicted in Figure 1 as the semi-transparent circle surrounding the informed robot). For example, the informed robot of Figure 1 perceives its four neighbouring positions and the four diagonal ones. The eight numbers surrounding the robot represent its current perception of the environment: it perceives 1 robot above it, 1 robot in position down-left, and 0 in the other six directions. The positions up, right, down and left are reachable with a single move, while the diagonal ones are reachable with two moves. However, the perception of the diagonal positions is also useful for the computation of the next action, as a robot located there (e.g. the one perceived in down-left) could move towards the same position chosen by the informed robot (e.g. up, if the informed robot moves left).

The rest of the paper is structured as follows. Section 2 introduces SCEL and its implementation in rewriting logic MISSCEL, and briefly describes the reasoner PIRLO. Section 3 provides a general methodology to enrich SCEL components with reasoning capabilities by resorting to explicit *reasoner integrators*, together with a concrete instantiation for MISSCEL, PIRLO and their use for the implementation of the robotic scenario. Finally, Section 4 presents the analytical activities performed to validate our approach, while Section 5 wraps up and discusses related and future work.

Personal Note: The fourth author has known Kokichi for a long time. Kokichi and MW are both members of IFIP WG 1.3 on Foundations of System Specification; in 1996 - 1998 MW has participated in the CafeOBJ project. CafeOBJ [10,14,15] is a very well designed advanced algebraic specification language developed by Kokichi and his group. Together with Maude and Elan [7], CafeOBJ is among the three main implementations of rewriting logic. The CafeOBJ project had also been coordinated by Kokichi and had the purpose of making formal methods accessible to practising software engineers. MW and his group were especially concerned with case studies and were able to show that CafeOBJ is well-suited for specifying and analysing complex concurrent systems such as a model of the airport "Munich II" [21] and the operational semantics of multi-threaded Java [22]. Our paper here explores these ideas and is written in the spirit of Kokichi's project: it uses rewriting logic for tackling a case study on concurrent autonomic systems and aims at making formal methods useful for software engineers.

Discussing and cooperating with Kokichi is always a pleasant experience; we are looking forward to many further inspiring exchanges.

2   Preliminaries

Section 2.1 introduces SCEL and shows how the robotic scenario can be modelled with it, while Section 2.2 discusses how PIRLO exploits the environment perceptions of robots to reason about their next steps and suggest optimal choices.

2.1 SCEL

SCEL [13] is a kernel formal language developed for modelling adaptive systems. It brings together programming abstractions to directly address aggregations (how different components interact to form ensembles and systems), behaviors (how components progress) and knowledge manipulation, according to specific policies. This allows to program interaction, adaptation and self- and context-awareness.

SCEL specifications are made of possibly cooperating SCEL *components* which, as de- picted in Figure 2, are composed by an inter- face, a knowledge repository, a set of policies, and a process. The role of an interface is that of publishing and making available to other components selected parts of the local knowl- edge. A knowledge repository manages compo- nent's data, and offers high-level primitives for

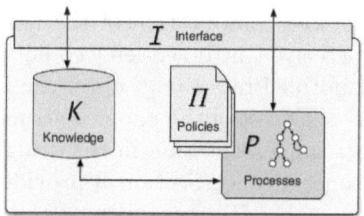

Fig. 2. A SCEL component

adding, retrieving and *withdrawing* it. Policies regulate the interaction between the internal parts of a component (*interaction policy*) and with other compo- nents (*authorization predicate*). Finally, a process executing actions in the style of process calculi is used to explicitly represent the behaviour of a component. Processes execute local computations, coordinate the interaction with the local knowledge or interact with remote repositories according to the interfaces and policies of the involved components. In particular, three actions are provided to interact with repositories: **put**, **qry** and **get**, paired, respectively, with the *adding, retrieving* and *withdrawing* primitives. Noteworthy, the target of these actions can be either **self**, or the id of a component, or a target predicate al- lowing, respectively, to access the local knowledge, the knowledge of another component in a point-to-point fashion, or to perform an attribute-based com- munication with any (**qry** or **get**) or all (**put**) components satisfying the target predicate.

An in depth presentation of SCEL is out of the scope of this paper, we refer the reader to [13], while a preliminary version of SCEL can be found in [12]. In this paper we consider SCEL$_{TS}$, a SCEL dialect where repositories are tuple spaces, and policies are omitted: intra-component processes evolve in a pure interleaving fashion, while extra-component interactions are always authorized. Note that policies are supported by MISSCEL (in particular the authorization predicates), but no policy language has been integrated yet.

MISSCEL: A Maude Interpreter and Simulator for SCEL. SCEL comes with solid semantics foundations laying the basis for formal reasoning. MISS- CEL, a faithful rewriting logic-based implementation of SCEL's operational semantics is a first step in this direction. MISSCEL is written in Maude [11], an instantiation of rewriting logic which allows to execute rewrite theories. What we obtain is then an executable operational semantics for SCEL, that is an

```
1  SC(I( tId('SCId)),
2    K( < tId('SCId) ; av(id('robot-normal-1)) >, < tId('type) ; av('normal)
                                                                        >,
3        < tId('pos) ; av(1) av(2) >, < tId('collisions) ; av(13) >),
4    Pi(INTERLEAVING-INTERACTION-PREDICATE),
5    P( qry(< tId('pos) ; ?x('x) ?x('y) >)@ self .
6       put(< tId('dir) ; randomDirection(x('x), x('y)) >)@ self .
7       put(< av('terminated) >)@ self [ get(< av('terminated) >)@ self .
8                                        pDef('PnormalRobot)] )
```

Listing 1.1. A (MIS)SCEL component representing a normal robot

interpreter. Given a SCEL specification, thanks to MISSCEL it is possible to exploit the rich Maude toolset [11] to perform:

- automatic state-space generation,
- qualitative analysis via Maude's invariant and LTL model checkers,
- debugging via probabilistic simulations and animations generation,
- quantitative analysis via the recently proposed MULTIVESTA [26], a distributed statistical analyzer extending VESTA [28] and PVESTA [2].

A further advantage of MISSCEL is that SCEL specifications can now be intertwined with raw Maude code, exploiting its great expressiveness. This allows to obtain cleaner specifications in which SCEL is used to model behaviours, aggregations, and knowledge manipulation, leaving scenario-specific details like environment sensing abstractions or robots movements to Maude.

Robots of our scenario are modelled as SCEL components. Listing 1.1 provides the MISSCEL representation of the normal robot of Figure 1 with label 13.

In MISSCEL, a SCEL component is defined as a Maude term with sort `ServiceComponent` built with the operation `op SC : Interface Knowledge Policies Processes -> ServiceComponent` . The interface exposes the id of the robot (line 1), while, as depicted in lines 2-3, the knowledge contains the id (`'robot-normal-1`), the type (`'normal`), the position (`1,2`) and the current number of collisions (`13`). Line 4 specifies that the default policy of SCEL_{TS} is enforced. Finally, lines 5-8 contain the behaviour specification of the robot. The robot first queries its position from the local knowledge (line 5) and then adds a randomly selected direction to its knowledge. Here we have two examples showing that it might be useful to mix SCEL and Maude specifications: `randomDirection` is a Maude operation which probabilistically selects one of

```
1  ceq SC(I, K(< tId('pos) ; av(x)  av(y)  >, < tId('dir) ; av(dir)
2     >, k), Pi,P)
3     = SC(I, K(< tId('pos) ; av(x2) av(y2) >                        , k), Pi
         ,P)
4     if av(x2) av(y2) := computeNeighbouringPosition(av(x),av(y),av(dir)) .
```

Listing 1.2. The Maude equation to actuate robot movements

$$P \downarrow_\circ P \quad a.P \downarrow_a P \quad \frac{P \downarrow_\alpha P'}{P + Q \downarrow_\alpha P'} \quad \frac{Q \downarrow_\alpha Q'}{P + Q \downarrow_\alpha Q'}$$

Fig. 3. Four of the rules of SCEL's semantics of processes

```
1   op commit : Process -> Commitment . rl commit(P) =>
2   commitment(inaction,P) . rl commit(a . P) => commitment(a,P) . crl
3   commit(P + Q) => commitment(a, P1) if commit(P) => commitment(a,
4   P1) .
```

Listing 1.3. The rules of Figure 3 implemented in MISSCEL

the possible directions in which the robot can move. This direction is then consumed by the Maude equation of Listing 1.2 to actuate the movement (where `computeNeighbouringPosition` simply increases or decreases x or y depending on the direction `dir`). We similarly defined an equation to abstract the environment sensing of informed robots. Then, in line 7 the token `terminated` is added to the local repository to signal completion of the movement. This token can now be consumed by the process enclosed is squared brackets (in parallel with the one just described), and finally the process definition `pDef('PnormalRobot)` is invoked, meaning that it is replaced with its body, which actually corresponds to the whole described process.

Coming to semantics-related aspects, the operational semantics of SCEL[13] is defined in two steps: the semantics of processes, and the semantics of systems. First, the semantics of processes specifies their commitments, ignoring the structure of SCEL components. Namely, issues like allocation of processes to a component, available data in the knowledge, and regulating policies are ignored at this level. Then, by taking process commitments and system configuration into account, the semantics of systems provides a full description of systems behavior. The same happens in MISSCEL. Due to space constraints we now exemplify the correspondence of SCEL semantics and its implementation in MISSCEL for the semantics of processes only.

Figure 3 depicts four of the rules defining SCEL's semantics of processes, specifying, respectively from left to right, that: a process can commit in itself executing an inaction, a process composed by P prefixed by an action a can commit in P by executing a, a process $P + Q$, in which P can commit in P' executing an action, or Q can commit in Q' executing another action, can commit either in P' or in Q' executing the corresponding action.

Listing 1.3 depicts (omitting unnecessary details) how we implemented the rules of Figure 3 in MISSCEL. Where P, Q and P1 are Maude variables with sort `Process` (i.e. place-holders for any term with the specified sort), while a is an `Action` variable. The correspondence is straightforward. Note that we need only one rule for the + operator, as we defined it with the `comm` axiom, meaning that it has the commutative property, meaning the when applying a rule to P + Q, Maude will try to match the rule also with Q + P.

2.2 Pirlo

For specification and execution of reasoning about which move to execute in order to minimize collision probability we use Pirlo, an implementation of action programming in rewriting logic [5]. The general idea is to write a non-deterministic action program that captures agents' behavioural alternatives. The effects of these alternatives are then computed by the Pirlo reasoning system and can subsequently be evaluated, e.g. by computing the probability of avoiding collisions when moving in a specific direction.

For Pirlo being able to reason about domain dynamics, the current state perceived by the agent is represented in terms of fluents, i.e. properties of the environment that are object to change due to actions executed by an agent or other events. Additionally, a specification of domain dynamics is provided in terms of rewrite rules which encode the effects of actions on the environment, i.e. they encode the changes that happen to fluents upon action execution. This specification of domain dynamics can be augmented by other assumptions about the environment, like general laws or invariants, to form an exhaustive background knowledge that can be used to predict the effects of action execution. Note that dynamics can be encoded on first-order level using variables for domain objects, thus allowing for concise specification of knowledge and efficient computation of action effects.

Pirlo uses specified knowledge about domain dynamics to compute the possible effects of non-deterministic programs that encode various action alternatives for an agent. These programs are constructed by means of procedural operations as well as non-deterministic operators, e.g. choice of action and choice of argument. For example, given a non-deterministic

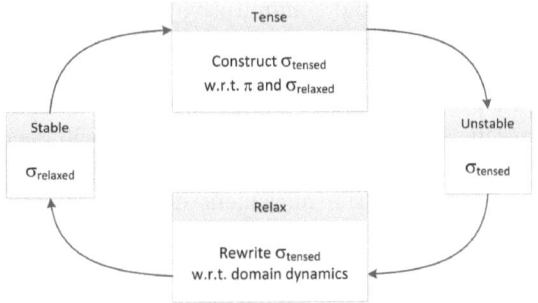

Fig. 4. Action programming in rewriting logic

choice operator # and two distinct actions a and a', the program a # a' will lead to the computation of the effects of executing either a or a'. Actions induced by programs are used to rewrite a fluent term representing the current state and computing its normal form w.r.t. domain dynamics and background knowledge which have been specified in terms of rewrite rules. This approach is roughly outlined in Figure 4. For example, given an agent that perceives a state s and s', and that has been provided with a specification for actions a and a' defining s and a -> s'' and s' and a' -> s''', the computation of possible effects of executing the program a # a' will result in two new state terms according to action execution; namely, these are s and s' and a that rewrites to s'' and s' when executing action a and s and s' and a' rewriting to s and s''' when

```
1  sorts Agent Position Probability .
2
3  op pos : Agent Int Int -> Position .
4  op p : Float -> Probability .
```

Listing 1.4. Example domain fluents

```
1  var A : Agent .
2  vars X, Y, DX, DY : Int .
3
4  crl pos(A, X      , Y     ) and move(A, DX, DY)
5  => pos(A, X + DX, Y + DY)
6  if X + DX and Y + DY are in grid area .
```

Listing 1.5. Specification of the effects of the move action

executing a', respectively. For a more detailed discussion of action programming in rewriting logic, the reader is referred to [5].

Domain specification. For our scenario, the system state is represented by fluents as shown in Listing 1.4 denoting an agent's position and the probability of the system being in a certain state, respectively. Fluents are conjoined to states by an associative and commutative operator op and : State State -> State

denoting logical conjunctions of fluents and/or states respectively. Fluents are considered a sub-sort of sort state. For example, pos(a,1,0) and pos(a',2,2) and p(0.8) denotes a state with two agents a and a' being located at the specified positions, and that this state will occur with a probability of 0.8.

In the presented scenario, agents only have a move action that takes the moving agent and the movement delta in x- and y-direction as parameters. For example, move(a,1,0) denotes that agent a will move one step to the right on the grid area.

When specifying action domains in rewriting logic, system dynamics (i.e. action effects) are modelled in terms of (conditional) rewrite laws that specify the action's precondition and the affected portion of the current state as a fluent formula that is conjoined with the action representation. The effect of a move action is thus represented by a rewrite law as shown in Listing 1.5. An action program that allows an agent to move in any direction or to stand still can then be defined as shown in Listing 1.6.

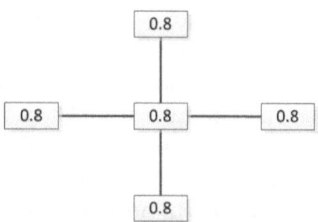

Fig. 5. Probability of agent position after one step

Lookup tables. In order to allow an agent to compute the probability of colliding with another agent, it is useful to provide to the reasoning agent information about the probability that a perceived agent will be at a certain position in the future. As the movement of uncontrolled agents is assumed to be random (with

```
1  op moveProgram : Agent -> Program . eq moveProgram(A)
2  = move(A,0,0) # move(A,1,0) # move(A,-1,0) # move(A,0,1) # move(A,0,-1) .
```

Listing 1.6. Specification of agent movement alternatives

```
1  op update : Agent -> Action .
2
3  var CA : ControlledAgent . var A : Agent .
4  vars X, Y, X', Y' : Int . vars P, P' : Float.
5
6  crl pos(CA, X, Y) and pos(A, X', Y') and update(A) and p(P)
7   => pos(CA, X, Y) and pos(A, X', Y') and p(P * P')
8   if P' := lookup(X, Y, X', Y') .
```

Listing 1.7. Specification of collision probability update

a uniform probability distribution, i.e. each of the five actions is chosen with a probability of 0.2), this information can be precomputed and used as a lookup table for computation of collision avoidance probability at run-time. Figure 5 graphically represents this lookup table when no borders are considered. The centered point is considered to be the current position of a perceived agent. The numbers denote the probability that this agent will *not* be at the given position after one step. Note that the lookup table does not take into account situations where borders are present; however, for these cases, it could be precomputed as well.

To allow an agent to compute the probability of not colliding with a certain other agent, an action `update` is defined as shown in Listing 1.7. `CA` denotes a controlled agent (being specified as a subsort of agent to allow distinction from uncontrolled agents).

Example. Consider the state `pos(ca,1,1) and pos(a,1,2)`, ca being the controlled agent, and a an uncontrolled one. In order to compute the probabilities of avoiding collisions when performing a certain `move` action, agent `ca` invokes the reasoner by passing to it the current state. Then, the reasoner computes the results of the sequential program `moveProgram(ca);update(a)`, that first chooses a possible move (and performs it hypothetically), and finally updates the probability of avoiding a collision in the resulting state. The given program will compute a probability of 0.8 of avoiding a collision when standing still or moving up, and a probability of 1.0 for all other moves. In the example situation, the reasoner thus will propose to either move down, left or right to achieve the best result. If the informed robot perceives multiple other agents in its environment, the update is performed for each of them, resulting in a cumulated computation of the probability that a particular move will avoid collision.

3   Enriching SCEL with Reasoning Capabilities

SCEL has been defined to deal with components behaviours and interactions, while PIRLO has been conceived to express and perform reasoning. Even if it would be possible to directly enrich SCEL with reasoning capabilities, this would not be convenient from a *separation of concerns* perspective. Here we present a general approach to enrich SCEL with external reasoning capabilities (Section 3.1), we instantiate it for MISSCEL (Section 3.2), and then show how to integrate MISSCEL with PIRLO for dealing with the robotic scenario (Section 3.3).

3.1   Methodology

We aim at enriching SCEL components with a reasoner to be *invoked* when necessary. Ideally, this should be done by minimally extending SCEL. In Figure 2 we depicted the constituents of a component: interfaces, policies, processes and repositories. Interfaces and policies will not be involved in the extension, as the former only exposes the local knowledge to other components, and the latter are not considered in SCEL$_{TS}$. Processes store and retrieve data (tuples in SCEL$_{TS}$) in repositories. The interaction between a process and its local repository is a natural choice to plug a reasoner: we can use special data (*reasoning request tuples*) whose addition to the local knowledge triggers the reasoner. Reasoning results can then be stored in the knowledge as *reasoning result tuples*, allowing local processes to access them as any other data. We could have either passive reasoners invoked when necessary, or active ones that continuously monitor the repositories. In Sections 3.2, 3.3 we exemplify the first case.

Figure 6 depicts such an *enriched* SCEL *component*. With respect to Figure 2, now local communications are filtered by *RI*, a *reasoner integrator*. As depicted by the grey arrow between *RI* and *R* (a *reasoner*), in case of reasoning requests, *RI* invokes *R*, which evaluates the request and returns back the result of the reasoning phase. *RI* then stores the obtained result in the knowledge, allowing the local processes to access it via common **get** or **qry** actions.

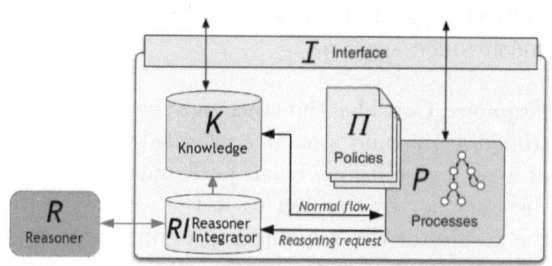

Fig. 6. Enriched SCEL component

In case of normal data, the flow goes instead directly to the knowledge.

Actually, *RI* has the further fundamental role of translating data among the internal representations used by SCEL and by the reasoner, acting hence as an adapter between them. To sum up, *RI* performs three tasks: it first translates the reasoning request from SCEL's representation to the reasoner's one (*scel2reasoner*), then it invokes the reasoner (*invokeReasoner*), and finally translates back the results (*reasoner2scel*). Clearly, each reasoner requires its own implementation of the three operations. Hence, as depicted in Figure 7, we separate the *RI* component into an *abstract reasoning interface* and a *concrete adapter*. The former is given just once and contains the definition of the three operations, while the latter is reasoner- and domain-specific, and provides the

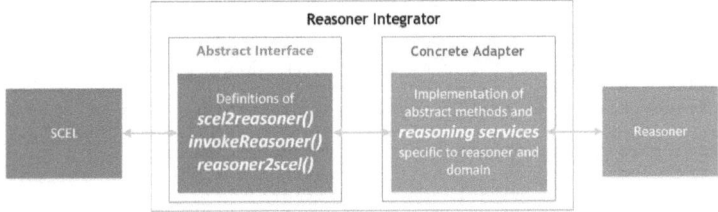

Fig. 7. An architectural perspective of the reasoner integrator

actual implementation of the three operations. In Section 3.2 we discuss the instantiation for MISSCEL of the abstract reasoning interface. The three operations implemented by a concrete adapter provide a connection from SCEL to a particular reasoner taking care of the translation of syntactical representations and of the actual execution of the reasoning operation. As discussed in Section 3.3, in our running case study these steps consist of: (*i*) providing to the reasoner the information about nearby robots perceived by proximity sensors; (*ii*) invoking PIRLO's reasoning service to calculate the optimal action w.r.t. this information; (*iii*) returning an optimal action to the SCEL program.

3.2   Providing the Abstract Interface in MISSCEL

We now discuss how we enriched MISSCEL to provide components with abstract reasoning interfaces.

Listing 1.8 depicts MISSCEL's abstract reasoning interface (omitting unnecessary details). Line 3 defines the reasoner-side sorts and variables for reasoning requests and results. Constructors for these sorts are provided in the concrete adapter. Line 4 defines the variables used to match the SCEL-side parameters of the reasoning results and requests (lists of values like e.g. integers or strings). Lines 6-8 define the three operations discussed in Section 3.1. Note how `scel2reasoner` goes from SCEL-side to reasoner-side values, `reasoner2scel` does the opposite, and `invokeReasoner` deals with reasoner-side values only. Lines 10-16 show how our methodology is actuated: in case of a local put of a tuple t, we actually store the result of `invokeReasonerIfNecessary(t)`. If t is a reasoning request tuple (i.e. has id `'reasoningRequest`, line 11), then its parameters are translated by `scel2reasoner` (line 13), the reasoner is invoked (line 14), and the obtained result is translated back by `reasoner2scel` (line 15). Note that the result is enclosed in a reasoning result tuple (line 12). Finally, if t is not a reasoning request tuple, the equation of line 16 is applied (due to the `owise` clause standing for *otherwise*), leaving it unchanged.

3.3   Integrating MISSCEL and PiRLo for the Robotic Scenario

We now discuss the integration of MISSCEL and PiRLo for the robotic scenario, i.e. we present the defined concrete adapter.

```
1   mod ABSTRACT-REASONING-INTERFACE is
2    --- importings of modules are omitted
3    sorts RRequest RRequestParameters RResult RResultParameters .
4    var rReq : RRequest . var rRes : RResult .
5    var requestParameter resultParameter : List{Value} . var t : Tuple .
6
7    op scel2reasoner  : List{Value} -> RRequestParameters .
8    op invokeReasoner : RRequest -> RResultParameters .
9    op reasoner2scel  : RResult -> List{Value} .
10   op invokeReasonerIfNecessary : Tuple -> Tuple .
11   ceq invokeReasonerIfNecessary(< tId('reasoningRequest) ;
               requestParameter >)
12       =                         < tId('reasoningResult)  ; resultParameter
               >
13    if rReq := scel2reasoner(requestParameter)
14    /\ rRes := invokeReasoner(rReq)
15    /\ resultParameter := reasoner2scel(rRes) .
16   eq invokeReasonerIfNecessary(t) = t [ owise ] .
17   endm
```

Listing 1.8. The MISSCEL's abstract reasoning interface.

As PIRLO needs as input a state term and an action program as outlined in Section 2.2, these have to be constructed from the parameters of a reasoning request. While these input parameters are required by PIRLO regardless of the underlying problem, their representation is very much depending on the domain specification (see Section 2.2). Thus, the following paragraph outlines an instantiation of `scel2Reasoner` for the robotics scenario to illustrate the approach. The resulting implementation of `scel2Reasoner` is shown in Listing 1.9.

The `buildState` operation takes the parameters of the reasoning request and transforms them to a state term and an action program according to the requested reasoning service. Namely, proximity sensor data is translated into the fluent representation that was introduced in Section 2.2. For example, if a robot is perceived on direction up, a position fluent `pos(<some id>, ownX, ownY + 1)` is constructed and conjoined with the current state term. This construction is performed recursively by the operation `buildPosOfPerceivedRobots` for all the perceived robots. Finally, the built state is annotated with a fluent `p(1.0)`, which is exploited by PIRLO to encode the probability of not colliding with another robot after one step. Note that, if necessary, information about error rates of proximity sensors could be encoded here. Listing 1.9 shows the general outline of `buildState` for reasoning services regarding four perceived positions only.

The action program used to update collision probability as described in Section 2.2 is constructed by the operation `buildProgram` depicted in Listing 1.9. In general, it produces a non-deterministic program that will compute the effects for all possible actions of the controlled agent, and subsequently will deduce the probability for each action of not colliding with another agent. To do so, an action program only consisting of the operation `update(<some id>)` is sequentially added to the final reasoner program for each robot perceived by the proximity sensor (i.e. for each position fluent in the state term that is not encod-

```
1   var rReqParams : List{Value} . var S : State . var P : Program .
2
3   ceq scel2reasoner(rReqParams) = reasoningRequest(S, P)
4    if S := buildState(rReqParams)
5    /\ P := buildProgram(S) .
6
7   op buildState : List{Value} -> State .
8   eq buildState(av('reasonWith4Directions) av(id(SCID)) av(ownX) av(ownY)
9                 av(#Up) av(#Right) av(#Down) av(#Left))
10  = pos(SCID, ownX, ownY) and p(1.0) and
11    buildPosOfPerceivedRobots(ownX, ownY, #Up, #Right, #Down, #Left) .
12
13  op buildProgram : State -> Program .
14  eq buildProgram(pos(CA,X,Y) and S) = moveProgram(R) ; buildUpdateProgram(
      S) .
15
16  op buildUpdateProgram : State -> Program .
17  eq buildUpdateProgram(pos(R,X,Y) and S)= update(R,0) ; buildUpdateProgram
      (S).
18  eq buildUpdateProgram(pos(R,X,Y)) = update(R,0) .
```

Listing 1.9. Concrete implementation of `scel2Reasoner`.

```
1   eq invokeReasoner(reasoningRequest(S, P))
2   = reasoningResult(maxProb(metaExec(S, P))) .
3
4   var A : PrimitiveAction .
5   eq reasoner2scel(reasoningResult(A ; P)) = av(translateAction(A)) .
6
7   op translateAction : PrimitiveAction -> Qid .
8   eq translateAction(move(SCID, 0, 0)) = 'standStill .
9   eq translateAction(move(SCID, 1, 0)) = 'right .
10  --- Other directions are translated similarly.
```

Listing 1.10. Concrete implementation of `invokeReasoner` and `reasoner2scel`.

ing the controlled agent). As described in Section 2.2, distinction of controlled and uncontrolled agents can be realized via sub-sorting.

Lines 1-2 of Listing 1.10 show the implementation of `invokeReasoner`, which takes as parameters the state term and program constructed in the previous steps. Here, `maxProb` and `metaExec` are operations provided by PIRLO. Finally, lines 4-9 of Listing 1.10 show the implementation of `reasoner2scel`, i.e. how the result provided by the reasoner is translated to SCEL's syntactic representation.

4 Methodology Validation: Analysis of the Scenario

We now describe the analysis activities performed on the robotic scenario by resorting to MISSCEL and its integration with PIRLO. We have performed two kind of analysis. An informal analysis of videos generated out of probabilistic simulations (Section 4.2); and statistical model checking (Section 4.3). In particular, in the early development stages of the scenario we mainly concentrated on informally analysing single simulations and their automatically generated animations. This can be considered as a debugging phase. A couple of trial-and-error iterations were enough for the model to acquire sufficient maturity to undergo a more rigorous analysis in terms of statistical model checking. Qualitative analysis of SCEL specifications is possible in MISSCEL by resorting to the rich Maude framework [11] (e.g. via Maude's reachability analysis capabilities, or LTL model checker) but it suffers from the state-space explosion problem, and it is limited to small scenarios. To tackle larger scenarios, and to gain more insights into the model by dealing with *probabilities* and *quantities*, rather than *possibilities*, we resorted to quantitative statistical analysis techniques. The work presented in this section greatly benefited from the previous experience done by the third author in the line of research of [24,8] where PMAUDE [1] (a probabilistic extension of MAUDE) and PVESTA (a tool extended by MULTIVESTA, used in this paper) have been used to model and analyze robotic self-assembly strategies.

4.1   From Non-determinism to Probabilistic Simulations

MISSCEL is an executable operational semantics for SCEL. As such, given a SCEL specification representing a system's state (i.e. a set of SCEL components), MISSCEL *executes* it by applying a rule of SCEL's semantics to (part of) the state. According to such semantics a system evolves non-deterministically by executing the process of one of its components, and in particular by consuming one of its actions. We will call *active* the component triggering the execution step. Clearly, depending on the action (e.g. a **get** or a group **put**) a single execution step may involve more than one component (e.g. the sender and the receivers), the execution is however triggered by one of them (the active one).

As usual (especially in the Maude context, e.g. [6,8,1,17]), in order to obtain probabilistic behaviours out of non-deterministic ones we need to resolve this non-determinism. Two main approaches exist in the literature, one where MAUDE specifications are enriched with probabilities and quantities (obtaining *probabilistic rewrite theories* [1]) and schedulers are used to solve the remaining non-determinism (see e.g. [8,1,17]), and the other approach, where probabilistic strategy languages [6] are used to associate probabilities to rule applications. Both approaches resolve non-determinism by probabilistic choices.

In a way, our proposal can be associated with both approaches. Intuitively, it belongs to the first approach because we rely on a (Java) scheduler that exploits MISSCEL to generate all one-step next states, and then probabilistically selects one of them. From another point of view it can be seen as taking the second approach, as we implicitly specify the same probability to every rule application. As a last remark, our approach can be considered as "conservative", as we did not modify MISSCEL itself, but we exploited an external scheduler in order to resolve non-determinism. However, nothing would prevent us from taking different choices in the lines of [1].

Apart from efficiency and scalability concerns, the above outlined *naive* scheduler does not fit well with the considered scenario, where components are robots moving independently: it leads to unrealistic executions in which robots "evolve with different frequencies". In order to have a more realistic abstraction we need *fair* executions, i.e. we need to consider execution iterations (or rounds) in which

```
1  performSimulation(state,numberOfIterations)
2    while(numberOfIterations have been performed)
3    listOfIds := getIds(state);
4    shuffledIds := shuffleProbabilistically(listOfIds);
5    while(shuffledIds contains further ids)
6      states := oneStepNextStates(state,shuffledIds.getNext());
7      state := chooseProbabilistically(states);
```

Listing 1.11. The pseudo-code for simulations with fair scheduling

each component executes in turn. Listing 1.11 provides the pseudo-code to perform simulations with *fair* scheduling. Provided the fair scheduler with an initial state and a maximal number of iterations (line 1), for every iteration it first obtains the list of components' identifiers (line 3), then iteratively executes the system forcing the choice of active components according to their order in the list (lines 5-7). Noteworthy, the list is shuffled probabilistically at every iteration (line 4), so that conflicts among components (e.g. willingness to consume the same tuple) are implicitly resolved with dynamic priorities. Furthermore, this solution offers better performances, as at each step of an iteration only the next states triggered by an active component are generated (line 6).

Recall that a step of the system does not correspond to a movement of a robot, but to the consumption of a SCEL action. In order to mimic simultaneous movements, we provided robots with processes of the same length, so that they move in the same iteration. Intuitively, we added some actions to normal robots (querying the current position), and now robots move every 8 iterations.

4.2   Animated Probabilistic Simulations

Simulations are performed by using the fair simulator of Section 4.1. In order to obtain animated simulations we implemented an exporter from SCEL terms to DOT graphs [16], offering the automatic generation of images from states, and of animations from images: they have greatly facilitated the debugging of MISSCEL, PiRLo and of the specification of the robotic scenario.

In order to detail the dynamics of the robotic scenario, we now discuss a simulation regarding ten normal robots and an informed one using the reasoner. We performed 4400 execution steps (i.e. 400 execution iterations for the 11 robots), requiring in average around 30 milliseconds per step. Given that each robot executes 400 actions, and that robots perform a movement (or stand still) every 8 actions, we have that each robot performs at most 50 movements, and the reasoner is invoked 50 times by the informed robot. Six interesting states of the simulation are depicted in the automatically generated images of Figure 8.

Given the number of robots, the initial state of a simulation is computed by probabilistically distributing them in the arena. An example is depicted in the top-left of Figure 8, where we notice an informed robot (the black circle) and only nine normal ones (white circles), meaning that two robots are colliding. During the simulation each robot counts its collisions with others (depicted in their labels), but ignores those of the initial state. As we will discuss, during

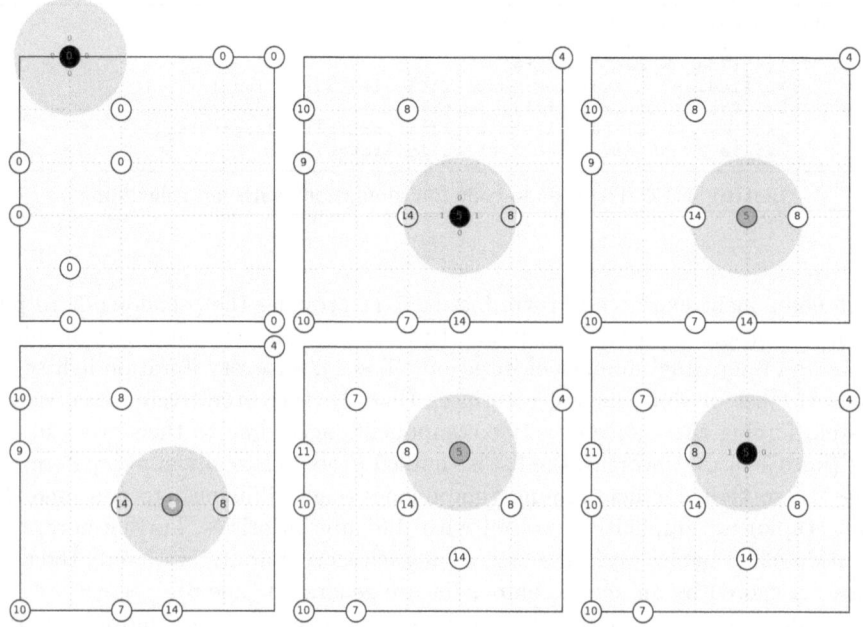

Fig. 8. Six states of a simulation of the robotic scenario

the execution the informed robot changes its "internal state" among *monitoring,*
wait for reason result and *actuating reason result*. The informed robot is initially
black, meaning that it is *monitoring* the environment. As depicted by its perception range (the semi-transparent circle surrounding it) it perceives only the
four surrounding positions (up, right, down and left). In other simulations and
in Section 4.3 we considered greater perception ranges allowing e.g. to perceive
also the four surrounding diagonal positions.

After several iterations we reach the configuration depicted in the top-middle
of Figure 8. Even if not appreciable in the figure, the number of collisions of
the informed robot is five, while the normal ones have an average of more than
nine. The informed robot perceives a robot on its left and one on its right.
Further execution leads to the state in the top-right of Figure 8. The informed
robot changed its color to grey, meaning that it froze its current perception of
the environment and passed it to the reasoner (state *waiting for reason result*).
Given that the informed robot perceived a robot on its right and one on its
left, we can expect that if either an up or a down movement will be chosen,
as movements in other directions may lead to collisions. Furthermore, also the
choice of not moving should be avoided, as the perceived robots could move
towards the informed one.

In the bottom-left part of Figure 8 we notice that the informed robot is labelled
with a yellow light (state *actuating reason result*), symbolizing the reception of
the reasoning result. As expected, in the bottom-centre part of Figure 8 we

see that the informed robot moved up. Finally (bottom-left of Figure 8), the informed robot enters again in state *monitoring*.

4.3   Statistical Model Checking

By performing different simulations by varying the number and distribution of robots we noticed that normal robots tend to collide more than informed ones. We can measure and quantify this phenomenon via statistical analysis techniques.

We perform a quantitative analysis by resorting to statistical model checking (see e.g. [27,28,2]). This technique does not yield the absolute confidence of qualitative or probabilistic model checking, but allows to analyze (up to some statistical errors) larger scenarios and to deal with the stochastic nature of probabilistic systems. Statistical model checking does not exhaustively explore systems state-spaces, but rather performs n independent simulations, with n large enough to statistically estimate quantitative properties. More precisely, properties are estimated for a given confidence interval specified by two parameters α and δ: if a property is estimated as the real number $\bar{x}$, then with probability $(1 - \alpha)$ the actual value of the property belongs to the interval $[\bar{x} - \delta/2, \bar{x} + \delta/2]$. Clearly, the coarser is the confidence interval, the less accurate is the estimation, and hence the smaller number of simulations are required. In all our experiments we fixed 0.05 for both α and δ, meaning that with probability 0.95 the actual value of a property estimated as $\bar{x}$ belongs to $[\bar{x} - 0.025, \bar{x} + 0.025]$.

We exploited MULTIVESTA [26], a distributed statistical analyzer and model checker which performs Monte Carlo based evaluations of quantitative temporal multi-expressions (MULTIQUATEX) [26,1], allowing to query expected values of real-typed parametric expressions like the *number of collisions of an informed robot at the growing of the number steps, fixing* 5000 *as maximum number of steps*. A presentation of MULTIVESTA and of MULTIQUATEX is out of the scope of this paper, we refer the interested reader to [26,25,2,28,1].

Figure 9 presents the results of some of the performed experiments. We considered two scenarios concerning an arena with 5×5 cells containing ten normal robots and an informed one; all are probabilistically distributed. In the first scenario the informed robot perceives only the four surrounding positions (up, right, down, left). In the second scenario the informed robot has a wider perception range allowing to perceive also the positions in the four diagonal directions (upright, down-right, down-left, up-left). Figure 8 and Figure 1 depict, respectively, some possible configurations of the first and second scenario.

For both scenarios we first studied the expected value of the average number of collisions of the normal robots when varying of the number of execution steps from 1 to 5000 (i.e. 455 iterations). Not surprisingly, we obtain very similar measures for both the scenarios, and hence we use only one plot in Figure 9 ("Avg collisions of random walkers"). Noteworthy, after 5000 steps, the average of the number of collisions of the normal robots is near to 26.8 in both the scenarios.

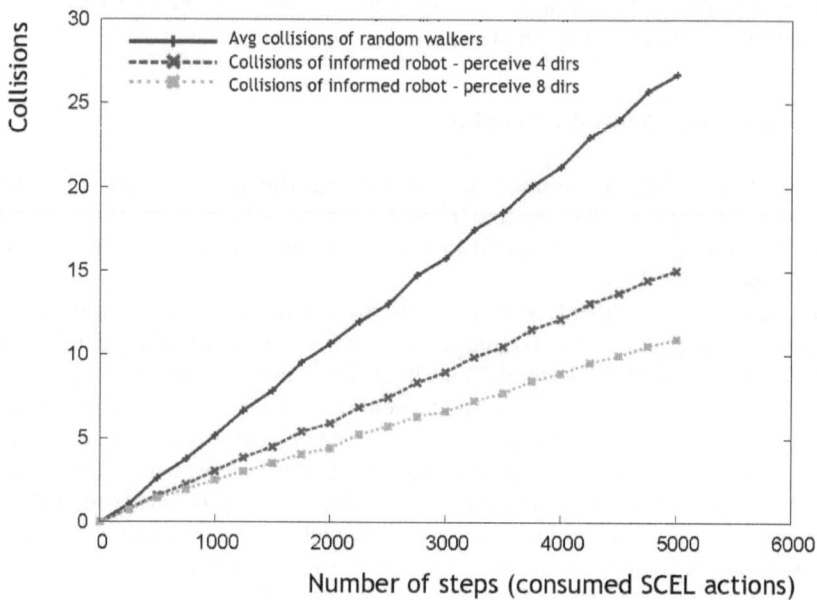

Fig. 9. Collisions of normal and informed robots at varying of the number of steps

More interesting is the comparison of the expected value of the number of collisions of informed robots when varying the perception range. For both scenarios we thus also studied the number of collisions of the informed robot at steps from 1 to 5000. As depicted by the plots "Collisions of informed robot - perceive 4 dirs" and "Collisions of informed robot - perceive 8 dirs", informed robots do significantly less collisions than the normal ones. In particular, after 5000 steps we observe 15 collisions for the informed robot that perceives only four positions, and 10.9 for the one that perceives also the additional four diagonal positions. Hence, the perception of the four surrounding positions leads to reducing by 44% the number of collisions when compared to random walking. A doubly richer perception reaching also the diagonal positions leads to reducing by 60% the number of collisions.

All the described analysis have been performed on a machine equipped with four Intel Xeon E7540 and 64GB of RAM, running Linux 2.6.32 and Java 1.7.0 04-b20 64bit, requiring in total less then one hour and an half.

5   Conclusions

Future software systems will have to cope with dynamically changing environments rendering difficult any static approach to their design. To this end, *service component ensembles*, i.e. systems with a massive number of autonomous (service) components which adapt to changing requirements at run-time were proposed.

This paper discussed a methodology for the integration of service components and reasoners, enabling components to evaluate their current state at run-time to optimize their behaviour, thus making them autonomous. The proposed approach aims at a *separation of concerns* between behavioural and reasoning aspects by explicitly providing component parts with clearly distinguished responsibilities.

Coordination and execution of service components behaviour, together with distribution of knowledge among them is specified in terms of SCEL, a process description language that exploits the notion of distributed tuple spaces, and offers attribute-based communication, where the set of participants to a communication is evaluated at run-time as those satisfying a given predicate.

The processing of knowledge to produce information used to autonomously adapt behaviour is performed by particular reasoning parts of the component. Such elaboration is explicitly triggered by a SCEL process whenever there is a need for additional information, e.g. to obtain optimal behavioural alternatives.

The presented methodology is not restricted to a particular reasoner. Moreover, many reasoners could be used at the same time, each performing particular reasoning tasks for which they are best suited. To this end, particular *reasoning services* can be requested by a SCEL process according to the task at hand.

In order to allow for a clear integration of SCEL components and reasoners, we added a so-called *reasoner integrator* to the original constituents of a SCEL component. The reasoner integrator is composed by an *abstract interface* offered by SCEL components, and by a *concrete adapter* that has to be implemented for any integrated reasoner and considered scenario. The adapter has to perform the translation of knowledge between the representations used by SCEL components and by the one of the reasoner. Moreover it has to implement the reasoning services specific to the scenario at hand.

In an example scenario regarding colliding robots, we provided the behavioural specification with MISSCEL, the MAUDE implementation of SCEL. Reasoning capabilities have been instead specified exploiting PIRLO, a MAUDE implementation of action programming. Given that we provided rewriting logic and MAUDE as formal environment, we can perform formal evaluation of modelled systems by resorting to the MAUDE tool framework. As an exemplary analysis, we performed statistical model checking of the robotic scenario by exploiting MULTIVESTA, a recently proposed statistical analyser for probabilistic systems.

In this paper we did not study the computational cost of providing autonomous components with reasoning capabilities. Reasoning is an external feature invoked by SCEL components at need, and, indeed, its cost depends on the considered scenario and reasoner, and on the kind of reasoning and the frequency of its invocation. For example, it has only a slight impact in our robotic scenario. This is due to two main reasons: the required reasoning is relatively simple and has been efficiently implemented in PIRLO and it is not invoked frequently. A step of the system corresponds to the consumption of a SCEL action; robots perform 8 actions in order to perform a movement, and only informed robots resort to reasoning, which is thus invoked every 88 steps of the system. In order to provide an informal idea of the overhead introduced by the reasoning phases, we run simulations that are based on 400 iterations (i.e. 4400 steps) for three scenarios: one with 11 random walkers, and two with 10 random walkers and an informed robot perceiving, respectively, 4 and 8 positions. By performing 5 simulations of each of the three scenario, we obtained an average execution time in seconds of 135 (30.7 milliseconds per step), 136.2 (31.0 milliseconds per step) and 138.2 (31.4 milliseconds per step), respectively.

Due to the simplicity of the considered reasoning, in this paper we did not investigate how to introduce approximations in the reasoning procedures. However, the reasoning performed by robots perceiving the 4 surrounding positions can be considered as an approximation of the case with 8 perceptions, as less information is taken into account when choosing the next movement. Moreover, the decisions taken by random walkers can be considered as a further approximation, as no information at all is used, and the next movement is chosen randomly. What we have shown in this paper is that, for the considered scenario, exploiting a perception of a small portion of the surrounding environment (i.e. the 4 surrounding positions) leads to an almost halved number of collisions, in average. Perceiving a doubly larger portion of the environment (i.e. the 4 surrounding positions, and the 4 diagonal ones) further decreases the number of collisions, but does not provide an improvement comparable to the one introduced by the case of 4 perceptions w.r.t. the random walkers case.

Related Work. Other MAUDE-based approaches to autonomic and adaptive systems exist in the literature. Among these we mention MESSI [24,8,9] and PAGODA [30], which propose modular architectures for specifying and prototyping systems of autonomous cooperating agents.

Both approaches are based on the Russian Dolls architectures [23,29] and propose to hierarchically structure components, where the component of a layer can be seen as a sort of *adaptation manager* of the one of the inner layer (i.e. the *managed component*). MESSI achieves adaptation via meta-programming mechanisms based on computational reflection, i.e. a manager component executes the managed one changing its code, filtering its inputs and elaborating its outputs. PAGODA, instead, achieves adaptation mainly by intercepting and manipulating messages while they cross the layers of a component.

The two approaches are more generic than the one proposed in this paper, as we focus on a MAUDE implementation of a specific programming language (SCEL), and show how its components can be enriched with reasoning capabilities. In SCEL each component has an explicit representation of its behaviour (i.e. its process description), which can be executed and modified at run time by loading other process descriptions stored in the distributed repositories. Thus, in a sense, we have a two-layer architecture based on meta-programming (in fact programs are data which can be modified and executed at run-time).

However, this paper, and in particular Section 4, is related to the research line of MESSI, where a probabilistic extension of MAUDE and PVeStA (a tool extended by MultiVeStA) have been used to model and analyze robotic self-assembly strategies. In a broad sense, this work can be considered as a follow-up of that research line.

Future Work. While the integration of behaviour and reasoning is clearly defined from a service component point of view, our approach does not take into account yet the structure of knowledge that is used as input and provided as output for reasoning services. The use of specific knowledge representation formalisms will further enhance the clarity of integration of elaboration and execution. Especially when multiple reasoners are employed, a component managing the flow of information between a SCEL process and the different reasoners would clearly benefit from a clean formalization of the different internal representations. Of course, the choice of using $SCEL_{TS}$ rather than any other variant of SCEL simplified the methodology and its implementation.

In this paper we did not consider policies, another important component of SCEL that uses them at the level of operational semantics: before executing a SCEL action it is checked whether the action is permitted by the policies defined for the components under consideration. The current MISSCEL implementation does not consider any policy language and simply assumes that all actions are permitted. However, we do not foresee any problem in implementing in MISSCEL authorization predicates described by means of a specific policy language. Moreover, for more complicated policies, possibly involving structured and advanced reasoning, we can envisage the possibility of resorting to specific reasoners, by following the methodology proposed in this paper.

Another issue worth investigating is the explicit distribution and coordination of knowledge among the different service components forming an ensemble. The challenge is how to integrate the results provided by the individual reasoners of each component, to obtain a global outcome from the distributed local ones. This is especially important in presence of shared resources, or in case some form of consensus has to be reached.

The presented approach for enhancing behavioural specifications of service components with reasoning capabilities relies on the explicit invocation of the reasoner by a requesting process. This means that for the moment only *passive reasoners* are used that can be invoked at needs. An alternative approach would be enabling reasoners to have a more active role by continuously elaborating the information they have access to and providing components with appropriate suggestions for decision to take.

References

1. Agha, G.A., Meseguer, J., Sen, K.: PMaude: Rewrite-based specification language for probabilistic object systems. In: Cerone, A., Wiklicky, H. (eds.) QAPL 2005. ENTCS, vol. 153(2), pp. 213–239. Elsevier (2006)
2. AlTurki, M., Meseguer, J.: PVeStA: A parallel statistical model checking and quantitative analysis tool. In: Corradini, A., Klin, B., Cîrstea, C. (eds.) CALCO 2011. LNCS, vol. 6859, pp. 386–392. Springer, Heidelberg (2011)
3. ASCENS Autonomic Service-Component ENSembles, http://www.ascens-ist.eu

4. Beckert, B., Damiani, F., de Boer, F.S., Bonsangue, M.M. (eds.): FMCO 2011. LNCS, vol. 7542. Springer, Heidelberg (2013)
5. Belzner, L.: Action programming in rewriting logic (technical communication). Theory and Practice of Logic Programming, On-line Supplement (2013)
6. Bentea, L., Ölveczky, P.C.: A probabilistic strategy language for probabilistic rewrite theories and its application to cloud computing. In: Martí-Oliet, N., Palomino, M. (eds.) WADT 2012. LNCS, vol. 7841, pp. 77–94. Springer, Heidelberg (2013)
7. Borovanský, P., Kirchner, C., Kirchner, H., Moreau, P.E.: Elan from a rewriting logic point of view. Theor. Comput. Sci. 285(2), 155–185 (2002)
8. Bruni, R., Corradini, A., Gadducci, F., Lluch Lafuente, A., Vandin, A.: Modelling and analyzing adaptive self-assembly strategies with Maude. In: Durán, F. (ed.) WRLA 2012. LNCS, vol. 7571, pp. 118–138. Springer, Heidelberg (2012)
9. Bruni, R., Corradini, A., Gadducci, F., Lluch Lafuente, A., Vandin, A.: A conceptual framework for adaptation. In: de Lara, J., Zisman, A. (eds.) FASE 2012. LNCS, vol. 7212, pp. 240–254. Springer, Heidelberg (2012)
10. CafeOBJ, http://www.ldl.jaist.ac.jp/cafeobj
11. Clavel, M., Durán, F., Eker, S., Lincoln, P., Martí-Oliet, N., Meseguer, J., Talcott, C.L.: All About Maude - A High-Performance Logical Framework. LNCS, vol. 4350. Springer, Heidelberg (2007)
12. De Nicola, R., Ferrari, G.L., Loreti, M., Pugliese, R.: A language-based approach to autonomic computing. In: Beckert, et al (eds.) [4], pp. 25–48
13. De Nicola, R., Loreti, M., Pugliese, R., Tiezzi, F.: SCEL: A language for autonomic computing. Tech. rep. (January 2013), http://rap.dsi.unifi.it/scel/pdf/SCEL-TR.pdf
14. Diaconescu, R., Futatsugi, K.: CafeOBJ Report. The Language, Proof Techniques, and Methodologies for Object-Oriented Algebraic Specification. AMAST Series in Computing, vol. 6. World Scientific (1998)
15. Diaconescu, R., Futatsugi, K., Ogata, K.: CafeOBJ: Logical foundations and methodologies. Computers and Artificial Intelligence 22(3-4), 257–283 (2003)
16. GraphViz – Graph Visualization Software, http://www.graphviz.org
17. Eckhardt, J., Mühlbauer, T., AlTurki, M., Meseguer, J., Wirsing, M.: Stable availability under denial of service attacks through formal patterns. In: de Lara, J., Zisman, A. (eds.) FASE 2012. LNCS, vol. 7212, pp. 78–93. Springer, Heidelberg (2012)
18. Hölzl, M., Rauschmayer, A., Wirsing, M.: Software engineering for ensembles. In: Wirsing, M., Banâtre, J.-P., Hölzl, M., Rauschmayer, A. (eds.) Software-Intensive Systems. LNCS, vol. 5380, pp. 45–63. Springer, Heidelberg (2008)
19. IBM: An architectural blueprint for autonomic computing. Tech. rep., 3rd edn (June 2005)
20. Project InterLink (2007), http://interlink.ics.forth.gr
21. Knapp, A., Wirsing, M.: Specifying an airport with CafeOBJ: A case study. In: 2nd CafeOBJ Workshop, Tokio, Japan (1997)
22. Knapp, A., Wirsing, M.: An event space-based operational semantics of multi-threaded Java and its formalisation in CafeOBJ. In: 3rd CafeOBJ Workshop, Kanazawa, Japan (1998)
23. Meseguer, J., Talcott, C.: Semantic models for distributed object reflection. In: Magnusson, B. (ed.) ECOOP 2002. LNCS, vol. 2374, pp. 1–36. Springer, Heidelberg (2002)
24. MESSI Maude Ensemble Strategies Simulator and Inquirer (2012), http://sysma.lab.imtlucca.it/tools/ensembles

25. Pianini, D., Sebastio, S., Vandin, A.: Statistical analysis of chemical computational systems with MultiVeStA and Alchemist, http://eprints.imtlucca.it/1697
26. Sebastio, S., Vandin, A.: MultiVeStA: Statistical Model Checking for Discrete Event Simulators. In: 7th International Conference on Performance Evaluation Methodologies and Tools (ValueTools 2013), http://eprints.imtlucca.it/1798, doi:10.4108/icst.valuetools.2013.254377
27. Sen, K., Viswanathan, M., Agha, G.: On statistical model checking of stochastic systems. In: Etessami, K., Rajamani, S.K. (eds.) CAV 2005. LNCS, vol. 3576, pp. 266–280. Springer, Heidelberg (2005)
28. Sen, K., Viswanathan, M., Agha, G.A.: Vesta: A statistical model-checker and analyzer for probabilistic systems. In: Baier, C., Chiola, G., Smirni, E. (eds.) QEST 2005, pp. 251–252. IEEE Computer Society (2005)
29. Talcott, C.L.: Coordination models based on a formal model of distributed object reflection. In: Brim, L., Linden, I. (eds.) MTCoord 2005. ENTCS, vol. 150(1), pp. 143–157. Elsevier (2006)
30. Talcott, C.L.: Policy-based coordination in PAGODA: A case study. In: Boella, G., Dastani, M., Omicini, A., van der Torre, L.W., Cerna, I., Linden, I. (eds.) CoOrg 2006 & MTCoord 2006. ENTCS, vol. 181, pp. 97–112. Elsevier (2007)
31. Wirsing, M., Hölzl, M.M., Tribastone, M., Zambonelli, F.: Ascens: Engineering autonomic service-component ensembles. In: Beckert, et al. (eds.) [4], pp. 1–24

Dynamic Validation of Maude Prototypes of UML Models

Francisco Durán, Manuel Roldán, Antonio Moreno, and José María Álvarez

Dpto. Lenguajes y Ciencias de la Computación, Universidad de Málaga, Spain
{duran,mrc,amoreno,alvarezp}@lcc.uma.es

Abstract. We propose an approach for the validation of UML models annotated with OCL constraints. Specifically, we provide support for dynamically validating class invariants and operation pre/post conditions during the execution of prototypes automatically obtained from UML diagrams. The supported UML models specify both static and dynamic aspects, specifically, we focus on class and sequence diagrams. The proposal is based on Maude: UML models and OCL expressions are represented as Maude specifications, which allows us to evaluate OCL expressions on UML models by term rewriting. A model transformation allows us to accomplish this transformation automatically, and represents a first step towards the integration of the proposed facilities into development environments. The Maude specifications thus obtained can be seen as high-level executable prototypes of the annotated UML models.

1 Introduction

The benefits of early prototyping and checking at design time have for long been advocated by the software community. Specifically, different tools support the validation and verification of UML models [4], both static and dynamic ones. However, very little exists on the verification and validation of OCL constraints [40] on them, and almost nothing when we look to their dynamic behavior (see, e.g., [10,9], and discussion on related work in Section 4).

We propose a system for the validation of UML diagrams with OCL constraints, where these models include both static and dynamic specifications. Specifically, we provide support for a modeler who specifies the behavior of a system by means of UML sequence diagrams to use Maude [11,12] capabilities to validate the invariants, pre- and post-conditions specified for classes and operations using OCL.

We have developed an EMF-based model transformation that takes a UML model (currently we only support class and sequence diagrams), annotated with constraints expressed in OCL, and generates a corresponding Maude specification. For us, the behavior of a system is specified by its sequence diagrams, and the OCL constraints specified in the class diagrams provide a *contract*, the invariants each class must satisfy at any time, and the pre- and post-conditions that operations must respect. If the source sequence diagrams is an executable specification of a system, the Maude specification automatically generated will

S. Iida, J. Meseguer, and K. Ogata (Eds.): Futatsugi Festschrift, LNCS 8373, pp. 212–228, 2014.

be an executable prototype of it, and will be susceptible of being used for the automated validation of the given constraints. If the source sequence diagram were not executable, the Maude specification generated could still be seen as a skeleton of it, which could then be completed with Maude code to model the behavior of the different operations. This is the approach followed for generating final code, say Java or C++, and was the proposal in [35] and in previous works as, e.g., [41]. We however assume we are at a very abstract level of design, and do not need to have all the details that would have to be available for generating a full implementation. We believe that any UML modeler would prefer adding the missing pieces of his specification in UML, and not having to do it in Maude, a language he may be not familiar with, and if so he would be working on automatically-generated skeletons that would require a considerable amount of work before being able to complete them. The possibility of completing Maude code is even less attractive if we think on an incremental-iterative methodology were we would have to repeatedly complete the Maude specifications, or if we were able to apply other automated transformations on the (incomplete) UML models with different purposes.

Maude [11,12] is an executable formal specification language based on rewriting logic, with a rich set of validation and verification tools [12,13], increasingly used as support of UML, MDA, and OCL (see, e.g., [39,33,6,5,14]). Furthermore, Maude has demonstrated to be a good environment for rapid prototyping, a good logical and semantic framework, and also good for application development (see surveys [12,29]).

Several authors have already explored how to represent different UML diagrams in Maude (see, e.g., [23,18,30]). We currently focus on class and sequence diagrams, and we provide a basic scheme for specifying UML dynamic models as rewrite systems. The use of the proposed scheme allows us, not only to simulate UML models by executing their corresponding Maude specifications, but also to dynamically validate their OCL constraints. Furthermore, our Maude prototypes are not restricted to these uses, we could use the tools of the Maude environment to perform other kinds of analyses. For example, we have already explored the use of our Maude prototypes in conjunction with the Maude reachability-analysis tool to locate scenarios which fulfill or violate given constraints [16].

Basically, the dynamic validation of the constraints of a model requires two tasks: the identification of those states on which constraints must be satisfied, and the evaluation of the satisfaction of such constraints on them. Our approach provides support for the location of relevant states by using a given *scheme* to specify system prototypes, and the evaluation of the OCL constraints on such states is accomplished by using mOdCL [35], our OCL interpreter for Maude, which can evaluate, not only OCL constraints, but OCL expressions in general.

Our aim is to be able to directly verify UML models by extending existing modeling environments. Our transformation from UML models to Maude specifications has been developed using state-of-the-art MDE tools, namely ATL [22] and Acceleo.[1] A model-to-text transformation is used to get mOdCL Maude

---

[1] Acceleo's web site: http://www.eclipse.org/acceleo/

configurations from Ecore object models, using mOdCL as infrastructure to manage OCL constraints along execution and as a back-end tool to evaluate OCL expressions.

We have developed the transformation from UML models to Maude specifications for the Papyrus tool, which is a modeling tool inside the Eclipse environment that provides support for OCL. Thus, given a UML model (class and sequence diagrams) defined using Papyrus, we are able to automatically generate a Maude specification which can be executed and analyzed in the Maude system. Although our transformation is in theory usable with different UML environments, since it takes UML models conforming to its metamodel [31], the different possibilities offered in UML makes the portability between commercial tools tricky.

The ATL+Acceleo transformation presented in this paper together with several medium size case studies, including the complete cinema example in [35] and the classical Royal & Loyal example from [40], is available at http://maude.lcc.uma.es/mOdCL. The implementation of mOdCL, together with its documentation and some examples, may be found in the same site.

The paper is structured as follows. Section 2 serves as a brief introduction to the main technologies used in the paper, namely rewriting logic and Maude, and model-driven software development, ATL y Acceleo. Section 3 presents our proposal to represent UML class and sequence diagrams as Maude prototypes, considering their static and dynamic aspects. Section 4 revises some related work, and Section 5 draws some conclusions and anticipates some future work.

2   Technological Background

We make in this section brief presentations to the main technologies used in our approach. We assume basic knowledge of UML and OCL—we refer the interested reader to appropriate references, e.g., [4] for an introduction to UML and [40,9] for one to OCL. Section 2.1 introduces rewriting logic and the Maude language. Section 2.2 introduces model-driven software development and the transformation languages ATL and Acceleo.

2.1   Rewriting Logic and Maude

Maude [11,12] is a high-performance reflective language and system that integrates an equational style of functional programming with rewriting logic computation, supporting specification and programming for a wide range of applications [29].

Rewriting logic [28] is a logic of change that can naturally deal with state and with highly nondeterministic concurrent computations. In rewriting logic, the state space of a distributed system is specified as an algebraic data type in terms of an equational specification (Σ, E), where Σ is a signature of sorts (types) and operations, and E is a set of equational axioms. The dynamics of a system in rewriting logic is then specified by rewrite *rules* of the form $t \to t'$, where t and t' are Σ-terms. This rewriting happens modulo the equations E, describing in fact local transitions $[t]_E \rightarrow [t']_E$. These rules describe the local, concurrent transitions possible in the system, i.e., when a part of the system state fits the pattern t (modulo the equations E) then it can change to a new state in which t has been replaced by t'.

Maude supports the modeling of object-based systems by providing sorts representing the essential concepts of object (`Object`), message (`Msg`), and configuration (`Configuration`). A configuration is a multiset of objects and messages (with the empty syntax, associative commutative, union operator `__`) that represents a possible system state.

Although the user is free to define any syntax for representing objects and messages, several additional sorts and operators are introduced as a common notation. Maude provides sorts `Oid` for object identifiers, `Cid` for class identifiers, `Attribute` for attributes of objects, and `AttributeSet` for multisets of attributes (with `_,_` as union operator). Given a class C with attributes a_i of types S_i, the objects of this class are then record-like structures of the form

$$< O : C \mid a_1 : v_1, ..., a_n : v_n >$$

where O is the identifier of the object, and v_i are the current values of its attributes (with appropriate types). Class inheritance is directly supported by Maude's order-sorted type structure.

2.2   Model-Driven Software Development, ATL and Acceleo

Model-Driven Software Development (MDSD) is a methodology that proposes the use of models as the main artifacts in the software lifecycle. One of the main goals of this methodology is to maximize the compatibility between systems, simplifying the design process, and promoting the communication between the different software stakeholders.

Models, metamodels, and model transformations are the key ingredients of MDSD. Metamodels are used to describe modeling languages. Basically, a metamodel is a model that specifies, at a higher level of abstraction, the concepts of a modeling language and the relationships between them. A concept is any abstract or concrete *thing of interest*, and with a specific purpose, for the system being modeled.

If models are important in MDSD, so are the different ways of manipulating them, being model transformations the most significant one. A model-to-model transformation allows the mapping between two models. Different languages (declarative, imperative, and hybrid ones) exist in the context of MDSD for the definition of model transformations. In all cases, model transformations are defined at the metamodel level, and applied on models that conform to these metamodels. Figure 1 illustrates the typical architecture of model transformations.

We have defined a model transformation from UML models (that conform to the UML metamodel in [31]) to Maude models (that conform to the Maude

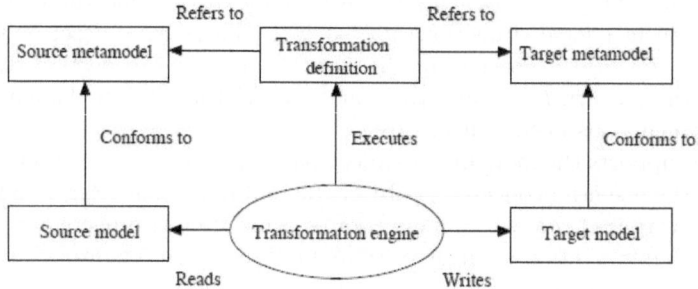

Fig. 1. Model transformation architecture (borrowed from [15])

metamodel in [32]). Such a transformation has been defined using the model transformation language ATL [21].

ATL can be used to develope exogenous—source and target models may conform to different metamodels—and unidirectional—transformation rules are executed in one direction, one of the models is the input and the other one the output—transformations. It is a hybrid language, in the sense that it has declarative and imperative constructors. Basically, an ATL model-to-model transformation is defined in terms of rules that specify relations between elements in the input model and elements in the output model. Although imperative contructs may allow us to optimize the efficiency of our transformations, declarative ones will typically be closer to how developers understand the transformations. This declarative style allows us focusing on the transformation, hiding details as the selection of input elements, the rule execution order, etc.

Once we have our Maude model, conforming to its metamodel, we need to transform it to text so that it can be loaded into the Maude system. For this purpose, there are different model-to-text transformation languages. We use Acceleo, because it follows the OMG standard for model-to-text transformations, and because its operational semantics is given by OCL, as for other tools in our setting. A model-to-text transformation in Acceleo basically consists in a mapping between each object in the input model and a string of characters that represents the output.

3   UML Prototyping with Maude

We describe in this section the Maude representation of UML models that we use, and give a very high-level description of our ATL+Acceleo transformation. The interested reader may find these details at http://maude.lcc.uma.es/mOdCL.

3.1   A Maude Representation of Class Diagrams

In UML, the structure of systems is basically specified by class diagrams. To define the concrete representation of the elements in class diagrams in Maude,

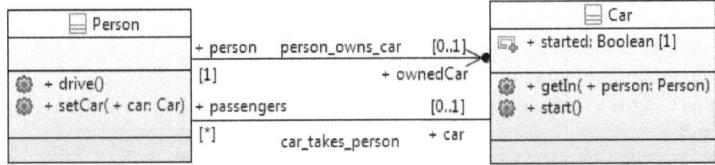

Fig. 2. Class diagram *PersonCar*

we follow an approach similar to those used in the metamodeling frameworks MOMENT-2 [5] and e-Motions [34], where class diagrams are represented as Maude modules, and system states are represented as configurations of objects. However, since these approaches deal with Ecore models, and not proper UML ones, and since we are interested in the dynamic validation of our models, our representation presents some differences with these ones: on the representation of attributes, associations and operations, as explained below; since we deal with interactions between objects, our configurations are of objects and messages, and not only of objects; and, since OCL plays a significant role in our setting, we use OCL sorts to represent the elements of class diagrams.

UML classes are represented as Maude classes (see Section 2.1). There are however a few minor differences with respect to the common Maude object-based notation. For instance, attributes and associations are represented as constants of the sort `AttributeName`, and its values are represented by OCL types.

```
op _:_ : AttributeName OclType -> Attribute [ctor] .
```

Let us consider the class diagram in Figure 2. The diagram represents a very simple system with two classes, namely `Person` and `Car`. A person can have either no car or one car, and a car can have passengers. A person is supposed to be inside no car or one car. A car has a boolean attribute `started` which indicates whether it is started or not. A person has an operation `drive()`, and a car has operations `getIn(person: Person)`, which adds a new passenger to the car, and `start()`, which toggles the starting state of the car.

The class diagram must be completed with appropriate OCL constraints. E.g., a car without passengers should always be stopped.

```
context Car inv EmptyCarIsStopped :
    started implies passengers->size() > 0
```

Similarly, pre- and post conditions may be specified for each of the operations in the class diagram. E.g., for the `getIn` operation to be executed, the person to get on the car should not be in any car, and there should be at least one available seat in the car. Once the operation is completed, the person should be one of the passengers of the car, and the number of passengers should have been increased by one.

```
context Car::getIn(person: Person)
```

```
pre:    person.car.oclIsUndefined()
        and
        passengers->size() < 5
post:   passengers->includes(person)
        and
        passengers@pre->size()+1 = passengers->size()
```

The ATL transformation is straightforward: we basically say how each element in the UML metamodel is mapped into elements in the Maude metamodel.

For each class C in the diagram the transformation produces a sort declaration for sort C, makes it subsort of Cid, and declares a constant C of sort C. Thus, for class Person we get the following declarations:

```
sort Person .
subsort Person < Cid .
op Person : -> Person [ctor] .
```

For each attribute or association A, a constant of sort AttributeName is produced. For our example we get the following declarations:

```
op started : -> AttributeName [ctor] .
op car : -> AttributeName [ctor] .
op passengers : -> AttributeName [ctor] .
op ownedCar : -> AttributeName [ctor] .
```

Notice that with these declarations, terms of sort Configuration that do not respect the corresponding model may be constructed, i.e., we could, e.g., have a Person object with an attribute started of sort Integer. This is a situation already present in the Maude representation of object-based systems, and, as for them, it may be handled by appropriate membership constraints.

Associations are represented as references to objects. Thus, associations with multiplicity 1 are represented as attributes of sort Oid, and associations with multiplicity * as attributes of sort Set (for Oid sets). Constraints as ordered, unique, other multiplicities, etc. on the associations will adjust this rule appropriately; e.g., if the association is ordered, a sequence will be used instead of a set. Restrictions on the cardinality of associations will lead to appropriate OCL constraints on them. Association classes and other features we may find in UML class diagrams are also supported.

An operation $op(arg_1 : type_1, \ldots, arg_n : type_n): type$ is represented as a constant op, of sort OpName (of operation names), and constants $arg_1, \ldots, arg_n$, of sort Arg (of arguments). Types of operation arguments are specified by using OCL sorts. For the operations in our *PersonCar* example we get the following declarations:

```
op start : -> OpName [ctor] .
op getIn : -> OpName [ctor] .
op person : -> Arg [ctor] .
op drive : -> OpName [ctor] .
op setCar : -> OpName [ctor] .
op car : -> Arg [ctor] .
```

The mOdCL evaluator will handle invariants, pre- and post-conditions as given,[2] since the appropriate mechanisms are included in the infrastructure managing the execution stack. For details, see Section 3.2 and [35].

3.2   Representation of System Behavior

In UML, the behavior of a system may be specified in several diagrams: sequence diagrams, activity diagrams, collaboration diagrams, etc. These diagrams specify the behavior of systems as the behavior of the operations specified in their class diagrams. Each of these operations may invoke other operations, perform actions, or produce changes in the states of the systems. In what follows, we focus on the behavior described by sequence diagrams, and assume synchronous messages and a single thread of execution (see [17] for its generalization to asynchronous messages and multithreaded execution).

In the Maude representation of sequence diagram, the behavior of each operation will be specified as a sequence of Maude rewrite rules. These rules may require access to information related to their invocation or computation, as the objects invoking the operations or the actual parameters used in their invocation. To gather this information, we assume that the execution context for the running operation is represented by an object of class Context with the form

```
< ctx : Context | opN : m, obj : id, args : vars, seq : N >
```

where m is the name of the active operation, id is the identifier of the current object ($self$), $vars$ is a set of pairs, each of which has the name of a parameter or a local variable and its actual value, and N is a list of pairs which guides the execution of the rules—messages are to be executed in the order established in the sequence diagram. Although for sequence diagrams without nested blocks a single natural number is enough, using a list of pairs allows us to handle alternatives and loops.

Operations may be invoked by other operations, so the possibly recursive chaining of invocations must be supported. Our proposal provides, as part of its infrastructure, an execution stack, which will keep the sequence of contexts of the pending operations. To allow the user not to have to directly manage such an execution stack, the system just need to know about the invocation and termination of operations. To this end, we assume that the rules specifying the behavior of an operation follow a basic scheme with three successive messages, namely, call, return, and resume.

Messages are assumed to be sent with the call operator:

```
op call : OpName Oid ArgsList -> Msg [ctor] .
```

When a message $m(args\text{-}list)$ is to be sent to an object obj, a message call(m, obj, $args\text{-}list$) that represents the state of the system is placed in

---

[2] For mOdCL to be able to tokenize OCL expressions, white spaces must be placed around its operators.

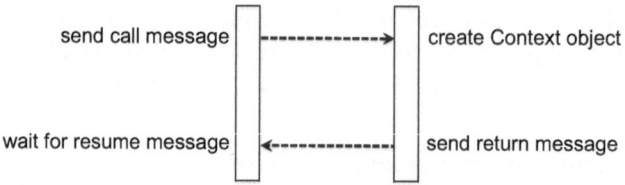

Fig. 3. Operation behavior specification scheme

the configuration of objects and messages. This `call` message is then processed by the execution stack infrastructure, which creates a `Context` object with the identifier of the object sending the message, the name of the invoked operation, and the values of its parameters.

Figure 3 shows how a `Context` object is generated when a `call` message shows up in the system configuration. The execution of the sender object gets blocked until the operation is completed, waiting for a `resume(m, result)` message. The invoked operation is then executed until a `return(result)` message is sent. When the stack infrastructure detects such a `return` message, it pulls the context on the top of the execution stack and puts a `resume` message in the configuration.

```
op return : OclType -> Msg [ctor] .
op resume : OpName OclType -> Msg [ctor] .
```

The parameter of the `return` operation is the value to be returned as result, which is then set as second parameter of the corresponding `resume` message.

The stack infrastructure includes the definition of classes `Stack` and `Context`. A stack object has a single attribute `state` that stores the stack of pending context objects. Respective equations `CALL` and `RETURN` are in charge of dealing with the `call` and `return` messages as explained above, pushing and pulling contexts into the stack as expected. To make the user completely unaware of the underlying stack, an initialization equation `INIT` is in charge of adding an empty stack to the initial configuration.

Given the scheme proposed in Sections 3.1 and 3.2, we know that `CALL` and `RETURN` equations are executed to handle, respectively, `call` and `return` messages. This allows us to locate states before and after the execution of operations. We will make use of that to check pre-conditions and invariants before the execution of operations, and post-conditions and invariants after their completion.

Finally, given the Maude prototype thus obtained, we can define an initial state and use the Maude rewriting commands to execute our system (see Section 3.5). Thanks to the infrastructure managing the execution stack and the generic behavior scheme described above, the validation of OCL constraints is accomplished automatically. If all constraints are respected, the execution terminates as any normal execution. However, if some constraint is violated, the system execution gets stopped and an `error` message is provided.

3.3   OCL Expressions and the Behavior of Systems

Traditionally, UML sequence diagrams model interactions between objects. However, different extensions available since UML 2.0 allow us to use them for more than that. The possibility of using OCL expressions as arguments in method invocations, and as assignments in found messages[3] allow us to specify the complete behavior of systems using sequence diagrams.

We explain here the transformation for simple sequence diagrams. See the documentation at `http://maude.lcc.uma.es/mOdCL` for details on the transformation for diagrams with blocks, conditionals and loops.

Our transformation generates a Maude rule per message in the sequence diagram. All these rules are top rules, with an operator `{_}` grabbing the entire configuration. The basic structure of the lefthand side of each of these rules, intended for handling a message m sent to an object of class C is as follows:

```
{  < ctx : Context | opN : m, obj : Self:Oid, args : vars, seq : N >
   < Self:Oid : C | Attrs >
   Cf:Configuration  }
```

The same components will appear in the righthand side of the rule. Several specific cases are to be considered:

(call) If the rule represents an invocation to another method, the righthand side of the rule will include

```
call(iMethod, iMethodClass, (methodArgsList))
```

where *iMethod* is the name of the method being invoked, *iMethodClass* is the name of the class the method is defined in—possibly a variable in the *args* list in the context object—and *methodArgsList* is a (possibly empty) list or arguments of the invoked method.

(resume) If the rule is representing an invocation to a method m in the sequence diagram and this invocation is preceded by an invocation to another operation, the resume operator is to be added to the lefthand side of the rule

```
resume(previousMethod, Rst:OclType)
```

where *previousMethod* is the name of the operation called in the previous message.

(return) If the rule represents either the last rule in the sequence diagram being transformed or a lost message,[4] the righthand side of the rule will include

```
return(returnValue)
```

where *returnValue* is the value to be returned, which is supposed to agree with the type of the method.

---

[3] In UML, a *found message* is a message whose caller is not shown.
[4] In UML, a *lost message* is a message whose callee is not shown.

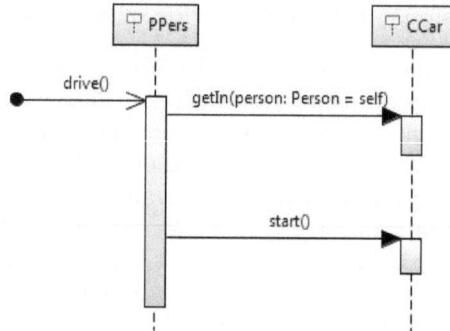

Fig. 4. Sequence diagram of the operation `Person::drive()`

As indicated above, OCL expressions may be used as method arguments and return values. To handle them properly, all method arguments and return values are evaluated using the `eval` mOdCL operation. The use of the `{_}` operator in the rules specifying the behavior of the system allows us to use the entire system to evaluate OCL expressions.

3.4   Transformation Example: The *PersonCar* Case

We show in this section the UML specification of the behavior of operations in the class diagram in Figure 2, and illustrate the Maude code obtained by the transformation.

The sequence diagram shown in Figure 4 represents the behavior of the `drive()` operation. In it, we see two lifelines, namely `PPers`, of class `Person`, and `CCar`, of class `Car`. The objects that represent these lifelines are related by the `person_owns_car` association (see Figure 2). The first message in the sequence, `getIn`, has a single parameter, `person`, of type `Person`. We can see in the figure how the parameter `person` receives the OCL expression 'self' as value. Note that the OCL expression is quoted: it is handled as such by the mOdCL `eval` function. The `drive()` operation is completed by invoking the `start()` operation once the `getIn` one has concluded. The code generated by the transformation for the `Person::drive()` operation is shown in Figure 5.

Note how the generated code follows the structure presented in the previous section:

1. The first rule, `1:GETIN::CAR`, corresponds to the first message addressed to `CCar` in the sequence diagram. Notice the `call` operation in the righthand side of this rule representing the invocation of the method, and how the parameter of the message is evaluated using the `eval` mOdCL operation (the ellipsis replaces the entire configuration in the lefthand side).
2. The second rule, `2:START::CAR`, corresponds to the second message in the diagram. Since it has no parameters, the arguments list of the `call` operation in its righthand side is set to `empty`.

```
rl [1:GETIN::CAR] :
 { < ctx : Context | opN : drive, obj : Self:Oid, args : (AL-1:ArgsList),
     seq : [ ( 1 | 1 ) ] >
     < Self:Oid : P:Person | ownedCar : VAR7:OclType, car : VAR5:OclType,
       AS-1:AttributeSet >
     Cf:Configuration}
 =>
 { < ctx : Context | opN : drive, obj : Self:Oid, args : (AL-1:ArgsList),
     seq : [ ( 1 | 2 ) ] >
     < Self:Oid : P:Person | ownedCar : VAR7:OclType, car : VAR5:OclType,
       AS-1:AttributeSet >
     call(getIn, VAR7:OclType, (arg(person, eval(self, ...))))
     Cf:Configuration } .
rl [2:START::CAR] :
 { < ctx : Context | opN : drive, obj : Self:Oid, args : (AL-1:ArgsList),
     seq : [ ( 1 | 2 ) ] >
     < Self:Oid : P:Person | ownedCar : VAR7:OclType, car : VAR5:OclType,
       AS-1:AttributeSet >
     resume(getIn, Rst:OclType)
     Cf:Configuration }
 =>
 { < ctx : Context | opN : drive, obj : Self:Oid, args : (AL-1:ArgsList),
     seq : [ ( 1 | 3 ) ] >
     < Self:Oid : P:Person | ownedCar : VAR7:OclType, car : VAR5:OclType,
       AS-1:AttributeSet >
     call(start, VAR7:OclType, empty)
     Cf:Configuration } .
rl [3:RETURN] :
 { < ctx : Context | opN : drive, obj : Self:Oid, args : (AL-1:ArgsList),
     seq : [ ( 1 | 3 ) ] >
     < Self:Oid : P:Person | ownedCar : VAR7:OclType, car : VAR5:OclType,
       AS-1:AttributeSet >
     resume(start, Rst:OclType)
     Cf:Configuration }
 =>
 { < ctx : Context | opN : drive, obj : Self:Oid, args : (AL-1:ArgsList),
     seq : [ ( 1 | 4 ) ] >
     < Self:Oid : P:Person | ownedCar : VAR7:OclType, car : VAR5:OclType,
       AS-1:AttributeSet >
     return(null)
     Cf:Configuration } .
```

Fig. 5. Maude code generated for the operation `Person::drive()`

3. The third and last rule `3:RETURN` models the return of the `drive` operation. Although the operation returns no value, we must send the `return` message to unblock other potential rules waiting on the corresponding `resume`.

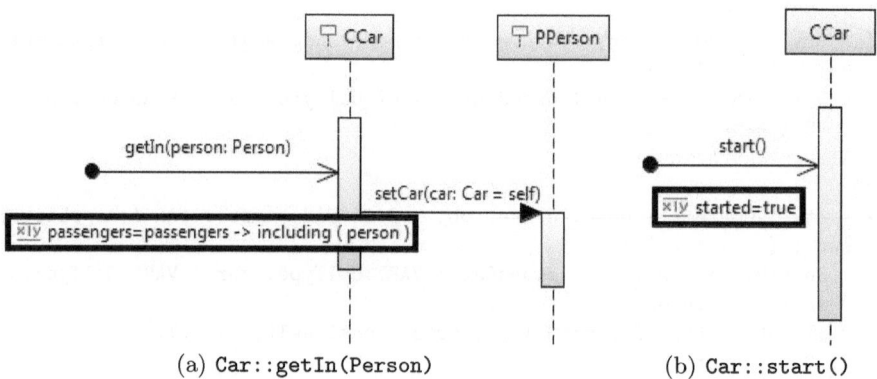

(a) `Car::getIn(Person)`   (b) `Car::start()`

Fig. 6. Sequence diagrams for operations `Car::getIn(Person)` and `Car::start()`

The sequence diagrams for operations `getIn` and `start` are shown in Figures 6(a) and 6(b), respectively. Note how these operations change attribute values. This is done by using found messages. For each attribute to be modified, the found message has a parameter with name the name of the attribute to be modified and as value an OCL expression. The transformation of the entire UML model of the system produces a Maude specification which can be executed (see Section 3.5).

3.5   Execution of the Diagrams

UML models described as explained in the previous sections can be automatically transformed into a Maude specification by using our ATL and Acceleo transformations. The resulting specification is a collection of Maude modules which specify in Maude the structure and behavior modeled by UML class and sequence diagrams.

To be able to use the thus obtained specification to rewrite, we just need an initial configuration. We plan to get this initial configuration from object diagrams, but currently it has to be provided directly as a Maude term.

Given `Oid` constants `ada` and `ferrari`, we may ask `ada` to drive her `ferrari` with the following command:

```
rewrite
  [ < ada : Person | car : ferrari >
    < ferrari : Car | started : false, passengers : Set{mt-ord} >
    call(drive, ada, empty) ] .
result Configuration+:
  { resume(drive, null)
    < stack : Stack | state : nil >
    < ada : Person | car : ferrari >
    < ferrari : Car | started : true, passengers : Set{ada} > }
```

The given initial configuration has been executed using the rewrite rules in the Maude specification obtained by the transformation, taking into account the OCL constraints specified for the different operations. Note that, in the resulting term, the `ferrari` object has its `started` attribute to `true`, and `ada` appears in its set of passengers. The drive operations has returned `null` as result, which appears in the `resume` message.

4 Related Work

An increasing number of commercial UML tools provide some kind of support for OCL. However, they are in general limited to parsing, type checking, and evaluation of expressions or checking of instances or models (see, e.g. the discussion on tool support in [9]).

There are also many contributions providing some analysis of OCL constraints on UML diagrams. Tools like USE [19], Dresden OCL [38], MDT [27] or the evaluator mOdCL, can be used to check OCL constraints on concrete system states (snapshots), that is, can evaluate OCL expressions on UML object diagrams. In USE, systems can also be simulated, and properties like constraint consistency or independency can be checked. Although reasoning on OCL is undecidable in general, some support for verification is provided by tools like HOL-OCL [7], based on the HOL-Isabelle theorem prover, approaches looking at OCL constraints as satisfiability problems using Alloy [3,24,37], or tools expressing them as constraint satisfaction problems [8]. Some of them use sequence diagrams as input describing test cases to be validated [19] or as output that shows scenarios demonstrating given properties [36].

Hamann, Hofrichter and Gogolla propose in [20] an extension of the USE tool for validating OCL constraints on state diagrams. In such a work, the semantics of operations is described by using their SOIL language, and the USE tool is responsible for the execution and the validation of the OCL constraints.

UML static and dynamic diagrams, without OCL constraints, have been formalized and used to reason about them by different authors using, e.g., the B-method [1], Petri Nets [2], Rewriting Logic [25], or finite automata [42].

The idea of using Maude specifications as executable prototypes of systems is not new (see, e.g., [12] for a revision on the literature). In the context of UML, different authors have proposed the use of Maude to formalize UML models [18] or some of its diagrams [23,26,30], and as support for prototyping. E.g., Wirsing and Knapp propose in [41] a formal approach to design object-oriented systems based on the use of rewriting logic and UML diagrams. In their proposal, diagrams are semi-automatically translated into incomplete Maude specifications which then have to be completed by hand. The resulting specifications would be used as prototypes of the systems. In our opinion, this proposal requires an experimented Maude user to complete the generated Maude specifications.

5   Conclusions and Future Work

We have presented a proposal to dynamically validating OCL constraints on high level Maude prototypes of UML models. Our dynamic validator relies on the use of mOdCL, our evaluator of OCL expressions, to validate constraints on concrete states. The mOdCL evaluator has been designed as an external component, and can also be used for statically validating OCL constraints. Thus, we provide the possibility of validating either statically or dynamically OCL constraints on UML models.

Given the specification of a system and its OCL constraints, many possibilities are opened inside the Maude formal environment: theorem proving, model checking, reachability analysis, invariant analyzing, etc. We have already explored some of the possibilities, e.g., using our validator in conjunction with the reachability tools of Maude to automatically generate test case violating the OCL constraints [16]. But mechanisms to prove the independence or inconsistency of constraints, and the static validation of dynamic constraints using the Maude's invariant analyzer have already been initiated, and we plan to advance on them in the near future.

Acknowledgements. This work was partially supported by Research Project TIN2011-23795 and by Universidad de Málaga (Campus de Excelencia Internacional Andalucía Tech).

References

1. UML-B, http://wiki.event-b.org/index.php/UML-B
2. Ameedeen, M.A., Bordbar, B.: A model driven approach to represent sequence diagrams as free choice Petri Nets. In: 12th Intl. IEEE Enterprise Distributed Object Computing Conf., ECOC 2008, pp. 213–221. IEEE (2008)
3. Anastasakis, K., Bordbar, B., Georg, G., Ray, I.: On challenges of model transformation from UML to Alloy. Software and System Modeling 9(1), 69–86 (2010)
4. Booch, G., Rumbaugh, J., Jacobson, I.: The Unified Modeling Language User Guide, 2nd edn. Addison-Wesley (2005)
5. Boronat, A., Meseguer, J.: An Algebraic Semantics for MOF. In: Fiadeiro, J.L., Inverardi, P. (eds.) FASE 2008. LNCS, vol. 4961, pp. 377–391. Springer, Heidelberg (2008)
6. Boronat, A., Meseguer, J.: Algebraic semantics of ocl-constrained metamodel specifications. In: Oriol, M., Meyer, B. (eds.) TOOLS EUROPE 2009. LNBIP, vol. 33, pp. 96–115. Springer, Heidelberg (2009)
7. Brucker, A.D., Wolff, B.: HOL-OCL: A Formal Proof Environment for UML/OCL. In: Fiadeiro, J.L., Inverardi, P. (eds.) FASE 2008. LNCS, vol. 4961, pp. 97–100. Springer, Heidelberg (2008)
8. Cabot, J., Clarisó, R., Riera, D.: Verification of uml/ocl class diagrams using constraint programming. In: First Intl. Conf. on Software Testing, Verification, and Validation, ICST 2008, pp. 73–80. IEEE (2008)
9. Cabot, J., Gogolla, M.: Object constraint language (OCL): A definitive guide. In: Bernardo, M., Cortellessa, V., Pierantonio, A. (eds.) SFM 2012. LNCS, vol. 7320, pp. 58–90. Springer, Heidelberg (2012)

10. Cabot, J., Teniente, E.: Constraint support in MDA tools: A survey. In: Rensink, A., Warmer, J. (eds.) ECMDA-FA 2006. LNCS, vol. 4066, pp. 256–267. Springer, Heidelberg (2006)

11. Clavel, M., Durán, F., Eker, S., Lincoln, P., Martí-Oliet, N., Meseguer, J., Quesada, J.F.: Maude: Specification and Programming in Rewriting Logic. Theoretical Computer Science 285(2), 187–243 (2002)

12. Clavel, M., Durán, F., Eker, S., Lincoln, P., Martí-Oliet, N., Meseguer, J., Talcott, C.: All About Maude - A High-Performance Logical Framework. LNCS, vol. 4350. Springer, Heidelberg (2007)

13. Clavel, M., Durán, F., Hendrix, J., Lucas, S., Meseguer, J., Ölveczky, P.: The Maude Formal Tool Environment. In: Mossakowski, T., Montanari, U., Haveraaen, M. (eds.) CALCO 2007. LNCS, vol. 4624, pp. 173–178. Springer, Heidelberg (2007)

14. Clavel, M., Egea, M.: ITP/OCL: A rewriting-based validation tool for UML+OCL static class diagrams. In: Johnson, M., Vene, V. (eds.) AMAST 2006. LNCS, vol. 4019, pp. 368–373. Springer, Heidelberg (2006)

15. Czarnecki, K., Helsen, S.: Feature-based survey of model transformation approaches. IBM Syst. J. 45(3), 621–645 (2006)

16. Durán, F., Gogolla, M., Roldán, M.: Tracing Properties of UML and OCL Models with Maude. In: Durán, F., Rusu, V. (eds.) Proc. of Intl. Workshop on Algebraic Methods in Model-Based Software Engineering, AMMSE 2011, Electronic Proceedings in Theoretical Computer Science (2011)

17. Durán, F., Roldán, M.: Validating OCL constraints on Maude prototypes of UML models (2012), http://maude.lcc.uma.es/mOdCL/docs/mOdCL-validation.pdf

18. Fernández-Alemán, J.L., Toval-Álvarez, A.: Seamless Formalizing the UML Semantics through Metamodels. In: Siau, K., Halpin, T. (eds.) Unified Modeling Language: Systems Analysis, Design and Development Issues, pp. 224–248. Idea Group Publishing (2001)

19. Gogolla, M., Büttner, F., Richters, M.: USE: A UML-based Specification Environment for Validating UML and OCL. Science of Computer Programming 69(1-3), 27–34 (2007)

20. Hamann, L., Hofrichter, O., Gogolla, M.: On integrating structure and behavior modeling with OCL. In: France, R.B., Kazmeier, J., Breu, R., Atkinson, C. (eds.) MODELS 2012. LNCS, vol. 7590, pp. 235–251. Springer, Heidelberg (2012)

21. Jouault, F., Allilaire, F., Bézivin, J., Kurtev, I.: ATL: A model transformation tool. Science of Computer Programming 72(1-2), 31–39 (2008)

22. Jouault, F., Kurtev, I.: Transforming models with ATL. In: Bruel, J.-M. (ed.) MoDELS 2005. LNCS, vol. 3844, pp. 128–138. Springer, Heidelberg (2006)

23. Knapp, A.: Generating Rewrite Theories from UML Collaborations. In: Futatsugi, K., Nakagawa, A., Tamai, T. (eds.) CAFE: An Industrial-Strength Algebraic Formal Method, pp. 97–120. Elsevier (2000)

24. Kuhlmann, M., Gogolla, M.: From UML and OCL to relational logic and back. In: France, R.B., Kazmeier, J., Breu, R., Atkinson, C. (eds.) MODELS 2012. LNCS, vol. 7590, pp. 415–431. Springer, Heidelberg (2012)

25. Lund, M.S.: Operational Analysis of Sequence Diagram Specifications. PhD thesis (2007)

26. Lund, M.S., Stølen, K.: Deriving tests from UML 2.0 sequence diagrams with neg and assert. In: Intl. Workshop on Automation of Software Test, AST 2006, pp. 22–28. ACM (2006)

27. MDT-OCL-Team. MDT OCL (2008), http://www.eclipse.org/modeling/mdt/?project=ocl/

28. Meseguer, J.: Conditional Rewriting Logic as a Unified Model of Concurrency. Theoretical Computer Science 96, 73–155 (1992)
29. Meseguer, J.: 20 years of rewriting logic. Technical report, University of Illinois at Urbana-Champaign (2012), `http://hdl.handle.net/2142/32096`
30. Mokhati, F., Badri, M.: Generating Maude Specifications from UML Use Case Diagrams. Journal of Object Technology 8(2), 136–319 (2009)
31. Object Management Group. OMG unified modeling language (OMG UML), superstructure, v2.1.2 (formal/2007-11-02) (2007), `http://atenea.lcc.uma.es/index.php/Main_Page/Resources/MaudeMM`
32. Rivera, J.E., Durán, F., Vallecillo, A.: A metamodel for Maude, `http://atenea.lcc.uma.es/index.php/Main_Page/Resources/MaudeMM`
33. Rivera, J.E., Durán, F., Vallecillo, A.: Formal Specification and Analysis of Domain Specific Models Using Maude. Simulation 85(11-12), 778–792 (2009)
34. Rivera, J.E., Durán, F., Vallecillo, A.: A Graphical Approach for Modeling Time-Dependent Behavior of DSLs. In: 2009 IEEE Symposium on Visual Languages and Human-Centric Computing, VL/HCC 2009, pp. 51–55. IEEE (2009)
35. Roldán, M., Durán, F.: Dynamic validation of OCL constraints with mOdCL. ECEASST 44 (2011)
36. Soeken, M., Wille, R., Drechsler, R.: Verifying dynamic aspects of UML models. In: Design, Automation and Test in Europe, DATE 2011, pp. 1077–1082. IEEE (2011)
37. Soeken, M., Wille, R., Kuhlmann, M., Gogolla, M., Drechsler, R.: Verifying UML/OCL models using boolean satisfiability. In: Design, Automation and Test in Europe, DATE 2010, pp. 1341–1344. IEEE (2010)
38. Software Technology Group. DresdenOCL, `http://www.dresden-ocl.org/`
39. Troya, J., Vallecillo, A.: A rewriting logic semantics for ATL. Journal of Object Technology 10(5), 1–29 (2011)
40. Warmer, J., Kleppe, A.: The Object Constraint Language: Getting Your Models Ready for MDA. Addison-Wesley (2003)
41. Wirsing, M., Knapp, A.: A formal approach to object-oriented software engineering. Theoretical Computer Science 285, 519–560 (2001)
42. Zhang, C., Duan, Z.: Specification and verification of UML 2.0 sequence diagrams using event deterministic finite automata. In: Fifth Intl. Conf. on Secure Software Integration and Reliability Improvement, SSIRI 2011, pp. 41–46. IEEE (2011)

Inspecting Rewriting Logic Computations
(in a Parametric and Stepwise Way)[*]

María Alpuente[1], Demis Ballis[2], Francisco Frechina[1], and Julia Sapiña[1]

[1] DSIC-ELP, Universitat Politècnica de València,
Camino de Vera s/n, Apdo 22012, 46071 Valencia, Spain
[2] CLIP Lab, Technical University of Madrid,
E-28660, Boadilla del Monte, Madrid, Spain

Abstract. Trace inspection is concerned with techniques that allow the trace content to be searched for specific components. This paper presents a rich and highly dynamic, parameterized technique for the trace inspection of Rewriting Logic theories that allows the non-deterministic execution of a given unconditional rewrite theory to be followed up in different ways. Using this technique, an analyst can browse, slice, filter, or search the traces as they come to life during the program execution. Starting from a selected state in the computation tree, the navigation of the trace is driven by a user-defined, inspection criterion that specifies the required exploration mode. By selecting different inspection criteria, one can automatically derive a family of practical algorithms such as program steppers and more sophisticated dynamic trace slicers that facilitate the dynamic detection of control and data dependencies across the computation tree. Our methodology, which is implemented in the Anima graphical tool, allows users to capture the impact of a given criterion thereby facilitating the detection of improper program behaviors.

1 Introduction

Dynamic analysis is crucial for understanding the behavior of large systems. Dynamic information is typically represented using execution traces whose analysis is almost impracticable without adequate tool support. Existing tools for analyzing large execution traces rely on a set of visualization techniques that facilitate the exploration of the trace content. Common capabilities of these tools include stepping the program execution while searching for particular components and having the option to simplify the traces by hiding some specific contents.

[*] This work has been partially supported by the EU (FEDER), the Spanish MEC project ref. TIN2010-21062-C02-02, the Spanish MICINN complementary action ref. TIN2009-07495-E, and by Generalitat Valenciana ref. PROMETEO2011/052. This work was carried out during the tenure of D. Ballis' ERCIM "Alain Bensoussan" Postdoctoral Fellowship. The research leading to these results has received funding from the European Union Seventh Framework Programme (FP7/2007-2013) under grant agreement n. 246016. F. Frechina was supported by FPU-ME grant AP2010-5681.

S. Iida, J. Meseguer, and K. Ogata (Eds.): Futatsugi Festschrift, LNCS 8373, pp. 229–255, 2014.
© Springer-Verlag Berlin Heidelberg 2014

Program animation or *stepping* refers to the very common debugging technique of executing code one step at a time, allowing the user to inspect the program state and related data before and after the execution step. This allows the user to evaluate the effects of a given statement or instruction in isolation and thereby gain insight into the program behavior (or misbehavior). Nearly all modern IDEs, debuggers, and testing tools currently support this mode of execution optionally, where animation is achieved either by forcing execution breakpoints, code instrumentation, or instruction simulation.

Rewriting Logic (RWL) is a very general *logical* and *semantic framework*, which is particularly suitable for formalizing highly concurrent, complex systems (e.g., biological systems [7] and Web systems [2,6]). RWL is efficiently implemented in the high-performance system Maude [9]. Roughly speaking, a *rewriting logic theory* seamlessly combines a *term rewriting system* (TRS) with an *equational theory* that may include equations and axioms (i.e., algebraic laws such as commutativity, associativity, and unity) so that rewrite steps are performed *modulo* the equations and axioms. In recent years, debugging and optimization techniques based on RWL have received growing attention [1,15,19,20], but to the best of our knowledge, no versatile program animator or trace inspection tool for RWL/Maude has been formally developed to date.

To debug Maude programs, Maude has a basic tracing facility that allows the user to advance through the program execution stepwise with the possibility to set break points, and lets him/her select the statements to be traced, except for the application of algebraic axioms that are not under user control and are never recorded explicitly in the trace. All rewrite steps that are obtained by applying the equations or rules for the selected function symbols are shown in the output trace so that the only way to simplify the displayed view of the trace is by manually fixing the traceable equations or rules. Thus, the trace is typically huge and incomplete, and when the user detects an erroneous intermediate result, it is difficult to determine where the incorrect inference started. Moreover, this trace is either directly displayed or written to a file (in both cases, in plain text format) thus only being amenable for manual inspection by the user. This is in contrast with the enriched traces described in this work, which are complete (all execution steps are recorded by default) and can be sliced automatically so that they can be dramatically simplified in order to facilitate a specific analysis. Also, the trace can be directly displayed or delivered in its meta-level representation, which is very useful for further automated manipulation.

Contributions. This paper presents the first semantic-based, parametric trace exploration technique for RWL computations that involve rewriting modulo associativity (A), commutativity (C), and unity (U) axioms. Our technique is based on a generic animation algorithm that can be tuned to work with different modalities, including *incremental stepping* and *automated forward slicing*, which drastically reduces the size and complexity of the traces under examination. The algorithm is fully general and can be applied for debugging as well as for optimizing any RWL-based tool that manipulates unconditional RWL theories. Our formulation takes into account the precise way in which Maude mechanizes the equational rewriting process modulo B, where B may contain any combination of associativity, commutativity, and unity axioms for different binary operators, and revisits all those rewrite steps in an informed, fine-grained way where each small step corresponds to the application of an equation, equational axiom, or rule. This allows us to explain the input execution trace with regard to the set of symbols of interest (input symbols) by tracing them along the execution trace so that, in the case of the forward slicing modality, all data that are not descendants of the observed symbols are filtered out. The ideas are implemented and tested in a graphical tool called Anima that provides a skillful and highly dynamic interface for the dynamic analysis of RWL computations.

Related Work. Program animators have existed since the early years of programming. Although several steppers have been implemented in the functional programming community (see [10] for references), none of these systems applies to the animation and dynamic forward slicing of Maude computations. An algebraic stepper for Scheme is defined and formally proved in [10], which is included in the DrScheme programming environment. The stepper reduces Scheme programs to values (according to the reduction semantics of Scheme) and is useful for explaining the semantics of linguistic facilities and for studying the behavior of small programs. In order to discover all of the steps that occur during the program evaluation, the stepper rewrites (or "instruments") the code, which is in contrast to our technique which does not rely on program instrumentation.

In [4,5], an incremental, backward trace slicer was presented that generates a trace slice of an execution trace $\mathcal{T}$ by tracing back a set of symbols of interest along (an instrumented version of) $\mathcal{T}$, while data that are not required to produce the target symbols are simply removed. This can be very helpful in debugging since any information that is not strictly needed to deliver a critical part of the result is discarded, which helps answer the question of "what program components might effect a selected computation". However, for the dual problem of "what program components might be effected by a selected computation", a kind of forward expansion is needed (which has been overlooked to date in RWL research).

Plan of the paper. After some preliminaries in Section 2 that describe basic notions of RWL, Section 3 summarizes the rewriting modulo equational theories defined in Maude and provides a convenient trace instrumentation technique that facilitates the stepwise inspection of Maude computations. Section 4 formalizes trace inspection as a semantics-based procedure that is parameterized by the criterion for the inspection. Section 5 formalizes three different exploration techniques that are mechanically obtained as an instance of the generic scheme: 1) an interactive program stepper that allows rewriting logic theories to be stepwisely animated; 2) a partial stepper that is able to work with partial inputs; and 3) an automated, forward slicing technique that is suitable for analyzing complex, textually-large system computations by filtering out the irrelevant data that do not derive from some selected terms of interest. The Anima tool is described in Section 6, and Section 7 concludes.

2   Preliminaries

Let us recall some important notions that are relevant to this work. We assume some basic knowledge of term rewriting [21] and Rewriting Logic [16]. Some familiarity with the Maude language [9] is also required.

We consider an *order-sorted signature* Σ, with a finite poset of sorts $(S, <)$ that models the usual subsort relation [9]. We assume an S-sorted family $\mathcal{V} = \{\mathcal{V}_s\}_{s \in S}$ of disjoint variable sets. $\tau(\Sigma, \mathcal{V})_s$ and $\tau(\Sigma)_s$ are the sets of terms and ground terms of sort s, respectively. We write $\tau(\Sigma, \mathcal{V})$ and $\tau(\Sigma)$ for the corresponding term algebras. The set of variables that occur in a term t is denoted by $Var(t)$. In order to simplify the presentation, we often disregard sorts when no confusion can arise.

A *position* w in a term t is represented by a sequence of natural numbers that addresses a subterm of t (Λ denotes the empty sequence, i.e., the root position). By notation $w_1.w_2$, we denote the concatenation of positions (sequences) w_1 and w_2. Positions are ordered by the prefix ordering; that is, given the positions w_1 and w_2, $w_1 \leq w_2$ if there exists a position u such that $w_1.u = w_2$.

Given a term t, we let $Pos(t)$ denote the set of positions of t. By $t_{|w}$, we denote the *subterm* of t at position w, and $t[s]_w$ specifies the result of *replacing* the subterm $t_{|w}$ by the term s.

A *substitution* $\sigma \equiv \{x_1/t_1, x_2/t_2, \ldots, x_n/t_n\}$ is a mapping from the set of variables $\mathcal{V}$ to the set of terms $\tau(\Sigma, \mathcal{V})$ which is equal to the identity almost everywhere except over a set of variables $\{x_1, \ldots, x_n\}$. The *domain* of σ is the set $Dom(\sigma) = \{x \in \mathcal{V} \mid x\sigma \neq x\}$. By id we denote the *identity* substitution. The application of a substitution σ to a term t, denoted $t\sigma$, is defined by induction on the structure of terms:

$$t\sigma = \begin{cases} x\sigma & \text{if } t = x, x \in \mathcal{V} \\ f(t_1\sigma, \ldots, t_n\sigma) & \text{if } t = f(t_1, \ldots, t_n), n \geq 0 \end{cases}$$

Given two terms s and t, a substitution σ is the *matcher* of t in s, if $s\sigma = t$. The term t is an *instance* of the term s, iff there exists a matcher σ of t in s. By $match_s(t)$, we denote the function that returns a matcher of t in s if such a matcher exists.

A labelled *equation* (or simply *equation*) is an expression of the form $[l] : \lambda = \rho$, where $\lambda, \rho \in \tau(\Sigma, \mathcal{V})$, $Var(\rho) \subseteq Var(\lambda)$, and l is a label, i.e., a name that identifies the equation. A labelled *rewrite* rule (or simply *rewrite* rule) is an expression of the form $[l] : \lambda \Rightarrow \rho$, where $\lambda, \rho \in \tau(\Sigma, \mathcal{V})$, $Var(\rho) \subseteq Var(\lambda)$, and l is a label. When no confusion can arise, rule and equation labels are often omitted. The term λ (resp., ρ) is called *left-hand side* (resp. *right-hand side*) of the rule $\lambda \Rightarrow \rho$ (resp. equation $\lambda = \rho$).

A *Term Rewriting System* (TRS for short) R is a finite set of rewrite rules. We formalize the rewrite relation $\rightarrow_R$ w.r.t. a TRS R as follows. A rewrite step is the application of a rewrite rule to a term t that replaces a *redex* (reducible expression) of t by its contracted version, or *contractum*. Formally, a term t *rewrites* to a term t' (in symbols $t \overset{r,\sigma,w}{\rightarrow}_R t'$) iff there exists a rewrite rule $[r] :$

$(\lambda \Rightarrow \rho) \in R$, a substitution σ, and a position w of t such that the redex $t_{|w} = \lambda\sigma$ and $t' = t[\rho\sigma]_w$.

3   Rewriting Modulo Equational Theories

Roughly speaking, a rewriting logic theory [20] seamlessly combines a term rewriting system with an equational theory that may include equations and axioms (i.e., algebraic laws such as commutativity, associativity, and unity) so that rewrite steps are applied modulo the equations and axioms. Within this framework, the system states are typically represented as elements of an algebraic data type that is specified by the equational theory, while the system computations are modeled via the rewrite rules, which describe transitions between states.

More formally, an *order-sorted equational theory* is a pair (Σ, E), where Σ is an order-sorted signature, $E = \Delta \cup B$ with Δ a collection of (oriented) equations, and B a collection of equational axioms (i.e., algebraic laws such as associativity, commutativity, and unity) that can be associated with any binary operator of Σ^1. The equational theory (Σ, E) induces a congruence relation on the term algebra $\tau(\Sigma, \mathcal{V})$, which is denoted by $=_E$. A *rewrite theory* is a triple $\mathcal{R} = (\Sigma, \Delta \cup B, R)$, where $(\Sigma, \Delta \cup B)$ is an order-sorted equational theory, and R is a TRS.

Example 1. The following rewrite theory, encoded in Maude, specifies a buggy version of the fault-tolerant client-server communication protocol of [17].

```
mod CLIENT-SERVER-TRANSF is inc NAT  .          var C S H : Host .
                                                var Q : Question .
  sorts Content State Msg Cli Serv Host         var A : Answer .
    Data CliName ServName Question Answer .      var D : Data .
                                                var CNT : Content .
  subsorts Msg Cli Serv < State .
  subsorts CliName ServName < Host .            eq [inc] : f(S, C, Q) = (Q + 1) .
  subsorts Nat < Question Answer < Data .
                                                rl [req]   : [C, S, Q, na] =>
  ops Srv-A Srv-B : -> ServName .                            [C, S, Q, na] &
  ops Cli-A Cli-B : -> CliName .                             S <- {C, Q} .
  op null : -> State .                          rl [reply] : S <- {C, Q} & [S] =>
  op _&_ : State State -> State [assoc comm                  [S] &
                      id: null] .                            C <- {S, f(S, C, Q)} .
  op _<-_ : Host Content -> Msg .               rl [rec]   : C <- {S, D} &
  op {_,_} : Host Data -> Content .                          [C, S, Q, A] =>
  op [_,_,_,_] : CliName ServName                            [C, S, Q, A] .
                Question Answer -> Cli .        rl [dupl]  : (H <- CNT) =>
  op na : -> Answer .                                        (H <- CNT) & (H <- CNT) .
  op [_] : ServName -> Serv .                   rl [loss]  : (H <- CNT) => null .
  op f : ServName CliName Question -> Answer .  endm
```

The specification models an environment where several clients and servers interact. Each server can serve many clients. However, for the sake of simplicity, we assume that each client communicates with a single server.

The names of clients and servers belong to the sorts CliName and ServName, respectively. Clients are represented as 4-tuples of the form [C, S, Q, A], where C is the client's name, S is the name of the server it wants to communicate with,

---

[1] Equational specifications in Maude can be theories in membership equational logic, which may include conditional membership axioms not addressed in this paper.

Q is a natural number that identifies a client request, and D is either a natural number that represents the server response, or the constant value na (not available) when the response has not yet been received. Servers are stateless and are represented as structures [S], with S being the server's name. All messages are represented as pairs of the form H <- CNT, where H is either the client or server host name, and CNT stands for the message contents. These contents are pairs {H,D}, with H being the host's name and D being a data value that represents either a request or a response.

The server S uses a function f (only known to the server itself) that takes a question Q from client C as input. This function is defined by means of the equation inc, which specifies that the call $f(S, C, Q)$ computes $Q + 1$.

Program states are formalized as a soup (multiset) of clients, servers, and messages, whereas the system behavior is formalized through five rewrite rules that model a faulty communication environment in which messages can arrive out of order, can be duplicated, and can be lost. Specifically, the rule req allows a client C to send a message with request Q to the server S. The rule reply lets the server S consume the client request Q and send a response message that is computed by means of the function f. The rule rec specifies the client reception of a server response D that should be stored in the client data structure. However, the right-hand side [C, S, Q, A] of the rule rec includes an intentional, barely perceptible bug that does not let the client structure be correctly updated with the incoming response D. The correct right-hand side should be [C, S, Q, D]. Finally, the rules dupl and loss model the faulty environment and have the obvious meaning: messages can either be duplicated or lost.

Given a rewrite theory (Σ, E, R), with $E = \Delta \cup B$, the rewriting modulo E relation (in symbols, $\rightarrow_{R/E}$) can be defined by lifting the usual rewrite relation on terms $\rightarrow_R$ [14] to the E-congruence classes $[t]_E$ on the term algebra $\tau(\Sigma, \mathcal{V})$ that are induced by $=_E$ [8]; that is, $[t]_E$ is the class of all terms that are equal to t modulo E. Hence the rewrite relation $\rightarrow_{R/E}$ is defined as $=_E \circ \rightarrow_R \circ =_E$. Unfortunately, $\rightarrow_{R/E}$ is, in general, undecidable since a rewrite step $t \rightarrow_{R/E} t'$ involves searching through the possibly infinite equivalence classes $[t]_E$ and $[t']_E$.

The exploration technique formalized in this work is formulated by considering the precise way in which Maude proves the rewrite steps modulo an equational theory $E = \Delta \cup B$ (see Section 5.2 in [9]). Actually, the Maude interpreter implements rewriting modulo E by means of two much simpler relations, namely $\rightarrow_{\Delta,B}$ and $\rightarrow_{R,B}$. These allow rewrite rules and equations to be intermixed in the rewriting process by simply using an algorithm of matching modulo B.

Roughly speaking, the relation $\rightarrow_{\Delta,B}$ uses the equations of Δ (oriented from left to right) as simplification rules: thus, for any term t, by repeatedly applying the equations as simplification rules, we eventually reach a normalized term $t\downarrow_{\Delta,B}$ to which no further equations can be applied. The term $t\downarrow_{\Delta,B}$ is called a *canonical form* of t w.r.t. Δ modulo B. On the other hand, the relation $\rightarrow_{R,B}$ implements rewriting with the rules of R, which might be non-terminating and non-confluent, whereas Δ is required to be terminating and Church-Rosser modulo B in order to guarantee the existence and unicity (modulo B) of a canonical form w.r.t. Δ for any term [9].

Formally, $\rightarrow_{R,B}$ and $\rightarrow_{\Delta,B}$ are defined as follows: given a rewrite rule $[r]$:
$(\lambda \Rightarrow \rho) \in R$ (resp., an equation $[e] : (\lambda = \rho) \in \Delta$), a substitution σ, a term
t, and a position w of t, $t \overset{r,\sigma,w}{\rightarrow}_{R,B} t'$ (resp., $t \overset{e,\sigma,w}{\rightarrow}_{\Delta,B} t'$) iff $\lambda\sigma =_B t_{|w}$ and
$t' = t[\rho\sigma]_w$. When no confusion can arise, we simply write $t \rightarrow_{R,B} t'$ (resp.
$t \rightarrow_{\Delta,B} t'$) instead of $t \overset{r,\sigma,w}{\rightarrow}_{R,B} t'$ (resp. $t \overset{e,\sigma,w}{\rightarrow}_{\Delta,B} t'$).

Under appropriate conditions on the rewrite theory, a rewrite step $s \rightarrow_{R/E} t$
modulo E on a term s can be implemented without loss of completeness by
applying the following rewrite strategy [11]:

1. **Equational simplification of s in Δ modulo B**, that is, reduce s using
   $\rightarrow_{\Delta,B}$ until the canonical form w.r.t. Δ modulo B ($s \downarrow_{\Delta,B}$) is reached;
2. **Rewrite $(s \downarrow_{\Delta,B})$ in R modulo B** to t' using $\rightarrow_{R,B}$, where $t' \in [t]_E$.

A *computation* (trace) $\mathcal{C}$ for s_0 in the rewrite theory $(\Sigma, \Delta \cup B, R)$ is then
deployed as the (possibly infinite) rewrite sequence

$$s_0 \rightarrow^*_{\Delta,B} s_0 \downarrow_{\Delta,B} \rightarrow_{R,B} s_1 \rightarrow^*_{\Delta,B} s_1 \downarrow_{\Delta,B} \rightarrow_{R,B} \cdots$$

that interleaves $\rightarrow_{\Delta,B}$ rewrite steps and $\rightarrow_{R,B}$ rewrite steps following the strategy mentioned above. Note that, following this strategy, after each rewriting step
using $\rightarrow_{R,B}$, generally the resulting term s_i, $i = 1, \ldots, n$, is not in canonical normal form and is thus normalized before the subsequent rewrite step using $\rightarrow_{R,B}$
is performed. Also in the precise strategy adopted by Maude, the last term of a
finite computation is finally normalized before the result is delivered.

Therefore, any computation can be interpreted as a sequence of juxtaposed
$\rightarrow_{R,B}$ and $\rightarrow^*_{\Delta,B}$ transitions, with an additional equational simplification $\rightarrow^*_{\Delta,B}$
(if needed) at the beginning of the computation, as depicted below.

$$s_0 \quad \rightarrow^*_{\Delta,B} s_0 \downarrow_{\Delta,B} \rightarrow_{R,B} s_1 \rightarrow^*_{\Delta,B} s_1 \downarrow_{\Delta,B} \rightarrow_{R,B} s_2 \rightarrow^*_{\Delta,B} s_2 \downarrow_{\Delta,B} \cdots$$

We define a *Maude step* from a given term s as any of the sequences $s \rightarrow^*_{\Delta,B}$
$s \downarrow_{\Delta,B} \rightarrow_{R,B} t \rightarrow^*_{\Delta,B} t \downarrow_{\Delta,B}$ that head the non-deterministic Maude computations
for s. Note that, for a canonical form s, a Maude step for s boils down to
$s \rightarrow_{R,B} t \rightarrow^*_{\Delta,B} t \downarrow_{\Delta,B} t$. We define $m\mathcal{S}(s)$ as the set of all such non-deterministic
Maude steps stemming from s.

3.1   Instrumented Computations

In this section, we introduce an auxiliary technique for instrumenting computation traces. The instrumentation allows the relevant information of the rewrite
steps, such as the selected redex and the contractum produced by the step, to
be traced despite the fact that terms are rewritten modulo equational axioms
that may cause their components to be implicitly reordered. Given a computa-
tion $\mathcal{C}$, let us show how $\mathcal{C}$ can be expanded into an *instrumented* computation $\mathcal{T}$

in which each application of the matching modulo B algorithm that is used in $\rightarrow_{R,B}$-steps and $\rightarrow_{\Delta,B}$-steps is explicitly mimicked by the specific application of a bogus equational axiom, which is oriented from left to right and then applied as a rewrite rule in the standard way.

Typically hidden inside the B-matching algorithms, some pertinent term transformations allow terms that contain operators obeying equational axioms to be rewritten into supportive B-normal forms that facilitate the matching modulo B. In the case of AC-theories, these transformations allow terms to be reordered and correctly parenthesized in order to enable subsequent rewrite steps. Basically, this is achieved by producing a single, auxiliary representative of their AC congruence class (i.e., the AC-normal form) [3]. An AC-normal form is typically generated by replacing nested occurrences of the same AC operator by a flattened argument list under a variadic symbol, sorting these arguments under some linear ordering and combining equal arguments using multiplicity superscripts [13]. For example, the congruence class containing $f(f(\alpha, f(\beta, \alpha)), f(f(\gamma, \beta), \beta))$ where f is an AC symbol and subterms α, β and γ belong to alien theories might be represented by $f^*(\alpha^2, \beta^3, \gamma)$, where f^* is a variadic symbol that replaces nested occurrences of f. A more formal account of this transformation is given in [12].

As for purely associative theories, we can get an A-normal form by just flattening nested function symbol occurrences without sorting the arguments. This case has practical importance because it corresponds to lists. C-normal forms are just obtained by properly ordering the arguments of a commutative binary operator. Finally, for function symbols that satisfy the unit axiom U, the identity element of U is not included in the U-normal form, and variables under a U symbol can always be assigned the identity element through U-matching [12].

Then, rewriting modulo B in Maude proceeds by using the special form of matching called B-matching on the internal representation of terms as B-normal forms, where B may contain, among others, any combination of associativity, commutativity, and unity axioms for different binary operators. Moreover, in a Maude step, all terms in the sequence are shown in B-normal form (without multiplicity superscripts).

In the following, we discuss how we can simulate B-matching in our framework by means of specific "fake" axioms that mimic the B-matching transformation of terms that occur internally in Maude. This allows these transformations to be unhidden and explicitly revealed in the output trace.

Example 2. Consider a binary AC operator f together with a simple, standard lexicographic ordering over constant symbols. Given the term $f(b, f(f(b,a), c))$, let us reveal how this term matches modulo AC the left-hand side of the rule $[r]: f(f(x,y), f(z,x)) \Rightarrow x$ with AC-matching substitutions $\{x/b, y/a, z/c\}$ and $\{x/b, y/c, z/a\}$. For the first solution, this is mimicked by the transformation sequence $f(b, f(f(b,a), c)) \xrightarrow{\texttt{toACnf}} f^*(a, b^2, c) \xrightarrow{\texttt{fromACnf}} f(f(b,a), f(c,b))$, where 1) the first step corresponds to a term transformation that obtains the AC-normal form $f^*(a, b^2, c)$, and 2) the second step corresponds to the inverse, unflattening transformation that delivers the AC-equivalent term $f(f(b,a), f(c,b))$ that syntacti-

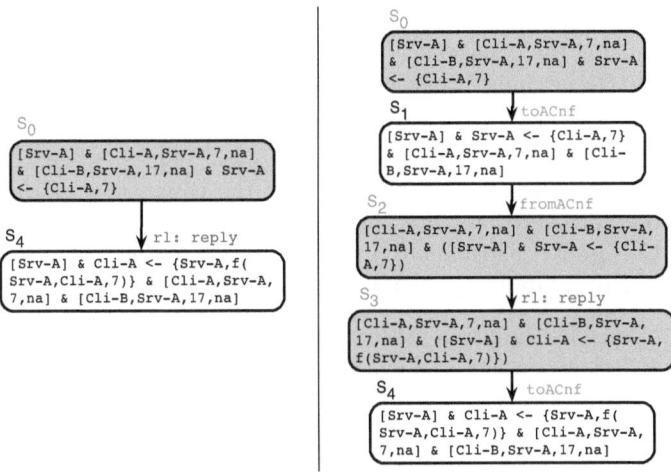

Fig. 1. A rewrite step and its instrumented version

cally matches the left-hand side of rule r with substitution $\{x/b, y/a, z/c\}$. Note that an alternative unflattening transformation is possible $f^*(a, b^2, c) \overset{\text{fromACnf}}{\longrightarrow} f(f(b,c), f(a,b))$ that actually delivers the second AC-matcher $\{x/b, y/c, z/a\}$.

Obviously, in our implementation, rewriting modulo B proceeds by using the standard form of B-matching on B-normal forms supported by Maude, where B-normalization is applied both to the states and to the (left-hand sides and right-hand sides) of the rules. The artifice described above is only a means to reveal the term transformations of subterms forced by the step so that any position can be properly traced across rewriting steps. Let us see an example.

Example 3. Consider the rewrite theory of Example 1 together with the rewrite step and corresponding instrumentation shown in Figure 1, where B-normalized nodes are represented in white, whereas nodes not in B-normal form are shown shaded in grey. The instrumented version of the rewrite step reveals that the normalized rule[2]

```
rl [reply] : [S] & S <- {C, Q}  => [S] & C <- {S, f(S, C, Q)} .
```

is not actually applied into the term s_0, but rather into a B-equivalent term s_2 that is chosen to syntactically match the left-hand side of the applied rule. As a result, all the information we collect from the application of the rule (e.g., the position where the rule was applied) corresponds to the s_1, s_2, and s_3 states, which are omitted in the non-instrumented version of the rewrite step.

---

[2] Note that, in this specific case, the B-normalization of the **reply** rule simply consists of a reordering of arguments in the left-hand side of the rule. Given any program rule, when no confusion can arise we always use the same label for the original rule and for the B-normalized version of the rule that is internally used by Maude.

Therefore, any given instrumented computation consists of a sequence of rewrite steps using the equations ($\to_\Delta$), rewrite rules ($\to_R$), equational axioms, and (internal) B-matching transformations ($\to_B$). More precisely, each rewrite step $s \overset{r,\sigma,w}{\to}_{R,B} t$ (resp., $s \overset{e,\sigma,w}{\to}_{\Delta,B} t$) is broken down into a rewrite sequence $s \to_B^* s' \overset{r,\sigma,w}{\to}_{R,\emptyset} t' \to_B^* t$ (resp., $s \to_B^* s' \overset{e,\sigma,w}{\to}_{\Delta,\emptyset} t' \to_B^* t$), where $s' =_B s$ and s' syntactically matches the left-hand side of the equation e or rule r that is applied in the considered rewrite step. We define the rewrite relation $\to_K$ as $\to_R \cup \to_\Delta \cup \to_B$. By $instrument(\mathcal{C})$ we denote a function that takes a computation $\mathcal{C}$ and delivers its instrumented counterpart.

Example 4. Consider the rewrite theory of Example 1 together with the following computation $\mathcal{C}$ that consists of a single Maude step (note that the last term is normalized):

$$\mathcal{C} = \text{[Srv-A] \& Cli-A <- \{Srv-A, f(Srv-A, Cli-A, 7)\}}$$
$$\text{\& [Cli-A, Srv-A, 7, na]} \overset{\text{inc}}{\longrightarrow}_{\Delta,B}$$
$$\text{[Srv-A] \& Cli-A <- \{Srv-A, 8\} \& [Cli-A, Srv-A, 7, na]} \overset{\text{rec}}{\longrightarrow}_{R,B}$$
$$\text{[Srv-A] \& [Cli-A, Srv-A, 7 , na]}$$

The corresponding instrumented computation $\mathcal{T}$, produced by $instrument(\mathcal{C})$, is given by suitably parenthesizing and reordering the arguments of the second term by applying ACU-matching transformations for the operator _&_.

These internal transformations allow the rec rule to be applied by syntactically matching the third term of $\mathcal{T}$ within its left-hand side.

$$\mathcal{T} = \text{[Srv-A] \& Cli-A <- \{Srv-A, f(Srv-A, Cli-A, 7)\}}$$
$$\text{\& [Cli-A, Srv-A, 7, na]} \overset{\text{inc}}{\longrightarrow}_\Delta$$
$$\text{[Srv-A] \& Cli-A <- \{Srv-A, 7+1\}}$$
$$\text{\& [Cli-A, Srv-A, 7, na]} \overset{\text{builtIn}(+)}{\longrightarrow}_\Delta$$
$$\text{[Srv-A] \& Cli-A <- \{Srv-A, 8\} \& [Cli-A, Srv-A, 7, na]} \overset{\text{fromACUnf}}{\longrightarrow}_B$$
$$\text{[Srv-A] \& (Cli-A <- \{Srv-A, 8\} \& [Cli-A, Srv-A, 7, na])} \overset{\text{rec}}{\longrightarrow}_R$$
$$\text{[Srv-A] \& [Cli-A, Srv-A, 7, na]}$$

The second rewrite step of the instrumented trace is simply proven with the bogus rule:

```
rl [fromACUnf] :  [Srv-A] & Cli-A <- {Srv-A, 8}
                      & [Cli-A, Srv-A, 7, na] =>
                  [Srv-A] & (Cli-A <- {Srv-A, 8}
                      & [Cli-A, Srv-A, 7, na]) .
```

In order to improve readability, we omit B-matching transformations and built-in evaluations when displaying Maude steps (unless explicitly stated otherwise). This is consistent with the strategy adopted by Maude and is the default option in our tool. As described in Section 6, by using the tool Anima, the user can visualize either the simplified view of a rewrite step or the complete and detailed instrumented version of the step.

4   Exploring Computation Trees

Given a rewrite theory $\mathcal{R}$, the transition space of all computations in $\mathcal{R}$ from the initial term s can be represented as a *computation tree*[3], $\mathcal{T}_{\mathcal{R}}(s)$. RWL computation trees are typically large and complex objects to deal with because of the highly-concurrent, nondeterministic nature of rewrite theories. Also, their complete generation and inspection are generally not feasible since some of their branches may be infinite as they encode nonterminating computations.

Example 5. Consider the rewrite theory of Example 1 together with the initial term [Srv-A] & [Cli-A,Srv-A,7,na] & [Cli-B,Srv-A,17,na]. In this case, the computation tree consists of several infinite computations that start from the considered initial term and model interactions between clients Cli-A, Cli-B and server Srv-A. A fragment of the computation tree is depicted in Figure 2 where we only display the equations and rules that have been applied at each rewrite step, while other information such as the computed substitution and the rewrite position are omitted in the depicted tree. Also for simplicity, note that we merge the two edges leading from s_1 to the same node s_4 with the rules req and dup, respectively.

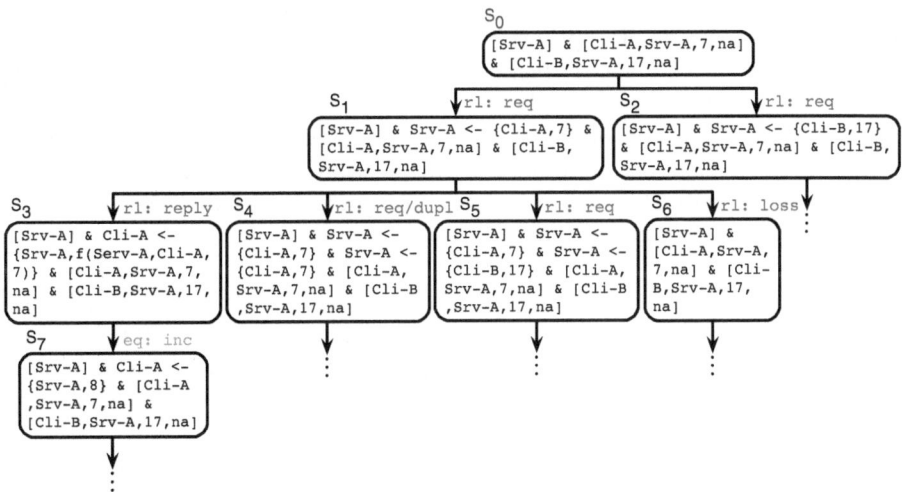

Fig. 2. Computation tree

---

[3] In order to facilitate trace inspection, computations are visualized as trees, although they are internally represented by means of more efficient graph-like data structures that allow common subexpressions to be shared.

Note that the instrumented version of a computation tree $\mathcal{T}_\mathcal{R}(s)$ can be constructed from $\mathcal{T}_\mathcal{R}(s)$ by expanding each computation in $\mathcal{T}_\mathcal{R}(s)$ into its corresponding instrumented counterpart as explained in Section 3.1. Also, it is possible to switch from the instrumented computation tree to the non-instrumented one by simply hiding the intermediate B-matching transformations and algebraic axiom applications that occur in the instrumented tree. In the sequel, we let $\mathcal{T}_\mathcal{R}^+(s)$ denote the instrumented computation tree that originates from the state s.

The rest of this section presents a slicing-based exploration technique that allows the user to incrementally generate and inspect a portion of the instrumented computation tree $\mathcal{T}_\mathcal{R}^+(s)$ by expanding (slices of) its computation states into their descendants starting from the root node. The exploration is an interactive procedure that can be completely controlled by the user, who is free to choose the computation states to be expanded. Roughly speaking, in our slices certain subterms of a term are omitted, leaving "holes" that are denoted by special variable symbols.

4.1 Term Slices and Instrumented Computation Slices

A term *slice* of the term s is a term $s^\bullet$ that hides part of the information in s; that is, the irrelevant data in s that we are not interested in are simply replaced by special $\bullet$-variables of appropriate sort, denoted by $\bullet_i$, with $i = 0, 1, 2, \ldots$. Given a term slice $s^\bullet$, a *meaningful* position p of $s^\bullet$ is a position $p \in \mathcal{P}os(s^\bullet)$ such that $s^\bullet_{|p} \neq \bullet_i$, for all $i = 0, 1, \ldots$.

By $\mathcal{MP}os(s^\bullet)$, we denote the set that contains all the meaningful positions of $s^\bullet$. Symbols that occur at meaningful positions of a term slice are called *meaningful* symbols. Basically, a term slice records just the information the user wants to observe of a given term.

Example 6. Consider the client-server specification of Example 1. Then, the term slice [Cli-A, Srv-A, $\bullet_1$, $\bullet_2$] represents any request from client Cli-A to communicate with server Srv-A where the request and response identification numbers are irrelevant. For this term slice, the set of meaningful positions is $\{\Lambda, 1, 2\}$.

The next auxiliary definition formalizes the function $Tslice(t, P)$ that allows a term slice of t to be constructed w.r.t. a set of positions P of t. The function $Tslice$ relies on the function $fresh^\bullet$ whose invocation returns a (fresh) variable $\bullet_i$ of appropriate sort that is distinct from any previously generated variable $\bullet_j$.

Definition 1 (Term Slice). *Let $t \in \tau(\Sigma, \mathcal{V})$ be a term and let P be a set of positions s.t. $P \subseteq \mathcal{P}os(t)$. Then, the term slice $Tslice(t, P)$ of t w.r.t. P is computed as follows.*

$$Tslice(t, P) = recslice(t, P, \Lambda), \; where$$

$$(\text{frag})\frac{V^\bullet = \mathcal{I}(U^\bullet, U \to V) \quad \wedge \quad V^\bullet \neq \mathsf{fail}}{\langle U \to V \to^* W, S^\bullet \leftrightarrow^* U^\bullet \rangle \Longrightarrow \langle V \to^* W, S^\bullet \leftrightarrow^* U^\bullet \leftrightarrow V^\bullet \rangle}$$

Fig. 3. The inference rule frag of the transition system $(Conf, \Longrightarrow)$

$$recslice(t, P, p) = \begin{cases} f(recslice(t_1, P, p.1), \ldots, recslice(t_n, P, p.n)) \\ \qquad if\ t = f(t_1, \ldots, t_n), n \geq 0,\ and\ p \in \bar{P} \\ t \qquad if\ t \in \mathcal{V}\ and\ p \in \bar{P} \\ fresh^\bullet \qquad otherwise \end{cases}$$

and $\bar{P} = \{u \mid u \leq p \wedge p \in P\}$ is the prefix closure of P.

Roughly speaking, the function $Tslice(t, P)$ yields a term slice of t w.r.t. a set of positions P that includes all symbols of t that occur within the paths from the root of t to any position in P, while each maximal subterm $t_{|p}$, with $p \notin P$, is replaced by means of a freshly generated $\bullet$-variable.

Example 7. Let $t = d(f(g(a, h(b)), c), a)$ be a term, and let $P = \{1.1,\ 1.2\}$ be a set of positions of t. By applying Definition 1, we get the term slice $t^\bullet = Tslice(t, P) = d(f(g(\bullet_1, \bullet_2), c), \bullet_3)$ and the set of meaningful positions $MPos(t^\bullet) = \{\Lambda, 1, 1.1, 1.2\}$.

Definition 2 (Inspection criterion). *An* inspection criterion *is a function* $\mathcal{I}(s^\bullet, s \to_K t)$ *that, given a* $\to_K$*-rewrite step* $s \to_K t$*, and a term slice* $s^\bullet$ *of* s*, computes a term slice* $t^\bullet$ *of* t.

Roughly speaking, inspection criteria allow us to control the information content conveyed by term slices resulting from the execution of $\to_K$-rewrite steps. It is worth noting that distinct implementations of the inspection criteria may produce distinct slices of the considered rewrite step. Several examples of inspection criteria are discussed in Section 5. We assume that the special value fail is returned by the inspection criterion whenever no slice $t^\bullet$ can be computed by $\mathcal{I}$. Actually, for any sensible criterion $\mathcal{I}$, $\mathcal{I}(\bullet, s \to_K t) = \mathsf{fail}$ (i.e., no meaningful result can be derived when no relevant information is considered).

Given the instrumented computation $\mathcal{T} = (s_0 \to_K s_1 \ldots \to_K s_n)$, with $n \geq 1$, an *instrumented computation slice* of $\mathcal{T}$ w.r.t. the inspection criterion $\mathcal{I}$ is the sequence $\mathcal{T}_\mathcal{I}^\bullet = (s_0^\bullet \leftrightarrow s_1^\bullet \leftrightarrow \ldots \leftrightarrow s_n^\bullet)$ that can be generated by sequentially applying $\mathcal{I}$ to the steps that compose $\mathcal{T}$. We often write $\mathcal{T}^\bullet$ for an instrumented computation slice $\mathcal{T}_\mathcal{I}^\bullet$ when the inspection criterion $\mathcal{I}$ is clear from the context.

Let us formalize a calculus to generate instrumented computation slices by means of a transition system $(Conf, \Longrightarrow)$ [18] where

- *Conf* is a set of *configurations* of the form $\langle \mathcal{T}, \mathcal{F}^\bullet \rangle$, where $\mathcal{T}$ is a an instrumented computation and $\mathcal{F}^\bullet$ is an instrumented computation slice of a prefix of $\mathcal{T}$;

– the transition relation $\Longrightarrow$ implements the calculus of instrumented computation slices and is the smallest relation that satisfies the inference rule frag given in Figure 3. By $\Longrightarrow^*$, we denote the usual transitive and reflexive closure of the relation $\Longrightarrow$.

Roughly speaking, the rule frag transforms the configuration $\langle U \rightarrow_K V \rightarrow_K^* W, S^\bullet \bullet\!\!\rightarrow_K^* U^\bullet \rangle$ into the configuration $\langle V \rightarrow_K^* W, S^\bullet \bullet\!\!\rightarrow^* U^\bullet \bullet\!\!\rightarrow V^\bullet \rangle$ where the first step $U \rightarrow_K V$ has been consumed and its corresponding slice $U^\bullet \bullet\!\!\rightarrow V^\bullet$ w.r.t. $\mathcal{I}$ has been added to $S^\bullet \bullet\!\!\rightarrow^* U^\bullet$. The rule frag only applies when the inspection criterion $\mathcal{I}$ generates a term slice $V^\bullet$ that is not the fail value.

The sequential application of the considered inference rule allows the instrumented computation $\mathcal{T}$ to be traversed in order to produce the sliced counterpart $\mathcal{T}^\bullet$ of $\mathcal{T}$ w.r.t. $\mathcal{I}$. More formally,

Definition 3 (Computation slice). *Given the instrumented computation* $\mathcal{T} = (s_0 \rightarrow_K s_1 \rightarrow_K \ldots \rightarrow_K s_n)$, *with* $n \geq 1$, *the instrumented computation slice* $\mathcal{T}^\bullet$ *of* $\mathcal{T}$ *w.r.t. the inspection criterion* $\mathcal{I}$ *and term slice* $s_0^\bullet$ *of* s_0 *is defined by the function* $Cslice(s_0^\bullet, \mathcal{T}, \mathcal{I})$ *which is defined as follows.*

$$Cslice(s_0^\bullet, \mathcal{T}, \mathcal{I}) = \textbf{if } \langle \mathcal{T}, s_0^\bullet \rangle \Longrightarrow^* \langle \varepsilon, \mathcal{T}^\bullet \rangle \textbf{ then } \mathcal{T}^\bullet \textbf{ else } fail$$

where ε *denotes the empty computation. Note that the second component* $s_0^\bullet$ *of the initial configuration* $\langle \mathcal{T}, s_0^\bullet \rangle$ *matches the sequence* $S^\bullet \bullet\!\!\rightarrow^* U^\bullet$ *in rule frag by taking* $s_0^\bullet$ *for* $U^\bullet$ *and considering a sequence* $S^\bullet \bullet\!\!\rightarrow^* U^\bullet$ *consisting of zero steps.*

4.2   Instrumented Computation Tree Slices

Instrumented computation tree slices are formally defined as follows.

Definition 4 (Instrumented Computation Tree Slice). *Let* $\mathcal{T}_\mathcal{R}^+(s_0)$ *be an instrumented computation tree for the term* s_0 *in the rewrite theory* $\mathcal{R} = (\Sigma, \Delta \cup B, R)$; *let* $s_0^\bullet$ *be a term slice of* s_0; *and let* $\mathcal{I}$ *be an inspection criterion. An instrumented computation tree slice for* $s_0^\bullet$ *in* $\mathcal{R}$ *w.r.t.* $\mathcal{I}$ *is a tree* $\mathcal{T}_{\mathcal{R},\mathcal{I}}^+(s_0^\bullet)$ *(simply denoted by* $\mathcal{T}_\mathcal{R}^+(s_0^\bullet)$ *when no confusion can arise) such that:*

1. *the root of* $\mathcal{T}_\mathcal{R}^+(s_0^\bullet)$ *is* $s_0^\bullet$;
2. *each branch of* $\mathcal{T}_\mathcal{R}^+(s_0^\bullet)$ *is an instrumented computation slice* $\mathcal{T}^\bullet$ *w.r.t.* $\mathcal{I}$ *and* $s_0^\bullet$ *of a computation* $\mathcal{T}$ *in* $\mathcal{T}_\mathcal{R}^+(s_0)$.
3. *for each instrumented computation* $\mathcal{T}$ *in* $\mathcal{T}_\mathcal{R}^+(s_0)$, *there is one, and only one, instrumented computation slice* $\mathcal{T}^\bullet$ *of* $\mathcal{T}$ *in* $\mathcal{T}_\mathcal{R}^+(s_0^\bullet)$.

In the following section, we show how tree slices of a given instrumented computation tree in $\mathcal{R} = (\Sigma, \Delta \cup B, R)$ can be generated by repeatedly unfolding the nodes of the original tree.

```
function expand(s, s•, R, I)
1.  A = ∅
2.  for each M ∈ mS(s)
3.      M• = Cslice(s•, instrument(M), I)
4.      if M• ≠ fail then A = A ∪ {M•}
5.  end
6.  return A
endf
```

Fig. 4. The one-step *expand* function

4.3 Exploring the Computation Tree

In our methodology, instrumented computation tree slices are incrementally constructed by expanding tree nodes (i.e., term slices), starting from the root node (i.e., the initial term slice). Formally, given the term s and the term slice $s^\bullet$ of s, the expansion of s in the rewrite theory $\mathcal{R} = (\Sigma, \Delta \cup B, R)$ w.r.t. the inspection criterion $\mathcal{I}$ is defined by the function $expand(s, s^\bullet, \mathcal{R}, \mathcal{I})$ of Figure 4 which unfolds the term slice $s^\bullet$ by deploying and then slicing all the possible instrumented Maude computation steps stemming from s that are given by $mS(s)$. In other words, for each Maude step $\mathcal{M} = s \to^*_{\Delta,B} s\downarrow_{\Delta,B} \to_{R,B} t \to^*_{\Delta,B} t\downarrow_{\Delta,B}$, we first compute its instrumented version and then the corresponding instrumented Maude step slice $\mathcal{M}^\bullet$ is generated, which is then added to the set of arcs $\mathcal{A}$.

The overall construction methodology for instrumented computation tree slices is specified by the function *explore*, defined in Figure 5. Given a rewrite theory $\mathcal{R}$, a term slice $s_0^\bullet$ of the initial term s_0, and an inspection criterion $\mathcal{I}$, the function *explore* essentially formalizes an interactive procedure that is driven by the user starting from an elemental tree slice fragment, which only consists of the sliced root node $s_0^\bullet$. The instrumented computation tree slice $\mathcal{T}_\mathcal{R}^+(s_0^\bullet)$ is built by choosing, at each loop iteration of the algorithm, the tree leaf that represents the term slice to be expanded by means of the auxiliary function $pickLeaf(\mathcal{T}_\mathcal{R}^+(s_0^\bullet))$, which allows the user to freely select a leaf node from the frontier of the current tree $\mathcal{T}_\mathcal{R}^+(s_0^\bullet)$. Then, $\mathcal{T}_\mathcal{R}^+(s_0^\bullet)$ is augmented by calling $addPaths(\mathcal{T}_\mathcal{R}^+(s_0^\bullet), s^\bullet, expand(s, s^\bullet, \mathcal{R}, \mathcal{I}))$. This function call adds all the instrumented computation slices w.r.t. $\mathcal{I}$ and $s^\bullet$ that correspond to the Maude steps that originate from the term s.

The special value **EoE** (End of Exploration) is used to terminate the inspection process: when the function $pickLeaf(\mathcal{T}_\mathcal{R}^+(s_0^\bullet))$ is equal to **EoE**, no term to be expanded is selected and the exploration terminates delivering (a fragment of) the computation tree slice $\mathcal{T}_\mathcal{R}^+(s_0^\bullet)$.

5 Particularizing the Exploration

The methodology given in Section 4 provides a generic scheme for the exploration of (instrumented) computation trees w.r.t. a given inspection criterion $\mathcal{I}$ that

```
function explore(s_0, s_0^•, R, I)
1.  T_R^+(s_0^•) = s_0^•
2.  while((s^• = pickLeaf(T_R^+(s_0^•))) ≠ EoE) do
3.      T_R^+(s_0^•) = addPaths(T_R^+(s_0^•), s^•, expand(s, s^•, R, I))
4.  od
5.  return T_R^+(s_0^•)
endf
```

Fig. 5. The interactive *explore* function

must be selected or provided by the user. In this section, we show three implementations of the criterion I that produce three distinct exploration strategies. In the first case, the considered criterion allows an interactive program stepper to be derived in which rewriting logic theories can be stepwisely animated. In the second case, we implement a partial stepper that allows computations with partial inputs to be stepped. Finally, in the last instantiation of the framework, the chosen inspection criterion implements an automated, forward slicing technique that simplifies the traces and allows relevant control and data information to be easily identified within the computation trees.

5.1 Interactive Stepper

Given an instrumented computation tree $T_R^+(s_0)$ for an initial term s_0 and a rewrite theory R, the stepwise inspection of the computation tree can be directly implemented by instantiating the exploration scheme of Section 4 with the basic inspection criterion $I_{step}(s, s \xrightarrow{r,\sigma,w}_K t) = t$ which simply returns the reduced term t of the rewrite step $s \xrightarrow{r,\sigma,w}_K t$.

This way, by starting the exploration from a term slice that corresponds to the whole initial term s_0 (i.e., $s_0^• = s_0$), the call $explore(s_0, s_0^•, R, I_{step})$ generates (a fragment of) the instrumented computation tree $T_R^+(s_0)$ whose topology depends on the program states that the user decides to expand during the exploration process.

Example 8. Consider the rewrite theory R in Example 1 and the computation tree in Example 5. Assume the user starts the exploration by calling $explore(s_0, s_0^•, R, I_{step})$, with $s_0 = s_0^•$, which allows all the Maude steps that stem from the initial term s_0 to be expanded w.r.t. the inspection criterion I_{step}. This generates the instrumented computation tree fragment $T_R^+(s_0)$ in Figure 6.

Now, the user can either quit or carry on with the exploration of nodes s_3 and s_5, which would result in the instrumented version of the tree fragment that is shown in Figure 2.

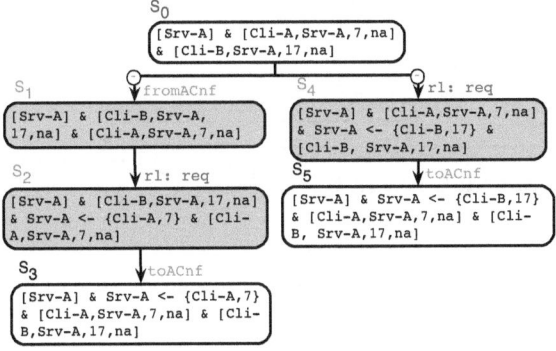

Fig. 6. Inspection of the state s_0 w.r.t. $\mathcal{I}_{step}$

5.2   Partial Stepper

The computation states produced by the program stepper defined above do not include •-variables. However, sometimes it may be useful to work with partial information and hence with term slices that "abstract some data" by using •-variables. This may help the user focus on those parts of the program state that he/she wants to observe, while disregarding pointless information or unwanted rewrite steps.

We define the following inspection criterion

$$\mathcal{I}_{pstep}(s^{\bullet}, s \overset{r,\sigma,w}{\rightarrow}_K t) = \textbf{if } s^{\bullet} \overset{r,\sigma^{\bullet},w}{\rightarrow}_K t^{\bullet} \textbf{ then } t^{\bullet} \textbf{ else } \textsf{fail}$$

Roughly speaking, given a rewrite step $s \overset{r,\sigma,w}{\rightarrow}_K t$, the criterion $\mathcal{I}_{pstep}$ returns a term slice $t^{\bullet}$ of the reduced term t, whenever $s^{\bullet}$ can be rewritten to $t^{\bullet}$ using the very same rule r at the same position w with the corresponding matching substitution $\sigma^{\bullet}$.

The particularization of the exploration scheme given by the criterion $\mathcal{I}_{pstep}$ allows an interactive, partial stepper to be derived, in which the user can work with state information of interest, thereby producing more compact and focused representations of the visited slices of the (instrumented) computation trees.

Example 9. Consider the computation tree of Example 5 whose initial term is $s_0 =$ [Srv-A] & [Cli-A,Srv-A,7,na] & [Cli-B,Srv-A,17,na]. Let $s_0^{\bullet} =$ ($\bullet_1$ & [Cli-A,Srv-A,7,na] & $\bullet_2$) be a term slice of s_0 where only client Cli-A data structure is considered of interest. Assume that the inspection criterion $\mathcal{I}_{pstep}$ is used to generate computation tree slice fragments. The computation tree slice fragment shown in Figure 7 is obtained by first expanding the node $s_0^{\bullet}$ into $s_1^{\bullet}$, and then the node $s_1^{\bullet}$ into $s_2^{\bullet}$, $s_3^{\bullet}$. The expanded nodes have been highlighted in the figure. Note that the adopted partial stepping strategy allows a simplified view of (a part of) the considered computation tree to be constructed. Specifically, the generated computation tree slice fragment isolates client Cli-A's behavior. More precisely, given the input encoded in the initial term slice $s_0^{\bullet}$, the

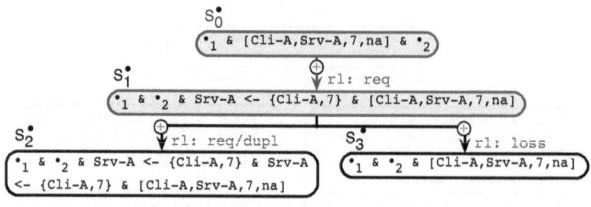

Fig. 7. Computation tree slice fragment for $s_0^\bullet$ w.r.t. $\mathcal{I}_{pstep}$

computation can evolve by only applying either the rule `req` to the `Cli-A` data structure, or the rules `dupl` and `loss` to `Cli-A`'s request messages.

In other words, this amounts to saying that a client-server protocol interaction cannot be successfully carried out when the input term does not specify a sever data structure (in this specific case, `[Srv-A]` should be included in $s_0^\bullet$), since its presence is essential to fire the `reply` rule that is in charge of producing server responses.

5.3   Forward Trace Slicer

Forward trace slicing is a program analysis technique that allows computations to be simplified w.r.t. a selected slice of their initial term. More precisely, given an instrumented computation $\mathcal{T}$ with initial term s_0 and a term slice $s_0^\bullet$ of s_0, forward slicing yields a simplified view $\mathcal{T}^\bullet$ of $\mathcal{T}$ in which each term s of the original instrumented computation is replaced by the corresponding term slice $s^\bullet$ that only records the information that depends on the meaningful symbols of $s_0^\bullet$, while irrelevant data are simply pruned away.

In the following, we define an inspection criterion $\mathcal{I}_{slice}$ that implements the forward slicing for a single rewrite step. Given a rewrite step $\mu = (s \xrightarrow{r,\sigma,w}_K t)$ (with $r = \lambda \Rightarrow \rho$) and a term slice $s^\bullet$ of the term s, it delivers the term slice $t^\bullet$ that results from "rewriting" $s^\bullet$ at position w with the rule r and a suitable substitution that abstracts any irrelevant information of the computed substitution σ with •-variables. A precise formalization of the inspection criterion $\mathcal{I}_{slice}$ is provided by the algorithm in Figure 8.

Note that, by adopting the inspection criterion $\mathcal{I}_{slice}$, the exploration scheme of Section 4 automatically turns into an interactive, forward trace slicer that expands computation states using the slicing methodology encoded into the inspection criterion $\mathcal{I}_{slice}$. In other words, given an instrumented computation tree $\mathcal{T}_{\mathcal{R}}^+(s_0)$ and a user-defined term slice $s_0^\bullet$ of the initial term s_0, any computation slice $s_0^\bullet \leftrightarrow s_1^\bullet \ldots \leftrightarrow s_n^\bullet$ in the tree $\mathcal{T}_{\mathcal{R}}^+(s_0^\bullet)$, which is computed by the *explore* function, is the sliced counterpart of an instrumented computation $s_0 \to s_1 \ldots \to s_n$ (w.r.t. the term slice $s_0^\bullet$) in the instrumented computation tree $\mathcal{T}_{\mathcal{R}}^+(s_0)$.

Roughly speaking, the inspection criterion $\mathcal{I}_{slice}$ works as follows. When the rewrite step μ occurs at a position w that is not a meaningful position of $s^\bullet$

$$\textbf{function } \mathcal{I}_{slice}(s^\bullet, s \xrightarrow{\lambda \Rightarrow \rho, \sigma, w}_K t)$$
1. **if** $w \in \mathcal{MPos}(s^\bullet)$ **then**
2. $\quad \theta = \{x/fresh^\bullet \mid x \in Var(\lambda)\}$
3. $\quad \lambda^\bullet = Tslice(\lambda, \mathcal{MPos}(s^\bullet_{|w}) \cap Pos(\lambda))$
4. $\quad \psi_\lambda = \langle\!\langle \theta, match_{\lambda^\bullet}(s^\bullet_{|w}) \rangle\!\rangle$
5. $\quad t^\bullet = s^\bullet[\rho\psi_\lambda]_w$
6. **else**
7. $\quad t^\bullet = \textsf{fail}$
8. **fi**
9. **return** $t^\bullet$
endf

Fig. 8. Inspection criterion that models the forward slicing of a rewrite step

(in symbols, $w \notin \mathcal{MPos}(s^\bullet)$), trivially μ does not contribute to producing the meaningful symbols of $t^\bullet$. This amounts to saying that no relevant information descends from the term slice $s^\bullet$ and, hence, the function returns the fail value.

On the other hand, when $w \in \mathcal{MPos}(s^\bullet)$, the computation of $t^\bullet$ involves a more in-depth analysis of the rewrite step, which is based on a refinement process that allows the descendants of $s^\bullet$ in $t^\bullet$ to be computed.

The following definition is auxiliary and is used to update (override) a substitution σ_1 with the substitution σ_2, where both σ_1 and σ_2 may contain •-variables.

Definition 5 (substitution update). *Let σ_1 and σ_2 be two substitutions,. The update of σ_1 w.r.t. σ_2 (in symbols $\langle\!\langle \sigma_1, \sigma_2 \rangle\!\rangle$) is defined by $\langle\!\langle \sigma_1, \sigma_2 \rangle\!\rangle = \sigma_{\restriction Dom(\sigma_1)}$, where the substitution σ is given by*

$$x\sigma = \begin{cases} x\sigma_2 & \text{if } x \in Dom(\sigma_1) \cap Dom(\sigma_2) \\ x\sigma_1 & \text{otherwise} \end{cases}$$

The main idea behind the operator $\langle\!\langle \_, \_ \rangle\!\rangle$ is that, in order to compute a rewrite step from the term slice $s^\bullet$ using the rule r, all variables in r are naïvely assumed to be initially bound to •-variables that model irrelevant data, and the bindings are incrementally updated as we apply the rule r.

More specifically, given the rewrite step $\mu : s \xrightarrow{r, \sigma, w} t$, with $r = \lambda \Rightarrow \rho$, and the term slice $s^\bullet$, we initially define the substitution $\theta = \{x/fresh^\bullet \mid x \in Var(\lambda)\}$ that binds each variable in $\lambda \Rightarrow \rho$ to a fresh •-variable. This corresponds to assuming that all the information in μ, which is introduced by the substitution σ, can be marked as irrelevant. Then, θ is refined as follows.

We first compute the term slice $\lambda^\bullet = Tslice(\lambda, \mathcal{MPos}(s^\bullet_{|w}) \cap Pos(\lambda))$ that filters the meaningful symbols of the left-hand side λ of the rule r w.r.t. the set of meaningful positions of $s^\bullet_{|w}$. Then, by matching $s^\bullet_{|w}$ into $\lambda^\bullet$, we generate a matcher $match_{\lambda^\bullet}(s^\bullet_{|w})$ that extracts the meaningful symbols from $s^\bullet_{|w}$. Such a matcher is then used to compute ψ_λ, which is an update of θ w.r.t. $match_{\lambda^\bullet}(s^\bullet_{|w})$ containing the meaningful information to be propagated across the rewrite step. Finally, the term slice $t^\bullet$ is computed from $s^\bullet$ by replacing its subterm at position

w with the instance $\rho\psi_\lambda$ of the right-hand side of the applied rule r. This way, we can transfer all the relevant information marked in $s^\bullet$ into the slice of the resulting term $t^\bullet$.

Example 10. Consider the rewrite theory in Example 1 together with the following rewrite step

$$s \stackrel{\text{req}}{\to} t : \texttt{[Srv-A]} \ \& \ \texttt{[Cli-A,Srv-A,7,na]} \stackrel{\text{req}}{\to}$$
$$\texttt{[Srv-A]} \ \& \ \texttt{Srv-A <- \{Cli-A,7\}} \ \& \ \texttt{[Cli-A,Srv-A,7,na]}$$

that applies (at position $w = 2$) the rule $\texttt{req}: \lambda \Rightarrow \rho$, with $\lambda = \texttt{[C,S,Q,na]}$ and $\rho = \texttt{[C, S, Q, na]} \ \& \ \texttt{S <- \{C, Q\}}$.

Let $s^\bullet = \bullet_1 \ \& \ \texttt{[Cli-A,}\bullet_2\texttt{,7,} \ \bullet_3 \texttt{]}$ be a term slice of s. The execution of the inspection criterion $\mathcal{I}_{slice}(s^\bullet, s \stackrel{\text{req}}{\to} t)$ that computes a term slice $t^\bullet$ of t proceeds as follows.

First, the substitution θ is initialized to $\{\texttt{C}/\bullet_4, \ \texttt{S}/\bullet_5, \ \texttt{Q}/\bullet_6\}$ and the slice $\lambda^\bullet$ of λ is computed w.r.t. the meaningful positions of $s^\bullet_{|\Lambda.2}$ that also appear in λ. Specifically, $\lambda^\bullet = Tslice(\lambda, \{\Lambda, 1, 3\}) = \texttt{[C,}\bullet_7\texttt{,Q,}\bullet_8\texttt{]}$. Then, the update ψ_λ of θ is calculated. More precisely, $match_{\lambda^\bullet}(s^\bullet_{|w}) = match_{\texttt{[C,}\bullet_7\texttt{,Q,}\bullet_8\texttt{]}}(\texttt{[Cli-A,}\bullet_2\texttt{,7,}\bullet_3\texttt{]})$ $= \{\texttt{C}/\texttt{Cli-A}, \ \bullet_7 \ /\bullet_2, \ \texttt{Q}/7, \ \bullet_8 \ /\bullet_3\}$ and $\psi_\lambda = \langle\!\langle\theta, match_{\lambda^\bullet}(s^\bullet_{|w})\rangle\!\rangle = \{\texttt{C}/\texttt{Cli-A}, \ \texttt{S}/\bullet_5,$
$\texttt{Q}/7\}$. Roughly speaking, the computed update ψ_λ refines θ by replacing the uninformed bindings $\texttt{C}/\bullet_4$ and $\texttt{Q}/\bullet_6$ with $\texttt{C}/\texttt{Cli-A}$ and $\texttt{Q}/7$, respectively. Finally, $\mathcal{I}_{slice}(s^\bullet, s \stackrel{\text{req}}{\to} t)$ returns the term slice $t^\bullet = s^\bullet[\rho\psi_\lambda]_2 = \bullet_1 \ \& \ \texttt{[Cli-A,} \ \bullet_5$ $\texttt{,7,na]} \ \& \ \bullet_5 \texttt{<-\{Cli-A,7\}}$.

The following example describes the interactive construction process of a fragment of an instrumented computation tree slice based on the $\mathcal{I}_{slice}$ criterion. To improve its readability, we omit the transformation steps that are required to mimick the behavior of the Maude B-matching algorithm. The example also demonstrates how forward trace slicing can be fruitfully employed to debug RWL specifications.

Example 11. Consider the computation tree of Example 5 whose initial term is $s_0 = \texttt{[Srv-A]} \ \& \ \texttt{[Cli-A,Srv-A,7,na]} \ \& \ \texttt{[Cli-B,Srv-A,17,na]}$. Let $s_0^\bullet = (\bullet_1 \ \& \ \texttt{[Cli-A,}\bullet_2\texttt{,7,} \ \bullet_3 \texttt{]} \ \& \ \bullet_4)$ be a term slice of s_0 where only request 7 of client $\texttt{Cli-A}$ is considered of interest. We get the computation tree slice fragment shown in Figure 9 by first expanding (w.r.t. the inspection criterion $\mathcal{I}_{slice}$) the node $s_0^\bullet$ into $s_1^\bullet$; the node $s_1^\bullet$ into $s_2^\bullet$, $s_3^\bullet$ (which is automatically normalized to $s_5^\bullet$ using the equation $\texttt{inc}$), and $s_4^\bullet$; and finally the node $s_5^\bullet$ into $\{s_6^\bullet \ldots s_9^\bullet\}$. The branch leading from $s_0^\bullet$ to $s_9^\bullet$ is highlighted.

Note that the intermediate node $s_3^\bullet$ does not have to be expanded since it is an intermediate node generated by the expansion of node $s_1^\bullet$ that is automatically normalized into $s_5^\bullet$. Indeed, the computation slice generated by expanding the node $s_1^\bullet$ is $s_1^\bullet \stackrel{\text{reply}}{\leftrightarrow} s_3^\bullet \stackrel{\text{inc}}{\leftrightarrow} s_5^\bullet$, which corresponds to the forward slicing of a Maude step from s_1.

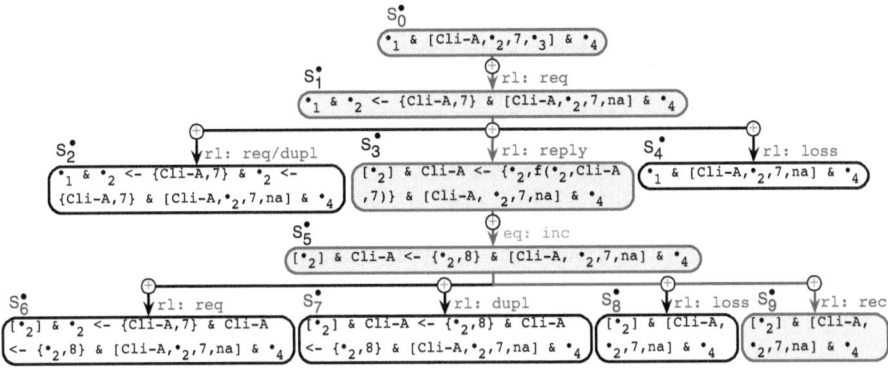

Fig. 9. Computation tree slice fragment for •$_1$ & [Cli-A,•$_2$,7, •$_3$] & •$_4$ w.r.t. $\mathcal{I}_{slice}$

The slicing process automatically computes a computation tree slice fragment that represents a partial view of the protocol interactions from client Cli-A's perspective. Actually, irrelevant information is hidden and rules applied on irrelevant positions are directly ignored, which allows a simplified slice to be obtained thus favoring its inspection for debugging and analysis purposes. In fact, if we observe the highlighted branch in Figure 9, we can easily detect the wrong behavior of the rule **rec**. Specifically, by inspecting the term slice $s_9^{\bullet} = ([\bullet_2]$ & [Cli-A,•$_2$, 7,na] & •$_4$), which is generated by an application of the rule **rec**, we immediately realize that response 8 produced in the parent node $s_5^{\bullet}$ has not been stored in $s_9^{\bullet}$, which clearly reveals the bug in the applied rule **rec**.

Finally, it is worth noting how the forward trace slicer implemented via the criterion $\mathcal{I}_{slice}$ differs from the partial stepper given at the end of Section 5.1. Given a term slice $s^{\bullet}$ and a rewrite step $s \xrightarrow{r,\sigma,w}_K t$, $\mathcal{I}_{slice}$ always yields a slice $t^{\bullet}$ when the rewrite step occurs at a meaningful position, whereas the inspection criterion $\mathcal{I}_{pstep}$ encoded in the partial stepper may fail to provide a computed slice $t^{\bullet}$ when $s^{\bullet}$ does not rewrite to $t^{\bullet}$, which allows the user to identify those states that can be reached, from any instance of the sliced input state, by standard rewriting.

Example 12. Consider the computation tree of Example 5 whose initial term is s_0 — [Srv A] & [Cli A,Srv A,7,na] & [Cli B,Srv A,17,na], and the initial term slice $s_0^{\bullet} = (\bullet_1$ & [Cli-A,•$_2$,7, •$_3$] & •$_4$) of Example 11. Then, no expansion of node $s_0^{\bullet}$ is possible using the inspection criterion $\mathcal{I}_{pstep}$, since the input encoded in $s_0^{\bullet}$ does not suffice to enable the application of any protocol rule, whereas the forward slicing strategy specified by the criterion $\mathcal{I}_{slice}$ allows

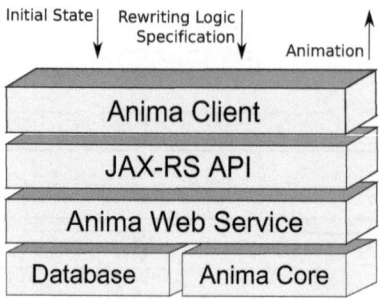

Fig. 10. Anima architecture

the computation tree fragment in Figure 9 to be generated. Nevertheless, tree fragments computed by forward slicing do not generally describe valid computations, that is, computations that can be proven for any instance of the sliced input state.

6   Implementation

The exploration methodology developed in this paper has been implemented in the Anima tool, which is publicly available at http://safe-tools.dsic.upv.es/anima/. The underlying rewriting machinery of Anima is written in Maude and consists of about 250 Maude function definitions (approximately 2000 lines of source code). Anima also comes with an intuitive Web user interface based on AJAX technology, which allows users to graphically animate their programs and display fragments of computation trees. The core exploration engine is specified as a RESTful Web service by means of the Jersey JAX-RS API.

The architecture of Anima is depicted in Figure 10 and consists of five main components: Anima Client, JAX-RS API, Anima Web Service, Database, and Anima Core. The Anima Client is purely implemented in HTML5 Canvas[4] and JavaScript. It represents the front-end layer of our tool and provides an intuitive, versatile Web user interface, which interacts with the Anima Web Service to invoke the capabilities of the Anima Core and save partial results in the MongoDB Database component, which is a scalable, high-performance, open source NoSQL database that perfectly fits on our needs.

Figure 11 displays a screenshot that shows the Anima tool at work on the case study that is described in Example 11. The figure depicts (a fragment of) the computation tree slice for this example program and several capabilities offered by the tool.

---

[4] For the sake of efficiency, browsers limit the maximum dimensions of a canvas object (eg., Chrome limits a canvas to a maximum width or height of 8192 pixels). Exceeding these limits may cause the inability to properly display the current exploration.

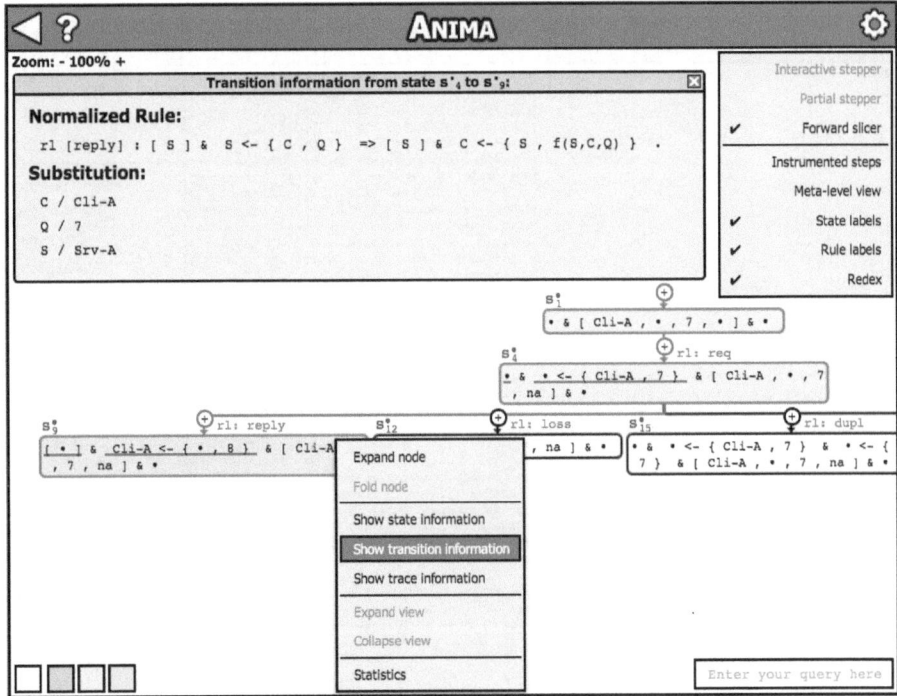

Fig. 11. Anima at work

These are the main features provided by Anima:

1. *Inspection strategies.* The tool implements the three inspection strategies described in Section 5. As shown in Figure 11, the user can select the desired strategy by using the selector provided in the option pane.
2. *Select meaningful symbols for slicing.* State slices can be specified by highlighting with the mouse the state symbols of interest directly on the tree.
3. *Expand/Fold program states.* The user can expand or fold states of the tree by double-clicking or right-clicking on them with the mouse and then selecting either the *Expand Node* option or *Fold Node* option that are offered in the contextual menu. For instance, in Figure 11, a state slice on the frontier of the computed tree slice fragment has been selected and is ready to be expanded through the *Expand Node* option that will add all the possible slices of the Maude steps to the tree starting from the selected node. The whole branch leading from the root to the selected node of the tree is highlighted. Common actions like dragging, zooming, and navigating the tree are allowed. Also, when a tree node is selected, the position of the tree on the screen is automatically rearranged to keep the chosen node at the center of the scene.
4. *Display instrumented trace.* The user can freely choose to display either a default, simplified view of a rewrite step (where only the applied rewrite rule is displayed), or the complete and detailed sequence of steps in the

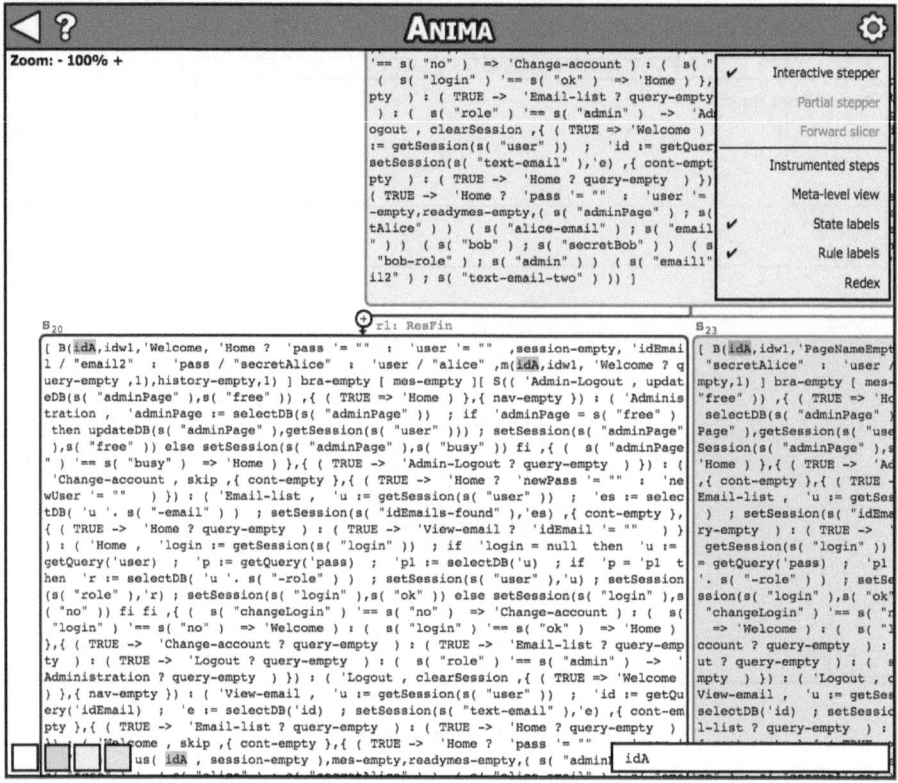

Fig. 12. Anima search mechanism

corresponding instrumented trace that simulates the step. This facility can be locally accessed by clicking in the +/− symbols that respectively adorn the standard/instrumented view of the rewrite step, or by checking/unchecking the *Instrumented steps* option in the Anima option pane for the entire computation tree.

5. *Tree Query mechanism.* The search facility illustrated in Figures 11 and 12 implements a pattern language that allows the selected information of interest to be searched on huge states of complex computation trees. The user only has to provide a filtering pattern (the query) that specifies the set of symbols that he/she wants to search for, and then all the states matching the query are automatically highlighted in the computation tree.

6. *Show rewrite step information.* Anima facilitates the inspection of any rewrite step $s \rightarrow t$ of the computation tree by underlining the differences between the two states (typically the selected redex of s and its contractum in t). In the case of a non-instrumented step $s \rightarrow_{\Delta,B} t$ (resp. $s \rightarrow_{R,B} t$), we cannot highlight in general the redex and contractum of the step as they might not exist in s and t because of the matching modulo B that precedes the rewrite step, and the normalization that occurs after the rewrite step. Actually, recall

Trace information

Step	RuleName	Execution trace
1	'Start	[Srv-A] & [Cli-A , Srv-A , 7 , na] & [Cli-B , Srv-A , 17 , na]
2	flattening	[Srv-A] & [Cli-A , Srv-A , 7 , na] & [Cli-B , Srv-A , 17 , na]
3	unflattening	[Srv-A] & [Cli-B , Srv-A , 17 , na] & [Cli-A , Srv-A , 7 , na]
4	req	[Srv-A] & [Cli-B , Srv-A , 17 , na] & Srv-A <- { Cli-A , 7 } & [Cli-A , Srv-A , 7 , na]
5	flattening	[Srv-A] & Srv-A <- { Cli-A , 7 } & [Cli-A , Srv-A , 7 , na] & [Cli-B , Srv-A , 17 , na]
6	unflattening	[Cli-A , Srv-A , 7 , na] & [Cli-B , Srv-A , 17 , na] & [Srv-A] & Srv-A <- { Cli-A , 7 }
7	reply	[Cli-A , Srv-A , 7 , na] & [Cli-B , Srv-A , 17 , na] & [Srv-A] & Cli-A <- { Srv-A , f(Srv-A,Cli-A,7) }
8	inc	[Cli-A , Srv-A , 7 , na] & [Cli-B , Srv-A , 17 , na] & [Srv-A] & Cli-A <- { Srv-A , 7 + 1 }
9	builtIn	[Cli-A , Srv-A , 7 , na] & [Cli-B , Srv-A , 17 , na] & [Srv-A] & Cli-A <- { Srv-A , 8 }
10	flattening	[Srv-A] & Cli-A <- { Srv-A , 8 } & [Cli-A , Srv-A , 7 , na] & [Cli-B , Srv-A , 17 , na]
Total size:		884

Back   Export trace

Fig. 13. Anima trace information

that s and t are eventually reordered, augmented with identity elements, and parenthesised, yielding the B-equivalent terms s' and t' that star in an intermediate rewrite step $s' \to_\Delta t'$ (resp., $s' \to_R t'$). In this case, we underline the antecedents in s of the reduced redex in s' (and the descendants in t of the contractum that appears in t').

Furthermore, by clicking on the corresponding edge label of the tree, additional transition information is also displayed in the *transition information* window that shows up at the top, including the computed substitution and the normalized rule/equation applied.

7. *Show trace information.* By right-clicking a tree node and by selecting the *Show trace information* option, the user can obtain the complete information of the execution trace from the root to the selected node. This information is presented in a table that includes the labels of the rules and equations applied, the terms that result from the application of each rule or equation and the computed trace slice (if applicable) as shown in Figure 13. Moreover, Anima offers the possibility to export the displayed trace into meta-level representation, so the user can easily transfer the selected trace to any other Maude trace analyzer tool like, for example, *i*JULIENNE [4].

8. *Show statistics.* Finally, detailed statistics of the current computation tree can be accessed by selecting the *Statistics* option that appears in the contextual menu for any node in the tree. This shows, among others, the number of terms (normalized or not) that are reachable from this node, its number of children and depth in the tree, and the global size of the computation tree.

7   Conclusions

The analysis of execution traces plays a fundamental role in many program analysis approaches, such as runtime verification, monitoring, testing, and specification mining. We have presented a parametrized exploration technique that can be applied to the inspection of rewriting logic computations and that can work in different ways. Three instances of the parameterized exploration scheme (an incremental stepper, an incremental partial stepper, and a forward trace slicer) have been formalized and implemented in the Anima tool, which is a novel program animator for RWL. The tool is useful for Maude programmers in two ways. First, it graphically exemplifies the semantics of the language, allowing the evaluation rules to be observed in action. Secondly, it can be used as a debugging tool, allowing the users to step forward and backward while slicing the trace in order to validate input data or locate programming mistakes.

As already mentioned, the present version supports the instrumentation of matching modulo associativity, commutativity, and (left-, right- or two-sided) unity. Nevertheless, Anima has an extensible design so that instrumentation for other equational axioms such as idempotency can be easily added in the future.

As future work, we intend to apply our exploration technique to more sophisticated rewrite theories that may include membership axioms as well as conditional rules and equations. Furthermore, we plan to integrate the analysis capabilities of the backward trace slicer iJULIENNE [4] in Anima. The idea is to first apply forward trace slicing to a given computation in order to remove all the information that does not affect the observed symbols. This procedure may produce "incorrect" computation slices, that is, computation slices that do not precise all the concrete input data that are required to generate the relevant symbols in the output/final state of the computation slice, as seen in Example 12. Hence, backward trace slicing might be applied to the generated computation slice to enrich it with new input symbols computed as antecedents of the relevant output with the aim of ensuring the correctness of the slice.

Finally, we envisage to equip Anima with dynamic program slicing techniques to extract the minimal program slice that is needed to generate any selected execution trace of the computation tree.

References

1. Alpuente, M., Ballis, D., Baggi, M., Falaschi, M.: A Fold/Unfold Transformation Framework for Rewrite Theories extended to CCT. In: Proc. PEPM 2010, pp. 43–52. ACM (2010)
2. Alpuente, M., Ballis, D., Espert, J., Romero, D.: Model-checking Web Applications with Web-TLR. In: Bouajjani, A., Chin, W.-N. (eds.) ATVA 2010. LNCS, vol. 6252, pp. 341–346. Springer, Heidelberg (2010)
3. Alpuente, M., Ballis, D., Espert, J., Romero, D.: Backward Trace Slicing for Rewriting Logic Theories. In: Bjørner, N., Sofronie-Stokkermans, V. (eds.) CADE 2011. LNCS, vol. 6803, pp. 34–48. Springer, Heidelberg (2011)
4. Alpuente, M., Ballis, D., Frechina, F., Sapiña, J.: Slicing-Based Trace Analysis of Rewriting Logic Specifications with iJULIENNE. In: Felleisen, M., Gardner, P. (eds.) ESOP 2013. LNCS, vol. 7792, pp. 121–124. Springer, Heidelberg (2013)
5. Alpuente, M., Ballis, D., Frechina, F., Romero, D.: Using Conditional Trace Slicing for improving Maude programs. Science of Computer Programming (2013) (to appear)

6. Alpuente, M., Ballis, D., Romero, D.: A Rewriting Logic Approach to the Formal Specification and Verification of Web applications. Science of Computer Programming (2013) (to appear)
7. Baggi, M., Ballis, D., Falaschi, M.: Quantitative Pathway Logic for Computational Biology. In: Degano, P., Gorrieri, R. (eds.) CMSB 2009. LNCS, vol. 5688, pp. 68–82. Springer, Heidelberg (2009)
8. Bruni, R., Meseguer, J.: Semantic Foundations for Generalized Rewrite Theories. Theoretical Computer Science 360(1-3), 386–414 (2006)
9. Clavel, M., Durán, F., Eker, S., Lincoln, P., Martí-Oliet, N., Meseguer, J., Talcott, C.: Maude Manual (Version 2.6). Technical report, SRI Int'l Computer Science Laboratory (2011), http://maude.cs.uiuc.edu/maude2-manual/
10. Clements, J., Flatt, M., Felleisen, M.: Modeling an Algebraic Stepper. In: Sands, D. (ed.) ESOP 2001. LNCS, vol. 2028, pp. 320–334. Springer, Heidelberg (2001)
11. Durán, F., Meseguer, J.: A Maude Coherence Checker Tool for Conditional Order-Sorted Rewrite Theories. In: Ölveczky, P.C. (ed.) WRLA 2010. LNCS, vol. 6381, pp. 86–103. Springer, Heidelberg (2010)
12. Eker, S.: Associative-Commutative Matching via Bipartite Graph Matching. The Computer Journal 38(5), 381–399 (1995)
13. Eker, S.: Associative-Commutative Rewriting on Large Terms. In: Nieuwenhuis, R. (ed.) RTA 2003. LNCS, vol. 2706, pp. 14–29. Springer, Heidelberg (2003)
14. Klop, J.W.: Term Rewriting Systems. In: Abramsky, S., Gabbay, D., Maibaum, T. (eds.) Handbook of Logic in Computer Science, vol. I, pp. 1–112. Oxford University Press (1992)
15. Martí-Oliet, N., Meseguer, J.: Rewriting Logic: Roadmap and Bibliography. Theoretical Computer Science 285(2), 121–154 (2002)
16. Meseguer, J.: Conditional Rewriting Logic as a Unified Model of Concurrency. Theoretical Computer Science 96(1), 73–155 (1992)
17. Meseguer, J.: The Temporal Logic of Rewriting: A Gentle Introduction. In: Degano, P., De Nicola, R., Meseguer, J. (eds.) Montanari Festschrift. LNCS, vol. 5065, pp. 354–382. Springer, Heidelberg (2008)
18. Plotkin, G.D.: The Origins of Structural Operational Semantics. The Journal of Logic and Algebraic Programming 60-61(1), 3–15 (2004)
19. Riesco, A., Verdejo, A., Caballero, R., Martí-Oliet, N.: Declarative Debugging of Rewriting Logic Specifications. In: Corradini, A., Montanari, U. (eds.) WADT 2008. LNCS, vol. 5486, pp. 308–325. Springer, Heidelberg (2009)
20. Riesco, A., Verdejo, A., Martí-Oliet, N.: Declarative Debugging of Missing Answers for Maude. In: Proc. RTA 2010. LIPIcs, vol. 6, pp. 277–294 (2010)
21. TeReSe. Term Rewriting Systems. Cambridge University Press (2003)

The Semantics of Datalog for the Evidential Tool Bus[*]
(Extended Abstract)

Simon Cruanes[1], Stijn Heymans[2], Ian Mason[3],
Sam Owre[3], and Natarajan Shankar[3]

[1] Ecole Polytechnique, Palaiseau, France
[2] Artificial Intelligence Center, SRI International, Menlo Park, CA 94025, USA
[3] Computer Science Laboratory, SRI International, Menlo Park, CA 94025, USA
simon.cruanes.2007@polytechnique.org,
Stijn.Heymans@sri.com,
{Iam,Owre,Shankar}@csl.sri.com

Dedicated to Kokichi Futatsugi for his inspiring vision and generous spirit.

Abstract. The Evidential Tool Bus (ETB) is a distributed framework
for tool integration for the purpose of building and maintaining assurance cases. ETB employs Datalog as a metalanguage both for defining
workflows and representing arguments. The application of Datalog in
ETB differs in some significant ways from its use as a database query
language. For example, in ETB Datalog predicates can be tied to external tool invocations. The operational treatment of such external calls is
more expressive than the use of built-in predicates in Datalog. We outline the semantic characteristics of the variant of Datalog used in ETB
and describe an abstract machine for evaluating Datalog queries.

1 Introduction

Software is an important component of many modern safety-critical systems, and
its reliability must therefore be certified to very high levels of assurance. It is
quite common for an assurance case for software to be developed using workflows
that integrate multiple formal, semi-formal, and informal tools. The capabilities
offered by these tools span the software lifecycle from requirements capture and
validation, to design and verification, and eventually system integration and
testing. At SRI, we have been developing a framework for software assurance
called the Evidential Tool Bus (ETB) [5]. The ETB middleware can be used
to integrate external tools through tool wrappers, to define workflows, and to

[*] This work was supported by NSF Grant CSR-EHCS(CPS)-0834810, NASA Cooperative Agreement NNA10DE73C, and by DARPA under agreement number FA8750-
12-C-0284. The views and conclusions contained herein are those of the authors and
should not be interpreted as necessarily representing the official policies or endorse-
ments, either expressed or implied, of NSF, NASA, DARPA or the U.S. Government.
We are grateful for the insightful feedback we received from the anonymous referees
and from Mark Utting of the University of Waikato.

S. Iida, J. Meseguer, and K. Ogata (Eds.): Futatsugi Festschrift, LNCS 8373, pp. 256–275, 2014.
© Springer-Verlag Berlin Heidelberg 2014

collect claims and evidence in support of a well-defined argument. The Datalog fragment of Horn clause programming is at the core of ETB. Datalog is used as the metalanguage, both for scripting workflows that incorporate multiple tools, and for representing assurance arguments. ETB differs from other application of Datalog in some subtle but significant ways. Since we are using Datalog for developing assurance cases, it is important to capture the semantic details of the language in a rigorous manner. We outline the semantic peculiarities of ETB Datalog and define an abstract machine for the evaluation of Datalog programs in the context of a distributed computation.

Workflows for software assurance involve *semi-formal* steps for validation, testing, and hazard analysis; *formal* steps for verification, synthesis, and test generation; and *informal* steps such as checklists and human inputs. From the viewpoint of assurance, the end result of such a workflow must be a certifiable assurance case consisting of claims supported by arguments and evidence. Many verification workflows involve multiple tools: type checkers, static analyzers, SAT and SMT solvers, interactive and automated theorem provers, and symbolic and explicit-state model checkers. The tools and inference rules used in the argument must be expressly qualified for use in the assurance case. Each of the different tools might work only with certain languages and representations, so that translations between different representations will also be a key part of the workflow. An assurance case constructed from the workflow is a collection of artifacts (files, properties, metrics, etc.) along with claims about these artifacts, and arguments in support of these claims. For the purpose of certification, it is desirable that arguments representing the assurance case be replayable. It should also be possible to maintain the argument against changes to inputs (e.g., requirements) as well as modifications to the tools.

The Evidential Tool Bus framework has been outlined in an earlier paper [5]. We summarize the key points below. ETB is a distributed framework for tool integration. An ETB installation is a network of ETB servers as shown in Figure 1, where each server can offer specific services. ETB uses Datalog as the scripting language for defining workflows as well as the metalanguage for building arguments. Services are packaged as Datalog predicates. Each ETB server runs a Datalog engine that can be used to implement workflows integrating different services. The claims are maintained together with their proofs. A service is associated with a Datalog predicate by means of a wrapper. For example, the Yices SMT solver can be offered as a service through the Datalog predicate $yices(F, S, M)$, where the variable[1] F represents a file containing a formula in the Yices input language, S is the result, *sat* or *unsat*, of the satisfiability check, and M is the model when S is *sat*. If $a.ys$ is a Yices file containing a formula, then the query $yices(a.ys, S, M)$ invokes the Yices solver to bind the variables S and M.

A workflow is defined as a Datalog program consisting of Horn clauses. For example, a workflow that generates a test input from a formula in a file F and executes it on a program P can be defined by the Horn clause below, where

---

[1] As is conventional in logic programming, identifiers starting with uppercase letters are variables.

$A :- B, C, D$ represents the clause $(B \wedge C \wedge D) \implies A$.

$$gentest(F, P, Result) :- yices(F, S, M), equal(S, sat), test(P, M, Result)$$

If $a.ys$ is a file defining a Yices formula and b is a file containing a program, then $gentest(a.ys, b, Result)$ executes the workflow on these files and binds the test results to the variable $Result$. A query is invoked by a client and is evaluated by a Datalog engine at a server in the ETB network. The server can invoke services that are available at other nodes in the network. The $gentest$ query above is evaluated at a specific server, but might use the $yices$ service at a remote server by copying the input files to the remote server and copying back any files representing the results.

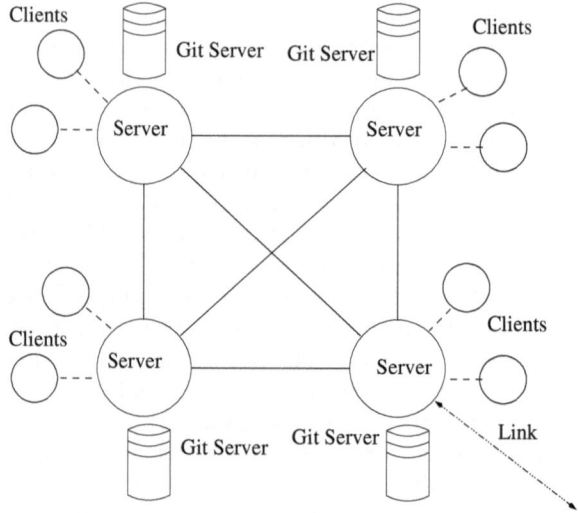

Fig. 1. The ETB Client-Server Architecture

The Datalog variant used in ETB serves as an integration language for a distributed network of services. It is also used as a representation language for assurance arguments that build in calls to certain trusted services. External services are invoked through queries with external predicates such as the $yices$ predicate. Such invocations are operationally quite similar to the evaluation of internal predicates, e.g., $gentest$, in the sense that the evaluation step returns a (possibly empty) set of clauses whose head atoms are instances of the query atom. This leads to a richer notion of external predicates than the traditional *built-in* predicates in Datalog. Furthermore, the similarity between the evaluation of internal and external predicates yields a somewhat uniform denotational and operational semantics for the Datalog variant used in ETB.

There is a large volume of work on Datalog related to its use in Databases. This work has its origins in a workshop on *Logic and Data Bases* organized by

Gallaire and Minker [6]. Details of the use and implementation of Datalog as a programming language are covered in the book *Foundations of Databases* by Abiteboul, Hull, and Vianu [1], and in several survey articles [3,7,8]. Our focus here is on Datalog extended with a specific mechanism for service invocation that is richer than the interpretation of *built-in* predicates. We present the semantics of this version of Datalog that is suitable for use in the ETB framework. The abstract machine we present employs *tabling* to memoize the computation of repeated subgoals, and the presentation here is somewhat related to the abstract machine for tabled Datalog defined by Sagonas and Swift [10].

We describe the peculiarities of ETB Datalog in Section 3. We then present the semantics of ETB Datalog in Section 4. Concluding observations and future work are presented in Section 6.

2   A Brief Overview of Datalog

Though Datalog was first introduced as a deductive language for defining database queries, it has found applications in a number of other areas such as declarative networking [9], static analysis [12], distributed computing[2], and parallel programming [4]. The core of Datalog is a Horn clause programming language where the terms are either variables or constants. Typical applications of Datalog employ a fragment that includes a notion of negation, but we restrict ourselves to the positive fragment.

The Datalog language is specified relative to a set of *constants* C, a set of *variables* V, and a set of *predicates* Σ, where each predicate has an arity. An *atom* is of the form $p(a_1, \ldots, a_n)$, where p is an n-ary predicate in Σ, and each a_i is a *term*, i.e., either a variable in V or a constant in C. A *ground* atom is an atom that contains no variables. A *rule* is of the form $A :- Q$, where A is the *head* atom of the rule, and the *body* Q is a (possibly empty) sequence of atoms $A_1, \ldots, A_n$. The set of variables occurring in the head A must be a subset of those occurring in the body Q. A program R is a set of rules. A predicate p is defined in R by the set of rules in R of the form $p(a_1, \ldots, a_n) :- Q$.

For example, the program below defines a *sibling* relation given the *father* and *mother* relations. The parent relation is defined as the union of the father and mother relations.

$$sibling(X, Y) :- parent(Z, X), parent(Z, Y)$$
$$parent(X, Y) :- father(X, Y)$$
$$parent(X, Y) :- mother(X, Y)$$

A Datalog program will contain both rules, such as the definitions shown above, as well as facts which are just ground atoms such as

$$father(joe, bill)$$
$$mother(mary, joe)$$
$$father(jim, mary)$$
$$father(jim, bob)$$

Informally, a Datalog program R consisting of rules and facts entails a set of ground atoms H, i.e., every atom in H holds in every model of R. A query is a negated atom of the form $\neg p(a_1, \ldots, a_n)$. The answers to such a query are the ground instances of $p(a_1, \ldots, a_n)$ in H, namely, the refutations of the query. For example, if the query is $\neg sibling(mary, x)$, then the answers are $sibling(mary, mary)$ (which is counterintuitive, but what the definition implies) and $sibling(mary, bob)$.

The definition of the *sibling* relation can already be formulated in first-order logic, but Datalog can also capture recursive definitions that are not expressible in first-order logic. The *ancestor* relation can be given the recursive Horn clause definition shown below.

$$ancestor(X, Y) :- parent(X, Y)$$
$$ancestor(X, Y) :- parent(Z, Y), ancestor(X, Z)$$

For example, the query $\neg ancestor(X, bill)$ yields the answers

1. $ancestor(joe, bill)$
2. $ancestor(mary, bill)$
3. $ancestor(jim, bill)$

3   Datalog as Used in ETB

As a metalanguage for ETB, Datalog offers a simple semantic framework for expressing claims, composing arguments, and defining workflows that direct the flow of information and work to and from the external tools. For example, the following ETB Datalog program generates all the satisfying assignments for a Boolean formula.

$$sat(F, M) :- yices(F, S, M), equal(S, sat)$$
$$unsat(F) :- yices(F, S, M), equal(S, unsat)$$
$$allsat(F, Answers) :- sat(F, M),$$
$$negateModel(F, M, NewF),$$
$$allsat(NewF, T),$$
$$cons(M, T, Answers)$$
$$allsat(F, Answers) :- unsat(F), nil(Answers)$$

The query $\neg yices(f, S, M)$ triggers the invocation of the Yices SMT solver on the Yices formula in the file corresponding to the file handle f to return the result *sat* or *unsat* binding S. In the latter case, the model M is irrelevant and is bound to the Yices formula *false*. In the former case, the variable M is bound to the model which is given as a Yices formula that is a conjunction of literals. The program for the predicate *allsat* invokes the Yices solver to compute a model M for the formula in the file f. Its negation is conjoined with the formula in F and placed in a new file with the handle $NewF$. The *allsat* procedure is repeated on $NewF$ until the formula becomes unsatisfiable. The list of all the assignments is bound to the variables *Answers*. Note that even the list operations of binding *Answers* to *nil* and the pairing operation $cons(M, T, Answers)$ are implemented as external calls.

Let f be the file handle for the file containing the input Yices formula. A goal query, e.g., $\neg allsat(f, Answers)$ is evaluated with respect to a set of rules by means of backward chaining. The goal is resolved with all the program clauses where *allsat* is the head predicate, i.e., the predicate of the head atom. There are two such clauses. In both cases, unification binds the variable F with the file handle f. The leading atoms of the body, namely, $sat(f, M)$ and $unsat(f)$, then become new goals. Backward chaining on these goals leads to the evaluation of $yices(f, S, M)$. Although the subgoal $yices(f, S, M)$ occurs twice in the evaluation, it is only evaluated once. If Yices finds the formula in the file (handle) f to be satisfiable, then it binds S to *sat* and M to the resulting model which we can label as m_1. Since the evaluation of $unsat(F)$ returns no bindings, we can terminate the evaluation of the second clause in the definition of *allsat*. The evaluation of the body of the first clause continues with the evaluation of $negateModel(F, M, NewF)$. This creates a new file where the contents of the file handle f have been augmented with the assertion of the negation of the formula corresponding to model m_1. The *allsat* program is now evaluated recursively on this new file. The answer m_1 is added to the list of assignments $m_2, \ldots, m_n$ returned by the recursive evaluation.

The bulk of the computation is carried out by these external tools. Predicates, like *yices*, that invoke external tools are called *interpreted* or *external* predicates. They are similar to built-in predicates in Datalog. However, built-in predicates are usually invoked on ground arguments whereas the invocation in ETB of an interpreted predicate will involve binding the variables to zero or more bindings. The typical evaluation of a query involving an interpreted predicate, such as *yices* will return at most one binding, but there are predicates that can return multiple bindings. Another difference with built-in predicates is that the evaluation of an interpreted predicate can generate further queries. For example, an interpreted query for computing a definite integral of a function over an interval using Risch's algorithm might return a result with the qualification that the function must be defined and continuous over the interval. Queries returned by the external procedure can be used to guard the answers with side conditions or reflect the case analysis in the computation.

We employ standard mathematical notation in presenting the details of ETB Datalog. The metavariables a and b range over Datalog terms, i.e., variables and constants. The metavariable p ranges over Datalog predicates, the metavariable A ranges over atoms, and Q ranges over conjunctions of atoms. In running text, a clause is bracketed for ease of reading and is represented as $A :\quad Q$, with head A and body Q.

The Datalog variant used in ETB has several distinctive features:

1. The basic evaluation scheme is backward chaining on rules through resolution with queries. The body literals in the rule are evaluated through backward chaining, left-to-right order. This order of evaluation is significant. Backward chaining is needed to ensure that only the relevant external predicate calls

are evaluated. The left-to-right order of evaluation on the body of a rule ensures that external predicates are not evaluated until their preconditions have been verified. For example, it does not make sense to invoke the PVS prover on a formula that has not yet been typechecked.

2. As in tabled evaluation [10], the searches are memoized to avoid repeated computation.

3. An external predicate corresponds to a service that might be available only from specific servers. In order to provide this service, the corresponding server has one or more wrappers associated with the predicate. Each wrapper covers a specific mode for the predicate. The modes specify the arguments to the predicate that are provided as inputs, and some subset of the remaining arguments might be computed through the evaluation of the wrappers. For example, the invocation of the *yices* predicate has the mode $\langle +, -, - \rangle$ in the *allsat* program.

4. Though the external calls can return multiple bindings (i.e., substitutions) for the outputs, most wrappers are expected to return at most one binding. This means that we can adopt a Prolog-style, tuple-at-a-time mode of evaluation rather than computing with sets of tuples.

5. External calls can generate further queries. This means that the evaluation of an external call, e.g., $p(a_1, \ldots, a_n)$ can return clauses of the form $p(b_1, \ldots, b_n) :- Q$. Most implementations of Datalog restrict external calls to ground atoms, i.e., atoms of the form $p(b_1, \ldots, b_n)$ for ground terms $b_1, \ldots, b_n$.

6. The evaluation of Datalog queries relative to a program returns a set of claims. Each claim is supported by a derivation or a proof. The derivation should be replayable, and it should be possible to identify the evidence artifacts such as files (and file contents) that are used in the derivation.

7. For the purpose of developing an assurance argument, we can restrict the external predicates and Datalog rules that are sanctioned for use in the construction of a derivation.

8. Query evaluation is distributed in the sense that the evaluation of external calls can take place at a remote ETB server. This means that the evaluation must be asynchronous — at any given point in the computation, a server can be awaiting results from multiple external calls. In some cases, a service might fail during evaluation or might only become available after a delay.

The above features of ETB Datalog require special treatment that are not offered by existing implementations of Datalog. We present the semantics of ETB Datalog and describe an abstract machine that captures the evaluation of Datalog queries in this framework.

4   Semantics of ETB Datalog

The semantics of the Datalog language can be given by a traditional first-order structure M that maps each element c of C to an element $\mathbf{c}$ in the domain $|M|$, and each n-ary predicate to a subset of the set $|M|^n$ of the n-tuples from $|M|$. The meaning of a rule set R can be given by a set H of ground atoms such that for any model M of R: $M \models A$ for $A \in H$. In this case, we say $R \models A$. Given a goal query $\neg p(a_1, \ldots, a_n)$ and a rule set R, a Datalog computation should return the set of valid ground instances of the goal query, i.e., those atoms A that are instances of $p(a_1, \ldots, a_n)$ such that $R \models A$.

One way to check $R \models A$ is by computing the minimal Herbrand model for R. This is done starting with H_0 as the empty set. Each successive H_{i+1} is computed by closing under the application of rules from R so that

$$H_{i+1} = \{\hat{B} | \hat{B} = \sigma(B) \text{ for ground } \hat{B}, \sigma(Q) \subseteq H_i, B :- Q \in R\}.$$

Then $H = H_i$ for the least i such that $H_i = H_{i+1}$. It can be checked that $R \models A$ iff $A \in H$. Note also that for a given R, the set H is finite, even if the set of constants C is infinite.

An operational way to compute the valid ground instances of the goal query is through depth-first backward search. We introduce the operations of substitution and unification as a prelude to the operational semantics. A substitution σ is a partial map from variables in V to terms, e.g., $[v_1 \mapsto a_1, v_2 \mapsto a_2]$. For such a partial map, $\sigma(x) = a$ if σ maps x to a, and $\sigma(x) = x$, otherwise. A substitution σ can be applied to an atom A as $\sigma(A)$, a rule body Q as $\sigma(Q)$, or a rule K as $\sigma(K)$. In each case, the result is obtained by substituting $\sigma(x)$ for each occurrence of a variable x. A substitution σ is at least as general as another substitution σ' if $\sigma(x) = \sigma'(x)$ whenever $\sigma(x)$ is defined. An atom A is an *instance* of an atom B if there is a substitution σ such that $\sigma(B) = A$. Conversely, B is said to be a *generalization* of A. A substitution σ is at least as general as another substitution σ' if $\sigma(A)$ is at least as general than $\sigma'(A)$, for any atom A. A substitution σ is a *unifier* of two atoms A and B if $\sigma(B)$, i.e., the *unification*, is an instance of A. We have given an asymmetric definition of unification so that we can avoid renaming the variables in A and B apart. A substitution σ is the *most general* unifier of two atoms A and B if it yields a unification $\sigma(B)$ that is at least as general as the unification resulting from another unifier. The operation $mgu(A, B)$ is the most general unifier of A and B when it exists, and is $\perp$, otherwise.

Unification is used to compute $D_R(A)$, the valid ground instances of A given the rule set R. It is defined mutually recursively with the operation $D_R(Q)$ that computes the valid ground instances of a sequence of atoms Q. We define $D_R(Q)$ as

$$D_R(A, Q) = \{A', Q' | A' \in D_R(A), \sigma(A) = A', Q' \in D_R(\sigma(Q))\},$$

and $D_R(\epsilon) = \epsilon$, where ϵ is the empty sequence. Let $R(A)$ be the set of clauses $\{\sigma(B :- Q) | B :- Q \in R, \sigma = mgu(A, B) \neq \perp\}$. We can complete the mutual recursion by defining $D_R(A)$ as

$$\{B' | B :- Q \in R(A), Q' \in D_R(Q), \sigma(Q) = Q', B' = \sigma(B)\}.$$

The sets $D_R(A)$ and $D_R(Q)$ are finite and contain all and only the ground instances of A and Q, respectively, that are valid in R.

In ETB, we also include an external oracle E that interprets the *external predicates*, which we take as any predicate that is not defined in R.[2] With external predicates, we give up the property that there is a finite Herbrand model. For example, if we have an external predicate *successor* such that $successor(0, Y)$ returns the binding of 1 to Y, and $successor(K, Y)$ is the successor of the numeral K, then we can write a Datalog program that computes all of the natural numbers:

$$nat(0)$$
$$nat(X) :- nat(Y), successor(Y, X)$$

We can in fact recover the full power of Prolog through external oracles that perform unification.

Examples of atoms in external predicates can range from simple built-in operations such as $less(x, y)$ and $subrange(low, high, i)$ to wrapper calls such as $yices(f, S, M)$. The interpretation $E(p(a_1, \ldots, a_n))$ for an atom is performed by a *wrapper*. For example, the evaluation of the external predicate

$$yices(filename.ys, s, m)$$

invokes a wrapper that executes the Yices SMT solver on the input from the file $filename.ys$, and binds the result, sat or $unsat$, to the variable s, and a model, if one exists to the variable m. In general, the interpretation $E(p(a_1, \ldots, a_n))$ returns a (possibly empty) list of clauses where each clause has the form

$$p(b_1, \ldots, b_n) :- Q.$$

The head atom $p(b_1, \ldots, b_n)$ must be an instance of the query atom $p(a_1, \ldots, a_n)$, and the variables in the head must also occur in the body. Most Datalog variants admit only a limited interpretation of external predicates where the queries must be fully grounded, whereas in ETB, we allow a more liberal and expressive interpretation of external predicates that allows further queries to be spawned. This interpretation also makes the behavior of E and R similar with respect to the operational semantics.

Each external predicate can be evaluated under one or more *modes*. An n-ary mode for an n-ary predicate is a sequence of symbols length n, where each symbol is either $+$ or $-$. The positions marked by $+$ are the input arguments for the predicate, and these have to be grounded in the query, whereas the positions marked $-$ are the outputs that are bound during the evaluation of the query. For an atom $p(a_1, \ldots, a_n)$, $mode(p(a_1, \ldots, a_n))$ is the sequence $m_1, \ldots, m_n$, where each m_i is either $+$ or $-$, and a_i is a variable exactly when m_i is $-$. An external predicate might have wrappers associated only with specific modes. For example, the query $subrange(0, High, 3)$ is not sensible since the set of bindings for $High$ is infinite. Similarly, $yices(F, unsat, M)$ should not have a wrapper associated

---

[2] We disallow the possibility of a predicate being defined both in R and E since in our semantics, the same effect can be achieved solely through external oracles.

with it since it requires finding a file containing an unsatisfiable formula, and there could be unboundedly many such files.

There is a partial ordering on the modes of an external predicate so that one mode is narrower than another if the set of input arguments of the first mode is a superset of the set of input arguments of the second mode. If a mode is interpretable for an external predicate, then any narrowing of this mode obtained by turning outputs arguments into input arguments must also be interpretable. This can be satisfied by interpreting p with a more general mode, i.e., one where some of the input arguments are outputs, and filtering the results relative to the additional input arguments. For example, to compute $E(p(c_1, \ldots, c_n))$, we can instead compute $E(p(a_1, \ldots, a_n))$, where each a_i is either c_i or a fresh variable v_i. The resulting clauses can then be instantiated and filtered so that the head atom is always an instance of $p(c_1, \ldots, c_n)$. This ensures, for example, that it is always possible to invoke an external call on a fully grounded atom.

The wrappers for the different modes of an external predicate have to be *compatible*, so that even if there are multiple wrappers for p that can be used to compute $E(p(a_1, \ldots, a_n))$, the set of clauses returned is the same. In ETB, we do not check the compatibility of the wrappers for a given external predicate. Instead, we assume that every external predicate has a wrapper for the fully grounded mode, i.e., one where all the arguments are inputs. This is the only wrapper that needs to be trusted since it will be used to check the arguments associated with the final set of claims.

Herbrand models do not make sense for external oracles since new constants can be generated when an oracle is invoked. We can instead construct a relatively closed Herbrand model where an oracle generates a set of ground external atoms Ω and $E[\Omega]$ is $\bigcup\{E(A)|A \in \Omega\}$. Then, a ground atom A is a consequence of R and E (relative to the oracle Ω) if $R \cup E[\Omega] \models A$. The minimal Herbrand model can be constructed by defining H_0 as the empty set and $H_{i+1} = \{\hat{B}|\hat{B} = \sigma(B)$ for ground $\hat{B}, \sigma(Q) \subseteq H_i, B :- Q \in R \cup E[\Omega]\}$. We can then say that the ground atom A is a consequence of R and E if for *some* set of ground external atoms Ω, A is a consequence of $R \cup E[\Omega]$. The abstract machine in Section 5 defines a specific set Ω from which Herbrand models can be constructed.

The model-theoretic semantics and the minimal Herbrand model do not yield effective operational methods for computing the set of answers to a query relative to a rule set R and an external oracle E. In the next section, we present an abstract machine for answering Datalog queries.

5   An Abstract Machine for ETB Datalog

We define an abstract machine for the ETB Datalog engine and argue for its correctness relative to the semantics given in the previous section. The engine evaluates a goal query of the form $\neg p(a_1, \ldots, a_n)$ against a set of rules R and external oracle E. The goal is to return all and only those ground instances of $p(a_1, \ldots, a_n)$ that are entailed by the rules R together with the external oracle E.

In order to easily check for equality, all the expressions are maintained in normalized form so that variables are ordered by occurrence so that v_i names the i'th distinct variable occurring in the expression. For example, the atom $p(X, c_1, Y)$ is normalized as $p(v_1, c_1, v_2)$. Similarly, a clause $p(X, c_1, Y)$:− $p(X, c_2, Z), p(Z, c_3, Y)$ is represented as $p(v_1, c_1, v_2)$:− $p(v_1, c_2, v_3), p(v_3, c_3, v_2)$.

5.1   An Abstract Inference System

We can first capture the Datalog computation as an abstract inference system [11]. For this we define a *logical state* is a pair $\langle G, J \rangle$, where

1. The set G consists of goals so that G is $\{\neg A_1, \ldots, \neg A_n\}$
2. The set J consists of clauses of the form B :− Q or of the form B, where Q is a nonempty list of atoms. A *claim* is a clause of the form B in J. It must be ground because of the condition that any variables in the head must occur in the body, and the body here is empty.

In each inference step, we perform one of the following steps:

1. **Backchain:** For a clause of the form B :− $A_1, \ldots, A_n$ in J, we add the goal $\neg A_1$ to G if it is not already in G.
2. **Resolve:** For a goal $\neg A$ in G and clause B :− Q in R, we add a new clause K to J, where $\sigma = mgu(A, B) \neq \bot$ and $K = \sigma(B$:− $Q)$.
3. **External:** For a goal $\neg A$ in G where A is an external atom and a clause K in $E(A)$, we add a new clause K to J.
4. **Propagate:** For a clause in J of the form B :− A, Q and another clause in J of the form A', with σ such that $\sigma(A) = A'$, we add the new clause $\sigma(B$:− $Q)$ to J.

The initial logic state consists of $G = \{\neg A\}$ where $\neg A$ is the initial goal. The inference procedure terminates when no further inference steps can be applied, i.e., when the logic state is *irreducible*. The result of the computation is the set $\{B \in J | \sigma(A) = B\}$.

The abstract inference system described here is sound and complete with respect to the semantics given above. Given an irreducible state $\langle G, J \rangle$, the set Ω is the set of all claims of the form $\{B \in J | B$ is an external atom$\}$. Then, each claim in J is a consequence of $R \cup E[\Omega]$. Additionally, for an initial goal $\neg A$, expanding Ω does not add any new claims of the B to J, where B is an instance of A.

5.2   An Abstract Machine

The abstract inference system above captures the basic idea of using resolution to compute with Datalog programs, but it has a major source of inefficiency. The logic state is not suitably indexed so that the number of steps for finding an applicable inference step can be quadratic in the number of formulas in the state. The number of formulas can itself be exponential in the size of the universe.

We can improve the performance of the abstract machine through better indexing and structuring.

Another problem with the abstract inference system is that our Datalog engine works in a distributed setting where new queries can be added from other nodes in the network. In this case, we might be done processing one goal query but the state might not be irreducible because other goals are still being processed. A termination check is needed to determine if a goal has been fully processed and all of the associated claims have been generated.

We modify the inference system to address these drawbacks. In the extended system, the state now consists of goal nodes G, clause nodes J, and an index T. The goal and clause nodes are enriched with annotations. Each entry g in G now consists of

1. *Literal:* The actual goal literal.
2. *Parents:* A set of the clauses in J from which the goal originated. This entry can be empty if the goal was introduced at the top level. Note that a goal can have multiple parents.
3. *Index:* The index that uniquely identifies a goal node. The *Index* slot is used in timestamps for checking termination.
4. *Claims:* A *sequence* of claims, i.e., clause nodes j where $j.Clause$ is of the form B, instantiating the goal.
5. *Children:* The set of clause nodes obtained by applying R or E to the Atom.
6. *Status: Open, Resolved, Closed,* or *Completed.*[3]

Each entry j in J consists of

1. *Clause:* The actual clause corresponding to the entry.
2. *Goal:* The parent goal in G from which the clause node originates.
3. *Subgoal:* A pointer to the subgoal in G generated from the clause. This slot could be empty. If $j.Clause$ is of the form $B :- A, Q$, then the $j.Subgoal.Literal$ is $\neg A$. Furthermore, $j.Subgoal.Parents$ contains j.
4. *Subclause:* A set of clause nodes that are derived by propagating from j.
5. *SubgoalIndex:* The number of claims corresponding to the subgoal that have already been propagated. It is initially zero when node j is created and is bumped up by one for each claim that is propagated from the subgoal.

We say that one goal h is an *immediate subgoal* of another goal g if there is some j such that $j.Goal = g$ and $j.Subgoal = h$. The inference steps can now be rewritten to operate on the annotated logic state.

1. **Backchain:** For a clause node j in J with $j.Clause$ of the form $B :- A_1, \ldots, A_n$, where $j.Subgoal$ is empty,
   (a) If there is already a goal node g in G with $g.Atom$ slot of the form $\neg A_1$, we add j to $g.Parents$ and set $j.Subgoal$ to g and $j.SubgoalIndex$ to 0.

---

[3] In the implementation, a goal may also be *Stuck* if there is neither a rule nor a wrapper associated with it. This can happen, for example, if the server providing the wrapper is temporarily unavailable.

(b) Otherwise, if there is no goal node g in G with $g.Atom$ of the form $\neg A_1$, we create a new goal node g' so that
   i. $g'.Literal$ is $\neg A_1$,
   ii. $g'.Parents$ is $\{j\}$,
   iii. $g'.Index$ is $T + 1$,
   iv. $g'.Claims$ is the empty sequence,
   v. $g'.Status$ is $Open$.
   All the other fields of g are left empty, and the global time parameter T in the state is incremented by one.

2. **Resolve:** For a goal node g in G with $g.Status = Open$, and $g.Literal = \neg A$, and each clause $B :- Q$ in R, we add a new clause node j to J, where $j.Clause = K = \sigma(B :- Q)$ with $\sigma = mgu(A, B) \neq \bot$, $j.Goal = g$, and $j.SubgoalIndex = 0$, with all the other fields empty. We also set $g.Status$ to $Resolved$.

3. **External:** For a goal node g in G with $g.Status = Open$, and $g.Literal = \neg A$, and for each clause K returned by $E(A)$, where $g.Literal = \neg A$, we add a new clause node j to J, where $j.Clause = K$, $j.Goal = g$, and $j.SubgoalIndex = 0$, with all the other fields empty. We also set $g.Status$ to $Resolved$.

4. **Propagate:** For some goal node g and for some clause node j' in $g.Parents$, where $j'.Clause$ is $B :- A, Q$ and $j'.SubgoalIndex$ is smaller than the length of $g.Claims$,
   let $j = g.Claims[j'.SubgoalIndex]$ with $j.Clause$ of the form A', we create a clause node j'' with
   (a) $j''.Clause$ set to $\sigma(B :- Q)$ where $A' = \sigma(A)$,
   (b) $j''.Goal$ set to $j'.Goal$, and
   (c) $j''.SubgoalIndex$ set to 0.
   Also, add j'' to $j'.Subclause$, set $j''.Subclause$ to the empty set, and increment $j'.SubgoalIndex$ by one.

5. **Claim:** For a clause j where $j.Claim$ is of the form B, we add j to the end of $j.Goal.Claims$ unless B is already present as $j'.Claim$ for some j' in $j.Goal.Claims$. We assume that this step is done immediately after a **Propagate**, **Resolve**, or **External** step whenever a claim is generated.

The abstract machine is initialized with a single initial goal node g with $g.Literal = \neg A$ with $g.Index = 1$ and with $T = 1$. The evaluation is terminated when no rule is applicable. In the next subsection, we augment the abstract machine with support for detecting termination. The key modifications in the machine defined above are

1. The clauses in J are no longer maintained as a set. This is to simplify the termination check.
2. The **Propagate** step does not scan all the claims but is instead triggered by the addition of a claim to the goal.

5.3   Abstract Machine with Termination Check

The abstract machine with the inference steps **Backchain**, **Resolve**, **External**, **Propagate**, and **Claim** is a refinement of the abstract inference system in

Subsection 5.1. However, it lacks a way of checking that a subgoal g has been fully evaluated, i.e., no further claims can be added to $g.Claims$. There is a simple but impractical way to do this that is already implicit in the abstract inference system: if the computation is stuck so that no further inference steps can be applied, then the computation has terminated. This only works if we are evaluating a single query in a sequential setting. However, ETB is a distributed system where the Datalog engine is evaluating many queries simultaneously and these computations could be sharing subgoals. Some of these subgoals might be fully evaluated even while new queries are being added and other parts of the computation have only be partially completed. A global termination check will not work in this context. We still need a termination check so that completed subgoals can be garbage collected.

Checking termination is not straightforward since the evaluation graph consisting of goal and clause nodes can contain cycles. Swift and Sagonas [10] interleave the evaluation with a check for strongly connected components (SCCs) to identify the fully evaluated nodes. We present a more fine-grained method for checking termination that can be run alongside the normal evaluation. For this purpose, we augment the state of the goals g with

1. A map $g.T$ from goals to sets of clauses such that $g.T(h)$ is nonempty only when h is an immediate subgoal of the goal g, and $g.T(h)$ is the set of clauses $\{j | j.Goal = g \land j.Subgoal = h\}$.
2. A partial map $g.D$ from goals to a number so that $g.D(h)$ is defined only when $h.Index < g.Index$ and h is not closed. The entry $g.D(h)$ is the number of claims from h that have been fully propagated in the derivation rooted at g. This means that every sub-derivation of g has propagated at least k claims from h for $k = g.D(h)$. The partial map $g.D$ contains the unclosed subgoals of g at the point when the **Close** rule (defined below) is applied.
3. A slot $g.Unclosed$ which, when defined, is the maximal index of an unclosed subgoal h of g such that $h.Index < g.Index$. In particular, $g.Unclosed$ is defined when g is closed, and it is the maximal index of a goal h such that $g.D$ is defined.

We modify the **Backchain** step of the abstract machine so that whenever it is applied to a clause j to set $j.Subgoal$ to h, we also add j to $g.T(h)$, where $g = j.Goal$.

Define $min(i_1, i_2)$ for two possibly undefined numeric values i_1 and i_2 as

1. *undefined*, if both i_1 and i_2 are undefined
2. i_1, if i_2 is undefined or $i_1 \leq i_2$, and
3. i_2 if i_1 is undefined or $i_2 < i_1$.

For a set of indices I, $min(i, I)$ is i if I is empty, or it is the minimal index in $\{i\} \cup I$. If I is a nonempty set of indices, then $min(I)$ is the minimal index in I.

Close: The **Close** rule performs a step in the termination check computation. We say that g is *closed* if $g.Status$ is *Closed* or *Completed*. When $g.Status = Closed$, then the only way a new claim can be added to g is if it is the result of adding a new claim to some subgoal h of g such that $h.Index < g.Index$. When $g.Status = Completed$, then no further claims can be added to g.

The **Close** rule is applied to a goal g where

1. $g.Status \in \{Resolved, Closed\}$, and for all $j \in g.Children$, $j.Clause$ is a claim or $j.Subgoal$ has been set. This ensures that the immediate children of g are either claims or have generated subgoals. Note that the **Backchain** rule registers a subgoal in $g.T$ as soon as it is generated.
2. For all h we check that either $g.T(h)$ is empty, $h.Index \le g.Index$, or $h.Status$ is $Closed$ and $h.Unclosed \le g.Index$ when $h.Unclosed$ is defined. In the latter two cases, we also check that for all j in $g.T(h)$, $j.SubgoalIndex = |h.Claims|$ and for all $j' \in j.Subclause$, either $j'.Clause$ is a claim or $j'.Subgoal$ has been set. This check ensures that we have a complete set of subgoals that have propagated all their claims, and the resulting clauses have also generated their subgoals (if any).

When this check is valid for a goal g, we compute the value of $g.D(h)$ for h such that $h.Index < g.Index$. We first compute for any h such that $h.Index \le g.Index$, the set

$$\tau(g)(h) = \{h'.D(h)|h' \text{ is closed}, g.T(h') \text{ is nonempty}, h'.D(h) \text{ is defined}\}.$$

If $\tau(g)(g)$ is either empty or $min(\tau(g)(g)) = |g.Claims|$, then we mark $g.Status$ as $Closed$ and then set $g.D(h)$ as below for unclosed h such that $h.Index < g.Index$. If $g.T(h)$ is nonempty, $g.D(h)$ is set to $min(|h.Claims|, \tau(g)(h))$. Otherwise, we set $g.D(h)$ to $min(\tau(g)(h))$. In any remaining case, $g.D(h)$ is undefined. Note that because of the way that τ is computed, $g.D(h)$ is defined only when h is not closed and $h.Index < g.Index$.

Once $g.D$ is set, we can recompute $g.Unclosed$ as the maximal unclosed h such that $g.D(h)$ is defined. If $g.D$ is everywhere undefined, then $g.Unclosed$ is also undefined. The information that g is closed needs to be propagated to any goal node h such that $h.Unclosed = g$, and this happens when the **Close** rule is applied to h.

Complete: The rule **Complete** marks nodes as completed. If for some g, $g.Status$ is $Closed$ then $g.Status$ can be set to $Completed$ if either

1. $g.D(h)$ is everywhere undefined, or
2. For some goal h such that g is an immediate subgoal of h, $h.Status = Completed$. Recall that g is an immediate subgoal of h when for some j in $g.Parents$, $j.Goal = h$.

5.4   An Example

We illustrate the abstract machine on a simple example using the program in Figure 2 consisting of clauses C_1 through C_7.

The derivation is summarized in the goal table and the clause table in Figures 3 and 4, respectively. The **Backchain** rule is implicit in the $Parent$ column

C_1	$black(a, b)$
C_2	$white(b, c)$
C_3	$white(b, a)$
C_4	$blackpath(X, Y) :- \qquad\qquad black(X, Y)$
C_5	$blackpath(X, Y) :- black(X, Z), whitepath(Z, Y)$
C_6	$whitepath(X, Y) :- \qquad\qquad white(X, Y)$
C_7	$whitepath(X, Y) :- white(X, Z), blackpath(Z, Y)$

Fig. 2. An Example Datalog Program

and the **Claim** rule is implicit in the *Claims* column of the goal table. The derivation steps for **Resolve** and **Propagate** are marked in the clause table. are marked in the

Goal	Literal	Parents	Claims	Children	Status
G_1	$\neg blackpath(a, Y)$	J_{13}	J_4, J_{17}, J_{18}	J_1, J_2	Resolved
G_2	$\neg black(a, Z)$	J_1, J_2	J_3	J_3	Resolved
G_3	$\neg whitepath(b, Y)$	J_5	$J_{10}, J_{11}, J_{19}, J_{20}$	J_{12}, J_{13}	Resolved
G_4	$\neg white(b, Z)$	J_6, J_7	J_8, J_9	J_8, J_9	Resolved
G_5	$\neg blackpath(c, Y)$	J_{12}		J_{15}, J_{16}	Resolved
G_6	$\neg black(c, Z)$	J_{16}			Resolved

Fig. 3. The Goal nodes

We can now look at the termination process. The map $G_6.T$ is everywhere empty since it has no immediate subgoals. We can therefore mark it as *Closed* with $G_5.Unclosed$ undefined, and then mark G_6 as *Completed* since $G_6.D$ is also everywhere undefined.

The map $G_5.T$ is only defined at G_6 and $G_5.T(G_6) = \{J_{15}\}$. The preconditions of the **Close** rule hold for G_65 since $G_6.Status$ is *Closed*, $G_6.Unclosed$ is undefined, and $J_{15}.Subgoals$ is empty. G_5 can therefore be marked as *Closed* and *Completed*, and $G_5.D$ is everywhere undefined, and $G_5.Unclosed$ is also undefined.

The map $G_4.T$ is also everywhere empty since it has no subgoals, and it can also be marked as *Closed* and *Completed* with $G_4.D$ everywhere undefined.

The map $G_3.T$ is nonempty on G_4, G_5, and G_1 so that $G_3.T(G_1) = \{J_{13}\}$, $G_3.T(G_4) = \{J_7\}$, $G_3.T(G_5) = \{J_{12}\}$. Since both G_4 and G_5 are closed, we set $G_3.D(G_1) = 3$, leave $G_3.D$ undefined on other arguments, and mark G_3 as *Closed*.

The goal G_2 has no immediate subgoals and can be marked as *Completed*. The goal G_1 has subgoals G_2 and G_3 as immediate subgoal so that $G_1.T(G_2) = \{J_2, J_2\}$ and $G_1.T(G_3) = \{J_5\}$. The τ definition for G_1 has $\tau(G_1)(G_1) = 3$, and since $\tau(G_1)(G_1) = |G_1.Claims|$, we can mark $G_1.Status$ as *Closed*, and

$Node$	$Clause$	$Derivation$
J_1	$blackpath(a, Y) :- black(a, Y)$	**Resolve**(G_1, C_4)
J_2	$blackpath(a, Y) :- black(a, Z), whitepath(Z, Y)$	**Resolve**(G_1, C_5)
J_3	$black(a, b)$	**Resolve**(G_2, C_1)
J_4	$blackpath(a, b)$	**Propagate**(J_3, J_1)
J_5	$blackpath(a, Y) :- whitepath(b, Y)$	**Propagate**(J_3, J_2)
J_6	$whitepath(b, Y) :- white(b, Y)$	**Resolve**(G_3, C_6)
J_7	$whitepath(b, Y) :- white(b, Z), blackpath(Z, Y)$	**Resolve**(G_3, C_7)
J_8	$white(b, c)$	**Resolve**(G_4, C_2)
J_9	$white(b, a)$	**Resolve**(G_4, C_3)
J_{10}	$whitepath(b, c)$	**Propagate**(J_8, J_6)
J_{11}	$whitepath(b, a)$	**Propagate**(J_9, J_6)
J_{12}	$whitepath(b, Y) :- blackpath(c, Y)$	**Propagate**(J_8, J_7)
J_{13}	$whitepath(b, Y) :- blackpath(a, Y)$	**Propagate**(J_9, J_7)
J_{14}	$whitepath(b, b)$	**Propagate**(J_4, J_{13})
J_{15}	$blackpath(c, Y) :- black(c, Y)$	**Resolve**(G_5, C_4)
J_{16}	$blackpath(c, Y) :- black(c, Z), whitepath(Z, Y)$	**Resolve**(G_5, C_5)
J_{17}	$blackpath(a, c)$	**Propagate**(J_{10}, J_5)
J_{18}	$blackpath(a, a)$	**Propagate**(J_{11}, J_5)
J_{19}	$whitepath(b, c)$	**Propagate**(J_{17}, J_{13})
J_{20}	$whitepath(b, a)$	**Propagate**(J_{18}, J_{13})

Fig. 4. The Clause nodes

since there are no goals with smaller indices, $G_1.Status$ can also be marked as *Completed*. This is then propagated to G_3, so that every goal node is now marked as completed.

5.5   Correctness

The new abstract machine can be simulated by the abstract inference procedure, but it is not easy to see why the termination check works. The termination check marks a goal node as *Closed* when it has been completely evaluated modulo the goal nodes with smaller indices. Each closed node also tracks its open subgoals in $g.D$ along with the minimal number of claims propagated from these subgoals. The **Close** step ensures that a goal node is closed only when it is current with respect to all its immediate subgoals. These subgoals can add new claims but this has to be initiated by the addition of a claim to an open subgoal. We can then make the following claims.

Theorem 1. *Let g be a goal node with $g.Status = Closed$ and let $Pr(g)(h)$ represent the number of claims propagated from an immediate subgoal h of g in the derivation of g at the point when $g.Status$ was last set to Closed. If a* *new claim is added to g, then for some subgoal h different from g, $|h.Claims| >$ $Pr(g)(h)$.*

This is because a closed goal node is fully evaluated in terms of propagating claims from its subgoals and applying the **Backchain** rule to the clauses resulting from the propagation. The only way a new claim can be added to g is through a **Propagate** step applied to some subgoal of g other than g.

Theorem 2. *When a goal node g is marked with g.Status = Closed, its evaluation is complete modulo the evaluation of the goals h such that g.D(h) is defined.*

This means that no new claims can be added to g unless there are new claims (beyond the number recorded in $g.D(h)$) are added to some goal h such that $g.D(h)$ is defined. We maintain the invariant that if $g.D(h)$ is defined, then $g.Index > h.Index$ and h is not closed. If we look at the subgoal relation in the derivation of g, then the entry $g.D(h)$ is defined for every unclosed subgoal h of g, and $g.D(h)$ is the minimum number of claims that have been propagated in the derivation of g. By Theorem 1, the only way g can add a new claim is if some immediate subgoal propagates a new claim. By induction, the only way that a claim can be propagated to g is if a new claim is added to some unclosed subgoal h of g, i.e., one where $g.D(h)$ is defined. Hence, the theorem.

Theorem 3. *When a goal node g is marked as completed, no further claims can be added for it.*

This is because for such a node, $g.D$ is everywhere undefined, and hence by Theorem 2, it is not waiting on new claims from any other nodes. In fact, such a node can be seen as the root node of a strongly connected component (SCC) in the evaluation graph. If every node in the strongly connected component is closed modulo other completed nodes or other closed nodes in the strongly connected component, then the entire component has been completely evaluated.

Note that the **Close** step can be interleaved with other steps in the evaluation. It would also make sense to run the **Close** computation in rounds by scanning the goals that are not marked as completed from the highest index downwards.

The implementation of the ETB Datalog engine builds an an Application Programming Interface (API) that can be used to implement the goals. The API includes the following operations for adding goal nodes, processing a goal by either resolving it against the rules or through external evaluation, processing a clause node, propagating a new claim, and closing the evaluation.

We have thus defined an abstract machine for evaluating Datalog programs that operates in a distributed setting.

6   Conclusions

The Evidential Tool Bus (ETB) is a framework for defining distributed workflows that construct claims supported by arguments, where some of the subclaims can be established by external services. ETB uses a variant of Datalog as the scripting language for defining workflows and as the metalanguage for representing arguments. The main novelty of ETB Datalog is that it enhances the basic Datalog language with external predicates for defining computations that invoke external services over a distributed network. We have presented a denotational semantics for ETB Datalog and defined an abstract machine that captures the evaluation of programs using both internal and external predicates. This abstract machine is the basis for the implementation of the Datalog engine used in ETB.

The novel contributions of our work include

1. A powerful mechanism for external predicates that incorporates distributed services.
2. A semantics for Datalog extended with external predicates.
3. An abstract machine that works in a distributed setting.
4. A novel termination check for the abstract machine that indicates when the evaluation of a subgoal has been completed.

The semantic treatment of ETB Datalog given here is a step toward a richer language for defining distributed workflows. The semantics we have given works in a distributed setting where new goals can be added, but the evaluation is still sequential. The body of a clause is evaluated in left-to-right order even when there is no dependency. Since we would like to allow the definition of workflows that exploit parallelism, we are working on extending the language to include annotations for parallel evaluation.

References

1. Abiteboul, S., Hull, R., Vianu, V.: Foundations of Databases. Addison-Wesley, Reading (1995)
2. Alvaro, P., Marczak, W.R., Conway, N., Hellerstein, J.M., Maier, D., Sears, R.: Dedalus: Datalog in time and space. Springer (2011)
3. Ceri, S., Gottlob, G., Tanca, L.: What you always wanted to know about Datalog (and never dared to ask). IEEE Transactions on Knowledge and Data Engineering 1(1), 146–166 (1989)
4. Cleary, J.G., Utting, M., Clayton, R.: Datalog as a parallel programming language. Technical Report ISSN 1177-777X, University of Waikato, Department of Computer Science (2010)
5. Cruanes, S., Hamon, G., Owre, S., Shankar, N.: Tool integration with the Evidential Tool Bus. In: Giacobazzi, R., Berdine, J., Mastroeni, I. (eds.) VMCAI 2013. LNCS, vol. 7737, pp. 275–294. Springer, Heidelberg (2013)
6. Gallaire, H., Minker, J.: Logic and data bases. Perseus Publishing (1978)
7. Hellerstein, J.M.: The declarative imperative: Experiences and conjectures in distributed logic. ACM SIGMOD Record 39(1), 5–19 (2010)
8. Huang, S.S., Green, T.J., Loo, B.T.: Datalog and emerging applications: An interactive tutorial. In: Sellis, T.K., Miller, R.J., Kementsietsidis, A., Velegrakis, Y. (eds.) SIGMOD Conference, pp. 1213–1216. ACM (2011)
9. Loo, B.T., Condie, T., Garofalakis, M., Gay, D.E., Hellerstein, J.M., Maniatis, P., Ramakrishnan, R., Roscoe, T., Stoica, I.: Declarative networking: Language, execution and optimization. In: Proceedings of the 2006 ACM SIGMOD International Conference on Management of Data, pp. 97–108. ACM (2006)

10. Sagonas, K., Swift, T.: An abstract machine for tabled execution of fixed-order stratified logic programs. ACM Transactions on Programming Languages and Systems (TOPLAS) 20(3), 586–634 (1998)
11. Shankar, N.: Inference systems for logical algorithms. In: Sarukkai, S., Sen, S. (eds.) FSTTCS 2005. LNCS, vol. 3821, pp. 60–78. Springer, Heidelberg (2005)
12. Whaley, J., Avots, D., Carbin, M., Lam, M.S.: Using Datalog with binary decision diagrams for program analysis. In: Yi, K. (ed.) APLAS 2005. LNCS, vol. 3780, pp. 97–118. Springer, Heidelberg (2005)

Synthesis of Infinite-State Abstractions and Their Use for Software Validation

Carlo Ghezzi*, Andrea Mocci, and Mario Sangiorgio

Politecnico di Milano
Dipartimento di Elettronica, Informazione e Bioingegneria,
P.za Leonardo Da Vinci 32, 20131 Milano (MI) Italy
{ghezzi,mocci,sangiorgio}@elet.polimi.it

Abstract. In the recent years, several research efforts have been devoted to developing approaches to synthesize specifications of software behavior. Most of the proposed approaches addressed the inference of finite-state abstractions. The synthesized abstractions have been integrated in different validation scenarios, such as testing. While finite-state models can be effectively used as models of a software component's behavior for certain specific purposes, they can hardly be used as full-fledged specifications. Because of their very limited expressive power, they cannot represent some of the component behaviors and may lead to synthesizing too coarse abstractions. In this paper, we survey a set of approaches that instead infer infinite-state abstractions, which can be used to express richer sets of behaviors of a software component in a black-box manner. For such approaches, we also discuss the few existing applications to software validation. In particular, we discuss the limitations and identify how, in principle, they can be used in different validation scenarios and how this opens new research directions.

1 Introduction

A formal specification is a description of the behaviors of a given software expressed in a certain mathematical notation with a clear semantics. Formal specifications are important and often essential for many validation activities. Examples of such activities are testing [1], where specifications can be used as oracles to check the correctness of an implementation for a certain set of inputs, or model checking [2], where specifications have both the role of models of software artifacts and properties to be checked on the model itself.

In practice, the cost of producing a component's specification is often as high as code writing, and thus producing the component itself. Moreover, a formal specification requires mathematical skills that may not be possessed by developers. These are among the reasons why specifications are often absent for real-world software components. When present, specifications are given through

---

* This research has been partially funded by the European Commission, Programme IDEAS-ERC, Pro ject 227977-SMScom.

S. Iida, J. Meseguer, and K. Ogata (Eds.): Futatsugi Festschrift, LNCS 8373, pp. 276–295, 2014.
© Springer-Verlag Berlin Heidelberg 2014

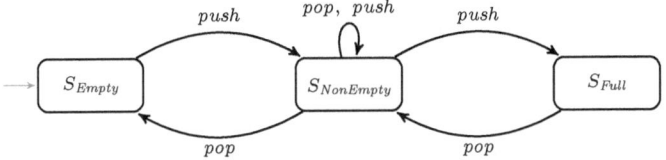

Fig. 1. A behavior model of a bounded stack

natural language in an informal way, that is not amenable to the automatic validation approaches described above. In addition, no guarantee can be assumed that the specification and the implementation are synchronized. Very often, they diverge because implementations are maintained without making the corresponding changes to the specification.

A recent branch of research activity in software engineering has been devoted to addressing the problems due to a missing specification by proposing the automatic synthesis through the analysis of existing software. The pioneering work described in DAIKON [3] goes exactly in this direction. Most of the work involving software specification synthesis has focused on finite-state abstractions of software behavior [4]. Finite-state abstractions may capture an important behavioral aspect of software components, that is, the protocol of interaction with the component. Intuitively, an interaction protocol describes the legal sequences of operations that are valid from the client's point of view when the client calls operations available through the component's interface.

Properties of the interaction protocol typically express precedence relations. For example, a component that represents a file requires that the file should be open before a write operation can be performed; that is, write can only be called after (a successful) open operation. Such properties are naturally expressible with an automaton, or in general with a finite-state abstraction that may not possess all the properties of an automaton. Semiautomata, that is, automata with no final states, are typically used to express interaction protocols, since the notion of a final state is not useful to express component behaviors.

Examples of finite-state models of software components are the ones inferred by ADABU [5,6], which uses dynamic analysis, and CONTRACTOR [7], which uses static analysis to derive behavior models from C programs. Figure 1 shows a behavior model of a bounded stack as inferred by CONTRACTOR; for example, the model describes the fact that the *pop* operation is not enabled in S_{Empty}, imposing a precedence relation on the legal sequences of operations on the component, that requires at least a *push* operation to be called before any call of *pop*.

Inferred behavior models have been used for many validation activities; examples include test case generation [8,6], integration in model checking [9], and runtime verification [10]. However, behavior models are formalisms that capture only a subset of the possible behaviors of the analyzed component. In particular, being finite-state machines, they must abstract away any collection-like behavior, like LIFO or FIFO behaviors, because these cannot be represented with a finite-state abstraction. For this reason, finite-state machines are most of the times *models* of certain behaviors exhibited by a given software, rather than full-fledged specifications of it.

The motivation of this paper is twofold. First, we critically survey the field, focusing on techniques that infer specifications that instead consist of infinite-state abstractions, which potentially may achieve the role of full-fledged specifications of software components. For example, such abstractions are contracts [11] or algebraic specifications [12,13], which potentially can capture such infinite-state behaviors, like collection-like behaviors, that finite-state machines may represent only in a very imprecise way, yielding very coarse abstractions.

Finally, we are interested in exploring the potential usages of inferred infinite-state abstractions that may reveal new research directions. In fact, while several approaches to validation that use inferred behavior models have been studied and proposed, very few exist that use inferred infinite-state abstractions in similar scenarios. To this aim, we first critically analyze such existing works, and then we outline possible future work considering the existing literature where infinite-state abstractions are considered to be present, and where an inference step could be potentially integrated.

For the sake of clarity, hereafter we discuss some of the assumptions we make in this paper and we describe the main terms we use. First, we refer to software components that define *abstract data types* (ADT), implemented as *classes*. We assume that the class only exports *methods* through its *interface*. A method represents an operation that can be used to operate on instances of the ADT (also called objects). Client components can only use these exported operations to interact with a given component. We distinguish among the following kinds of operations:

Observers : These are operations that return to the client some information related to the state of the object upon which they are invoked. Observers may be *pure* or not. A pure observer can only observe and cannot modify the internal state of the object.

Modifiers : These are operations that change the state of the object they are applied upon. If a class exports modifiers, the instantiated objects are said to be *mutable*.

Terms, or *traces*, represent sequences of operations. While the two words are often used interchangeably in formal approaches to software specification, in the area of software testing and analysis usually a trace denotes an *execution trace*, that is, an executed sequence of operations of a given implemented software component. In this paper, for the sake of clarity, we will always refer to such notion as execution trace.

Structure of the Paper. The paper is organized as follows. Section 2 discusses the state of the art about synthesis of infinite-state abstractions from software components. We classify the existing approaches by the classes of infinite state abstractions that they can synthesize, like contracts and algebraic

Table 1. Works surveyed on the State of the Art

Approach	Ref.	Specification	Abstract	Input	Analysis
DAIKON	[3,14]	Contract	No	Ex.Traces	Dynamic
DYSY	[15]	Contract	No	Code + Ex.Traces	Dynamic + Static
AXIOM MEISTER	[16]	Contract	Yes	Code	Static
AUTOINFER	[17]	Contract	Yes	Tests	Dynamic
KINDSPEC	[18]	Contract	Yes	Code	Static
HEUREKA	[19]	Algebraic Spec	Yes	Tests	Dynamic
ADIHEU	[20]	Algebraic Spec	Yes	Tests	Dynamic
SABICU	[21]	Algebraic Spec	Yes	Tests	Dynamic
ABSSPEC	[22]	Algebraic Spec	Yes	Code	Static
SPY	[23]	Intensional BM	Yes	Tests	Dynamic

specifications. Then, Section 3 identifies possible validation scenarios where such inferred infinite-state abstractions could be used, considering existing approaches and outlining promising research directions. Finally, Section 4 derives conclusions of this paper.

2   Synthesis of Infinite-State Abstractions: State of the Art

In this section, we will introduce the existing synthesis approaches that address infinite-state abstractions. Table 1 reports the main features of the surveyed approaches, classified mainly according to the class of infinite-state abstraction (specification) they synthesize. Moreover, we distinguish whether the specification is *abstract* (that is, expressed in terms of what a client can observe externally), what is the *source artifact* of the analysis, and what kind of analysis (static or dynamic) is used to infer the specification.

The section is structured according to the kind of specification synthesized by each of the surveyed approaches. We start by describing approaches that infer contracts (Section 2.1), then approaches that synthesize algebraic specifications (Section 2.2), and finally specifications based on trace assertions (Section 2.3).

2.1   Inferring Contracts

Contracts are a popular methodology to specify the behavior of software components in general, and they have been successfully applied to infinite-state components too. Basically, a *contract* [11,24] uses pre/post-conditions to specify the behavior of each operation in isolation. The pre-condition states what has to be true to invoke the operation (i.e., it states an obligation for the client); the post-condition states what has to be true when the operation terminates (i.e., it states an obligation for the object onto which the operation is applied).

There are five main approaches that implement inference of contracts for infinite-state components:

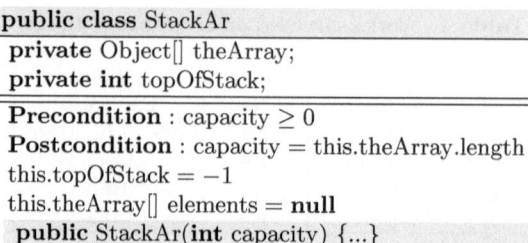

Fig. 2. The contract inferred by DAIKON for the STACKAR constructor

- DAIKON, an invariant detector that can be used to infer contracts of data abstractions;
- DYSY, which integrates dynamic analysis and symbolic execution to infer contracts;
- AXIOM MEISTER, which infers contracts for modifiers, expressed in terms of observer return values, using symbolic execution;
- AUTOINFER, that infers abstract postconditions of modifiers for components written in the EIFFEL language;
- KINDSPEC, which infers pre- and post-condition like specifications of C programs using the MATCHING LOGIC semantic framework [25].

Daikon. The DAIKON [3,14] invariant detector has been a pioneering work in the area of specification inference. DAIKON analyses the values of program variables at specific program points as a result of test case invocations. Starting from the results of these test case invocations, DAIKON infers invariant properties that hold at the recorded program points. For example, it may infer that the value of variable x is always greater than or equal to 10 before a statement that contains a division by s. An invariant holding at the entry point of an operation represents its preconditions, while an invariant holding at exit points represents a postcondition.

The inferred invariants predicate about program variables, including internal fields of classes. Consider, for example, a reference implementation of a bounded stack in JAVA, called STACKAR; this ADT is typically implemented with an array and an integer value pointing to the top of the stack. Figure 2 shows an example of invariants inferred by DAIKON, representing likely preconditions and postconditions of a STACKAR constructor which initializes it with a specific capacity.

Daikon works by generating candidate invariants out of a rich grammar of patterns, and then checking if they hold at specific program points. Invariants are reported only if there is enough statistical evidence that they do not hold by chance, and several optimizations are performed to get better results in terms of performance and relevance of reported invariants. Such optimizations include, for example, suppression of weaker invariants, that is, invariants that are logically implied by other ones.

DySy. One of the main problems with DAIKON and in general of dynamic invariant detection is that it is hard, sometimes, to know in advance what are the possible patterns of invariants to be detected, and so the approach could fail in deriving interesting behaviors of the component to be analyzed. To overcome this limitation, the DYSY approach [15] integrates black box dynamic analysis with symbolic execution, which is a white box, static analysis technique. By using symbolic execution, DYSY is able to derive operation pre- and post-conditions based on the actual code behavior; in this sense, DYSY is able to infer a method specification without using invariant patterns. However, symbolic execution is unable to generalize code behavior in the presence of loops or recursive operations; in this case, the approach uses some ad-hoc heuristics to support common iterative structures.

In the case of both DAIKON and DYSY, there are some fundamental problems in applying specification synthesis approaches to extract contracts of data abstractions. The main problem is that the state must be expressed in function of some variables that represent the state of the component. In principle, the specification of a component must be *abstract*, that is, *implementation independent*. In other words, specifications should respect the *information hiding* [26] principle. It should be expressed only in terms of the operations that are visible at the component's interface. Although useful for many development activities like testing, the invariants extracted by DAIKON and DYSY are not abstract and they represent code behavior expressed in terms of the component internals.

Axiom Meister. This tool [16] infers contracts from the static analysis of .NET programs. The tool requires the developer to choose the modifier methods he wants to analyze and its related observers. The tool requires observers to be *observationally pure*, i.e. they are only allowed to change the state in a way that it is invisible to clients. Then, AXIOM MEISTER produces an abstract description of the modifier behavior in terms of the values returned by observer methods. Figure 3 shows the specification inferred by AXIOM MEISTER for the push operation of a bounded stack.

AXIOM MEISTER's inference approach is based on symbolic execution of the modifier method under analysis, which tries to explore all the possible execution paths; in symbolic execution, for each path, there is a corresponding path condition stating the symbolic constraints required for its execution. In general, path conditions express constraints over the data structures used to implement the operation and its enclosing class. The tool aims at producing a specification for an ADT and thus it has to find an abstraction of path conditions relying only on class observers. This process produces many path specific axioms, which are finally merged and simplified to obtain the more compact and readable specification. The inferred specification can be either used by humans or by SPEC#.

AutoInfer. The AUTOINFER approach presented in [17] provides another interesting approach that partially infers contracts with dynamic analysis but without using component internals. In fact, AUTOINFER expresses behavior in function of

```
void push(Object x)
    requires size()<capacity() otherwise FullStackException
    ensures top() = x
    ensures size() = old(size()) + 1
    ensures capacity() = old(capacity())
```

Fig. 3. The SPEC# contract inferred by AXIOM MEISTER for the PUSH method of a bounded stack

observer return values. The approach targets Eiffel, an object-oriented language that supports *design by contract* [11], a development methodology that focuses on specifying the behavior of software components through contracts. The inference approach proposed by the authors uses novel dynamic inference techniques to infer modifier postconditions. Intuitively, such postconditions are properties that express how observers change their returned values after the invocation of an operation[1].

In particular, the approach supports the inference of two peculiar kind of assertions in modifier postconditions:

- assertions that involve quantification, that are useful to express frame properties, like that all the elements of a collection are still present after an operation invocation;
- assertions that involve implications, useful to identify which conditions trigger a particular different behavior.

AUTOINFER is based on dynamic analysis like DAIKON; the test cases used as inference base are generated by using random testing. The approach uses a modified version of AUTOTEST [27], which prunes generated test cases when they satisfy the operation preconditions. The operation preconditions are essentially assumed to be (correctly) written by the developer.

The main limitation of the approach is that it just focuses on the inference of postconditions of modifiers; the authors tailored the proposed inference techniques to postconditions because a previous work identifies preconditions as normally well written in contract-based development approaches. For this reason, the approach is not easily extensible to preconditions.

KindSpec. The KINDSPEC approach presented in [18] uses a static analysis technique based on the K framework to infer specifications for KERNELC programs. In particular, the tool focuses on modeling the behavior of heap-manipulating code. For each modifier operation, the tool finds a specification in the form of a set of facts represented by logic implications. Figure 4 shows an example of a specification inferred by KINDSPEC. An important difference with respect to the specifications produced by other tools is that KINDSPEC only

---

[1] In the Eiffel jargon, the specific language targeted by the approach, observers are called queries and modifiers are called commands.

isnull(s) = 1	$\implies$	isnull(s') = 1
isnull(s) = 0 $\quad\wedge$ size(s) = capacity(s)	$\implies$	top(s) = top(s')
isnull(s) = 0 $\quad\wedge$ size(s) < capacity(s)	$\implies$	isnull(s') = 0 $\wedge$ top(s') = x $\wedge$ size(s') = size(s) + 1

Fig. 4. The contract inferred by KINDSPEC for the push(Stack s, Object x) function for a bounded Stack

looks for invariants involving calls to observer functions and the return value of the analyzed modifier. It does not produce invariants containing predicates over the implementation details of a class. It is worth to say that, since it is not possible to guarantee that a KERNELC observer is pure, each function call in the logic formulas is assumed to be evaluated independently from the others, under the same initial conditions, to avoid the need of making assumptions on possible side effects.

The inference algorithm implemented in KINDSPEC relies on the symbolic execution engine of the MATCHING LOGIC verifier MATCHC. This choice makes it possible for KINDSPEC to statically analyze the source code instead of concrete execution traces. The framework also ensures the correctness of the inferred specifications. In fact, they can check the inferred specifications with the MATCHC verifier. A peculiarity of this approach is that KINDSPEC does not reason about the whole heap. It instead separates the different parts of the heap and its algorithms can reason only about the relevant ones for a specific function.

KINDSPEC is interesting from a particular point of view, which serves as a bridge from contracts to algebraic specifications for our classification of inference approaches. It is important to emphasize that while the MATCHC verifier – on which the programs are interpreted to infer specifications – is based on algebraic rewrite rules, the inferred specifications themselves are not presented and interpreted with an algebraic style. In fact, each inferred fact represents the pre- and the post-state of the component itself explicitly, in a style that is typical of contracts, justifying our classification. However, by using only observers, such facts could be easily rewritten, and possibly interpreted, as conditional axioms in a typical algebraic specification style.

2.2   Synthesis of Algebraic Specifications

When specifying components with contracts, the focus is on each operation in isolation, and some kind of model is used to predicate about the state of the component to be specified. This can be the value of internal variables, as in the case of DAIKON, or the return value of observers, like in the case of AUTOINFER. Both, however, have pitfalls. The former case leads to a violation of the information hiding principle, since the specification ends up referring to implementation details that should instead remain hidden. The latter instead assumes that enough observers are available to support the effect of any other operation. A different point of view is adopted in the case of algebraic specifications, where

$$
\begin{array}{ll}
\forall x : Stack, c : Integer, e : Object \mid & \\
pop.state(push.state(x, e)) & = x \\
size.retval(Stack(c)) & = 0 \\
size.retval(push.state(x, e)) & = size.retval(x) + 1 \\
top.retval(push.state(x, e)) & = e \\
contains.retval(Stack(c), e) & = \textbf{false} \\
contains.retval(push(x, e), e) & = \textbf{true}
\end{array}
$$

Fig. 5. An algebraic specification of an unbounded Stack as inferred by HEUREKA

the focus is on the whole component to be specified, and the behavior of operations is specified implicitly (and not explicitly) through algebraic axioms.

Each axiom in an algebraic specification is an equation that prescribes when two different sequences of operations, for a certain state and for certain parameters, are *equal*. The interpretation of this equality depends on the semantics of the algebraic specifications; for example, the semantics may impose that the sequences of operations are equivalent in the sense that they will expose the same observable behavior to the component clients.

Several approaches have been investigated to synthesize specifications that fall in the area of algebraic specification. The main ones are surveyed below.

Heureka. HEUREKA [19] is the main existing approach that infers algebraic specifications. HEUREKA explicitly targets JAVA classes and uses dynamic analysis. Furthermore, HEUREKA uses a particular semantics for algebraic axioms, called *behavioral* or *hidden semantics* [28], which is based on the concept of *behavioral equivalence*. Intuitively, a behavioral equivalence relation clusters elements of the algebra which cannot be distinguished by any possible sequence of operations.

Figure 5 shows an algebraic specification of an unbounded stack as inferred by HEUREKA. Because the synthesis approach targets JAVA, each method is potentially modeled with two operations: i) an operation modeling how state is changed, if the method is not pure – the operation is denoted with the .**state** suffix; ii) an operation modeling the return value of the method, if this is not **void** – the operation is denoted with the .**retval** suffix. This is a typical choice when modeling classes of object-oriented languages with algebraic specifications.

The technique operates with a fully black-box approach; the input consists of a class' public interface and a set of actual values for method parameters, called *instance pool*. HEUREKA starts by generating terms, that is, sequences of operations, and then groups them by checking if they are behaviorally equivalent. Behavioral equivalence is in general undecidable, so the tool checks it up to a certain maximum depth of contexts. Once equivalent terms have been detected, the tools tries to generalize them by introducing universally quantified variables, obtaining candidate axioms. Axioms are then tested and reported if no counterexample is found.

HEUREKA has been evaluated against implementations of data abstractions mainly from the Java Development Kit (JDK).

Adiheu. Another work that infers algebraic specifications is ADIHEU [20]. The approach uses behavior models to improve the inference process of HEUREKA. Essentially, behavior models are used to reduce the checks needed to establish if two terms are behaviorally equivalent. In the case of ADIHEU, the finite-state abstraction of the component is used as an intermediate model that is easier to synthesize, but whose synthesis dramatically improves the performance of the algebraic specification synthesizer of HEUREKA. The approach reduces the needed number of method invocations for the component under analysis from 50% to almost one order of magnitude.

Sabicu. SABICU [21] proposed an approach to infer algebraic specification similar to HEUREKA, but supporting also the inference of conditional algebraic axioms. Compared to HEUREKA, it is less general in the sense that the structure of possible axiom is derived from predefined templates, not from the generalization of equations classified by behavioral equivalence. Such predefined patterns may be enriched with *conditional extensions*, that represent specific conditions for the axiom to be applied. For example, consider the *contains* method of the stack example; then, the following axiom can be inferred by SABICU:

$$\forall x : Stack, e, f : Object \mid \quad contains.retval(push.state(x, e), f) = \textbf{true if } e = f$$
$$\textbf{else } contains.retval(x, f)$$

The axiom expresses the fact that if *contains* is called after a *push*, it returns true if the parameter value for both methods is the same; otherwise, it returns the return value of *contains* called on the rest of the stack.

Another important aspect of SABICU is that it keeps track of a statistical metric of axioms, that is, the number of instances that satisfy the axiom itself. Thus, it not only derives common properties, that is, properties that hold for every possible instance of an ADT, but also special axioms that hold only for a subset of the tested instances. This aspect is useful to derive axioms whose holding conditions are too complex and not supported by the inference patterns of SABICU, but that could be potentially derived manually.

AbsSpec. ABSSPEC [22] is a tool to automatically infer high level, property-oriented specifications in the form of algebraic equations for CURRY, a lazy functional logic programming language. These features of CURRY require a careful definition of program semantics. The nature of the language requires different equality relations to be defined in order to support features like free variables in formulas.

Like other algebraic specification recovery tools, ABSSPEC produces specifications in the form of sets of equations relating (nested) operation calls that have the same behavior. ABSSPEC is based on a white box static inference mechanism that is guaranteed to generate correct specifications. The inference technique is

```
data Stack a = S [a]

new       :: Stack a
isEmpty   :: Queue a -> Bool
push      :: a -> Stack a -> Stack a
pop       :: Stack a -> Stack a
top       :: Stack a -> a

--- Inferred algebraic specification
--- contextual equivalence
(pop (push x (pop y))) = (pop (pop (push x y)))
(top (push x (push y z))) = (top (push x (pop (push y z))))
(pop (push x (pop (pop y)))) = (pop (pop (pop (push x y))))
(pop (push x (pop (push y z)))) = (pop (pop (push y (push x z))))
(pop (push x (pop (push y z)))) = (pop (pop (push x (push y z))))
(top (push x1 (push x3 (push x2 x4)))) =
   (top (push x1 (push x2 (push x3 x4))))

--- computed result equivalence
(top (push x new)) = x
```

Fig. 6. A two-sided queue algebraic specification inferred by AbsSpec

based on an abstract semantics for the CURRY language: a condensed goal-independent fix-point semantics that has been specifically designed to model the small-step behavior of rewriting [29] for logic functional programming languages.

The completeness of the inferred specifications depends on the analysis bounds in term of trace length and analyzed functions the user decides to set. The tool is guaranteed to infer correct and complete specifications within these bounds.

Figure 6 shows the inferred algebraic specification for a stack. For the example we selected to consider the push, pop, top, and isEmpty functions. The inferred algebraic specification includes two different kinds of logic formulas. The first set of equations uses the contextual equivalence, which checks whether two terms are equal within any context. The last formula instead uses the *computed result* equivalence relation, in which all the possible outcomes for the left side equals to the results for the right side. The latter is the usual equality relation for functional languages.

2.3 A Synthesis Approach Based on Trace Assertions

Algebraic specifications are useful to infer some interesting properties of operation interaction (like idempotent and equivalent traces), but in some cases it is hard to use them as a specification language. In some cases, algebraic specifications require *hidden functions*, that is, operations that are used only for specification purposes and that are not exposed to the clients to be accessible.

For many reasons, the use of hidden functions has been criticized as a problem with respect to information hiding, and some authors have considered this necessity of algebraic specifications as a violation of the principle (see for example [30] and also some early work on software specification [31]). In fact, they may convey design and implementation decisions.

Obviously, this problem also hinders the capability of algebraic specifications to be inferred in the case of components that would require hidden functions.

Canonical Traces : $Stack(c).push^N(d_i) \mid N \le c$

operation	Pattern	Equivalence
$t.pop()$	$t = s.push(d)$	s
$t.push(e)$	$t = Stack(c).push^c(d_i)$	t
$t.capacity() : c$	$t = Stack(c).s$	t
$t.size() : 0$	$t = Stack(c)$	t
$t.size() : k$	$t = Stack(c).push^k(d_i)$	t
$t.top() : d$	$t = s.push(d)$	t
$t.contains(e) : $ **true**	$t = s.push(e).q$	t
$t.contains(e) : $ **false**	$t = Stack(c).push^c(d_i) \mid d_i \ne e$	t

Fig. 7. A TAM specification of a bounded stack

Hidden functions, in general, encapsulate an abstract state that depends on the component behavior itself.

The trace assertion method (TAM) [32,30] is a specification formalism and notation introduced to deal with the problems of information hiding violation in algebraic specifications. A particular set of traces, called *canonical traces*, is chosen to uniquely identify the state of the component, and assertions (that is, predicates) on canonical traces are used to the behavior of operations.

In TAM, an operation is specified in a tabular notation which maps a given pattern in the trace to the behavior of the operation. For this reason, equations describing the behavior of operations are explicit, in the sense that they explicitly describe their behavior in terms of the canonical trace model.

Figure 7 shows the TAM specification of a stack with a tabular notation. By allowing arbitrary predicates to specify the structure of traces, TAM solves the problem of hidden functions.

We are not aware of published work that directly targets trace assertions as a specification formalism for synthesized specifications. We have instead developed the SPY approach [23], which uses a closely related method to model the state of an infinite-state data abstraction.

Spy. SPY [23] is a specification synthesis method that targets JAVA classes like HEUREKA, but it uses a different class of target specifications. SPY synthesizes so-called *intensional behavior models*. As we discussed briefly in the introduction, a behavior model is a finite-state abstraction where each transition represents a modifier invocation and the states describe, with a certain level of abstraction, observer return value in a particular state. An intensional behavior model is a generalization of a particular kind of behavior model, called *behavioral equivalence model (*BEM), where each state represents a class of behaviorally equivalent objects, and it represents a subset of all the possible behaviors of the component (e.g., for a subset of possible parameters for methods, or for terms up to a certain length). An intensional behavior model generalizes a BEM by using an

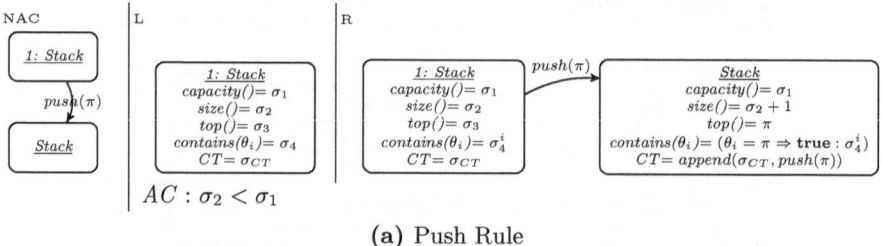

(a) Push Rule

Fig. 8. An intensional behavior model rule describing the behavior of a *push* operation in a non-full bounded Stack

generative approach, similar to a graph grammar: each operation is described by a rule which describes how new states, and new transitions, can be added to an existing BEM to explain new behaviors. The generalization is possible because each state is uniquely identified by a canonical trace, as in TAM.

Figure 8 shows a rule describing the behavior of the *push* operation of a stack. Essentially, it describes how a new state on a BEM can be generated after the invocation of a push operation. First, the rule describes how the observer return values change – that is, *size* is incremented by 1 and *top* returns the inserted element; second, the rule describes the value of the new canonical trace for the state by appending the last operation to the previous canonical trace.

SPY first infers a BEM from the dynamic analysis of a JAVA class, as in HEUREKA. Essentially, it has three steps:

- for a user-specified instance pool, it generates terms up to a certain length and classifies them by behavioral equivalence, generating a BEM;
- then, SPY uses heuristics based on a metric for object distance to identify a candidate set of canonical traces for an inferred BEM;
- finally, a generalization step uses invariant detection (à la DAIKON) to detect both trace assertions describing the behavior of modifiers and other invariants describing the behavior of observers; such invariants are used to generalize BEMs to intensional behavior models.

The use of trace assertions, essentially, makes SPY able to infer specifications where methods like HEUREKA would explicitly require hidden functions.

3   Use of Inferred Specifications for Validation

In the introduction of this paper we discussed how inferred specifications may play a role beyond specification recovery and documentation improvement. We mentioned, in particular, their use in software validation. Hereafter we first survey and discuss existing work that uses inferred infinite-state models for validation purposes (Section 3.1). Then we outline some possible research directions (Section 3.2).

3.1   Existing Approaches

Hereafter, we explore the related work that uses the results of inference of infinite-state abstractions to perform different kinds of validation – either of the inferred specifications themselves or of the artifacts under analysis. Existing work in this area is reviewed below for the classes of specification we identified in this paper.

Contracts. Most existing validation approaches that use inferred infinite-state specifications involve contracts. A number of such techniques embed contract inference in more complex workflow that includes static analysis and testing. The use of DAIKON, in this context, has been pretty intense [33]. A full survey of all the usages of DAIKON is outside the scope of this paper, mainly because the contracts inferred by DAIKON are in general not abstract, that is, they normally express pre- and post-conditions in term of a class' internal representation.

A notable example is provided by DSD-CRASHER [34], which combines dynamic contract inference, static code analysis, and testing. The first phase of the approach relies on DAIKON for specification inference. In this context, the inferred specification acts as an oracle of the intended program behavior. The next phases of DSD-CRASHER focus on detection of possible bugs, which is performed in two separate steps. First, static analysis is used to find counterexamples that possibly violate the inferred contracts. Second, testing is performed to confirm that the issues found with static analysis are actually bugs. Both steps are important because static analysis may return an over-approximated set of issues containing some bugs that are not reachable in real executions.

A research approach that uses abstract contract inference for bug finding is STATEFUL TESTING [35], which is based upon AUTOINFER-synthesized EIFFEL contracts. By using STATEFUL TESTING it is possible to produce a suitable test suite that is both able to uncover bugs in the code and that can lead to the inference of more accurate contracts. The approach starts from the AUTOTEST random test case generation; the initial test suite is then improved by leveraging the contracts inferred with AUTOINFER. The underlying hypothesis of the approach is that the initial test suite, which is generated randomly, likely misses to cover some behavior of the component under test. Thus, it is desirable to enrich such initial test suite to cover more behaviors and obtain a more complete test suite. Inferred contracts indeed provide an effective way to enhance a test suite. STATEFUL TESTING leverages the information encoded in the inferred contracts to find test cases that violate their preconditions and postconditions. Adding these new test cases improves the number of faults that it can expose and thus, in the end, likely leads to the inference of more precise contracts.

Algebraic Specifications. Inference approaches like HEUREKA [19], [36], or SPY [23] interleave automated test generation with specification inference. For example, HEUREKA uses test generation also after algebraic axiom generation to prune invalid axioms generated by the generalization phase. In [36] the authors propose an iterative approach where testing and specification inference are mutually enhanced by each other. Essentially, the approach starts from an initial set of tests that guide specification inference. Then such specifications are used to guide the automatic generation of new tests. In the initial iterations, such approach is very likely to generate test cases that violate the previously inferred specifications. The violating tests might be exercising either new program behaviors or exposing some fault that was not exercised in initial iterations of the approach. The technique has been implemented by considering both contracts as inferred by DAIKON, and algebraic specifications inferred with a mechanism that is closely related to the one of SABICU.

Through testing, it is also possible to provide an empirical comparison of the quality of inferred specifications by different methods. For example, the experimental validation of SPY against HEUREKA [23] has been performed by generating test cases and using the component under analysis as an oracle against the prediction of both inferred specifications, to compute the numbers of correct, wrong, or undetermined predictions.

Comparing inferred specifications is also the subject of [37]. This paper proposes a technique to automatically check the mutual consistency of two different infinite-state abstractions, that is, algebraic specifications and intensional behavior models of the same software component. The approach reduces the consistency problem to model checking. The evaluation considers (and simulates) typical situations that may arise in the context of specification inference. For example, different inference bases may get different (and inconsistent) behavior predicted by the two different inferred specifications; the approach is able to derive such inconsistencies that may potentially arise in the context of specification inference.

3.2   Potential Future Research Directions

The works analyzed so far demonstrate that specification inference can be the basis for interesting validation activities. Hereafter, we briefly analyze potentially interesting research directions that can be further. To this aim, we briefly discuss examples of existing literature that use non-inferred infinite state abstractions, and we discuss how inferred specifications could play a role. We explore two areas of possible applications: testing and debugging, and validation in the so-called *open world*.

Testing and Debugging. Testing and debugging techniques can get significant improvements in their effectiveness when accurate specifications are available. For example, specifications may act as oracles of the intended behavior of a piece of code. Testing tools can rely on this information to discriminate between the expected and actual behavior of the code under analysis.

Many existing works use contracts to enable the automatic generation of test cases that try to find input values violating them. For example, EIFFEL natively supports *design by contract*, and the research community developed several techniques to leverage such specification for automatic test case generation. These approaches rely on contracts as oracles to drive the search performed by random testing techniques [27] or evolutionary algorithms [38]. These approaches explore the input spaces trying to find test cases that violate the precondition of a method, or that satisfy the precondition but violate the postcondition.

ASTOOT [39] uses algebraic specifications and term rewriting to automatically generate test cases for object-oriented software. The tool produces test cases to ensure the equivalence of all the sequence of operations that should bring an object in a given abstract state. It generates different sequences of operations and the assertions on the value returned by observer methods needed to check that the object is in the right abstract state. The presence of specifications is also useful to optimize an existing test suite. ROSTRA [40] relies on algebraic specifications to minimize the number of test cases contained in a test suite. Minimization is performed by eliminating redundant test cases, i.e. the test cases that cover the same abstract states, and removing the ones dealing with equivalent objects.

The aforementioned approaches work in the presence of an existing specification. Since very often in practice specifications are missing, incomplete, or unreliable, inference techniques can help to fill this gap. However, existing methods that apply to human-produced specifications cannot be simply transferred as they are to inferred specifications. The latter, in fact, reflect the actual behavior of observed code, plus generalizations; they do not express, per se, the *intended* program behavior. To enable application of approaches like the ones we reviewed above, one should first inspect the extracted specifications to ensure that they actually reflect the intended component behavior. This inspection can be non-trivial for infinite-state abstractions.

A different approach views specification inference and validation as integrated steps that mutually influence each other. In fact, it is also possible to envision a feedback loop in which specifications are built starting from existing test cases and, at the same time, they are used to construct new relevant test cases, reaching a point where the likelihood of finding new mismatching test cases from the implementation and the specification is relatively low. This approach has been explored by STATEFUL TESTING and can be traced back to the pioneering work on finite-state abstraction learning and testing approach called L^* [41]. If one applies such a technique to a reference implementation, then the specification is likely to capture the intended behavior and can be used, for example, for precise regression testing or even for program verification.

Service-Oriented Architectures and Open-World Software. Inference of infinite-state abstractions may play a relevant role in the context of modern software architectures, like service-oriented architectures, living in the so-called open world [42]. Such applications, in fact, are composed by using third-party components or services on which the developer has no control. Composition may even occur dynamically, at run time. In such contexts, the value of an inferred specification is particularly critical, since a service client has no possibility to inspect the implementation of a service.

The work by Bianculli et. al. [43] uses infinite-state abstractions in the context of a service-oriented environment. Specifically, algebraic specifications are used to monitor the behavior of a stateful service, like a typical shopping cart used by most e-commerce Web applications. The proposed approach uses aspect-oriented programming [44] to monitor a BPEL service and the operations that are invoked on it. An algebraic specification interpreter (either the HEUREKA [45] or CAFEOBJ [46] one) is used to evaluate the monitored terms and check it against the observed operation result. In this work, the specification is assumed to be provided. However, this assumption may be irrealistic, considering the current state of the practice in the specification of service-oriented applications. Although a specification (both for functional and non-functional aspects) should in principle be available to support *service-level agreement* between service providers and users, in practice descriptions are informal and compliance with their evolving implementation may not be ensured.

Existing inference techniques may not be straightforwardly applied in this context. For example, the techniques for algebraic specifications, like HEUREKA, are computationally expensive and the number of method invocations required to infer a specification is relatively high. If these method invocations have to be applied to an existing service, they would negatively affect non-functional properties of the service to be analyzed. Furthermore, it can be unreasonable to expect each client should perform analysis on the same exposed service to obtain the specification. Instead, one should perhaps envision specific discovery services and mechanisms to perform specification inference. In addition, inference should apply to both functional and non-functional interface properties.

4   Conclusions

Infinite-state abstractions can provide very precise descriptions of behaviors that finite-state machines would instead ignore. However, it is hard to produce them and keep them consistent with implementations. Thus they are seldom used in the practice of software development. In this paper, we surveyed the research literature on specification inference for infinite-state abstractions, focusing in particular on two existing classes: pre-/post-condition based contracts and algebraic specifications. Furthermore, we outlined interesting validation scenarios where an inference step can play an important role, extending the applicability of existing work. Although very promising initial work has been focusing on the interplay between specification inference and validation, more research is needed to make it applicable and to pave the way for use of infinite-state abstractions in the practice of software engineering.

References

1. Young, M., Pezze, M.: Software Testing and Analysis: Process, Principles and Techniques. John Wiley & Sons (2007)
2. Burch, J.R., Clarke, E.M., McMillan, K.L., Dill, D.L., Hwang, L.J.: Symbolic model checking: 10^{20} states and beyond. Information and Computation 98(2) (1992)
3. Ernst, M.D.: Dynamically Discovering Likely Program Invariants. Ph.D. thesis, University of Washington, Seattle, Washington (August 2000)

4. Robillard, M., Bodden, E., Kawrykow, D., Mezini, M., Ratchford, T.: Automated api property inference techniques. IEEE Transactions on Software Engineering 39(5), 613–637 (2013)
5. Dallmeier, V., Lindig, C., Wasylkowski, A., Zeller, A.: Mining object behavior with adabu. In: Proceedings of the 2006 International Workshop on Dynamic Systems Analysis, WODA 2006, pp. 17–24. ACM, New York (2006)
6. Dallmeier, V., Knopp, N., Mallon, C., Hack, S., Zeller, A.: Generating test cases for specification mining. In: Proceedings of the 19th International Symposium on Software Testing and Analysis, ISSTA 2010, pp. 85–96. ACM, New York (2010)
7. De Caso, G., Braberman, V., Garbervetsky, D., Uchitel, S.: Program abstractions for behaviour validation. In: 2011 33rd International Conference on Software Engineering (ICSE), pp. 381–390 (2011)
8. Xie, T., Notkin, D.: Tool-assisted unit-test generation and selection based on operational abstractions. Automated Software Engineering 13(3), 345–371 (2006)
9. Peled, D., Vardi, M.Y., Yannakakis, M.: Black box checking. In: Proceedings of the IFIP TC6 WG6.1 Joint International Conference on Formal Description Techniques for Distributed Systems and Communication Protocols (FORTE XII) and Protocol Specification, Testing and Verification (PSTV XIX). FORTE XII / PSTV XIX 1999, pp. 225–240. Kluwer, The Netherlands (1999)
10. Mocci, A., Sangiorgio, M.: Detecting component changes at run time with behavior models. Computing 95(3), 191–221 (2013)
11. Meyer, B.: Applying "Design by Contract". IEEE Computer 25(10), 40–51 (1992)
12. Guttag, J.V., Horning, J.J.: The algebraic specification of abstract data types. Acta Informatica 10, 27–52 (1978), http://dx.doi.org/10.1007/BF00260922
13. Goguen, J., Malcolm, G.: Algebraic Semantics of Imperative Programs. Foundations of Computing Series. Mit Press (1996)
14. Ernst, M.D., Perkins, J.H., Guo, P.J., McCamant, S., Pacheco, C., Tschantz, M.S., Xiao, C.: The Daikon system for dynamic detection of likely invariants. Science of Computer Programming 69(1-3), 35–45 (2007); Special issue on Experimental Software and Toolkits
15. Csallner, C., Tillmann, N., Smaragdakis, Y.: DySy: Dynamic symbolic execution for invariant inference. In: Proceedings of the 30th International Conference on Software Engineering, ICSE 2008, pp. 281–290. ACM, New York (2008)
16. Tillmann, N., Chen, F., Schulte, W.: Discovering likely method specifications. In: Liu, Z., He, J. (eds.) ICFEM 2006. LNCS, vol. 4260, pp. 717–736. Springer, Heidelberg (2006)
17. Wei, Y., Furia, C.A., Kazmin, N., Meyer, B.: Inferring better contracts. In: Proceedings of the 33rd International Conference on Software Engineering, ICSE 2011, pp. 191–200. ACM, New York (2011)
18. Alpuente, M., Feliú, M.A., Villanueva, A.: Automatic inference of specifications using matching logic. In: Proceedings of the ACM SIGPLAN 2013 Workshop on Partial Evaluation and Program Manipulation, PEPM 2013, pp. 127–136. ACM, New York (2013)
19. Henkel, J., Reichenbach, C., Diwan, A.: Discovering documentation for Java container classes. IEEE Trans. Software Eng. 33(8), 526–543 (2007)
20. Ghezzi, C., Mocci, A., Monga, M.: Efficient recovery of algebraic specifications for stateful components. In: Ninth International Workshop on Principles of Software Evolution: In Conjunction with the 6th ESEC/FSE Joint Meeting, IWPSE 2007, pp. 98–105. ACM, New York (2007)

21. Xie, T., Notkin, D.: Automatically identifying special and common unit tests for object-oriented programs. In: Proc. 16th IEEE International Symposium on Software Reliability Engineering (ISSRE 2005), pp. 277–287 (November 2005)

22. Bacci, G., Comini, M., Feliú, M.A., Villanueva, A.: Automatic synthesis of specifications for first order Curry programs. In: Proceedings of the 14th Symposium on Principles and Practice of Declarative Programming, PPDP 2012, pp. 25–34. ACM, New York (2012)

23. Ghezzi, C., Mocci, A., Monga, M.: Synthesizing intensional behavior models by graph transformation. In: IEEE 31st International Conference on Software Engineering, ICSE 2009, pp. 430–440. IEEE (2009)

24. Meyer, B.: Design by Contract: The Eiffel Method. In: International Conference on Technology of Object-Oriented Languages, p. 446 (1998)

25. Roşu, G., Ştefănescu, A.: Matching Logic: A New Program Verification Approach (NIER Track). In: ICSE 2011: Proceedings of the 30th International Conference on Software Engineering, pp. 868–871. ACM (2011)

26. Parnas, D.L.: On the criteria to be used in decomposing systems into modules. Commun. ACM 15, 1053–1058 (1972)

27. Meyer, B., Fiva, A., Ciupa, I., Leitner, A., Wei, Y., Stapf, E.: Programs that test themselves. Computer 42(9), 46–55 (2009)

28. Goguen, J., Malcolm, G.: A hidden agenda. Theoretical Computer Science 245(1), 55–101 (2000)

29. Comini, M., Torella, L.: A condensed goal-independent fixpoint semantics modeling the small-step behavior of rewriting. In: Kovacs, L., Kutsia, T. (eds.) SCSS 2013. EPiC Series, vol. 15, pp. 31–49. EasyChair (2013)

30. Janicki, R., Sekerinski, E.: Foundations of the trace assertion method of module interface specification, vol. 27, pp. 577–598. IEEE Press, Piscataway (2001)

31. Bartussek, W., Parnas, D.L.: Using assertions about traces to write abstract specifications for software modules. In: Bracchi, G., Lockemann, P. (eds.) Information Systems Methodology. LNCS, vol. 65, pp. 211–236. Springer, Heidelberg (1978)

32. Parnas, D.L.: A technique for software module specification with examples. Commun. ACM 15(5), 330–336 (1972)

33. Ernst, M.: Daikon-related invariant detection publications (2013), http://groups.csail.mit.edu/pag/daikon/pubs/#daikon-methodology

34. Csallner, C., Smaragdakis, Y., Xie, T.: DSD-Crasher: A hybrid analysis tool for bug finding. ACM Trans. Softw. Eng. Methodol. 17(2), 8:1–8:37 (2008)

35. Wei, Y., Roth, H., Furia, C., Pei, Y., Horton, A., Steindorfer, M., Nordio, M., Meyer, B.: Stateful testing: Finding more errors in code and contracts. In: 2011 26th IEEE/ACM International Conference on Automated Software Engineering (ASE), pp. 440–443 (2011)

36. Xie, T., Notkin, D.: Mutually enhancing test generation and specification inference. In: Petrenko, A., Ulrich, A. (eds.) FATES 2003. LNCS, vol. 2931, pp. 60–69. Springer, Heidelberg (2004)

37. Ghezzi, C., Mocci, A., Salvaneschi, G.: Automatic cross validation of multiple specifications: A case study. In: Rosenblum, D.S., Taentzer, G. (eds.) FASE 2010. LNCS, vol. 6013, pp. 233–247. Springer, Heidelberg (2010)

38. Silva, L.S., Wei, Y., Meyer, B., Oriol, M.: Evotec: Evolving the best testing strategy for contract-equipped programs. In: APSEC, pp. 290–297 (2011)

39. Doong, R.K., Frankl, P.G.: The astoot approach to testing object-oriented programs. ACM Transactions on Software Engineering and Methodology 3(2), 101–130 (1994)

40. Xie, T., Marinov, D., Notkin, D.: Rostra: A framework for detecting redundant object-oriented unit tests. In: 26th IEEE/ACM International Conference on Automated Software Engineering (ASE 2011), pp. 196–205 (2004)
41. Angluin, D.: Learning regular sets from queries and counterexamples. Inf. Comput. 75(2), 87–106 (1987)
42. Baresi, L., Di Nitto, E., Ghezzi, C.: Toward open-world software: Issues and challenges. IEEE Computer 39(10), 36–43 (2006)
43. Bianculli, D., Ghezzi, C.: Monitoring conversational web services. In: 2nd International Workshop on Service Oriented Software Engineering: in Conjunction with the 6th ESEC/FSE Joint Meeting, IW-SOSWE 2007, pp. 15–21. ACM, New York (2007)
44. Kiczales, G., Lamping, J., Mendhekar, A., Maeda, C., Lopes, C., Loingtier, J.M., Irwin, J.: Aspect-oriented programming. In: Akşit, M., Matsuoka, S. (eds.) ECOOP 1997. LNCS, vol. 1241, pp. 220–242. Springer, Heidelberg (1997)
45. Henkel, J., Reichenbach, C., Diwan, A.: Developing and debugging algebraic specifications for java classes. ACM Trans. Softw. Eng. Methodol. 17(3), 14:1–14:37 (2008)
46. Diaconescu, R., Futatsugi, K., Iida, S.: Component-based algebraic specification and verification in CafeOBJ. In: Wing, J.M., Woodcock, J., Davies, J. (eds.) FM 1999. LNCS, vol. 1709, pp. 1644–1663. Springer, Heidelberg (1999)

Behavioral Rewrite Systems and Behavioral Productivity

Grigore Roşu[1,2] and Dorel Lucanu[2]

[1] University of Illinois at Urbana-Champaign, USA
grosu@illinois.edu
[2] Alexandru Ioan Cuza University, Iaşi, Romania
dlucanu@info.uaic.ro

Abstract. This paper introduces *behavioral rewrite systems*, where rewriting is used to evaluate experiments, and *behavioral productivity*, which says that each experiment can be fully evaluated, and investigates some of their properties. First, it is shown that, in the case of (infinite) streams, behavioral productivity generalizes and may bring to a more basic rewriting setting the existing notion of stream productivity defined in the context of infinite rewriting and lazy strategies; some arguments are given that in some cases one may prefer the behavioral approach. Second, a behavioral productivity criterion is given, which reduces the problem to conventional term rewrite system termination, so that one can use off-the-shelf termination tools and techniques for checking behavioral productivity in general, not only for streams. Finally, behavioral productivity is shown to be equivalent to a proof-theoretic (rather than model-theoretic) notion of behavioral well-specifiedness, and its difficulty in the arithmetic hierarchy is shown to be Π_2^0-complete. All new concepts are exemplified over streams, infinite binary trees, and processes.

1 Introduction

Behavioral abstraction, or the process of understanding how a system behaves under a given set of relevant observations or experiments, is a fundamental problem in formal methods: like information hiding, behavioral abstraction provides the capability to abstract away from internal implementation details to better capture and reason about the actual system behavior.

Behavioral equivalence, also informally called *indistinguishability under experiments* in the literature [18, 13, 2, 19], is an important example of behavioral abstraction. CafeOBJ [4], an executable specification language developed under the leadership and vision of Kokichi Futatsugi, was one of the first systems that provided explicit support for specifying and verifying behavioral equivalence.

We briefly explain behavioral equivalence using a very simple example. The two (infinite) processes represented in Figure 1 can be behaviorally specified by the following terminating term rewriting system R (behavioral specifications typically use equations, but we here tacitly use rewriting instead):

S. Iida, J. Meseguer, and K. Ogata (Eds.): Futatsugi Festschrift, LNCS 8373, pp. 296–314, 2014.

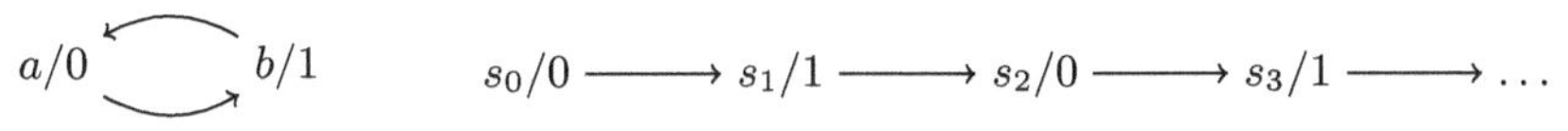

$a/0 \quad b/1 \qquad\qquad s_0/0 \longrightarrow s_1/1 \longrightarrow s_2/0 \longrightarrow s_3/1 \longrightarrow \dots$

Fig. 1. Two behavioraly equivalent processes

$$out(a) \to 0 \qquad out(b) \to 1 \qquad next(a) \to b \qquad next(b) \to a$$

$$out(s_i) \to i \bmod 2 \qquad\qquad next(s_i) \to s_{i+1}$$

Each state has an output value, represented in the figure by a pair *state/output*. The output is modeled by the operation *out(state)* and the transitions are modeled by the operation *next(state)*. We can observe that the states a and s_0 are behaviorally indistinguishable by experimenting with them:

1. We first check if the output values for the two states are equal:
   $out(a) \xrightarrow{*}_R 0$ and $out(s_0) \xrightarrow{*}_R 0$.
2. We check the equality of the output values after one transition:
   $out(next(a)) \xrightarrow{*}_R 1$ and $out(next(s_0)) \xrightarrow{*}_R 1$.
3. We check the equality of the output values after two transitions:
   $out(next^2(a)) \xrightarrow{*}_R 0$ and $out(next^2(s_0)) \xrightarrow{*}_R 0$. And so on.

So, for each experiment $out(next^i(*))$ respectively applied on the two states, we obtain $out(next^i(a)) \xrightarrow{*}_R v$ and $out(next^i(s_0)) \xrightarrow{*}_R v$ for certain $v \in \{0,1\}$ and thus conclude that a and s_0 are indistinguishable under experiments. Obviously, a and s_1 are distinguishable under experiments (e.g., $out(s_1) \xrightarrow{*}_R 1$).

Lazy rewriting is an alternative, more operational approach to study infinite-behavior objects. The idea here is to use lazy rewriting to only extract as much information from the infinite behavior of an object or data-structure as needed in the given context, this way avoiding the infinite nature of the object or data-structure. In this approach, the notion of *productivity* [5, 10, 24] plays a crucial rule. It captures the intuition of *unlimited progress*, that is, that the term under analysis can be continuously evaluated (or rewritten) in such a way that its infinite behavior is uniquely determined as the limit of this evaluation process.

Both behavioral equivalence and productivity were proposed in the early 1980's, the former by Reichel [18] and the later by Dijkstra [5]. Since then, attracted by the benefits and elegance of each of the two approaches, there have been many related approaches, reasoning techniques and tool prototypes proposed for each of them, e.g. [2, 4, 7–10, 13, 14, 16, 17, 19, 22, 24–26, 28, 29] among many others. However, up to now, in spite of common intuitions and ultimate goals, these two approaches to infinite behavior have lived separate lives. In this paper we make a first step towards bringing the two approaches closer. To make this possible, we first introduce the general notion of a behavioral rewrite system, and then formally define our notion of behavioral productivity for such systems. Note that almost any two papers in the aforementioned lists defines different variants of behavioral equivalence or productivity. We are not attempting to consolidate all these different variations in this paper. Instead, our objective is to capture the *essence* of these important concepts in order to highlight their relationships. We believe that our results can be adapted to each particular approach, but this is beyond our scope here.

A *behavioral rewrite system* (BRS) is a term rewrite system (TRS) together with a set of *derivative* operations (or *observers*) which are used to formally define *experiments*, where the rewriting relation is used to compute the results of the experiments. The usual productivity makes sense for those TRS's defining infinite data structures[1]: R is productive for a ground term t, intended to represent an infinite data structure $[\![t]\!]$, if the rewriting relation $\rightarrow_R$ can be used to obtain any approximation of $[\![t]\!]$ starting from t. We propose *behavioral productivity* as another example of a behavioral abstraction: it says that each experiment applied on t can be computed in finite time by means of ordinary rewriting. Behavioral productivity captures the idea that the behavior of a given term can be gradually "produced"; since the set of experiments that need to be applied on the term in order to potentially yield the term's behavior is recursively enumerable, behavioral productivity means, in fact, that each of the experiments applied on the term can be "evaluated", or in our rewrite context, can be rewritten to a data term. For the above process example, R is behaviorally productive for a state s if and only if each experiment of the form $out(next^i(*))$ can be rewritten to a data value term (here 0 or 1) when applied in any state. It is easy to see that R is behaviorally productive for all states of the two processes. However, if we add a new state c and only the transition $next(b) \rightarrow c$, then we observe that R is not behaviorally productive for c because $out(next^i(c))$ is irreducible.

We show that for streams, behavioral productivity for BRS's generalizes the productivity for TRS's in several ways: it can be defined for a larger class of specifications, there are non-productive TRS's for which their behavioral versions are behaviorally productive, and it can be defined for non-ground terms as well. Behavioral productivity plays for coinductive specifications a role which is dual to that played by sufficient completeness for inductive specifications. We show that if a BRS (not necessarily defining streams) is productive for a term t, then it behaviorally well-specifies the object represented by t; moreover, under mild conditions the two notions coincide. We also show that the problem of saying whether a given BRS is behaviorally productive is Π_2^0-complete. Our main practical result in this paper is a criterion that reduces the checking of behavioral productivity of a "coinductive" BRS to the termination of the rewriting relation (in the usual sense) of its underlying TRS. That means that one can use off-the-shelf termination techniques and tools developed and continuously improved by the rewriting community (see, e.g., [12, 6]) to test for behavioral productivity.

All results reported in this paper lead us to the belief that behavioral rewrite systems may be more suitable than term rewrite systems when we want to

---

[1] Again, formal definitions of productivity differ from paper to paper, mixing the conceptual notion with operational or technical limitations (e.g., requiring the terms to only be streams, or requiring orthogonality of the TRS, or both). We drop all those limitations here and focus on the essence of the concept.

analyze the behavioral properties of infinite data structures/processes. We summarize the arguments supporting this idea: 1) behavioral productivity is uniformly defined for all BRS's , 2) a TRS can be associated with various BRS's and hence we can capture various definitions for the productivity of TRS's , 3) some anomalies like "productive for t but does not well-specify t" are avoided, and 4) productivity can be defined for a larger class of terms.

Section 2 introduces the notation used in the paper and recalls the definitions of stream productivity and of behavioral specifications. Section 3 introduces behavioral rewrite systems and behavioral productivity. Section 4 discusses how behavioral productivity captures stream productivity as a special instance. Two main properties of the behavioral productivity are studied in the next two sections: Section 5 shows that the termination in the standard sense of the term rewriting relation of a coinductive BRS yields behavioral productivity; Section 6 shows that behavioral productivity implies behavioral well-definedness and that, under some reasonable conditions, the two notions coincide. The hardness of of the behavioral productivity problem is studied in Section 8.

2   Background, Preliminary Notions, and Notations

A *many-sorted signature* (S, Σ), or just *signature* Σ, is a set of *sorts* S together with a set Σ of *operations* $\sigma : s_1 \times \cdots \times s_n \to s$, where $s_1, \ldots, s_n, s \in S$. We let $T_\Sigma(X)$ denote the set of Σ-*terms* built with operation symbols in Σ and with variables in the S-indexed set X. A Σ-*context for sort* $s \in S$ is a Σ-term $C \in T_\Sigma(X \cup \{* : s\})$ having precisely one occurrence of the special variable $*$ of sort s; to emphasize that C is such a context we may write $C[*{:}s]$, and if t is a term of sort s then we let $C[t]$ denote the term obtained replacing $*$ by t in C.

Fix a set $\mathcal{X}$ of S-sorted variables. A Σ-*rewrite rule* is a triple $(\forall X) l \to r$, where $X \subseteq \mathcal{X}$ is an S-indexed set of *variables* and $l, r \in T_\Sigma(X)$ such that l is not a variable and each variable in r also occurs in l. We often simply write $l \to r$ for a rewrite rule and then X is the set of the variables occurring in l. A *term rewriting system (TRS)* is a pair (Σ, R), where Σ is a many-sorted signature and R is a set of Σ-rewrite rules. The *rewrite relation* $\to_R$ is defined as usual: $t \to_R t'$ for $t, t' \in T_\Sigma(\mathcal{X})$ iff there exists a Σ-context C, a rule $(\forall X) l \to r$, and a substitution $\theta : X \to T_\Sigma(\mathcal{X})$ such that $t = C[\theta(l)]$ and $t' = C[\theta(r)]$. We let $\xrightarrow{*}_R$ denote the reflexive and transitive closure of $\to_R$, and $\leftarrow_R$ the inverse of $\to_R$.

A Σ-*equation* is a triple $(\forall X) t = t'$, where X has the same meaning as that for rewrite rules and $t, t' \in T_\Sigma(X)$. A *many-sorted equational specification* is a pair (Σ, E), where Σ is a many-sorted signature and E a set of Σ- equations.

2.1   Stream Productivity

Although there are attempts to define productivity more generally, e.g. [10], so far productivity was mainly used for streams (or infinite lists), with lazy (infinite) rewriting [5, 24, 7–10, 26, 28, 29]. Here we remind the reader this particular but conventional notion of productivity. To clearly emphasize its limited scope to stream rewrite systems and to distinguish it from our more general notion of behavioral productivity, we will call it *stream productivity* from here on. Also, to avoid the difficult task of unifying the various definitions of streams and productivity in the papers listed above, we adopt the least restricted definition that we were able to find in the literature, which in our view best captures the intuition underlying the concept originally proposed by Dijskstra in [5]. This is the definition proposed in [10], but without the orthogonally requirement. Orthogonality ensures unique normal forms, so well-definedness, but that seems to be unnecessary for productivity. In our view, productivity is the capability of producing an element of the stream on any position, not necessarily of producing a unique such element. Adding the orthogonality restriction brings no technical difficulty, but since some of the papers above do not require it, we find it more appropriate to keep our notions and results as unrestricted as possible.

A *stream-TRS* [10] is a TRS (Σ, R) having a special sort *Data* for stream elements, a sort *Stream* for streams, and an "implicit" operation $\_:\_ : Data \times Stream \to Stream$ that allows to regard a stream as its "head" element followed by its "tail" stream. A stream-TRS may contain operations together with rewrite rules defining the data and may contain operations together with rewrite rules defining the streams of interest and desired operations on them. For instance, the constant stream $zeros := 0 : 0 : 0 : \ldots$ containing only 0's, the sub-stream consisting only of the elements on odd positions of a stream, and the stream obtained by zipping two streams can be defined by the following rewrite rules:

$$zeros \to 0 : zeros \quad odd(B_1 : B_2 : S) \to B_1 : odd(S) \quad zip(B : S, S') \to B : zip(S', S)$$

where B, B_1, B_2 are variables of sort *Data* and S, S' are variables of sort *Stream*. The above TRS is non-terminating, so termination is not the right concept for stream-TRS's. Stream productivity aims at capturing the notion of *unlimited progress*. Informally, a stream is productive iff it can be continuously evaluated (or rewritten), element by element. Formally, a stream-TRS (Σ, R) is **stream productive** [10] for the stream (ground term) s iff $Prod_R(s) = \infty$, where the *stream production function* $Prod_R$ is defined by $Prod_R(s) = \sup\{n \mid s \xrightarrow{*}_R d_1 : d_2 : \ldots : d_n : t\}$, where d_i are data terms. In practice, to avoid non-termination, stream productivity is typically used in combination with lazy rewriting.

2.2 Behavioral Signatures, Experiments and Behavioral Equivalence

Here we recall several folklore behavioral concepts, following for uniformity the notation and approach in [22] but without claiming any novelty or ownership. These concepts have been introduced under various names and notations in earlier works by fathers of behavioral specification, such as Sannella, Tarlecki, Wirsing, Reichel, Goguen, Futatsugi, Bidoit, Hennicker, to only mention a few.

A *behavioral signature* is a pair (Σ, Δ), where Σ is a signature and Δ is a set of Σ-contexts, which we call *derivatives*. If $\delta[*:h] \in \Delta$ then the sort h is called a *hidden sort*. Let $H \subseteq S$ be the set of all hidden sorts of (Σ, Δ). The remaining sorts in $V = S - H$ are called *data, or visible sorts*. A *data operation* is an operation in Σ taking and returning only visible sorts; we let $\Sigma\!\restriction_V \subseteq \Sigma$

denote the sub-signature of data sorts and operations. A Σ-sentence/-equation is called a *data sentence/equation* iff it is a $\Sigma\restriction_V$-sentence/-equation. A Σ-equation $(\forall X)\, t = u$ is called a *hidden equation* when the sort of t, u is hidden. A *behavioral (equational) specification* $\mathcal{B}$ is a pair $((\Sigma, \Delta), E)$, where (Σ, Δ) is a behavioral signature and E is a set of Σ-equations. A Δ-*experiment* is a Δ-context (i.e., one formed only with contexts in Δ) of visible result sort. If Δ is clear, we may write experiment for Δ-experiment and context for Δ-context.

In the case of streams, the most straightforward choice for derivatives is $\Delta = \{hd[*:Stream], \ tl[*:Stream]\}$, which is the one we will consider for our stream examples in the rest of the paper. However, the following are also possible choices for derivatives, as they allow to reach any element of a stream:

$\{hd[*:Stream], \ hd(tl[*:Stream]), \ tl(tl[*:Stream])\}$,

$\{hd[*:Stream], \ odd[*:Stream], \ even[*:Stream]\}$,

$\{hd[*:Stream], \ zip(tl([*:Stream]), S)\}, \ \{hd(tl^n[*:Stream]) \mid n \in Nat\}$, etc.

Many examples of derivative sets are discussed in [19], there called *cobases*.

Given a behavioral signature (Σ, Δ), the Δ-experiments allow us to "observe" hidden terms, and thus state and prove *behavioral properties*. A common behavioral property is the *behavioral equivalence*, stating that two hidden terms are behaviorally equivalent iff they are indistinguishable under experiments: $\mathcal{B}$ *behaviorally satisfies* hidden equation e, written $\mathcal{B} \Vdash e$, iff $\mathcal{B} \vdash C[e]$ for each experiment C, where $C[t = u]$ is $C[t] = C[u]$. Another behavioral property is the *behavioral productivity*, which is the main concept introduced and investigated in this paper, stating that a hidden term has "producible" behaviors, that is, it rewrites to some data element under each experiment.

3   Behavioral Rewrite Systems and Productivity

In this section we introduce our main notions in this paper and discuss them by means of examples. Our first notion, that of a *behavioral rewrite system*, has the same relationship to behavioral equational specifications as rewrite systems have to equational specifications: they orient the equations into rewrite rules.

Definition 1. *A* **behavioral rewrite system (BRS)** $\mathcal{B}$ *is a pair* $((\Sigma, \Delta), R)$, *where* (Σ, Δ) *is a behavioral signature and* (Σ, R) *is a TRS.* $\mathcal{B}$ **terminates** *iff* (Σ, R) *terminates as a TRS, and is* **coinductive** *iff* $\delta[f(\overline{x})]$ *is not a normal form for any* $f : \overline{s} \to h$ *in* $\Sigma - \Delta$ *and* $\delta[*:h]$ *in* Δ *($\overline{x}$ are variables of sort $\overline{s}$).*

Our notion of coinductive rewrite system is reminiscent of earlier beahavioral concepts, such as "observer completeness" in [1] and "cobasis" in [21]. It is in fact dual to the folklore notion of "inductive rewrite system", that is, one where there is a subset of operations called "constructors" such that $f(\gamma(\overline{x}))$ is rewritable (typically the left-hand side term of some rewrite rule) for any non-constructor (or defined) operator f and any constructor γ; such rules guarantee that, in the presence of termination, each non-constructor operation is fully defined in terms of constructors. Dually, the fact that the terms $\delta[f(\overline{x})]$ in a coinductive rewrite system are rewritable will guarantee that, in the presence of termination, each non-derivative operation can be fully observed (Theorem 3). We next introduce our general notion of behavioral productivity, inspired from the more particular but insightful notion of stream productivity [5, 10, 24]:

Definition 2. *BRS* $\mathcal{B} = ((\Sigma, \Delta), R)$ *is* **productive for a hidden term** t *iff for each* Δ-*experiment* C *there is some* $(\Sigma\restriction_V \cup \Delta)$-*term* d *such that* $C[t] \xrightarrow{*}_R d$. $\mathcal{B}$ *is* **productive** *iff it is productive for any hidden term, and it is* **ground productive** *iff it is productive for any ground hidden term.*

Therefore, productivity for a hidden term t means that a result of applying any experiment C on t can be eventually "produced", or in other words, since the experiments can typically be easily enumerated, that a behavior of t can be incrementally approximated without getting stuck on any particular experiment. Following the duality induction/coinduction above, note that productivity plays the dual role of sufficient completeness [15]. Indeed, sufficient completeness implies that a term $u[x]$ (for simplicity, suppose that u has only one variable, x) can be shown equal to a constructor ground term under any substitution of its variable x by a constructor ground term c, that is, all the non-constructor operations in $u[c]$ can be eventually eliminated; dually, productivity implies that a term t can be shown equal to a derivative term under any derivation (or experiment) C of it, that is, all the non-derivative operations in $C[t]$ can be eventually eliminated. This duality between productivity and sufficient completeness is technically irrelevant in this paper, therefore we do not bother to formalize it, but we find it interesting and thus worthwhile noting.

Note that the "result" $(\Sigma\restriction_V \cup \Delta)$-term d in Definition 2 can use the operations in Δ only as Δ-experiments applied to variables of hidden sort, because no other non-data operations are allowed in d and because the sort of d is visible. In particular, if t has no hidden variables then d is a $\Sigma\restriction_V$-term. To avoid confusion with "stream productivity", we take the freedom to tacitly call our productivity for BRS's *behavioral productivity* whenever we feel that clarifies the presentation.

In the sequel we illustrate the notions above on several examples.

Example 1. (*Streams*) A behavioral rewrite system of bit streams (or infinite lists) may include a sort *Bit* with two constants 0 and 1, a sort *Stream* for bit streams with operations $hd : Stream \to Bit$ (head) and $tl : Stream \to Stream$ (tail), and as many stream operations and defining rewriting rules as desired. For instance, the constant stream *zeros*, the sub-stream on odd positions *odd*, and the stream merging *zip* can be behaviorally defined as:

$$hd(zeros) \to 0 \qquad hd(odd(S)) \to hd(S) \qquad hd(zip(S, S')) \to hd(S)$$
$$tl(zeros) \to zeros \qquad tl(odd(S)) \to odd(tl(tl(S))) \qquad tl(zip(S, S')) \to zip(S', tl(S))$$

One can also define a stream operation returning the sub-stream on even positions as $even(S) \to odd(tl(S))$. The set Δ of derivatives consists of the two contexts $hd[*:Stream]$ and $tl[*:Stream]$. Thus, *Stream* is a hidden sort and *Bit* is visible. The stream experiments are contexts of the form $hd(tl^i[*:Stream])$, where $i \geq 0$. It is not hard to check that this behavioral rewrite system for streams is terminating, coinductive, and behaviorally productive. For instance, *zeros* is behaviorally productive because $hd(tl^i(zeros)) = 0$ for any $i > 0$. Also, $odd(S)$ is productive because $hd(tl^i(odd(S))) \xrightarrow{*} hd(tl^{2i}(S))$ for any $i > 0$.

Example 2. (Non-Deterministic Streams) Consider now a bit stream *random*, which can produce any sequence of 0 and 1 bits. It can be defined as follows:

$$hd(random) \to 0 \qquad hd(random) \to 1 \qquad tl(random) \to random$$

This BRS terminates and is both coinductive and productive. The stream *random* is *not* productive according to existing formal definitions of stream productivity [10], as those require, in our view unjustified, that the stream elements are not only producible, but also *unique*. We believe that productivity and unique normal forms of experiments are orthogonal issues, so we do not mix them.

Example 3. (Non-Terminating Streams) Let us extend the stream BRS in Example 1 with a new constant *ones*, an operation _:_ : $Bit \times Stream \to Stream$, and the rewrite rules:

$$ones \to 1 : ones \qquad hd(B : S) = B \qquad tl(B : S) = S$$

Obviously, the resulting BRS is not terminating. It is coinductive, however, because $hd(ones) \to hd(1 : ones)$ and $tl(ones) \to tl(1 : ones)$. It is also productive, because there is some rewriting sequence $hd(tl^i(ones)) \xrightarrow{*} 1$ for each $i \geq 0$; even though a lazy strategy may be needed in order to generate such rewriting sequences, it is important to note that for each experiment on *ones* there is some finite rewriting sequence computing it, so the BRS is productive on *ones*.

Example 4. (Non-Coinductive Streams) Let us replace the two defining rules of *zeros* in the stream BRS in Example 1 with the following three rules:

$$hd(zeros) \to 0 \qquad hd(tl(zeros)) = 0 \qquad tl(tl(zeros)) = zeros$$

Obviously, the resulting BRS is not coinductive, because $tl(zeros)$ is now a normal form. It remains both terminating and productive, though. However, if we instead choose Δ to be $\{hd[*:Stream], hd(tl[*:Stream]), tl(tl[*:Stream])\}$, then the stream BRS becomes also coinductive.

Example 5. (Non-Productive Streams) All the example BRS's above were productive. One can also have non-productive BRS's ; however, since Theorem 3 tells us that coinductive and terminating BRS's are also productive, it must be the case that any non-productive BRS must either not be coinductive or not terminate. We show an example of each. An example of non-coinductive non-productive BRS can be obtained from the BRS in Example 1 by dropping any of its rules. The other case is trickier. Let us extend the stream BRS in Example 1 with a stream a (constant of sort *Stream*) defined with the rules $hd(a) \to 0$ and $tl(a) \to odd(a)$. Then the resulting BRS is not productive for a, because there is no way to "evaluate" $hd(tl^2(a))$: indeed, $hd(tl^2(a)) \to hd(tl(odd(a))) \to hd(odd(tl^2(a))) \to hd(tl^2(a)) \to \dots$. This rewrite sequence shows that this stream BRS is also non-terminating. Note, however, that it is coinductive.

Let us next also discuss some non-stream examples of BRS's .

Example 6. (*Infinite Binary Trees*) A BRS defining infinite binary trees over bits consists of a definition of bits (similar to that of streams), a sort *Tree* for infinite binary trees together with the operations *root* : *Tree* → *Bit* (the root of the tree), *left* : *Tree* → *Tree* (the left subtree), *right* : *Tree* → *Tree* (the right subtree), and other operations over trees and their defining rewriting rules. Here are several examples of such operations inspired from [25]:

$$root(ones) \rightarrow 1 \qquad root(\neg T) \rightarrow \overline{root(T)} \qquad root(thue) \rightarrow 0$$
$$left(ones) \rightarrow ones \qquad left(\neg T) \rightarrow \neg left(T) \qquad left(thue) \rightarrow thue$$
$$right(ones) \rightarrow ones \quad right(\neg T) \rightarrow \neg right(T) \quad right(thue) \rightarrow thue + ones$$

$$root(T1 + T2) \rightarrow root(T1) \oplus root(T2)$$
$$left(T1 + T2) \rightarrow left(T1) + left(T2)$$
$$right(T1 + T2) \rightarrow right(T1) + right(T2)$$

where the addition ($\oplus$) and the negation ($\overline{\cdot}$) over bits are defined as usual: $0 \oplus B \rightarrow B$, $1 \oplus 1 \rightarrow 0$, $\overline{0} \rightarrow 1$, $\overline{1} \rightarrow 0$. The set Δ of derivatives consists of three contexts: $root(*:Tree)$, $left(*:Tree)$, and $right(*:Tree)$. So, the sort *Tree* is hidden and the sort *Bit* is visible. This behavioral rewrite system for infinite binary trees is terminating, coinductive and productive. Moreover, one can show that, for example, the infinite binary trees *thue + ones* and *¬thue* are indistinguishable under Δ-experiments; indeed, the behavioral prover CIRC [16] can prove them behaviorally equivalent, but this is beyond our scope in this paper.

Example 7. (*Processes*) The BRS defining the processes presented in Section 1 consists of a visible sort *Int* for integers, visible operations over integers and their defining rewriting rules, a hidden sort *State* for the states, two hidden constants a, b of sort *State* describing the states of the first process, an operation (generalized hidden constant) $s : Int \rightarrow State$ for the states of the second process, and two operations *out* : *State* → *Int* and *next* : *State* → *State*, which together with their rewrite rules describe the behaviors of the two processes. The set of derivatives Δ consists of two contexts: $out(*:State)$ and $next(*:State)$. It is easy to see that this BRS of processes is terminating, coinductive and productive.

Example 8. (*Non-Deterministic, or Non-Confluent Processes*) Here is an example of BRS which is productive but is not confluent. Add to the BRS in Example 7 one more hidden constant of sort *State*, say c, together with the following rules:

$$next(a) \rightarrow c \qquad next(c) \rightarrow a \qquad out(c) \rightarrow 1$$

The resulting BRS is productive (for each of a, b, c) but is not confluent (the critical pair $b \leftarrow next(a) \rightarrow c$ is not join-able). However, $out(next^i(b)) \xrightarrow{*}_R v_i$ and $out(next^i(c)) \xrightarrow{*}_R v_i$ for some $v_i \in \{0, 1\}$, so b and c are indistinguishable under experiments. Hence each experiment on a is uniquely determined, in spite of the lack of confluence of this BRS.

The various examples above showed that neither termination, nor coinductivity, nor confluence is a requirement for productivity. As shown in Section 5, termination and coinductivity imply productivity; confluence, however, appears to play no role for productivity.

4 Behavioral Productivity Generalizes Stream Productivity

In this section we discuss the relationship between productivity in the usual sense of stream-TRS definitions and behavioral productivity of stream BRS definitions, essentially showing that nothing is lost wrt productivity when using the latter. On the contrary, the BRS approach to define streams has the benefit that one can use our termination-based technique in Theorem 3 to prove stream productivity.

We start by defining a transformation, given in Definition 3, which shows the immediate correspondence between stream productivity and behavioral productivity, namely that the former falls as a special case of the latter for particular behavioral rewrite systems, namely ones of streams.

Definition 3. *Let $\mathcal{R} = (\Sigma, R)$ be a stream-TRS (see Section 2.1). We let $\mathcal{B}_0(\mathcal{R})$ be the BRS $((\Sigma \cup \{hd, tl\}, \{hd, tl\}), R \cup \{hd(B : S) \to B, tl(B : S) \to S\})$.*

To avoid interfering with the head/tail operations that may already be defined and used in the original stream-TRS $\mathcal{R}$, we assume that the hd/tl added to the BRS $\mathcal{B}_0(\mathcal{R})$ are fresh. To achieve this, one may need to rename the potentially homonymous operations in $\mathcal{R}$.

Theorem 1. *Let $\mathcal{R}$ be a stream-TRS and let s be a ground stream term. Then $s \xrightarrow{*}_{\mathcal{R}} d_1 : d_2 : \ldots : d_n : t$ iff $hd(s) \xrightarrow{*}_{\mathcal{B}_0(\mathcal{R})} d_1, \ldots, hd(tl^{n-1}(s)) \xrightarrow{*}_{\mathcal{B}_0(\mathcal{R})} d_n$, and $tl^n(s) \xrightarrow{*}_{\mathcal{B}_0(\mathcal{R})} t$. Therefore, $\mathcal{R}$ is productive for s if and only if $\mathcal{B}_0(\mathcal{R})$ is behaviorally productive for s.*

Proof. Straightforward by induction on n, noting that $s \xrightarrow{*}_{\mathcal{R}} h : t$ if and only if $hd(s) \xrightarrow{*}_{\mathcal{B}_0(\mathcal{R})} h$ and $tl(s) \xrightarrow{*}_{\mathcal{B}_0(\mathcal{R})} t$. □

The transformation $\mathcal{R} \mapsto \mathcal{B}_0(\mathcal{R})$ above is so trivial that it should not be surprising that $\mathcal{B}_0(\mathcal{R})$, in spite of capturing stream productivity as an instance of the more general concept of behavioral productivity, does not add much behavioral value; in particular, it is not coinductive and, if the original stream-TRS $\mathcal{R}$ does not terminate, $\mathcal{B}_0(\mathcal{R})$ does not terminate either. Therefore, our termination-based technique in Theorem 3 cannot be applied to prove stream productivity if we follow this simplistic approach.

We next give a converse transformation, from stream-BRS's to stream-TRS's, also trivial and also productivity preserving:

Definition 4. *Let $\mathcal{B}$ be a stream-BRS. We let $\mathcal{R}_0(\mathcal{B})$ be the stream-TRS obtained from $\mathcal{B}$ by adding the lazy constructor[2] $\_:\_$ and the rule $S \to hd(S) : tl(S)$.*

Like in the previous transformation, to avoid interfering with the stream construct that may already be defined and used in the original stream-BRS $\mathcal{B}$, we assume that the $\_:\_$ added to the TRS $\mathcal{R}_0(\mathcal{B})$ is fresh. If one does not like the fact that the rule added to $\mathcal{R}_0(\mathcal{B})$ has a variable (S, of sort *Stream*) as left hand side, then one can instantiate the rule above for the stream operations defined in $\mathcal{B}$. This rule, however, is not problematic for lazy rewriting, because it is not applied indefinitely under the hd/tl operations that it generates.

---

[2] We refer the reader to [10] for precise stream-TRS definitions and terminology.

Theorem 2. *Let $\mathcal{B}$ be a stream-BRS. Then $s \xrightarrow{*}_{\mathcal{R}_0(\mathcal{B})} d_1 : d_2 : \ldots : d_n : t$ iff $hd(s) \xrightarrow{*}_{\mathcal{B}} d_1, \ldots, hd(tl^{n-1}(s)) \xrightarrow{*}_{\mathcal{B}} d_n$, and $tl^n(s) \xrightarrow{*}_{\mathcal{B}} t$. Therefore, $\mathcal{B}$ is behaviorally productive for a ground stream term s if and only if $\mathcal{R}_0(\mathcal{B})$ is stream productive for s.*

Proof. Straightforward again, by induction on n, noting that $s \xrightarrow{*}_{\mathcal{R}_0(\mathcal{B})} h : t$ if and only if $hd(s) \xrightarrow{*}_{\mathcal{B}} h$ and $tl(s) \xrightarrow{*}_{\mathcal{B}} t$. □

As explained in Section 2.1, existing variants of stream-TRS and stream productivity definitions are more restricted than ours. If one wants to adapt our results above to those variants, then one needs to add similar restrictions to the corresponding stream-BRSes. For example, if one strongly believes that or absolutely needs that stream-TRSes must be orthogonal (in order to ensure unique normal forms), as it is the case in several stream-TRS variants, then one can require that same orthogonality restriction on the stream-BRS.

In addition to its theoretical significance, the transformation above may also have practical value. Supposing that one prefers to use lazy rewriting to define streams, one may admittedly be reluctant to use our "behavioral style" because, even if one proves productivity using behavioral techniques (e.g., Theorem 3), one still cannot directly use the BRS in one's lazy rewriting framework. The transformation $\mathcal{B} \mapsto \mathcal{R}_0(\mathcal{B})$ above says that all one needs to do to take advantage of *both* our behavioral approach and one's lazy rewriting framework is to define one's streams as a BRS $\mathcal{B}$, prove it behaviorally productive, then transform it into the stream-TRS $\mathcal{R}_0(\mathcal{B})$ by adding the lazy construct and rule as in Definition 4, and finally use it in one's lazy rewrite framework knowing that it is productive.

While we agree that the stream-TRS definitional style is compact, elegant, and the required lazy rewriting strategy to evaluate them is well supported by several programming languages, we conclude this section by warning the reader that the more conventional stream-TRS style may sometimes, rather unexpectedly, lead to situations of what one may call *accidental non-productivity*. Consider, for example, the following stream-TRS from [29]:

$$zeros \to 0 : zeros \qquad f(x : s) \to g(f(s)) \qquad g(x : s) \to zeros$$

This stream-TRS follows the lazy definitional style and it is easy to see that $f(zeros)$ can only be the stream $zeros$, which is productive. However, unfortunately, $f(zeros)$ is *not productive in the original sense*, because $f(zeros) \to f(0:zeros) \to g(f(zeros)) \to^* g^2(f(zeros)) \to \ldots$ and there is no way to produce a first 0 element. The problem here is that the lazy stream construct in the definition of g prevents the rule from matching, because $f(zeros)$ cannot be split in a head and tail. Such a situation would have not appeared if one followed a behavioral rewriting style, aiming at defining a terminating and coinductive BRS like the following, which is immediately productive by Theorem 3:

$$hd(zeros) \to 0 \qquad hd(f(s)) \to hd(g(f(tl(s)))) \qquad hd(g(s)) \to 0$$
$$tl(zeros) \to zeros \qquad tl(f(s)) \to tl(g(f(tl(s)))) \qquad tl(g(s)) \to zeros$$

One could argue that accidental non-productive situations like above are not an artifact of lazy TRS rewriting as we are implying, but instead desirable. Even if one agrees with that, we think that one may still want to eliminate accidental non-productivity whenever possible, preferably even through automatic equivalent TRS-transformations. We believe that the behavioral rewriting approach proposed in this paper could help with this aspect, but our results in this direction are preliminary and so are only informally discussed in Section 7.

The idea is to devise more involved (stream-semantics preserving) transformations $\mathcal{R} \mapsto \mathcal{B}_i(\mathcal{R})$ (for different i indexes - $i = 0$ is the most basic, starting point transformation) from stream-TRS's into BRS's , more precisely ones where $\mathcal{B}_i(\mathcal{R})$ may be behaviorally productive also in situations where $\mathcal{R}$ is not necessarily productive. Then one can use Theorem 3 and termination tools to check the behavioral productivity of $\mathcal{B}_i(\mathcal{R})$, and finally report back the equivalent stream-TRS $\mathcal{R}_0(\mathcal{B}_i(\mathcal{R}))$ which is now stream productive. One can also devise different transformations $\mathcal{B} \mapsto \mathcal{R}_i(\mathcal{B})$ that make the resulting stream-TRS follow the more common style that one uses when defining stream-TRS's (e.g., replacing pairs of behavioral rules $hd(l) \to h$ and $tl(l) \to t$ by lazy rules $l \to h : t$,etc.). Such transformations are beyond our scope in this paper.

5   Termination and Coinductivity Imply Productivity

Productivity is an inherently difficult problem (see Section 8) and there are no tools available that can check productivity in general. It is therefore important to reduce the problem of checking productivity to other problems with better tool support. In this section we give a practical criterion that reduces behavioral productivity to termination in the standard sense, so that one can use off-the-shelf termination tools to check productivity.

Theorem 3. *Let $\mathcal{B} = ((\Sigma, \Delta), R)$ be a BRS such that $\Sigma - (\Sigma\restriction_V \cup \Delta)$ contains only operations of hidden result sort. Then $\mathcal{B}$ terminating and coinductive implies $\mathcal{B}$ productive.*

Proof. Let t be a hidden term and let C be a Δ-experiment for t. If t is a $(\Sigma\restriction_V \cup \Delta)$-term then we are done. If t contains some operation in $\Sigma - (\Sigma\restriction_V \cup \Delta)$, which by hypothesis must be of hidden result sort, then since the result sort of $C[t]$ is visible it must be the case that $C[t]$ contains a subterm of the form $\delta[f(\overline{u})]$ for some $f : \overline{s} \to h$ in $(\Sigma\restriction_V \cup \Delta)$, some $\delta[*:h]$ in Δ, and some tuple term $\overline{u}$ of tuple sort $\overline{s}$. Hence, by coinductivity, $C[t]$ cannot be in normal form, so it can be rewritten to some other term of visible sort. If the resulting term contains any operation in $\Sigma - (\Sigma\restriction_V \cup \Delta)$, then we can apply the same arguments above and reduce it to another term of visible sort. Since R terminates, eventually the resulting term will contain no operations in $\Sigma - (\Sigma\restriction_V \cup \Delta)$, which proves that $\mathcal{B}$ is productive for t.   □

The condition "$\Sigma - (\Sigma\restriction_V \cup \Delta)$ contains only operations of hidden result sort" in Theorem 3 is, unfortunately, necessary. Indeed, consider a stream BRS defining a stream a with rules $hd(a) \to vis(a)$ and $tl(a) \to a$, where $vis : Stream \to Bit$ is some artificially included operation of visible result in $\Sigma - (\Sigma\restriction_V \cup \Delta)$. This

BRS obviously terminates and is coinductive, but it is not productive because $hd(a)$ cannot be evaluated.

Fortunately, both this condition and the coinductivity of a BRS are trivial syntactic checks. The only non-trivial hypothesis of Theorem 3 is the termination, but since all that is required is standard termination of a TRS, this theorem allows for the use of off-the-shelf termination tools (e.,g., [12, 6]) for checking productivity of behavioral rewrite systems. Note that this would not be possible if we allowed rules of the form $zeros \to 0 : zeros$; the point here is that such non-terminating rules are unnecessary, because they can be replaced with their coinductive variants and then productivity can be checked using conventional termination techniques and tools.

Theorem 3 is reminiscent of a recent result by Zantema [29] which states that, for some restricted variants of stream rewrite systems, termination implies well-definedness; however, well-definedness of streams is formalized as a rather intricate, model-theoretical concept in [29], while our formalization is based on simple proof-theoretical/operational arguments.

Finally, Theorem 3 may find applications in deciding that certain classes of stream TRS-es are productive, provided that one can decide termination for the corresponding BRS-es; it would be interesting to see whether one can find this way an alternative proof for the decidability of productivity result by Endrullis et al. [10] for the particular class of stream constant specifications.

6 Behavioral Productivity Means Well-Specified Behavior

Behavioral productivity suggests, intuitively, well-specified behavior, that is, behavior which is not under-specified. However, it is not immediate what it means for a term to be well-specified in our general behavioral context. To avoid the complications and diversity that come with particular choices of models over behavioral signatures (see [19] for several of them), we prefer to take an operational, or proof-theoretical approach here: we say that a term t is well-specified iff it is indistinguishable by means of experiments (and rewriting) from a clone t' of it using cloned operations defined the same way as the original operations. This notion of behavioral well-specifiedness is somehow dual to constructor-based well-definedness. In this section we give an alternative but equivalent way to understand productivity by means of well-specified behavior.

Definition 5. *Given BRS $\mathcal{B}$, let $\mathcal{B} \Vdash t = t'$ denote the **behavioral join equivalence** of $\mathcal{B}$: for any experiment C there is some term u with $C[t] \to^* u \leftarrow^* C[t']$.*

Consider the stream term $zeros$ in Example 1. BRS STREAM behaviorally well-specifies $zeros$ because one can show that STREAM $\Vdash zeros = zeros'$ for any other stream $zeros'$ specified the same way as $zeros$ (i.e., STREAM includes $hd(zeros') \to 0$ and $tl(zeros') \to zeros'$). Similarly, STREAM well-specifies the stream operation odd in Example 1, because one can behaviorally prove STREAM $\Vdash (\forall S)\, odd(S) = odd'(S)$ for any operation odd' defined the same way as odd (i.e., $hd(odd'(S)) \to hd(S)$ and $tl(odd'(S)) \to odd'(tl^2(S))$). The CIRC tool [16] can prove these properties automatically by circular coinduction. However, **STREAM** does not well-specifies a constant stream a specified without any rule, because there is no way to show that $a = a'$ for another constant a'. Also, it does not well-specifies a constant stream a specified with rules $hd(a) \to 0$ and $tl(a) \to odd(a)$, since $hd(tl^2(a)) \to hd(tl(odd(a))) \to hd(odd(tl^2(a))) \to hd(tl^2(a)) \to \ldots$ and similarly for a clone a' of a, with no chance to show that $hd(tl^2(a)) = hd(tl^2(a'))$.

Interestingly and perhaps intriguingly at first, the *random* stream in Example 2 defined as $hd(random) \to 0$, $hd(random) \to 1$, and $tl(random) \to random$ is in fact well-specified. It is non-deterministic, but that is intended in its specification; its non-determinism is not a consequence of under- or lack of specification.

As it is usually the case with "equality" relations defined in terms of joint rewriting, one should be aware of the fact that non-confluent rewriting might lead to equalities which are not semantically valid. For example in our case here, since *random* can rewrite its bits to either 0 or 1, it is behaviorally join equivalent to any other stream, in particular to *zeros*. To avoid such phenomena, we advice the reader to only use the notion of behavioral join equivalence in combination with term cloning, which is described below.

Definition 6. *Given behavioral specification $\mathcal{B} = ((\Sigma, \Delta), R)$, let $\mathcal{B}'$ extend $\mathcal{B}$ by adding to Σ a copy σ' of each $\sigma \in \Sigma - (\Sigma\restriction_V \cup \Delta)$ and to R a copy $l' \to r'$ of each $l \to r \in R$, where l' (resp. r') is obtained by replacing each $\sigma \in \Sigma - (\Sigma\restriction_V \cup \Delta)$ in l (resp. r) with σ'. $\mathcal{B}$ (**behaviorally) well-specifies term t iff $\mathcal{B}' \Vdash t = t'$, where t' is obtained by replacing each $\sigma \in \Sigma - (\Sigma\restriction_V \cup \Delta)$ in t with σ'.*

Hence, $\mathcal{B}'$ "clones" each operation which is not a data operation or a derivative, as well as all the rules referring to those operations. Behavioral well-specifiedness of a term t states that t is behaviorally equivalent to its corresponding clone t', so from a behavioral point of view, t can have only one meaning.

Theorem 4. $\mathcal{B} = ((\Sigma, \Delta), R)$ *productive for t implies $\mathcal{B}$ well-defines t. Conversely, if the rules in R "do not introduce" operations in $\Sigma - (\Sigma\restriction_V \cup \Delta)$, that is, if for each $(l \to r) \in R$ it is the case that if l does not contain operations in $\Sigma - (\Sigma\restriction_V \cup \Delta)$ then r does not contain operations in $\Sigma - (\Sigma\restriction_V \cup \Delta)$ either, then $\mathcal{B}$ well-defines t implies $\mathcal{B}$ productive for t.*

Proof. Suppose that $\mathcal{B} = ((\Sigma, \Delta), R)$ is productive on term t and let $\mathcal{B}' = ((\Sigma', \Delta), R')$ and t' be the clone extension of $\mathcal{B}$ and the clone of t, respectively, as explained in Definition 6. Let C be a Δ-experiment for t. Since $\mathcal{B}$ is productive, there is some $(\Sigma\restriction_V \cup \Delta)$-term d such that $C[t] \xrightarrow{*}_R d$. We get $C[t'] \xrightarrow{*}_{R'} d$ using the copies of the rules used in the above reduction. Hence, $\mathcal{B} \vdash C[t] = C[t']$. Since the experiment C is arbitrary, $\mathcal{B}' \Vdash t = t'$.

Suppose now that $\mathcal{B}$ well-defines t and let $\mathcal{B}'$ and t' be the clone extension of $\mathcal{B}$ and the clone of t, respectively, as explained in Definition 6. Let C be a Δ-experiment for t. Since $\mathcal{B}$ well-defines t, there is some term u such that $C[t] \xrightarrow{*}_R u$ and $C[t'] \xrightarrow{*}_R u$. Since $C[t] \xrightarrow{*}_R u$ and the rules of R do not introduce operations in $\Sigma - (\Sigma\restriction_V \cup \Delta)$, it follows that u cannot contain any clone operation in $\Sigma' - (\Sigma\restriction_V \cup \Delta)$. For the same reason, since $C[t'] \xrightarrow{*}_R u$, it follows that u cannot contain any operation in $\Sigma - (\Sigma\restriction_V \cup \Delta)$. The only possibility is then that u is a $(\Sigma\restriction_V \cup \Delta)$-term, which proves that $\mathcal{B}$ is productive for t.   □

Note that all the productivities in Section 3 follow by Theorem 4.

7   Towards More Pragmatic Transformations

We have the following situation: on the one hand, term rewriting systems are more compact and elegant for specifying infinite data structures or systems; on the other hand, behavioral rewrite systems are more suitable for analyzing the behavioral well-definedness (which is implied by the behavioral productivity). The question is whether we can have the advantages of both approaches. We strongly believe that the answer is yes, provided that we are able to define appropriate mechanisms to safely translate from one approach to the other. In this section we discuss some initial steps towards such mechanisms.

The transformation $\mathcal{R} \mapsto \mathcal{B}_0(\mathcal{R})$ taking a stream-TRS into a BRS (see Definition 3) typically yields neither terminating nor coinductive BRS's , so it is not very practical. However, we have seen in Section 4 that there are non-productive stream-TRS's $\mathcal{R}$ for which we can find behavioral versions $\mathcal{B}(\mathcal{R})$ which are productive. So, we may aim at finding transformations $\mathcal{R} \mapsto \mathcal{B}(\mathcal{R})$ which avoid the accidental non-productivity. A partial positive answer is given by the algorithm described in [29, 28]. That algorithm works fine only on a particular subclass of stream-TRS's and associates a BRS $\mathcal{B}_1(\mathcal{R})$ with a stream-TRS $\mathcal{R}$ such that $\mathcal{R}$ is well-defined (has a unique model) if and only if $\mathcal{B}_1(\mathcal{R})$ is terminating. The conditions on $\mathcal{R}$ ensures the fact $\mathcal{B}_1(\mathcal{R})$ is coinductive and, by Theorem 3, we obtain that if $\mathcal{B}_1(\mathcal{R})$ is terminating then it is productive. We may further assume that we have a transformation $\mathcal{R}_1$ associating a stream-TRS $\mathcal{R}_1(\mathcal{B})$ with each coinductive and terminating stream-BRS $\mathcal{B}$ such that the productivity is preserved. Then the composition of the two transformations $\mathcal{R} \mapsto \mathcal{R}_1(\mathcal{B}_1((R)))$ may transform a non-productive stream-TRS into a productive one. For instance, if $\mathcal{R}_1(\mathcal{B})$ includes rules of the form $f(x : s) \to h : t$ with h and t $\mathcal{B}$-normal forms of $hd(f(x : s))$ and respectively $tl(f(x : s))$, then the stream-TRS considered in Section 4 is transformed in

$$zeros \to 0 : zeros \qquad f(x : s) \to 0 : zeros \qquad g(x : s) \to 0 : zeros$$

which is productive (the anomalies are away).

Not only the streams can be specified as TRS's with infinite rewriting. For instance, the infinite binary trees defined in Example 6 are specified by the following TRS:

$$ones \to 1/ones, ones\backslash$$
$$\neg B/T_1, T_2\backslash \to \overline{B}/\neg T_1, \neg T_2\backslash$$
$$B/T_1, T_2\backslash + B'/T_1'', T_2'\backslash \to B \oplus B'/T_1 + T_1', T_2 + T_2'\backslash$$
$$thue \to 0/thue, thue + ones\backslash$$

where $\_/\_, \_\backslash : Bit\ Tree\ Tree \to Tree$ is a constructor. Similarly, the two processes defined in Section 1 can be specified by the rewrite rules

$$a \to 0; b \quad b \to 1; a \quad s_{2i} \to 0; s_{2i+1} \quad s_{2i+1} \to 0; s_{2i+2}$$

where $\_; \_ : Int\ State \to State$ is a constructor.

The algorithm defining the transformation $\mathcal{B}_1$ can be adapted, e.g., for trees or for processes. Like for streams, only a subclass of tree-TRS's or process-TRS's can be transformed with such an algorithm; these subclasses can be defined by adapting the conditions from Definition 1 in [29]. Unfortunately, a transformation which can be applied in the general case may be hard or impossible to define. The main reason is given by the fact that it is hard or impossible to formally state at this level of generality what it means for a BRS to be a "correct behavioral version" of a given TRS.

We suggest the following methodology in order to have both the compactness and the elegance of the TRS definitional style, as well as the behavioral well-definedness/productivity for a given class of specifications:

1. formally define when a BRS is a correct behavioral version (e.g., specifies the same data structure or system) of a given TRS from your class;
2. define a transformation $\mathcal{B}$ which associate a BRS $\mathcal{B}(\mathcal{R})$ with a given TRS $\mathcal{R}$ from your class and prove that $\mathcal{B}(\mathcal{R})$ is a correct version of $\mathcal{R}$;
3. when checking if a given TRS $\mathcal{R}$ is behaviorally productive, show that $\mathcal{B}(\mathcal{R})$ is coinductive and terminating;
4. eventually, define a transformation $\mathcal{R}$ which associate a TRS with each coinductive and terminating TRS in order to have a way to transform non-productive TRS's into productive ones.

8   Behavioral Productivity Is a Π_2^0-Complete Problem

Behavioral equivalence is known to be a Π_2^0-complete problem, both for streams [20] and in general [3]. Also, a series of recent results show that many rewriting problems, including termination and stream productivity, are Π_2^0-complete [9, 7, 26, 11]. Here we show that the behavioral productivity problem is no exception.

Π_2^0 is the class, or degree, in the arithmetic hierarchy consisting of predicates $\pi(z)$ of the form $(\forall x)(\exists y)\ r(x, y, z)$, where r is a recursive (or decidable) predicate and x, y, z range over natural numbers (or, equivalently, over recursively enumerable domains). Π_2^0 contains predicates which are strictly harder than recursively enumerable or co-recursively enumerable. A canonical Π_2^0-complete problem is TOTALITY$(M) := (\forall x)(\exists n)\ \text{STOP}(x, n, M)$, asking whether computational device (Turing machine, program, rewrite system, etc.) M stops on all its inputs; here $\text{STOP}(x, n, M)$ is the recursive predicate saying that machine M stops in at most n steps on input x. The reader is referred to [23] for more details on the arithmetic hierarchy and the class Π_2^0.

To see why, for example, the terminating problem for a rewrite system is Π_2^0-complete [9, 26], consider TRS's computing r.e. functions (see, e.g., Section 3.2 in Terese book [27]) instead of Turing machines and interpret $\text{STOP}(x, n, M)$ by "the TRS M finds in at most n steps" all normal forms of the term x; then TOTALITY becomes exactly the terminating problem for TRS's .

Theorem 5. *The behavioral productivity problem is Π_2^0-complete.*

Proof. We first show the membership to the class Π_2^0. Let $\mathcal{B} = ((\Sigma, \Delta), R)$ be a BRS and let t be a hidden term. The predicate $\text{SEARCH}(t \overset{?}{\to} u, n, R)$, telling that there is a reduction $t \overset{*}{\to}_R u$ of length at most n, is recursive. The set of $(\Sigma|_V \cup \Delta)$-terms d is r.e. and therefore the predicate $(\exists d) C[t] \overset{*}{\to}_R d$ is equivalent to $(\exists \langle n, d \rangle) \text{SEARCH}(C[t] \overset{?}{\to} d, n, R)$. Then the productivity problem is equivalent to $(\forall C)(\exists \langle n, d \rangle) \text{SEARCH}(C[t] \overset{?}{\to} d, n, R)$.

The Π_2^0-hardness of the behavioral productivity problem over behavioral rewrite systems is proved using the reduction given by the transformation $\mathcal{R} \mapsto \mathcal{B}_0(\mathcal{R})$, defined over stream-TRS's in Section 4: The productivity problem for stream-TRS's is Π_2^0-hard [9] and this problem is reduced to the productivity problem for the stream behavioral specifications by Theorem 1. We can now conclude with the main result. □

9   Conclusion

This paper investigates the role of term rewriting in behavioral reasoning. The notion of term rewriting system is extended to that of behavioral rewrite system, and a proper notion of productivity, called behavioral productivity, is given for the new systems. Various aspects of the new notion are largely exemplified on streams, infinite binary trees and processes. It is shown that behavioral productivity plays a similar role for coinductive specifications to that played by sufficient completeness for inductive specifications. Behavioral productivity generalizes the existing notion of productivity defined over stream rewriting systems. Two main properties of the proposed behavioral approach are proved (under mild conditions): termination yields behavioral productivity, and behavioral productivity is equivalent to behavioral well-specification. The former property allows us to use the existing tools for rewrite termination [12, 6] for checking behavioral productivity. It was also shown that behavioral productivity has the same complexity as many other rewriting-related problems, namely it is Π_2^0-complete.

Even if behavioral productivity is defined for behavioral rewrite systems, it can be extended to term rewrite systems by means of algorithms similar to that described in [29], which associate behavioral versions to term rewrite systems. Finding such algorithms for more general cases than that of streams is one of the future work directions.

Productivity was defined for the first time for streams [5]. Then it was extended for infinite data structures used in functional programming [24]. See, e.g., [8] for a review of the main approaches dealing with productivity. Recently, productivity was intensively studied in the context of term rewriting systems [10, 26]. Behavioral specifications were first introduced in [18]. Then behavioral reasoning was intensively studied in different algebraic/logic frameworks [13, 2, 4, 19, 17, 14]. The behavioral rewrite systems introduced in this paper are an instance of the parametric definition given in [22].

Acknowledgment. The work presented in this paper was supported by the Romanian Contract 161/15.06.2010, SMISCSNR 602-12516 (DAK), and by the USA grants NSF CCF-1218605, NSA H98230-10-C-0294, DARPA HACMS (SRI subcontract) 19-000222, and Rockwell Collins 4504813093.

References

1. Bidoit, M., Hennicker, R.: Observer complete definitions are behaviourally coherent. In: OBJ/CAFEOBJ/MAUDE AT FORMAL METHODS 1999, pp. 83–94. THETA (1999)
2. Bidoit, M., Hennicker, R., Kurz, A.: Observational logic, constructor-based logic, and their duality. Theoretical Computer Science 3(298), 471–510 (2003)
3. Buss, S., Roşu, G.: Incompleteness of behavioral logics. In: Proceeding of CMCS 2000. ENTCS, vol. 33, pp. 61–79. Elsevier (2000)
4. Diaconescu, R., Futatsugi, K.: CafeOBJ Report. AMAST Series in Computing, vol. 6. World Scientific (1998)
5. Dijkstra, E.W.: On the productivity of recursive definitions. EWD749 (September 1980)
6. Durán, F., Lucas, S., Meseguer, J.: Mtt: The maude termination tool (system description). In: Armando, A., Baumgartner, P., Dowek, G. (eds.) IJCAR 2008. LNCS (LNAI), vol. 5195, pp. 313–319. Springer, Heidelberg (2008)
7. Endrullis, J., Geuvers, J., Zantema, H.: Degrees of undecidability in term rewriting. In: Grädel, E., Kahle, R. (eds.) CSL 2009. LNCS, vol. 5771, pp. 255–270. Springer, Heidelberg (2009)
8. Endrullis, J., Grabmayer, C., Hendriks, D.: Data-oblivious stream productivity. In: Cervesato, I., Veith, H., Voronkov, A. (eds.) LPAR 2008. LNCS (LNAI), vol. 5330, pp. 79–96. Springer, Heidelberg (2008)
9. Endrullis, J., Grabmayer, C., Hendriks, D.: Complexity of fractran and productivity. In: Schmidt, R.A. (ed.) CADE 2009. LNCS (LNAI), vol. 5663, pp. 371–387. Springer, Heidelberg (2009)
10. Endrullis, J., Grabmayer, C., Hendriks, D., Isihara, A., Klop, J.W.: Productivity of stream definitions. Theor. Comput. Sci. 411(4-5), 765–782 (2010)
11. Endrullis, J., Hendriks, D., Bakhshi, R.: On the Complexity of Equivalence of Specifications of Infinite Objects. In: Proc. ACM SIGPLAN Int. Conf. on Functional Programming (ICFP 2013), pp. 153–164. ACM (2012)
12. Giesl, J., Thiemann, R., Schneider-Kamp, P., Falke, S.: Automated Termination Proofs with AProVE. In: van Oostrom, V. (ed.) RTA 2004. LNCS, vol. 3091, pp. 210–220. Springer, Heidelberg (2004)
13. Goguen, J.A., Diaconescu, R.: Towards an algebraic semantics for the object paradigm. In: Ehrig, H., Orejas, F. (eds.) Abstract Data Types 1992 and COMPASS 1992. LNCS, vol. 785, pp. 1–29. Springer, Heidelberg (1994)
14. Hausmann, D., Mossakowski, T., Schröder, L.: Iterative Circular Coinduction for CoCASL in Isabelle/HOL. In: Cerioli, M. (ed.) FASE 2005. LNCS, vol. 3442, pp. 341–356. Springer, Heidelberg (2005)
15. Kapur, D., Narendran, P., Rosenkrantz, D.J., Zhang, H.: Sufficient-completeness, ground-reducibility and their complexity. Acta Inf. 28(4), 311–350 (1991)
16. Lucanu, D., Goriac, E.-I., Caltais, G., Roşu, G.: CIRC: A behavioral verification tool based on circular coinduction. In: Kurz, A., Lenisa, M., Tarlecki, A. (eds.) CALCO 2009. LNCS, vol. 5728, pp. 433–442. Springer, Heidelberg (2009)

17. Mossakowski, T., Schröder, L., Roggenbach, M., Reichel, H.: Algebraic-coalgebraic specification in CoCASL. J. Log. Alg. Program. 67(1-2), 146–197 (2006)
18. Reichel, H.: Behavioural equivalence – a unifying concept for initial and final specifications. In: The 3rd Hungarian Comp. Sci. Conference, Akademiai Kiado (1981)
19. Roşu, G.: Hidden Logic. PhD thesis, University of California at San Diego (2000)
20. Roşu, G.: Equality of streams is a Π_2^0-complete problem. In: Proceedgins of ICFP 2006, pp. 184–191. ACM (2006)
21. Roşu, G., Goguen, J.: Hidden congruent deduction. In: Caferra, R., Salzer, G. (eds.) FTP 1998. LNCS (LNAI), vol. 1761, pp. 251–266. Springer, Heidelberg (2000)
22. Roşu, G., Lucanu, D.: Circular Coinduction – A Proof Theoretical Foundation. In: Kurz, A., Lenisa, M., Tarlecki, A. (eds.) CALCO 2009. LNCS, vol. 5728, pp. 127–144. Springer, Heidelberg (2009)
23. Rogers, H.: Theory of Recursive Functions and Effective Computability. Paperback edn. The MIT Press (1987)
24. Sijtsma, B.A.: On the productivity of recursive list definitions. ACM Trans. Program. Lang. Syst. 11(4), 633–649 (1989)
25. Silva, A., Rutten, J.: Behavioural differential equations and coinduction for binary trees. In: Leivant, D., de Queiroz, R. (eds.) WoLLIC 2007. LNCS, vol. 4576, pp. 322–336. Springer, Heidelberg (2007)
26. Simonsen, J.G.: The Π_2^0-completeness of most of the properties of rewriting systems you care about (and productivity). In: Treinen, R. (ed.) RTA 2009. LNCS, vol. 5595, pp. 335–349. Springer, Heidelberg (2009)
27. Terese: Term Rewriting Systems. Cambridge Tracts in Theoretical Computer Science, vol. 55. Cambridge University Press (2003)
28. Zantema, H.: A tool proving well-definedness of streams using termination tools. In: Kurz, A., Lenisa, M., Tarlecki, A. (eds.) CALCO 2009. LNCS, vol. 5728, pp. 449–456. Springer, Heidelberg (2009)
29. Zantema, H.: Well-definedness of streams by termination. In: Treinen, R. (ed.) RTA 2009. LNCS, vol. 5595, pp. 164–178. Springer, Heidelberg (2009)

Functional Logic Programming in Maude*

Santiago Escobar

DSIC-ELP, Universitat Politècnica de València, Spain
sescobar@dsic.upv.es

Abstract. Functional logic programming languages combine the most important features of functional programming languages and logic programming languages. Functional logic programming applied to the Maude specification language would replace the functional viewpoint by an equational viewpoint while retaining the logic features. This paper tries to bridge the gap between functional logic languages and the current implementation of narrowing as symbolic reachability in Maude. It illustrates how many features available in modern functional logic languages are easily definable and simulated in Maude but also shows how Maude goes beyond standard practices in the functional logic area by using, e.g. equational properties such as associativity and commutativity or order-sorted information. As a practical application we use the *Missionaries and Cannibals* equational logic program given by Goguen and Meseguer for Eqlog in the eighties.

1 Introduction

Functional logic programming languages combine the most important features of functional programming languages such as Haskell and logic programming languages such as Prolog. From the functional paradigm they borrow algebraic data types, advanced typing, evaluation strategies, and higher-order functions among other features; and from the logic paradigm they borrow logical variables, computing with partial information, constraint solving, and nondeterministic search for solutions among other features. Functional logic programming in the Maude specification language combines logical variables, computing with partial information, and constraint solving with reasoning modulo equational properties, advanced data types, order-sorted typing, efficient equational evaluation, distinction between concurrent and functional parts, and parameterised modules.

The Eqlog programming language [22] developed by Goguen and Meseguer in the eighties was a first attempt to combine both equational programming with logic programming. Eqlog unified equational programming and Horn-logic programming into one paradigm. Its logic design task was to embed order-sorted equational logic and Horn logic without equality into a suitable Horn logic with equality [23]. During the eighties, also the japanese *Fifth Generation Computer System* project started and it is claimed that failed because of the choice of

---

* This paper has been partially supported by the EU (FEDER) and the Spanish MEC/MICINN under grant TIN 2010-21062-C02-02, and by Generalitat Valenciana PROMETEO2011/052.

S. Iida, J. Meseguer, and K. Ogata (Eds.): Futatsugi Festschrift, LNCS 8373, pp. 315–336, 2014.

concurrent constraint logic programming as the bridge between the parallel computer and the programming language, but probably it failed because most of the appropriate technology was missing. Many researchers in the functional logic programming area (see [39,21,11,33,24]) have tried, since the eighties, to combine the best features of both paradigms into a concurrent constraint functional logic programming paradigm and many possibilities have been explored (see [24,25] for a survey). Nowadays there is a remarkable body of programming languages and tools in the functional logic area. Maude with logic features may easily be an excellent choice in the near future for an effective and efficient concurrent constraint functional logic programming language, in the spirit of the original japanese *Fifth Generation Computer System* project.

Modern concurrent constraint functional logic programming languages, such as Curry [26], combine different features of both functional and logic paradigms using an evaluation mechanism called narrowing. *Narrowing* is a generalization of term rewriting that allows free variables in terms (as in logic programming) and replaces pattern matching by unification in order to (non-deterministically) reduce these terms. Narrowing was originally introduced for automated theorem proving [41], then used as a mechanism for solving equational unification problems [20], it became the "de facto" evaluation mechanism for functional logic programming languages [5], and it was generalized from equational unification problems to solve the more general problem of symbolic reachability [35]. The narrowing mechanism has a number of important applications including automated proofs of termination [7], execution of functional-logic programming languages [6], program transformation [1], verification of cryptographic protocols [35], and equational unification [28], to mention just a few.

An essential aspect in concurrent constraint functional logic programming is the choice of an effective and efficient narrowing evaluation strategy. Several approaches have been defined in the literature [5,2,4,15,16,18,12]. The *needed narrowing* strategy [5] and the *parallel needed narrowing* strategy [4], both extended with the *residuation* principle, are applicable to left-linear constructor rewrite systems and are lazy (or demand-driven), obtaining interesting properties and performance. The *natural narrowing* strategy [15,16] is applicable to left-linear constructor rewrite systems too, and is extended to rewrite systems in general [18]. It is also demand-driven with similar interesting properties and performance. The development of narrowing in Maude as symbolic reachability [9,12] is applicable to any unconditional rewrite theory without memberships (up to some extra conditions [35,9,12]). This version of narrowing in Maude is not demand-driven and it is still an open problem to develop demand-driven narrowing evaluation strategies dealing with equational properties such as associativity and commutativity.

This paper tries to bridge the gap between functional logic languages such as Curry and the current implementation of narrowing as symbolic reachability in Maude. It illustrates how many features available in modern functional logic languages are easily definable and simulated in Maude; we consider: (i) a semantics of values, (ii) a call-time choice semantics, (iii) conditional rules,

(iv) strict equality, (v) extra variables, (vi) constraint solving, and (vii) residuation. Many other features of functional logic languages are not considered in this paper because of lack of space. However, this paper shows how Maude goes beyond standard practices in the functional logic area by using features not available to functional logic languages, e.g. reasoning modulo and an order-sorted setting.

As a motivating example for the reader, in Section 2 we present how the *Missionaries and Cannibals* equational logic program of [22] can be written using the narrowing features available nowadays in Maude. This is an example requiring some constraint solving features, logical variables, order-sorted types, and associativity–commutativity–identity, thus it cannot be specified in current functional logic languages. In Section 3 we introduce some basic concepts on rewriting logic. In Section 4 we recall the narrowing mechanism and how it is made available in Maude. In Section 5 we present how features available in Curry are easily definable and simulated in Maude and demonstrate in Section 6 how queries on the motivating example are executed. Finally, we conclude in Section 7.

2   Example: Missionaries and Cannibals

As a motivating example for the reader, we present how the *Missionaries and Cannibals* equational logic program of [22] can be written using the narrowing features currently available in Maude. The equational logic program[1] of [22] used a syntax proposed for Eqlog where a functional syntax very close to Maude was combined with some syntax for Horn-clauses using symbol ":-".

```
module MAC[T :: MACTH] using NAT, TRIPLIST = LIST[trip] is
  preds
    boatok : trip
    solve, good : triplist
  fns
    boat : pred -> trip
    lb,rb : triplist -> pset
    mset,cset : pset -> pset
  vars
    PS:pset, L:triplist, P:person, T:trip
  axioms
    boatok(boat(PS)) :- # PS = 1.
    boatok(boat(PS)) :- # PS = 2.
    mset(PS) = PS /\ m0.
    cset(PS) = PS /\ c0.
    lb(nil) = m0 + c0.
    rb(nil) = empty.
    lb(L * boat(PS)) = lb(L) - PS :- even # L.
    rb(L * boat(PS)) = rb(L) + PS :- even # L.
    rb(L * boat(PS)) = rbQ - PS :- odd # L.
    lb(L * boat(PS)) = lb(L) + PS :- odd # L.
    good(L * T) :- # cset(lb(L * T)) =< # mset(lb(L * T)) or mset(lb(L * T)) = 0,
                   # cset(rb(L * T)) =< # mset(rb(L * T)) or mset(rb(L * T)) = 0,
```

---

[1] The original program in [22] had an error because the number of cannibals has to be lower than or equal to the number of missionaries in both sides unless there is no missionary. We discovered this error thanks to the new narrowing-based executability in Maude.

```
                    good(L), boatok(T).
    good(nil).
    solve(L) :- good(L), lb(L) = empty.
endmod MAC
```

This module is parametric on a theory T :: MATCH for the names of the mission-aries and cannibals, which are instantiated to m0 = taylor, helen, william and c0 = umugu, nzwave, amoc. Also a module for lists is imported[2], where _*_ is the constructor symbol for lists and #_ is the length operation for lists. The system is configured as a list of trips (sort triplist) where each trip is a term rooted by a predicate boat with a set of names of missionaries and can-nibals. Each trip in the list is considered good if it satisfies some properties. Odd positions in the list represent moving from left to right and even positions from right to left. There are some extra symbols for set manipulation: _+_ for union, _-_ for removal, and _/_ for intersection; indeed (multi-)sets are the only data structure in this example with extra equational properties, namely associativity, commutativity and identity for the multiset. There are also some symbols for lists: even indicates whether a list has an even number of elements and odd indicates whether a list has an odd number of elements. Finally, the predicate boatok checks whether a trip is ok and solve is the general predicate for checking/generating the triplist solution.

This is an example requiring some constraint solving features, logical variables, order-sorted types, and associativity, commutativity, and an identity symbol for multisets. For instance, it requires constraint solving features because of the numerical conditions for length of lists in the conditions of predicate good; this would be solved by using a generator function and using these length functions by residuation. Also, the program considers equational properties, since the problem is represented by a list of trips and each element is the boat with a multiset of missionaries and cannibals; this would be easily handled by narrowing modulo these properties. And it clearly includes order-sorted information in the sense of having people which are specialized into missionaries and cannibals. Also, note that some functional logic features described in Section 5 are necessary here; for instance, this example considers a semantics of values instead of all reachable terms, predicates are just conditional rules evaluated into a special sort different from Bool that only contains positive (or successful) cases, and conditions in conditional rules are indeed strict equalities instead of syntactic equality.

3   Background on Rewriting Logic and Term Rewriting

We follow the classical notation and terminology from [42] for term rewriting, and from [32] for rewriting logic and order-sorted notions. We assume an order-sorted signature $\Sigma = (S, \leq, \Sigma)$ with poset of sorts $(S, \leq)$ and such that for each sort $s \in S$ the connected component of s in $(S, \leq)$ has a top sort, denoted $[s]$, and all $f : s_1 \cdots s_n \to s$ with $n \geq 1$ have a top sort overloading $f : [s_1] \cdots [s_n] \to [s]$.

---

[2] The original program assumes lists are created using an associative symbol but unification modulo associativity is infinitary and it is not available in Maude.

We also assume an S-sorted family $\mathcal{X} = \{\mathcal{X}_s\}_{s \in S}$ of disjoint variable sets with each $\mathcal{X}_s$ countably infinite. $\mathcal{T}_{\Sigma}(\mathcal{X})_s$ is the set of terms of sort s, and $\mathcal{T}_{\Sigma,s}$ is the set of ground terms of sort s. We write $\mathcal{T}_{\Sigma}(\mathcal{X})$ and $\mathcal{T}_{\Sigma}$ for the corresponding order-sorted term algebras. For a term t, $Var(t)$ denotes the set of all variables in t.

Positions are represented by sequences of natural numbers denoting an access path in the term when viewed as a tree. The top or root position is denoted by the empty sequence Λ. We define the relation $p \leq q$ between positions as $p \leq p$ for any p; and $p \leq p.q$ for any p and q. Given $U \subseteq \Sigma \cup \mathcal{X}$, $Pos_U(t)$ denotes the set of positions of a term t that are rooted by symbols or variables in U. The set of positions of a term t is written $Pos(t)$, and the set of non-variable positions $Pos_{\Sigma}(t)$. The subterm of t at position p is $t|_p$ and $t[u]_p$ is the term t where $t|_p$ is replaced by u.

A *substitution* $\sigma \in Subst(\Sigma, \mathcal{X})$ is a sorted mapping from a finite subset of $\mathcal{X}$ to $\mathcal{T}_{\Sigma}(\mathcal{X})$. Substitutions are written as $\sigma = \{X_1 \mapsto t_1, \ldots, X_n \mapsto t_n\}$ where the domain of σ is $Dom(\sigma) = \{X_1, \ldots, X_n\}$ and the set of variables introduced by terms $t_1, \ldots, t_n$ is written $Ran(\sigma)$. The identity substitution is id. Substitutions are homomorphically extended to $\mathcal{T}_{\Sigma}(\mathcal{X})$. The application of a substitution σ to a term t is denoted by $t\sigma$. For simplicity, we assume that every substitution is idempotent, i.e., σ satisfies $Dom(\sigma) \cap Ran(\sigma) = \emptyset$. Substitution idempotency ensures $t\sigma = (t\sigma)\sigma$. The restriction of σ to a set of variables V is $\sigma|_V$; sometimes we write $\sigma|_{t_1,\ldots,t_n}$ to denote $\sigma|_V$ where $V = Var(t_1) \cup \cdots \cup Var(t_n)$. Composition of two substitutions σ and σ' is denoted by $\sigma\sigma'$.

A Σ-*equation* is an unoriented pair $t = t'$, where $t, t' \in \mathcal{T}_{\Sigma}(\mathcal{X})_s$ for some sort $s \in S$. Given an order-sorted signature Σ and a set $\mathcal{E}$ of Σ-equations, order-sorted equational logic induces a congruence relation $=_{\mathcal{E}}$ on terms $t, t' \in \mathcal{T}_{\Sigma}(\mathcal{X})$ (see [34]). The $\mathcal{E}$-equivalence class of a term t is denoted by $[t]_{\mathcal{E}}$ and $\mathcal{T}_{\Sigma/\mathcal{E}}(\mathcal{X})$ and $\mathcal{T}_{\Sigma/\mathcal{E}}$ denote the corresponding order-sorted term algebras modulo $\mathcal{E}$. Throughout this paper we assume that $\mathcal{T}_{\Sigma,s} \neq \emptyset$ for every sort s, because this affords a simpler deduction system.

An *equational theory* $(\Sigma, \mathcal{E})$ is a pair with Σ an order-sorted signature and $\mathcal{E}$ a set of Σ-equations. The $\mathcal{E}$-*subsumption* preorder $\sqsupseteq_{\mathcal{E}}$ (or just $\sqsupseteq$ if $\mathcal{E}$ is understood) holds between $t, t' \in \mathcal{T}_{\Sigma}(\mathcal{X})$, denoted $t \sqsupseteq_{\mathcal{E}} t'$ (meaning that t is *more general* than t' modulo $\mathcal{E}$), if there is a substitution σ such that $t\sigma =_{\mathcal{E}} t'$; such a substitution σ is said to be an $\mathcal{E}$-*match* from t to t'.

An $\mathcal{E}$-*unifier* for a Σ-equation $t = t'$ is a substitution σ such that $t\sigma =_{\mathcal{E}} t'\sigma$. For $Var(t) \cup Var(t') \subseteq W$, a set of substitutions $CSU_{\mathcal{E}}^W(t = t')$ is said to be a *complete* set of unifiers for the equality $t = t'$ modulo $\mathcal{E}$ away from W iff: (i) each $\sigma \in CSU_{\mathcal{E}}^W(t = t')$ is an $\mathcal{E}$-unifier of $t = t'$; (ii) for any $\mathcal{E}$-unifier ρ of $t = t'$ there is a $\sigma \in CSU_{\mathcal{E}}^W(t = t')$ such that $\sigma|_W \sqsupseteq_{\mathcal{E}} \rho|_W$; (iii) for all $\sigma \in CSU_{\mathcal{E}}^W(t = t')$, $Dom(\sigma) \subseteq (Var(t) \cup Var(t'))$ and $Ran(\sigma) \cap W = \emptyset$. If the set of variables W is irrelevant or is understood from the context, we write $CSU_{\mathcal{E}}(t = t')$ instead of $CSU_{\mathcal{E}}^W(t = t')$. An $\mathcal{E}$-unification algorithm is *complete* if for any equation $t = t'$ it generates a complete set of $\mathcal{E}$-unifiers. A unification algorithm is said to be *finitary* and complete if it always terminates after generating a finite and complete set of solutions.

A *rewrite rule* is an oriented pair $l \rightarrow r$, where[3] $l \notin \mathcal{X}$ and $l, r \in \mathcal{T}_\Sigma(\mathcal{X})_s$ for some sort $s \in S$. An *(unconditional) order-sorted rewrite theory* is a triple $(\Sigma, \mathcal{E}, R)$ with Σ an order-sorted signature, $\mathcal{E}$ a set of Σ-equations, and R a set of rewrite rules.

The rewriting relation on $\mathcal{T}_\Sigma(\mathcal{X})$, written $t \rightarrow_R t'$ or $t \rightarrow_{p,R} t'$ holds between t and t' iff there exist $p \in Pos_\Sigma(t)$, $l \rightarrow r \in R$ and a substitution σ, such that $t|_p = l\sigma$, and $t' = t[r\sigma]_p$. The relation $\rightarrow_{R/\mathcal{E}}$ on $\mathcal{T}_\Sigma(\mathcal{X})$ is $=_\mathcal{E}; \rightarrow_R; =_\mathcal{E}$, i.e., $t \rightarrow_{R/\mathcal{E}} t'$ iff there exists u, u' s.t. $t =_\mathcal{E} u \rightarrow_R u' =_\mathcal{E} t'$. Note that $\rightarrow_{R/\mathcal{E}}$ on $\mathcal{T}_\Sigma(\mathcal{X})$ induces a relation $\rightarrow_{R/\mathcal{E}}$ on the free $(\Sigma, \mathcal{E})$-algebra $\mathcal{T}_{\Sigma/\mathcal{E}}(\mathcal{X})$ by $[t]_\mathcal{E} \rightarrow_{R/\mathcal{E}} [t']_\mathcal{E}$ iff $t \rightarrow_{R/\mathcal{E}} t'$. The transitive (resp. transitive and reflexive) closure of $\rightarrow_{R/\mathcal{E}}$ is denoted $\rightarrow^+_{R/\mathcal{E}}$ (resp. $\rightarrow^*_{R/\mathcal{E}}$).

The application of one $\rightarrow_{R/\mathcal{E}}$ step is undecidable in general since $\mathcal{E}$-congruence classes can be arbitrarily large. Therefore, $R/\mathcal{E}$-rewriting is usually implemented [29] by $R,\mathcal{E}$-rewriting. A relation $\rightarrow_{R,\mathcal{E}}$ on $\mathcal{T}_\Sigma(\mathcal{X})$ is defined as: $t \rightarrow_{p,R,\mathcal{E}} t'$ (or just $t \rightarrow_{R,\mathcal{E}} t'$) iff there exist $p \in Pos_\Sigma(t)$, a rule $l \rightarrow r$ in R, and a substitution σ such that $t|_p =_\mathcal{E} l\sigma$ and $t' = t[r\sigma]_p$.

We assume that the relation $\rightarrow_{R,\mathcal{E}}$ is local $\mathcal{E}$-*coherent* [29], i.e., $\forall t_1, t_2, t_3$ we have $t_1 \rightarrow_{R,\mathcal{E}} t_2$ and $t_1 =_\mathcal{E} t_3$ implies $\exists t_4, t_5$ such that $t_2 \rightarrow^*_{R,\mathcal{E}} t_4$, $t_3 \rightarrow^+_{R,\mathcal{E}} t_5$, and $t_4 =_\mathcal{E} t_5$. Let us recall how coherence works at least for the common associative-commutative (AC) case. The best way to illustrate it is by its *absence*. Consider a symbol $\_+\_$ declared as AC. Now consider the rule $b + b \rightarrow c$, where b and c are constants. This rule, if not completed by another, is *not* coherent modulo AC. What this means is that there will be term *contexts* in which the rule *should* be applied, but it cannot be applied. Consider, for example, the term $b + (a + b)$, where a is also a constant. Intuitively, we should be able to apply to it the above rule to simplify it to the term $a + c$ in one step. However, since we are using the weaker rewrite relation $\rightarrow_{R,AC}$ instead of the stronger but much harder to implement relation $\rightarrow_{R/AC}$, we cannot! The problem is that the rule cannot be applied (even if we match modulo AC) to either the top term $b + (a + b)$ or the subterm $a + b$. We can however make our rule *coherent* modulo AC by adding the extra rule $b + b + Y \rightarrow c + Y$. This extended version of our rule will now apply to the term $b + (a + b)$, giving the simplification $b + (a + b) \longrightarrow_{R,AC} a + c$. Technically, what coherence means is that the weaker relation $\rightarrow_{R,\mathcal{E}}$ becomes semantically equivalent to the stronger relation $\rightarrow_{R/\mathcal{E}}$.

Coherence can be handled implicitly or explicitly, i.e., either the matching mechanism is modified to take care of this issue or the rules are explicitly extended, which is the option shown above; see [43] for a comparison between

---

[3] Note that we do not impose here the standard condition $Var(r) \subseteq Var(l)$, necessary for executability of rewriting in practice. Rewriting with extra variables in right-hand sides is handled at a theoretical level by allowing the matching substitution to instantiate these extra variables in any possible way. Extra variables do no pose any problem to narrowing and are part of the nondeterministic search of solutions typical of logic programming.

implicit and explicit extensions. For rewriting, implicit extensions are sufficient in many cases, as the implicit $\mathcal{E}$-coherence completion provided by the Maude tool [10] for any combination of associativity (A), commutativity (C), and identity (U) axioms. For narrowing, implicit extension is more complicated and it is sufficient to consider explicit single-variable extensions in common cases such as combinations of C, AC, and ACU axioms, i.e., given a rule $s \rightarrow t$ one considers $s + x \rightarrow t + x$ where x is a new variable. The method is as follows for AC. For any symbol f which is AC, and for any rule of the form $f(u, v) \rightarrow w$ in $\mathcal{E}$, we add also the equation $f(f(u, v), X) \rightarrow f(w, X)$, where X is a new variable not appearing in u, v, w. In an order-sorted setting, we should give to X *the biggest sort possible*, so that it will apply in all generality. As an additional optimization, note that some rules may already be coherent modulo AC, so that we need not add the extra equation. See [13] for further information.

We also assume that the equational theory is split into $\mathcal{E} = E \cup Ax$ such that E is a set of equations oriented into rules and Ax is a set of equational axioms satisfying:

1. Ax is *regular*, i.e., for each $t = t'$ in Ax, we have $Var(t) = Var(t')$, and *sort-preserving*, i.e., for each substitution σ, we have $t\sigma \in \mathcal{T}_\Sigma(\mathcal{X})_\mathsf{s}$ iff $t'\sigma \in \mathcal{T}_\Sigma(\mathcal{X})_\mathsf{s}$; furthermore, for each equation $t = t'$ in Ax, all variables in $Var(t)$ have a top sort.
2. Ax has a finitary and complete unification algorithm, which implies that Ax-matching is finitary and complete.
3. For each $t \rightarrow t'$ in E we have $Var(t') \subseteq Var(t)$.
4. E is *sort-decreasing*, i.e., for each $t \rightarrow t'$ in E, each $\mathsf{s} \in \mathsf{S}$, and each substitution σ, $t'\sigma \in \mathcal{T}_\Sigma(\mathcal{X})_\mathsf{s}$ implies $t\sigma \in \mathcal{T}_\Sigma(\mathcal{X})_\mathsf{s}$.
5. The relation $\rightarrow_{E,Ax}$ is confluent, terminating, and local Ax-*coherent*, i.e., for each term t, the relation terminates and produces a unique irreducible term (up to Ax-equivalence) denoted by $t\downarrow_{E,Ax}$.

Given an order-sorted equational theory $(\Sigma, E \cup Ax)$, (t', θ) is an E, Ax-*variant* [19] (or just a variant) of term t if $t\theta\downarrow_{E,Ax} =_{Ax} t'$ and $\theta\downarrow_{E,Ax} =_{Ax} \theta$. An order-sorted equational theory $(\Sigma, E \cup Ax)$ has the *finite variant property* [19] iff for each Σ-term t, a complete set of its most general variants is finite. A finitary and complete unification algorithm is defined for order-sorted equational theories with the finite variant property [19].

4   Narrowing in Maude

Logic programming languages are well suited for goal solving. Functional programming languages are equipped with equational definition of operations. Several approaches have been considered in the literature for combining the funcional and logic paradigms, see [24]. On the one hand, it is a natural idea to add an equality predicate to logic programs, leading to equational logic programming [27]. On the other hand, it is also a natural idea to add logical variables to functional programs, leading to narrowing-based equational reasoning [20].

Logic variables are also valuable at the level of model checking rather than functional programming, as proposed for symbolic reachability in [35] and extended to *logical* model checking in [17,8].

At each rewriting step one must choose which subterm of the subject term and which rule of the specification are going to be considered. Similarly, at each narrowing step one must choose which subterm of the subject term, which rule of the specification, and which instantiation[4] on the variables of the subject term and the rule's left-hand side are going to be considered. The difference between a rewriting step and a narrowing step is that in both cases we use a rewrite rule $l \to r$ to rewrite t at a position p in t, but narrowing unifies the left-hand side l and the chosen subject term $t|_p$ before actually performing the rewriting step. Narrowing is restricted[5] to non-variable positions of t, whereas rewriting does not require such a restriction.

Let $\mathcal{R} = (\Sigma, E \cup Ax, R)$ be an order-sorted rewrite theory where R is a set of unconditional rewrite rules, specified with the `rl` keyword, E is a set of unconditional equations specified with the `eq` and `variant` keywords, and Ax is a set of commonly occurring axioms —declared in Maude as equational attributes— such that an $E \cup Ax$-unification procedure is available in Maude. Unification algorithms already available in Maude are divided in two groups: (i) Ax-unification for order-sorted signatures with any combination of free, C, AC, or ACU function symbols [9], and (ii) $E \cup Ax$-unification for order-sorted equational theories with the finite variant property [12].

Let $CSU_{E \cup Ax}(u = u')$ provide[6] a finitary and complete set of unifiers for any pair of terms u, u' with the same top sort. The $R,(E \cup Ax)$-*narrowing* relation on $\mathcal{T}_\Sigma(\mathcal{X})$ is defined as $t \leadsto_{\sigma,p,R,E \cup Ax} t'$ (or $\leadsto_\sigma$ when p, R, E, Ax are understood) if there is a non-variable position $p \in Pos_\Sigma(t)$, a (possibly renamed) rule $l \to r$ in R, and a unifier $\sigma \in CSU_{E \cup Ax}(t|_p = l)$ such that $t' = (t[r]_p)\sigma$. We denote by $t \leadsto^+_{\sigma,R,E \cup Ax} t'$ (resp. $t \leadsto^*_{\sigma,R,E \cup Ax} t'$) the transitive (resp. reflexive-transitive) closure of the narrowing relation, where σ is obtained as the composition of the substitutions for each narrowing step in the sequence.

Consider the following system module defining the addition function `_+_` on natural numbers built from 0 and `s`:

```
mod NAT-NARROWING is
  sort Nat .
  op 0 : -> Nat [ctor] .
```

---

[4] Demand-driven narrowing strategies may require instantiations of a term that do not correspond to a most general unifier of a subterm and a left-hand side of a rule, see [5,2].

[5] The *paramodulation* inference rule used in paramodulation-based theorem proving [37] is similar to narrowing and does not require non-variable positions.

[6] In the present implementation of Maude, we are not interested in a minimal set of unifiers, but only in a finite and complete set. Minimality is easily achieved in syntactic unification (see [31]) but it is very costly in Ax-unification or $E \cup Ax$-unification, e.g., the ACU-unification available in Maude does not always provide a minimal set of unifiers.

```
op s : Nat -> Nat [ctor] .
op _+_ : Nat Nat -> Nat .
vars X Y : Nat .
rl [base] : 0 + Y => Y .
rl [ind] : s(X) + Y => s(X + Y) .
endm
```

Consider the term X + s(0) and the two rules base and ind. Narrowing will instantiate variable X with 0 and s(X') respectively in order to be able to apply each of these rules, i.e., the following two narrowing steps are generated:

$$X + s(0) \rightsquigarrow_{\{X \mapsto 0\}, \text{base}} s(0)$$

$$X + s(0) \rightsquigarrow_{\{X \mapsto s(\#1:\text{Nat})\}, \text{ind}} s(\#1:\text{Nat} + s(0))$$

Note that, for simplicity, we show only the bindings of the unifier that affect the input term. There are infinitely many narrowing derivations starting at the input expression X + s(0) (at each step the reduced subterm is underlined):

1. $\underline{X + s(0)} \rightsquigarrow_{\{X \mapsto 0\}, \text{base}} s(0)$
2. $\underline{X + s(0)} \rightsquigarrow_{\{X \mapsto s(\#1:\text{Nat})\}, \text{ind}} s(\underline{\#1:\text{Nat} + s(0)}) \rightsquigarrow_{\{\#1:\text{Nat} \mapsto 0\}, \text{base}} s(s(0))$
3. $\underline{X + s(0)} \rightsquigarrow_{\{X \mapsto s(\#1:\text{Nat})\}, \text{ind}} s(\underline{\#1:\text{Nat} + s(0)})$
   $\rightsquigarrow_{\{\#1:\text{Nat} \mapsto s(\#2:\text{Nat})\}, \text{ind}} s(s(\underline{\#2:\text{Nat} + s(0)})) \rightsquigarrow_{\{\#2:\text{Nat} \mapsto 0\}, \text{base}} s(s(s(0)))$

And some of those infinitely many narrowing derivations are infinite in length, e.g. by applying rule ind infinitely many times:

$$\underline{X + s(0)} \rightsquigarrow_{\{X \mapsto s(\#1:\text{Nat})\}, \text{ind}} s(\underline{\#1:\text{Nat} + s(0)})$$
$$\rightsquigarrow_{\{\#1:\text{Nat} \mapsto s(\#2:\text{Nat})\}, \text{ind}} s(s(\underline{\#2:\text{Nat} + s(0)}))$$
$$\rightsquigarrow_{\{\#2:\text{Nat} \mapsto s(\#3:\text{Nat})\}, \text{ind}} s(s(s(\underline{\#3:\text{Nat} + s(0)})))$$
$$\cdots$$

The classical application of narrowing modulo an equational theory is to perform $E \cup Ax$-unification by E, Ax-narrowing (see [20,19]) when the equations E are oriented into rules and are confluent, terminating and coherent modulo Ax (see Section 3). When the theory also satisfies the *finite variant property* [19], a finitary and complete unification algorithm based on a narrowing strategy called *folding variant narrowing* is provided in [19]. This unification algorithm is available in Maude, see [12].

The modern application of narrowing modulo an equational theory is that of *symbolic reachability analysis* [35], when the rules R are understood as *transition rules*. Given an order-sorted rewrite theory of the form $\mathcal{R} = (\Sigma, E \cup Ax, R)$ where: (i) $E \cup Ax$ has a finitary and complete $E \cup Ax$-unification algorithm (for instance, the ACU-unification algorithm available in Maude or the $E \cup Ax$-unification algorithm based on folding variant narrowing) and (ii) the transition rules R are $E \cup Ax$-coherent and *topmost* (see [35]), then narrowing is a *complete* deductive method for symbolic reachability analysis, i.e., for solving existential queries of the form $\exists \overline{x} : t(\overline{x}) \rightarrow^* t'(\overline{x})$ in the sense that the formula holds for $\mathcal{R}$ iff there is a sequence of narrowing steps $t \rightsquigarrow_{\sigma_1, R, E \cup Ax} t_1 \rightsquigarrow_{\sigma_2, R, E \cup Ax} t_2 \cdots t_{n-1} \rightsquigarrow_{\sigma_n, R, E \cup Ax}$ t_n such that t_n and t' have a $E \cup Ax$-unifier. This symbolic reachability is available also in Maude, see [12]. The standard search command of Maude uses the syntax search $Term_1$ arrow $Term_2$ where the arrows can be =>1, =>+, =>*, =>! for just one rewriting step, one or more rewriting steps, zero or more rewriting steps, or until no more rewriting steps are possible. This feature is extended to narrowing in Full Maude by allowing variables both in $Term_1$ and $Term_2$ (possibly sharing variables) and allowing extra arrows ~>1, ~>+, ~>*, ~>! for just one narrowing step, one or more narrowing steps, zero or more narrowing steps, or until no more narrowing steps are possible.

The current use of narrowing and unification in Maude is distributed as follows: (i) Ax-unification available in Maude for order-sorted signatures with any combination of free, C, AC, or ACU function symbols (see [9]); (ii) $E \cup Ax$-unification available in Full Maude (and soon in Maude) using the folding variant narrowing strategy for theories with the finite variant property (see [12]); and (iii) narrowing-based reachability analysis using rules R modulo $E \cup Ax$ (see [12]).

The narrowing relation currently available in Maude is slightly different than the standard one formally defined above. Let $\mathcal{R} = (\Sigma, G \cup E \cup Ax, R)$ be an order-sorted rewrite theory where R, E, and Ax are defined as above and G are the remaining equations. Note that equations in G do not have the variant attribute and have no restriction, i.e., they can be conditional equations, with the owise attribute, etc. Each narrowing step of the form $t \rightsquigarrow_{\sigma, p, R, E \cup Ax} t'$ is followed by simplification $t' \downarrow_{G, Ax}$, i.e., the combined relation is defined as $t \rightsquigarrow_{\sigma, p, R, E, G, Ax} t''$ iff $t \rightsquigarrow_{\sigma, p, R, E \cup Ax} t'$ and $t'' = t' \downarrow_{G, Ax}$. Note that this combined relation may be incomplete because equations G are not considered for unification, i.e., given a reachability problem of the form $\exists \overline{x} : t(\overline{x}) \rightarrow^* t'(\overline{x})$ and a solution σ (i.e., $t\sigma \rightarrow^*_{R, G \cup E \cup Ax} t'\sigma$), the relation $\rightsquigarrow_{\sigma, p, R, E, G, Ax}$ may not be able to find a more general solution.

5   Functional Logic Programming in Maude

We define a functional logic program in Maude as a rewrite theory $\mathcal{R} = (\Sigma, G \cup E \cup Ax, R)$ where R defines[7] the rules used by narrowing, $E \cup Ax$ is the equational theory for unification purposes and $G \cup Ax$ is the equational theory for simplification only. A functional logic computation consists of a reachability problem of the form $\exists \overline{x} : t(\overline{x}) \rightarrow^* t'(\overline{x})$ and a narrowing sequence with a computed substitution σ where σ is a solution. Note that we are interested in a semantics[8]

---

[7] In reality, one would expect two sets R_{rew} and R_{narr}, one for rewriting only and one for narrowing only, as in the equational case with E and G, but we leave this for future implementations.

[8] A well-versed reader may believe we are interested in a semantics of both computed answers and normal forms instead of only normal forms but this is arguable, e.g. the different solutions found by narrowing for the reachability problem $f(x) \rightarrow^* 0$ using programs (i) $f(x) \rightarrow 0$ and $f(0) \rightarrow 0$ and (ii) $f(x) \rightarrow 0$ are irrelevant for the folding

of normal forms and assume that the term $t'(\overline{x})$ is *strongly irreducible w.r.t.* $\rightarrow_{R,G \cup E \cup Ax}$, i.e., for any irreducible substitution $\rho : \mathcal{T}_{\Sigma}(\mathcal{X}) \rightarrow \mathcal{T}_{\Sigma}$, $t'\rho$ is irreducible. Indeed, we are interested in a semantics of values rather than normal forms but the concept of a value in Maude is not just as simple as a constructor term in Haskell or Curry. As an example, take the rule double(X) $\rightarrow$ X + X using the built-in Maude addition operator on natural numbers. For the reachability problem double(1) $\rightarrow^*$ X, the expression double(1) is just evaluated to 2 and assigned to X. If we take the reachability problem double(1+2) $\rightarrow^*$ Y, there are different evaluation orders depending on whether 1+2 is evaluated before the symbol double or not, but the normal form assigned to Y is 6.

In this section, we consider several features that are common in functional logic languages such as Curry. In Section 5.1 we consider a call-time choice semantics for computing values. Then equality in this semantics is adapted to the notion of *strict equality* in Section 5.2 and this allows us to consider conditional rules with conditions using only strict equality in Section 5.3 and extra variables in right-hand sides of rules in Section 5.4. Finally, all these features provide us with all the ingredients for constraint solving capabilities in Section 5.5, including the concept of residuation.

5.1   Non-deterministic Functional Logic Computations and Kinds in Order-Sorted Equational Logic

An interesting property of functional logic programming languages is that they do not assume confluence of the equational specification. For instance, consider the non-deterministic function coin with two rules coin $\rightarrow$ 0 and coin $\rightarrow$ 1. When we consider the expression double(coin), the obtained results are 0, 1, and 2 even if the reader would expect only 0 and 2. Different semantics give different results to the previous expression:

1. If the expression coin is passed without evaluation to the function double, we obtain the expression coin+coin, which has four possible derivations to values 0, 1, 1, and 2. This behaviour corresponds to *run-time choice*, which means that the choice of the value associated to a function parameter may be determined later. This is the standard semantics associated to rewrite theories in Maude.

2. If the expression coin is evaluated before passing it to the function double, we obtain the expressions 0+0 and 1+1, which return 0 and 2. This behaviour corresponds to *call-time choice* in functional/equational programming, which means that the choice of the value associated to a function parameter is determined when calling the function symbol. This behaviour corresponds also to *variable sharing* when non-determinism is present. Sharing in rewriting and narrowing are captured by the idea of graph rewriting [38] and graph narrowing [14]. This is the intended semantics accepted by the functional logic community. See [36] for elaborated interactions on non-determinism

---

variant narrowing strategy [19], which returns *only* the most general solution using the common rule $f(x) \rightarrow 0$, and similarly for this paper.

and non-right-linear equations (or rules). Some bizarre behaviours are still possible when combining it with demand-driven evaluation and solutions have been recently developed [40].

All these behaviours are easily representable in rewriting logic by using kinds. Since functional logic programs are interested only in values and not in normal forms, constructor symbols would be the only ones belonging to a concrete sort and defined symbols will belong to the kind. For example, let us consider a definition of natural numbers using the sort Nat, without any algebraic property; where the kind of Nat, [Nat], is used for terms that are not natural numbers.

```
sort Nat .
op 0 : -> Nat [ctor] .
op s_ : Nat -> Nat [ctor] .
```

Operations, for example addition and the function double would be defined on the kind of Nat, since they are not considered as valid terms of sort Nat.

```
op _+_ : [Nat] [Nat] -> [Nat] .
rl 0 + M:[Nat] => M:[Nat] .
rl s N:[Nat] + M:[Nat] => s (N:[Nat] + M:[Nat]) .

op double : [Nat] -> [Nat] .
rl double(N:[Nat]) => N:[Nat] + N:[Nat] .
```

Similarly, the function coin is defined on the kind.

```
op coin : -> [Nat] .
rl coin => 0 .
rl coin => s 0 .
```

Now we can search for all possible normal forms, corresponding to a typical run-time choice semantics.

```
search double(coin) =>! N:[Nat] .
Solution 1          Solution 2          Solution 3
N:[Nat] --> 0       N:[Nat] --> s 0     N:[Nat] --> s s 0
No more solutions.
```

We can force a call-time choice semantics by imposing variables and constructor symbols of sort Nat instead of the kind [Nat], which forces arguments to be evaluated first.

```
op double : Nat -> [Nat] .          search double(coin) =>! N:[Nat] .
rl double(N:Nat) => N:Nat + N:Nat . Solution 1          Solution 2
                                    N:[Nat] --> 0   N:[Nat] --> s s 0
                                    No more solutions.
```

As a typical example of non-determinism in functional logic programming with a call-time choice, we include the function permute based on a function insert that non-deterministically inserts an element in any position of a listof natural numbers.

```
mod PERMUTE is
  sort Nat .                        sort NatList .
  op 0 : -> Nat [ctor] .            op nil : -> NatList [ctor] .
  op s_ : Nat -> Nat [ctor] .        op _:_ : Nat NatList -> NatList [ctor] .
  vars N E : Nat . var NL : NatList .

  op permute : NatList -> [NatList] .
  rl permute(nil) => nil .
  rl permute(N : NL) => insert(N,permute(NL)) .

  op insert : Nat NatList -> [NatList] .
  rl insert(E,nil) => E : nil .
  rl insert(E,N : NL) => E : N : NL .
  rl insert(E,N : NL) => N : insert(E,NL) .
endm
```

A typical evaluation would return all the permutations of a given list of natural numbers.

```
search permute(0 : s 0 : s s 0 : nil) =>! NL:NatList .
Solution 1                          Solution 2
NL:NatList --> 0 : s 0 : s s 0 : nil NL:NatList --> s 0 : 0 : s s 0 : nil
Solution 3                          Solution 4
NL:NatList --> 0 : s s 0 : s 0 : nil NL:NatList --> s 0 : s s 0 : 0 : nil
Solution 5                          Solution 6
NL:NatList --> s s 0 : 0 : s 0 : nil NL:NatList --> s s 0 : s 0 : 0 : nil
No more solutions.
```

We can already use the narrowing capabilities to solve some symbolic reachability problems, for instance give a fully instantiated final term and include logical variables in the initial term, so that narrowing searches for solutions; note that the inclusion of the variable Z:NatList makes the search space infinite even if there is only one solution, which is obtained by restricting the search to the first solution found using the extra option [1].

```
search [1] permute(0 : X:Nat : (s s 0) : Z:NatList)
       ~>! 0 : (s 0) : (s s 0) : nil .
Solution 1
X:Nat --> s 0 ; Z:NatList --> nil
No more solutions.
```

5.2 Strict Equality

Since functional logic programs are interested on values instead of normal forms, the standard Maude equality is not useful and we need a *strict equality*[9] [26]. That is, an expression coin == 0 will always be evaluated to false because it

---

[9] Strict not in the sense of argument evaluation but in the sense of checking only for values (normal forms).

requires a rule application of `coin` before checking for equality. We would like to have a built-in strict equality, as in major functional logic languages, but we have to define it explicitly in this paper. Indeed, since we want narrowing to be able to instantiate variables in a proper way, we must implement an explicit strict equality in every program written in Maude. We use the symbol =:= along[10] the paper to denote this strict equality, which is explicitly defined for each sort in the following form, when there are no algebraic properties, using also the boolean symbol **and**:

$$f(X_1, \ldots, X_n) \mathtt{=:=} g(Y_1, \ldots, Y_m) \to false \qquad \text{if } f \neq g, n \geq 0, m \geq 0$$
$$c \mathtt{=:=} c \qquad\qquad\qquad \to true$$
$$f(X_1, \ldots, X_n) \mathtt{=:=} f(Y_1, \ldots, Y_n) \to X_1\mathtt{=:=}Y_1 \text{ and } \cdots \text{ and } X_n\mathtt{=:=}Y_n \quad \text{if } fn > 1$$

Symbols f and g, and constant c above correspond to constructor symbols associated to the normal forms of interest, which is more delicate in the presence of an order-sorted setting with kinds, as shown in the previous section.

When we have algebraic properties such as associativity, commutativity and identity, strict equality is not so well-studied and different formulations are possible; however we do not further discuss strict equality here because in the next section we are going to simplify it to just a rule X =:= X → **true**. Now we can search for equality with the desired behaviour, where `coin` is evaluated to 0 and, then, =:= checks that it is equal to 0 in order to reduce to **true**.

```
search coin =:= 0 =>* true .
Solution 1
empty substitution
No more solutions.
```

5.3 Conditional Equations

Another relevant feature of functional logic programming languages is the use of conditional rules. The current implementation of narrowing in Maude deals only with unconditional rules but we transform conditional rules into unconditional ones using a standard technique in functional logic languages such as Curry (see [2,26] for details). Conditional means that a rule has an extra element, apart from the left-hand and right-hand sides, which contains conditions and, intuitively, these conditions must be satisfied before the rule is applied. These conditions can be of different form in Maude but we restrict ourselves to just equality conditions. Note that modern functional logic programming languages use conditions of the form "$t == t'$" and "$t =:= t'$" for both syntactic and strict equality, respectively. However, we will simplify it here to conditions of the form "$t =:= t'$". In Maude syntax, a definition of the membership function for multisets of natural numbers is of the form:

```
sort NatSet .
op empty : -> NatSet . subsort Nat < NatSet .
```

---

[10] The symbol =:= is original from the system Curry where it is a built-in operation.

```
op _;_ : NatSet NatSet -> NatSet [assoc comm id: empty] .
vars N E : Nat . var NS : NatSet .

op member : Nat NatSet -> [Bool] .
rl member(E, empty) => false .
crl member(E, N ; NL) => true if E =:= N == true .
```

Functional logic languages assume that, when there is a conditional rule, the only valuable case is usually when the condition is true and the case where the condition is false is irrelevant, due to problems of negation in functional logic programs [3]. We implement this idea in the paper. First, a new sort Success and a new constant symbol success are defined in Maude. Note that there is no symbol for the negative counterpart. Second, the =:= symbol is simply defined for the positive case returning success, e.g. for the sort Nat is defined as follows:

```
sort Success .
op success : -> Success [ctor] .
op _=:=_ : Nat Nat -> [Success] [comm] .
rl X:Nat =:= X:Nat => success .
```

Note that variable X must be of a specific sort but not a kind, in order to obtain the call-time choice semantics of Section 5.1. Third, we replace the conditional expression by a new operator ">>" with just the positive case, where we restrict reductions on the second argument using the attributes frozen (2) and strat (1 0), as in the standard Maude if-then-else-fi symbol. Again, this transformation is standard in functional logic languages such as Curry, see [2,26] where the symbol >> is also known as if-then (without an else branch).

```
op _>>_ : [Success] [Nat] -> [Nat] [frozen (2) strat (1 0)] .
rl success >> X:[Nat] => X:[Nat] .
```

Note that Maude expects conditions to be boolean expressions but we consider here conditions to be of sort Success just because we consider only the positive cases. The transformation of the previous definition of member is as follows:

```
op member : Nat NatSet -> [Bool] .
rl member(E, empty) => false .
rl member(E, N ; NS) => E =:= N >> true .
```

We can search for solutions to membership in the following form:

```
search member(N:Nat,0 ; s 0 ; s s 0) ~>! true .
Solution 1          Solution 2          Solution 3
N:Nat --> 0         N:Nat --> s 0       N:Nat --> s s 0
No more solutions.
```

5.4   Extra Variables

As in logic programming, rules have extra variables not appearing in the left-hand side. There are different characterizations of rules with extra variables but

we do not impose any restriction here, since extra variables are simply part
of the right-hand side when using >> expressions. An interesting example is
the definition of the function last returning the last element of a given list of
natural numbers, but using the function append (++) instead of traversing the
list to decompose the argument NL into a new list NL' and the last element E:

```
op _++_ : NatList NatList -> [NatList] .
rl nil ++ NL' => NL' .
rl (N : NL) ++ NL' => N : (NL ++ NL') .

op last : NatList -> [Nat] .
rl last(NL) => NL' ++ (E : nil) =:= NL >> E [nonexec] .
```

Note that variables E and NL' are extra variables not appearing in the left-hand
side and are quantified existentially. The nonexec label is necessary[11] because
Maude accepts only rules and equations without extra variables. The execution
of a query to last would be as follows, where we restrict to just the first solution:

```
search [1] in last(0 : s 0 : s s 0 : nil) ~>! X:Nat .
Solution 1
X:Nat --> s s 0
No more solutions.
```

5.5   Constraint Solving and Residuation

Logic programming is quite effective in solving goals and many strategies have
been defined in the literature to speed up that process. A typical optimization
in logic programming is to combine different goals where some of them are suspended until an instantiation is provided by another goal. This procedure is
called *residuation* in functional logic programming languages such as Curry [26]
and Escher [30] and it is easy to achieve in Maude. That is, residuation is based on
the idea to delay or suspend function calls until they are ready for deterministic
evaluation. Since the residuation principle evaluates function calls by deterministic reduction steps, nondeterministic search is usually encoded by predicates
or disjunctions. Moreover, if some part of a computation might suspend, one
needs a primitive to execute computations concurrently. For instance, we include a symbol "&" for the conjunction of constraints using the sort Success
so that both arguments are evaluated concurrently, i.e., if the evaluation of one
argument suspends, the other one is evaluated. This requires very little in Maude.

```
op _&_ : [Success] [Success] -> [Success] [assoc comm id: success] .
```

The trick in Maude is that we will be using equations, with a rewriting semantics,
for those suspended function calls while we will be using rules, with a narrowing
semantics in this paper, for the others (see Footnote 7).

For instance, if we define a predicate for generating natural numbers through
narrowing:

---

[11] A new attribute extra-vars(E,NL') may be used in the future to denote a rule with
extra variables.

```
op nat : Nat -> [Success] .
rl nat(0) => success .
rl nat(s N) => nat(N) .
```

And change the former specification of addition to use equations, so that addition will be evaluated by rewriting (residuation) and never by narrowing:

```
op _+_ : Nat Nat -> [Nat] .
eq 0 + M = M .
eq (s N) + M = s (N + M) .
```

Now we can solve the conjunction of two goals very effectively, since narrowing will be used only for nat and once this function instantiates some variable of an addition expression, the equations of addition will be used.

```
search [1] nat(X:Nat) & (X:Nat + 0) =:= s 0 ~>! success .
Solution 1
X:Nat --> s 0
No more solutions.
```

In the context of Maude, the narrowing search space is very much reduced, since only the evaluation of nat by narrowing generates new states and the evaluation of addition and equality is done by equations, which is very efficient in Maude. However, in many situations we have to reduce the search space by imposing an order of evaluation among different constraints, i.e., Curry provides a symbol &> that forces an evaluation of constraints from left to right, but this symbol is indeed our symbol >> defined above. Now we can run the previous query slightly faster.

```
search [1] nat(X:Nat) >> (X:Nat + 0) =:= s 0 ~>! success .
Solution 1
X:Nat --> s 0
No more solutions.
```

However, if we swap the constraints, (X:Nat + 0) =:= s 0 >> nat(X:Nat) does not return any value, whereas (X:Nat + 0) =:= s 0 & nat(X:Nat) does.

6   Executing the Motivating Example

The specification of the equational logic program in Section 2 by using the features and functionalities described in Section 5 is as follows.

```
mod MAC is
  pr SUCCESS . pr TRIPLIST . pr PSET .

  ops taylor helen william : -> Elem [ctor] .      ops umugu nzwawe amoc : -> Elem [ctor] .
  var L : TripList . var T : Trip . var PS : PSet .

  op gen : Elem -> [Success] .
  rl gen(taylor) => success .          eq gen(taylor) = success .
  rl gen(helen) => success .           eq gen(helen) = success .
```

```
rl gen(william) => success .          eq gen(william) = success .
rl gen(umugu) => success .            eq gen(umugu) = success .
rl gen(nzwawe) => success .           eq gen(nzwawe) = success .
rl gen(amoc) => success .             eq gen(amoc) = success .

op m0 : -> [PSet] .                   op c0 : -> [PSet] .
eq m0 = taylor helen william  .       eq c0 = umugu nzwawe amoc  .

op mset : PSet -> [PSet] .            op cset : PSet -> [PSet] .
eq mset(PS) = PS /\ m0 .              eq cset(PS) = PS /\ c0 .

op boatok : Trip -> [Success] .       op boat : PSet -> Trip [ctor] .
eq boatok(boat(X:Elem)) = gen(X:Elem) .
eq boatok(boat(X1:Elem X2:Elem))
  = gen(X1:Elem) >> gen(X2:Elem) >> ((X1:Elem =/= X2:Elem) =:= true) .

ops lb rb : TripList -> [PSet] .
eq lb(nil) = m0 c0 .
eq lb(L * boat(PS)) = if (even # L) then (lb(L) - PS) else (lb(L) PS) fi .
eq rb(nil) = empty .
eq rb(L * boat(PS)) = if (even # L) then (rb(L)  PS) else (rb(L) - PS) fi .

op good : TripList -> [Success] .
eq good(nil) = success .
eq good(L * T)
  = boatok(T) >> good(L) >> ( (# cset(lb(L * T)) =< # mset(lb(L * T))
                               or (# mset(lb(L * T)) == 0))
                             and
                             (# cset(rb(L * T)) =< # mset(rb(L * T))
                               or (# mset(rb(L * T)) == 0))          ) =:= true .

op solve : TripList -> [Success] .
eq solve(L) = good(L) >> (lb(L) == empty) =:= true .
endm
```

We have used a specific generator function **gen** which is the only function using rules apart from =:=; and both have rules and equations, both for narrowing and rewriting (residuation). Predicates are indeed considered as conditional equations evaluated into **success** and the conditions have been transformed using the **>>** operator. The remaining code is encoded into equations, thus speeding up the execution. We have also used **>>** to order the evaluation of constraints, thus speeding up the execution too. We omit[12] the specification of the auxiliary modules for list of trips and sets of missionaries and cannibals, but they are defined with equations and following the description of this paper.

One of the possible solutions is

```
search  solve(nil * boat(taylor umugu) * boat(taylor) * boat(nzwawe amoc) * boat(umugu) *
              boat(william helen) * boat(helen nzwawe) * boat(taylor helen) *
              boat(amoc) * boat(umugu amoc) * boat(helen) * boat(helen nzwawe) )
        =>! success .
Solution 1
empty substitution
No more solutions.
```

We can search for solutions to queries using variables, for instance the person chosen in the last two steps, e.g. **helen**, is irrelevant and we use variable E:

```
search solve(nil * boat(taylor umugu) * boat(taylor) * boat(nzwawe amoc) * boat(umugu) *
             boat(william helen) * boat(helen nzwawe) * boat(taylor helen) *
```

---

[12] The experiments are available at http://www.dsic.upv.es/~sescobar/MAC.html.

```
                    boat(amoc) * boat(umugu amoc) * boat(E) * boat(E nzwawe) ) ~>! success .
Solution 1        Solution 2          Solution 3          Solution 4          Solution 5
E:Elem --> amoc  E:Elem --> helen  E:Elem --> taylor  E:Elem --> umugu  E:Elem --> william
No more solutions.
```

The cannibal chosen in steps $9th$ and $10th$ is irrelevant and we use variable E1:

```
search  solve(nil * boat(taylor umugu) * boat(taylor) * boat(nzwawe amoc) * boat(umugu) *
               boat(william helen) * boat(helen nzwawe) * boat(taylor helen) *
               boat(E1) * boat(umuguE1) * boat(E) * boat(E nzwawe) ) ~>! success .
Solution 1                                  Solution 2
E1:Elem --> amoc ; E:Elem --> amoc          E1:Elem --> amoc ; E:Elem --> helen
Solution 3                                  Solution 4
E1:Elem --> amoc ; E:Elem --> taylor        E1:Elem --> amoc ; E:Elem --> umugu
Solution 5                                  Solution 6
E1:Elem --> amoc ; E:Elem --> william       E1:Elem --> nzwawe ; E:Elem --> amoc
Solution 7
E1:Elem --> nzwawe ; E:Elem --> umugu
No more solutions.
```

The current implementation of narrowing as symbolic reachability in Full Maude is not able to handle the most general and powerful query search solve(L) ~>* success due to its huge execution time and big memory consumption.

The well-versed reader of narrowing features in Maude may wonder whether this equational logic program can be used with the latest variant-generation features recently available in Maude [12]. The answer is yes. First, this program has no nondeterministic computation and no extra variables in right-hand sides, so it can be turned into a confluent, terminating and coherent equational theory modulo associativity, commutativity, and an identity symbol. Then, variant generation can be tried on the different input terms of the search commands shown above and the generated variants contain the expected results shown above. Indeed, this program and the output can be found in the url given above. This process runs faster than symbolic reachability, but the results are the same and are not discussed in this paper. Note that the expression solve(L) does not have a finite number of most general variants and, thus, symbolic reachability would be able to find the solution given enough time and memory while the variant generation is incapable of finding it.

7   Conclusions

We have tried to illustrate how concurrent constraint functional logic programs can be written and executed by using the novel infrastructure of narrowing as symbolic reachability in Maude. This paper shows how Maude goes beyond standard practices in the functional logic area by using, e.g. equational properties such as associativity and commutativity or an order-sorted setting. A detailed comparison of features that are available in Curry or Maude is outside of this paper, as well as a performance comparison between both languages.

References

1. Alpuente, M., Ballis, D., Falaschi, M.: Transformation and debugging of functional logic programs. In: Dovier, A., Pontelli, E. (eds.) 25 Years of Logic Programming. LNCS, vol. 6125, pp. 271–299. Springer, Heidelberg (2010)
2. Antoy, S.: Evaluation strategies for functional logic programming. Journal of Symbolic Computation 40, 875–903 (2005)
3. Antoy, S.: Programming with narrowing: A tutorial. Journal of Symbolic Compututation 45(5), 501–522 (2010)
4. Antoy, S., Echahed, R., Hanus, M.: Parallel evaluation strategies for functional logic languages. In: Naish, L. (ed.) ICLP, pp. 138–152. MIT Press (1997)
5. Antoy, S., Echahed, R., Hanus, M.: A needed narrowing strategy. J. ACM 47(4), 776–822 (2000)
6. Antoy, S., Hanus, M.: Functional logic programming. Commun. ACM 53(4), 74–85 (2010)
7. Arts, T., Zantema, H.: Termination of logic programs using semantic unification. In: Proietti, M. (ed.) LOPSTR 1995. LNCS, vol. 1048, pp. 219–233. Springer, Heidelberg (1996)
8. Bae, K., Escobar, S., Meseguer, J.: Abstract logical model checking of infinite-state systems using narrowing. In: van Raamsdonk, F. (ed.) RTA. LIPIcs, vol. 21, pp. 81–96. Schloss Dagstuhl - Leibniz-Zentrum fuer Informatik (2013)
9. Clavel, M., Durán, F., Eker, S., Escobar, S., Lincoln, P., Martí-Oliet, N., Meseguer, J., Talcott, C.L.: Unification and narrowing in maude 2.4. In: Treinen, R. (ed.) RTA 2009. LNCS, vol. 5595, pp. 380–390. Springer, Heidelberg (2009)
10. Clavel, M., Durán, F., Eker, S., Lincoln, P., Martí-Oliet, N., Meseguer, J., Talcott, C.: All About Maude - A High-Performance Logical Framework. LNCS, vol. 4350. Springer, Heidelberg (2007)
11. Dershowitz, N.: Goal Solving as Operational Semantics. In: International Logic Programming Symposium, Portland, OR, pp. 3–17. MIT Press, Cambridge (1995)
12. Durán, F., Eker, S., Escobar, S., Meseguer, J., Talcott, C.L.: Variants, unification, narrowing, and symbolic reachability in maude 2.6. In: Schmidt-Schauß, M. (ed.) RTA. LIPIcs, vol. 10, pp. 31–40. Schloss Dagstuhl - Leibniz-Zentrum fuer Informatik (2011)
13. Durán, F., Meseguer, J.: On the church-rosser and coherence properties of conditional order-sorted rewrite theories. J. Log. Algebr. Program. 81(7-8), 816–850 (2012)
14. Echahed, R., Peltier, N.: Narrowing data-structures with pointers. In: Corradini, A., Ehrig, H., Montanari, U., Ribeiro, L., Rozenberg, G. (eds.) ICGT 2006. LNCS, vol. 4178, pp. 92–106. Springer, Heidelberg (2006)
15. Escobar, S.: Refining weakly outermost-needed rewriting and narrowing. In: PPDP, pp. 113–123. ACM Press, New York (2003)
16. Escobar, S.: Implementing natural rewriting and narrowing efficiently. In: Kameyama, Y., Stuckey, P.J. (eds.) FLOPS 2004. LNCS, vol. 2998, pp. 147–162. Springer, Heidelberg (2004)
17. Escobar, S., Meseguer, J.: Symbolic model checking of infinite-state systems using narrowing. In: Baader, F. (ed.) RTA 2007. LNCS, vol. 4533, pp. 153–168. Springer, Heidelberg (2007)
18. Escobar, S., Meseguer, J., Thati, P.: Natural narrowing for general term rewriting systems. In: Giesl, J. (ed.) RTA 2005. LNCS, vol. 3467, pp. 279–293. Springer, Heidelberg (2005)

19. Escobar, S., Sasse, R., Meseguer, J.: Folding variant narrowing and optimal variant termination. Journal of Logic and Algebraic Programming 81(7-8), 898–928 (2012)
20. Fay, M.: First-order unification in an equational theory. In: Joyner, W.H. (ed.) Proceedings of the 4th Workshop on Automated Deduction, Austin, Texas, USA, pp. 161–167. Academic Press (1979)
21. Goguen, J., Meseguer, J.: Eqlog: Equality, Types and Generic Modules for Logic Programming. In: de Groot, D., Lindstrom, G. (eds.) Logic Programming, Functions, Relations and Equations, pp. 295–363. Prentice-Hall (1986)
22. Goguen, J.A., Meseguer, J.: Equality, types, modules, and (why not?) generics for logic programming. J. Log. Program. 1(2), 179–210 (1984)
23. Goguen, J.A., Meseguer, J.: Models and equality for logical programming. In: Ehrig, H., Levi, G., Montanari, U. (eds.) TAPSOFT 1987 and CFLP 1987. LNCS, vol. 250, pp. 1–22. Springer, Heidelberg (1987)
24. Hanus, M.: The Integration of Functions into Logic Programming: From Theory to Practice. Journal of Logic Programming 19&20, 583–628 (1994)
25. Hanus, M.: Multi-paradigm declarative languages. In: Dahl, V., Niemelä, I. (eds.) ICLP 2007. LNCS, vol. 4670, pp. 45–75. Springer, Heidelberg (2007)
26. Hanus, M.: Functional logic programming: From theory to curry. In: Voronkov, A., Weidenbach, C. (eds.) Ganzinger Festschrif. LNCS, vol. 7797, pp. 123–168. Springer, Heidelberg (2013)
27. Hölldobler, S.: Foundations of Equational Logic Programming. LNCS, vol. 353. Springer, Heidelberg (1989)
28. Hullot, J.-M.: Canonical forms and unification. In: Bibel, W., Kowalski, R.A. (eds.) CADE 1980. LNCS, vol. 87, pp. 318–334. Springer, Heidelberg (1980)
29. Jouannaud, J.-P., Kirchner, H.: Completion of a set of rules modulo a set of equations. SIAM J. Comput. 15(4), 1155–1194 (1986)
30. Lloyd, J.W.: Programming in an integrated functional and logic language. Journal of Functional and Logic Programming 1999(3) (1999)
31. Martelli, A., Montanari, U.: An Efficient Unification Algorithm. ACM Transactions on Programming Languages and Systems 4, 258–282 (1982)
32. Meseguer, J.: Conditional rewriting logic as a unified model of concurrency. Theoretical Computer Science 96(1), 73–155 (1992)
33. Meseguer, J.: Multiparadigm logic programming. In: Kirchner, H., Levi, G. (eds.) ALP 1992. LNCS, vol. 632, pp. 158–200. Springer, Heidelberg (1992)
34. Meseguer, J.: Membership algebra as a logical framework for equational specification. In: Parisi-Presicce, F. (ed.) WADT 1997. LNCS, vol. 1376, pp. 18–61. Springer, Heidelberg (1998)
35. Meseguer, J., Thati, P.: Symbolic reachability analysis using narrowing and its application to verification of cryptographic protocols. Higher-Order and Symbolic Computation 20(1-2), 123–160 (2007)
36. Moreno, J.C.G., Hortalá-González, M.T., López-Fraguas, F.J., Rodríguez-Artalejo, M.: An approach to declarative programming based on a rewriting logic. J. Log. Program. 40(1), 47–87 (1999)
37. Nieuwenhuis, R., Rubio, A.: Paramodulation-based theorem proving. In: Robinson, J.A., Voronkov, A. (eds.) Handbook of Automated Reasoning, pp. 371–443. Elsevier and MIT Press (2001)
38. Plump, D.: Essentials of term graph rewriting. Electr. Notes Theor. Comput. Sci. 51, 277–289 (2001)
39. Reddy, U.S.: Narrowing as the Operational Semantics of Functional Languages. In: Proceedings of Second IEEE Int'l Symp. on Logic Programming, pp. 138–151. IEEE Computer Society Press (1985)

40. Riesco, A., Rodríguez-Hortalá, J.: Singular and plural functions for functional logic programming. CoRR, abs/1203.2431 (2012)
41. Slagle, J.R.: Automated theorem-proving for theories with simplifiers commutativity, and associativity. J. ACM 21(4), 622–642 (1974)
42. TeReSe (ed.): Term Rewriting Systems. Cambridge University Press, Cambridge (2003)
43. Vigneron, L.: Automated deduction techniques for studying rough algebras. Fundamenta Informaticae 33(1), 85–103 (1998)

Confluence: The Unifying, Expressive Power of Locality*

Jiaxiang Liu[1,2,4,5] and Jean-Pierre Jouannaud[1,2,3]

[1] School of Software and Software Chair, Tsinghua University, Beijing, China
[2] LIX, École Polytechnique, Palaiseau, France
[3] Université Paris-Sud, Orsay, France
[4] Key Laboratory for Information System Security, Ministry of Education, Beijing, China
[5] Tsinghua National Laboratory for Information Science and Technology (TNList), Beijing, China

1 Introduction

Scientific fields undergo successive phases of specialization and unification.

The field of programming languages is in a phase of specialization. Among the main programming paradigms are imperative programming, functional programming, logic programming, object oriented programming, concurrent programming and distributed programming. Each of these fields is further specialized. For example, there are many different paradigms for functional programming: LISP, Mac Carthy's original functional programming paradigm based on pure lambda-calculus for lists enriched with recursion; ML, Milner's paradigm based on a typed lambda-calculus enriched with data types, a let construct and recursion which has become a standard; O'Donnel's paradigm based on orthogonal rewriting; and OBJ, Goguen's paradigm based on terminating rewriting in first-order algebra to cite a few. Similarly, logic programming has given rise to constraint logic programming, as well as query languages for data bases.

Bridges have also been built across these programming languages: OCaml is a functional programming language with modules, objects, inheritance, and more [18]. MAUDE is a functional, rewriting-based, programming language supporting concurrency [16]. Similar to MAUDE, CafeOBJ [3] supports in addition behavioural descriptions [17]. Functional, logic and constraint programming coexist in CoqMT [20]. Bridges have also been built at the more abstract level of programming paradigms. For one example, Kirchner's rho-calculus is an attempt to unify lambda-calculus and rewriting [12]. Meseguer's rewriting logic can be seen as an attempt to unify terminating rewriting with process algebra [15]. Concurrent logic programming is constraint logic programming with concurrent access to a store representing the current state of shared logical facts [19]. Attempts of unifying functional and logic programming are numerous, although not entirely conclusive so far.

In the area of functional programming, we think that a unification phase has started, and our goal in this paper is to contribute to this trend.

The theory of functional programming languages relies on two major properties of *rewriting*, its computation mechanism: a syntactic property, called confluence, and a

* This work is supported in part by NSFC grant (No. 61272002, 91218302), 973 Program (No. 2010CB328003) and National Key Technologies R&D Program (No. SQ2012BAJY4052) of China.

S. Iida, J. Meseguer, and K. Ogata (Eds.): Futatsugi Festschrift, LNCS 8373, pp. 337–358, 2014.

semantic property, called type preservation. Rewriting is a recursive relation on two expressions of the same type, such as arithmetic on natural numbers. Such a relation is usually non-deterministic, hence the result could depend on particular choices made by the interpreter or compiler. Confluence is the property expressing that rewriting is deterministic, that is, the result does not actually depend upon a particular evaluation path. Type preservation expresses the property that the input and the output have the same functional behaviour. Our interest in this paper is in confluence, and our goal is to unify techniques for checking confluence of a given rewriting relation, independently of the rewriting mechanism itself, and of its termination properties.

1.1 Confluence Checking: The Principles

Historically, confluence checking has been influenced by a few foundational works, for terminating rewriting, and for non-terminating rewriting independently. In both cases, there are abstract results at the level of relations on a set, and concrete results elaborating upon the abstract one in the case of a concrete structure on which the computation takes place.

Let $\longrightarrow$ be a binary relation on an abstract set S, called rewriting. We denote by $\longrightarrow^=$ its reflexive closure, by $\longrightarrow^*$ its reflexive, transitive closure called *derivation*, and by $\longleftrightarrow^*$ its reflexive, symmetric, transitive closure called *conversion*. A triple s, u, v is called a *local peak* if $u \longleftarrow s \longrightarrow v$, a *peak* if $u \; {}^*\!\!\longleftarrow s \longrightarrow^* v$. A conversion $u \longleftrightarrow^* v$ is *joinable* if $u \longrightarrow^* t \; {}^*\!\!\longleftarrow v$ for some t and strongly joinable if $u \longrightarrow^= t \; {}^=\!\!\longleftarrow v$. The rewriting relation $\longrightarrow$ is Church-Rosser (resp., confluent, locally confluent) if every conversion (resp., peak, local peak) is joinable. It is strongly confluent if every local peak is strongly joinable.

As for the terminating case, Newman proved that confluence of an abstract rewriting relation is reducible to local confluence, while Knuth and Bendix, followed by Huet, proved that local confluence of a rewriting relation on terms is reducible to the join-ability of specific local peaks called *critical*. For the non-terminating case, Hindley proved that confluence of an abstract rewriting relation is reducible to its strong confluence, while Tait proved that parallel rewriting in lambda-calculus is strongly confluent, which implies confluence. Driven by the many applications, the terminating branch of rewriting specialized further into rewriting modulo, constraint rewriting, higher-order rewriting and normal rewriting to cite a few. On the other hand, the non-terminating branch kept its unity by generalizing Tait's result to orthogonal rewriting systems, an important class of strongly confluent, concrete rewriting systems.

In the recent years, techniques for proving confluence have been revisited so as to start the unification process.

First, van Oostrom succeeded to capture Newman's and Hindley's results under a unique, more expressive new approach in which each rewrite step on a given abstract set is decorated by elements belonging to an abstract set of *labels* equipped with a well-founded order $\rhd$. Define a decreasing diagram for a local peak $u \longleftarrow_l s \longrightarrow_m v$ as a conversion $u \xrightarrow[(\lhd l)^*]{*} \xrightarrow[m]{=} \xrightarrow[(\lhd l,m)^*]{*} \xleftarrow[(\lhd l,m)^*]{*} \xleftarrow[l]{=} \xleftarrow[(\lhd m)^*]{*} v$. Then rewriting is confluent if every local peak has a decreasing diagram. It is easy to see that joinability for terminating relations and strong joinability for arbitrary relations are particular decreasing diagrams. A general form of decreasing diagram is described in [24], which is more flexible for practical use.

Second, all important results belonging to the terminating branch have been unified by Jouannaud and Li under the concept of a Normal Abstract Rewriting System [8]. There are two main ideas behind NARSes. Rewriting is defined again on an abstract set, but each rewrite step is now decorated by a subset P_p of an abstract set $\mathcal{P}$ of *positions* equipped with a well-founded order $>$, p being the minimum of P_p. It is then possible to characterize whether a local peak $u \xleftarrow{P_p} s \xrightarrow{Q_q} v$ is a *disjoint peak* ($p\#q$), an *ancestor peak* ($q > P_p$), or a *critical peak* ($q \in P_p$) and to reduce confluence of a NARS to the joinability of its abstract critical peaks. The framework of NARSes appears therefore to be intermediate between abstract and concrete rewriting. Indeed, normal rewriting can specialize to all important concrete rewriting relations that have been introduced in the terminating case, and the associated notions of critical pairs are indeed instances of the abstract ones defined for a NARS.

1.2   Weaknesses of Decreasing Diagrams

Van Oostrom showed that the method of decreasing diagrams is complete under the countability assumption, that is, every confluent countable system can be labelled in such a way that its local peaks have a decreasing diagram. The proof uses Klop's notion of cofinal derivation for each convertibility class, which is a (possibly infinite) sequence $\{t_i\}_{i < I \leq \omega}$ of terms such that $(\forall i \neq 0)\, t_{i-1} \longrightarrow t_i$, and $(\forall s \in \mathcal{O})\, s \longrightarrow^* t_i$ for some $i < I$. Then, a step $s \longrightarrow t$ is labelled by 0 if it belongs to the cofinal derivation, and by 1 plus the minimum distance of t to the cofinal derivation otherwise. It is quite easy to verify that all peaks have a decreasing diagram for that labelling.

Since Klop's notion of cofinal derivation is non-constructive, this result does not tell us how to guess the labelling we need. On the other hand, it could give us hints. Unfortunately, this is not the case if we look for a *local* labelling, that is a mapping from rewrite steps to labels. Consider for example a confluent system made of two distinct convertibility classes C_1 and C_2, the first having a cofinal derivation reduced to a single element a, and the second having an infinite one $\{t_i\}_{i < \omega}$. Let us add the rewrite step $a \rightarrow t_{1000}$. Then, the resulting system is still confluent, but the union of both cofinal derivations is not a cofinal derivation. Of course, $\{t_i\}_{i < \omega}$ is a cofinal derivation for the union, but the labels of all steps in C_1 must be increased by one. $\{a, t_{i \geq 1000}\}$ is another with a similar effect on many steps in C_2. This shows that labelling can hardly be local.

A major strength of decreasing diagrams is that they capture Hindley's Lemma as well as Newman's Lemma. To prove it, it suffices to label the rewrite steps by the same label in the first case, and by the origin s of the step $s \rightarrow t$ in the second. Doing so, we obtain a *constructive* labelling, rather than using the completeness result itself (which we could do). Of course, *all* known criteria for confluence of abstract relations are covered by van Oostrom's result, as a result of completeness. It however comes as a surprise to us that in each case, a labelling can be built. Assume P is a recursive set of confluent relations. Then, we would like to exhibit a recursive function L_P taking as input a relation $R \in P$ and returning a labelling function for R which satisfies van Oostrom's assumptions. If such a function exists for every P, then we say that van Oostrom decreasing diagrams method is *constructively complete*. We suspect a negative answer to the open question whether this holds. Indeed, no constructive labelling is known for Huet's generalization [7, Lemma 2.5] of Hindley's Lemma.

To overcome this particular weakness, van Oostrom introduced a generalization of decreasing diagrams for local peaks that he calls *commutation diagrams*. The idea is to duplicate the original rewrite relation $\longrightarrow$ as $\longrightarrow$ and $\longrightarrow$. Then any step in a conversion is painted in blue if heading to the left, and in red if heading to the right. We shall prefix all notions by the word *coloured*. The coloured version of van Oostrom's theorem says that coloured confluence (or commutation) follows from the coloured joinability of coloured local peaks. Coloured confluence implies confluence provided the transitive closures of both relations coincide with the transitive closure of the starting relation. Refining Tait's idea for showing confluence of the lambda-calculus, we can indeed paint in blue the starting relation, and in red its transitive closure. Coloured confluence can be much easier to prove than confluence of the original relation, because the two coloured relations can have very different labellings, giving more flexibility. Whether the coloured version of van Oostrom's method is constructively complete for abstract relations is open, but there is now a constructive labelling for the commutation version of Huet's generalization [7, Lemma 2.5] of Hindley's Lemma. We shall indeed prove that the most important criteria among those we know of can be proved with a constructive labelling when using coloured diagrams, which shows their importance.

The situation gets more complex when it comes to rewrite systems. Van Oostrom's framework is abstract, only constants are rewritten. The framework therefore allows for *critical peaks* only: a constant a rewriting to constants b and c. Disjoint peaks enjoy a decreasing diagram for any well-behaved labelling. Our experience is that difficulties come essentially from ancestor peaks, which exist when terms have a nested structure. Ancestor peaks are joinable in various ways, depending on whether or not a given variable may have multiple occurrences in the lefthand or righthand sides of a given rule. These joinability diagrams are not decreasing in general, unless the rules are both left- and right-linear, or simply left-linear, but the technicalities get more complex. Indeed, another result of Huet, called *parallel closedness* criterion, says that a left-linear system is confluent if all its critical peaks $s \longleftarrow u \longrightarrow t$ satisfy the condition $s \longrightarrow^{p_1} \ldots \longrightarrow^{p_n} t$ where $\{p_i\}_{i \in [1..n]}$ is a set of pairwise disjoint occurrences. We shall prove it, as well as its generalization [22], by blending coloured *multi-labelled* diagrams with positional rewriting in order to abstract these results from a particular term structure. Multi-labelling refers to a powerful extension of van Oostrom's technique allowing for global interpretations defined locally by a sequence of labels.

1.3 Organization

Our goal is to lift van Oostrom's result to abstract positional rewriting, so as to capture the concrete results in both the terminating and the non-terminating case. Our abstract framework of (multi-) labelled abstract positional rewriting systems is described in Section 2 together with our strategy for proving confluence. We will review in subsequent sections several important results which are characteristic of the literature on confluence, and derive them as concrete cases of a same schema. On this journey, we are not going to consider all rewriting notions captured by a NARS, but only plain and parallel rewriting, the general case of NARS being left for future work.

2   Labelled Positional Rewriting

Labelled positional rewriting brings together labelled rewriting as defined by van Oostrom and positional rewriting as introduced by Jouannaud and Li. As a consequence, our notations are possibly heavier than usual, and sometimes heavier than needed. We assume given:

- a set $\mathcal{L}$, which elements are called labels, equipped with a partial quasi-order $\unrhd$ which strict part $\rhd$ is well-founded. We write $m = n$ (resp., $m\#n$) for equivalent (resp., incomparable) labels m, n, and $\alpha \rhd l$ (resp., $l \rhd \alpha$) if $m \rhd l$ (resp., $l \rhd m$) for all m in the multiset (or sequence) α of labels ;
- a set $\mathcal{P}$ which elements are called *positions*, equipped with a partial well-founded order $>_{\mathcal{P}}$, writing $p\#q$ for incomparable positions p, q, satisfying the axiom: $p'\#q$ if $p' >_{\mathcal{P}} p$ and $p\#q$, a binary (infix) *concatenation* operation $\cdot$, and a minimum Λ satisfying the axioms: $p \cdot \Lambda = \Lambda \cdot p = p$ and $p \cdot q >_{\mathcal{P}} p$ provided $q \neq \Lambda$. Given a set of positions Q, we let $p \cdot Q := \{p \cdot q \mid q \in Q\}$;
- a set $\mathcal{O}$ which elements are called *terms*.

2.1   Domains

A *domain* P_p is any non-empty, *downward closed* set of positions $p' \geq_{\mathcal{P}} p$, that is, such that $p' \in P_p$ and $p' \geq_{\mathcal{P}} q \geq_{\mathcal{P}} p$ imply $q \in P_p$ (hence, $p \in P_p$). In some cases, p will not be mentioned, writing then P instead of P_p. Given a position p and a domain Q_q, it is easy to verify that $p \cdot Q_q$ is a domain of minimum $p \cdot q$. In practice, a domain is meant to be the set of non-variable positions of some left-hand side of rule in a term. We denote by $\mathcal{D}_{\mathcal{P}}$ the set of domains over $\mathcal{P}$. We use the letters p, q for positions and the notations P_p, Q_q (or P, Q) for domains.

We write $p >_{\mathcal{P}} Q$ if $(\exists q \in Q)\, p >_{\mathcal{P}} q$ and $(\forall q \in Q)\, q \not\geq_{\mathcal{P}} p$, and $Q_q >_{\mathcal{P}} P_p$ if $q >_{\mathcal{P}} P_p$. Two domains P_p, Q_q are *parallel* or *disjoint*, written $P_p\#Q_q$ if $p\#q$.

We use the letters Γ, Δ for multisets (or sequences) of domains, and specifically Π, Θ for sets (or sequences) of *pairwise parallel* domains, which set is denoted by $\mathcal{D}_{//\mathcal{P}}$.

We write: $\Gamma\#P_p$ if $(\forall Q_q \in \Gamma)\, Q_q\#P_p$; $\Gamma\#\Delta$ if $(\forall P_p \in \Gamma)\, P_p\#\Delta$; $\Gamma \in P_p$ if $(\forall Q_q \in \Gamma)\, q \in P_p$; $\Gamma \geq_{\mathcal{P}} p$ if $(\forall Q_q \in \Gamma)\, q \geq_{\mathcal{P}} p$; $\Gamma >_{\mathcal{P}} P_p$ if $(\forall Q_q \in \Gamma)\, Q_q >_{\mathcal{P}} P_p$; $P_p \bowtie Q_q$ if $p \notin Q_q \wedge q \notin P_p$; $\Gamma \bowtie \Delta$ if $(\forall P_p \in \Gamma)(\forall Q_q \in \Delta)\, P_p \bowtie Q_q$.

We shall freely use the following straightforward key property of domains, which first three cases are called respectively "*disjoint case*", "*critical case*" and "*ancestor case*" in the literature:

Lemma 1. $(\forall p, q \in \mathcal{P})(\forall P_p \in \mathcal{D}_{\mathcal{P}})(q\#p \vee q \in P_p \vee q >_{\mathcal{P}} P_p \vee p >_{\mathcal{P}} q)$.

2.2 Rewriting

We now consider relations generated by *labelled, positional rewrite steps* of the form $s \xrightarrow[P_p]{l} t$ for $s, t \in \mathcal{O}$, $l \in \mathcal{L}$ and $P_p \in \mathcal{D}_{\mathcal{P}}$, and may omit any of l, s, t or P_p. Given an arbitrary labelled positional rewrite step $\xrightarrow[P_p]{l}$, we denote its projection on $\mathcal{O} \times \mathcal{O}$ by $\longrightarrow$, its inverse by $\xleftarrow[P_p]{l}$, its reflexive closure by $\xRightarrow[P_p]{l}$, its symmetric closure by $\xleftrightarrow[P_p]{l}$, its reflexive, transitive closure, called *derivation* or *reachability*, by $\xtwoheadrightarrow[\Gamma]{\alpha}$ for some sequences α of labels and Γ of domains, and its reflexive, symmetric, transitive closure, called *convertibility* by $\xtwoheadleftrightarrow[\Gamma]{\alpha}$. Mention of l, P_p, α, Γ may be altogether omitted, or abbreviated appropriately, in general by the property that they satisfy, as in $\xrightarrow[\geq_{\mathcal{P}} p]{l}$.

We call *conversion*, the sequence $u_0 \xleftrightarrow[P_{p_1}^1]{l_1} \dots \xleftrightarrow[P_{p_n}^n]{l_n} u_n$ of steps witnessing the membership of a convertible pair (u_0, u_n) to $\xtwoheadleftrightarrow[\Gamma]{\alpha}$ for some α, Γ.

The triple (v, u, w) is called a *local peak* if $v \xleftarrow[P_p]{m} u \xrightarrow[Q_q]{n} w$, a *peak* if $v \xtwoheadleftarrow[\Gamma_1]{\alpha} u \xtwoheadrightarrow[\Gamma_2]{\beta} w$, and a *valley* if $v \xtwoheadrightarrow[\Gamma_1]{\alpha} u \xtwoheadleftarrow[\Gamma_2]{\beta} w$, and the pair (v, w) is then said to be *locally divergent*, *divergent* and *joinable* respectively. The relation $\longrightarrow$ is said to be (locally) *confluent* if every (locally) divergent pair is joinable, and *Church-Rosser* if every convertible pair is joinable.

Conversions can be coloured as explained in the introduction, rewrites heading left in blue and those heading right in red. All notions have therefore a coloured version, which is from now on the one we consider, the uncoloured one being obtained by taking identical labellings for both colours.

2.3 Rewriting Axioms

According to Lemma 1, there are three kinds of local peaks: *disjoint peaks* if $q \# p$, *ancestor peaks* if $q >_{\mathcal{P}} P_p$, and *critical peaks* if $q \in P_p$.

We classically assume that rewriting satisfies three (unlabelled) axioms, one for disjoint peaks, one for ancestor peaks and one for parallel steps, which are displayed in Figure 1, where Π_1 and Π_2 are supposed to be sequences of pairwise parallel domains. The (universally quantified) assumptions are pictured with plain arrows, while the (existentially quantified) conclusions are pictured with dashed arrows.

In case rewrites are coloured, there are indeed two versions of the ancestor peak axiom, depending which colour is above the other.

The following lemma follows from the parallel steps axiom:

Lemma 2. *Given a set of domains $\Pi \in \mathcal{D}_{//\mathcal{P}}$, and two enumerations Π_1 and Π_2 of Π, then $s \xtwoheadrightarrow[\Pi_1]{} t$ iff $s \xtwoheadrightarrow[\Pi_2]{} t$.*

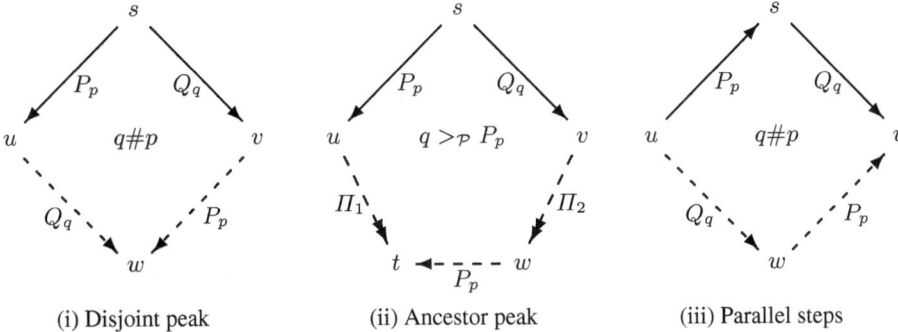

(i) Disjoint peak (ii) Ancestor peak (iii) Parallel steps

Fig. 1. Positional rewriting axioms

We can therefore define *parallel, positional rewriting* as the relation such that $s \underset{\Pi}{\Longrightarrow} t$ iff $s \underset{\Pi_1}{\longrightarrow} t$ for an arbitrary enumeration Π_1 of the set Π of parallel domains. The following straightforward properties of parallel rewriting are important:

Lemma 3. $s \underset{\{P_p\}}{\Longrightarrow} t$ *iff* $s \underset{P_p}{\longrightarrow} t$.

Lemma 4. *Assume that* $\Pi \# \Theta$. *Then* $s \underset{\Pi \cup \Theta}{\Longrightarrow} t$ *iff* $s \underset{\Pi}{\Longrightarrow} u \underset{\Theta}{\Longrightarrow} t$ *for some* u.

2.4 Local Diagrams

Given a *rewriting* relation $\longrightarrow$ on a set $\mathcal{O}$, we first consider specific sub-relations of $\twoheadleftarrow\!\!\twoheadrightarrow$ made of a local peak and an associated conversion called *local diagrams* and recall the important subclass of van Oostrom's decreasing (local) diagrams and their main property: a relation all whose local diagrams are decreasing enjoys the Church-Rosser property, hence confluence.

Decreasing diagrams were introduced in [23]. In this paper, we use their most general incarnation defined in [24], where it is shown that they imply confluence. Since these notions relate to labels and not to positions, we shall omit positions in the coming definitions. Further, we shall only consider coloured diagrams as already announced.

Definition 1 (Coloured local diagram). *A coloured local diagram D is a pair made of a coloured local peak $D_{peak} = v \longleftarrow u \longrightarrow w$ and a coloured conversion $D_{conv} = v\twoheadleftarrow\!\!\twoheadrightarrow w$. We call diagram rewriting the rewriting relation $\Longrightarrow_D$ on coloured conversions associated with a set $\mathcal{D}$ of coloured local diagrams, in which a local peak is replaced by one of its associated coloured conversions:*

$$P \, D_{peak} \, Q \Longrightarrow_D P \, D_{conv} \, Q \text{ for some } D \in \mathcal{D}$$

Note that rewriting a coloured conversion yields indeed a coloured conversion. In the sequel, the colouring will remain implicit.

Definition 2 (Decreasing local diagram).

A local diagram with peak $v \xleftarrow{m} u \xrightarrow{n} w$ is decreasing if its conversion has the form $v \xleftarrow{\alpha}\!\!\twoheadleftarrow s \xrightarrow{n}\!\!\twoheadrightarrow s' \xleftarrow{\gamma}\!\!\twoheadleftarrow\!\!\twoheadrightarrow t' \xleftarrow{m}\!\!\twoheadleftarrow t \xleftarrow{\beta}\!\!\twoheadrightarrow w$, with labels in α (resp. β) strictly smaller than m (resp. n), and each label in γ strictly smaller than m or n. $s \xrightarrow{n}\!\!\twoheadrightarrow s'$ and $t' \xleftarrow{m}\!\!\twoheadleftarrow t$ are called the facing steps of the conversion. We often talk of decreasing diagrams, omitting the word local.

Theorem 1 ([24]). *A labelled, abstract rewriting relation is coloured Church-Rosser (hence coloured confluent) if all its coloured local peaks have a decreasing diagram.*

In [11], Jouannaud and van Oostrom proved Theorem 1 by diagram rewriting. Despite the fact that it is proved there for uncoloured conversions, the proof applies without any change to coloured conversions, since rewriting a coloured conversion yields a coloured conversion. This is not quite the case of van Oostrom's original proofs which adaptation requires duplicating the lemmas relating to his lexicographic maximum measure used for carrying inductive proofs [23]. The idea of the proof based on diagram rewriting is to define a measure on conversions that decreases when replacing a local peak by the conversion associated to its decreasing diagram. Termination of diagram rewriting then implies the Church-Rosser property, thus confluence. A simpler measure is introduced in [9]. Yet another, related measure is given in [6]. We shall give here a simple measure which blends the latter two:

Definition 3. *The interpretation of a conversion P is defined as the multiset $\|P\| :=$ $\{\langle l, T \rangle \mid P = T \xrightarrow{l} H$ or $P = H \xleftarrow{l} T\}$. Conversions are compared in the quasi-order $P \succcurlyeq Q$ iff $\|P\| ((\trianglerighteq, \succcurlyeq)_{lex})_{mul} \|Q\|$, which equivalence is the equality $P == Q$ iff $\|P\| ((=, ==)_{lex})_{mul} \|Q\|$.*

Here is the main property of the above order, implying Theorem 1:

Lemma 5. $\succcurlyeq$ *is a partial quasi-order, which strict part $\succ\!\!\!\succ$ is well-founded, and such that $PD_{peak}Q \succ\!\!\!\succ PD_{conv}Q$ for any decreasing diagram D and conversions P, Q.*

This property is proved first in [11] with a complex order, in [9] with a simpler, related order, and in [6] with a slightly different, albeit more complex order. The order given here is the simplest possible, and its proof is very similar to [9].

We now consider *multi-labelled* abstract rewrite systems, for which each single rewrite step is labelled by a sequence $[l_1, \ldots, l_n]$, each label l_i belonging to a set $\mathcal{L}_i$ equipped with an order $\trianglerighteq_i$ which strict part $\triangleright_i$ is well-founded. The sequence itself is not a label, this would then be a labelled system as before and we would use the word tuple instead.

Definition 4. *Given a labelled rewrite system R, a local diagram D is stable if for any two conversions $P, Q, PD_{peak}Q == PD_{conv}Q$.*

The existence of stable diagrams depends on the properties of the order on conversions. If this order is monotone, as is the one introduced in [6], then the above condition reduces to $D_{peak} == D_{conv}$. If it is not, as are the present one and those introduced in [11,9], then the property must be checked whether it holds or not for a given diagram. The following simple stable diagram is used in Theorem 8:

Lemma 6. *Let* $D_{peak} = v \xleftarrow{m} u \xrightarrow{n} w$ *and* $D_{conv} = v \xleftarrow{m} u' \xrightarrow{n} w$. *Then* D *is a stable diagram.*

Theorem 2. *An* n-*labelled abstract rewriting relation is coloured Church-Rosser (hence coloured confluent) if, for each local peak there exists some* $j \leq n$ *such that the local peak enjoys a stable diagram for every* ith*-label with* $i < j$ *and a decreasing diagram for its* jth*-label.*

Proof. Conversions now decrease in the order $(\succcurlyeq_1, \ldots, \succcurlyeq_n)_{lex}$ when a local peak is replaced by its associated conversion.   □

The use of an n-labelled relation is actually different from the use of the tuple $\langle l_1, \ldots, l_n \rangle$ as a (single) label, since the order $(\succcurlyeq_1, \ldots, \succcurlyeq_n)_{lex}$ is different from the order $\succcurlyeq$ generated by the n-tuple of labels. Multi-labelled systems are indeed a way to use labelling as a complex global interpretation on conversions, while still concentrating on local peaks.

We will show the important impact of this seemingly small extension of van Oostrom's technique in Theorem 8.

3   Terminating Systems

In this first application of Theorem 2, we assume a single colour and a single label, which means rewriting relations are 1-labelled, that is, van Oostrom's original labelling technique as described by Theorem 1 suffices. We further make three key assumptions throughout this section:

(i) rewriting satisfies the axioms for disjoint and ancestor peaks;
(ii) the rewrite relation is terminating;
(iii) we use *self-labelling*: a rewrite step $u \longrightarrow v$ is labelled by u.

Note that self-labelling is made possible by assumption (ii), labels being compared in the order $\longrightarrow\!\!\!\!\!\twoheadrightarrow$. The following important lemma is straightforward:

Lemma 7. *Joinable local peaks enjoy a decreasing diagram.*

The result then follows:

Theorem 3. *A terminating labelled positional rewriting relation satisfying the axioms for disjoint and ancestor peaks is confluent iff all its critical peaks are joinable.*

Proof. Using Lemma 7.   □

Terminating, first-order rewriting satisfies Theorem 3, possibly the most celebrated result on the topic [14]. So do Church's simply typed λ-calculus [1], another celebrated result, and more generally orthogonal systems [13] and algebraic, functional languages [10].

4   Linear Systems

In this second application of Theorem 2, we assume two colours and a single label. We further make a key assumption about the labelling and joinability of disjoint and (duplicated) ancestor peaks, which is displayed at Figure 2.

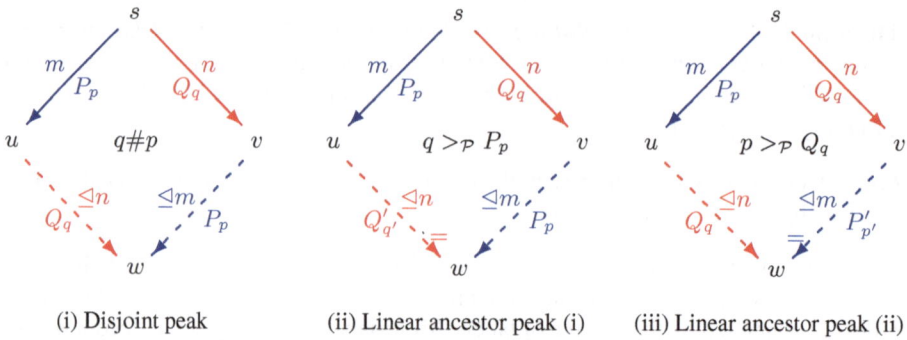

(i) Disjoint peak   (ii) Linear ancestor peak (i)   (iii) Linear ancestor peak (ii)

Fig. 2. Linear axiom for disjoint and ancestor peaks

These revised axioms for disjoint and linear ancestor peaks are indeed decreasing diagrams. Note that comparing rewrite positions breaks the symmetry between the two colours, which results in two different axioms for ancestor peaks.

We still need to care about critical peaks, and again, comparing positions will break the symmetry between two colours, which will result this time in three kinds of critical peaks, the new kind corresponding to the case where the two rewrite positions are equal.

- *top critical peaks*: $u \xleftarrow[P_p]{m} s \xrightarrow[Q_q]{n} v$ with $q = p$
- *red subterm critical peaks*: $u \xleftarrow[P_p]{m} s \xrightarrow[Q_q]{n} v$ with $q \in P_p \setminus \{p\}$
- *blue subterm critical peaks*: $u \xleftarrow[P_p]{m} s \xrightarrow[Q_q]{n} v$ with $p \in Q_q \setminus \{q\}$

The following result follows easily from Theorem 2 and Lemma 1:

Theorem 4. *A labelled positional rewriting relation satisfying the axioms for disjoint and linear ancestor peaks is coloured Church-Rosser if all its critical peaks enjoy a decreasing diagram.*

This result applies to any concrete system satisfying these axioms, which are very restrictive since they are true of *linear systems* only. In case the two coloured relations are identical, then we can conclude that the original relation is confluent. The particular case of first-order linear rewriting appears in [25], with a similar uni-coloured analysis.

Notice that critical peaks need be duplicated in the coloured version, unless the superposition is at the top, but not anymore if the two colours are identical, as is the case when we are interested in a direct proof of confluence of a given relation. On the other hand, having two colours gives more flexibility for the labelling, hence may help in finding decreasing diagrams for some critical pairs.

Theorem 4 implies Huet's generalization [7, Lemma 2.5] of Hindley's Lemma. Both are actually direct applications of the coloured version of Theorem 1, as first noted by van Oostrom [23].

5   Left-Linear Systems

In this section, we relax the previous assumption for ancestor peaks, by allowing for rewriting in parallel at a set of disjoint occurrences on the right. To this end, we shall need the full power of Theorem 2 with two colours and sequences of labels. Technically, we shall follow Tait's steps that we refine with an original variation by taking the given rewriting relation as blue, and its parallel rewriting version as red. This choice will be easier to carry out than taking parallel rewriting for both the blue and red relations as done by Tait and his many followers.

We first introduce several kinds of local peaks needed in presence of parallel rewriting:

Definition 5. *A local peak* $u \xleftarrow{P_p} s \xrightarrow{\Pi} v$ *is called a* disjoint peak *if* $P_p \# \Pi$, *a* (parallel) blue/red ancestor peak *if* $\Pi >_{\mathcal{P}} P_p$, *a* parallel blue/red critical peak *if* $\Pi \in P_p$ *and a* plain blue/red critical peak *if* $\Pi = \{Q_q\}$ *and* $q \in P_p$. *A local peak* $u \xleftarrow{P_p} s \xrightarrow{\{Q_q\}} v$ *is called a* (plain) red/blue ancestor peak *if* $p >_{\mathcal{P}} Q_q$, *and a* (plain) red/blue critical peak *if* $p \in Q_q$.

Throughout this section, we revise the axioms for disjoint and ancestor peaks as in Figure 3, and make four assumptions on the labels used:

- red labels are strictly larger than blue labels;
- the set of red labels is a sup-semi-lattice;
- given a parallel step $s \xrightarrow[\Pi]{m} t$, we assume that its label is the sup of the labels of its elementary parallel steps. Therefore, given any Π_1, Π_2 s.t. $\Pi = \Pi_1 \cup \Pi_2$ and $s \xrightarrow[\Pi_1]{m_1} u \xrightarrow[\Pi_2]{m_2} t$ for some u, then $m = sup\{m_1, m_2\}$;
- given $s \xrightarrow[\Pi_1]{m_1} u \xrightarrow[\Pi_2]{m_2} t$ with $\Pi_1 \# \Pi_2$, by Lemma 4 we have $s \xrightarrow[\Pi_2]{} v \xrightarrow[\Pi_1]{} t$ for some v, we further assume the labels satisfy $s \xrightarrow[\Pi_2]{m_2} v \xrightarrow[\Pi_1]{m_1} t$.

We use Σ to denote sequence of elements in $\mathcal{D}_{//\mathcal{P}}$, writing $\Sigma \# \Gamma$ if $(\forall \Pi \in \Sigma) \Pi \# \Gamma$, and $\Sigma \geq_{\mathcal{P}} p$ if $(\forall \Pi \in \Sigma) \Pi \geq_{\mathcal{P}} p$.

To prepare the proof of the main theorem of this section, we need three auxiliary lemmas:

Lemma 8. *Given a derivation* $s \xrightarrow[\Sigma]{\alpha} u \xrightarrow[\Pi]{n} t$ *s.t.* $\Sigma \# \Pi$, *then* $s \xrightarrow[\Pi]{n} v \xrightarrow[\Sigma]{\alpha} t$ *for some* v.

Proof. By induction on the number of steps in $s \xrightarrow[\Sigma]{\alpha} u$ and application of Lemma 4 and our assumptions on labels.   □

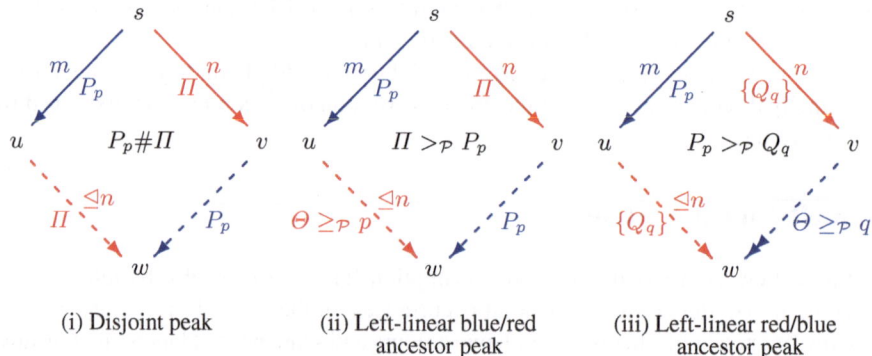

(i) Disjoint peak   (ii) Left-linear blue/red   (iii) Left-linear red/blue
                          ancestor peak   ancestor peak

Fig. 3. Left-linear axioms for disjoint and ancestor peaks

Lemma 9. *Given a peak $u \xleftarrow[\Gamma]{} s \xrightarrow[\Pi]{n} v$ s.t $\Gamma \# \Pi$, then $u \xrightarrow[\Pi]{n'} t \xleftarrow[\Gamma]{} v$ for some t, n' with*
$n' \trianglelefteq n$.

Proof. By induction on the number of steps in $u \xleftarrow[\Gamma]{} s$ and application of the axiom for disjoint peaks.   □

Lemma 10. *Given a peak $u \xleftarrow[\Theta]{} s \xrightarrow[\Pi]{n} v$ s.t. $\Theta \bowtie \Pi$, then $u \xrightarrow[\Pi']{n'} t \xleftarrow[\Gamma]{} v$ for some t, Π', Γ and n' with $n' \trianglelefteq n$. If $\Theta \cup \Pi \geq_{\mathcal{P}} p$ is satisfied for some position p, then $\Pi' \cup \Gamma \geq_{\mathcal{P}} p$. Π' is called the residual of Π after the derivation $s \twoheadrightarrow u$, denoted by Π/Θ.*

The notion of residual is quite old. It is the key to many results, like the finite development theorem and the standardization theorem, see [21].

Proof. The proof is by induction on the number of steps in $s \xrightarrow[\Theta]{} u$.

Selecting the first step $s \xrightarrow[P_{p_1}^1]{} u'$ of $s \twoheadrightarrow u$, we have $u \xleftarrow[\Theta']{} u' \xleftarrow[P_{p_1}^1]{} s \xrightarrow[\Pi]{n} v$ where $\Theta' = \Theta \setminus \{P_{p_1}^1\}$. To analyze the local peak $u' \xleftarrow[P_{p_1}^1]{} s \xrightarrow[\Pi]{n} v$, we split Π as $\Pi = \Pi_1 \cup \Pi_2$ s.t. $\Pi_1 \# P_{p_1}^1$ and Π_2 satisfying either $\Pi_2 >_{\mathcal{P}} P_{p_1}^1$ or $(\forall Q_q \in \Pi_2) p_1 >_{\mathcal{P}} Q_q$, in which case Π_2 contains one element or is empty. It follows in both cases that $s \xrightarrow[\Pi_1]{n_1} v' \xrightarrow[\Pi_2]{n_2} v$. By the axiom for disjoint peaks, $u' \xrightarrow[\Pi_1]{n'_1} w' \xleftarrow[P_{p_1}^1]{} v'$ for some w' with $n'_1 \trianglelefteq n_1$. Using now the axiom for ancestor peaks, $w' \xleftarrow[P_{p_1}^1]{} v' \xrightarrow[\Pi_2]{n_2} v$ can be joined by $w' \xrightarrow[\Pi'_2]{n'_2} w \xleftarrow[\Gamma]{} v$ for some Π'_2, Γ, w with $n'_2 \trianglelefteq n_2$, where $\Pi'_2 \geq_{\mathcal{P}} p_1$ if $\Pi_2 >_{\mathcal{P}} P_{p_1}^1$, or $\Pi'_2 = \Pi_2$ otherwise. In both cases, $\Pi'_2 \# \Pi_1$ and $\Pi'_2 \bowtie \Theta'$, thus $u' \xrightarrow[\Pi_1 \cup \Pi'_2]{n'} w \xleftarrow[\Gamma]{} v$, with $n' = sup\{n'_1, n'_2\} \trianglelefteq sup\{n_1, n_2\} = n$ and $\Theta' \bowtie (\Pi_1 \cup \Pi'_2)$. If there exists some p s.t. $\Theta \cup \Pi \geq_{\mathcal{P}} p$, it is easy to see $\Theta' \cup \Pi_1 \cup \Pi'_2 \cup \Gamma \geq_{\mathcal{P}} p$.

Applying the induction hypothesis to the peak $u \overset{n'}{\underset{\Theta'}{\longleftarrow}} u' \xrightarrow[\Pi_1 \cup \Pi_2']{} w$ yields the result.   □

The following result follows:

Theorem 5. *Assuming that parallel steps have labels which are strictly larger than the labels of plain steps, a labelled positional rewriting relation satisfying the axioms for disjoint and left-linear ancestor peaks is confluent if its critical peaks satisfy the decreasing diagrams in Figure 4:*

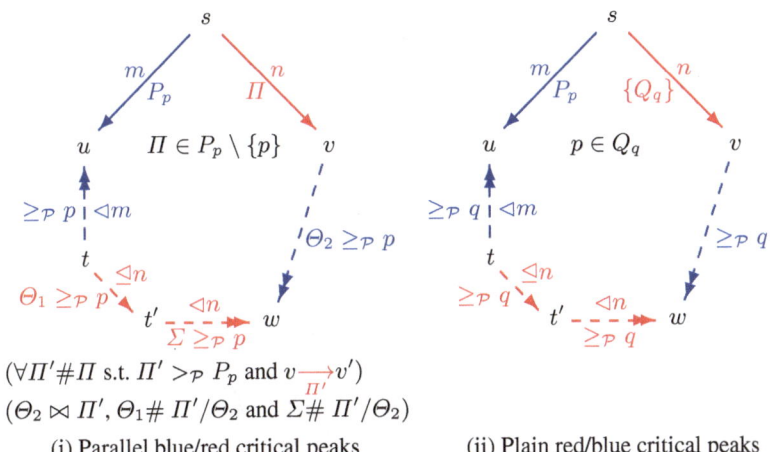

$$(\forall \Pi' \# \Pi \text{ s.t. } \Pi' >_{\mathcal{P}} P_p \text{ and } v \xrightarrow[\Pi']{} v')$$
$$(\Theta_2 \bowtie \Pi', \Theta_1 \# \Pi'/\Theta_2 \text{ and } \Sigma \# \Pi'/\Theta_2)$$

(i) Parallel blue/red critical peaks   (ii) Plain red/blue critical peaks

Fig. 4. Assumptions for critical peaks

Proof. We show that every local peak $u \overset{m}{\underset{P_p}{\longleftarrow}} s \xrightarrow[\Pi]{n} v$ has a decreasing diagram. There are three cases according to the comparison between P_p and Π:

(i): $(\forall Q_q \in \Pi) P_p \bowtie Q_q$. We conclude by Lemma 10.

(ii): $(\exists Q_q \in \Pi) q \in P_p \setminus \{p\}$. The proof is represented in Figure 5. We first split Π into $\Pi = \Pi_1 \cup \Pi_2 \cup \Pi_3$ with $\Pi_1 := \{Q_q \in \Pi \mid q \in P_p\}$, $\Pi_2 := \{Q_q \in \Pi \mid q >_{\mathcal{P}} P_p\}$ and $\Pi_3 := \{Q_q \in \Pi \mid q \# p\}$, hence $s \xrightarrow[\Pi_1]{n_1} v_1 \xrightarrow[\Pi_2]{n_2} v_2 \xrightarrow[\Pi_3]{n_3} v$ by Lemma 4, and $n = sup\{n_1, n_2, n_3\}$ by assumption on labels of parallel steps. By assumption, the blue/red critical peak $u \overset{m}{\underset{P_p}{\longleftarrow}} s \xrightarrow[\Pi_1]{n_1} v_1$ has a conversion $u \overset{\lhd m}{\underset{\Theta_1}{\longleftarrow}} t \xrightarrow[]{n_1'} t_1' \overset{\alpha}{\underset{\Sigma}{\twoheadrightarrow}} w_1 \overset{}{\underset{\Theta_2}{\longleftarrow}} v_1$, with $\Theta_2 \bowtie \Pi_2, \Theta_1 \cup \Theta_2 \geq_{\mathcal{P}} p, \Sigma \geq_{\mathcal{P}} p, n_1' \trianglelefteq n_1$ and $\alpha \lhd n_1 \trianglelefteq n$. By Lemma 10, the peak $w_1 \overset{}{\underset{\Theta_2}{\longleftarrow}} v_1 \xrightarrow[\Pi_2]{n_2} v_2$ can be joined by $w_1 \xrightarrow[\Pi_2']{n_2'} w_2 \overset{}{\underset{\Gamma}{\longleftarrow}} v_2$ where $n_2' \trianglelefteq n_2$ and $\Pi_2' \cup \Gamma \geq_{\mathcal{P}} p$. For the peak $w_2 \overset{}{\underset{\Gamma}{\longleftarrow}} v_2 \xrightarrow[\Pi_3]{n_3} v$, since $P_p \# \Pi_3$ by definition, we have $\Gamma \# \Pi_3$, hence $w_2 \xrightarrow[\Pi_3]{n_3'} w \overset{}{\underset{\Gamma}{\longleftarrow}} v$ by Lemma 9 with $n_3' \trianglelefteq n_3$. By assumption in Figure 4(i), $\Sigma \# \Pi_2'$, hence $t_1' \xrightarrow[\Pi_2']{n_2'} t_2' \overset{\alpha}{\underset{\Sigma}{\twoheadrightarrow}} w_2$ by Lemma 8. We also have $t_2' \xrightarrow[\Pi_3]{n_3'} t' \overset{\alpha}{\underset{\Sigma}{\twoheadrightarrow}} w$ since $\Sigma \geq_{\mathcal{P}} p$ and $P_p \# \Pi_3$.

Thanks to the assumption in Figure 4(i), $\Theta_1 \# \Pi_2'$. Since $\Theta_1 \geq_P p$, $\Pi_2' \geq_P p$ and $P_p \# \Pi_3$, $t \xrightarrow[\Theta_1 \cup \Pi_2' \cup \Pi_3]{n'} t'$ by Lemma 4, where $n' = sup\{n_1', n_2', n_3'\} \trianglelefteq sup\{n_1, n_2, n_3\} = n$. The local peak $u \xleftarrow[P_p]{m} s \xrightarrow[\Pi]{n} v$ has therefore a decreasing conversion, namely

$$u \xleftarrow{\trianglelefteq m} t \xrightarrow[\Theta_1 \cup \Pi_2' \cup \Pi_3]{n'} t' \xrightarrow[\Sigma]{\trianglelefteq n} w \xleftarrow[\Gamma]{} v.$$

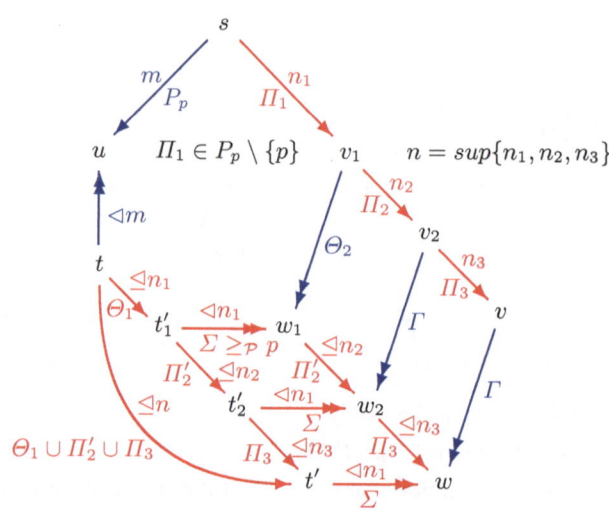

Fig. 5. Proof of Theorem 5. Case(ii)

(iii): $(\exists Q_q \in \Pi)p \in Q_q$. We first split the step $s \xrightarrow[\Pi]{n} v$ into $s \xrightarrow[\{Q_q\}]{n_1} v' \xrightarrow[\Pi_3]{n_3} v$ where $p \in Q_q$ and $\Pi_3 = \Pi \setminus \{Q_q\}$. By assumption, the plain red/blue critical peak $u \xleftarrow[P_p]{m} s \xrightarrow[\{Q_q\}]{n_1} v'$ admits the conversion $u \xleftarrow{\trianglelefteq m} t \xrightarrow[\Theta_1]{\trianglelefteq n_1} t_1' \xrightarrow[\Sigma]{\trianglelefteq n_1} w_1 \xleftarrow[\Gamma]{} v'$ where $\Gamma \geq_P q$, $\Sigma \geq_P q$ and $\Theta_1 \geq_P q$. Since $Q_q \# \Pi_3$, we have $\Gamma \# \Pi_3$, $\Sigma \# \Pi_3$ and $\Theta \# \Pi_3$. Then the proof continues similarly as in case (ii). □

Note that the rewrites from v to w in Figure 4(i) are pairwise disjoint, while those in Figure 4(ii) are arbitrary, making these two figures incompatible when $\Pi = \{Q_p\}$. In fact, we can define a more general, but also more complex condition than the one given in Figure 4(i).

Definition 6. *Given a derivation* $t \xleftarrow[\Gamma]{} s$ *and a set* Π *of pairwise parallel domains, we say that* Γ *and* Π *are* overlap-free, *written* $\Gamma \bowtie^* \Pi$, *iff* $\Gamma = nil$, *or* $t \xleftarrow[\Gamma']{} t_1 \xleftarrow[P_p]{} s$, $(\forall Q_q \in \Pi) P_p \bowtie Q_q$ *and one of the following three conditions holds:*
Case (i): $P_p \# \Pi$; *then* $\Gamma' \bowtie^* \Pi$.
Case (ii): $(\exists Q_q \in \Pi) p >_P Q_q$; *then* $\Gamma' \bowtie^* \Pi$.

Case (iii): $\Pi_1 := \{Q_q \in \Pi \mid Q_q >_{\mathcal{P}} P_p\} \neq \emptyset;$ *then* $\Gamma' \bowtie^* \Pi'_1 \cup \Pi_2$, *where* $\Pi_2 = \Pi \setminus \Pi_1$ *and* $\Pi'_1 := \Pi_1/\{P_p\}$.

Note that for any $\Theta, \Pi \in \mathcal{D}_{//\mathcal{P}}$, $\Theta \bowtie^* \Pi$ if $\Theta \bowtie \Pi$. Then extensions of Lemma 10 and Theorem 5 follow easily:

Lemma 11. *Given a peak* $u \xmathleftarrow[\Gamma]{} s \xrightarrow[\Pi]{n} v$ *s.t.* $\Gamma \bowtie^* \Pi$, *then* $u \xrightarrow[\Pi']{n'} t \xmathleftarrow[\Gamma']{} v$ *for some* $t, \Pi',$ Γ' *and* n' *with* $n' \trianglelefteq n$. *If* $\Gamma \cup \Pi \geq_{\mathcal{P}} p$ *is satisfied for some position* p, *then* $\Pi' \cup \Gamma' \geq_{\mathcal{P}} p$. *We shall overload the word* residual *and call* Π' *the residual of* Π *after the derivation* $s \xrightarrow[\Gamma]{} u$, *denoting it by* Π/Γ.

Theorem 6. *Assuming that parallel steps have labels which are strictly larger than the labels of plain steps, a labelled positional rewriting relation satisfying the axioms for disjoint and left-linear ancestor peaks is confluent if its critical peaks satisfy the decreasing diagrams in Figure 4, replacing in Figure 4(i) Θ_2 with Γ, and the bottom condition with the following one:*

$$(\forall \Pi' \# \Pi \; s.t. \; \Pi' >_{\mathcal{P}} P_p \; and \; v \xrightarrow[\Pi']{} v')$$
$$(\Gamma \bowtie^* \Pi', \Theta_1 \# \Pi'/\Gamma \; and \; \Sigma \# \Pi'/\Gamma).$$

Proof. Same proof as for Theorem 5, replacing Lemma 10 by Lemma 11.   □

With this new condition, take $\Pi = \{Q_q\}$ with $p = q$ in Figure 4(i), giving then birth to a top critical peak. Then, the set Π' satisfying the condition above would be empty and the condition be trivially satisfied, making both figures identical in this case. This explains the condition $\Pi \in P_p \setminus \{p\}$ in Figure 4(i), to avoid the duplication that would occur with $p = q$.

The overlap-free condition on Γ and Π' given in the theorem is somewhat complicated, because we cannot talk about variables at the abstract level. On the other hand, the condition will become quite simple at the concrete level where the notion of variable is available. This lack of expressivity of the abstract language is an obstacle for obtaining a better result. However, Theorem 6 can be improved to the price of an even more complex definition of overlap-freeness. More precisely, in the diagram of Figure 4, the conversion from t' to v could use an alternation of red steps at positions in Σ_i and blue steps at positions in Γ_i. We did not try to formulate the necessary adaptation of the notions of overlap-freeness $\bowtie^*$ and residual $\_/\_$, therefore left to the interested reader. The improvement enabled by such a machinery would be marginal.

5.1 First-Order Left-Linear Systems

Theorem 6 gives sufficient conditions for an abstract rewriting relation to be confluent. We shall now consider the concrete case of first-order rewrite systems. To this end, we need to show that first-order rewriting satisfies our axioms, and that the abstract notion of critical peak leads to the usual concrete notion of critical pair. We refer to [2] for the basics of first-order term rewriting.

Accordingly, we denote by: $\mathcal{V}ar(s)$ the set of variables occurring in s; $\#_x(s)$ the number of occurrences of the variable x in s; $\mathcal{P}os(s)$, the set of positions of the term

s ; $s|_p$ the subterm of s at position $p \in \mathcal{P}os(s)$; $s[u]_p$ the term obtained by replacing $s|_p$ by u ; $s[u_1, \ldots, u_n]_{p_1, \ldots, p_n}$ the term obtained by replacing $s|_{p_i}$ by u_i for $i \in [1..n]$; $s\sigma$ the instance of s by the substitution σ ; $|s|$ the size of the term s ; $l \to r$ the rewrite rule of lefthand side l and righthand side r. Rewriting a term s with a rule $l \to r$ at position p with the substitution σ is the relation between the terms $s[l\sigma]_p$ and $s[r\sigma]_p$. $l\sigma$ is called a redex and $r\sigma$ its associated reduct.

We shall assume that the label of a plain rewrite step $v \xleftarrow[P_p]{} u$ is the integer 0 while the label of a parallel step $u \xrightarrow[\Pi]{} v$ is the integer 1, which satisfies our abstract assumption that the labels of parallel steps are strictly larger than that of plain steps. It also satisfies obviously the properties of labels for parallel steps.

Definition 7. *Given a rule* $l \to r$, *a set of rules* $\{g_i \to d_i\}_{i \leq n}$ *and a set of disjoint positions* $\{p_i \in \mathcal{P}os(l)\}$ *such that the unification problem* $l|_{p_i} = g_i$ *has most general unifier* γ, *then the pair* $(r\gamma, l\gamma[\ldots d_i\gamma \ldots]_{\ldots p_i \ldots})$ *is a* parallel red/blue critical pair *(a* plain critical pair *if* $n = 1$) *of the rules* $g_1 \to d_1, \ldots, g_n \to d_n$ *onto* $l \to r$ *at positions* $p_1, \ldots, p_n$. *A* top critical pair *is a plain critical pair with* $p_1 = \Lambda$. *Others are* subterm critical pairs. *Plain blue/red critical pairs are defined as expected.*

There is no need for duplicating top critical pairs, we shall therefore consider that they are plain blue/red pairs, as in the abstract case. Decreasing diagrams for these pairs are obtained by instantiating the diagrams of Figure 4 and formulating their conditions appropriately:

Definition 8. *Plain blue/red critical pairs are said to be* decreasing *if they satisfy the diagram of Figure 4 (ii).*

Parallel red/blue critical pairs are said to be decreasing *if they satisfy the diagram of Figure 4 (i), replacing* Θ_2 *by* Γ, *allowing domains that are not disjoint, with the conditions* $Var(t'|_{\Theta_1}) \subseteq Var(s|_\Pi)$ *and* $(\forall s_i \xrightarrow[\Theta_i]{} t_i \in t' \xrightarrow[\Sigma]{} w)(Var(t_i|_{\Theta_i}) \subseteq Var(s|_\Pi))$.

This elegant condition is due to Bertram Felgenhauer [5]. It indeed follows quite naturally in the case of first-order terms from the abstract condition given at Figure 4. Note however that Felgenhauer's decreasing diagrams are different from ours since the labelling technique is not the same: he uses rule-labelling, each rule coming with an integer index. Rewrite steps, whether plain or parallel, use as label the set of rule indexes implied in the rewrite (a singleton set in case of plain rewrites). As a consequence, plain steps may have a bigger label than parallel steps, which gives more flexibility for building decreasing diagrams: in particular the steps between u and t in Figure 4 could be red as well as blue in this case. An interesting question is whether our approach is compatible with a more flexible schema for labelling plain and parallel steps.

Theorem 7. *A first-order term rewriting system R is confluent if all its parallel red/blue subterm critical pairs, plain blue/red subterm critical pairs and top critical pairs are decreasing.*

Proof. We simply need to verify the axioms and apply Theorem 6.   □

Considering (plain) higher-order systems would actually not make much difference in the case where there are no critical peaks with beta. Such a restriction is true of pure lambda-calculus with explicit substitutions, since no rule has an abstraction as its lefthand side. We do not substantiate this claim here.

5.2 When Plain Critical Pairs Suffice

The question we now investigate is whether parallel critical pairs are really needed, or if plain critical pairs are enough. This question has received quite a lot of attention in the past [7,22,4] under the name of parallel-closedness. Proofs all follow the same proof pattern introduced by Huet, by induction via a quite smart well-founded order. We will show how to obtain it, and generalize it, in van Oostrom's coloured labelled framework, therefore hiding this induction within the use of the labelling technique. We shall as before state and prove our result at the abstract level of labelled rewrite relations, therefore making it available to a wider range of rewriting applications.

In this subsection, we use $\widetilde{\Sigma}$ to denote heterogeneous sequences consisting of domains and sets of pairwise parallel domains, since an arbitrary conversion $\twoheadleftarrow\!\!\!\longrightarrow\!\!\!\twoheadrightarrow_{\widetilde{\Sigma}}$ may contain both (plain) blue steps and (parallel) red steps at the same time. We write $\widetilde{\Sigma}\#\Gamma$ if $((\forall P_p \in \widetilde{\Sigma})P_p\#\Gamma)\wedge((\forall\Pi \in \widetilde{\Sigma})\Pi\#\Gamma)$, $\widetilde{\Sigma} \geq_\mathcal{P} p$ if $((\forall P_p \in \widetilde{\Sigma})P_p \geq_\mathcal{P} p)\wedge((\forall\Pi \in \widetilde{\Sigma})\Pi \geq_\mathcal{P} p)$. We also use specific color to denote components or properties of steps in that specific color, for example, $s\twoheadleftarrow\!\!\overset{\alpha}{\underset{\widetilde{\Sigma}}{\longrightarrow}}\!\!\twoheadrightarrow t$ meaning α is the sequence of labels of red steps in $s\twoheadleftarrow\!\!\!\underset{\widetilde{\Sigma}}{\longrightarrow}\!\!\!\twoheadrightarrow t$. All related abbreviations come as expected.

We need a lemma blending Lemma 8 with Lemma 9 before to show the main result.

Lemma 12. *Given conversion* $u\twoheadleftarrow\!\!\overset{\alpha}{\underset{\widetilde{\Sigma}}{\longrightarrow}}\!\!\twoheadrightarrow s\overset{n}{\underset{\Pi}{\longrightarrow}}v$ *s.t.* $\widetilde{\Sigma}\#\Pi$*, then* $u\overset{n'}{\underset{\Pi}{\longrightarrow}}t\twoheadleftarrow\!\!\overset{\alpha}{\underset{\widetilde{\Sigma}}{\longrightarrow}}\!\!\twoheadrightarrow v$ *for some* t, n'*, with* $n' \trianglelefteq n$*.*

Proof. By induction on the number of steps in $u\twoheadleftarrow\!\!\overset{\alpha}{\underset{\widetilde{\Sigma}}{\longrightarrow}}\!\!\twoheadrightarrow s$ and application of the axiom for disjoint peaks, Lemma 4 and our assumptions on labels.   □

The main result of this section states that decreasingness of plain critical peaks implies the Church-Rosser property of rewriting:

Theorem 8. *A labelled, positional rewriting relation satisfying (i) our assumptions on labels and (ii) the axioms for disjoint and left-linear ancestor peaks is coloured Church-Rosser, hence confluent, if its plain critical peaks enjoy the following local diagrams in Figure 6:*

Proof. We apply Theorem 2 with two labels. To this end, we define an appropriate labelling for the rewrite steps before to analyze the local peaks.

We (re-) label the plain step $s\overset{m}{\underset{P_p}{\longrightarrow}}t$ by the sequence $[m, 0]$, and the parallel step $s\overset{m}{\underset{\Pi}{\longrightarrow}}t$ by $[m, |\Pi|]$ where $|\Pi|$ denotes the size of the set Π. These labels for plain and parallel rewriting have the following structure: the first label remains the same as the original one in $\mathcal{L}$, and is compared in the order $\trianglerighteq$, while the second label is a natural number, which is compared in the familiar order $>_N$ on natural numbers.

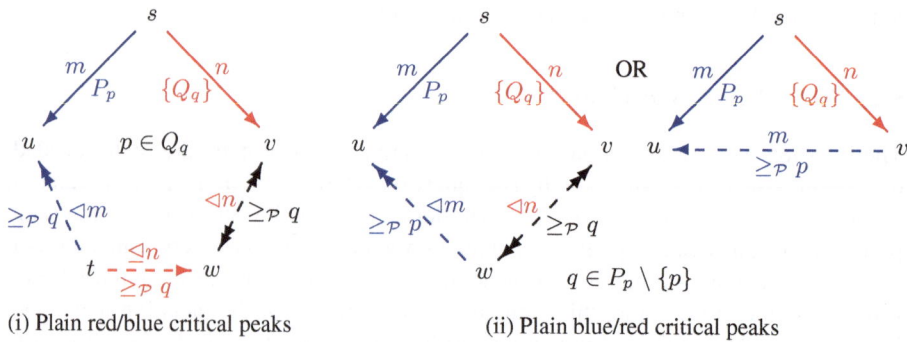

(i) Plain red/blue critical peaks   (ii) Plain blue/red critical peaks

Fig. 6. Assumptions for plain critical peaks

The first label satisfies our assumptions on labels—in particular, the (first) label for parallel rewrites is strictly larger than the (first) label for plain rewrites—, the axioms for disjoint and left-linear ancestor peaks, and the assumptions for plain critical peaks. The second label will be used in case the first fails to conclude. It turns out that it does not need to satisfy (and actually does not satisfy) the axioms and assumptions that are required from the first. Theorem 2 allows us to use a sequence of labels possibly satisfying different assumptions, which is impossible with Theorem 1 even if grouping different labels as a single tuple of labels.

In the sequel, we shall omit the second label when the first allows to conclude.

Given a local peak $v \xleftarrow[P_p]{[m,0]} u \xrightarrow[\Pi]{[n,|\Pi|]} w$, we distinguish three cases:

(i): $(\forall Q_q \in \Pi)\, P_p \bowtie Q_q$. Using the first label, Lemma 10 concludes this case.

(ii): $(\exists Q_q \in \Pi)\, p \in Q_q$. The proof is similar to Case (iii) of the proof of Theorem 5, using Lemma 12 instead of Lemma 8 and 9.

(iii): $(\exists Q_q \in \Pi)\, q \in P_p \setminus \{p\}$. As shown in Figure 7(i), we first select $Q_q \in \Pi$ s.t. $q \in P_p \setminus \{p\}$ and split the local peak into $v \xleftarrow[P_p]{m} u \xrightarrow[\{Q_q\}]{n_1} w' \xrightarrow[\Pi']{n_2} w$ according to Lemma 4, where $\Pi' := \Pi \setminus \{Q_q\}$. Since $n = sup\{n_1, n_2\}$ by assumption on labels, we get $n_1 \trianglelefteq n, n_2 \trianglelefteq n$. By assumption, we have either $v \xleftarrow{\alpha} t' \xleftarrow[\widetilde{\Sigma}]{\beta} \twoheadrightarrow w'$ for some $t', \alpha, \beta, \widetilde{\Sigma}$ with $\alpha \lhd m, \beta \lhd n_1$ and $\widetilde{\Sigma} \geq_{\mathcal{P}} q$, or $v \xleftarrow{m} w'$. The proof for the former case is represented in Figure 7(ii). Since $\widetilde{\Sigma} \geq_{\mathcal{P}} q$, $\widetilde{\Sigma} \# \Pi'$, hence $t' \xrightarrow[\Pi']{n_2'} t \xleftarrow[\widetilde{\Sigma}]{\beta} \twoheadrightarrow w$ for some t, n_2' with $n_2' \trianglelefteq n_2$ by Lemma 12. It then results in a decreasing diagram (using the first label only) shown in the figure. In the latter case, the conversion $v \xleftarrow{[m,0]} w' \xrightarrow[\Pi']{[n_2,|\Pi'|]} w$ is either decreasing for the first label if $n_2 \lhd n$, or is stable for the first label by Lemma 6 while decreasing for the second, as displayed at Figure 7(iii), which concludes the whole proof.

□

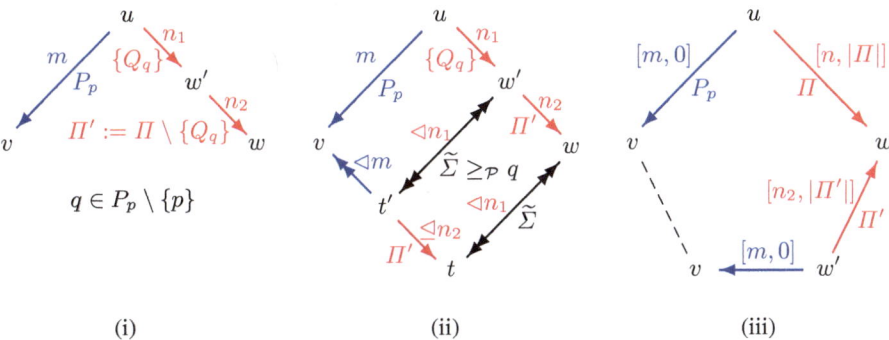

Fig. 7. Proof of Theorem 8. Case (iii)

The black dashed lines here relate two copies of a same term in order to make the picture looking better.

Following Felgenhauer [4], the right diagram of Figure 6(ii) can probably be relaxed by adding extra blue steps from v at arbitrary positions larger than q. We have not yet succeeded capturing this improvement in our setting.

Now we can turn our attention to concrete, first-order rewriting systems, using the above abstract result to prove Toyama's generalization [22] of Huet's parallel closedness criterion [7]. We still use two kinds of rewriting relations: the original one as blue, and the parallel one as red.

Lemma 13 ([22]). *A left-linear term rewriting system R is confluent if for every plain subterm critical pair $\langle u, v \rangle$ we have $v \longrightarrow u$, and for every top critical pair $\langle u, v \rangle$ we have $v \longrightarrow t \twoheadleftarrow u$ for some t.*

Proof. We label a plain step $v \longleftarrow u$ rewritten at position p by $\langle 0, |v|_p| \rangle$ and all parallel steps by tuple $\langle 1, 0 \rangle$. Then to apply Theorem 8, we simply need to verify the assumptions on labels and the axioms on peaks.   □

Toyama's proof is very different, based on a slight generalization of Hindley's Lemma that we already alluded to. As a result, it is much more involved. A further advantage of our proof, using colours and labels, is that it makes clear the origin of these different criteria for top and subterm critical pairs. We are indeed very surprised that Toyama was able to come up with the right condition using Huet's proof technique. Here, it follows quite naturally, we believe.

Our proof technique actually shows that it is possible to generalize a little bit Toyama's condition for top critical pairs, as we do now.

Definition 9. *A rewrite rule $l \to r$ is called size-increasing if $(\forall x \in \mathcal{V}ar(l)) \#_x(l) \le \#_x(r)$ and $|l| \le |r|$. Given a term rewriting system R, we denote by $R_{s\uparrow}$ its maximum subset of size-increasing rules, and by $\longrightarrow_{R_{s\uparrow}}$ the corresponding rewrite steps.*

Lemma 14. *A left-linear term rewriting system R is confluent if for every plain sub-term critical pair $\langle u, v \rangle$ we have $v \longrightarrow u$, and for every top critical pair $\langle u, v \rangle$ we have*

$$v \overset{(\neq \Lambda)^*}{\underset{R_{s\uparrow}}{\longleftarrow}} t' \overset{(\neq \Lambda)^*}{\longleftarrow} t \longrightarrow w \longleftarrow u \text{ for some } t, t', w \text{ provided the rewrite positions of}$$

$t' \overset{(\neq \Lambda)^*}{\longleftarrow} t$ *are pairwise disjoint.*

In fact, there are various ways to generalize Toyama's condition, based on our proof technique, using in particular variations of the size-increasing notion. We however prefer the present notion, which is clear and simple enough, and leave the possible variations to the interested reader.

6 Conclusion

We have described a general framework for proving confluence (actually Church-Rosser) properties of rewriting systems. Our approach is axiomatic, in the sense that we hide the term structure as long as possible, and derive concrete results from the abstract ones by first verifying the axioms and then instantiating the abstract conditions.

This abstract framework is based on a generalization of van Oostrom's approach which turns local labels into global measures on proofs by defining appropriate orders on conversions. It further blends this framework with the abstract notion of positions recently introduced by Jouannaud and Li. Thanks to the abstract notion of positions, we can reduce Church-Rosser properties of abstract rewriting relations to simple labelling properties of certain local peaks called critical. Thanks to the use of several labels, we can use complex inductive arguments which are actually hidden in the order used on conversions. Finally, the use of colours to generalize the Church-Rosser property allows us to encode and simplify old techniques based on the use of parallel rewriting to study the properties of plain rewriting.

We have devoted limited effort to instantiate our abstract results to concrete cases, since these instantiations are mostly straightforward in the plain rewriting setting, whether first- or higher-order. These simple technicalities should of course be carried out carefully in future work. Indeed, our ultimate goal is to capture the entire field of confluence (or Church-Rosser) proofs with a single abstract theorem reducing the Church-Rosser property of a NARS to the existence of decreasing diagrams for its critical peaks, classified with respect to the three manageable sub-components of NARSes, the terminating, linear non-terminating, and left-linear non-terminating ones.

The case of conditional rewriting is another potential subject for future work. However, since conditions serve filtering out critical pairs instances, this issue is somehow orthogonal to our effort. In this respect, the general case of NARSes is more important to us. This is the direction we want to investigate first. Such a result could become the basis of a very general implementation in which different concrete cases would be implemented via appropriate plug-ins.

Acknowledgements. To a referee for his very careful reading.

References

1. Church, A., Rosser, J.B.: Some properties of conversion. Transactions of the American Mathematical Society 39, 472–482 (1936)
2. Dershowitz, N., Jouannaud, J.-P.: Rewrite systems. In: Handbook of Theoretical Computer Science, Volume B: Formal Models and Sematics (B), pp. 243–320. North-Holland (1990)
3. Diaconescu, R., Futatsugi, K.: An overview of cafeobj. Electr. Notes Theor. Comput. Sci. 15, 285–298 (1998)
4. Felgenhauer, B.: Personnal communication (2013)
5. Felgenhauer, B.: Rule labeling for confluence of left-linear term rewrite systems. In: International Workshop on Confluence (2013)
6. Felgenhauer, B., van Oostrom, V.: Proof orders for decreasing diagrams. In: van Raamsdonk, F. (ed.) RTA. LIPIcs, vol. 21, pp. 174–189. Schloss Dagstuhl - Leibniz-Zentrum fuer Informatik (2013)
7. Huet, G.P.: Confluent reductions: Abstract properties and applications to term rewriting systems. J. ACM 27(4), 797–821 (1980)
8. Jouannaud, J.-P., Li, J.: Church-rosser properties of normal rewriting. In: Cégielski, P., Durand, A. (eds.) CSL. LIPIcs, vol. 16, pp. 350–365. Schloss Dagstuhl - Leibniz-Zentrum fuer Informatik (2012)
9. Jouannaud, J.-P., Liu, J.: From diagrammatic confluence to modularity. Theor. Comput. Sci. 464, 20–34 (2012)
10. Jouannaud, J.-P., Okada, M.: A computation model for executable higher-order algebraic specification languages. In: LICS, pp. 350–361. IEEE Computer Society (1991)
11. Jouannaud, J.-P., van Oostrom, V.: Diagrammatic confluence and completion. In: Albers, S., Marchetti-Spaccamela, A., Matias, Y., Nikoletseas, S., Thomas, W. (eds.) ICALP 2009, Part II. LNCS, vol. 5556, pp. 212–222. Springer, Heidelberg (2009)
12. Kirchner, C.: Rho-calculi for computation and logic (invited talk). In: Tiwari, A. (ed.) RTA. LIPIcs, vol. 15, pp. 2–4. Schloss Dagstuhl - Leibniz-Zentrum fuer Informatik (2012)
13. Klop, J.W.: Combinatory Reduction Systems. Mathematical Centre Tracts 127. Mathematisch Centrum, Amsterdam (1980)
14. Knuth, D.E., Bendix, P.B.: Simple word problems in universal algebras. In: Leech, J. (ed.) Computational Problems in Abstract Algebra, pp. 263–297. Elsevier (1970)
15. Meseguer, J.: Rewriting logic and maude: Concepts and applications. In: Bachmair, L. (ed.) RTA 2000. LNCS, vol. 1833, pp. 1–26. Springer, Heidelberg (2000)
16. Meseguer, J.: Maude. In: Padua, D.A. (ed.) Encyclopedia of Parallel Computing, pp. 1095–1102. Springer (2011)
17. Nakamura, M., Kong, W., Ogata, K., Futatsugi, K.: A specification translation from behavioral specifications to rewrite specifications. IEICE Transactions 91-D(5), 1492–1503 (2008)
18. Pottier, F.: An overview of *Calpha*ml. Electr. Notes Theor. Comput. Sci. 148(2), 27–52 (2006)
19. Saraswat, V.A.: The paradigm of concurrent constraint programming. In: ICLP, pp. 777–778 (1990)
20. Strub, P.-Y.: Coq modulo theory. In: Dawar, A., Veith, H. (eds.) CSL 2010. LNCS, vol. 6247, pp. 529–543. Springer, Heidelberg (2010)
21. Terese: Term rewriting systems. In: Klop, J.W., et al. (eds.) Cambridge Tracts in Theoretical Computer Science, vol. 55. Cambridge University Press (2003)
22. Toyama, Y.: Commutativity of term rewriting systems. Programming of future generation computers II, pp. 393–407 (1988)

23. van Oostrom, V.: Confluence by decreasing diagrams. Theor. Comput. Sci. 126(2), 259–280 (1994)
24. van Oostrom, V.: Confluence by decreasing diagrams converted. In: Voronkov, A. (ed.) RTA 2008. LNCS, vol. 5117, pp. 306–320. Springer, Heidelberg (2008)
25. Zankl, H., Felgenhauer, B., Middeldorp, A.: Labelings for decreasing diagrams. In: Schmidt-Schauß, M. (ed.) RTA. LIPIcs, vol. 10, pp. 377–392. Schloss Dagstuhl - Leibniz-Zentrum fuer Informatik (2011)

Foundations for Ensemble Modeling –
The HELENA Approach
Handling Massively Distributed Systems with ELaborate ENsemble Architectures*

Rolf Hennicker and Annabelle Klarl

Ludwig-Maximilians-Universität München
Germany

Abstract. Ensembles are groups of active entities that collaborate to perform a certain task. Modeling software systems for ensemble execution is challenging since such applications are highly dynamic involving complex interaction structures of concurrently running individuals. In this work, we propose a formal foundation for ensemble modeling based on a rigorous semantic framework. Our approach is centered around the notion of a role expressing the capabilities that a component needs when participating in a specific ensemble. We use ensemble structures to model the structural aspects of collaborations and labeled transition systems to specify the dynamic behavior typical for performing a certain role. Our approach is driven by a clear discrimination between types, used on the specification level, and instances, which form concrete ensembles in an ensemble automaton. The semantics of an ensemble specification is given by the class of all ensemble automata which adhere to the properties of an ensemble structure such that any ensemble member, playing a certain role, exhibits a behavior that is allowed by the role behavior specification.

1 Introduction

1.1 Motivation

The continuously increasing potential of new computer technologies paves the way for developing advanced applications in which huge numbers of distributed nodes collaborate to accomplish various tasks under changing environments. Application domains are, for instance, environmental monitoring and simulation, robotics, e-mobility and cloud computing. Such applications are typically highly dynamic involving a complex interaction behavior between nodes. Nodes may join or leave a collaboration, they may change location and they may autonomously adapt to new conditions. Systems supporting such applications are extremely software-intensive. In contrast to available hardware, current software engineering practices are not sufficiently developed to support such scenarios in

---

* This work has been partially sponsored by the EU project ASCENS, 257414.

S. Iida, J. Meseguer, and K. Ogata (Eds.): Futatsugi Festschrift, LNCS 8373, pp. 359–381, 2014.

a reliable way on a semantically solid basis with sound formal specification and verification techniques.

On this background, the EU project ASCENS [1,34] pursues the goal to develop foundations, techniques and tools to support the whole life cycle for the construction of Autonomic Service-Component ENSembles [9]. An ensemble is understood as a collection of autonomic entities that collaborate for some global goal. Following [27,2], a goal can be an "achieve goal", such that the ensemble will terminate when the goal (specified, e.g., by a particular state) is reached, or a "maintenance goal", such that a certain property (specified, e.g., by a system invariant) is maintained while the system is running.

The inherent complexity and dynamics of ensembles exhibiting a collective, goal-oriented behavior is a huge challenge. Well-known techniques, like component-based software engineering [33,31], are not sufficient for modeling ensembles, but must be augmented with other features that allow to focus on the particular characteristics of ensembles. While a component model describes the architectural and dynamic properties of a (complex) target system, ensembles are dynamically formed on demand as specific, goal-oriented communication groups running on top of a target system and different ensembles may run concurrently on the same system (dealing with different tasks). The target platform of the system can be component-based, but it is crucial to recognize that the same component instance may take part in different ensembles under particular, ensemble-specific *roles*. A component instance can play different roles at the same time and it can dynamically change its role. Therefore, we propose to center our approach around the notion of a role [21] and to model an ensemble in terms of roles and their interactions to collectively pursue a certain goal.

Ensemble modeling is particularly important in the analysis phase of the development life cycle since it allows us to concentrate only on parts of the capabilities that a component must finally support. Each role a component can fill represents a particular view on the component needed to solve a specific collaborative task. In this way complexity of system modeling can be significantly reduced.

1.2 The HELENA Approach

In this paper, we propose a rigorous formal foundation for ensemble modeling that can be used during requirements elicitation and as a basis for the development of designs. In the HELENA approach, we assume given a set of component types. The component types define basic attributes and operations that are commonly available. Each role (more precisely, role type) is defined for a subset of component types whose instances can fill the role. A role specifies particular capabilities in terms of role attributes and role operations that are only relevant when performing the role. The structural aspects of a collaboration are determined by an *ensemble structure* which consists of a set of roles (constrained by multiplicities) and a set of role connectors determining which roles may interact in terms of which operations. This introduces a level of security since other interactions are not legal; i.e. an interaction requested by a component which does not fit to its current role would be a failure. For visualizing ensemble structures, we use UML-like notations [30]. Additionally, we use labeled transition systems to determine the dynamic aspects of a collaboration in terms of role behaviors such that collaboration is directed towards a specific task.

Our framework supports specialization in the sense that different extensions and interpretations of an ensemble model are possible. For instance we do not fix any particular paradigm for interaction on the level of an ensemble structure. Interaction could be performed by accessing knowledge in the repositories of components, like in SCEL [17,18], it could be realized by implicit knowledge exchange managed by the runtime infrastructure, like in DEECo [12], or it could be based on explicit synchronous or asynchronous communication.

To provide semantics for an ensemble specification, the interaction paradigm must be instantiated. In this paper, we show how this can be done for the case of synchronous message passing systems. For a given ensemble specification, we consider the class of its semantic models given by particular labeled transition systems called *ensemble automata*. Each state of the system determines a set of component instances which are currently participating in the ensemble and a set of role instances which are currently adopted by the component instances. Both component and role instances have a current data state determined by their attribute values respectively. The attribute values of a component instance ci determine the (basic) information that is shared by all role instances that ci is currently playing. Moreover, to each role instance a control state is associated that determines its current progress according to the behavior specification of the corresponding role type. Transitions between ensemble states are caused either by communication between role instances according to a role connector or when certain management operations are performed such that component instances join or leave an ensemble, change their role or adopt an additional role.

In the following sections, we first consider, in Sect. 2, the syntactic notions for ensemble structures and ensemble specifications. In Sect. 3, we define their semantic interpretations: we consider ensemble states, formed by collections of component and role instances, and we focus on the particular case of synchronous message passing systems for which we introduce ensemble automata as semantic models of ensemble specifications. In Sect. 4, we discuss related work and, in Sect. 5, we give a short summary and point out ideas how our approach will be extended towards a comprehensive, semantically well-founded ensemble development methodology.

Dedication. Our approach is strongly influenced by the school of algebraic specifications and institutions [20], including the seminal work of Prof. Futatsugi as one of the leading architects of prominent algebraic specification languages like OBJ2 [19] and CafeOBJ [29]. Indeed, an ensemble structure in HELENA can be considered as a signature, ensemble automata as models of that signature, ensemble states as (higher-order) algebras, ensemble specifications as presentations and the satisfaction relation is implicitly given by the notion of a model of an ensemble specification. We would like to thank Prof. Futatsugi very cordially for his important contributions to the field and for his very friendly attitude in scientific and private discussions. In particular, it was always a great pleasure to discuss with him new ideas for the observational interpretation of algebraic specifications, as supported by CafeOBJ and implemented in the CafeOBJ environment [28]. It is a pleasure for us to dedicate this work to Prof. Futatsugi and we want to wish him many more new exciting ideas and experiences in the future.

2   Ensemble Structures and Specifications

In the HELENA approach, we tackle systems with a large number of entities which collaborate towards a specific goal. The foundation for those systems are components which are presented in the first subsection. To cope with the complexity of systems with large numbers of components, we afterwards introduce the notion of an ensemble structure as a view on a component-based system. Lastly, we outline the specification of the dynamic behavior of roles collaborating in such an ensemble structure to direct behavior towards the intended task.

Throughout the paper, we use a peer-2-peer network as running example which supports the distributed storage of files that can be retrieved upon request. Several peers of the network will work together when a file is requested. One peer will play the role of the requester of the file, other peers will act as routers and finally, the peer storing the requested file will appear in the role of a provider.

Notation. Whenever we consider tuples $t = (t_1, \ldots, t_n)$, in the following we use the notation $t_i(t)$ to refer to t_i.

2.1   Components

First, we introduce the concepts of rudimentary components providing basic information usable in all roles the component can fill. Component types are characterized by *attributes* and *operations*. Attributes and parameters of operations are not (necessarily) typed.

Definition 1 (Attributes and Operations). *An* attribute *is a named variable. An* operation *op is of the form op = opname(params) such that opname is the name of the operation and params is a list of formal parameters.*

Definition 2 (Attribute Values). *Let A be a set of attributes and $\mathcal{D}$ a universe of data values. An A-state is a function $\delta : A \to \mathcal{D}$ which assigns a value in $\mathcal{D}$ to each attribute in A. The set of all A-states is denoted by $DStates_A$.*

Let us consider this definition in the context of our running example of a peer-2-peer network. Typical attributes in such an environment are the network address of an entity and the list of filenames and their content which an entity stores. The set of attributes can thus be defined as $A = \{$address, fileNames, contents$\}$. The function δ_1 may, for example, assign the value 198.121.1.3 to the attribute address, [1.txt, 2.pdf] to the attribute fileNames, and some file contents to the attribute contents.

To classify components according to their capabilities, we introduce *component types*. A component type defines the attributes and operations for all components of that type. It forms the basis for more specialized and complex capabilities. A component instance is a concrete instantiation of its component type.

Definition 3 (Component Type). *A component type* ct *is a tuple* $ct = (nm, attrs, ops)$ *such that* nm *is the name of the component type, attrs is a set of attributes, and* $ops = \langle ops_{out}, ops_{in}, ops_{int} \rangle$ *with* ops_{out}, ops_{in}, *and* ops_{int} *are sets of outgoing, incoming, and internal operations respectively.*

The basic component type in a peer-2-peer network is $peer = (\text{Peer}, \{\text{address}, \text{fileNames}, \text{contents}\}, \langle \emptyset, \emptyset, \emptyset \rangle)$. Each component of component type $peer$ has the attributes address, fileNames, and contents and no (basic) operations, since all $peer$ operations introduced in the sequel will only be relevant for particular roles. For visualization, we introduce a graphical notation for component types like in UML (cf. Fig. 1).

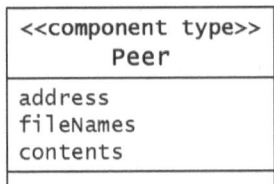

Fig. 1. Component type *peer* in graphical notation

2.2   Ensemble Structures

Components can collaborate to perform certain tasks. For this purpose, they team up in *ensembles*. Each participant in the ensemble contributes specific functionalities to the collaboration, we say, the participant plays a certain *role* in the ensemble. A role (more precisely, role type) defines which types of components can contribute the desired functionality to the overall collaboration and enhances them with role-specific capabilities. Firstly, the role specifies the component types of entities which are able to fill this role. Secondly, it defines role-specific attributes to store data that is relevant for performing the role and role-specific operations which are required to fulfill the responsibilities of the role.

Definition 4 (Role). *Let* CT *be a set of component types. A role* r *over* CT *is a tuple* $r = (head, roleattrs, roleops)$ *such that*

- *head* $= \langle nm, ctypes \rangle$ *declares the name* nm *of the role together with a finite, non-empty set* $ctypes \subseteq CT$ *of component types (whose instances can fill the role* r*),*
- *roleattrs specifies the role specific attributes, and*
- *roleops* $= \langle roleops_{out}, roleops_{in}, roleops_{int} \rangle$ *specifies outgoing, incoming, and internal operations provided by the role* r*.*

In the context of our peer-2-peer network, we consider the task of requesting and transferring a file. To perform this task, we envision three roles: requester, router, and provider. The requester wants to download the file. First, it needs to request the address of the peer storing the file from the network, while using the routers as forwarding peers of its request. Once the requester knows the address, it directly requests the file from the provider for download. Each role can be adopted by instances of component type *peer*, but exhibits different capabilities to take over responsibility for the transfer task. The requester must be able to request the address of the provider from a router and receive the reply. Afterwards, it must be able to request the file from the provider and receive the content. The router must be able to receive a request for the address, forward it to another router, receive the reply from another router, and send it back. The provider of a certain file must be able to receive a request for the file and send back the content. Formally, the role of the provider peer is defined as follows:

$$provider = ((\langle \texttt{ Provider}, \{peer\} \rangle, \emptyset,$$
$$\langle \{\texttt{sndFile(cont)}\}, \{\texttt{reqFile(fn)}\}, \emptyset \rangle))$$

Note that for this role neither specific attributes nor internal operations are necessary, but the requester role stores the name of the requested file in its role-specific attribute `fileName`.

We use a UML-like visualization of roles annotated with the stereotype «role type». The diagrams for the roles in the peer-2-peer network are given in Fig. 2. They consist of three parts: the name of the role followed by the set of component types which can fill the role, the role attributes, and the role operations together with the modifiers out, in, and int.

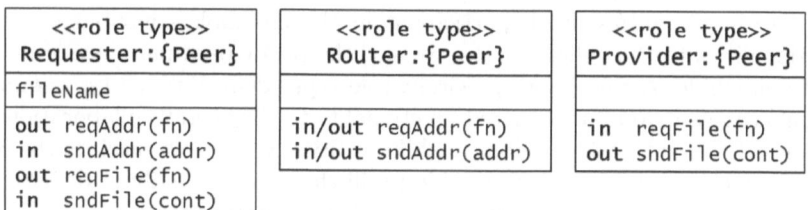

Fig. 2. Roles *requester*, *router*, and *provider* in graphical notation

To collaborate on tasks, roles need to communicate. A role initiates the information transfer via the call of an outgoing operation and receives information via the reception of an incoming operation. However, for the specification of collaborations we do not only want to declare communication abilities of a single role, but also to specify which roles are meant to interact by which messages. This information is specified by a *role connector* (or more precisely, role connector type). Role connectors are directed such that they can also support multicast sending of messages.

Definition 5 (Role Connector). *Let CT be a set of component types and R be a set of roles over CT. A role connector rc over R is a tuple rc = (nm, src, trg, ops, rcconstraints) such that*

- *nm is the name of the role connector,*
- *src ∈ R denotes the source role from which information is transferred along rc,*
- *trg ∈ R denotes the target role to which information is transferred along rc, and*
- *ops is a set of operations such that ops ⊆ roleops$_{out}$(src) ∩ roleops$_{in}$(trg) determine which messages can be sent along rc.*

In our running example, a requester peer needs to send a download request for a file to the provider peer. For that communication, we introduce the role connector rfc = (ReqFileConn, $requester$, $provider$, {reqFile(fn)}). In Fig. 2 we can verify that rfc is well-formed according to Def. 5 since reqFile is an outgoing operation for the role $requester$ and an incoming operation for the role $provider$. For the reply, we introduce the role connector sfc = (SndFileConn, $provider$, $requester$, {sndFile(cont)}). Role connectors are visualized as shown in Fig. 3. The first box shows the name of the role connector, the second one the source and target role, and the last one the exchanged messages. Although in our example rfc and sfc are only responsible for one message, role connectors can in general allow a set of messages, some of which could also be declared as multicast messages.

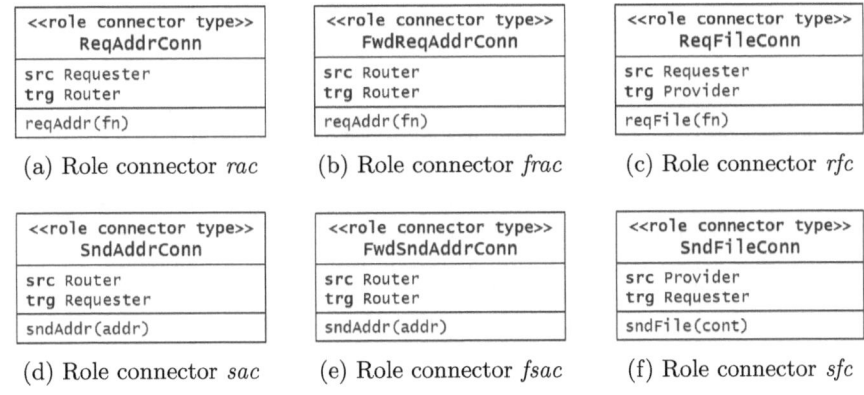

Fig. 3. Role connectors providing interaction abilities in graphical notation

Roles and role connectors form the basic building blocks for collaborations in ensembles. An *ensemble structure* determines the kind of teams needed to perform a task. An ensemble structure specifies which roles contribute to the collaboration and which role connectors are required for interaction. Additionally, in an ensemble structure roles are equipped with a multiplicity which determines how many instances may contribute. Thus, an ensemble structure specifies the structural aspects of a collaboration.

Definition 6 (Ensemble Structure). *Let CT be a set of component types. An* ensemble structure Σ over CT *is a pair* $\Sigma = (roles, conns)$ *such that*

- *roles is a set of roles over CT such that each* $r \in roles$ *has a multiplicity* $mult(r) \in Mult$ *and Mult is the set of multiplicities available in UML, like* 0..1 *or* *,*
- *conns is a set of role connectors over roles such that for each* $rc \in conns$, *it holds* $src(rc), trg(rc) \in roles$.

The ensemble structure Σ *is* closed *if all operations are used in connectors, i.e. if*

$$\bigcup_{rc \in conns} ops(rc) = \bigcup_{r \in roles} (roleops_{out}(r) \cup roleops_{in}(r));$$

otherwise it is open.

For our peer example, we define an ensemble structure $\Sigma_{transfer}$. The ensemble structure is composed of a requester role (with at most one instance participating in the ensemble), a router role (with arbitrarily many instances participating in the ensemble), and a provider role (with at most one instance participating in the ensemble). Communication between those roles is needed to request and receive the provider address from the network (possibly involving several forwarding steps via routers) and finally to request and receive the file from the provider itself. Formally, the ensemble structure $\Sigma_{transfer} = (roles, conns)$ embraces the two sets:

$$roles = \{\langle requester, 0..1\rangle, \langle router, *\rangle, \langle provider, 0..1\rangle\}$$
$$conns = \{rac, sac, frac, fsac, sfc, rfc\}$$

In the set *roles*, we find each role associated with a multiplicity as mentioned before. The role connectors in the set *conns* provide the means to request and send address and file (cf. Fig. 3). We visualize ensemble structures similarly to collaborations in composite structure diagrams in UML 2. Fig. 4 shows the ensemble structure $\Sigma_{transfer}$ in graphical notation. Roles are depicted as boxes with the multiplicity written in the upper right corner. Role connectors are represented as arrows between source and target roles labeled with the connector name.

2.3   Ensemble Specifications

After having modeled the structural aspects of an ensemble, we move on to the specification of dynamic behaviors. A role itself declares the particular capabilities needed to perform a certain task in the form of its operations. How these operations are used to model role behavior is formalized by a *labeled transition system*. Starting from an initial state, the role behavior specifies which sequences of operations can be executed to contribute the required responsibilities of this role to the overall collaboration.

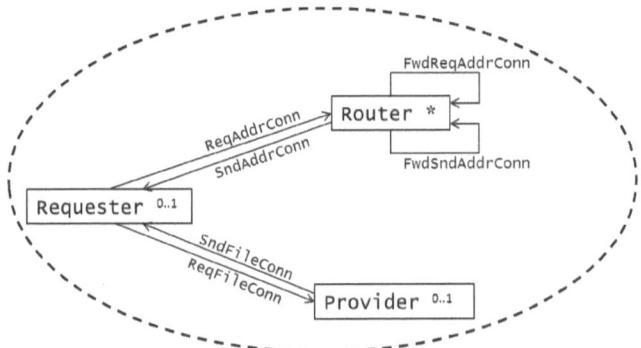

Fig. 4. Ensemble structure $\Sigma_{transfer}$

Definition 7 (Labeled Transition System). *A labeled transition system* (LTS) *is a tuple* $(Q, q_0, \Lambda, \Delta)$ *such that* Q *is a set of states,* $q_0 \in Q$ *is the initial state of the LTS,* Λ *is a set of labels, and* $\Delta \subseteq Q \times \Lambda \times Q$ *is a transition relation. For* $(q, l, q') \in \Delta$, *we also write* $(q \xrightarrow{l} q') \in \Delta$.

A *role behavior* is a labeled transition system whose labels denote sending an operation (expressed by the operation followed by an exclamation mark "!") or receiving an operation (expressed by the operation followed by a question mark "?") or executing an internal operation (expressed just by the operation).

Definition 8 (Role Behavior). *Let* $\Sigma = (roles, conns)$ *be an ensemble structure and* $r \in roles$. *A role behavior of* r *is given by a labeled transition system* $RoleBeh_r = (Q, q_0, \Lambda, \Delta)$ *such that*

- Q *is a set of control states,*

- $q_0 \in Q$ *is the initial state,*

- Λ *is the set of labels given by*
  $\{nm(rc).op! \mid \exists rc \in conns : r = src(rc),\ op \in ops(rc)\} \cup$
  $\{nm(rc).op? \mid \exists rc \in conns : r = trg(rc),\ op \in ops(rc)\}$,

- $\Delta \subseteq Q \times \Lambda \times Q$ *is a transition relation.*

Following our notational convention, we write $Q(RoleBeh_r)$ for Q, $q_0(RoleBeh_r)$ for q_0, $\Lambda(RoleBeh_r)$ for Λ, and $\Delta(RoleBeh_r)$ for Δ.

The full specification of an ensemble comprises the architecture of the collaboration in terms of an ensemble structure Σ and the set of all role behavior specifications.

Definition 9 (Ensemble specification). *An* ensemble specification *is a pair* $EnsSpec = (\Sigma, RoleBeh)$ *such that*

- $\Sigma = (roles, conns)$ *is an ensemble structure over a set CT of component types, and*
- $RoleBeh = (RoleBeh_r)_{r \in roles}$ *is a family of role behaviors RoleBeh$_r$ for each* $r \in roles$.

Let us illustrate the specification of ensembles with our running example. We specify the dynamic behavior of the *requester*, *router* and *provider* roles by the three role behaviors $RoleBeh_{requester}$, $RoleBeh_{router}$, and $RoleBeh_{provider}$ shown in Fig. 5. All three behaviors terminate since in this application we consider an achieve goal such that an ensemble stops when it has fulfilled its task.

The router role exhibits the most interesting behavior. Its responsibility is to provide the address of the provider to a requesting peer. A router can first receive a request `reqAddr(fn)?` to search for the address where the file with name `fn` is located from a requester, using the connector *rac*, or from (another) router, using the forward request address connector *frac*. Since the router may or may not store the file itself, in each case it has two possibilities to proceed: either it has the file and thus sends its own address back to the requester with the message `sndAddr(addr)!`, or it does not have the file and thus requests the address from a neighboring peer by issuing the call `reqAddr(fn)!`. In the first case, it has immediately met its responsibility according to the router role while in the second case it has to wait for a response and then to forward it to the requesting peer. Note that on the instance level considered later on in Sect. 3, the peer instance playing the router will adopt the role of a provider when it detects that it stores the file itself (cf. the transition from state σ_5 to σ_6 in Fig. 9).

With this example we want to illustrate that the separate consideration of roles facilitates significantly the task of system specification for ensembles. If we had directly started with component-based modeling of a peer component, it would have been necessary to specify the full component behavior at once. This behavior would have to model all possible behaviors which a component instance should be able to perform. In particular, one would have to decide whether a component instance should administrate several threads for concurrent executions of different tasks at the same time or whether a component is only able to perform different tasks in a sequential order.

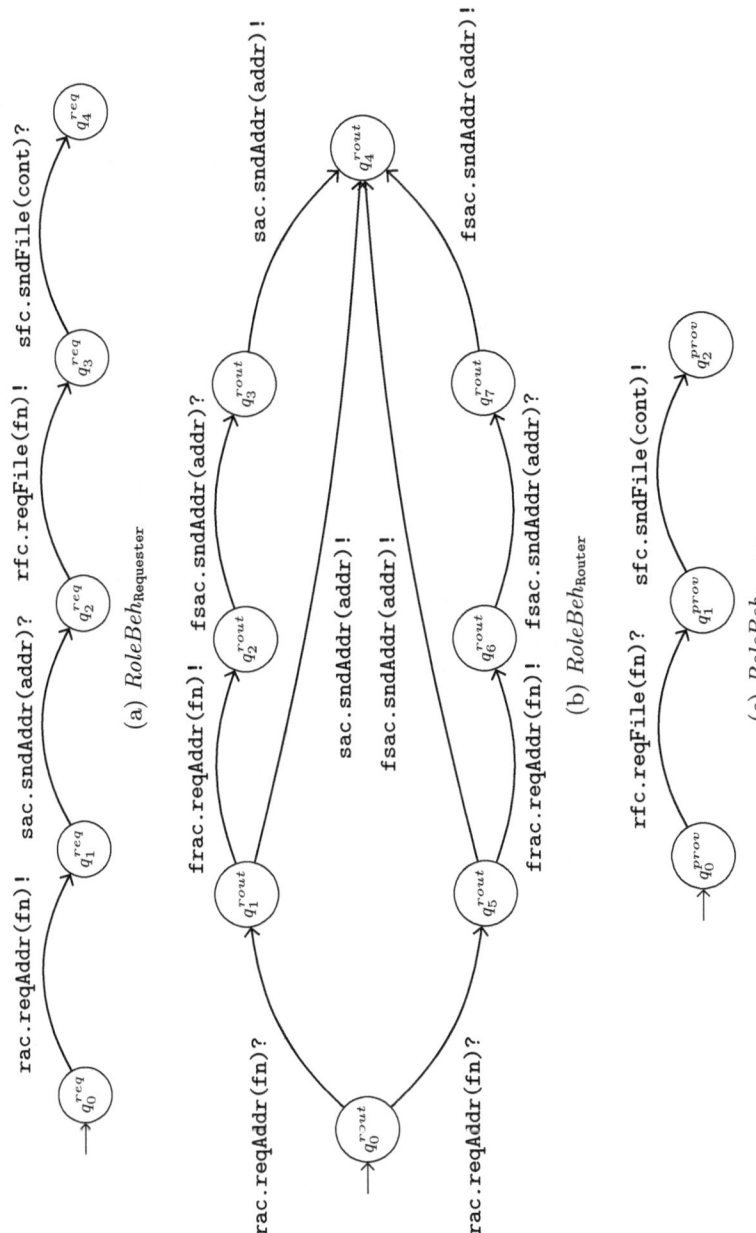

Fig. 5. Behaviors specifications

3   Semantics of Ensemble Specifications

3.1   Ensemble States

An ensemble structure $\Sigma = (roles, conns)$ over a set CT of component types specifies which roles and role connectors are needed to perform a task. The actual execution of an ensemble will be performed by collaborating component instances. We assume that before an ensemble is started there exists already a repository of component instances which can potentially contribute. Formally, this repository is given by a family $INST = (INST_{ct})_{ct \in CT}$ of pairwise disjoint sets $INST_{ct}$ of component instances for each component type ct. For an ensemble state σ, the currently participating component instances are determined by the sets $insts = (insts_{ct})_{ct \in CT}$ shown in Def. 10 below. The situation is different for roles. Role instances are only created when a component instance adopts that role. Formally, we assume given a family $RID = (RID_r)_{r \in roles}$ of countably infinite and pairwise disjoint sets RID_r of role identifiers for role r. These sets determine a space of names which can be instantiated when a new role instance is created. An ensemble state σ has not only to record which are the current component members of the ensemble, but also which role instances currently exist. These are determined by the sets $roleinsts = (roleinsts_r)_{r \in roles}$ below. Any existing role instance must be adopted by exactly one component instance and any participating component instance must at least adopt one role instance. For the formalization of these relationships we use the surjective mappings $adoptedBy = (adoptedBy_r)_{r \in roles}$ whose functionalities are defined below.

To fully specify a Σ-ensemble state, we additionally need to determine the data states of component and role instances (given by valuations of component and role attributes resp.), and also the control state of a role instance showing the current progress of its execution. For this purpose, we use the families of functions $data$, $roledata$, and $control$ as indicated below.

Definition 10 (Σ-ensemble state). *Let CT be a set of component types, $INST$ be a family of sets of component instances and RID be a universe of role identifiers as explained above. A Σ-ensemble state (over $INST$) is a tuple*

$$\sigma = (insts, roleinsts, adoptedBy, data, roledata, control)$$

such that

- *$insts = (insts_{ct})_{ct \in CT}$ is a family of sets $insts_{ct} \subseteq INST_{ct}$ of component instances currently participating in the ensemble,*
- *$roleinsts = (roleinsts_r)_{r \in roles}$ is a family of sets $roleinsts_r \subseteq RID_r$ of role instances currently existing in the ensemble such that the multiplicities of $r \in roles$ in Σ are respected, i.e. $|roleinsts_r| \leq 1$ if $mult(r) = 0..1$,*
- *$adoptedBy = (adoptedBy_r)_{r \in roles}$ is a family of surjective functions $adoptedBy_r : roleinsts_r \rightarrow \bigcup_{ct \in ctypes(r)} insts_{ct}$ such that each role instance is associated to a unique component instance,*

- $data = (data_{ct})_{ct \in CT}$ *is a family of functions*
  $data_{ct} : insts_{ct} \to DStates_{attrs(ct)}$,
- $roledata = (roledata_r)_{r \in roles}$ *is a family of functions*
  $roledata_r : roleinsts_r \to DStates_{roleattrs(r)}$,
- $control = (control_r)_{r \in roles}$ *is a family of functions*
  $control_r : roleinsts_r \to CStates_r$ *with a set* $CStates_r$ *of control states.*

The set of all Σ-ensemble states is denoted by $States_\Sigma$.

Following our notational conventions, for a Σ-ensemble state $\sigma = (insts, roleinsts, adoptedBy, data, roledata, control)$ we write $insts(\sigma)$ for $insts$, $insts_{ct}(\sigma)$ for $insts_{ct}$, and similarly for all other parts of σ.

To illustrate the meaning of the *adoptedBy* functions, we visualize the mapping for two different Σ-ensemble states σ_1 and σ_2 in Fig. 6. Both states are based on the set $INST = \{ci1, ci1', ci2'\}$ of component instances of type CT and CT' resp.. The idea is that there are two ensembles running in parallel such that σ_1 is a state of the first ensemble and σ_2 is a state of the second. The given component instances should be able to participate at the same time in both ensembles. For instance in σ_1, ci1 adopts the role instances ri1 and ri1' of different role types R and R'. In σ_2, ci1 adopts, at the time, another role instance ri3 of type R. Being surjective, each function *adoptedBy$_r$* associates each component instance ci which is participating in an ensemble with at least one role instance. The inverse image of one component instance ci in a particular state is thus the set of all role instances which ci is currently playing in that state. Only component instances that do currently not participate in an ensemble, like ci1' in Fig. 6, have no associated role instance.

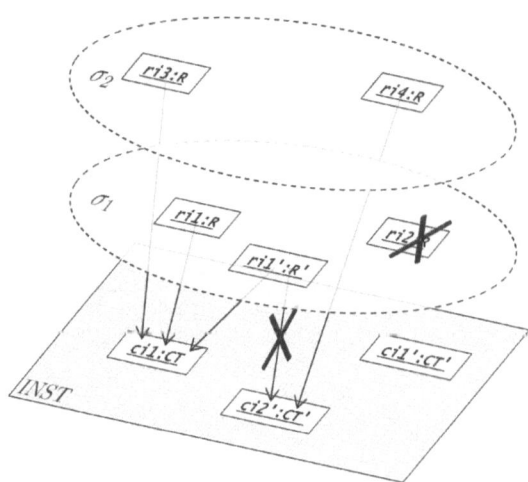

Fig. 6. Visualization of the function *adoptedBy*

Let us illustrate the definition of a Σ-ensemble state at our peer-2-peer network. Consider the ensemble structure $\Sigma_{transfer}$ and four component instances of type *peer* such that $INST = INST_{peer} = \{p1, p2, p3, p4\}$, i.e. we have given a system with four peers. A valid ensemble state over $INST$ could be that $p1$ has adopted the role of a requester that requests a file with name `"song.mp3"`, $p2$ and $p3$ work as routers, and $p3$ provides the file; $p4$ is not involved in this collaboration. The formal representation of such a $\Sigma_{transfer}$-ensemble state $\sigma = (insts, roleinsts, adoptedBy, data, roledata, control)$ is given in Fig. 7; a graphical representation of this state is shown in Fig. 8. The current control state of each role instance is shown in a circle and taken from the role behavior specifications. For instance, $rout1$ being in control state q_2^{rout} has just sent out a request address message to another router via the role connector $frac$, and $rout2$ being in control state q_5^{rout} has just received this message. We assume that the component $p3$ stores the requested file and therefore adopts, in the current state, also the role of a provider being in the initial provider state q_0^{prov}.

$$
\begin{aligned}
insts_{peer} &= \{p1, p2, p3\} & data_{peer}(p1) &= \{(\texttt{address} \mapsto \texttt{198.121.1.1},\\
roleinsts_{requester} &= \{req\} & & \quad \texttt{fileNames} \mapsto \dots)\}\\
roleinsts_{router} &= \{rout1, rout2\} & & \quad \texttt{contents} \mapsto \dots)\}\\
roleinsts_{provider} &= \{prov\} & data_{peer}(p2) &= \dots\\
adoptedBy_{requester}(req) &= \{p1\} & data_{peer}(p3) &= \dots\\
adoptedBy_{router}(rout1) &= \{p2\} & roledata_{requester}(req) &= \{\texttt{fileName} \mapsto \texttt{"song.mp3"}\}\\
adoptedBy_{router}(rout2) &= \{p3\} & roledata\_(\_) &= \emptyset\\
adoptedBy_{provider}(prov) &= \{p3\} & control_{requester}(req) &= q_1^{req}\\
& & control_{router}(rout1) &= q_2^{rout}\\
& & control_{router}(rout2) &= q_5^{rout}\\
& & control_{provider}(prov) &= q_0^{prov}
\end{aligned}
$$

Fig. 7. A $\Sigma_{transfer}$-ensemble state σ

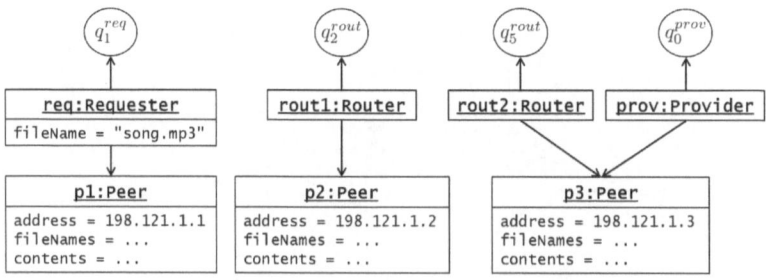

Fig. 8. $\Sigma_{transfer}$-ensemble state σ in graphical notation

3.2 Ensemble Automata

A system evolves over time by execution of operations of component instances. To model the precise collaborative behavior we have to fix how interaction is performed. In this paper, we consider the case of message passing systems with synchronous communication. Two communication partners must synchronize whenever they want to execute a shared input/output operation; otherwise they cannot proceed. We define a formal execution model for ensembles in terms of ensemble automata. Their states are ensemble states as defined in the last section. We consider two kinds of actions that can cause state transitions. First, we consider communication actions which express synchronous communication betweeen role instances. These actions are represented by operation labels of the form $opname(actparams)(rc, ri, ri')$ meaning that a role instance ri sends a message determined by an operation with name $opname$ and with actual parameters $actparams$ via a role connector rc to a role instance ri'. Of course, the message must be supported by the role connector and the role types of the communicating role instances must fit to the source and target roles of the connector. For technical simplicity, we assume that ensemble structures are closed and that roles and component types do not declare internal operations. The general case could be modeled by simple variants of the form of operation labels. The second kind of actions are represented by management labels of the form $adopt(ci, r)$ or $giveUp(ci, ri)$. The first label expresses that a component instance ci adopts a role r, either because ci is joining the ensemble or because ci adopts an additional role. In any case, a new role instance will be created (cf. Eq. (1)), and the $adoptedBy$ function will be updated accordingly (cf. Eq. (2)). The second management label expresses that a component instance ci gives up a role instance ri. The role instance is then deleted from the ensemble and the component instance must leave the ensemble if this was the only role played by the component. For all kinds of labels, appropriate pre- and postconditions are provided that are respected by the transitions. The postconditions specify the effect of the operation for the different constituent parts of an ensemble state. If no effect is specified then the interpretation is loose leaving room for non-deterministic behavior.

Definition 11 (Σ-ensemble automaton). *Let CT be a set of component types and let $INST = (INST_{ct})_{ct \in CT}$ be a family component instances as in Def. 10. Let $\Sigma = (roles, conns)$ be an ensemble structure over CT. A Σ-ensemble automaton (over INST) is a labeled transition system $M = (S, \sigma_0, L, T)$ such that*

- $S \subseteq States_\Sigma$,
- $\sigma_0 \in S$ *is the initial state,*
- $L = oplabels \cup mgmtlabels$ *such that*
  - $oplabels = \{ opname(actparams)(rc, ri, ri') \mid$
    $rc \in conns, ri \in RID_{src(rc)}, ri' \in RID_{trg(rc)},$
    $opname(params) \in ops(rc)$ *such that* $actparams \in \mathcal{D}^*$ *is a list of actual parameters instantiating params* $\}$

- $mgmtlabels =$
  $\{adopt(ci, r) \mid ci \in INST_{ct}, r \in roles \ such \ that \ ct \in ctypes(r)\} \cup$
  $\{giveUp(ci, ri) \mid ci \in INST_{ct}, ri \in RID_r$
  $such \ that \ r \in roles \ and \ ct \in ctypes(r)\}$
- for each $(\sigma_1, l, \sigma_2) \in T$, one of the following holds:
  - if $l = opname(actparams)(rc, ri, ri')$ then

    $(pre) \qquad ri \in roleinsts_{src(rc)}(\sigma_1), ri' \in roleinsts_{trg(rc)}(\sigma_1),$

    $(post) \qquad insts(\sigma_2) = insts(\sigma_1), roleinsts(\sigma_2) = roleinsts(\sigma_1),$

    $\qquad\qquad\quad adoptedBy(\sigma_2) = adoptedBy(\sigma_1)$

- if $l = adopt(ci, r)$ with $ci \in INST_{ct}, r \in roles$ then

  $(post) \qquad insts_{ct}(\sigma_2) = insts_{ct}(\sigma_1) \cup \{ci\},$

  $\qquad\qquad\quad insts_{ct'}(\sigma_2) = insts_{ct'}(\sigma_1) \ for \ all \ ct' \neq ct,$

  $\qquad\qquad\quad roleinsts_r(\sigma_2) = \qquad\qquad\qquad\qquad\qquad\qquad\qquad\qquad\quad (1)$

  $\qquad\qquad\qquad roleinsts_r(\sigma_1) \cup \{ri\} \ with \ ri \in RID_r, ri \notin roleinsts_r(\sigma_1),$

  $\qquad\qquad\quad roleinsts_{r'}(\sigma_2) = roleinsts_{r'}(\sigma_1) \ for \ all \ r' \neq r,$

  $\qquad\qquad\quad adoptedBy_r(\sigma_2)(ri) = ci \ for \ the \ new \ role \ instance \ ri, \qquad (2)$

  $\qquad\qquad\quad adoptedBy_{r'}(\sigma_2)(ri') =$

  $\qquad\qquad\qquad adoptedBy_{r'}(\sigma_1)(ri') \ for \ all \ r' \in roles, ri' \neq ri,$

  $\qquad\qquad\quad data(\sigma_2) = data(\sigma_1),$

  $\qquad\qquad\quad roledata_{r'}(\sigma_2)(ri') =$

  $\qquad\qquad\qquad roledata_{r'}(\sigma_1)(ri') \ for \ all \ r' \in roles, ri' \neq ri,$

  $\qquad\qquad\quad control_{r'}(\sigma_2)(ri') =$

  $\qquad\qquad\qquad control_{r'}(\sigma_1)(ri') \ for \ all \ r' \in roles, ri' \neq ri,$

- if $l = giveUp(ci, ri)$ with $ci \in INST_{ct}, ri \in RID_r$ then

  $(pre) \qquad\qquad ci \in insts_{ct}(\sigma_1), ri \in roleinsts_r(\sigma_1),$

  $\qquad\qquad\qquad adoptedBy_r(\sigma_1)(ri) = ci,$

  $(post) \quad insts_{ct}(\sigma_2) = \begin{cases} insts_{ct}(\sigma_1) \setminus \{ci\} \ , \ if \ \nexists ri' \neq ri. \\ \qquad\qquad\qquad\qquad adoptedBy_r(\sigma_1)(ri') = ci \\ insts_{ct}(\sigma_1) \qquad , \ otherwise \end{cases}$

  $\qquad\quad insts_{ct'}(\sigma_2) = insts_{ct'}(\sigma_1) \ for \ all \ ct' \neq ct,$

  $\qquad\quad roleinsts_r(\sigma_2) = roleinsts_r(\sigma_1) \setminus \{ri\},$

  $\qquad\quad roleinsts_{r'}(\sigma_2) = roleinsts_{r'}(\sigma_1) \ for \ all \ r' \neq r,$

  $\qquad\quad adoptedBy(\sigma_2) = adoptedBy(\sigma_1)|_{roleinsts(\sigma_2)},$

  $\qquad\quad data(\sigma_2) = data(\sigma_1),$

  $\qquad\quad roledata(\sigma_2) = roledata(\sigma_1)|_{roleinsts(\sigma_2)},$

  $\qquad\quad control(\sigma_2) = control(\sigma_1)|_{roleinsts(\sigma_2)}.$

The class of all ensemble automata for an ensemble structure Σ is denoted by **EAut**(Σ).

Fig. 9 shows an example of an ensemble automaton for the peer-2-peer net-work. The state σ_6 corresponds to the $\Sigma_{transfer}$-state σ in Fig. 8. The peer instance $p1$ starts the task by joining the ensemble as a *requester* which creates a new role instance *req* for the *requester*. Then $p2$ joins the ensemble in the role of a *router* and the role instance *rout1* for the first router is created in σ_2. The role instance *req* then sends to the router *rout1* a request for the address of the peer who stores file "song.mp3". Since *rout1* is currently adopted by $p2$ which does not store the requested file, another peer $p3$ needs to join the ensemble in state σ_4 as a router. It adopts the new role instance *rout2*. Now, *rout1* forwards the request for the address to *rout2* leading to state σ_5. The component $p3$ stores the file and therefore additionally adopts the role of a *provider* realized by the role instance *prov* which is depicted in Fig. 8. Afterwards, the component $p3$, in its role as a router *rout2*, sends its address to the forwarding router *rout1* and then the component $p3$ abandons its role as a router leading to state σ_8. Another forwarding step transmits the address from *rout1* to *req*. The requester *req* can now directly request the file from the provider *prov* who sends the content of the file back to the requester. At this point, the task is finished in state σ_{11}.

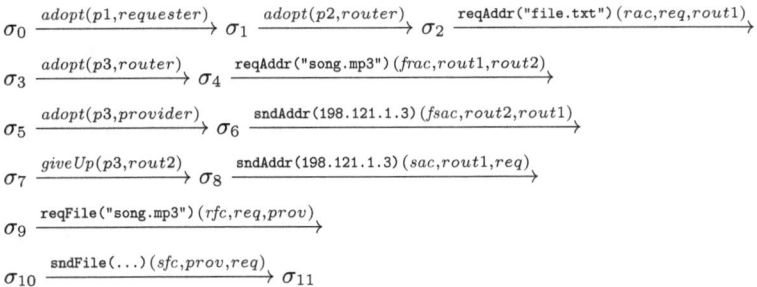

Fig. 9. Valid sequence of transitions in the $\Sigma_{transfer}$-model

In a Σ-ensemble automaton, the ensemble can behave arbitrarily as long as it uses legal transitions between Σ-ensemble states. However, we want role in-stances to act according to their specified role behaviors such that the ensemble works towards reaching a particular goal. These role behaviors restrict the Σ-ensemble automaton such that that only sequences of actions adhering to the behavior specifications of the roles are allowed. This leads to our notion of a *model of an ensemble specification.*.

Definition 12 (Model of an Ensemble Specification). *Let CT and INST be as in Def. 11. Let $\Sigma = (roles, conns)$ be an ensemble structure over CT, let EnsSpec $= (\Sigma, RoleBeh)$ with RoleBeh $= (RoleBeh_r)_{r \in roles}$ be an ensemble specification and let $M = (S, \sigma_0, L, T)$ with $L = oplabels \cup mgmtlabels$ be a Σ-ensemble automaton (over INST).*

M is a model of *EnsSpec, if the following conditions are satisfied:*

(1) *for all opname(actparams)(rc, ri, ri′) ∈ oplabels, $\sigma_1, \sigma_2 \in S$, it holds:*

If $\sigma_1 \xrightarrow{opname(actparams)(rc,ri,ri')} \sigma_2 \in T$, *then*

    (a) $control_{r''}(\sigma_1)(ri'') = control_{r''}(\sigma_2)(ri'')$ *for all $r'' \in$ roles, $ri'' \notin \{ri, ri'\}$,*

    (b) *there exists $ri \in roleinsts_r(\sigma_1)$, $r \in roles$ such that*

$$control_r(\sigma_1)(ri) \xrightarrow{nm(rc).opname(params)!} control_r(\sigma_2)(ri) \in$$
$$\Delta(RoleBeh_r), \text{ and}$$

    (c) *it exists $ri' \in roleinsts_{r'}(\sigma_1)$, $r' \in roles$ such that*

$$control_{r'}(\sigma_1)(ri') \xrightarrow{nm(rc).opname(params)?} control_{r'}(\sigma_2)(ri') \in$$
$$\Delta(RoleBeh_{r'})$$

such that actparams $\in \mathcal{D}^*$ is a list of actual parameters instantiating params,

(2) *for all adopt(ci, r) ∈ mgmtlabels, $\sigma_1, \sigma_2 \in S$, it holds:*

If $\sigma_1 \xrightarrow{adopt(ci,r)} \sigma_2 \in T$ *with $roleinsts_r(\sigma_2) = roleinsts_r(\sigma_1) \cup \{ri\}$,*
$ri \notin roleinsts_r(\sigma_1)$, *then $control_r(\sigma_2)(ri) = q_0(RoleBeh_r)$.*

The class of all models of EnsSpec is denoted by **Mod**(*EnsSpec*).

Condition (1a) says that control states of role instances that are not involved in the communication do not change. The rules (1b) and (1c) express that a communication between two role instances is only allowed if the role instances are in a control state of their respective role behaviors such that both roles are allowed to communicate. There are no restrictions on the particular instances that want to communicate since role behaviors are specified on the type and not on the instance level. Condition (2) requires that whenever a role instance is created its control state is the initial state of its role behavior. There are no particular constraints for the occurrence of management operations since those are not considered in role behaviors and therefore can always occur when their pre- and postconditions of Def. 11 are satisfied.

As an example, consider the ensemble specification in Sect. 2.3 with the three role behaviors specified in Fig. 5. The ensemble automaton shown in Fig. 9 respects the role behavior specifications and is therefore a model of the ensemble specification.

4   Related Work

Our framework is driven by a rigorous discrimination between instances and types. Formally, an ensemble is composed by a set of component instances such that each component instance, participating in the ensemble, adopts at least one role instance representing a role that the component currently plays in a collaboration. Of course, sets of interacting components are considered in any reasonable component model. They occur in the form of architectures [4,10,13], networks [5], assemblies [11,22], team automata [8], etc. Mostly, components and their behaviors are described on the type level such that the dynamic creation of individual instances, their identification and the evolution of systems is not supported. Exceptions are component interaction automata [11], which identify components by names such that individual communications naming sender and receiver of a message are possible (similarly to communication between role instances in ensemble automata), and SCEL [18] which additionally allows dynamic creation of components. This is possible since SCEL considers two levels of operational semantics, the component level and the system level. Similarly, the HELENA approach distinguishes between role behaviors (on the type level) and ensemble behaviors (on the instance level). We do not create new component instances during the run of an ensemble because we assume them to be already given by an overall system management when an ensemble is started. However, component instances can dynamically join and leave an ensemble while role instances are dynamically created (and adopted by a component instance) during an ensemble execution. Also in the DEECo model [12] for ensemble-based component systems the membership of components in ensembles is dynamically changing which is realized by the DEECo runtime framework. Interaction of ensemble members is implicit in DEECo and performed via knowledge exchange triggered by the DEECo infrastructure. A computational model for DEECo is defined in terms of automata [3] that express knowledge exchange by buffered updating of components' knowledge. A general mathematical system model for ensembles based on input/output relations has been presented in [24]. It aims at general applicability such that, e.g., also physical parts based on differential equations can be integrated. HELENA is more concrete since at least explicit notions of interaction and collaboration (on the type and on the instance level) are involved.

In contrast to the other component models HELENA is centered around the notion of a role which allows to focus only on those capabilities of a component that is actually needed in a particular collaboration. The use of roles has already been proposed in [21,26] as an additional concept to classes and objects in object-oriented programming. In [26] it is stated that "a role of an object is a set of properties which are important for an object to be able to behave in a certain way expected by a set of other objects". In these approaches the consideration of role instances is already recommended and, in [26], a diagrammatic specification of role behaviors is suggested. Experiments with implementing roles in Smalltalk are also discussed. In [32] a formal definition for "model specifications" in the language LODWICK is proposed consisting of a signature, a static model and a dynamic model. The signature relates types and roles; the static model comprises all instances of types and their relationships to roles that may potentially exist; the dynamic model consist of sequences of sets of objects and their associated roles similar to state transitions in ensemble automata. LODWICK is designed as a rudimentary modeling language which does not contain collaboration specifications and does not support object interactions in the dynamic models. Apparently the ideas of role-based modeling did not have much influence on new methodologies for component-based systems engineering. Although

UML2 has explicitly established a conceptual role layer between types and in-stances (for context dependent modeling), our impression is that its potential has not been sufficiently recognized yet.

The situation is different in the community of (multi-)agent systems where the modeling of roles is incorporated as a central part in methodologies for analysis and design. For instance, the GAIA methodology [35] and its extensions [15] con-sider a multi-agent system as a computational organization consisting of various interacting roles; this is very similar to our interpretation of ensembles. Most specifications in this methodologies are, however, rather informal or at most semi-formal, like the UML-based notation Agent UML [6]. Agent UML models collaborations by interaction protocols which combine sequence diagrams with state diagrams. Another approach has been pursued in the ROPE project [7], which proposes to use "cooperation processes" represented by Petri nets for the specification of collaborative behavior. A model-driven approach to the develop-ment of role-based open multi-agent software is presented in [36]. It uses Object-Z notation and focuses merely on structural properties of role organizations and agent societies and not on interaction behavior. The structural concepts involve, however, specifications of role spaces as containers of role instances (that can be taken by agents), which resembles ensemble states in HELENA. All these methods are not based on a formal semantics and do not provide verification techniques which will be a central topic of our approach in the near future. In particular, they do not formalize concurrent executions which is built-in in our ensemble automata expressed by interleaving.

5   Conclusion

In this paper, we presented the HELENA approach for modeling ensemble-based systems. HELENA extends the component-based approach by the notion of roles teaming up in ensemble to collaborate for some global goal. We introduced en-semble structures to capture the static architecture of such teams composed of roles and role connectors for communication between roles. For the dynamic as-pects, an ensemble specification adds role behaviors to ensemble structures. The formal semantics and execution model of an ensemble specification was given as an ensemble automaton for the evolving ensemble with synchronous commu-nication. We illustrated our approach by the running example of a peer-2-peer network for storing and downloading files.

We consider our work as a first step towards a comprehensive methodology for the development of ensemble systems founded on a precise semantic basis. We have not yet considered an infrastructure for the administration of ensembles. Several variants are possible dependent on the choice of a concrete interaction and/or communication model. For instance, we will define also an execution model for asynchronous communication which can be realized by message pass-ing via event queues. A further important issue concerns the transition from ensemble specifications to designs and implementations. One possibility is to use component-based architectures for the target systems and to map ensemble specifications (semi-automatically) to a component-based design for concurrent executions of ensembles. The mapping depends again on the choice of particular interaction models like synchronous and buffered communication including multicast message passing. We also plan to study an interaction model based on knowledge repositories and knowledge exchange like in SCEL and DEECo. Since SCEL can be considered as an abstract programming language we envisage to implement ensemble specifications by abstract SCEL programs. The semantic foundations of both languages should be appropriate to verify the correctness of the implementation. Another possibility is a direct implementation of ensemble specifications by using an appropriate framework, a prototype of which has currently been developed [25]. As a next step, we want to investigate under which conditions properties of communication compatibility (see e.g. [23]) valid for role behaviors can be propagated to ensemble automata and implementations. The challenge here is that role behavior specifications are formalized for types while ensemble automata (and implementations) concern concurrently executing instances.

Concerning the first phase of the development life cycle our methodology should still be augmented with explicit interaction specifications. Currently our behavioral descriptions are local to single role behaviors, but do not explicitly model the interactions to achieve a goal on a global level. For that purpose, we want to investigate appropriate notations, for instance on the basis of communication protocols used for specifying global interactions in multi-party sessions [14], [16]. The transition from an interaction specification to an ensemble specification must be formalized by an appropriate refinement relation. Then we want to consider properties of interaction specifications (expressed in some logic) and to prove that they are preserved by refinement. Also the explicit integration of adaptation and awareness requirements, which are central to autonomously evolving systems, must be considered. We need techniques to specify goals, for instance in the style of KAOS [27], and we need verification techniques for goal satisfaction. The validation of HELENA w.r.t. the case studies of the ASCENS project (e-mobility, robotics rescue scenario, autonomic cloud platform) is currently ongoing.

Acknowledgment. We would like to thank Lenz Belzner, Giulio Iacobelli, Nora Koch and Rocco De Nicola for intensive and stimulating discussions and Philip Mayer for reading and commenting a draft version of this paper. We would also like to thank the anonymous reviewers for their constructive and helpful comments on the first version of this paper.

References

1. The ASCENS Project, http://www.ascens-ist.eu
2. Abeywickrama, D., Bicocchi, N., Zambonelli, F.: SOTA: Towards a General Model for Self-Adaptive Systems. In: 21st IEEE International Workshop on Enabling Technologies: Infrastructure for Collaborative Enterprises, pp. 48–53. IEEE CS Press, Toulouse (2012)

3. Ali, R.A., Bures, T., Gerostathopoulos, I., Hnetynka, P., Keznikl, J., Kit, M., Plasil, F.: DEECo Computational Model - I. Tech. Rep. D3S-TR-2013-01, Charles University in Prague (2013)
4. Allen, R., Garlan, D.: A Formal Basis for Architectural Connection. ACM Trans. Softw. Eng. Methodol. 6(3), 213–249 (1997)
5. Barros, T., Ameur-Boulifa, R., Cansado, A., Henrio, L., Madelaine, E.: Behavioural models for distributed Fractal components. Annales des Télécommunications 64(1-2), 25–43 (2009)
6. Bauer, B., Müller, J.P., Odell, J.: Agent UML: A formalism for specifying multiagent software systems. Int. Journal of Software Engineering and Knowledge Engineering 11, 91–103 (2000)
7. Becht, M., Gurzki, T., Klarmann, J., Muscholl, M.: ROPE: Role Oriented Programming Environment for Multiagent Systems. In: Proceedings of the Fourth IECIS International Conference on Cooperative Information Systems, COOPIS 1999, pp. 325–333. IEEE Computer Society, Washington, DC (1999)
8. ter Beek, M.H., Ellis, C.A., Kleijn, J., Rozenberg, G.: Synchronizations in Team Automata for Groupware Systems. Computer Supported Cooperative Work 12(1), 21–69 (2003)
9. Bensalem, S., Bures, T., Combaz, J., De Nicola, R., Hölzl, M., Koch, N., Loreti, M., Tuma, P., Wirsing, M., Zambonelli, F.: A Life Cycle for the Development of Autonomic Systems. In: 3rd Awareness Workshop at SASO 2013 (2013) (submitted)
10. Bernardo, M., Ciancarini, P., Donatiello, L.: Architecting families of software systems with process algebras. ACM Trans. Softw. Eng. Methodol. 11(4), 386–426 (2002)
11. Brim, L., Černá, I., Vařeková, P., Zimmerova, B.: Component-interaction automata as a verification-oriented component-based system specification. SIGSOFT Softw. Eng. Notes 31(2), 4 (2006)
12. Bures, T., Gerostathopoulos, I., Hnetynka, P., Keznikl, J., Kit, M., Plasil, F.: DEECo: An ensemble-based component system. In: Proceedings of CBSE 2013, pp. 81–90. ACM, Vancouver (2013)
13. Bures, T., Hnetynka, P., Plasil, F.: SOFA 2.0: Balancing Advanced Features in a Hierarchical Component Model. In: SERA, pp. 40–48 (2006)
14. Castagna, G., Dezani-Ciancaglini, M., Padovani, L.: On global types and multiparty sessions. In: Bruni, R., Dingel, J. (eds.) FORTE 2011 and FMOODS 2011. LNCS, vol. 6722, pp. 1–28. Springer, Heidelberg (2011)
15. Cernuzzi, L., Juan, T., Sterling, L., Zambonelli, F.: The Gaia Methodology: Basic Concepts and Extensions. In: Bergenti, F., Gleizes, M.P. (eds.) Methodologies and Software Engineering for Agent Systems, Multiagent Systems, Artificial Societies, and Simulated Organizations, vol. 11, pp. 69–88. Springer, Heidelberg (2004)
16. Coppo, M., Dezani-Ciancaglini, M., Padovani, L., Yoshida, N.: Inference of global progress properties for dynamically interleaved multiparty sessions. In: De Nicola, R., Julien, C. (eds.) COORDINATION 2013. LNCS, vol. 7890, pp. 45–59. Springer, Heidelberg (2013)
17. De Nicola, R., Ferrari, G., Loreti, M., Pugliese, R.: A Language-Based Approach to Autonomic Computing. In: Beckert, B., Bonsangue, M.M. (eds.) FMCO 2011. LNCS, vol. 7542, pp. 25–48. Springer, Heidelberg (2012)
18. De Nicola, R., Loreti, M., Pugliese, R., Tiezzi, F.: SCEL: A Language for Autonomic Computing. Tech. rep., IMT, Institute for Advanced Studies Lucca, Italy (2013)

19. Futatsugi, K., Goguen, J.A., Jouannaud, J.P., Meseguer, J.: Principles of OBJ2. In: Van Deusen, M.S., Galil, Z. (eds.) POPL, pp. 52–66. ACM Press (1985)
20. Goguen, J.A., Burstall, R.M.: Institutions: Abstract Model Theory for Specification and Programming. J. ACM 39(1), 95–146 (1992)
21. Gottlob, G., Schrefl, M., Röck, B.: Extending Object-Oriented Systems with Roles. ACM Trans. Inf. Syst. 14(3), 268–296 (1996)
22. Hennicker, R., Knapp, A.: Modal Interface Theories for Communication-Safe Component Assemblies. In: Cerone, A., Pihlajasaari, P. (eds.) ICTAC 2011. LNCS, vol. 6916, pp. 135–153. Springer, Heidelberg (2011)
23. Hennicker, R., Knapp, A.: Modal interface theories for communication-safe component assemblies. In: Cerone, A., Pihlajasaari, P. (eds.) ICTAC 2011. LNCS, vol. 6916, pp. 135–153. Springer, Heidelberg (2011)
24. Hölzl, M., Wirsing, M.: Towards a System Model for Ensembles. In: Agha, G., Danvy, O., Meseguer, J. (eds.) Talcott Festschrift. LNCS, vol. 7000, pp. 241–261. Springer, Heidelberg (2011)
25. Klarl, A., Hennicker, R.: The Helena Framework, http://www.pst.ifi.lmu.de/Personen/team/klarl/papers/helena.jar
26. Kristensen, B.B., Østerbye, K.: Roles: Conceptual Abstraction Theory and Practical Language Issues. TAPOS 2(3), 143–160 (1996)
27. van Lamsweerde, A.: Requirements Engineering: From System Goals to UML Models to Software Specifications. Wiley (2009)
28. Mori, A., Futatsugi, K.: Verifying Behavioural Specifications in CafeOBJ Environment. In: Wing, J.M., Woodcock, J., Davies, J. (eds.) FM 1999. LNCS, vol. 1709, pp. 1625–1643. Springer, Heidelberg (1999)
29. Nakajima, S., Futatsugi, K.: An Object-Oriented Modeling Method for Algebraic Specifications in CafeOBJ. In: Adrion, W.R., Fuggetta, A., Taylor, R.N., Wasserman, A.I. (eds.) ICSE, pp. 34–44. ACM (1997)
30. OMG (Object Management Group): OMG Unified Modeling Language Superstructure. Specification, OMG (Object Management Group) (2011), http://www.omg.org/spec/UML/2.4.1/Superstructure/
31. Rausch, A., Reussner, R., Mirandola, R., Plášil, F. (eds.): The Common Component Modeling Example. LNCS, vol. 5153. Springer, Heidelberg (2008)
32. Steimann, F.: On the representation of roles in object-oriented and conceptual modelling. Data Knowl. Eng. 35(1), 83–106 (2000)
33. Szyperski, C.: Component Software: Beyond Object-Oriented Programming, 2nd edn. Addison-Wesley Longman Publishing Co., Inc., Boston (2002)
34. Wirsing, M., Hölzl, M., Tribastone, M., Zambonelli, F.: ASCENS: Engineering Autonomic Service-Component Ensembles. In: Beckert, B., Damiani, F., de Boer, S., Bonsangue, M.M. (eds.) FMCO 2011. LNCS, vol. 7542, pp. 1–24. Springer, Heidelberg (2013)
35. Wooldridge, M., Jennings, N.R., Kinny, D.: The Gaia Methodology for Agent-Oriented Analysis and Design. Autonomous Agents and Multi-Agent Systems 3(3), 285–312 (2000)
36. Xu, H., Zhang, X., Patel, R.J.: Developing Role-Based Open Multi-Agent Software Systems. International Journal of Computational Intelligence Theory and Practice 2 (2007)

Behaviour, Interaction and Dynamics[*]

Roberto Bruni[1], Hernán Melgratti[2], and Ugo Montanari[1]

[1] Dipartimento di Informatica, Università di Pisa, Italy
[2] Departamento de Computación, FCEyN, Universidad de Buenos Aires - Conicet, Argentina

Abstract. The growth and diffusion of reconfigurable and adaptive systems motivate the foundational study of models of software connectors that can evolve dynamically, as opposed to the better understood notion of static connectors. In this paper we investigate the interplay of behaviour, interaction and dynamics in the context of the BIP component framework, here denoted BI(P), as we disregard priorities. We introduce two extensions of BIP: 1) *reconfigurable* BI(P) allows to reconfigure the set of admissible interactions, while preserving the set of interacting components; 2) *dynamic* BI(P) allows to spawn new components and interactions during execution. Our main technical results show that reconfigurable BI(P) is as expressive as BI(P), while dynamic BI(P) allows to deal with infinite state systems. Still, we show that reachability remains decidable for dynamic BI(P).

1 Introduction

Recent years have witnessed an increasing interest about a rigorous modelling of (different classes of) connectors. The term *connector*, as used here, has been coined within the area of component-based software architectures, to name entities that can regulate the interaction of a collection of components [15]. This has led to the development of different mathematical frameworks that are used to specify, design, analyse, compare, prototype and implement suitable connectors. Our previous efforts have been focused at unifying different frameworks, in particular, the BIP component framework [2], Petri nets with boundaries [16] and the algebras of connectors [7,1] based on the tile model [12]. In [8] we have shown that BIP without priorities, written BI(P) in the following, is equally expressive as nets with boundaries. Thanks to the correspondence results in [16,10], we can define an algebra of connectors as expressive as BI(P), where a few basic connectors can be composed in series and parallel to generate any BI(P) system.

All above approaches deal with systems that have static structures, i.e., systems in which the possible interactions among components are all defined at design time and remain unchanged during runtime. Nevertheless, when shifting to connectors for systems that adapt their behaviour to changing environments,

---

[*] Research supported by the EU Integrated Project 257414 ASCENS, the Italian MIUR Project CINA (PRIN 2010/11), ANPCyT Project BID-PICT-2008-00319, and EU FP7-project MEALS 295261.

S. Iida, J. Meseguer, and K. Ogata (Eds.): Futatsugi Festschrift, LNCS 8373, pp. 382–401, 2014.

the situation is less well-understood. For example, approaches based on mobile calculi (like the π-calculus [14]) are not suited, because there the notion of connector / component is lost. In fact, a general and uniform theory for dynamic connectors is still lacking. On the one hand, static structures of connectors can be studied and executed efficiently. On the other hand, systems that can traverse a large or infinite number of connector configurations are better dealt with concise computational models that are tailored to dynamic structures.

Some recent progress has been done in [6], where Dy-BIP is proposed. We remind that an ordinary BIP component is defined by a set of ports P and a finite automaton whose transitions carry subsets of P as labels. An ordinary BIP system consists of a finite number of components (fixing the "Behaviour") whose ports are disjoint, together with a set of admissible synchronisations between the transitions of components (fixing the "Interaction"). Neither the set of components, nor the set of interactions can change over time. In contrast to BIP, the set of interactions can change dynamically in Dy-BIP, but this is obtained by ad-hoc design choices. As a consequence, the definition of Dy-BIP systems can be error-prone or lead to incomplete specifications unless the complex methodology outlined in [6] is adopted.

In order to contribute to the development of a general theory for dynamic connectors, in this paper we study two other extensions of the BI(P) framework with different degrees of "dynamism" that allow enhanced conciseness, modularity and expressiveness.

As a first step, we focus on a *reconfigurable* version of BI(P), analogous to but simpler than Dy-BIP. A reconfigurable BI(P) system allows for the dynamic modification of interactions among components, i.e., the set of available interactions changes as a side-effect of an interaction between components. Our first result proves that any reconfigurable BI(P) system is equivalent to an ordinary BI(P) system. This result is achieved by introducing a "controller" component for each interaction that can be added or removed at run-time. Roughly, the controller keeps track of whether the managed interaction is currently available or not and forces the components willing to use that interaction to synchronise also with the controller. This mapping shows that the reconfiguration capabilities provided by reconfigurable BI(P) do not increase the expressive power of BI(P). In fact, reconfigurable BI(P) only provides a more compact representation of ordinary systems, while ordinary BI(P) representations may require an exponential blow up in the number of components (it requires one controller for each possible interaction, and the interactions are subsets of ports). The crux of the proof is the fact that the set of controller components can be defined statically. In fact, the interfaces of components in reconfigurable BI(P) are static, i.e., the set of available ports in every component is fixed. As a consequence, the set of all possible interactions in a system are determined at design time (despite the fact that they can be enabled/disabled at run-time).

Our next step is to explore situations in which the interfaces of the components may change dynamically (i.e., to support the creation/elimination of ports). This requirement also imposes the necessity of handling interactions that can be created/removed dynamically, as in reconfigurable BI(P). We take as an inspiring example the notion of correlation sets in web services [17,13], that is used to keep separate sessions between clients and servers. In these cases, when a partner call is made, then an instance of the session is initialised with suitable correlation data (e.g., specific message fields) gathered for the partner. To this aim we exploit *coloured* tokens, where the colours are freshly created session identifiers. This way, we do not need to replicate the ports and structure of components, instead we keep all the coloured tokens within the same instance of the component, distributed along its states: as in general it can happen that two or more replicas are in the same state, then it is possible that two or more coloured tokens mark the same state at the same time. An interaction is possible only when all the involved components carry correlated colours, i.e., identifiers for the same session. In fact, while session identifiers are created locally to each component (e.g., s_1 in a first component and s_2 in a second component), a new interaction is also created that correlates them (e.g., s_1s_2). Possibly many sessions are opened with the same partners involved. In subsequent interactions, correlation tokens are then exploited to identify the session that interaction is part of. When the session ends, the correlation tokens are discarded. At the beginning, when the system is initialised, we assume that all components carry correlated tokens, i.e., that they are all part of the same session. Correspondingly, we introduce an extension of BI(P), called *dynamic* BI(P), in which component instances and new interactions can be added/removed dynamically. In this case we obtain systems that are possibly infinite state and more expressive than ordinary BI(P) systems. However, our second main result shows that reachability is decidable for dynamic BI(P).

Structure of the paper. Section 2 recalls the basics of BI(P) systems. Section 3 introduces reconfigurable BI(P) systems and shows that they are as expressive as ordinary BI(P) systems. Section 4 introduces dynamic BI(P) systems and shows their correspondence with Place/Transition (P/T) Petri nets. Due to space limitation and to the fact that P/T Petri nets are mainly used here as a technical tool for the decidability proof, we assume the reader has some familiarity with P/T Petri nets and refer to the standard literature [11] otherwise. Both reconfigurable and dynamic BI(P) systems are illustrated over small motivating examples. Section 5 gives some concluding remarks.

2   The BIP Component Framework, and BI(P)

BIP [2] is a component framework that exploits a three-layered architecture: 1) the lower level is called *Behaviour* and it fixes the activities of individual atomic components; 2) the middle layer is called *Interaction* and it defines the handshaking mechanisms between components; and 3) the top level is called *Priority* and it assigns a partial order of preferences to the admissible interactions. This section recalls the formal definition of BIP using the notation from [4]. Here we disregard priorities and write BI(P) to avoid confusion.

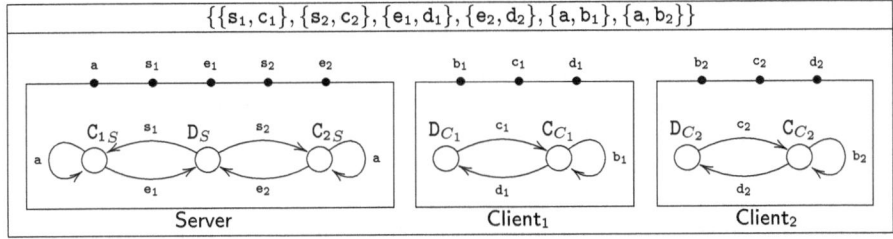

Fig. 1. A simple BI(P) system

The lower layer consists of a set of atomic components with ports. The sets of ports of components are pairwise disjoint, i.e., each port is uniquely assigned to a component. Components are automata whose transitions are labelled by sets of their ports.

Definition 1 (Component). *A component $B = (Q, P, \rightarrow)$ is a transition system where Q is a set of states (ranged over by $p, q, \ldots$), P is a set of ports (ranged over by $a, b, \ldots$), and $\rightarrow \subseteq Q \times 2^P \times Q$ is the set of labelled transitions.*

As usual, we write $q \xrightarrow{a} q'$ to denote the transition $(q, a, q') \in \rightarrow$. We say that a is enabled in q, denoted $q \xrightarrow{a}$, iff there exists q' s.t. $q \xrightarrow{a} q'$. We assume that for all q, q' it holds $q \xrightarrow{\varnothing} q'$ iff $q = q'$.

The second layer consists of connectors that specify the allowed interactions between components.

Definition 2 (Interaction). *Given a set of ports P, an interaction over P is a non-empty subset $a \subseteq P$.*

We write $a_1 a_2 \ldots a_n$ for the interaction $\{a_1, a_2, \ldots, a_n\}$ and $a \downarrow_{P_i}$ for the projection of $a \subseteq P$ over the set of ports $P_i \subseteq P$, i.e., $a \downarrow_{P_i} = a \cap P_i$.

Definition 3 (BI(P) system). *A BI(P) system $B = \gamma(B_1, \ldots, B_n)$ is the composition of a finite set $\{B_i\}_{i=1}^{n}$ of transitions systems $B_i = (Q_i, P_i, \rightarrow_i)$ such that their sets of ports are pairwise disjoint, i.e., $P_i \cap P_j = \varnothing$ for $i \neq j$, parametrized by a set $\gamma \subset 2^P$ of interactions over the set of ports $P = \biguplus_{i=1}^{n} P_i$. We call P the underlying set of ports of B, written $\iota(B)$.*

The semantics of a BI(P) system $\gamma(B_1, \ldots, B_n)$ is given by the transition system $(Q, P, \rightarrow_\gamma)$, with $Q = \Pi_i Q_i$, $P = \biguplus_{i=1}^{n} P_i$ and $\rightarrow_\gamma \subseteq Q \times 2^P \times Q$ is the least set of transitions satisfying the following inference rule

$$\frac{a \in \gamma \qquad \forall i \in 1..n : q_i \xrightarrow{a \downarrow_{P_i}} q_i'}{(q_1, \ldots, q_n) \xrightarrow{a}_\gamma (q_1', \ldots, q_n')}$$

Example 1. Consider the BI(P) system shown in Fig. 1, which contains a component Server that sequentially interacts with two clients Client$_1$ and Client$_2$. The Server starts a connection with Client$_i$ thanks to the interaction $s_i c_i$. Once the session is initiated, the server and the connected client synchronise over the interaction ab_i. The session ends when the server and the connected client perform $e_i d_i$. Note that the server has dedicated ports for handling the connections of different clients (s_i and e_i), but it interacts analogously with all of them. The next section introduces an extension of BI(P) that allows for a more compact description of this kind of systems.

3   Reconfigurable BI(P)

Our first extension is concerned with the possibility of enabling and disabling specific interactions dynamically, as proposed in an internal document of the ASCENS project. An interaction a can be enabled/disabled when all components involved in the interaction a agree to do so. After a is enabled, it can be used as an ordinary interaction until it gets disabled. Transitions in a reconfigurable BI(P) component are decorated with either (i) ϵ for ordinary actions over (a set of) ports (like the actions of ordinary BI(P) components), (ii) $+$ to add a new interaction, and (iii) $-$ to remove an interaction.

Definition 4 (Reconfigurable Component). *Let $\mathcal{P}$ be a set of ports. A reconfigurable component $B = (Q, P, \longrightarrow)$ is a transition system where Q is a set of states, $P \subset \mathcal{P}$ is a finite set of ports, and $\longrightarrow \subseteq Q \times 2^{\mathcal{P}} \times \{+, -, \epsilon\} \times Q$ is the set of labelled transitions such that $(q, a, \rho, q') \in \longrightarrow$ implies:*

1. *if $\rho = \epsilon$ then $a \in 2^P$;*
2. *if $\rho \in \{+, -\}$ then $a \cap P \neq \varnothing$.*

The annotation ρ indicates if the interaction a must be added $(+)$ to the set γ of global interactions, be removed $(-)$ from γ, or be already present (ϵ) in γ. Condition (1) states that the ports involved in any ordinary transition (i.e., $\rho = \epsilon$) are ports of the component, i.e., $a \in 2^P$. A transition that adds/removes a global interaction a may also refer to ports belonging to other components (Condition 2).

We write $q \xrightarrow{a\rho} q'$ to denote the transition $(q, a, \rho, q') \in \longrightarrow$. We say that a is enabled in q, denoted $q \xrightarrow{a}$, iff there exists q' s.t. $q \xrightarrow{a\epsilon} q'$. We assume that for all q, q' it holds $q \xrightarrow{\varnothing\epsilon} q'$ iff $q = q'$. Given a set of ports P, we write $a\#P$ if $a \cap P = \varnothing$.

Definition 5 (Reconfigurable BI(P) system). *A reconfigurable BI(P) system $B = \gamma(B_1, \ldots, B_n)$ is the composition of a finite set $\{B_i\}_{i=1}^n$ of reconfigurable components $B_i = (Q_i, P_i, \longrightarrow_i)$ such that their sets of ports are pairwise disjoint, i.e., $P_i \cap P_j = \varnothing$ for $i \neq j$, parametrized by a set $\gamma \subset 2^P$. We call $P = \biguplus_{i=1}^n P_i$ the underlying set of ports of B, written $\iota(B)$.*

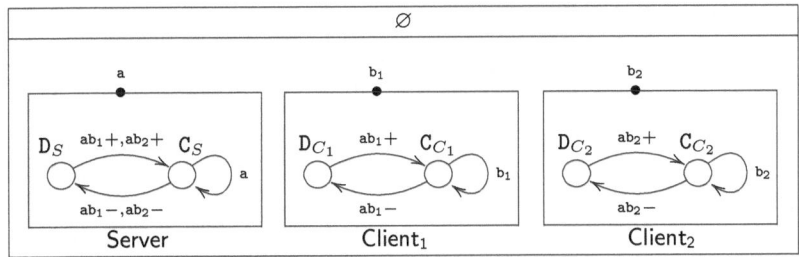

Fig. 2. A simple reconfigurable BI(P) system

$$\frac{a \in \gamma \quad \forall i \in 1..n : q_i \xrightarrow{\;a\downarrow_{P_i}\epsilon\;} q_i'}{\gamma(q_1,\ldots,q_n) \xrightarrow{\;a\;} \gamma(q_1',\ldots,q_n')}\,[\text{INT}]$$

$$\frac{a \in 2^P \smallsetminus \gamma \quad \neg(a\#P_i) \implies q_i \xrightarrow{\;a+\;} q_i' \quad (a\#P_i) \implies q_i' = q_i \quad \gamma' = \gamma \cup \{a\}}{\gamma(q_1,\ldots,q_n) \xrightarrow{\;a\;} \gamma'(q_1',\ldots,q_n')}\,[\text{ADD}]$$

$$\frac{a \in \gamma \quad \neg(a\#P_i) \implies q_i \xrightarrow{\;a-\;} q_i' \quad (a\#P_i) \implies q_i' = q_i \quad \gamma' = \gamma \smallsetminus \{a\}}{\gamma(q_1,\ldots,q_n) \xrightarrow{\;a\;} \gamma'(q_1',\ldots,q_n')}\,[\text{DEL}]$$

Fig. 3. Operational semantics of reconfigurable BI(P) systems

Example 2. The client/server scenario introduced in Example 1 can be modelled as the reconfigurable BI(P) system depicted in Fig. 2. Now, the server and the clients have the transitions ab_i+ and ab_i- that respectively allow for the dynamic enabling/disabling of the interaction ab_i. In this case, the connection of a client to a server is modelled by the dynamic enabling of the interaction ab_i. Analogously, the disconnection is modelled as the dynamic disabling of the interaction ab_i.

The semantics of a reconfigurable BI(P) system $B = \gamma(B_1,\ldots,B_n)$ with $\iota(B) = P$ and $\gamma \subseteq 2^P$ is given by the transition system $(Q, \longrightarrow)$ where

- $Q = 2^P \times \Pi_i Q_i$ (we write $\gamma(q_1,\ldots,q_n)$ for $\langle \gamma, \langle q_1,\ldots,q_n\rangle\rangle \in Q$), and
- $\longrightarrow \subseteq Q \times 2^P \times Q$ is the least set of transitions satisfying the inference rules in Fig. 3.

Each state of the transition system keeps, not only the states of all components but also, the set γ of all enabled interactions. Rule [INT] stands for ordinary interactions and it is analogous to the inference rule for ordinary BI(P) systems. Rule [ADD] accounts for the addition of a new global interaction a to the set of enabled interactions γ. Note that all components affected by the interaction a, i.e., the ones that have ports in a (condition $a\#P_i$), need to agree on the

addition of the new interaction a (i.e., all of them perform the transition $\xrightarrow{a+}$).
Remaining components do not move. Rule [DEL] specifies the removal of an
enabled interaction and is analogous to [ADD].

Example 3. Consider the reconfigurable BI(P) system in Example 2. The initial state in which no connection has been established is given by the term
$\varnothing(D_S, D_{C_1}, D_{C_2})$. In this state, the system can start a session between the Server
and either Client$_1$ or Client$_2$. Assuming that a session with Client$_1$ is established, then the system can move as follows

$$\varnothing(D_S, D_{C_1}, D_{C_2}) \xrightarrow{\text{ab}_1+} s \quad \text{with } s = \{\text{ab}_1\}(C_S, C_{C_1}, D_{C_2})$$

After session initiation, Server and Client$_1$ can repeatedly synchronise with
interaction ab$_1$ as any ordinary BI(P) system, i.e.,

$$s \xrightarrow{\text{ab}_1} s \xrightarrow{\text{ab}_1} \dots \xrightarrow{\text{ab}_1} s$$

At some point, both Server and Client$_1$ decide to close the session and the
system returns to the initial state by removing the interaction ab$_1$, i.e.,

$$s \xrightarrow{\text{ab}_1-} \varnothing(D_S, D_{C_1}, D_{C_2})$$

3.1   Reconfigurable BI(P) in BI(P)

This section shows that Reconfigurable BI(P) is as expressive as BI(P), i.e., that
adding the possibility of dynamically changing the set of interactions does not
increase the expressiveness, even if a price is paid in terms of the combinatorial
explosion of global states.

We start by introducing some auxiliary notation and definitions.

Let $B = (Q, P, \longrightarrow)$ be a reconfigurable component. The set of reconfigurable
interactions of B is defined as follows

$$\mathcal{R}(B) = \{a \mid (q, a, \rho, q') \in \longrightarrow \text{ and } \rho \neq \epsilon\}$$

For any reconfigurable interaction of a BI(P) component, i.e., $a \in \mathcal{R}(B)$, we
add two additional ports in the encoded component, which are denoted by $\tilde{a}^B+$
and $\tilde{a}^B-$. We remark that we add some decoration to the interaction a in order
to avoid port clashes between the different components of a system. Note that
the same dynamic interaction may appear in different components of a system
(e.g., ab$_1$ and ab$_2$ in Fig. 2) and we need to ensure that a port appears in one
component at most. Although different choices for decoration would be possible,
we will use the following in the rest of the paper.

$$\tilde{a}^B = (a \cap P) \cup \{\tilde{p} \mid p \in a \smallsetminus P\}.$$

We write $\widetilde{\mathcal{R}(B)}$ for the set of all decorated reconfigurable interactions, i.e.,
$\widetilde{\mathcal{R}(B)} = \{\tilde{a}^B \mid a \in \mathcal{R}(B)\}$. For example, $\widetilde{\mathcal{R}(\text{Server})} = \{\widetilde{\text{ab}_1}, \widetilde{\text{ab}_2}\}$.

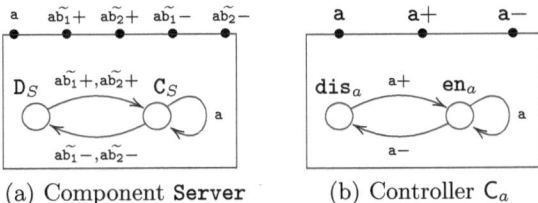

(a) Component **Server**   (b) Controller C_a

Fig. 4. Encoding reconfigurable BI(P) in BI(P)

The notion of reconfigurable interaction is straightforwardly extended to reconfigurable BI(P) systems. Let $B = \gamma(B_1, \ldots, B_n)$ be a reconfigurable BI(P) system, then the set of reconfigurable interactions is defined as

$$\mathcal{R}(B) = \bigcup_{1 \le i \le n} \mathcal{R}(B_i).$$

Definition 6. *Let $B = (Q, P, \longrightarrow)$ be a reconfigurable component. The corresponding BI(P) component $[\![B]\!]$ is $(Q, P \cup (\widetilde{\mathcal{R}(B)} \times \{+, -\}), \rightarrow)$ with $\rightarrow$ defined such as $(q, a, q') \in \rightarrow$ iff*

- *$(q, a, \rho, q') \in \longrightarrow$ and $\rho = \epsilon$; or*
- *$(q, a', \rho, q') \in \longrightarrow$, $\rho \ne \epsilon$ and $a = (\widetilde{a'}^B, \rho)$*

Figure 4(a) shows the BI(P) component corresponding to the reconfigurable component **Server** depicted in Fig. 2. For simplicity, we write $\widetilde{a}^B \rho$ for a port $(\widetilde{a}^B, \rho)$, e.g., we write $\widetilde{ab_1}+$ instead of $(\widetilde{ab_1}, +)$. Note that we extend the interface of the component by adding two ports for each reconfigurable interaction, one for signalling the addition of the interaction and the other for the removal. Besides, the transition relation of the component remains unchanged but transitions corresponding to dynamic interactions are renamed to use the added ports.

The following result states a correspondence between the behaviour of a reconfigurable component and its encoded version.

Lemma 1. *Let $B = (Q, P, \longrightarrow)$ be a reconfigurable component and $[\![B]\!] = (Q, P, \rightarrow)$ its encoded version. Then, $q \xrightarrow{a\rho} q'$ if and only if*

- *$\rho = \epsilon$ and $q \xrightarrow{a} q'$, or*
- *$\rho \ne \epsilon$ and $q \xrightarrow{\widetilde{a}^B \rho} q'$*

Proof. It follows directly from the definition of $[\![B]\!]$.

We now address the encoding of the behaviour of reconfigurable interactions. We will associate any reconfigurable interaction with a BI(P) component that models the dynamics of an interaction that can be dynamically enabled and disabled.

Definition 7. *Let a be an interaction. A controller for a is the BI(P) component* $C_a = (Q_{C_a}, P_{C_a}, \rightarrow)$ *defined in Fig. 4(b).*

Note that the net C_a has two places, one for an enabled interaction, named a_{en}, and the other for a disabled one, named a_{dis}. The only possible transition for a disable interaction is the enabling (i.e., $a+$). After being enabled, the interaction can be used as a usual one (a) until it is disabled ($a-$). We remark that each of these behaviours is observed over a dedicated port.

Definition 8. *Let* $B = \gamma(B_1, \ldots, B_n)$ *be a reconfigurable BI(P) system with* $\mathcal{R}(B) = \{a_0, \ldots, a_j\}$. *The corresponding BI(P) system is defined as follows*

$$[\![\gamma(B_1, \ldots, B_n)]\!] = [\![\gamma]\!]([\![B_1]\!], \ldots, [\![B_n]\!], C_{a_0}, \ldots, C_{a_j})$$

where

$$[\![\gamma]\!] = (\gamma \setminus \mathcal{R}(B)) \cup \left(\bigcup_{a \in \mathcal{R}(B), \rho \in \{\epsilon, +, -\}} \{[\![a]\!]_\rho\} \right)$$

with

$$[\![a]\!]_\rho = \begin{cases} \{a\rho\} \cup \{\widetilde{a}^{B_i}\rho \mid 1 \leq i \leq n \text{ and } a \in \mathcal{R}(B_i)\} & \text{if } \rho \in \{+, -\} \\ \{a\} \cup \{p \mid 1 \leq i \leq n \text{ and } p \in a \downarrow_{P_i}\} & \text{if } \rho = \epsilon \end{cases}$$

Moreover, any state $\gamma(q_1, \ldots, q_n)$ *of* B *will be associated with a state* $[\![\gamma(q_1, \ldots, q_n)]\!]$ *of* $[\![B]\!]$ *where*

$$[\![\gamma(q_1, \ldots, q_n)]\!] = (q_1, \ldots, q_n, s_0, \ldots, s_j)$$

with

$$s_i = \begin{cases} en_{a_i} & \text{if } a_i \in \gamma \\ dis_{a_i} & \text{if } a_i \notin \gamma \end{cases}$$

Example 4. The reconfigurable system introduced in Example 2 is encoded as the BI(P) system shown in Fig. 5, which contains five components: the encoded versions of the components Server, Client$_1$ and Client$_2$, and the two interaction controllers (i.e., one for each reconfigurable interaction ab$_1$ and ab$_2$). The set γ contains six interactions, three for each reconfigurable interaction. The initial state of the system in Example 2 corresponds to $(D_S, D_{C_1}, D_{C_2}, ab_{1dis}, ab_{2dis})$. Then, the transition that starts a session between Server and Client$_1$ is simulated by

$$(D_S, D_{C_1}, D_{C_2}, ab_{1dis}, ab_{2dis}) \xrightarrow{\{ab_1+, \widetilde{ab_1}+, \widetilde{ab}_1+\}}_\gamma (C_S, C_{C_1}, D_{C_2}, ab_{1en}, ab_{2dis})$$

The synchronisation between Server and Client$_1$ with the interaction ab$_1$ is

$$(C_S, C_{C_1}, D_{C_2}, ab_{1en}, ab_{2dis}) \xrightarrow{\{ab_1, a, b_1\}}_\gamma (C_S, C_{C_1}, D_{C_2}, ab_{1en}, ab_{2dis})$$

Similarly, Server and Client$_1$ jointly disconnect with the following transition

$$(C_S, C_{C_1}, D_{C_2}, ab_{1en}, ab_{2dis}) \xrightarrow{\{ab_1-, \widetilde{ab_1}-, \widetilde{ab}_1-\}}_\gamma (D_S, D_{C_1}, D_{C_2}, ab_{1dis}, ab_{2dis})$$

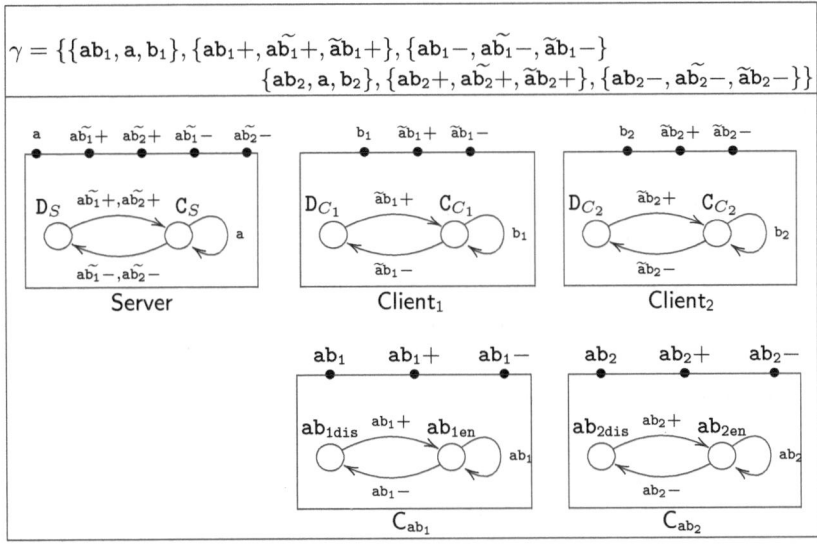

Fig. 5. A simple reconfigurable BI(P) system encoded in ordinary BI(P)

As illustrated by the above example, the transitions of a reconfigurable BI(P) system and its corresponding BI(P) system are in one-to-one correspondence, as formalised by the following result.

Theorem 1 (Correspondence). *Let* $B = \gamma(B_1, \ldots, B_n)$ *be a reconfigurable BI(P) system with* $\mathcal{R}(B) = \{a_0, \ldots, a_j\}$. *Then,* $\gamma(q_1, \ldots, q_n) \xrightarrow{a} \gamma'(q_1', \ldots, q_n')$ *iff* $\exists b \in \{a, \gamma_a, \gamma_{a+}, \gamma_{a-}\}$ *s.t.* $[\![\gamma(q_1, \ldots, q_n)]\!] \xrightarrow{b}_{[\![\gamma]\!]} [\![\gamma'(q_1', \ldots, q_n')]\!]$.

Proof. $\Rightarrow$) By case analysis on the derivation of $\gamma(q_1, \ldots, q_n) \xrightarrow{a} \gamma'(q_1', \ldots, q_n')$.
$\Leftarrow$) Follows by case analysis on the shape of a.

4   Dynamic BI(P)

In this section we further extend BI(P) by allowing the dynamic replication of components as result of the interaction of existing components. The idea is that upon certain interactions, where each involved component forks an instance of itself with some given initial state, some sort of session is established among (all and only) the spawned replicas that can thus interact in a sandboxed way, isolated from the rest of the system. For example, this is useful when the same server component must serve a possibly unbounded number of client requests separately but concurrently. As another example, some form of publish-subscribe mechanism can also be represented, where each subscriber has a dedicated notification handler. As explained in the Introduction, the mechanism underlying dynamic BI(P) resembles, to some extent, the use of correlation tokens in web service computing.

Technically, we rely on an infinite set of port names $\mathcal{P}$ ranged over by $\mathsf{a}, \mathsf{b}, \ldots$, an infinite set of port variable names $\mathcal{X}$ ranged over by $x, y, \ldots$, and an infinite set of state names $\mathcal{Q}$ ranged over by $\mathsf{p}, \mathsf{q}, \ldots$. We assume $\mathcal{P}$, $\mathcal{Q}$ and $\mathcal{X}$ pairwise disjoint. As in general an interaction is related to a specific session, we sometimes decorate ports and interactions with specific correlation tokens as their subscripts. For example, for $a = \mathsf{ab}$ we write a_c for $\mathsf{a_c b_c}$.

Definition 9 (Dynamic Component). *A* dynamic component *is a tuple* $B = (Q, P, \rightarrow)$ *where* $Q \subset \mathcal{Q}$ *is a set of places,* $P \subset \mathcal{P}$ *is a set of ports, and* $\rightarrow$ *is a finite set of transitions, each having one of the following shapes:*

- $\mathsf{q}(x) \xrightarrow{a_x} \mathsf{q}'(x)$, *i.e., (a coloured version of) a BI(P) transition;*
- $\mathsf{q}(x) \xrightarrow{a_x y+} \mathsf{q}'(x) \oplus \mathsf{q}''(y)$, *i.e., a port creation;*
- $\mathsf{q}(x) \xrightarrow{x-} \varnothing$, *i.e., a port removal;*
- $\mathsf{q}(x) \xrightarrow{x} \mathsf{q}'(x)$, *i.e., an interaction over a dynamically created port.*

Ports that appear in labels of the form a_x are parametric to the correlation token and are called *static* ports; the other ports are called *dynamic*. We assume static ports cannot be used as correlation tokens. In the following we denote by P_x the set of static ports of P, by P_a the set of static ports in P parametrized by the token a and by $\delta(P)$ the set of dynamic ports. For example, if $P = \{\mathsf{a}, \mathsf{b}\}$ with a static and b dynamic, then $P_\mathsf{c} = \{\mathsf{a_c}\}$. Note that if all transitions have the form $\mathsf{q}(x) \xrightarrow{a_x} \mathsf{q}'(x)$ then B is essentially an ordinary BI(P) component.

The current state of a dynamic component $B = (Q, P, \rightarrow)$ takes the form $\langle P, f \rangle$ with $P \subset \mathcal{P}$ defining the current ports of the component (that includes opened sessions) and $f : Q \rightarrow 2^P$ such that $f(\mathsf{q_1}) \cap f(\mathsf{q_2}) = \varnothing$ for $\mathsf{q_1} \neq \mathsf{q_2}$. The function f represents the current internal state of the component replicas. For example, if $f(\mathsf{q}) = \{\mathsf{a}, \mathsf{b}\}$ then there are two replicas of the component, one involved in session a and one in b both with current state q. The condition $f(\mathsf{q_1}) \cap f(\mathsf{q_2}) = \varnothing$ for $\mathsf{q_1} \neq \mathsf{q_2}$ guarantees that each replica is associated with a different session and that to each session corresponds exactly one state.

As a matter of notation we denote $f \oplus \mathsf{p}(\mathsf{a})$ the function defined as

$$(f \oplus \mathsf{p}(\mathsf{a}))(\mathsf{q}) = \begin{cases} f(\mathsf{q}) & \text{if } \mathsf{q} \neq \mathsf{p} \\ f(\mathsf{q}) \cup \{\mathsf{a}\} & \text{if } \mathsf{q} = \mathsf{p} \end{cases}$$

Remark 1. Initially there is only one session opened for each component, i.e., for each component there is only one state p such that $f(\mathsf{p}) \neq \varnothing$ and such $f(\mathsf{p})$ must be a singleton. To shorten the notation but without loss of generality, we shall assume that such initial session identifier is void, i.e. $f(\mathsf{p}) = \{\bullet\}$ and omit the corresponding port $\bullet$ from the drawing of components.

The operational semantics of components is given by the three rules in Fig. 6.

The first rule ([CINT]) deals with both: i) the case of an ordinary interaction a_a (here coloured by the token a); and ii) the case of a dynamic interaction over the session associated with a.

$$\frac{\mathsf{q}(x) \xrightarrow{\alpha} \mathsf{q}'(x) \qquad \mathsf{a} \in \delta(P) \qquad \alpha \in \{a_x, x\}}{\langle P, \mathsf{q}(\mathsf{a}) \oplus f \rangle \xrightarrow{\alpha\{\mathsf{a}/x\}} \langle P, \mathsf{q}'(\mathsf{a}) \oplus f \rangle} [\text{CInt}]$$

$$\frac{\mathsf{q}(x) \xrightarrow{a_x y+} \mathsf{q}'(x) \oplus \mathsf{q}''(y) \qquad \mathsf{a} \in \delta(P) \qquad \mathsf{b} \notin P}{\langle P, \mathsf{q}(\mathsf{a}) \oplus f \rangle \xrightarrow{a_{\mathsf{a}}\mathsf{b}+} \langle P \cup \{\mathsf{b}\} \cup P_{\mathsf{b}}, \mathsf{q}'(\mathsf{a}) \oplus \mathsf{q}''(\mathsf{b}) \oplus f \rangle} [\text{COpen}]$$

$$\frac{\mathsf{q}(x) \xrightarrow{x-} \varnothing \qquad \mathsf{a} \in \delta(P)}{\langle P, \mathsf{q}(\mathsf{a}) \oplus f \rangle \xrightarrow{\mathsf{a}-} \langle P \setminus (\{\mathsf{a}\} \cup P_{\mathsf{a}}), f \rangle} [\text{CClose}]$$

Fig. 6. Operational semantics of dynamic components

The second rule ([COPEN]) is the most complex one, as it deals with component spawning and port creation. Here the freshly created session identifier is b, which is then used as a fresh dynamic port, together with suitable instances P_{b} of the static ports of the component. The spawned instance of the component has initial state $\mathsf{q}''(\mathsf{b})$. Ports in P_{b} will allow the spawned instance of the component to interact on static ports with some other spawned components that are part of the same session. Moreover, the spawned instance of the component will be able to interact on the port b by synchronising with all the other spawned components that are part of the same session. Note that although the token b has been created within the session a, such information is not maintained in the state, i.e., sessions a and b will run independently.

Finally, the third rule ([CCLOSE]) deals with session closure, where the token a and all the ports $\{\mathsf{a}\} \cup P_{\mathsf{a}}$ associated with the closed session a are discarded.

Example 5. Consider a server component that interacts with a possibly unbounded number of clients by keeping different/separate sessions. Any session starts with a client request for a new connection. After the initial connection, each client synchronises with the server by using a dedicated, private port until the client disconnects from the server. This behaviour can be modelled as the component depicted in Fig. 7(a). We rely on the standard graphical representation of coloured Petri nets, in which places are represented by circles and transitions are drawn as rectangles connected to their pre and post-set by direct arcs which are decorated with the colours of the involved tokens. In addition, we show the ports of the component as bullets drawn on the boundaries, like in BIP notation. The component in Fig. 7(a) has one static port cnt, two places accept and open with the following three transitions:

- $t_0 = \mathsf{accept}(x) \xrightarrow{\mathsf{cnt}_x \, y+} \mathsf{accept}(x) \oplus \mathsf{open}(y)$: if the server can accept a new connection (i.e., a token can be consumed from the place accept), then it performs the action cnt that creates a new dynamic port (to be associated with the symbol y). After performing this action, the server will still accept new connections because the token x is put back to the place accept. Now, the component has a new session (i.e., a dedicated port) for interacting with

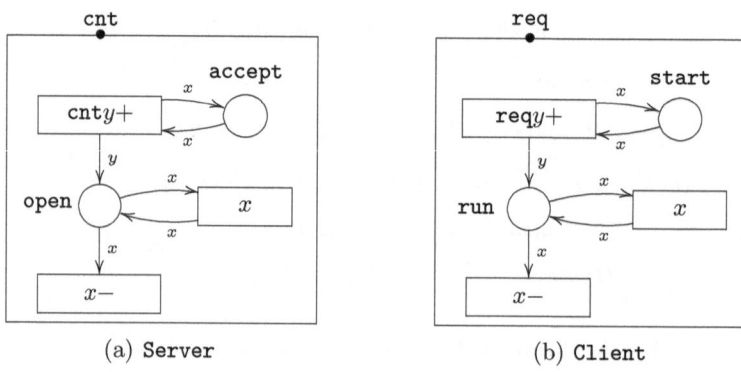

Fig. 7. Two dynamic components

the recently connected client as represented by the token y containing the fresh created port name in the place open.

- $t_1 = \mathrm{open}(x) \xrightarrow{x} \mathrm{open}(x)$: For any open session x, the server can repeatedly perform an action on the corresponding dynamic port. This transition does not alter the set of ports of the component.
- $t_2 = \mathrm{open}(x) \xrightarrow{x-} \varnothing$: An already opened session x is closed after performing the corresponding action $x-$, that synchronises with a request from the client to close the same session.

The component modelling the behaviour of a client is depicted in Fig. 7(b), which is analogous to Fig. 7(a).

Definition 10 (Dynamic BI(P) system). *A* dynamic BI(P) system $B = \gamma(B_1, \ldots, B_n)$ *is the composition of a finite set* $\{B_i\}_{i=1}^n$ *of dynamic BI(P) components* $B_i = (Q_i, P_i, \rightarrow_i)$ *such that their sets of ports are pairwise disjoint, i.e.,* $P_i \cap P_j = \varnothing$ *for* $i \neq j$, *parametrized by a set* $\gamma \subset 2^P$ *of interactions over the set of ports* $P = \biguplus_{i=1}^n P_i$.

Without loss of generality, we assume that for any $a \in \gamma$ it is either the case that a contains static ports only and we call it *static* or it contains no static port at all and we call it *dynamic*. Moreover, if $a \downarrow_{P_i}$ is made of static ports, then $a \downarrow_{P_i} = a'_{\mathbf{a}_i}$ for some a' and $\mathbf{a}_i \in P_i$, i.e., all static ports in $a \downarrow_{P_i}$ are parametrized by the same session identifier $\mathbf{a}_i$. In such case, we let $ids_i(a)$ denote $\mathbf{a}_i$

In the following we write $I(a)$ to denote the set $\{i \mid \neg(a \# P_i)\}$ of indices of the components involved in a and $\overline{I(a)}$ to denote its complement $[1, n] \setminus I(a) = \{i \mid a \# P_i\}$. If a is static, we denote by $ids(a)$ the set $\{ids_i(a) \mid i \in I(a)\}$, otherwise we let $ids(a) = \varnothing$.

Given a set of substitutions $\sigma = \{\mathbf{b}_i / \mathbf{a}_i\}_{i \in I}$ and a static interaction $a \in \gamma$ such that $ids(a) \subseteq \{\mathbf{a}_i\}_{i \in I}$ we write a_σ for the interaction obtained by replacing in a each parameter $\mathbf{a}_i$ by the corresponding parameter $\mathbf{b}_i$. Moreover, we write γ_σ for the set of renamed static interactions $\{a_\sigma \mid a \in \gamma \wedge ids(a) \subseteq \{\mathbf{a}_i\}_{i \in I}\}$. Finally, given a dynamic interaction a we write $\gamma \ominus a$ for the set of interactions

$$\frac{a \in \gamma \qquad \forall i.s_i \xrightarrow{a \downarrow P_i} s_i'}{\gamma(s_1, \ldots, s_n) \xrightarrow{a} \gamma(s_1', \ldots, s_n')} [\text{SINT}]$$

$$\frac{a \in \gamma \qquad i \in I(a) \implies s_i \xrightarrow{a \downarrow P_i, b_i +} s_i' \qquad b_i \text{ fresh}}{i \in \overline{I(a)} \implies s_i' = s_i \qquad \sigma = \{b_i/ids_i(a)\}_{i \in I(a)}} [\text{SOPEN}]$$
$$\gamma(s_1, \ldots, s_n) \xrightarrow{a} (\gamma \cup \{b_i\}_{i \in I(a)} \cup \gamma_\sigma)(s_1', \ldots, s_n')$$

$$\frac{a \in \gamma \qquad i \in I(a) \implies s_i \xrightarrow{a \downarrow P_i -} s_i' \qquad i \in \overline{I(a)} \implies s_i' = s_i}{\gamma(s_1, \ldots, s_n) \xrightarrow{a} (\gamma \ominus a)(s_1', \ldots, s_n')} [\text{SCLOSE}]$$

Fig. 8. Operational semantics of dynamic BI(P) systems

in γ where the ports in a do not appear. Formally, $\gamma \ominus a = \{a' \in \gamma \mid a' \cap a = \varnothing \wedge ids(a') \cap a = \varnothing\}$

Let s_i range over $2^{P_i} \times P_i^{Q_i}$ representing a generic state of the component B_i. The semantics of a dynamic BI(P) system $\gamma(B_1, \ldots, B_n)$ is defined by the three rules in Fig. 8.

Example 6. Consider the dynamic BI(P) components introduced in Example 5. We illustrate one possible run of the server with two clients in Fig. 9. Roughly, it corresponds to the series of transitions in Fig. 10, where $\gamma, \gamma', \gamma''$ are the ones indicated in Fig. 9. The first transition is obtained by combining the server transition

$$\langle \{\text{cnt}\}, \text{accept}(\bullet) \rangle \xrightarrow{\text{cnt v} +} \langle \{\text{cnt}, \text{cnt}_v, v\}, \text{accept}(\bullet) \oplus \text{open}(v) \rangle$$

with the following transition of the first client:

$$\langle \{\text{req}_1\}, \text{start}_1(\bullet) \rangle \xrightarrow{\text{req}_1 \text{ m} +} \langle \{\text{req}_1, \text{req}_{1m}, m\}, \text{start}_1(\bullet) \oplus \text{run}_1(m) \rangle$$

Analogously, for the second transition. Note that suitable replicas cnt_v, cnt_w, req_{1m}, req_{2n} of the static ports cnt, req_1, req_2 have been created locally to each component, and that the set of interactions has been enriched with suitable replicas $\text{cnt}_v \text{req}_{1m}$ and $\text{cnt}_w \text{req}_{2n}$ of the static interactions $\text{cnt} \text{req}_1$ and $\text{cnt} \text{req}_2$ together with freshly created dynamic interactions $v m$ and $w n$.

Let s denote the last state reached. Then, the server can interact with the clients by performing the interactions $v m$ and $w n$ as many times as needed, with the system remaining in the same state s:

$$s \xrightarrow{v m} s \xrightarrow{w n} s \cdots$$

The above transitions are obtained by combining dynamic transitions of the server (labels v and w) with dynamic transitions of the clients (labels m and n).

Finally, we illustrate the case when the session between the server and the second client is closed:

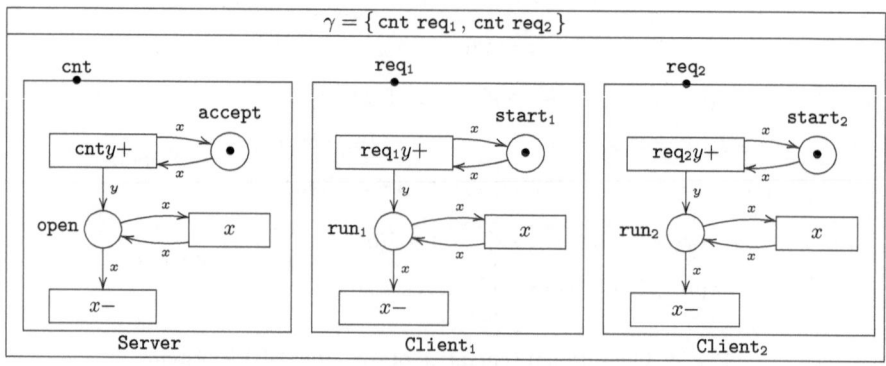

(a) Initial State

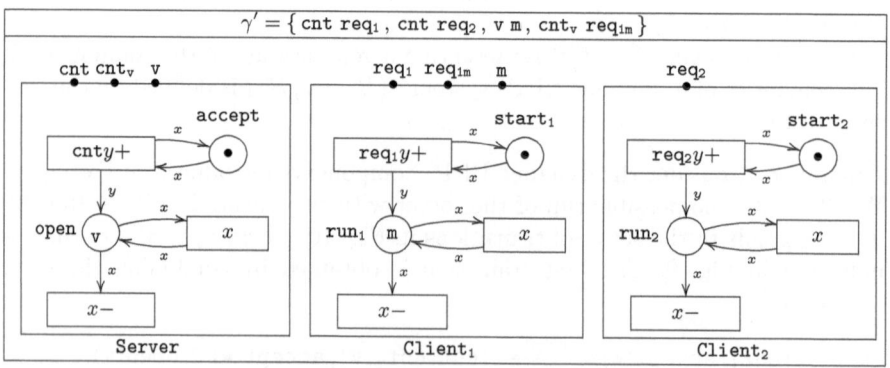

(b) First Synchronisation

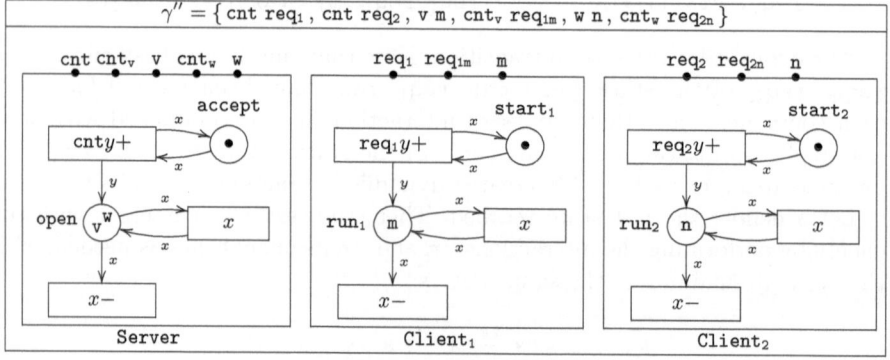

(c) Second Synchronisation

Fig. 9. A run of the server with two clients

$$\gamma \left(\begin{array}{l} \langle\{\mathtt{cnt}\}, \mathtt{accept}(\bullet)\rangle, \\ \langle\{\mathtt{req}_1\}, \mathtt{start}_1(\bullet)\rangle, \\ \langle\{\mathtt{req}_2\}, \mathtt{start}_2(\bullet)\rangle \end{array} \right)$$

$$\xrightarrow{\mathtt{cnt\ req}_1} \gamma' \left(\begin{array}{l} \langle\{\mathtt{cnt}, \mathtt{cnt}_v, v\}, \mathtt{accept}(\bullet) \oplus \mathtt{open}(v)\rangle, \\ \langle\{\mathtt{req}_1, \mathtt{req}_{1m}, m\}, \mathtt{start}_1(\bullet) \oplus \mathtt{run}_1(m)\rangle, \\ \langle\{\mathtt{req}_2\}, \mathtt{start}_2(\bullet)\rangle \end{array} \right)$$

$$\xrightarrow{\mathtt{cnt\ req}_2} \gamma'' \left(\begin{array}{l} \langle\{\mathtt{cnt}, \mathtt{cnt}_v, v, \mathtt{cnt}_w, w\}, \mathtt{accept}(\bullet) \oplus \mathtt{open}(v) \oplus \mathtt{open}(w)\rangle, \\ \langle\{\mathtt{req}_1, \mathtt{req}_{1m}, m\}, \mathtt{start}_1(\bullet) \oplus \mathtt{run}_1(m)\rangle, \\ \langle\{\mathtt{req}_2, \mathtt{req}_{2n}, n\}, \mathtt{start}_2(\bullet) \oplus \mathtt{run}_2(n)\rangle \end{array} \right)$$

Fig. 10. Transitions representing a run of the server with two clients

$$s \xrightarrow{\mathtt{w\ n}} \gamma' \left(\begin{array}{l} \langle\{\mathtt{cnt}, \mathtt{cnt}_v, v\}, \mathtt{accept}(\bullet) \oplus \mathtt{open}(v)\rangle, \\ \langle\{\mathtt{req}_1, \mathtt{req}_{1m}, m\}, \mathtt{start}_1(\bullet) \oplus \mathtt{run}_1(m)\rangle, \\ \langle\{\mathtt{req}_2\}, \mathtt{start}_2(\bullet)\rangle \end{array} \right)$$

The above transition is obtained by combining a closing transitions of the server (label $w-$) with a closing transition of the second client (label $n-$). Note that the set of ports of the server and of the second client are updated consequently, by removing all ports that refer to the session identifiers w and n. Similarly, the set of interactions is $\gamma' = \gamma'' \ominus w\ n$.

4.1 Dynamic BI(P) vs BI(P) vs P/T Nets

Unlike reconfigurable BI(P) systems, dynamic BI(P) systems are strictly more expressive than ordinary BI(P) systems. This can be immediately seen by noting that BI(P) systems are finite state (see, e.g., [8], where it was shown that any BI(P) system corresponds to a safe Petri net), while this is not the case for dynamic BI(P) systems (see, e.g., Example 6).

In this section we outline a correspondence between dynamic BI(P) systems and Place/Transition Petri nets. This is interesting because: i) it shows that properties like reachability remains decidable and ii) it draws a nice analogy with the correspondence between ordinary BI(P) systems and safe Petri nets shown in [8].

Roughly, given a dynamic BI(P) system $B = \gamma(B_1, ..., B_n)$ we define a P/T Petri net $N(B)$ whose places are tuples of states from components $B_1, ..., B_n$ and whose transitions represent the possible interactions. Note that $N(B)$ is determined statically and may contain more places and transitions than those strictly necessary, i.e., $N(B)$ may contains places that will never be marked as well as transitions that will never be enabled. Still $N(B)$ is finite and it is neither an ordinary automata nor a safe Petri net because: i) it may contain transitions that are attached to two output places; and ii) during a run it may produce more than one token in the same place.

Places of $N(B)$. The places of the net will be named like pairs $(I, \{p_i\}_{i \in I})$, where $\varnothing \subset I \subseteq [1, n]$ and $\forall i \in I.p_i \in Q_i$. Intuitively, the place $(I, \{p_i\}_{i \in I})$ represents a session that involves replicas of the components B_i such that $i \in I$, where the ith component is in state p_i.

The initial marking of $N(B)$ has one token in the place $([1, n], \{p_{0i}\}_{i \in [1,n]})$, where p_{0i} denotes the initial state of the ith component.

Transitions of $N(B)$. The transitions will be named like pairs (p, t) for p a place like described above and t one of the following: an ordinary interaction a or an interaction with spawning a^+, with $a \in \gamma$; a dynamic interaction I or a closing interaction I^- with $\varnothing \subset I \subseteq [1, n]$. However not all combinations of p and t are considered. A pair (p, t) where $p = (I, \{p_i\}_{i \in I})$ is included in $N(B)$ if:

1. $t = a$, $I(a) \subseteq I$ and for all $i \in I(a)$ then $p_i(x) \xrightarrow{a_{ix}} q_i(x)$ is a transition of B_i with $a \downarrow_{P_i} = a_{i\,ids_i(a)}$. In this case we let $^\bullet(p, t) = p$ and $(p, t)^\bullet = (I, \{q_i\}_{i \in I})$ such that $q_i = p_i$ whenever $i \in I \setminus I(a)$.

2. $t = a^+$, $I(a) \subseteq I$ and for all $i \in I(a)$ then $p_i(x) \xrightarrow{a_{ix}y+} q_i(x) \oplus q'_i(y)$ is a transition of B_i with $a \downarrow_{P_i} = a_{i\,ids_i(a)}$. In this case we let $^\bullet(p, t) = p$ and $(p, t)^\bullet = (I, \{q_i\}_{i \in I}) \oplus (I(a), \{q'_i\}_{i \in I(a)})$ such that $q_i = p_i$ whenever $i \in I \setminus I(a)$.

3. $t = I$ and for all $i \in I$ then $p(x) \xrightarrow{x} q(x)$ is a dynamic transitions of B_i. In this case we let $^\bullet(p, t) = p$ and $(p, t)^\bullet = (I, \{q_i\}_{i \in I})$.

4. $t = I^-$ and for all $i \in I$ then $p(x) \xrightarrow{x-} \varnothing$ is a dynamic transitions of B_i. In this case we let $^\bullet(p, t) = p$ and $(p, t)^\bullet = \varnothing$.

Example 7. Consider the dynamic BI(P) system B introduced in Example 6. The corresponding P/T Petri net $N(B)$ contains, e.g., the places:

$(\{1\}, \{\text{accept}\})$ $(\{1\}, \{\text{open}\})$ $(\{2\}, \{\text{start}_1\})$ $(\{2\}, \{\text{run}_1\})$ $(\{3\}, \{\text{start}_2\})$
$(\{3\}, \{\text{run}_2\})$ $(\{1, 2\}, \{\text{accept}, \text{start}_1\})$ $(\{1, 2\}, \{\text{accept}, \text{run}_1\})$
$(\{1, 2\}, \{\text{open}, \text{start}_1\})$ $(\{1, 2\}, \{\text{open}, \text{run}_1\})$ $(\{1, 3\}, \{\text{accept}, \text{start}_2\})$
$(\{1, 3\}, \{\text{accept}, \text{run}_2\})$ $(\{1, 3\}, \{\text{open}, \text{start}_2\})$ $(\{1, 3\}, \{\text{open}, \text{run}_2\})$
$(\{2, 3\}, \{\text{start}_1, \text{start}_2\})$ $(\{2, 3\}, \{\text{start}_1, \text{run}_2\})$ $(\{2, 3\}, \{\text{run}_1, \text{start}_2\})$
$(\{2, 3\}, \{\text{run}_1, \text{run}_2\})$ $(\{1, 2, 3\}, \{\text{accept}, \text{start}_1, \text{start}_2\})$ . . .

The initial marking of $N(B)$ is $(\{1, 2, 3\}, \{\text{accept}, \text{start}_1, \text{start}_2\})$.
The net $N(B)$ contains the transitions:

$((\{1\}, \{\text{open}\}), \{1\})$ $((\{1, 2, 3\}, \{\text{accept}, \text{start}_1, \text{start}_2\}), (\text{cnt req}_1)^+)$
$((\{1\}, \{\text{open}\}), \{1\}^-)$ $((\{1, 2, 3\}, \{\text{accept}, \text{start}_1, \text{run}_2\}), (\text{cnt req}_1)^+)$
$((\{2\}, \{\text{run}_1\}), \{2\})$ $((\{1, 2, 3\}, \{\text{accept}, \text{start}_1, \text{start}_2\}), (\text{cnt req}_2)^+)$
$((\{2\}, \{\text{run}_1\}), \{2\}^-)$ $((\{1, 2, 3\}, \{\text{accept}, \text{run}_1, \text{start}_2\}), (\text{cnt req}_2)^+)$
$((\{3\}, \{\text{run}_2\}), \{3\})$ $((\{1, 2, 3\}, \{\text{open}, \text{run}_1, \text{run}_2\}), \{1, 2, 3\})$
$((\{3\}, \{\text{run}_2\}), \{3\}^-)$ $((\{1, 2, 3\}, \{\text{open}, \text{run}_1, \text{run}_2\}), \{1, 2, 3\}^-)$
$((\{1, 2\}, \{\text{open}, \text{run}_1\}), \{1, 2\})$ $((\{1, 2\}, \{\text{accept}, \text{start}_1\}), (\text{cnt req}_1)^+)$
$((\{1, 3\}, \{\text{open}, \text{run}_2\}), \{1, 3\})$ $((\{1, 3\}, \{\text{accept}, \text{start}_2\}), (\text{cnt req}_2)^+)$
$((\{1, 2\}, \{\text{open}, \text{run}_1\}), \{1, 2\}^-)$ $((\{1, 3\}, \{\text{open}, \text{run}_2\}), \{1, 3\}^-)$
$((\{2, 3\}, \{\text{run}_1, \text{run}_2\}), \{2, 3\})$ $((\{2, 3\}, \{\text{run}_1, \text{run}_2\}), \{2, 3\}^-)$

Since for all transitions (p, t) we have ${}^\bullet(p, t) = p$, we omit to define the presets of transitions. Since for all transitions of the form (p, I) we have $(p, I)^\bullet = p$ and for all transitions of the form (p, I^-) we have $(p, I^-)^\bullet = \varnothing$, we omit to define the postsets of such transitions. Then we have:

$$(p, (\mathtt{cnt}\,\mathtt{req}_1)^+)^\bullet = p \oplus (\{1, 2\}, \{\mathtt{open}, \mathtt{run}_1\})$$
$$(p, (\mathtt{cnt}\,\mathtt{req}_2)^+)^\bullet = p \oplus (\{1, 3\}, \{\mathtt{open}, \mathtt{run}_2\})$$

As already said, $N(B)$ can contain dead transitions (never enabled) as well as dead places (never marked). A simple inspection reveals that the only places and transitions that are not dead are:

$p_1 = (\{1, 2, 3\}, \{\mathtt{accept}, \mathtt{start}_1, \mathtt{start}_2\})$ $(p_1, (\mathtt{cnt}\,\mathtt{req}_1)^+)$ $(p_1, (\mathtt{cnt}\,\mathtt{req}_2)^+)$
$p_2 = (\{1, 2\}, \{\mathtt{open}, \mathtt{run}_1\})$ $(p_2, \{1, 2\})$ $(p_2, \{1, 2\}^-)$
$p_3 = (\{1, 3\}, \{\mathtt{open}, \mathtt{run}_2\})$ $(p_3, \{1, 3\})$ $(p_3, \{1, 3\}^-)$

Theorem 2. *Reachability is decidable for any dynamic BI(P) system B.*

Proof. The proof exploits the P/T Petri net encoding $N(B)$ of B and the fact that reachability is decidable for P/T Petri nets.

Let $s = \gamma(s_1, ..., s_n)$ be a state of B with $s_i = \langle P_i, f_i \rangle$ for $i \in [1, n]$, and let $\delta(\gamma)$ denote the set of dynamic interactions of γ (i.e., the opened sessions). Then we denote by $N(s)$ the marking defined as follows:

$$N(s) = \bigoplus_{a \in \delta(\gamma)} (I(a), \{\mathtt{p}_i \in B_i \mid i \in I(a) \wedge f_i(\mathtt{p}_i) \cap a \neq \varnothing\})$$

Next, we prove separately the two implications:

1. if there is a transition from s to s' in B, then there is a transition from $N(s)$ to $N(s')$ in $N(B)$;
2. if there is a transition from $N(s)$ to m in $N(B)$, then there is a state s' such that there is a transition from s to s' in B with $N(s') = m$.

1st implication. Assume there is a transition $s \xrightarrow{a} s'$ in B. Then, there are four cases to consider, but due to space limitation, we show only the second case ([SINT]), which is the more interesting one.

- $s \xrightarrow{a} s'$ is a static transition obtained via rule [SINT].
- $s \xrightarrow{a} s'$ is a dynamic transition obtained via rule [SINT]. Since $a \in \gamma$, then there is a token $p = (I(a), \{\mathtt{p}_i \in B_i \mid i \in I(a) \wedge f_i(\mathtt{p}_i) \cap a \neq \varnothing\}) \in N(s)$. Moreover, there must be transitions $\mathtt{p}_i(x) \xrightarrow{x} \mathtt{q}_i(x)$ of B_i for each $i \in I(a)$. Therefore, there is a transition $(p, I(a))$ with ${}^\bullet(p, I(a)) = p$ and $(p, I(a))^\bullet = (I(a), \{\mathtt{q}_i\}_{i \in I(a)})$. It is immediate to see that $(p, I(a))$ is enabled in $N(s)$ and that its firing leads to $N(s')$.
- $s \xrightarrow{a} s'$ is a spawning transition obtained via rule [SOPEN].
- $s \xrightarrow{a} s'$ is a closing transition obtained via rule [SCLOSE].

2nd implication. Assume that there is a transition (p, t) in $N(B)$ that is enabled in $N(s)$ and whose firing leads to a marking m. Since t is enabled, then $p \in N(s)$, i.e., it must be the case that $p = (I(a'), \{\mathbf{p}_i \in B_i \mid i \in I(a') \wedge f_i(\mathbf{p}_i) \cap a' \neq \varnothing\})$ for some $a' \in \delta(\gamma)$. Then, there are four cases to consider, but due to space limitation, we show only the third case, which is the more interesting one.

- $t = a$, $I(a) \subseteq I(a')$ and $\forall i \in I(a)$ then $\mathbf{p}_i(x) \xrightarrow{a_{ix}} \mathbf{q}_i(x)$ is a transition of B_i with $a \downarrow_{P_i} = a_{i\,ids_i(a)}$.
- $t = a^+$, $I(a) \subseteq I(a')$ and $\forall i \in I(a)$ then $\mathbf{p}_i(x) \xrightarrow{a_{ix}y+} \mathbf{q}_i(x) \oplus \mathbf{q}'_i(y)$ is a transition of B_i with $a \downarrow_{P_i} = a_{i\,ids_i(a)}$.
- $t = I(a')$ and $\forall i \in I(a')$ then $\mathbf{p}(x) \xrightarrow{x} \mathbf{q}(x)$ is a dynamic transitions of B_i. In this case we have ${}^\bullet(p, t) = p$ and $(p, t)^\bullet = (I(a'), \{\mathbf{q}_i\}_{i \in I(a')})$. Then, by rule [CINT], we know that $a' \downarrow_{P_i} = \mathbf{a}_i \in \delta(P_i)$ and $s_i = (P_i, \mathbf{p}_i(\mathbf{a}_i) \oplus f'_i) \xrightarrow{\mathbf{a}_i} (P_i, \mathbf{q}_i(\mathbf{a}_i) \oplus f'_i) = s'_i$ for each $i \in I(a')$ and by rule [SINT] we have that $s \xrightarrow{a'} \gamma(s'_1, ..., s'_n) = s'$ for $s'_i = s_i$ when $i \in [1, n] \setminus I(a')$. It is immediate to see that $N(s') = m$.
- $t = I(a')^-$ and $\forall i \in I(a')$ then $\mathbf{p}(x) \xrightarrow{x-} \varnothing$ is a dynamic transitions of B_i.

The thesis follows by the fact that reachability is decidable for $N(B)$. □

5   Concluding Remarks

In this paper we have investigated two suitable extensions of BI(P) with dynamically defined behaviour and interaction. The first extension, called reconfigurable BI(P), has evolved from a previous proposal of the VERIMAG research group within the project ASCENS, before Dy-BIP was proposed in [6]. Here we prove that reconfigurable BI(P) is equally expressive as ordinary BI(P). The second extension, called dynamic BI(P), has been inspired by the use of correlation sets in web services and can be used to define systems with infinitely many states (contrary to ordinary BI(P) systems), but ensures that state reachability is decidable. Therefore, both extensions still preserve key BI(P) features in terms of analysis and verification. Notably the encodings exploited in our expressiveness results are obtained without a considerable change of the basic components, in the spirit of the glue expressiveness introduced in [3].

With respect to Dy-BIP, we think dynamic BI(P) has some advantages. While Dy-BIP imposes ad hoc restrictions (e.g., transitions of atomic components are labelled with only one single local port instead of a set of local ports) and extensions (e.g. transitions of atomic components are decorated with non-local architecture constraints that may involve port names of other components, thus compromising the modularity of the specification and moreover history variables are introduced to store the identity of interacting components), this is not necessary for dynamic BI(P). Furthermore, the number of component instances cannot change in Dy-BIP, contrary to dynamic BI(P).

In the future we plan to study the interplay between probabilities, priorities and dynamics, possibly in the compositional setting offered by the algebra of

Petri nets with boundaries [9]. We are confident that our proposals can fit well with the priorities based on the offer predicate semantics defined in [5].

Acknowledgments. We thank Simon Bliudze for several suggestions and comments on a preliminary version of this paper.

References

1. Arbab, F., Bruni, R., Clarke, D., Lanese, I., Montanari, U.: Tiles for Reo. In: Corradini, A., Montanari, U. (eds.) WADT 2008. LNCS, vol. 5486, pp. 37–55. Springer, Heidelberg (2009)
2. Basu, A., Bozga, M., Sifakis, J.: Modeling heterogeneous real-time components in BIP. In: Fourth IEEE International Conference on Software Engineering and Formal Methods (SEFM 2006), pp. 3–12. IEEE Computer Society (2006)
3. Bliudze, S., Sifakis, J.: A notion of glue expressiveness for component-based systems. In: van Breugel, F., Chechik, M. (eds.) CONCUR 2008. LNCS, vol. 5201, pp. 508–522. Springer, Heidelberg (2008)
4. Bliudze, S., Sifakis, J.: Causal semantics for the algebra of connectors. Formal Methods in System Design 36(2), 167–194 (2010)
5. Bliudze, S., Sifakis, J.: Synthesizing glue operators from glue constraints for the construction of component-based systems. In: Apel, S., Jackson, E. (eds.) SC 2011. LNCS, vol. 6708, pp. 51–67. Springer, Heidelberg (2011)
6. Bozga, M., Jaber, M., Maris, N., Sifakis, J.: Modeling dynamic architectures using Dy-BIP. In: Gschwind, T., De Paoli, F., Gruhn, V., Book, M. (eds.) SC 2012. LNCS, vol. 7306, pp. 1–16. Springer, Heidelberg (2012)
7. Bruni, R., Lanese, I., Montanari, U.: A basic algebra of stateless connectors. Theor. Comput. Sci. 366(1-2), 98–120 (2006)
8. Bruni, R., Melgratti, H., Montanari, U.: Connector algebras, Petri nets, and BIP. In: Clarke, E., Virbitskaite, I., Voronkov, A. (eds.) PSI 2011. LNCS, vol. 7162, pp. 19–38. Springer, Heidelberg (2012)
9. Bruni, R., Melgratti, H., Montanari, U., Sobociński, P.: Connector algebras for C/E and P/T nets' interactions. Logical Methods in Comp. Sci. 9(3)(2013).
10. Bruni, R., Melgratti, H., Montanari, U.: A connector algebra for P/T nets interactions. In: Katoen, J.-P., König, B. (eds.) CONCUR 2011. LNCS, vol. 6901, pp. 312–326. Springer, Heidelberg (2011)
11. Esparza, J., Nielsen, M.: Decidability issues for Petri nets. Petri Nets Newsletter 94, 5–23 (1994)
12. Gadducci, F., Montanari, U.: The tile model. In: Proof, Language, and Interaction, pp. 133–166. The MIT Press (2000)
13. Lapadula, A., Pugliese, R., Tiezzi, F.: A formal account of ws-bpel. In: Lea, D., Zavattaro, G. (eds.) COORDINATION 2008. LNCS, vol. 5052, pp. 199–215. Springer, Heidelberg (2008)
14. Milner, R., Parrow, J., Walker, D.: A calculus of mobile processes, I–II. Inf. Comput. 100(1), 1–77 (1992)
15. Perry, D.E., Wolf, E.L.: Foundations for the study of software architecture. ACM SIGSOFT Software Engineering Notes 17, 40–52 (1992)
16. Sobociński, P.: Representations of Petri net interactions. In: Gastin, P., Laroussinie, F. (eds.) CONCUR 2010. LNCS, vol. 6269, pp. 554–568. Springer, Heidelberg (2010)
17. Viroli, M.: A core calculus for correlation in orchestration languages. J. Log. Algebr. Program. 70(1), 74–95 (2007)

Partially Ordered Knowledge Sharing and Fractionated Systems in the Context of other Models for Distributed Computing

Mark-Oliver Stehr, Minyoung Kim, and Carolyn Talcott

SRI International
{stehr,mkim,clt}@csl.sri.com

Abstract. The latest sensor, actuator, and wireless communication technologies make it feasible to build systems that can operate in challenging environments, but we argue in this paper that the foundations needed to support the design of such systems are not well developed. Traditional models based on strong computing primitives, such as atomic transactions, should be replaced by weaker models such as the *partially ordered knowledge sharing model*, which we motivate in this paper and put into context of existing research. We also introduce a general *probabilistic semantics* for our model and the flavor of its specialization to characterize *fractionated systems*, an interesting class of systems with a potentially large number of redundantly operating components that can be programmed independently of the actual number that is deployed or operational at runtime.

1 Introduction

A wide variety of distributed computing models have been proposed and are being successfully used in practice, but in this paper we would like to argue that with a few exceptions most models are not well aligned with the current technological trends. This is especially indicated by the lack of unified models and the astonishing degree of diversity of mostly incompatible point solutions and protocols for emerging technologies with applications in rapidly growing areas such as mobile networking, sensor networks, networked cyber-physical systems, instrumented spaces, space and maritime networking, intelligent ensembles, biologically-inspired computing, and mobile social networking. A general observation is that in many application domains there is a trend from powerful centralized or tightly coupled solutions to decentralized and loosely-coupled architectures.

Given such powerful trends it is often instructive to look at extreme cases. In our context, we envision open networked systems consisting of a large number of nodes that are continuously evolving, with nodes and groups of nodes joining or leaving, or more generally a network exhibiting merging/partitioning of all kinds. Wireless communication will be prevalent, but spectrum remains limited, and

S. Iida, J. Meseguer, and K. Ogata (Eds.): Futatsugi Festschrift, LNCS 8373, pp. 402–433, 2014.

with the proliferation of wireless devices, interference becomes an increasingly serious problem. The highly dynamic network may be physically controllable to some degree, e.g., through mobility, transmission power control, or advanced technologies such as smart antennas and beam forming. Various wireless communication technologies will be used in combination and together with traditional wired and new emerging communication technologies. Additional challenges may arise from the environment, leading to potentially high and unpredictable loss rates, asymmetric connectivity, and windows of communication opportunities that may be very short due to relative mobility. Unreliability and heterogeneity of the nodes and limited resources, especially bandwidth and energy lead to further difficulties. Intermittent and opportunistic connectivity can be expected to be the common forms of communication in the future, given that the huge number of personal devices and sensors cannot be continuously connected. Safety- and mission-critical systems will need to exploit large amounts of redundancy to ensure correct operation in such noisy environments. Nevertheless, with the large number of nodes there is also the expectation that the distributed system as a whole has capabilities, e.g., in terms of performance and reliability, that are beyond those of any monolithic system.

Given the potentially highly transient and unreliable nature of the topological neighborhood (in fact the notion of neighbor becomes hard to define for many emerging technologies), we propose the partially ordered knowledge sharing model, which tries to avoid exposing this concept to applications and instead uses a logical broadcast model (with a partial order semantics) that does not rely on addressing individual nodes. The notion of locality is implicit but remains essential, because knowledge can be shared over several hops. How knowledge is shared is not defined by the model. Protocols based on shared memory, message passing, broadcasting, gossiping, network coding and their combinations can be used in implementations. The model does not assume any form of atomic interactions, because they are not implementable in the environments that we envision. Clearly, this has a significant impact on how the nodes need to cooperate and what problems can be solved while remaining within the scope of model.

As summarized in Section 6, in spite of key differences our work is related to a wide range of ideas, most notably the knowledge-based view of distributed algorithms [51], the classical asynchronous message-passing and broadcast models and corresponding impossibility results [42], the study of group communication in the presence of network partitions [75], the work on semantically reliable multicast [81,80], delay- and disruption-tolerant networking [39,88], distributed blackboard models [27], and the idea of functionally accurate, cooperative distributed systems [70]. As discussed in Section 6, our work is also closely related to various flavors of gossip protocols and generalizations [16]. Various informal models for gossip protocols have been proposed, but given the diversity and the fact that new variants of gossip-style algorithms keep emerging an exact formal characterization seems difficult if we do not want to simply identify gossip protocols in terms of their power with the entire class of distributed algorithms, say based on the message passing model.

The partial order knowledge sharing model is not intended to be associated with a fixed set of architectures or protocols, let it be shared memory, broadcasting, overlay networks, gossip-style protocols, or distributed hashing. Instead, the knowledge sharing model is intended as the weakest sensible distributed computing model on which applications can be built. The mapping of the model into a protocol or more realistically into a combination of protocols can depend on application requirements and is typically influenced by the environment in which the model is deployed. A deployment on a set of hosts in the Internet would use different protocols than a deployment on a sensor network. Furthermore, a deployment on wireless mobile nodes such as personal-digital assistants would use different protocols than a computing cluster on a local area network. Nevertheless, applications or functions can be developed at a level that enables code to be reused in a wide range of environments and ultimately in heterogenous systems of systems.

Ideally, applications make use of the partially ordered knowledge sharing model for all of their purposes, but since the model must be necessarily weak, applications may exploit additional capabilities of the underlying platform, e.g., specific networking capabilities for more efficient communication, access to large databases, or interfaces of specific cyber-physical devices.

Overview of this Paper. In the following Section 2 we motivate the partially ordered knowledge sharing model, a model for losely coupled distributed computing, which is subsequently formalized in Section 3. It serves as a basis for other models introduced in this paper, namely its probabilistic refinement in Section 4 and a more restricted model for the particularly interesting class of fractionated systems introduced in Section 5. Some examples of fractionated systems are informally given in Section 5.1 to illustrate to broad scope of this notion. Since one goal of this paper is to put these models in the context of existing research, we review various related models in Section 6, before we conclude in Section 7.

2   Knowledge Sharing as a Basis for Distributed Computing

Our *partially ordered knowledge sharing model* is a generalization of a distributed computing model that we have used in earlier work [88] as the basis for disruption-tolerant networking. In that work we have used knowledge sharing with specific orderings as a support layer for disruption-tolerant routing algorithms. The knowledge sharing model is asynchronous and can make explicit the structure of a distributed computation in space and time, and hence is less abstract than many other models of distributed computing, e.g., those abstracting from the network topology by assuming direct end-to-end channels.

In a nutshell, we assume a *networked cyber-physical system* with a finite set of so called *cyber-nodes* that provide *computing* resources, can have volatile and/or persistent *storage*, and are all equipped with *networking* capabilities. Cybernodes can have additional devices such as *sensors* and *actuators*, through which they can observe and control their environment, but only to a limited degree (including possibly their own physical state, e.g., their orientation/position). Cyber-nodes can be fixed or mobile, and for the general model no assumption is made about the computing or storage resources or about the network and the communication capabilities or opportunities that it provides. Hence this model covers a broad range of *heterogeneous* technologies (e.g., wireless/wired, unicast/broadcast) and potentially challenging environment conditions, where networking characteristics can range from high-quality persistent connectivity to intermittent/episodic connectivity. The cyber-physical system is *open* in the sense that new nodes can join and leave the network at any time. Permanent or temporary communication or node *failures* are admitted by this model. As a consequence, many forms of network dynamics including partitioning, merging, message ferrying, group mobility, etc. are possible.

In the following, we give an informal characterization of an individual cyber-node that will be sufficient for the our purposes. First of all, each cyber-node has a unique *name*, but different from most models of distributed computing, names are not used for communication between nodes, thereby allowing applications that do not make use of names and hence maintain a certain degree of anonymity or indistinguishability. Each cyber-node has a *local clock*, which increases monotonically by at least a fixed smallest unit in each instruction and is only loosely synchronized with other nodes in the network if admitted by the networking conditions. We also assume that each node has access to a source of randomness (e.g., a fair coin), with the idea that typical applications of this model make heavy use of randomization techniques.

Locally, each cyber-node uses an event-based sequential and universal computation model. The model is based on the dual notions of local events and distributed knowledge. Two key services are provided by each node. First, timed events can be posted, i.e., scheduled to be executed at any local time (possibly randomized) in the future. Second, knowledge can be posted, i.e., submitted for dissemination in the network. All local computation is event-based, where corresponding to the two services above, events can be either *timed events* or *knowledge events*, with the latter representing the reception of a new unit of knowledge. Similar to existing middleware frameworks for messaging or group communication, knowledge dissemination can take place independently in different logical *cyber-spaces*, but a unit of knowledge is a more state-like entity that should not be confused with the notion of a message. Furthermore, no reliability, delivery order, or atomicity guarantees are provided to the applications, because they would severely limit the scalability of the model in terms of the network size.

Partially ordered knowledge sharing is asynchronous and each node can use some of its storage as a cache, which we also refer to as a *knowledge base*. Network caching allows the system to support communication even if no end-to-end path exists at a single point in time. Different from a shared-memory model, partially ordered knowledge sharing allows each node to have its own (typically partial and delayed) view of the distributed state of knowledge. Different from an asynchronous message-passing model, knowledge is not directed towards a particular destination. Instead each node decides based on the knowledge content (or its embedded type) if it wants to use the unit of knowledge that it receives.

Epidemic and (spatial) gossiping techniques can be used to implement knowledge sharing, but unlike gossiping, which is based on the exchange of cache summaries, knowledge sharing can also be implemented by single-message protocols based on unidirectional unicast or broadcast communication [88]. Epidemic computing covers a very broad class of algorithms, whereas partially ordered knowledge sharing is a more restricted model that makes use of the abstract semantics of knowledge that is given in a very specific way, namely in terms of an equivalence relation and a partial order. The consideration of the partial-order semantics of knowledge by intermediate nodes is of key importance for scalable implementations and also the reason why knowledge sharing is fundamentally different from asynchronous/unreliable or even epidemic/probabilistic broadcast.

To partially capture the semantics of knowledge for the purpose of distributed knowledge sharing, we assume an application-specific partial order $\leq$ on all knowledge items together with its induced equivalence relation. We refer to $\leq$ as the *subsumption order* given that the intuitive meaning of $k \leq k'$ is that k' contains at least the information contained in k. With this interpretation the induced equivalence $k \equiv k'$, defined as $k \leq k'$ and $k \geq k'$, means that k and k' have the same semantics, even if they are represented in different ways. In this situation, the knowledge sharing model may (but does not have to) discard k' without delivering it to the application, if k has already been delivered. In addition to $\leq$, we assume an application-specific strict partial order $\prec$ that is compatible with $\leq$ and we refer to as *replacement order*, with the intuition that $k \prec k'$ means that k' replaces/overwrites k, and hence if k has not been delivered yet to the application, the knowledge sharing model may (but does not have to) discard it without delivering it to the application, if k' has already been received. Subsumption equivalence can be important in actual implementations, but we identify elements that are subsumption-equivalent for the purpose of the formal treatment in this paper.

The use of a locally sequential model may seem quite restrictive but it encourages a programming discipline where large monolithic programs are broken up into small units that are distributed over the network, a process that we call *software fractionation*. Concurrent execution techniques can be used as long as they are consistent with the sequential model. This is similar to the approach to multi-programming advocated in [74]. The use of a sequential model also means that the application code does not use any explicit concurrency control, e.g., semaphores, monitors, locks, which implies that all application code will be wait-free by definition. This also means that typical concurrent programs cannot be expressed in the model, but conversely a mapping of the partially ordered knowledge sharing model to networked shared memory nodes, each with multiple threads and/or processes, constitutes a possible implementation in today's space of technologies.

The partially ordered knowledge sharing model can be specialized by imposing local and global resource bounds as well by more specific environment (and hence network) models. This paper, however, will not impose such technical restrictions, but rather focuses on the motivation and rationale behind our basic model, its probabilistic and fractionated variants, and their relationship to other models for distributed computing.

3   Formalization of the Partially Ordered Knowledge Sharing Model

Each cyber-node x can assume a local state from a set $\mathcal{Q}_x$, it can generate and handle local events from a set $\mathcal{E}_x$, and it can generate and handle knowledge from a set $\mathcal{K}_x$. Note that no finiteness requirements are imposed on $\mathcal{Q}_x$, $\mathcal{E}_x$, and $\mathcal{K}_x$. To avoid confusion, assume that the sets $\mathcal{Q}, \mathcal{E}, \mathcal{K}$, defined as the union of $\mathcal{Q}_x, \mathcal{E}_x, \mathcal{K}_x$ over all nodes x, respectively, are disjoint. Since states and event are local, we can without loss of generality assume that the sets $\mathcal{Q}_x$ are disjoint and we also assume that the sets $\mathcal{E}_x$ are disjoint. The sets $\mathcal{K}_x$ are generally not disjoint, because knowledge can be shared between the nodes.

Since knowledge can be used to represent non-local events, it is possible to treat knowledge and events in a uniform way for many purposes. For instance, like knowledge, events can be equipped with an ordering capturing their abstract semantics, and hence we assume that $\mathcal{K}_x$ and $\mathcal{E}_x$ are both equipped with a *replacement order*, a strict partial order that we denote by $\prec$. In concrete applications, the definition of $\prec$ may involve a subsumption ordering, but for the following it is only the replacement ordering that matters. We use $\preceq$ to denote the reflexive closure of $\prec$. We should note, however, that different from knowledge, events are local and hence the replacement order on events is local to each node.

Each unit of knowledge $k \in \mathcal{K}_x$ has a creator $x_c(k)$ and a time $t_c(k)$ defining the node where it was created and the local time of creation. Furthermore, it has an activation time $t_a(k)$, defining the earliest time the knowledge should be handled, and an expiration time $t_e(k)$, after which it is too late to handle the knowledge so that it can be discarded. Note that the ordering on knowledge may but does not have to use any of this information. Similarly, each local event $e \in \mathcal{E}_x$ has a creator $x_c(e)$, which can only be x, a creation time $t_c(e)$, an activation time $t_a(e)$ defining the local time at which it is scheduled, and an expiration time $t_e(e)$, after which it will not be scheduled anymore. We always require that $t_c(k) \leq t_a(k) < t_e(k)$ and similarly $t_c(e) \leq t_a(e) < t_e(e)$. An equality $t_c(k) = t_a(k)$ is useful and common for knowledge, but for events we typically have $t_c(e) < t_a(e)$.

We will not require that knowledge and events are handled in a particular order, e.g., in the order defined by activation time. In fact, they can be handled at any time between activation and expiration, and if several units satisfy this condition, the selection is nondeterministic, i.e., unspecified in the general model. Clearly, this does not preclude the use of the model together with a more constrained implementation or policy.

In the following we define the set $\mathcal{A}_x$ of *actions* as $\mathcal{K}_x \cup \mathcal{E}_x$, with the idea that the handling of a unit of knowledge or an event can be considered as an action. We generally use a to range over single actions and A to range over sets of actions. We also assume a set $\mathcal{Z}_x$ of random values for each node x, without making any assumptions on their distribution at this point. In this paper, we use $FS(X)$ to denote the set of finite (not necessarily proper) subsets of X. Now, the local behavior of each node x is specified by an *initializer*, i.e., a relation $\bullet \rightarrow_{t,x,z} \subseteq (\mathcal{Q}_x \times FS(\mathcal{A}_x))$ and by a *handler*, i.e., a relation $\rightarrow_{t,x,z} \subseteq (\mathcal{A}_x \times \mathcal{Q}_x) \times (\mathcal{Q}_x \times FS(\mathcal{A}_x))$. The meaning of $\bullet \rightarrow_{t,x,z} q', A'$ is that node x is initialized at time t with randomness z to a state q' and initially generates a set of actions $A' = E' \cup K'$, representing a finite set of events E' and/or knowledge K'. Similarly, the meaning of $a, q \rightarrow_{t,x,z} q', A'$ is that processing a in state q by node x at time t with randomness z leads to state q' and the generation of a set of actions $A' = E' \cup K'$. In these cases, we require $x_c(a') = x$ and $t_c(a') = t$ for all $a' \in A'$. We should note that any of the sets A', E', and K' can be empty.

We assume that, given t, x, and $z \in \mathcal{Z}_x$, there is a unique (q', A') such that $\bullet \rightarrow_{t,x,z} q', A'$, and we define $h_{t,x,z}(\bullet)$ as this unique (q', A'). Similarly, for all a and q we require that there is at most one (q', A') such that $a, q \rightarrow_{t,x,z} q', A'$. We define $h_{t,x,z}(a, q)$ as this unique (q', A') if it exists and as $(q, \emptyset)$ otherwise. Hence, $h_{t,x,z}(\bullet)$ and $h_{t,x,z}(a, q)$ are always well defined.

The state of a cyber-node is of the form $K, E, q \ @ \ t, x$, where x is the name of the node, t is an element of the time domain $\mathcal{T} \subseteq \mathbb{R}$ representing its local time, $K \subseteq \mathcal{K}$ is a set of knowledge units cached at x, $E \subseteq \mathcal{E}_x$ is a set of local events pending at x, and $q \in \mathcal{Q}_x$ is the local state of x. Note that a node can store knowledge that is not relevant for itself, and hence K is not restricted to $\mathcal{K}_x$.

The rules of the partially ordered knowledge sharing model are presented in Figure 1. We view each unit of knowledge and each event as a singleton set and use juxtaposition (empty syntax) to denote set union. If such a union is used in the premise of a proof rule, we always assume that it denotes the union of disjoint sets, i.e., Kk implies $k \notin K$ if it occurs in a premise.

A configuration of a cyber-physical system S is a set of local states $K, E, q \ @ \ t, x$, one for each cyber-node x of S. Given a configuration c containing $K, E, q \ @ \ t, x$, we write $K_x(c)$ to denote K. The set of configurations is denoted by $\mathcal{C}$. The rules in Fig. 1 define a labeled transition relation $\rightarrow$ on configurations of the cyber-physical system S in the following (non-standard) sense: For configurations c and c', we have $c \rightarrow_r c'$ iff there exist an instance r of a rule such that c contains the premises of r and c' is obtained by an update of c with the conclusion which is defined as below. In this case, we also say that r is *applicable* in c, and we write $r(c) = c'$, viewing r as a partial function $r : \mathcal{C} \rightarrow_p \mathcal{C}$. A $\bullet$ is used to denote the empty set of premises and the empty conclusion. If one of the premises is $K, E, q \ @ \ t, x$ and the conclusion is $K', E', q' \ @ \ t', x$ then c' is obtained from c by replacing this premise by the conclusion (not removing any other premises). If the conclusion is $\bullet$ then c' is simply obtained by removing the premises from c.

$$\mathsf{Intro}(t,x,z) \ \frac{\bullet}{K',E',q' \ @ \ t,x} \quad \text{if} \ \bullet \rightarrow_{t,x,z} q', E'K'$$

$$\mathsf{KDel}(x,k) \ \frac{Kk,E,q \ @ \ t,x}{K,E,q \ @ \ t,x}$$

$$\mathsf{KExp}(x,k) \ \frac{Kk,E,q \ @ \ t,x}{K,E,q \ @ \ t,x} \quad \text{if} \ t \geq t_e(k)$$

$$\mathsf{EExp}(x,e) \ \frac{K,Ee,q \ @ \ t,x}{K,E,q \ @ \ t,x} \quad \text{if} \ t \geq t_e(e)$$

$$\mathsf{KRepl}(x,k,k') \ \frac{Kkk',E,q \ @ \ t,x}{Kk',E,q \ @ \ t,x} \quad \text{if} \ k \prec k'$$

$$\mathsf{ERepl}(x,e,e') \ \frac{K,Eee',q \ @ \ t,x}{K,Ee',q \ @ \ t,x} \quad \text{if} \ e \prec e'$$

$$\mathsf{KComp}(x,k,z,\Delta t) \ \frac{K,E,q \ @ \ t,x}{KK',EE',q' \ @ \ t',x} \quad \text{if} \ \begin{array}{l} k \in K, \ t_a(k) \leq t < t_e(k), \\ k,q \rightarrow_{t,x,z} q', E'K', \ t' = t + \Delta t \end{array}$$

$$\mathsf{EComp}(x,e,z,\Delta t) \ \frac{K,E,q \ @ \ t,x}{KK',EE',q' \ @ \ t',x} \quad \text{if} \ \begin{array}{l} e \in E, \ t_a(e) \leq t < t_e(e), \\ e,q \rightarrow_{t,x,z} q', E'K', \ t' = t + \Delta t \end{array}$$

$$\mathsf{Comm}(x,y,k,\Delta t) \ \frac{K_x,E_x,q_x \ @ \ t_x,x \quad K_yk,E_y,q_y \ @ \ t_y,y}{K_xk,E_x,q_x \ @ \ t'_x,x} \quad \text{if} \ \begin{array}{l} x \neq y, \\ t_x \leq t'_x \geq t_y, \\ t'_x = t_x + \Delta t \end{array}$$

$$\mathsf{Sleep}(x,\Delta t) \ \frac{K,E,q \ @ \ t,x}{K,E,q \ @ \ t',x} \quad \text{if} \ t' = t + \Delta t$$

$$\mathsf{Elim}(x) \ \frac{K,E,q \ @ \ t,x}{\bullet}$$

Fig. 1. Rules of the Partially Ordered Knowledge Sharing Model

By inspection of the rules we can see that, given a configuration c, applicable rule instances r are uniquely determined by a subset of their variables. Using the same variables as in the rules to denote the binding, we define a rule instance as one of the following: $\mathsf{Intro}(t,x,z)$, $\mathsf{KDel}(x,k)$, $\mathsf{KExp}(x,k)$, $\mathsf{EExp}(x,e)$, $\mathsf{KRepl}(x,k,k')$, $\mathsf{ERepl}(x,e,e')$, $\mathsf{KComp}(x,k,z,\Delta t)$, $\mathsf{EComp}(x,e,z,\Delta t)$, $\mathsf{Comm}(x,y, k,\Delta t)$, $\mathsf{Sleep}(x,\Delta t)$, and $\mathsf{Elim}(x)$. All rules have an implicit constraint that $\Delta t \geq \tau$ where $\tau > 0$ is the *minimum time duration*, a constant fixed for the system. The set of all rules instances will be denoted by $\mathcal{R}$.

We briefly convey the intuition behind these rules in the following. The *introduction and elimination rules* $\mathsf{Intro}(t,x,z)$ and $\mathsf{Elim}(x)$ express that nodes can be added and removed, respectively, from the system dynamically at any time in the absence of other constraints on the execution. This allows us to model dynamic scaling of the system size as well as node failures. The *deletion rule* $\mathsf{KDel}(x,k)$

expresses that shared knowledge can be discarded or lost at any time in constrast to events which are local. In practice, some (probabilistic) constraints may be placed on this rule depending on the actual environment. The *expiration rules* $\mathsf{KExp}(x, k)$ and $\mathsf{EExp}(x, e)$ model the internal expiration of knowledge and events. Although $\mathsf{KExp}(x, k)$ is subsumed by $\mathsf{KDel}(x, k)$ it is important to distinguish these two rules so that the environment can impose constraints on the latter only. Similar to expiration, the *replacement rules* $\mathsf{KRepl}(x, k, k')$ and $\mathsf{ERepl}(x, e, e')$ model the internal replacement of knowledge and events, respectively. The *computation rules* $\mathsf{KComp}(x, k, z, \Delta t)$ and $\mathsf{EComp}(x, e, z, \Delta t)$ model a computational step triggered by a unit of knowledge k or an event e, respectively. The *communication rule* $\mathsf{Comm}(x, y, k, \Delta t)$ expresses the transmission of knowledge k from any node y to any node x, and just like the deletion rules it is typically subject to environmental constraints, e.g. the feasible communication possibilities may depend on network topology or a probabilistic transmission model. Note that according to our definition of rule application the transmitting node y remains unchanged in this step. Finally, the *sleep rule* $\mathsf{Sleep}(x, \Delta t)$ simply allows time to pass locally but monotonically in each node.

An (unconstrained) execution in the partially ordered knowledge sharing model is a finite sequence $\pi = c_0, r_0, c_1, r_1, c_2, \ldots, c_n$ or an infinite sequence $\pi = c_0, r_0, c_1, r_1, c_2, \ldots$ of configurations such that c_0 is the empty configuration and $c_i \rightarrow_{r_i} c_{i+1}$ for all i. For each r_i above we say that the index i is a *step* of the execution π. We say that a rule r is *applied* in π at j iff $r = r_j$. For the following definition and the subsequent weak fairness properties, we abstract from the passage of time and hence identify instances of proof rules that only differ in t, t' (or the corresponding indexed variables). We say that r is *permanently applicable* in π at i iff r is applicable in all steps $j \geq i$ of π.

Depending on the properties on interest, additional constraints imposed by the environment must be made explicit, e.g. regarding the underlying network model as pointed out above. Furthermore, in order to establish liveness properties, gloabal fairness as defined subsequently is the weakest sensible requirement that an environment may impose on executions. An execution is *computationally fair* iff each instance of a *computation rule* that is permanently applicable at i is applied at some $j \geq i$. Similarly, an execution is *replacement fair* iff each instance of a *replacement rule* that is permanently applicable at i is applied at some $j \geq i$. An execution is *communication fair* iff each instance of a *communication* rule that is permanently applicable at i is applied at some $j \geq i$. Note that an applicable communication rule can lose applicability if the conclusion has been reached already, which means that direct communication between each pair is not required if the information can be exchanged over multiple hops by other instantiations of the communication rules. An execution π is *locally fair* iff it is computationally fair and replacement fair. An execution is *globally fair* iff it is locally fair and communication fair.

For convenience, we introduce a few more abstract local transition relations. We write $a, q \rightarrow_{x,t} q', A'$ iff there exists z such that $a, q \rightarrow_{t,x,z} q', A'$. Similarly, we write $a, q \rightarrow_x q', A'$ iff there exists t such that $a, q \rightarrow_{t,x} q', A'$. We write

$a, q \rightarrow_{t,x} q'$ iff there exists A' such that $a, q \rightarrow_x q', A'$. Finally, we write $q \rightarrow_x q'$ iff there exists a such that $a, q \rightarrow_x q'$. Similarly, we write $\bullet \rightarrow_x q'$ iff there exists A' such that $\bullet \rightarrow_x q', A'$. We also use the reflexive and transitive versions, that is, we write $q \rightarrow_x^* q'$ to denote the existence of a possibly trivial chain $q \rightarrow_x \cdots \rightarrow_x q'$, and we write $\bullet \rightarrow_x^* q'$ to denote $\bullet \rightarrow_x q \rightarrow_x^* q'$. Similarly, we write $a', q \rightarrow_x^+ q''$ iff $a', q \rightarrow_x q' \rightarrow_x^* q''$. Finally, we write $a, q \rightarrow_x$ iff there exists q', A' such that $a, q \rightarrow_x q', A'$.

The initialization and handler relations need to be defined so that they are *consistent* with the replacement order in the following sense: If $\bullet \rightarrow_x^* q$ and $a', q \rightarrow_x^+ q'$ and $a \preceq a'$ then it is not the case that $a, q' \rightarrow_x$. Furthermore, we require that the handler relation is *complete* in the following sense: If $\bullet \rightarrow_x^* q$ and $a \in \mathcal{A}_x$ then $a, q \rightarrow_x$ if there is no action $a' \in \mathcal{A}_x$ with $a \preceq a'$ such that $\bullet \rightarrow_x^* q'$ and $a', q' \rightarrow_x^+ q$. Consistency means that actions corresponding to knowledge or events that have already been processed are obsolete and are ignored. Completeness means that new knowledge and events can always be processed if they are not obsolete. Consistency implies, in particular, that an instance of a computation rule will not remain applicable after the corresponding event or knowledge has been processed. As a consequence of the consistency condition, it is possible to define the replacement relation as a relation derived from the application, thereby making part of the application semantics available at other nodes of the network. The use of this information outside of the application to discard knowledge in an implementation can be essential if resources are limited but is not strictly required (e.g., may only take place at some nodes) in the partially ordered knowledge sharing model.

A *generic implementation* that satisfies consistency assuming a handler relation that already satisfies completeness can be defined as follows. Without loss of generality we assume that each local state $q \in \mathcal{Q}_x$ is of the form $q = (\bar{K}, \bar{E}, \bar{q})$ with the idea that a finite set $\bar{K} \subseteq \mathcal{K}_x$ is used to keep track of all knowledge units processed by node x and a finite set $\bar{E} \subseteq \mathcal{E}_x$ keeps track of all pending events, i.e., events that have not yet been processed. Now the generic implementation is inductively defined below. As defined by Rule (1) the implementation starts with the empty set of processed knowledge and the intially pending events yet to be processed. Rules (2) and (3) capture the processing of a unit of knowledge or an event, respectively. To concisely keep track of all knowledge processed in the past (usually an unbounded set) and all events to be processed in the future it is sufficient to store the maximum of these sets (obsolete items are ignored in line with the replacement rules).

(1) $\bullet \rightarrow_{t,x} (\emptyset, \max(F'), q'), E'K'$
      if $\bullet \rightarrow_{t,x} q', E'K'$.
(2) $k, (\bar{K}, \bar{E}, q) \rightarrow_{t,x} (\max(\bar{K}k), \max(\bar{E}E'), q'), E'K'$
      if $k, q \rightarrow_{t,x} q', E'K'$ and $k \notin \downarrow\bar{K}$.
(3) $e, (\bar{K}, \bar{E}e, q) \rightarrow_{t,x} (\bar{K}, \max(\bar{E}E'), q'), E'K'$
      if $e, q \rightarrow_{t,x} q', E'K'$ and $e \notin \bar{E}$.

In this definition, we use the maximum $\max(\ldots)$ of a set of knowledge units or events, which is defined as the set of maximal elements w.r.t. the replacement ordering $\prec$. In addition, $\downarrow\bar{K}$ denotes the downward closure of a set of knowledge units K, i.e. the set of all k with $k \preceq \bar{k}$ for some $\bar{k} \in \downarrow\bar{K}$.

4 Probabilistic Refinement of the Model

In this section we show how our model can be enriched to take into account probabilisitic effects, which are often important to adequately model and verify networked cyber-physical systems. Two sources of nondeterminism exist in our model and need to be equipped with probabilities: nondeterminism due to local random choices of the algorithm (formalized by instantiation of z in the rules) and nondeterminism due to choices of the environment, under which we subsume any other choices such as location and time of execution (formalized by x, t, and other variables in the rules).

For a general probabilistic treatment, only measurable subsets are of interest. Hence, we assume that each of the sets $\mathcal{T}$, $\mathcal{Q}_x$, $\mathcal{K}_x$, $\mathcal{E}_x$, $\mathcal{Z}_x$ is equipped with a σ-algebra defining which subsets are measurable. This naturally gives rise to σ-algebras on $\mathcal{Q}$, $\mathcal{K}$, $\mathcal{E}$, $\mathcal{Z}$, and finally $\mathcal{R}$ (the set of rule instances) and $\mathcal{C}$ (the set of configurations). We always use $\mathcal{B}(S)$ to denote a suitable σ-algebra associated with S to capture the measurable sets of interest. If S is a topological space, the Borel σ-algebra would be a natural choice and used in most practical cases, but the following construction does not depend on it.

In the probabilistic version of the model, the behavior of each node x is specified by a time-independent probability measure $P_x : \mathcal{B}(\mathcal{Z}_x) \to [0,1]$. If more than one random value is needed, $\mathcal{Z}_x$ can be a finite or infinite product (in which case z would be a tuple). For most practical purposes, P_x can be simply defined as a uniform distribution or the joint probability of independent uniform distributions.

In this way, we define probability distributions over the local choices in the nondeterministic model. However, there are many other choices in the knowledge sharing model that remain nondeterministic. In order to equip system executions with probabilities, all nondeterminism needs to be resolved. This is done, in the following, by means of an environment, a more neutral term to subsume what is often called a strategy, a scheduler, a policy, or an adversary.

We use C and R to range over $\mathcal{B}(\mathcal{C})$ and $\mathcal{B}(\mathcal{R})$, respectively. The probabilistic model can only consider executions that lie within measurable sets. Hence, in order to cover all executions starting from a measurable set C_0, we require that for each C the set of rule instances applicable in C, i.e., applicable in some $c \in C$, must be measurable. In this case, we also require that this set R is a measurable function (recall that rule instances are viewed as partial functions on configurations, which can be naturally lifted to sets of configurations). Now measurable executions are defined as finite sequences of the form $(C_0, (R_0, C_1), (R_1, C_2), \ldots, (R_{n-1}, C_n))$ subject to the condition $C_{i+1} = R_i(C_i)$. We denote by $\mathcal{B}(\mathcal{E}^n)$ the product σ-algebra of all measurable executions and use Π to range over this set.

We now formalize the environment as a family of functions $P_n : \mathcal{E}^n \times \mathcal{B}(\mathcal{R}) \to [0,1]$ such that $P_n(\cdot, R)$ is measurable, $P_n(\pi, \cdot)$ is a probability measure, and $P_n(\pi, R) > 0$ implies that there exists a rule instance $r \in R$ that is applicable in the last configuration of π. We denote by $\mathsf{Comp}(x)$ the set of all instances of computation rules for node x, and by $\mathsf{Comp}(x, z)$ the subset for a given choice of z. We now require that P_n accurately reflects the local probabilities P_x at each node x, i.e., $P_n(\pi, \mathsf{Comp}(x, Z)) = P_n(\pi, \mathsf{Comp}(x))P_x(Z)$ for all $Z \in \mathcal{B}(\mathcal{Z}_x)$. In this way, we can uniformly treat all nondetermism (internal and external) through the notion of an environment.

Given these assumptions, we are now prepared to construct the execution semantics of our probabilistic model as a particular stochastic process. To this end, we first inductively define a family of probability measures $P_n : \mathcal{B}(\mathcal{E}^n) \to [0,1]$ as follows: $P_0(C_0) = \delta_{c_0}(C_0)$ and $P_{n+1}(\Pi, (R, C)) = \int_\Pi P_n(d\pi) \int_R P_n(\pi, dr)$ for $\Pi, (R, C) \in \mathcal{B}(\mathcal{E}^{n+1})$. For the base case, we have used the Dirac measure δ_{c_0} as the initial probability measure. In the induction step, we use the Lebesgue integral, exploiting the fact that $P_n(\cdot, R)$ is measurable. Note that C is uniquely determined by Π and R.

Since P is defined as a finite-dimensional composition of probability kernels we can apply the Ionescu Tulcea extension theorem (see e.g. [67]) to construct a probability space $(\Omega, \mathcal{F}, P)$ and random variables $\bar{C}_0 : \Omega \to \mathcal{C}$ and $(\bar{R}_i, \bar{C}_{i+1}) : \Omega \to \mathcal{R} \times \mathcal{C}$ such that $\bar{C}_0, (\bar{R}_0, \bar{C}_1), \ldots$ constitutes an infinite stochastic process satisfying $P(\bar{C}_0, (\bar{R}_0, \bar{C}_1), \ldots, (\bar{R}_{n-1}, \bar{C}_n) \in C_0, (R_0, C_1), \ldots, (R_{n-1}, C_n)) = P_n(C_0, (R_0, C_1), \ldots, (R_{n-1}, C_n))$ for each n.

Note that the execution semantics of our probabilistic model is a general construction of a probability measure on product spaces that is very concise, because it does not depend on the nature of the underlying probability distributions, e.g. wether they are discrete or continuous. As a direction for future work, it would be important to work out specializations and more generally define a simple language that captures practically relevant subclasses with more specific environment models (e.g. templates for specific distributions) that can be supported by automated tools for verification and analysis.

5 Fractionated Knowledge Sharing Model

The fractionated knowledge sharing model imposes additional conditions on the (probabilistic) knowledge sharing model. In view of our motivation to serve as a basis for highly dynamic and robust systems, it seems natural to require that the fractionated model limits the use of node names (especially avoiding the problematic notion of neighborhood) and local state by requiring that the knowledge generated by a node is only a nondeterministic or randomized function of local time and all knowledge that has been processed, but disregarding obsolete knowledge. This is however too strong, because each unit of knowledge generated is equipped with the name of its creator, which clearly violates this condition. Furthermore, we may want to keep track of names, e.g., contributors in sensor information fusion, without making use of the specific names themselves. Hence, we use a more general definition based on a notion of symmetry, which generally allows names to appear in generated knowledge units, but limits their use.

Given an execution $\pi = c_0, r_0, c_1, r_1, c_2, \ldots$ we denote by $K_x(\pi, i)$ the set of all knowledge units available (received and posted) at node x before step i, i.e., the union of all k and K appearing in applications of introduction or computation rules. Given t, x, and $z \in \mathcal{Z}_x$, we recall that $h_{t,x,z}(\bullet)$ and $h_{t,x,z}(a, q)$ are always well defined and of the form (q', A') with $A' = E' \cup K'$. In this case, we also use $h^{\mathrm{k}}_{t,x,z}(\bullet)$ or $h^{\mathrm{k}}_{t,x,z}(a, q)$, respectively, to denote the unique K'.

A *(permutation) symmetry* is a bijective mapping $\sigma : \mathcal{X} \to \mathcal{X}$ on the node identifiers. We assume that a symmetry σ can be lifted to local states and actions a (and sets thereof) such that $\sigma(x_c(a)) = x_c(\sigma(a))$. In a syntactic representation, a possible (although limited) way to achieve this is by replacing all occurrences of x by $\sigma(x)$. Category theory is the right tool for a more general treatment but beyond the scope of this paper, which only gives the flavor of how we approach fractionated systems.

For the *homogeneous fractionated model*, we now require that the following conditions hold for each node x, time t, $z \in \mathcal{Z}_x$, local state $q \in \mathcal{Q}_x$ such that • $\to^*_x q$, and each symmetry $\sigma : \mathcal{X} \to \mathcal{X}$. **(1)** $\sigma(h_{t,x,z}(\bullet)) = h_{t,\sigma(x),z}(\bullet)$. **(2)** $\sigma(h_{t,x,z}(k, q)) = h_{t,\sigma(x),z}(\sigma(k), \sigma(q))$. **(3)** $\sigma(h_{t,x,z}(e, q)) = h_{t,\sigma(x),z}(\sigma(e), \sigma(q))$. These conditions express that the initializer and handlers at x are independent of x (location-independence) and do not distinguish between the remaining nodes.

We say that a family of functions $f_{t,x,z} : \mathrm{FS}(\mathcal{K}_x) \to \mathrm{FS}(\mathcal{K}_x)$ for $z \in \mathcal{Z}_x$ is *homogeneous* iff $\sigma(f_{t,x,z}(K)) = f_{t,\sigma(x),z}(\sigma(K))$ for each symmetry $\sigma : \mathcal{X} \to \mathcal{X}$. For the *homogeneous functional model*, we now require in addition to the conditions above that there exists a homogeneous family $f_{t,x,z}$ such that the following conditions hold for each execution π, where the introduction or a computation rule is applied at step i for node x with time t and $z \in \mathcal{Z}_x$. **(1)** $h^{\mathrm{k}}_{t,x,z}(\bullet) \subseteq f_{t,x,z}(\emptyset)$. **(2)** $h^{\mathrm{k}}_{t,x,z}(k, q) \subseteq f_{t,x,z}(\max(K_x(\pi, i) \cup \{k\}))$. **(3)** $h^{\mathrm{k}}_{t,x,z}(e, q) \subseteq f_{t,x,z}(\max(K_x(\pi, i)))$. These conditions express that the generated knowledge must match the resulting knowledge defined by the family $f_{t,x,z}$, and hence is independent of q and, by the homogeneity condition, independent of x (up to a symmetry). Note that we do not have a corresponding functionality requirement for generated events.

For practical purposes we need to relax these conditions in two ways. First, full fractionation as defined by the condition above, implies complete anonymity or indistinguishability of nodes, which is clearly not a realistic requirement for nodes that can model identifiable users or cyber-physical devices. A hybrid approach that allows a mix of conventional identifiable and fractionated nodes would address this problem. This is not sufficient, however, because even the fractionated part will not be homogenous in practice, because in complex systems different fractions will often implement different functions. In other words, anonymity/indistinguishability can at best be partial in practical systems and our fractionated model needs to capture this.

A straightforward solution is to partition the set of fractionated nodes into equivalence classes and to restrict the symmetries to symmetries that respect the equivalence relation, i.e., $h(x) \equiv x$. This leads the a definition of the general *fractionated model*, which can capture a heterogeneous set of equivalence classes, with homogeneity within each class, which can be a singleton to express full distinguishability. To establish a connection to traditional concepts, an equivalence class may also be also be thought of as the role of a type of nodes.

In this section we have only given a flavor of our fractionated model, which together with the following examples should be sufficient to convey the intution. The general definition and theory of fractionated systems is being further studied and will be subject of a future publication.

5.1   Examples of Fractionated Systems

The need to operate in very general environments makes it impossible to solve many traditional problems such as consensus in the original sense. However, by relaxing the problem specifications it is often possible to find fractionated solutions with weaker guarantees. A number of typical examples that may also be thought of as design patterns of fractionated systems are informally discussed in the following.

Distributed Task Execution. A task that is ready for execution is represented by a unit of knowledge. A number of anonymous nodes will execute this task after a random delay (using a timed event) and post the execution status of the task as knowledge, replacing the knowledge unit that triggered the execution by means of a suitable ordering. The execution is preempted at any time if knowledge about the execution of the task at some other node is received. Depending on the timing there is the possibility of redundant execution, but the system is tolerant to temporary or permanent node or communication failures.

Sensor Information Fusion. In this example we assume a set of identifiable sensor nodes that inject their measurements as time-stamped knowledge streams into the network. Another set of anonymous nodes in the network is performing sensor fusion computations based on what knowledge is available to them. In the simplest case, each such node is time-triggered, performing one computation per event, computing a function of all knowledge received so far and generating a new piece of time-stamped aggregated knowledge. Aggregated knowledge is equipped by an ordering that is consistent with the order of the knowledge it depends on so that obsolete knowledge can be discarded at the earliest point in the network.

Distributed Optimization. We assume that each node has the capability to compute the objective function that specifyies the optimization objective. The best known solution is represented as knowledge using the ordering on the value domain of the objective function. The ordering can be a total ordering in which case a converged distributed state represents a single solution, or a partial ordering representing multi-objective optimization problems, where the distributed state should converge to the set of Pareto-optimal solutions as in our study on parallel and distributed optimization [65]. Each node can use any method, e.g., periodic sampling the parameter space, to initialize the parameters and to incrementally improve the objective, in which case knowledge with the improved solution will be posted. Each node takes into account the available knowledge about the best current solution.

Distributed Consensus. While solving the consensus problem is not possible in our model, a weaker version which makes a best effort to converge to an agreement if connectivity allows it, can be expressed. In the simplest solution, each node proposes a random value (e.g., 0 or 1) posted as knowledge and keeps track of the proposals from other nodes. Whenever it detects a tie, it will change and post its proposal to break the tie. Note that it is essential to distinguish different proposals from other nodes, but it is only the number of proposals (with a specific value) that matters for the decision.

Sensor/Actor Virtualization. Sensor and actuator nodes implement a minimal interface based on two kinds of knowledge: facts and goals, representing observations and control goals, respectively. Fact and goals are equipped with an ordering based on their timestamps, so that new observations/controls will replace previous ones. Any other node in the network can perform computations on behalf or any sensor/actuator, so that the system functionality will not be affected by a missing computation node.

Declarative Control. The transformation of facts/goals into new facts/goals, respectively, is a form of computation. A sample logical framework that can support a notion of distributed proofs with applications to sensor/actor networks can be found in [66]. In the simplest case all computational nodes are anonymous and performing deductions in a single logical theory that is shared and assumed to be known to all nodes. Other nodes may be identifiable and correspond to physical devices such as sensors and actuators, respectively.

Cyber-Physical Workflows. A cyber-physical workflow is an operational description of the dynamics of a cyber-physical system with sensors and actuators. Similar to a logical framework, control goals evolve over time based on feedback from observations (facts). The workflow is executed in a distributed and fault-tolerant fashion, so that each step of the workflow can be executed by any node in the network who has the knowledge available.

In all these examples, the communication can be subject to delays or disruptions or the network may be even partitioned and the system will continue to operate in a useful and meaningful way. If the network heals or partitions merge, separately evolving components can resynchronize. The system can also be scaled up and down incrementally at runtime by adding and or removing nodes. A faulty or disappearing node does not lead to loss of essential state, which is represented as knowledge that is redundantly cached. No notion of a neighborhood is exposed to applications, thereby avoiding a concept that is highly dynamic, often not well-defined, and may exposed node identities. Nevertheless, the model uses a notion of locality by propagating knowledge through the network with potentially unbounded delays.

6 Related Work

Epistemic View of Distributed Systems. Knowledge sharing is a well known idea that has been investigated in Halpern and Moses' groundbreaking paper [51] and in many subsequent works. Since then epistemic approaches have received renewed interest due to their capability to put the concept of partial information into the hands of the programmer (see, e.g., the SCEL language for autonomic computing [78]) and their potential to serve as as unifying framework for modalities such as time, location, and probability (see, e.g., [79]).

Initially, understanding knowledge sharing in distributed environments has lead to a complementary view providing new insights into distributed algorithms and a logical justification for their fundamental limitations. For instance, attaining common knowledge, i.e., complete knowledge about the knowledge of other agents (and hence about the global state) in a distributed system is not feasible in a strict sense, and hence problems like the coordinated attack problem is unsolvable in asynchronous systems. In practice, approximations of common knowledge can be used by making various assumptions of synchrony, but the fundamental problem in asynchronous systems remains.

Halpern's concept of knowledge is based on a modal logic, which expresses facts and the state of knowledge of individual agents. A key axiom is the knowledge axiom which states that if an agent knows a fact that fact must be true. The use of knowledge in the partially ordered knowledge sharing model is not limited to facts. For instance, knowledge can represent goals as in [87]. Consequently, we do not assume a particular modal logic, which means that knowledge about knowledge must be explicitly represented if it is needed. Our model is centered around the partial order structure of knowledge (which can also capture information content) and how it enables distributed knowledge sharing and replacement. Our subsumption relation has a logical interpretation (which in a sufficiently expressive logic can be defined in terms of a logical implication), but the replacement ordering is of a different nature in that it cannot be reduced to a simple logical relationship.

Asynchronous Message Passing and Broadcasting. Asynchronous message passing was the basis for one of the early models of concurrent computation, the actor model [2], and the key feature that distinguishes it from synchronous message passing models is that maximum delay of messages in transit is unbounded. The FLP-model [43] captures the essence of asynchronous message passing and has been used to study many impossibility results of distributed computing [42]. Each message carries the name of the intended destination. Messages are placed in a message buffer (modeled as a multiset) by a send operation. A message in the buffer may be delivered if the destination process invokes a receive operation, but the receive operation may be unsuccessful and return without a message. If the receive operation is successful the message is deleted from the buffer. From this description it is clear that message integrity and absence of duplication is assumed. In addition, we have the following fairness requirement: If a receive operation is performed infinitely many times by a given process then every message with this process as its destination is eventually delivered.

Asynchronous broadcast differs from the message passing model only in that the send operation generates a copy of the message for each process as a destination. All these messages are placed in the buffer and are received asynchronously with an unbounded maximum delay. The synchronous version of broadcast is also known as atomic broadcast, which involves an unbounded number of parties and hence is inherently non-scalable. On the other hand, it has been shown that a probabilistic version of broadcast [17], has good scalability properties under realistic assumptions. It is also known as bimodal multicast, because with high probability either all or none of the non-faulty processes will receive the message.

Group communication systems provide group membership and communication services (usually including reliable atomic multicast with or without message ordering guarantees) that were initially based on the virtual synchrony semantics that essentially allows them to operate as replicated state machines as long as sufficient synchronization can be maintained. Virtual synchrony can handle fail-stop faults and considers a recovered process as a new one. Due to its limitations, a more relaxed extended virtual synchrony semantics has been proposed [75] to support more general fault models such as network partitioning and remerging. Practical implementations such as Spread perform very well and provide range of powerful primitives, but the inevitable drawback is the need for tight synchronization (e.g., by means of a virtual token ring) which limits the scalability and the capability to deal with highly unstable/dynamic networks.

Gossiping and Epidemic Algorithms. Bimodal multicast and various other approaches to probabilistic broadcast fall into the broad class of gossip protocols [16], which have been initially studied in [28] and have been shown to exhibit a dynamics similar to the spread of epidemics [38], which is why they are often referred to as epidemic protocols. Due to their loosely-coupled nature, fault-tolerance, and weak assumptions, gossip protocols are closely related to our partially ordered knowledge sharing model (which lives at a higher level of abstraction), and hence this body of research deserves a careful review. The class of gossip protocols is quite diverse and new gossip-style protocols continue to emerge, which makes it difficult to capture their essence in a formal definition. In the informal characterization of [16] a gossip protocol is based on pairwise, periodic interactions exchanging information of (small) bounded size so that the information exchanged reflects the state of the peer. Communication can be unreliable and the frequency of interactions is relatively low. Also the selection of peers for pairwise interactions needs to involve a form of randomness. According to [16] it is useful to distinguish three styles of gossip protocols. There are information dissemination protocols concerned with or supporting the end-to-end delivery of data (e.g., bimodal multicast [17], rumor spreading [60]), and protocols for reconciling replicas (e.g., [28,82,47,92]), which reduce the entropy of the global system and hence are also known as anti-entropy protocols, and protocols that use in-network computation for information aggregation/fusion (e.g., [62]). Gossip protocols are often used to implement services e.g., for membership, resource, reputation, key management, systems for distributed monitoring, management, and data mining [91], and can serve as a foundation for higher-level protocols, e.g., routing protocols, as their are used in the Internet, in mobile ad hoc networking, in delay-/disruption-tolerant networking [40], and peer-to-peer networking [5]. More recently, general programming frameworks for gossip-style algorithms such as [37] have been developed.

Probabilistic Information Dissemination. Based on the observation that a peer-sampling service [58] is at the core of many gossip protocols, a general conceptual framework has been proposed in [64] and further refined in [21]. A similar framework with an informal discussion of various system and network parameters can be found in [41]. In [21] a gossip protocol is defined in as the iteration of three operations (executed once within a fixed period), namely randomized peer selection (i.e., sampling peers from the current view), data exchange, and data processing. Data exchange is considered a two-way synchronous exchange of information initiated by the active (i.e., sampling) peer. This model express push, pull, and push-pull data exchanges, and like in [58] can be simplified to a one-way message passing in the push case. Some limitations of this model are already pointed out by the authors in [64]. In particular, it is questioned if this model is sufficiently general to capture protocols that involve e.g., asynchronous broadcast. For instance, [11] does not use explicit peer-selection and pairwise interactions, but uses iterative broadcasting (with limited range and message loss). The answer may depend on the level of abstraction and on the network model. In [21], it is assumed that links are reliable, which is different from the model in [17], which allows for probabilistic message loss. It is shown that with reliable links, the model is equivalent to a model with atomic pairwise interactions. The reference further identifies a subclass of anonymous gossip protocols that are oblivious to the selected peers and establish an equivalence (in terms of their capability to compute functions) to so-called population protocols that are also based on atomic pairwise interactions. In the generic peer-sampling service [58], random-peer selection is based on the current view, which is a suitable random subset of all nodes in the network. In more general models, this view can be spatially-biased as for instance in spatial gossiping protocols [63] for networks with mobile nodes or in the topology sensitive epidemic algorithm [1]. Clearly, this deviates from the common assumption in the analysis of gossip protocols that node select their peers uniformly randomly among all nodes in the network.

In contrast to anti-entropy gossip protocols (see below), which are reconciling local state, gossip-based dissemination protocols provide logically a broadcasting service for streams of messages, which are typically buffered only for short periods of time so that buffer space is available for new messages coming in. The network model is critical in gossip-based dissemination. For instance, network partitioning is usually not considered, and it has been observed that gossip-based dissemination is not robust under correlated losses [16]. Partially ordered knowledge sharing, on the other hand, is targeting such uncooperative environments and hence more closely related to the following remaining two classes of gossip/epidemic algorithms.

Reconciling Replicas. According to the definition in [92] anti-entropy protocols perform pairwise exchanges of so-called deltas, that is, differences in the local states of the two peers partcipating in an interaction. At the core of the model it is assumed that each peer has a set of variables (keys) which not only have a value but also a version number. The ordering on version numbers is then be used by the anti-entropy protocol to discard old versions in favor of new versions whenever information is merged and cached in the network. It is noteworthy that the concept of versions with their total order is a special case of partially ordered knowledge sharing. In fact, partially ordered knowledge sharing, which is reconciling the content of local knowledge bases, can be naturally implemented as a generalization of anti-entropy gossiping (with the partial order providing additional structure to exploit for reconcilation).

In-network Computing. The last category of gossip protocols aim at the distributed computation of functions (such as min, max, number of votes, weighted sums, averages) of the individual node states so that the result (or an approximation) is eventually available at all nodes. For instance, a simple approach to compute averages using gossip in the abovementioned framework is to define the data exchange function so that the intermediate results, say v_i and v_j at the two participating nodes i and j is replaced by the local average $(v_i + v_j)/2$ at each node. Under fairly general conditions the network will converge to the exact result, but it has also been shown in [12] that message loss can easily lead to errors of several orders of magnitude. This shows that the model based on atomic pairwise interactions is an idealization and more refined models are needed for a detailed analysis. Using the broadcast gossip model, [11] shows that distributed averaging (as a special case of consensus) can be achieved simply by mixing, where each node periodically (locally) broadcasts its current value and all receivers compute their new value as the weighted average (the weight is called mixing parameter) of their current value and the received value. The algorithm is robust to failures, but the analysis is done under the assumption of reliable broadcast. Related approaches are the computation of separable functions, i.e., linear combinations of local functions, in [76] and the computation of frequent elements [69] in a fully distributed way. The partially ordered knowledge sharing model can model in-network computations, but imposes some additional structure, namely the partial order, which allow us to naturally organize such computations to operate on asynchronous and unreliable streams, using ordered timestamped elements in the simplest case.

Semantic Networking. Semantically reliable multicast [81] is designed to make use of the semantics of messages to discard obsolete messages in overload situations. To this end the authors assume that messages are equipped with an obsolescence relation that is coherent with the causal order of events. As suggested by the authors, this can be implemented by simply tagging each message at its source with all messages that it makes obsolete. The obsolescence relation is hence defined independently for each stream of messages by the sender and generalizes the idea of stubborn channels. Stubborn channels [49] between non-faulty processes have the property that if a message is sent without sending another message that it is guaranteed that this message will eventually be received.

Probabilistic reliable multicast [80] is a combination of semantically reliable multicast and gossip-based probabilistic multicast, but instead of a tight integration the authors argue in favor of a layering of probabilistic multicast on top of semantically reliable multicast for performance reasons and to reduce the likelihood of problematic correlated losses. Different from partially ordered knowledge sharing, messages are buffered only for a (typically short) finite duration in probabilistic multicast, which justifies this layered approach. Replacement in the knowledge-based model is not necessarily limited to overload situations. A more important difference, however, is that the replacement ordering does not have to be coherent with the causal order. This enables the use of more powerful partial (and total) orders which break ties in the distributed system in a consistent way. A single total order for instance is a common pattern that implements a distributed and hence potentially inconsistent shared memory abstraction.

An idea related to semantically reliable multicast is used in the implementation of realtime UDP [4], a protocol that can improve VoIP quality by in-network buffering with hop-to-hop retransmission. While this has been applied to a specific class of applications, it is an instance of a more general intuitive idea of buffered information that is "overtaken by events" [3], which is similar to the obsolescence relation of semantically reliable multicast and hence can also be captured by a replacement relation in the partially ordered knowledge sharing model. Semantics-aware networking is only recently gaining attention in the context of networked cyber-phyxial systems. For example, [59] focusses on continuous data sources and exploits their underlying models to improve the quality of real-time dissemination in unreliable networks using a broker-based publish/subscribe architecture.

Delay- and Disruption-Tolerant Networking. Delay-tolerant networking (DTN) [39,40,97] evolved from early ideas on an interplanetary Internet architecture [22] and uses late binding and a store-and-forward approach (potentially utilizing persistent storage) to deal with episodic and intermittent connectivity and to overcome delays and temporary disconnections. Network partitioning and merging is usually considered part of the normal operation, especially when nodes (or groups of nodes) are used as data mules or message ferries [98] to transport stored messages by means of physical mobility. A related concept are throw-boxes [99], which can be placed in the environment as buffers to further improve temporal decoupling of nodes. More generally, and in contrast to traditional Internet or MANET protocols, DTN aims to support communication even if a simultaneous end-to-end path does not exist. Even without network partitioning, the possibility of hop-to-hop (instead of end-to-end) retransmissions in DTN can offer significant performance advantages and resource savings. Instead of operating at the packet level, its units of information are semantically meaningful bundles (or fragments) of variable and typically large size. In content-centric networking [57] the semantically meaningful unit is referred to as content, and the network is viewed as a content cache which is queried by the user. The DARPA-funded program on DTN [36,88] combined both lines of research to support multi-party communication with late-binding. It integrates distributed content caching and intelligent routing with the primary objective of overcoming failures, delays, and disruptions of all kinds, especially in wireless networks with mobile nodes.

Distributed Hashing. Instead of using a so-called unstructured approach, that does not impose any systematic structure on top of the network, it is sometimes useful to impose specific virtual topologies through which queries for information and replies can be efficiently routed (usually in a number of steps logarithmic in the network size). For instance, a common technique to store information in peer-to-peer networks [5] are distributed hash tables (DHT) [14] that can rely on the specific properties of the network structure to ensure resiliency and efficiency of information access. Apart from limitations on the form of queries, the efficient mapping of the overlay into the physical network is a difficult problem [84] that partly conflicts with the objective of hashing so that useful tradeoffs have to be identified. Further difficulties arise in resource-heterogeneous, highly dynamic, and mobile networks, especially with node instabilities and partitioning. Some discussion and partial solutions can be found in [52]. On the other end, it is argued in [71] that DHT should support atomic data access and updates (sometimes referred to as a transactional DHT), but most proposals only attempt to make a best effort towards this property or avoid the problem using a write-once semantics. Strong consistency is useful for many applications and indeed practical as for instance demonstrated in [89], but it is also clear that, beyond the challenges mentioned above, it imposes further limitations on the environments in which it can be deployed.

Asynchronous Shared-Memory Models. Several asynchronous shared memory models have been proposed. Many of them evolved from the traditional (synchronous) parallel random access machine (PRAM) model. For instance, the asynchronous PRAM (APRAM) model [25] has been introduced to make explicit the cost of synchronization. The APRAM is a variation of the PRAM model, where each processor is equipped with its own local clock and the execution time of each instruction is unbounded. Shared memory is modeled as a set of atomic registers with atomic read and write operations. Several models for APRAMs have been studied. The early model [45] had an explicit instruction for barrier synchronization. An extension of the APRAM model with probabilistic delays has been introduced in [26]. Looking beyond the objective of computing functions, impossibility results for the APRAM model have been studied in [53]. An orthogonal direction, namely the use of storage redundancy to accelerate randomized computations has been studied in [73] in the context of the distributed memory machine (DMM), a further refinement of the PRAM that organizes globally shared memory into memory modules (still supporting shared access).

Parallel programs with shared variables based on Lamport's sequential consistency model have been extensively used in formal program verification. The semantics of parallel execution is defined by nondeterministic interleavings of their statements. For instance, in UNITY [23] (which stands for Unbounded Nondeterministic Iterative Transformations) a program is a set of Dijkstra-style guarded commands subject to a weak fairness condition, a simple and elegant representation amenable to rigorous formalization. Various extensions in terms of compositionality, fairness, and probabilities have been proposed [83]. It is also interesting to note that ideas behind UNITY can be applied at higher levels of granularity [74] leading to a discipline of multiprogramming based on the view that parallel programs should ideally use a simple nondeterministic model and parallel execution is simply a semantics-preserving mapping of this model to the computing resources (by means of a scheduler).

Closely related, but studied in a language independent context, are asynchronous iterative transformations [44], a very general model in which conceptually a function is iterated on the global state of the system (represented simply as a vector of local states), but instead of performing synchronous global updates, each component of the global state is updated independently (allowing for possibly unbounded communication delays). Various convergence results have been established in this (non-probabilistic) setting [44].

Distributed shared memory (DSM) models [35] provide the programmer with the abstraction of shared memory without relying on physical shared memory. This can be achieved, for instance, by implementing DSM on top of an asynchronous message passing model [10], but the overhead of maintaining consistency, the key feature of a shared memory abstraction, can be substantial. Various DSM models are compared in [13]. A well-known model are Linda tuple spaces, which combine access to shared variables with synchronization (discussed below). An interesting but less general model, which avoids inconsistencies by design, is the Agora shared memory architecture [18] based on write-once objects which are replicated when referenced.

Self-stabilizing Algorithms. Motivated by similar notions in control theory, self-stabilizing algorithms [86,31] have been originally studied using the nondeterministic parallel program model, where communication in a network is modeled by shared variables with atomic operations. Starting with Dijkstra's seminal work [30] on self-stabilizing algorithms for unidirectional token rings, self-stabilizing algorithms have been proposed for many problems including mutual exclusion, leader election, consensus, graph coloring, clustering, routing, and overlay construction. The key characteristic of self-stabilizing algorithms is that they eventually have to reach a legitimate state, given by the program specification, if they start with or are put into an arbitrary state (e.g., by a transient memory failure).

Generalizations of self-stabilization, e.g., based on closure (a set including all faulty states) and convergence (the legitimate set of states), have been proposed as a foundation for fault-tolerant distributed computing [8]. Even in this generalized sense, self-stabilization is a very strong property. Motivated by efficiency concerns and impossibility results in the deterministic setting, weaker notions of self-stabilization have been introduced, in particular probabilistic self-stabilization, which only requires convergence with probability one [29]. Some general principles and techniques for designing self-stabilizing algorithms have been developed such as local checkability and counter flushing [9,93].

The idea of self-stabilizing systems has also been extended to message passing systems (asynchronous and with unbounded delays). For instance, the approach in [61] can transform any distributed message-passing algorithm into a self-stabilizing algorithm by recognizing failures using a (self-stabilizing) distributed snapshot (collected at a single node) and initiating a global reset if necessary. Nevertheless, some results indicate that self-stabilization does not fit well with the concept of asynchronous message passing with unbounded delays [48,55]. Even weak concepts of self-stabilizing are very strong in the sense that recovery is required even if all nodes fail. One significant drawback of self-stabilizing algorithms is that they are not required to make progress in dynamic environments with continuous failures, a situation which becomes more likely with the scale of the network. In other words, they may be unproductive during failures and rely on periods of global stability to reach legitimate states.

Anonymity in Self-stabilizing Algorithms. Self-stabilizing algorithms differ in their assumptions on the availability of process identifiers which allow to break symmetries. As pointed out by Dijkstra [30], a self-stabilizing algorithm for token rings does not exist iff all processors are identical, but his proposed algorithm is almost uniform, by singling out one exceptional machine which runs a different algorithm than all others. In this context, a distributed algorithm is said to be uniform if all processes locally execute the same algorithm. Clearly, uniformity is not a real restriction if the program can be conditional on unique process identifiers. Hence, a system is called anonymous iff all processes have the same identifier. Other ways to break the symmetry include access to network topology [6] or randomness. The latter, however, cannot be used to guarantee unique process identities in an anonymous system, because a self-stabilizing algorithm (in the strongest sense) can be initialized to any state. Generally, randomization is essential to break symmetries for the purpose of e.g., leader selection. For instance, a probabilistic algorithm for scalable leader election in non-anonymous networks based on bimodal multicast can be found in [50]. By storing local pointers to neighbors (a partial form of identification), leader election becomes solvable [56] in an anonymous network by a randomized self-stabilizing algorithm. On the other hand, in the population protocol model [7], which is fully anonymous (i.e., without any local identification of neighbors), leader election cannot be solved. The advantage of fully anonymous self-stabilizing algorithms is that they are also stabilizing with respect to topology changes. A very general result in this context is the existence of a universal self-stabilizing algorithm [19], which can operate under very few assumptions on the underlying network, but clearly only if a self-stabilizing algorithm exists at all.

A lot of work on self-stabilization is centered around generalizing Dijkstra's token-passing algorithm, but the chatty nature of this style is not suitable in resource-constrained environments such as sensor networks where locally checkable self-stabilization is highly preferable. Also the atomic operations of the shared variable model is not implementable in such environments, which are often characterized by high message loss/collision rates [90,54,68]. Based on the cached sensor net transform of [54], where each node caches the state of all its neighbors, the work [90] shows how self-stabilizing algorithms (for locally checkable properties) can be transformed to operate in wireless sensor network based on asynchronous broadcast with message loss, but some difficulties remain to establish all desirable features simultaneously. Furthermore, although the model uses anonymous nodes, local identification of neighbors is still assumed. The challenge of extending this work to highly dynamic environments is left as an open problem. More recently, self-stabilizing algorithms that are robust to network topology changes have also been studied under the title of self-stabilizing and self-organizing algorithms [32].

Petri Nets and Related Models. As the earliest model for concurrent systems, Petri nets are inherently asynchronous and based on two key concepts, namely places and transitions. The global state of the system is usually defined as a marking that by definition assigns a number of indistinguishable tokens to each place. The sequential semantics is defined by the so-called token game in which transitions can remove tokens from their input places and produce tokens on their output places in an atomic step. Petri nets, more precisely compact high-level representations such as algebraic Petri nets, where tokens can carry data, have been successfully used for modeling and verification of distributed algorithms [85]. Their natural partial-order semantics, which can itself be represented as a net, can yield intuitive presentations and new insights. For instance, impossibility results regarding mutual exclusion or consensus and their connection to conspiration have been studied in [95]. Various extensions of the Petri net model, namely fairness, randomization, and quasi-synchrony to overcome the limitations of the basic model have been studied.

Although conceptually simple, the use of atomic transitions is very powerful and has to be used with care to make sure that this abstraction is accurate or implementable in a given system context. Implementations of transitions can be captured by transition refinement, which is one of the lines of research where the power of atomicity has been observed. With partially ordered knowledge sharing we are investigating a weaker model that intentionally avoids any assumption of atomic transitions. A unit of data is not modeled as a token, which can be moved by an atomic transition. Instead, data can be copied to a new place and the original can be discarded, but in two separate operations. More generally, a computation can generate new data (output) from existing data (input), but the input does not disappear in this step. It is straightforward to generalize a computation to multiple inputs and multiple outputs by performing multiple computations sequentially or concurrently, but it is important to understand that inputs might disappear, before the computation can take place.

It should be noted that Petri nets can be found as special cases at the core of many other formalisms such as linear logic [46] and rewriting logic [72], and hence our remarks apply accordingly. Another model closely related to Petri nets are (Linda) tuple spaces [20], where the atomic data units take the form of tuples, and atomic in/get and out/put operations are available to remove and add tuples to the space, respectively, and hence, like in Petri nets, mutual exclusion can be directly expressed. For instance, the LIME (Linda in a Mobile Environment) [77] is based on the idea that the tuple spaces of individual host conceptually merge when they come into contact, which can partition again when the connection is lost. Since tuple space operations must be implemented using an atomic transaction protocol, disconnections must be announced or somehow anticipated by the system before they happen to make sure that tuples (like tokens) are not lost or duplicated, which is difficult in practice and limits the applicability in disruptive environments. A different approach is taken in the space-based computing architecture of [15] which organizes tuple spaces using distributed hash tables. In addition to the in/get operation, Linda tuple spaces also support a non-destructive read, similar to extensions of Petri nets with read arcs [24,94].

Multi-Agent Systems. Blackboard systems [33] are a well-known paradigm in multi-agent systems that allows multiple agents to interact and collaborate by sharing knowledge through a so-called blackboard. The knowledge on the blackboard can be modified and agents can register for blackboard events of interest. Originally used as a sequential model together with Lisp, parallel and distributed implementations have been proposed in [27] and [34]. Consistency maintenance among replicated blackboard data and the implementation of blackboard transactions, which can modify data and possibly involve an entire region, i.e., a set of data units, of the blackboard have been identified as major challenges, and addressed by locking at different levels of granularity in [27]. Interestingly, it has been pointed out that an alternative might be to structure the blackboard and the algorithms so that blackboard objects are never modified and instead new versions are created to reflect changes. Another variation which handles errors, uncertainty, and temporal inconsistencies as part of the overall problem solving process are the functionally accurate, cooperative distributed systems that have been informally characterized and explored in [70]. This work is interesting not only because it is far ahead of its time, but also because most the patterns discussed (ranging from abstraction, aggregation, and parallelism) can be naturally realized on top of the partially ordered knowledge sharing model.

A key distinguishing feature from many of the models discussed in this section is that the partially ordered knowledge sharing model is not closely tied to a particular implementation or class of protocols. Depending on available networking technologies and performance requirements (e.g., latency, scalability, robustness) the model can be implemented by a wide range of approaches (and combinations) including shared memory, physical broadcasting, overlay networks, and gossip-style protocols.

7 Conclusions

The partially ordered knowledge sharing model, its probabilistic and fractionated instantiations, are an attempt to build foundations that can be directly mapped into the latest emerging technologies and possible future technologies that give up the notions of reliable computing and communication as primitives. Special cases of our partially ordered knowledge sharing model have found applications in practical systems for disruption-tolerant networking [88] and, more recently, content-based networking [96], where content can be equipped with user-defined orderings. Wireless mobile networks, sensor networks, and more generally networked cyber-physical systems are current applications that are often mission-critical and urgently need better theoretical foundations. Future technologies based on biological or nano-computing will require a fundamentally different kind of software. Even in the short-term we expect that the trend to further miniaturization, e.g., of current VLSI technologies, can only be maintained if the foundations for ensembles of unreliable computing elements are sufficiently developed. In this paper, we have made a small contribution by motivating and defining our basic models and informally discussing their relation to existing and mostly well-known models of distributed computing.

We believe that further work is needed in at least two directions, namely (1) the application, validation, and refinement of our models using case studies based on simulations or experiments with broad range of technologies, and (2) the development of a methodology, theory, and tools to support the design and construction of systems based on these models. Some initial progress has been made on both fronts with applications ranging from content-based mobile ad-hoc networking with Android devices to cyber-physical networked systems such as our heterogeneous mobile robot and quadcopter testbed that we have been building at SRI (see `http://ncps.csl.sri.com`). Increasing the scale in terms of the numbers of nodes (in simulations and deployments) and reducing the granularity at which the model is applied are important engineering challenges that we are trying to address in these applications.

Acknowledgments. Support from National Science Foundation Grant 0932397 (A Logical Framework for Self-Optimizing Networked Cyber-Physical Systems) and Office of Naval Research Grant N00014-10-1-0365 (Principles and Foundations for Fractionated Networked Cyber-Physical Systems) is gratefully acknowledged. Any opinions, findings, and conclusions or recommendations expressed in this material are those of the authors and do not necessarily reflect the views of NSF or ONR.

References

1. Acosta-Elías, J., Luna-Rivera, J.M., Recio-Lara, M., Gutiérrez-Navarro, O., Pineda-Reyes, B.: Topology-sensitive epidemic algorithm for information spreading in large-scale systems. In: Guo, M., Yang, L.T., Di Martino, B., Zima, H.P., Dongarra, J., Tang, F. (eds.) ISPA 2006. LNCS, vol. 4330, pp. 439–450. Springer, Heidelberg (2006)
2. Agha, G.: Actors: a model of concurrent computation in distributed systems. MIT Press, Cambridge (1986)
3. Amir, Y.: Overtaken by events. In: Personnal Communication (April 2010)
4. Amir, Y., Danilov, C., Goose, S., Hedqvist, D., Terzis, A.: 1-800-overlays: using overlay networks to improve VoIP quality. In: NOSSDAV 2005: Proceedings of the International Workshop on Network and Operating Systems Support for Digital Audio and Video, pp. 51–56. ACM, New York (2005)
5. Androutsellis-Theotokis, S., Spinellis, D.: A survey of peer-to-peer content distribution technologies. ACM Comput. Surv. 36(4), 335–371 (2004)
6. Angluin, D.: Local and global properties in networks of processors (extended abstract). In: STOC 1980: Proceedings of the Twelfth Annual ACM Symposium on Theory of Computing, pp. 82–93. ACM, New York (1980)
7. Angluin, D., Aspnes, J., Fischer, M.J., Jiang, H.: Self-stabilizing population protocols. ACM Trans. Auton. Adapt. Syst. 3(4), 1–28 (2008)
8. Arora, A., Gouda, M.: Closure and convergence: A foundation of fault-tolerant computing. IEEE Transactions on Software Engineering 19, 1015–1027 (1993)
9. Arora, A., Gouda, M., Varghese, G.: Constraint satisfaction as a basis for designing nonmasking fault-tolerance. J. High Speed Netw. 5(3), 293–306 (1996)
10. Attiya, H., Welch, J.: Distributed Computing: Fundamentals, Simulations, and Advanced Topics. Wiley-Interscience (2004)
11. Aysal, T.C., Yildiz, M.E., Sarwate, A.D., Scaglione, A.: Broadcast gossip algorithms for consensus. Trans. Sig. Proc. 57(7), 2748–2761 (2009)
12. Babaoglu, O., Canright, G., Deutsch, A., Caro, G.D., Ducatelle, F., Gambardella, L., Ganguly, N., Jelasity, M., Montemanni, R.: Design patterns from biology for distributed computing. ACM Transactions on Autonomous and Adaptive Systems 1, 26–66 (2006)
13. Bal, H.E., Tanenbaum, A.S.: Distributed programming with shared data. Comput. Lang. 16(2), 129–146 (1991)
14. Balakrishnan, H., Kaashoek, M.F., Karger, D., Morris, R., Stoica, I.: Looking up data in p2p systems. Commun. ACM 46(2), 43–48 (2003)
15. Bessler, S., Fischer, A., Khn, E., Mordinyi, R., Tomic, S.: Using tuple-spaces to manage the storage and dissemination of spatial-temporal content. Journal of Computer and System Sciences (2009)
16. Birman, K.: The promise, and limitations, of gossip protocols. SIGOPS Oper. Syst. Rev. 41(5), 8–13 (2007)
17. Birman, K.P., Hayden, M., Ozkasap, O., Xiao, Z., Budiu, M., Minsky, Y.: Bimodal multicast. ACM Trans. Comput. Syst. 17(2), 41–88 (1999)
18. Bisiani, R., Forin, A.: Multilanguage parallel programming of heterogeneous machines. IEEE Trans. Comput. 37(8), 930–945 (1988)
19. Boldi, P., Vigna, S.: Self-stabilizing universal algorithms. In: Self–Stabilizing Systems (Proc. of the 3rd Workshop on Self–Stabilizing Systems), pp. 141–156. Carleton University Press (1997)

20. Bruni, R., Montanari, U.: Concurrent models for linda with transactions. Mathematical. Structures in Comp. Sci. 14(3), 421–468 (2004)
21. Busnel, Y., Bertier, M., Kermarrec, A.-M.: Bridging the Gap between Population and Gossip-based Protocols. Research Report RR-6720, INRIA (2008)
22. Cerf, V., Burleigh, S., Hooke, A., Torgerson, L., Durst, R., Scott, K., Travis, E., Weiss, H.: Status of this memo interplanetary internet (ipn): Architectural definition, Internet Draft (May 2001)
23. Chandy, K.M.: Parallel program design: a foundation. Addison-Wesley Longman Publishing Co. Inc. (1988)
24. Christensen, S., Hansen, N.D.: Coloured petri nets extended with place capacities, test arcs and inhibitor arcs. In: Ajmone Marsan, M. (ed.) ICATPN 1993. LNCS, vol. 691, pp. 186–205. Springer, Heidelberg (1993)
25. Cole, R., Zajicek, O.: The APRAM: incorporating asynchrony into the PRAM model. In: SPAA 1989: Proceedings of the First Annual ACM Symposium on Parallel Algorithms and Architectures, pp. 169–178. ACM (1989)
26. Cole, R., Zajicek, O.: The expected advantage of asynchrony. J. Comput. Syst. Sci. 51(2), 286–300 (1995)
27. Corkill, D.D.: Design alternatives for parallel and distributed blackboard systems. In: Jagannathan, V., Dodhiawala, R., Baum, L.S. (eds.) Blackboard Architectures and Applications, pp. 99–136. Academic Press (1989)
28. Demers, A., Greene, D., Hauser, C., Irish, W., Larson, J., Shenker, S., Sturgis, H., Swinehart, D., Terry, D.: Epidemic algorithms for replicated database maintenance. In: PODC 1987: Proceedings of the Sixth Annual ACM Symposium on Principles of Distributed Computing, pp. 1–12. ACM, New York (1987)
29. Devismes, S., Tixeuil, S., Yamashita, M.: Weak vs. self vs. probabilistic stabilization. In: ICDCS 2008: Proceedings of the 2008 The 28th International Conference on Distributed Computing Systems, pp. 681–688. IEEE Computer Society, Washington, DC (2008)
30. Dijkstra, E.W.: Self-stabilizing systems in spite of distributed control. Commun. ACM 17(11), 643–644 (1974)
31. Dolev, S.: Self-stabilization. MIT Press, Cambridge (2000)
32. Dolev, S., Tzachar, N.: Empire of colonies: Self-stabilizing and self-organizing distributed algorithm. Theor. Comput. Sci. 410(6-7), 514–532 (2009)
33. Engelmore, R.S., Morgan, A. (eds.): Blackboard Systems. Addison-Wesley (1988)
34. Ensor, J.R., Gabbe, J.D.: Transactional blackboards. In: IJCAI 1985: Proceedings of the 9th International Joint Conference on Artificial Intelligence, pp. 340–344. Morgan Kaufmann Publishers Inc. (1985)
35. Eskicioglu, M.R.: A comprehensive bibliography of distributed shared memory. SIGOPS Oper. Syst. Rev. 30(1), 71–96 (1996)
36. R. K et al.: The spindle disruption tolerant networking system. In: Proceedings of IEEE Military Communications Conference (2007)
37. Eugster, P., Felber, P., Le Fessant, F.: The "art" of programming gossip-based systems. SIGOPS Oper. Syst. Rev. 41(5), 37–42 (2007)
38. Eugster, P.T., Guerraoui, R., Kermarrec, A.M., Massouli, L.: From epidemics to distributed computing. IEEE Computer 37, 60–67 (2004)
39. Fall, K.: A delay-tolerant network architecture for challenged internets. In: SIGCOMM 2003: Proceedings of the 2003 Conference on Applications, Technologies, Architectures, and Protocols for Computer Communications, pp. 27–34. ACM (2003)
40. Farrell, S., Cahill, V.: Delay- and Disruption-Tolerant Networking. Artech House, Inc., Norwood (2006)

41. Fernandess, Y., Fernández, A., Monod, M.: A generic theoretical framework for modeling gossip-based algorithms. SIGOPS Oper. Syst. Rev. 41(5), 19–27 (2007)
42. Fich, F., Ruppert, E.: Hundreds of impossibility results for distributed computing. Distrib. Comput. 16(2-3), 121–163 (2003)
43. Fischer, M.J., Lynch, N.A., Paterson, M.S.: Impossibility of distributed consensus with one faulty process. J. ACM 32(2), 374–382 (1985)
44. Frommer, A., Szyld, D.B.: On asynchronous iterations. J. Comput. Appl. Math. 123(1-2), 201–216 (2000)
45. Gibbons, P.B.: A more practical PRAM model. In: SPAA 1989: Proceedings of the First Annual ACM Symposium on Parallel Algorithms and Architectures, pp. 158–168. ACM (1989)
46. Girard, J.-Y.: Linear logic. Theor. Comput. Sci. 50, 1–102 (1987)
47. Golding, R.A., Long, D.D.E.: The performance of weak-consistency replication protocols. Technical Report UCSC-CRL-92-30, Santa Cruz, CA, USA (1992)
48. Gouda, M.G., Multari, N.J.: Stabilizing communication protocols. IEEE Trans. Comput. 40(4), 448–458 (1991)
49. Guerraoui, R., Olivera, R., Schiper, A.: Stubborn communication channels. Technical report, LSE, D'epartement d'Informatique, Ecole Polytechnique F'ed'erale de (1996)
50. Gupta, I., Renesse, R.V., Birman, K.P.: A probabilistically correct leader election protocol for large groups. In: Herlihy, M.P. (ed.) DISC 2000. LNCS, vol. 1914, pp. 89–103. Springer, Heidelberg (2000)
51. Halpern, J.Y., Moses, Y.: Knowledge and common knowledge in a distributed environment. Journal of the ACM 37, 549–587 (1984)
52. Heer, T., Gotz, S., Rieche, S., Wehrle, K.: Adapting distributed hash tables for mobile ad hoc networks. In: PERCOMW 2006: Proceedings of the 4th Annual IEEE International Conference on Pervasive Computing and Communications Workshops, p. 173. IEEE Computer Society (2006)
53. Herlihy, M.: Impossibility results for asynchronous PRAM (extended abstract). In: SPAA 1991: Proceedings of the Third Annual ACM Symposium on Parallel Algorithms and Architectures, pp. 327–336. ACM, New York (1991)
54. Herman, T.: Models of self-stabilization and sensor networks. In: Das, S.R., Das, S.K. (eds.) IWDC 2003. LNCS, vol. 2918, pp. 205–214. Springer, Heidelberg (2003)
55. Howell, R.R., Nesterenko, M., Mizuno, M., Mizuno, M.: Finite-state self-stabilizing protocols in message-passing systems. In: Proceedings of the Fourth Workshop on Self-Stabilizing Systems, pp. 62–69 (1999)
56. Itkis, G., Levin, L.: Fast and lean self-stabilizing asynchronous protocols. In: SFCS 1994: Proceedings of the 35th Annual Symposium on Foundations of Computer Science, pp. 226–239. IEEE Computer Society, Washington, DC (1994)
57. Jacobson, V., Smetters, D.K., Thornton, J.D., Plass, M.F., Briggs, N.H., Braynard, R.L.: Networking named content. In: CoNEXT 2009: Proceedings of the 5th International Conference on Emerging Networking Experiments and Technologies, pp. 1–12. ACM (2009)
58. Jelasity, M., Voulgaris, S., Guerraoui, R., Kermarrec, A.-M., van Steen, M.: Gossip-based peer sampling. ACM Trans. Comput. Syst. 25(3), 8 (2007)
59. Kang, W., Kapitanova, K., Son, S.H.: RDDS: A real-time data distribution service for cyber-physical systems. IEEE Trans. Industrial Informatics 8(2), 393–405 (2012)
60. Karp, R., Schindelhauer, C., Shenker, S., Vocking, B.: Randomized rumor spreading. In: FOCS 2000: Proceedings of the 41st Annual Symposium on Foundations of Computer Science, p. 565. IEEE Computer Society (2000)

61. Katz, S., Perry, K.: Self-stabilizing extensions for message-passing systems. In: PODC 1990: Proceedings of the Ninth Annual ACM Symposium on Principles of Distributed Computing, pp. 91–101. ACM (1990)

62. Kempe, D., Dobra, A., Gehrke, J.: Gossip-based computation of aggregate information. In: FOCS 2003: Proceedings of the 44th Annual IEEE Symposium on Foundations of Computer Science, p. 482. IEEE Computer Society, Washington, DC (2003)

63. Kempe, D., Kleinberg, J., Demers, A.: Spatial gossip and resource location protocols. In: STOC 2001: Proceedings of the Thirty-Third Annual ACM Symposium on Theory of Computing, pp. 163–172. ACM (2001)

64. Kermarrec, A.-M., van Steen, M.: Gossiping in distributed systems. SIGOPS Oper. Syst. Rev. 41(5), 2–7 (2007)

65. Kim, J., Kim, M., Stehr, M.-O., Oh, H., Ha, S.: A parallel and distributed metaheuristic framework based on partially ordered knowledge sharing. ELSEVIER Journal of Parallel and Distributed Computing (JPDC) 72(4), 564–578 (2012)

66. Kim, M., Stehr, M.-O., Talcott, C.: A distributed logic for networked cyberphysical systems. ELSEVIER Journal of Science of Computer Programming (2013), http://dx.doi.org/10.1016/j.scico.2013.01.011

67. Klenke, A.: Probability Theory: A Comprehensive Course. Springer, London (2008)

68. Kulkarni, S.S., Arumugam, M.: Transformations for write-all-with-collision model. Comput. Commun. 29(2), 183–199 (2006)

69. Lahiri, B., Tirthapura, S.: Computing frequent elements using gossip. In: Shvartsman, A.A., Felber, P. (eds.) SIROCCO 2008. LNCS, vol. 5058, pp. 119–130. Springer, Heidelberg (2008)

70. Lesser, V.R., Corkill, D.D.: Functionally accurate, cooperative distributed systems. In: Distributed Artificial Intelligence, pp. 295–310. Morgan Kaufmann Publishers Inc. (1988)

71. Lynch, N.A., Malkhi, D., Ratajczak, D.: Atomic data access in distributed hash tables. In: Druschel, P., Kaashoek, M.F., Rowstron, A. (eds.) IPTPS 2002. LNCS, vol. 2429, pp. 295–305. Springer, Heidelberg (2002)

72. Meseguer, J.: Conditioned rewriting logic as a united model of concurrency. Theor. Comput. Sci. 96(1), 73–155 (1992)

73. auf der Heide, F.M., Scheideler, C., Stemann, V.: Exploiting storage redundancy to speed up randomized shared memory simulations. Theor. Comput. Sci. 162(2), 245–281 (1996)

74. Misra, J.: A discipline of multiprogramming: programming theory for distributed applications. Springer-Verlag New York, Inc., Secaucus (2001)

75. Moser, L.E., Amir, Y., Melliar-Smith, P.M., Agarwal, D.A.: Extended virtual synchrony. In: Proceedings of the IEEE 14th International Conference on Distributed Computing Systems, pp. 56–65. IEEE Computer Society Press (1994)

76. Mosk-Aoyama, D., Shah, D.: Computing separable functions via gossip. In: PODC 2006: Proceedings of the Twenty-Fifth Annual ACM Symposium on Principles of Distributed Computing, pp. 113–122. ACM, New York (2006)

77. Murphy, A.L., Picco, G.P., Roman, G.-C.: Lime: A coordination model and middleware supporting mobility of hosts and agents. ACM Trans. Softw. Eng. Methodol. 15(3), 279–328 (2006)

78. De Nicola, R., Ferrari, G., Loreti, M., Pugliese, R.: A language-based approach to autonomic computing. In: Beckert, B., Damiani, F., de Boer, F.S., Bonsangue, M.M. (eds.) FMCO 2011. LNCS, vol. 7542, pp. 25–48. Springer, Heidelberg (2012)

79. Panangaden, P.: Knowledge and information in probabilistic systems. In: van Breugel, F., Chechik, M. (eds.) CONCUR 2008. LNCS, vol. 5201, p. 4. Springer, Heidelberg (2008)

80. Pereira, J., Oliveira, R., Rodrigues, L., Kermarrec, A.-M.: Probabilistic semantically reliable multicast. In: NCA 2001: Proceedings of the IEEE International Symposium on Network Computing and Applications, p. 100. IEEE Computer Society, Washington, DC (2001)

81. Pereira, J., Rodrigues, L., Oliveira, R.: Semantically reliable multicast: Definition, implementation, and performance evaluation. IEEE Trans. Comput. 52(2), 150–165 (2003)

82. Petersen, K., Spreitzer, M.J., Terry, D.B., Theimer, M.M., Demers, A.J.: Flexible update propagation for weakly consistent replication. In: SOSP 1997: Proceedings of the Sixteenth ACM Symposium on Operating Systems Principles, pp. 288–301. ACM (1997)

83. Rao, J.R.: Extensions of the Unity Methodology: Compositionality, Fairness and Probability in Parallelism. Springer-Verlag New York, Inc., Secaucus (1995)

84. Ratnasamy, S., Stoica, I., Shenker, S.: Routing algorithms for dhts: Some open questions. In: Druschel, P., Kaashoek, M.F., Rowstron, A. (eds.) IPTPS 2002. LNCS, vol. 2429, pp. 45–52. Springer, Heidelberg (2002)

85. Reisig, W.: Elements of distributed algorithms: modeling and analysis with Petri nets. Springer-Verlag New York, Inc. (1998)

86. Schneider, M.: Self-stabilization. ACM Comput. Surv. 25(1), 45–67 (1993)

87. Stehr, M.-O., Kim, M., Talcott, C.: Toward distributed declarative control of networked cyber-physical systems. In: Proc. of the 7th Intl. Conf. on Ubiquitous Intelligence and Computing (to appear). Full version available http://www.csl.sri.com/~stehr/CPS/cpslogic.pdf

88. Stehr, M.-O., Talcott, C.: Planning and learning algorithms for routing in disruption-tolerant networks. In: Proceedings of IEEE Military Communications Conference (2008)

89. Temkow, B., Bosneag, A.-M., Li, X., Brockmeyer, M.: PaxonDHT: Achieving consensus in distributed hash tables. In: SAINT 2006: Proceedings of the International Symposium on Applications on Internet, pp. 236–244. IEEE Computer Society, Washington, DC (2006)

90. Turau, V., Weyer, C.: Fault tolerance in wireless sensor networks through self-stabilisation. Int. J. Commun. Netw. Distrib. Syst. 2(1), 78–98 (2009)

91. Van Renesse, R., Birman, K.P., Vogels, W.: Astrolabe: A robust and scalable technology for distributed system monitoring, management, and data mining. ACM Trans. Comput. Syst. 21(2), 164–206 (2003)

92. van Renesse, R., Dumitriu, D., Gough, V., Thomas, C.: Efficient reconciliation and flow control for anti-entropy protocols. In: LADIS 2008: Proceedings of the 2nd Workshop on Large-Scale Distributed Systems and Middleware, pp. 1–7. ACM (2008)

93. Varghese, G.: Self-stabilization by counter flushing. In: PODC 1994: Proceedings of the Thirteenth Annual ACM Symposium on Principles of Distributed Computing, pp. 244–253. ACM (1994)

94. Vogler, W.: Partial order semantics and read arcs. Theor. Comput. Sci. 286(1), 33–63 (2002)

95. Völzer, H.: Fairneß, Randomisierung und Konspiration in verteilten Algorithmen. PhD thesis, Humboldt-Universität zu Berlin, Mathematisch-Naturwissenschaftliche Fakultät II (2000)

96. Wood, S., Mathewson, J., Joy, J., Stehr, M.-O., Kim, M., Gehani, A., Gerla, M., Sadjadpour, H., Garcia-Luna-Aceves, J.: ICEMAN: A system for efficient, robust and secure situational awareness at the network edge. In: Proceedings of IEEE Military Communications Conference (2013)

97. Zhang, Z., Zhang, Q.: Delay-/disruption tolerant mobile ad hoc networks: latest developments: Research articles. Wirel. Commun. Mob. Comput. 7(10), 1219–1232 (2007)

98. Zhao, W., Ammar, M.H.: Message ferrying: Proactive routing in highly-partitioned wireless ad hoc networks. In: FTDCS 2003: Proceedings of the The Ninth IEEE Workshop on Future Trends of Distributed Computing Systems, p. 308. IEEE Computer Society, Washington, DC (2003)

99. Zhao, W., Chen, Y., Ammar, M., Corner, M., Levine, B., Zegura, E.: Capacity enhancement using throwboxes in dtns. In: Proc. IEEE Intl Conf on Mobile Ad hoc and Sensor Systems (MASS), pp. 31–40 (2006)

Extending Operation Semantics to Enhance the Applicability of Formal Refinement*

Shaoying Liu

Department of Computer Science
Faculty of Computer and Information Sciences
Hosei University, Japan

Abstract. This paper proposes an extension of operation semantics and discusses its benefits in enhancing the applicability of Morgan's formal refinement calculus in practical software development.

1   Introduction

Morgan established the refinement rule for developing sequential programs in [1]. Let $A : s\ [A_{pre}, A_{post}]$ be an operation that changes the the initial state s (a set of variables subject to change) to a final state s' satisfying the postcondition A_{post}, provided that the precondition A_{pre} is true before the operation. If operation $B : s\ [B_{pre}, B_{post}]$ refines operation A, denoted by $A \sqsubseteq B$, then the refinement rule containing the following two conditions must be satisfied by A and B:

(1) $A_{pre} \Rightarrow B_{pre}$

(2) $A_{pre} \wedge B_{post} \Rightarrow A_{post}$

The rule states that operation B weakens the precondition and strengthens the postcondition of A. The rational behind the rule has been well described by Morgan in [1] and the rule has been widely accepted by the formal methods community [2,3,4,5].

While the application of the rule disallows an operation to be refined into an incorrect executable program, it allows a feasible (or satisfiable) operation to be refined into an infeasible operation in the process of a successive refinements leading to code. By infeasible operation we mean that the operation is impossible to be satisfied by any normally executable program (i.e., a program defining a function). Such a refinement may have a negative impact on software development in practice. For example, consider the operation

$F : \{x\}[x \neq 0,\ x > 0 \wedge x' = x + 1 \vee x < 0 \wedge x' = x + 2]$

where x is an integer. F can be refined into the operation

$H : \{x\}[true,\ x > 0 \wedge x' = x + 1]$

because both operations F and H satisfy the refinement rule, that is,

$F_{pre} \Rightarrow H_{pre}$

$F_{pre} \wedge H_{post} \Rightarrow F_{post}$

---

* This work is supported in part by the SCAT research foundation and Hosei University.

S. Iida, J. Meseguer, and K. Ogata (Eds.): Futatsugi Festschrift, LNCS 8373, pp. 434–440, 2014.

However, there are two problems with operation H. Firstly, it is not desired with respect to operation F because it does not do exactly what F requires (e.g., when $x < 0$, F requires that the state variable x be increased by 2, that is $x' = x + 2$, but operation H offers no definition). Secondly, H is infeasible, that is, it is impossible to refine H into a normally executable program (An extreme example is to refine operation H into a "miracle" : $H^m : \{x\}[true, false])$.

This situation has the following three implications for real software development:

- The refinement rule does not guarantee that an operation will be refined into a correct program (i.e., a program that is both normally executable and satisfying its operation specification), although it guarantees that the operation will not be refined into an incorrect program (i.e., a program that is either not normally executable or not satisfying its operation specification). For this reason, the refinement rule must be used with caution; otherwise, the developer (i.e., a person who carries out operation refinements) may waste time and efforts in finding a correct program.
- It is possible to form a sequence of operations F, H, H_1, ..., H_n ($n \geq 1$) by a successive refinements from F, i.e., $F \sqsubseteq H \sqsubseteq H_1 \sqsubseteq \cdots \sqsubseteq H_n$, and at the point of trying to refining H_n the developer realizes that there does not exist a normally executable program to implement H_n. For this reason, the developer has to trace back along the operation sequence to check where he or she made a mistake at some point (i.e., creating an infeasible operation). This can be extremely time-consuming and frustrating. Alternatively, when an abstract operation is refined into a concrete one, the developer can check whether the concrete operation is feasible or not. If it is not, he can trace back to the latest abstract operation to find the mistake. However, this also requires that developer check both whether the refinement rule is satisfied and whether the concrete operation is feasible. Although this may not be as time-consuming as the previous situation involving a sequence of operations, it is still undesirable for real software development because the feasibility of an operation (especially a complex operation) is difficult to verify in general.

Our experience in software development [6] suggests that it is desirable that successful refinements (i.e., the refinements that obey the refinement rule) always lead to a correct program. Thus, the developer can concentrate on refinement without the need to check the feasibility (or satisfiability) of refined operations. Fortunately, this can be done by properly extending the semantics of operations.

Carefully analyzing operations F and H above, we understand that the undesirable situation above is actually influenced by the following two points:

- The postcondition of F does not contain non-determinism in defining the final state x'. Since refinement aims to resolve non-determinism (in the way of weakening precondition and strengthening postcondition), the refinement rule should not be applied to operation F. However, if we restrict the application of refinement to only non-deterministic operations, it will require a checking of the nondeterministic property before the refinement is carried out. This again will incur additional cost and efforts, and possibly technical difficulty.

– Operation H is *interpreted* as a *partial* relation (in this case, a partial function) under the *restricted domain* by its precondition. The restricted domain of H is a subset of its domain that contains only the values satisfying the precondition H_{pre}. The rational behind the partial relation interpretation is that we inherit the convention for defining partial relations or functions in mathematics.

In fact, treating H as a partial relation is the root of the problem. To solve this problem, we propose to interpret operations like H as a total relation under its restricted domain.

2   Extending Operation Semantics

The underlying principle for extending the operation semantics is that we treat every operation as a total relation under its restricted domain. Specifically, we define the semantics of operation A introduced in the beginning of this paper as followings:

$$\forall_{s \in \Sigma} \cdot A_{pre}(s) \Rightarrow \exists_{s' \in \Sigma} \cdot (A_{post}(s, s') \Rightarrow A_{post}(s, s')) \wedge (\neg A_{post}(s, s') \Rightarrow s' = s)$$

where Σ denotes the set of all states.

If operation A cannot change the initial state s to a final state s' satisfying its postcondition A_{post} (i.e., $A_{post}(s, s')$ is false), then it will only maintain the state s (i.e., $s' = s$, like *skip* in some programming languages); otherwise, A will change s to a s' satisfying by A_{post}. Thus, operation H defined previously, for example, will be equivalent to the following operation H^t:

$H^t : \{x\}[true, \, x > 0 \wedge x' = x + 1 \vee x \leq 0 \wedge x' = x]$

Apparently, H^t is not a refinement of operation F because the postcondition of H^t does not strengthen that of F.

In fact, the extension is quite supportive to real software development and consistent with the corresponding mechanism in programming languages. In a real software development, it is often the case that an operation remains only partially specified in early phases [7,6], possibly because there is a lack of understanding of the real requirements or design decisions. Therefore, it is quite possible that the developer defines an operation like H above. With the extended semantics, the operation will produce no "harm" with respect to the desired requirement, because the operation will do nothing obvious except preserving the current state for "undefined" input states (this is pretty similar to the situation that an operation for drawing a rectangle will draw nothing if the command for drawing a rectangle is not defined in the operation specification). Compared to treating the "undefined" input states as "undefined", this extension in semantics is also "safer", because it avoids the situation of implementing the "undefined" function as a program that may "crash" or not terminate. Moreover, the semantic extension also maintains a consistency between an operation like H and a "if-then" statement in most procedural programming languages. That is, "if-then" is a natural implementation of an operation like H^t. For example, the following program segment in Java implements H^t:

if (x > 0)

    x = x + 1;

Since the semantic extension makes any operation as a total relation under its restricted domain and there exists a program to implement a total relation, we will have the following benefit in refinement:

A successful refinement will definitely lead to a correct program.

In other words, application of Morgan's refinement rule will not be possible to refine a feasible operation into an infeasible operation under the extended operation semantics (no need to mention the "miracle")

Furthermore, the extension will also facilitate the developer in writing a formal operation specification. It is no longer necessary to explicitly write the identical relation between the initial and the final states, such as $s' = s$, if it is required as part or the whole function of the operation. This will save the developer considerable amount of time for writing formal specifications and have tremendous impact on the introduction of formal methods to industry because it would be more efficient to write formal specifications without the need to define variables whose values are not expected to change before and after the operation (possibly under certain conditions). For example, assuming we define an operation called *Withdraw* for an Automated Teller Machine (ATM) [8]. The operation takes a requested *amount* of money to be withdrawn and the *account_file* as input and modifies only the *balance* of the corresponding account. Suppose we have the types

$Account = ID \times Password \times Balance \times Available\_Amount;$
$AllAccounts = \textbf{set of } Account;$

where **set of** *Account* denotes a set type with element type as *Account*, then, we may define the operation as follows:

$Withdraw : \{account : Account, account\_file : AllAccounts\}$
$[true,$
$account'.balance = account.balance - amount \wedge$
$account\_file' = (account\_file \setminus \{account\}) \cup \{account'\}]$

Although several items, such as *account'.ID*, *account'.Password*, and *account'.Available_Amount*, are not explicitly defined in the postcondition, under the extended operation semantics the specification implies that all those items are the same as those of the same account before the operation (i.e., *account.ID*, *account.Password*, and *account.Available_Amount*).

The advantage of this semantics will be obvious if only small parts of variables of more complex types need to be updated and all the rest parts remain the same. This advantage becomes even more obvious in specifying and refining object-oriented systems. Due to potential side effects of calling a method of an object in an expression, method calls are not appropriate to use in pre- and postconditions of operations. For example, Object-Z does not permit the appearance of method calls in pre- and postconditions of an operation schema [9]. To define the relation between the initial state and the final state of an operation (say A) involving objects (say a, b, c) as the attributes of its corresponding object (say obj, where a, b, and c are its attributes and A is its method), a reasonable way is to treat each object as a value of a composite type and then define the relation in terms of the object attributes before and after the operation, as used by Utting in [10] and Cavalcanti and Naumann in [11]. For instance, we can treat object a as a value of a composite type that has three attributes (fields) x, y, and z (treat b and c similarly). Then the relation between the initial state (including a, b, and c) and the final state (including $a\prime$, $b\prime$, and $c\prime$) modelled by operation A can be defined in the postcondition of A in terms of the attributes of the initial objects (in the initial state) and those of the final objects (in the final state). It is often the case that the change from the initial state to the final state made by a single operation needs to be defined by only updating some attributes of the objects involved. Imagining how complex it would be if attributes of objects are other objects and the depth of such a nested definition is great. As pointed out by Hall in [12], developing large-scale object-oriented software using the current formal methods is still a tremendous challenge in practice. Our experience in several previous projects [13,6,8] has convinced us that our proposal in this paper is a useful solution.

3   Discussion

In spite of the practical advantages of our proposed semantic extension, one may argue that such an extension may create a possibility for ambiguity in a specification. Let us take the operation H introduced in Section 1 as an example. If we interpret its semantics the same as that of operation H^t defined in Section 2, that is, considering the final state $x\prime$ being equal to the initial state x under the condition $x \leq 0$, then we may mess it up with a possible situation that the specifier forgets to define $x\prime$ as something else (e.g., $x\prime = x+2$) under the same condition. However, this problem can be resolved by a proper validation of the specification. There are many techniques that can be applied for this purpose, such as review and analysis [14,15], animation [16,17,18], simulation [19], and testing [20,21]. Since validation has been a routine activity in industrial projects [22], checking the ambiguities above will not add extra cost to software processes. Of course, since important decisions in a requirements or design specification must ultimately be made by humans, there is no guarantee that all the ambiguities can be eliminated by a validation activity. This is similar to the situation that no guarantee can be provided to ensure that no mistakes will be made in software development using formal methods. However, our proposal in this paper can at least help to simplify formal specifications by omitting "tedious" and "trivial" definitions, and make refinement as a more encouraging and practical technique for practitioners to use.

4   Conclusion

We have proposed to extend operation semantics so that every operation is treated as a total relation under its domain restricted by its precondition. This extension ensures that a successful refinement of an operation will definitely lead to a correct program; it also allows the developer to simplify and write formal specifications more efficiently. We believe that these advantages over the original operation semantics will enhance the applicability of the refinement approach in practice, and perhaps produce a great economic impact on real software development in industry. This is because there is no need to conduct feasibility checking during a successive refinement process and no need to spend time for writing equations in an operation specification to define variables that are supposed not to change by the operation.

References

1. Morgan, C.: Programming from Specifications, 2nd edn. Prentice-Hall (1994)
2. Woodcock, J., Davies, J.: Using Z: Specification, Refinement, and Proof. Prentice-Hall (1996)
3. Abrial, J.R.: The B-Book: Assigning Programs to Meanings. Cambridge University Press (1996)
4. Leuschel, M., Butler, M.: Automatic Refinement Checking for B. In: Lau, K.-K., Banach, R. (eds.) ICFEM 2005. LNCS, vol. 3785, pp. 345–359. Springer, Heidelberg (2005)
5. Boiten, E.A.: Loose specification and refinement in Z. In: Bert, D., Bowen, J.P., Henson, M.C., Robinson, K. (eds.) B 2002 and ZB 2002. LNCS, vol. 2272, pp. 226–241. Springer, Heidelberg (2002)
6. Liu, S., Shibata, M., Sat, R.: Applying SOFL to Develop a University Information System. In: Proceedings of 1999 Asia-Pacific Software Engineering Conference (APSEC 1999), Takamatsu, Japan, pp. 404–411. IEEE Computer Society Press (1999)
7. Hall, A.: Seven Myths of Formal Methods. IEEE Software, 11–19 (1990)
8. Liu, S.: A Case Study of Modeling an ATM Using SOFL. Technical Report HCIS-2003-01, CIS, Hosei University, Koganei-shi, Tokyo, Japan (2003)
9. Smith, G.: The Object-Z Specification Language. In: Advances in Formal Methods. Kluwer Academic (2000)
10. Utting, M.: An Object-Oriented Refinement Calculus with Modular Reasoning. PhD thesis, University of New South Wales, Australia (1992)
11. Cavalcanti, A., Naumann, D.A.: Forward Simulation for Data Refinement of Classes. In: Eriksson, L.-H., Lindsay, P.A. (eds.) FME 2002. LNCS, vol. 2391, pp. 471–490. Springer, Heidelberg (2002)
12. Hall, A.: Realising the Benefits of Formal Methods. In: Lau, K.-K., Banach, R. (eds.) ICFEM 2005. LNCS, vol. 3785, pp. 1–4. Springer, Heidelberg (2005)
13. Liu, S., Asuka, M., Komaya, K., Nakamura, Y.: An Approach to Specifying and Verifying Safety-Critical Systems with Practical Formal Method SOFL. In: Proceedings of the Fourth IEEE International Conference on Engineering of Complex Computer Systems (ICECCS 1998), Monterey, California, USA, pp. 100–114. IEEE Computer Society Press (1998)

14. Parnas, D.L., Weiss, D.M.: Active Design Reviews: Principles and Practices. Journal of Systems and Software 7, 259–265 (1987)
15. Heitmeyer, C.L., Bull, A., Gasarch, C., Labaw, B.: SCR*: A Toolset for Specifying and Analyzing Requirements. In: COMPASS 1995: 10th Annual Conference on Computer Assurance, pp. 109–122. National Institute of Standards and Technology (1995)
16. Gargantini, A., Riccobene, E.: Automatic Model Driven Animation of SCR Specifications. In: Pezzé, M. (ed.) FASE 2003. LNCS, vol. 2621, pp. 294–309. Springer, Heidelberg (2003)
17. Morrey, I., Siddiqi, J., Hibberd, R., Buckberry, G.: A Toolset to Support the Construction and Animation of Formal Specifications. Journal of Systems and Software 41, 147–160 (1998)
18. Hazel, D., Strooper, P.A., Traynor, O.: Possum: An Animator for the SUM Specification Language. In: Proceedings of 1997 Asia-Pacific Software Engineering Conference (APSEC 1997), pp. 42–51. IEEE CS Press (1997)
19. Leveson, N.G., Reese, J.D., Heimdahl, M.P.E.: SpecTRM: A CAD System for Digital Automation. In: Proceedings of 17th Digital Avionics System Conference (DASC 1998), Seattle, USA (1998)
20. Miller, T., Strooper, P.: A Framework and Tool Support for the Systematic Testing of Model-Based Specifications. ACM Transactions on Software Engineering and Methodology 12, 409–439 (2003)
21. Liu, S.: Verifying Consistency and Validity of Formal Specifications by Testing. In: Wing, J.M., Woodcock, J. (eds.) FM 1999. LNCS, vol. 1708, pp. 896–914. Springer, Heidelberg (1999)
22. Bekbay, S., Liu, S.: A Study of Japanese Software Process Practices and a Potential for Improvement Using SOFL. In: Proceedings of Third International Conference on Quality Software (QSIC 2003), Dallas, Texas, USA. IEEE Computer Society Press (2003)

An Institution for Imperative RSL Specifications

Anne E. Haxthausen

DTU Compute, Technical University of Denmark,
DK-2800 Kgs. Lyngby, Denmark
aeha@dtu.dk

Abstract. The RAISE Specification Language (RSL) is a wide-spectrum specification language having a very complex semantics. This paper defines an institution for an imperative subset RSL_I of RSL such that this subset can be given a much simpler semantics in terms of that institution. The subset allows model-oriented type definitions, declaration of state variables, axiomatic specification of values (including functions), and explicit function definitions. Functions may be imperative. The semantics of an RSL_I specification is defined to be the loose semantics of a theory presentation consisting of a signature Σ and a set of sentences E that can easily be derived from the specification.

Keywords: Institutions, formal specification languages, RSL, algebraic semantics, state based specifications.

1 Introduction

The RAISE Specification Language (RSL) [15] is the formal specification language associated with the RAISE development method [16]. The language is a rich, wide-spectrum language that encompasses and integrates different specification styles in a common conceptual framework. Hence, RSL enables the formulation of modular specifications which are algebraic or model-oriented, applicative/functional or imperative, and sequential or concurrent, or even a mixture of these specification styles.

RSL has been given a denotational semantics [12]. The construction of the denotational model and a demonstration of its existence has also been presented in [2]. The semantics is very complex and difficult to read. One reason for this is the expressiveness of RSL and the unified integration of aspects of the different specification styles. Especially the concurrency aspects complicate the semantics. As many RSL specifications are only expressed in well-defined subsets of RSL, not involving concurrency, e.g. in a sequential, applicative subset or a sequential, imperative subset, an idea could be to provide simpler semantics for such subsets. At the same time, the way the semantics is given could be improved. To make it more accessible, we suggest to provide institution based semantics. The concept of *institutions* [7] formalises the informal notion of logical systems with signatures, sentences, and models. To give an institution based semantics for a specification language, first an underlying institution for the language should be

S. Iida, J. Meseguer, and K. Ogata (Eds.): Futatsugi Festschrift, LNCS 8373, pp. 441–464, 2014.

defined, and then on top of that the semantics of specifications should be given in terms of the underlying institution. An institution based semantics has many advantages. For instance, institutions and various kinds of mappings between institutions provide a framework for comparing and relating them. Institutions have primarily been used for giving semantics to algebraic specification languages like CafeOBJ [5,4], Maude [3], and CASL [14,13].

An institution for an applicative subset $mRSL$ of RSL has already been defined and used to give semantics to that subset in [10,11]. The goal of this paper is, in the line of that, to show how one can define an institution for an imperative subset RSL_I of RSL such that this subset can be given a semantics in terms of that institution.

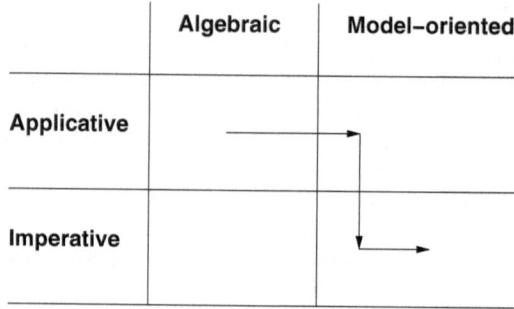

Fig. 1. Specification styles through a typical RAISE development

According to the RAISE method a typical development (see Fig. 1) of imperative software starts with an applicative, algebraic specification which is refined into an applicative, model-oriented specification. Then the applicative, model-oriented specification is transformed (as defined in [9]) into an imperative, model-oriented specification (which might be further refined). It is our goal to let RSL_I cover the imperative, model-oriented specifications that can be achieved by the transformation step (the target of the second arrow in Fig. 1).

1.1   Outline of the Paper

The core of the paper is Section 3 in which an institution for an imperative subset of RSL is defined. Section 2 introduces an imperative subset of RSL, RSL_I, and explains the principles for how specifications of this subset can be given a semantics in terms of that institution. Finally, achievements, related work, and future work are summarised in Section 4. Appendix A defines the mathematical background: the category theoretical notion of institutions and the notation used in the semantic definitions of the RSL_I institution.

2   An Imperative Subset of RSL

This section presents RSL_I: an imperative, deterministic subset of RSL. First, in Section 2.1, a kernel of RSL_I is informally presented, and then, in Section 2.2, it is explained how additional RSL_I constructs can be derived as shorthands for kernel constructs. An example of an RSL_I specification is given in Section 2.3. Finally, in Section 2.4, the principles for how RSL_I specifications can be given a semantics are explained.

2.1   The Kernel

A basic RSL_I *specification* takes the form

scheme id = ce

where *id* is an identifier that gives name to the specification and *ce* is a flat class expression. A flat *class expression* consists of abbreviation type definitions, variable declarations, value declarations, and axioms surrounded by the keywords **class** and **end**. The identifiers introduced by the type definitions, variable declarations, and value declarations of a class expression are assumed to be distinct.

An *abbreviation type definition*

type id = te

defines a type name *id* to be an abbreviation for a type expression *te*, i.e. in any type expression occurrences of *id* and *te* are interchangeable. Recursive abbreviation type definitions are not allowed.

Type expressions are constructed in a model-oriented way, as in VDM[6], from declared type names, declared variable names, type literals, and type operators. The kernel comprises the following type expressions

- type names *id* (introduced in abbreviation type definitions),
- type literals: **Unit, Char, Int, Real**, and **Bool**,
- composite types: $t_1 \times t_2$ (for Cartesian products), $t - \textbf{infset}$ (for sets), t^ω (for lists), $t_1 \overrightarrow{m} t_2$ (for maps), and $t_1 \overset{\sim}{\rightarrow} acc\ t_2$ (for possibly partial functions from t_1 to t_2), where t, t_1, and t_2 are type expressions, and *acc* consists of a read access description of the form **read** $\{id_1, ..., id_n\}$ and a write access description of the form **write** $\{id_1, ..., id_n\}$, where $id_1, ..., id_n$ are names of declared variables. Functions in the type denoted by $t_1 \overset{\sim}{\rightarrow} acc\ t_2$ may read the contents of the variables stated in its read access description and make assignments to variables stated in its write access description. In the kernel it is assumed that the variable set in the write access description is a subset of the variable set in the read access description.

Note that the type expressions include higher order type expressions. Type expressions that do not contain type names are called *canonical type expressions*.

A type expression denotes a *type* which is a set of values. More about that in Section 3.4.

A *variable declaration*

variable id : te

introduces a (state) variable with a name *id* that can store values of the type denoted by type expression *te*. The type expression is not allowed to contain function types having variable accesses[1]. In Section 2.2 it will be explained how initial values of variables can be specified.

A *(basic) value declaration*

value id : te

introduces a name *id* for a value belonging to the type denoted by type expression *te*. Note, that *te* is allowed to be any type expression, so it can also be a function type. It is assumed that value names are not overloaded.

An *axiom* is of the form

axiom e

where *e* is a Boolean value expression. Axioms are used to constrain the possible interpretations of declared values and possible initial values of variables.

In RSL there is no syntactic distinction between value expressions and statements. What is traditionally considered as statements are just special cases of value expressions. *Value expressions* in the kernel include

- value names *id* of declared values,
- variable names *id* of declared variables,
- integer literals representing **Int** values: ..., $-1, 0, 1, ...$
- literals representing **Real** values: ..., -5.2, ..., 0.0, ..., 108.77, ...
- literals representing **Bool** values: **true** and **false**
- literals representing **Char** values: ..., 'c', ..., '+', ...
- **skip** representing the only value in the **Unit** type,
- **chaos** representing non-termination,
- product expressions of the form $(e_1, \ldots e_n)$, where $n \geq 2$,
- set enumerations of the form $\{e_1, \ldots e_n\}$, where $n \geq 0$,
- list enumerations of the form $\langle e_1, \ldots e_n \rangle$, where $n \geq 0$,
- map enumerations of the form $[e_1 \mapsto e_1', \ldots, e_n \mapsto e_n']$, where $n \geq 0$,
- function applications of the form $fe(e)$,
- prefix expressions *prefixop e*, where *prefixop* is a built-in prefix operator like **hd**,
- infix expressions e_1 *infixop* e_2, where *infixop* is a built-in infix operator like $+$ and $=$,
- quantified expressions[2] $\forall \ id : t \cdot eb$ and $\exists \ id : t \cdot eb$,
- equivalence expressions $e_1 \equiv e_2$,
- if-then-else expressions **if** eb **then** e_1 **else** e_2 **end**,

---

[1] This is a restriction compared to full RSL. In Section 4.3 it will be discussed how this restriction can be loosened.

[2] Note that it is allowed to quantify over values of *any* type expression *t*, and hence also to quantify over imperative functions and higher-order functions.

- assignments $id := e$, where id is the name of a declared variable,
- the initialise expression **initialise** that represents the effect of initialising each declared variable to its initial value, and
- statement sequencing expressions $eu; e$.

where e, e_1, e_2, ..., e_n, e'_1, ..., e'_n, eb, fe, eu are value expressions, id is an identifier, and t is a type expression. The requirements for a value expression to be *well-formed* will be formally defined in Section 3.2 in terms of some typing and variable access rules.

A value expression is said to be *canonical* if all constituent type expressions are canonical.

Note that iterative constructs like while loops are not included in the kernel language as they do not occur in the imperative specifications that we are targeting (i.e. those that can be obtained by applying the transformations described in [9], as mentioned in Section 1).

Intuitively, the execution of a value expression may either diverge (not terminate) or it has the effect of returning a value after possibly having updated the contents of the variables. In Section 3.6 a formal denotational semantics of canonical RSL_I kernel value expressions will be given.

2.2 Derived Constructs

There are also derived constructs that can be described as shorthands for the kernel constructs mentioned above. It is out of the scope of this paper to mention all derived constructs, but we will give some important examples.

Explicit Function Definitions. For instance, an *explicit function definition*

> **value**
>   id : tfun
>   id(x) ≡ e

where $tfun$ is a function type expression, id and x are identifiers, and e is a value expression (in which the formal parameter x may occur), is a shorthand for the basic *value declaration*

> **value** id : tfun

and the *axiom*

> **axiom** $\forall$ x : t • id(x) ≡ e

where t is the formal parameter type of the function type expression $tfun$.

If the formal parameter type t is a Cartesian product type $te_1 \times \dots \times te_n$, then the left-hand side of the equivalence can also be written in the form $id(id_1, \dots, id_n)$. In that case the derived axiom will be

> **axiom** $\forall$ (id$_1$, ..., id$_n$) : t • id(id$_1$, ..., id$_n$) ≡ e

An explicit function definition can also have a precondition *eb* which is a Boolean value expression that may refer to the formal parameter(s) and the declared variables:

value
   id : tfun
   id(x) ≡ e
   pre eb

This is a shorthand for the following value declaration and axiom

value id : tfun
axiom ∀ x : t • (eb ≡ **true** ⇒ id(x) ≡ e)

Subtypes in Value Declarations. To simplify the presentation in this paper, the kernel does not comprise RSL subtype expressions that denote subtypes[3] of other types. An example of an RSL subtype expression is **Nat** that denotes the subset of integers $i \geq 0$ in **Int**.

However, a value declaration, specifying a value to be in a subtype is a derived construct that is a shorthand for a value declaration specifying the value to be in its super-type and an axiom expressing that the value is in its subtype. For instance,

value id : **Nat**

is a shorthand for

value id : **Int**
axiom id $\geq$ 0

Initialisation of Variables. A variable declaration can also contain a specification of its initial value by an expression *e* that must not refer to any variables:

variable id : te := e

This is a shorthand for

variable id : te
axiom (**initialise** ; id := e) ≡ **initialise**

The axiom states that assigning the initial value *e* to the variable *id* right after an initialisation, would not change the values stored in the variables. In other terms **initialise** will result in a state where the value of *id* is *e*.

If a variable declaration does not contain a specification of its initial value (and there are no axioms like the one stated above) then its initial value is underspecified.

---

[3] In RSL types are sets and subtype means subset.

Variable Access Descriptions in Function Type Expressions. In the kernel it is required that there is a read access description and a write access description in function type expressions, however, in full RSL it is allowed to leave out read and/or write access descriptions. If there is no read access description, it is a shorthand for the read access description

read {}

and if there is no write access description, it is a shorthand for the write access description

write {}

In the kernel it is required that the variable set in the write access description is a subset of the variable set in the read access description. However, in full RSL a shorthand is allowed: variables that are in the write access description need not to be repeated in the read access description. The meaning is as if they had been repeated. Furthermore, in full RSL the curly brackets in the access descriptions may be left out.

2.3   Example of an Imperative Specification

Fig. 2 contains an example of an imperative specification having a variable *stack* that can store a *Stack* value. According to the type abbreviation, a *Stack* value is a list of integers. All the functions are allowed to read the *stack* variable, as they have a **read** *stack* access description in their function type, while only the *push* and *pop* functions are allowed to write (assign new values to) the *stack* variable, as only these functions have a **write** *stack* access description in their function type. **hd**, **tl** and ^ are RSL built-in operators for taking the head of a list, taking the tail of a list, and for concatenating two lists, respectively. The initial value of the variable is not specified and it is not specified what happens when the functions are applied to arguments that do not fulfil the preconditions. Everything else is completely specified. Note that it is also possible to give axiomatic specifications of functions, obtaining more loose specifications.

   Larger examples can be found e.g. in [16].

2.4   Semantics

A (well-formed) RSL$_I$ specification *determines* a signature, Σ, and a set of Σ-sentences, E, of the underlying institution (that will be described in Section 3). In order to determine the signature and sentences of a specification, first derived constructs (like explicit function definitions) should be expanded into the constructs they are shorthands for. Furthermore, all occurrences of type abbreviation names in type expressions should be expanded into their *canonical type expressions*, i.e. type expressions not referring to any type identifiers, by recursively expanding type identifiers according to their abbreviations. For the

```
scheme I_STACK =
    class
        type
            Stack = Int^ω

        variable
            stack : Stack

        value
            is_empty : Unit →̃ read stack Bool
            is_empty() ≡ stack = ⟨⟩,

            push : Int →̃ read stack write stack Unit
            push(elem) ≡ stack := ⟨elem⟩ ^ stack,

            pop : Unit →̃ read stack write stack Unit
            pop() ≡ stack := tl stack
            pre ∼ is_empty(),

            top : Unit →̃ read stack Int
            top() ≡ hd stack
            pre ∼ is_empty()
    end
```

Fig. 2. Example of an RSL$_I$ specification

resulting specification it is straightforward to determine the signature and axioms: The signature captures the type definitions, the variable declarations, and the value declarations of the specification, and the sentences are the Boolean value expressions of the axioms. We will give examples of this later.

The *semantics* of a specification that determines a signature Σ and a set of Σ-sentences E, is the loose semantics of the theory presentation (Σ, E), i.e. the semantics is the class of those Σ-models that satisfy all the sentences in E.

3 An Institution for an Imperative Subset of RSL

In this section, we define an institution I_{RSL_I} for the imperative subset RSL$_I$ of RSL described in Section 2. The definition of the notion of institutions and the meta notation used in the semantic definitions of the RSL$_I$ institution can be found in Appendix A.

3.1   Signatures

In the following, let Id denote the set of allowed RSL identifiers for types, values and variables.

Definition 1. *The set of* canonical type expressions *over a set of variable identifiers $Id_V \subseteq Id$ is the least set $T(Id_V)$ that satisfies:*

- **Unit, Char, Int, Real, Bool** $\in T(Id_V)$,
- $t_1 \times t_2 \in T(Id_V)$, *if* $t_1 \in T(Id_V)$ *and* $t_2 \in T(Id_V)$,
- $t-$**infset** $\in T(Id_V)$, *if* $t \in T(Id_V)$,
- $t^\omega \in T(Id_V)$, *if* $t \in T(Id_V)$,
- $t_1 \overset{\sim}{\underset{m}{\to}} t_2 \in T(Id_V)$, *if* $t_1 \in T(Id_V)$ *and* $t_2 \in T(Id_V)$,
- $t_1 \overset{\sim}{\to}$ **read** rs **write** $ws\ t_2 \in T(Id_V)$, *if* $t_1 \in T(Id_V)$, $t_2 \in T(Id_V)$, $rs \subseteq Id_V$, *and* $ws \subseteq rs$.

An RSL_I *signature* is intended to capture information given in the type, value and variable declarations of an RSL_I specification.

Definition 2. *An* RSL$_I$ signature *is a triple $\Sigma = (A, OP, V)$ where*

- $A \in Id \underset{m}{\to} T(\mathbf{dom}\ V)$ *is a map representing a set of type abbreviation definitions. It maps type names to canonical type expressions they abbreviate.*
- $OP \in Id \underset{m}{\to} T(\mathbf{dom}\ V)$ *is a map representing a set of value declarations. It maps value names to their canonical type expressions.*
- $V \in Id \underset{m}{\to} T(\emptyset)$ *is a map representing a set of variable definitions. It maps variable names to their canonical type expressions. It is assumed that the type expressions do not contain function types having variable accesses[4].*

such that **dom** A, **dom** OP *and* **dom** V *are disjoint.*

The type expressions in $T(\mathbf{dom}\ V)$ are also called *canonical Σ type expressions*.

Note that OP could alternatively have been defined as a family of $T(\mathbf{dom}\ V)$ sorted sets of value names, more in tradition of signatures for many other institutions. However, we choose to use a map from value names to their types in $T(\mathbf{dom}\ V)$ as this is more close to the original RSL semantics. This choice was possible because we have assumed that value names are not overloaded.

A signature is said to be *applicative* if $V = [\ ]$.

Example 1. The signature of the specification shown in Section 2.3 is the triple $\Sigma = (A, OP, V)$ where

$A = [\,\text{Stack} \mapsto \mathbf{Int}^\omega\,]$,
$OP =$
$\quad [\ \text{is\_empty} \mapsto \mathbf{Unit} \overset{\sim}{\to} \mathbf{read}\ \{\text{stack}\}\ \mathbf{write}\ \{\}\ \mathbf{Bool},$
$\qquad \text{push} \mapsto \mathbf{Int} \overset{\sim}{\to} \mathbf{read}\ \{\text{stack}\}\ \mathbf{write}\ \{\text{stack}\}\ \mathbf{Unit},$
$\qquad \text{pop} \mapsto \mathbf{Unit} \overset{\sim}{\to} \mathbf{read}\ \{\text{stack}\}\ \mathbf{write}\ \{\text{stack}\}\ \mathbf{Unit},$
$\qquad \text{top} \mapsto \mathbf{Unit} \overset{\sim}{\to} \mathbf{read}\ \{\text{stack}\}\ \ \mathbf{write}\ \{\}\ \mathbf{Int}$
$\quad],$
$V = [\,\text{stack} \mapsto \mathbf{Int}^\omega\ ]$

---

[4] In Section 4.3 it will be discussed how this restriction can be loosened.

3.2   Sentences

In the following, let $\Sigma = (A, OP, V)$ be an arbitrary signature.

In this section we will define Σ-sentences to be canonical, Boolean RSL_I kernel value expressions that are well-formed with respect to Σ, i.e. they only refer to value names and variable names in Σ and follow certain typing rules and variable access rules.

In order to formally define what "well-formed" means, we first give a static semantics for canonical RSL_I kernel value expressions (the syntax of which was given in Section 2).

The static semantics for selected[5] canonical RSL_I kernel value expressions is given in Fig. 3. It is defined by a set of inference rules for assertions of the form $\Sigma \vdash e \rhd t$, rs, ws, where e is a canonical RSL_I kernel value expression, t is a canonical RSL_I type expression, and rs, and ws are sets of (variable) identifiers. Such an assertion states that e is well-formed, has type t, potentially reads the variables in rs and potentially writes in (i.e. makes assignments to) the variables in ws. The inference rules for infix expressions and prefix expressions depend on type assertions for the RSL infix operators and the RSL prefix operators, respectively. These type assertions take the form $infixop : t_1 \times t_2 \overset{\sim}{\to} t$ and $prefixop : t_1 \overset{\sim}{\to} t_2$, respectively, where t, t_1 and t_2 are canonical RSL_I type expressions, and they are defined by $37 + 12$ type assertion rules that can be found in [15].

In Section 4.3 it will be discussed how the static semantics can be loosened by adding some sub-typing rules.

Definition 3. *An* RSL_I Σ *value expression is a canonical* RSL_I *kernel value expression e that is well-formed with respect to Σ, i.e. for which $\Sigma \vdash e \rhd t$, rs, ws holds for some t, rs, and ws. The set of all Σ value expressions is denoted* $ValueExpr(\Sigma)$.

Definition 4. *An* RSL_I Σ-*sentence is a Boolean* RSL_I Σ *value expression e that does not potentially write in variables, i.e. for which $\Sigma \vdash e \rhd$ **Bool**, rs, $\emptyset$ holds for some rs.*

Example 2. The specification shown in Section 2.3 determines a sentence for each function definition. For instance, the sentence determined by the definition of the push function is the following:

$$\forall \ elem : \mathbf{Int} \bullet push(elem) \equiv stack := \langle elem \rangle \ \widehat{} \ stack$$

Note that according to the static semantic rules, equivalence expressions have an empty write access set (and as we shall see later in the dynamic semantics

---

[5] The static semantics for set, list and map enumerations is not shown as it is similar to that for product expressions, the static semantics for prefix expressions is not shown as it is similar to that of infix expressions, and the static semantics for existential quantifications is not shown as it is just as for universal quantifications. The static semantics shown for product expressions having two elements can be generalised in the obvious way to products having more than two elements.

$$\frac{id \in \mathbf{dom}\ OP\quad t = OP(id)}{(A, OP, V) \vdash id \rhd t,\ \emptyset,\ \emptyset}\quad \frac{id \in \mathbf{dom}\ V\quad t = V(id)}{(A, OP, V) \vdash id \rhd t,\ \{id\},\ \emptyset}$$

$$\Sigma \vdash c \rhd \mathbf{Char},\ \emptyset,\ \emptyset\quad \Sigma \vdash i \rhd \mathbf{Int},\ \emptyset,\ \emptyset\quad \Sigma \vdash r \rhd \mathbf{Real},\ \emptyset,\ \emptyset\quad \Sigma \vdash b \rhd \mathbf{Bool},\ \emptyset,\ \emptyset$$

$$\Sigma \vdash \mathbf{skip} \rhd \mathbf{Unit},\ \emptyset,\ \emptyset\quad \Sigma \vdash \mathbf{chaos} \rhd t,\ \emptyset,\ \emptyset$$

$$\frac{\Sigma \vdash e_1 \rhd t_1,\ rs_1,\ ws_1\quad \Sigma \vdash e_2 \rhd t_2,\ rs_2,\ ws_2}{\Sigma \vdash (e_1, e_2) \rhd t_1 \times t_2,\ rs_1 \cup rs_2,\ ws_1 \cup ws_2}$$

$$\frac{\Sigma \vdash e \rhd t_1,\ rs_1,\ ws_1\quad \Sigma \vdash fe \rhd t_1 \overset{\sim}{\to} \mathbf{read}\ rs\ \mathbf{write}\ ws\ t_2,\ rs_2,\ ws_2}{\Sigma \vdash fe(e) \rhd t_2,\ rs \cup rs_1 \cup rs_2,\ ws \cup ws_1 \cup ws_2}$$

$$\frac{\Sigma \vdash e_1 \rhd t_1,\ rs_1,\ ws_1\quad \Sigma \vdash e_2 \rhd t_2,\ rs_2,\ ws_2\quad infixop : t_1 \times t_2 \overset{\sim}{\to} t}{\Sigma \vdash e_1\ infixop\ e_2 \rhd t,\ rs_1 \cup rs_2,\ ws_1 \cup ws_2}$$

$$\frac{t \in T(\mathbf{dom}\ V)\quad (A \setminus \{id\}, OP \dagger [id \mapsto t], V \setminus \{id\}) \vdash eb \rhd \mathbf{Bool},\ rs,\ \emptyset}{(A, OP, V) \vdash \forall\ id : t \bullet eb \rhd \mathbf{Bool},\ rs,\ \emptyset}$$

$$\frac{\Sigma \vdash e_1 \rhd t,\ rs_1,\ ws_1\quad \Sigma \vdash e_2 \rhd t,\ rs_2,\ ws_2}{\Sigma \vdash e_1 \equiv e_2 \rhd \mathbf{Bool},\ rs_1 \cup rs_2 \cup ws_1 \cup ws_2,\ \emptyset}$$

$$\frac{\Sigma \vdash eb \rhd \mathbf{Bool},\ rs,\ ws\quad \Sigma \vdash e_1 \rhd t,\ rs_1,\ ws_1\quad \Sigma \vdash e_2 \rhd t,\ rs_2,\ ws_2}{\Sigma \vdash \mathbf{if}\ eb\ \mathbf{then}\ e_1\ \mathbf{else}\ e_2\ \mathbf{end} \rhd t,\ rs \cup rs_1 \cup rs_2,\ ws \cup ws_1 \cup ws_2}$$

$$\frac{id \in \mathbf{dom}\ V\quad t = V(id)\quad \Sigma \vdash e \rhd t,\ rs,\ ws}{(A, OP, V) \vdash id := e \rhd \mathbf{Unit},\ rs,\ ws \cup \{id\}}\quad (A, OP, V) \vdash \mathbf{initialise} \rhd \mathbf{Unit},\ \emptyset,\ V$$

$$\frac{\Sigma \vdash eu \rhd \mathbf{Unit},\ rs_1,\ ws_1\quad \Sigma \vdash e_2 \rhd t_2,\ rs_2,\ ws_2}{\Sigma \vdash eu; e_2 \rhd t_2,\ rs_1 \cup rs_2,\ ws_1 \cup ws_2}$$

Fig. 3. Static semantics of selected canonical RSL$_I$ kernel value expressions. In the inference rules, the following meta variables are used: Σ and (A, OP, V) for signatures, id for identifiers in Id, c, i, r and b for char, integer, real and Bool literals, respectively, fe, e, eb, eu, e_1, and e_2 for canonical RSL$_I$ kernel value expressions, t, t_1 and t_2 for canonical RSL$_I$ type expressions, and rs, rs_1, rs_2, ws, ws_1, and ws_2 for sets of (variable) identifiers.

equivalence expressions do not have any side effects, they compare the returned values and side effects of its two arguments and gives true, if these are the same) even their sub-expressions contain assignments, as it is the case in this example. Therefore, the value expression in this example can be used as a sentence.

3.3 Semantic Domains

This section defines some semantic domains that are needed when giving semantics to type expressions and value expressions. The semantics of type expressions and value expressions are in turn needed when defining the notion of models and the satisfaction relation, respectively.

In the following, let $\Sigma = (A, OP, V)$ be an arbitrary signature.

For each canonical type expression $t \in T(\mathbf{dom}\ V)$, there is a value domain $Value_t$ (of values of type t), for each set of variables $vs \subseteq \mathbf{dom}\ V$, there is a store domain $Store_{vs}$, for each canonical type expression $t \in T(\mathbf{dom}\ V)$ and set of variables $ws \subseteq \mathbf{dom}\ V$, there is a process domain $Procs_{ws,t}$, and for each $t \in T(\mathbf{dom}\ V)$ and sets of variables $rs, ws \subseteq \mathbf{dom}\ V$, there is an effect domain $Effect_{rs,ws,t}$. The domains are sets defined as follows, where vs, rs, ws are subsets of variables in $\mathbf{dom}\ V$, and t, t_1 and t_2 are canonical type expressions in $T(\mathbf{dom}\ V)$:

- $Value_{\mathbf{Unit}} = \{skip\}$
- $Value_{\mathbf{Char}} = \{'A',...\}$
- $Value_{\mathbf{Int}} = \mathbb{Z}$ (the set of all Integers)
- $Value_{\mathbf{Real}} = \mathbb{R}$ (the set of all Real numbers)
- $Value_{\mathbf{Bool}} = \mathbb{B} = \{tt, ff\}$
- $Value_{t_1 \times t_2} = Value_{t_1} \times Value_{t_2}$
- $Value_{t-\mathbf{infset}} = (Value_t)-\mathbf{infset}$
- $Value_{t^\omega} = (Value_t)^\omega$
- $Value_{t_1 \overrightarrow{\widetilde{m}} t_2} = (Value_{t_1} \times Value_{t_2})-\mathbf{infset}$
- $Value_{t_1 \overset{\sim}{\to}\ \mathbf{read}\ rs\ \mathbf{write}\ ws\ t_2} = Value_{t_1} \to Effect_{rs,ws,t_2}$
  That is, a value of type $t_1 \overset{\sim}{\to} \mathbf{read}\ rs\ \mathbf{write}\ ws\ t_2$ is a function f from values of type t_1 to effects of type t_2 such that f only reads variables in rs and writes variables in ws.
- $Store_{vs} = \{\varrho : Id \overrightarrow{m} Value \mid \mathbf{dom}\ \varrho = vs \wedge \forall v \in vs \bullet \varrho(v) \in Value_{V(v)}\}$
  That is, a store ϱ maps each variable identifier v of vs to a value in the type denoted by the type expression $V(v)$ of v.
- $Procs_{ws,t} = (Store_{ws} \times Value_t) \cup \{\bot\}$. That is, a process[6] is either a pair consisting of a store and a value, or it is a diverging process represented by $\bot$.
- $Effect_{rs,ws,t} = Store_{rs} \to Procs_{ws,t}$. That is, an effect is a function that returns a process for a given store. Effects are used as denotations for value expressions in the context of a given model.

The domain $Type$ of all Σ-types, the domain $Value$ of all Σ-values, and the domain $Store$ of all Σ-stores are defined in terms of the domains above:

- $Type = \bigcup_{t \in T(\mathbf{dom}\ V)} Value_t-\mathbf{infset}$. That is, a type is a subset[7] of values in $Value_t$ for some canonical type expression $t \in T(\mathbf{dom}\ V)$.
- $Value = \bigcup_{t \in T(\mathbf{dom}\ V)} Value_t$
- $Store = \bigcup_{vs \subseteq \mathbf{dom}\ V} Store_{vs}$

As it can be seen most of the domains depend on the V component of the signature. If it is not clear from the context, with right to which signature the domains are defined, the domains will be tagged with the signature like in $Store(\Sigma)$ and $Type(\Sigma)$.

---

[6] The term *process* is a reminiscence of the terminology used for the full RSL language. For the imperative RSL_I the process domain is a very degenerated domain compared to the process domain for full RSL.

[7] We allow subsets in order, in future work, to be able to give semantics to subtype expressions.

3.4   Dynamic Semantics of Type Expressions

In the following, let $\Sigma = (A, OP, V)$ be an arbitrary signature.

The semantics of canonical Σ type expressions in $T(\mathbf{dom}\ V)$ is given by a meaning function $M(\Sigma) : T(\mathbf{dom}\ V) \to Type(\Sigma)$ mapping type expressions t into the types they denote. $M(\Sigma)$ is defined by:

$$M(\Sigma)(t) = Value_t$$

When Σ is clear from the context, we sometimes just write M instead of $M(\Sigma)$.

3.5   Models

In the following let $\Sigma = (A, OP, V)$ be a signature.

Definition 5. *An* RSL$_I$ Σ-model *is a triple* $m = (m_A, m_{OP}, st_{init})$ *where*

- $m_A \in Id \rightarrowtail Type$, *such that* $\mathbf{dom}\ m_A = \mathbf{dom}\ A$ *and* $m_A(a) = M(A(a))$ *for* $a \in \mathbf{dom}\ A$. *That is,* m_A *maps each type name* a *of* A *into the type denoted by its abbreviation* $A(a)$.
- $m_{OP} \in Id \rightarrowtail Value$, *such that* $\mathbf{dom}\ m_{OP} = \mathbf{dom}\ OP$ *and* $m_{OP}(op) \in M(OP(op))$ *for* $op \in \mathbf{dom}\ OP$. *That is,* m_{OP} *maps each value name* op *of* OP *into a value in the type denoted by the type expressions* $OP(op)$ *of* op.
- $st_{init} \in Store$, *such that* $\mathbf{dom}\ st_{init} = \mathbf{dom}\ V$ *and* $st_{init}(v) \in M(V(v))$ *for* $v \in \mathbf{dom}\ V$. *That is,* st_{init} *denotes the initial store that maps each variable name* v *of* V *to its initial value that must be in the type of the variable.*

Note that all Σ-models have the same m_A component.[8]

Note that as aliasing (two variable names representing the same location in the storage) is not possible in RSL and only global variables are allowed in the considered RSL$_I$ subset, it has not been necessary to introduce a notion of locations for variables and in each model include a map from value names to their locations and let a store be a map from locations to values. It has been sufficient to define a store to be a map from variable names to values.

Definition 6. *For each signature* Σ, $Mod(\Sigma)$ *is the discrete category having the* RSL$_I$ Σ-models m *as its objects and the identities* id_m *on these objects as its only morphisms.*

3.6   Dynamic Semantics of Value Expressions

The dynamic semantics of well-formed mRSL value expressions was defined in [10,11]. Here we generalise and extend it to cover well-formed RSL$_I$ kernel value expressions.

---

[8] Note that this would not have been the case if signatures had a component being a set of sorts and canonical type expressions of abbreviation type definitions could refer to these sorts.

In the following, let $\Sigma = (A, OP, V)$ be an arbitrary signature.

The meaning of an RSL$_I$ Σ value expression e in the context of a Σ-model m is a Σ-effect. Hence, the semantics of Σ value expressions is given by a meaning function

$$M(\Sigma) : |Mod(\Sigma)| \to ValueExpr(\Sigma) \to Effect(\Sigma)$$

where $|Mod(\Sigma)|$ is the set of all Σ-models, $ValueExpr(\Sigma)$ is the set of RSL$_I$ Σ value expressions, and $Effect(\Sigma) = \bigcup_{t \in T(\mathbf{dom}\ V)} Effect_{V,V,t}$ is the union of all effect domains $Effect_{V,V,t} = Store_V \to Procs_{V,t}$.

$M(\Sigma)$ is defined below such that for each Σ-model m and each Σ value expression e of type t, $M(\Sigma)(m)(e) \in Effect_{V,V,t}$.

In the following let $m = (m_A, m_{OP}, st_{init})$ be a Σ-model and $st \in Store_V$ be a Σ-store. For each kind of expression e, $M(\Sigma)(m)(e)(st)$ is defined as follows, where it is assumed that e is well-formed with respect to Σ:

- For value names $id \in \mathbf{dom}\ OP$

  $$M(\Sigma)(m)(id)(st) = (st,\ m_{OP}(id))$$

- For variable names $id \in \mathbf{dom}\ V$

  $$M(\Sigma)(m)(id)(st) = (st,\ st(id))$$

- For integer literals i

  $$M(\Sigma)(m)(i)(st) = (st,\ i)$$

  Other kinds of literals are given semantics in a similar way.
- For basic expressions

  $$M(\Sigma)(m)(\mathbf{skip})(st) = (st,\ skip)$$

  $$M(\Sigma)(m)(\mathbf{chaos})(st) = \bot$$

- For product expressions

  $$
  \begin{aligned}
  &M(\Sigma)(m)((e_1,\ e_2))(st) = \\
  &\quad \mathbf{case}\ \ M(\Sigma)(m)(e_1)(st)\ \mathbf{of} \\
  &\qquad \bot \to \bot, \\
  &\qquad (st',\ v') \to \\
  &\qquad\qquad \mathbf{case}\ \ M(\Sigma)(m)(e_2)(st')\ \mathbf{of} \\
  &\qquad\qquad\quad \bot \to \bot, \\
  &\qquad\qquad\quad (st'',\ v'') \to (st'',\ (v',\ v'')) \\
  &\qquad\qquad \mathbf{end} \\
  &\quad \mathbf{end}
  \end{aligned}
  $$

The semantics above for product expressions having two elements generalises in the obvious way to product expressions having more than two elements. Enumeration value expressions for sets, lists and maps are given semantics in a similar way.

– For function applications $fe(e)$, where the expression fe has a function type $t_1 \overset{\sim}{\to}$ **read** rs **write** ws t_2 and e has type t_1 (according to the static semantics):

$$M(\Sigma)(m)(fe(e))(st) =$$
$$\quad \textbf{case}\ \ M(\Sigma)(m)(fe)(st)\ \textbf{of}$$
$$\qquad \bot \to \bot,$$
$$\qquad (st',\ vfe) \to$$
$$\qquad\qquad \textbf{case}\ \ M(\Sigma)(m)(e)(st')\ \textbf{of}$$
$$\qquad\qquad\quad \bot \to \bot,$$
$$\qquad\qquad\quad (st'',\ ve) \to$$
$$\qquad\qquad\qquad \textbf{case}\ \ vfe(ve)(st''/rs)\ \textbf{of}$$
$$\qquad\qquad\qquad\quad \bot \to \bot,$$
$$\qquad\qquad\qquad\quad (st''',\ vres) \to\ (st'' \dagger st''',\ vres)$$
$$\qquad\qquad\qquad \textbf{end}$$
$$\qquad\qquad \textbf{end}$$
$$\quad \textbf{end}$$

Note that $vfe(ve)$ is applied to the store st'' restricted to the set of the function's read variables rs as $vfe \in Value_{t1} \to (Store_{rs} \to Proc_{ws,t2})$. If the application terminates, it returns a store st''' that only contains the write variables, so in that case the store returned by $M(\Sigma)(m)(fe(e))(st)$ must be $st'' \dagger st'''$.

– For infix expressions

$$M(\Sigma)(m)(e_1\ infixop\ e_2)(st) =$$
$$\quad \textbf{case}\ \ M(\Sigma)(m)(e_1)(st)\ \textbf{of}$$
$$\qquad \bot \to \bot,$$
$$\qquad (st',\ v') \to$$
$$\qquad\qquad \textbf{case}\ \ M(\Sigma)(m)(e_2)(st')\ \textbf{of}$$
$$\qquad\qquad\quad \bot \to \bot,$$
$$\qquad\qquad\quad (st'',\ v'') \to (st'',\ M(infixop)(v',\ v''))$$
$$\qquad\qquad \textbf{end}$$
$$\quad \textbf{end}$$

where

$$M(infixop) \in Value \times Value \overset{\sim}{\to} Value$$

is a function that respects the types of infixop. For instance, $M(+)(i1, i2) = i1 + i2$, for values $i1, i2 \in Value_{Int}$

Prefix expressions are given semantics in a similar way.

– For quantified expressions

$$M(\Sigma)(m)(\forall\ id : t \bullet eb)(st) =$$
$$\quad \textbf{let}$$
$$\qquad \Sigma'' = (A \backslash \{id\},\ OP \dagger [id \mapsto t],\ V \backslash \{id\}),$$
$$\qquad b = \forall\ v \in M(\Sigma)(t) \bullet M(\Sigma'')(m \dagger [id \mapsto v])(eb)(st \backslash \{id\}) = (st,\ tt)$$
$$\quad \textbf{in}\ (st,\ b)\ \textbf{end}$$
$$\quad \textit{where}\ m \dagger [id \mapsto v] = (m_A \backslash \{id\},\ m_{OP} \dagger [id \mapsto v],\ m_V \backslash \{id\})$$

Existential qualified expressions are given semantics in a similar way.

- For equivalence expressions

$$M(\Sigma)(m)(e_1 \equiv e_2)(st) =$$
$$(st, M(\Sigma)(m)(e_1)(st) = M(\Sigma)(m)(e_2)(st))$$

- For structured expressions

$M(\Sigma)(m)(\textbf{if } eb \textbf{ then } e_1 \textbf{ else } e_2 \textbf{ end})(st) =$
    case $M(\Sigma)(m)(eb)(st)$ **of**
        $\perp \rightarrow \perp,$
        $(st', tt) \rightarrow M(\Sigma)(m)(e_1)(st')$
        $(st', f\!f) \rightarrow M(\Sigma)(m)(e_2)(st')$
  end

- For assignments

$M(\Sigma)(m)(x := e)(st) =$
    case $M(\Sigma)(m)(e)(st)$ **of**
        $\perp \rightarrow \perp,$
        $(st', v') \rightarrow (st' \dagger [x \mapsto v'], skip)$
  end

- For the initialise expression

$$M(\Sigma)(m)(\textbf{initialise})(st) = (st_{init}, skip)$$

- For sequence expressions

$M(\Sigma)(m)(eu \; ; \; e_2)(st) =$
    case $M(\Sigma)(m)(eu)(st)$ **of**
        $\perp \rightarrow \perp,$
        $(st', v') \rightarrow M(\Sigma)(m)(e_2)(st')$
  end

3.7   The Satisfaction Relation

In the following, let $\Sigma = (A, OP, V)$ be an arbitrary signature.

The I_{RSL_I} satisfaction relation $\models_\Sigma$ is defined in terms of the meaning function $M(\Sigma)$ for Σ value expressions:

Definition 7. *For any Σ-model m and any Σ-sentence e*

$$m \models_\Sigma e$$

if and only if

$$\forall st \in Store_V \bullet M(\Sigma)(m)(e)(st) = (st, tt).$$

That is, a Σ-model m satisfies a Σ-sentence e, if and only if the effect of e in any store st is to return the truth value tt and leave the store unchanged. Note that the store will actually always be unchanged as it is required that e does not potentially write in variables.

For an applicative signature, the condition reduces to:

$$M(\Sigma)(m)(e)([]) = ([], tt).$$

3.8   Signature Morphisms

Let $\Sigma = (A, OP, V)$ and $\Sigma' = (A', OP', V')$ be signatures.

Definition 8. *An* RSL_I *signature morphism* $\sigma : \Sigma \to \Sigma'$ *is a triple* $\sigma = (\sigma_A, \sigma_{OP}, \sigma_V)$ *where*

- $\sigma_A \in \mathbf{dom}\ A \to \mathbf{dom}\ A'$ *is a mapping of abbreviation type names*
- $\sigma_{OP} \in \mathbf{dom}\ OP \to \mathbf{dom}\ OP'$ *is a mapping of value names*
- $\sigma_V \in \mathbf{dom}\ V \to \mathbf{dom}\ V'$ *is an injective[9] mapping of variable names*

such that the following conditions hold

1. $A'(\sigma_A(a)) = \sigma(A(a))$ *for all* $a \in \mathbf{dom}\ A$
2. $OP'(\sigma_{OP}(op)) = \sigma(OP(op))$ *for all* $op \in \mathbf{dom}\ OP$
3. $V'(\sigma_V(v)) = \sigma(V(v))$ *for all* $v \in \mathbf{dom}\ V$

where σ *is lifted to a function* $\sigma : T(\mathbf{dom}\ V) \to T(\mathbf{dom}\ V')$ *mapping* Σ *type expressions* t *to* Σ' *type expressions* $\sigma(t)$ *by replacing all variable names* $v \in \mathbf{dom}\ V$ *occurring in variable accesses in* t *with corresponding variable names* $\sigma_V(v) \in \mathbf{dom}\ V'$.

The three conditions mean that a type/value/variable name having type t in Σ can only be mapped to a type/value/variable name having type $\sigma(t)$ in Σ', so types are preserved. In other terms, the following diagrams must commute:

$$
\begin{array}{ccc}
\mathbf{dom}\ A & \xrightarrow{\ \sigma_A\ } & \mathbf{dom}\ A' \\
\downarrow{\scriptstyle A} & & \downarrow{\scriptstyle A'} \\
T(\mathbf{dom}\ V) & \xrightarrow{\ \sigma\ } & T(\mathbf{dom}\ V')
\end{array}
$$

$$
\begin{array}{ccc}
\mathbf{dom}\ OP & \xrightarrow{\ \sigma_{OP}\ } & \mathbf{dom}\ OP' \\
\downarrow{\scriptstyle OP} & & \downarrow{\scriptstyle OP'} \\
T(\mathbf{dom}\ V) & \xrightarrow{\ \sigma\ } & T(\mathbf{dom}\ V')
\end{array}
$$

$$
\begin{array}{ccc}
\mathbf{dom}\ V & \xrightarrow{\ \sigma_V\ } & \mathbf{dom}\ V' \\
\downarrow{\scriptstyle V} & & \downarrow{\scriptstyle V'} \\
T(\emptyset) & \xrightarrow{\ \sigma\ } & T(\emptyset)
\end{array}
$$

---

[9] This restriction is necessary in order to define the model reduct functor in Section 3.10.

3.9 Sentence Morphisms

Signature morphisms σ can be lifted to work on sentences:

Definition 9. *Let $\Sigma = (A, OP, V)$ and $\Sigma' = (A', OP', V')$ be signatures, and $\sigma = (\sigma_A, \sigma_{OP}, \sigma_V) : \Sigma \to \Sigma'$ a signature morphism. $Sen(\sigma) : Sen(\Sigma) \to Sen(\Sigma')$ is defined to be the function translating Σ-sentences into Σ'-sentences by replacing occurrences of value names and variable names as prescribed by σ_{OP}, and σ_V, respectively, and furthermore for quantified expressions $\forall id : t \bullet eb$, the constituent id and all free occurrences of id in eb must be replaced with an identifier $id^\bullet \in Id$ which does not occur in $\mathbf{dom}\ A' \cup \mathbf{dom}\ V' \cup \mathbf{dom}\ OP'$ in order to avoid unintended name clashes in the translated version of eb.*

3.10 Model Reduct Functor

In the following, let $\Sigma = (A, OP, V)$ and $\Sigma' = (A', OP', V')$ be arbitrary signatures, and let $\sigma = (\sigma_A, \sigma_{OP}, \sigma_V) : \Sigma \to \Sigma'$ be an arbitrary signature morphism.

In this section we are going to define the model reduct functor for the I_{RSL_I} institution. In order to do that we first need to define some auxiliary constructions lifting signature morphisms to functions that can make conversions between Σ-stores and Σ'-stores, and between Σ-values and Σ'-values.

For later use, we introduce the following lemmas.

Lemma 1. $Value_{\sigma(t)} = Value_t$ for $t \in T(\emptyset)$.

Proof. The lemma follows from the fact that $\sigma(t) = t$ for $t \in T(\emptyset)$.

Lemma 2. $st(v) \in Value_{V'(\sigma_V(v))}$ for $st \in Store(\Sigma)_{vs}$, $v \in vs$ and $vs \subseteq \mathbf{dom}\ V$.

Proof. $st(v) \in Value_{V(v)}$ by the Σ-stores definition in Section 3.3, $Value_{V(v)} = Value_{\sigma(V(v))}$ by Lemma 1 and the assumption $V(v) \in T(\emptyset)$, and $Value_{\sigma(V(v))} = Value_{V'(\sigma_V(v))}$ by condition 3 in Definition 8.

In the following, for any $vs \subseteq \mathbf{dom}\ V$, let $\sigma_V(vs)$ denote $\{\sigma_V(v) | v \in vs\}$.

First for any $vs \subseteq \mathbf{dom}\ V$, we lift the signature morphism σ to a function σ_{vs} translating Σ-stores to Σ'-stores, and we define an inverse function σ_{vs}^{-1} too:

Definition 10. $\sigma_{vs} : Store(\Sigma)_{vs} \to Store(\Sigma')_{\sigma_V(vs)}$ *is the function defined by* $\sigma_{vs}(st) = [\sigma_V(v) \mapsto st(v) | v \in \mathbf{dom}\ st]$ *for* $st \in Store(\Sigma)_{vs}$

This definition is well-formed as σ_V is injective and $st(v) \in Value_{V'(\sigma_V(v))}$. The first follows from Definition 8 and the latter follows from Lemma 2.

Definition 11. $\sigma_{vs}^{-1} : Store(\Sigma')_{\sigma_V(vs)} \to Store(\Sigma)_{vs}$ *is the function defined by* $\sigma_{vs}^{-1}(st') = [v \mapsto st'(\sigma_V(v)) | v \in vs]$ *for* $st' \in Store(\Sigma')_{\sigma_V(vs)}$

This definition is well-formed as one can in a similar way prove that $st'(\sigma_V(v)) \in Value_{V(v)}$.

We now lift the signature morphism σ to a family of functions translating Σ values to Σ' values: $\sigma = (\sigma_t)_{t \in T(\mathbf{dom}\ V)}$, where $\sigma_t : Value_t \rightarrow Value_{\sigma(t)}$, and we define an inverse function $\sigma^{-1} = (\sigma_t^{-1})_{t \in T(\mathbf{dom}\ V)}$, where $\sigma_t^{-1} : Value_{\sigma(t)} \rightarrow Value_t$.

Definition 12. *The functions $\sigma_t : Value_t \rightarrow Value_{\sigma(t)}$ and $\sigma_t^{-1} : Value_{\sigma(t)} \rightarrow Value_t$ are defined for $t \in T(\mathbf{dom}\ V)$ as follows:*

- *For basic types t **Char**, **Bool**, **Int**, **Real**, and **Unit**, σ_t and σ_t^{-1} are the identity functions. (This is possible due to the property stated in Lemma 1.)*
- *For composite types t, $\sigma_t(v)$ and $\sigma_t^{-1}(v')$ are defined by recursively applying σ and σ^{-1} to sub-values of v an v', respectively. For instance, $\sigma_{t_1 \times t_2}((v_1, v_2)) = (\sigma_{t_1}(v_1), \sigma_{t_2}(v_2))$ for $v_1 \in Value_{t_1}$ and $v_2 \in Value_{t_2}$.*
- *For function types $t = t_1 \xrightarrow{\sim} \mathbf{read}\ rs\ \mathbf{write}\ ws\ t_2$, $\sigma_t(f)$, where $f \in Value_t$, and $\sigma_t^{-1}(f')$, where $f' \in Value_{\sigma(t)}$ and $\sigma(t) = t_1' \xrightarrow{\sim} \mathbf{read}\ rs'\ \mathbf{write}\ ws'\ t_2'$, are defined as follows:*

$$\sigma_t(f) =$$
$$\lambda\ v' \in\ Value_{t_1'}\ \bullet$$
$$\lambda\ st' \in Store_{rs'}\ \bullet$$
$$\mathbf{case}\ f(\sigma_{t_1}^{-1}(v'))(\sigma_{rs}^{-1}(st'))\ \mathbf{of}$$
$$\bot \rightarrow \bot,$$
$$(st,\ v) \rightarrow (\sigma_{ws}(st)\ ,\ \sigma_{t_2}(v))$$
$$\mathbf{end}$$

$$\sigma_t^{-1}(f) =$$
$$\lambda\ v \in\ Value_{t_1}\ \bullet$$
$$\lambda\ st \in Store_{rs}\ \bullet$$
$$\mathbf{case}\ f'(\sigma_{t_1}(v))(\sigma_{rs}(st))\ \mathbf{of}$$
$$\bot \rightarrow \bot,$$
$$(st',\ v') \rightarrow (\sigma_{ws}^{-1}(st')\ ,\ \sigma_{t_2}^{-1}(v'))$$
$$\mathbf{end}$$

From the definition it can be seen that for applicative types $t \in T(\emptyset)$, the functions are just the identities. If t is an imperative function type (i.e. the function type has a non empty variable access description), then σ_t^{-1} convert function values f' of type $\sigma(t)$ to a corresponding function value f of type t. f behaves like f', except that it accesses a variable x whenever f' accesses variable $\sigma_V(x)$.

Now we are ready to define the model reduct functor.

Definition 13. *Let $\Sigma = (A, OP, V)$ and $\Sigma' = (A', OP', V')$ be signatures, and let $\sigma : \Sigma \rightarrow \Sigma'$ be a signature morphism. The model reduct functor $Mod(\sigma) : Mod(\Sigma') \rightarrow Mod(\Sigma)$ is defined to*

- *map each Σ'-model $m' = (m_A', m_{OP}', st_{init}')$ in $Mod(\Sigma')$ to a Σ-model $m = (m_A, m_{OP}, st_{init})$ where*
  - *m_A is uniquely determined by the signature Σ, cf. Definition 5.*

- $m_{OP}(op) = \sigma_{OP(op)}^{-1}(m'_{OP}(\sigma_{OP}(op)))$ *for* $op \in \mathbf{dom}\ OP$, *where* $\sigma_{OP(op)}^{-1}$ *is defined by Definition 12.*
- $st_{init}(v) = st'_{init}(\sigma_V(v))$ *for all* $v \in \mathbf{dom}\ V$, *(i.e.* $st_{init} = \sigma_{\mathbf{dom}\ V}^{-1}(st'_{init})$, *where* $\sigma_{\mathbf{dom}\ V}^{-1}$ *is the function defined in Definition 11).*
- *and to map each morphism* $id_{m'}$ *(for* $m' \in |Mod(\Sigma')|$*) in* $Mod(\Sigma')$ *to a morphism* $Mod(\sigma)(id_{m'}) = id_{Mod(\Sigma')(m')}$ *in* $Mod(\Sigma)$.

Above the application $\sigma_{OP(op)}^{-1}(m'_{OP}(\sigma_{OP}(op)))$ is well-formed, as the argument $m'_{OP}(\sigma_{OP}(op)) \in M(OP'(\sigma_{OP}(op))) = Value_{OP'(\sigma_{OP}(op))} = Value_{\sigma(OP(op))}$, (by Definition 5, by the definition of M in Section 3.4, and by Definition 8). The value $\sigma_{OP(op)}^{-1}(m'_{OP}(\sigma_{OP}(op))) \in Value_{OP(op)} = M(Op(op))$ (by Definition 12 and by the definition of M in Section 3.4) and can therefore be used for $m_{OP}(op)$.

3.11 Satisfaction Condition and the I_{RSL_I} Institution

The following proposition states that satisfaction is invariant with respect to changes of signatures.

Proposition 1. *Satisfaction condition: For all signatures* Σ *and* Σ', *signature morphisms* $\sigma : \Sigma \to \Sigma'$, Σ'*-models* m', *and* Σ*-sentences* e:

$$m' \models_{\Sigma'} Sen(\sigma)(e) \qquad iff \qquad Mod(\sigma)(m') \models_{\Sigma} e$$

Proof. It is straightforward to prove the proposition by induction over the structure of e.

To sum up, the I_{RSL_I} institution is defined as follows.

Definition 14. *The* I_{RSL_I} *institution is a quadruple* $(Sign, Sen, Mod, \models)$ *where*

- *Sign is a category of signatures and signature morphisms as defined in Definitions 2 and 8, respectively.*
- $Sen : Sign \to Set$ *is the functor defined by Definitions 4 and 9, respectively.*
- $Mod : Sign \to Cat^{op}$ *is the functor that maps each signature* Σ *in* $Sign$ *to the category* $Mod(\Sigma)$ *defined in Definition 6, and maps each signature morphism* $\sigma : \Sigma \to \Sigma'$ *in* $Sign$ *to the reduct functor* $Mod(\sigma) : Mod(\Sigma') \to Mod(\Sigma)$ *defined in Definition 13.*
- *For each* $\Sigma \in |Sign|$, $\models_{\Sigma} \subseteq |Mod(\Sigma)| \times Sen(\Sigma)$ *is the satisfaction relation defined in Definition 7.*

The required satisfaction condition (see Definition 15) holds for I_{RSL_I} due to Proposition 1 and so the above definition of I_{RSL_I} yields an institution.

4 Conclusion

In this section we summarise achievements, related work and future work.

4.1   Achievements

The contribution of the work reported in this paper is the provision of an institution for an imperative subset, RSL_I, of RSL, and a description of the principles for defining a semantics of the subset in terms of that institution.

4.2   Related Work

Compared with the original semantics[12] of RSL, our new semantics is more elegant and easy to understand as simpler semantic domains are used (this is possible as we only consider a subset of the full language) and a clear structure is provided by the institutional setting. Moreover, an advantage of defining the semantics in an institutional way is the institution-independent concepts and results that then come for free.

Our RSL_I subset extends the mRSL subset in [10,11], by allowing variable declarations, explicit function definitions, more type expressions, and more value expressions, but we have removed sort declarations.

Co-algebraic approaches have been suggested for the semantics of state-based specifications, but these are based on terminal semantics, while for RSL we need loose semantics. An observational logic suited for state-based systems specifications having loose semantics has been suggested in [8], but the observational approach does not fit the original semantics of RSL. In [1] a state-based extension of CASL has been suggested. Specifications in this extension also have loose semantics, but the specification approach differs in several ways from ours. For instance, the state-as-algebra approach of Gurevich is used to specify the possible states of a system, while we use explicit state variables, and also a syntactic and semantic distinction between applicative functions (called static functions), state dependent functions and state-changing functions (called procedures) is made, while we have a unified syntactic and semantic integration of such functions.

4.3   Future Work

It is planned to extend the considered RSL subset and adapt the institution for that.

An obvious extension would be to allow sort declarations and to allow sorts in type expressions. The adaption of the institution for that should be done as for the applicative subset mRSL in [10,11].

It could also be nice to allow subtype expressions in the type expressions of abbreviation type definitions (subtype expressions in value expressions and value declarations can be expanded away as shorthands for constructs without subtype expressions). To allow subtype expressions in type expressions would at least mean that the meaning function for type expressions should be changed.

It could be interesting to loosen the second condition in Definition 8 for signature morphisms to allow $OP'(\sigma_{OP}(op))$ to have variable access descriptions that are subsets of the corresponding ones in $\sigma(OP(op))$. This is possible, but will complicate the definition of the model reduct function in Definition 13 considerably. Similarly, one could add suitable sub-typing rules to the typing rules in Fig. 3 loosening the type requirements for value expressions to allow type coercions from function types to function types allowing more variable accesses. The latter would also imply that the meaning function for expressions should be modified to include application of coercion functions at places where type coercions would be allowed.

One could also allow variables to have types referring to variables, as long as there are no cyclic self references. Apart from changing the definition of signatures accordingly, it would require a change in the definitions of the auxiliary functions in Definitions 10–11 for making conversions (wrt. a given signature morphism $\sigma : \Sigma \to \Sigma'$) between Σ-stores and Σ'-stores.

One could also take a further step to consider a kernel for full RSL. Including the concurrency would mean that the semantics domains would be considerably more complicated.

For RAISE, a transformation of applicative specifications into imperative specifications have been defined [9]. We plan to use the framework of institutions to define a formal refinement relation between applicative and imperative RSL specifications and prove that the defined transformation maps applicative specifications into refinements of them.

Acknowledgements. I would like to thank Morten P. Lindegaard for great discussions and comments to an earlier version of this paper, Chris George and Jan Storbank Pedersen for helpful discussions on the typing rules for RSL, and Hubert Baumeister for interesting discussions on the differences between his approach to state-based specifications in [1] and my approach. Finally, I would like to thank the anonymous reviewers for useful comments.

The diagrams in this paper were created using Paul Taylor's diagrams package for drawing diagrams.

References

1. Baumeister, H., Zamulin, A.V.: State-Based Extension of CASL. In: Grieskamp, W., Santen, T., Stoddart, B. (eds.) IFM 2000. LNCS, vol. 1945, pp. 3–24. Springer, Heidelberg (2000)
2. Bolignano, D., Debabi, M.: Higher Order Communicating Processes with Value-passing, Assignment and Return of Results. In: Ibaraki, T., Iwama, K., Yamashita, M., Inagaki, Y., Nishizeki, T. (eds.) ISAAC 1992. LNCS, vol. 650, pp. 319–331. Springer, Heidelberg (1992)
3. Clavel, M., Durán, F., Eker, S., Lincoln, P., Martí-Oliet, N., Meseguer, J., Talcott, C.: All About Maude - A High-Performance Logical Framework. LNCS, vol. 4350. Springer, Heidelberg (2007)
4. Diaconescu, R., Futatsugi, K.: CafeOBJ Report: The Language, Proof Techniques, and Methodologies for Object-Oriented Algebraic Specification. AMAST Series in Computing. World Scientific Publishing (1998)
5. Diaconescu, R., Futatsugi, K., Ogata, K.: CafeOBJ: Logical Foundations and Methodologies. Computing and Informatics 22, 257–283 (2003)

6. Fitzgerald, J., Larsen, P.G.: Modelling Systems: Practical Tools and Techniques for Software Development, 2nd edn. Cambridge University Press (2009)
7. Goguen, J.A., Burstall, R.M.: Institutions: Abstract Model Theory for Specification and Programming. Logic of Programs 1983 39, 95–146 (1992); Predecessor in: LNCS vol. 164, pp. 221–256 (1984)
8. Hennicker, R., Bidoit, M.: Observational Logic. In: Haeberer, A.M. (ed.) AMAST 1998. LNCS, vol. 1548, pp. 263–277. Springer, Heidelberg (1998)
9. Jørgensen, T.D.: Transformation of Applicative Specifications into Imperative Specifications. IMM-Thesis-2005-30, Informatics and Mathematical Modelling. Technical University of Denmark, DTU, Richard Petersens Plads, Building 321, DK-2800 Kgs. Lyngby, Supervised by Associate Professor. Ph.D. Anne E. Haxthausen and Associate Professor Hans Bruun (2004)
10. Lindegaard, M.P.: Proof Support for RAISE – by a Reuse Approach Based on Institutions. IMM-PHD-2004-132, Informatics and Mathematical Modelling. Technical University of Denmark, DTU, Richard Petersens Plads, Building 321, DK-2800 Kgs. Lyngby, Supervised by Assoc. Prof. Anne E. Haxthausen (2004)
11. Lindegaard, M.P., Haxthausen, A.E.: Proof Support for RAISE – by a Reuse Approach based on Institutions. In: Rattray, C., Maharaj, S., Shankland, C. (eds.) AMAST 2004. LNCS, vol. 3116, pp. 319–333. Springer, Heidelberg (2004)
12. Milne, R.E.: Semantic Foundations of RSL. Technical Report RAISE/CRI/DOC/4/V1, CRI A/S (1990)
13. Mossakowski, T., Haxthausen, A., Sannella, D., Tarlecki, A.: CASL, the Common Algebraic Specification Language: Semantics and proof theory. Computing and Informatics 22(3-4), 285–322 (2003)
14. Mosses, P.D. (ed.): CASL Reference Manual. LNCS, vol. 2960. Springer, Heidelberg (2004)
15. The RAISE Language Group. The RAISE Specification Language. The BCS Practitioners Series. Prentice Hall Int. (1992)
16. The RAISE Method Group. The RAISE Development Method. The BCS Practitioners Series. Prentice Hall Int. (1995)

A   Formal Background

A.1   Notation

This section summarises some of the basic meta notation used for describing the RSL_I institution.

For (possibly infinite) sets $S, S_1, \ldots, S_n$, S-**infset** denotes the power set of S, i.e. the set of all (possibly infinite) subsets of S, S^ω denotes the set of all (possibly infinite) lists (sequences) with elements in S, $S_1 \times \ldots \times S_n$ denotes the set of n-tuples $(v_1, \ldots, v_n)$ where the $v_i \in S_i$ for $i = 1, \ldots, n$, $S_1 \to S_2$ denotes the set of total functions from S_1 to S_2, $S_1 \overset{\sim}{\to} S_2$ denotes the set of potentially partial functions from S_1 to S_2, and $S_1 \overrightarrow{m} S_2$ denotes the set of finite maps from S_1 to S_2, i.e. the set of total functions from finite subsets of S_1 to S_2.

For sets we use standard notation like $\cup$ for the union operation and $\emptyset$ for the empty set.

For maps m, **dom** m denotes the domain of m. For maps $m, m' \in S_1 \overrightarrow{m} S_2$, $m \dagger m'$ (m overwritten by m') denotes the map m'' for which

dom $m'' =$ **dom** $m \cup$ **dom** m'
$m''(x) = m'(x)$ for $x \in$ **dom** m'
$m''(x) = m(x)$ for $x \in$ **dom** $m \wedge x \notin$ **dom** m'

and for maps $m \in S_1 \xrightarrow{m} S_2$ and a subset s of S_1, m/s (m restricted to s) denotes the map m' for which

dom $m' = s \cap$ **dom** m
$m'(x) = m(x)$ for $x \in$ **dom** m'

and $m \setminus s$ (m restricted by s) denotes the map m' for which

dom $m' = ($**dom** $m) \setminus s$
$m'(x) = m(x)$ for $x \in$ **dom** m'

A.2   Institutions

This section presents the definition of the concept of *institutions* [7] that formalises the informal notion of a logical system. The definition is made using *category theory*, and for a category C, its collection of objects will be denoted by $|C|$.

Definition 15. *An* institution I *is a quadruple* $(Sign, Sen, Mod, \models)$ *where*

- *Sign is a category of signatures and signature morphisms*
- *Sen : Sign $\to$ Set is a functor giving, for each signature Σ, a set of sentences $Sen(\Sigma)$ over the signature, and for each signature morphism $\sigma : \Sigma \to \Sigma'$, a sentence translation map $Sen(\sigma) : Sen(\Sigma) \to Sen(\Sigma')$, where $Sen(\sigma)(e)$ is often written $\sigma(e)$,*
- *Mod : Sign $\to$ Cat^{op} is a functor that maps each signature Σ to the category of models $Mod(\Sigma)$ over the signature, and for each signature morphism $\sigma : \Sigma \to \Sigma'$, a reduct functor $Mod(\sigma) : Mod(\Sigma') \to Mod(\Sigma)$, where $Mod(\sigma)(m')$ is often written $m'|_\sigma$,*
- *$\models_\Sigma \subseteq |Mod(\Sigma)| \times Sen(\Sigma)$ is a satisfaction relation for each $\Sigma \in |Sign|$*

so that
$$m' \models_{\Sigma'} Sen(\sigma)(e) \qquad iff \qquad Mod(\sigma)(m') \models_\Sigma e$$
for each $\sigma : \Sigma \to \Sigma'$ in Sign, $m' \in |Mod(\Sigma')|$, and $e \in Sen(\Sigma)$. This requirement is known as the satisfaction condition.

8*k*-ary Grid Graph Models of Tabular Forms

Takeo Yaku[1], Koichi Anada[2], Koushi Anzai[3], Shinji Koka[4],
Youzou Miyadera[5], and Kensei Tsuchida[6]

[1] Dept. Information Science
Nihon University
Tokyo, Japan
yaku.takeo@nihon-u.ac.jp
[2] Waseda Research Institute for Science and Engineering
Waseda University
Tokyo, Japan
anada-koichi@waseda.jp
[3] Dept. Economics
Kanto Gakuen University
Gunma, Japan
kanzai@kanto-gakuen.ac.jp
[4] College of Humanities and Sciences
Nihon University
Tokyo, Japan
koka.shinji@yakulab.net
[5] Div. Natural Science
Tokyo Gakugei University
Tokyo, Japan
miyadera@u-gakugei.ac.jp
[6] Dept. Information Sciences and Arts
Toyo University
Kawagoe, Japan
kensei@toyo.jp

Abstract. Tabular forms are commonly used in software. Those tabular forms
are represented as rectangular dissections. In rectangular dissections, ruled line
oriented operations such as cell merge, line and column operations are often
used. With respect to ruled line oriented operations, 8*k*-ary grid graphs have
been introduced as models of rectangular dissections that provide fast algorithms. This paper surveys octal and hexa-decimal grid graph models of rectangular dissections. First, octal grids, called octgrids, for single layer rectangular
dissections and related algorithms are introduced. Next, hexa-decimal grid
graphs for multiple layer rectangular dissections, called hexadeci-grids, and related algorithms are introduced. Furthermore, tetraicosa-grid graphs for rectangular solid dissections for CG applications, called tetraicosa-grids and related
algorithms are introduced.

Keywords: modeling of spreadsheets, rectangular dissections, rectangular
piped dissections, ruled line oriented transformations.

S. Iida, J. Meseguer, and K. Ogata (Eds.): Futatsugi Festschrift, LNCS 8373, pp. 465–477, 2014.
© Springer-Verlag Berlin Heidelberg 2014

1   Introduction

Tabular forms are widely used in user interfaces of visual languages (see e.g., [4]). Among them are tables in document processing, sheets in spread sheet processing, land forms in GIS and raster data in CG. However, it is known that you sometimes get unexpected results in tabular processing by transformation commands such as cell/row/column insertion/deletion for tabular forms. For example, if you insert a row or a column for some heterogeneous tabular form, you will sometimes find unexpected cells in unexpected locations. Those systems also often require rather long computation time for editing. Accordingly, reliable and efficient models of tabular forms are required.

We note that in rectangular dissections, ruled line oriented operations such as cell merge, line and column operations are often used. Thus, this paper deals with graph models of rectangular dissections with respect to ruled line oriented operations.

J. L. Bentley introduced quadtrees in 1975 [1], and K. Kozminsky and E. Kinnen introduced properties of rectangular duals in 1985 [2] as data structures of rectangular dissections.

Yaku introduced in 2002 octal degree grid graph, later called octgrids, for ruled line preserving transformation of rectangular dissections. It was shown that octgrids are effective for ruled line oriented operations (e.g., [9]).

Octgrids are generalized to hexadecimal grids and to tetraicosa grids in order to manipulate multiple layer rectangular dissections and rectangular solid dissections.

This paper surveys $8k$-ary ($k = 1, 2, 3$) grid graph models of rectangular and rectangular solid dissections [15]. In Section II, octal grid graphs, called octgrids, for single layer rectangular dissections and related algorithms are introduced.

Next, in Section III, octgrids are generalized to the 2.5 dimension. Hexadecimal grid graphs for multiple layer rectangular dissections, called hexadeci-grids, and related algorithms are introduced. We note that transformation operations over tabular forms, stratum maps and 2.5D facility layouts of buildings often preserve ruled lines. Furthermore, in Section IV, we apply above results to CG data structures and tetraicosa-grid graphs for rectangular solid dissections, called tetraicosa-grids, and related algorithms are introduced.

2   Octal Grid Graphs for the Single Layer Rectangular Dissections [6, 7, 10, 11]

In [6], Yaku introduced "octgrids" based on octal grid graphs for heterogeneous rectangular dissections such as Figure 1 (left). And it was shown that the octgrid model provides algorithms that run faster than well-known data structures such as rectangular duals (e.g. [7]).

We introduce octal degree heterogeneous grid graphs (see e.g. [7]) called *octgrids*, that represent heterogeneous rectangular dissections, and provide efficient algorithms for mesh preserving transformation of CG objects. We first provide the definition of the octgrids.

2.1   Octgrids

The "octgrid" for a rectangular dissection D is defined informally as follows: Each node in "octgrid" corresponds to a rectangle (cell) in D. Two nearest nodes are connected if corresponding two cells in D have ruled line in common as in Figure 1. Figure 1 shows a rectangular dissection and the corresponding "octgrid".

Definition 2.1

Let D be a rectangular dissection. An octgrid $G = (V_D, L, E_D, A_D, \alpha_D)$ for D is a multiple edge undirected grid graph, where V_D is identified as the set of   rectangles in D. $L = \{enw, esw, eew, eww\}$, E_D $(E_D \subseteq V_D \times L \times V_D)$ is a set of undirected *labeled* edges of V_D of the form $[v_c, l, v_d]$, where v_c and v_d are in V_D and l is in L. E_D is defined by the following **Rules** 1-4, $A_D = R^4$ and $\alpha_D : V_D \to R^4$ are defined for $v_c \in V_D$ by $\alpha_D = (nw(c), sw(c), ew(c), ww(c))$. Function $nw(c), sw(c), ew(c)$ and $ww(c)$ are defined for v_c which corresponds to a rectangle in D by the north wall location, the south wall location, the east wall location and the west wall location of the rectangle respectively.

Rule 1. If $nw(c) = nw(d)$, that is, c and d have the equal north wall, and there is no cell between c and d which have the equal north wall, then $[v_c, enw, v_d]$ is in E_D and $\lambda_D = enw$. In this case $[v_c, enw, v_d]$ is called a *north wall edge*.

Rule 2. If $sw(c) = sw(d)$, that is, c and d have the equal south wall, and there is no cell between c and d which have the equal south wall, then $[v_c, esw, v_d]$ is in E_D and $\lambda_D = esw$. In this case $[v_c, esw, v_d]$ is called a *south wall edge*.

Rule 3. If $ew(c) = ew(d)$, that is, c and d have the equal east wall, and there is no cell between c and d which have the equal east wall, then $[v_c, eew, v_d]$ is in E_D and $\lambda_D = eew$. In this case $[v_c, eew, v_d]$ is called an *east wall edge*.

Rule 4. If $ww(c) = ww(d)$, that is, c and d have the equal west wall, and there is no cell between c and d which have the equal west wall, then $[v_c, eww, v_d]$ is in E_D and $\lambda_D = eww$. In this case $[v_c, eww, v_d]$ is called a *west wall edge*.

Figure 1 shows a heterogeneous rectangular dissections and its corresponding octgrid. Two nodes are linked if they are nearest and have a ruled line in common. We note that the inner nodes have eight edges and the degrees of nodes are at most 8. Rectangular dissections are surrounded by "perimeter cells" in this paper, for convenience of algorithms.

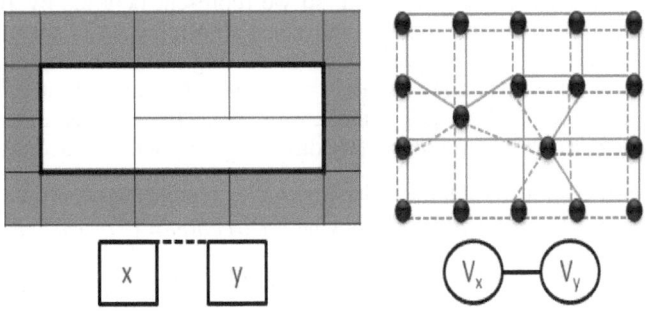

Fig. 1. A rectangular dissection D (left) and its corresponding octgrid G_D (right)

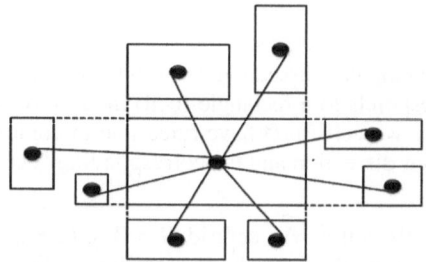

Fig. 2. Links around a node in an octgrid

Figure 3 shows another example of rectangular dissections and the corresponding octgrid.

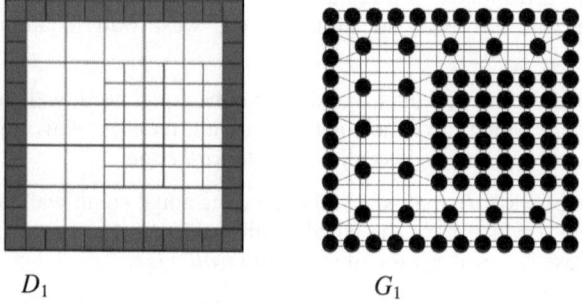

D_1 G_1

Fig. 3. A rectangular dissection D_1 and the corresponding octrid G_1

We have the following proposition.

Proposition 2.1. *Let D be a rectangular dissection with width n and depth m, E_D be the edges in the octgrid G_D for D, and k be the number of inner cells of D. The, the following equation holds*:

$$2|E_D| = 6(2n\text{-}4) + 6(2m\text{-}4) + 8k + 16.$$

2.2   Algorithms [7]

An octgrid is an undirected grid graph, so we represent octgrids by 16-ary directed grid graphs as follows. After that, we introduce algorithms. And we introduce "*Forward*" and "*Backward*" because the actual processing becomes difficult if you do not know the direction of the edges. By this, each cell refers to each other with 8 edges. Therefore, each cell has 16 edges at most. This is the 16-ary directed grid graph. The 32-ary directed grid graph and the 48-ary directed grid graph are also the same.

The octgrid G_D for a rectangular dissection D is represented by 16-ary directed grid graph. $G_{DD} = (V_D, L, Direction, A, E_{DD})$, where $Direction = \{Forward, Backward\}$,

$E_{DD} \subseteq V_D \times L \times Direction \times V_D$ is defined as follows.

If a undirected edge [s, edge, t] is in E_D, then

(1) a directed edge(s, *edge*, *Forward*, t) is in E_{DD} ($s_x < t_x$)

and

(2) (s, *edge*, *Backward*, t) is in E_{DD} ($s_x \geqq t_x$),

for *edge* L_D.

Now, we introduce a cell unification algorithm.

ALGORITHM *CellUnification*8(G_D, v_x, v_y, G_F)
INPUT
> $G_D = (V_D, L, E_D, A_D, \alpha_D)$: an octgrid for a rectangular dissection D.
> v_x, v_y: adjacent nodes in G_D with $ww(x) = ww(y)$, $ew(x) = ew(y)$, and $sw(x) = nw(y)$.

OUTPUT
> $G_F = (V_F, L, E_F, A_F, \alpha_F)$: the octgrid for the rectangular dissection F, where F is obtained from D by the unification of cells x and y into x.

METHOD
> 1. Change edges around v_x and v_y.
> 2. Delete edges around v_y.
> 3. Delete node v_y.

COMPLEXITY
> This algorithm runs in $O(1)$ time, since the numbers of links around   nodes are at most 8.

We show an algorithm that delete the northern side row from the focused cell. Following Figure 4 illustrates an example.

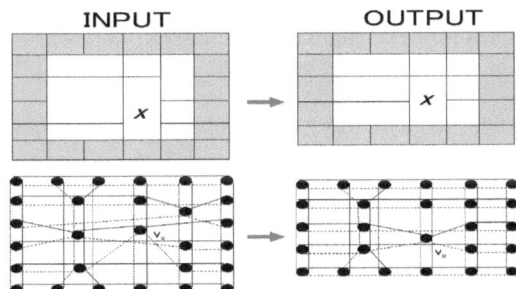

Fig. 4. Deletion of the northern side row at the focused cell

ALGORITHM *DeleteSingleRow*8(G_D, v_x, G_E)
INPUT
> G_D: An octgrid for a rectangular dissection D.
> v_x: The node (not in perimeters) in G_D for a focused cell x.

OUTPUT
> G_E: The octgrid deleted the northern side row of the cell v_x.

METHOD
> 1. Put the west side perimeter node linked with north wall edge to v_x, v_0.
> 2. Mark "N" to all nodes linked with north wall edge to v_0.

3. Delete inner node, which are marked "N" and linked with south wall edge to v_0.
4. Change north wall edge of the inner node linked to v_0.
5. Change south wall edge of the inner node linked to v_0.
6. Change north-south links of the east side perimeter node linked to v_0 and the links of v_0, and delete the two nodes with east-west edges.
7. Change the height by the height of the deleted row.

We construct an algorithm that delete all rows intersected to the focused cell. The following Figure 5 illustrates an example.

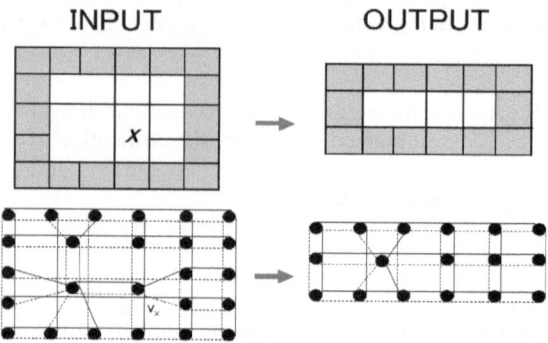

Fig. 5. Deletion of multiple rows intersected with the cell x

ALGORITHM *DeleteMultipleRows8(G_D, v_x, G_E)*
INPUT
  G_D: The octgrid for a rectangular dissection D.
  v_x: A node in G_D, which is not in perimeters at the north and the south ends.
OUTPUT
  G_E: The octgrid deleted with rows, the number of rows is equivalent to the height of v_x.
METHOD
  1. Put the west side perimeter node linked by south wall edge to v_x, v_0.
  2. Put the south side node adjacent to v_0, v_h.
  3. Put the west side perimeter node linked by north wall edge to v_x, v_i.
  4. Put the lower node adjacent to v_i, v_{i+1}.
  5. DeleteRow(G_D, v_x, G_E).
  6. Add 1 to i.
  7. If $sw(v_i) < sw(v_h)$ then return to Step 4.

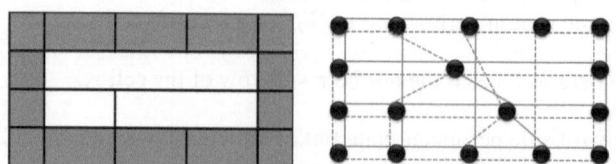

Fig. 6. A rectangular dissection and its corresponding octgrid

Cell unification algorithm runs in $O(1)$ time. From these properties, we obtain efficient resolution reduction algorithms that provide 3D maps with the appropriate resolution [10].

3   Hexadecimal Grid Graphs for the Multiple Layer Rectangular Dissections [10, 13, 15]

In this section, we consider *multiple layer rectangular dissections* with cells of heterogeneous sizes. The following Figure 7 shows an example of multiple layer rectangular dissection. Multiple layer rectangular dissections illustrate multiple page books of spread sheets.

We note that multiple layer rectangular dissections are effective tools to represent multiple page books in spreadsheets, facility layouts and stratum maps, for examples.

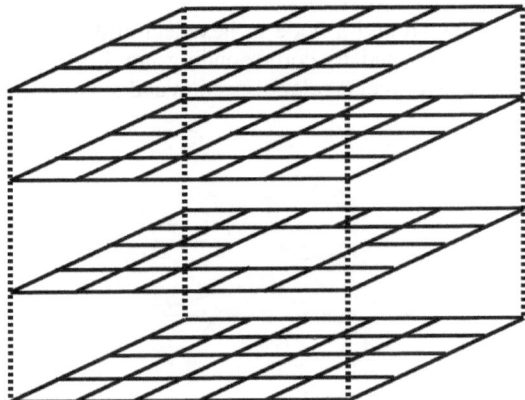

Fig. 7. An example of multiple layer rectangular dissections (two layers)

3.1   The Hexadeci-Grids

Next, we introduce hexadecimal grids.

Definition 3.1.
Let $D = (T, P, l)$ be a k-layered rectangular dissection. A h*exadeci-grid* $G_D = (V_D, L, E_D, A_D, \alpha_D)$ for D is a multi-edge undirected grid graph. We provide definitions of L, E_D, A_D, and α_D. First, we define the nodes V_D. We put a node corresponding to each cell.   Next, we define the labels L ($L = \{enw, esw, eew, eww, nec, nwc, sec, swc\}$). Next, we define the edges E_D. $E_D \subseteq V_D \times L \times V_D$ is the following set of undirected labeled edges of V_D of the form $[v_c, l, v_d]$, where v_c and v_d are in V_D and l is in L. (i) We define edges in E_D between nearest cells in D that have corner horizontally in common by **Rules 1 − 4** similarly to octgrids. (ii) We define edges in E_D between nearest cells in D that have corners vertically in common by the following rules.

Rule 5. It is assumed that cells c and d are located in the different layer. If $nec(c) = nec(d)$ and there is no cell between c and d which have the equal x - y coordinate of a northeastern, then $[v_c, nec, v_d]$ is in E_D. In this case, $[v_c, nec, v_d]$ is called *northeastern corner edge*.

Rule 6. It is assumed that cells c and d are located in the different layer. If $nwc(c) = nwc(d)$ and there is no cell between c and d which have the equal x - y coordinate of a northwestern, then $[v_c, nwc, v_d]$ is in E_D . In this case, $[v_c, nwc, v_d]$ is called *northwestern corner edge*.

Rule 7. It is assumed that cells c and d are located in the different layer. If $sec(c) = sec(d)$ and there is no cell between c and d which have the equal x - y coordinate of a southeastern, then $[v_c, sec, v_d]$ is in E_D. In this case, $[v_c, sec, v_d]$ is called *southeastern corner edge*.

Rule 8. It is assumed that cells c and d are located in the different layer. If $swc(c) = swc(d)$ and there is no cell between c and d which have the equal x - y coordinate of a southwestern, then $[v_c, swc, v_d]$ is in E_D. In this case, $[v_c, swc, v_d]$ is called *southwestern corner edge*.

$A_D = R^8$ and $\alpha_D\colon V_D \to R^8$ are defined for $v_c \in V_D$ by $\alpha_D = (nw(c), sw(c), ew(c), ww(c), nec(c), nwc(c), sec(c), swc(c))$.

Figure 8 shows links around a node in hexadeci-grid. Figure 9 shows a multiple layer rectangular dissection and its corresponding hexadeci-grid. Figure 10 shows a concept of the multiple layer rectangular dissection and a multiple page book.

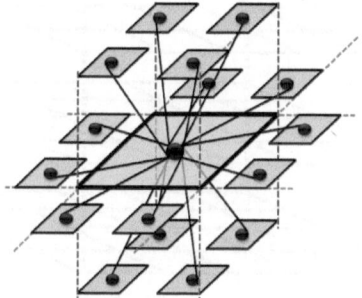

Fig. 8. Links around a node in a hexadecimal grid

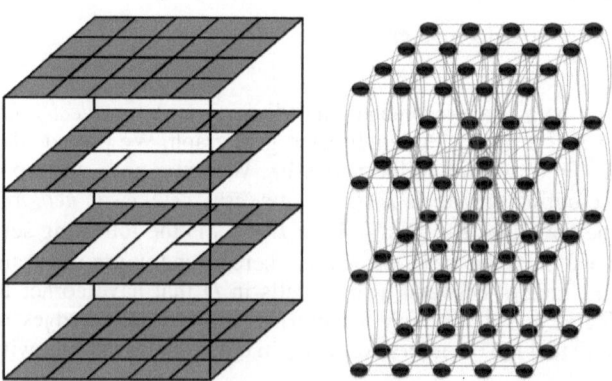

Fig. 9. A multiple layer rectangular dissection (left) and its corresponding hexadeci-grid (right)

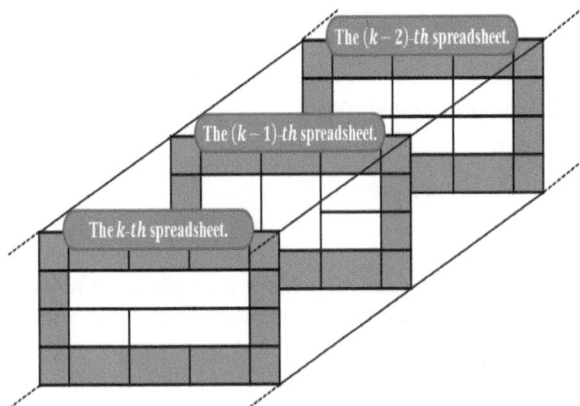

Fig. 10. A concept of multiple layer rectangular dissection of a multiple page book

3.2   Algorithms

This subsection introduces algorithms for hexadeci-grids. A hexadeci-grid G_D is represented by the following 32-ary directed grid graph. $G_{DD} = (V_D, L, Direction, A, E_{DD})$, where $Direction = \{Forward, Backward\}$.

$E_{DD} \subseteq V_D \times L \times Direction \times V_D$ is defined as follows.

If $[s, edge, t]$ is in E_D, then

(1) $(s, edge, Forward, t)$ is in E_{DD} $(s_x < t_x)$

and

(2) $(s, edge, Backward, t)$ is in E_{DD} $(s_x \geqq t_x)$,

for $edge$ L_D.

We modify *UnifyCells*8 and obtain a cell unification algorithm for hexadeci-grids.

ALGORITHM *CellUnification*16(G_D, v_x, v_y, G_F)
INPUT
    $G_D = (V_D, L, E_D, A_D, \alpha_D)$: a hexadeci-grid for a multiple   layer rectangular dissec-
                tion D.
    v_x, v_y: nodes in G_D with $ww(x) = ww(y)$, $ew(x) = ew(y)$, and $sw(x) = nw(y)$.
OUTPUT
    $G_F = (V_F, L, E_F, A_F, \alpha_F)$: the hexaeci-grid for the multiple layer rectangular dissec-
                tion D, where F is obtained from D by unify cells x and y
                into x.
METHOD
    1. Change edges of the horizontal direction around v_x and v_y.
        2. Delete edges of the horizontal direction around v_y.
        3. Change edges of the vertical direction around v_x and v_y.

4. Delete edges of the vertical direction around v_y.
5. Delete node v_y.

ALGORITHM *LayerDeletion*16(G_D, v_x, G_F)
INPUT
  $G_D = (V_D, L, E_D, A_D, \alpha_D)$: a hexadeci-grid for multiple layer rectangular dissection
                     D.
  v_x: a node in G_D.
OUTPUT
  $G_F = (V_F, L, E_F, A_F, \alpha_F)$: a Hexadeci-grid for multiple layer rectangular dissection
                     D, where F is obtained from D by delete k-th layer.
METHOD
  1. Delete edges of the horizontal direction around v_x.
  2. Delete edges of the vertical direction around v_x.
  3. Delete node v_x in G_D.
  4. Repeat 1~3 steps for all cells in G_D.

We have the following proposition.

Proposition 3.1. *Let D be a multiple layer rectangular dissection with width n, depth m, and layer l, E_D be the edges in the hexadeci-grid G_D for D, and k be the number of inner cells of D. The following equation holds*:

$$2|E_D| = 8 \times 8 + 12(n\text{-}2)(m\text{-}2) + 14(m\text{-}2)(l\text{-}2)$$
$$+ 14(l\text{-}2)(n\text{-}2) + 10(n\text{-}2) + 10(m\text{-}2) + 12(l\text{-}2) + 16k$$

4   Tetra-Icosa Grids for the Rectangular Solid Dissections [9]

Next, apply concepts of octgrids to CG data structures. We introduce a 24-ary grid graph representation for rectangular solid graphics.
    A *rectangular solid dissection* is a collection $D = \{S_1, S_2, ..., S_N\}$ of mutually disjoint rectangular solids, where $S_1 \cup S_2 \cup ... \cup S_N = D$.

Definition 4.1.
A *tetraicosa-grid* for D is an undirected labeled multi-edge grid graph $G_D = (V_D, L, E_D, A)$, defined as follows: (1) $V_D = \{v_s \mid s$ is in D; v_s corresponds to $s\}$ is a set of nodes, (2) $L = \{EquivalentUpwardNorthEastCornerPole,$ $EquivalentDownwardNorthEastCornerPole, ..., EquivalentBackwardFloorWe\text{-}stBeam\}$ ($|L| = 24$) is the set of *edge labels*, (3) E_D is a set of undirected labeled edges defined as follows; if s and t are the nearest solids in D such that s and t have an upper north beam in common, then [s, *EquivalentForwardCeilingNorthBeam*, t] is in E_D (Figure 11). Edges for other beams and corner poles are similarly defined.
    Figure 12 illustrates links around a node in a tetraicosa-grid. Furthermore, Figure 13 shows a rectangular solid dissection (left) and the corresponding tetraicosa-grid (right).

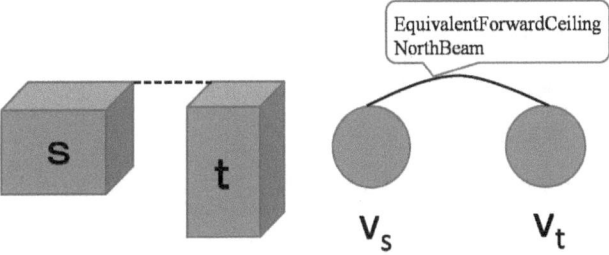

Fig. 11. Example of labels for Eedges

Figure 12 illustrates links around a node in a tetraicosa-grid. Furthermore, Figure 13 shows a rectangular solid dissection (left) and the corresponding tetraicosa-grid (right).

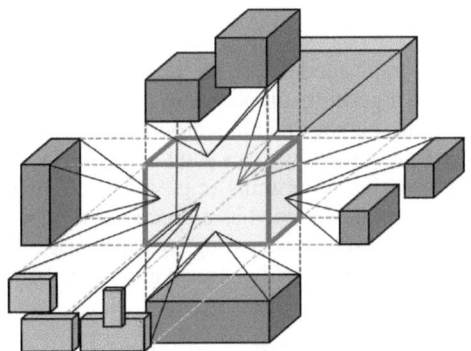

Fig. 12. Links around a node in a hexadecimal grid

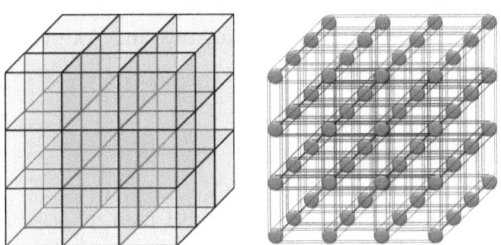

Fig. 13. A rectangular piped dissection (left) and its corresponding teraicose-grid (right)

Proposition 4.1. *Let D be a rectangular piped dissection with width k, depth l, and height m, E_D be the edges in the tetraicosa-grid G_D for D, and i be the number of inner voxels of D. The following equation holds*:

$$2|E_D| = 12 \times 8 + 16 \times 4(k\text{-}2) + 16 \times 4(l\text{-}2)$$
$$+ 16 \times 4(m\text{-}2) + 20 \times 2(k\text{-}2)(l\text{-}2)$$
$$+ 20 \times 2(k\text{-}2)(m\text{-}2) + 20 \times 2(l\text{-}2)(m\text{-}2) + 24i$$

G_D is represented by 48-ary directed grid graph $G_{DD} = (V_D, L, Direction, A_D, E_{DD})$, where $Direction = \{Forward, Back\text{-}ward\}$, as follows.

$E_{DD} \subseteq V_D \times L \times Direction \times V_D$ is defined as follows.

If $[s, edge, t]$ is in E_D, then

(1) $(s, edge, Forward, t)$ is in E_{DD} $(s_x < t_x)$

and

(2) $(s, edge, Backward, t)$ is in E_{DD} $(s_x \geqq t_x)$,

for $edge$ L_D.

Then, the similar $O(1)$ time voxel unification algorithm can be given as cell unification algorithms octgrids and in hexadeci-grids.

5   Conclusion

We surveyed $8k$-ary grid graph models for the rectangular and rectangular piped dissections. Cell unification algorithm of octgrids, hexadeci-grids and tetraicosa-grids runs in $O(1)$ time, since the number of links around a node is bounded by 8, 16, 24, respectively. From these properties, we can show that $8k$-ary grid graph models provide rapid ruled line preserving algorithms (e.g., [8, 9, 13, 14]). Data formats and processing systems have been developped as a successor of a program diagram system [3]. As future works, we consider processing systems (e.g., [7, 8, 12, 14], and a graph grammar that characterizes octgrids (see e.g., [5, 13, 16]).

Acknowledgment. The authors would like to thank Professors Kimio Sugita of Tokai University, Takaaki Goto of the University of Electro Communications, Tomokazu Arita of Obirin University, Tomoe Motohashi of Kanto Gakuin University and Goro Akagi of Kobe University for their valuable suggestions. They also thank Messrs. Kenshi Nomaki, Yuki Shindo, Shunichi Nakagawa and Akira Kureha of Nihon University, for their valuable suggestions.

References

1. Bentley, J.L.: Multidimensional binary search trees used for associative searching. Communications of the ACM 18(9), 509–517 (1975)
2. Kozminsky, K., Kinnen, E.: Rectangular Duals of Planar Graphs. Networks 16, 145–157 (1985)
3. Yaku, T., Futatsugi, K., Adachi, A., Moriya, E.: Hichart-A hierarchical flowchart description language. In: Proc. IEEE COMPSAC, vol. 11, pp. 157–163 (1987)
4. Burnett, M.M., Sheretov, A., Rothermel, G.: Scaling up a "What You See Is What You Test" Methodology to Spreadsheet Grids. In: Proc. VL, pp. 30–37 (1999)
5. Adachi, Y., Kobayashi, S., Tsuchida, K., Yaku, T.: An NCE Context-Sensitive Graph Grammar for Visual Design Languages. In: Proc. VL, pp. 228–235 (1999)

6. Yaku, T.: Representation of heterogeneous tessellation structures by graphs. Memoir of WAAP Meetings 108, 1–6 (2001), http://www.waap.gr.jp/waap-memoir/waap108/waap108_02-yaku/011201waap108tabl-e-rep-doc.pdf
7. Kirishima, T., Motohashi, T., Tsuchida, K., Yaku, T.: Table processing based on attribute graphs. In: Proc. 6th IASTED Internat. Conf. Software Engin. & Appli., pp. 131–136 (2002)
8. Arita, T., Kishira, S., Motohashi, T., Nomaki, K., Sugita, K., Tsuchida, K., Yaku, T.: Implementation of 24-ary grid representation for rectangular solid dissections. In: Proc. 4th GRAPP, pp. 103–106 (2009)
9. Koka, S., Anada, K., Nomaki, K., Shindo, Y., Yaku, T.: Row Manipulation in the Heterogeneous Tabular Forms with a Hexadecimal Grid Graph Model. In: Proc. ACM SAC, pp. 710–711 (2012)
10. Akagi, G., Anada, K., Koka, S., Nakayama, Y., Nomaki, K., Yaku, T.: A Resolution Reduction Method Multi-resolution Terrain Maps. In: SGIGRAPH 2012 Poster (2012) (to appear)
11. Yaku, T., Anada, K., Koka, S., Shindo, Y.: Kensei Tsuchida, Row Manipulation in the Heterogenous Tabular Forms with an Octal Grid Model. In: Proc. IEEE VL/HCC 2011, pp. 269–270 (2011)
12. Koka, S., Anada, K., Nomaki, K., Yaku, T.: Tabular Form Editing with a Hexadecimal Grid Graph Model. In: Proc. IEEE VL/HCC, pp. 253–254 (2011)
13. Shindo, Y., Anada, K., Anzai, K., Koka, S.: A Graph Grammar Model for Syntaxes of Financial Statements. In: Proc. IEEE VL/HCC, pp. 265–266 (2011)
14. Anada, K., Anzai, K., Koka, S., Yaku, T.: An Implementation of the 16-ary Grid Graphs for the Multiply Layered Rectangular Dissections. In: Proc. MSV 9, WORLDCOMP (2012), extended abstract
15. Yaku, T., Anzai, K., Anada, K., Koka, S.: 8k-ary Grid Graph Modeling of the Rectangular Meshes. In: Proc. MSV 9 (2012), extended abstract
16. Yaku, T., Anada, K., Anzai, K., Koka, S., Shimizu, M., Shindo, Y.: A Graph Grammar Model of Financial Statements with Heterogeneous Parts. In: Proc. MSV 9 (2012), extended abstract

Everlasting Challenges with the OBJ Language Family

Shin Nakajima*

National Institute of Informatics
Tokyo, Japan
nkjm@nii.ac.jp

Abstract. Algebraic specification languages of the OBJ family are quite flexible in providing adequate means by which to delineate software abstractions. Although originally developed in the late 1970s, these languages are applied to new problems that have arisen with emerging software-intensive systems. As an example of continuing efforts to tackle those problems, the present paper considers the application of the OBJ family language, specifically Realtime Maude, to model-based analysis of power consumption in Android smartphones. Hereby, it demonstrates that the language is powerful enough to be a basis for dealing with this new problem.

Keywords: Realtime Maude, Sampling Abstraction, Energy Bugs, Android Smartphone.

1 Introduction

Software is an enabler for innovation, and its frontier is expanding rapidly as a result of best practices in the marketplace. Despite the strong need for solid basis for safe and reliable software systems, the advancement of scientific grounds is always behind the rapid evolution of practices (cf. [27]). Software research is barely able to cope with the increased complexity of such systems. A key to understanding such problems is modeling at the right level of abstraction, without which system development is arduous.

Unambiguously delineating the software models requires concise notation or language for rigorous expression at an appropriate level of abstraction. Since the model characteristics are divergent, no language is universal, and languages are elaborated as new problems are encountered. Searching for such appropriate languages is often the most important task of scientists. For example, Sir Issac Newton, while formulating particle dynamics, introduced the concept of the point mass as an abstraction of apples and planets, and differential calculus as means by which to describe their essential properties (cf. [16]).

Formal methods or formal specification languages have their roots in the 1970s (cf. [25]). These languages are to software abstraction as differential calculus is

---

* Also affiliated with The Graduate University for Advanced Studies.

S. Iida, J. Meseguer, and K. Ogata (Eds.): Futatsugi Festschrift, LNCS 8373, pp. 478–493, 2014.

to Newtonian dynamics. Specifically, algebraic specification languages, which appeared in the late 1970s, are quite flexible in providing adequate abstractions, thanks to the property-oriented specification writing style [33]. Extensive research led to the development of the OBJ language family [14], which includes OBJ2 [12], Maude [9], and CafeOBJ [11]. These languages are applied to new problems that have arisen with emerging software-intensive systems. They include, even limited to my personal experience, object-oriented design [20][22], software architecture with mobility [22], multi-paradigm software modeling [21], and policies to govern user behavior [23]. Software technology is continuously evolving and new research areas, such as self-adaptive systems [13][17][24][29] and smartphones [1][28][31], are of great interest today.

As an example of continuing efforts to challenge new problems, the present paper focuses on energy bugs in Android smartphones [31], in which unexpected power consumption has become a major concern because of limited battery capacity. Although smartphones are compact and small, they are complex systems in which hardware components, the Linux operating system, the Android frameworks, and applications (*app*) are inter-related. All of these components have much impact on the power consumption, but their causal relationships remain unclear due to the complexity of the multi-layered architecture.

We herein describe the OBJ language approach, specifically Realtime Maude [30], to model-based analysis of power consumption in Android smartphones. It is true that much must be done before applying the proposed method to dealing with *ebugs* [31] in real-world Android applications. The reported approach, however, demonstrates that the language is powerful enough to deal with these new problems.

The paper is structured as follows. Section 2 describes the problem of energy bugs in smartphones, using the Wi-Fi component as a concrete example. Section 3 proposes a model-based approach using the power consumption automaton (PCA). Section 4 explains a method for the representation and analysis of PCA using Realtime Maude. Section 5 presents discussions and some remarks on future research directions. Section 6 summarizes research related to the power consumption problems, and conclusions are presented in Section 7.

2   Energy Bugs in Smartphones

2.1   Power Management in Android Smartphones

Power consumption of smartphone applications such as *Android apps* is a major concern because smartphones have batteries with limited power capacity. Some apps, although functionally correct, suffer from unexpected power consumption, which is referred to as an *energy bug (ebugs)* [31]. Debugging such ebugs currently makes use of the energy profiler (cf. [32]), which monitors the program execution at runtime to check whether power drains exist.

Figure 1 shows an overview of an Android smartphone with regard to power consumption. The Android framework together with the Linux kernel provides

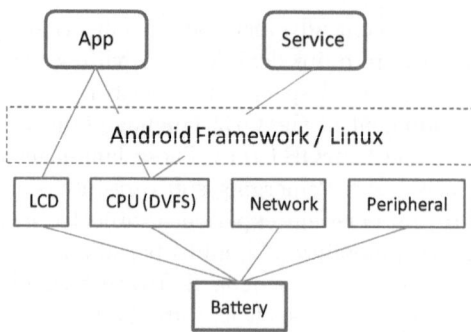

Fig. 1. Overview of an Android Smartphone

basic features to the application tasks, apps and services. Android apps are application processes that provide GUI to the user, whereas the Android service does not use a GUI and is a background process. They are multi-threaded programs. In addition, the application processes use other hardware components such as networks or peripherals, all of which consumes battery power.

The Android framework encapsulates the underlying components to allow programming tasks to be accessible. However, the framework is not transparent for application developers with regard to the precise power consumption behavior. The framework adapts an aggressive power saving strategy; the power control subsystem automatically forces the system to sleep when the user does not touch the screen for some period of time.

While adapting this aggressive strategy, the Android framework provides wake locks for power management. An app can request CPU resources through wake locks, and the CPU is kept awake while some active locks are in place. An acquired wake lock should have a matching release call. Otherwise, the wake lock is kept active even after the caller program is destroyed. Such improper uses of wake locks result in ebugs [31], which can, in principle, be eliminated in the early stages of development because these are design bugs.

2.2 Wi-Fi Subsystem

This section explains the Wi-Fi subsystem, which is used as a concrete example to illustrate the motivation and approach to addressing energy bugs in smartphones. Figure 2 is an example of a measured energy profile of a Wi-Fi client in Nexus One operating in the power save mode (PSM) [3]. The figure is taken from [18] and is modified slightly for illustrative purposes. We refer to the paper for the detailed measurement conditions.

The Wi-Fi client, or station (STA), is in the passive scan mode. The access point (AP) periodically sends beacon signals to notify the STA to start data transfer. Figure 2 shows that STA is in the Deep Sleep state, and then goes to the High Power state to send or receive various frames. STA occasionally stays in the Idle Listen state to see whether there are further frames to come. In the case

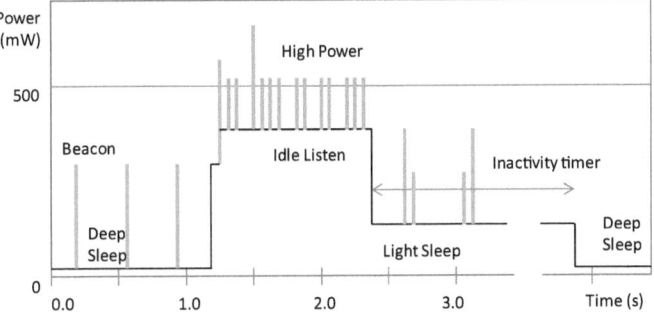

Fig. 2. Wi-Fi Energy Profile (Adapted from [18])

of data transfer, STA moves to the Light Sleep state if it detects a no-more-data flag. STA stays in this state for a while with the expectation that further data transfer will be occurring soon. It can respond to beacon signals more quickly in the Light Sleep state than in the Deep Sleep state because enough current is provided. Last, STA is forced into the Deep Sleep state by a time-out event of an inactivity timer.

The Wi-Fi subsystem, as well as the other hardware components, adopts the concept of wake locks for power management. `WifiManager` is the key library class to provide a method of controlling `WifiLock` [1], and allows an application process to keep the Wi-Fi radio awake. Section 4.3 will discuss this topic in detail.

2.3 Power Consumption Model

Let $F(t)$ be an energy consumption function of the graph in Figure 2. Then, the total power consumption $(P(T))$ from time 0 to time T is obtained by the accumulation, or the integral of $F(t)$.

$$P(T) \;=\; \int_0^T F(t)dt$$

As the above explanation using Figure 2 suggests, the states of STA are changed in both event-trigger (signal or frame) and time-trigger (periodic or timeout) manners. Such changes can be represented by a state-transition system, and the concept of the power state is introduced here. Figure 3 shows an example of a state-transition system of Wi-Fi STA operating in the PSM.

While $P(T)$ above is formulated as the integral of a function $F(t)$, it can be simplified if the power consumption is approximated by a linear function of time in each power state. Such an approximation can mostly reproduce the energy profile in Figure 2.

Let $P(t_S, t_E)^{PS}$ be the consumed power in the state PS from t_S to t_E such that $P(t_S, t_E)^{PS}=C^{PS}\times(t_E - t_S)$ if we know a constant C^{PS}. The consumed

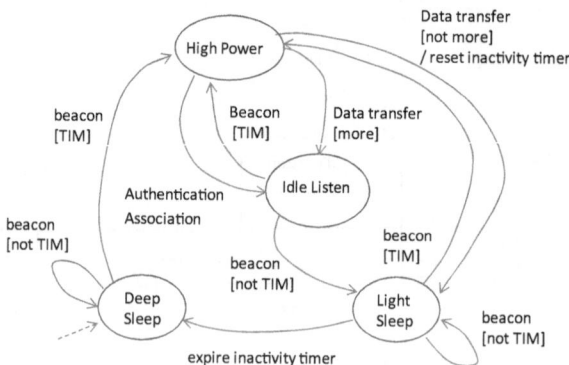

Fig. 3. Behavioral Model of STA

power is proportional to the period of time that STA dwells on the particular power state. Then, $P(T)$ becomes the sum of the power consumption in all states that the STA transition system visits.

$$P(T) = \sum_{i=0}^{n-1} P(t_i, \ t_{i+1})^{PS}$$

where $t_0 = 0$ and $t_n = T$. With $t = t_E - t_S$, $P(t_S, t_E)^{PS}$ can be written as $P(t)^{PS}$, which is equal to $C^{PS} \times t$. For example, $P(t)^{DeepSleep}$ refers to the sum of the power consumed as the drain currents of the radio circuits and the power needed to process the beacon signals. The *DeepSleep* state is visited many times while the Wi-Fi subsystem is enabled.

3   Model-Based Analysis of Power Consumption

3.1   Power Consumption Automaton

As mentioned above, the behavior of STA is modeled in terms of a state-transition system. A state transition sequence generates a trace consisting of the power states that the STA visits. $P(T)$ can be calculated by accumulating the power consumed in all such visited states. Here, we introduce a state transition system, the power consumption automaton, to express the power consumption formally.

The power consumption automaton (PCA) is a six-tuple. We give its formal definition by following the presentation of the linear hybrid system in [5], $\langle\ Loc, Var, Lab, Edg, Act, Inv\ \rangle$. The components are explained below.

1. *Loc* is a finite set of locations to represent the power states.
2. *Var* is a finite set of real-valued variables, A valuation v for the variables is a function to assign a real-value $v(x) \in R$ to each variable $x \in Var$, and V represents a set of valuations.

3. *Lab* is a finite set of synchronization labels containing the stutter label $\tau \in Lab$.

4. *Edg* is a finite set of transitions. Each transition e is a tuple $\langle l, a, \mu, l' \rangle$ where $l \in Loc$ and $l' \in Loc$ are a source and a target location respectively, $a \in Lab$ is a synchronization label, and μ is an action defined by a guarded set of assignments (referred to as updates)

$$\psi \Rightarrow \{ \, x := \alpha_x \mid x \in Var \, \},$$

where the guard ψ is a linear formula over the variables, and α_x is also a linear term.

5. *Act* is a mapping from locations in *Loc* to a set of activities to represent the flow dynamics. $Act(l)$ is a differential equation of the form $dP/dt = K$ with an integer K $(K \in Z)$ for a variable $P \in Var$. K is either C^j for the case of power consumption $(P(t)^l)$ or 1 for the clock.

6. *Inv* is a mapping from locations in *Loc* to invariants $Inv(l) \subseteq V$. $Inv(l)$ is defined by a linear formula ϕ over Var.

Two PCAs are synchronized on the common set of labels $Lab_1 \cap Lab_2$. Whenever PCA_1 makes a discrete transition with a synchronization label $a \in (Lab_1 \cap Lab_2)$, PCA_2 also performs a discrete transition.

The PCA is a strict subclass of the linear hybrid automaton (LHA) [6]. Informally, the LHA is a hybrid automaton, the guards (ψ), updates (μ), and invariants (ϕ) of which are only linear expressions, and the dynamics are specified using differential inequalities that are linear constraints over first-order derivatives ($C_1 \leq dx/dt \leq C_2$). The dynamics of the PCA are differential equalities of the form, $dP/dt = C^l$ for the case of the power consumption variable P, and $dX/dt = 1$ for the clock variable X, both of which are linear equality constraints over first-order derivatives. Therefore, the PCA is a subclass of the LHA.

3.2   Analysis of Power Consumption Automaton

This section reviews the algorithmic analysis methods, which were studied extensively for the linear hybrid automaton (LHA) [5]. Here, we focus on a reachability analysis over an infinite state space generated by the labeled transition system (LTS) associated with the LHA.

The LHA has several special cases such as a timed automaton (TA), a multirate timed system (MTS), an n-rate timed system (nRTS), and a stopwatch automaton (SWA). An LHA is *simple* if the location invariants (ϕ) and transition guards (ψ) are of the form $x \leq k$ or $k \leq x$ for $x \in Var$ and $k \in Z$.

A variable x is a clock if $Act(l, x) = 1$ for each location l and $\mu(e, x) \in \{0, x\}$ for each edge. A skewed clock is a clock to change with time at a rate k $(k \in Z)$; $Act(l, x) = k$ and $\mu(e, x) \in \{0, x\}$. k can be different from 1.

A TA is a simple linear hybrid automaton, whose variables are clocks. An MTS is a linear hybrid automaton, whose clocks are skewed. An nRTS is an MTS, each skewed clock of which proceeds at n different rates. An SWA is a TA, in which $Act(l, x) \in \{0, 1\}$ and $\mu(e, x) \in \{0, x\}$. The reachability problem is known to be decidable for the TA and *simple* MTS, but undecidable for other cases even though they are *simple*.

A naive question regarding the PCA would be to ask whether a PCA model can reproduce an energy profile such as that in Figure 2. The profile shows just one particular trace instance. Although test executions of the model PCA might reproduce the trace, this is not useful for design-level debugging. Analyzing the PCA using various scenarios is desirable, and some static analysis methods such as symbolic model-checking would be better than test executions. Furthermore, although precise numerical values are needed, for example, in the optimization problems, the focus here is to detect anomalies and systematic analyses are preferred. Because of the decidability of the reachability problem, a close look at the PCA is needed.

Imagine that we have a PCA model with M power states, each of which consumes different amounts of electric power as $P(t)^j = C^j \times t$ $(j = 0 \ldots M - 1)$. We also assume that the property to check takes the form of $\Box(Pow \leq Max)$, which indicates that the total power (Pow) is within a given Max.

In discussing the decidability of the reachability problem, we consider how the PCA is encoded in some subclass of LHA. A naive method is to encode the PCA as an M-rate timed system. A skewed clock Pow is introduced, which changes with time at the rate of C^j in the power state j, namely proceeds at M different rates. Pow can record the total power consumption as the PCA changes its power states.

Alternatively, the PCA can be regarded as an MTS. Since $P(t)^j$ is linear in time, the power consumption in one power state j is essentially the period of time that the PCA stays in that state. We may regard each $P(t)^j$ as a skewed clock X^j that changes with time at a fixed rate of C^j. Since X^j changes with time only when the PCA is in that particular state j, X^j must be stopped in all the other states. Therefore, the PCA is regarded as a multirate SWA, where the total power consumption is calculated such that $Pow = \sum_{j=0}^{M-1} X^j$. The PCA is more expressive than either the MTS or the SWA.

As mentioned above, the reachability problem is undecidable for either an nRTS or a *simple* SWA. The reachability problem of the PCA is also undecidable even if we restrict the PCA to be *simple*. We may consider using an over-approximation analysis method, which is complete with respect to finding bugs.

PCA may be encoded in another variant of TA, priced timed automaton (PTA) [7]. A PTA has *observer* variables $(ObsVar)$ that change their values at locations or transition edges, but that are not used in guards nor invariants. The observer variables are computed by a sum of *weights* along transition sequnces, but not as dynamics of LHA. In the PTA theory, the analysis is aimed for the optimization problems They deal with questions, for example, to find minimum paths along which the observer variable has a specified value.

Although our problem is to find anomalies in power consumption behavior, which is different from optimizations, we may encode PCA as an PTA in which the variable *Pow* is regarded as an *observer* variable not used in guards nor invariants ($Pow \in ObsVar$ and $Pow \notin Var$).

4   Analysis Using Realtime Maude

4.1   Realtime Maude

Realtime Maude [2][30] is an extension of Maude [9] for the application of rewriting logic [19] to the executable specifications of realtime and hybrid systems. Realtime Maude adapts *explicit* time model as compared to an *implicit* or symbolic representation of time. The latter is used in the reachability analysis methods for the LHA [5][6].

Realtime Maude provides two types of rewrite rules, instantaneous rules and tick rules. The instantaneous rules are inherited from Maude, and rewrite terms in a concurrent manner without delay, namely instantaneously. A general form is introduced as a rewriting of concurrent objects [9][19]. The present paper, however, uses a simplified presentation just for sketching how the PCA is encoded in Realtime Maude.

Let $T(A)$ be a term with argument A. Then, a conditional instantaneous rule with label r takes the following form:

$$r : T(A) \longrightarrow T'(A') \text{ if } C \ .$$

The term on the left-hand side ($T(A)$) is rewritten to the term on the right-hand side ($T'(A')$). This rule is fired or enabled to make transitions only when the side condition C is satisfied.

The rewrite rule can represent synchronous communications between two parties. Let $T_1(A_1)$ and $T_2(A_2)$ be terms for the parties involved, and let M be a message term to trigger the communication. The following rewrite rule can be considered to describe synchronous communications between the two parties because both $T_1(A_1)$ and $T_2(A_2)$ change their internal status simultaneously with M:

$$r : T_1(A_1) \ T_2(A_2) \ M \longrightarrow T_1(A'_1) \ T_2(A'_2) \ M' \text{ if } C \ .$$

This example also shows that the rule generates a new message term M'.

The tick rules are introduced in Realtime Maude [30] to be responsible for passage of time. There might be a situation in which the firing of instantaneous rules interferes with that of tick rules. Realtime Maude adapts a rewriting strategy to control the firing of instantaneous rules and tick rules. All of the instantaneous rules are fired at some point in time until no such rule to be enabled is found. The net result is that the entire system is in a *stable* state. Then, the tick rules are checked if they are enabled.

Let T be a set of terms to represent a snapshot of the entire system. A tick rule works on T enclosed with curly brackets ({ and }), where T is a term of sort *System* pre-defined in Realtime Maude.

$1 : \{\, T\, \} \longrightarrow \{\, T'\, \}$ **in time** τ_l **if** C

The rule states that the amount of the time τ_l passes in rewriting T to T'. Here, C may refer to a condition related to time τ_l, and such tick rules advance the time nondeterministically as long as τ_l satisfies the condition C. For example, the rule below, with a given constant u, advances time by any amount so long as the condition $\tau_l \leq u$ is satisfied:

$1 : \{\, T\, \} \longrightarrow \{\, T'\, \}$ **in time** τ_l **if** $\tau_l \leq u$

The amount of time to advance is not chosen exactly, but rather can be any value that satisfies the condition. It needs a sound method by which to choose an adequate time value because time is continuous in general.

Realtime Maude adapts *sampling abstractions* for such time-nondeterministic systems, in which the notion of the maximum time elapsed (mte) plays an important role. Each term T is accompanied by two functions, δ and *mte*, where δ is described so as to return a new term T' which is a modification of T after the passage of time τ_l, and *mte* returns information on the sampling point, at which the tick rules regarding to this T are supposed to fire.

The tick rules are then written as shown below where the side condition refers to $mte(T)$:

$1 : \{\, T\, \} \longrightarrow \{\, \delta(T, \tau_l)\, \}$ **in time** τ_l **if** $\tau_l \leq mte(T)$

$mte(T)$ is the upper limit of the advancement of time, and thus instructs the formal analysis method to consider transitions at some particular time to satisfy the side condition. This means that the transition from T to T' is fired at least once in the time interval specified by $mte(T)$.

The sampling abstraction is effective in the time-bounded model-checking. The property to check is expressed as a *formula* in linear temporal logic (LTL), and the following command invokes the model-checker.

mc $initState \models^t formula$ **in time** $\leq B$

The model checking method is feasible even for the case of continuous time because of the sampling abstraction.

4.2   Encoding PCA in Realtime Maude

Realtime Maude is expressive enough to represent a wide range of realtime and hybrid systems such as timed automaton and hybrid automaton. Since the power consumption automaton (PCA) is a subclass of the linear hybrid automaton (Section 3.1), the PCA can be encoded in Realtime Maude.

First, we introduce two reserved variables *loc* and *pow*. The value of *loc* refers to a location $L \in Loc$, and *pow* represents the total consumed power (Section 3.2). We then have a set of variables, $Var \cup \{loc, pow\}$. A PCA is a term with K+2 arguments that takes the following form:

$$pca(LOC, POW, N_1, \ldots, N_K)$$

where $N_j \in Var$.

Each synchronization label in *Lab* is turned into a message A_i in Realtime Maude. *Edge* describes how the transition occurs, and thus is encoded in the rewrite rule. An edge $\langle L, A, \mu, L' \rangle$ with μ taking the form of $\psi \Rightarrow \{\ x := \alpha_x | x \in Var \}$ is encoded in a rewrite rule with a side condition. ψ is defined over Var, and does not refer to *loc* or *pow*. Particularly, *pow* is an observer variable. If a PCA has only one variable X, for simplicity, the transition is translated into an instantaneous rule.

$$r : A \ \ pca(L, POW, X) \ \longrightarrow \ pca(L', POW, \alpha_X) \ \ \textbf{if} \ \psi$$

Although the location L may be changed, the power does not. The value of X is updated to be α_X.

The edge with the stutter label *tau* is encoded as a rewrite rule just to change the location (L) to a new location (L') without any message term being involved. L' is possibly the same as L.

$$r : pca(L, POW, X) \ \longrightarrow \ pca(L', POW, \alpha_X) \ \ \textbf{if} \ \psi$$

Act is responsible for the flow dynamics in the power state and is concerned with the time-dependent behavior of the PCA. This aspect is encoded in tick rewrite rules. We define $\delta(T, \tau_l)$ as follows:

$$\delta(pca(L, POW, X), \tau_l) = pca(L, POW + C^L \times \tau_l, X')$$

X' is defined in a proper manner. For an example case of a regular clock variable, it calculates the effects on the time progress; $X' = X + \tau_l$. Realtime Maude supports the linear arithmetic for time such as $POW + C^L \times \tau_l$ with a constant C^L.

In the PCA, *Inv* is essentially a time constraint representing that the state transition does not occur from state L while the specified temporal conditions φ are satisfied, where φ does not refer to the observer variable *pow*. This situation is the same as that in which the state transition occurs only when $\neg \varphi$ becomes satisfied. The new term is also calculated using the associated δ:

$$r : \{\ pca(L, POW, X)\ \} \ \longrightarrow \ \{\ \delta(pca(L, POW, X), \tau_l)\ \} \ \ \textbf{in time} \ \ \tau_l \ \ \textbf{if} \ \neg \varphi$$

Once the PCA is encoded as a set of instantaneous rules and tick rules, its time-dependent behavior is checked with the time-bounded model-checking method As mentioned earlier, the property to check is $\square(Pow \leq Max^{total})$ within a given time interval of 0 to B.

$$\textbf{mc} \ initState \models^t \square(Pow \leq Max^{total}) \ \textbf{in time} \leq B$$

The analysis is performed under the sampling abstraction, which is dependent on the function *mte*.

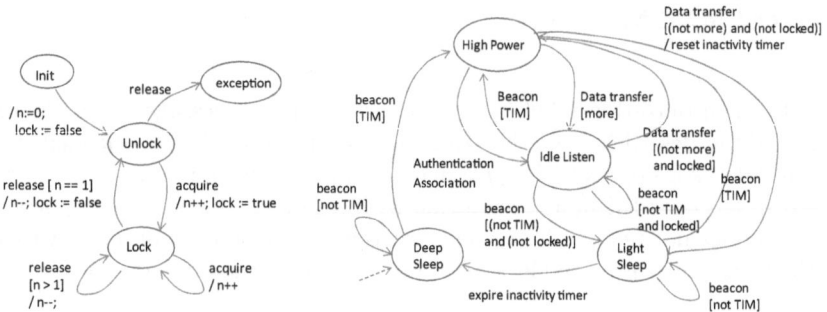

Fig. 4. Wi-Fi PSM with Wake Lock

4.3 Wi-Fi PCA Model in Realtime Maude

Based on the encoding method in Section 4.2, we present Realtime Maude descriptions of PCA examples. Figure 4 shows two PCA models, Wi-Fi Wake Lock (left) and Wi-Fi STA (right), in diagrammatic forms.

The wake lock is not time-dependent, but changes its states in response to the acquire and release events. This is a good example for illustrating the instantaneous rules of Realtime Maude. A *wakeLock* term has two internal variables: *LCK* of sort *Bool* for representing its locking status and *N* of sort *Nat* for storing the reference counts:

op *wakeLock* : *Bool   Nat → System*

Let *Acquire* and *Release* be message terms for the corresponding events. The behavior of *wakeLock* is specified by a set of instantaneous rules.

> $a1$: *Acquire wakeLock*$(false, 0) \longrightarrow$ *wakeLock*$(true, 1)$ *Locked*
> $a2$: *Acquire wakeLock*$(true, N) \longrightarrow$ *wakeLock*$(true, N + 1)$
> $r1$: *Release wakeLock*$(false, 0) \longrightarrow$ *Exception*
> $r2$: *Release wakeLock*$(true, 1) \longrightarrow$ *wakeLock*$(false, 0)$ *Unlocked*
> $r3$: *Release wakeLock*$(true, N) \longrightarrow$ *wakeLock*$(true, N - 1)$ **if** $N>1$

In the rules $a1$ and $r2$, appropriate message terms, *Locked* or *Unlocked*, are also generated while the *wakeLock* term changes internal values.

The Wi-Fi PCA in Figure 4 has four power states with numerous transitions. Since a transition is turned into a set of rewrite rules in Realtime Maude, the description becomes lengthy. In the following, we describe some of the behavior only.

First, we introduce a term *wifiSTA* with four arguments. In addition to *loc* (sort *Loc*) and *pow* (sort *Time*), the *wifiSTA* term has a Boolean flag to indicate the status of the Wi-Fi WakeLock, and an inactivity timer of sort *Time*.

op *wifiSTA* : *Loc Time Bool Time → System*

The value of the Boolean flag is flipped in response to the *Locked* and *Unlocked* messages sent by the *wakeLock*. Two instantaneous rules, $w1$ and $w2$, are responsible for these messages.

w1: $wifiSTA(L, P, false, X)$ *Locked* $\longrightarrow wifiSTA(L, P, true, X)$
w2: $wifiSTA(L, P, true, X)$ *Unocked* $\longrightarrow wifiSTA(L, P, false, X)$

Next we consider three transitions from the *HighPower* state when $wifiSTA$ receives *Data* messages with the *More* flag. We assume that these occur instantaneously and do not consume any electric power. When the *More* flag is not on, the destination locations differ depending on the wake lock flag value (rules $h2$ and $h3$).

h1: $wifiSTA(HighPower, P, B, X)$ *Data(More)*
$\qquad \longrightarrow wifiSTA(IdleListen, P, B, X)$
h2: $wifiSTA(HighPower, P, false, X)$ *Data(NoMore)*
$\qquad \longrightarrow wifiSTA(LightSleep, P, false, 0)$
h3: $wifiSTA(HighPower, P, true, X)$ *Data(NoMore)*
$\qquad \longrightarrow wifiSTA(IdleListen, P, true, X)$

Rule $h2$ sets the fourth argument to 0 to reset the inactivity timer (Figure 4).

The access point (AP), which is not shown here, periodically sends beacon frames. They have the TIM flag on when the AP notifies $wifiSTA$ to start exchanging additional frames. The transitions from the *IdleListen* state go to different destinations based on the combination of the TIM flag and the status of the wake lock (Figure 4). We assume that the message term *Beacon* has an argument to designate the TIM flag value.

i1: $wifiSTA(IdleListen, P, B, X)$ *Beacon(TIM)*
$\qquad \longrightarrow wifiSTA(HighPower, P, B, X)$
i2: $wifiSTA(IdleListen, P, false, X)$ *Beacon(noTIM)*
$\qquad \longrightarrow wifiSTA(LightSleep, P, false, X)$
i3: $wifiSTA(IdleListen, P, true, X)$ *Beacon(noTIM)*
$\qquad \longrightarrow wifiSTA(IdleListen, P, true, X)$

The time-dependent behavior of $wifiSTA$ is related to the accumulated power consumption values in each power state (pow) and the inactivity timer in the *LightSleep* state. The power consumptions in states other than *LightSleep* are almost the same: The power consumption P is updated to be $P + C^{DS} \times \tau$ with a constant value for that power state, for example C^{DS} in the *DeepSleep* state. The power state *loc* is not changed since $wifiSTA$ stays there.

$\delta(wifiSTA(DeepSleep, P, B, X), \tau)$
$\qquad = wifiSTA(DeepSleep, P + C^{DS} \times \tau, B, X)$

The definition of δ involving the *LightSleep* takes into account of the inactivity timer. Let *Timeout* be a constant to represent the timeout count of the inactivity

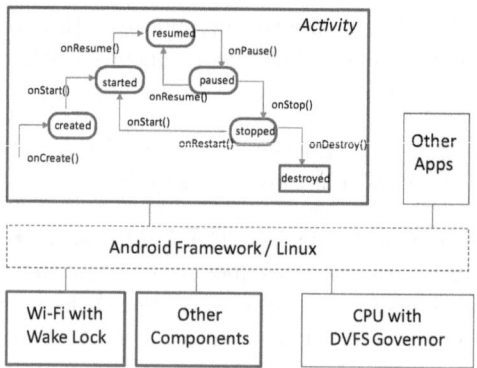

Fig. 5. Android Application

timer. When δ is called before the timeout is reached, the power consumption is calculated just as in the above cases. It, however, makes a slightly different calculation when the inactivity timeout occurs, in which case the state is also changed to the *DeepSleep* state.

$$\delta(wifiSTA(LightSleep, P, B, X), \tau)$$
$$= wifiSTA(LightSleep, P + C^{LS} \times \tau, B, X + \tau)$$
$$\text{if } X < Timeout - \tau$$
$$\delta(wifiSTA(LightSleep, P, B, X), \tau)$$
$$= wifiSTA(DeepSleep, P + C^{LS} \times (Timeout - X), B, 0)$$
$$\text{if } X \geq Timeout - \tau$$

Last, *mte* in the *LightSleep* state, where the inactivity timer is effective, returns the value $(Timeout - X)$ to indicate that the tick rules for $wifiSTA$ must be consulted after the specified ticks. In the other states, *mte* returns infinity (inf) to indicate that *mte* does not provide any useful information on the time point of interest.

$$mte(wifiSTA(L, P, B, X)) = Timeout - X \text{ if } (L = LightSleep)$$
$$mte(wifiSTA(L, P, B, X)) = inf \text{ if } not(L = LightSleep)$$

The access point (AP) may be responsible for further time-dependencies and introduces appropriate definitions of its own *mte*.

5 Discussion

The example PCA presented in this paper is the Wi-Fi subsystem, which is not an application, whereas the motivation of the present study is removing ebugs from Android applications at the design stage. As illustrated in Figure 5, the target application may use several hardware subsystems such as Wi-Fi. The power consumption of these subsystems is attributed to this application. The other applications to be executed concurrently may also affect the execution time of that particular application. The model-based analysis framework must take into account these components.

PCAs for all of the power consumers in the system are needed as a kind of *library* for the analysis of applications. The Wi-Fi PCA is a first example of such library components. Second, an Android application is implemented as an activity, as a subclass of `Activity`. An activity consists of a set of callback methods, and the behavior of the activity is modeled by the state-transition system to follow the life-cycle. Since the PCA, being a subclass of the LHA, subsumes discrete transition systems, such behavioral specifications can also be captured by the PCA. Thus, model-based analysis using the PCA is useful for the design-level debugging of ebugs in Android applications.

Figure 5 also shows that Android smartphones are equipped with ARM core processors to allow dynamic voltage-frequency scaling (DVFS) [15]. The DVFS governor in Android changes the voltage and frequency based on the CPU usage. Changing the voltage and frequency has an impact on the CPU power consumption, and it also affects the execution time of a program as the CPU performance changes. If the CPU clock rate decreases, the physical time that the program executes becomes long and the components used by the program are occupied longer resulting in more power consumption.

The CPU usage is related to the number of active processes, which is not known beforehand. The power consumption affected by the DVFS is difficult to predict, but may be considered to be probabilistic. Therefore, the behavior of the PCA is considered a stochastic process as in the statistical model-checking [34] or the statistical runtime checking [26]. In regard to the OBJ language family, especially Maude, PMaude [4] was proposed as an approach to the modeling of probabilistic object systems. PMaude may be a first step needed to solve the problem at hand.

6   Related Research

A. Pathak et al [31] pointed out the importance of eliminating energy bugs in smartphones, which they referred to as *ebugs*. They also proposed the use of state-transition systems for modeling of the power consumption and developed Eprof [32]. Eprof is an energy profiler to monitor the program execution at runtime to detect potential ebugs. The concept of using an automaton-based representation of the PCA was inspired by their work.

MoVES [8] uses the stopwatch-extension of UPPAAL [10] for modeling and analyzing embedded systems such as the schedulability or the power consumption. The power consumption model is, however, that $P(t) = C \times t$ without considering the difference in power states.

The Power consumption automaton (PCA) was introduced in [28]. They encoded the PCA in the stopwatch automaton (SWA) and used the stopwatch-extension of UPPAAL for the reachability analysis. PCA, however, is not fully represented because the SWA is not multirated. Therefore, query checking is performed separately for each clock. Checking of $A\square((\sum_{PS} P^{PS}) \leq Max^{Total})$ is not possible. It is because the sum of clock variables does not make sense due to the symbolic model-checking algorithm. Although $\bigwedge_{PS} A\square((P^{PS} \leq Max^{PS})$ is possible, this is different from the above property.

7   Conclusion

Modeling at the right level of abstraction is necessary in order to capture the fundamental properties of software systems, and requires concise notations or languages. The languages of the OBJ family are quite flexible and were adopted herein due to their property-oriented specification method. We demonstrated how the power consumption of smartphones, one of the recent hot topics, was dealt with using the notion of power consumption automaton and its encoding in Realtime Maude. Furthermore, we also pointed out that stochastic or probabilistic methods would be needed for the power consumption analysis of smartphone applications. In summary, quantitative methods will play an important role in addressing new problems in emerging software-intensive systems.

References

1. Android, http://developer.android.com
2. Realtime Maude, http://heim.ifi.uio.no/peterol/RealTimeMaude/
3. IEEE Standard 802.11, Wireless LAN Medium Access Control (MAC) and Physical Layer (PHY) Specifications (1999)
4. Agha, G., Meseguer, J., Sen, K.: PMaude: Rewrite-based Specification Language forf Probabilistic Object Systems. ENTCS 153, 213–239 (2006)
5. Alur, R., Courcoubetis, C., Halbwachs, N., Henzinger, T.A., Ho, P.-H., Nicollin, X., Olivero, A., Sifakis, J., Yovine, S.: The Algorithmic Analysis of Hybrid Systems. Theor. Comp. Sci. (138), 3–24 (1995)
6. Alur, R.: Formal Verification of Hybrid Systems. In: Proc. EMSOFT 2011, pp. 273–278 (2011)
7. Bouyer, P., Fahrenberg, U., Larsen, K.G., Markey, N.: Quantative Analysis of Real-Time Systems Using Priced Timed Automata. Comm. ACM 54(9), 78–87 (2011)
8. Brekling, A., Hansen, M.R., Madsen, J.: MoVES – A Framework for Modeling and Verifying Embedded Systems. In: Proc. ICM 2009, pp. 149–152 (2009)
9. Clavel, M., Durán, F., Eker, S., Lincoln, P., Martí-Oliet, N., Meseguer, J., Talcott, C.: All About Maude - A High-Performance Logical Framework. LNCS, vol. 4350. Springer, Heidelberg (2007)
10. David, A., Illum, J., Larsen, K.G., Skou, A.: Model-based Framework for Schedulability Analysis Using UPPAAL 4.1, Aalborg University (2009)
11. Diaconescu, R., Futatsugi, K.: CafeOBJ Report. World Scientific (1998)
12. Futatsugi, K., Goguen, J., Jouannaud, J.-P., Meseguer, J.: Principles of OBJ2. In: Proc. 12th POPL, pp. 52–66 (1985)
13. Ghezzi, C.: Adaptive Software – the fading boundary between development time and run time. An invited Talk at SEAMS 2011, Waikiki (May 2011)

14. Goguen, J., Malcolm, G.: Algebraic Semantics of Imperative Programs. The MIT Press (1996)
15. Hennessy, J.L., Patterson, D.A.: Computer Architecture: A Quantitative Approach, 5th edn. Morgan Kaufmann (2011)
16. Hiroshige, T.: History of Physics, Baihukan, vol. 1 (1968) (in Japanese)
17. Kephart, J., Chess, D.: The Vision of Autonomic Computing. IEEE Computer 36(1), 41–50 (2003)
18. Manweiler, J., Choudhury, R.R.: Avoiding the Rush Hours: WiFi Energy Management via Traffic Isolation. In: Proc. MobiSys 2011 (2011)
19. Meseguer, J.: Conditional Rewriting Logic as a Unified Model of Concurrency. ENTCS 96, 73–155 (1992)
20. Nakajima, S., Futatsugi, K.: An Object-Oriented Modeling Method for Algebraic Specifications in CafeOBJ. In: Proc. ICSE 1997, pp. 34–44 (1997)
21. Nakajima, S.: Using Algebraic Specification Techniques in Development of Object-Oriented Frameworks. In: Wing, J.M., Woodcock, J., Davies, J. (eds.) FM 1999, vol. II. LNCS, vol. 1709, p. 1664. Springer, Heidelberg (1999)
22. Nakajima, S.: An Algebraic Approach to Object-Oriented Software Engineering. Ph.D. Dissertation, The University of Tokyo (2000)
23. Nakajima, S., Ishiguro, M., Tanaka, K.: Rewriting Logic Approach to Modeling and Analysis of Client Behavior in Open Systems. In: Min, S.L., Pettit, R., Puschner, P., Ungerer, T. (eds.) SEUS 2010. LNCS, vol. 6399, pp. 83–94. Springer, Heidelberg (2010)
24. Nakajima, S.: An Architecture of Dynamically Adaptive PHP-based Web Applications. In: Proc. APSEC 2011, pp. 203–210 (2011)
25. Nakajima, S.: Introduction to Formal Methods – Logic-based Software Development, Ohm-sya (2012) (in Japanese)
26. Nakajima, S.: Importance Sampling of Runtime Interference. In: Proc. APSEC 2012, pp. 693–696 (2012)
27. Nakajima, S., Miwa, Y.: Soft Edge – Searching for Sciences of Software Development. Maruzen (2013) (in Japanese)
28. Nakajima, S., Ueda, Y.: Power Consumption Analysis of Smartphone Applications using UPPAAL, Orally presented at WIP session of 1st CPSNA (August 2013)
29. Nakajima, S.: Safe Substitution of Components in Self-adaptive Web Applications. To appear in Proc. APSEC 2013 (2013)
30. Ölveczky, P.C., Meseguer, J.: Semantics and Pragmatics of Real-Time Maude. Higher-Order and Symbolic Computation 20(1-2), 161–196 (2007)
31. Pathak, A., Hu, Y.C., Zhang, M.: Bootstrapping Energy Debugging on Smartphones: A First Look at Energy Bugs in Mobile Devices. In: Proc. Hotnets 2011 (2011)
32. Pathak, A., Hu, Y.C., Zhang, M.: Where is the energy spent inside my app?: Fine Grained Energy Accoutning on Smartphones with Eprof. In: Proc. EuroSys 2012 (2012)
33. Wing, J.: A Specifier's Introduction to Formal Methods. IEEE Computer, 8–24 (1990)
34. Zuliani, P., Baier, C., Clarke, E.M.: Rare-Event Verification for Stochastic Hybrid Systems. In: Proc. HSCC 2012, pp. 217–225 (2012)

Formal Modeling and Analysis of Google's Megastore in Real-Time Maude*

Jon Grov[1,2] and Peter Csaba Ölveczky[1,3]

[1] University of Oslo
[2] Bekk Consulting AS
[3] University of Illinois at Urbana-Champaign

Abstract. Cloud systems need to replicate data to ensure scalability and high availability. To enable their use for applications where consistency of the data is important, cloud systems should provide transactions. Megastore, developed and widely applied at Google, is one of very few cloud data stores that provide transactions; i.e., both data replication, fault tolerance, and data consistency. However, the only publicly available description of Megastore is short and informal. To facilitate the widespread study, adoption, and further development of Megastore's novel approach to transactions on replicated data, a much more detailed and precise description is needed. In this paper, we describe an executable formal model of Megastore in Real-Time Maude that we have developed. Our model is the result of many iterations resulting from correcting design flaws uncovered during Real-Time Maude analysis. We describe our model and explain how it can be simulated for QoS estimation and model checked to verify functional correctness.

1 Introduction

Cloud systems enable customers to deploy applications in a highly scalable and available infrastructure. Key to these features is *replication*: several copies of customer data in geographically distributed data centers allow cloud services to cope with peaks in system load, as well as with network and site failures.

Many applications require database facilities for storing valuable data. Databases provide *transactions*: for a given sequence of read and write operations on data items, the user is assured *atomicity*, which means that either no operation is completed or all operations are completed, and *serializability*, which means that the execution of concurrent transactions must provide the same result as some sequential execution. Transactions are necessary protection against inconsistency due to interleaved operations on shared data. For example, if two transactions t_1 and t_2 both read and write bank account x to deposit \$20, it is crucial to avoid both the execution $t_1 : read(x) = 10$; $t_2 : read(x) = 10$; $t_1 : x := 10 + 20$; $t_2 : x := 10 + 20$; $t_1 : write(x, 30)$; $t_2 : write(x, 30)$, where t_1's deposit is lost, and the execution $t_1 : read(x) = 10$; $t_1 : x := 10 + 20$; $t_1 : write(x, 30)$; $t_2 : read(x) =$

* This work was partially supported by AFOSR Grant FA8750-11-2-0084.

S. Iida, J. Meseguer, and K. Ogata (Eds.): Futatsugi Festschrift, LNCS 8373, pp. 494–519, 2014.

30; $t_2 : x := 30 + 20$; $t_2 : write(x, 50)$; $abort(t_1)$, where t_2 was allowed to read t_1's update which was later aborted.

Some applications, such as newspaper content management and social networks like Facebook, can tolerate lower degrees of consistency. Other applications have strict consistency requirements; notable examples include stock exchange systems, online auctions, banking, and medical systems: it is clear that a lost update due to concurrent transactions could have serious consequences in a system recording the medication of hospital patients.

Transactions are among the most important features of a database management system (DBMS), since a correct implementation of atomicity and serializability impose significant challenges. To quote Michael Stonebraker [20]:

> "It is possible to build your own [transaction support] on any of these systems, given enough additional code. However, the task is so difficult, we wouldn't wish it on our worst enemy. If you need [transaction support], you want to use a DBMS that provides them; it is much easier to deal with this at the DBMS level than at the application level."

Transaction management in the cloud, with geographical distribution and data replication, involves additional challenges because of:

- Performance: Concurrent access to replicas at different locations requires costly network coordination.
- Availability: The complexity of coordinating transactions across network sites increases significantly due to possible network and site failures.

Given the difficulties of transaction management on replicated data, we believe that formal methods are crucial to enable the use of cloud-based data stores also for applications where strong data consistency is required. First of all, formal analysis should be used to catch subtle "corner case" errors during design and development of the data store. Second, because of the complexity and criticality of such systems, it is necessary for application providers to be convinced that the cloud system indeed provides transaction support. Formal verification could be a major component in providing such assurance to application providers, just like formal methods can be used in Level A certification of critical avionics systems.

There are currently only a few cloud data stores with transaction support. Microsoft's SQL Azure [4] uses a master-based approach to coordination, which reduces fault-tolerance and gives worse performance for clients far from the master site. Google's Spanner [6] demands a complex infrastructure involving GPS hardware and atomic clocks, which reduces its applicability. Google's Megastore [2] provides replication and transactions through a replicated transaction log. Despite its relatively low performance, Megastore is used by Google for many well-known services such as GMail, Android Market, and Google+ [6], and is offered to customers using Google's cloud-based application platform AppEngine.

In this paper, we use the rewriting-logic-based Real-Time Maude language and tool [17] to formally model, simulate, and model check Megastore. The design of Megastore is informally described in the paper [2]. However, designing a complete fault-tolerant protocol requires much more detail than publicly available. Our contributions are:

1. We provide a precise, formal model of Megastore, which includes many details and aspects not even described informally in [2]. Because of the ambiguity and the lack of detail in the informal specification, we had to make a number of assumptions and design choices in our formalization. Our model is the result of several modifications resulting from extensive model checking during this formalization process.
2. We show how Megastore can be model checked and probabilistically simulated using Maude and Real-Time Maude.
3. We provide a general method for analyzing serializability in distributed transactional systems with replicated data.

Our formal model should facilitate further research on the Megastore approach. In particular, we are working on combining Megastore with the FLACS approach [8] to provide serializable transactions also across partitions.

The rest of the paper is organized as follows: Section 2 gives some background on Maude and Real-Time Maude. Section 3 presents an overview of Megastore and its approach to fault-tolerance. Section 4 describes our formal model of Megastore. Section 5 explains how we have formally analyzed our model. Finally, Section 6 discusses related work and gives some concluding remarks.

2   Maude and Real-Time Maude

Real-Time Maude [13] is a language and tool that extends Maude [5] to support the formal specification and analysis of real-time systems. The specification formalism emphasizes *ease* and *generality* of specification, and is particularly suitable for modeling distributed real-time systems in an object-oriented style. Real-Time Maude specifications are executable, and the tool provides a variety of formal analysis methods, including simulation, reachability analysis, and LTL and timed CTL model checking.

2.1   Maude

Maude [5] is a rewriting-logic-based formal language and high-performance simulation and model checking tool. A Maude module specifies a *rewrite theory* [10,3] $(\Sigma, E \cup A, R)$, where:

- Σ is an algebraic *signature*; that is, a set of declarations of *sorts*, *subsorts*, and *function symbols*.
- $(\Sigma, E \cup A)$ is a *membership equational logic theory* [11], with E a set of possibly conditional equations and membership axioms, and A a set of equational axioms such as associativity, commutativity, and identity, so that equational deduction is performed *modulo* the axioms A. The theory $(\Sigma, E \cup A)$ specifies the system's state space as an algebraic data type.

- R is a collection of *labeled conditional rewrite rules* specifying the system's local transitions, each of which has the form[1] $[l] : t \longrightarrow t'$ **if** $\bigwedge_{j=1}^{m} cond_j$, where each $cond_j$ in the condition is either an equality $u_j = v_j$ (u_j and v_j have the same normal form) or a rewrite $t_j \longrightarrow t'_j$ (t_j rewrites to t'_j in zero or more rewrite steps), and l is a *label*. Such a rule specifies a *one-step transition* from a substitution instance of t to the corresponding substitution instance of t', *provided* the condition holds. The rules are universally quantified by the variables appearing in the Σ-terms t, t', u_j, v_j, t_j, and t'_j, and are applied *modulo* the equations $E \cup A$.[2]

We briefly summarize the syntax of Maude and refer to [5] for more details. Operators are introduced with the op keyword: op $f : s_1 \ldots s_n$ -> s. They can have user-definable syntax, with underbars '_' marking the argument positions. Some operators can have equational *attributes*, such as assoc, comm, and id, stating, for example, that the operator is associative and commutative and has a certain identity element. Such attributes are used by the Maude engine to match terms *modulo* the declared axioms. An operator can also be declared to be a constructor (ctor) that defines the carrier of a sort. Equations and rewrite rules are introduced with, respectively, keywords eq, or ceq for conditional equations, and rl and crl. The mathematical variables in such statements are declared with the keywords var and vars, or can be introduced on the fly in a statement without being declared previously, in which case they have the form *var* : *sort*. An equation $f(t_1, \ldots, t_n) = t$ with the owise (for "otherwise") attribute can be applied to a subterm $f(\ldots)$ only if no other equation with left-hand side $f(u_1, \ldots, u_n)$ can be applied.

In object-oriented Maude modules, a *class* declaration

class C | $att_1 : s_1,$ ... , $att_n : s_n$.

declares a class C with attributes att_1 to att_n of sorts s_1 to s_n. An *object* of class C in a given state is represented as a term < $O : C$ | $att_1 : val_1, ..., att_n : val_n$ > of sort Object, where O, of sort Oid, is the object's *identifier*, and where val_1 to val_n are the current values of the attributes att_1 to att_n. A *message* is a term of sort Msg, where the declaration msg $m : s_1 \ldots s_n$ -> Msg defines the syntax of the message (m) and the sorts ($s_1 \ldots s_n$) of its parameters.

The state is a term of the sort Configuration in a concurrent object-oriented system, and has the structure of a *multiset* made up of objects and messages. Multiset union for configurations is denoted by a juxtaposition operator (empty syntax) that is declared associative and commutative, so that rewriting is *multiset rewriting* supported directly in Maude. Since a class attribute may have sort Configuration, we can have *hierarchical* objects which contain a subconfiguration of other (possibly hierarchical) objects and messages.

---

[1] An equational condition $u_i = w_i$ can also be a *matching equation*, written $u_i := w_i$, which instantiates the variables in u_i to the values that make $u_i = w_i$ hold, if any.

[2] Operationally, a term is reduced to its E-normal form modulo A before any rewrite rule is applied in Real-Time Maude.

The dynamic behavior of concurrent object systems is axiomatized by specifying each of its transition patterns by a rewrite rule. For example, the rule

```
rl [1] :  m(O,w)
          < O : C | a1 : x, a2 : O', a3 : z >
       =>
          < O : C | a1 : x + w, a2 : O', a3 : z >
          m'(O',x) .
```

defines a parameterized family of transitions (one for each substitution instance) in which a message m, with parameters O and w, is read and consumed by an object O of class C, the attribute a1 of the object O is changed to x + w, and a new message m'(O',x) is generated. The message m(O,w) is *removed* from the state by the rule, since it does *not* occur in the right-hand side of the rule. Likewise, the message m'(O',x) is *generated* by the rule, since it *only* occurs in the right-hand side of the rule. By convention, attributes whose values do not change and do not affect the next state of other attributes or messages, such as a3, need not be mentioned in a rule. Similarly, attributes whose values influence the next state of other attributes or the values in messages, but are themselves unchanged, such as a2, can be omitted from right-hand sides of rules.

A *subclass* inherits all the attributes and rules of its superclasses.

Formal Analysis in Maude. A Maude module is executable under some conditions, such as the equations being confluent and terminating, possibly modulo some structural axioms, and the theory being coherent [5].

Maude's *rewrite command* simulates *one* of the many possible system behaviors from the initial state by rewriting the initial state. Maude's *search* command uses a breadth-first strategy to search for states that are reachable from the initial state, match the *search pattern*, and satisfy the *search condition*.

Maude's *linear temporal logic model checker* analyzes whether each behavior satisfies a temporal logic formula. *State propositions*, possibly parametrized, are operators of sort Prop, and their semantics is defined by equations of the form

```
ceq statePattern |= prop = b if cond
```

for b a term of sort Bool, which defines the state proposition *prop* to hold in all states t such that t |= *prop* evaluates to true. A temporal logic *formula* is constructed by state propositions and temporal logic operators such as True, False, ~ (negation), /\, \/, -> (implication), [] ("always"), <> ("eventually"), U ("until"), and W ("weak until"). The command

```
(red modelCheck(t, formula) .)
```

then checks whether the temporal logic formula *formula* holds in all behaviors starting from the initial state t. Such model checking terminates if the state space reachable from the initial state t is finite.

2.2 Real-Time Maude

A Real-Time Maude [17] *timed module* specifies a *real-time rewrite theory* [16], that is, a rewrite theory $\mathcal{R} = (\Sigma, E \cup A, R)$, such that:

1. $(\Sigma, E \cup A)$, contains a specification of a sort Time defining the (discrete or dense) time domain.
2. The rules in R are decomposed into:
   - "ordinary" rewrite rules that model *instantaneous* change that is assumed to take zero time, and
   - *tick (rewrite) rules* of the form

     crl [l] : {t} => {t'} in time u if *cond*

     that model the elapse of time in a system, where { _ } is a constructor of a new sort GlobalSystem and u is a term of sort Time denoting the *duration* of the rewrite.

The initial state of a system must be equationally reducible to a term {t_0}. The form of the tick rules then ensures uniform time elapse in all parts of a system.

Real-Time Maude extends Maude's analysis features to the real-time setting. Real-Time Maude's *timed fair rewrite* command simulates *one* behavior of the system *up to a certain duration*. It is written with syntax

(tfrew t in time <= *timeLimit* .)

where t is the term to be rewritten ("the initial state"), and *timeLimit* is a ground term of sort Time. Real-Time Maude extends Maude's *search* command to search for states that can be reached within a given time interval from the initial state.

Real-Time Maude provides both *unbounded* and *time-bounded* LTL model checking. The unbounded model checking command

(mc t |=u *formula* .)

checks whether the temporal logic formula *formula* holds in all behaviors starting from the initial state t. When the reachable state space is infinite, *time-bounded* LTL model checking, in which each behavior starting in t is only analyzed up to a certain time bound, can be used to ensure termination of the model checking.

3 Overview of Megastore

A *data store* is a system providing functionality to write and access persistent data. Data stores are used to offload the complexity of data management from individual applications by providing transaction support, access control, and/or fault recovery. A data store often uses *replication* to ensure high availability in the presence of site and/or network failures: several copies of the same data are stored at different locations.

Megastore [2] is a data store offering very high availability and transaction support. It is deployed within Google's own cloud infrastructure. In addition to being widely used internally at Google, Megastore is also used by Google's customers through the cloud-based application platform AppEngine. Megastore handles more than three billion write and 20 billion read transactions daily and stores nearly a petabyte of data across many global data centers [2].

Data are replicated among sites (data centers), and Megastore can tolerate failure of up to $n-1$ replicas, with n the total number of replicas. A *transaction* is a sequence of read and write operations on entities, followed by a commit request. Clients can issue transaction requests from any site replicating the relevant data, and updates are propagated to the other replicas before the transaction commits.

In Megastore, data are stored as *entities*, each entity being a set of key-value pairs. Entities are organized into *entity groups*. Transactional serializability is only guaranteed for operations within the same entity group.

Initially, all operations in a transaction are executed locally at the receiving site. When a commit request is issued, a coordination procedure between the sites is used to decide whether or not the transaction is valid and can be committed. If not, usually due to some concurrent update of the same data, the entire transaction is aborted and must be restarted from the beginning.

Megastore uses the Paxos protocol [9] for coordinating updates. This allows most transactions to complete even in the presence of site and/or network failures. Section 3.1 explains the behavior of Megastore in more detail, and Section 3.2 explains how Megastore deals with recovery from faults.

3.1   Transaction Execution in Megastore

Any Megastore site S may receive transaction requests for entities replicated at S. Entities are versioned, and Megastore provides reads with different levels of consistency. We focus here on *current reads*, which give the most recent version written. Any transaction updating an entity must perform a current read before performing the update.

Each site has a *coordinator*, which is always informed about whether the local replica is up-to-date. When a current read is issued, it is executed locally if and only if granted by the local coordinator. Otherwise, a majority read is required, as explained in Section 3.2.

During the execution of a transaction t, read operations are completed immediately, while write operations are buffered. When receiving the commit request, the site receiving t, denoted the *originating site* of t, initiates the coordination procedure. Megastore's approach to combine availability with serializability is to partition data into relatively small units (entity groups), and maintain a separate transaction log for each entity group. This log is replicated, and serializability within the entity group is ensured, since, at any given time, only one transaction is allowed to update the log.

A transaction t accessing an entity group eg reads entities in eg from a given log position lp. t's updates are buffered during transaction execution. When all operations of t are completed and t is ready for commit, the originating site of t prepares a log entry for eg containing t's updates and runs *Paxos* [9] to request that this log entry becomes entry $lp + 1$ in the replicated log.

Paxos is a generic consensus protocol for distributed systems which consists of the following phases:

1. Agree on a leader.
2. The leader then proposes a value to the participating processes.
3. Once the proposed value is acknowledged by at least a majority of the processes, the leader informs all participants about the decision.

In the presence of failures, this may be insufficient to reach consensus, in which case a new round is initiated where another process becomes the leader.

Megastore optimizes Paxos by including in each log entry the Paxos leader for the *next* log entry. Phase 1 is therefore replaced by a request from the originating site directly to the leader. In the case of conflict, i.e., if multiple sites request different log entries for the same log position, Paxos ensures that only one is elected, and the others are aborted.

After a successful Paxos round, each site replicating eg then appends the chosen log entry for position $lp + 1$ to the local copy of the transaction log for eg, and subsequently updates the local data store.

3.2   Fault Tolerance and Failure Recovery

Failures may cause some processes to stop responding and/or may block network messages from being delivered. Fault tolerance implies that a transaction execution must be able to proceed even if some replicating sites are unable to apply the update. This means that a previously failed site may have missed updates on some entity groups.

To provide fault tolerance, Megastore requires that even if a site is unable to apply an update for some entity group, the site's coordinator must be informed and then mark the entity group as invalid. This is part of the Paxos coordination procedure, and means that the coordinator of a failed site must be reachable. Otherwise the update is blocked until the entire site is confirmed to be down by Megastore's underlying failure detection mechanism.

If a site, upon executing a current read, sees that the entity group in question is invalid, it performs a *majority read* and a *catchup* before proceeding. During the majority read, the local site s_l requests from each other replicating site s_r the most recent log position known to be valid by s_r. When s_l has received a reply from a majority of the replicating sites, it performs catchup as follows: any log position missing at s_l is requested from some updated site. When the catchup is complete, the local coordinator marks the replica as valid, and the current read operation can proceed.

4   Formalizing Megastore in Real-Time Maude

This section explains how we have formalized Megastore in Real-Time Maude. Our model contains 56 rewrite rules, of which we only present 15 in this paper. The entire executable formal specification is available at `http://folk.uio.no/jongr/megastore/maude.html`. Section 4.1 lists our system assumptions, Section 4.2 presents our model of Megastore in the absence of failures, and Section 4.3 shows our model in the presence of failures.

4.1   System Assumptions

Based on the description in [2], we make the following system assumptions:

- Megastore is deployed across geographically distant sites connected by a wide-area network. The network delays between two nodes can therefore vary significantly, and we do not assume FIFO delivery between the same pair of nodes.
- A site always knows all the other replicating sites for an entity group.
- Sites can fail and recover spontaneously, and messages can be dropped due to site or network failures.
- Coordinators are supposed to be very stable. Furthermore, Megastore requires that the coordinator of each running site is accessible; otherwise update transactions are blocked until the given replica is confirmed down and can be excluded. We therefore assume that coordinators are always available.
- Small time differences caused by clock skews of the local clocks are ignored.

4.2   The Model without Failure Handling

We model Megastore in an object-oriented way, where the global state consists of a multiset of site objects and messages traveling between them. Each site is modeled as an object instance of the following class:

```
class Site |
   entityGroups : Configuration,
   localTransactions : Configuration,
   coordinator : EntGroupLogPosPairSet .
```

The attribute `entityGroups` contains one `EntityGroup` object for each entity group replicated at the site, and the attribute `localTransactions` contains one `Transaction` object for each active transaction originating at the site. The attribute `coordinator` denotes the local coordinator state for each entity group, and is a ;-separated set of terms *eg* `upToDateAt` *lp*, denoting that the entity group *eg* is up-to-date at log position *lp*, and terms *eg* `invalidAt` *lp*, denoting that the local replica of *eg* may be missing some log entries at or before *lp*.

Entity Groups. Each local entity group copy is modeled as an object instance of the following class:

```
class EntityGroup |
   entitiesState : EntitySet,
   transactionLog : LogEntryList,
   replicas : EntityGroupReplicaSet,
   proposals : PaxosProposalSet,
   pendingWrites : PendingWriteList .
```

The attribute `entitiesState` describes the available versions of each entity in the entity group. Each such record is a term `entity(eg,i)` `|->` `(lpos(p_1),v_1)` `::` ... `::` `(lpos(p_k),v_k)`, where `entity(eg,i)` denotes the ith entity of the entity group eg, and `(lpos(p_j),v_j)` is an entity version containing the value v_j, created at log position p_j.

The attribute `transactionLog` denotes the local copy of the replicated transaction log which is the core of Megastore's replication protocol. Each log entry belongs to a given *log position*. A log entry $(t\ lp\ s\ ol)$ contains the identity t of the originating transaction, the log position lp, the leader site s for the *next* log entry, and the list ol of write operations executed by t.

The attribute `replicas` denotes the set of sites replicating this entity group. The attribute `proposals` denotes the local state in ongoing Paxos processes involving this entity group. It contains two types of values: `proposal(s,t,lp,pn)`, which represents a request from site s to become the leader for log position lp on behalf of transaction t, and `accepted(s,le,pn)`, which states that this site has accepted Paxos proposal number pn containing the log entry le from site s.

Megastore executes write operations in two steps: (i) write to the log, which occurs immediately when the chosen log entry is committed; and (ii) updating the actual data in the `entityState`. The attribute `pendingWrites` maintains a list of write operations waiting to be applied to the `entityState`.

Transactions. A transaction request is a `::`-separated list of current read operations `cr(e)` and write operations `w(e,v)`. Transactions being executed are modeled as object instances of the following class:

```
class Transaction |
    operations : OperationList,
    reads : EntitySet,
    writes : OperationList,
    status : TransStatus,
    readState : ReadStateSet,
    paxosState : PaxosStateSet .
```

The attribute `operations` initially contains the transaction request. During execution, operations are removed from this list. For a read operation the resulting entity is stored in the attribute `reads`. The attribute `writes` is used to buffer write operations. `status` denotes the overall transaction status: `idle`, `executing(lp,t)` (the transaction is executing at log position lp and will continue executing for time t), and `in-paxos`, which is used during the commit process. The attributes `readState` and `paxosState` store transient data for each entity group accessed by the transaction execution.

Modeling Communication. We assume that the communication delay is non-deterministic. The *set* of possible delays depends on the sender and receiver, and is given by `possibleMsgDelays(s_1, s_2)` as a '`;`'-separated set of time values:

```
sort TimeSet .     subsort Time < TimeSet .
op emptyTimeSet : -> TimeSet .
```

```
op _;_ : TimeSet TimeSet -> TimeSet [ctor assoc comm id: emptyTimeSet] .
op possibleMsgDelays : SiteId SiteId -> TimeSet [comm] .
```

A "ripe" message has the form

> msg *mc* from *sender* to *receiver*

where *mc* is the *message content*. A message in transit that will be delivered after t time units is modeled by a term dly(msg *mc* from *sender* to *receiver*, t):

```
sort DlyMsg .
subsort Msg < DlyMsg < NEConfiguration .
op dly : Msg Time -> DlyMsg [ctor right id: 0] .
msg msg_from_to_ : MsgContent Oid Oid -> Msg .
```

Nondeterministically selecting *any* possible delay from possibleMsgDelays(s_1, s_2) can be done using a matching equation in the condition of the rewrite rule. A rule creating a single message with nondeterministic delay should have the form[3]

```
var T : Time .    var TS : TimeSet .

crl [sendMsgAnd...] :
    < SID : Site | ... >   ...
  =>
    < SID : Site | ... >   ...
    dly(msg mc from SID to SID', T)
 if ... /\ T ; TS := possibleMsgDelays(SID,SID') .
```

A site must often *multicast* a message to all other sites replicating an entity group. The delay of each single message must of course be selected nondeterministically. A naïve solution to model such multicast by generating the corresponding single messages in any order would be prohibitively expensive from a model checking perspective: if there are n recipients, there would be $n!$ different orders in which these messages could be *created*. We can therefore use a "partial order reduction" technique, in which the messages are sent in a certain order. In particular, the replicas attribute of an EntityGroup object contains sets of tuples egrs(SID,N), where the second component is unique in the group. We can therefore order the set of recipients, and generate the single messages in this order, reducing the number of possible orders of sending the messages from $n!$ to 1. The following rewrite rule is used to "dissolve" a "multicast message"

> multiCast *mc* from SID to EGRS

into single messages with nondeterministically selected delays:

```
op multiCast_from_to_ : MsgContent Oid EntityGroupReplicaSet
    -> Configuration [ctor] .
eq multiCast MC from SID to noEGR = none .
crl [multiCastToUnicast] :
```

---

[3] We do not show most variable declarations, but follow the Maude convention that variables are written with capital letters.

```
multiCast MC from SID to (egrs(SID', N) ; EGRS)
=>
 dly(msg MC from SID to SID', T)
 (multiCast MC from SID to EGRS)
if N == smallest(egrs(SID', N) ; EGRS)
  /\ T ; TS := possibleMsgDelays(SID, SID') .
```

Therefore, to multicast a message with message content mc to all other sites replicating the entity group EG, a rule of the following form *could* be used:

```
rl [multicastReplicatingSites]
   < SID : Site | entityGroups : < EG : EntityGroup | replicas : EGRS, ... > ...
=>
   < SID : Site | .... >  ...
(multiCast mc from SID to EGRS) .
```

However, this would still involve $n + 1$ rewrite steps needed to get to a state where all the single messages have been generated, unnecessarily increasing the state space explored during model checking. By using rewrite conditions, we can replace the above rewrite rule with a rule

```
var SINGLE-MSGS : NEConfiguration .

crl [multicastReplicatingSitesEfficient]
      < SID : Site | entityGroups : < EG : EntityGroup | replicas : EGRS, ... > ...
      =>
      < SID : Site | .... >  ...
      SINGLE-MSGS
      if (multiCast mc from SID to EGRS) => SINGLE-MSGS .
```

where SINGLE-MSGS is a variable of some sort containing sets of delayed messages, but no occurrences of the multiCast operator. In this rewrite rule, all the single messages are created in *one* rewrite step, drastically reducing the reachable state space. (The local "partial order reduction" is still important, since it significantly reduces the number of behaviors explored by Maude during the evaluation of the rewrite condition; however, it does not reduce the reachable state space.)

Dynamic Behavior. The dynamic behavior of Megastore *without* fault tolerance features is modeled by 16 rewrite rules, 7 of which are given below. A transaction request with operations ol and name t is sent to a site s by a message newTrans(s, t, ol). When a site gets such a transaction request, the site adds a corresponding transaction object to its localTransactions.

```
rl [newTrans] :
   newTrans(SID, TID, OL)
   < SID : Site | localTransactions : LOCALTRANS >
   =>
   < SID : Site | localTransactions : LOCALTRANS
        < TID : Transaction | operations : OL, readState : emptyReadState,
                              paxosState : emptyPaxosState, reads : emptyEntitySet,
                              writes : emptyOpList, status : idle > .
```

If the next operation in an `idle` transaction TID is a current read (`cr`) of an entity `entity(EG,N)` in entity group EG, the transaction goes to the local state `executing(LP,readDelay)`, where LP is the local coordinator's current log position for EG, and `readDelay` is the time it takes to perform a read operation:

```
crl [startCurrentLocalRead] :
   < SID : Site | coordinator : (EG upToDateAt LP ; CES),
                     entityGroups : EGROUPS
                        < EG : EntityGroup | pendingWrites : emptyPWList >
                     localTransactions : LOCALTRANS
                        < TID : Transaction | operations : cr(entity(EG,N)) :: OL,
                                              status : idle > >
   =>
   < SID : Site | localTransactions : LOCALTRANS
                        < TID : Transaction | operations : cr(entity(EG,N)) :: OL,
                                              status : executing(LP, readDelay) > >
   if not (containsUpdate(entity(EG,N), OL) and
           inConflictWithRunning(EG, LOCALTRANS)) .
```

To avoid locals conflicts, a site only allows one active update transaction for each entity group. The condition of the rewrite rule blocks the read request if the transaction TID contains an update operation on `entity(EG,N)` until there are no other active conflicting transactions.

When the `executing` timer expires (i.e., becomes zero), the read operation completes and adds the version read at the given log position to `reads`. The transaction status is then set to `idle`, allowing execution to proceed:

```
rl [endCurrentLocalRead] :
   < SID : Site |
      entityGroups : EGROUPS
         < EG : EntityGroup | entitiesState : (entity(EG,N) |-> EVERSIONS) ; BSTATE >,
      localTransactions : LOCALTRANS
         < TID : Transaction | operations : cr(entity(EG,N)) :: OL, readState : RSTATE,
                               status : executing(LP, 0), reads : READS > >
   =>
   < SID : Site | localTransactions : LOCALTRANS
         < TID : Transaction |
                  operations : OL, readState : readpos(EG, LP) ; RSTATE, status : idle,
                  reads : READS ; (entity(EG,N) |-> getVersion(LP, EVERSIONS)) > > .
```

A write operation is moved to the buffer `writes`, and will be executed once the transaction is committed:

```
rl [bufferWriteOperation] :
   < SID : Site | localTransactions : LOCALTRANS
         < TID : Transaction | operations : w(EID, VAL) :: OL, writes : WRITEOPS,
                               status : idle > >
   =>
   < SID : Site | localTransactions : LOCALTRANS
         < TID : Transaction | operations : OL, writes : WRITEOPS :: w(EID, VAL) > > .
```

When all operations in the `operations` list are completed (reads) or buffered (writes), the transaction is ready to commit. All buffered updates are merged into a candidate log entry. If the transaction updates entities from several entity groups, one log entry is created for each group.

For each such entity group, the first step is to send the candidate log entry to the leader for the *next* log position, which was selected during the previous coordination round. The rule for initiating Paxos is modeled as follows:

```
crl [initiateCommit] :
  < SID : Site |
       entityGroups : EGROUPS,
       localTransactions : LOCALTRANS
           < TID : Transaction | operations : emptyOpList,
                                 writes : WRITEOPS, status : idle
                                 readState : RSTATE, paxosState : PSTATE > >
  =>
  < SID : Site |
       localTransactions : LOCALTRANS
           < TID : Transaction | paxosState : NEW-PAXOS-STATE,
                                 status : in-paxos > >
  ACC-LEADER-REQ-MSGS
  if EIDSET := getEntityGroupIds(WRITEOPS) /\
     NEW-PAXOS-STATE := initiatePaxosState(EIDSET, TID, WRITEOPS,
                                           SID, RSTATE, EGROUPS)
  /\ (createAcceptLeaderMessages(SID, NEW-PAXOS-STATE)) => ACC-LEADER-REQ-MSGS .
```

getEntityGroupIds(WRITEOPS) contains entity groups accessed by operations in WRITEOPS, and NEW-PAXOS-STATE contains one record for each entity group. These records contain the log position that TID requests to update and the candidate log entry *le*. The operator createAcceptLeaderMessages generates an acceptLeaderReq message to the leader of each entity group containing the transaction id TID and candidate log entry *le*.

The execution then proceeds as follows for each entity group:

1. When the leader s_l receives an acceptLeaderReq message from the originating site s_o for the transaction TID, the leader site inspects the proposals set for the given entity group, to check whether it has previously accepted some value for this log position and entity group. If so, there is a conflict, and s_l signals this with a message to the originating site of TID, which aborts the transaction. Otherwise, s_l sends an acceptLeaderRsp message to s_o.
2. When it receives an acceptLeaderRsp message, the originating site proceeds by multicasting the log entry to the other replicating sites. Each recipient of this message must verify that it has not already granted an accept for this log position. If so, the recipient replies with an accept message to the originating site. We show this rule below.
3. After receiving an acceptAllRsp message from all replicating sites, the originating site confirms the commit by multicasting an applyReq message. When receiving this message, a recipient appends the proposed log entry to the transactionLog of the entity group, and the update operations are added to the pendingWrites list. With this, the transaction is committed.

The following rule shows the rule from step 2 where a replicating site receives an acceptAllReq message. The site verifies that it has not already granted an accept for this log position (since messages could be delayed for a long time, it checks both the transaction log and received proposals). If there are no such conflicts, the site responds with an accept message, and stores its accept in `proposals` for this entity group. The record (`TID' LP SID OL`) represents the candidate log entry, containing the transaction identifier `TID'`, the log position `LP`, the proposed leader site `SID`, and the list of update operations `OL`.

```
crl [rcvAcceptAllReq] :
   (msg acceptAllReq(TID, EG, (TID' LP SID OL), PROPNUM) from SENDER to THIS)
   < THIS : Site |
     entityGroups : EGROUPS
       < EG : EntityGroup | proposals : PROPSET, transactionLog : LEL > >
   =>
   < THIS : Site |
     entityGroups : EGROUPS
       < EG : EntityGroup |
         proposals : accepted(SENDER, (TID' LP SID OL), PROPNUM) ;
                   removeProposal(LP, PROPSET) > >
   dly(acceptAllRsp(TID, EG, LP, PROPNUM) from THIS to SENDER), T)
   if not (containsLPos(LP, LEL) or hasAcceptedForPosition(LP, PROPSET))
     /\ T ; TS := possibleMessageDelay(THIS, SENDER) .
```

Modeling Time and Time Elapse. We follow the guidelines in [17] for modeling time in object-oriented specifications. Since an action can only be triggered by the arrival of a message, the expiration of a timer, or by another event, we use the following tick rule to advance time until the next event will take place:

```
crl [tick] : {SYSTEM} => {delta(SYSTEM, mte(SYSTEM))}
            if mte(SYSTEM) > 0 /\ mte(SYSTEM) =/= INF .
```

The function `mte` denotes the minimum time that can elapse until the next event will take place, and `delta` defines the effect of time elapse on the state. For example, `mte(dly(M,T) REST) = min(T, mte(REST))`, which means that `mte`(m) is zero for a ripe message m (since m is identical to `dly`(m,0)). Therefore, time cannot advance when there are ripe messages in the configuration.

We import the built-in module `NAT-TIME-DOMAIN-WITH-INF`, which defines the time domain `Time` to be the natural numbers, with an additional constant `INF` (for ∞) of a supersort `TimeInf`.

4.3   Modeling Megastore's Fault Tolerance Mechanisms

Megastore is supposed to tolerate: (i) site failures (except for the coordinators); (ii) message loss; and (iii) arbitrarily long message delays. We have formalized these fault tolerance features using 37 rewrites rules, out of which we show only 1 rule in this paper. Our model provides fault tolerance and consistency through the following mechanisms:

- A Paxos-based commit protocol to ensure that even in the presence of multiple failure and recovery events, all available replicas agree on the value for the

next log position. If the originating site s_o, after sending an `acceptLeaderReq`
message for log position lp, does not receive a response from the leader of lp
within a certain amount of time, it attempts to become the leader itself by
sending a `prepareAllReq` message to all replicating sites. When receiving a
positive response from a majority of sites, s_o proceeds with the accept phase
by multicasting an `acceptAllReq` message to all replicating sites. If at this
point s_o fails to receive an `acceptAllRsp` message from a majority of sites, it
re-initiates the prepare step after a nondeterministic backoff.

 - If a replicating site s_r is unable to apply an update, the coordinator at
   s_r must ensure that the site avoids serving invalid data. After obtaining a
   `acceptAllRsp` message from a majority of the replicating sites, the originating site sends an `invalidateCoordinator` message to each site which did not
   respond in time to the `acceptAllReq` message.
 - A majority read and catchup procedure is used to bring a replica up-to-
   date in case of failures. When executing a current read operation requesting
   an entity from an invalid entity group eg (according to the coordinator),
   the originating site s_o broadcasts a `majorityRead` request to all sites replicating eg. Each available recipient responds with the highest log position
   seen so far. When a majority of replicating sites have responded, s_o sends
   a `catchupRequest` containing the highest received log position to *one* of the
   responding sites. If this site does not have a complete log, s_o sends several
   catchup requests. Once s_o's log is complete, the entity group is marked as
   valid in the coordinator.

The following rule belongs to the first mechanism above, and shows how we
meet a requirement of Paxos: after a site has accepted a log entry, it can never
accept another log entry for this log position. Therefore, if a replicating site
receives a `prepareAllReq` message for a log position where it has already accepted a log entry, the entry is sent to the originating site in a `prepareAllRsp`
message. At the originating site, the log entry for the highest proposal number
seen so far is stored within the `prepare` record of `paxosState`. If the originating site has received `prepareAllRsp` from a majority of the participating sites
(`hasQuorum(size(SIS ; SENDER), REPLICAS)`), it initiates the `acceptAll` step by
multicasting an `acceptAllReq` to all sites replicating the entity group `EG`:

```
crl [rcvPrepareAllRspWithValue] :
    (msg prepareAllRsp(TID,EG, (TID2 LP MSID1 OL1), PROPNUM, PN)
        from SENDER to THIS)
    < THIS : Site |
        entityGroups : < EG : EntityGroup | replicas : EGRS > EGROUPS,
        localTransactions : LOCALTRANS
            < TID : Transaction | status : in-paxos,
                paxosState : prepare(EG, (TID3 LP MSID2 OL2),
                                      PROPNUM, SEEN-PROPNUM, SIS, EXP) ; PSTATE > >
  =>
    < THIS : Site |
        localTransactions : LOCALTRANS
            (if hasQuorum(size(SIS ; SENDER), REPLICAS) then
                < TID : Transaction | status : in-paxos, paxosState :
```

```
                        acceptAll(EG, NEW-LE, PROPNUM, THIS, defTimeout) ; PSTATE >
            else
              < TID : Transaction | paxosState :
                        prepare(EG, NEW-LE, PROPNUM, maxPn(PN, SEEN-PROPNUM),
                                (SIS ; SENDER), EXP) ; PSTATE >
            fi) >
    MSGS
  if REPLICAS := getSites(EGRS) /\
     NEW-LE := chooseValue(PN, SEEN-PROPNUM,
                           (TID2 LP MSID1 OL1),(TID3 LP MSID2 OL2))
     /\ (if hasQuorum(size(SIS ; SENDER), REPLICAS) then
            multiCast acceptAllReq(TID, EG, NEW-LE, PROPNUM) from THIS to EGRS
            else none fi) => MSGS .
```

Site Failures. All processing is blocked and incoming messages are dropped when a site has failed. The exception is that the (co-located) coordinator of the site is supposed to be available, and be able to receive and respond to `invalidateCoordinator` messages even when the site is otherwise failed.

We model site failures in a modular way by enclosing the failed site object by a "wrapper": a failed site is modeled as a term `failed(< s : Site | ... >)`. This wrapper is declared to be a *frozen* operator (see [5])

```
op failed : Object -> Object [ctor frozen (1)] .
```

which ensures that no activity takes place inside the failed object.

A message arriving at a failed site is dropped, unless it is a message to the coordinator:

```
crl [msgWhenSiteFailure] :
    (msg MC from SENDER to SID)  failed(< SID : Site | >)
    =>
    failed(< SID : Site | >)
    if not isInvalidateCoordinator(MC) .

crl [invalidateCoordinator] :
    (msg invalidateCoordinator(EG, LP) from SENDER to THIS)
    failed(< THIS : Site | coordinator : CES >)
    =>
    failed(< THIS : Site | coordinator : applyInvalidate(EG, LP, CES) >)
    (dly invalidateConfirmed(EG, LP) from THIS to SENDER, T)
    if T ; TS := possibleMsgDelays(THIS,SENDER) .
```

In our analysis, we use "messages" `siteFailure(s)` and `siteRepair(s)` to inject failures and repairs as follows:

```
msgs siteFailure siteRepair : SiteId -> Msg .

crl [siteDown] :
    siteFailure(SID) < SID : Site | > => failed(< SID | >) dly(siteRepair(SID), T)
  if T ; TS := possibleSiteRepairTimes .

rl [siteUp] :
    siteRepair(SID) failed(< SID : Site | >) => < SID : Site | > .
```

5   Formally Analyzing our Model of Megastore

We used both simulation and temporal logic model checking throughout the development of our formal model from the description in [2]. Simulation provided quick feedback; allowed us to analyze large systems with many sites, transactions, and failures; and "probabilistic" simulation was used for quality of service (QoS) estimation of the model. Model checking, which explores all possible system behaviors, turned out to be very useful to find a number of subtle design flaws that were not uncovered during extensive simulations.

This section shows how our model of Megastore can be formally analyzed in (Maude and) Real-Time Maude. In particular, Section 5.1 lists the main properties to analyze; Section 5.2 gives some parameters of our model; Section 5.3 shows how we can simulate our model for QoS estimation; Section 5.4 explains our model checking of the model *without* fault-tolerance features; and Section 5.5 describes the model checking of the entire model. Finally, Section 5.6 presents a general technique for formally analyzing the *serializability* property of transactional systems: each execution is equivalent to one in which all operations of a transaction are completed before the next transaction begins.

5.1   Properties to Analyze

We use Real-Time Maude to analyze both *quality of service* and *correctness* properties of our model. The important quality of service parameters are:

1. Transaction latency: the delay between the reception of a transaction request and the response to the caller.
2. The fraction of received transactions that are committed and aborted, respectively.

If there are a *finite* number of transactions to be executed, then the main correctness properties that the system should satisfy are:

3. All transactions will eventually finish their execution.
4. All replicas of an entity must eventually have the same value.
5. All logs for the same entity group must eventually contain the same entries.
6. The execution is serializable; i.e., it gives the same result as some execution where the transactions are executed one after the other.
7. Furthermore, from some point on, the properties 3-6 above must hold for all future states.

5.2   System Parameters

There are a number of system parameters in our model, including:

- the number of sites;
- the set of possible message delays between each pair of sites;
- the number of transactions and their arrival times;

- the set of operations in each transaction;
- the number of entities and their organization into entity groups;
- the degree of replication of the different entity groups;
- the number and time distribution of site failures, and the set of possible durations of a site failure;
- the amount of message losses; and
- the duration of the timeouts before initiating fault handling procedures.

Changing these parameters allows us to analyze the model under different scenarios. For example, to define the set of possible message delays, we need to define the function `possibleMsgDelays`. In some of the model checking commands, we use three sites and the following message delays:

```
eq possibleMsgDelays(PARIS, LONDON) = (10 ; 30 ; 80) .
eq possibleMsgDelays(PARIS, NEW-YORK) = (30 ; 60 ; 120) .
eq possibleMsgDelays(LONDON, NEW-YORK) = (30 ; 60 ; 120) .
```

Transactions and failures are injected into the system by (delayed) messages `dly(newTrans(`s,t,ol`),`$startTime$`)` and `dly(siteFailure(`s`),`$failureTime$`)`. For example, some of our analyses use `initTransactions` and `initFailures`, where the start time of each transaction is nondeterministically selected from the set of possible start times `transStartTime`, and the time of each failure is nondeterministically selected from the set `ttf`:

```
vars T1 T2 T3 : Time .     vars TS1 TS2 TS3 : TimeSet .

crl [delayTransactions] :
   initTransactions
   =>
   dly(newTrans(PARIS, T-K, cr(entity(EG1,0)) :: w(entity(EG1,0),value(2))), T1)
   dly(newTrans(LONDON, T-L, cr(entity(EG1,0)) :: w(entity(EG1,0),value(5))), T2)
   dly(newTrans(NEW-YORK, T-M, cr(entity(EG2,0)) :: w(entity(EG2,0),value(4))), T3)
   if T1 ; TS1 := transStartTime /\ T2 ; TS2 := transStartTime
   /\ T3 ; TS3 := transStartTime .

eq transStartTime = (10 ; 50 ; 200) .

crl [delayFailures] :
   initFailures => dly(siteFailure(LONDON), T1) dly(siteFailure(NEW-YORK), T2)
   if T1 ; TS1 := ttf /\ (T2 ; TS2) := ttf .

eq ttf = (40 ; 100) .
```

The initial state `initMegastore` can then be defined as follows:

```
op initMegastore : -> GlobalSystem .
eq initMegastore = {initSites initTransactions initFailures} .

eq initSites =
  < PARIS : Site | coordinator : EG1 upToDateAt lpos(0) ; EG2 upToDateAt lpos(0),
                   entityGroups : entityGroupsParis, localTransactions : none >
  < LONDON : Site | coordinator : EG1 upToDateAt lpos(0) ; EG2 upToDateAt lpos(0),
                    entityGroups : entityGroupsLondon, localTransactions : none >
  < NEW-YORK : Site | coordinator : EG1 upToDateAt lpos(0) ; EG2 upToDateAt lpos(0),
                      entityGroups : entityGroupsNY, localTransactions : none > .
```

5.3   Simulation

We can use Real-Time Maude's timed rewrite command to simulate the system for a certain duration:

```
Maude> (tfrew initMegastore in time <= 850 .)

{< LONDON : Site | coordinator : EG1 upToDateAt lpos(0) ; EG2 upToDateAt lpos(1),
  entityGroups : (
   < EG1 : EntityGroup |
     entitiesState : entity(EG1,0) |-> lpos(0)value(0) ; entity(EG1,1) |-> lpos(0)value(0),
     pendingWrites : emptyPWList,
     proposals : accepted(LONDON,T-L lpos(1) LONDON w(entity(EG1,0),value(5)),2),
     replicas : egr(LONDON,0,lpos(0)) ; egr(NEW-YORK,2,lpos(0)) ; egr(PARIS,1,lpos(0)),
     transactionLog : initTrans lpos(0) PARIS emptyOpList >
   < EG2 : EntityGroup | ... >),
  localTransactions :
   < T-L : Transaction | operations : emptyOpList,
       paxosState : acceptAll(EG1,T-L lpos(1) LONDON w(entity(EG1,0),value(5)),
                    1,LONDON ; NEW-YORK, 240),
       reads : entity(EG1,0)|-> lpos(0)value(0), writes : w(entity(EG1,0),value(5)),
       readState : readpos(EG1,lpos(0)), status : in-paxos > >
< NEW-YORK : Site | ... >
< PARIS : Site | ... >} in time 850
```

Although this gives very quick and useful feedback, each application of a rule which selects a value nondeterministically will select the same value. To simulate more random behaviors, and to obtain more realistic QoS estimates, we have also defined a "probalistic" version of our model where the different delays are given by discrete probability distributions. We then add an object containing the seed to Maude's built-in `random` function to the configuration, and use this random value to sample a message delay from the probability distribution. Our probability distribution for the network delays is as follows:[4]

	30%	30%	30%	10%
London ↔ Paris	10	15	20	50
London ↔ New York	30	35	40	100
Paris ↔ New York	30	35	40	100

We generate transactions with a *transaction generator* for each site, which generates transaction requests at random times, with an adjustable average rate measured in *transactions per second (TPS)*. We simulated two fully replicated entity groups. We assume a delay of 10 ms for a local read operation in accordance with the real-world measurements reported in [2].

Simulation without Fault Injection. With an average of 2.5 TPS and no failures, we observe the following results in a run of 200 seconds:

	Avg. latency (ms)	Commits	Aborts
London	122	149	15
New York	155	132	33
Paris	119	148	18

---

[4] The delays New York–Paris and New York–London are the same, assuming transatlantic backbone links from each of these cities. The delay between Paris and London reflect that network equipment and local lines increase delivery times.

The relatively high abort rate is expected, since we have only two entity groups. While our calibration data are estimates based on a typical setup for this type of cloud service combined with information given in [2], our measured latency appears fairly consistent with Megastore itself [2]: "Most users see average write latencies of 100–400 milliseconds, depending on the distance between datacenters, the size of the data being written, and the number of full replicas."

Simulation with Fault Injection. We have modified the above experiment by adding a fault injector that randomly injects short outages in the sites. The mean time to failure and the mean time to repair for each site was set to 10 and 2 seconds, respectively. This is a challenging scenario where a large fraction of the transactions will experience failure on one or multiple sites. The results from our simulation are given in the following table.

	Avg. latency (ms)	Commits	Aborts
London	218	109	38
New York	336	129	16
Paris	331	116	21

Although both the average latency and the abort rate increase significantly, these results indicate that Megastore is able to maintain an acceptable quality of service under this challenging failure scenario.

5.4   Model Checking the Model without Fault Tolerance

We use linear temporal logic model checking to verify that all possible executions from a given initial state satisfy the correctness properties 3-5 and 7 in Section 5.1 (the serializability analysis is explained in Section 5.6).

The state proposition `allTransFinished` is `true` in all states where all transactions have finished executing. That is, there are no `Transaction` objects remaining in a site's `localTransactions` and there are no messages in the system:

```
vars SYSTEM REST LOCALTRANS EGS1 EGS2 : Configuration .
var M : Msg .       vars ES1 ES2 : EntitySet .       vars TL1 TL2 : LogEntryList .

op allTransFinished : -> Prop [ctor] .
eq {initTransactions REST}  |= allTransFinished = false .
eq {< S1 : Site | localTransactions : < TID : Transaction | > LOCALTRANS > REST}
    |= allTransFinished = false .
eq {M REST}  |= allTransFinished = false .
eq {SYSTEM}  |= allTransFinished = true [owise] .
```

This definition first characterizes the states where `allTransFinished` does *not* hold; the last equation, with the `owise` attribute, then defines `allTransFinished` to be `true` for all other states.

The following proposition `entityGroupsEqual` is `true` for all states where all replicas of each entity have the same value:

```
op entityGroupsEqual : -> Prop [ctor] .
ceq {< S1 : Site | entityGroups : < EG1 : EntityGroup | entitiesState : ES1 > EGS1 >
     < S2 : Site | entityGroups : < EG1 : EntityGroup | entitiesState : ES2 > EGS2 >
     REST}  |= entityGroupsEqual = false if ES1 =/= ES2 .
eq  {SYSTEM}  |= entityGroupsEqual = true [owise] .
```

In the same way, we can define when all transitions logs for each entity group are equal:

```
op transLogsEqual : -> Prop [ctor] .
ceq {< S1 : Site | entityGroups : < EG1 : EntityGroup | transactionLog : TL1 > EGS1 >
     < S2 : Site | entityGroups : < EG1 : EntityGroup | transactionLog : TL2 > EGS2 >
     REST}  |= transLogsEqual = false if TL1 =/= TL2 .
eq  {SYSTEM}  |= transLogsEqual = true [owise] .
```

The temporal logic formula

```
<> [] (allTransFinished /\ entityGroupsEqual /\ transLogsEqual)
```

says that in *all possible executions* from the initial state, a state satisfying Properties 1–3 and where all subsequent states also satisfy those properties, will eventually be reached.

In the absence of the sophisticated failure handling, this formula should hold for all possible message delays and transaction (start and execution) times. We have therefore abstracted from the real-time features of our model, such as message delays, execution times, and timers, and have transformed our model into an *untimed model* that will exhibit *all possible* behaviors of the system. Model checking this property for the initial state initMegastore (without delays) with the three sites and three transactions can be done in Maude as follows:

```
Maude> (red modelCheck(initMegastore,
              <> [] (allTransFinished /\ entityGroupsEqual /\ transLogsEqual)) .)

result Bool :  true
```

That is, the desired property holds. The model checking took 950 seconds on an Intel Xeon 1.87Ghz CPU with 128 GB RAM. Reachability analysis showed that this untimed model has 992,992 states reachable from initMegastore. Both model checking and reachability analysis from initMegastore extended with a fourth transaction were aborted due to lack of memory after 11 hours.

5.5 Model Checking the Model with Failure Handling

The analysis in Section 5.4 shows that model checking the *untimed* model is unfeasible for four transactions even *without* the large fault-tolerance part. Furthermore, the fault-tolerance features of Megastore require an extensive use of timers. Therefore, we model check only the real-time version described in Section 4 when including the fault-tolerance part.

Since we consider a finite number of transactions, the desired property must now also take into account the following possibility: if a failure causes one or more of the sites to miss the *last* update, leaving its coordinator invalidated, then no further transactions will arrive to initiate a majority read. Therefore, we use modified versions of the propositions in Section 5.4, that make sure that we only require equal `entitiesState` and `transactionLog` among sites where the coordinator indicates that the given entity group is up-to-date:

```
op entityGroupsEqualOrInvalid : -> Prop [ctor] .
ceq  {< S1 : Site | coordinator : eglp(EG1, LP) ; EGLP,
                    entityGroups : < EG1 : EntityGroup | entitiesState : ES1 > EGS1 >
       < S2 : Site | coordinator : eglp(EG1, LP) ; EGLP,
                    entityGroups : < EG1 : EntityGroup | entitiesState : ES2 > EGS2 >
     REST} |= entityGroupsEqual = false if ES1 =/= ES2 .
eq {SYSTEM} |= entityGroupsEqualOrInvalid = true [owise] .
```

We have model checked a number of scenarios, all with three sites, two entity groups, three transactions (each accessing one item in each entity group). The parameters we modify are: the number of possible message delays, the possible start times of a transaction, and the number of failures and their start times. In the case with possible message delays $\{20, 100\}$, possible transaction start times $\{10, 50, 200\}$, and one failure at time 60, the following (unbounded) Real-Time Maude model checking command verifies the desired property in 1164 seconds:

```
Maude: (mc initMegastore |=u <> [] (allTransFinished /\ entityGroupsEqualOrInvalid
                                  /\ transLogsEqualOrInvalid) .)

result Bool :   true
```

We summarize the execution time of the above model checking command for different system parameters, where $\{n_1, \ldots, n_k\}$ means that the corresponding value is selected nondeterministically from the set. All the model checking commands that finished executing returned `true`. *DNF* means that the execution was aborted after more than 4 hours.

Msg. delay	#Trans	Trans. start time	#Fail.	Fail. time	Run (sec)
$\{20, 100\}$	4	$\{19, 80\}$ and $\{50, 200\}$	0	–	1367
$\{20, 100\}$	3	$\{10, 50, 200\}$	1	60	1164
$\{20, 40\}$	3	20, 30, and $\{10, 50\}$	2	$\{40, 80\}$	872
$\{20, 40\}$	4	20, 20, 60, and 110	2	70 and $\{10, 130\}$	241
$\{20, 40\}$	4	20, 20, 60, and 110	2	$\{30, 80\}$	DNF
$\{10, 30, 80\}$, and $\{30, 60, 120\}$	3	20, 30, 40	1	$\{30, 80\}$	DNF
$\{10, 30, 80\}$, and $\{30, 60, 120\}$	3	20, 30, 40	1	60	DNF

5.6   Model Checking Serializability

The *serialization graph* for a given execution of a set of committed transactions is a directed graph where each transaction is represented by a node, and where there is an edge from a node t_1 to another node t_2 iff the transaction t_1 has executed an operation on entity e before transaction t_2 executed an operation on the same entity, and at least one of the operations was a write operation. It is well known that an execution of multiple transactions is serializable if and only if its *serialization graph* is acyclic [21].

If there is only one version of each entity, and every update therefore overwrites the previous version, the *before* relation follows real time. In a multi-versioned replicated data store like Megastore, we require a defined *version order* $<<$ on the written entity values to decide the *before* relation when constructing the serialization graph. For example: a write operation $w(e,v)$ which creates a version k of entity e occurs *before* a current read $cr(e)$ iff $cr(e)$ reads a version l where $k << l$ according to the selected version order.

Since we require serializability within each entity group only, and every committed transaction is assigned a unique log position for each entity group it updates, we use log positions for the version order. This means that if, for example, t_i reads from log position lp and t_k commits an update at log position lp', then $t_i \rightarrow t_k$ in the serialization graph iff $lp < lp'$.

When an update transaction t_i commits, it produces a message containing:

- the log position and value of each entity it has read; and
- the set of entities written, all of them have the log position assigned to t_i.

We therefore add to the state an object of class `TransactionHistory` containing the current serialization graph. Each time a transaction commits, this object reads the above message and updates its serialization graph.

The sort `SerGraph` defines a set of edges:

```
var E : Edge .
sort SerGraph .        sort Edge .       subsort Edge < SerGraph .
op _<->_ : TransId TransId -> Edge [ctor] .
op emptyGraph : -> SerGraph [ctor] .
op _;_ : SerGraph SerGraph -> SerGraph [ctor assoc comm id: emptyGraph] .
eq E ; E = E .

class TransactionHistory | graph : SerGraph .
```

The proposition `isSerializable` can then be defined as expected:

```
op isSerializable : -> Prop [ctor] .
eq {< th : TransactionHistory | graph : GRAPH > REST}
        |= isSerializable = not hasCycle(GRAPH) .
```

We can therefore verify that for each state, the execution up to the current state is serializable:

```
Maude: (mc initMegastore |=u [] isSerializable .)

result Bool :  true
```

6   Related Work and Concluding Remarks

Despite the importance of transactional data stores, we are not aware of any work on formalizing and verifying such systems. We are also not aware of any detailed description of Megastore itself beyond [2].

The paper [18] addresses the need for formal analysis of replication and concurrency control in transactional cloud data stores. Using Megastore as a motivating example, the authors propose a generic framework for concurrency control based on Paxos, and include a pseudo-code description of Paxos and a proof of how it can be used to ensure serializability. In contrast, we provide a much more detailed and formal model not only of Paxos, but of Megastore itself.

The value of Maude for formally analyzing other cloud mechanisms is demonstrated in [19], where the authors point out possible bottlenecks in a naïve implementation of ZooKeeper for key distribution, and in [7], where the authors analyze denial-of-service prevention mechanisms using Maude and PVeStA.

Real-Time Maude has been used to model and analyze a wide range of advanced state-of-the-art systems, including multicast protocols [14], wireless sensor network algorithms [15], and scheduling protocols [12]. In all these applications, Real-Time Maude analysis uncovered significant design errors that could be traced back to flaws in the original system. The work presented in this paper differs fundamentally from those applications of Real-Time Maude: in this case, our starting point was a fairly brief and informal overview paper on Megastore – in addition to a number of papers describing the underlying Paxos protocol. We therefore had to "fill in" a lot of details, in essence developing and formalizing our own version of the Megastore approach. The available source on Megastore was not detailed enough to allow us to map flaws found during Real-Time Maude model checking to flaws in the original description of Megastore. Instead, we used Real-Time Maude simulation and model checking extensively throughout our development of this very complex system to improve our model to the point where we cannot find any flaws during our model checking analyses.

Our main contribution is therefore this fairly detailed executable formal model of (our version of) Megastore. Minor contributions include general techniques for: (i) efficiently modeling multicast with nondeterministic message delays in Real-Time Maude; and (ii) model checking the serializability property of distributed transactions on replication data in (Real-Time) Maude.

We hope that our formalization contributes to further research on the Megastore approach to transactional data stores. In particular, we are planning on combining Megastore with the FLACS approach [8] to provide serializability also for transactions accessing multiple entity groups. Other future work includes defining a probabilistic version of our model in a probabilistic extension of Maude, and use the PVeStA tool [1] for statistical model checking and more advanced QoS estimation.

Acknowledgments. We are grateful to the Festschrift editors for giving us the opportunity to honor Kokichi Futatsugi, an excellent researcher and a true gentleman. The second author and his family still have many fond memories from Kokichi and Junko's visit to Oslo a few years ago. We would also like to thank the anonymous reviewers for very insightful comments which have helped us improve the paper.

References

1. AlTurki, M., Meseguer, J.: PVeStA: A parallel statistical model checking and quantitative analysis tool. In: Corradini, A., Klin, B., Cîrstea, C. (eds.) CALCO 2011. LNCS, vol. 6859, pp. 386–392. Springer, Heidelberg (2011)
2. Baker, J., et al.: Megastore: Providing scalable, highly available storage for interactive services. In: CIDR (2011), http://www.cidrdb.org
3. Bruni, R., Meseguer, J.: Semantic foundations for generalized rewrite theories. Theoretical Computer Science 360(1-3), 386–414 (2006)
4. Campbell, D.G., Kakivaya, G., Ellis, N.: Extreme scale with full SQL language support in Microsoft SQL Azure. In: SIGMOD 2010, pp. 1021–1024. ACM (2010)
5. Clavel, M., Durán, F., Eker, S., Lincoln, P., Martí-Oliet, N., Meseguer, J., Talcott, C.: All About Maude - A High-Performance Logical Framework. LNCS, vol. 4350. Springer, Heidelberg (2007)
6. Corbett, J.C., et al.: Spanner: Google's globally-distributed database. In: OSDI 2012, pp. 251–264. USENIX Association, Berkeley (2012)
7. Eckhardt, J., Mühlbauer, T., AlTurki, M., Meseguer, J., Wirsing, M.: Stable availability under denial of service attacks through formal patterns. In: de Lara, J., Zisman, A. (eds.) FASE 2012. LNCS, vol. 7212, pp. 78–93. Springer, Heidelberg (2012)
8. Grov, J., Ölveczky, P.C.: Scalable and fully consistent transactions in the cloud through hierarchical validation. In: Hameurlain, A., Rahayu, W., Taniar, D. (eds.) Globe 2013. LNCS, vol. 8059, pp. 26–38. Springer, Heidelberg (2013)
9. Lamport, L.: Paxos made simple. ACM Sigact News 32(4), 18–25 (2001)
10. Meseguer, J.: Conditional rewriting logic as a unified model of concurrency. Theoretical Computer Science 96, 73–155 (1992)
11. Meseguer, J.: Membership algebra as a logical framework for equational specification. In: Parisi-Presicce, F. (ed.) WADT 1997. LNCS, vol. 1376, pp. 18–61. Springer, Heidelberg (1998)
12. Ölveczky, P.C., Caccamo, M.: Formal simulation and analysis of the CASH scheduling algorithm in Real-Time Maude. In: Baresi, L., Heckel, R. (eds.) FASE 2006. LNCS, vol. 3922, pp. 357–372. Springer, Heidelberg (2006)
13. Ölveczky, P.C., Meseguer, J.: Semantics and pragmatics of Real-Time Maude. Higher-Order and Symbolic Computation 20(1-2), 161–196 (2007)
14. Ölveczky, P.C., Meseguer, J., Talcott, C.L.: Specification and analysis of the AER/NCA active network protocol suite in Real-Time Maude. Formal Methods in System Design 29(3), 253–293 (2006)
15. Ölveczky, P.C., Thorvaldsen, S.: Formal modeling, performance estimation, and model checking of wireless sensor network algorithms in Real-Time Maude. Theoretical Computer Science 410(2-3), 254–280 (2009)
16. Ölveczky, P.C., Meseguer, J.: Specification of real-time and hybrid systems in rewriting logic. Theor. Comput. Sci. 285(2), 359–405 (2002)
17. Ölveczky, P.C., Meseguer, J.: Semantics and pragmatics of Real-Time Maude. Higher-Order and Symbolic Computation 20(1-2), 161–196 (2007)
18. Patterson, S., Elmore, A.J., Nawab, F., Agrawal, D., El Abbadi, A.: Serializability, not serial: concurrency control and availability in multi-datacenter datastores. Proc. VLDB Endow. 5(11), 1459–1470 (2012)
19. Skeirik, S., Bobba, R.B., Meseguer, J.: Formal analysis of fault-tolerant group key management using ZooKeeper. In: IEEE International Symposium on Cluster Computing and the Grid, pp. 636–641 (2013)
20. Stonebraker, M., Cattell, R.: 10 rules for scalable performance in 'simple operation' datastores. Commun. ACM 54(6), 72–80 (2011)
21. Weikum, G., Vossen, G.: Concurrency Control and Recovery in Database Systems. Morgan Kaufman Publishers (2001)

EHRA: Specification and Analysis
of Energy-Harvesting Wireless Sensor Networks

Anh-Dung Phan, Michael R. Hansen, and Jan Madsen

DTU Compute, Technical University of Denmark
{padu,mire,jama}@dtu.dk

Abstract. Although energy consumption of wireless sensor network has been studied extensively, we are far behind in understanding the dynamics of the power consumption along with energy production using harvesters. We introduce Energy Harvesting Routing Analysis (EHRA) as a formal modelling framework to study wireless sensor networks (WSN) with energy-harvesting capabilities. The purpose of the framework is to analyze WSNs at a high level of abstraction, that is, before the protocols are implemented and before the WSN is deployed. The conceptual basis of EHRA comprises the environment, the medium, computational and physical components, and it captures a broad range of energy-harvesting-aware routing protocols. The generic concepts of protocols are captured by a many-sorted signature, and concrete routing protocols are specified by corresponding many-sorted algebras.

A first analysis tool for EHRA is developed as a simulator implemented using the functional programming language F#. This simulator is used to analyze global properties of WSNs such as network fragmentation, routing trends, and energy profiles for the nodes. Three routing protocols, with a progression in the energy-harvesting awareness, are analyzed on a network that is placed in a heterogeneous environment.

1 Introduction

A Cyber-Physical System (CPS) is a system featuring a tight combination of its computational and physical elements and the coordination between them. The term CPS is used to emphasize the importance of the intense link between the computational and physical elements, rather than focussing on just the computational elements, which often is the case for embedded systems. This heterogeneous nature is recognized as a main challenge in modelling CPSs [5]. We study a special class of CPSs namely Wireless Sensor Networks.

A Wireless Sensor Network (WSN) is a distributed network of *sensor nodes*, deployed in a *physical environment*. Each node collects information, also called *observations*, about its environment, e.g. environmental monitoring and control, healthcare monitoring and traffic control, to name a few. This information is processed either at the node, in the network, at a so-called *base station*, or in any combination of these. Collected information is ultimately gathered at the base station, where it is further analysed.

S. Iida, J. Meseguer, and K. Ogata (Eds.): Futatsugi Festschrift, LNCS 8373, pp. 520–540, 2014.

Each node provides two functionalities: sensing and transmitting information of its local environment, and relaying sensed information from neighbouring nodes. Fig. 1a shows an architecture of a classical node as well as its environment comprising the physical environment, where information is sensed, and the medium through which information is exchanged with neighbouring nodes.

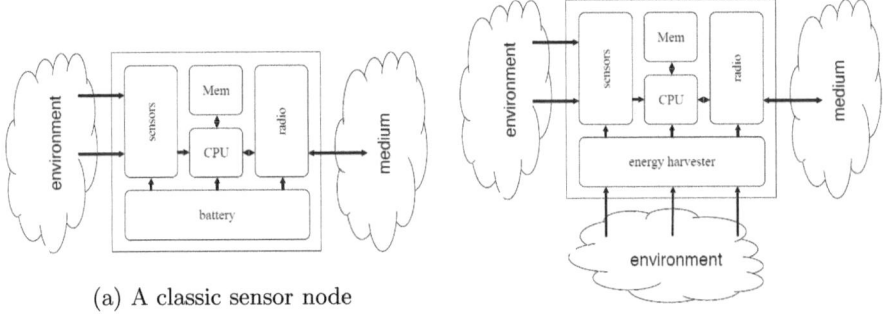

(a) A classic sensor node

(b) An energy-harvesting sensor node

Fig. 1. Architecture of a sensor node

A key issue of a WSN is the unpredictable behaviour of the environment. For the communication medium, this is handled in the Media Access Control (MAC) protocol, and for the physical sensing, nothing particular is needed, as this is just a sampling of information. The requirement of long lifetime of the WSN is the real challenge. In a classical sensor node, the components (sensor, radio, computer and memory) are all fuelled from a battery, which means that energy is used whenever they are active. In order to sustain long lifetime, components must be designed for low power and they have to be active only when needed. When sensor nodes are idle most of the time, another challenge is to synchronize their information exchange. This is typically handled in the MAC protocol.

We are considering WSNs based on *zero-power devices*, where the battery is substituted by an *energy harvester*, which is able to gather energy from the environment (see Fig. 1b) through light, temperature differences or vibrations, for example. This adds an extra dimension to the problem because energy is harvested over time with varying rates that are difficult to predict. This has a profound impact on how the network is managed, i.e. how information is routed to the base station. This could be handled by energy-aware routing protocols trying to balance the traffic to keep nodes alive for as long as possible. For this to be efficient, a model of energy consumption within a node is needed. This will allow the routing protocol to predict when a node has too little energy to be used and hence another sensor node has to be selected. When having energy harvesting, sensor nodes can regain energy and when fully charged, energy is "free", which means that it should be used. Each node then has to have a model of the dynamics of the energy to be able to balance the usage of nodes.

An example network showing the challenge with energy-harvesting-aware protocols is given in Fig. 2, where the nodes are placed in a 7×7 grid. There is a hole of size 3×3 where no node is present. Each node can communicate with (at most) four neighbours which are the closest ones either vertically or horizontally. Throughout this paper we consider energy harvesters that are based on solar power. The shade of a node is, therefore, relevant, because that influences

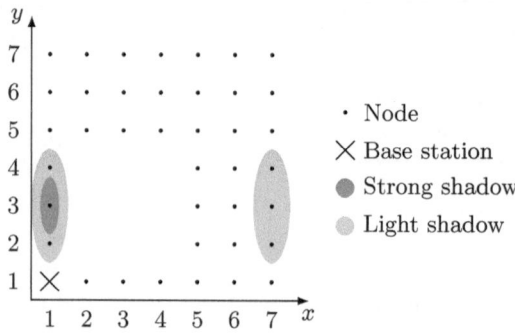

Fig. 2. A network structure with shadowed nodes

the ability to harvest energy. The node at position $(1, 1)$ is the base station and the purpose of the network is to route observations from the individual nodes to this base station. To reach the base station, many messages are passing through two routes along the axes. The challenge of an energy-harvesting-aware routing protocol is to dynamically adapt the routes to avoid that nodes on "bottleneck routes" get drained.

This paper, which extends [6], has the following main contributions:

- A formal semantical framework for energy-harvesting-aware wireless sensor networks, including energy-harvesting-aware protocols. In [6], the presentations are at an informal level only.
- The framework [6] is extended to deal with probabilistic protocols and it is shown to capture the probabilistic protocol Energy Aware Routing [17].
- A discrete-event simulator is developed and used to compare three routing protocols with a progression of energy-harvesting awareness. This is the first tool development for EHRA. So far these protocols have been analysed using different dedicated simulators making comparison of results difficult.

We have experimented with model-checking techniques for our framework. These experiments showed severe scalability problems due to the huge number of parallel components in the nodes as well as in the network and, therefore, a simulation-based approach was chosen. Our plan is to extend the framework with statistical model-checking techniques.

Related Work. Discrete-event simulation has often been used to simulate WSNs and some discrete-event simulators are tailored for WSNs' characteristics. Avrora, for example, offers both efficiency and accuracy in instruction-level simulation [19]. We are interested in more high-level properties. Another approach is taken by [16], where ReactiveML, a variant of OCaml with reactive programming constructs [13], is used as a basis for simulating ad-hoc sensor networks. The environment is expressed in Lucky, a declarative domain-specific language to describe physical conditions. Energy consumption of a node is described in an automata-based model. In their framework, global properties of WSNs are analyzed but energy harvesting is not considered.

There are also work applying formal methods to the analysis of WSNs. In [3], a single sensor node is modelled in HyTech, a hybrid automata model checker, and safety properties are analyzed. At the network level, to alleviate scalability issues of model-checking, they simulate a network of hybrid automata corresponding to the WSN and take energy consumption into account. A similar approach is taken in [15], where Real-Time Maude is used to analyze the Optimal Geographical Density Control algorithm for WSNs. They use model-checking techniques to verify functional properties and resort to the corresponding simulator for performance evaluation. An interesting trade-off between model checking and simulation is statistical model checking approach. While it gives more reliable results than simulation, the approach is more scalable than model checking. For example, Uppaal SMC, a statistical model checker, has been used to verify properties of the Lightweight Media Access Control protocol [2]. However, none of the above referred articles addresses energy-harvesting issues.

Several empirical approaches to energy-harvesting WSNs have been proposed, e.g. [4,10,11,14,18]. In [11], for example, local energy management is used to reduce latency on routing messages to the base station. But these approaches do not consider dynamic routes which are essential to energy-harvesting scenarios. In [12], a mathematical framework is given for examining energy-harvesting-aware routing in multi-hop WSNs. But this approach is based on the unrealistic assumption that each node has global knowledge of the whole network.

The Structure of the Paper. Our thesis is that a broad class of energy-harvesting-aware protocols can be described within a unified conceptual framework. A suggestion of such a unified conceptual framework is presented in the next section, where we develop: A semantical framework for energy-harvesting-aware WSNs, the basic concepts of energy-harvesting-aware protocols, and the generic behaviour of an energy-harvesting-aware node. The basic concepts of energy-harvesting-aware protocols are expressed as a many-sorted signature, that is, in terms of a collection of types and specifications of operations. A protocol is expressed as a corresponding many-sorted algebra.

In Section 3 some evidence supporting the above thesis is collected by expressing three protocols in the framework. More examples are, of course, needed to give substantial support for the thesis. Analysis support for such a framework has many advantages: New protocols can be developed within an existing conceptual basis and different protocols can be compared on "equal term", that is, by using the same model of the environment and communication medium, for example. Furthermore, experiments can be conducted with configurations of nodes before the nodes are implemented and deployed in a physical environment. Section 4 provides a description of a discrete-event simulator for the framework and the three considered protocols are analyzed in Section 5.

2   The Generic Modelling Framework

We consider networks where nodes are uniquely identified using identifiers $id \in$ Id. The purpose of a network is to forward *observations* $o \in$ Observation from nodes to a so-called *base station*, see Fig. 2, where an observation could be a temperature measurement or a recording of a car passing.

In the following we consider a network with N sensor nodes. Each node id has a *local state* $s \in S_{id} =$ CompState$_{id} \times$ PhysState$_{id}$ comprising two parts:

- A *computational state* $cs \in$ CompState$_{id}$. A node is equipped with a CPU (see Fig. 1b) and computations could concern local treatment of observations and processing related to the protocol.
- A *physical state* $ps \in$ PhysState$_{id}$. In order to make the routing energy-harvesting aware, a node must have the possibility to sample its physical state, for example, to be able to make decisions on the basis of the actual energy level of a battery.

A *network state* $\bar{s} = (s_1, \ldots, s_N) \in S = S_{id_1} \times \cdots \times S_{id_N}$ is a vector of N local states, where s_i is a local state of node id_i for $1 \leq i \leq N$. A *timed network state* is a pair $(t, \bar{s})$, where $t \in \mathbb{R}_{\geq 0}$ is the time stamp of the network state $\bar{s}$.

A node id can broadcast a *message* $m \in$ Msg using the *output event* send$_{id}(m)$. Messages relate to observations and to the energy awareness of the nodes (see Section 2.2). The asynchronous broadcast of messages is handled as follows:

- A relation $t, \bar{s}, id \vdash_S d,$ send$_{id}(m)$ expresses that node id can send message m after delay $d \in \mathbb{R}_{\geq 0}$, i.e. at time $t + d$, in the timed network state $(t, \bar{s})$.
- Two functions initSend$_{id}$, completeSend$_{id} : S_{id} \times$ Msg $\rightarrow S_{id}$ are used to handle the sending of messages from a node id by expressing the state change when the sending is initiated and when it is completed. Details about these functions are deferred until Section 4.2.

Furthermore, $\bar{s} \vdash_E id$ expresses that the node id is *enabled* in the network state $\bar{s}$. This relation is used to model energy requirement of equipment in nodes.

We model the environments (see Fig. 1b) for observations and energy harvesting, and for the medium by three relations $\vdash_O, \vdash_H$ and $\vdash_M$:

- Observation environment: $id, t \vdash_O d, o$, where $t, d \in \mathbb{R}_{\geq 0}$, expresses that node id can make the observation o at time $t + d$.
- Energy harvesting environment: $id, t \vdash_H d, ps$, where $t, d \in \mathbb{R}_{\geq 0}$, expresses that node id has physical state ps at time $t + d$.
- Medium: $\bar{s}, id \vdash_M id'$ expresses that node id' can receive a message from node id in the network state $\bar{s}$. We call id' a *neighbour* of id in $\bar{s}$.

A node id can react to the following *input events*:

– Sample the physical state. At the sample time, there is an exact match between physical state of a node and the "real" physical state. The effect of this event is described by a function:

$$\mathsf{samplePS}_{id} : S_{id} \times \mathsf{PhysState} \to S_{id}$$

– Sense observation. The effect of this event is described by a function:

$$\mathsf{senseObs}_{id} : S_{id} \times \mathsf{Observation} \to S_{id}$$

– Receive message. The effect of this event is given by a function:

$$\mathsf{treatMsg}_{id} : S_{id} \times \mathsf{Msg} \to S_{id}$$

The semantics of a network is given in terms of a labelled transition system where we use labels of the following form:

$$\mathsf{Label} = \mathbb{R}_{\geq 0} \times (\{\epsilon\} \cup \{\mathsf{send}(m)_{id_i} \mid m \in \mathsf{Msg} \text{ and } 1 \leq i \leq N\})$$

Definition 1. *The semantics of a network of N sensor nodes, given the relations: $\vdash_O, \vdash_H, \vdash_M, \vdash_S$ and $\vdash_E$, is a labelled transition system $(TS, (0, s_0), \longrightarrow)$, where $S = S_{id_1} \times \cdots \times S_{id_N}$, $TS = \mathbb{R}_{\geq 0} \times S$, $\bar{s}_0 \in S$ is the initial network state, and $\longrightarrow \subseteq TS \times \mathsf{Label} \times TS$ is the transition relation such that:*
$(t, \bar{s}) = (t, (s_1, \ldots, s_N)) \xrightarrow{d, e} (t'(s'_1, \ldots, s'_N)) = (t', \bar{s}')$ *if* $t' = t + d$ *and*

– *either $e = \epsilon$ and some node id_{j_0} performs an internal event in the form of sensing an observation or sampling the physical state:*

   1. $s'_k = s_k$, *for every node id_k that is different from id_{j_0}*
   2. *and either*
      • *node id_{j_0} is enabled and sensing an observation o at time $t + d$:*

$$\bar{s} \vdash_E id_{j_0}, id_{j_0}, t \vdash_O d, o \text{ and } s'_{j_0} = \mathsf{senseObs}_{id_{j_0}}(s_{j_0}, o)$$

      • *or node id_{j_0} is sampling its physical state at time $t + d$:*

$$id_{j_0}, t \vdash_H d, ps \text{ and } s'_{j_0} = \mathsf{samplePS}_{id_{j_0}}(s_{j_0}, ps)$$

– *or $e = \mathsf{send}_{id_{j_0}}(m)$ and node id_{j_0} is enabled and performs a send event at time $t + d$, and its enabled neighbours perform internal receive-message events:*

   1. $\bar{s} \vdash_E id_{j_0}, s, id_{j_0}, t \vdash_S d, \mathsf{send}_{id_{j_0}}(m), s'_{j_0} - \mathsf{completeSend}(s_{j_0}, m),$
   2. *for every enabled neighbour id_k of id_{j_0} (i.e. $\bar{s}, id_{j_0} \vdash_M id_k$ and $\bar{s} \vdash_E id_k$):*

$$s'_k = \mathsf{treatMsg}_{id_k}(s_k, m) \text{ and}$$

   3. *For any other node id_k (i.e. $id_k \neq id_{j_0}$ and $(\bar{s}, id_{j_0} \nvdash_M id_k$ or $\bar{s} \nvdash_E id_k))$:*

$$s'_k = s_k$$

Notice that even disabled nodes can sample their physical states. This allows drained nodes to recover when the energy-harvesting conditions allow so.

An *execution* is described by a possibly infinite transition sequence:

$$(t_0, \bar{s}_0) \xrightarrow{d_1, e_1} (t_1, \bar{s}_1) \xrightarrow{d_2, e_2} (t_2, \bar{s}_2) \xrightarrow{t_3, e_3} (t_3, \bar{s}_3) \cdots$$

where $t_{i-1} \leq t_i$. We require that infinite executions diverge, that is, $t_i \to \infty$ when $i \to \infty$. Further restrictions could be imposed, for example, that enabled transitions are not ignored, that is, it is not the case that $\bar{s}_{i-1} \xrightarrow{t'_i, e'_i} \bar{s}'_i$ and $t_{i-1} \leq t'_i < t_i$ (where $t_0 = 0$). Notice that such requirements impose restrictions on $\vdash_H, \vdash_O$ and $\vdash_S$.

2.1   Basic Concepts of Energy-Harvesting-Aware Protocols

Basic concepts that are used when expressing energy-harvesting-aware protocols are introduced now. They are presented as the many-sorted signature in Fig. 3. The operations are specific to the node under consideration, but subscripts for the identity of the node will be left out.

$id \in \mathsf{Id}$	unique node identifier
$o \in \mathsf{Observation}$	observation
$ps \in \mathsf{PhysState}$	physical state
$cs \in \mathsf{CompState}$	computational state
$as \in \mathsf{AbsState}$	abstract state
$m \in \mathsf{Msg}$	message having one of the forms:
$\mathsf{obsMsg}(dst, o)$	observation message with node $dst \in \mathsf{Id}$ as destination
$\mathsf{nbMsg}(src, as)$	neighbour message message from node $src \in \mathsf{Id}$

next	: CompState → Id
updateEnergyState	: CompState × PhysState → CompState
updateRoutingState	: CompState → CompState
consistent?	: CompState → {true, false}
abstractView	: CompState → AbsState
updateNeighbourView	: CompState × Id × AbsState → CompState
transmitChange?	: CompState × CompState → {true, false}

Fig. 3. Fundamental types and operations

The function next: CompState → Id determines the best neighbour to whom observations should be forwarded in a given computational state.

The computational state may contain data representing the perception of the physical state and the function updateEnergyState: CompState × PhysState → CompState synchronizes this perception with the "real" physical state.

Information about available energy in nodes must be exchanged between neighbours. This local information usually comprises just a condensed version of the computational state to limit costly traffic (exchange of huge messages). Such a condensed computation state is named an *abstract state as* $\in$ AbsState and the function abstractView: CompState $\rightarrow$ AbsState computes the abstract version of a computational state. A predicate transmitChange?: CompState $\times$ CompState $\rightarrow$ {true, false} is used to determines whether a change in the computational state is significant enough to cause a message exchange and the function updateNeighbourView: CompState $\times$ Id $\times$ AbsState $\rightarrow$ CompState updates the computational state with a new abstract state of a given neighbour.

The routing from a node is determined by knowledge about the energy in the node itself and in neighbour nodes. When this energy knowledge changes either due to an internal update of the energy state or to an update of a view of a neighbour, then the computational state may become *inconsistent* in the sense that all neighbours seem "further away" from the base station than the node itself. It is essential to be able to detect this undesirable situation where there is no "natural choice" for routing observations and the predicate consistent?: CompState $\rightarrow$ {true, false} is used for that purpose.

The routing part of the computational state is updated by use of the function updateRoutingState : CompState $\rightarrow$ CompState with the purpose of creating a consistent computational state. Hence, it is required that:

$$consistent?(updateRoutingState(cs)) = true \qquad (1)$$

The Link to the Physical World

A node has an exact perception of its physical state just at the time instants where it samples its physical state. Between sampling points when sensing observations or exchanging messages, the perception of the available energy is maintained by using a family of cost functions:

$$cost f : PhysState \rightarrow PhysState$$

where f is any of the resource-demanding operation specified in Section 2.1.

2.2   The Generic Behaviour of a Node

A major thesis of this work is that the generic behaviour of a node id can be defined by composition of the functions in Fig. 3. In particular, we give definitions for the functions:

$$samplePS_{id} : S_{id} \times PhysState_{id} \rightarrow S_{id}$$
$$senseObs_{id} : S_{id} \times Observation \rightarrow S_{id}$$
$$treatMsg_{id} : S_{id} \times Msg \rightarrow S_{id}$$

These definitions are given in Fig. 4. Each function definition can be partitioned into a computational part relating to the operations in the node and a cost part updating the perception of the physical state. The applications of the cost

$$
\begin{aligned}
&\mathsf{samplePS}_{id}((cs, ps), ps') \;= \\
&\quad \mathtt{let}\ cs' = \mathsf{updateRoutingState}(\mathsf{updateEnergyState}(cs, ps')) \\
&\quad \mathtt{let}\ ps'' = \mathsf{costUpdateEnergyState}(\mathsf{costUpdateRoutingState}(ps')) \\
&\quad \mathtt{if}\ \neg\mathsf{transmitChange?}(cs, cs')\ \mathtt{then}\ (cs, ps'') \\
&\quad \mathtt{else\ let}\ m = \mathsf{nbMsg}(id, \mathsf{abstractView}(cs')) \\
&\qquad \mathsf{initSend}_{id}(m, (cs', \mathsf{costSend}(\mathsf{costAbstractView}(ps'')))) \\[4pt]
&\mathsf{senseObs}_{id}((cs, ps), o) \;= \\
&\quad \mathsf{initSend}_{id}((cs, \mathsf{costSend}(\mathsf{costNext}(ps'))), \mathsf{obsMsg}(\mathsf{next}(cs), o)) \\[4pt]
&\mathsf{treatMsg}_{id}((cs, ps), m) = \mathtt{case}\ m\ \mathtt{of} \\
&\qquad\qquad\qquad\quad \mathsf{obsMsg}(dst, o)\ \rightarrow\ \mathsf{TreatObsMsg}_{id}(dst, o, cs, ps) \\
&\qquad\qquad\qquad\quad \mathsf{nbMsg}(src, as)\ \rightarrow\ \mathsf{TreatNbMsg}_{id}(src, as, cs, ps) \\[4pt]
&\mathtt{where}\ \mathsf{TreatObsMsg}_{id}(dst, o, cs, ps) = \\
&\qquad \mathtt{if}\ id \neq dst\ \mathtt{then}\ (cs, ps) \\
&\qquad \mathtt{else}\ \mathsf{initSend}_{id}((cs, \mathsf{costSend}(\mathsf{costNext}(ps))), \mathsf{obsMsg}(\mathsf{next}(cs), o)) \\[4pt]
&\mathtt{and}\quad \mathsf{TreatNbMsg}_{id}(src, as, cs, ps) = \\
&\qquad \mathtt{let}\ cs' = \mathsf{updateNeighbourView}(cs, src, as) \\
&\qquad \mathtt{let}\ cs'' = \mathsf{updateRoutingState}(cs') \\
&\qquad \mathtt{let}\ ps' = \mathsf{costUpdateNeighbourView}(\mathsf{costUpdateRoutingState}(ps)) \\
&\qquad \mathtt{if}\ \neg\mathsf{transmitChange?}(cs, cs'') \wedge \mathsf{consistent?}(cs')\ \mathtt{then}\ (cs', ps') \\
&\qquad \mathtt{else\ let}\ m = \mathsf{nbMsg}(id, \mathsf{abstractView}(cs'')) \\
&\qquad\quad \mathsf{initSend}_{id}((cs'', \mathsf{costSend}(\mathsf{costAbstractView}(ps'))), m)
\end{aligned}
$$

Fig. 4. The generic behaviour of node id

functions follow directly the computational part of the definitions, so we just consider the computational part here.

When the physical state is sampled ($\mathsf{samplePS}_{id}((cs, ps), ps')$), the energy state must be updated and the routing state is updated as well to preserve consistency of the computational state. If this change is insignificant, then nothing is broadcasted and just the physical state has changed. (The computational state cs is kept to preserve the consistency with the neighbours' view of the node.) Otherwise, a *neighbour message* is broadcasted containing the identity of the node and an abstract view of its new computational state.

When an observation is sensed ($\mathsf{senseObs}_{id}((cs, ps), o)$), then an *observation message* $\mathsf{obsMsg}(\mathsf{next}(cs), o)$ is broadcasted having the best neighbour for routing observations, i.e. $\mathsf{next}(cs)$, as destination.

If the node is the destination of an observation message, then the observation is relayed to the best neighbour. If the incoming message is a neighbour message, then updates of the neighbour view and the routing state are performed, and if this causes a significant change, then a neighbour message is broadcasted.

Notice that the resulting computational is consistent.

3   Three Routing Protocols

We study three routing protocols: Directed Diffusion (DD) [8], Energy Aware Routing (EAR) [17], and Distributed Energy Harvesting Aware Routing (DE-HAR) [9]. Models of DD and DEHAR using our framework are given in [6] so they are just informally discussed below, where we also give a formal definition of EAR. The rationale for choosing these protocols is to examine the framework under increasing energy-harvesting awareness, where:

- DD is the simplest protocol without any energy-harvesting awareness. It is used for comparison purpose only.
- EAR has an energy-harvesting awareness that is limited to knowledge of its immediate neighbours. Furthermore, EAR is using a probabilistic routing protocol.
- DEHAR has an energy-harvesting awareness that goes beyond its immediate neighbours.

We use cost functions uniformly on all three protocols. Each operation e.g. updateRoutingState, updateNeighbourView, send, next and abstractView has an associated amount of energy consumption. We assume that costs are independent of message sizes. The protocols will be analyzed using the example network in Fig. 2.

3.1   Directed Diffusion

The DD protocol is very simple as it always forwards an observation to the neighbour having the shortest distance (in the number of hops) to the base station. For example, the node in position $(4, 6)$ in Fig. 2 will always direct its observations to either node $(3, 6)$ or node $(4, 5)$. All nodes to the left of the diagonal $x = y$ being above the hole, i.e. $x \leq 4$, will definitely use routes that pass through the "problematic" node $(1, 3)$ in the dark shadow. Such use of the same low-energy path often leads to energy depletion and network partition.

Since DD uses the shortest routes, it will use less energy than the other two protocols considered. DD does not make any routing adaptation based on changes of energy levels. Any energy-harvesting-aware protocol should exhibit a better exploitation of "free" energy than DD.

We refer to [6] for a formalization of DD using our modelling framework.

3.2   Energy Aware Routing

The main idea behind the EAR protocol is to make a node aware of the energy level of its immediate neighbours. This knowledge is used

- to avoid sending observations to neighbours having energy levels below a certain threshold, and
- to use a random selection, based on the current energy metric, of routes to "energy-sound" neighbours that are closer to the base station.

This should prevent a systematic use of low-energy paths and, in this way, the network should degrade globally, not locally, and the lifetime of the network should be extended. But notice that the addition of energy-harvesting awareness will lead to more network communication due to the exchange of information about energy levels. Hence, the traffic in the network will increase and an analysis of energy-harvesting-aware protocols must take these costs into account.

A computational state is a 6-tuple $(c, e, ft, pt, rt, nt) \in$ CompState, where

- $c \in R_{\geq 0}$ is a *cost* of choosing the node for forwarding messages,
- $e \in$ Energy is an *energy level*,
- $ft \in$ ForwardingMap $=$ Id $\to R_{\geq 0}$ is a *forwarding map* that contains costs of using links to its neighbours,
- $pt \in$ ProbabilityMap $=$ Id $\to R_{[0,1]}$ is a *probability distribution*, where $pt(j)$ is the probability for choosing neighbour j as the receiver of an observation. It is required that $\Sigma_{j \in \text{dom}(pt)} pt(j) = 1$,
- $rt \in$ EnergyMap $=$ Id $\to$ Energy is an *energy map* that describes the energy required for communication with the neighbours, and
- $nt \in$ NeighbourMap $=$ Id $\to$ AbsState is a *neighbour map* containing an abstract view of the state of the neighbours. In this case, the abstract state is simply the cost equivalent of the energy level AbsState $= R_{\geq 0}$.

The domains of the maps ft, pt and rt are restricted to identifiers for neighbours that are closer to the base station (in terms of hop count) than the node under consideration.

The physical state just comprises the stored energy $e \in$ Energy and we assume that there is a conversion function from energy level to a cost, that is a non-negative real number. This function is used when the physical state is sampled and synchronized with the computational state. The cost function is extended from the physical state to the computational and abstract states in a trivial way:

$$\text{cost}(c, e, ft, pt, rt, nt) = \text{cost}(\text{abstractView}(c, e, ft, pt, rt, nt)) = c$$

The function $\text{next}(c, e, ft, pt, rt, nt)$ will make a random choice for the destination of observations on the basis of the probability distribution pt.

The main idea when updating the routing map is to avoid neighbours with high costs (determined by the constant δ below). The probability distribution is updated accordingly. The cost of the current node is the weighted cost obtained using the probability distribution and the routing map [17]:

$$
\begin{aligned}
&\text{updateRoutingState}(c, e, ft, pt, rt, nt) = \\
&\quad \text{let } ft' = ft \setminus \{id \in \text{dom}(ft) \mid ft(id) < \delta \cdot \min_k ft(k)\} \\
&\quad \text{let } pt' = \text{probabilityDist}(ft') \\
&\quad \text{let } c' = \Sigma_{k \in \text{dom}(pt)} pt'(k) \cdot ft'(k) \\
&\quad (c', e, ft', pt', rt, nt)
\end{aligned}
$$

where the probability distribution $pt' = \text{probabilityDist}(ft')$ is defined as follows:

$$pt'(id) = \frac{\frac{1}{ft'(id)}}{\Sigma_{k \in \text{dom}(ft')} \frac{1}{ft'(k)}}$$

for $id \in \text{dom}(ft)$. In this distribution neighbours with low costs are more likely to be chosen than those with high costs.

A computational state (c, e, ft, pt, rt, nt) is consistent if pt is a genuine probability distribution, that is, if at least one neighbour closer to the base station has a sufficient energy level.

The function synchronizing the physical state and the computational state is defined by:

$$\mathsf{updateEnergyState}((c, e, \mathit{ft}, \mathit{pt}, \mathit{rt}, \mathit{nt}), e') = (\mathsf{cost}(e'), e', \mathit{ft}, \mathit{pt}, \mathit{rt}, \mathit{nt})$$

and the function converting a computational state to an abstract one has a similar simple definition:

$$\mathsf{abstractView}(c, e, \mathit{ft}, \mathit{pt}, \mathit{rt}, \mathit{nt}) = c$$

The following function updates the abstract state of a neighbour:

$$\begin{aligned}
\mathsf{updateNeighbourView}&((c, e, \mathit{ft}, \mathit{pt}, \mathit{rt}, \mathit{nt}), \mathit{id}, \mathit{as}) = \\
&\texttt{let } r = \mathit{rt}(\mathit{id}) \\
&\texttt{let } C = \mathsf{cost}(\mathit{as}) + e^{\alpha} \cdot r^{\beta} \\
&\texttt{let } \mathit{ft}' = \mathit{ft} + [\mathit{id} \to C] \\
&\texttt{let } \mathit{nt}' = \mathit{nt} + [\mathit{id} \to \mathit{as}] \\
&(c, e, \mathit{ft}', \mathit{pt}, \mathit{rt}, \mathit{nt}')
\end{aligned}$$

where α and β are weighing factors for finding minimum-energy paths, and $m + [a \to b]$ is the map obtained from m letting a be mapped to b. The constants α and β are chosen so that nodes with highest residual energy have smallest costs, and the cost C of using a link is a sum of the cost of sender and the residual energy of receiver. We refer to [17] for further details.

A change of a computational state is transmitted to the neighbours just when the cost difference of the change is above some threshold $K_{\mathrm{change}} \in R_{\geq 0}$:

$$\mathsf{transmitChange?}(cs, cs') = |\mathsf{cost}(cs) - \mathsf{cost}(cs')| > K_{\mathrm{change}}$$

3.3   Distributed Energy Harvesting Aware Routing

The energy-harvesting awareness of EAR is limited to just knowing the energy levels of the neighbours. The DEHAR protocol [9] develops a technique to distribute knowledge about energy deficits of nodes in order to avoid heavy traffic through drained nodes further away in the network.

The main idea behind DEHAR is presented using the example in Fig. 5. The computational state of each node is initialized to its distance to the base station and observations are forwarded to the neighbour being closest to the base station.

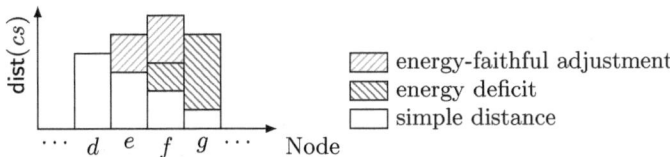

Fig. 5. DEHAR protocol with consistent nodes using energy-faithful adjustments

So initially DEHAR works just like DD. For the example in Fig. 5, observations from d will initially be routed as follows: $d \rightarrow e \rightarrow f \rightarrow g$.

When the energy of a node is depleted, its distance is adjusted with an *energy deficit* so that it appears further away from the base station. This is the case for nodes f and g in the figure. When e receives this adjusted distance of f in a neighbour message, the computational state of e becomes *inconsistent* since both (all) of its neighbours, that is d and f, have further distances to the base station than e. In this inconsistent state, node e has no neighbour to whom it is natural to forward observations, and it must update its routing state in order to regain a consistent state (cf. (1). This is done by adjusting e's distance with a so-called *energy-faithful adjustments* [9], so that it appears further away from the base station than d and f does. When this adjusted distance of e is communicated to the neighbours, then f needs a similar energy-faithful adjustment to regain a consistent state. Now each node is in a consistent state where it can forward observations in a meaningful manner.

This example shows that the energy deficiencies of nodes f and g are distributed and they have an influence of routes from node d, which is neither a neighbour of f nor of g.

We refer to [6] for a formalization of DEHAR using our modelling framework.

4   The F# Model for EHRA

In this section we describe the basic ideas behind the F#-model of the EHRA framework, with emphasis on the environments, the timing and the communication parts. The functional programming language F# [7] belongs to the SML family and F# models resemble models expressed in the constructive parts of specification languages like VDM and RAISE. The network behaviour is modelled using discrete-event simulation techniques [1].

4.1   The General Setup

We present models for the *network topology*, the *timing of events* and the *environment*. In particular, we explain how the relations $\vdash_H, \vdash_O, \vdash_M, \vdash_E$ and $\vdash_S$ are represented.

The model for the energy harvesting $id, t \vdash_H d, ps$ is focussing on available light as described by the polymorphic object interface type `Environment<'Id>`, which is parameterized with the types `'Id` for identities of nodes:

```
type Environment<'Id> =
  abstract light : 'Id -> Time -> float
  abstract harvest : 'Id -> Time -> Time -> Energy
```

Here the `light` function indicates shadow levels of nodes over time, and the `harvest` function estimates an amount of energy that a node can harvest between two time points. The energy is given by a percentage indication of a relative energy level:

```
type [<Measure>] percent
type Energy = float<percent>
```

and we use a discrete-time model of time:

```
type Time = int64<ms>
```

The unit of measures shows that we use clocks on the millisecond level in the examples. We assume in the following that a type Id is given for identifiers.

A node is modelled by a polymorphic type using type variables for the computational state 'CS, the physical state 'PS, the abstract state 'AS and for observations 'Obs:

```
type Node<'CS,'PS,'AS,'Obs> =
  { ComputationalState : 'CS
    PhysicalState : 'PS
    Position : Position
    Neighbours : Set<Id>
    Obs : 'Obs
    Ops : Operations<'CS,'PS,'AS,'Obs> }
```

The object interface type Operations<'CS,'PS,'AS,'Obs> corresponds to the signature in Fig. 3 and a value of the field Ops denotes a corresponding algebra. A value of the node type captures the local state of a node. The positions of nodes are not essential for the approach, but they are often convenient in calculations of reachable neighbours. In the network in Fig. 2 two nodes are neighbours if the distance between them is 1. Note that a node maintains a set of the identifiers of neighbours it can reach. This is used to decide $\bar{s}, id \vdash_M id'$ is an efficient manner.

A network state is modelled as a map from identifiers to nodes:

```
Map<Id, Node<'CS, 'PS, 'AS, 'Obs>>
```

and a timed network state is called a *world* and captured by the type:

```
type World<'CS, 'PS, 'AS, 'Obs> =
  { Time : Time
    Network : Map<Id, Node<'CS, 'PS, 'AS, 'Obs>>
    Env : Environment<Id> }
```

Messages and internal events are modelled using algebraic datatypes closely following the definitions in Section 2:

```
type Message<'AS, 'Obs> = | ObservationMsg of Id * 'Obs
                          | NeighbourMsg of Id * 'AS

type InternalEvent<'AS, 'Obs> = | SamplePS of Energy
                                | SenseObs of 'Obs
                                | MessageEvt of Message<'AS, 'Obs>
```

4.2   Discrete-Event Simulation in a Functional Setting

The notion *time hopping* is central to discrete-event simulation. It is based on a facility that keeps track of the current time and whenever an event occurs, one immediately jumps to the start of the next event. This skip of durations, where no event occurs, is essential for obtaining efficient simulations. To implement this, we use time-stamped internal events:

```
type Event<'AS,'Obs> = Event of Time * Id * InternalEvent<'AS,'Obs>
```

and organize scheduled events as a priority queue with type `PQueue<Event>`, ordered by time stamps. The priority queue is maintained using the standard operations:

```
minimum : PQueue<'T> -> 'T
extractMin : PQueue<'T> -> 'T * PQueue<'T>
insert : PQueue<'T> -> 'T -> PQueue<'T>
isEmpty : PQueue<'T> -> bool
```

The transition steps of Definition 1 are simulated using two functions:

```
executeInternalEvent : InternalEvent -> Id -> Time -> World -> World
```

```
scheduleNextEvent : Id -> World * PQueue<Event> -> PQueue<Event>
```

where `executeInternalEvent` $e\,id\,t\,w$ returns the new world obtained from w by execution of internal event e at time t in node id and `scheduleNextEvent` $id\,(w,q)$ gives the new priority queue obtained from q by scheduling the next event from node id in world w.

The implementation of the function `executeInternalEvent` follows directly the definition of the generic behaviour of a node as given in Fig. 4, and this definition is based on an implementation of the signature specified in Fig. 3.

An implementation of the function `scheduleNextEvent` is based on implementations of $t,\bar{s},id \vdash_S d, \mathsf{send}_{id}(m)$, $id,t \vdash_O d,o$ and $id,t \vdash_H d,ps$. In the current version, delays between observations at a given node id are generated as random numbers on the basis of a specified mean value μ and a standard deviation σ. Delays in connection with the other relations are generated similarly possibly using other mean values and standard deviations.

By function composition, the one-step simulation function

```
doEvent : Event -> World * PQueue<Event> -> World * PQueue<Event>
```

is expressed as follows:

```
let doEvent (Event(t, id, ievt)) (w, pq) =
        let w' = executeInternalEvent ievt id t w
        (w', scheduleNextEvent id (w', pq))
```

The discrete-event simulation function

```
simulate: World * PQueue<Event> -> World * PQueue<Event>
```

is defined by repeated application of `doEvent` until the event queue is empty:

```
let rec simulate(w, evts) = if isEmpty evts then (w, evts)
                            else let (evt, evts') = extractMin evts
                                 simulate(doEvent evt (w, evts'))
```

In order to start up a "proper" simulation process for a given initial world, an initialized event queue is used where every node has a scheduled event. This will ensure that every node is active during the simulation. It is, of course, easy to make variants of `simulate` function, where the simulation terminates after a specified time or after a predefined number of simulation steps, as well as variants where a trace of the simulation is saved in a file.

5   Experimental Results

In this section we present simulation results for the network shown in Fig. 2 on the basis of the three protocols in Section 3. These protocols are simulated using identical node specifications. We assume that each node has a radio range of 1; that means a node has at most 4 neighbours in the mesh. A simulation day consists of 12 hours of full light and 12 hours of no light. The light shadow gives 75% efficiency of energy harvesting while the dark shadow reduces energy-harvesting efficiency to 25%. Observations are generated using a mean value of 900 seconds while mean of energy measure is 1800 seconds. The standard deviation for generating these events is 10 seconds. Arrivals of events are calculated based on these values. It gives non-deterministic execution, but different simulation runs are quite similar in terms of their general behaviours. For the EAR protocol, we choose the following values $\delta = 3$, $\alpha = -2$, $\beta = 1$ and $K_{change} = 1$. The simulation time is 30 days equivalent to 720 hours. Fig. 6a shows initial energy levels, where all sensor nodes are fully charged.

We illustrate energy changes by coloured heatmaps on energy levels for DD, EAR and DEHAR in Fig. 6b, 6c and 6d. There are five, three and two drained nodes after 720 simulation hours for DD, EAR and DEHAR respectively. From the heatmaps of DD and EAR we see fragmented networks where a majority of nodes cannot send messages to the base station because energy levels of nodes along the two axes are exhausted. This can easily happen when routing algorithms do not choose paths in an intelligent way.

Although it is not visible in the heatmaps above, network fragmentation happens early for the DD and EAR protocols. To quantify this, we recorded accumulated number of drained nodes over time in each experiment. The simulations showed that after 720 hours the DD protocol drained 1.5× as many nodes as EAR did and 3.5× as many as DEHAR did. In DEHAR experiments, some nodes might temporarily be out of energy, but they quickly recovered. The reason is that these nodes are free of duty until they become healthy again.

For DD and EAR protocols, no recovery of nodes was observed. For these two protocols all observations from nodes at the left side of the line $x = 5$ (when $y > 1$) will pass through the nodes with low energy along the y-axis. The reason for this is that an EAR node is never sending observations to the neighbour to the right or the neighbour above as it is making a probabilistic choice between neighbours that are closer to the base station only. Therefore, EAR can make probabilistic choices between all shortest paths from a node to the base station; but it can never choose a longer path. In the EAR-network, observations from

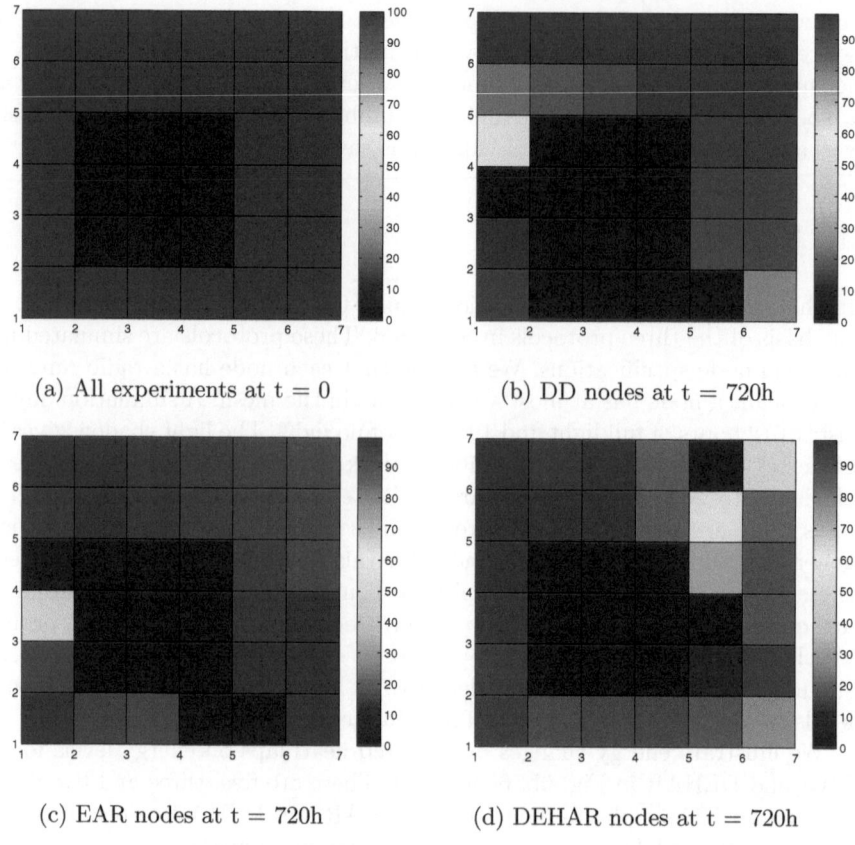

(a) All experiments at t = 0   (b) DD nodes at t = 720h

(c) EAR nodes at t = 720h   (d) DEHAR nodes at t = 720h

Fig. 6. Energy levels

the nine nodes in the upper right corner (where $x \geq 5$ and $y \geq 5$) are either following paths to the base station along the x-axis or the y axis according to probabilistic choices. But this is insufficient for preventing a fragmentation of the network.

The DEHAR nodes have more lively changes in energy levels than the DD and EAR nodes. To understand the dynamic behaviour of DEHAR, we visualize the amount of messages passing through each node over the simulation period in Fig. 7a. This visualization demonstrates flow trend of messages from the colder regions to the warmer ones in the network (see Fig. 7b). Although node $(1, 5)$ is just 4 hops away from the base station, it often chooses a longer route for messages. By using longer routes with high-energy nodes, the DEHAR protocol is able to give low-energy nodes a chance to regain their energy.

To study the protocols further, we analyzed the number of messages sent by the protocols and the amount of energy they harvested as functions of time. We will not present the graphs for these experiments to save space, but just present the main observations.

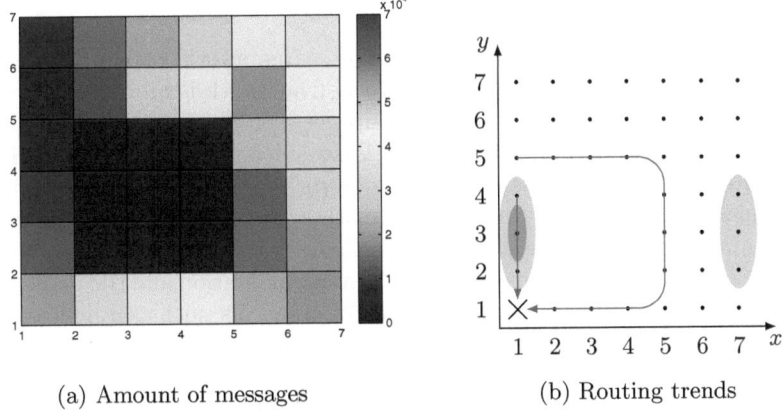

(a) Amount of messages

(b) Routing trends

Fig. 7. DEHAR nodes at t = 720h

Each protocol exhibited a linear growth in the number of sent messages y_s as a function of time t:

$$y_s = c \cdot t$$

where $c = 1180$ for DD, $c = 1389$ for EAR, and $c = 2083$ for DEHAR in *messages/h* unit. Hence the DEHAR protocol exchanged almost twice as many messages as the DD protocol did. The extra overhead of DEHAR paid off because fragmentation was never observed for DEHAR simulations and the protocol allowed depleted nodes to recover. The EAR protocol exchanged about 18% more messages than that of DD; but the EAR protocol just maintained a connected network slightly longer than the DD protocol did, and there was no clear indication of an advantage of using a probabilistic protocol.

Although the three protocols were simulated in the same conditions, they behaved quite differently in terms of energy harvesting. In general, DEHAR harvested 50% and 40% more energy than DD and EAR, respectively. A node can only harvest energy up to its capacity. That is, when it is fully charged, no further energy is harvested. Because the trend of DEHAR is to use routes with high-energy nodes, DEHAR tends to use energy where it is available and allows nodes that otherwise would not be fully charged to harvest energy.

Two remarks on the setup of the experiments should be emphasized:

- A simple 7 × 7 network was used to be able to interpret the results and assess the correctness. Much larger networks can be analyzed efficiently by the tool.
- Homogeneous nodes (same radio range and functionality) were used for transparency and convenience only. An individual setup of the nodes can be established when that is desirable.

6   Conclusions

In this paper, we have presented our analysis framework EHRA for energy-harvesting WSNs. The conceptual part of the framework is an improvement of that in [6] in the sense that the relationship between computational parts and physical parts of systems is clarified, and it is extended to cope with probabilistic routing protocols. A formal semantical framework for EHRA is presented it is accompanied with a discrete-event simulator that is developed in the functional programming language F# in a manner that is very close to the formal model – this gives confidence about correctness of the implementation and the model. The simulator is used to analyze global properties of protocols, such as fragmentation, routing trends and energy-harvesting behaviours in the network.

The EHRA framework was used to model and analyze three routing protocols Directed Diffusion (DD), Energy Aware Routing (EAR), and Distributed Energy Harvesting Aware Routing (DEHAR) listed in the increasing order of energy-harvesting awareness. In particular, DD does not take energy harvesting into account. In EAR-based networks, a node has energy knowledge of its immediate neighbours only and will route messages based on a probabilistic choice where neighbours with more energy are more likely to be chosen than low-energy ones. Just neighbours being closer to the base station are candidates of this selection process. In DEHAR-based networks, each node also has knowledge of the energy levels of its immediate neighbours; but condensed information about the energy on neighbours' routes to the base station is added to that knowledge.

These protocols were analyzed on a network having two bottlenecks on routes to the base station, where the nodes on one of these routes have particular low energy-harvesting capabilities. The simulations showed that the DD-based network soon became fragmented because nodes on both problematic routes ran out of energy. The EAR-based network operated slightly longer before it became fragmented. An advantage of using a probabilistic protocol to guarantee that at least some observations would reach the base station could *not* be observed. The DEHAR-based network did not get fragmented during the simulation. Furthermore, it exhibited a routing trend where longer routes were used to prevent low-energy nodes on shorter routes to be drained. This ability to find energy-efficient detours, i.e. routes that are longer than a shortest path to the base station, is the main feature of DEHAR that prevented the network from fragmentation in our experiments. The DEHAR-based network harvested the most energy of the three networks and it is the only one that showed an ability to help drained nodes recover.

This work, therefore, validates the formal conceptual framework and shows that global properties of interesting energy-harvesting-aware routing protocols can be analyzed using the simulator.

Acknowledgments. This research has partially been funded by the IDEA4CPS project granted by the Danish Research Foundation for Basic Research. Furthermore, we are grateful for discussions with Mikkel Koefoed Jakobsen.

References

1. Banks, J., Carson, J., Nelson, B.L., Nicol, D.: Discrete-Event System Simulation, 5th edn. Prentice Hall (2010)
2. Bulychev, P.E., David, A., Larsen, K.G., Mikucionis, M., Poulsen, D.B., Legay, A., Wang, Z.: UPPAAL-SMC: Statistical model checking for priced timed automata. In: Proceedings 10th Workshop on Quantitative Aspects of Programming Languages and Systems. EPTCS, vol. 85, pp. 1–16 (2012)
3. Coleri, S., Ergen, M., Koo, T.J.: Lifetime analysis of a sensor network with hybrid automata modelling. In: Proceedings of the 1st ACM International Workshop on Wireless Sensor Networks and Applications, WSNA 2002, pp. 98–104. ACM (2002)
4. Corke, P., Valencia, P., Sikka, P., Wark, T., Overs, L.: Long-duration solar-powered wireless sensor networks. In: Proceedings of the 4th Workshop on Embedded Networked Sensors, EmNets 2007, pp. 33–37. ACM (2007)
5. Derler, P., Lee, E.A., Sangiovanni-Vincentelli, A.L.: Modeling Cyber-Physical Systems. Proceedings of the IEEE 100(1), 13–28 (2012)
6. Hansen, M.R., Jakobsen, M.K., Madsen, J.: A Modelling Framework for Energy Harvesting Aware Wireless Sensor Networks. In: Sustainable Energy HarvestingTechnologies - Past, Present and Future, pp. 3–24. INTECH (2011)
7. Hansen, M.R., Rischel, H.: Functional Programming Using F#. Cambridge University Press (2013)
8. Intanagonwiwat, C., Govindan, R., Estrin, D., Heidemann, J., Silva, F.: Directed diffusion for wireless sensor networking. IEEE/ACM Transactions on Networking 11(1), 2–16 (2003)
9. Jakobsen, M.K., Madsen, J., Hansen, M.R.: DEHAR: A distributed energy harvesting aware routing algorithm for ad-hoc multi-hop wireless sensor networks. In: Proceedings of the 2010 IEEE International Symposium on A World of Wireless, Mobile and Multimedia Networks, WOWMOM 2010, pp. 1–9. IEEE (2010)
10. Jiang, X., Polastre, J., Culler, D.: Perpetual environmentally powered sensor networks. In: Proceedings of the 4th International Symposium on Information Processing in Sensor Networks, IPSN 2005, pp. 463–468. IEEE (2005)
11. Kansal, A., Potter, D., Srivastava, M.B.: Performance aware tasking for environmentally powered sensor networks. In: Proceedings of the Joint International Conference on Measurement and Modeling of Computer Systems, SIGMETRICS 2004/Performance 2004, pp. 223–234. ACM (2004)
12. Lin, L., Shroff, N.B., Srikant, R.: Asymptotically optimal energy-aware routing for multihop wireless networks with renewable energy sources. IEEE/ACM Transactions on Networking 15(5), 1021–1034 (2007)
13. Mandel, L., Benbadis, F.: Simulation of mobile ad hoc network protocols in ReactiveML. In: Proceedings of Synchronous Languages, Applications, and Programming (SLAP 2005), Edinburgh, Scotland. Electronic Notes in Theoretical Computer Science (April 2005)
14. Moser, C., Thiele, L., Benini, L., Brunelli, D.: Real-time scheduling with regenerative energy. In: Proceedings of the 18th Euromicro Conference on Real-Time Systems, ECRTS 2006, pp. 261–270. IEEE Computer Society (2006)
15. Ölveczky, P.C., Thorvaldsen, S.: Formal modeling, performance estimation, and model checking of wireless sensor network algorithms in Real-Time Maude. Theoretical Computer Science 410(2-3), 254–280 (2009)

16. Samper, L., Maraninchi, F., Mounier, L., Mandel, L.: GLONEMO: Global and accurate formal models for the analysis of ad-hoc sensor networks. In: Proceedings of the First International Conference on Integrated Internet Ad Hoc and Sensor Networks (InterSense 2006). ACM (2006)
17. Shah, R.C., Rabaey, J.M.: Energy aware routing for low energy ad hoc sensor networks. In: IEEE Wireless Communications and Networking Conference Record, pp. 350–355 (2002)
18. Simjee, F., Chou, P.H.: Everlast: Long-life, supercapacitor-operated wireless sensor node. In: Proceedings of the International Symposium on Low Power Electronics and Design, ISLPED 2006, pp. 197–202. ACM (2006)
19. Titzer, B.L., Lee, D.K., Palsberg, J.: Avrora: Scalable sensor network simulation with precise timing. In: Proceedings of the 4th International Symposium on Information Processing in Sensor Networks (IPSN 2005), pp. 477–482. IEEE (2005)

Some Engineering Applications of the OTS/CafeOBJ Method

Petros Stefaneas, Iakovos Ouranos, Nikolaos Triantafyllou, and Katerina Ksystra

National Technical University of Athens
petros@math.ntua.gr,
{iouranos,nitriant,katksy}@central.ntua.gr

Abstract. In this paper we present briefly some of the engineering applications of the OTS/CafeOBJ method, conducted by researchers of the National Technical University of Athens in recent years. Such domains of applications include reactive rule-based systems, context-aware adaptive systems and the design by contract paradigm. Other case studies conducted include modeling and verification of Social Networks, Semantic Web and Mobile Digital Rights Management Systems.Finally, we present a summary of the lessons learned from these applications.

Keywords: OTS/CafeOBJ method, Case studies.

1   Introduction

Specification with the OTS/CafeOBJ methodology is a very powerful approach for the verification of systems design [9]. The abstraction level provided by the hidden algebra formalization allows the engineer to work at a very high level, and to focus on the design rather than the implementation details [16]. This can drastically reduce the complexity of the verification effort. Also, CafeOBJ uses theorem proving which is based on rewriting. Rewriting is an efficient way of implementing equational logic and we believe that this approach is easier to learn than other verification techniques based on higher logic.

This paper presents in brief some of the ongoing research under deployment at the National Technical University of Athens, Greece (CafeOBJ@NTUA). For more details please consult the blog http://cafeobjntua.wordpress.com/. The research on the engineering applications of the algebraic specification language CafeOBJ [15] and the OTS/CafeOBJ method [29] at NTUA, began at 2004 (six doctoral dissertationsand ten final year Diploma theses have either been completed or are still in progress at various stages). Historically, the first results were published in conference proceedings and the main topic of these early conference papers was about the modeling and verification of mobile systems [31-32]. The main journal publication of this first period of research was [30]. This was followed by case studies about modeling and verification of authentication protocols for sensor networks, which were conducted [33-35] with some interesting results; from them, valuable lessons were learned about the

S. Iida, J. Meseguer, and K. Ogata (Eds.): Futatsugi Festschrift, LNCS 8373, pp. 541–559, 2014.
© Springer-Verlag Berlin Heidelberg 2014

OTS/CafeOBJ method and its real-time extension.More diploma theses followed that focused on the verification of mobile DRM standards and the formal analysis of the MPEG-2 encoding algorithm and their results were presented in [43] and [25-26], respectively. A formal approach to detect malicious users in Social Networks by adapting the Confidant protocol of ad-hoc networksis an example of a domain application currently under consideration.

1.1   Prerequisites

OTS. An Observational Transition System (OTS) [29] is a distributed system that can be written in terms of equations. Assuming that there exists a universal state space Y and that each datatype D we need to use (including their equivalence relationship) has been declared in advance, an OTS S is formally defined as a triplet S = <O,I,T> where:

- O is a finite set of observers. Each o ϵ O is a functiono : Y → D, where D is a data type that may differ from observer to observer. Given an OTS S and two states u_1, u_2, the equivalence u_1 =s u_2 between them with respect to S is defined as; for all o ϵ O, $o(u_1) = o(u_2)$, i.e. two states are considered behaviorally equivalent if all the observers return for these states the same data values.
- I is the set of initial states such that I is a subset of Y.
- T is a set of conditional transitions. Each $\tau \epsilon$ T is a function τ : Y → Yand preserves the equivalence between two states;if u_1 =s u_2 then $\tau(u_1)$ =s $\tau(u_2)$. For each u ϵ Y, $\tau(u)$ is called the successor state of u wrt τ. The condition c_τ is called the effective condition of τ. Also, $\tau(u) = u$ if not $c_\tau(u)$. Finally, observers and transitions may be parameterized by data type values.

CafeOBJ. CafeOBJ is an algebraic specification language and processor [9]. In a CafeOBJ module we can declare sorts, operators, variables and equations. There exists two kinds of sorts; visible sortsthat denote abstract data types and hidden sorts that denote the state space of an abstract machine. Two kinds of behavioral operators can be applied to hidden sorts: action and observation operators. An observation operator can only be used to observe the inside of an abstract machine while an action operator can change its state. Declarations of observation operators and action operators start with the keywords `bop` or `bops`, and those of other operators start with `op` or `ops`. Finally, declarations of equations start with `eq`, and those of conditional ones with `ceq`.

OTS in CafeOBJ. Observational transition systems can be described as behavioral specifications in CafeOBJ [29]. The universal state space Y of an OTS is denoted in CafeOBJ by a hidden sort and an observer by an observation operator. Any initial state in I is denoted by a constant and a transition by an action operator. The transitions are defined by describing what the value, returned by each observer in the successor state becomes, when the transitions are applied in an arbitrary state u. For expressing the effective conditions, conditional equations are used. Finally, in the OTS/CafeOBJ theorem proving technique the CafeOBJ system verifies the desiredproperties by using the equations of the theory that defines the OTS as left to right rewrite rules.

Behavioral Object Composition. A methodology for behavioral object composition,which is naturally supported by CafeOBJ, has been defined in [8, 40]. This methodology is hierarchical, since the composition of behavioral objects yields another behavioral object. One of the most important contributions of this methodology is that it enables the reuse of not only the specifications of the composing objects but their proofs as well. The main technical concept underlying the composition method is projection operators; these are special observers defined for each composing object to obtain its state from the state of the composed object. There are several ways to compose an object. Parallel Composition (without synchronization),dynamic composition (in which component objects are created and deleted dynamically), and composition with synchronization, generalizing both former operators [8].

2   Ongoing Research

The first topic we present briefly in this section is the modeling of reactive rule-based systems, which are systems that react to the detection of events with appropriate actions, and are defined by reactive rules. The second is context-aware adaptive systems and the need for their formal specification and verification.These systems use information from their context and adapt their behavior to cope with changes on it. The third topic is on-going research on how to combine the OTS/CafeOBJ approach with the Design by Contract paradigm to create a new software development methodology. The forth case study is about the Semantic Web and an attempt to reason about its technologies in a unified way [27]. The fifth is about the formalization of Social networks and the verification of some critical properties these should enjoy [22].The final topic presents several results[45,41 and 42] from the application of algebraic specifications to the mobile Digital Rights Management standard of the Open Mobile Alliance.

2.1   Reactive Rule-Based Systems

Reactive rules expressed by Rule Markup Languages are used to define reactive rule-based systems/agents. Such systems are needed for bridging the gap between the existing Web, where data sources can only be accessed to obtain information, and the dynamic Web, where data sources are enriched with reactive behavior. Examples of reactive rule-based systems are e-commerce platforms that react to user actions (put an item in the basket), web services that react to notifications (SOAP messages) and active databases. The use of reactive rules to specify such reactive systems in a declarative way seems promising. They can supportad-hoc, flexible and dynamic workflows that can change at run-time. This allows the system designer to modifythe system if the requirements change.

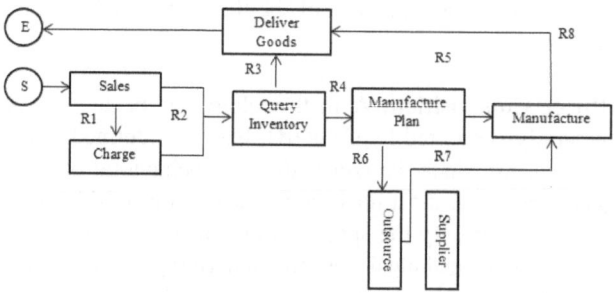

Fig. 1. Inter-business processes of a supply chain

However, reactive rules have no formal verification tools; alsothese rules can interact during execution, thus making the task of verifying their behaviordifficult.To overcome these issues, we have proposed in[24] an approachtoformalizethe most common families of reactive rules. In particular, we have presentedOTS semantics for Production (PR), Event Condition Action (ECA) and Knowledge Representation (KR) rules, as well as for Complex Event Processing. This semantics allows the mapping between reactive rules and algebraic specification languages,through whichverification support for such rules can be obtained.

As a next step, we have used CafeOBJ for the specification of reactive rule-based systems [21]. We have presented a methodology for expressing Production and Event Condition Action rules (the main reactive rules families) in CafeOBJ terms that captures the semantics of such rules and allows the verification of their behavior. Finally, we have applied the proposed method to an industrial case study that uses reactive rules to control the activities of its business agents [28].

The case study refers to the business processes between the manufacturing agent of a motorcycle corporation and one of its suppliers in terms of Event Condition Action rules. These business processes are presented in figure 1, where Ri denotes an Event Condition Action rule. For example rule R1 states that:"After the sales department accepts an order from a customer, a charge activity is initiated to wait for payment from the customer". After formalizing the system in OTS/CafeOBJ terms we were able to verify safety properties for it. An example of a property proved with the help of the OTS/CafeOBJ method is the invariant property shown in table 1. We believe that the results from this first case study were promising and that a tool that will automatically translate a set of reactive rules, written in a Rule Markup language, to an OTS/CafeOBJ specification will greatly facilitate the verification of complex rule-based systems.

Table 1. Invariant property of the maunufacturer agent

Informal Definition	CafeOBJ notation
It is not possible the payment of the customer not to be greater or equal from the order price and the goods to be delivered to the customer.	`eq inv1(S,C) = not(not(payment(S,C)>= cost(S,C)) and (deli- vered(S,C) = true))` `.`

Table 2. Invariant properties of the traffic monitoring system

CafeOBJ notation

```
eq inv1(S,N1,N2) =           eq inv2(S,N1,N2) =
not(received(camera(S,N1),   not(received(camera(S,N1),
N2) and received(camera      N2) and cansend(camera
(S,N2),N1)) .                (S,N1),N2)) .
```

2.2   Context-Aware Adaptive Systems

Context-aware adaptive systems are new-technology mobile systems that can sense their physical environment (context) and adapt their behavior accordingly. Context can be defined as any information that is used to characterize the situation of an entity [7]. In the above definition, an entity can be a person, place, or object that is considered relevant to the interaction between a user and an application, including the user and application themselves. Recently, context-awareness has been adopted in the development of critical applications. Thus, the need for modeling and verifying the behavior of such systems has become stronger.

In [23] we have applied the OTS/CafeOBJ method to context-aware adaptive systems.We usedthe methodology of behavioral object composition for the modeling of context-aware systems.It wasthen possible to define separately the functionalities of the components of the system but also define their interaction. We argue that in this way, the proposed framework can naturally express the entity-context dependency and the adaptation of the system to cope with changes in the context.A case study of a context-aware adaptive system fora decentralized traffic monitoring system is presented in [20]. This system consists of cameras that monitor the road and communicate through ping-echo messages in order to report failures of cameras. To demonstrate the expressiveness of our framework we applied it to this traffic monitoring system and proved some security properties using the OTS/CafeOBJ methodology.

Two of the safety properties that were required for the system are shown in table 2. The first property states that it is not possible for two cameras to have received ping messages from each other at the same time (this would result in a system deadlock). The second property declares that it is not possible for a camera to have received a ping message from another camera and to be able to send a ping message to that camera. Thisproperty was used as a lemma in order to prove invariant 1. These properties are important for the purpose of this system, i.e. the communication of the cameras through messages in order to report failures and traffic conditions.

2.3   Design by Contract

Algebraic specifications in general can be used in at least two ways. The first and most commonly used is to take an existing system, specify it and verify the properties that are crucial to the behavior of the system. A disadvantage of this use is that it is usually very costly to redesign/implement an already working system if it does not satisfy the desired properties. However this is necessary when we are concerned with critical systems. The second, and most cost efficient use, is to apply algebraic specifications to design the system and verify its behavior before it is created. In this case if an error is found, i.e. the system does not satisfy the desired behavior, then, only its specification needs to be refined and not the implementation. A disadvantage of this use is that there is no guarantee that the final implementation of the system will respect the specification. To this end, there has been some research to use CafeOBJ specifications to generate Java code [11, 12]. However, due to the behavioral nature of CafeOBJ specifications, in many cases the generated Java code is not usable [12]. This makes the previous methodology not a feasible solution to the problem of obtaining an implementation of a CafeOBJ specification which is a model of it. In particular the problem in generating code from OTS/CafeOBJ specifications can be tracked to the way observation functions are defined. These observations can be thought of as experiments conducted to a black box, i.e. only the values they return are observable not the way they are calculated. These values are used to characterize the state of the system. Thus, OTS/CafeOBJ specifications can be thought of as denoting models which only satisfy the specifications behaviorally, i.e. satisfy them for all given experiments. Despite the difficulties of generating code from OTS/CafeOBJ specifications, such a methodology is highly valuable when reasoning about real life systems because many clever implementations used in practice only satisfy their specifications in this sense. A typical example is the traditional implementation of sets by lists, where union implemented by append fails to strictly satisfy basic laws like commutativity and idempotency, but does satisfy them behaviorally [9].

On the other hand, there exist specification languages based on the idea of Design by Contract (DbC), like the Java Modeling Language (JML [39]), which were created to allow the development of tools able to automatically verify that an implementation satisfies the specification [6]. These languages use pre- and post- conditions to describe the intended behavior of an object's methods in the style of Hoare logic. The goal of DbC languages is to verify that the methods satisfy their specifications and not to reason about the specifications themselves (i.e. the design of the system). An obvious disadvantage of this approach is that such languages are tied to a single programming language (e.g. Java) and cannot be used to reason about systems whose implementation requires the combination of languages. Creating such tools for all possible combinations of languages does not seem feasible [16]. Additionally, the verification of high level security properties and the verification of infinite state systems is often not possible using solely DbC methods like JML [14, 38]. High level security properties usually depend on design decisions that span across several classes located in several packages and writing appropriate JML annotations for such properties is tedious and error-prone because these annotations have to spread all over the application, and thus it is not possible to verify their overall correct behavior with the JML tools. This is due to the fact that DbC specifications are restricted to a single class. Additionally, reasoning about safety properties with JML is based on modeling the system as a finite state automaton and thus this approach is unsuitable for many real life systems due to the state explosion problem.

We have observed that the two approaches, DbC and OTS/CafeOBJ, are complementary. Thus, despite the fact that in most cases it is not possible to generate code directly from an OTS/CafeOBJ specification we argue that it is possible to obtain an implementation that is a model of the CafeOBJ specification by first translating it to an equivalent JML specification. In particular we propose a software development methodology that allows the development of verified critical Java applications consisting of the following steps:

- The design of the system is specified using the OTS/CafeOBJ method, and the desired safety properties are verified by a design engineer using this specification.
- Next, (some part of) the specification is translated to an equivalent JML.
- The JML specification is given to a programmer for implementation
- The Java implementation is verified against the JML specification using the existing tools.

The equivalence between OTS/CafeOBJ and JML specifications of step 2 denotes that all models of the generated JML specification are models of the original OTS/CafeOBJ specification, i.e. showing that the translation is a refinement between the two specifications in the sense of [43]. To this end we have been working on a translation, from OTS/CafeOBJ to JML (cafe2JML). A preliminary version of this translation is presentedin [45]. With this methodology, the design of the system is verified using the OTS/CafeOBJ approach which has proved its effectiveness in very difficult properties and systems. Also, because the specification is independent of the actual programming language it can be implemented using any combination of languages. Additionally, due to the nature of the original CafeOBJ specification, the JML specification can be implemented in a number of ways, allowing for code optimization. For example consider the following OTS/CafeOBJ specification of a simple counter, consisting of one observation operation, read, and one transition, add:

```
mod* COUNTER{
protecting(INT + BOOL)
*[Counter]*
opinit : -> Counter
bop add : Int Counter -> Counter
bop read : Counter->Int
var I :Int .
varC : Counter .
op c-add : Int ->Bool .
eq c-add(⊥)= I>= 0 .
eq read(init)= 0   .
ceq read(add(I,C))= I + read(C) if c-add(I) .
ceq add(I,C) = C if not c-add(I).}
```

The previous OTS/CafeOBJ specification will generate based on the cafe2JML translation the following JML specification which defines one method for the observation (that does not change the state of the object) and one for the transition (the value ofthe observation when the transition is successfully applied is defined in the contract of add):

```
public class Counter {
//@initially (read() == 0) ;
public Counter(){}
public /*@ pure @*/ int read(){}
/*@ public normal_behavior
@ ensures( I>=0 ==> read()== \old(I + read())) ;
@ also
@ ensures I < 0 ==>read() == \old(read()) ; */
public void add(int I){}}
```

This JML specification can now be implemented in several ways, however if the implementation does satisfy the specification then it will retain the properties of the CafeOBJ specification since the JML specification is a refinement of it;

```
public class Counter {//@initially read() == 0) ;
privateintthe_read_value ;

public Counter(int UID){the_read_value = 0;}
public /*@ pure @*/int read(){return the_read_value ;}/*@


/*@ public normal_behavior
@ ensures (I>=0 ==>read()== \old(I + read())) ;
@ also
@ ensures I<0 ==>read() == \old(read()) ; */
public void add(intI){
if(I>=0)the_read_value=the_read_value + I ; } }
```

To evaluate the effectiveness of this methodology we have used cafe2JML to translate an OTS/CafeOBJ specification (based on the specification of [40]) of a moderately complex ATM system. Next, we created a Java implementation based on the generated JML specification and successfully verified its compliance using the KEY-project [6] plugin for Eclipse Juno. A necessary next step in this research is the development of similar translations into other DbC languages (e.g. Spec#, a DbC language for C#). Applications of this methodology could also be applied to proof carrying code techniques as we discuss in [44].

2.4   The Semantic Web and Algebraic Reasoning: Some First Applications Using Behavioral Specifications

The Semantic Web aims at converting the current web into a "web of data" that can be processed directly and indirectly by humans and machines. There exists a strongneed for reasoning between and within the various components of the Semantic Web and we believe that behavioral algebraic specifications could fill that gap.

As a first step towards this direction, we have created an abstract specification of the Semantic Web stack using CafeOBJ [27].To demonstratehow our approach can be used to specifythe interaction between different SW technologies, we have modeled a system consisting of a set of rules and an ontology(two basic SW technologies)as a composite Observational Transition System (OTS).Also we showed how reasoning about the behavior of the rules in conjunction to the information that can be derived from the ontology can be performed.

First, we specified a simple ontology consisting of the following classes: class Persons, Adults, Drivers, Vehicles and Grownups. These classes describe when someone is a person, an adult and so on and the ontology defines the relationships between these classes. One such relationship is the following;*Driver is a person that drives a vehicle.*

Each class was specified as an OTS.For example, a part of the specification of the class Personis presented below; according to this specification, classes are collections of objects and individuals are instances of objects. The observer / in observes if an individual belongs to a class or not. The operator assertis a transition that changes the state of the class by asserting that an individual belongs to that class. Finally, the sort thing is used to express the fact that every individual is a member of the class owl:Thing.

```
mod* PersonCLASS{
pr(THINGS)
*[personSet]*
bop _\in_ : thing personSet ->Bool
bop assert : thing personSet ->personSet }
```

Then,the ontology wasmodeled as a composed OTS that is created from classes OTSswith the use of projection operators.

```
mod* Ontology{
pr(Things + AdultClass + DriverClass + PersonCLASS + Ve-
chicleClass + GrownupCLASS)
-- projections
bop adults  : onto ->adultSet
bop drivers : onto ->driverSet
bop persons : onto ->personSet
bopvechicles : onto ->vechicleSet}
```

Using appropriate observers we defined class memberships(i.e. describewhensomeone is a person, an adult or a member of a certain class in general), subclass and equivalence (i.e. two classes that contain the same individuals) relationships.In this way, class inferences (i.e. from a given class membership discover new class membership) performed by ontologies' inference methodswere simulated by CafeOBJ's rewriting system.One class inference that can be derived from this ontology is the following;*Drivers are grownups*, which wasreduced to true using our approach.

Second, to demonstrate how reasoning can be performed between rules and ontologies, we defined another higher level composed OTS, called System, which has the ontology as component and as transitions the following rules;*If someone is a grown up assert that his/her age is greater than 18 years*, and *On a register request, successfully register the user if he/she is older than 18 years old.*

In this higher level OTS, more complex reasoning can be performed by combining information from the ontology and the rules.For example one inference that can be madeis that;*if someone is a driver he/she can register to the desired service*, which was successfully derived using the OTS/CafeOBJ method.To conclude, we believe that the OTS/CafeOBJ method and its abstraction level provided by the hidden algebra approachcan be particularly effective for modeling and verifying heterogeneous systems such as the Semantic Web.

2.5   An Algebraic Specification of Social Networks

We havecreated a formalization of an abstract social network as the composition of behavioral objects by using OTS/CafeOBJ [22].The composed OTS represents the social network thatconsists of an arbitrary number of Profile OTSs, which correspond to the profiles of the various users. Then, we verified some security properties every social network should enjoy,like the one shown in table 3 below.

Following the proof scores methodology, we successfully verified that the specification of the Profile OTS satisfies invariant 1, but its verification failed for the network OTS [22]. For a sub-case of the tag transition (a transition of the social network OTS), CafeOBJ returned false. This case was reachable for our system and thus could not use any lemma to discard it.

The problem was derived from the fact that when a user "tags" another user in a photo (i.e. publishes a photo with the names of the users that appear in the photo) in a real social network, this photo belongs to both users. This property was transferred to our specification and caused the violation of invariant 1.

Table 3. A desired safety property of a social network

Informal definition	CafeOBJ notation
A user A can see your photo P if your profile is open to public, or if your profile is visible to your friends and A belongs to your friends or if your profile is visible to the friends of your friends and A belongs either to your friends or to the friends of your friends or if your profile is open to a special list only and user A belongs to that list or finally if user A is yourself.	`eq inv1(S,A,P)=((P /in pho-toalbum(S))and not((type(S) = public)or((type(S) = friend) and (A //in friends(S)))or ((type(S) = ffriend)and((A //in friendoffriends(S)or(A //in friends(S))))))or(myid(S) = A)or((type(S) =splist)and(A //in specialist(S))))))implies not view3(S,A,P) .`

The equations defining the transition tag were:

```
1.op c-tagFB : AccountidAccountid Placeholder Nat Content
Sys ->Bool
2. eq c-tagFB(A1,A2,PH,N,C1,S) = (A1 /in accounts(S)) and
(A2 /in accounts(S)) and (placetype?(PH) = phototype)
and ( type?(C1) = picture) and (A1&N&C1//in photoal-
bum(profile(A1,S))) .
3. ceq profile(A3,tagFB(A1,A2,C1,PH, N,S)) = re-
ceive(C1,A2,PH, profile(A2,S)) if (c-
tagFB(A1,A2,PH,N,C1,S) and (A3 = A2)) .
4. ceq profile(A3,tagFB(A1,A2,C1,PH,N,S)) = profile(A3 ,
S) if (not(A3 = A1) and c-tagFB(A1,A2,PH,N,C1,S) ) .
```

Lines 1 and 2 define the effective condition and state that a user can tag another user in a content, if that content is a photo and is located in his photo album. Line 3 states that if user A2 gets tagged by user A1 then the state of user A2 changes to the state of receiving this photo as content and storing it into his photo album. This is achieved by stating that the projected state of A2 changes to `re-ceive(C1,A2,PH,profile(A2,S))`.Line 4 states that the profile remains unchanged if the effective condition of the transition rule does not hold.

By separating the specification of the network from the specifications of the profiles the problem was isolated to the design of the composed OTS, not the components. This knowledge could then be used to refine the specification of the network while maintaining the same specification for the profile OTSs, significantly speeding up the refinement.

2.6   Mobile Digital Rights Management Systems

Digital Rights Management systems (DRMs) control many aspects of the life cycle of digital contents including consumption, management and distribution. The software responsible for these actions is called the DRM agent.Two key components of DRM systems are the language in which the permissions and constraints on the contents are expressed,and the allocation algorithm responsible for determining when an action on a content is authorized [13]. The languages are referred to as Rights Expression Languages (RELs) [13]. A set of permissions and constraints expressed in such a language is called a license. In a typical scenario a user will have multiple such licenses installed in his agent. The Open Mobile Alliance (OMA) is a well-know DRM standard organization responsible for the creation of DRM standards in the mobile environment [10, 13]. The research presented here is mainly focused on the specification and verification of these standards.

The first problem we attempted to solve was the lack of formal semantics of the OMA-REL [13]. The non-existence of this semantics leads to the use of licenses whose behavior is uncertain, i.e. they might not behave in the way that the creator of the license intended. To solve this problem we defined a formal semantics for

Table 4. CafeOBJ specification of the constraints permitted by OMA REL

```
mod* CONS{
pr(CONSTRAINT-SET+NAT+INDIV+SYSTEM+DATE+INTERV)
op timeCount[ _ , _ ,_ ,_ ] : Nat NatNatNat -> Cons
op count[_ , _]: Nat Nat -> Cons
op True : -> Cons
op accumulated[ _ , _ ] : Nat Nat -> Cons
op individual[_ , _] : IndInd -> Cons
op System [_ , _ ] : Sys Sys -> Cons
op datetime[ _ , _ ] : DtDt -> Cons
op interval[_] : Interv -> Cons}
```

OMA-REL and specified it by using CafeOBJ [41]. For example the CafeOBJ specification of the various constraints that can be expressed by OMA REL is shown on table 4. This semantics together with its specification permitted the use of the rewriting logic implemented by CafeOBJ to reason about when an action on a content is allowed (for a given set of licenses and under a set of assumptions that define the environment in which the query is to be executed). In this way, it was possible to reason and verify the behavior of a license by eliminating any doubts about its behavior [41].

Table 5. Safety property of the original OMA algorithm

Informal Definition	CafeOBJ notation
Whenever a license is chosen for a given content, then the license is valid at that specific time.	`eq inv1(S,L)= ((L= bes-tLic(S)) and not (L = nil)) implies valid(S,L)`

Table 6. The property verified for the proposed algorithm

Informal Definition	CafeOBJ notation
If there exists a permission P in the set of the originally permitted actions by a set of licenses LS, and after a series of satisfactions of user requests P is no longer allowed, then the color of P is not white.	`eq inv1(S,P) = (P/in al-lowed (S)) and (P/in dep-leted (S)) implies not(color(S,P)= white)`

A key component of the OMA-DRM standard is the algorithm which is responsible for selecting what license to use when there are multiple licenses installed referring to the same content [13]. It has already been argued that this algorithm causes the loss of rights on contents under certain circumstances [5]. We redesigned this algorithm so as to minimize these losses [42]. To reduce the implementation cost, the OMA algorithm remained at the core of the redesigned algorithm. However, we had first to verify that it satisfied a minimum safety property, which is shown in table 5. This was achieved by specifying the DRM agent as an OTS written in CafeOBJ terms and verifying the desired safety property with the proof scores method [46]. Next, to ensure that the algorithm we proposed did in fact solve the loss of rights problem, it was specified using the OTS/CafeOBJ method as well, and we successfully verified that indeed the loss of rights is minimized, the property verified can be seen in table 6.

Additional Remarks. The Timed Observational Transition System (TOTS)/CafeOBJ method is a version of the OTS/CafeOBJ method for modeling, specificationand verification of distributed systems and protocols with real time constraints.We have worked on a case study from the field of source authenticationprotocols, TESLA protocol, to show the application of the method to suchcomplex systems. Our approach to TESLA and a summary of the experiences gained have been published at [33,37].

In another paper [36] we sketch some first steps towards the definition of a protocol algebra based on the framework of behavioral algebraic specification. Following the tradition of representing protocols as state machines, we use the notion of Observational Transition System to express them in an executable algebraic specification language such as CafeOBJ.

Finally, we believe that the enrichment of engineering standards and notations (such as ASN.1) with algebraic specification techniques will help the smoother adoption of formal methodologies in the community of networking. We have been working towards a software environment that can translate a protocol to an executable algebraic specification language such as CafeOBJ to check critical properties of systems. More on CafeOBJ/OTS, standards and ASN1 can be found at [2-4].

3   Some Lessons Learned and Future Work

3.1   Lessons Learned

In contrast to other fully automated verification approaches the proof score methodology is computer/human interactive [29]. This allows the designer to understand why the design fails to meet the desired properties, if it does. So it is easier to refine the specification if the need arises. Proof scoresare used to verify that a property is invariant by induction on the state space of the OTS. The CafeOBJ system verifies the inductive steps by using the equations of the theory that defines the OTS as left to right rewrite rules[15].However, very often the engine will stop the rewriting process before reaching a conclusion. It is then required from the user to split the equations defining the state where the rewriting stopped [29]. One of the biggest challenges wefaced working with the OTS/CafeOBJ methodology was to make sure that no cases were omitted in the proof scores. In real case studies like the above, case splitting can be repeated many times and, in doing so, generate proof passages (sub-proof scores) in the range of hundreds. For example, a relatively simple subcase that needed to be verified in [46] was defined by the following equations in CafeOBJ terms:

```
eq s' = use1(s) .
eq (useReq(s) = null) = false .
eq (best(s) = emptyLic) = false .
eq type3?(labelCP?(find3(useReq(s),best(s))))= once .
eq (type3?(label?(find4(useReq(s),best(s)))=once)=false .
eqpossLic(s) = emptyLic .
eq p /in allowed(s) = true .
eq (p= perm3?(useReq(s),find3(useReq(s),best(s))))=
false.
eq (belong3?(makeReq(p),find3(useReq(s),best(s)))=false .
eq color(s,p) = white .
eq p /in depleted(s) = false .
eq p /in buildPS1(find3(useReq(s),best(s)))= true .
```

The engineer has to manually verify that all symmetrically defined states are accounted for, i.e. check that the case defined by the following equations is also covered and so on.

```
eq s' = use1(s) .
eq(useReq(s) = null) = false.
eq (best(s) = emptyLic) = false .
eq type3?(labelCP?(find3(useReq(s),best(s))))= once .
eq (type3?(label?(find4(useReq(s),best(s))))= once)=
false .
eqpossLic(s) = emptyLic .
eq p /in allowed(s) = true .
eq (p=perm3?(useReq(s),find3(useReq(s),best(s))))=false .
eq (belong3?(makeReq(p),find3(useReq(s),best(s)))=false .
eq color(s,p) = white .
eq p /in depleted(s) = false .
eq p /in buildPS1(find3(useReq(s),best(s)))= false .
```

Checking that no case was overlooked is a tedious task, but one very important for the correctness of the verification. We believe that a way to systematically keep track of all the cases, denoting which cases are still open,would lift a big weight off the shoulders of the engineers.

Typically in a behavioral specification you define how the values of the observers change after the successful application of a transition rule to an arbitrary state. The values of these observers may be subject to other constraints as well (in addition to the effective condition). An interesting lesson learned during the case studies above-was that the specifications must be as complete as possible in order to speed up the verification process. This means that it is equally important to define what the values of the observers become when these extra constraints hold as well as when they do not hold, although it may seem irrelevant to the specification. For example, it may seem sufficient to define only the value of an observer after the application of a transition as follows [22]:

```
ceq view3(acceptfriendrequest(A1,P),A3,Pi) = true if
((type(P) = friend) and (A3 = A1)) or ((type(P) =
ffriend) and ((A3 = A1) or (A3 //in friendsoffriends
(P,friends(P))))) and c-acceptfriendrequest(A1,P) .
```

Nevertheless, defining explicitly what the value of the observer is when the conditions do not hold can significantly speed up the verification. In the case above this can be done by using the following equation:

```
ceq view3(acceptfriendrequest(A1,P),A3,Pi)= view3(P,A3
,Pi) if not (((type(P) = friend) and (A3 = A1)) or
((type(P) = ffriend) and ((A3 = A1) or (A3 //in friend-
soffriends(P,friends(P))))) andc-
acceptfriendrequest(A1,P)) .
```

Otherwise, these unspecified cases will appear as clauses to case splitting in the verification or even make the discovery of extra lemmas necessary. A specification is rather complete when the CafeOBJ engine successfully proves that the default behavioral equivalence (=*=) is congruent with the specification.

Finally, during the case splitting stage of the verification it is possible to define a state that is unreachable w.r.t. the OTS specification. In such cases, if CafeOBJ returns false as the conclusion of the induction, a lemma must be generated to discard this case. However, one of the advantages of the case splitting process being computerhuman interactive is that an attentive engineer can reason that the proof score is heading towards an unreachable state at a very earlier stage, before CafeOBJ returns either true or false. For instance, in the following proof passage CafeOBJ returned neither true nor false [46].

```
open ISTEP
eq ((subl,l) = errLic) = false .
eq belong3?(makeReq(p),find3(r,(subl , l))) = true .
eq belong3?(makeReq(p),find3(r,subl)) = true .
eq belong3?(makeReq(p),find3(r,(subl ,(subl' , l)))) =
false .
red inv7(p,r,(subl,l),subl') implies istep9 .
close
```

Nonetheless, we were able to reason that the following equations could not hold simultaneously in our specification, and we used them to define invariant 7. The formulation of a lemma at this early stage is usually easier and can greatly reduce the size of the case splitting thus saving valuable time.

```
belong3?(makeReq(p),find3(r,subl)) and
```

```
notbelong3?(makeReq(p),find3(r,(subl,subl',l)))) .
```

3.2   Future Work

Algebraic specification languages such as CafeOBJ, Maude [19] and CASL [18] have well-known advantages for modeling digital systems. In some cases, it is useful to attempt to prove that the model—usually couched as a transition system—has certain properties. For that purpose, some algebraic specification languages have been coupled with interactive theorem-proving systems; CASL, for instance, has been interfaced with HOL/Isabelle [1]. We propose that CafeOBJ should be likewise coupled with the interactive proof environment Athena[17] (Athena+CafeOBJ). Then, we plan to use Athena+CafeOBJ in various domains of applications such as Semantic Web, e-services, social networks and braid groups. This research will be part of the research project "THALIS" already approved by the Greek Government to promote research excellence.

Acknowledgments. This research has been co-financed by the European Union (European Social Fund – ESF) and Greek national funds through the Operational Program "Education and Lifelong Learning" of the National Strategic Reference Framework (NSRF) - Research Funding Program: THALIS.

References

1. Autexier, S., Mossakowski, T.: Integrating HOL-CASL into the Development Graph Manager MAYA. In: Armando, A. (ed.) FroCos 2002. LNCS (LNAI), vol. 2309, pp. 2–17. Springer, Heidelberg (2002)
2. Barlas, K., Koletsos, G., Ouranos, I., Stefaneas, P.: From ASN.1 into CafeOBJ: Some first steps. In: Fourth SEE Workshop on Formal Methods, pp. 66–72. IEEE Computer Society CPS (2009)
3. Barlas, K., Koletsos, G., Stefaneas, P., Ouranos, I.: Towards a correct Translation from ASN.1 into CafeOBJ. Special Issue on Innovations in Intelligent Systems and Applications of the International Journal of Reasoning-based Intelligent Systems (IJRIS) 2(3-4), 300–309 (2010)
4. Barlas, K., Koletsos, G., Stefaneas, P.: Extending Standards with Formal Methods: Open Document Architecture. In: Proc. Innovations in Intelligent Systems and Applications (INISTA), 2012 International Symposium on Innovations in Intelligent Systems and Applications (INISTA), pp. 1–5 (2012)
5. Barth, A., Mitchell, J.C.: Managing digital rights using linear logic. In: 21st Annual IEEE Symposium on Logic in Computer Science, pp. 127–136. IEEE press, Seattle (2006)

6. Beckert, B., Hähnle, R., Schmitt, P.H. (eds.): Verification of Object-Oriented Software. LNCS, vol. 4334. Springer, Heidelberg (2007)
7. Dey, A.K., Abowd, G.D.: Towards a Better Understanding of Context and Context-Awareness. In: The First International Symposium on Handheld and Ubiquitous Computing (HUC), Karlsruhe, Germany (1999)
8. Diaconescu, R.: Behavioural specification for hierarchical object composition. Theoretical Computer Science 343(3), 305–331 (2005)
9. Diaconescu, R., Futatsugi, K., Iida, S.: CafeOBJ Jewels. In: Futatsugi, K., Nakagawa, A.T., Tamai, T. (eds.) CAFE: An Industiral-Strength Algebraic Formal Method, pp. 33–60. Elsevier (2000)
10. Digital Rights Management 2.1. Technical Report, Open Mobile Alliance (2008)
11. Doungsaard, C., Suwannasart, T.: A Semantic Part Generated Java Statement from a CafeOBJ Specification. In: IEEE International Conference on Electro/Information Technology (2006)
12. Doungsaard, C., Suwannasart, T.: An Automatic Approach to Transform CafeOBJ Specifications to Java Template Code. In: International Conference on Software Engineering Research and Practice, SERP 2003, Las Vegas, Nevada, USA, June 23-26, vol. 1 (2003)
13. DRM Rights Expression Language 2.1. Technical Report, Open Mobile Alliance (2010)
14. Dulaj, I.: Specification of Security policies by JML (2010), http://www.divaportal.org/smash/get/diva2:353056/FULLTEXT01.pdf
15. Futatsugi, K., Diaconescu, R.: CafeOBJ Report. World Scientific, AMAST Series (1998)
16. Futatsugi, K., Goguen, J.A., Ogata, K.: Verifying Design with Proof Scores. In: Meyer, B., Woodcock, J. (eds.) Verified Software. LNCS, vol. 4171, pp. 277–290. Springer, Heidelberg (2008)
17. http://www.proofcentral.org/athena/
18. http://www.informatik.uni-bremen.de/cofi/wiki/index.php/CASL
19. http://maude.cs.uiuc.edu/
20. Iftikhar, M.U., Weyns, D.: A Case Study on Formal Verification of Self-Adaptive Behaviors in a Decentralized System. In: 11th International Workshop on Foundations of Coordination Languages and Self-Adaptation (FOCLASA), Newcastle, UK (2012)
21. Ksystra, K., Stefaneas, P., Frangos, P.: An Algebraic Framework for Modeling of Reactive rule-based Intelligent Agents. In: Geffert, V., Preneel, B., Rovan, B., Štuller, J., Tjoa, A.M. (eds.) SOFSEM 2014. LNCS, vol. 8327, pp. 407–418. Springer, Heidelberg (2014)
22. Ksystra, K., Triantafyllou, N., Barlas, K., Stefaneas, P.S.: An Algebraic Specification of Social Networks. In: BCS Quality SG SQM/INSPIRE Conference, Tampere, Finland (2012)
23. Ksystra, K., Stefaneas, P.S., Frangos, P.: A behavioral framework for context aware adaptive systems (submitted for publication 2014)
24. Ksystra, K., Triantafyllou, N., Stefaneas, P.: On the Algebraic Semantics of Reactive Rules. In: Bikakis, A., Giurca, A. (eds.) RuleML 2012. LNCS, vol. 7438, pp. 136–150. Springer, Heidelberg (2012)
25. Ksystra, K., Stefancas, P., Ouranos, P., Frangos, P.: A Parallel Version of the MPEG-2 Encoding Algorithm Formally Analyzed using Algebraic Specifications. In: International Conference on Signal Processing and Multimedia Applications (SIGMAP), pp. 35–38 (2010)
26. Ksystra, K., Stefaneas, P., Triantafyllou, N., Ouranos, I.: An Algebraic Specification for the MPEG-2 Encoding Algorithm. In: Fourth South-East European Workshop on Formal Methods (SEEFM), pp. 46–52 (2009)

27. Ksystra, K., Triantafyllou, N., Stefaneas, P.S., Frangos, P.: Semantic Web and Algebraic Reasoning: Some First Applications Using Behavioral Specifications. In: Seventh International Workshop on Semantic and Social Media Adaptation and Personalization, Luxembourg, pp. 81–86 (2012)

28. Liua, J., Zhangb, J., Hub, J.: A case study of an inter-enterprise workflow-supported supply chain management system. Information and Management 42, 441–454 (2005)

29. Ogata, K., Futatsugi, K.: Some Tips on Writing Proof Scores in the OTS/CafeOBJ method. In: Futatsugi, K., Jouannaud, J.-P., Meseguer, J. (eds.) Goguen Festschrift. LNCS, vol. 4060, pp. 596–615. Springer, Heidelberg (2006)

30. Ouranos, I., Stefaneas, P., Frangos, P.: An Algebraic Framework for Modeling of Mobile Systems. IEICE Trans. Fund. E90-A(9), 1986–1999 (2007)

31. Ouranos, I., Stefaneas, P., Frangos, P.: An Algebraic Specification of Mobile IPv6 Protocol. In: 1st Conf. Principles of Software Engineering (PRISE), Buenos Aires, Argentina (2004)

32. Ouranos, I., Stefaneas, P., Frangos, P.: A Formal Specification Framework for Ad Hoc Mobile Communication Networks. In: SOFSEM 2007, pp. 91–102 (2007)

33. Ouranos, I., Ogata, K., Stefaneas, P.: Formal Analysis of TESLA protocol in the Timed OTS/CafeOBJ method. In: Margaria, T., Steffen, B. (eds.) ISoLA 2012, Part II. LNCS, vol. 7610, pp. 126–142. Springer, Heidelberg (2012)

34. Ouranos, I., Stefaneas, P., Ogata, K.: Formal Modeling and Verification of Sensor Network Encryption Protocol in the OTS/CafeOBJ Method. In: Margaria, T., Steffen, B. (eds.) ISoLA 2010, Part I. LNCS, vol. 6415, pp. 75–89. Springer, Heidelberg (2010)

35. Ouranos, I., Stefaneas, P.: Verifying Security Protocols for Sensor Networks using Algebraic Specification Techniques. In: Bozapalidis, S., Rahonis, G. (eds.) CAI 2007. LNCS, vol. 4728, pp. 247–259. Springer, Heidelberg (2007)

36. Ouranos, I., Stefaneas, P.: Towards a Protocol Algebra Based on Algebraic Specifications. In: Lee, R. (ed.) SERA 2013. SCI, vol. 496, pp. 85–98. Springer, Heidelberg (2013)

37. Ouranos, I., Ogata, K., Stefaneas, P.: TESLA source authentication protocol verification experiment in the Timed OTS/CafeOBJ method: Experiences and Lessons Learned (2013) (submitted for publication)

38. Pavlova, M., Barthe, G., Burdy, L., Huisman, M., Lanet, J.L.: Enforcing High-Level Security Properties for Applets. In: Sixth Smart Card Research and Advanced Application IFIP Conference, pp. 1–16 (2003)

39. Chalin, P., Kiniry, J.R., Leavens, G.T., Poll, E.: Beyond assertions: Advanced specification and verification with JML and ESC/Java2. In: de Boer, F.S., Bonsangue, M.M., Graf, S., de Roever, W.-P. (eds.) FMCO 2005. LNCS, vol. 4111, pp. 342–363. Springer, Heidelberg (2006)

40. Iida, S., Matsumoto, M., Diaconescu, R., Futatsugi, K., Lucanu, D.: Concurrent Object Composition in CafeOBJ. Technical Report IS-RR-98-0009S, Japan Advanced Institute of Science and Technology, JAIST (1998)

41. Triantafyllou, N., Ouranos, I., Stefaneas, P.: Algebraic Specifications for OMA REL Licenses. In: IEEE International Conference on Wireless and Mobile Computing, Networking and Communications, pp. 376–381. IEEE Press, Marrakech (2009)

42. Triantafyllou, N., Stefaneas, P., Frangos, P.: An Algorithm for Allocating User Requests to Licenses in the OMA DRM System. IEICE Transactions on Information and Systems E96-D(6), 1258–1267 (2013)

43. Triantafyllou, N., Ksystra, K., Stefaneas, P., Frangos, P.: Applying Algebraic Specifications on Digital Right Management Systems. In: Imperial College Computing Student Workshop, ICCSW 2011, pp. 94–100 (2011)

44. Triantafyllou, N., Ksystra, K., Stefaneas, P., Frangos, P.: Proof Carrying Code using Algebraic Specifications. Journal of Applied Mathematics & Bioinformatics 3(1), 43–56 (2013)
45. Triantafyllou, N., Stefaneas, P., Frangos, P.: OTS/CafeOBJ2JML: An attempt to combine Design By Contract with Behavioral Specifications. Technical report (2012)
46. Triantafyllou, N., Ouranos, I., Stefaneas, P., Frangos, P.: Formal Specification and Verification of the OMA License Choice Algorithm in the OTS/CafeOBJ Method. In: ICETE the International Joint Conference on e-Business and Telecommunications (WINSYS), pp. 173–180. SciTe Press, Athens (2010)

Verifying the Design of Dynamic Software Updating in the OTS/CafeOBJ Method

Min Zhang, Kazuhiro Ogata, and Kokichi Futatsugi

Research Center for Software Verification
Japan Advanced Institute of Science and Technology (JAIST)
{zhangmin,ogata,futatsugi}@jaist.ac.jp

Abstract. Dynamic Software Updating (DSU) is a technique for updating running software systems without incurring downtime. However, a challenging problem is how to design a correct dynamic update so that the system after being updated will run as expected instead of causing any inconsistencies or even crashes. The OTS/CafeOBJ method is an effective and practical approach to specifying and verifying the design of software. In this paper, we propose an algebraic way of specifying and verifying the design of dynamic updates in the OTS/CafeOBJ method. By verifying the design of a dynamic update, we can (1) gain a better understanding of the update, e.g., how the behavior of the running system is affected by the update, (2) identify updating points where the dynamic update can be safely applied, (3) detect potential errors, and hence (4) design a safer dynamic update.

1 Introduction

Software systems are inevitably subject to changes in order to fix bugs, or add new functionality, etc. A traditional way of deploying such changes is first shutting down a running system, then installing new version or applying patches, and finally relaunching the system. However, there are a class of systems that provide non-stoppable services such as financial transaction systems, and traffic control systems. To update such systems, dynamic software updating DSU [1] is an effective approach in which running software can be updated on the fly without being shut down and relaunched.

A challenging problem with dynamic updating is how to ensure their correctness and safety so that a system after being updated will behave as expected instead of causing any inconsistencies or even crashes in the worst case. To make sure a system can be correctly updated, it is important that the update should be correctly designed, e.g., how state and behavior are changed, at which points update can be safely applied, and what properties should be satisfied by updated systems.

Several studies have been conducted on the correctness of dynamic software updating. Duggan *et al.* proposed that dynamic update should be type safe in that functions must refer to the data of desired types [2,3]. Neamtiu *et al.* introduced the notion of *version consistency*, meaning that the calls between functions

S. Iida, J. Meseguer, and K. Ogata (Eds.): Futatsugi Festschrift, LNCS 8373, pp. 560–577, 2014.

in different versions should be consistent [4]. These properties are necessary to make sure that dynamic update is correctly performed at the code leve, but not sufficient. A correct dynamic update also depends upon its logical design, such as how an old system's state and behavior are changed, and when update should be applied. Gupta *et al.* proposed a formal framework to analyze the *validity* of dynamic update [5] by studying whether a reachable state of the new system can be finally reached by the updated system. However, it is generally undecidable to check the validity of an update. Hayden *et al.* proposed an approach to analyzing how the behavior of a system is affected by an update and whether the change of the behavior satisfies the requirement [6]. Their approach is designed for the updates in C programs.

Little attention has been paid to the correctness of dynamic updating at the design level. Our previous work has shown that a correct design of an update is equally important to its implementation, and proposed an approach to formalizing dynamic updating based on three updating models called *invoke model*, *interrupt model*, and *relaxed consistency model* [7]. In this paper, we classify dynamic updates into two classes, i.e., *instantaneous updating model*, and *incremental updating model* in terms of how state and behavior of old system is changed by update. We propose an approach to formalizing dynamic updates that conform to either of the two models in the OTS/CafeOBJ method. The OTS/CafeOBJ method is an algebraic approach to formalizing and verifying the design of software systems [8,9]. We choose the OTS/CafeOBJ method for its flexibility in formalization such as the support of user-defined abstract data types, and systematic verification approaches, i.e., by compositionally writing proof scores and *searching* (or model checking) [10,11]. It also supports the formalization and verification of infinite-state systems. Several case studies have been conducted to demonstrate its effectiveness [12,13,14,15].

By verifying the design of dynamic updates, we can gain a better understanding of the design, identify updating points where the dynamic update can be safely applied, detect potential errors in update, and hence design a safer one. To demonstrate the feasibility of our approach, we formalize and verify a system, which is dynamically updated from a flawed mutual exclusion protocol to a correct one. By verification, we find the update may cause the system into a deadlock state. The verification result helps us find the problem that causes the deadlock. Compared with other existing approaches [5,6], our approach is more general in that it is not specific to some concrete dynamic updates and how they are implemented. Those that conform to the instantaneous or incremental updating model can be specified and verified in this approach. Moreover, it is not specific to dynamic updates that are designed and implemented in certain programming languages.

The rest of this paper is organized as follows. Section 2 presents the two models of dynamic updating. Section 3 briefly introduces the OTS/CafeOBJ method. Section 4 describes our approach to formalizing dynamic updates in the OTS/CafeOBJ method. Section 5 shows a demonstrating example. Section 6 discusses some related work, and Section 7 concludes the paper.

2   Models of Dynamic Software Updating

We classify dynamic updates into two classes according to how they change the behavior and state of running systems. In one model, a running system may be interrupted by a DSU system first before being updated. After update, it is resumed from where it is interrupted to run the new-version code. In the other model, there can be a period during which both the old system and the new system run in parallel. After update is completed, the old system stops, while the new system keeps running. We call them *instantaneous updating model* and *incremental updating model*. In this section, we describe the two models and introduce some typical DSU systems that conform to either of them.

2.1   Instantaneous Updating Model

In instantaneous updating model, a system that is running an old version is first temporarily interrupted in some state when updating condition is satisfied. Updating is then applied, e.g., loading new-version code into memory, and converting the current old state into a corresponding new one that is consistent the new version. After updating is completed, the system is resumed from the generated state to run the new-version code. Thus, the system will behave as a new system.

Instantaneous updating model is quite suited to dynamic updating to single-threaded applications, such as web servers *vsftpd* (a commonly used FTP daemon) and *sshd* (secure shell daemon). Many DSU systems support instantaneous dynamic updating. Gupta *et al.* proposed a way of dynamic updating by using state transfer [16]. They first suspend the running process, copy it to a new one using state transfer, and upgrade it with new code. Hicks *et al.* proposed a framework for dynamic update based on patches and state transformation [1]. Neamtiu *et al.* developed a tool called Ginseng for the dynamic update to single-threaded C programs [17]. Although these DSU systems are different in terms of their ways of implementing dynamic updates, the ways of how the behavior of systems is affected by updating are the same. Namely, dynamic updates supported by these DSU systems conform to the instantaneous updating model.

2.2   Incremental Updating Model

In incremental updating model, an old system is gradually updated to running the new-version code. There is a period during which the old system and the new one can run in parallel. After updating starts, the old system keeps running, and a part of the old system can be separately updated once it satisfies the specified updating condition. The updated part will start to run the new-version code, with the other part of the system is still running the old-version code. After all the system is updated, updating is completed, and the whole system behaves like a new-version system.

Incremental updating model is well suited to dynamic updates of multi-threaded programs and distributed systems. For instance, when updating a multi-threaded program, there may be some threads that cannot be updated when update is started, e.g., because they are occupying some critical resources. These threads have to keep running the old version until they reach some state where updating condition is satisfied. After all threads are updated, the updating process is completed, and the whole system executes the new version. Updating distributed systems can be considered similar to updating multi-threaded programs by viewing each node in systems as thread.

There are some typical DSU systems supporting incremental updating. For instance, POLUS [18] is designed and implemented for dynamic updating to multi-threaded C programs. In POLUS, they proposed a relaxed consistency model for dynamic updating. It allows the parallel execution of both the old version and new version after updating starts. The states of the two versions are bidirectionally transformable. The consistency between the two versions is ensured by the bidirectional write-through synchronization. Podus is suited to dynamic updating to distributed systems [19]. Kitsune [20] is a general-purpose dynamic updating tool for both single- and multi-threaded C applications. One common feature of them is that they all allow the co-existence of the states of old and new versions during updating, which is different from the instantaneous updating model. During updating, a system is partially updated when updating condition is satisfied. Updating is gradually completed when all parts in the system are updated.

3   The OTS/CafeOBJ Method

The OTS/CafeOBJ method is an algebraic way of formalizing, specifying and verifying the design of software systems [8,9]. OTS is abbreviated for observational transition system, a mathematical model of state transition systems. CafeOBJ is an executable algebraic specification language [21], which is well suited to specify OTS. The basic idea of the OTS/CafeOBJ method is modeling a software system as an OTS, specifying the OTS in CafeOBJ, and verifying system's properties using CafeOBJ's theorem proving or searching facilities.

3.1   Observational Transition System (OTS)

In OTS, abstract data types are used to formalize values such as natural numbers, Boolean values, and strings in software systems. System's states are characterized by the values that are returned by a special class of functions called *observers*, unlike traditional state transition systems where states are represented as sets of variables. Transitions between states are also specified by functions which we call *transitions* to differ them from ordinary functions.

We suppose that all abstract data types have been predefined for the values used in a system and denote them by D with different subscripts. Let Υ denote a universal state space.

Definition 1 (OTSs). *An OTS S is a triple $\langle \mathcal{O}, \mathcal{I}, \mathcal{T} \rangle$ such that:*

- $\mathcal{O}$: A set of observers. Each observer is a function $o : \Upsilon \times D_{o1} \times \ldots \times D_{om} \to D_o$. Two states v_1, v_2 are equal (denoted by $v_1 =_S v_2$) if each observer returns the same value with the same arguments from the two states.
- $\mathcal{I}$: A set of initial states s.t. $\mathcal{I} \subseteq \Upsilon$.
- $\mathcal{T}$: A set of transitions. Each transition is a function $t : \Upsilon \times D_{t1} \times \ldots \times D_{tn} \to \Upsilon$. Each t preserves the equivalence between two states in that if $v_1 =_S v_2$, then for each $y_i (i = 1, \ldots, n)$ in D_{ti}, $t(v_1, y_1, \ldots, y_n) =_S t(v_2, y_1, \ldots, y_n)$. Each t has an effective condition $c\text{-}t : \Upsilon \times D_{t1} \times \ldots \times D_{tn} \to \mathcal{B}$, s.t. for any state v if $\neg c\text{-}t(v, y_1, \ldots, y_n)$, $t(v, y_1, \ldots, y_n) =_S v$.

OTSs can be specified in CafeOBJ as equational specifications. Each equation defined for initial states is in the form of:

```
eq o(v_0, x_1, ..., x_m) = T[x_1, ..., x_m] .
```

Keyword `eq` is used to declare an equation in CafeOBJ. The above equation is defined for an observer in the form of $o : \Upsilon \times D_{o1} \times \ldots \times D_{om} \to D_o$, where v_0, $x_j (j = 1, \ldots, m)$ are variables of Υ and D_{oj} respectively. T is a term of D_o, representing the value observed by o with arguments $x_1, \ldots, x_m$ in all initial states.

Each equation defined for an observer $o : \Upsilon \times D_{o1} \times \ldots \times D_{om} \to D_o$ and a transition $t : \Upsilon \times D_{t1} \ldots \times D_{tn} \to \Upsilon$ is in the following form:

```
ceq o(t(v, y_1, ..., y_n), x_1, ..., x_m) = T[v, y_1, ..., y_n, x_1, ..., x_m]
    if  c-t(v, y_1, ..., y_n) .
```

Keyword `ceq` is used to declare a conditional equation. The equation specifies all the values observed by o in the state $t(v, y_1, \ldots, y_n)$, where $y_i (j = 1, \ldots, n)$ is a variable of D_{ti}. The condition part is the effective condition of t, which says if the effective condition holds, the values observed by o in the state $t(v, y_1, \ldots, y_n)$ are equal to those represented by the term T. If the effective condition does not hold, the state $t(v, y_1, \ldots, y_n)$ is equal to v, which is formalized by the following equation:

```
ceq t(v, y_1, ..., y_n) = v if not  c-t(v, y_1, ..., y_n)   .
```

3.2   Verification in the OTS/CafeOBJ Method

Generally, there are two ways of verifying systems' properties in the OTS/CafeOBJ method. One is by theorem proving and the other is by searching (or model checking).

Verification by Theorem Proving. The basic idea of verification by theorem proving in CafeOBJ is to construct proof scores for an invariant property by using CafeOBJ as a proof assistant. Proof scores are instructions that can be executed in CafeOBJ. Verifying a system's property is actually a process of writing proof scores with humans creating the proof plan in which proof should be performed and CafeOBJ evaluating proof scores based on the proof plan. If proof scores are successfully completed and they are evaluated by CafeOBJ as expected, a desired property is proved.

The strategy of constructing proof scores is by structural induction on system states and case analysis. In the base case, we check whether the property being proved holds in the initial states defined in an OTS. If it holds, we continue to deal with the induction case. Otherwise, the proof fails. In the induction case, we make a hypothesis that the property being proved holds for a state v, and check whether it holds for all possible successor states of v. If it is true, the proof is finished, and otherwise fails. During proving, we may need to prove some lemmas, which are necessary to prove the main property. Interested readers can refer to [22] for more details of how to construct proof scores in the OTS/CafeOBJ method.

Verification by Searching (or Model Checking). Searching is another way of verifying invariant properties in CafeOBJ. By searching, CafeOBJ traverses the states (or a bounded number of states if the states are infinite) that are reachable from a given initial state, and check which states satisfy a specific condition. The condition is the negation of the property in order to find counterexamples of it. Once CafeOBJ returns a solution, it means that there exists an execution path from an initial state to a state where the property does not hold, which is considered as a counterexample for the failure of the property.

Searching in CafeOBJ is an effective way to find counterexamples, and particularly useful when the size of system's states is reasonably small. A more efficient searching functionality is implemented in Maude [23], a sibling language of CafeOBJ. Besides searching, Maude also provides model checking facilities which are more efficient to find counterexamples of invariant properties and even liveness properties. An OTS can also be specified in Maude, so that we can use Maude's searching and model checking facilities. Some approaches have been proposed to automatically translate a CafeOBJ specification that specifies an OTS into Maude for the same purpose [24,25].

Instead of using either theorem proving or searching (or model checking) for verification, the combination of them is also useful. During constructing proof scores for an invariant property, we can immediately stop proving once we find a counterexample for it or for some lemma which is necessary to prove the property. An approach called induction-guided falsification (IGF) has been proposed to combine theorem proving and model checking based on modeling a system as an OTS (see [26] for the details).

4   Formalization of Dynamic Updating by OTS

To design a dynamic update, we should consider five factors, i.e., the old system S_{old} which is running and waiting for updating, the new system S_{new} which will run after updating, updating model (instantaneous or incremental), updating condition φ specifying under which condition update can be applied, and a state transformation function f which is used to convert an old-version state into a new-version state.

To formalize an update, we assume that both the old and new systems S_{old} and S_{new} have been formalized by two OTSs, i.e., $S_{\text{old}} = \langle \mathcal{O}_{\text{old}}, \mathcal{I}_{\text{old}}, \mathcal{T}_{\text{old}} \rangle$, and $S_{\text{new}} = \langle \mathcal{O}_{\text{new}}, \mathcal{I}_{\text{new}}, \mathcal{T}_{\text{new}} \rangle$.

4.1 Formalization of Instantaneous Updating

Suppose that there is an instantaneous update designed to update S_{old} by S_{new}. We define an OTS S_{ins} with S_{old} and S_{new} to formalize an instantaneous update. S_{ins} is defined as follows:

Definition 2 (OTS S_{ins} of instantaneous update). $S_{\text{ins}} = \langle \mathcal{O}_{\text{ins}}, \mathcal{I}_{\text{ins}}, \mathcal{T}_{\text{ins}} \rangle$:

- $\mathcal{O}_{\text{ins}} = \mathcal{O}_{\text{old}} \uplus \mathcal{O}_{\text{new}} \cup \{status : \varUpsilon \to \mathcal{B}\}$
- $\mathcal{I}_{\text{ins}} = \{v_0 | status(v_0) = false, v_0 \in \mathcal{I}_{\text{old}}\}$
- $\mathcal{T}_{\text{ins}} = \mathcal{T}_{\text{old}} \uplus \mathcal{T}_{\text{new}} \cup \{update : \varUpsilon \to \varUpsilon\}$.

Operator $\uplus$ denotes a disjoint union of two sets, e.g., $\mathcal{O}_{\text{old}} \uplus \mathcal{O}_{\text{new}} = \{(o, v) | v \in \{\text{old}, \text{new}\}, o \in \mathcal{O}_v\}$. In the paper we write o_v instead of (o, v) for convenience. $\mathcal{O}_{\text{ins}}$ is a disjoint union of $\mathcal{O}_{\text{old}}$ and $\mathcal{O}_{\text{new}}$, plus a new observer $status$. We view the old system, the new system, and updating from the old system to the new one as a whole system. In that sense, updating can be considered as an internal adapting process in adaptive program [27]. We call the states of the whole system *super states*, each of which consists of an old state and a new state, plus a flag indicating whether the old system is updated or not. In $\mathcal{O}_{\text{ins}}$, observers that are from $\mathcal{O}_{\text{old}}$ are used to represent the states in old system, and those from $\mathcal{O}_{\text{new}}$ represent the states in new system. We use the observer $status$ to represent the status of update. It returns false in a given state if it is a state before update, and otherwise true.

Initial states v_0 in $\mathcal{I}_{\text{ins}}$ are those initial states in $\mathcal{I}_{\text{old}}$ and their $status$ is false, i.e., $status(v_0) = false$, indicating that update cannot take place before the old system starts. Initial states of the new system are undefined in the initial states in $\mathcal{I}_{\text{ins}}$. That is because new system runs from a state which is transformed from an old state where update takes place. Thus, the initial states of the new system do not affect how a system is updated.

Set $\mathcal{T}_{\text{ins}}$ includes both the transitions in the old system and those in the new one. We introduce a new transition $update$ to formalize the behavior of updating from S_{old} to S_{new}. The effective condition of $update$ is represented by a state predicate $c\text{-}update : \varUpsilon \to \mathcal{B}$. We assume that the updating condition is represented by a state predicate φ, which returns true for a given old state when the updating condition is satisfied, and otherwise false. We enhance φ. Given a super state v, φ returns true if it is true for the old state in v, and otherwise false. The effective condition of $update$ can be defined by the following equation:

eq $c\text{-}update(v) = (\textbf{not } status(v)) \textbf{ and } \varphi(v)$.

The equation says that the effective condition holds in those states before up-dating where the updating condition is satisfied. Transition *update* only takes affect in those states where *c-update* is true.

After *update* takes affect in a super state v, the old state in v is transformed into a new one. It is equal to say that the new state in v is initialized according to the old state and transformation function. The transformation can be formalized as a set of equations. Each of them is defined for an observer in o_{new} in the following from:

```
ceq  o_new(update(v), x_1, ..., x_m) = T  if c-update(v)  .
```

The equation specifies the values observed by o_{new} in the state *update(v)*. Given parameters $x_1, \ldots, x_m$, the left-hand term represents the value observed by o_{new} in state *update(v)* with respect to $x_1, \ldots, x_m$. The value equals the one of term T which usually contains the values in the old state in v. Especially, some values in the new state are copies of the corresponding values in the old state. In that case, we use the following equation to specify the new values:

```
ceq  o_new(update(v), x_1, ..., x_m) = o_old(v, x_1, ..., x_m)  if c-update(v)  .
```

The values in the old state in v are not affected by updating. Thus, old values in the state *update(v)* are the same as those in v. Thus, the values observed by each observer o_{old} are not changed. They can be defined by the following equation:

```
eq  o_old(update(v), x_1, ..., x_m) = o_old(v, x_1, ..., x_m)  .
```

Note that the above equation is unconditional. That is because no matter the effective condition holds or not in v, the values in the old state in v are not affected by transition *update*.

Update only takes place once in instantaneous updating model. Thus, after an update takes affect the status of the states afterwards is set true to indicate update has taken place. The following equation specifies the change of status when update takes affect:

```
ceq  status(update(v)) = true  if  c-update(v)  .
```

State status is only affected by update. Transitions in both old and new systems do not change the status. For each transition $t : \Upsilon \times D_1 \ldots \times D_n \to \Upsilon$ in $\mathcal{T}_v$, we have the following equation:

```
eq  status(t(v, y_1, ..., y_n)) = status(v)  .
```

If the effective condition is not satisfied by a state v, e.g., v is a state after updating, or the updating condition φ is not satisfied by v, transition *update* takes no effect on v. This fact is specified by the following equation:

```
ceq  update(v) = v  if not c-update(v)  .
```

The definition of each transition that is from $\mathcal{T}_{\text{old}}$ or $\mathcal{T}_{\text{new}}$ should be slightly revised in $\mathcal{T}_{\text{ins}}$. That is because transitions from $\mathcal{T}_{\text{old}}$ only take effect before updating, while those from $\mathcal{T}_{\text{new}}$ take effect after updating. Thus, $status(v) = false$ should be a part of the effective conditions for the transitions from $\mathcal{T}_{\text{old}}$ in state v. Similarly, $status(v) = true$ should be a part of the effective conditions for the transitions from $\mathcal{T}_{\text{new}}$. We also need to specify the facts that the values in the old state are not affected by any transitions from $\mathcal{T}_{\text{new}}$, and similarly those in the new state are not affected by the transitions from $\mathcal{T}_{\text{old}}$. Therefore, for each observer o_{old} and a transition t_{new}, they satisfy the following equation:

eq $o_{\text{old}}(t_{\text{new}}(v, y_1, \ldots, y_n), x_1, \ldots, x_m) = o_{\text{old}}(v, x_1, \ldots, x_m)$.

Similarly, for each observer o_{new} and transition t_{new}, they satisfy the equation:

eq $o_{\text{new}}(t_{\text{old}}(v, y_1', \ldots, y_{n'}'), x_1', \ldots, x_m') = o_{\text{new}}(v, x_1', \ldots, x_{m'}')$.

In this way, we define an OTS $\mathcal{S}_{\text{ins}}$ that specifies an instantaneous update from S_{old} to S_{new}.

4.2   Formalization of Incremental Updating

Incremental updates allow concurrent execution of both old and new systems, which makes the formalization more complicated than that of instantaneous updates. During the current execution, an old state is gradually transformed into new one. Each transformation may change a fragment of old state. After all fragments of the old state are transformed, an update is completed. We divide an old state of system S_{old} into a set of *sub-states*. Each sub-state is an updating unit, meaning that a sub-state is either completely transformed into new one or completely not transformed.

We make some assumptions on the old systems in order to formalize dynamic update on it. We assume that in an old state there is a sub-set of such sub-states they have the same data fields in an old state. To differentiate such sub-states, let P be a set of index, and each sub-state is indexed with an element in P. We called them *indexed* sub-states. We further assume that other sub-states that are not in the sub-set must be transformed at the same time. We call them *unindexed* sub-states. These assumptions are reasonable for the dynamic updates on multi-threaded software systems or distributed systems. Each indexed sub-state represents the state of a thread or node, while unindexed sub-states represent shared values and resources in systems.

Suppose that an incremental update is designed for an old system S_{old} to make it updated to a new one S_{new}. We define an OTS $\mathcal{S}_{\text{inc}}$ to formalize incremental updates from S_{old} to S_{new}. We further suppose that $\mathcal{S}_{\text{old}}$ and $\mathcal{S}_{\text{new}}$ are two OTSs modeling S_{old} and S_{new} respectively.

Definition 3 (OTS $\mathcal{S}_{\text{inc}}$ of incremental update). $\mathcal{S}_{\text{inc}} = \langle \mathcal{O}_{\text{inc}}, \mathcal{I}_{\text{inc}}, \mathcal{T}_{\text{inc}} \rangle$:

- $\mathcal{O}_{\text{inc}} = \mathcal{O}_{\text{old}} \uplus \mathcal{O}_{\text{new}} \cup \mathcal{O}'$
- $\mathcal{I}_{\text{inc}} = \{v_0 | v_0 \in \mathcal{I}_{\text{old}}, \neg started(v_0), \neg updated(v_0, p), \neg updated'(v_0)\}$

– $\mathcal{T}_{\text{inc}} = \mathcal{T}_{\text{old}} \uplus \mathcal{T}_{\text{new}} \cup \mathcal{T}'$

where, $\mathcal{O}' = \{started : \Upsilon \to \mathcal{B}, updated : \Upsilon \times P \to \mathcal{B}, updated' : \Upsilon \to \mathcal{B}\}$, and $\mathcal{T}' = \{start : \Upsilon \to \Upsilon, update' : \Upsilon \to \Upsilon, update : \Upsilon \times P \to \Upsilon\}$.

$\mathcal{O}_{\text{inc}}$ consists of the observers in $\mathcal{O}_{\text{old}}$ and $\mathcal{O}_{\text{new}}$, and three new observers in $\mathcal{O}'$, i.e., *started*, *updated* and *updated'*. Observer *started* returns a Boolean value for a given state, representing whether an update has been started or not. Observer *updated* returns a Boolean value for a given indexed sub-state to indicate whether the sub-state is updated or not. Observer *updated'* returns true if sub-states are updated by *update'* in v, and otherwise false. We assume that updates do not start from initial states of the old system, i.e., $started(v_0) = false$, and each sub-state is not yet updated, i.e., $updated(v_0, i) = false$ for each $i \in P$, and $updated(v_0) = false$.

The set $\mathcal{T}_{\text{inc}}$ is a disjoint union of $\mathcal{T}_{\text{old}}$ and $\mathcal{T}_{\text{new}}$, plus four transitions in $\mathcal{T}'$. Transition *start* specifies the starting of an incremental update. One of the condition of *start* is that in the current state updating must have not been started. There may be some other conditions in concrete systems to start updating. Such conditions should also be specified as part of the effective condition of *start*.

Next, we explain transitions *update* and *update'*, which formalize the updating of indexed and unindexed sub-states respectively. Suppose that there is an updating condition of updating indexed sub-states. We use a state predicate $\varphi : \Upsilon \times P \to \mathcal{B}$ to specify the condition. Namely, φ returns true for a given super state v and a sub-state whose identifier is i if the sub-state satisfies the condition, and otherwise false. The effective condition of transition *update* can be specified by the following equation:

eq $c\text{-}update(v, i) = \varphi(v, i)$ **and not** $updated(v, i)$.

By updating, an indexed sub-state is transformed into new corresponding ones. We define a set of equations to specify the transformation. Each is defined for an observer in $\mathcal{O}_{\text{new}}$ whose observed value is initialized by the transformation. The equation is of the following form:

ceq $o_{\text{new}}(update(v, i), x_1, \ldots, x_m) = T$ **if** $c\text{-}update(v, i)$.

The above equation says in the state $update(v, i)$, the values observed by o_{new} equals T, where T is a term representing the relation between the values observed by o_{new} and some values in the old state.

Transition *update'* can be defined likewise. We assume that there is an updating condition of unindexed sub-states according to the design of the update, and we define a state predicate $\varphi' : \Upsilon \to \mathcal{B}$ to specify the condition. The effective condition of transition *update'* can be specified by the following equation:

eq $c\text{-}update'(v) = \varphi'(v)$ **and not** $updated'(v)$.

Unindexed sub-states are transformed at the same time into new corresponding ones. We define a set of equations to specify the transformation. Each is defined for an observer in $\mathcal{O}_{\text{new}}$ whose observed value is initialized by the transformation.

Since it is similar to the equations defined for *update*, we omit the details in the paper.

The definitions of transitions in $\mathcal{T}_{\text{inc}}$ that are from $\mathcal{T}_{\text{old}}$ and $\mathcal{T}_{\text{new}}$ need slight revision, like the formalization of instantaneous updates.

5   A Demonstrating Example

In this section, we use an example to demonstrate how to use the proposed approach to formalize and verify a concrete dynamic updating. We assume that a system is running a flawed mutual exclusion protocol, and it is dynamically updated with a correct one. We design a dynamic update that conforms to the incremental updating model. By verification, we found that the system after being updated satisfies mutual exclusion property. However, we also found it may go to a deadlock state. A counterexample is found. By analyzing the counterexample, we give two solutions to solve the deadlock problem by modifying the update.

5.1   An Update of a Mutual Exclusion Protocol

First, we explain the flawed mutual protocol, which is being executed by the running system. The pseudo-code of the protocol is shown as follows:

A flawed mutual exclusion protocol and its state transition diagram

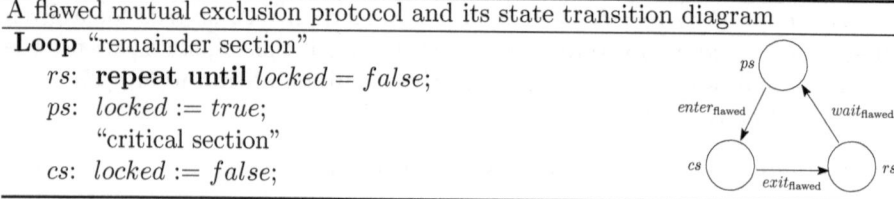

Loop "remainder section"
  rs: **repeat until** *locked* = *false*;
  ps: *locked* := *true*;
       "critical section"
  cs: *locked* := *false*;

Initially, each process is at the remainder section (*rs*). A process waits at the pre-critical section (*ps*) to enter the critical section (*cs*) until *locked* becomes false. It sets *locked* true, and enters the critical section. It sets *locked* false when it is leaving the critical section.

The protocol does not satisfy mutual exclusion because of the non-atomicity of the action of setting *locked* true and entering the critical section. It can be solved by using an atomic operation *fetch&store*, which takes a variable x and a value d, and atomically sets x to d and returns the previous value of x. The revised protocol and the behavior of each process in it are depicted as follows:

A correct mutual exclusion protocol and its state transition diagram

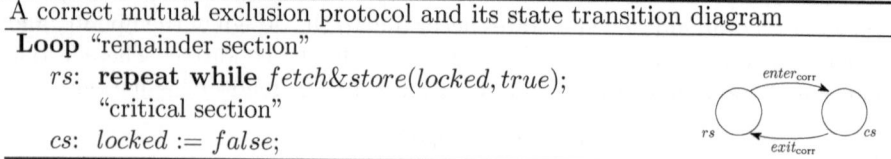

Loop "remainder section"
  rs: **repeat while** *fetch&store(locked, true)*;
       "critical section"
  cs: *locked* := *false*;

When *locked* is false, a process atomically sets *locked* true and enters the critical section. The revised protocol has been proved to satisfy mutual exclusion in OTS/CafeOBJ method. We omit the details of the proof in the paper.

5.2   A Dynamic Updating and Its Formalization

We consider dynamically updating the system that is running the flawed mutual exclusion protocol to run the correct one. The update is performed in the incremental updating model, and can be started at any moment. When update takes place, the value of *locked* in the correct protocol is initialized with the one of the flawed protocol. After update starts, an old process will switch to executing the new protocol once it is at the remainder section. If an old process is not in the remainder section, it has to continue to execute the flawed protocol until it returns back to the remainder section. The updating is completed after all processes are updated to the correct protocol.

To formalize the update, we first formalize the flawed protocol and the correct one as OTSs $\mathcal{S}_{\text{flawed}}$ and $\mathcal{S}_{\text{corr}}$ respectively. Let L be the set $\{rs, ps, cs\}$, and P be a set of processes' identifiers. The definition of $\mathcal{S}_{\text{flawed}}$ is as follows:

Definition of OTS $\mathcal{S}_{\text{flawed}}$ for the flawed mutual exclusion protocol: $\mathcal{S}_{\text{flawed}} \triangleq \langle \mathcal{O}_{\text{flawed}}, \mathcal{I}_{\text{flawed}}, \mathcal{T}_{\text{flawed}} \rangle$.

- $\mathcal{O}_{\text{flawed}} \triangleq \{pc_{\text{flawed}} : \Upsilon \times P \to L, locked_{\text{flawed}} : \Upsilon \to \mathcal{B}\}$
- $\mathcal{I}_{\text{flawed}} \triangleq \{v_0 | pc_{\text{flawed}}(v_0, p) = rs_{\text{flawed}} \wedge \neg locked_{\text{flawed}}(v_0)\}$
- $\mathcal{T}_{\text{flawed}} \triangleq \{wait_{\text{flawed}} : \Upsilon \times P \to \Upsilon, enter_{\text{flawed}} : \Upsilon \times P \to \Upsilon, exit_{\text{flawed}} : \Upsilon \times P \to \Upsilon\}$

There are two observers pc_{flawed} and $locked_{\text{flawed}}$. Given a state v and a process identifier p, $pc_{\text{flawed}}(v, p)$ returns a value in L, indicating the location of process p in v, and $locked_{\text{flawed}}(v)$ represents the value of the shared Boolean variable *locked* in v. $\mathcal{I}_{\text{flawed}}$ define the set of initial states, where all processes are at the remainder section, and *locked* is false. Three transitions are used to specify the corresponding three actions of each process, i.e., waiting for, entering and leaving the critical section. We only take $enter_{\text{flawed}}$ for example to explain the definitions of the transitions.

The effective condition is represented by a state predicate $c\text{-}enter_{\text{flawed}} : \Upsilon \times P \to \mathcal{B}$. A process p can enter the critical section if it is at the ps, which can be specified by the following equation:

eq $c\text{-}enter_{\text{flawed}}(v, p) = (pc_{\text{flawed}}(v, p) = ps)$.

When $c\text{-}enter_{\text{flawed}}(v, p)$ is true, p enters the critical section, and *locked* is set *true* in the state $enter_{\text{flawed}}(v, p)$. The changes are specified by the following two equations:

ceq $pc_{\text{flawed}}(enter_{\text{flawed}}(v, p), p') = (\text{if } p = p' \text{ then } cs \text{ else } pc_{\text{flawed}}(v, p') \text{ fi})$
         if $c\text{-}enter_{\text{flawed}}(v, p)$.
ceq $locked_{\text{flawed}}(enter_{\text{flawed}}(v, p)) = true \text{ if } c\text{-}enter_{\text{flawed}}(v, p)$.

In the above equation p' is a variable of P, representing an arbitrary process. It can be the same as p or others. The equation says that only p's location is changed by the transition from v to $enter_{\text{flawed}}(v, p)$. The other two transitions can be defined likewise.

The definition of $\mathcal{S}_{\text{corr}}$ is similar to $\mathcal{S}_{\text{flawed}}$, except that we only need two transitions $enter_{\text{corr}}$ and $exit_{\text{corr}}$ to formalize process's behavior because of the atomicity of the operation $fetch\&store$. We omit the detailed definition of the two transitions.

Definition of OTS $\mathcal{S}_{\text{corr}}$ of the correct mutual exclusion protocol: $\mathcal{S}_{\text{corr}} \triangleq \langle \mathcal{O}_{\text{corr}}, \mathcal{I}_{\text{corr}}, \mathcal{T}_{\text{corr}} \rangle$.

- $\mathcal{O}_{\text{corr}} \triangleq \{pc_{\text{corr}} : \Upsilon \times P \to L, locked_{\text{corr}} : \Upsilon \to \mathcal{B}\}$
- $\mathcal{I}_{\text{corr}} \triangleq \{v_0 | pc_{\text{corr}}(v, p) = rs_{\text{corr}} \wedge \neg locked_{\text{corr}}(v_0)\}$
- $\mathcal{T}_{\text{corr}} \triangleq \{enter_{\text{corr}} : \Upsilon \times P \to \Upsilon, exit_{\text{corr}} : \Upsilon \times P \to \Upsilon\}$

Having the two OTSs $\mathcal{S}_{\text{flawed}}$ and $\mathcal{S}_{\text{corr}}$, we can formalize the dynamic update based on Definition 3, since the update conforms to the incremental updating model.

Definition of OTS $\mathcal{S}_{\text{upd}}$ for the dynamic update: $\mathcal{S}_{\text{upd}} \triangleq \langle \mathcal{O}_{\text{upd}}, \mathcal{I}_{\text{upd}}, \mathcal{T}_{\text{upd}} \rangle$.

- $\mathcal{O}_{\text{upd}} = \mathcal{O}_{\text{flawed}} \uplus \mathcal{O}_{\text{corr}} \cup \mathcal{O}'$
- $\mathcal{I}_{\text{upd}} = \{v_0 | v_0 \in \mathcal{I}_{\text{flawed}}, \neg started(v_0), \neg updated(v_0, p), \neg updated'(v_0)\}$
- $\mathcal{T}_{\text{upd}} = \mathcal{T}_{\text{flawed}} \uplus \mathcal{T}_{\text{corr}} \cup \mathcal{T}'$

$\mathcal{O}'$ and $\mathcal{T}'$ are the sets of observers and transitions, which are the same as the ones in Definition 3. The set P in the arity of observers in $\mathcal{O}'$ and transitions $\mathcal{T}'$ in $\mathcal{S}_u$ is the same as the one in $\mathcal{S}_{\text{flawed}}$ and $\mathcal{S}_{\text{corr}}$, indicating a set of process's identifiers. Namely, the state of each process in the old system is considered as an indexed sub-state, and there is only one unindexed sub-state, i.e., the value of $locked$. The update of each process and the shared Boolean variable $locked$ is specified by $update$ and $update'$, respectively. Transition $start$ formalizes the starting of the update. We explain how the three transitions are defined to specify the dynamic update.

In the example, we assume that the dynamic update can be started at any moment. Thus, there is no extra condition for the transition $start$ except that the update has not been started. After the transition $start$, the system starts to be updated. Thus, the effective condition of $start$ and the change of the value observed by $started$ can be defined by the following two equations:

```
eq c-start(v) = not started(v)  .
ceq started(start(v)) = true if c-start(v)  .
```

After an update starts, a process must be updated if it is in the remainder section and not yet updated. Thus, we declare the following equation to define the effective condition of $update$:

```
eq c-update(v, p) =
    started(v) and not updated(v, p) and pc_flawed(v, p) = rs  .
```

Once a process is updated, it goes into the remainder section of the correct protocol, and is marked as updated. The following two equations specify this updating.

```
ceq pccorr(update(v, p), p') =
     (if p = p' then rscorr else pccorr(v, p') fi) if c-update(v, p) .
ceq updated(update(v, p), p') =
     (if p = p' then true else updated(v, p') fi) if c-update(v, p) .
```

Transition $update'$ can be defined likewise. It specifies the updating of the unindexed sub-state, i.e., the value observed by $locked_{\text{flawed}}$. We assume that the value can be updated at any state after the update has been started. After being updated, the value observed by $locked_{\text{corr}}$ is initialized by the value observed by $locked_{\text{flawed}}$. The following two equations specify the effective condition and the initialization of the value observed by $locked_{\text{corr}}$ due to the updating.

```
eq c-update'(v) = started(v) and not updated'(v) .
ceq lockedcorr(update'(v)) = lockedflawed(v) if c-update'(v) .
```

5.3   Verification of the Dynamic Update

One basic property the system should enjoy after being updated is mutual exclusion. Another property is *deadlock freedom* in that the system after being updated should never reach to a deadlock state. A deadlock state is that the value of $locked_{\text{corr}}$ is true but no process is at the critical section. Thus, no process can enter the critical section and the value observed by $locked_{\text{corr}}$ is always true, leading to deadlock.

Verification by Theorem Proving. For the mutual exclusion property, it is equal to say that for any state v which is reachable from an initial state in $\mathcal{I}_u$ and any two processes p_1 and p_2, if both p_1 and p_2 are at the critical section of the correct protocol after the system is updated, p_1 and p_2 must be the same one. We use a state predicate $\mu : \Upsilon \times P \times P \rightarrow \mathcal{B}$ to formalize it.

```
eq μ(v, p1, p2) =
     (pccorr(v, p1) = cscorr and pccorr(v, p2) = cscorr implies p1 = p2) .
```

We prove in CafeOBJ that $\mu(v, p_1, p_2)$ is true for any p_1, p_2 in P, and any v which is reachable from initial states in $\mathcal{I}_{\text{upd}}$. The proof is based on structural induction. Three lemmas are used in the proof. The lemmas are also proved in the same way in CafeOBJ. We omit the details of the proof since it is not the emphasis of the paper.

Verification by Searching. For the deadlock freedom property, we verify that a deadlock state can never be reached from any initial state in $\mathcal{I}_u$ by using *searching* in CafeOBJ. If there are a limited number of processes running in the system, it is feasible to search all possible states that are reachable from initial states, and check whether there is a deadlock state.

In the example, we assumed that there are only two processes in the system and denoted them by p_i and p_j, respectively. Let v_0 be the corresponding initial state in the old system. We want to verify that from v_0 there is no such a state where p_i and p_j are not in the critical section of the correct protocol but the value of *locked* in the correct protocol is true.

We define a state predicate $\rho : \Upsilon \to \mathcal{B}$ which returns true if a given state v is a deadlocked state.

eq $\rho(v) = (pc_{\text{corr}}(v, p_i) = rs$ **and** $pc_{\text{corr}}(v, p_j) = rs$ **and** $locked_{\text{corr}}(v))$.

We use the following CafeOBJ command to search a state v from v_0 such that $\rho(v)$ is true.

red v_0 =(*,*)=>* v **suchThat** $\rho(v)$.

CafeOBJ returns a state as shown by D in Fig. 1, which means that from the initial state v_0 there is a path for the system to reach a deadlocked state.

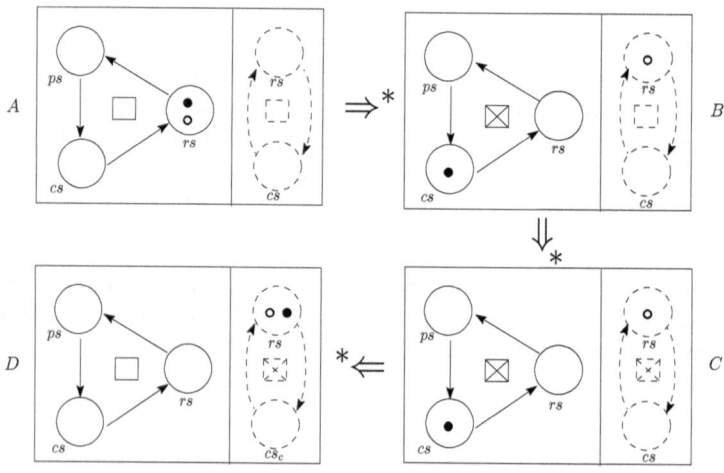

The meaning of notations:
$\bullet : p_i, \circ : p_j, \bigcirc :$ location, $\square : true,$ $\boxtimes : false,$ $\Rightarrow^*:$ n-step transition $(n \geq 0)$.
Solid symbols:the flawed mutual exclusion protocol, dashed symbols: the correct protocol.

Fig. 1. A counterexample for the deadlock freedom property caused by the updating

The dynamic update is obviously not safe because the system after being updated may go into a deadlocked state, though the correct mutual exclusion protocol is deadlock free. From the counterexample shown in Fig. 1, we recognize the reason why deadlock happens. Diagram A in the figure denotes the initial state. It goes to B after p_i enters the critical section, and *locked* in the flawed protocol is true in B. Then, updating happens. Process p_j goes to the remainder section of the correct protocol, and *locked* in the correct protocol is set to be the value of *locked* in the flawed protocol, i.e., true, as shown in C. From C, p_i leaves the critical section in the flawed protocol, and gets updated at remainder section. The whole system reaches D, which is a deadlocked state. One solution is to set an updating condition for the update of *locked*. Namely, *locked* in the flawed mutual exclusion protocol can be updated only if it is false. We revised the OTS $\mathcal{S}_{corr}$ based on this change, and verified the deadlock freedom property again with the new OTS. CafeOBJ returns no solutions, meaning that the revised dynamic update does not cause deadlock after the system is updated.

6   Related Work

Several studies have been conducted on the correctness of dynamic software updating. They can be grouped into two classes. One studies the correctness at the code level, such as type safety [2,3] and version consistency [4] as described in Section 1. They are necessary properties that should be satisfied by any dynamic updates to make sure systems after being updated can run correctly. The other class is about the correctness at a higher abstract level, such as validity [16] and behavioral correctness [6]. They are also useful to analyze how a running system's behavior is changed due to updating. However, their formalization is still at the code level, which may bring difficulties for verification, e.g., the undecidability of validity due to the halting problem of programs [16]. In our earlier work, we classified dynamic updates into three classes according to how they are implemented, i.e., *interrupt model*, *invoke model*, and *relaxed consistency model* [7]. Regardless of the difference in implementation, updates in interrupt model and invoke model can be considered as instantaneous updates, and those in relaxed consistency model as incremental updates. In that sense, the classification of dynamic updates as instantaneous and incremental updates is more general.

A similar approach has been proposed to study the correctness of adaptive programs [27], i.e., the adaption of a system between programs due to the surrounding environment. They classified adaptions into different models such as one-point adaption, guided adaption and overlap adaption. They used a concrete example to illustrate their idea of how to formalize the adaptions. At the behavior level, the adaption of a system can be viewed as a special kind of "updating", and thus we believe that our formalization approach can also be used to formalize the adaption of systems.

7   Conclusion

We have presented an approach to formalizing and verifying the design of dynamic software updates in the OTS/CafeOBJ method. We classified dynamic updates into two models, i.e., *instantaneous updating model* and *incremental updating model*. A dynamic update that conforms to either of the two models can be formalized as an OTS, with which we can formally analyze the update by verifying whether it satisfies the desired properties. By verification we can understand better how a system's behavior is affected by an update, find updating points where an update can be safely applied, and detect some potential errors in an update such as errors in state transformation or updating condition. Our approach is general in that it is neither specific to a concrete update nor to the updates that are specific to a concrete programming language.

We are considering conducting more case studies on practical dynamic updates with the proposed approach. Potential cases are dynamic updates to some prevalent web applications such as *vsftpd* and *sshd*. Updates to these applications confirm to instantaneous updating model. Some are dynamic updates to multi-threaded applications such as *Apache* HTTP server. They have been used as benchmarks by some DSU systems such as POLUS [18], Ginseng [17]. However, they focus on the implementation of these updates, but pay little attention to their correctness such as whether the system after being updated satisfies the properties that are supposed to be satisfied by the system of the new version. Such questions can be answered by verifying these dynamic updates in our proposed approach.

References

1. Hicks, M., Nettles, S.: Dynamic software updating. ACM TOPLAS 27, 1049–1096 (2005)
2. Duggan, D.: Type-based hot swapping of running modules. In: Functional Programming, vol. 36, pp. 62–73. ACM (2001)
3. Stoyle, G., Hicks, M., Bierman, G., et al.: Mutatis mutandis: safe and predictable dynamic software updating. ACM TOPLAS 40, 183–194 (2005)
4. Neamtiu, I., Hicks, M., Foster, J., et al.: Contextual effects for version-consistent dynamic software updating and safe concurrent programming. In: POPL, vol. 43, pp. 37–49. ACM (2008)
5. Gupta, D., Jalote, P., Barua, G.: A formal framework for on-line software version change. IEEE Transactions on Software Engineering 22(2), 120–131 (1996)
6. Hayden, C.M., Magill, S., Hicks, M., Foster, N., Foster, J.S.: Specifying and verifying the correctness of dynamic software updates. In: Joshi, R., Müller, P., Podelski, A. (eds.) VSTTE 2012. LNCS, vol. 7152, pp. 278–293. Springer, Heidelberg (2012)
7. Zhang, M., Ogata, K., Futatsugi, K.: Formalization and verification of behavioral correctness of dynamic software updates. Electr. Notes Theor. Comput. Sci. 294, 12–23 (2013)
8. Futatsugi, K., Goguen, J.A., Ogata, K.: Verifying design with proof scores. In: Meyer, B., Woodcock, J. (eds.) Verified Software. LNCS, vol. 4171, pp. 277–290. Springer, Heidelberg (2008)
9. Ogata, K., Futatsugi, K.: Proof scores in the OTS/CafeOBJ method. In: Najm, E., Nestmann, U., Stevens, P. (eds.) FMOODS 2003. LNCS, vol. 2884, pp. 170–184. Springer, Heidelberg (2003)
10. Ogata, K., Futatsugi, K.: Compositionally writing proof scores of invariants in the OTS/CafeOBJ method. J. UCS 19, 771–804 (2013)
11. Ogata, K., Futatsugi, K.: Simulation-based verification for invariant properties in the OTS/CafeOBJ method. Electr. Notes Theor. Comput. Sci. 201, 127–154 (2008)
12. Kong, W., Ogata, K., Futatsugi, K.: Towards reliable E-Government systems with the OTS/CafeOBJ method. IEICE Transactions 93-D, 974–984 (2010)
13. Hasebe, K., Okada, M.: Formal analysis of the *i*kp electronic payment protocols. In: Okada, M., Babu, C. S., Scedrov, A., Tokuda, H. (eds.) ISSS 2002. LNCS, vol. 2609, pp. 441–460. Springer, Heidelberg (2003)

14. Ogata, K., Futatsugi, K.: Formal verification of the horn-preneel micropayment protocol. In: Zuck, L.D., Attie, P.C., Cortesi, A., Mukhopadhyay, S. (eds.) VMCAI 2003. LNCS, vol. 2575, pp. 238–252. Springer, Heidelberg (2002)

15. Ogata, K., Futatsugi, K.: Formal analysis of the bakery protocol with consideration of nonatomic reads and writes. In: Liu, S., Araki, K. (eds.) ICFEM 2008. LNCS, vol. 5256, pp. 187–207. Springer, Heidelberg (2008)

16. Gupta, D., Jalote, P.: On-line software version change using state transfer between processes. Software: Practice and Experience 23, 949–964 (1993)

17. Neamtiu, I., Hicks, M.W., Stoyle, G., et al.: Practical dynamic software updating for c. In: PLDI, ACM SIGPLAN, pp. 72–83 (2006)

18. Chen, H., Yu, J., Hang, C., et al.: Dynamic software updating using a relaxed consistency model. IEEE Transactions on Software Engineering (99), 679–694 (2011)

19. Segal, M., Frieder, O.: On-the-fly program modification: Systems for dynamic updating. IEEE Software 10, 53–65 (1993)

20. Hayden, C.M., Smith, E.K., Denchev, M., Hicks, M., Foster, J.S.: Kitsune: Efficient, general-purpose dynamic software updating for c. In: Proceedings of the ACM International Conference on Object Oriented Programming Systems Languages and Applications, pp. 249–264. ACM (2012)

21. Diaconescu, R., Futatsugi, K.: CafeOBJ report: The language. In: Proof Techniques, and Methodologies for Object-Oriented Algebraic Specification, vol. 6 (1998)

22. Ogata, K., Futatsugi, K.: Some tips on writing proof scores in the OTS/CafeOBJ method. In: Futatsugi, K., Jouannaud, J.-P., Meseguer, J. (eds.) Goguen Festschrift. LNCS, vol. 4060, pp. 596–615. Springer, Heidelberg (2006)

23. Clavel, M., Durán, F., Eker, S., Lincoln, P., Martí-Oliet, N., Meseguer, J., Talcott, C.: All About Maude - A High-Performance Logical Framework. LNCS, vol. 4350. Springer, Heidelberg (2007)

24. Zhang, M., Ogata, K., Nakamura, M.: Translation of state machines from equational theories into rewrite theories with tool support. IEICE Transactions on Information and Systems 94-D, 976–988 (2011)

25. Nakamura, M., Kong, W., et al.: A specification translation from behavioral specifications to rewrite specifications. IEICE Transactions 91-D, 1492–1503 (2008)

26. Ogata, K., Nakano, M., Kong, W., Futatsugi, K.: Induction-guided falsification. In: Liu, Z., Kleinberg, R.D. (eds.) ICFEM 2006. LNCS, vol. 4260, pp. 114–131. Springer, Heidelberg (2006)

27. Zhang, J., Cheng, B.H.C.: Model-based development of dynamically adaptive software. In: ICSE, pp. 371–380. IEEE (2006)

On Automation of OTS/CafeOBJ Method

Daniel Găină[1], Dorel Lucanu[2], Kazuhiro Ogata[1], and Kokichi Futatsugi[1]

[1] Japan Advanced Institute of Science and Technology (JAIST)
{daniel,ogata,futatsugi}@jaist.ac.jp
[2] Alexandru Ioan Cuza University
dlucanu@info.uaic.ro

Abstract. The proof scores method is an interactive verification method in algebraic specification that combines manual proof planning and reduction (automatic inference by rewriting). The proof score approach to software verification coordinates efficiently human intuition and machine automation. We are interested in applying these ideas to transition systems, more concretely, in developing the so-called OTS/CafeOBJ method, a modelling, specification, and verification method of observational transition systems. In this paper we propose a methodology that aims at developing automatically proof scores according to the rules of an entailment system. The proposed deduction rules include a set of generic rules, which can be found in other proof systems as well, together with a set of rules specific to our working context. The methodology is exhibited on the example of the alternating bit protocol, where the unreliability of channels is faithfully specified.

1 Introduction

This paper is focused on developing the OTS/CafeOBJ method, a modeling, specification and verification method of Observational Transition Systems (OTS), which has been previously explored in many case studies [22,8,21,7]. The logical framework used to develop the methodology is that of constructor-based order-sorted preorder algebra. The signatures are enhanced with a set of constructor operators, the sorts of constructors are called *constrained*, and the sorts that are not constrained are called *loose*. The models are those algebras that are reachable w.r.t. given constructors [1]. For example, given an algebraic signature (S, F), where S is the set of sorts and F is the family of function symbols, an (S, F)-algebra A is reachable w.r.t constructors $F^c \subseteq F$ if for any element $a \in A$ there exists a set Y of variables of loose sorts, an evaluation $f : Y \to A$, and a *constructor term* $t \in T_{(S,F^c)}(Y)$ such that $\overline{f}(t) = a$, where $\overline{f} : T_{(S,F^c)}(Y) \to A$ is the unique extension of $f : Y \to A$ to a (S, F^c)-morphism. The formulas consist of universally quantified conditional atoms, where the atomic sentences are of three types: equations, membership and preorder axioms. [1]

The advantages provided by the expressiveness of constructor-based logics have been previously explored in [2,1], where a method for proving coinductive

---

[1] In Maude literature preorder axioms are known as rewrite rules.

S. Iida, J. Meseguer, and K. Ogata (Eds.): Futatsugi Festschrift, LNCS 8373, pp. 578–602, 2014.
© Springer-Verlag Berlin Heidelberg 2014

properties is presented. We propose a methodology for proving inductive properties of OTS specified with constructor-based logics. Only universally quantified conditional sentences are considered, a restriction that makes it possible to use term rewriting to verify system properties. We are interested in reaching a greater level of automation than in [21,8,7,22] by designing proof rules meant to be used for developing more complex proof tactics, which are implemented in Constructor-based Inductive Theorem Prover (CITP) [11]. In comparison with the previous approaches to verifying OTS, the proof scores consist of simple CITP commands. This has the advantage of making the proofs shorter and allowing automated reasoning. The present paper presents the verification methodology supported by CITP.

In [17] a subset of authors give a set of proof rules for constructor-based logics at the abstract level of institutions [13], and a quasi-completeness result is proved. [2] In [9], the proof rules are lifted up at the level of specifications such that quasi-completeness is preserved for the specifications with loose semantics denotation. [3] The entailment relation is constructed as follows: a basic entailment relation between specifications and atomic sentences is assumed which, in applications, is given by the system that assists the proof, for example CafeOBJ [5] or Maude [4]. This relation is then extended with proof rules for the quantification over variables of both constrained and loose sorts, logical implication, and case analysis.

In applications, the specifications are often declared with initial semantics (see [10] for details about the initial semantics in logics with constructors). Roughly speaking, less models means more properties to prove, which sometimes require new inference rules. In order to make the specification calculus defined in [9] effective in practice, it must be enriched with specialized proof rules for the initial data types that are often used in our methodology, and supported by proof tactics that can often be completed automatically. A first such enrichment is proposed in this paper.

In our approach, a goal $SP \vdash E$ consists of a specification SP and a set of formulas E rather than a single formula. By applying a proof rule to a goal $SP \vdash E$ we obtain a set of goals $SP_1 \vdash E_1, \ldots, SP_n \vdash E_n$ if some preconditions are satisfied. If it is not the case, the proof rule leaves the goal unchanged. This slightly general view captures a natural phenomenon related to verification: not only the formula of the initial goal is changing in the proof process but also the specification. It is crucial for automation to design proof tactics that preserve the confluence and termination properties in the proof process. Below we describe the contributions to the development of OTS/CafeOBJ method:

(1) The simplest tactics implement the proof rules of the specification calculus. We revise the entailment system defined in [9] to increase its efficiency in

---

[2] Some proof rules contain infinite premises which can only be checked with induction schemes. As a consequence, the resulting entailment system is not compact.

[3] Loose semantics is meant to capture all models that satisfy the axioms of a specification while initial semantics describes the initial (or standard) model of the axioms of a specification.

applications: we propose a more general *simultaneous induction* scheme, and we refine *case analysis* such that it can be applied automatically. The entailment system obtained is then enriched with *specialised proof rules* for the predefined data types declared with initial semantics.

(2) We define also *derived inference rules* which are built by combination of other tactics. For example, each of the proof rules is coupled with the reduction of the ground terms occurring in the formulas to prove to their normal forms. This has the advantage of preserving the confluence property of the specifications. We define a simple but efficient tactic to avoid non-termination processes during verification. The underlying assumption is the existence of a BOOL specification of boolean values which are protected since they are used to establish the truth. This tactic reduces a goal of the form $SP \vdash t = t'$ if $C \wedge b = not\ b \wedge C'$ to the empty goal set, where b is a boolean ground term.

(3) We propose a *proof strategy* to build automatically a complete proof of a goal, which basically establishes an application order of the "basic" tactics. This proof procedure is closely linked to term rewriting and it preserves the confluence property of specifications during verification.

The strength of the proposed methodology is exhibited on a non-trivial case study, the alternating bit protocol (ABP). The unreliability of the communication channels is faithfully modelled by specifying dropping of elements in arbitrary positions of the communication channels. This technique of modelling non-determinism with underspecified operators and then exploiting that in theorem proving is possible due to the expressivity of constructor-based logics.

Structure of the paper. In Section 2, we define the proof rules of the method and the proof strategy. In Section 3.1, we specify the ABP with unreliable communication channels; the verification methodology is explained by proving a safety property for ABP. In Section 4, we summarise the conclusions and we give some future directions for research.

2   Proving Methodology

In this section we revise the entailment system in [9], and we enrich it with specialised proof rules for the initial data types that are often used in our methodology. We also propose tactics to construct proof scores automatically.

2.1   The Underlying Logic

We describe the logical framework underlying the verification methodology. The logic presented here is more expressive than the one in [9] as it includes membership and preorder axioms besides equations.

*Order-Sorted Algebra (**OSA**) [20].* An *order-sorted signature* is a triple $(S, \leq, F)$ with $(S, \leq)$ a preorder, i.e. reflexive and transitive, and (S, F) a many-sorted signature. Let $\widehat{S} = S/_{\equiv_\leq}$ be the set of connected components of S under the equivalence relation $\equiv_\leq$ generated by $\leq$. The equivalence $\equiv_\leq$ can be extended to sequences in the usual way. An order-sorted signature is called *sensible* if for any two operators $\sigma : w \to s$ and $\sigma : w' \to s'$ such that $w \equiv_\leq w'$ we have $s \equiv_\leq s'$. Hereafter, we assume that all signatures are sensible.

An *order-sorted signature morphism* $\varphi : (S, \leq, F) \to (S', \leq', F')$ is a many-sorted signature morphism $\varphi : (S, F) \to (S', F')$ which

(1) preserves subsort overloading (i.e. for all $\sigma \in F_{w \to s} \cap F_{w' \to s'}$ with $w \equiv_\leq w'$ we have $\varphi^{op}_{(w,s)}(\sigma) = \varphi^{op}_{(w',s')}(\sigma)$, where $\varphi^{op}_{(w,s)} : F_{w \to s} \to F'_{\varphi(w) \to \varphi(s)}$), and such that

(2) $\varphi^{st} : (S, \leq) \to (S', \leq')$ is monotonic.

An *order-sorted Σ-algebra* M, where $\Sigma = (S, \leq, F)$, is a many-sorted (S, F)-algebra such that $s \leq s'$ implies $M_s \subseteq M_{s'}$, and for all $\sigma \in F_{w \to s} \cap F_{w' \to s'}$ with $w \equiv_\leq w'$ and $m \in M^w \cap M^{w'}$ we have $M_{\sigma:w \to s}(m) = M_{\sigma:w' \to s'}(m)$. For each connected component $[s] \in \widehat{S}$ we let $M_{[s]}$ denote the set $\bigcup_{s' \in [s]} M_{s'}$. An *order-sorted Σ-homomorphism* $h : M \to N$ is a many-sorted (S, F)-homomorphism such that for all $s \equiv_\leq s'$ and $m \in M_s \cap M_{s'}$ we have $h_s(m) = h_{s'}(m)$. This defines a category $\mathrm{Mod}^{\mathbf{OSA}}(\Sigma)$.

Proposition 1. *[20] The category* $\mathrm{Mod}^{\mathbf{OSA}}(\Sigma)$ *has an initial term algebra* T_Σ *defined as follows:*

- *if* $(w, s) \in S^* \times S$, $\sigma \in F_{w \to s}$ *and* $t \in (T_\Sigma)^w$ *then* $\sigma(t) \in (T_\Sigma)_s$,
- *if* $s_0 \leq s$, $t \in (T_\Sigma)_{s_0}$ *then* $t \in (T_\Sigma)_s$.

*Order-Sorted Preorder Algebra (***OSPA***) [6].* An *order-sorted preorder Σ-algebra* M, where $\Sigma = (S, \leq, F)$, is an order-sorted algebra with an additional preorder structure $(M_{[s]}, \leq_{[s]})$ for each connected component $[s] \in \widehat{S}$. An *order-sorted preorder Σ-homomorphism* $h : M \to N$ is an order-sorted homomorphism which preserves the preorder structure. This defines a category $\mathrm{Mod}^{\mathbf{OSPA}}(\Sigma)$.

A signature morphism $\varphi : (S, \leq, F) \to (S', \leq', F')$ induces a forgetful functor $\mathrm{Mod}^{\mathbf{OSPA}}(\varphi) : \mathrm{Mod}^{\mathbf{OSPA}}(S', \leq', F') \to \mathrm{Mod}^{\mathbf{OSPA}}(S, \leq, F)$ defined as follows:

- for each order-sorted preorder algebra $M' \in |\mathrm{Mod}^{\mathbf{OSPA}}(S', \leq', F')|$,
  - $\mathrm{Mod}^{\mathbf{OSPA}}(\varphi)(M')_s = M'_{\varphi(s)}$ for all $s \in S$,
  - $\mathrm{Mod}^{\mathbf{OSPA}}(\varphi)(M')_\sigma = M'_{\varphi(\sigma)}$ for all $(w, s) \in S^* \times S$ and $\sigma \in F_{w \to s}$,
  - $m_1 \leq_{[s]} m_2$ whenever $m_1 \leq_{[\varphi(s)]} m_2$ for all $[s] \in \widehat{S}$ and $m_1, m_2 \in \mathrm{Mod}^{\mathbf{OSPA}}(\varphi)(M)_{[s]}$.
- for each order-sorted preorder homomorphism $h' \in \mathrm{Mod}^{\mathbf{OSPA}}(\Sigma')$,
  - $\mathrm{Mod}^{\mathbf{OSPA}}(\varphi)(h')_s = h'_{\varphi(s)}$ for all $s \in S$.

We denote by $\_\!\restriction_\varphi$ the functor $\mathrm{Mod}^{\mathbf{OSPA}}(\varphi)$. If $M'\!\restriction_\varphi = M$ then we say that M' is a φ-expansion of M, and M is the φ-reduct of M. If φ is a signature inclusion then we may write $M'\!\restriction_{(S, \leq, F)}$ instead of $M'\!\restriction_\varphi$.

For each order-sorted signature $\Sigma = (S, \leq, F)$ there are three kinds of atomic sentences:

(1) equational atoms $t = t'$, where $t, t' \in (T_\Sigma)_{[s]}$ and $[s] \in \widehat{S}$,
(2) membership atoms $t : s$, where $t \in (T_\Sigma)_{[s]}$ and $[s] \in \widehat{S}$,
(3) preorder atoms $t \Rightarrow t'$, where $t, t' \in (T_\Sigma)_{[s]}$ and $[s] \in \widehat{S}$.

The set $\mathbb{S}en^{\mathbf{OSPA}}(\Sigma)$ of sentences consists of universally quantified conditional atoms of the form $(\forall X)\mathtt{atm}$ if $\mathtt{atm}_1 \wedge \ldots \wedge \mathtt{atm}_n$, where X is a finite set of variables for Σ, and $\mathtt{atm}, \mathtt{atm}_i$ are atoms. Each order-sorted signature morphism $\varphi : \Sigma \to \Sigma'$ determines a function $\mathbb{S}en^{\mathbf{OSPA}}(\varphi) : \mathbb{S}en^{\mathbf{OSPA}}(\Sigma) \to \mathbb{S}en^{\mathbf{OSPA}}(\Sigma')$ which translates the sentences symbol-wise. When there is no danger of confusion we denote $\mathbb{S}en^{\mathbf{OSPA}}(\varphi)$ simply by φ.

The satisfaction of a sentence by a model $M \in \mathbb{M}od^{\mathbf{OSPA}}(\Sigma)$, where $\Sigma = (S, \leq, F)$, is defined by induction on the structure of the sentences:

- $M \models_\Sigma t = t'$ iff $M_t = M_{t'}$,
- $M \models_\Sigma t : s$ iff $M_t \in M_s$,
- $M \models_\Sigma t \Rightarrow t'$ iff $M_t \leq_{[s]} M_{t'}$,
- $M \models_\Sigma \mathtt{atm}$ if $\mathtt{atm}_1 \wedge \ldots \wedge \mathtt{atm}_n$ iff $M \models_\Sigma \mathtt{atm}_i$ for all $i \in \{1, \ldots, n\}$ implies $M \models_\Sigma \mathtt{atm}$,
- $M \models_\Sigma (\forall X)\rho$ iff for all ι_X-expansions M' of M we have $M' \models_{\Sigma[X]} \rho$.

where $t, t' \in (T_\Sigma)_{[s]}$ are terms, $s \in S$ is a sort, $\mathtt{atm}$ if $\mathtt{atm}_1 \wedge \ldots \wedge \mathtt{atm}_n \in \mathbb{S}en^{\mathbf{OSPA}}(\Sigma)$ is a quantifier-free sentence, $(\forall X)\rho \in \mathbb{S}en^{\mathbf{OSPA}}(\Sigma)$ is any sentence, $\iota_X : \Sigma \hookrightarrow \Sigma[X]$ is the extension of Σ with constants from X.

Proposition 2 (The satisfaction condition). *For all signature morphisms $\varphi : \Sigma \to \Sigma'$, models $M' \in \mathbb{M}od^{\mathbf{OSPA}}(\Sigma')$ and sentences $\rho \in \mathbb{S}en^{\mathbf{OSPA}}(\Sigma)$ we have $M'\restriction_\varphi \models_\Sigma \rho$ iff $M' \models_{\Sigma'} \varphi(\rho)$.*

Proof. Straightforward, by induction on the structure of the sentences.   □

*Constructor-based Order-Sorted Preorder Algebra (**COSPA**).* We apply the ideas from [17] to define the constructor-based version of **OSPA**. A *constructor-based order-sorted signature* $(S, \leq, F, F^c)$ consists of an order-sorted signature $(S, \leq, F)$ and a subfamily of sets of operation symbols $F^c \subseteq F$. A sort $s \in S$ is *constrained* if there exists $w \in S^*$ such that $F^c_{w \to s} \neq \emptyset$. Let S^c be the set of constrained sorts and $S^l = S - S^c$ the set of *loose* sorts. $M \in \mathbb{M}od^{\mathbf{OSPA}}(\Sigma)$ is *reachable* w.r.t. the constructors in F^c if there exists a function $f : Y \to M$, where Y is a set of variables of loose sorts, such that $f^\# : (T_{(S, \leq, F^c)}(Y))_s \to M_s$ is surjective for all $s \in S^c$, where $f^\# : T_{(S, \leq, F^c)}(Y) \to M\restriction_{(S, \leq, F^c)}$ is the unique extension of f to a $(S, \leq, F^c)$-homomorphism. The notion of reachability generalises the one in [1] to the order-sorted case. Let $\mathbb{M}od^{\mathbf{COSPA}}(S, \leq, F, F^c) \subseteq \mathbb{M}od^{\mathbf{OSPA}}(S, \leq, F)$ be the full subcategory of reachable order-sorted preorder algebras.

A *constructor-based order-sorted signature morphism* $\varphi : (S, \leq, F, F^c) \to (S', \leq', F', F'^c)$ consists of an order-sorted signature morphism $\varphi : (S, \leq, F) \to (S', \leq', F')$ such that

(1) constructors are preserved along the signature morphisms, i.e. if $\sigma \in F^c$ then $\varphi(\sigma) \in F'^c$,

(2) no "new" constructors are introduced for "old" constrained sorts, i.e. if $s \in S^c$ and $\sigma' \in (F'^c)_{w' \to \varphi(s)}$ then there exists $\sigma \in F^c_{w \to s}$ such that $\varphi(\sigma) = \sigma'$, and

(3) if $s_0' \in S'$ and $s \in S^c$ such that $s_0' \leq' \varphi(s)$ then there exists $s_0 \in S$ such that $s_0 \leq s$ and $\varphi(s_0) = s_0'$.

Proposition 3. *For all constructor-based order-sorted signature morphisms φ : $(S, \leq, F, F^c) \to (S', \leq', F', F'^c)$, $M' \in |\mathrm{Mod}^{\mathbf{COSPA}}(S', \leq', F', F'^c)|$ implies $M'|_\varphi \in |\mathrm{Mod}^{\mathbf{COSPA}}(S, \leq, F, F^c)|$.*

Proof. Let $\varphi^c : (S, \leq, F^c) \to (S', \leq, F'^c)$ be the restriction of φ to constructors. It suffices to prove that for all sets Y' of variables for $(S', \leq', F'^c, F')$ of loose sorts there exists a set Y of variables for $(S, \leq, F, F^c)$ of loose sorts and an assignment $f : Y \to T_{(S', \leq', F'^c)}(Y')|_{\varphi^c}$ such that the unique extension $f^\# : T_{(S, \leq, F^c)}(Y) \to T_{(S', \leq', F'^c)}(Y')|_{\varphi^c}$ of f to a $(S, \leq, F^c)$-homomorphism is a surjection.

Let Y' be a set of loose variables for $(S', \leq', F', F'^c)$. We define $f : Y \to T_{(S', \leq', F'^c)}(Y')|_{\varphi^c}$ as follows:

- for all $s \in S^c$ let $Y_s = \emptyset$.
- for all $s \in S^l$ let Y_s be a set of fresh variables such that
  - if $\varphi(s) \in S'^l$ then there exists a bijection $f_s : Y_s \to Y'_{\varphi(s)}$, and
  - if $\varphi(s) \in S'^c$ then there exists a bijection $f_s : Y_s \to T_{(S', \leq', F'^c)}(Y')_{\varphi(s)}$.

We prove by induction on the structure of the terms $t' \in (T_{(S', \leq', F'^c)}(Y'))_{s'}$ that if $s' \in \varphi(S)$ then for all $s \in \varphi^{-1}(s')$ there exists $t \in (T_{(S, \leq, F)}(Y))_s$ such that $f_s^\#(t) = t'$.

(1) **For $y' \in Y'_{s'}$:** Assume that $s' \in \varphi(S)$, and fix $s \in \varphi^{-1}(s')$. Then take $t = f^{-1}(y')$.

(2) **For $\sigma'(t') \in T_{(S', \leq', F'^c)}(Y')_{s'}$:** Assume that $s' \in \varphi(S)$, and fix $s \in \varphi^{-1}(s')$. There exists $w \in S^*$ and $\sigma \in F_{w \to s}$ such that $\varphi(\sigma) = \sigma'$. By the induction hypothesis, there exists $t \in (T_{(S, \leq, F)}(Y))^w$ such that $f^\#(t) = t'$. It follows that $f^\#(\sigma(t)) = \sigma'(t')$.

(3) **For $s_0' \leq' s'$ and $t' \in T_{(S', \leq', F'^c)}(Y')_{s_0'}$:** Assume that $s' \in \varphi(S)$, and fix $s \in \varphi^{-1}(s')$. There are two cases.
  (a) **For $s \in S^c$:** There exists $s_0 \in S$ such that $s_0 \leq s$ and $\varphi(s_0) = s_0'$. By the induction hypothesis, there exists $t \in T_{(S, \leq, F^c)}(Y)_{s_0}$ such that $f^\#(t) = t'$. It follows that $t \in T_{(S, \leq, F^c)}(Y)_s$ and we have $f^\#(t) = t'$.
  (b) **For $s \in S^l$:** it follows easily by the definition of f.

$\square$

Hereafter, we work within the context of **COSPA**, which is the underlying logic of the methodology presented in this paper. For the sake of simplicity, we will make the following notations.

Notation 1. *For all constructor-based order-sorted signatures $(S, \leq, F, F^c)$,*

1. $\mathrm{Sen}(S, \leq, F, F^c) = \mathrm{Sen}^{\mathbf{OSPA}}(S, \leq, F)$ *and*

2. $\mathrm{Mod}(S, \leq, F, F^c) = \mathrm{Mod}^{\mathbf{COSPA}}(S, \leq, F, F^c)$.

For all constructor-based order-sorted signature morphisms $\varphi : (S, \leq, F, F^c) \to (S', \leq', F', F'^c)$,

1. $\mathrm{Sen}(\varphi) = \mathrm{Sen}^{\mathbf{OSPA}}(\varphi)$, and
2. $\mathrm{Mod}(\varphi)$ *is the restriction of the functor*

$$\mathrm{Mod}^{\mathbf{OSPA}}(\varphi) : \mathrm{Mod}^{\mathbf{OSPA}}(S', \leq', F') \to \mathrm{Mod}^{\mathbf{OSPA}}(S, \leq, F)$$

to the subcategory $\mathrm{Mod}^{\mathbf{COSPA}}(S', \leq', F', F'^c)$.

For all $M \in |\mathrm{Mod}(S, \leq, F, F^c)|$ *and* $\rho \in \mathrm{Sen}(S, \leq, F, F^c)$ *we write* $M \models_{(S, \leq, F, F^c)} \rho$ *instead of* $M \models_{(S, \leq, F)} \rho$. *When there is no danger of confusion we drop the subscript* $(S, \leq, F, F^c)$ *from* $\models_{(S, \leq, F, F^c)}$, *and we write simply* $M \models \rho$.

The following corollary of Propositions 2 and 3 says that **COSPA** defined above is an institution [13].

Corollary 1. *For all signature morphisms* $\varphi : (S, \leq, F, F^c) \to (S', \leq', F', F'^c)$, *models* $M' \in \mathrm{Mod}(S', \leq', F', F'^c)$ *and sentences* $\rho \in \mathrm{Sen}(S, \leq, F, F^c)$ *we have* $M'\!\upharpoonright_\varphi \models_{(S, \leq, F, F^c)} \rho$ *iff* $M' \models_{(S', \leq', F', F'^c)} \varphi(\rho)$.

A *substitution* of Σ-terms with variables in Y for variables in X, where $\Sigma = (S, \leq, F, F^c)$, is a S-sorted function $\theta : X \to T_\Sigma(Y)$. Note that θ can be canonically extended to $\theta^{term} : T_\Sigma(X) \to T_\Sigma(Y)$ and $\theta^{sen} : \mathrm{Sen}(\Sigma[X]) \to \mathrm{Sen}(\Sigma[Y])$, where $\Sigma[X]$ and $\Sigma[Y]$ are the extensions of Σ with (non-constructor) constants from X and Y, respectively. When there is no danger of confusion we may drop the superscripts *term* and *sen* from notations. On the semantic side θ, determines a forgetful functor $\_\!\upharpoonright_\theta : \mathrm{Mod}(\Sigma[Y]) \to \mathrm{Mod}(\Sigma[X])$ such that for all $M \in \mathrm{Mod}(\Sigma[Y])$, $M\!\upharpoonright_\theta$ interprets all symbols in Σ as M, and $(M\!\upharpoonright_\theta)_x = M_{\theta(x)}$ for all $x \in X$.

Proposition 4 (The satisfaction condition for substitutions). *For all substitutions* $\theta : X \to T_\Sigma(Y)$, *sentences* $\rho \in \mathrm{Sen}(\Sigma[X])$ *and models* $M \in |\mathrm{Mod}(\Sigma[Y])|$ *we have* $M\!\upharpoonright_\theta \models_{\Sigma[X]} \rho$ *iff* $M \models_{\Sigma[Y]} \theta(\rho)$.

Proof. Straightforward, by induction on the structure of the sentences. ☐

Notation 2. *Given* $t \in T_\Sigma(X)$ *and* $\theta : X \to T_\Sigma(Y)$ *such that* $X = \{x_1, \ldots, x_n\}$ *and* $\theta(x_i) = t_i$ *for all* $i \in \{1, \ldots, n\}$ *then we may write the term* $\theta(t)$ *in the form* $t[x_1 \leftarrow t_1, \ldots, x_n \leftarrow t_n]$.

2.2 General Proof Rules

The entailment system in [9] is generalised to **COSPA**. In addition, we propose a *simultaneous induction* scheme which is more general than the structural induction [9], and *case analysis* is refined such that it can be applied automatically.

A specification SP consists of a signature $\mathrm{Sig}(\mathrm{SP})$, a set of sentences $\mathrm{Ax}(\mathrm{SP}) \subseteq \mathrm{Sen}(\mathrm{Sig}(\mathrm{SP}))$, and a class of models $\mathrm{Mod}(\mathrm{SP}) \subseteq \mathrm{Mod}(\mathrm{Sig}(\mathrm{SP}))$ such that $M \models \mathrm{Ax}(\mathrm{SP})$ for all $M \in |\mathrm{Mod}(\mathrm{SP})|$. A specification morphism $\varphi : \mathrm{SP}_1 \to \mathrm{SP}_2$ consists of a signature morphism $\varphi : \mathrm{Sig}(\mathrm{SP}_1) \to \mathrm{Sig}(\mathrm{SP}_2)$ such that

(a) $\mathbb{A}x(\text{SP}_2) \models \varphi(\mathbb{A}x(\text{SP}_1))$, and
(b) for all $M_2 \in |\mathbb{M}od(\text{SP}_2)|$ we have $M_2\!\restriction_\varphi \in |\mathbb{M}od(\text{SP}_1)|$.

This defines a category of specifications SPEC. Below we recall some of the specification-building operators introduced in [23].

Basic Specification. Any pair (Σ, E) of signature Σ and set of sentences E is a basic specification with the signature $\mathbb{S}ig(\Sigma, E) = \Sigma$, set of sentences $\mathbb{A}x(\Sigma, E) = E$, and class of models $\mathbb{M}od(\Sigma, E)$ consisting of all Σ-models which satisfy E.

Sum. For any specifications SP_1 and SP_2 such that $\mathbb{S}ig(\text{SP}_1) = \mathbb{S}ig(\text{SP}_2)$, $\text{SP}_1 \cup \text{SP}_2$ is a specification such that $\mathbb{S}ig(\text{SP}_1 \cup \text{SP}_2) = \mathbb{S}ig(\text{SP}_1)$, $\mathbb{A}x(\text{SP}_1 \cup \text{SP}_2) = \mathbb{A}x(\text{SP}_1) \cup \mathbb{A}x(\text{SP}_2)$, and $\mathbb{M}od(\text{SP}_1 \cup \text{SP}_2) = \mathbb{M}od(\text{SP}_1) \cap \mathbb{M}od(\text{SP}_2)$.

Translation. Let SP be a specification and $\varphi : \mathbb{S}ig(\text{SP}) \hookrightarrow \Sigma$ a signature morphism. $\text{SP} * \varphi$ is a specification such that $\mathbb{S}ig(\text{SP} * \varphi) = \Sigma$, $\mathbb{A}x(\text{SP} * \varphi) = \varphi(\mathbb{A}x(\text{SP}))$, and $\mathbb{M}od(\text{SP} * \varphi)$ consisting of all Σ-models M' such that the reduct of M' along φ is a SP-model, in symbols, $M'\!\restriction_\varphi \in \mathbb{M}od(\text{SP})$.

Initiality. Given a class $\mathcal{H}$ of model morphisms, for any two specifications SP_0 and SP and any signature morphism $\varphi : \mathbb{S}ig(\text{SP}_0) \to \mathbb{S}ig(\text{SP})$, the *free restriction* of SP to SP_0 through φ, denoted $\text{SP!}_{\mathcal{H}}(\varphi, \text{SP}_0)$, is a specification such that $\mathbb{S}ig(\text{SP!}_{\mathcal{H}}(\varphi, \text{SP}_0)) = \mathbb{S}ig(\text{SP})$, $\mathbb{A}x(\text{SP!}_{\mathcal{H}}(\varphi, \text{SP}_0)) = \mathbb{A}x(\text{SP})$, and
$\mathbb{M}od(\text{SP!}_{\mathcal{H}}(\varphi, \text{SP}_0)) = \{M \in \mathbb{M}od(\text{SP}) \mid \text{there exists } M_0 \in \mathbb{M}od(\text{SP}_0) \text{ and}$
$\eta : M_0 \to M\!\restriction_\varphi \in \mathcal{H} \text{ such that for all}$
$h_0 : M_0 \to N\!\restriction_\varphi \text{ with } N \in \mathbb{M}od(\text{SP})$
$\text{there exists a unique arrow}$
$h : M \to N \text{ that satisfies } \eta; h\!\restriction_\varphi = h_0\}$

If $\mathcal{H}$ consists of identity morphisms then no "junk" and no "confusion" is added to the models of SP_0. In this case we say that SP_0 is imported by SP in *protecting mode.* Importations in protecting mode can be realized also by the operator *Translation.*

Definition 3. *[3] An entailment system for deducing the logical consequences of specifications is a family of predicates* $\vdash \overset{def}{=} \{\text{SP} \vdash \_\}_{\text{SP} \in |\text{SPEC}|}$ *on the sets of sentences with the following properties:*

$$[lemma] \frac{\text{SP} \cup (\mathbb{S}ig(\text{SP}), E_0) \vdash E \quad \text{SP} \vdash E_0}{\text{SP} \vdash E}$$

$$[union] \frac{\text{SP} \vdash E_0 \quad \text{SP} \vdash E}{\text{SP} \vdash E_0 \cup E} \qquad [trans] \frac{\text{SP} \vdash E \text{ and } \varphi : \mathbb{S}ig(\text{SP}) \to \Sigma}{\text{SP} * \varphi \vdash \varphi(E)}$$

$$[sum1] \frac{\text{SP}_1 \vdash \Gamma}{\text{SP}_1 \cup \text{SP}_2 \vdash \Gamma} \qquad [sum2] \frac{\text{SP}_2 \vdash \Gamma}{\text{SP}_1 \cup \text{SP}_2 \vdash \Gamma}$$

where $\text{SP}, \text{SP}_1, \text{SP}_2 \in |\text{SPEC}|$, $\Gamma \subseteq \mathbb{S}en(\mathbb{S}ig(\text{SP}_1))$, *and* $E_0, E \subseteq \mathbb{S}en(\mathbb{S}ig(\text{SP}))$.

Definition 4. *[3] An entailment system* $\vdash = \{\text{SP} \vdash \_\}_{\text{SP} \in |\text{SPEC}|}$ *is sound if* $\text{SP} \vdash E$ *implies* $\text{SP} \models E$ *for all specifications* SP *and sets of sentences* E.

Below we define the proof rules that support our verification methodology.

Simultaneous Induction [SI]. This proof rule is a generalization of the structural induction, and it can be applied to a goal of the form $\mathsf{SP} \vdash \{(\forall X)\rho_i \mid i = \overline{1, m}\}$, where X is a set of constrained variables for Σ, where $\Sigma = \mathbb{S}ig(\mathsf{SP})$, and for all $i \in \{1, \ldots, m\}$, ρ_i is a $\Sigma[X]$-sentence [4]. Let F^c be the constructors of the signature Σ. We let CON range over all sort-preserving mappings $X \to F^c$, i.e. for every $x \in X$, the sort of $\mathsf{CON}(x)$ is less or equal than the sort of x. For each mapping $\mathsf{CON} : X \to F^c$ and variable $x \in X$ let $Z_{x,\mathsf{CON}} = z_{x,\mathsf{CON}}^1 \cdots z_{x,\mathsf{CON}}^n$ be a string of arguments for the constructor $\mathsf{CON}(x)$. By an abuse of notation, we let $Z_{x,\mathsf{CON}}$ denote both the string $z_{x,\mathsf{CON}}^1 \cdots z_{x,\mathsf{CON}}^n$ and the set $\{z_{x,\mathsf{CON}}^1, \ldots, z_{x,\mathsf{CON}}^n\}$. We define the set of variables $Z_{\mathsf{CON}} = \bigcup_{x \in X} Z_{x,\mathsf{CON}}$ and the substitution $\mathsf{VAR}_{\mathsf{CON}}^\# : X \to T_\Sigma(Z_{\mathsf{CON}})$ by $\mathsf{VAR}_{\mathsf{CON}}^\#(x) = \mathsf{CON}(x)(Z_{x,\mathsf{CON}})$. Let $\mathsf{VAR}_{\mathsf{CON}}$ range over all substitutions $X \to T_\Sigma(Z_{\mathsf{CON}})$ with the following properties:

(a) $\mathsf{VAR}_{\mathsf{CON}}(x) \in Z_{x,\mathsf{CON}}$ or $\mathsf{VAR}_{\mathsf{CON}}(x) = \mathsf{CON}(x)(Z_{x,\mathsf{CON}})$ for all $x \in X$, and
(b) $\mathsf{VAR}_{\mathsf{CON}}(x) \in Z_{x,\mathsf{CON}}$ for some $x \in X$.

Since any substitution is sort-decreasing, the sort of $\mathsf{VAR}_{\mathsf{CON}}(x)$ is less or equal than the sort of x. The function CON gives the induction cases, while the function $\mathsf{VAR}_{\mathsf{CON}}$ is used to define the induction hypothesis for each case. For all sort-preserving mappings $\mathsf{CON} : X \to F^c$ we define the following specification:

$$\mathsf{SP}_{\mathsf{CON}} = \mathsf{SP} * \iota_{Z_{\mathsf{CON}}} \cup (\Sigma[Z_{\mathsf{CON}}], \{\mathsf{VAR}_{\mathsf{CON}}(\rho_i) \mid \mathsf{VAR}_{\mathsf{CON}} : X \to T_\Sigma(Z_{\mathsf{CON}}) \text{ and } i = \overline{1, m}\})$$

where $\iota_{Z_{\mathsf{CON}}} : \Sigma \hookrightarrow \Sigma[Z_{\mathsf{CON}}]$. *Simultaneous Induction* is defined as follows:

$$[SI] \frac{\mathsf{SP}_{\mathsf{CON}} \vdash \mathsf{VAR}_{\mathsf{CON}}^\#(\rho_i) \text{ for all } \mathsf{CON} : X \to F^c \text{ and } i = \overline{1, m}}{\mathsf{SP} \vdash \{(\forall X)\rho_i \mid i = \overline{1, m}\}}$$

Note that $\mathsf{SP}_{\mathsf{CON}}$ consists of the specification SP refined by the induction hypothesis $\{\mathsf{VAR}_{\mathsf{CON}}(\rho_i) \mid \mathsf{VAR}_{\mathsf{CON}} : X \to T_\Sigma(Z_{\mathsf{CON}}) \text{ and } i = \overline{1, m}\}$.

Lemma 1. *[9] Consider a specification SP and a sentence $(\forall X)\rho \in \mathbb{S}en(\mathbb{S}ig(\mathsf{SP}))$. Let $\Sigma = \mathbb{S}ig(\mathsf{SP})$ and Σ^c be the sub-signature of constructors of Σ. We have*

(1) $\mathsf{SP} \models (\forall X)\rho$ iff $\mathsf{SP} * \iota_X \models \rho$, where $\iota_X : \Sigma \hookrightarrow \Sigma[X]$, and
(2) if X is a set of variables of constrained sorts then $\mathsf{SP} \models (\forall X)\rho$ iff $\mathsf{SP} \models (\forall Y)\theta(\rho)$ for all substitutions $\theta : X \to T_\Sigma(Y)$ such that
  (a) Y is a finite set of variables of loose sorts, and
  (b) $\theta(x) \in T_{\Sigma^c}(Y)$ for all $x \in X$.

The above lemma is used to prove the soundness of $[SI]$.

Proposition 5. Simultaneous Induction *is sound.*

Proof. Assume that $\mathsf{SP}_{\mathsf{CON}} \models \mathsf{VAR}_{\mathsf{CON}}^\#(\rho_i)$ for all $\mathsf{CON} : X \to F^c$ and $i = \overline{1, m}$. Let $\Sigma^c = (S, \leq, F^c)$ be the sub-signature of constructors, where $\Sigma = (S, \leq, F, F^c)$. By Lemma 1(2) it suffices to show that $\mathsf{SP} \models (\forall Y)\theta(\rho_i)$ for all $i = \overline{1, m}$ and $\theta : X \to T_\Sigma(Y)$ such that

---

[4] Note that $(\forall X)(\forall Y)\rho = (\forall X \cup Y)\rho$.

(1) Y is a finite set of variables of loose sorts, and
(2) $\theta(x) \in T_{\Sigma^c}(Y)$ for all $x \in X$.

Let $\theta : X \to T_{\Sigma}(Y)$ be such a substitution. We proceed by induction on the sum of depths of terms in $\{\theta(x) \mid x \in X\}$, which exists as a consequence of X being finite. Let $\text{CON} : X \to F^c$ be the sort-preserving mapping such that for all $x \in X$ the topmost constructor of $\theta(x)$ is $\text{CON}(x)$. For all $x \in X$ let $T_x = t_x^1 \ldots t_x^n$ be the string of the intermediate subterms of $\theta(x)$. We define the substitution $\psi : Z_{\text{CON}} \to T_{\Sigma^c}(Y)$ by $\psi(z_{x,\text{CON}}^j) = t_x^j$.

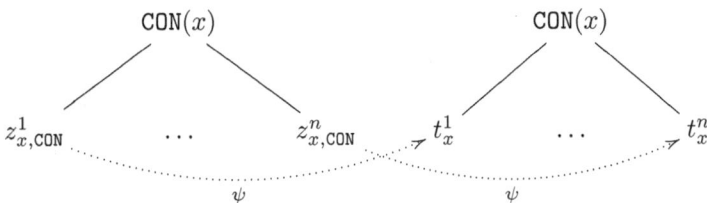

By our assumptions we have

$$\text{SP}*\iota_{Z_{\text{CON}}}\cup(\Sigma[Z_{\text{CON}}], \{\text{VAR}_{\text{CON}}(\rho_j) \mid \text{VAR}_{\text{CON}} : X \to T_{\Sigma}(Z_{\text{CON}}), j = \overline{1,m}\}) \models \text{VAR}_{\text{CON}}^{\#}(\rho_i)$$

for all $i = \overline{1,m}$. Since substitutions preserve satisfaction, we obtain

$$\text{SP}*\iota_Y\cup(\Sigma[Y], \{\psi(\text{VAR}_{\text{CON}}(\rho_j)) \mid \text{VAR}_{\text{CON}} : X \to T_{\Sigma}(Z_{\text{CON}}), j = \overline{1,m}\}) \models \psi(\text{VAR}_{\text{CON}}^{\#}(\rho_i))$$

for all $i = \overline{1,m}$. Since $\text{VAR}_{\text{CON}}^{\#}; \psi = \theta$ we have

$$\text{SP} * \iota_Y \cup (\Sigma[Y], \{\psi(\text{VAR}_{\text{CON}}(\rho_j)) \mid \text{VAR}_{\text{CON}} : X \to T_{\Sigma}(Z_{\text{CON}}), j = \overline{1,m}\}) \models \theta(\rho_i)$$

for all $i = \overline{1,m}$.

   For all substitutions $\text{VAR}_{\text{CON}} : X \to T_{\Sigma}(Z_{\text{CON}})$, the sum of depths of terms in $\{\psi(\text{VAR}_{\text{CON}}(x)) \mid x \in X\}$ is strictly less than the sum of depths of terms in $\{\theta(x) \mid x \in X\}$. By the induction hypothesis, $\text{SP} \models (\forall Y)\psi(\text{VAR}_{\text{CON}}(\rho_j))$ for all $\text{VAR}_{\text{CON}} : X \to T_{\Sigma}(Z_{\text{CON}})$ and $j = \overline{1,m}$. By Lemma 1(1), $\text{SP} * \iota_Y \models \psi(\text{VAR}_{\text{CON}}(\rho_j))$ for all $\text{VAR}_{\text{CON}} : X \to T_{\Sigma}(Z_{\text{CON}})$ and $j = \overline{1,m}$. Since

$$\text{SP} * \iota_Y \models \{\psi(\text{VAR}_{\text{CON}}(\rho_j)) \mid \text{VAR}_{\text{CON}} : X \to T_{\Sigma}(Z_{\text{CON}}), j = \overline{1,m}\}$$

and

$$\text{SP} * \iota_Y \cup (\Sigma[Y], \{\psi(\text{VAR}_{\text{CON}}(\rho_j)) \mid \text{VAR}_{\text{CON}} : X \to T_{\Sigma}(Z_{\text{CON}}), j = \overline{1,m}\}) \models \theta(\rho_i)$$

where $i = \overline{1,m}$. We obtain $\text{SP} * \iota_Y \models \theta(\rho_i)$, where $i = \overline{1,m}$. By Lemma 1(1), $\text{SP} \models (\forall Y)\theta(\rho_i)$, where $i = \overline{1,m}$. $\qquad\square$

Case Analysis [CA]. This proof rule divides a goal into a sufficient number of separate cases. Analysing each such case individually may be enough to prove the initial goal. We say that $E = \{(\forall X)(\forall Y^i)u = v^i \text{ if } \text{Cond}^i \mid i = \overline{1,n}\} \subseteq \mathbb{A}x(SP)$ is a *[CA]-set of sentences*, where SP is a specification, if

- X is the set of all variables occurring in u, and
- $\text{SP} \models \bigvee\limits_{i=1}^{i \leq n} (\exists Y^i)\psi(\text{Cond}^i)$ for all substitutions $\psi : X \to T_\Sigma$.

Consider a goal $\text{SP} \vdash \rho$, and a $[CA]$-set of sentences $E \subseteq \mathbb{A}x(\text{SP})$ as above. Let t be a ground term occurring in ρ, and t_1 a subterm of t which is matched by u, i.e. there exists a substitution $\theta : X \to T_{\mathbb{S}ig(\text{SP})}$ such that $\theta(u) = t_1$. We define *Case Analysis* as follows:

$$[CA]\frac{\text{SP} * \iota_{Y^i} \cup (\Sigma[Y^i], \theta(\text{Cond}^i)) \vdash \rho \text{ for all } i = \overline{1,n}}{\text{SP} \vdash \rho}$$

where $\iota_{Y^j} : \Sigma \hookrightarrow \Sigma[Y^j]$ is the signature inclusion.

In our case study, X consists of a single variable of the sort representing the state space of the transitional system, and Y^j consists of variables added by the matching equations. The specification SP obviously satisfies the disjunction $\bigvee\limits_{i=1}^{i \leq n} (\exists Y^i)\psi(\text{Cond}^i)$ as the conditions Cond^i describe all possible patterns of a sequence.

Proposition 6. Case Analysis *is sound.*

Proof. Assume that $\text{SP} * \iota_{Y^i} \cup (\Sigma[Y^i], \theta(\text{Cond}^i)) \models \rho$ for all $i \in \{1, \ldots, n\}$ and let $M \in \mathbb{M}od(\text{SP})$. We prove that $M \models_\Sigma \rho$. By our assumptions, there exists $j \in \{1, \ldots, n\}$ and a ι_{Y^j}-expansion M' of M, where $\iota_{Y^j} : \Sigma \hookrightarrow \Sigma[Y^j]$, such that $M' \models_{\Sigma[Y^j]} \theta(\text{Cond}^j)$. Notice that $M' \in \mathbb{M}od(\text{SP} * \iota_{Y^j} \cup (\Sigma[Y^j], \theta(\text{Cond}^j)))$, and since $\text{SP} * \iota_{Y^j} \cup (\Sigma[Y^j], \theta(\text{Cond}^j)) \models \rho$, we have $M' \models_{\Sigma[Y^j]} \rho$. Hence $M \models_\Sigma \rho$. $\square$

Substitutivity [ST]. We can infer new sentences by substituting terms for variables. This proof rule is used during the verification process to instantiate sentences that are not executable by rewriting.

$$[ST]\frac{(\forall Y)\rho \in \mathbb{A}x(\text{SP}) \quad \theta : Y \to T_{\mathbb{S}ig(\text{SP})}(Z)}{\text{SP} \vdash (\forall Z)\theta(\rho)}$$

Proposition 7. Substitutivity *is sound.*

Proof. The proof is a direct consequence of the satisfaction condition for substitutions (see Proposition 4). $\square$

Subterm Replacement [SR]. A specialized rule of inference using subterm replacement is the basis for *term rewriting*. Let SP be a specification and $(\forall X)\rho$ a Σ-sentence, where $\Sigma = \mathbb{S}ig(\text{SP})$. Suppose that $X = Y \cup \{z\}$, where $z \notin Y$, and $\theta, \psi : X \to T_\Sigma(Y)$ are two substitutions such that $\theta(y) = \psi(y) = y$ for all $y \in Y$.

$$\frac{\text{SP} \vdash (\forall Y)\psi(\rho) \quad \text{SP} \vdash (\forall Y)\theta(z) = \psi(z)}{\text{SP} \vdash (\forall Y)\theta(\rho)}$$

The following result is a generalisation of soundness of *Subterm Replacement* for many-sorted algebra [12].

Proposition 8. Subterm Replacement *is sound.*

Theorem of Constants [TC]. We define the following proof rule for the quantification over variables of loose sorts:

$$[TC]\frac{\text{SP} * \iota_Y \vdash \rho}{\text{SP} \vdash (\forall Y)\rho}$$

where SP is a specification, $(\forall Y)\rho$ is a sentence, and $\iota_Y : \mathbb{S}ig(\text{SP}) \hookrightarrow \mathbb{S}ig(\text{SP})[Y]$. Note that even if not all of the variables in Y are of loose sorts if we have proved $\text{SP} * \iota_Y \vdash \rho$ then we conclude $\text{SP} \vdash (\forall Y)\rho$. This means that there are cases in practice when we apply $[TC]$ to goals with sentences quantified over variables of constrained sorts. The following proposition is a corollary of Lemma 1(1).

Proposition 9. Theorem of Constants *is sound.*

Remark 1. In the verification process we separate variables that are handled with $[SI]$ from the variables that are dealt with $[TC]$, rather than distinguishing variables of constrained sorts from variables of loose sorts. In general, this choice cannot be automated and is entirely up to the user to make.

Implication. The following proof rule is defined for the logical implication:

$$[IP]\frac{\text{SP} \cup (\mathbb{S}ig(\text{SP}), \text{Cond}) \vdash \text{atm}}{\text{SP} \vdash \text{atm if Cond}}$$

where SP is a specification, atm is an atom, and Cond is a conjunction of atoms.

Proposition 10. *[9]* Implication *is sound.*

The following theorem is a corollary of Propositions 5-10.

Theorem 1. *Consider a sound entailment relation* $\vdash^b = \{\text{SP} \vdash^b \_\}_{\text{SP}\in|\text{SPEC}|}$ *for proving quantifier-free unconditional atoms. The least entailment relation* $\vdash = \{\text{SP} \vdash \_\}_{\text{SP}\in|\text{SPEC}|}$ *over* $\vdash^b$ *closed to* $[SI], [CA], [ST], [SR], [TC]$ *and* $[IP]$ *is sound.*

Proof. By Proposition 5-10, the semantic entailment relation $\{\text{SP} \models \_\}_{\text{SP}\in|\text{SPEC}|}$ is closed to $[SI], [CA], [ST], [SR], [TC]$ and $[IP]$. Then the least entailment relation $\{\text{SP} \vdash \_\}_{\text{SP}\in|\text{SPEC}|}$ closed to $[SI], [CA], [ST], [SR], [TC]$ and $[IP]$ is included in $\{\text{SP} \models \_\}_{\text{SP}\in|\text{SPEC}|}$. □

2.3   Specialised Proof Rules

When initial semantics is used the above rules are not enough to prove the desired properties of the specifications. Specialised proof rules (that cannot be derived from the general inference rules defined in Section 2.2) are needed to complete the verification process. Since algebraic specification languages have libraries defining the initial data types often used in applications, it is natural for the theorem prover supporting the verification to be equipped with deduction rules for the predefined data types declared with initial semantics.

Contradiction [CT]. In algebraic specification the boolean data type is often used to establish the truth. The boolean specification BOOL is defined with initial semantics and it is imported by any other specification in protecting mode. The following proof rule is valid for any specification that protects the boolean values. For any specification morphisms ι : BOOL $\hookrightarrow$ SP such that ι : $\mathbb{S}ig$(BOOL) $\hookrightarrow$ $\mathbb{S}ig$(SP) is an inclusion, we define the following proof rule:

$$[CT]\frac{\text{SP} \vdash \text{true => false}}{\text{SP} \vdash \rho}$$

Proposition 11. Contradiction *is sound.*

Proof. For any specification morphisms ι : BOOL $\hookrightarrow$ SP and $M \in |\mathbb{M}od(\text{SP})|$ we have $M \not\models$ true => false. If SP $\models$ true => false then SP has no models, which implies SP $\models \rho$ for any sentence $\rho \in \mathbb{S}en(\mathbb{S}ig(\text{SP}))$. □

It follows that negation has been somehow introduced, in a weaker form. For example, the following sentence $(\forall Y)$true = false if $t_1 = t_2$ says that the term t_1 is different from t_2.

Less-Equal [LE]. Let NAT denote the specification defined with initial semantics which includes a sort Nat with two constructors 0 :$\to$ Nat and s_ : Nat $\to$ Nat, and an ordinary operators <= : Nat Nat $\to$ Bool defined by the following sets of equations:

$$\begin{array}{lll} (\forall M) & \text{M <= M} = \text{true,} \\ (\forall M) & \text{0 <= s M} = \text{true,} \\ (\forall M) & \text{s M <= 0} = \text{false,} \\ (\forall M, N) & \text{s M <= s N} = \text{M <= N.} \end{array}$$

For any specification morphism NAT $\hookrightarrow$ SP such that we have $\{(\text{s}^m\text{0 <= t} = \text{true}), (\text{t <= s}^n\text{0} = \text{true})\} \subseteq \mathbb{A}x(\text{SP})$ and $n < m$, where $t \in T_{\mathbb{S}ig(\text{SP})}$ and $n, m \in \mathbb{N}$, we define the following proof rule

$$[LE]\frac{}{\text{SP} \vdash \rho}$$

where ρ is any sentence.[5]

Proposition 12. Less-Equal *rule is sound.*

Proof. For any specification morphism NAT $\hookrightarrow$ SP such that $\{\text{s}^m\text{0 <= t, t <= s}^n\text{0}\} \subseteq \mathbb{A}x(\text{SP})$, we have SP $\models$ s^{m}0 <= s^{n}0. For any $M \in \mathbb{M}od(\text{SP})$ if $n < m$ then $M \not\models$ s^{n}0 <= s^{m}0 and $M \not\models$ s^{n}0 = s^{m}0, which is a contradiction with SP $\models$ s^{m}0 <= s^{n}0. It follows that SP has no models. Hence, for any sentence ρ we have SP $\models \rho$. □

---

[5] Note that for all natural numbers $n, m \in \mathbb{N}$ we have $n \leq m$ iff s^{n}0 <= s^{m}0, where s^{n}0 = $\underbrace{s \ldots s}_{n \text{ times}}$ 0 and s^{n}0 <= s^{m}0 stands for s^{n}0 <= s^{m}0 = true.

Sequence Case Analisys [SC]. Our approach to support the automation of case analysis is to consider specialized proof rules for various patterns over the data types. Here we consider the example of sequences. Let SEQUENCE denote the specification defined with initial semantics which includes a sort Sequence together with the following constructors: empty denoting the empty sequence, and an associative operation _,_ denoting the concatenation. The elements of the sequences are of sort Elt. Let ι : SEQUENCE $\hookrightarrow$ SP be a specification morphism, where ι : $\mathbb{S}ig$(SEQUENCE) $\hookrightarrow$ $\mathbb{S}ig$(SP) is an inclusion of signatures. Suppose we want

$$\text{SP} \vdash (\forall Y)\text{atm if Cond} \wedge \text{L1}, \text{E1}, \text{L2}, \text{E2}, \text{L3} = \text{t1}, \text{t2} \wedge \text{Cond}'$$

where Li are variables of sort Sequence, Ei are variables of sort Elt, $Y \supseteq \{\text{L1}, \text{L2}, \text{L3}, \text{E1}, \text{E2}\}$ is a set of variables, atm is an atom, Cond and Cond' are conjunctions of atoms, and $t_1, t_2 \in T_{\mathbb{S}ig(\text{SP})}(Y - \{\text{L1}, \text{E1}, \text{L2}, \text{E2}, \text{L3}\})_{\text{Sequence}}$ are terms that do not contain the variables L1, E1, L2, E2, L3. [SC] divides the above goal into the following cases:

(1) SP $\vdash$ $(\forall Y)$atm[L3 $\leftarrow$ L3, t2] if Cond[L3 $\leftarrow$ L3, t2] $\wedge$ L1, E1, L2, E2, L3 = t1 $\wedge$ Cond'[L3 $\leftarrow$ L3, t2],
(2) SP $\vdash$ $(\forall Y')$atm[L2 $\leftarrow$ L2, L2'] if Cond[L2 $\leftarrow$ L2, L2'] $\wedge$ L1, E1, L2 = t1 $\wedge$ L2', E2, L3 = t2 $\wedge$ Cond'[L2 $\leftarrow$ L2, L2'], where Y' = Y $\cup$ {L2'},
(3) SP $\vdash$ $(\forall Y)$atm[L1 $\leftarrow$ t1, L1] if Cond[L1 $\leftarrow$ t1, L1] $\wedge$ L1, E1, L2, E2, L3 = t2 $\wedge$ Cond'[L1 $\leftarrow$ t1, L1]

The above three subgoals describe the following three possibilities: either both E1 and E2 are in t1, or E1 is in t1 and E2 is in t2, or E1 and E2 are in t2. The rule [SC] is specific to SEQUENCE, which is declared with initial semantics, and it cannot be derived from the general proof rules.

Proposition 13. Sequence Case Analysis *is sound.*

Proof. Assume that

(1) SP $\models$ $(\forall Y)$atm[L3 $\leftarrow$ L3, t2] if Cond[L3 $\leftarrow$ L3, t2] $\wedge$ L1, E1, L2, E2, L3 = t1 $\wedge$ Cond'[L3 $\leftarrow$ L3, t2],
(2) SP $\models$ $(\forall Y')$atm[L2 $\leftarrow$ L2, L2'] if Cond[L2 $\leftarrow$ L2, L2'] $\wedge$ L1, E1, L2 = t1 $\wedge$ L2', E2, L3 = t2 $\wedge$ Cond'[L2 $\leftarrow$ L2, L2'], where Y' = Y $\cup$ {L2'},
(3) SP $\models$ $(\forall Y)$atm[L1 $\leftarrow$ t1, L1] if Cond[L1 $\leftarrow$ t1, L1] $\wedge$ L1, E1, L2, E2, L3 = t2 $\wedge$ Cond'[L1 $\leftarrow$ t1, L1].

We show SP $\models$ $(\forall Y)$t = t' if Cond $\wedge$ L1, E1, L2, E2, L3 = t1, t2 $\wedge$ Cond'. Let $M \in \mathbb{M}od(\text{SP})$.

We denote by Σ the signature $\mathbb{S}ig(\text{SP})$. Let N be a ι_y-expansion of M, where $\iota_y : \Sigma \hookrightarrow \Sigma[Y]$, such that $N \models_{\Sigma[Y]}$ Cond, $N \models_{\Sigma[Y]}$ L1, E1, L2, E2, L3 = t1, t2 and $N \models_{\Sigma[Y]}$ Cond'. Since the sequences are protected, there are three possibilities:

(a) N_{E1} and N_{E2} are in N_{t1},
(b) N_{E1} is in N_{t1}, and N_{E2} is in N_{t2}, and

(c) N_{E1} and N_{E2} are in N_{t2}.

We will focus on the first case as the rest of the cases are similar. Without danger of confusion the interpretation of $\_,\_$ into the model N will be denoted also by $\_,\_$. Since $N_{L1}, N_{E1}, N_{L2}, N_{E2}, N_{L3} = N_{t1}, N_{t2}$ and both N_{E1} and N_{E2} are in N_{t1}, there exists $n \in N_{\text{Sequence}}$ such that $N_{L3} = n, N_{t2}$. Let $\theta : Y \to T_\Sigma(Y)$ be the substitution which is the identity on $Y - \{L3\}$ and $\theta(L3) = L3, t2$. Let N' be a ι_Y-expansion of M such that $N'_{L3} = n$ and $N'_y = N_y$ for all $y \in Y - \{L3\}$. Since t_2 does not contain L3 we have $N'_{t2} = N_{t2}$. Note that $(N'\restriction_\theta)_{L3} = N'_{\theta(L3)} = N'_{L3,t2} = n, N'_{t2} = n, N_{t2} = N_{L3}$. We obtain $N'\restriction_\theta = N$, and since $N \models_{\Sigma[Y]}$ Cond and $N \models_{\Sigma[Y]}$ Cond$'$, by the satisfaction condition for substitutions, $N' \models_{\Sigma[Y]}$ Cond[L3 $\leftarrow$ L3, t2] and $N' \models_{\Sigma[Y]}$ Cond$'$[L3 $\leftarrow$ L3, t2]. We have

$$N'_{L1}, N'_{E1}, N'_{L2}, N'_{E2}, N'_{L3}, N'_{t2} = N_{L1}, N_{E1}, N_{L2}, N_{E2}, n, N_{t2} =$$
$$N_{L1}, N_{E1}, N_{L2}, N_{E2}, N_{L3} = N_{t1}, N_{t2} = N'_{t1}, N'_{t2}$$

Since the sequences are protected, $N'_{L1}, N'_{E1}, N'_{L2}, N'_{E2}, N'_{L3} = N'_{t1}$. We obtain $N' \models_{\Sigma[Y]}$ L1, E1, L2, E2, L3 = t1. By assumption (1), $N' \models_{\Sigma[Y]}$ atm[L3 $\leftarrow$ L3, t2], and by the satisfaction condition for substitutions, $N \models_{\Sigma[Y]}$ atm.   □

[SC] simplifies the formula to prove while [CA] refines the specification of the goal by adding new equations. The following theorem is a corollary of Theorem 1 and Propositions 11, 12 and 13.

Theorem 2. *Consider a sound entailment relation* $\vdash^b = \{$SP $\vdash^b$ $\_\}_{\text{SP} \in |\text{SPEC}|}$ *for proving quantifier-free unconditional atoms. Then the least entailment relation* $\vdash = \{$SP $\vdash$ $\_\}_{\text{SP} \in |\text{SPEC}|}$ *over* $\vdash^b$ *closed to* [SI], [CA], [ST], [SR], [TC], [IP], [CT], [LE] *and* [SC] *is sound.*

2.4 Tactics

This methodology is designed for algebraic specification languages which are executable by rewriting. Given a goal SP $\vdash$ E, the underlying assumption is that $\mathbb{A}x(\text{SP})$ forms a term rewriting system which is terminating and possibly confluent. By applying a tactic to a goal it is desirable to preserve termination and confluence. Note that the proof rules of the specification calculus can be regarded, upside down, as tactics for decomposing problems.

Reduction [RD]. The basic entailment relation $\vdash^b$ from Theorem 2 is provided by the system which supports the description of constructor-based specifications. The present methodology is implemented in CITP [11] which is built on top of Maude. Given a specification SP, any goal of the form (1) SP $\vdash$ $t = t'$, (2) SP $\vdash$ $t : s$ and (3) SP $\vdash$ $t \Rightarrow t'$, where t, t' are ground terms and s is a sort, is reduced to the empty goal set if (1) t and t' can be rewritten to the same normal form by the system using the equations and membership axioms of $\mathbb{A}x(\text{SP})$, (2) the sort of t is a subsort of s, (3) t can be rewritten to t' by applying the preorder axioms of $\mathbb{A}x(\text{SP})$, respectively. Maude search engine is invoked in the third case.

Inconsistency [*IC*]. Let BOOL $\hookrightarrow$ SP be a specification morphism. One can easily prove by induction that SP $\vdash (\forall B)t = t'$ if Cond $\wedge\ B =$ not $B \wedge$ Cond$'$, where B is a variable of sort Bool. By [*ST*], SP $\vdash t = t'$ if Cond $\wedge\ b =$ not $b \wedge$ Cond$'$ for all ground terms b of sort Bool. It follows that the entailment system defined above is closed to the following rule of inference

$$[IC]\frac{}{\text{SP} \vdash t = t' \text{ if Cond} \wedge b = \text{not } b \wedge \text{Cond}'}$$

where BOOL $\hookrightarrow$ SP is a specification morphism and $(t = t'$ if Cond $\wedge\ b =$ not $b \wedge$ Cond$')$ is a quantifier-free sentence such that b is a ground term of sort Bool. [*IC*] is crucial for the automation since the equation $b =$ not b might cause a non-terminating process when added to SP by the [*IP*] rule.

Normal Forms [*NF*]. Algebraic specification languages executable by rewriting are equipped with a partial function $nf_{\text{SP}} : T_{\mathbb{S}ig(\text{SP})} \to T_{\mathbb{S}ig(\text{SP})}$ for all specifications SP such that for all $t \in T_{\mathbb{S}ig(\text{SP})}$, $nf_{\text{SP}}(t)$ is a normal form of t w.r.t. $\mathbb{A}x(\text{SP})$ if one exists, and $nf_{\text{SP}}(t)$ is undefined, otherwise. Note that SP $\vdash^b t = t'$ iff $nf_{\text{SP}}(t)$ and $nf_{\text{SP}}(t')$ are defined and equal.

Let $nf_{\text{SP}} : \mathbb{S}en(\text{SP}) \to \mathbb{S}en(\text{SP})$ be the canonical extension of $nf : T_{\mathbb{S}ig(\text{SP})} \to T_{\mathbb{S}ig(\text{SP})}$. The following rule of inference can be obtained by a successive application of [*SR*]:

$$[NF]\frac{\text{SP} \vdash nf_{\text{SP}}(\rho)}{\text{SP} \vdash \rho}$$

where ρ is any sentence.

Proposition 14. *The entailment system defined in Theorem 1 is closed to* [*NF*].

Proof. Let t_1 be a ground term occurring in ρ. Since SP $\vdash^b t_1 = nf(t_1)$, by [*SR*] the entailment system of Theorem 1 is closed to the following rule of inference: $\frac{\text{SP} \vdash \rho[t_1 \leftarrow nf(t_1)]}{\text{SP} \vdash \rho}$. Let $\{t_1, \ldots, t_n\}$ be all ground terms occurring in ρ. Note that $nf(\rho) = \rho[t_1 \leftarrow nf(t_1), \ldots, t_n \leftarrow nf(t_n)]$. By applying n times the rule [*SR*] we get that the entailment system defined in Theorem 1 is closed to [*NF*].   □

In order to preserve the confluence property of specifications in the proof process, each application of any of the proof rules above is preceded by a reduction of the ground terms occurring in the formulas to prove to their normal forms. In practice, the proof of a goal SP $\vdash \rho$ stops if $nf_{\text{SP}}(\rho)$ is undefined. The following simple example illustrates the benefit of this tactic.

Example 1. Consider a specification SP with three constant symbols a b c : $\to$ s and one equation a = b. If we apply [*IP*] to SP $\vdash b = c$ if a = c we get SP $\cup$ $(\mathbb{S}ig(\text{SP}), \{a = c\}) \vdash b = c$, and SP $\cup (\mathbb{S}ig(\text{SP}), \{a = c\})$ is not confluent because the critical pair c $\leftarrow$ a $\to$ b is not joinable. On the other hand, if a reduction to the normal forms is performed then the new goal is SP $\vdash b = c$ if b = c, which is reduced to SP $\cup (\mathbb{S}ig(\text{SP}), \{b = c\}) \vdash b = c$ by [*IP*]. By applying [*NF*] we get SP $\cup (\mathbb{S}ig(\text{SP}), \{b = c\}) \vdash c = c$; finally SP $\cup (\mathbb{S}ig(\text{SP}), \{b = c\}) \vdash c = c$ is discharged by [*RD*].

Since $[NF]$ is coupled with any other proof rule, it will be omitted from the discussions.

Case Analysis (revisited). In practice, we give labels to conditional equations used for case analysis. It follows that the $[CA]$-sets of sentences are part of the specification. Given a specification SP let $CA(\text{SP}) = (\{(\forall X_j)(\forall Y_j^i)u_j = v_j^i \text{ if Cond}^i \mid i = \overline{1, n_j}\})_{j \in J} \subseteq \mathcal{P}(\mathbb{A}x(\text{SP}))$ be the family of all $[CA]$-sets of sentences of SP. Consider a ground term $t \in T_{\mathbb{S}ig(\text{SP})}$. We say that t_1 is a $[CA]$-*subterm* of t if there exists $j_{t_1} \in J$ such that

(1) $u_{j_{t_1}}$ matches t_1, i.e. there exists a substitution $\theta_{t_1} : X \to T_{\mathbb{S}ig(\text{SP})}$ such that $\theta(u_{j_{t_1}}) = t_1$, and

(2) there is no $j \in J$ such that u_j matches a proper subterm of t_1.

Assume a goal SP $\vdash \rho$ and a ground term t occurring in ρ. Consider the tactic which consists of successive applications of $[CA]$, one for each $[CA]$-subterm of t. This tactic will replace $[CA]$ defined above. In applications, t is selected automatically from the list of all ground terms which occur in ρ.

Example 2. Consider the specification morphism NAT $\hookrightarrow$ FUN, where FUN is a specification with two functions over the natural numbers:

(1) F is defined by the following $[CA]$-set: $\begin{cases} \text{F}(\text{X}) = 5 \text{ if X} \texttt{<=} 7, \\ \text{F}(\text{X}) = 1 \text{ if } 8 \texttt{<=} \text{X}. \end{cases}$

(2) G is defined by the following $[CA]$-set: $\begin{cases} \text{G}(\text{Y}) = 2 \text{ if Y} \texttt{<=} 4, \\ \text{G}(\text{Y}) = 7 \text{ if } 5 \texttt{<=} \text{Y}. \end{cases}$

Suppose we want to prove FUN $\vdash (\forall \text{X}) 9 \texttt{<=} \text{G}(\text{F}(\text{X})) + \text{G}(\text{X}) = \textbf{true}$. By $[TC]$ the new goal is FUN $* \iota_{\text{X1}} \vdash 9 \texttt{<=} \text{G}(\text{F}(\text{X1})) + \text{G}(\text{X1}) = \textbf{true}$, where $\iota_{\text{X1}} : \mathbb{S}ig(\text{FUN}) \hookrightarrow \mathbb{S}ig(\text{FUN})[\text{X1}]$ is the inclusion of signatures. Case analysis is performed with respect to the $[CA]$-subterms F(X1) and G(X1) of the term $9 \texttt{<=} \text{G}(\text{F}(\text{X1})) + \text{G}(\text{X1})$. There are four cases:

(a) X1 $\texttt{<=}$ 4, (c) 8 $\texttt{<=}$ X1 $\texttt{<=}$ 4,
(b) 5 $\texttt{<=}$ X1 $\texttt{<=}$ 7, (d) 8 $\texttt{<=}$ X1.

Note that the cases (a), (b) and (d) are discharged by $[RD]$ while the case (c) is discharged by $[LE]$. The corresponding proof tree is depicted in the figure below, where the circles represent the empty goal set.

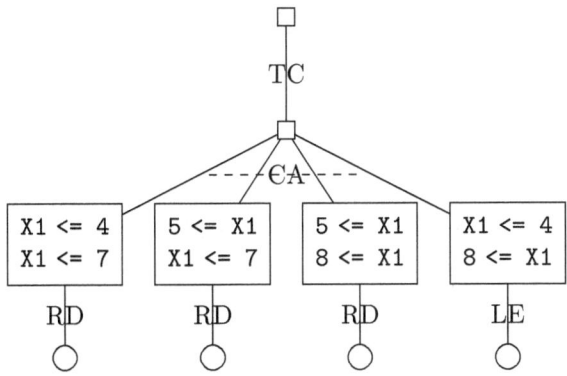

Remark 2. The proof of FUN $\vdash (\forall X)9 <= G(F(X))+G(X) = true$ can be performed automatically by CITP by giving the command (apply TC CA RD .).

Note that $[LE]$ is applied automatically by CITP without giving an explicit command. The idea is that the interaction with the user is not needed to discharge goals with inconsistent specifications. Hence, $[IC]$ and $[CT]$ are applied also automatically by CITP.

Proof Strategy. Except $[SI]$, all basic tactics are designed for goals consisting of a specification and a single formula. We make the following convention: if a tactic different from $[SI]$ is applied to a goal of the form $SP \vdash \{\rho_1, \ldots, \rho_n\}$, the goal is decomposed into a set of subgoals $\{SP \vdash \rho_1, \ldots, SP \vdash \rho_n\}$, and then the tactic is applied to each $SP \vdash \rho_i$.

The application order of the basic tactics is crucial for automating the proof process. $[SI]$ is applied first. $[TC]$ is performed before $[IC]$ as $[IC]$ can be applied only to goals with quantifier-free formulas. $[IC]$ discharges any goal of the form $SP \vdash atm$ if $Cond \wedge b = not\ b \wedge Cond'$, otherwise $[IC]$ leaves the goal unchanged. An application of $[IP]$ is preceded by an application of $[IC]$. $[RD]$ attempts to discharge any goal with an atomic formula. If $[RD]$ fails to complete the proof then $[CT]$ and $[LE]$ tactics are used.

The order of tactic applications described above is well-established for all goals. However, the application of case analysis depends on the problem to solve. Based on the case studies, we have two proof strategies:

(1) $[SI]$, $[CA]$, $[SC]$, $[TC]$, $[IC]$, $[IP]$, $[RD]$, $[CT]$, $[LE]$, and
(2) $[SI]$, $[TC]$, $[CA]$, $[IC]$, $[IP]$, $[RD]$, $[CT]$, $[LE]$.

A tactic can be applied to a goal if it has a certain pattern, otherwise the tactic leaves the goal unchanged. Note that not all OTS are modelled using sequences. In such a case the application of $[SC]$ leaves the goal unchanged. The advantages of these proof strategies can be noticed clearly in concrete examples which can be found at http://www.jaist.ac.jp/~danielmg/citp.html.

The present methodology does not include automatic lemma discovery. It is for the user to find the appropriate induction scheme for the problem to solve, and the constrained variables for induction.

3   Methodology at Work: ABP Case Study

Alternating Bit Protocol is a communication protocol that enables to send reliable messages on unreliable channels. It is often used as a case study, either for some algebraic formalisms or for tools dedicated to analysis or verification of concurrent systems. Even if the protocol seems to be simple, its complete algebraic specification is quite complex and its formal correctness proof is very large. We show that using our methodology, most of the proving process can be automated.

Since this section involves the operational semantics of the system that assists the proofs, we write the formulas in Maude-like notation, meaning that we omit the universal quantifier and we distinguish ordinary equations from matching equations.

3.1   The ABP Protocol

We describe briefly the protocol. Two processes, *Sender* and *Receiver*, that do not share any common memory use two channels to communicate with each other. Sender sends repeatedly a pair `< bit1,pac >` of a bit and a packet to the receiver over one of the channels, let's say `channel1`. When Sender gets `bit1` from Receiver over the other channel, let's say `channel2`, it is a confirmation from Receiver that the packet sent was received. In this case Sender alternates `bit1` and selects the next packet for sending. Receiver puts `bit2` into `channel2` repeatedly. When Receiver gets a pair `< b,p >` such that `b` is different from `bit2` it stores `p` into a `list` and alternates `bit2`. Initially both channels are empty and the Sender's bit is different from the Receiver's bit. We assume that the channels are unreliable, meaning that the data in the channels may be lost, but not exchanged or damaged.

The packets sent by Sender to Receiver through `channel1` are indexed by the natural numbers and are of the form $pac(0), pac(s0), \ldots, pac(s^n0)$, where `op pac : Nat -> Packet` is the constructor for packets. The bits sent by both Sender and Receiver into the communication channels are modelled by the boolean values `true` and `false`. The communication channels and the packets received by the Receiver are modelled by sequences.

(a) `channel1` consists of sequences of pairs of bits and packets of the form $< b_1, p_1 >, \ldots, < b_n, p_n >$.
(b) `channel2` consists of sequences of bits of the form $b_1, \ldots, b_n$.
(c) The `list` of packets received by Receiver consists of sequences of packets of the form $p_1, \ldots, p_n$.

In the OTS/CafeOBJ method the transitions between the states of the system are modelled with constructor operators. For the ABP specification, the constructors are the following ones:

Constructor	Meaning
`init : -> Sys`	Initial state
`rec1 : Sys -> Sys`	Sender receives bits
`rec2 : Sys -> Sys`	Receiver receives pairs of bits & packets
`send1 : Sys -> Sys`	Sender sends pairs of bits & packets
`send2 : Sys -> Sys`	Receiver sends bits
`drop1 : Sys -> Sys`	Dropping one element of channel1
`drop2 : Sys -> Sys`	Dropping one element of channel2

The structure of a state is abstracted by the following observers, each one returning an observable information about the state:

Observer	Meaning
`channel1 : Sys -> Channel1`	Sender-to-Receiver channel
`channel2 : Sys -> Channel2`	Receiver-to-Sender channel
`bit1 : Sys -> Bit`	Sender's bit
`bit2 : Sys -> Bit`	Receiver's bit
`next : Sys -> Nat`	Number of packet sent by Sender
`list : Sys -> List`	Lists of packets received by Receiver

The meaning of an observer is formally described by means of (conditional) equations. For instance, the value of `bit1` after the application of `rec1` is described by the following $[CA]$-set of conditional equations:

```
bit1(rec1(S))= bit1(S)     if channel2(S)= empty
bit1(rec1(S))= bit1(S)     if B,C2 := channel2(S)/\ B = not bit1(S)
bit1(rec1(S))= not bit1(S) if B,C2 := channel2(S)/\ B = bit1(S)
```

More tricky is the specification of loosing data from the channels, because the dropped elements are arbitrarily chosen. We use "underspecified" operations to model the dropping actions. For instance, the value of `channel1` after the application of `drop1` is specified by two operations `p1 r1 : Sys -> Channel1` and the following $[CA]$-set of conditional equations:

```
channel1(drop1(S))= p1(S),r1(S) if p1(S),< B,P >,r1(S) := channel1(S)
channel1(drop1(S))= channel1(S) if match(channel1(S),p1(S),r1(S))= false
```

Roughly speaking, the arguments of `p1` and `r1` are constructor terms of the form $\sigma_n(\ldots\sigma_1(\text{init}))$, where $\sigma_i \in \{\text{rec1},\ldots,\text{drop2}\}$, and the values returned are sequences because the communication channels are protected. There are no equations to define `p1` and `r1`, meaning that each model has its own interpretation of `p1` and `r1`. If `channel1(S)` is matched by `p1(S),< B,P >,r1(S)` then the element `< B,P >` is dropped, otherwise, `drop1` does not affect the system state. Each model of the specification is deterministic but the non-deterministic behaviour consists of the different interpretations of the functions `p1` and `r1` into the models. An application of `drop1` to a given state does not change the values of `bit1`, `bit2`, `next` and `list`.

3.2 The Correctness Proof

We will explain our methodology by proving a safety property for ABP. The protocol is specified using only conditional equations. In order to avoid non-termination in the proof process, we use preorder axioms with the semantic of equality. The proof begins with the following four lemmas:

(1) If `channel1` contains `bit1` then all bits before `bit1` are equal to `bit1`.

$$\text{inv1} \overset{def}{=} \text{B' => bit1(S) if}$$
$$\text{C1,< B,P >,C2,< B',P' >,C3 := channel1(S)} \bigwedge \text{B = bit1(S)}$$

(2) All bits of `channel1` are equal to `bit1` when `bit2` is equal to `bit1`.

$$\text{inv2} \overset{def}{=} \text{B => bit1(S) if}$$
$$\text{C1,< B,P >,C2 := channel1(S)} \bigwedge \text{bit2(S) = bit1(S)}$$

(3) `bit2` is equal to `bit1` when `channel2` contains `bit1`.

$$\text{inv3} \overset{def}{=} \text{bit2(S) = bit1(S) if}$$
$$\text{D1,B,D2 := channel2(S)} \bigwedge \text{B = bit1(S)}$$

(4) If `channel2` contains `bit1` then all the bits before `bit1` are equal to `bit1`.

$$\text{inv4} \overset{def}{=} \text{B' => bit1(S) if}$$
$$\text{D1,B,D2,B',D3 := channel2(S)} \bigwedge \text{B = bit1(S)}$$

Remark 3. The invariants inv1, inv2 and inv4 are specified as preorder axioms. As equations the above invariants would cause non-termination: when [*SI*] is applied to the goal ABP ⊢ {inv1, inv2, inv3, inv4}, invi are added as hypotheses to the specification ABP; then an application of inv1, for example, to reduce a term implies the evaluation of the condition C1,< B,P >,C2,< B',P' >,C3 := channel1(S) that requires another application of inv1, which produces a non-termination process. Since these hypotheses are needed in the verification process, i.e., they must be executable, we choose to formalise them as preorder axioms. In this way, the termination property is preserved and the new (equational and preorder) axioms are executable.

The invariants cannot be proved independently (without a simultaneous induction scheme) since the proof of each invariant depends on the rest.

Secondly, we prove the following invariant by (ordinary) structural induction using the invariants above.

$$\text{inv5} \overset{def}{=} \text{P => pac(next(S)) if C1,< B,P >,C2 := channel1(S)} \bigwedge \text{B = bit1(S)}$$

The invariant inv5 says that if `channel1` contains a pair < B,P > and B is equal to `bit1` then P is equal to `pac(next)`.

When Receiver gets the nth packet it has received $pac(0), \ldots, pac(n)$, in this order. Each $pac(i)$ for $i = 0, \ldots, n$ has been received only once, and no other packet have been received. This property is formalised below.

$$\text{goal1} \overset{def}{=} \text{mk(next)(S) = pac(next(S)),list(S) if bit1(S) = not bit2(S)}$$
$$\text{goal2} \overset{def}{=} \text{mk(next)(S) = list(S) if bit1(S) = bit2(S)}$$

where $\mathtt{mk}$: $\mathtt{Nat}$ $\rightarrow$ $\mathtt{List}$ is defined by $\begin{cases} \mathrm{mk}(0) = \mathrm{pac}(0), \\ \mathrm{mk}(\mathrm{s}\ \mathrm{n}) = \mathrm{pac}(\mathrm{s}\ \mathrm{n})\mathrm{mk}(\mathrm{n}). \end{cases}$ The formulas $\mathtt{goal1}$ and $\mathtt{goal2}$ are proved by simultaneous induction using $\mathtt{inv2}$, $\mathtt{inv3}$ and $\mathtt{inv5}$. We present the proof of the four invariants as the rest of the proof is similar.

Let $\mathtt{INV} = \mathtt{ABP} \cup (\mathbb{S}ig(\mathtt{ABP}), \{\mathtt{lemma-inc}\})$, where

$$\mathtt{lemma-inc} \overset{def}{=} \mathtt{true} \ \Rightarrow \ \mathtt{false} \ \mathtt{if} \ \mathtt{not} \ \mathtt{bit1(S)} \ \Rightarrow \ \mathtt{bit1(S)}$$

The above axiom says that $\mathtt{not}$ $\mathtt{bit1(S)}$ and $\mathtt{bit1(S)}$ are different for all system states $\mathtt{S}$. Note that $\mathtt{lemma-inc}$ is not executable since the left-hand side term is ground and the condition contains the variable $\mathtt{S}$. The proof of $\mathtt{INV} \vdash \{\mathtt{inv1}, \mathtt{inv2}, \mathtt{inv3}, \mathtt{inv4}\}$ is performed with CITP using the proof strategy $[SI]$, $[CA]$, $[SC]$, $[TC]$, $[IC]$, $[IP]$, $[RD]$, $[CT]$. The goal is generated by the following command:

```
(goal INV |-
crl [inv1]: B1:Bit => bit1(S:Sys) if
 C1:Channel1,< B:Bit,P:Packet >,C2:Channel1,< B1:Bit,P1:Packet >,C3:Channel1
 := channel1(S:Sys) ∧ B:Bit = bit1(S:Sys) ;
crl [inv2]: B:Bit => bit1(S:Sys) if
 C1:Channel1,< B:Bit,P:Packet >,C2:Channel1 := channel1(S:Sys) ∧
 bit2(S:Sys) = bit1(S:Sys) ;
ceq [inv3]: bit2(S:Sys) = bit1(S:Sys) if
 C2:Channel2,B:Bit,C3:Channel2 := channel2(S:Sys) ∧ B:Bit = bit1(S:Sys)
 [metadata "enhanced"];
crl [inv4]: B':Bit => bit1(S:Sys) if
 D1:Channel2,B:Bit,D2:Channel2,B':Bit,D3:Channel2 := channel2(S:Sys) ∧
 B:Bit = bit1(S:Sys) ; )
```

CITP discharges an equation $t_1 = t_2$ with the attribute $\mathtt{"enhanced"}$ by proving $t_1 \Rightarrow t_2$. The proof consists of the sequence of commands described below.

```
(set ind on S:Sys .)        --- rec1 ---
(apply SI .)                (init lemma-inc by S:Sys <- X1 .) (auto .)

--- init ---                --- rec2 ---
(auto .)                    (init lemma-inc by S:Sys <- X1 .) (auto .)

--- drop1 ---               --- send1 ---
(auto .)                    (auto .)

--- drop2 ---               --- send2 ---
(auto .)                    (auto .)
```

The variable $\mathtt{S}$ is selected for induction. By applying $[SI]$ we obtain seven subgoals corresponding to each of the seven constructors:

$$\mathtt{INV} * \iota_{X1} \cup (\mathbb{S}ig(\mathtt{INV})[X1], \Gamma[S \leftarrow X1]) \vdash \Gamma[S \leftarrow \sigma(X1)]$$

where $\iota_{X1} : \mathbb{S}ig(\mathtt{INV}) \hookrightarrow \mathbb{S}ig(\mathtt{INV})[X1]$, $\mathtt{X1}$ is a constant representing an arbitrary state of the system, $\sigma \in \{\mathtt{init}, \mathtt{rec1}, \mathtt{rec2}, \mathtt{send1}, \mathtt{send2}, \mathtt{drop1}, \mathtt{drop2}\}$, and

$\Gamma = \{\texttt{inv1}, \texttt{inv2}, \texttt{inv3}, \texttt{inv4}\}$. For the cases $\sigma = \texttt{rec1}$ and $\sigma = \texttt{rec2}$, $\texttt{lemma-inc}$ is instantiated by substituting $\texttt{X1}$ for $\texttt{S}$. Then each of the remaining goals is split into four subgoals corresponding to each invariant. We obtain 28 subgoals that are discharged automatically by the command ($\texttt{auto .}$) which uses the proof strategy $[SI]$, $[CA]$, $[SC]$, $[TC]$, $[IC]$, $[IP]$, $[RD]$, $[CT]$. Note that the application of $[SI]$ at this point leaves the goal unchanged. The proof tree corresponding to $\texttt{INV} * \iota_{\texttt{X1}} \cup (\mathbb{S}ig(\texttt{INV})[\texttt{X1}], \Gamma[S \leftarrow \texttt{X1}], \texttt{lemma-inc}[S \leftarrow \texttt{X1}]) \vdash \texttt{inv2}[S \leftarrow \texttt{rec1}(\texttt{X1})]$ is depicted in the figure below:

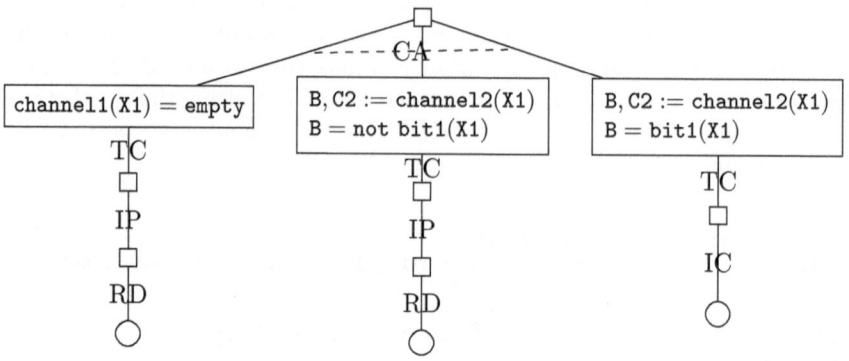

Note that $[CA]$ is performed w.r.t. the $[CA]$-subterm $\texttt{bit1(rec1(X1))}$. There are three cases given by the conditions of the $[CA]$-set of sentences which defines the value of $\texttt{bit1}$ after the execution of $\texttt{rec1}$ at a given state. The proof tree corresponding to $\texttt{INV} * \iota_{\texttt{X1}} \cup (\mathbb{S}ig(\texttt{INV})[\texttt{X1}], \Gamma[S \leftarrow \texttt{X1}]) \vdash \texttt{inv2}[S \leftarrow \texttt{drop1}(\texttt{X1})]$ is depicted in the following figure.

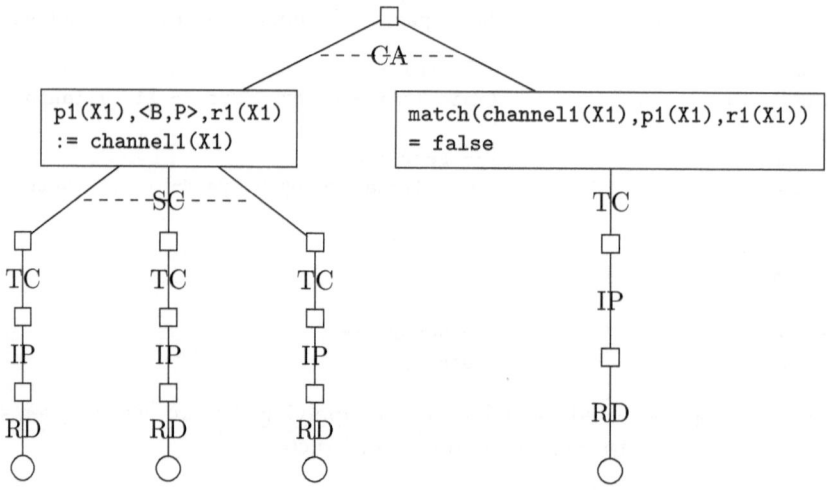

In this case, CA is performed w.r.t. the $[CA]$-subterm $\texttt{channel1(drop1(X1))}$. The interested reader can look into $\texttt{http://www.ldl.jaist.ac.jp/citp/}$ for tool demonstration.

4   Conclusions

We presented a methodology for proving inductive properties of OTS. The proposed method aims at automating the proof score approach to verification. We revise the entailment system in [9] to increase its efficiency in applications and we enrich it with a set of specific proof rules for initial data types that are often used in our methodology. We define proof tactics that preserve confluence and termination of the specifications in the proof process, and we propose a proof strategy to apply the tactics automatically. The viability of the methodology is demonstrated by CITP, a prototype tool implementing the methodology. We used the ABP example in order to exhibit the main strong points of the proposed methodology. Algebraic specification languages have standard libraries with predefined modules. In order to perform verification of complex software systems it is crucial to have tactics for the initial data types that are often used in practice such as booleans, sequences or natural numbers. The challenge is how to integrate these tactics with the ones for loose semantics and to push the boundaries of automation.

The logical frameworks underlying tools like Circ [19,16] or Maude ITP [18] do not include preorder axioms, and are not based on constructors. Circ implements a similar tactic with the *Case Analysis* proposed here. *Case analysis* is interactive in Maude ITP. Another paper that uses the ABP as a benchmark example is [14]. The proof in [14] is coinductive and it is based on the circular coinductive rewriting algorithm [15] implemented in the BOBJ system. In [14], the unreliability of the communication channels is modelled by "fair streams", while here it is modelled by a special dropping operation that is closer to a real description. With the OTS approach, the ABP specification is closer to a faithful representation, and since all data types are specified in detail, the proof becomes more complex.

Future work includes testing of the methodology on other case studies, and increasing the automation level.

Acknowledgements. The work presented in this paper has been partially supported by the Japanese Contract Kakenhi 23220002, and by the Romanian Contract 161/15.06.2010, SMISCSNR 602-12516 (DAK).

References

1. Bidoit, M., Hennicker, R.: Constructor-based observational logic. J. Log. Algebr. Program. 67(1-2), 3–51 (2006)
2. Bidoit, M., Hennicker, R., Kurz, A.: Observational logic, constructor-based logic, and their duality. Theor. Comput. Sci. 3(298), 471–510 (2003)
3. Borzyszkowski, T.: Logical systems for structured specifications. Theor. Comput. Sci. 286(2), 197–245 (2002)
4. Clavel, M., Durán, F., Eker, S., Lincoln, P., Martí-Oliet, N., Meseguer, J., Talcott, C.: All About Maude - A High-Performance Logical Framework. LNCS, vol. 4350. Springer, Heidelberg (2007)

5. Diaconescu, R., Futatsugi, K.: CafeOBJ Report: The Language, Proof Techniques, and Methodologies for Object-Oriented Algebraic Specification. AMAST Series in Computing, vol. 6. World Scientific (1998)
6. Diaconescu, R., Futatsugi, K.: Logical foundations of CafeOBJ. Theor. Comput. Sci. 285(2), 289–318 (2002)
7. Futatsugi, K.: Verifying Specifications with Proof Scores in CafeOBJ. In: ASE, pp. 3–10. IEEE Computer Society (2006)
8. Futatsugi, K., Goguen, J.A., Ogata, K.: Verifying Design with Proof Scores. In: Meyer, B., Woodcock, J. (eds.) Verified Software. LNCS, vol. 4171, pp. 277–290. Springer, Heidelberg (2008)
9. Futatsugi, K., Găină, D., Ogata, K.: Principles of proof scores in CafeOBJ. Theor. Comput. Sci. 464, 90–112 (2012)
10. Găină, D., Futatsugi, K.: Initial Semantics in Logics with Constructors. J. Log. Comput (2013), http://dx.doi.org/10.1093/logcom/exs044
11. Găină, D., Zhang, M., Chiba, Y., Arimoto, Y.: Constructor-based Inductive Theorem Prover. In: Heckel, R. (ed.) CALCO 2013. LNCS, vol. 8089, pp. 328–333. Springer, Heidelberg (2013)
12. Goguen, J.: Theorem Proving and Algebra (1994)
13. Goguen, J.A., Burstall, R.: Institutions: Abstract Model Theory for Specification and Programming. Journal of the Association for Computing Machinery 39(1), 95–146 (1992)
14. Goguen, J.A., Lin, K.: Behavioral Verification of Distributed Concurrent Systems with BOBJ. In: 3rd International Conference on Quality Software (QSIC), p. 216 (2003)
15. Goguen, J.A., Lin, K., Rosu, G.: Circular Coinductive Rewriting. In: ASE, pp. 123–132 (2000)
16. Goriac, E.-I., Lucanu, D., Roşu, G.: Automating Coinduction with Case Analysis. In: Dong, J.S., Zhu, H. (eds.) ICFEM 2010. LNCS, vol. 6447, pp. 220–236. Springer, Heidelberg (2010)
17. Găină, D., Futatsugi, K., Ogata, K.: Constructor-based Logics. J. UCS 18(16), 2204–2233 (2012)
18. Hendrix, J.D.: Decision Procedures for Equationally Based Reasoning. Technical Report, UIUC (2008)
19. Lucanu, D., Goriac, E.-I., Caltais, G., Roşu, G.: CIRC: A Behavioral Verification Tool based on Circular Coinduction. In: Kurz, A., Lenisa, M., Tarlecki, A. (eds.) CALCO 2009. LNCS, vol. 5728, pp. 433–442. Springer, Heidelberg (2009)
20. Meseguer, J.: Order-Sorted Parameterization and Induction. In: Palsberg, J. (ed.) Mosses Festschrift. LNCS, vol. 5700, pp. 43–80. Springer, Heidelberg (2009)
21. Ogata, K., Futatsugi, K.: Flaw and modification of the iKP electronic payment protocols. Inf. Process. Lett. 86(2), 57–62 (2003)
22. Ogata, K., Futatsugi, K.: Simulation-based Verification for Invariant Properties in the OTS/CafeOBJ Method. Electr. Notes Theor. Comput. Sci. 201, 127–154 (2008)
23. Sannella, D., Tarlecki, A.: Specifications in an Arbitrary Institution. Inf. Comput. 76(2/3), 165–210 (1988)

Mechanical Analysis of Reliable Communication in the Alternating Bit Protocol Using the Maude Invariant Analyzer Tool

Camilo Rocha[1] and José Meseguer[2]

[1] Escuela Colombiana de Ingeniería, Bogotá, Colombia
[2] University of Illinois at Urbana-Champaign, Urbana IL, USA

Abstract. The InvA tool supports the deductive verification of safety properties of infinite-state concurrent systems. Given a concurrent system specified as a rewrite theory and a safety formula to be verified, InvA reduces such a formula to inductive properties of the underlying equational theory by means of the application of a few inference rules. Through the combination of various techniques such as unification, narrowing, equationally-defined equality predicates, and SMT solving, InvA achieves a significant degree of automation, verifying automatically many proof obligations. Maude Inductive Theorem Prover (ITP) can be used to discharge the remaining obligations which are not automatically verified by InvA. Verification of the reliable communication ensured by the Alternating Bit Protocol (ABP) is used as a case study to explain the use of the InvA tool, and to illustrate its effectiveness and degree of automation in a concrete way.

1   Introduction

The late Amir Pnueli entitled his invited talk at FM'99 "Deduction is Forever" [22]. Pnueli, who had pioneered the use of temporal logic in computer science as well as many model checking techniques, wanted to remind us that algorithmic verification methods are not enough by themselves and should always be complemented by deductive verification methods. What is actually happening is that model checking and theorem proving methods are increasingly used in tandem, and the borderline between both is becoming more tenuous. Verification of temporal logic properties, particularly for infinite-state systems, is an area where both algorithmic and deductive methods can be used, sometimes together.

In the rewriting logic research program [16], model checking methods and tools have been extensively developed. However, deductive techniques, while well-supported for equational specifications with an initial algebra semantics, do not directly apply to temporal logic formulas. One important exception is the deductive verification approach with *proof scores* and the *OTS/CafeOBJ method* [9,19], pioneered by Kokichi Futatsugi and his collaborators, for the verification of *invariants* of concurrent systems. By using such an approach quite

S. Iida, J. Meseguer, and K. Ogata (Eds.): Futatsugi Festschrift, LNCS 8373, pp. 603–629, 2014.

sophisticated systems have been verified [20,21]. Work on the OTS/CafeOBJ method has stimulated our own work on deductive verification of concurrent systems. Indeed, the work presented here is a concrete example of the way in which we have responded to such an encouraging stimulus. Our main purpose has been to advance the following goals:

1. **Deductive Support for Temporal Logic**. Beyond invariants, deductive reasoning about other temporal logic properties should be supported. For the moment we have advanced this to support a useful subset of *safety properties*, but we hope to extend the methods to also support liveness properties.
2. **Reduction of Temporal Verification to Equational Verification**. As much as possible, temporal logic properties should be construed as "syntactic sugar" for inductive properties of an algebraic specification corresponding to the system's states and the predicates satisfied by such states. In this way, all the wealth of techniques and tools already available to verify properties of algebraic specifications with an initial algebra semantics can be leveraged.
3. **Increased automation**. To reduce the verification effort, the level of automation should be increased as much as possible, both at the level of reasoning about temporal properties, and after reducing such properties to inductive proof obligations in equational logic.

Our way to advance goals (1)–(3) has been to develop new deductive verification techniques, embody them in the InvA tool [23,24] as part of the Maude formal environment, and test the practical advancement of goals (1)–(3) through case studies. We can summarize our present advances as follows. Goals (1) and (2) have been advanced by (i) identifying a class of commonly used safety properties; and (ii) developing and proving correct a set of inference rules that reduce the verification of such safety properties to inductive equational reasoning. A key technique for this reduction has been the use of unification and narrowing to prove stability properties in an inductive way. The development of Goal (3) has been advanced by a combination of automation techniques including: (i) automation of narrowing and unification in the underlying Maude system; (ii) automation of certain conditional inferences; (iii) systematic use of equationally-defined equality predicates [12]; (iv) use of SMT solvers; and (v) use of proof tactics in the Maude ITP.

Although still work in progress and amenable to many subsequent improvements and extensions, it seems fair to say that the advances in goals (1)–(3) supported by the InvA tool have been significant. A good way to give a feeling for such advances is to explain how they have helped in automating a remarkable amount of proof tasks when verifying a well-known benchmark verified by other systems, and in particular by the OTS/CafeOBJ methodology and tool, namely, the reliable communication ensured by the Alternating Bit Protocol. This also makes it possible to compare our proof efforts with those in OTS/CafeOBJ and measure advances in Goal (3) in a concrete and meaningful way.

In summary, therefore, this work should be seen in the context of a very long and broader exchange of ideas with Kokichi Futatsugi and his collaborators in the CafeOBJ group, which has stimulated advances in both Maude and

CafeOBJ. In particular, it has been a pleasure to discuss our ideas about InvA with Kokichi Futatsugi and Kazuhiro Ogata, and to benefit from their experience in the deductive verification of invariants. This work is cordially dedicated to Kokichi Futasugi in the spirit of such a long term and very fruitful exchange of ideas.

2   Preliminaries

This paper follows notation and terminology from [15] for order-sorted equational logic and from [5] for rewriting logic.

An *order sorted signature* Σ is a tuple $\Sigma = (S, \leq, F)$ with finite poset of sorts $(S, \leq)$ and a finite S-index set of function symbols $F = \{F_{w,s}\}_{(w,s) \in S^* \times S}$. It is assumed that: (i) each connected component of a sort $s \in S$ in the poset ordering has a top sort, denoted by k_s, and (ii) for each operator declaration $f \in F_{s_1 \ldots s_n, s}$ there is also a declaration $f \in F_{k_{s_1} \ldots k_{s_n}, k_s}$. The collection $X = \{X_s\}_{s \in S}$ is an S-sorted family of disjoint sets of variables with each X_s countably infinite. The set of terms of sort s is denoted by $T_\Sigma(X)_s$ and the set of ground terms of sort s is denoted by $T_{\Sigma,s}$, which are assumed nonempty for each s. The expressions $T_\Sigma(X)$ and T_Σ denote the respective term algebras. The set of variables of a term t is written $vars(t)$ and is extended to sets of terms in the natural way. A *substitution* θ is a sorted map from a finite subset $dom(\theta) \subseteq X$ to $T_\Sigma(X)$ and extends homomorphically in the natural way; $ran(\theta)$ denotes the set of variables introduced by θ and $t\theta$ the application of θ to a term t. Substitution $\theta_1\theta_2$ is the composition of substitutions θ_1 and θ_2. A substitution θ is called *ground* iff $ran(\theta) = \varnothing$.

A *Σ-equation* is a Horn clause $t = u$ **if** γ, where $t = u$ is a *Σ-equality* with $t, u \in T_\Sigma(X)_s$ for some sort $s \in S$, and the *condition* γ is a finite conjunction of Σ-equalities $\bigwedge_{i \in I} t_i = u_i$. An *equational theory* is a tuple (Σ, E) with order-sorted signature Σ and finite set of Σ-equations E. For φ a Σ-equation, $(\Sigma, E) \vdash \varphi$ iff φ can be proved from (Σ, E) by the deduction rules in [15] iff φ is valid in all models of (Σ, E); assuming $T_{\Sigma,s} \neq \varnothing$ for each $s \in S$, (Σ, E) induces the congruence relation $=_E$ on $T_\Sigma(X)$ defined for any $t, u \in T_\Sigma(X)$ by $t =_E u$ iff $(\Sigma, E) \vdash t = u$. The expressions $T_{\Sigma/E}(X)$ and $T_{\Sigma/E}$ denote the quotient algebras induced by $=_E$ over the algebras $T_\Sigma(X)$ and T_Σ, respectively; $T_{\Sigma/E}$ is the *initial algebra* of (Σ, E). An *E-unifier* for a Σ-equality $t = u$ is a substitution θ such that $t\theta =_E u\theta$. A *complete* set of E-unifiers for a Σ-equality $t = u$ is written $CSU_E(t = u)$ and it is called *finitary* if it contains a finite number of E-unifiers. The expression $CU_E(t = u)$ denotes the set of ground E-unifiers of a Σ-equality $t = u$. A theory inclusion $(\Sigma, E) \subseteq (\Sigma', E')$ is *protecting* iff the unique Σ-homomorphism $T_{\Sigma/E} \longrightarrow T_{\Sigma'/E'}|_\Sigma$ to the Σ-reduct of the initial algebra $T_{\Sigma'/E'}$ is an isomorphism.

A *Σ-rule* is a sentence $t \to u$ **if** γ, where $t \to u$ is a *Σ-sequent* with $t, u \in T_\Sigma(X)_s$ for some sort $s \in S$ and the *condition* γ is a finite conjunction of Σ-equalities. A *rewrite theory* is a tuple $\mathcal{R} = (\Sigma, E, R)$ with equational theory $\mathcal{E}_\mathcal{R} = (\Sigma, E)$ and a finite set of Σ-rules R. A *topmost rewrite theory* is a rewrite theory $\mathcal{R} = (\Sigma, E, R)$ such that for some top sort $\mathfrak{s}$ and for each $t \to u$ **if** $\gamma \in R$, the terms t, u satisfy $t, u \in T_\Sigma(X)_\mathfrak{s}$ and $t \notin X$, and no operator in Σ has $\mathfrak{s}$ as argument sort. For $\mathcal{R} = (\Sigma, E, R)$ and φ a Σ-rule, $\mathcal{R} \vdash \varphi$ iff φ can be obtained from $\mathcal{R}$ by the deduction rules in [5] iff φ is valid in all models of $\mathcal{R}$. For φ a Σ-equation, $\mathcal{R} \vdash \varphi$ iff $\mathcal{E}_\mathcal{R} \vdash \varphi$. A rewrite theory $\mathcal{R} = (\Sigma, E, R)$ induces the rewrite relation $\to_\mathcal{R}$ on $T_{\Sigma/E}(X)$ defined for every $t, u \in T_\Sigma(X)$ by $[t]_E \to_\mathcal{R} [u]_E$ iff there is a *one-step* rewrite proof $\mathcal{R} \vdash t \to u$. The expressions $\mathcal{R} \vdash t \to u$ and $\mathcal{R} \vdash t \xrightarrow{*} u$ respectively denote a one-step rewrite proof and an arbitrary length (but finite) rewrite proof in $\mathcal{R}$ from t to u. The expression $\mathcal{T}_\mathcal{R} = (\mathcal{T}_{\Sigma/E}, \xrightarrow{*}_\mathcal{R})$ denotes the *initial reachability model* of $\mathcal{R} = (\Sigma, E, R)$ [5]. A Σ-sequent φ is an *inductive consequence* of $\mathcal{R}$ denoted $\mathcal{R} \Vdash \varphi$ iff $(\forall \theta : X \longrightarrow T_\Sigma) \mathcal{R} \vdash \varphi\theta$ iff $\mathcal{T}_\mathcal{R} \models \varphi$.

State predicates. A set of *state predicates* Π for $\mathcal{R} = (\Sigma, E, R)$ can be equationally-defined by an equational theory $\mathcal{E}_\Pi = (\Sigma_\Pi, E \uplus E_\Pi)$. Signature Σ_Π contains Σ, two sorts $Bool \leq [Bool]$ with constants $\top$ and $\bot$ of sort $Bool$, predicate symbols $p : \mathfrak{s} \longrightarrow [Bool]$ for each $p \in \Pi$, and optionally some auxiliary function symbols. Equations in E_Π define the predicate symbols in Σ_Π and auxiliary function symbols, if any; they protect (Σ, E) and the equational theory specifying sort $Bool$, constants $\top$ and $\bot$, and the Boolean operations. It is easy to define a state predicate $p \in \Pi$ as a Boolean combination of other already-defined state predicates $\{p_1, \ldots, p_n\}$ in Σ_Π. The reason why p has typing $p : \mathfrak{s} \longrightarrow [Bool]$ instead of $p : \mathfrak{s} \longrightarrow Bool$, is to allow partial definitions of p with equations that fully define the *positive* case by equations $p(t) = \top$ **if** γ, and either leave the *negative* case implicit or may only define some negative cases with equations $p(t') = \bot$ **if** γ' without necessarily covering all the cases.

LTL semantics. For $p \in \Pi$ and $[t]_E \in T_{\Sigma/E, \mathfrak{s}}$, $\mathcal{E}_\Pi$ defines the *semantics of* p in $\mathcal{T}_\mathcal{R}$ as follows: it is said that $p([t]_E)$ *holds* in $\mathcal{T}_\mathcal{R}$ iff $\mathcal{E}_\Pi \vdash p(t) = \top$. This defines a Kripke structure $\mathcal{K}_\mathcal{R}^\Pi = (T_{\Sigma/E, \mathfrak{s}}, \to_\mathcal{R}, L_\Pi)$ with labeling function L_Π such that, for each $[t]_E \in T_{\Sigma/E, \mathfrak{s}}$, the semantic equivalence $p \in L_\Pi([t]_E)$ iff $p([t]_E)$ holds in $\mathcal{T}_\mathcal{R}$. Then, all of LTL can be interpreted in $\mathcal{K}_\mathcal{R}^\Pi$ in the standard way [6], including the "always" ($\Box$), "next" ($\bigcirc$), and "strong implication" ($\Rightarrow$) operators.

Executability conditions. It is assumed that the set of equations of a rewrite theory $\mathcal{R}$ can be decomposed into a disjoint union $E \uplus B$, with B a collection of axioms (such as associativity, and/or commutativity, and/or identity) for which there exists a *matching algorithm modulo* B producing a finite number of B-matching substitutions, or failing otherwise. It is also assumed that the equations E can be oriented into a set of *ground sort-decreasing*, *ground confluent*, and *ground terminating* rules $\overrightarrow{E}$ modulo B. The expression $t \downarrow_{\Sigma, E/B} \in T_{\Sigma, s}(X)$ denotes the *E/B-canonical form* of $t \in T_\Sigma(X)$, which is guaranteed to exist under the executability conditions above mentioned. The rules R in $\mathcal{R}$ are assumed to be *ground coherent* relative to the equations E modulo B [28].

Free constructors. For $\mathcal{R} = (\Sigma, E \uplus B, R)$, the signature $\Omega \subseteq \Sigma$ is a signature of *free constructors* modulo B iff for each sort s in Σ and $t \in T_{\Sigma, s}$ there is $u \in T_{\Omega, s}$ satisfying $t =_{E \uplus B} u$, and $v \downarrow_{\Sigma, E/B} =_B v$ for any $v \in T_{\Omega, s}$. For the development in this paper it is required that $t \in T_{\Omega}(X)$ for each $t \to u$ if $\gamma \in R$ (see [23,24] for more details).

3   The Maude Invariant Analyzer Tool: An Overview

The *Maude Invariant Analyzer Tool* (InvA) is a tool designed for *interactively* proving two key safety properties of executable Maude specifications, namely, inductive stability and inductive invariance, plus their combination by strengthening techniques. The tool mechanizes an inference system that, without assuming finiteness of the set of initial or reachable states, uses rewriting and narrowing-based reasoning techniques, in which all temporal logic formulas eventually disappear and are replaced by purely equational conditional sentences. The InvA tool provides a substantial degree of mechanization and can automatically discharge many proof obligations without user intervention. It is implemented in the Maude language and exploits rewriting logic's reflection capabilities, i.e., it is a Maude specification that takes, as part of its input, a meta-representation of a Maude specification.

The concept of inductive stability for $\mathcal{R} = (\Sigma, E, R)$ is intimately related to the notion of the set of states $t \in T_{\Sigma,\mathfrak{s}}$ of $\mathcal{T}_{\mathcal{R}}$ that satisfy a state predicate $p \in \Pi$ and is closed under $\to_{\mathcal{R}}$. More precisely, for $p \in \Pi$ and $x \in X_{\mathfrak{s}}$, the property p being *inductively stable* for $\mathcal{R}$ is the safety property:

$$\mathcal{K}_{\mathcal{R}}^{\Pi} \models p(x) \Rightarrow \Box p(x)$$

meaning that if $p(t)$ holds in a state $t \in T_{\Sigma,\mathfrak{s}}$, then $p(u)$ holds in any state $u \in T_{\Sigma,\mathfrak{s}}$ that is reachable from t.

Invariants are among the most important safety properties. Given a set of initial states characterized by $I \in \Pi$, a state predicate $p \in \Pi$ being *inductively invariant* for $\mathcal{R}$ from the set of initial states I is the safety property

$$\mathcal{K}_{\mathcal{R}}^{\Pi} \models I(x) \Rightarrow \Box p(x)$$

meaning that if $I(t)$ holds in a state $t \in T_{\Sigma,\mathfrak{s}}$, then $p(u)$ holds in any state $u \in T_{\Sigma,\mathfrak{s}}$ reachable from t. In other words, the invariant p holds for all states reachable from I. Since the set of initial states is defined in $\mathcal{E}_{\Pi}$ as a state predicate $I \in \Pi$, an equational definition of I can of course capture an infinite set of initial states.

3.1   Inference System Mechanized in the InvA Tool

Given an inductive stability or inductive invariance property φ, the InvA tool generates equational proof obligations such that, if they hold, then $\mathcal{T}_{\mathcal{R}} \models \varphi$. For a topmost rewrite theory $\mathcal{R}$ and a set of state predicates Π specified in Maude, the InvA tool mechanizes inference rules ST, INV, STR1, STR2, C⇒, NR1, and NR2 depicted in Figure 1. Soundness proofs for each one of these inference rules can be found in [23]. The application of inference rules ST, INV, STR1, and STR2 to a given inductive stability or invariance LTL verification goal ultimately reduces such a goal to simpler inductive equational reasoning that can be handled by applying rules C⇒, NR1, and NR2.

Inference rule ST reduces the verification task of the inductive stability of a predicate p to the simpler condition $p \Rightarrow \bigcirc p$, which only involves 1-step search instead of arbitrary depth search. Inference rule INV reduces the verification task of inductive invariance to equational implication and inductive stability. Inference rules STR1 and STR2 are strengthening rules. Inference rule C⇒ handles equational implications, while rules NR1 and NR2 use 1-step narrowing modulo axioms to handle the symbolic 1-step search, for the temporal next operator, in formulae of the form $p \Rightarrow \bigcirc p$. Note that any inductive stability and invariance formula is ultimately reduced to equational reasoning. Thanks to the availability since Maude 2.6 of unification modulo commutativity (C), associativity and commutativity (AC), and modulo these theories plus identities (U), and to the narrowing modulo infrastructure, the InvA tool can handle modules with operators declared C, CU, AC, and ACU. Furthermore, since unification modulo the above theory combinations is decidable, and each one yields a *finite* set of complete unifiers, the set of proof obligations resulting from applying rules NR1 and NR2 is always finite.

Under the executability assumptions, $\mathcal{R}$ has a disjoint union $E \uplus B$ of equations, with B a collection of structural axioms on some function symbols in Σ such as associativity, commutativity, identity, etc., and E a set of ground sort-decreasing, ground confluent, ground terminating, and ground coherent (w.r.t. R) equations modulo B. Then, it is key to note that for rules NR1 and NR2 and for a combination of free and associative and/or commutative and/or identity axioms, except for symbols f that are associative but not commutative, a finitary B-unification algorithm exists. Instead, in general there is no finitary $E \uplus B$-unification algorithm, but for $\Omega \subseteq \Sigma$ a signature of free equational constructors modulo B and a Ω-equality $t = u$, $CSU_B(t = u)$ exactly characterizes as its ground instances the set $GU_B(t = u)$ (see [23, Lemma 2, Chapter 4] for more details).

3.2   Methodology and Commands Available to the User

The approach for proving inductive stability and invariance properties in the InvA tool is depicted in Figure 2.

Given a topmost rewrite theory $\mathcal{R}$, an equational specification $\mathcal{E}_\Pi$ for the state predicates Π, and an inductive safety property φ the InvA tool internally generates equational proof obligations according to the inference system in Figure 1 and tries to discharge as many of them as possible by using the heuristics described in Section 3.3. Any proof obligation that cannot be automatically discharged is output to the user so it can be handled interactively in an external tool such as Maude's Inductive Theorem Prover (ITP) [7,13] (an experimental interactive tool for proving properties of the initial algebra $\mathcal{T}_\mathcal{E}$ of an order-sorted equational theory $\mathcal{E}$ written in Maude).

$$\frac{\mathcal{R} \Vdash p(x) \Rightarrow \bigcirc p(x)}{\mathcal{R} \Vdash p(x) \Rightarrow \Box p(x)} \text{ St}$$

$$\frac{\mathcal{R} \Vdash I(x) \Rightarrow p(x) \qquad \mathcal{R} \Vdash p(x) \Rightarrow \Box p(x)}{\mathcal{R} \Vdash I(x) \Rightarrow \Box p(x)} \text{ Inv}$$

$$\frac{\begin{array}{cc} \mathcal{R} \Vdash I(x) \Rightarrow J(x) & \mathcal{R} \Vdash J(x) \Rightarrow \Box q(x) \\ \mathcal{R} \Vdash q(x) \Rightarrow p(x) \end{array}}{\mathcal{R} \Vdash I \Rightarrow \Box p} \text{ Str1}$$

$$\frac{\begin{array}{cc} \mathcal{R} \Vdash I(x) \Rightarrow p(x) & \mathcal{R} \Vdash I(x) \Rightarrow \Box q(x) \\ \mathcal{R} \Vdash q(x) \wedge p(x) \Rightarrow \bigcirc p(x) \end{array}}{\mathcal{R} \Vdash I(x) \Rightarrow \Box p(x)} \text{ Str2}$$

$$\frac{\bigwedge_{(q(v)=w \text{ if } \gamma') \in E_\Pi} \mathcal{E}_\Pi \Vdash p(v) = \top \text{ if } \gamma' \wedge w = \top}{\mathcal{R} \Vdash q(x) \Rightarrow p(x)} \text{ C}\Rightarrow$$

$$\frac{\bigwedge_{\substack{(l \to r \text{ if } \gamma) \in R \\ (\theta, w, \gamma') \in \Theta_l^p}} \mathcal{E}_\Pi \Vdash p(r\theta) = \top \text{ if } \gamma\theta \wedge \gamma'\theta \wedge w\theta = \top}{\mathcal{R} \Vdash p(x) \Rightarrow \bigcirc p(x)} \text{ Nr1}$$

$$\frac{\bigwedge_{\substack{(l \to r \text{ if } \gamma) \in R \\ (\theta, w, \gamma') \in \Theta_l^p}} \mathcal{E}_\Pi \Vdash p(r\theta) = \top \text{ if } \gamma\theta \wedge \gamma'\theta \wedge w\theta = \top \wedge q(l)\theta = \top}{\mathcal{R} \Vdash q(x) \wedge p(x) \Rightarrow \bigcirc p(x)} \text{ Nr2}$$

where $\Theta_l^p = \bigcup_{(p(v)=w \text{ if } \gamma') \in E_\Pi} \{(\theta, w, \gamma') \mid \theta \in CSU_B(l = v)\}.$

Fig. 1. Inference rules mechanized in the InvA tool

The user interacts with the InvA tool via commands; the commands available are the following:

- (help .) shows the list of commands available.
- (analyze-stable <pred> in <module> <module> .) generates the proof obligations for inference ST with inference NR1, for the given predicate. The first module equationally specifies the state predicate and the second one the topmost rewrite theory. This command tries to eagerly discharge the proof obligations; those that cannot be discharged are shown to the user.
- (analyze-stable <pred> in <module> <module> assuming <pred> .) generates the proof obligations for proving the third premise of inference STR2 with inference NR2, for the given predicate and the given modules. The first module equationally specifies the state predicates and the second one the topmost rewrite theory. This command tries to eagerly discharge the proof obligations; those that cannot be discharged are shown to the user.
- (analyze <pred> implies <pred> in <module> .) generates the proof obligations for proving the given implication in the given module, according to inference C⇒. This command tries to eagerly discharge the proof obligations; those that cannot be discharged are shown to the user.
- (show pos .) shows the proof obligations computed by the last analyze command that could not be discharged; those that were discharged are not shown.
- (show-all pos .) shows all the proof obligations computed by the last analyze command.

Observe that the analysis commands in InvA give direct tool support for deductive reasoning with *some* of the inference rules presented here, but not for all of them. For example, there is no command in InvA directly supporting deduction with inference rule INV. Nevertheless, deduction with *all* inference rules is supported by InvA via *combination of commands*. For example, deduction with inference rule INV can be achieved by combining the analyze and analyze-stable commands.

3.3 Proof-Search Heuristics in InvA

After applying rules ST, INV, STR1, STR2, C⇒, NR1, and NR2 according to the user commands, the InvA tool uses rewriting-based reasoning and narrowing procedures, and SMT decision procedures for automatically discharging as many of the generated equational proof obligations as possible. For an executable equational specification $\mathcal{E}_\Pi = (\Sigma_\Pi, E_\Pi \uplus B)$ and a conditional proof obligation φ of the form

$$t = u \text{ if } \gamma,$$

the InvA tool applies a proof-search strategy such that, if it succeeds, then the Kripke structure $\mathcal{K}_\mathcal{R}^\Pi$ associated to the initial reachability model $\mathcal{T}_\mathcal{R}$ satisfies

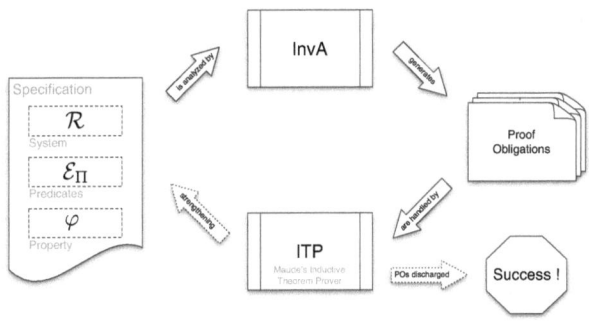

Fig. 2. Approach for checking inductive stability and invariance properties for rewrite theories

φ. Otherwise, if the proof-search fails, the proof obligation φ (or a logically equivalent variant) is output to the user.

For the proof-search process, the InvA tool first tries to simplify Boolean expressions in φ. During the simplification process, the tool assumes that any operator '$\sim$' is an equationally defined equality predicate, i.e., an *equality enrichment*. Given an order-sorted signature $\Sigma = (S, \leq, F)$ and an order-sorted equational theory $\mathcal{E} = (\Sigma, E)$ with initial algebra $\mathcal{T}_{\mathcal{E}}$, an equality enrichment [17] of $\mathcal{E}$ is an equational theory $\mathcal{E}^{\sim}$ that extends $\mathcal{E}$ by defining a Boolean-valued equality function symbol '$\sim$' that coincides with '=' in $\mathcal{T}_{\mathcal{E}}$.

Definition 1. *An equational theory $\mathcal{E}^{\sim} = (\Sigma^{\sim}, E^{\sim})$ is called an* equality enrichment *of $\mathcal{E} = (\Sigma, E)$, with $\Sigma^{\sim} = (S^{\sim}, \leq^{\sim}, F^{\sim})$ and $\Sigma = (S, \leq, F)$, iff*

- *$\mathcal{E}^{\sim}$ is a protecting extension of $\mathcal{E}$;*
- *the poset of sorts of $\Sigma^{\sim}$ extends $(S, \leq)$ by adding a new sort Bool that belongs to a new connected component, with constants $\top$ and $\bot$ such that $\mathcal{T}_{\mathcal{E}^{\sim}, Bool} = \{[\top], [\bot]\}$, with $\top \neq_{E^{\sim}} \bot$; and*
- *for each connected component in $(S, \leq)$ there is a top sort $k \in S^{\sim}$ and a binary commutative operator $\_ \sim \_ : k\ k \longrightarrow Bool$ in $\Sigma^{\sim}$, such that the following equivalences hold for any ground terms $t, u \in \mathcal{T}_{\Sigma, k}$:*

$$\mathcal{E} \vdash t = u \quad \Longleftrightarrow \quad \mathcal{E}^{\sim} \vdash (t \sim u) = \top,$$
$$\mathcal{E} \nvdash t = u \quad \Longleftrightarrow \quad \mathcal{E}^{\sim} \vdash (t \sim u) = \bot.$$

An equality enrichment $\mathcal{E}^{\sim}$ of $\mathcal{E}$ is called Boolean *iff it contains all the function symbols and equations making the elements of $\mathcal{T}_{\mathcal{E}^{\sim}, Bool}$ a two-element Boolean algebra.*

Using the information about '$\sim$', a Boolean transformation can be applied recursively to φ with the additional information of the equality enrichment, if any is defined.

The goal of the Boolean transformation process on a conditional proof obligation φ having the form $t = u$ **if** γ, is to obtain, if possible, an inductively equivalent proof obligation φ' for which the automatic search tests, explained below, have better chances of success. The following is a description of the Boolean transformations applied recursively by the InvA tool:

- If $t = u$ in φ is such that t is of the form $t_1 \sim t_2$ and u of the form $\bot$, then φ is transformed into $\top = \bot$ **if** $\gamma \wedge t_1 = t_2$.
- If $v_1 = v_2$, with $v_1, v_2 \in T_\Sigma(X)_{Bool}$, is any of the Σ-equalities in the condition γ of φ, then:
  - If v_1 is of the form $v_1^1 \sim v_1^2$ and v_2 of the form $\top$, then $v_1 = v_2$ is replaced by $v_1^1 = v_1^2$.
  - If v_1 is of the form $v_1^1 \sqcap \cdots \sqcap v_1^n$ and v_2 of the form $\top$, then $v_1 = v_2$ is replaced by $v_1^1 = \top \wedge \cdots \wedge v_1^n = \top$. Note that the v_1^i have sort *Bool*.
  - If v_1 is of the form $v_1^1 \sqcup \cdots \sqcup v_1^n$ and v_2 of the form $\bot$, then $v_1 = v_2$ is replaced by $v_1^1 = \bot \wedge \cdots \wedge v_1^n = \bot$. Note that the v_1^i have sort *Bool*.

Symbols $\sqcap$ and $\sqcup$ are used to represent, respectively, the conjunction and disjunction function symbols used by the Boolean equality enrichment in Definition 1. Also note that Σ-equalities are unoriented, and thus in the Boolean transformation the order of terms in the equalities is immaterial.

After the Boolean transformation process is completed, some automatic search tests are applied to the resulting proof obligation following the strategy described below. In what follows, it is assumed that φ has been already simplified by the abovementioned Boolean transformations. Furthermore, let $\bar{t}$, $\bar{u}$, $\bar{\gamma}$ be obtained from t, u, and γ, respectively, by replacing each variable $x \in X$ by a new constant $\bar{x} \in \overline{X}$, with $\Sigma \cap \overline{X} = \varnothing$.

1. *Equational simplification.* The strategy checks if φ holds *trivially*, i.e., if

$$t \downarrow_{\Sigma, E/B} =_B u \downarrow_{\Sigma, E/B}$$

or there is $t_i = u_i$ in γ such that $t_i \downarrow_{\Sigma, E/B}, u_i \downarrow_{\Sigma, E/B} \in T_\Sigma$ but

$$t_i \downarrow_{\Sigma, E/B} \neq_B u_i \downarrow_{\Sigma, E/B} .$$

Some simplifications in the form of reduction to canonical forms can be made to φ, even if they do not yield a trivial proof of φ. In some cases, such canonical reductions are incorporated into φ and the Boolean transformation is used again.

2. *Context joinability.* It checks whether φ is *context-joinable* [8]. The proof obligation φ is context-joinable iff $\bar{t}$ and $\bar{u}$ are joinable in the rewrite theory $\mathcal{R}_{\mathcal{E}}^{\varphi} = (\Sigma(\overline{X}), B, \overrightarrow{E} \uplus \overrightarrow{\gamma})$, obtained by making variables into constants and by orienting the equations E as rewrite rules $\overrightarrow{E}$ and *heuristically* orienting each equality $t_i = u_i$ in γ as a sequent $\bar{t_i} \to \bar{u_i}$ in $\overrightarrow{\gamma}$.

3. *Unfeasability.* It checks if the proof obligation is *unfeasible* [8]. The proof obligation φ is unfeasible if there is a conjunct $\overline{t_i} \to \overline{u_i}$ in $\overrightarrow{\gamma}$ and $v, w \in T_\Sigma(X)$ such that $\mathcal{R}_\mathcal{E}^\varphi \vdash \overline{t_i} \to \overline{v} \wedge \overline{t_i} \to \overline{w}$, $CSU_B(v = w) = \varnothing$, and v and w are *strongly irreducible* with $\overrightarrow{E}$ modulo B, i.e., if v and w are such that each one of its ground instances is in E-canonical form modulo B.

4. *SMT Solving.* It checks if the proof obligation can be proved by an SMT decision procedure. The condition γ of the proof obligation φ is analyzed and, if possible, a subformula consisting only of arithmetic subexpressions is extracted. This subformula has the following property: if it is a contradiction, then γ is unsatisfiable. Therefore, if the SMT decision procedure answers that the input subformula is unsatisfiable, then, as in the previous test, φ is unfeasible.

Because of the admissibility assumptions on $(\Sigma, E \uplus B)$, the first test of the strategy either succeeds or fails in finitely many equational rewrite steps. For the second and third tests, the strategy is not guaranteed to succeed or fail in finitely many rewrite steps because the oriented sequents $\overrightarrow{\gamma}$ can falsify a termination assumption. So, for these last two checks, InvA uses a bound on the depth of the proof-search. For the fourth test, InvA offers support for integer linear arithmetic constraints, which is known to be decidable and for which there are decision procedures already implemented in the SMT solver of choice.

The code in InvA for tests (2) and (3) was borrowed and adapted from the Church-Rosser Checker Tool [8]. For the test (4), the InvA tool relies on an extension of Maude with the CVC3 theorem prover available from the Matching Logic Project [25].

4   The Alternating Bit Protocol

The *Alternating Bit Protocol* (ABP) [2] is a data layer protocol. It was designed to achieve reliable full-duplex data transfer between two processes over an unreliable half-duplex transmission line in which messages can be lost or corrupted in a detectable way. The data link layer, the second lowest layer in the OSI seven layer model, splits data into frames for sending on the physical layer and receives acknowledgment frames. It performs error checking and re-transmits frames not received correctly. It provides an error-free virtual channel to the network layer, the third lowest layer in the OSI layer model.

The overall structure of ABP is illustrated in Figure 3. The protocol comprises an input stream of data to be transmitted, a *sender* and a *receiver* process, each having a data buffer and a one *bit* state, a *data channel* for data-bit pairs called *bit-packets*, an *acknowledgment channel* for bit-packets consisting of a single bit, and an output data stream. Here is how the protocol works:

- The sender process starts by repeatedly sending bit-packets (b, d_1) into the data channel, where b is the sender's bit and d_1 is the first element of the input stream.

- The receiver process starts by waiting until it receives the bit-packet (b, d_1), and then it repeatedly sends b over the acknowledgment channel.
- When the source process receives b, it begins repeatedly sending the bit-packet $(flip(b), d_2)$, where d_2 is the second element of the input stream, which is what the receiver process is now waiting for.
- When the target receives $(flip(b), d_2)$, it begins sending packets containing $flip(b)$.
- At any moment either channel can duplicate or lose its oldest packet, if any.
- And so on ...

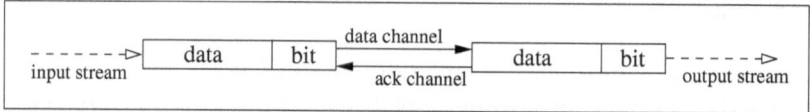

Fig. 3. The Alternating Bit Protocol

The protocol is highly concurrent and non-deterministic because, for instance, it is unknown how long will it take before a bit-packet gets through. To guarantee progress, it must be assumed that the channels are fair, in the sense that if the sender persists, eventually a bit-packet will get through. The reason is that without this assumption the algorithm is not correct because data transmission might fail forever. However, this is a fairness assumption that is not needed for analyzing the reliable communication enforced by the protocol. Remember that a safety property assures that "nothing bad happens", even when nothing ever happens.

4.1 Formal Modeling

The ABP specification in Maude has 9 modules. This section gives an overview; the full specification can be found in [23].

At the top level, the state space is represented by the top sort `Sys` defined in module `ABP-STATE`, which is a 6-tuple:

```
sort Sys .
op _:_>_|_<_:_ : iNat Bit BitPacketQueue BitQueue Bit iNatList
                -> Sys [ctor] .
```

The arguments of a state are the data from the input stream currently being transmitted by the sender (as `iNat`), the bit of the sender (as `Bit`), the data channel (as `BitPacketQueue`), the acknowledgment channel (as `BitQueue`), the bit of the receiver (as `Bit`), and the output stream (as `iNatList`).

The sort `iNat` is that of natural numbers in Peano notation, together with an equality enrichment. Natural numbers are used to represent packets in the potentially infinite input stream.

```
sort iNat .
op 0 : -> iNat [ctor] .
op s_ : iNat -> iNat [ctor] .
op _~_ : iNat iNat -> Bool [comm] .
```

Bits are defined in module BIT by sort Bit with two constructor constants, a 'flipping' operator, and an equality enrichment:

```
sort Bit .
ops on off : -> Bit [ctor] .
op flip : Bit -> Bit .
op _~_ : Bit Bit -> Bool [comm] .

eq flip(on)
 = off .
eq flip(off)
 = on .
```

Sort BitPacketQueue represents lists of bit-packets, sort BitQueue represents lists of bits, and sort iNatList represents lists of natural numbers. They are all lists defined in the usual way: an empty list is identified by the constructor constant nil, "cons" is a constructor binary symbol denoted by juxtaposition, and append is a defined binary symbol denoted by ';'. For instance, sort BitQueue defined in module BIT-QUEUE is specified as follows:

```
sort BitQueue .
op nil : -> BitQueue [ctor] .
op __ : Bit BitQueue -> BitQueue [ctor prec 61] .
op _;_ : BitQueue BitQueue -> BitQueue [prec 65] .

eq nil ; BQ:BitQueue
 = BQ:BitQueue .
eq B1:Bit BQ1:BitQueue ; BQ2:BitQueue
 = B:Bit (BQ1:BitQueue ; BQ2:BitQueue) .
```

Having covered the basic notation, consider the following ground term of sort Sys representing a state in the system:

```
s(0)  :  on  >  (off,0) nil  |  nil  <  off  :  (0 nil)
```

In this state, the packet from the input stream currently being sent is s(0), the sender's bit is on, the data channel contains only the bit-packet (off,0), the acknowledgment channel is empty, the receiver's bit is off, and the output stream consists only of the packet 0.

Finally, module ABP specifies the operation of the protocol with 15 rewrite rules. These rewrite rules model the transmission of the bit-packets through the data channel, the reception of acknowledgments from the receiver, data duplication and loss, among other behaviors of the system. For instance, consider the following five rewrite rules:

```
rl [send-1] :
```

```
    N:iNat : B1:Bit > BPQ:BitPacketQueue
                    | BQ:BitQueue < B2:Bit : NL:iNatList
=> N:iNat : B1:Bit > BPQ:BitPacketQueue ; ((B1:Bit, N:iNat) nil)
                    | BQ:BitQueue < B2:Bit : NL:iNatList .

rl [recv-1b] :
    N:iNat : on      > BPQ:BitPacketQueue
                    | off BQ:BitQueue < B2:Bit : NL:iNatList
=> s(N:iNat) : off > BPQ:BitPacketQueue
                    | BQ:BitQueue < B2:Bit : NL:iNatList .

rl [recv-1c] :
    N:iNat : off     > BPQ:BitPacketQueue
                    | on BQ:BitQueue < B2:Bit : NL:iNatList
=> s(N:iNat) : on >  BPQ:BitPacketQueue
                    | BQ:BitQueue < B2:Bit : NL:iNatList .

rl [recv-2a] :
    N:iNat : B1:Bit > (on,N2:iNat) BPQ:BitPacketQueue
                    | BQ:BitQueue < on : NL:iNatList
=> N:iNat : B1:Bit > BPQ:BitPacketQueue
                    | BQ:BitQueue < off : (N2:iNat NL:iNatList) .

rl [dup-1] :
    N:iNat : B1:Bit > BP:BitPacket BPQ:BitPacketQueue
                    | BQ:BitQueue < B2:Bit : NL:iNatList
=> N:iNat : B1:Bit > BP:BitPacket (BP:BitPacket BPQ:BitPacketQueue)
                    | BQ:BitQueue < B2:Bit : NL:iNatList .
```

The effects of these rules in a state can be summarized as follows:

[send-1] models the "fifo" placement of the current bit-packet in the data channel (the acknowledgment channel behaves in the same way).

[recv-1b] models the reception of the acknowledgment the sender was waiting for and thus the sender process immediately updates the packet to be transmitted with the next available packet from the input stream and flips its communication bit.

[recv-1c] models the reception of an acknowledgment the sender was not waiting for and thus the acknowledgment is ignored.

[recv-2a] models the reception of a bit-packet whose contents are put in the output stream.

[dup-1] duplicates the first message in the data channel.

Note that because of rule [recv-1c], for instance, the formal model of the ABP has potentially infinitely many reachable states: every time a packet is successfully transmitted, the sender's counter modeling the input stream is increased by one and then the whole sending process starts over again with the next packet.

5   Reliable Communication

The analysis that follows is based on the formal model explained in Section 4.1.

One of the main properties the ABP should enjoy is the reliable communication property. This means that the protocol makes possible to *reliably* communicate and deliver information from a source to a destination, even in the presence of unreliable channels of communication. The goal in this section is to report on the experience of using the InvA tool in the successful mechanical verification of this property.

5.1   Formal Specification of the Property

Reliable communication in ABP means that whenever n packets have been delivered, these were the first n packets sent in that particular order. Note that this is a property that must hold for each natural number n and that cannot be effectively checked by means of direct algorithmic techniques, such as model checking the ABP specification, even if the set of initial states is finite.

The reliable communication property is expressed by the state predicate inv-main and is defined as follows:

```
op inv-main : Sys -> Bool .

eq [inv-main-1] :
   inv-main(N:iNat : B:Bit  > BPQ:BitPacketQueue
                            | BQ:BitQueue < B:Bit : NL:iNatList)
 = (N:iNat NL:iNatList) ~ gen-list(N:iNat) .
ceq [inv-main-2] :
   inv-main(N:iNat : B1:Bit > BPQ:BitPacketQueue
                            | BQ:BitQueue < B2:Bit : NL:iNatList)
 = NL:iNatList ~ gen-list(N:iNat)
 if B1:Bit ~ B2:Bit = false .

op gen-list : iNat -> iNatList .

eq gen-list(0)
 = (0 nil) .
eq gen-list(s N)
 = (s N) gen-list(N) .
```

State predicate inv-main is fully defined by two equations and uses the auxiliary function gen-list. Equation [inv-main-1] considers the case in which the parity of the sender and receiver bits coincides. In this case, the reliable communication property holds if and only if the delivered packets correspond to all but the last packet sent and they are all in order. Equation [inv-main-2] considers the case in which the parity of the sender and receiver bits does not coincide. In this case, the reliable communication property holds if and only if the delivered packets correspond to all packets sent and they are all in order. Given a natural number n, function gen-list generates the list of the first n natural numbers in decreasing order.

Consider the rule [recv-2b] that models packet reception in ABP in order to motivate the correctness of the reliable communication property:

```
rl [recv-2b] :
   N:iNat : B:Bit > (off,N1:iNat) BPQ:BitPacketQueue
                    | BQ:BitQueue < off : NL:iNatList
=> N:iNat : B:Bit > BPQ:BitPacketQueue
                    | BQ:BitQueue < on : (N1:iNat NL:iNatList) .
```

Note that when a packet N1:iNat is received there is no assumption made about the relationship between N1:iNat and the current packet from the input stream N:iNat or the already delivered packets NL:iNatList. In this case, there is no obvious reason for the reliable communication property to hold, even if a state initially satisfies this property.

The goal is to prove the ABP inv-main-invariant from init. State predicate init defines the set of initial states as follows:

```
op init : Sys -> [Bool] .

eq [init-1] :
   init( 0 : on > nil | nil < on : nil)
 = true .
eq [init-2] :
   init( 0 : off > nil | nil < off : nil)
 = true .
```

The set of initial states for the verification task at hand, as defined by init, consists of exactly two states. Namely, those states where the packet to be transmitted is 0, the sender and receiver bits coincide, the communication channels are empty, and no packet has been delivered.

The following verification commands can be given to the InvA tool in order to check if state predicate inv-main is an inductive invariant from init:

```
(analyze init(S:Sys) implies inv-main(S:Sys) in ABP-PREDS .)

(analyze-stable inv-main(S:Sys) in ABP-PREDS ABP .)
```

It is assumed that module ABP-PREDS contains the state predicates and their corresponding auxiliary function symbols, and module ABP contains the specification of ABP, as explained in Section 4.1 and documented in [23].

When the above-mentioned commands, the InvA tool generates the following output:

```
Checking ABP-PREDS ||- init(S:Sys) => inv-main(S:Sys) ...
Proof obligations generated:   2
Proof obligations discharged: 2
Success!

Checking ABP-PREDS ||- inv-main(S:Sys) => 0 inv-main(S:Sys) ...
Proof obligations generated:   30
```

```
Proof obligations discharged: 22
The following proof obligations need to be discharged:
8. from inv-main-2 & recv-2b : pending
    inv-main(#7:iNat : #8:Bit > #10:BitPacketQueue
      | #11:BitQueue < on :(#9:iNat #12:iNatList)) = true
 if off ~ #8:Bit = false
 /\ #12:iNatList = gen-list(#7:iNat).
...
```

The tool generates 32 proof obligations and automatically discharges 24 of them. The remaining 8 proof obligations are returned to the user; in the snapshot, only one proof obligation for ground stability that was not automatically discharged is shown and it is identified by label 8.

Upon inspection of the InvA's output, it is relatively easy to observe that inv-main is not an inductive invariant for ABP. Indeed, consider the proof obligation identified by label 8, as show in the snapshot above, and a ground interpretation where #8:Bit is on, #7:iNat and #9:iNat are 0, and #12:iNatList is the singleton list 0 nil. For this particular ground instantiation, the condition in the proof obligation is satisfied because on ~ off reduces to false and the value returned by gen-list on input 0 is the ground list 0 nil. However, by equation [inv-main-2] in the definition of predicate inv-main, this proof obligation is false because the lefthand side of the conclusion reduces to the Boolean term 0 nil ~ 0 0 nil, which ultimately reduces to false. This is evidence of the fact that a stronger predicate is needed, that is, inv-main needs to be strengthened.

5.2   Strengthening the Invariant

The first observation to make is that the InvA tool would be able to automatically discharge more proof obligations and also return simpler ones if there were some mechanism for achieving case analysis on the sort Bit. Since the InvA internals do not yet offer this feature, a practical approach is to include the case splitting as part of the predicate's equational definition (similarly to what was done in the definition of state predicate init). For instance, state predicate inv is a finer-grained version of inv-main that exhibits the idea of case splitting on the sort Bit for the case of the bits in the sender and receiver.

```
op inv : Sys -> Bool .

eq [inv-1a] :
   inv(N:iNat : on  > BPQ:BitPacketQueue
                    | BQ:BitQueue < on : NL:iNatList)
 = (N:iNat NL:iNatList) ~ gen-list(N:iNat) .
eq [inv-1a] :
   inv(N:iNat : off > BPQ:BitPacketQueue
                    | BQ:BitQueue < off : NL:iNatList)
 = (N:iNat NL:iNatList) ~ gen-list(N:iNat) .
eq [inv-2a] :
```

```
      inv(N:iNat : on  > BPQ:BitPacketQueue
                          | BQ:BitQueue < off : NL:iNatList)
    = NL:iNatList ~ gen-list(N:iNat) .
  eq [inv-2a] :
      inv(N:iNat : off > BPQ:BitPacketQueue
                          | BQ:BitQueue < on : NL:iNatList)
    = NL:iNatList ~ gen-list(N:iNat) .
```

Since the case analysis on the sort Bit is already implemented in predicate
inv, and this is potentially useful for automation in the overall proof, this predicate is preferred over predicate inv-main. The idea is then to strengthen inv
instead of inv-main. Within the overall context of the verification task, the
change of predicate inv-main for inv requires a formal proof of the following
implications:

$$\text{ABP} \Vdash \text{init} \Rightarrow \text{inv} \qquad \text{and} \qquad \text{ABP} \Vdash \text{inv} \Rightarrow \text{inv-main}.$$

These two proof obligations can be analyzed with the help of inference rule C$\Rightarrow$
in Section 3.1. The InvA's mechanization of this inference rule can automatically
discharge the implications:

```
Checking ABP-PREDS ||- init(S:Sys) => inv(S:Sys) ...
Proof obligations generated:   2
Proof obligations discharged: 2
Success!

Checking ABP-PREDS ||- inv(S:Sys) => inv-main(S:Sys) ...
Proof obligations generated:   4
Proof obligations discharged: 4
Success!
```

Finding a strengthening for inv is not an easy task at first sight. The non-
obvious relationships between the channels and the alternating bits, and the
many rules that can concurrently apply to a state make this harder. But it is
the deep understanding of these relationships that guides the proof effort for
obtaining a useful, yet succinct and elegant, strengthening for inv.

The key to it all is that the channels behave under some sort of uniformity
that is parametric on the sender and receiver bits. This notion of uniformity
can be precisely captured with the help of some auxiliary predicates for the
two communication channels. Indeed, consider the following auxiliary predicates
all-packets and good-packet-queue:

```
op all-packets : BitPacketQueue Bit iNat -> Bool .

eq [ap-1] :
    all-packets(nil,B:Bit,N:iNat)
  = true .
eq [ap-2] :
    all-packets(BP:BitPacket BPQ:BitPacketQueue,B:Bit,N:iNat)
  = BP:BitPacket ~ (B:Bit,N:iNat) and
```

```
    all-packets(BPQ:BitPacketQueue,B:Bit,N:iNat) .

 op good-packet-queue : BitPacketQueue Bit iNat -> Bool .

 eq [gpq-1] :
    good-packet-queue(nil,B:Bit,N:iNat)
  = true .
ceq [gpq-2] :
    good-packet-queue((B1:Bit,N1:iNat) BPQ:BitPacketQueue,
                      B:Bit,N:iNat)
  = N:iNat ~ s(N1:iNat) and
    good-packet-queue(BPQ:BitPacketQueue,B:Bit,N:iNat)
 if B1:Bit = flip(B:Bit) .
 eq [gpq-3] :
    good-packet-queue((B:Bit,N1:iNat) BPQ:BitPacketQueue,
                      B:Bit,N:iNat)
  = N:iNat ~ N1:iNat and
    all-packets(BPQ:BitPacketQueue,B:Bit,N:Nat) .
```

Predicate `all-packets` on input `BPQ:BitPacketQueue` and `(B:Bit,N:iNat)` is true if and only if all bit-packets in `BPQ` have the form `(B,N)`. Predicate `good-packet-queue` on input `BPQ:BitPacketQueue` and `(B:Bit,N:iNat)` is true if and only if `BPQ` can be split into two parts, one of them possibly empty, where in the initial part of the channel all packets are of the form `(flip(B),N-1)` and in the second part of the form `(B,N)`. For example:

```
good-packet-queue((on,3) (off,4) (off,4) nil, off, 4) = true
good-packet-queue((on,3) (on,3) nil, off, 4) = true
good-packet-queue((off,4) nil, off, 4) = true
good-packet-queue((off,4) (on,4) nil, off, 4) = false
```

Auxiliary predicates `all-bits` and `good-bit-queue` are similar to the auxiliary predicates just discussed for channels of bit-packets, but they are about channels of bits.

```
 op all-bits : BitQueue Bit -> Bool .

 eq [ab-1] :
    all-bits(nil,B:Bit)
  = true .
 eq [ab-2] :
    all-bits(B1:Bit BQ:BitQueue,B:Bit)
  = B1:Bit ~ B:Bit and all-bits(BQ:BitQueue,B:Bit) .

 op good-bit-queue : BitQueue Bit -> Bool .

 eq [gbq-1] :
    good-bit-queue(nil,B:Bit)
  = true .
ceq [gbq-2] :
```

```
   good-bit-queue(B1:Bit BQ:BitQueue, B:Bit)
 = good-bit-queue(BQ:BitQueue,B:Bit)
 if B1:Bit = flip(B:Bit) .
 eq [gbq-3] :
   good-bit-queue(B:Bit BQ:BitQueue, B:Bit)
 = all-bits(BQ:BitQueue,B:Bit) .
```

The strengthening for `inv` is the state predicate `good-queues` that uses the auxiliary predicates above-mentioned:

```
op good-queues : Sys -> Bool .

eq [good-queues-1a] :
   good-queues(N:iNat : on > BPQ:BitPacketQueue |
               BQ:BitQueue < on : NL:iNatList)
 = all-bits(BQ:BitQueue,on) and
   good-packet-queue(BPQ:BitPacketQueue,on,N:iNat) .
eq [good-queues-1b] :
   good-queues(N:iNat : off > BPQ:BitPacketQueue |
               BQ:BitQueue < off : NL:iNatList)
 = all-bits(BQ:BitQueue,off) and
   good-packet-queue(BPQ:BitPacketQueue,off,N:iNat) .
eq [good-queues-2a] :
   good-queues(N:iNat : on > BPQ:BitPacketQueue |
               BQ:BitQueue < off : NL:iNatList)
 = good-bit-queue(BQ:BitQueue,off) and
   all-packets(BPQ:BitPacketQueue,on,N:iNat) .
eq [good-queues-2b] :
   good-queues(N:iNat : off > BPQ:BitPacketQueue |
               BQ:BitQueue < on : NL:iNatList)
 = good-bit-queue(BQ:BitQueue,on) and
   all-packets(BPQ:BitPacketQueue,off,N:iNat) .
```

State predicate `good-queues` is fully defined by four equations. It characterizes the patterns observed on the communication channels, and their relationship with the alternating bits, in four cases. For example, equation [good-queues-1a] states that a state in which both bits are `on` satisfies predicated `good-queues` if and only if all bits in the receiver's queue are `on` and the sender's channel can be split into two parts, where in the initial part of the channel all packets are of the form (`off`,N-1) and in the second part of the form (`on`,N).

As it will be shown, the strengthening `good-queues` of `inv` is enough to prove the correctness of ABP. Figure 4 depicts the full proof-tree for the inductive invariance of `inv-main` from `init` that uses state predicates `inv` and `good-queues`.

The next step in the proof is to check

ABP ⊩ good-queues ∧ inv ⇒ ◯inv   and

ABP ⊩ init ⇒ □good-queues,

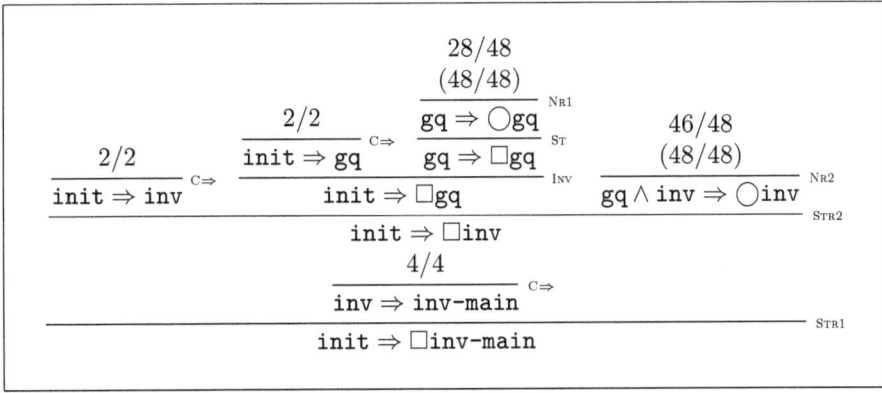

Fig. 4. Correctness proof of the Alternating Bit Protocol (gq stands for good-queues). The expression d/g denotes the number g of proof obligations generated and the number d of proof obligations automatically discharged by the InvA tool; the same expression in parenthesis has the same meaning but includes the use of the ITP and/or some auxiliary lemmata. Some trivial inferences have been omitted.

since the following two properties have been already proved:

$$\text{ABP} \Vdash \text{init} \Rightarrow \text{inv} \quad \text{and} \quad \text{ABP} \Vdash \text{inv} \Rightarrow \text{inv-main}.$$

When checking $\text{good-queues} \land \text{inv} \Rightarrow \bigcirc \text{inv}$, the following is the output given by the InvA tool:

```
rewrites: 97315 in 348ms cpu (346ms real) (279623 rewrites/second)
Checking ABP-PREDS ||- inv(S:Sys) => O inv(S:Sys)
  assuming good-queues(S:Sys) ...
Proof obligations generated:  48
Proof obligations discharged: 46
The following proof obligations could not be discharged:
8. from inv-1a & recv-2b : pending
    gen-list(#5:iNat)~(#6:iNat #9:iNatList) = true
 if #5:iNat = #6:iNat
 /\ all-bits(#8:BitQueue,off) = true
 /\ all-packets(#7:BitPacketQueue,off,#5:iNat) = true
 /\ gen-list(#5:iNat) = #5:iNat #9:iNatList .
46. from inv-1a & recv-2a : pending
    gen-list(#5:iNat)~(#6:iNat #9:iNatList) = true
 if #5:iNat = #6:iNat
 /\ all-bits(#8:BitQueue,on) = true
 /\ all-packets(#7:BitPacketQueue,on,#5:iNat) = true
 /\ gen-list(#5:iNat) = #5:iNat #9:iNatList .
```

The tool generates 48 proof obligations and automatically discharges 46 of them. The remaining two proof obligations are about properties of lists of natural numbers. Note that the Boolean transformation internally implemented by the InvA tool (explained in Section 3.1) splits the Boolean conjunctions in the specification of good-queues into conditions and the equality predicate '~' into '=', whenever it was possible. A proof script for proof obligations 8 and 46, that automatically discharges these proof obligations, can be given to the ITP as follows:

```
(goal po8 : ABP-PREDS |- A{ #5:iNat ; #6:iNat ; #9:iNatList ;
                            #8:BitQueue ; #7:BitPacketQueue }
 (
  (#5:iNat) = (#6:iNat) &
  (all-bits(#8:BitQueue,off)) = (true) &
  (all-packets(#7:BitPacketQueue,off,#5:iNat)) = (true) &
  (gen-list(#5:iNat)) = (#5:iNat #9:iNatList)
  =>
  (gen-list(#5:iNat) ~ (#6:iNat #9:iNatList)) = (true)
  )
.)
(auto .)

(goal po46 : ABP-PREDS |- A{ #5:iNat ; #6:iNat ; #9:iNatList ;
                             #8:BitQueue ; #7:BitPacketQueue }
 (
  (#5:iNat) = (#6:iNat) &
  (all-bits(#8:BitQueue,on)) = (true) &
  (all-packets(#7:BitPacketQueue,on,#5:iNat)) = (true) &
  (gen-list(#5:iNat)) = (#5:iNat #9:iNatList)
  =>
  (gen-list(#5:iNat) ~ (#6:iNat #9:iNatList)) = (true)
  )
.)
(auto .)
```

The following is the output of the ITP:

```
===================================
label-sel: po8#0@0
===================================
A{#5:iNat ; #6:iNat ; #7:BitPacketQueue ; #8:BitQueue ; #9:iNatList}
 gen-list(#5:iNat) = #5:iNat #9:iNatList
 & all-packets(#7:BitPacketQueue,off,#5:iNat) = true
 & all-bits(#8:BitQueue,off) = true & #5:iNat = #6:iNat
 ==> gen-list(#5:iNat)~(#6:iNat #9:iNatList) = true

+++++++++++++++++++++++++++++++++++

rewrites: 10751 in 173ms cpu (181ms real) (61990 rewrites/second)
Eliminated current goal.

q.e.d

+++++++++++++++++++++++++++++++++++

rewrites: 9172 in 51ms cpu (51ms real) (177962 rewrites/second)

===================================
label-sel: po46#1@0
===================================
```

```
A{#5:iNat ; #6:iNat ; #7:BitPacketQueue ; #8:BitQueue ; #9:iNatList}
 gen-list(#5:iNat) = #5:iNat #9:iNatList
 & all-packets(#7:BitPacketQueue,on,#5:iNat) = true
 & all-bits(#8:BitQueue,on) = true & #5:iNat = #6:iNat
 ==> gen-list(#5:iNat)~(#6:iNat #9:iNatList) = true
```

```
+++++++++++++++++++++++++++++++++++++
```

```
rewrites: 10751 in 179ms cpu (182ms real) (59745 rewrites/second)
Eliminated current goal.
```

```
q.e.d
```

```
+++++++++++++++++++++++++++++++++++++
```

This completes the proof of:

ABP ⊩ good-queues ∧ inv ⇒ ◯inv.

For the proof of init ⇒ □good-queues the InvA tool gives the following output:

```
rewrites: 10072 in 32ms cpu (35ms real) (314730 rewrites/second)
Checking ABP-PREDS ||- init(S:Sys) => good-queues(S:Sys) ...
Proof obligations generated:  2
Proof obligations discharged: 2
Success!
```

```
rewrites: 57223 in 284ms cpu (283ms real) (201476 rewrites/second)
Checking
  ABP-PREDS+LEMMATA ||- good-queues(S:Sys) => O good-queues(S:Sys) ...
Proof obligations generated:  48
Proof obligations discharged: 48
Success!
```

Note that in the proof of inductive stability, module ABP-PREDS+LEMMATA is used instead of ABP-PREDS. The former module contains 10 lemmata about the auxiliary predicates used by state predicate good-queues. Without these lemmata, the InvA tool discharges automatically only 26 of the 48 proof obligations. See [23] for a complete explanation of these lemmata and their mechanical proof in the ITP. This concludes the proof of the inductive invariance of good-queues from init for ABP.

The main result about the correctness of the ABP is then established mechanically in the InvA with help of the ITP. Namely, the following inductive property holds:

ABP ⊩ init ⇒ □inv-main.

See [23] for mechanical proofs of the admissibility of modules ABP, ABP-PREDS, ABP-PREDS+LEMMATA, and also for the ITP proof scripts used as part of the main result in this section.

6   Related Work and Concluding Remarks

The Alternating Bit Protocol (ABP) is a well-established benchmark in the proof technologies that address concurrent, non-deterministic systems. As such, it has been formally studied from different viewpoints using a wealth of formal techniques. They include process algebra [3,4], temporal Petri nets [27], the Calculus of Constructions [11], and timed rewriting logic [26], among many others.

In the framework of observational transition systems (OTS), ABP has been formally studied independently by K. Ogata and K. Futatsugi [20], and by K. Lin and J. Goguen [14]. In the former, the focus is on proving the same invariant property about reliable communication based on simultaneous induction. In the latter, the focus is on verifying liveness properties using conditional circular coinductive rewriting.

Figure 5 presents a comparison between the proof of the reliable communication property for ABP presented in [20], that uses proof scores, and the one presented here. This comparison is possible thanks to the authors of [20] who kindly shared the source code of their case study.

	Measure	[20]	This work
Model	LOC	286	208
Model + Predicates	LOC	286 + 63	208 + 200
State predicates	#	11	3
Lemmata	#	7	10
Proof scripts	LOC	5189	213
Proof scripts / # predicates	LOC	471.8	71

Fig. 5. Comparison of the ABP case study for the reliable communication property with a similar case study using proof scores in [20]

Note that the human proof effort in [20] is significantly higher than the one in proving the same property using the approach and tools of Section 3, as presented in this paper. However, this comparison needs to be taken with a grain of salt. In particular, the case study using proof scores in [20] does not benefit from automation techniques, not even for many proof obligations that are trivial base cases. In contrast, the combined power of InvA and ITP was of great help, not only because it automatically took care of many simple proof obligations, but also because of some of its equational inductive techniques such as cover-set induction [13].

This paper has presented a case study about the deductive analysis of inductive safety properties using the methodology, the proof system, and the Maude Invariant Analyzer tool (InvA) [23,24]. The subject of study is the Alterating Bit Protocol: a highly concurrent protocol for reliable data communication across a lossy channel. The invariant in this case study is about reliable communication, which is the main safety property of the ABP protocol. As a result of the case study, a fully mechanized proof for the correctness of the protocol is obtained with the InvA tool, and with help of Maude's ITP that was useful for discharging some equational proof obligations and auxiliary lemmata. The proof relies heavily on the specification and verification methods developed in [23,24], and their implementation in the InvA tool.

Future work should focus on improving the management of proof obligations in the InvA tool, specially when analyzing large specifications. There is also a need for improving the proof heuristics used by the tool. As explained in Section 3, a series of heuristics are employed by the InvA for discharging proof obligations. However, it should be possible to improve some of them and implement some new ones. For example, the InvA tool implements some basic heuristic for checking unsatisfiability of numeric conditions modulo SMT. This could perhaps be combined with equational narrowing, which is already available in Maude. This should increase the number of proof obligations automatically discharged by the tool, and thus lessen the proof effort of the user. There is also the need for improving the techniques available to the user in tools such as the ITP. For instance, inductive techniques such as cover-set induction modulo AC should be investigated, implemented, and offered to the user. The current ITP version supports cover-set induction [13] but for the moment *not* modulo AC. Finally, the comparison in Figure 5 could be taken a step further by (i) extending the InvA tool with (semi)automatic lemma discovery by means of symbolic simulation based on narrowing [1] and rewriting modulo SMT [23], and (ii) by comparing InvA's degree of automation with the OTS/CafeOBJ method assisted with automatic and interactive theorem proving tools such as CrÈme [18] and the newly developed CITP [10].

Acknowledgments. The authors would like to thank the anonymous referees for their comments that helped to improve the paper. This work was partially supported by NSF Grant CNS 13-19109.

References

1. Bae, K., Escobar, S., Meseguer, J.: Abstract logical model checking of infinite-state systems using narrowing. In: van Raamsdonk, F. (ed.) 24th International Conference on Rewriting Techniques and Applications, RTA 2013, Eindhoven, The Netherlands, June 24-26. LIPIcs, vol. 21, pp. 81–96. Schloss Dagstuhl - Leibniz-Zentrum fuer Informatik (2013)
2. Bartlett, K.A., Scantlebury, R.A., Wilkinson, P.T.: A note on reliable full-duplex transmission over half-duplex links. Commununications of the ACM 12(5), 260–261 (1969)
3. Bergstra, J., Klop, J.: Verification of an Alternating Bit Protocol by means of process algebra protocol. In: Bibel, W., Jantke, K. (eds.) Mathematical Methods of Specification and Synthesis of Software Systems 1985. LNCS, vol. 215, pp. 9–23. Springer, Heidelberg (1986)
4. Bezem, M., Groote, J.F.: Invariants in process algebra with data. In: Jonsson, B., Parrow, J. (eds.) CONCUR 1994. LNCS, vol. 836, pp. 401–416. Springer, Heidelberg (1994)
5. Bruni, R., Meseguer, J.: Semantic foundations for generalized rewrite theories. Theoretical Computer Science 360(1-3), 386–414 (2006)
6. Clarke, E.M., Grumberg, O., Peled, D.A.: Model Checking. The MIT Press, Cambridge (1999)

7. Clavel, M., Egea, M.: ITP/OCL: A rewriting-based validation tool for UML+OCL static class diagrams. In: Johnson, M., Vene, V. (eds.) AMAST 2006. LNCS, vol. 4019, pp. 368–373. Springer, Heidelberg (2006)
8. Durán, F., Meseguer, J.: A Church-Rosser checker tool for conditional order-sorted equational maude specifications. In: Ölveczky, P.C. (ed.) WRLA 2010. LNCS, vol. 6381, pp. 69–85. Springer, Heidelberg (2010)
9. Futatsugi, K., Gâinâ, D., Ogata, K.: Principles of proof scores in CafeOBJ. Theoretical Computer Science 464, 90–112 (2012)
10. Găină, D., Zhang, M., Chiba, Y., Arimoto, Y.: Constructor-based inductive theorem prover. In: Heckel, R. (ed.) CALCO 2013. LNCS, vol. 8089, pp. 328–333. Springer, Heidelberg (2013)
11. Giménez, E.: An application of co-inductive types in Coq: Verification of the Alternating Bit Protocol. In: Berardi, S., Coppo, M. (eds.) TYPES 1995. LNCS, vol. 1158, pp. 135–152. Springer, Heidelberg (1996)
12. Gutiérrez, R., Meseguer, J., Rocha, C.: Order-sorted equality enrichments modulo axioms. In: Durán, F. (ed.) WRLA 2012. LNCS, vol. 7571, pp. 162–181. Springer, Heidelberg (2012)
13. Hendrix, J.: Decision Procedures for Equationally Based Reasoning. PhD thesis, University of Illinois at Urbana-Champaign (April 2008)
14. Lin, K., Goguen, J.: A hidden proof of the Alternating Bit Protocol, http://cseweb.ucsd.edu/~goguen/pps/abp.ps
15. Meseguer, J.: Membership algebra as a logical framework for equational specification. In: Parisi-Presicce, F. (ed.) WADT 1997. LNCS, vol. 1376, pp. 18–61. Springer, Heidelberg (1998)
16. Meseguer, J.: Twenty years of rewriting logic. JLAP 81(7-8), 721–781 (2012)
17. Meseguer, J., Goguen, J.A.: Initially, induction and computability. Algebraic Methods in Semantics (1986)
18. Nakano, M., Ogata, K., Nakamura, M., Futatsugi, K.: Crème: an automatic invariant prover of behavioral specifications. International Journal of Software Engineering and Knowledge Engineering 17(6), 783–804 (2007)
19. Ogata, K., Futatsugi, K.: Proof scores in the OTS/CafeOBJ Method. In: Najm, E., Nestmann, U., Stevens, P. (eds.) FMOODS 2003. LNCS, vol. 2884, pp. 170–184. Springer, Heidelberg (2003)
20. Ogata, K., Futatsugi, K.: Simulation-based verification for invariant properties in the OTS/CafeOBJ method. Electronic Notes in Theorethical Computer Science 201, 127–154 (2008)
21. Ogata, K., Futatsugi, K.: Proof score approach to analysis of electronic commerce protocols. International Journal of Software Engineering and Knowledge Engineering 20(2), 253–287 (2010)
22. Pnueli, A.: Deduction is forever (1999) Invited talk at FM 1999 avaliable online at cs.nyu.edu/pnueli/fm99.ps
23. Rocha, C.: Symbolic Reachability Analysis for Rewrite Theories. PhD thesis, University of Illinois at Urbana-Champaign (2012), http://hdl.handle.net/2142/42200
24. Rocha, C., Meseguer, J.: Proving safety properties of rewrite theories. In: Corradini, A., Klin, B., Cîrstea, C. (eds.) CALCO 2011. LNCS, vol. 6859, pp. 314–328. Springer, Heidelberg (2011)
25. Roşu, G., Ştefănescu, A.: Matching Logic: A New Program Verification Approach (NIER Track). In: ICSE 211: Proceedings of the 30th International Conference on Software Engineering, pp. 868–871. ACM (2011)

26. Steggles, L., Kosiuczenko, P.: A timed rewriting logic semantics for SDL: A case study of the Alternating Bit Protocol. Electronic Notes in Theoretical Computer Science 15, 83–104 (1998)
27. Suzuki, I.: Formal analysis of the Alternating Bit Protocol by Temporal Petri Nets. IEEE Transactions on Software Engineering 16(11), 1273–1281 (1990)
28. Viry, P.: Equational rules for rewriting logic. TCS 285, 487–517 (2002)

Theorem Proving Based on Proof Scores
for Rewrite Theory Specifications of OTSs⋆

Kazuhiro Ogata and Kokichi Futatsugi

School of Information Science, JAIST
{ogata,futatsugi}@jaist.ac.jp

Abstract. We have intensively used proof scores to theorem prove that equational theory specifications of observational transition systems (OTSs) have properties. The paper describes a way to theorem prove that rewrite theory specifications of OTSs have invariant properties by proof score writing. The method may achieve a more faithfully seamless integration of model checking and theorem proving because no translation is needed for system specifications. The Lowe's modification (NSLPK) of NSPK authentication protocol is used to describe the method.

Keywords: (bounded) model checking, proof score, rewrite theory specification, search, theorem proving.

1 Introduction

Retrospect Let "I" refer to the first author in this paragraph. I first met the second author (Kokichi Futatsugi) at Tokyo in 1994, when I was finalizing my PhD project that was about an evolution of Smalltalk to a multiprocessor environment [1, 2]. When I gave a talk about my PhD project at JAIST in November, 1994, he asked me several questions. One question was in which way I had confirmed that my design and implementation worked as intended. I did not understand his true intention and then replied that a number of tests had been done. I joined his team in 1995, first working on design and implementation of rewrite engines [3–5]. I, together with him, started the research topic on formal verification of distributed concurrent systems with algebraic specification techniques in 1999 [6], still pursuing the topic, together with him and some others. One result is observational transition system (OTS) [7, 8]. I appreciate what he has done for me. One of the many things is to let me encounter that intriguing research topic. I have been still questing for an answer to his question that can convince him.

Let us start the technical part of the introduction of the present paper. OTSs are state transition systems (or state machines) that have emerged as a subclass of behavioral specifications [9, 10] based on UNITY [11]. The CafeOBJ [12] team led by the second author at JAIST has conducted a number of case studies

---

⋆ This work was partially supported by Kakenhi 23220002.

S. Iida, J. Meseguer, and K. Ogata (Eds.): Futatsugi Festschrift, LNCS 8373, pp. 630–656, 2014.

(among which are [13–20]) in which distributed concurrent systems are formalized as OTSs, OTSs are described as equational theory specifications in CafeOBJ and proof scores written in CafeOBJ are used to theorem prove that systems (formalized as OTSs) have properties. Proof scores are instructions such that when executed, if everything evaluates as expected, then some theorems are proved[21, 22]. Most properties verified are invariant properties, but a class of liveness ones can be treated[23]. OTS has been evolved into Timed OTS[24] that has been applied to a non-trivial case[25]. An automatic invariant prover called Creme has been designed and implemented[26]. The principle and logical foundation behind OTS and proof scores have been also constructed[21, 22, 27]. A proof assistant has been developed based on the logical foundation[28] and keeps evolving.

One research topic we have been pursuing is a seamless integration of model checking and (interactive) theorem proving[29, 30]. We have come up with a way to describe OTSs as rewrite theory specifications based on concurrent object-oriented rewrite theory specifications intensively used in the Maude[31] community so that OTSs can be model checked[32, 33]. We have then designed a way to translate a class of OTSs described as equational theory specifications into those as rewrite theory specifications and implemented a translator [34–37]. As imagined, the approach to the integration we have adopted so far needs two different system specifications for one system, and this is why translation from one to the other is required. We were thinking, however, that translation may prevent the two verification techniques from being integrated sufficiently well in a seamless way. We have then recognized that OTSs described as rewrite theory specifications can also be used for (interactive) theorem proving based on proof scores. The present paper describes a way to theorem prove that rewrite theory specifications of OTSs have invariant properties by proof score writing. The proposed method uses bounded model checking with depth 1 using rewriting-based search to discharge induction cases. The method may achieve a more faithfully seamless integration of model checking and theorem proving because no translation is needed for system specifications. The Lowe's modification (NSLPK)[38] of NSPK authentication protocol[39] is used to describe the method. Let us confess that we are not the first who have recognized that rewrite theory specifications can be used for theorem proving (see the related work section).

The rest of the paper is organized as follows. Sect. 2 mentions NSPK and gives a brief introduction to CafeOBJ. Sect. 3 describes integration of model checking and theorem proving. Sect. 4 outlines how to describe NSPK as a rewrite theory specification and to model check that NSPK has the nonce secrecy property with search. Sect. 5 uses NSLPK as an example to describe the proposed method. The two sections demonstrate that rewrite theory specifications of OTSs can be used for theorem proving as well as model checking. Sect. 6 mentions some related work. Sect. 7 concludes the paper.

2   Preliminaries

2.1   NSPK Authentication Protocol

NSPK[39] can be described as the three message exchanges:

Init: $p \to q$ $\{n_p, p\}_{k(q)}$
Resp: $q \to p$ $\{n_p, n_q\}_{k(p)}$
Ack: $p \to q$ $\{n_q\}_{k(q)}$

Each principal such as p and q is given a pair of keys (public and private keys). $\{m\}_{k(x)}$ is the ciphertext obtained by encrypting a message (or a tuple of messages) m with the principal x's public key. n_x is a nonce generated by a principal x. A nonce is a unique (and unguessable) number that is used once and may be implemented as a cryptographically secure pseudo random number.

One of the desired properties NSPK should have is the nonce secrecy property (NSP), which is that any nonces made in sessions that do not involve intruders are not leaked to the intruders, or equivalently that all nonces that can be gleaned by the intruders are those made by the intruders or by some other principals to authenticate the intruders.

Lowe reported on a counterexample showing that NSPK does not have NSP and proposed the modification [38]. The Lowe's modification is to include the sender's identification in the ciphertext used in a Resp message as follows:

Init: $p \to q$ $\{n_p, p\}_{k(q)}$
RevResp: $q \to p$ $\{n_p, n_q, q\}_{k(p)}$
Ack: $p \to q$ $\{n_q\}_{k(q)}$

The modified protocol is called the NSLPK authentication protocol.

We use the standard assumptions for protocol analysis to verify that NS(L)PK has NSP. Among them are that the cryptosystem used is perfect and the behaviors of malicious principals are formalized by the Dolev-Yao most general intruder[40]. Since we are only interested in NSP that can be expressed as an invariant property in this paper, it is not necessary to consider blocking of messages by the intruder.

2.2   CafeOBJ

CafeOBJ and Maude are direct successors of OBJ3 [41], and therefore can be considered language siblings. Hence, they have lots of features and functionalities in common. Since CafeOBJ has a large amounts of features and functionalities, it is impossible to introduce everything about CafeOBJ in this paper. Let us then describe only the features and functionalities of CafeOBJ that are required to read the paper.

A sort is a name given to a set of values. Sorts can be partially ordered, interpreted as subset relations among the sets corresponding to the sorts. Let PNat, PZero and PNzNat be the sorts given to the set of all natural numbers, the set of all non-zero natural numbers and the (singleton) set of zero, respectively.

PNat is the super-sort of PZero and PNzNat, and PZero and PNzNat are the sub-sorts of PNat. Operators are declared over sorts. Terms are inductively defined with operators and variables. Equations are used to define (standard) equivalence relations over terms.

Operators may be (data) constructors. Examples of constructors are as follows:

op true : → Bool {constr}
op false : → Bool {constr}
op z : → PZero {constr}
op s : PNat → PNzNat {constr}

where Bool is the sort given to the set of Boolean values. Operators with no arguments such as true are called constants. true and false are constants of Bool, denoting the usual Boolean values. z is a constant of PZero, denoting zero. Given a natural number n, $s(n)$ denotes the successor $(n+1)$ of n.

Basic units of specifications in CafeOBJ are modules. BOOL is a built-in module in which Boolean values are specified. Let PNAT be a module in which natural numbers are specified. BOOL is declared with tight semantics, and so is PNAT, which means that BOOL has one model "Boolean values" and PNAT has one model "natural numbers". We suppose that BOOL and PNAT are always protected in this paper.

Let RAND be a module declared with loose semantics, which means that RAND has a class of models. In RAND, both BOOL (that is automatically imported by almost all modules) and PNAT are imported, and the following operators are declared:

op seed : → PNat
op next : PNat → PNat

Note that they are not constructors. In RAND, we have the equations

eq $(\text{seed} = \text{next}(r)) = \text{false}$.
eq $(\text{next}(r) = \text{next}(r')) = (r = r')$.

where r and r' are variables of PNat. Note that two level equalities coexist in the two equations: (1) the meta-level (or the language-level) equality and (2) the object-level equality. The first occurrence of $=$ is the object-level equality and the second one is the meta-level equality in the first equation. The first and third occurrences of $=$ are the object-level equality and the second one is the meta-level equality in the second equation. The object-level equality operator (predicate) is declared in the built-in module EQL (that is part of BOOL) as follows:

op _ = _ : *Cosmos* *Cosmos* → Bool {comm}

where an underscore _ indicates the place in which an argument is put, and comm declares that the operator is commutative. *Cosmos* is a special sort in CafeOBJ and plays a wildcard sort. In EQL, the following equation is declared:

eq $(CUX = CUX) = \text{true}$.

where CUX is a variable of *Cosmos*.

Since RAND is declared with loose semantics, PNAT is protected and seed is not a constructor, seed denotes an arbitrary chosen natural number, and moreover since BOOL is protected, next generates an arbitrary chosen natural number that has not been generated due to the two equations in RAND. Hence, each model denoted by RAND is a permutation of all natural numbers. Some trivial permutations such as $0, 1, 2, \ldots$ and $99, 98, \ldots, 0, 199, 198, \ldots, \ldots 100, \ldots$ are not acceptable as cryptographically secure pseudo random numbers because they are predictable. But, unpredictableness of random numbers is implicitly specified in the behavior of protocols such that the intruder does not predict any nonces (random numbers), which works for verification purpose.

Let Intruder be the sort given to the set of intruders and intrdr a constant of Intruder, denoting the Dolev-Yao most general intruder. Let Prin&Intrdr be a super-sort of Prin and Intruder. A term of Prin&Intrdr denotes either a non-intruder principal or the intruder. Let Nonce be the sort given to the set of nonces. The constructor of nonces is declared as follows:

op n : Prin&Intrdr Prin&Intrdr PNat $\rightarrow$ Nonce {constr}

Given two principals p and q that may be the intruder and a random number r, $\mathrm{n}(p, q, r)$ denotes a nonce made by p to authenticate q, where r makes the nonce unique and unguessable. p and q in $\mathrm{n}(p, q, r)$ are meta-information in that they cannot be seen by any principals including the intruder. There are the (non-constructor) operators for nonces declared as follows:

op gen : Nonce $\rightarrow$ Prin&Intrdr
op forWhom : Nonce $\rightarrow$ Prin&Intrdr

The operators are defined in terms of equations as follows:

eq gen($\mathrm{n}(p, q, r)$) = p .
eq forWhom($\mathrm{n}(p, q, r)$) = q .

where p, q are variables of Prin&Intrdr and r is a variable of PNat.

Collections that are associative and commutative can be specified straightforwardly in CafeOBJ. Such collections are called soups. Let us consider soups of non-intruder principals. Let PrinSet be the sort given to the set of those soups. PrinSet is declared as a super-sort of Prin, which implies that a non-intruder principal is also the singleton soup that only consists of the principal. The constructors of PrinSet are declared as follows:

op noPrin : $\rightarrow$ PrinSet {constr}
op _ _ : PrinSet PrinSet $\rightarrow$ PrinSet {constr assoc comm **id** : noPrin}

The constant noPrin of PrinSet denotes the empty soup of Prin. The juxtaposition operator is associative and commutative as indicated by **assoc** and **comm**. noPrin is an identity of the juxtaposition operator as indicated by **id** : noPrin. Let a_1, a_2, a_3 be non-intruder principals. The term $a_1\ a_2\ a_3$ denotes the soup consisting of the three non-intruder principals. Since the juxtaposition operator is associative and commutative, $a_3\ a_2\ a_1$ and $a_2\ a_1\ a_3$ also denote the same soup. Since we would like to prohibit duplications in soups, we have the equation:

eq $a\ a = a$.

where a is a variable of **Prin**. For any type of soup, in the paper, the juxtaposition operator is used as a constructor, a constant denoting the empty soup is an identity of the juxtaposition operator and duplication is not allowed.

Let us consider a simple protocol (system) each of whose states consists of a soup of non-intruder principals, a soup of nonces and a random number. Those values are expressed as name/value pairs called observable values. Let **OVal** be the sort given to the set of observable values. The following constructors are used for observable values in the example:

op (prins : _) : PrinSet $\rightarrow$ OVal {constr}
op (nonces : _) : NonceSet $\rightarrow$ OVal {constr}
op (rand : _) : PNat $\rightarrow$ OVal {constr}

Terms that are in the forms (prins : ...), (nonces : ...) and (rand : ...) are called a **prins** observable value, a **nonces** observable value and a **rand** observable value, respectively. A state of the simple protocol is expressed as a soup of observable values. Let **Config** be the sort given to the set of those soups and a super-sort of **OVal**. But, not all terms of **Config** necessarily express states of the simple protocol. A term of **Config** expresses a state of the simple protocol if and only if **prins**, **nonces** and **rand** observable values appear in the term exactly once, respectively. The following operator (predicate) is used to check if a given term of **Config** expresses a state of the simple protocol:

op isValid : Config $\rightarrow$ Bool
eq isValid(s)
    = (#prins(s) = s(z) **and** #nonces(s) = s(z) **and** #rand(s) = s(z)) .

where **#prins**, **#nonces** and **#rand** returns the number of occurrences of the corresponding observable value in a given term of **Config**, respectively.

Initially, the soup of principals consists of given principals that participate in the simple protocol, the soup of nonces is empty (denoted as **noNonce**) and the random number is **seed**. An initial state (denoted as init(as), where as is the soup of given non-intruder principals) is specified as follows:

op init : PrinSet $\rightarrow$ Config
eq init(as) = (prins : as) (nonces : noNonce) (rand : seed) .

Let us consider one state transition (actually a set of state transitions) of the simple protocol such that two different non-intruder principals a, b are arbitrarily chosen, a nonce $n(a, b, r)$ is made with a, b and the random number r available and added into the soup of nonces, and a fresh random number is generated. The state transition is specified in transition rule (or rewrite rules) as follows:

ctrans [Rule1] :

$(\mathbf{prins}:(a\ b\ as))\ (\mathbf{nonces}:ns)\ (\mathbf{rand}:r)$

$\Rightarrow$

$(\mathbf{prins}:(a\ b\ as))\ (\mathbf{nonces}:(\mathbf{n}(a,b,r)\ ns))\ (\mathbf{rand}:\mathbf{next}(r))$
if $not(a=b)$.

where **Rule1** is the label of the transition rule, a,b are variables of **Prin**, as one of **PrinSet**, ns one of **NonceSet** and r one of **PNat**. Specifications that have transition rules are called rewrite theory (system) specifications, while those that do not have any transition rules (namely those that only have equations) are called equational theory specifications.

Given a rewrite theory system specification and a ground term that typically represents an initial state of the system, CafeOBJ makes it possible to exhaustively traverse all terms reachable from the ground term by zero (or one) or more state transitions with transition rules in a breadth first manner. This is called the search functionality (or just search). The search functionality that takes zero or more state transitions into account is in the form:

red $init\ =(n,d)\!\Rightarrow\!*\ pattern$ **suchThat** $cond$.

where $init$ is a ground term, $pattern$ a state pattern that may contain variables, $cond$ a Boolean term whose variables should occur in $pattern$, and n and d natural numbers or $*$ denoting the infinity. "**suchThat** $cond$" is an option. If $=(n,d)\!\Rightarrow\!+$ is used instead of $=(n,d)\!\Rightarrow\!*$, one or more state transitions are taken into account. The search functionality performs that traversal up to depth d and finds terms that match $pattern$ such that $cond$ holds. Substitutions (functions from variables to terms) obtained by matching those terms with $pattern$ such that $cond$ holds are called solutions. The search functionality provides at most n solutions.

If $cond$ is the negation of a state predicate to be proved invariant and $pattern$ contains enough information such that $cond$ can reduce to either **true** or **false**, then the search functionality can be used to model check that the state predicate is invariant with respect to the system specification under consideration. Let a, b be constants of **Prin** such that a does not equal b. The following search amounts to bounded model checking up to depth 5 that **isValid** is invariant with respect to the simple protocol:

red init(a b) $=(1,5)\!\Rightarrow\!*\ s$ **suchThat** (**not** isValid(s)) .

where s is a variable of **Config**. CafeOBJ reports that no solutions (no counterexamples) are found.

Unlike most existing model checkers, $init$ does not need to be made very concrete. $init$ may contain constants that denote arbitrary values. An arbitrary state of the simple protocol to which the transition rule **Rule1** can be applied is expressed as $(\mathbf{prins}:(\mathbf{a}\ \mathbf{b}\ \mathbf{as}))\ (\mathbf{nonces}:\mathbf{ns})\ (\mathbf{rand}:\mathbf{r})$, where a, b are constants of **Prin** denoting arbitrary non-intruder principals, a does not equal b, **as** is a constant of **PrinSet** denoting an arbitrary soup of non-intruder principals, **ns** is a constant of **NonceSet** denoting an arbitrary soup of nonces, and **r** is a constant of **PNat** denoting an arbitrary natural number (a random number). Let

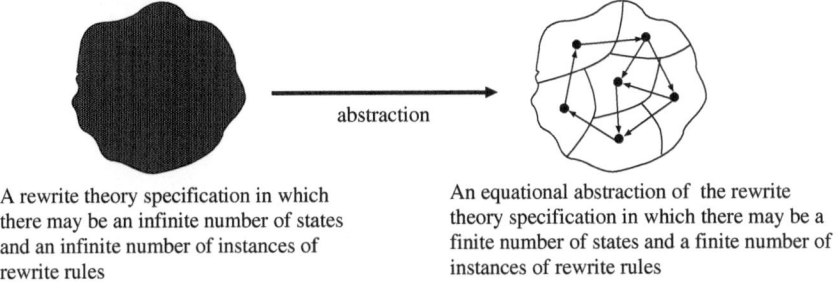

A rewrite theory specification in which there may be an infinite number of states and an infinite number of instances of rewrite rules

An equational abstraction of the rewrite theory specification in which there may be a finite number of states and a finite number of instances of rewrite rules

abstraction

Fig. 1. Equational (quotient) abstraction

s refer to the term. The following search finds all successor states of s obtained by applying **Rule1** to s:

red s $=(*, 1) \Rightarrow + s'$.

where s' is a variable of **Config**. There are two such successor states:

1. (**prins** : (a b as)) (**nonces** : (n(a, b, r) ns)) (**rand** : next(r))
2. (**prins** : (a b as)) (**nonces** : (n(b, a, r) ns)) (**rand** : next(r))

The following search proves that **isValid** is preserved by **Rule1**:

red s $=(*, 1) \Rightarrow + s'$ **suchThat** (not(isValid(s') == true)) .

Note that $t_1 == t_2$ reduces to **true** if both t_1 and t_2 reduce to a same term and **false** otherwise. If **isValid**(s') reduces to **true** for each s' of the two successor states, then the search does not find any solutions and **isValid** is preserved by **Rule1**. Otherwise, the search finds some solutions due to the use of "not" and "== **true**". Since there is no solution, **isValid** is preserved by **Rule1**. **isValid(init(as))** reduces to **true** for a constant **as** of **PrinSet** denoting an arbitrary soup of non-intruder principals, and then if state transitions specified by **Rule1** are only ones that happens in the simple protocol, **isValid** is invariant with respect to the simple protocol.

3   Integrations of Model Checking and Theorem Proving

Many attempts have been made to integrate model checking and theorem proving. This section mentions one attempt for verification and another for falsification in the algebraic specification community. We also mention two types of system specifications in CafeOBJ, system specification translation from one type into the other, and a possibility for a more faithfully seamless integration of model checking and theorem proving in the section.

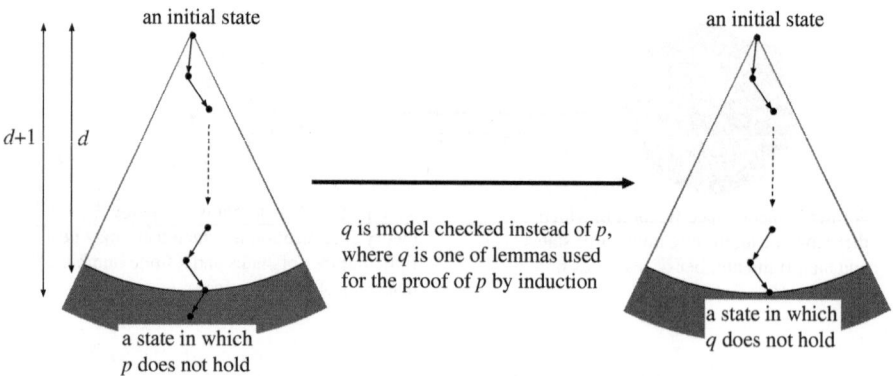

Fig. 2. Induction-guided falsification

3.1   Verification

Equational abstraction [42] is one way to integrate model checking and theorem proving. A system is described as a rewrite theory specification $\mathcal{R}$ in which there may be an infinite number of different states and a property is expressed as a linear temporal logic (LTL) formula φ. Equational abstraction adds a set E' of equations to $\mathcal{R}$, making the quotient specification $\mathcal{R}/E'$ that is called an equational abstraction of $\mathcal{R}$ (see Fig. 1). If (1) $\mathcal{R}/E'$ is executable such that the set of all equations in it are ground Church-Rosser and terminating, (2) φ is preserved by the quotient simulation from the (concrete) states in $\mathcal{R}$ to the (abstract) ones in $\mathcal{R}/E'$, and (3) there exist a finite number (a small enough number) of different states in $\mathcal{R}/E'$, then you can model check $\mathcal{R}/E' \models \varphi$ from which you conclude $\mathcal{R} \models \varphi$. You are supposed to discharge (1) and (2) with theorem proving. This is why equational abstraction is an integration of model checking and theorem proving. One case study with equational abstraction is the verification that a simplified version of the Lamport's bakery protocol in which there are two processes has the mutual exclusion and lockout freedom properties. Since the number given to processes may be increased unboundedly, the state space of the protocol is infinite even though there are two processes. The case study uses the observation that the relation between the two numbers owned by two processes in each state is essential but each actual number is not. The observation can be used to make an equational abstraction of a rewrite theory specification of the protocol that satisfies (1), (2) and (3).

3.2   Falsification

Induction-guided falsification (IGF) [29, 30] is another way to integrate model checking and theorem proving, precisely bounded model checking and induction often used in theorem proving. Suppose that you have a rewrite theory specification $\mathcal{R}$ and an equational theory specification $\mathcal{E}$ for one system to be

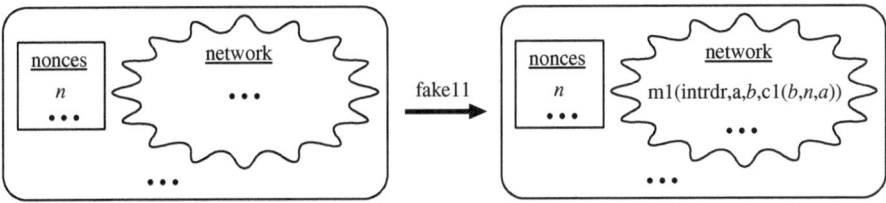

Fig. 3. A state transition in NSPK (faking an Init message using a nonce n gleaned by the intruder)

considered. For $\mathcal{R}$, an initial state s_0 of $\mathcal{R}$ and a state predicate p over $\mathcal{R}$, also suppose that it is possible to do bounded model checking up to depth d from s_0 in a reasonable amount of time for p, but not to do so up to depth $d+1$ or more. Suppose that there is no state such that p does not hold at depth d or any shallower positions, but such a state at depth $d+1$ From the assumptions, only bounded model checking cannot find the state such that p does not hold in a reasonable amount of time. If that is the case, you attempt to prove that a state predicate p' over $\mathcal{E}$ that corresponds to p is invariant with respect to $\mathcal{E}$ by induction, and conjecture lemmas. If each lemmas is a necessary one for the proof of p', there must be one lemma q' such that q' does not hold at depth d. Hence, you can find a state at depth d such that q' (precisely a state predicate over $\mathcal{R}$ that corresponds to q') does not hold, from which you can reach a state at depth $d+1$ such that p does not hold (see Fig. 2). One case study with IGF is the falsification that NSPK has the agreement (or authentication) property. For a rewrite theory specification of NSPK in which two non-intruder principals and the intruder participate, it is possible to do bounded model checking up to depth 5 for the property in a reasonable amount of time, but not up to depth 6 or any deeper positions. Hence, no state is found such that the property is broken with only bounded model checking. Then, the property attempts to be proved by induction and some lemmas are conjectured. One of the lemmas has a state at depth 5 in which the lemma does not hold, and such a state can be found by bounded model checking up to depth 5, from which you reach a state at depth 6 such that the agreement property is broken.

3.3 Two Types of System Specifications in CafeOBJ

In general, you need to have two types of system specifications for one system to integrate model checking and theorem proving. One is for model checking and the other for theorem proving. When writing them in CafeOBJ, the former is written as an equational theory specification and the latter as a rewrite theory specification.

Let us consider a state transition depicted in Fig. 3. The state transition called **fake11** is used in a state machine modeling the NS(L)PK authentication protocol and formalizes faking a message using a nonce n gleaned by the intruder. The state transition can be described in both equation and transition (rewrite) rule.

The state transition described in equation looks like

ceq nw(fake11(s, n, a, b)) = m1(intrdr, a, b, c1(b, n, a)) nw(s)
    if $n \in$ nonces(s) **and** not($a = b$) .
. . .

In this specification, the structure of a state is not explicit [7, 8]. Values that characterize a state can be observed only through operators called observation operators such as nonces and nw that are used to observe the nonces gleaned by the intruder and the network in a state. For example, s is a state and fake11(s, n, a, b) is the successor state of s after the state transition. nw(s) is the network in s, and nw(fake11(s, n, a, b)) is the one in fake11(s, n, a, b), which is defined in the equation.

The equation says that if the intruder intrdr has gleaned a nonce n in a state s ($n \in$ nonces(s)), a message m1(intrdr, a, b, c1(b, n, a)) may be faked, being put into the network nw(s). A network is formalized as a soup of messages. a is the seeming sender, b is the receiver but the actual sender is the intruder. c1(b, n, a) is the body of the message, a ciphertext made by encrypting n and a (the a's identification) with the b's public key. fake11(s, n, a, b) expresses the next state of the state transition, and nw(fake11(s, n, a, b)) expresses the network that consists of the newly faked one and those that reside in the previous network nw(s).

The state transition described in transition rule looks like

ctrans [fake11] :
(nonces : (n ns)) (nw : ms) · · ·
$\Rightarrow$
(nonces : (n ns)) (nw : (m1(intrdr, a, b, c1(b, n, a)) ms)) · · ·
if not($a = b$) .

In this specification, a state is expressed as a soup of observable values as described in Subsect. 2.2. (nonces : . . .) is a nonces observable value as described in Subsect. 2.2, but what is contained in it is a soup of nonces gleaned by the intruder. (nw : . . .) is called a nw observable value whose constructor is declared as follows:

op (nw : _) : Network → OVal {constr}

where Network is the sort given to the set of soups of messages.

3.4 System Specification Translation

One possible way to integrate model checking and theorem proving seamlessly is to translate one type of system specification into the other type. We have then designed and implemented a translator that takes a specific type of an equational theory system specification into a rewrite theory system specification [36]. For example, the state transition described in the equation shown in the previous subsection is translated into the one in transition rule shown in the previous subsection. We have proved that the rewrite theory system specification translated from an equational theory system specification has an invariant property if and only if the equational theory system specification has the property [37]. Let us note that the rewrite theory system specification translated may have unbounded number of reachable states and/or an unbounded length of terms may be needed to express states unless some parameters such as the number of processes are fixed. Therefore, even if an equational theory system specification has a counterexample such that the system specification does not have a property, the counterexample may not be revealed by conducting (bounded) model checking of the property for the rewrite theory system specification such that some parameters are fixed.

After we have proved that the design of the translator has the desired property, the translator has been implemented based on the design. Although the implementation has been done very carefully, however, there might be some unintended errors in the implementation because we have not verified that the implementation had the property. Moreover, there might be some slips in the proof that the design of the translator has the property because the proof has not been conducted formally but in a traditional mathematical way.

Let us note that even if you conducted code verification for the implementation, you would not conclude that the implementation does have the property because code verification assumes some idealized abstract machine but not a real machine that is out of scope of formal verification.

3.5   Towards a More Faithfully Seamless Integration

Translation (or transformation) is one of the successful and important techniques used in computer science. Compilers are the most prominent example. It would be much preferable, however, not to need to translate between two types of system specifications for model checking and theorem proving, respectively, because some unintended subtle errors might be introduced by translation. Hence, we would like to use one system specification for one system for both model checking and theorem proving if possible, which may lead to a more faithfully seamless integration of model checking and theorem proving. One possible candidate is rewrite theory specifications as we have shown some potential that rewrite theory specifications could be used for theorem proving in Subsect. 2.2. In the rest of the paper, NSPK and NSLPK are used to demonstrate that rewrite theory specifications can be used for both model checking and theorem proving.

4   Model Checking of NSPK

4.1   System Specification of NSPK

Specifications of random numbers, intruders, non-intruder principals, nonces, soups of non-intruder principals and soups of nonces are the same as those described in Subsect. 2.2.

Ciphertexts $\{n_p, p\}_{k(q)}$, $\{n_p, n_q\}_{k(p)}$ and $\{n_q\}_{k(q)}$ used in Init, Resp and Ack messages, respectively, are denoted by terms $\texttt{c1}(q, n_p, p)$, $\texttt{c2}(p, n_p, n_q)$ and $\texttt{c3}(q, n_q)$, respectively. Their sorts are $\texttt{Cipher}i$ for $i = 1, 2, 3$, respectively. Let $\texttt{non}(\texttt{c1}(q, n_p, p))$ and $\texttt{gen}(\texttt{c1}(q, n_p, p))$ be the nonce n_p used in the ciphertext $\texttt{c1}(q, n_p, p)$ and the principal p that must have made the ciphertext, respectively.

Init, Resp and Ack messages are denoted by terms $\texttt{m}i(p?, p, q, c_i)$ for $i = 1, 2, 3$, respectively. Their sorts are $\texttt{Msg}i$ for $i = 1, 2, 3$, respectively. The first argument $p?$ is the creator (the actual sender) of the message, the second argument p the seeming sender, the third argument q the receiver and the fourth argument c_i the ciphertext. The first argument is meta-information in that when q receives $\texttt{m}i(p?, p, q, e_i)$, q cannot look at $p?$. If $p?$ is different from p, then $p?$ is the intruder and the message has been faked by the intruder. One more sort $\texttt{Msg}$ is used for messages, which is a super-sort of $\texttt{Msg}i$ for $i = 1, 2, 3$.

The network is formalized as a soup of messages whose sort is $\texttt{Network}$. The empty network is expressed as a constant $\texttt{noMsg}$ of $\texttt{Network}$. We suppose that once a message $\texttt{m}i(p?, p, q, e_i)$ is put into the network, it will be never deleted, and if there exists such a message in the network, q can receive it. When q receives it, q thinks that it has been sent by p. Let c_i be a term whose sort is $\texttt{Cipher}i$ and ms be a term whose sort is $\texttt{Network}$, and then $c_i \in ms$ holds if and only if ms contains a term m_i whose sort is $\texttt{Msg}i$ such that m_i has c_i as its ciphertext.

A state is expressed as a soup of observable values mentioned in Subsect. 2.2 and Subsect. 3.3. The sort of states is $\texttt{Config}$ that is a super-sort of $\texttt{OVal}$, the sort of observable values. As in the simple protocol, not all terms of $\texttt{Config}$ necessarily express states of NSPK. A term of $\texttt{Config}$ expresses a state of NSPK if and only if $\texttt{nw}$, $\texttt{rand}$, $\texttt{prins}$ and $\texttt{nonces}$ observable values appear in the term exactly once, respectively[1]. Concretely, a state is in the form $(\texttt{nw} : ms)$ $(\texttt{rand} : r)$ $(\texttt{prins} : as)$ $(\texttt{nonces} : ns)$, where ms is a soup of messages that have been sent, r is a random number that will be used next to make a nonce, as is a soup of non-intruder principals and ns is a soup of nonces that have been gleaned by the intruder. In the initial state, ms is $\texttt{noMsg}$, the empty soup of messages, r is $\texttt{seed}$, a random number, as is a given soup of non-intruder principals that participate in the protocol and ns is $\texttt{noNonce}$. The initial state is referred to as $\texttt{init}(as)$.

23 transition rules are used to specify the behavior of NSPK. Five of them exactly obey the protocol and the rest of them fake messages based on nonces gleaned by the intruder and messages in the network. In the rest of the paper, let a, b be CafeOBJ variables of $\texttt{Prin}$, p, q, p', q' ones of $\texttt{Prin\&Intrdr}$, as one of $\texttt{PrinSet}$, ms one of $\texttt{Network}$, r one of $\texttt{PNat}$, n, n' ones of $\texttt{Nonce}$, ns one of $\texttt{NonceSet}$, s one of $\texttt{Config}$, $c1$ one of $\texttt{Cipher1}$, and $c2$ one of $\texttt{Cipher2}$, unless otherwise stated.

The following three transition rules formalize sending of Init messages by a non-intruder principal a to another non-intruder principal b, a non-intruder principal a to the intruder and the intruder to a non-intruder principal b, respectively, based on the protocol:

---

[1] The way to express states of NSLPK used in the paper is the same as that of NSPK.

ctrans [Init1] :
$(\mathtt{nw} : ms)\ (\mathtt{rand} : r)\ (\mathtt{nonces} : ns)\ (\mathtt{prins} : (a\ b\ as))$
$\Rightarrow$
$(\mathtt{nw} : (\mathtt{m1}(a, a, b, \mathtt{c1}(b, \mathtt{n}(a, b, r), a))\ ms))$
$(\mathtt{rand} : \mathtt{next}(r))\ (\mathtt{nonces} : ns)\ (\mathtt{prins} : (a\ b\ as))$
if $\mathrm{not}(a = b)$.

trans [Init2] :
$(\mathtt{nw} : ms)\ (\mathtt{rand} : r)\ (\mathtt{nonces} : ns)\ (\mathtt{prins} : (a\ as))$
$\Rightarrow$
$(\mathtt{nw} : (\mathtt{m1}(a, a, \mathtt{intrdr}, \mathtt{c1}(\mathtt{intrdr}, \mathtt{n}(a, \mathtt{intrdr}, r), a))\ ms))$
$(\mathtt{rand} : \mathtt{next}(r))\ (\mathtt{nonces} : (\mathtt{n}(a, \mathtt{intrdr}, r)\ ns))\ (\mathtt{prins} : (a\ as))$.

trans [Init3] :
$(\mathtt{nw} : ms)\ (\mathtt{rand} : r)\ (\mathtt{nonces} : ns)\ (\mathtt{prins} : (b\ as))$
$\Rightarrow$
$(\mathtt{nw} : (\mathtt{m1}(\mathtt{intrdr}, \mathtt{intrdr}, b, \mathtt{c1}(b, \mathtt{n}(\mathtt{intrdr}, b, r), \mathtt{intrdr}))\ ms))$
$(\mathtt{rand} : \mathtt{next}(r))\ (\mathtt{nonces} : ns)\ (\mathtt{prins} : (b\ as))$.

In the transition rule Init2, since the ciphertext $\mathtt{c1}(\mathtt{intrdr}, \mathtt{n}(a, \mathtt{intrdr}, r), a)$ can be decrypted by the intruder, the nonce $\mathtt{n}(a, \mathtt{intrdr}, r)$ is gleaned by the intruder.

The following transition rule formalizes replying to an Init message by sending a Resp message by the receiver q to the seeming sender p:

trans [Resp] :
$(\mathtt{nw} : (\mathtt{m1}(p', p, q, \mathtt{c1}(q, n, p))\ ms))\ (\mathtt{rand} : r)\ (\mathtt{nonces} : ns)\ (\mathtt{prins} : as)$
$\Rightarrow$
$(\mathtt{nw} : (\mathtt{m2}(q, q, p, \mathtt{c2}(p, n, \mathtt{n}(q, p, r)))\ \mathtt{m1}(p', p, q, \mathtt{c1}(q, n, p))\ ms))$
$(\mathtt{nonces} : (\mathbf{if}\ p = \mathtt{intrdr}\ \mathbf{then}\ \mathtt{n}(q, p, r)\ n\ ns\ \mathbf{else}\ ns\ \mathbf{fi}))$
$(\mathtt{rand} : \mathtt{next}(r))\ (\mathtt{prins} : as)$.

p' may be different from p. The transition rule says that if the ciphertext $\mathtt{c2}(p, n, \mathtt{n}(q, p, r))$ can be decrypted by the intruder, the intruder gleans the nonces n and $\mathtt{n}(q, p, r)$.

The following transition rule formalizes replying to a Resp message (which is a reply to an Init message sent by p to q) by sending an Ack message by the receiver p to the seeming sender q:

trans [Ack] :
$(\mathtt{nw} : (\mathtt{m2}(q', q, p, \mathtt{c2}(p, n, n'))\ \mathtt{m1}(p, p, q, \mathtt{c1}(q, n, p))\ ms))$
$(\mathtt{rand} : r)\ (\mathtt{nonces} : ns)\ (\mathtt{prins} : as)$
$\Rightarrow$
$(\mathtt{nw} : (\mathtt{m3}(p, p, q, \mathtt{c3}(q, n'))$
$\qquad \mathtt{m2}(q', q, p, \mathtt{c2}(p, n, n'))\ \mathtt{m1}(p, p, q, \mathtt{c1}(q, n, p))ms))$
$(\mathtt{nonces} : (\mathbf{if}\ q = \mathtt{intrdr}\ \mathbf{then}\ n'\ ns\ \mathbf{else}\ ns\ \mathbf{fi}))$
$(\mathtt{rand} : r)\ (\mathtt{prins} : as)$.

q' may be different from q. The transition rule says that if the ciphertext $c3(q, n')$ can be decrypted by the intruder, the intruder gleans the nonce n'.

Among the remaining 18 transition rules, nine of them formalize faking of messages based on nonces gleaned by the intruder and the rest formalize faking of messages based on messages in the network. Three transition rules from the former ones and one from the latter ones are shown in this paper.

ctrans [Fake11] :
$(\text{nw} : ms) \ (\text{rand} : r) \ (\text{nonces} : (n \ ns)) \ (\text{prins} :(a \ b \ as))$
$\Rightarrow$
$(\text{nw} : (\text{m1}(\text{intrdr}, a, b, \text{c1}(b, n, a)) \ ms))$
$(\text{rand} : r) \ (\text{nonces} : (n \ ns)) \ (\text{prins} : (a \ b \ as))$
if $\text{not}(a = b)$.

The transition rule Fake11 fakes the Init message $\text{m1}(\text{intrdr}, a, b, \text{c1}(b, n, a))$ based on a nonce n gleaned by the intruder. The message seems to have been sent by a non-intruder principal a to another non-intruder principal b, but is faked by the intruder.

trans [Fake11b] :
$(\text{nw} : ms) \ (\text{rand} : r) \ (\text{nonces} : (n \ ns)) \ (\text{prins} :(b \ as))$
$\Rightarrow$
$(\text{nw} : (\text{m1}(\text{intrdr}, \text{intrdr}, b, \text{c1}(b, n, \text{intrdr})) \ ms))$
$(\text{rand} : r) \ (\text{nonces} : (n \ ns)) \ (\text{prins} : (b \ as))$.

The transition rule Fake11b fakes the Init message $\text{m1}(\text{intrdr}, \text{intrdr}, b, \text{c1}(b, n, \text{intrdr}))$ based on a nonce n gleaned by the intruder.

ctrans [Fake21a] :
$(\text{nw} : ms) \ (\text{rand} : r) \ (\text{nonces} : (n \ n' \ ns)) \ (\text{prins} : (a \ as))$
$\Rightarrow$
$(\text{nw} : (\text{m2}(\text{intrdr}, \text{intrdr}, a, \text{c2}(a, n, n') \ ms))$
$(\text{rand} : r) \ (\text{nonces} : (n \ n' \ ns)) \ (\text{prins} : (a \ as))$
if $\text{not}(n = n')$.

The transition rule Fake21a fakes the Resp message $\text{m2}(\text{intrdr}, \text{intrdr}, a, \text{c2}(a, n, n'))$ based on two different nonces n, n' gleaned by the intruder.

trans [Fake22a] :
$(\text{nw} : (\text{m2}(q', q, p, c2) \ ms)) \ (\text{rand} : r) \ (\text{nonces} : ns) \ (\text{prins} : (a \ as))$
$\Rightarrow$
$(\text{nw} : (\text{m2}(\text{intrdr}, \text{intrdr}, a, c2) \ \text{m2}(q', q, p, c2) \ ms))$
$(\text{rand} : r) \ (\text{nonces} : ns) \ (\text{prins} : (a \ as))$.

The transition rule Fake22a fakes the Resp message $\text{m2}(\text{intrdr}, \text{intrdr}, a, c2)$ based on a Resp message $\text{m2}(q', q, p, c2)$ in the network.

4.2 Property Specification of NSP

NSP is expressed as an invariant property such that the following state predicate is invariant with respect to the system specification of NSPK:

op nonSec : Config Nonce $\rightarrow$ Bool
eq nonSec(s, n)
    $= n \in$ nonces(s) implies (gen(n) = intrdr or forWhom(n) = intrdr) .

where nonces(s) returns the soup of nonces that is contained in the nonces observable value in s^2. nonSec(s, n) says that if a nonce n has been gleaned by the intruder in a state s, n has been generated by the intruder or by a non-intruder principal to authenticate the intruder. Hence, the verification that NSPK has NSP is to show that nonSec(s, n) holds for all reachable states s and all nonces n.

4.3 Model Checking of NSP for NSPK

Let a, b be constants of Prin such that a does not equal b. The following search performs bounded model checking up to depth 5 that the rewrite theory system specification of NSPK in which two different non-intruder principals and the intruder participate has NSP:

red init(a b) $=(1, 5)\Rightarrow*$ ((nonces : (n ns)) s)
    suchThat (not nonSec((nonces : (n ns)) s, n)) .

The search finds a counterexample showing that NSPK does not have NSP, which is the same as the Lowe's counterexample (see Fig. 4)[3].

5 Theorem Proving of NSLPK

5.1 Modification of System Specification

The difference between NSPK and NSLPK is that the ciphertext used in a Resp message contains the identification of a principal that has made the ciphertext. That is, the ciphertext used in a revised Resp message is in the form c2(p, n_p, n_q, q). Let non(c2(p, n_p, n_q, q)) and gen(c2(p, n_p, n_q, q)) be the second nonce n_q used in the ciphertext c2(p, n_p, n_q, q) and the principal q that must have made the ciphertext, respectively. Accordingly, the system specification of NSPK is modified, becoming that of NSLPK. Among the nine transition rules shown in Subsect. 4.1, the three transition rules Resp, Ack and Fake21a are modified. The modified versions of the three transition rules are as follows:

---

[2] For a term s of Config, if there exists exactly one occurrence of nonces observable values in s, nonces(s) returns the soup of nonces in the observable value, and otherwise it returns noNonce.

[3] Let us confess that the model checking described in the subsection has been conducted with Maude instead of CafeOBJ because Maude search functionality is more efficient than CafeOBJ's.

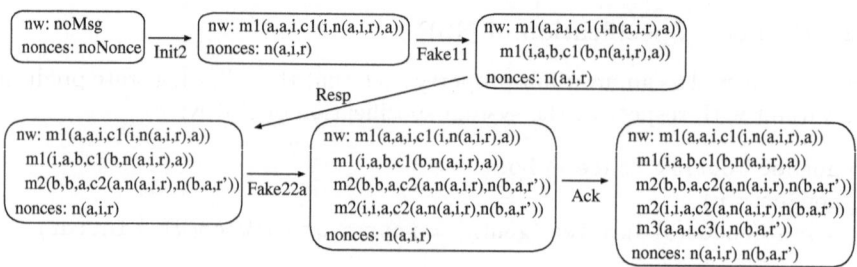

Fig. 4. A counterexample showing that NSPK does not have NSP (i stands for `intrdr`, r' stands for `next(r)`, and `rand` and `prins` observable values are omitted)

trans [RevResp] :
$(\text{nw} : (\text{m1}(p', p, q, \text{c1}(q, n, p))\ ms))\ (\text{rand} : r)\ (\text{nonces} : ns)\ (\text{prins} : as)$
$\Rightarrow$
$(\text{nw} : (\text{m2}(q, q, p, \text{c2}(p, n, \mathbf{n}(q, p, r), q))\ \text{m1}(p', p, q, \text{c1}(q, n, p))\ ms))$
$(\text{nonces} : (\text{if } p = \text{intrdr then } \mathbf{n}(q, p, r)\ n\ ns \text{ else } ns \text{ fi}))$
$(\text{rand} : \text{next}(r))\ (\text{prins} : as)$.

trans [RevAck] :
$(\text{nw} : (\text{m2}(q', q, p, \text{c2}(p, n, n', q))\ \text{m1}(p, p, q, \text{c1}(q, n, p))\ ms))$
$(\text{rand} : r)\ (\text{nonces} : ns)\ (\text{prins} : as)$
$\Rightarrow$
$(\text{nw} : (\text{m3}(p, p, q, \text{c3}(q, n'))$
$\qquad \text{m2}(q', q, p, \text{c2}(p, n, n', q))\ \text{m1}(p, p, q, \text{c1}(q, n, p))ms))$
$(\text{nonces} : (\text{if } q = \text{intrdr then } n'\ ns \text{ else } ns \text{ fi}))$
$(\text{rand} : r)\ (\text{prins} : as)$.

ctrans [RevFake21a] :
$(\text{nw} : ms)\ (\text{rand} : r)\ (\text{nonces} : (n\ n'\ ns))\ (\text{prins} : (a\ as))$
$\Rightarrow$
$(\text{nw} : (\text{m2}(\text{intrdr}, \text{intrdr}, a, \text{c2}(a, n, n', \text{intrdr})\ ms))$
$(\text{rand} : r)\ (\text{nonces} : (n\ n'\ ns))\ (\text{prins} : (a\ as))$
if $\text{not}(n = n')$.

Since the ciphertext used in a Resp message is modified as $\{n_p, n_q, q\}_{k(p)}$, the term denoting the ciphertext is modified as $\text{c2}(p, n_p, n_q, q)$. But, the transition rule Fake22a does not need to be modified.

5.2   Theorem Proving of NSP for NSLPK

The proof is conducted by induction on the number of transition rules applied. In this section, let `as` be a constant of `PrinSet` denoting an arbitrary soup of non-intruder principals, `m, n, n'` ones of `Nonce` denoting arbitrary nonces, `ms` one of `Network` denoting an arbitrary soup of messages, `r` one of `PNat` denoting an arbitrary natural number (a random number), ns one of NonceSet denoting an arbitrary soup of nonces, a, b ones of Prin denoting arbitrary non-intruder principals, and p, q, p', q' ones of Prin&Intrdr denoting arbitrary principals that may be the intruder.

First of all, an operator (predicate) check is declared and defined as follows:

op check : Bool Bool $\rightarrow$ Bool
eq check(pre, con)
    = **if** (pre **implies** con) == **true then true else false fi** .

where pre and con are variables of Bool. check takes as its first argument a conjunction of instances of lemmas and/or induction hypotheses and as its second argument a formula to prove in which variables are replaced with constants. If a sufficiently enough information is not given (cases are not sufficiently split), pre **implies** con may reduce to neither **true** nor **false**. If pre **implies** con does not reduce to **true**, we would like to have **false** as the result of check(pre, con). This is why we use _==_ in the right-hand side of the equation. Let us note that this is the only place in which _==_ is used.

For the base case, all we have to do is to check if the following term reduces to **true**:

check(**true**, nonSec(init(as), m))

Since the term reduces to **true**, the base case is discharged. We do not use any lemmas for the base case, this is why the first argument of check is **true**.

Let us consider the induction case in which the transition rule Init1 is taken into account. An arbitrary state of NSLPK to which Init1 can be applied is expressed as

(nw : ms) (rand : r) (nonces : ns) (prins : (a b as))

such that a does not equal b. Let s refer to the term. The following search finds all successor states of s obtained by applying Init1 to s:

red s =(*, 1)⇒+ s' .

where s' is a variable of Config. There are two such successor states[4]:

1. (nw : (m1(a, a, b, c1(b, n(a, b, r), a)) ms)) (rand : next(r)) (nonces : ns)
   (prins : (a b as))
2. (nw : (m1(b, b, a, c1(a, n(b, a, r), b)) ms)) (rand : next(r)) (nonces : ns)
   (prins : (a b as))

The following search is used to discharge the induction case concerned:

red s =(*, 1)⇒+ s' **suchThat** (not check(nonSec(s, m), nonSec(s', m))) .

---

[4] The search functionality is not allowed to specify transition rules used for search. Therefore, we prepare one module M for each transition rule t such that t is the only transition rule in M and all modules imported by M. This is how one transition rule is specified for search.

where nonSec(s, m) is an instance of the induction hypothesis and nonSec(s′, m) is the formula to prove in the induction case. No solution is found if and only if check(nonSec(s, m), nonSec(s′, m))) reduces to true for all successor states s′ of s with respect to Init1. If no solution is found, therefore, the induction case is discharged. In this case, no solution is found and then the induction case is discharged.

Let us consider the induction case in which the transition rule Init2 is taken into account. An arbitrary state s of NSLPK to which Init2 can be applied is expressed as

(nw : ms) (rand : r) (nonces : ns) (prins : (a as))

The search

red s =(*, 1)⟼+ s′ suchThat (not check(nonSec(s, m), nonSec(s′, m))) .

finds one solution (the substitution mapping s′ to the following term)

(nw : (m1(a, a, intrdr, c1(intrdr, n(a, intrdr, r), a)) ms))
(rand : next(r)) (nonces : (n(a, intrdr, r) ns)) (prins : (a as))

The reason why the search finds the solution is because CafeOBJ does not know whether m equals n(a, intrdr, r). We then need to split the case into two sub-cases: (1) m = n(a, intrdr, r) and (2) m ≠ n(a, intrdr, r). For both sub-cases, the search does not find any solutions. Hence, the induction case is discharged.

Let us consider the induction case in which the transition rule RevResp is taken into account. An arbitrary state s of NSLPK to which RevResp can be applied is expressed as

(nw : (m1(p′, p, q, c1(q, n, p)) ms)) (rand : r) (nonces : ns) (prins : as)

The case is split into the following four sub-cases:

1. p ≠ intrdr
2. p = intrdr, m = n(q, intrdr, r)
3. p = intrdr, m ≠ n(q, intrdr, r), m ≠ n
4. p = intrdr, m ≠ n(q, intrdr, r), m = n

The search (whose form is exactly the same as those used for the two induction cases described earlier) finds no solution for the first three sub-cases but one solution for the last sub-case. The solution is as follows:

(nw : (m2(q, q, intrdr, c2(intrdr, n, n(q, intrdr, r), q))
       m1(p′, intrdr, q, c1(q, n, intrdr)) ms))
(rand : next(r)) (nonces : (n(q, intrdr, r) n ns)) (prins : as)

The reason why the search finds the solution is because CafeOBJ knows neither who has made the nonce n nor for whom it has been made. We may do further case splitting, but the solution lets us conjecture the following lemma:

op nonInCiph1 : Config Cipher1 $\rightarrow$ Bool
eq nonInCiph1($s, c1$)
    = ($c1 \in$ msgs(s) and gen($c1$) = intrdr)
      implies
      (gen(non($c1$)) = intrdr or forWhom(non($c1$)) = intrdr) .

The lemma says that if there exists an Init message such that the cipher-text used in the message has been made by the intruder, say m1(p′, intrdr, q, c1(q, n, intrdr)) in the solution, then the nonce used in the ciphertext, say n in the solution, has been made by the intruder or for the intruder. When the lemmas is used, the search becomes

red s =(*, 1)$\Rightarrow$+ s'
    suchThat (not check(nonSec(s, m) and nonInCiph1(s, c1(q, n, intrdr)),
                       nonSec(s', m))) .

The search does not find any solutions for the fourth sub-cases. Then, the induction case is discharged as long as the lemma is proved.

Let us consider the induction case in which the transition rule RevAck is taken into account. An arbitrary state **s** of NSLPK to which RevAck can be applied is expressed as

(nw : (m2(q′, q, p, c2(p, n, n′, q)) m1(p, p, q, c1(q, n, p)) ms))
(rand : r) (nonces : ns) (prins : as)

The case is split into the following three sub-cases:

1. q $\neq$ intrdr
2. q = intrdr, m $\neq$ n′
3. q = intrdr, m = n′

The search that does not use any lemmas finds no solution for the first two sub-cases but one solution for the last sub-case. The solution is as follows:

(nw : (m3(p, p, intrdr, c3(intrdr, n′)) m2(q′, intrdr, p, c2(p, n, n′, intrdr))
      m1(p, p, intrdr, c1(intrdr, n, p)) ms))
(rand : r) (nonces : ns) (prins : as)

The reason why the search finds the solution is because CafeOBJ knows neither who has made the nonce n′ nor for whom it has been made. The solution lets us conjecture the following lemma:

op nonInCiph2 : Config Cipher2 $\rightarrow$ Bool
eq nonInCiph2($s, c2$)
    = ($c2 \in$ msgs(s) and gen($c2$) = intrdr)
      implies
      (gen(non($c2$)) = intrdr or forWhom(non($c2$)) = intrdr) .

The lemma says that if there exists a Resp message such that the cipher-text used in the message has been made by the intruder, say m2(q′, intrdr, p,

$c2(p, n, n', \mathtt{intrdr}))$ in the solution, then the second nonce used in the cipher-text, say n' in the solution, has been made by the intruder or for the intruder. When the lemmas is used, the search becomes

red s $=(*, 1)\Mapsto+$ s'
$\quad$ suchThat (not check(nonSec(s, m) and nonInCiph2$(s, c2(p, n, n', \mathtt{intrdr}))$,
$\qquad\qquad\qquad$ nonSec(s', m))) .

The search does not find any solutions for the third sub-case. Then, the induction case is discharged as long as the lemma is proved.

$\quad$ The remaining 19 induction cases can be discharged without use of any lemmas.

$\quad$ Let us consider the induction case in which the transition rule **Fake11b** is taken into account for the proof of nonInCiph1. An arbitrary state **s** of NSLPK to which **Fake11b** can be applied is expressed as

$(\mathtt{nw: ms})\ (\mathtt{rand: r})\ (\mathtt{nonces: (n\ ns)})\ (\mathtt{prins: (b\ as)})$

The case is split into the following two sub-cases: (1) $\mathtt{c1} \neq \mathtt{c1(b, n, intrdr)}$ and (2) $\mathtt{c1} = \mathtt{c1(b, n, intrdr)}$. The search

red s $=(*, 1)\Mapsto+$ s'
$\quad$ suchThat (not check(nonInCiph1$(s, \mathtt{c1})$, nonInCiph1$(s', \mathtt{c1})$)) .

finds no solution for the first sub-case but one solution for the second sub-case. The solution is as follows:

$(\mathtt{nw : (m1(intrdr, intrdr, b, c1(b, n, intrdr))\ ms)})$
$(\mathtt{rand : r})\ (\mathtt{nonces : (n\ ns)})\ (\mathtt{prins : (b\ as)})$

The reason why the search finds the solution is because CafeOBJ knows neither who has made the nonce **n** nor for whom it has been made. We can use **nonSec** to discharge the second sub-case, making the search become the following:

red s $=(*, 1)\Mapsto+$ s'
$\quad$ suchThat (not check(nonInCiph1$(s, \mathtt{c1})$ and nonSec(s, n),
$\qquad\qquad\qquad$ nonInCiph1$(s', \mathtt{c1})$)) .

The search does not find any solutions and so the induction case, as well as the sub-case, is discharged. The base case and the remaining 22 induction cases can be discharged without use of any lemmas.

$\quad$ Let us consider the induction case in which the transition rule **Fake21a** is taken into account for the proof of nonInCiph2. An arbitrary state of NSLPK to which **Fake21a** can be applied is expressed as

$(\mathtt{nw: ms})\ (\mathtt{rand: r})\ (\mathtt{nonces: (n\ n'\ ns)})\ (\mathtt{prins: (a\ as)})$

where **n** does not equal n'. The case is split into the following three sub-cases:

1. $\mathtt{c2} = \mathtt{c2(a, n, n', intrdr)}$
2. $\mathtt{c2} \neq \mathtt{c2(a, n, n', intrdr)}$, $\mathtt{c2} = \mathtt{c2(a, n', n, intrdr)}$

3. $c2 \neq c2(a, n, n', intrdr)$, $c2 \neq c2(a, n', n, intrdr)$

The search

red s $=(*, 1) \Rrightarrow + s'$
suchThat (not check(nonInCiph2(s, c2), nonInCiph1(s', c2))) .

finds no solution for the third sub-case but one solution for each of the first two sub-cases. The solution for the first sub-case is as follows:

(nw : (m2(intrdr, intrdr, a, c2(a, n, n', intrdr)) ms))
(rand : r) (nonces : (n n' ns)) (prins : (a as))

The reason why the search finds the solution is because CafeOBJ knows neither who has made the nonce n' nor for whom it has been made. We can use **nonSec** to discharge the first sub-case, making the search become the following:

red s $=(*, 1) \Rrightarrow + s'$
suchThat (not check(nonInCiph2(s, c2) and nonSec(s, n'),
                    nonInCiph2(s', c1))) .

The search does not find any solutions and then the first sub-case is discharged. The second sub-case can be discharged likewise with **nonSec(s, n)**. Then, the induction case is discharged. The base case and the remaining 22 induction cases can be discharged without use of any lemmas.

Accordingly, we have proved **nonSec**(s, n), together with two lemmas **nonInCiph1**$(s, c1)$ and **nonInCiph2**$(s, c2)$, for all reachable states s from the initial state **init**(as) with 23 transition rules, all nonces n, all ciphertexts $c1$ used in Init messages and all ciphertexts $c2$ used in Resp messages. That is, we have theorem proved that NSLPK has NSP based on the rewrite theory specification of NSLPK[5].

Let us note that since the agreement (or authentication) property can be described as an invariant property, we could theorem prove that the rewrite theory system specification of NSLPK has the property with the proof technique described in the paper.

6   Related Work

To the best of our knowledge, Rocha and Meseguer are the first who have proposed a way to theorem prove that rewrite theory specifications formalizing (concurrent) systems have properties. They have proposed a deductive (theorem proving) approach to verification that rewrite theory specifications have safety

---

[5] We also need to prove that whenever each transition rule is applied to each term of Config that expresses a state of NSLPK, it generates a term of Config that also expresses a state of NSLPK. The proof can be straightforwardly done as the one (described in Subsect. 2.2) that isValid is invariant with respect to the simple protocol.

(stable and invariant) properties [43]. The approach reduces temporal logic reasoning to equational inductive reasoning. To this end, they present seven proof rules called G-ST, NR1, G-INV, C⇒, STR1, STR2 and NR2. The first two and next two proof rules are used to reason about stable and invariant properties, respectively. It is often necessary to strengthen state predicates so that you can prove that the predicates are invariant with respect to state machines. The last three proof rules are used to strengthen state predicates. NR1 and NR2 use one-step narrowing modulo axioms (associativity and/or commutativity and/or identity) [44] to reduce temporal logic reasoning to equational inductive reasoning. Induction on the number of transition rules applied (used in the present paper) correspond to G-INV. G-INV has two premises. One premise is discharged by C⇒, which corresponds to the base case. The other premise is a stable property satisfaction relation that is discharged by G-ST and then NR1, which corresponds to the induction cases. Use of lemmas corresponds to STR1, STR2 and NR2. Although there are many things shared by the Rocha and Meseguer's approach and ours, theirs uses narrowing to conduct what correspond to induction cases, while ours uses search based on standard matching (but not unification). Moreover, we extensively use simultaneous induction [45], namely that each of the three proof scores for `nonSec`, `nonInCiph1` and `nonInCiph2` is compositionally written but uses all the three state predicates as induction hypotheses. If you use STR1, STR2 and NR2, you first need to prove that the conjunction of the state predicates is invariant and then reason about `nonSec` from the conjunction.

Bae, Escobar and Meseguer have proposed a logical model checking in which (concurrent) systems are specified as rewrite theory specifications [46]. The logical model checking uses a narrowing based logical Kripke structure in which states may contain logical variables and transition relations are basically one-step narrowing relations. Since a narrowing based logical Kripke structure may have an infinite number of states, they use two abstraction techniques called folding abstraction and equational abstraction such that an infinite number of states can be made finite. Although equational abstraction applied to a concrete Kripke structure can only deal with a simplified version of the Lamport's bakery protocol in which there are a fixed number of processes, the logical model checking, together with folding abstraction and equational abstraction, can also deal with the simplified version in which there are an arbitrary number of processes. Since folding abstraction and equational abstraction may not make an infinite number of states finite for any narrowing based logical Kripke structure, they also propose a logical bounded model checking. Our approach to theorem proving for invariant properties based on rewrite theory specifications uses bounded model checking with depth 1 with search. But the bounded model checking is not very concrete, and may have something to do with the (bounded) logical model checking. One piece of our future work is to clarify the relation between the (bounded) logical model checking and our approach.

k-induction [47] implemented in Symbolic Analysis Laboratory (SAL) [48] can verify that a state machine in which there are an infinite number of states has an invariant property. It uses an SMT based bounded model checker to confirm that there are no counterexamples showing that the state machine does not have the property in depth $k - 1$, and uses an SMT solver to show that for an arbitrary computation $s_0, \ldots, s_{k-1}, s_k$ that consists of $k + 1$ states, if the state predicate concerned holds in each s_i for $i = 0, \ldots, k - 1$, then the predicate holds in s_k. Our approach may be regarded as k-induction where $k = 1$ because bounded model checking with depth 1 is used to discharge induction cases. It may be worth pursuing a possibility that our approach can be made what corresponds to general k-induction.

7 Conclusion

We have described a way to theorem prove that rewrite theory specifications of OTSs have invariant properties by proof score writing. Our approach uses bounded model checking with depth 1 using rewriting-based (not narrowing-based) search, applying to an arbitrary state to which each transition rule can be applied, to discharge each induction case. The method may achieve a more faithfully seamless integration of model checking and theorem proving because no translation is needed for system specifications.

As usual, much work remains ahead to achieve a more faithfully seamless integration of the two verification techniques. One challenge is to automate proof score writing for rewrite theory specifications of OTSs. Proof score writing consists in case analysis/splitting and lemma discovery/use. Creme [26], an automatic invariant prover, automates both of them to some extent. Although some techniques may be used, however, Creme is dedicated to equational theory specifications of OTSs.

The second author has come up with a way to automate case analysis/splitting for rewrite theory specifications of OTSs. The method can be implemented in terms of order-sorted rewriting (not narrowing) modulo axioms and has been successfully applied to two non-trivial cases, Qlock, a mutual exclusion protocol, and ABP, a communication protocol, have some invariant properties. The method is one potential approach to automating proof score writing for rewrite theory specifications of OTSs.

As written in Sect. 1, OTSs have emerged as a sub-class of behavioral specifications, and OTSs described as equational theory specifications can be regarded as behavioral specifications. Behavioral equivalence [9, 10, 49, 50] is one main concern in behavioral specifications. We briefly discuss how to prove that a state predicate is invariant with respect to an OTS described as an equational theory specification through behavioral equivalence in [45]. It may be worth investigating how to prove that a state predicate is invariant with respect to an OTS described as a rewrite theory specification through behavioral equivalence. Before that, however, we need to clarify behavioral equivalence in rewrite theory specifications.

References

1. Ogata, K., Kurihara, S., Inari, M., Doi, N.: The design and implementation of HoME. In: PLDI 1992, pp. 44–54 (1992)
2. Ogata, K., Doi, N.: Object allocation and dynamic compilation in MultithreadSmalltalk. In: 9th SAC, pp. 452–456 (1994)
3. Ogata, K., Ohhara, K., Futatsugi, K.: TRAM: An abstract machine for order-sorted conditional term rewriting systems. In: Comon, H. (ed.) RTA 1997. LNCS, vol. 1232, pp. 335–338. Springer, Heidelberg (1997)
4. Ogata, K., Kondo, M., Ioroi, S., Futatsugi, K.: Design and implementation of Parallel TRAM. In: Lengauer, C., Griebl, M., Gorlatch, S. (eds.) Euro-Par 1997. LNCS, vol. 1300, pp. 1209–1216. Springer, Heidelberg (1997)
5. Ogata, K., Hirata, H., Ioroi, S., Futatsugi, K.: Experimental implementation of Parallel TRAM on massively parallel computer. In: Pritchard, D., Reeve, J. (eds.) Euro-Par 1998. LNCS, vol. 1470, pp. 846–851. Springer, Heidelberg (1998)
6. Ogata, K., Futatsugi, K.: Specification and verification of some classical mutual exclusion algorithms with CafeOBJ. In: OBJ/CafeOBJ/Maude Workshop at FM 1999, pp. 159–177 (1999)
7. Ogata, K., Futatsugi, K.: Proof scores in the OTS/CafeOBJ method. In: Najm, E., Nestmann, U., Stevens, P. (eds.) FMOODS 2003. LNCS, vol. 2884, pp. 170–184. Springer, Heidelberg (2003)
8. Ogata, K., Futatsugi, K.: Some tips on writing proof scores in the OTS/CafeOBJ method. In: Futatsugi, K., Jouannaud, J.-P., Meseguer, J. (eds.) Goguen Festschrift. LNCS, vol. 4060, pp. 596–615. Springer, Heidelberg (2006)
9. Goguen, J., Malcolm, G.: A hidden agenda. TCS 245, 55–101 (2000)
10. Diaconescu, R., Futatsugi, K.: Behavioural coherence in object-oriented algebraic specification. J. UCS 6, 74–95 (2000)
11. Chandy, K.M., Misra, J.: Parallel Program Design: A Foundation. Addison-Wesley (1988)
12. Diaconescu, R., Futatsugi, K.: CafeOBJ report. AMAST Series in Computing 6. World Scientific (1998)
13. Ogata, K., Futatsugi, K.: Formal verification of the MCS list-based queuing lock. In: Thiagarajan, P.S., Yap, R. (eds.) ASIAN 1999. LNCS, vol. 1742, pp. 281–293. Springer, Heidelberg (1999)
14. Ogata, K., Futatsugi, K.: Formal analysis of Suzuki&Kasami distributed mutual exclusion algorithm. In: Jacobs, B., Rensink, A. (eds.) Formal Methods for Open Object-Based Distributed Systems V. IFIP, vol. 81, pp. 181–195. Springer, Heildelberg (2002)
15. Xiang, J., Ogata, K., Futatsugi, K.: Formal fault tree analysis of state transition systems. In: 5th QSIC, pp. 124–131 (2005)
16. Kong, W., Ogata, K., Futatsugi, K.: Specification and verification of workflows with RBAC mechanism and SoD constraints. IJSEKE 17, 3–32 (2007)
17. Ogata, K., Futatsugi, K.: Formal analysis of the bakery protocol with consideration of nonatomic reads and writes. In: Liu, S., Maibaum, T., Araki, K. (eds.) ICFEM 2008. LNCS, vol. 5256, pp. 187–206. Springer, Heidelberg (2008)
18. Kong, W., Ogata, K., Futatsugi, K.: Towards reliable e-government systems with the OTS/CafeOBJ method. IEICE Transactions E93-D, 974–984 (2010)
19. Ogata, K., Futatsugi, K.: Proof score approach to analysis of electronic commerce protocols. IJSEKE 20, 253–287 (2010)

20. Zhang, M., Ogata, K., Futatsugi, K.: Formalization and verification of behavioral correctness of dynamic software updates. In: 2nd VSSE. ENTCS, vol. 294, pp. 12–23 (2013)
21. Futatsugi, K., Goguen, J., Ogata, K.: Verifying design with proof scores. In: Meyer, B., Woodcock, J. (eds.) VSTTE 2005. LNCS, vol. 4171, pp. 277–290. Springer, Heidelberg (2008)
22. Futatsugi, K., Găină, D., Ogata, K.: Principles of proof scores in CafeOBJ. TCS 464, 90–112 (2012)
23. Ogata, K., Futatsugi, K.: Proof score approach to verification of liveness properties. IEICE Transactions E91-D, 2804–2817 (2008)
24. Ogata, K., Futatsugi, K.: Modeling and verification of real-time systems based on equations. SCP 66, 162–180 (2007)
25. Ouranos, I., Ogata, K., Stefaneas, P.: Formal analysis of TESLA protocol in the Timed OTS/CafeOBJ method. In: Margaria, T., Steffen, B. (eds.) ISoLA 2012, Part II. LNCS, vol. 7610, pp. 126–142. Springer, Heidelberg (2012)
26. Nakano, M., Ogata, K., Nakamura, M., Futatsugi, K.: Creme: An automatic invariant prover of behavioral specifications. IJSEKE 17, 783–804 (2007)
27. Găină, D., Futatsugi, K., Ogata, K.: Constructor-based logics. J. UCS 18, 90–112 (2012)
28. Găină, D., Zhang, M., Chiba, Y., Arimoto, Y.: Constructor-based inductive theorem prover. In: Heckel, R., Milius, S. (eds.) CALCO 2013. LNCS, vol. 8089, pp. 328–333. Springer, Heidelberg (2013)
29. Ogata, K., Nakano, M., Kong, W., Futatsugi, K.: Induction-guided falsification. In: Liu, Z., He, J. (eds.) ICFEM 2006. LNCS, vol. 4260, pp. 114–131. Springer, Heidelberg (2006)
30. Ogata, K., Futatsugi, K.: A combination of forward & backward reachability analysis methods. In: Dong, J.S., Zhu, H. (eds.) ICFEM 2010. LNCS, vol. 6447, pp. 501–517. Springer, Heidelberg (2010)
31. Clavel, M., Durán, F., Eker, S., Lincoln, P., Martí-Oliet, N., Meseguer, J., Talcott, C.: All About Maude - A High-Performance Logical Framework. LNCS, vol. 4350. Springer, Heidelberg (2007)
32. Kong, W., Ogata, K., Futatsugi, K.: Model-checking observational transition system with Maudea. In: 20th ITC-CSCC, pp. 5–6 (2005)
33. Ogata, K., Kong, W., Futatsugi, K.: Falsification of OTSs by searches of bounded reachable state spaces. In: 18th SEKE, pp. 440–445 (2006)
34. Kong, W., Ogata, K., Seino, T., Futatsugi, K.: A lightweight integration of theorem proving and model checking for system verification. In: 12th APSEC, pp. 59–66 (2005)
35. Nakamura, M., Kong, W., Ogata, K., Futatsugi, K.: A specification translation from behavioral specifications to rewrite specifications. IEICE Transactions E91-D, 1492–1503 (2008)
36. Zhang, M., Ogata, K., Nakamura, M.: Translation of state machines from equational theories into rewrite theories with tool support. IEICE Transactions 94-D, 976–988 (2011)
37. Zhang, M., Ogata, K.: Invariant-preserved transformation of state machines from equations into rewrite rules. In: 18th APSEC, pp. 511–516 (2012)
38. Lowe, G.: An attack on the Needham-Schroeder public-key authentication protocol. IPL 56, 131–133 (1995)
39. Needham, R.M., Schroeder, M.D.: Using encryption for authentication in large networks of computers. CACM 21, 993–999 (1978)

40. Dolev, D., Yao, A.C.: On the security of public key protocols. IEEE TIT IT-29, 198–208 (1983)
41. Goguen, J., Winkler, T., Meseguer, J., Futatsugi, K., Jouannaud, J.P.: Introducing OBJ. In: Software Engineering with OBJ: Algebraic Specification in Action. Kluwer (2000)
42. Meseguer, J., Palomino, M., Martí-Oliet, N.: Equational abstractions. TCS 403, 239–264 (2008)
43. Rocha, C., Meseguer, J.: Proving safety properties of rewrite theories. In: Corradini, A., Klin, B., Cîrstea, C. (eds.) CALCO 2011. LNCS, vol. 6859, pp. 314–328. Springer, Heidelberg (2011)
44. Jouannaud, J.P., Kirchner, C., Kirchner, H.: Incremental construction of unification algorithms in equational theories. In: Diaz, J. (ed.) 10th ICALP. LNCS, vol. 154, pp. 361–373. Springer, Heidelberg (1983)
45. Ogata, K., Futatsugi, K.: Compositionally writing proof scores of invariants in the OTS/CafeOBJ method. J. UCS 19, 771–804 (2013)
46. Bae, K., Escobar, S., Meseguer, J.: Abstract logical model checking of infinite-state systems using narrowing. In: 24th RTA, pp. 81–96 (2013)
47. de Moura, L., Rueß, H., Sorea, M.: Bounded model checking and induction: From refutation to verification. In: Hunt Jr., W.A., Somenzi, F. (eds.) CAV 2003. LNCS, vol. 2725, pp. 14–26. Springer, Heidelberg (2003)
48. de Moura, L., Owre, S., Rueß, H., Rushby, J., Shankar, N., Sorea, M., Tiwari, A.: SAL 2. In: Alur, R., Peled, D.A. (eds.) CAV 2004. LNCS, vol. 3114, pp. 496–500. Springer, Heidelberg (2004)
49. Hennicker, R.: Context induction: A proof principle for behavioural abstractions. In: Miola, A. (ed.) DISCO 1990. LNCS, vol. 429, pp. 101–110. Springer, Heidelberg (1990)
50. Roşu, G., Lucanu, D.: Circular coinduction: A proof theoretical foundation. In: Kurz, A., Lenisa, M., Tarlecki, A. (eds.) CALCO 2009. LNCS, vol. 5728, pp. 127–144. Springer, Heidelberg (2009)

Author Index